T0190104

Learning with Kernels

Adaptive Computation and Machine Learning

Thomas Dietterich, Editor

Christopher Bishop, David Heckerman, Michael Jordan, and Michael Kearns, Associate Editors

Bioinformatics: The Machine Learning Approach, Pierre Baldi and Søren Brunak

Reinforcement Learning: An Introduction, Richard S. Sutton and Andrew G. Barto

Graphical Models for Machine Learning and Digital Communication, Brendan J. Frey

Learning in Graphical Models, Michael I. Jordan

Causation, Prediction, and Search, second edition, Peter Spirtes, Clark Glymour, and Richard Scheines

Principles of Data Mining, David Hand, Heikki Mannila, and Padhraic Smyth

Bioinformatics: The Machine Learning Approach, second edition, Pierre Baldi and Søren Brunak

Learning Kernel Classifiers: Theory and Algorithms, Ralf Herbrich

Learning with Kernels: Support Vector Machines, Regularization, Optimization, and Beyond, Bernhard Schölkopf and Alexander J. Smola

Learning with Kernels

Support Vector Machines, Regularization, Optimization, and Beyond

Bernhard Schölkopf
Alexander J. Smola

The MIT Press
Cambridge, Massachusetts
London, England

Typeset by the authors using LaTeX 2_ε

Library of Congress Cataloging-in-Publication Data

Learning with Kernels — Support Vector Machines,
Regularization, Optimization and Beyond / by Bernhard Schölkopf,
Alexander J. Smola.
p. cm.
Includes bibliographical references and index.
ISBN 978-0-262-53657-8 (paperback: alk. paper)
1. Machine learning. 2. Algorithms. 3. Kernel functions
I. Schölkopf, Bernhard. II. Smola, Alexander J.

To our parents

Contents

Series Foreword

The goal of building systems that can adapt to their environments and learn from their experience has attracted researchers from many fields, including computer science, engineering, mathematics, physics, neuroscience, and cognitive science. Out of this research has come a wide variety of learning techniques that have the potential to transform many scientific and industrial fields. Recently, several research communities have converged on a common set of issues surrounding supervised, unsupervised, and reinforcement learning problems. The MIT Press series on Adaptive Computation and Machine Learning seeks to unify the many diverse strands of machine learning research and to foster high quality research and innovative applications.

Learning with Kernels: Support Vector Machines, Regularization, Optimization, and Beyond is an excellent illustration of this convergence of ideas from many fields. The development of kernel-based learning methods has resulted from a combination of machine learning theory, optimization algorithms from operations research, and kernel techniques from mathematical analysis. These three ideas have spread far beyond the original support-vector machine algorithm: Virtually every learning algorithm has been redesigned to exploit the power of kernel methods. Bernhard Schölkopf and Alexander Smola have written a comprehensive, yet accessible, account of these developments. This volume includes all of the mathematical and algorithmic background needed not only to obtain a basic understanding of the material but to master it. Students and researchers who study this book will be able to apply kernel methods in creative ways to solve a wide range of problems in science and engineering.

Thomas Dietterich

Preface

One of the most fortunate situations a scientist can encounter is to enter a field in its infancy. There is a large choice of topics to work on, and many of the issues are conceptual rather than merely technical. Over the last seven years, we have had the privilege to be in this position with regard to the field of Support Vector Machines (SVMs). We began working on our respective doctoral dissertations in 1994 and 1996. Upon completion, we decided to combine our efforts and write a book about SVMs. Since then, the field has developed impressively, and has to an extent been transformed. We set up a website that quickly became the central repository for the new community, and a number of workshops were organized by various researchers. The scope of the field has now widened significantly, both in terms of new algorithms, such as kernel methods different to SVMs, and in terms of a deeper theoretical understanding being gained. It has become clear that kernel methods provide a framework for tackling some rather profound issues in machine learning theory. At the same time, successful applications have demonstrated that SVMs not only have a more solid foundation than artificial neural networks, but are able to serve as a replacement for neural networks that perform as well or better, in a wide variety of fields. Standard neural network and pattern recognition textbooks have now started including chapters on SVMs and kernel PCA (for instance, [235, 153]).

While these developments took place, we were trying to strike a balance between pursuing exciting new research, and making progress with the slowly growing manuscript of this book. In the two and a half years that we worked on the book, we faced a number of lessons that we suspect everyone writing a scientific monograph — or any other book — will encounter. First, writing a book is more work than you think, even with two authors sharing the work in equal parts. Second, our book got longer than planned. Once we exceeded the initially planned length of 500 pages, we got worried. In fact, the manuscript kept growing even after we stopped writing new chapters, and began polishing things and incorporating corrections suggested by colleagues. This was mainly due to the fact that the book deals with a fascinating new area, and researchers keep adding fresh material to the body of knowledge. We learned that there is no asymptotic regime in writing such a book — if one does not stop, it will grow beyond any bound — unless one starts cutting. We therefore had to take painful decisions to leave out material that we originally thought should be in the book. Sadly, and this is the third point, the book thus contains less material than originally planned, especially on the subject of theoretical developments. We sincerely apologize to all researchers who feel that their contributions should have been included — the book is certainly biased towards our own work, and does not provide a fully comprehensive overview of the field. We did, however, aim to provide all the necessary concepts and ideas to enable a reader equipped with some basic mathematical knowledge to enter the engaging world of machine learning, using theoretically well-founded kernel algorithms, and to understand and apply the powerful algorithms that have been developed over the last few years.

The book is divided into three logical parts. Each part consists of a brief introduction and a number of technical chapters. In addition, we include two appendices containing addenda, technical details, and mathematical prerequisites. Each chapter begins with a short discussion outlining the contents and prerequisites; for some of the longer chapters, we include a graph that sketches the logical structure and dependencies between the sections. At the end of most chapters, we include a set of problems, ranging from simple exercises (marked by •) to hard ones (•••); in addition, we describe open problems and questions for future research (○○○).[1] The latter often represent worthwhile projects for a research publication, or even a thesis. References are also included in some of the problems. These references contain the solutions to the associated problems, or at least significant parts thereof.

The overall structure of the book is perhaps somewhat unusual. Rather than presenting a logical progression of chapters building upon each other, we occasionally touch on a subject briefly, only to revisit it later in more detail. For readers who are used to reading scientific monographs and textbooks from cover to cover, this will amount to some redundancy. We hope, however, that some readers, who are more selective in their reading habits (or less generous with their time), and only look at those chapters that they are interested in, will benefit. Indeed, nobody is expected to read every chapter. Some chapters are fairly technical, and cover material included for reasons of completeness. Other chapters, which are more relevant to the central subjects of the book, are kept simpler, and should be accessible to undergraduate students.

In a way, this book thus contains several books in one. For instance, the first chapter can be read as a standalone "executive summary" of Support Vector and kernel methods. This chapter should also provide a fast entry point for practitioners. Someone interested in applying SVMs to a pattern recognition problem might want to read Chapters 1 and 7 only. A reader thinking of building their own SVM implementation could additionally read Chapter 10, and parts of Chapter 6. Those who would like to get actively involved in research aspects of kernel methods, for example by "kernelizing" a new algorithm, should probably read at least Chapters 1 and 2. A one-semester undergraduate course on learning with kernels could include the material of Chapters 1, 2.1–2.3, 3.1–3.2, 5.1–5.2, 6.1–6.3, 7. If there is more

1. We suggest that authors post their solutions on the book website www.learning-with-kernels.org.

time, one of the Chapters 14, 16, or 17 can be added, or 4.1–4.2. A graduate course could additionally deal with the more advanced parts of Chapters 3, 4, and 5. The remaining chapters provide ample material for specialized courses and seminars.

As a general time-saving rule, we recommend reading the first chapter and then jumping directly to the chapter of particular interest to the reader. Chances are that this will lead to a chapter that contains references to the earlier ones, which can then be followed as desired. We hope that this way, readers will inadvertently be tempted to venture into some of the less frequented chapters and research areas. Explore this book; there is a lot to find, and much more is yet to be discovered in the field of learning with kernels.

We conclude the preface by thanking those who assisted us in the preparation of the book. Our first thanks go to our first readers. Chris Burges, Arthur Gretton, and Bob Williamson have read through various versions of the book, and made numerous suggestions that corrected or improved the material. A number of other researchers have proofread various chapters. We would like to thank Matt Beal, Daniel Berger, Olivier Bousquet, Ben Bradshaw, Nicolò Cesa-Bianchi, Olivier Chapelle, Dennis DeCoste, Andre Elisseeff, Anita Faul, Arnulf Graf, Isabelle Guyon, Ralf Herbrich, Simon Hill, Dominik Janzing, Michael Jordan, Sathiya Keerthi, Neil Lawrence, Ben O'Loghlin, Ulrike von Luxburg, Davide Mattera, Sebastian Mika, Natasa Milic-Frayling, Marta Milo, Klaus Müller, Dave Musicant, Fernando Pérez Cruz, Ingo Steinwart, Mike Tipping, and Chris Williams.

In addition, a large number of people have contributed to this book in one way or another, be it by sharing their insights with us in discussions, or by collaborating with us on some of the topics covered in the book. In many places, this strongly influenced the presentation of the material. We would like to thank Dimitris Achlioptas, Luís Almeida, Shun-Ichi Amari, Peter Bartlett, Jonathan Baxter, Tony Bell, Shai Ben-David, Kristin Bennett, Matthias Bethge, Chris Bishop, Andrew Blake, Volker Blanz, Léon Bottou, Paul Bradley, Chris Burges, Heinrich Bülthoff, Olivier Chapelle, Nello Cristianini, Corinna Cortes, Cameron Dawson,Tom Dietterich, André Elisseeff, Oscar de Feo, Federico Girosi, Thore Graepel, Isabelle Guyon, Patrick Haffner, Stefan Harmeling, Paul Hayton, Markus Hegland, Ralf Herbrich, Tommi Jaakkola, Michael Jordan, Jyrki Kivinen, Yann LeCun, Chi-Jen Lin, Gabor Lugosi, Olvi Mangasarian, Laurent Massoulie, Sebastian Mika, Sayan Mukherjee, Klaus Müller, Noboru Murata, Nuria Oliver, John Platt, Tomaso Poggio, Gunnar Rätsch, Sami Romdhani, Rainer von Sachs, Christoph Schnörr, Matthias Seeger, John Shawe-Taylor, Kristy Sim, Patrice Simard, Stephen Smale, Sara Solla, Lionel Tarassenko, Lily Tian, Mike Tipping, Alexander Tsybakov, Lou van den Dries, Santosh Venkatesh, Thomas Vetter, Chris Watkins, Jason Weston, Chris Williams, Bob Williamson, Andreas Ziehe, Alex Zien, and Tong Zhang.

Next, we would like to extend our thanks to the research institutes that allowed us to pursue our research interests and to dedicate the time necessary for writing the present book; these are AT&T / Bell Laboratories (Holmdel), the Australian National University (Canberra), Biowulf Technologies (New York), GMD FIRST (Berlin), the Max-Planck-Institute for Biological Cybernetics (Tübingen), and Microsoft Research (Cambridge). We are grateful to Doug Sery from MIT Press for continuing support and encouragement during the writing of this book. We are, moreover, indebted to funding from various sources; specifically, from the Studienstiftung des deutschen Volkes, the Deutsche Forschungsgemeinschaft, the Australian Research Council, and the European Union.

Finally, special thanks go to Vladimir Vapnik, who introduced us to the fascinating world of statistical learning theory.

...the story of the sheep dog who was herding his sheep, and serendipitously invented both large margin classification and Sheep Vectors...

Illustration by Ana Martín Larrañaga

1 A Tutorial Introduction

This chapter describes the central ideas of Support Vector (SV) learning in a nutshell. Its goal is to provide an overview of the basic concepts.

Overview

One such concept is that of a kernel. Rather than going immediately into mathematical detail, we introduce kernels informally as similarity measures that arise from a particular representation of patterns (Section 1.1), and describe a simple kernel algorithm for pattern recognition (Section 1.2). Following this, we report some basic insights from statistical learning theory, the mathematical theory that underlies SV learning (Section 1.3). Finally, we briefly review some of the main kernel algorithms, namely Support Vector Machines (SVMs) (Sections 1.4 to 1.6) and kernel principal component analysis (Section 1.7).

Prerequisites

We have aimed to keep this introductory chapter as basic as possible, whilst giving a fairly comprehensive overview of the main ideas that will be discussed in the present book. After reading it, readers should be able to place all the remaining material in the book in context and judge which of the following chapters is of particular interest to them.

As a consequence of this aim, most of the claims in the chapter are not proven. Abundant references to later chapters will enable the interested reader to fill in the gaps at a later stage, without losing sight of the main ideas described presently.

1.1 Data Representation and Similarity

One of the fundamental problems of learning theory is the following: suppose we are given two classes of objects. We are then faced with a new object, and we have to assign it to one of the two classes. This problem can be formalized as follows:

Training Data

we are given empirical data

$$(x_1, y_1), \ldots, (x_m, y_m) \in \mathcal{X} \times \{\pm 1\}. \tag{1.1}$$

Here, $\mathcal{X}$ is some nonempty set from which the *patterns* x_i (sometimes called *cases, inputs, instances,* or *observations*) are taken, usually referred to as the *domain*; the y_i are called *labels, targets, outputs* or sometimes also *observations*.[1] Note that there are

1. Note that we use the term pattern to refer to individual observations. A (smaller) part of the existing literature reserves the term for a generic *prototype* which underlies the data. The

only two classes of patterns. For the sake of mathematical convenience, they are labelled by $+1$ and -1, respectively. This is a particularly simple situation, referred to as *(binary) pattern recognition* or *(binary) classification*.

It should be emphasized that the patterns could be just about anything, and we have made no assumptions on $\mathcal{X}$ other than it being a set. For instance, the task might be to categorize sheep into two classes, in which case the patterns x_i would simply be sheep.

In order to study the problem of learning, however, we need an additional type of structure. In learning, we want to be able to *generalize* to unseen data points. In the case of pattern recognition, this means that given some new pattern $x \in \mathcal{X}$, we want to predict the corresponding $y \in \{\pm 1\}$.[2] By this we mean, loosely speaking, that we choose y such that (x, y) is in some sense similar to the training examples (1.1). To this end, we need notions of *similarity* in $\mathcal{X}$ and in $\{\pm 1\}$.

Characterizing the similarity of the outputs $\{\pm 1\}$ is easy: in binary classification, only two situations can occur: two labels can either be identical or different. The choice of the similarity measure for the inputs, on the other hand, is a deep question that lies at the core of the field of machine learning.

Let us consider a similarity measure of the form

$$\begin{aligned} k : \mathcal{X} \times \mathcal{X} &\to \mathbb{R} \\ (x, x') &\mapsto k(x, x'), \end{aligned} \tag{1.2}$$

that is, a function that, given two patterns x and x', returns a real number characterizing their similarity. Unless stated otherwise, we will assume that k is *symmetric*, that is, $k(x, x') = k(x', x)$ for all $x, x' \in \mathcal{X}$. For reasons that will become clear later (cf. Remark 2.16), the function k is called a *kernel* [359, 4, 42, 62, 223].

General similarity measures of this form are rather difficult to study. Let us therefore start from a particularly simple case, and generalize it subsequently. A simple type of similarity measure that is of particular mathematical appeal is a *dot product*. For instance, given two vectors $\mathbf{x}, \mathbf{x}' \in \mathbb{R}^N$, the *canonical dot product* is defined as

Dot Product

$$\langle \mathbf{x}, \mathbf{x}' \rangle := \sum_{i=1}^{N} [\mathbf{x}]_i [\mathbf{x}']_i. \tag{1.3}$$

Here, $[\mathbf{x}]_i$ denotes the ith entry of $\mathbf{x}$.

Note that the dot product is also referred to as *inner product* or *scalar product*, and sometimes denoted with round brackets and a dot, as $(\mathbf{x} \cdot \mathbf{x}')$ — this is where the "dot" in the name comes from. In Section B.2, we give a general definition of dot products. Usually, however, it is sufficient to think of dot products as (1.3).

latter is probably closer to the original meaning of the term, however we decided to stick with the present usage, which is more common in the field of machine learning.

2. Doing this for every $x \in \mathcal{X}$ amounts to estimating a *function* $f : \mathcal{X} \to \{\pm 1\}$.

The geometric interpretation of the canonical dot product is that it computes the cosine of the angle between the vectors $\mathbf{x}$ and $\mathbf{x}'$, provided they are normalized to length 1. Moreover, it allows computation of the *length* (or *norm*) of a vector $\mathbf{x}$ as

Length

$$\|\mathbf{x}\| = \sqrt{\langle \mathbf{x}, \mathbf{x} \rangle}. \tag{1.4}$$

Likewise, the distance between two vectors is computed as the length of the difference vector. Therefore, being able to compute dot products amounts to being able to carry out all geometric constructions that can be formulated in terms of angles, lengths and distances.

Note, however, that the dot product approach is not really sufficiently general to deal with many interesting problems.

- First, we have deliberately not made the assumption that the patterns actually exist in a dot product space. So far, they could be any kind of object. In order to be able to use a dot product as a similarity measure, we therefore first need to represent the patterns as vectors in some dot product space $\mathcal{H}$ (which need not coincide with $\mathbb{R}^N$). To this end, we use a map

$$\begin{aligned} \Phi : \mathcal{X} &\to \mathcal{H} \\ x &\mapsto \mathbf{x} := \Phi(x). \end{aligned} \tag{1.5}$$

- Second, even if the original patterns exist in a dot product space, we may still want to consider more general similarity measures obtained by applying a map (1.5). In that case, Φ will typically be a nonlinear map. An example that we will consider in Chapter 2 is a map which computes products of entries of the input patterns.

Feature Space

In both the above cases, the space $\mathcal{H}$ is called a *feature space*. Note that we have used a bold face $\mathbf{x}$ to denote the vectorial representation of x in the feature space. We will follow this convention throughout the book.

To summarize, embedding the data into $\mathcal{H}$ via Φ has three benefits:

1. It lets us define a similarity measure from the dot product in $\mathcal{H}$,

$$k(x, x') := \langle \mathbf{x}, \mathbf{x}' \rangle = \langle \Phi(x), \Phi(x') \rangle . \tag{1.6}$$

2. It allows us to deal with the patterns geometrically, and thus lets us study learning algorithms using linear algebra and analytic geometry.
3. The freedom to choose the mapping Φ will enable us to design a large variety of similarity measures and learning algorithms. This also applies to the situation where the inputs x_i already exist in a dot product space. In that case, we *might* directly use the dot product as a similarity measure. However, nothing prevents us from first applying a possibly nonlinear map Φ to change the representation into one that is more suitable for a given problem. This will be elaborated in Chapter 2, where the theory of kernels is developed in more detail.

1.2 A Simple Pattern Recognition Algorithm

We are now in the position to describe a pattern recognition learning algorithm that is arguably one of the simplest possible. We make use of the structure introduced in the previous section; that is, we assume that our data are embedded into a dot product space $\mathcal{H}$.[3] Using the dot product, we can measure distances in this space. The basic idea of the algorithm is to assign a previously unseen pattern to the class with closer mean.

We thus begin by computing the means of the two classes in feature space;

$$\mathbf{c}_+ = \frac{1}{m_+} \sum_{\{i|y_i=+1\}} \mathbf{x}_i, \tag{1.7}$$

$$\mathbf{c}_- = \frac{1}{m_-} \sum_{\{i|y_i=-1\}} \mathbf{x}_i, \tag{1.8}$$

where m_+ and m_- are the number of examples with positive and negative labels, respectively. We assume that both classes are non-empty, thus $m_+, m_- > 0$. We assign a new point $\mathbf{x}$ to the class whose mean is closest (Figure 1.1). This geometric construction can be formulated in terms of the dot product $\langle \cdot, \cdot \rangle$. Half way between $\mathbf{c}_+$ and $\mathbf{c}_-$ lies the point $\mathbf{c} := (\mathbf{c}_+ + \mathbf{c}_-)/2$. We compute the class of $\mathbf{x}$ by checking whether the vector $\mathbf{x} - \mathbf{c}$ connecting $\mathbf{c}$ to $\mathbf{x}$ encloses an angle smaller than $\pi/2$ with the vector $\mathbf{w} := \mathbf{c}_+ - \mathbf{c}_-$ connecting the class means. This leads to

$$\begin{aligned} y &= \operatorname{sgn} \langle (\mathbf{x} - \mathbf{c}), \mathbf{w} \rangle \\ &= \operatorname{sgn} \langle (\mathbf{x} - (\mathbf{c}_+ + \mathbf{c}_-)/2), (\mathbf{c}_+ - \mathbf{c}_-) \rangle \\ &= \operatorname{sgn} (\langle \mathbf{x}, \mathbf{c}_+ \rangle - \langle \mathbf{x}, \mathbf{c}_- \rangle + b). \end{aligned} \tag{1.9}$$

Here, we have defined the offset

$$b := \frac{1}{2}(\|\mathbf{c}_-\|^2 - \|\mathbf{c}_+\|^2), \tag{1.10}$$

with the norm $\|\mathbf{x}\| := \sqrt{\langle \mathbf{x}, \mathbf{x} \rangle}$. If the class means have the same distance to the origin, then b will vanish.

Note that (1.9) induces a decision boundary which has the form of a hyperplane (Figure 1.1); that is, a set of points that satisfy a constraint expressible as a linear equation.

It is instructive to rewrite (1.9) in terms of the input patterns x_i, using the kernel k to compute the dot products. Note, however, that (1.6) only tells us how to compute the dot products between vectorial representations $\mathbf{x}_i$ of inputs x_i. We therefore need to express the vectors $\mathbf{c}_i$ and $\mathbf{w}$ in terms of $\mathbf{x}_1, \ldots, \mathbf{x}_m$.

Decision Function

To this end, substitute (1.7) and (1.8) into (1.9) to get the *decision function*

3. For the definition of a dot product space, see Section B.2.

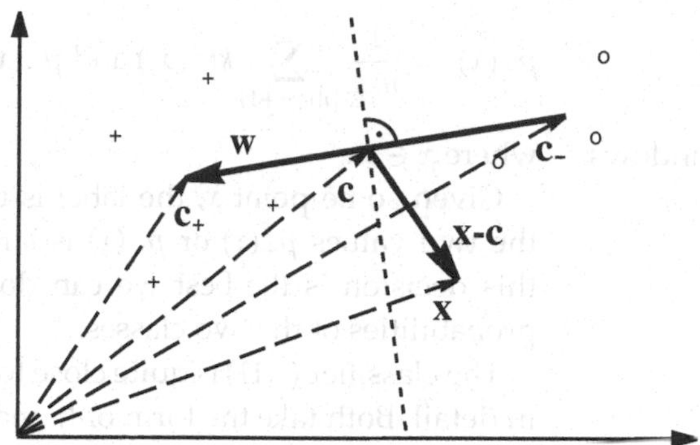

Figure 1.1 A simple geometric classification algorithm: given two classes of points (depicted by 'o' and '+'), compute their means $\mathbf{c}_+, \mathbf{c}_-$ and assign a test pattern $\mathbf{x}$ to the one whose mean is closer. This can be done by looking at the dot product between $\mathbf{x} - \mathbf{c}$ (where $\mathbf{c} = (\mathbf{c}_+ + \mathbf{c}_-)/2$) and $\mathbf{w} := \mathbf{c}_+ - \mathbf{c}_-$, which changes sign as the enclosed angle passes through $\pi/2$. Note that the corresponding decision boundary is a hyperplane (the dotted line) orthogonal to $\mathbf{w}$.

$$\begin{aligned} y &= \operatorname{sgn}\left(\frac{1}{m_+}\sum_{\{i|y_i=+1\}}\langle \mathbf{x}, \mathbf{x}_i\rangle - \frac{1}{m_-}\sum_{\{i|y_i=-1\}}\langle \mathbf{x}, \mathbf{x}_i\rangle + b\right) \\ &= \operatorname{sgn}\left(\frac{1}{m_+}\sum_{\{i|y_i=+1\}} k(x, x_i) - \frac{1}{m_-}\sum_{\{i|y_i=-1\}} k(x, x_i) + b\right). \end{aligned} \tag{1.11}$$

Similarly, the offset becomes

$$b := \frac{1}{2}\left(\frac{1}{m_-^2}\sum_{\{(i,j)|y_i=y_j=-1\}} k(x_i, x_j) - \frac{1}{m_+^2}\sum_{\{(i,j)|y_i=y_j=+1\}} k(x_i, x_j)\right). \tag{1.12}$$

Surprisingly, it turns out that this rather simple-minded approach contains a well-known statistical classification method as a special case. Assume that the class means have the same distance to the origin (hence $b = 0$, cf. (1.10)), and that k can be viewed as a probability density when one of its arguments is fixed. By this we mean that it is positive and has unit integral,[4]

$$\int_{\mathcal{X}} k(x, x')dx = 1 \text{ for all } x' \in \mathcal{X}. \tag{1.13}$$

In this case, (1.11) takes the form of the so-called Bayes classifier separating the two classes, subject to the assumption that the two classes of patterns were generated by sampling from two probability distributions that are correctly estimated by the

4. In order to state this assumption, we have to require that we can define an integral on $\mathcal{X}$.

Parzen windows estimators of the two class densities,

$$p_+(x) := \frac{1}{m_+} \sum_{\{i|y_i=+1\}} k(x, x_i) \text{ and } p_-(x) := \frac{1}{m_-} \sum_{\{i|y_i=-1\}} k(x, x_i), \tag{1.14}$$

Parzen Windows

where $x \in \mathcal{X}$.

Given some point x, the label is then simply computed by checking which of the two values $p_+(x)$ or $p_-(x)$ is larger, which leads directly to (1.11). Note that this decision is the best we can do if we have no prior information about the probabilities of the two classes.

The classifier (1.11) is quite close to the type of classifier that this book deals with in detail. Both take the form of kernel expansions on the input domain,

$$y = \operatorname{sgn}\left(\sum_{i=1}^{m} \alpha_i k(x, x_i) + b\right). \tag{1.15}$$

In both cases, the expansions correspond to a separating hyperplane in a feature space. In this sense, the α_i can be considered a *dual representation* of the hyperplane's normal vector [223]. Both classifiers are example-based in the sense that the kernels are centered on the training patterns; that is, one of the two arguments of the kernel is always a training pattern. A test point is classified by comparing it to all the training points that appear in (1.15) with a nonzero weight.

More sophisticated classification techniques, to be discussed in the remainder of the book, deviate from (1.11) mainly in the selection of the patterns on which the kernels are centered and in the choice of weights α_i that are placed on the individual kernels in the decision function. It will no longer be the case that *all* training patterns appear in the kernel expansion, and the weights of the kernels in the expansion will no longer be uniform within the classes — recall that in the current example, cf. (1.11), the weights are either $(1/m_+)$ or $(-1/m_-)$, depending on the class to which the pattern belongs.

In the feature space representation, this statement corresponds to saying that we will study normal vectors $\mathbf{w}$ of decision hyperplanes that can be represented as general linear combinations (i.e., with non-uniform coefficients) of the training patterns. For instance, we might want to remove the influence of patterns that are very far away from the decision boundary, either since we expect that they will not improve the generalization error of the decision function, or since we would like to reduce the computational cost of evaluating the decision function (cf. (1.11)). The hyperplane will then only depend on a subset of training patterns called *Support Vectors*.

1.3 Some Insights From Statistical Learning Theory

With the above example in mind, let us now consider the problem of pattern recognition in a slightly more formal setting [559, 152, 186]. This will allow us to indicate the factors affecting the design of "better" algorithms. Rather than just

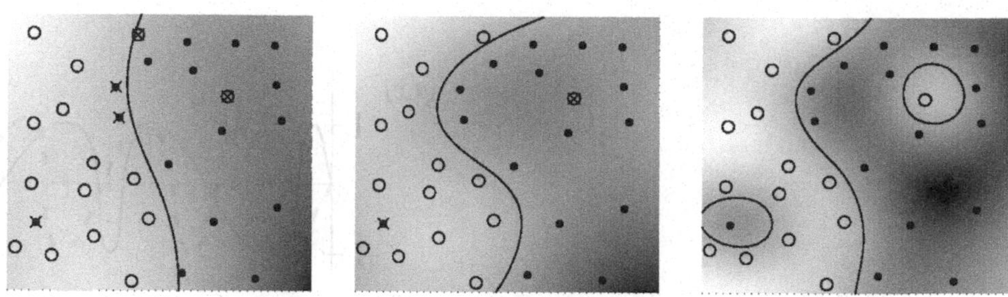

Figure 1.2 2D toy example of binary classification, solved using three models (the decision boundaries are shown). The models vary in complexity, ranging from a simple one *(left)*, which misclassifies a large number of points, to a complex one *(right)*, which "trusts" each point and comes up with solution that is consistent with all training points (but may not work well on new points). As an aside: the plots were generated using the so-called soft-margin SVM to be explained in Chapter 7; cf. also Figure 7.10.

providing tools to come up with new algorithms, we also want to provide some insight in how to do it in a promising way.

In two-class pattern recognition, we seek to infer a function

$$f : \mathcal{X} \rightarrow \{\pm 1\} \tag{1.16}$$

from input-output training data (1.1). The training data are sometimes also called the *sample*.

Figure 1.2 shows a simple 2D toy example of a pattern recognition problem. The task is to separate the solid dots from the circles by finding a function which takes the value 1 on the dots and -1 on the circles. Note that instead of plotting this function, we may plot the boundaries where it switches between 1 and -1. In the rightmost plot, we see a classification function which correctly separates all training points. From this picture, however, it is unclear whether the same would hold true for *test* points which stem from the same underlying regularity. For instance, what should happen to a test point which lies close to one of the two "outliers," sitting amidst points of the opposite class? Maybe the outliers should not be allowed to claim their own custom-made regions of the decision function. To avoid this, we could try to go for a simpler model which disregards these points. The leftmost picture shows an almost linear separation of the classes. This separation, however, not only misclassifies the above two outliers, but also a number of "easy" points which are so close to the decision boundary that the classifier really should be able to get them right. Finally, the central picture represents a compromise, by using a model with an intermediate complexity, which gets most points right, without putting too much trust in any individual point.

The goal of statistical learning theory is to place these intuitive arguments in a mathematical framework. To this end, it studies mathematical properties of learning machines. These properties are usually properties of the function class

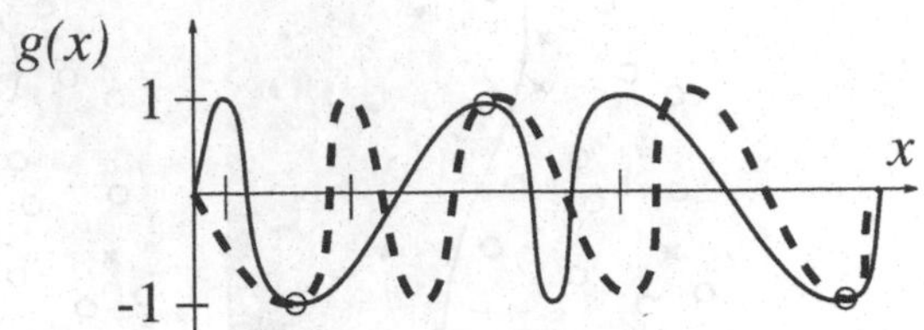

Figure 1.3 A 1D classification problem, with a training set of three points (marked by circles), and three test inputs (marked on the x-axis). Classification is performed by thresholding real-valued functions $g(x)$ according to $\text{sgn}(f(x))$. Note that *both* functions (dotted line, and solid line) perfectly explain the training data, but they give opposite predictions on the test inputs. Lacking any further information, the training data alone give us no means to tell which of the two functions is to be preferred.

that the learning machine can implement.

IID Data

We assume that the data are generated independently from some unknown (but fixed) probability distribution $\text{P}(x, y)$.[5] This is a standard assumption in learning theory; data generated this way is commonly referred to as *iid* (independent and identically distributed). Our goal is to find a function f that will correctly classify unseen examples (x, y), so that $f(x) = y$ for examples (x, y) that are also generated from $\text{P}(x, y)$.[6] Correctness of the classification is measured by means of the *zero-one*

Loss Function

loss function $c(x, y, f(x)) := \frac{1}{2}|f(x) - y|$. Note that the loss is 0 if (x, y) is classified correctly, and 1 otherwise.

Test Data

If we put no restriction on the set of functions from which we choose our estimated f, however, then even a function that does very well on the training data, e.g., by satisfying $f(x_i) = y_i$ for all $i = 1, \ldots, m$, might not generalize well to unseen examples. To see this, note that for each function f and any test set $(\bar{x}_1, \bar{y}_1), \ldots, (\bar{x}_{\bar{m}}, \bar{y}_{\bar{m}}) \in \mathcal{X} \times \{\pm 1\}$, satisfying $\{\bar{x}_1, \ldots, \bar{x}_{\bar{m}}\} \cap \{x_1, \ldots, x_m\} = \emptyset$, there exists another function f^* such that $f^*(x_i) = f(x_i)$ for all $i = 1, \ldots, m$, yet $f^*(\bar{x}_i) \neq f(\bar{x}_i)$ for all $i = 1, \ldots, \bar{m}$ (cf. Figure 1.3). As we are only given the training data, we have no means of selecting which of the two functions (and hence which of the two different sets of test label predictions) is preferable. We conclude that minimizing

Empirical Risk

only the *(average) training error* (or *empirical risk*),

$$R_{\text{emp}}[f] = \frac{1}{m} \sum_{i=1}^{m} \frac{1}{2} |f(x_i) - y_i|, \tag{1.17}$$

Risk

does not imply a small *test error* (called *risk*), averaged over test examples drawn from the underlying distribution $\text{P}(x, y)$,

5. For a definition of a probability distribution, see Section B.1.1.
6. We mostly use the term *example* to denote a pair consisting of a training pattern x and the corresponding target y.

$$R[f] = \int \frac{1}{2}|f(x) - y| \, d\mathrm{P}(x, y). \tag{1.18}$$

The risk can be defined for any loss function, provided the integral exists. For the present zero-one loss function, the risk equals the probability of misclassification.[7]

Statistical learning theory (Chapter 5, [570, 559, 561, 136, 562, 14]), or VC (Vapnik-Chervonenkis) theory, shows that it is imperative to restrict the set of functions from which f is chosen to one that has a *capacity* suitable for the amount of available training data. VC theory provides *bounds* on the test error. The minimization of these bounds, which depend on both the empirical risk and the capacity of the function class, leads to the principle of *structural risk minimization* [559].

Capacity

VC dimension

The best-known capacity concept of VC theory is the *VC dimension*, defined as follows: each function of the class separates the patterns in a certain way and thus induces a certain labelling of the patterns. Since the labels are in $\{\pm 1\}$, there are at most 2^m different labellings for m patterns. A very rich function class might be able to realize all 2^m separations, in which case it is said to *shatter* the m points. However, a given class of functions might not be sufficiently righ to shatter the m points. The VC dimension is defined as the largest m such that there exists a set of m points which the class can shatter, and ∞ if no such m exists. It can be thought of as a one-number summary of a learning machine's capacity (for an example, see Figure 1.4). As such, it is necessarily somewhat crude. More accurate capacity measures are the *annealed VC entropy* or the *growth function*. These are usually considered to be harder to evaluate, but they play a fundamental role in the conceptual part of VC theory. Another interesting capacity measure, which can be thought of as a scale-sensitive version of the VC dimension, is the *fat shattering dimension* [286, 6]. For further details, cf. Chapters 5 and 12.

Shattering

VC Bound

Whilst it will be difficult for the non-expert to appreciate the results of VC theory in this chapter, we will nevertheless briefly describe an example of a VC bound:

---

7. The risk based approach to machine learning has its roots in statistical decision theory [582, 166, 43]. In that context, $f(x)$ is thought of as an *action*, and the loss function measures the loss incurred by taking action $f(x)$ upon observing x when the true output (state of nature) is y.

Like many fields of statistics, decision theory comes in two flavors. The present approach is a *frequentist* one. It considers the risk as a function of the distribution P and the decision function f. The *Bayesian* approach considers parametrized families P_Θ to model the distribution. Given a prior over Θ (which need not in general be a finite-dimensional vector), the *Bayes risk* of a decision function f is the *expected* frequentist risk, where the expectation is taken over the prior. Minimizing the Bayes risk (over decision functions) then leads to a *Bayes decision function*. Bayesians thus act as if the parameter Θ were actually a random variable whose distribution is known. Frequentists, who do not make this (somewhat bold) assumption, have to resort to other strategies for picking a decision function. Examples thereof are considerations like *invariance* and *unbiasedness*, both used to restrict the class of decision rules, and the *minimax* principle. A decision function is said to be minimax if it minimizes (over all decision functions) the maximal (over all distributions) risk. For a discussion of the relationship of these issues to VC theory, see Problem 5.9.

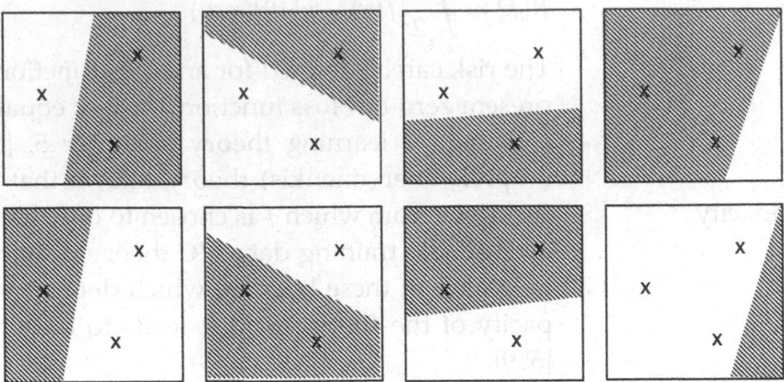

Figure 1.4 A simple VC dimension example. There are $2^3 = 8$ ways of assigning 3 points to two classes. For the displayed points in $\mathbb{R}^2$, all 8 possibilities can be realized using separating hyperplanes, in other words, the function class can shatter 3 points. This would not work if we were given 4 points, no matter how we placed them. Therefore, the VC dimension of the class of separating hyperplanes in $\mathbb{R}^2$ is 3.

if $h < m$ is the VC dimension of the class of functions that the learning machine can implement, then for all functions of that class, independent of the underlying distribution P generating the data, with a probability of at least $1 - \delta$ over the drawing of the training sample,[8] the bound

$$R[f] \leq R_{\mathrm{emp}}[f] + \phi(h, m, \delta) \tag{1.19}$$

holds, where the *confidence term* (or *capacity term*) ϕ is defined as

$$\phi(h, m, \delta) = \sqrt{\frac{1}{m}\left(h\left(\ln\frac{2m}{h} + 1\right) + \ln\frac{4}{\delta}\right)}. \tag{1.20}$$

The bound (1.19) merits further explanation. Suppose we wanted to learn a "dependency" where patterns and labels are statistically independent, $\mathrm{P}(x, y) = \mathrm{P}(x)\mathrm{P}(y)$. In that case, the pattern x contains no information about the label y. If, moreover, the two classes $+1$ and -1 are equally likely, there is no way of making a good guess about the label of a test pattern.

Nevertheless, given a training set of finite size, we can always come up with a learning machine which achieves zero training error (provided we have no examples contradicting each other, i.e., whenever two patterns are identical, then they must come with the same label). To reproduce the random labellings by correctly separating all training examples, however, this machine will necessarily require a large VC dimension h. Therefore, the confidence term (1.20), which increases monotonically with h, will be large, and the bound (1.19) will show

8. Recall that each training example is generated from $P(x, y)$, and thus the training data are subject to randomness.

that the small training error does not guarantee a small test error. This illustrates how the bound can apply independent of assumptions about the underlying distribution $P(x, y)$: it always holds (provided that $h < m$), but it does not always make a nontrivial prediction. In order to get nontrivial predictions from (1.19), the function class must be *restricted* such that its capacity (e.g., VC dimension) is small enough (in relation to the available amount of data). At the same time, the class should be large enough to provide functions that are able to model the dependencies hidden in $P(x, y)$. The choice of the set of functions is thus crucial for learning from data. In the next section, we take a closer look at a class of functions which is particularly interesting for pattern recognition problems.

1.4 Hyperplane Classifiers

In the present section, we shall describe a hyperplane learning algorithm that can be performed in a dot product space (such as the feature space that we introduced earlier). As described in the previous section, to design learning algorithms whose statistical effectiveness can be controlled, one needs to come up with a class of functions whose capacity can be computed. Vapnik et al. [573, 566, 570] considered the class of hyperplanes in some dot product space $\mathcal{H}$,

$$\langle \mathbf{w}, \mathbf{x} \rangle + b = 0 \text{ where } \mathbf{w} \in \mathcal{H}, b \in \mathbb{R}, \tag{1.21}$$

corresponding to decision functions

$$f(\mathbf{x}) = \operatorname{sgn}(\langle \mathbf{w}, \mathbf{x} \rangle + b), \tag{1.22}$$

and proposed a learning algorithm for problems which are separable by hyperplanes (sometimes said to be *linearly separable*), termed the *Generalized Portrait*, for constructing f from empirical data. It is based on two facts. First (see Chapter 7), among all hyperplanes separating the data, there exists a unique *optimal hyperplane*, distinguished by the maximum margin of separation between any training point and the hyperplane. It is the solution of

Optimal Hyperplane

$$\underset{\mathbf{w}\in\mathcal{H}, b\in\mathbb{R}}{\text{maximize}} \ \min\{\|\mathbf{x} - \mathbf{x}_i\| \,|\, \mathbf{x} \in \mathcal{H}, \langle \mathbf{w}, \mathbf{x} \rangle + b = 0, i = 1, \ldots, m\}. \tag{1.23}$$

Second (see Chapter 5), the capacity (as discussed in Section 1.3) of the class of separating hyperplanes decreases with increasing margin. Hence there are theoretical arguments supporting the good generalization performance of the optimal hyperplane, cf. Chapters 5, 7, 12. In addition, it is *computationally* attractive, since we will show below that it can be constructed by solving a quadratic programming problem for which efficient algorithms exist (see Chapters 6 and 10).

Note that the form of the decision function (1.22) is quite similar to our earlier example (1.9). The ways in which the classifiers are trained, however, are different. In the earlier example, the normal vector of the hyperplane was trivially computed from the class means as $\mathbf{w} = \mathbf{c}_+ - \mathbf{c}_-$.

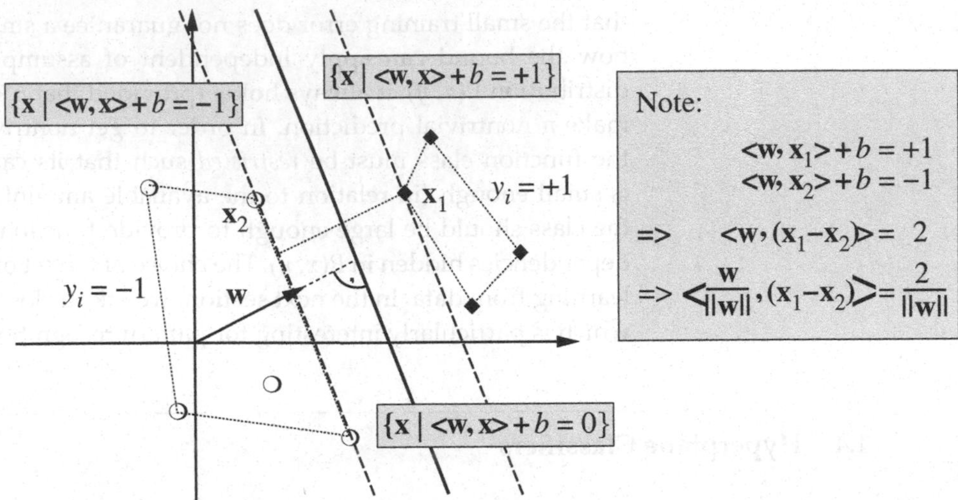

Figure 1.5 A binary classification toy problem: separate balls from diamonds. The *optimal hyperplane* (1.23) is shown as a solid line. The problem being separable, there exists a weight vector $\mathbf{w}$ and a threshold b such that $y_i(\langle \mathbf{w}, \mathbf{x}_i \rangle + b) > 0$ ($i = 1, \ldots, m$). Rescaling $\mathbf{w}$ and b such that the point(s) closest to the hyperplane satisfy $|\langle \mathbf{w}, \mathbf{x}_i \rangle + b| = 1$, we obtain a *canonical* form $(\mathbf{w}, b)$ of the hyperplane, satisfying $y_i(\langle \mathbf{w}, \mathbf{x}_i \rangle + b) \geq 1$. Note that in this case, the *margin* (the distance of the closest point to the hyperplane) equals $1/\|\mathbf{w}\|$. This can be seen by considering two points $\mathbf{x}_1, \mathbf{x}_2$ on opposite sides of the margin, that is, $\langle \mathbf{w}, \mathbf{x}_1 \rangle + b = 1$, $\langle \mathbf{w}, \mathbf{x}_2 \rangle + b = -1$, and projecting them onto the hyperplane normal vector $\mathbf{w}/\|\mathbf{w}\|$.

In the present case, we need to do some additional work to find the normal vector that leads to the largest margin. To construct the optimal hyperplane, we have to solve

$$\underset{\mathbf{w} \in \mathcal{H}, b \in \mathbb{R}}{\text{minimize}} \quad \tau(\mathbf{w}) = \frac{1}{2}\|\mathbf{w}\|^2 \tag{1.24}$$

$$\text{subject to} \quad y_i(\langle \mathbf{w}, \mathbf{x}_i \rangle + b) \geq 1 \text{ for all } i = 1, \ldots, m. \tag{1.25}$$

Note that the constraints (1.25) ensure that $f(\mathbf{x}_i)$ will be $+1$ for $y_i = +1$, and -1 for $y_i = -1$. Now one might argue that for this to be the case, we don't actually need the "≥ 1" on the right hand side of (1.25). However, without it, it would not be meaningful to minimize the length of $\mathbf{w}$: to see this, imagine we wrote "> 0" instead of "≥ 1." Now assume that the solution is $(\mathbf{w}, b)$. Let us rescale this solution by multiplication with some $0 < \lambda < 1$. Since $\lambda > 0$, the constraints are still satisfied. Since $\lambda < 1$, however, the length of $\mathbf{w}$ has decreased. Hence $(\mathbf{w}, b)$ cannot be the minimizer of $\tau(\mathbf{w})$.

The "≥ 1" on the right hand side of the constraints effectively fixes the scaling of $\mathbf{w}$. In fact, any other positive number would do.

Let us now try to get an intuition for why we should be minimizing the length of $\mathbf{w}$, as in (1.24). If $\|\mathbf{w}\|$ were 1, then the left hand side of (1.25) would equal the distance from $\mathbf{x}_i$ to the hyperplane (cf. (1.23)). In general, we have to divide

$y_i(\langle \mathbf{w}, \mathbf{x}_i \rangle + b)$ by $\|\mathbf{w}\|$ to transform it into this distance. Hence, if we can satisfy (1.25) for all $i = 1, \ldots, m$ with an $\mathbf{w}$ of minimal length, then the overall margin will be maximized.

A more detailed explanation of why this leads to the maximum margin hyperplane will be given in Chapter 7. A short summary of the argument is also given in Figure 1.5.

The function τ in (1.24) is called the *objective function*, while (1.25) are called *inequality constraints*. Together, they form a so-called *constrained optimization problem*. Problems of this kind are dealt with by introducing *Lagrange multipliers* $\alpha_i \geq 0$ and a *Lagrangian*[9]

Lagrangian

$$L(\mathbf{w}, b, \boldsymbol{\alpha}) = \frac{1}{2}\|\mathbf{w}\|^2 - \sum_{i=1}^{m} \alpha_i \left(y_i(\langle \mathbf{x}_i, \mathbf{w} \rangle + b) - 1 \right). \tag{1.26}$$

The Lagrangian L has to be minimized with respect to the *primal variables* $\mathbf{w}$ and b and maximized with respect to the *dual variables* α_i (in other words, a saddle point has to be found). Note that the constraint has been incorporated into the second term of the Lagrangian; it is not necessary to enforce it explicitly.

Let us try to get some intuition for this way of dealing with constrained optimization problems. If a constraint (1.25) is violated, then $y_i(\langle \mathbf{w}, \mathbf{x}_i \rangle + b) - 1 < 0$, in which case L can be increased by increasing the corresponding α_i. At the same time, $\mathbf{w}$ and b will have to change such that L decreases. To prevent $\alpha_i \left(y_i(\langle \mathbf{w}, \mathbf{x}_i \rangle + b) - 1 \right)$ from becoming an arbitrarily large negative number, the change in $\mathbf{w}$ and b will ensure that, provided the problem is separable, the constraint will eventually be satisfied. Similarly, one can understand that for all constraints which are not precisely met as equalities (that is, for which $y_i(\langle \mathbf{w}, \mathbf{x}_i \rangle + b) - 1 > 0$), the corresponding α_i must be 0: this is the value of α_i that maximizes L. The latter is the statement of the Karush-Kuhn-Tucker (KKT) complementarity conditions of optimization theory (Chapter 6).

KKT Conditions

The statement that at the saddle point, the derivatives of L with respect to the primal variables must vanish,

$$\frac{\partial}{\partial b} L(\mathbf{w}, b, \boldsymbol{\alpha}) = 0 \text{ and } \frac{\partial}{\partial \mathbf{w}} L(\mathbf{w}, b, \boldsymbol{\alpha}) = 0, \tag{1.27}$$

leads to

$$\sum_{i=1}^{m} \alpha_i y_i = 0 \tag{1.28}$$

and

$$\mathbf{w} = \sum_{i=1}^{m} \alpha_i y_i \mathbf{x}_i. \tag{1.29}$$

9. Henceforth, we use boldface Greek letters as a shorthand for corresponding vectors $\boldsymbol{\alpha} = (\alpha_1, \ldots, \alpha_m)$.

The solution vector thus has an expansion (1.29) in terms of a subset of the training patterns, namely those patterns with non-zero α_i, called *Support Vectors (SVs)* (cf. (1.15) in the initial example). By the KKT conditions,

Support Vector

$$\alpha_i \left[y_i \left(\langle \mathbf{x}_i, \mathbf{w}\rangle + b\right) - 1\right] = 0 \text{ for all } i = 1, \ldots, m, \tag{1.30}$$

the SVs lie on the margin (cf. Figure 1.5). All remaining training examples $(\mathbf{x}_j, y_j)$ are irrelevant: their constraint $y_j(\langle \mathbf{w}, \mathbf{x}_j\rangle + b) \geq 1$ (cf. (1.25)) could just as well be left out, and they do not appear in the expansion (1.29). This nicely captures our intuition of the problem: as the hyperplane (cf. Figure 1.5) is completely determined by the patterns closest to it, the solution should not depend on the other examples.

By substituting (1.28) and (1.29) into the Lagrangian (1.26), one eliminates the primal variables $\mathbf{w}$ and b, arriving at the so-called *dual optimization problem*, which is the problem that one usually solves in practice:

Dual Problem

$$\underset{\boldsymbol{\alpha}\in\mathbb{R}^m}{\text{maximize}} \quad W(\boldsymbol{\alpha}) = \sum_{i=1}^{m} \alpha_i - \frac{1}{2}\sum_{i,j=1}^{m} \alpha_i\alpha_j y_i y_j \langle \mathbf{x}_i, \mathbf{x}_j\rangle \tag{1.31}$$

$$\text{subject to} \quad \alpha_i \geq 0 \text{ for all } i = 1, \ldots, m \text{ and } \sum_{i=1}^{m} \alpha_i y_i = 0. \tag{1.32}$$

Decision Function

Using (1.29), the hyperplane decision function (1.22) can thus be written as

$$f(\mathbf{x}) = \operatorname{sgn}\left(\sum_{i=1}^{m} y_i\alpha_i \langle \mathbf{x}, \mathbf{x}_i\rangle + b\right), \tag{1.33}$$

where b is computed by exploiting (1.30) (for details, cf. Chapter 7).

The structure of the optimization problem closely resembles those that typically arise in Lagrange's formulation of mechanics (e.g., [206]). In the latter class of problem, it is also often the case that only a subset of constraints become active. For instance, if we keep a ball in a box, then it will typically roll into one of the corners. The constraints corresponding to the walls which are not touched by the ball are irrelevant, and those walls could just as well be removed.

Mechanical Analogy

Seen in this light, it is not too surprising that it is possible to give a mechanical interpretation of optimal margin hyperplanes [87]: If we assume that each SV $\mathbf{x}_i$ exerts a perpendicular force of size α_i and direction $y_j \cdot \mathbf{w}/\|\mathbf{w}\|$ on a solid plane sheet lying along the hyperplane, then the solution satisfies the requirements for mechanical stability. The constraint (1.28) states that the forces on the sheet sum to zero, and (1.29) implies that the torques also sum to zero, via $\sum_i \mathbf{x}_i \times y_i\alpha_i\mathbf{w}/\|\mathbf{w}\| = \mathbf{w} \times \mathbf{w}/\|\mathbf{w}\| = 0$.[10] This mechanical analogy illustrates the physical meaning of the term *Support* Vector.

10. Here, the $\times$ denotes the *vector* (or *cross*) *product*, satisfying $\mathbf{v} \times \mathbf{v} = 0$ for all $\mathbf{v} \in \mathcal{H}$.

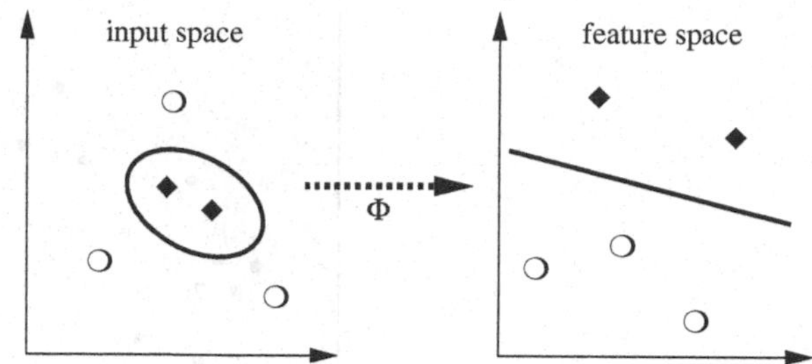

Figure 1.6 The idea of SVMs: map the training data into a higher-dimensional feature space via Φ, and construct a separating hyperplane with maximum margin there. This yields a nonlinear decision boundary in input space. By the use of a kernel function (1.2), it is possible to compute the separating hyperplane without explicitly carrying out the map into the feature space.

1.5 Support Vector Classification

We now have all the tools to describe SVMs (Figure 1.6). Everything in the last section was formulated in a dot product space. We think of this space as the feature space $\mathcal{H}$ of Section 1.1. To express the formulas in terms of the input patterns in $\mathcal{X}$, we thus need to employ (1.6), which expresses the dot product of bold face feature vectors $\mathbf{x}, \mathbf{x}'$ in terms of the kernel k evaluated on input patterns x, x',

$$k(x, x') = \langle \mathbf{x}, \mathbf{x}' \rangle . \tag{1.34}$$

This substitution, which is sometimes referred to as the *kernel trick*, was used by Boser, Guyon, and Vapnik [62] to extend the Generalized Portrait hyperplane classifier to nonlinear Support Vector Machines. Aizerman, Braverman, and Rozonoér [4] called $\mathcal{H}$ the *linearization space*, and used it in the context of the potential function classification method to express the dot product between elements of $\mathcal{H}$ in terms of elements of the input space.

The kernel trick can be applied since all feature vectors only occurred in dot products (see (1.31) and (1.33)). The weight vector (cf. (1.29)) then becomes an expansion in feature space, and therefore will typically no longer correspond to the Φ-image of a single input space vector (cf. Chapter 18). We obtain decision functions of the form (cf. (1.33))

Decision Function

$$f(x) = \operatorname{sgn}\left(\sum_{i=1}^{m} y_i \alpha_i \langle \Phi(x), \Phi(x_i) \rangle + b\right) = \operatorname{sgn}\left(\sum_{i=1}^{m} y_i \alpha_i k(x, x_i) + b\right), \tag{1.35}$$

and the following quadratic program (cf. (1.31)):

$$\underset{\alpha \in \mathbb{R}^m}{\text{maximize}} \quad W(\alpha) = \sum_{i=1}^{m} \alpha_i - \frac{1}{2} \sum_{i,j=1}^{m} \alpha_i \alpha_j y_i y_j k(x_i, x_j) \tag{1.36}$$

$$\text{subject to } \alpha_i \geq 0 \text{ for all } i = 1, \ldots, m, \text{ and } \sum_{i=1}^{m} \alpha_i y_i = 0. \tag{1.37}$$

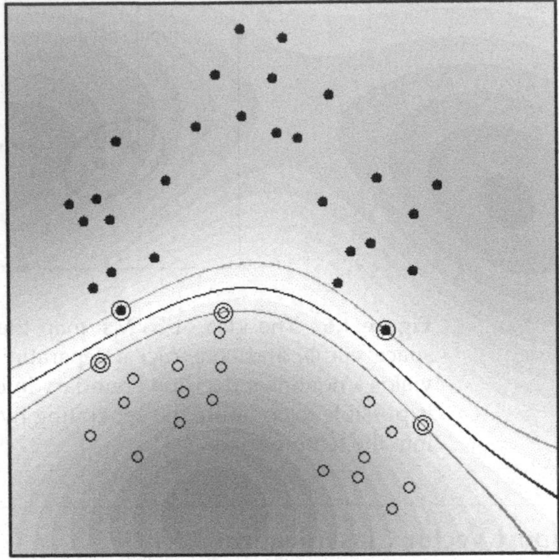

Figure 1.7 Example of an SV classifier found using a radial basis function kernel $k(x, x') = \exp(-\|x - x'\|^2)$ (here, the input space is $\mathcal{X} = [-1, 1]^2$). Circles and disks are two classes of training examples; the middle line is the decision surface; the outer lines precisely meet the constraint (1.25). Note that the SVs found by the algorithm (marked by extra circles) are not centers of clusters, but examples which are critical for the given classification task. Gray values code $|\sum_{i=1}^{m} y_i \alpha_i k(x, x_i) + b|$, the modulus of the argument of the decision function (1.35). The top and the bottom lines indicate places where it takes the value 1 (from [471]).

Figure 1.7 shows an example of this approach, using a Gaussian radial basis function kernel. We will later study the different possibilities for the kernel function in detail (Chapters 2 and 13).

Soft Margin Hyperplane

In practice, a separating hyperplane may not exist, e.g., if a high noise level causes a large overlap of the classes. To allow for the possibility of examples violating (1.25), one introduces slack variables [111, 561, 481]

$$\xi_i \geq 0 \text{ for all } i = 1, \ldots, m, \tag{1.38}$$

in order to relax the constraints (1.25) to

$$y_i(\langle \mathbf{w}, \mathbf{x}_i \rangle + b) \geq 1 - \xi_i \text{ for all } i = 1, \ldots, m. \tag{1.39}$$

A classifier that generalizes well is then found by controlling both the classifier capacity (via $\|\mathbf{w}\|$) and the sum of the slacks $\sum_i \xi_i$. The latter can be shown to provide an upper bound on the number of training errors.

One possible realization of such a *soft margin* classifier is obtained by minimizing the objective function

$$\tau(\mathbf{w}, \boldsymbol{\xi}) = \frac{1}{2}\|\mathbf{w}\|^2 + C\sum_{i=1}^{m} \xi_i \tag{1.40}$$

subject to the constraints (1.38) and (1.39), where the constant $C > 0$ determines the trade-off between margin maximization and training error minimization.[11] Incorporating a kernel, and rewriting it in terms of Lagrange multipliers, this again leads to the problem of maximizing (1.36), subject to the constraints

$$0 \leq \alpha_i \leq C \text{ for all } i = 1, \ldots, m, \text{ and } \sum_{i=1}^{m} \alpha_i y_i = 0. \tag{1.41}$$

The only difference from the separable case is the upper bound C on the Lagrange multipliers α_i. This way, the influence of the individual patterns (which could be outliers) gets limited. As above, the solution takes the form (1.35). The threshold b can be computed by exploiting the fact that for all SVs x_i with $\alpha_i < C$, the slack variable ξ_i is zero (this again follows from the KKT conditions), and hence

$$\sum_{j=1}^{m} \alpha_j y_j k(x_i, x_j) + b = y_i. \tag{1.42}$$

Geometrically speaking, choosing b amounts to shifting the hyperplane, and (1.42) states that we have to shift the hyperplane such that the SVs with zero slack variables lie on the ± 1 lines of Figure 1.5.

Another possible realization of a soft margin variant of the optimal hyperplane uses the more natural ν-parametrization. In it, the parameter C is replaced by a parameter $\nu \in (0, 1]$ which can be shown to provide lower and upper bounds for the fraction of examples that will be SVs and those that will have non-zero slack variables, respectively. It uses a primal objective function with the error term $(\frac{1}{\nu m} \sum_i \xi_i) - \rho$ instead of $C \sum_i \xi_i$ (cf. (1.40)), and separation constraints that involve a margin parameter ρ,

$$y_i(\langle \mathbf{w}, \mathbf{x}_i \rangle + b) \geq \rho - \xi_i \text{ for all } i = 1, \ldots, m, \tag{1.43}$$

which itself is a variable of the optimization problem. The dual can be shown to consist in maximizing the quadratic part of (1.36), subject to $0 \leq \alpha_i \leq 1/(\nu m)$, $\sum_i \alpha_i y_i = 0$ and the additional constraint $\sum_i \alpha_i = 1$. We shall return to these methods in more detail in Section 7.5.

1.6 Support Vector Regression

Let us turn to a problem slightly more general than pattern recognition. Rather than dealing with outputs $y \in \{\pm 1\}$, *regression estimation* is concerned with estimating real-valued functions.

To generalize the SV algorithm to the regression case, an analog of the soft margin is constructed in the space of the target values y (note that we now have

11. It is sometimes convenient to scale the sum in (1.40) by C/m rather than C, as done in Chapter 7 below.

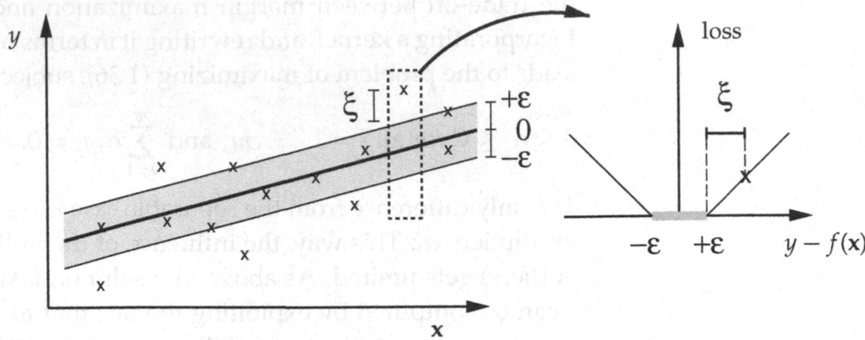

Figure 1.8 In SV regression, a tube with radius ε is fitted to the data. The trade-off between model complexity and points lying outside of the tube (with positive slack variables ξ) is determined by minimizing (1.47).

ε-Insensitive Loss

$y \in \mathbb{R}$) by using Vapnik's *ε-insensitive loss function* [561] (Figure 1.8, see Chapters 3 and 9). This quantifies the loss incurred by predicting $f(\mathbf{x})$ instead of y as

$$c(x, y, f(x)) := |y - f(\mathbf{x})|_\varepsilon := \max\{0, |y - f(\mathbf{x})| - \varepsilon\}. \tag{1.44}$$

To estimate a linear regression

$$f(\mathbf{x}) = \langle \mathbf{w}, \mathbf{x} \rangle + b, \tag{1.45}$$

one minimizes

$$\frac{1}{2}\|\mathbf{w}\|^2 + C\sum_{i=1}^{m} |y_i - f(\mathbf{x}_i)|_\varepsilon. \tag{1.46}$$

Note that the term $\|\mathbf{w}\|^2$ is the same as in pattern recognition (cf. (1.40)); for further details, cf. Chapter 9.

We can transform this into a constrained optimization problem by introducing slack variables, akin to the soft margin case. In the present case, we need two types of slack variable for the two cases $f(\mathbf{x}_i) - y_i > \varepsilon$ and $y_i - f(\mathbf{x}_i) > \varepsilon$. We denote them by $\boldsymbol{\xi}$ and $\boldsymbol{\xi}^*$, respectively, and collectively refer to them as $\boldsymbol{\xi}^{(*)}$.

The optimization problem is given by

$$\underset{\mathbf{w}\in\mathcal{H}, \boldsymbol{\xi}^{(*)}\in\mathbb{R}^m, b\in\mathbb{R}}{\text{minimize}} \quad \tau(\mathbf{w}, \boldsymbol{\xi}^{(*)}) = \frac{1}{2}\|\mathbf{w}\|^2 + C\sum_{i=1}^{m}(\xi_i + \xi_i^*) \tag{1.47}$$

$$\text{subject to} \quad f(\mathbf{x}_i) - y_i \le \varepsilon + \xi_i \tag{1.48}$$

$$y_i - f(\mathbf{x}_i) \le \varepsilon + \xi_i^* \tag{1.49}$$

$$\xi_i, \xi_i^* \ge 0 \qquad \text{for all } i = 1, \ldots, m. \tag{1.50}$$

Note that according to (1.48) and (1.49), any error smaller than ε does not require a nonzero ξ_i or ξ_i^* and hence does not enter the objective function (1.47).

Generalization to *kernel*-based regression estimation is carried out in an analogous manner to the case of pattern recognition. Introducing Lagrange multipliers, one arrives at the following optimization problem (for $C, \varepsilon \geq 0$ chosen a priori):

$$\begin{aligned}\underset{\boldsymbol{\alpha},\boldsymbol{\alpha}^*\in\mathbb{R}^m}{\text{maximize}} \quad W(\boldsymbol{\alpha},\boldsymbol{\alpha}^*) &= -\varepsilon\sum_{i=1}^m(\alpha_i^*+\alpha_i)+\sum_{i=1}^m(\alpha_i^*-\alpha_i)y_i \\ &\quad -\frac{1}{2}\sum_{i,j=1}^m(\alpha_i^*-\alpha_i)(\alpha_j^*-\alpha_j)k(x_i,x_j)\end{aligned} \tag{1.51}$$

$$\text{subject to} \quad 0 \leq \alpha_i, \alpha_i^* \leq C \text{ for all } i = 1, \ldots, m, \text{ and } \sum_{i=1}^m(\alpha_i - \alpha_i^*) = 0. \tag{1.52}$$

Regression Function

The regression estimate takes the form

$$f(x) = \sum_{i=1}^m(\alpha_i^* - \alpha_i)k(x_i, x) + b, \tag{1.53}$$

where b is computed using the fact that (1.48) becomes an equality with $\xi_i = 0$ if $0 < \alpha_i < C$, and (1.49) becomes an equality with $\xi_i^* = 0$ if $0 < \alpha_i^* < C$ (for details, see Chapter 9). The solution thus looks quite similar to the pattern recognition case (cf. (1.35) and Figure 1.9).

A number of extensions of this algorithm are possible. From an abstract point of view, we just need some target function which depends on $(\mathbf{w}, \boldsymbol{\xi})$ (cf. (1.47)). There are multiple degrees of freedom for constructing it, including some freedom how to penalize, or regularize. For instance, more general loss functions can be used for $\boldsymbol{\xi}$, leading to problems that can still be solved efficiently ([512, 515], cf. Chapter 9). Moreover, norms other than the 2-norm $\|.\|$ can be used to regularize the solution (see Sections 4.9 and 9.4).

Finally, the algorithm can be modified such that ε need not be specified a priori. Instead, one specifies an upper bound $0 \leq \nu \leq 1$ on the fraction of points allowed to lie outside the tube (asymptotically, the number of SVs) and the corresponding ε is computed automatically. This is achieved by using as primal objective function

ν-SV Regression

$$\frac{1}{2}\|\mathbf{w}\|^2 + C\left(\nu m\varepsilon + \sum_{i=1}^m|y_i - f(\mathbf{x}_i)|_\varepsilon\right) \tag{1.54}$$

instead of (1.46), and treating $\varepsilon \geq 0$ as a parameter over which we minimize. For more detail, cf. Section 9.3.

1.7 Kernel Principal Component Analysis

The kernel method for computing dot products in feature spaces is not restricted to SVMs. Indeed, it has been pointed out that it can be used to develop nonlinear generalizations of any algorithm that can be cast in terms of dot products, such as principal component analysis (PCA) [480].

Principal component analysis is perhaps the most common feature extraction algorithm; for details, see Chapter 14. The term *feature extraction* commonly refers to procedures for extracting (real) numbers from patterns which in some sense represent the crucial information contained in these patterns.

PCA in feature space leads to an algorithm called *kernel PCA*. By solving an eigenvalue problem, the algorithm computes nonlinear feature extraction functions

$$f_n(x) = \sum_{i=1}^{m} \alpha_i^n k(x_i, x), \tag{1.55}$$

where, up to a normalizing constant, the α_i^n are the components of the nth eigenvector of the kernel matrix $K_{ij} := (k(x_i, x_j))$.

In a nutshell, this can be understood as follows. To do PCA in $\mathcal{H}$, we wish to find eigenvectors $\mathbf{v}$ and eigenvalues λ of the so-called *covariance matrix* $\mathbf{C}$ in the feature space, where

$$\mathbf{C} := \frac{1}{m} \sum_{i=1}^{m} \Phi(x_i)\Phi(x_i)^\top. \tag{1.56}$$

Here, $\Phi(x_i)^\top$ denotes the transpose of $\Phi(x_i)$ (see Section B.2.1). In the case when $\mathcal{H}$ is very high dimensional, the computational costs of doing this directly are prohibitive. Fortunately, one can show that all solutions to

$$\mathbf{C}\mathbf{v} = \lambda \mathbf{v} \tag{1.57}$$

with $\lambda \neq 0$ must lie in the span of Φ-images of the training data. Thus, we may expand the solution $\mathbf{v}$ as

$$\mathbf{v} = \sum_{i=1}^{m} \alpha_i \Phi(x_i), \tag{1.58}$$

thereby reducing the problem to that of finding the α_i. It turns out that this leads to a dual eigenvalue problem for the expansion coefficients,

Kernel PCA Eigenvalue Problem

$$m\lambda \boldsymbol{\alpha} = K\boldsymbol{\alpha}, \tag{1.59}$$

where $\boldsymbol{\alpha} = (\alpha_1, \ldots, \alpha_m)^\top$.

Feature Extraction

To extract nonlinear features from a test point x, we compute the dot product between $\Phi(x)$ and the nth normalized eigenvector in feature space,

$$\langle \mathbf{v}^n, \Phi(x) \rangle = \sum_{i=1}^{m} \alpha_i^n k(x_i, x). \tag{1.60}$$

Usually, this will be computationally far less expensive than taking the dot product in the feature space explicitly.

A toy example is given in Chapter 14 (Figure 14.4). As in the case of SVMs, the architecture can be visualized by Figure 1.9.

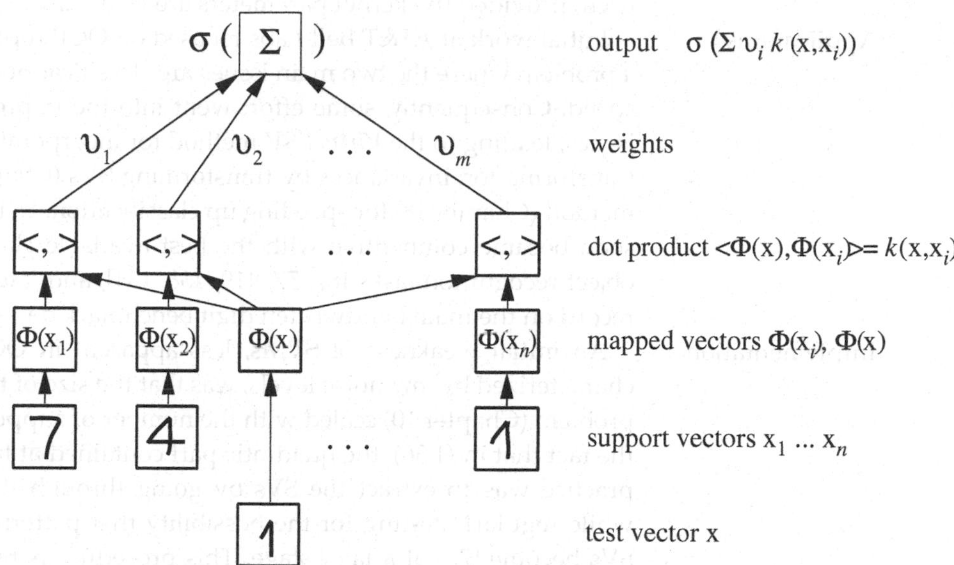

Figure 1.9 Architecture of SVMs and related kernel methods. The input x and the expansion patterns (SVs) x_i (we assume that we are dealing with handwritten digits) are nonlinearly mapped (by Φ) into a feature space $\mathcal{H}$ where dot products are computed. Through the use of the kernel k, these two layers are in practice computed in one step. The results are linearly combined using weights υ_i, found by solving a quadratic program (in pattern recognition, $\upsilon_i = y_i\alpha_i$; in regression estimation, $\upsilon_i = \alpha_i^* - \alpha_i$) or an eigenvalue problem (Kernel PCA). The linear combination is fed into the function σ (in pattern recognition, $\sigma(x) = \mathrm{sgn}\,(x + b)$; in regression estimation, $\sigma(x) = x + b$; in Kernel PCA, $\sigma(x) = x$).

1.8 Empirical Results and Implementations

Examples of Kernels

Having described the basics of SVMs, we now summarize some empirical findings. By the use of kernels, the optimal margin classifier was turned into a high-performance classifier. Surprisingly, it was observed that the polynomial kernel

$$k(x, x') = \langle x, x' \rangle^d, \tag{1.61}$$

the Gaussian

$$k(x, x') = \exp\left(-\frac{\|x - x'\|^2}{2\,\sigma^2}\right), \tag{1.62}$$

and the sigmoid

$$k(x, x') = \tanh\left(\kappa \langle x, x' \rangle + \Theta\right), \tag{1.63}$$

with suitable choices of $d \in \mathbb{N}$ and $\sigma, \kappa, \Theta \in \mathbb{R}$ (here, $\mathcal{X} \subset \mathbb{R}^N$), empirically led to SV classifiers with very similar accuracies and SV sets (Section 7.8.2). In this sense, the SV set seems to characterize (or *compress*) the given task in a manner which to some extent is independent of the type of kernel (that is, the type of classifier) used, provided the kernel parameters are well adjusted.

Applications

Initial work at AT&T Bell Labs focused on OCR (optical character recognition), a problem where the two main issues are classification accuracy and classification speed. Consequently, some effort went into the improvement of SVMs on these issues, leading to the *Virtual SV* method for incorporating prior knowledge about transformation invariances by transforming SVs (Chapter 7), and the *Reduced Set* method (Chapter 18) for speeding up classification. Using these procedures, SVMs soon became competitive with the best available classifiers on OCR and other object recognition tasks [87, 57, 419, 438, 134], and later even achieved the world record on the main handwritten digit benchmark dataset [134].

Implementation

An initial weakness of SVMs, less apparent in OCR applications which are characterized by low noise levels, was that the size of the quadratic programming problem (Chapter 10) scaled with the number of support vectors. This was due to the fact that in (1.36), the quadratic part contained at least all SVs — the common practice was to extract the SVs by going through the training data in chunks while regularly testing for the possibility that patterns initially not identified as SVs become SVs at a later stage. This procedure is referred to as *chunking*; note that without chunking, the size of the matrix in the quadratic part of the objective function would be $m \times m$, where m is the number of all training examples.

What happens if we have a high-noise problem? In this case, many of the slack variables ξ_i become nonzero, and all the corresponding examples become SVs. For this case, decomposition algorithms were proposed [398, 409], based on the observation that not only can we leave out the non-SV examples (the x_i with $\alpha_i = 0$) from the current chunk, but also some of the SVs, especially those that hit the upper boundary ($\alpha_i = C$). The chunks are usually dealt with using quadratic optimizers. Among the optimizers used for SVMs are LOQO [555], MINOS [380], and variants of conjugate gradient descent, such as the optimizers of Bottou [459] and Burges [85]. Several public domain SV packages and optimizers are listed on the web page http://www.kernel-machines.org. For more details on implementations, see Chapter 10.

Once the SV algorithm had been generalized to regression, researchers started applying it to various problems of estimating real-valued functions. Very good results were obtained on the Boston housing benchmark [529], and on problems of times series prediction (see [376, 371, 351]). Moreover, the SV method was applied to the solution of inverse function estimation problems ([572]; cf. [563, 589]). For overviews, the interested reader is referred to [85, 472, 504, 125].

I CONCEPTS AND TOOLS

The generic can be more intense than the concrete.

J. L. Borges[1]

We now embark on a more systematic presentation of the concepts and tools underlying Support Vector Machines and other kernel methods.

In machine learning problems, we try to discover structure in data. For instance, in pattern recognition and regression estimation, we are given a training set $(x_1, y_1), \ldots, (x_m, y_m) \in \mathcal{X} \times \mathcal{Y}$, and attempt to predict the outputs y for previously unseen inputs x. This is only possible if we have some measure that tells us how (x, y) is related to the training set. Informally, we want similar inputs to lead to similar outputs.[2] To formalize this, we have to state what we mean by *similar*.

A particularly simple yet surprisingly useful notion of similarity of *inputs* — the one we will use throughout this book — derives from embedding the data into a Euclidean feature space and utilizing geometrical concepts. Chapter 2 describes how certain classes of kernels induce feature spaces, and how one can compute dot products, and thus angles and distances, without having to explicitly work in these potentially infinite-dimensional spaces. This leads to a rather general class of similarity measure to be used on the inputs.

1. From *A History of Eternity*, in *The Total Library*, Penguin, London, 2001.
2. This procedure can be traced back to an old maxim of law: *de similibus ad similia eadem ratione procedendum est* — from things similar to things similar we are to proceed by the same rule.

On the *outputs*, similarity is usually measured in terms of a *loss function* stating how "bad" it is if the predicted y does not match the true one. The training of a learning machine commonly involves a *risk functional* that contains a term measuring the loss incurred for the training patterns. The concepts of loss and risk are introduced in depth in Chapter 3.

This is not the full story, however. In order to generalize well to the test data, it is not sufficient to "explain" the training data. It is also necessary to control the complexity of the model used for explaining the training data, a task that is often accomplished with the help of *regularization* terms, as explained in Chapter 4. Specifically, one utilizes objective functions that involve both the empirical loss term and a regularization term. From a *statistical* point of view, we can expect the function minimizing a properly chosen objective function to work well on test data, as explained by statistical learning theory (Chapter 5). From a *practical* point of view, however, it is not at all straightforward to *find* this minimizer. Indeed, the quality of a loss function or a regularizer should be assessed not only on a statistical basis but also in terms of the feasibility of the objective function minimization problem. In order to be able to assess this, and in order to obtain a thorough understanding of practical algorithms for this task, we conclude this part of the book with an in-depth review of optimization theory (Chapter 6).

The chapters in this part of the book assume familiarity with basic concepts of linear algebra and probability theory. Readers who would like to refresh their knowledge of these topics may want to consult Appendix B beforehand.

2 Kernels

In Chapter 1, we described how a kernel arises as a similarity measure that can be thought of as a dot product in a so-called feature space. We tried to provide an intuitive understanding of kernels by introducing them as similarity measures, rather than immediately delving into the functional analytic theory of the classes of kernels that actually admit a dot product representation in a feature space.

In the present chapter, we will be both more formal and more precise. We will study the class of kernels k that correspond to dot products in feature spaces $\mathcal{H}$ via a map Φ,

$$\Phi : \mathcal{X} \to \mathcal{H}$$
$$x \mapsto \mathbf{x} := \Phi(x), \tag{2.1}$$

that is,

$$k(x, x') = \langle \Phi(x), \Phi(x') \rangle . \tag{2.2}$$

Regarding the input domain $\mathcal{X}$, we need not make assumptions other than it being a set. For instance, we could consider a set of discrete objects, such as strings.

Overview

A natural question to ask at this point is what kind of functions $k(x, x')$ admit a representation of the form (2.2); that is, whether we can always construct a dot product space $\mathcal{H}$ and a map Φ mapping into it such that (2.2) holds true. We shall begin, however, by trying to give some motivation as to why kernels are at all useful, considering kernels that compute dot products in spaces of monomial features (Section 2.1). Following this, we move on to the questions of how, given a kernel, an associated feature space can be constructed (Section 2.2). This leads to the notion of a Reproducing Kernel Hilbert Space, crucial for the theory of kernel machines. In Section 2.3, we give some examples and properties of kernels, and in Section 2.4, we discuss a class of kernels that can be used as dissimilarity measures rather than as similarity measures.

Prerequisites

The chapter builds on knowledge of linear algebra, as briefly summarized in Appendix B. Apart from that, it can be read on its own; however, readers new to the field will profit from first reading Sections 1.1 and 1.2.

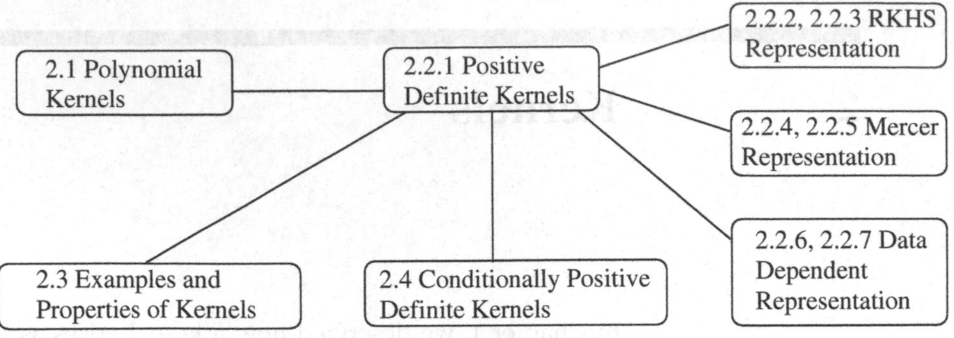

2.1 Product Features

In this section, we think of $\mathcal{X}$ as a subset of the vector space $\mathbb{R}^N$, ($N \in \mathbb{N}$), endowed with the canonical dot product (1.3).

Monomial Features

Suppose we are given patterns $x \in \mathcal{X}$ where most information is contained in the dth order products (so-called monomials) of entries $[x]_j$ of x,

$$[x]_{j_1} \cdot [x]_{j_2} \cdots [x]_{j_d}, \tag{2.3}$$

where $j_1, \ldots, j_d \in \{1, \ldots, N\}$. Often, these monomials are referred to as *product features*. These features form the basis of many practical algorithms; indeed, there is a whole field of pattern recognition research studying *polynomial classifiers* [484], which is based on first extracting product features and then applying learning algorithms to these features. In other words, the patterns are preprocessed by mapping into the feature space $\mathcal{H}$ of all products of d entries. This has proven quite effective in visual pattern recognition tasks, for instance. To understand the rationale for doing this, note that visual patterns are usually represented as vectors whose entries are the pixel intensities. Taking products of entries of these vectors then corresponds to taking products of pixel intensities, and is thus akin to taking logical "and" operations on the pixels. Roughly speaking, this corresponds to the intuition that, for instance, a handwritten "8" constitutes an eight if there is a top circle *and* a bottom circle. With just one of the two circles, it is not half an "8," but rather a "0." Nonlinearities of this type are crucial for achieving high accuracies in pattern recognition tasks.

Let us take a look at this feature map in the simple example of two-dimensional patterns, for which $\mathcal{X} = \mathbb{R}^2$. In this case, we can collect all monomial feature extractors of degree 2 in the nonlinear map

$$\Phi : \mathbb{R}^2 \to \mathcal{H} = \mathbb{R}^3, \tag{2.4}$$

$$([x]_1, [x]_2) \mapsto ([x]_1^2, [x]_2^2, [x]_1[x]_2). \tag{2.5}$$

This approach works fine for small toy examples, but it fails for realistically sized problems: for N-dimensional input patterns, there exist

$$N_{\mathcal{H}} = \binom{d+N-1}{d} = \frac{(d+N-1)!}{d!(N-1)!} \tag{2.6}$$

different monomials (2.3) of degree d, comprising a feature space $\mathcal{H}$ of dimension $N_{\mathcal{H}}$. For instance, 16×16 pixel input images and a monomial degree $d = 5$ thus yield a dimension of almost 10^{10}.

In certain cases described below, however, there exists a way of *computing dot products* in these high-dimensional feature spaces without explicitly mapping into the spaces, by means of kernels nonlinear in the input space $\mathbb{R}^N$. Thus, if the subsequent processing can be carried out using dot products exclusively, we are able to deal with the high dimension.

We now describe how dot products in polynomial feature spaces can be computed efficiently, followed by a section in which we discuss more general feature spaces. In order to compute dot products of the form $\langle \Phi(x), \Phi(x') \rangle$, we employ kernel representations of the form

Kernel

$$k(x, x') = \langle \Phi(x), \Phi(x') \rangle, \tag{2.7}$$

which allow us to compute the value of the dot product in $\mathcal{H}$ without having to explicitly compute the map Φ.

What does k look like in the case of polynomial features? We start by giving an example for $N = d = 2$, as considered above [561]. For the map

$$\Phi : ([x]_1, [x]_2) \mapsto ([x]_1^2, [x]_2^2, [x]_1[x]_2, [x]_2[x]_1), \tag{2.8}$$

(note that for now, we have considered $[x]_1[x]_2$ and $[x]_2[x]_1$ as separate features; thus we are looking at *ordered* monomials) dot products in $\mathcal{H}$ take the form

$$\langle \Phi(x), \Phi(x') \rangle = [x]_1^2[x']_1^2 + [x]_2^2[x']_2^2 + 2[x]_1[x]_2[x']_1[x']_2 = \langle x, x' \rangle^2. \tag{2.9}$$

In other words, the desired kernel k is simply the square of the dot product in input space. The same works for arbitrary $N, d \in \mathbb{N}$ [62]: as a straightforward generalization of a result proved in the context of polynomial approximation [412, Lemma 2.1], we have:

Proposition 2.1 *Define C_d to map $x \in \mathbb{R}^N$ to the vector $C_d(x)$ whose entries are all possible dth degree ordered products of the entries of x. Then the corresponding kernel computing the dot product of vectors mapped by C_d is*

Polynomial Kernel

$$k(x, x') = \langle C_d(x), C_d(x') \rangle = \langle x, x' \rangle^d. \tag{2.10}$$

Proof We directly compute

$$\langle C_d(x), C_d(x') \rangle = \sum_{j_1=1}^{N} \cdots \sum_{j_d=1}^{N} [x]_{j_1} \cdot \ldots \cdot [x]_{j_d} \cdot [x']_{j_1} \cdot \ldots \cdot [x']_{j_d} \tag{2.11}$$

$$= \sum_{j_1=1}^{N} [x]_{j_1} \cdot [x']_{j_1} \cdots \sum_{j_d=1}^{N} [x]_{j_d} \cdot [x']_{j_d} = \left(\sum_{j=1}^{N} [x]_j \cdot [x']_j \right)^d = \langle x, x' \rangle^d . \qquad \blacksquare$$

Note that we used the symbol C_d for the feature map. The reason for this is that we would like to reserve Φ_d for the corresponding map computing *unordered* product features. Let us construct such a map Φ_d, yielding the same value of the dot product. To this end, we have to compensate for the multiple occurrence of certain monomials in C_d by scaling the respective entries of Φ_d with the square roots of their numbers of occurrence. Then, by this construction of Φ_d, and (2.10),

$$\langle \Phi_d(x), \Phi_d(x') \rangle = \langle C_d(x), C_d(x') \rangle = \langle x, x' \rangle^d . \tag{2.12}$$

For instance, if n of the j_i in (2.3) are equal, and the remaining ones are different, then the coefficient in the corresponding component of Φ_d is $\sqrt{(d-n+1)!}$. For the general case, see Problem 2.2. For Φ_2, this simply means that [561]

$$\Phi_2(x) = ([x]_1^2, [x]_2^2, \sqrt{2}\,[x]_1[x]_2). \tag{2.13}$$

The above reasoning illustrates an important point pertaining to the construction of feature spaces associated with kernel functions. Although they map into different feature spaces, Φ_d and C_d are both valid instantiations of feature maps for $k(x, x') = \langle x, x' \rangle^d$.

To illustrate how monomial feature kernels can significantly simplify pattern recognition tasks, let us consider a simple toy example.

Toy Example

Example 2.2 (Monomial Features in 2-D Pattern Recognition) *In the example of Figure 2.1, a non-separable problem is reduced to the construction of a separating hyperplane by preprocessing the input data with Φ_2. As we shall see in later chapters, this has advantages both from the* computational *point of view (there exist efficient algorithms for computing the hyperplane) and from the* statistical *point of view (there exist guarantees for how well the hyperplane will generalize to unseen test points).*

In more realistic cases, e.g., if x represents an image with the entries being pixel values, polynomial kernels $\langle x, x' \rangle^d$ enable us to work in the space spanned by products of any d pixel values — provided that we are able to do our work solely in terms of dot products, without any explicit usage of a mapped pattern $\Phi_d(x)$. Using kernels of the form (2.10), we can take higher-order statistics into account, without the combinatorial explosion (2.6) of time and memory complexity which accompanies even moderately high N and d.

To conclude this section, note that it is possible to modify (2.10) such that it maps into the space of all monomials *up to* degree d, by defining $k(x, x') = (\langle x, x' \rangle + 1)^d$ (Problem 2.17). Moreover, in practice, it is often useful to multiply the kernel by a scaling factor c to ensure that its numeric range is within some bounded interval, say $[-1, 1]$. The value of c will depend on the dimension and range of the data.

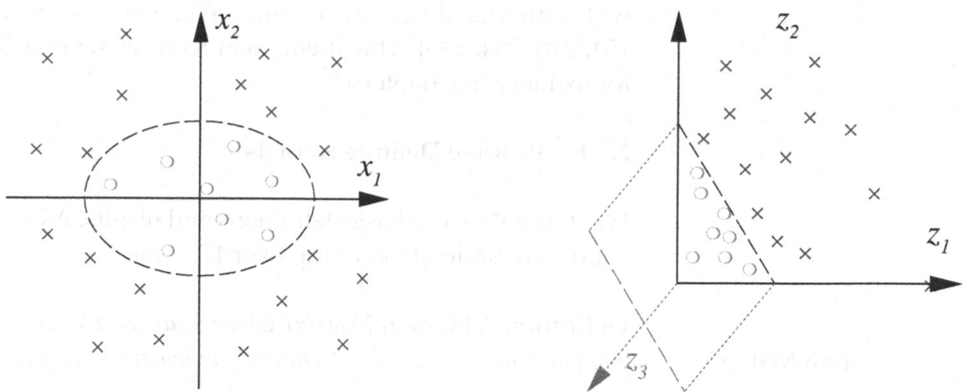

Figure 2.1 Toy example of a binary classification problem mapped into feature space. We assume that the true decision boundary is an ellipse in input space (left panel). The task of the learning process is to estimate this boundary based on empirical data consisting of training points in both classes (crosses and circles, respectively). When mapped into feature space via the nonlinear map $\Phi_2(x) = (z_1, z_2, z_3) = ([x]_1^2, [x]_2^2, \sqrt{2}\,[x]_1[x]_2)$ (right panel), the ellipse becomes a hyperplane (in the present simple case, it is parallel to the z_3 axis, hence all points are plotted in the (z_1, z_2) plane). This is due to the fact that ellipses can be written as linear equations in the entries of (z_1, z_2, z_3). Therefore, in feature space, the problem reduces to that of estimating a hyperplane from the mapped data points. Note that via the polynomial kernel (see (2.12) and (2.13)), the dot product in the three-dimensional space can be computed without computing Φ_2. Later in the book, we shall describe algorithms for constructing hyperplanes which are based on dot products (Chapter 7).

2.2 The Representation of Similarities in Linear Spaces

In what follows, we will look at things the other way round, and start with the kernel rather than with the feature map. Given some kernel, can we construct a feature space such that the kernel computes the dot product in that feature space; that is, such that (2.2) holds? This question has been brought to the attention of the machine learning community in a variety of contexts, especially during recent years [4, 152, 62, 561, 480]. In functional analysis, the same problem has been studied under the heading of *Hilbert space representations* of kernels. A good monograph on the theory of kernels is the book of Berg, Christensen, and Ressel [42]; indeed, a large part of the material in the present chapter is based on this work. We do not aim to be fully rigorous; instead, we try to provide insight into the basic ideas. As a rule, all the results that we state without proof can be found in [42]. Other standard references include [16, 455].

There is one more aspect in which this section differs from the previous one: the latter dealt with vectorial data, and the domain $\mathcal{X}$ was assumed to be a subset of $\mathbb{R}^N$. By contrast, the results in the current section hold for data drawn from domains which need no structure, other than their being nonempty sets. This generalizes kernel learning algorithms to a large number of situations where a vectorial representation is not readily available, and where one directly works with pairwise distances or similarities between non-vectorial objects [246, 467, 154, 210, 234, 585]. This theme will recur in several places throughout the book, for instance in Chapter 13.

2.2.1 Positive Definite Kernels

We start with some basic definitions and results. As in the previous chapter, indices i and j are understood to run over $1, \ldots, m$.

Gram Matrix

Definition 2.3 (Gram Matrix) *Given a function $k : \mathcal{X}^2 \to \mathbb{K}$ (where $\mathbb{K} = \mathbb{C}$ or $\mathbb{K} = \mathbb{R}$) and patterns $x_1, \ldots, x_m \in \mathcal{X}$, the $m \times m$ matrix K with elements*

$$K_{ij} := k(x_i, x_j) \tag{2.14}$$

is called the Gram matrix *(or* kernel matrix*) of k with respect to $x_1, \ldots, x_m$.*

PD Matrix

Definition 2.4 (Positive Definite Matrix) *A complex $m \times m$ matrix K satisfying*

$$\sum_{i,j} c_i \bar{c}_j K_{ij} \geq 0 \tag{2.15}$$

for all $c_i \in \mathbb{C}$ is called positive definite.[1] *Similarly, a real symmetric $m \times m$ matrix K satisfying (2.15) for all $c_i \in \mathbb{R}$ is called* positive definite.

Note that a symmetric matrix is positive definite if and only if all its eigenvalues are nonnegative (Problem 2.4). The left hand side of (2.15) is often referred to as the *quadratic form* induced by K.

PD Kernel

Definition 2.5 ((Positive Definite) Kernel) *Let $\mathcal{X}$ be a nonempty set. A function k on $\mathcal{X} \times \mathcal{X}$ which for all $m \in \mathbb{N}$ and all $x_1 \ldots, x_m \in \mathcal{X}$ gives rise to a positive definite Gram matrix is called a* positive definite (pd) kernel. *Often, we shall refer to it simply as a* kernel.

Remark 2.6 (Terminology) *The term* kernel *stems from the first use of this type of function in the field of integral operators as studied by Hilbert and others [243, 359, 112]. A function k which gives rise to an operator T_k via*

$$(T_k f)(x) = \int_{\mathcal{X}} k(x, x') f(x')\, dx' \tag{2.16}$$

is called the kernel of T_k.

In the literature, a number of different terms are used for positive definite kernels, such as reproducing kernel, Mercer kernel, admissible kernel, Support Vector kernel, nonnegative definite kernel, *and* covariance function. *One might argue that the term* positive definite kernel *is slightly misleading. In matrix theory, the term* definite *is sometimes reserved for the case where equality in (2.15) only occurs if $c_1 = \ldots = c_m = 0$.*

1. The bar in $\bar{c}_j$ denotes complex conjugation; for real numbers, it has no effect.

Simply using the term positive kernel, *on the other hand, could be mistaken as referring to a kernel whose* values *are positive. Finally, the term positive* semidefinite *kernel becomes rather cumbersome if it is to be used throughout a book. Therefore, we follow the convention used for instance in [42], and employ the term* positive definite *both for kernels and matrices in the way introduced above. The case where the value 0 is only attained if all coefficients are 0 will be referred to as* strictly *positive definite.*

We shall mostly use the term kernel. *Whenever we want to refer to a kernel $k(x, x')$ which is not positive definite in the sense stated above, it will be clear from the context.*

The definitions for positive definite kernels and positive definite matrices differ in the fact that in the former case, we are free to choose the points on which the kernel is evaluated — for every choice, the kernel induces a positive definite matrix.

Positive definiteness implies *positivity on the diagonal* (Problem 2.12),

$$k(x, x) \geq 0 \text{ for all } x \in \mathcal{X}, \tag{2.17}$$

and *symmetry* (Problem 2.13),

$$k(x_i, x_j) = \overline{k(x_j, x_i)}. \tag{2.18}$$

To also cover the complex-valued case, our definition of symmetry includes complex conjugation. The definition of symmetry of matrices is analogous; that is, $K_{ij} = \overline{K}_{ji}$.

Real-Valued Kernels

For real-valued kernels it is not sufficient to stipulate that (2.15) hold for real coefficients c_i. To get away with real coefficients only, we must additionally require that the kernel be symmetric (Problem 2.14); $k(x_i, x_j) = k(x_j, x_i)$ (cf. Problem 2.13).

It can be shown that whenever k is a (complex-valued) positive definite kernel, its real part is a (real-valued) positive definite kernel. Below, we shall largely be dealing with real-valued kernels. Most of the results, however, also apply for complex-valued kernels.

Kernels can be regarded as generalized dot products. Indeed, any dot product is a kernel (Problem 2.5); however, linearity in the arguments, which is a standard property of dot products, does not carry over to general kernels. However, another property of dot products, the Cauchy-Schwarz inequality, does have a natural generalization to kernels:

Proposition 2.7 (Cauchy-Schwarz Inequality for Kernels) *If k is a positive definite kernel, and $x_1, x_2 \in \mathcal{X}$, then*

$$|k(x_1, x_2)|^2 \leq k(x_1, x_1) \cdot k(x_2, x_2). \tag{2.19}$$

Proof For sake of brevity, we give a non-elementary proof using some basic facts of linear algebra. The 2×2 Gram matrix with entries $K_{ij} = k(x_i, x_j)$ $(i, j \in \{1, 2\})$ is positive definite. Hence both its eigenvalues are nonnegative, and so is their product, the determinant of K. Therefore

$$0 \leq K_{11}K_{22} - K_{12}K_{21} = K_{11}K_{22} - K_{12}\overline{K}_{12} = K_{11}K_{22} - |K_{12}|^2. \tag{2.20}$$

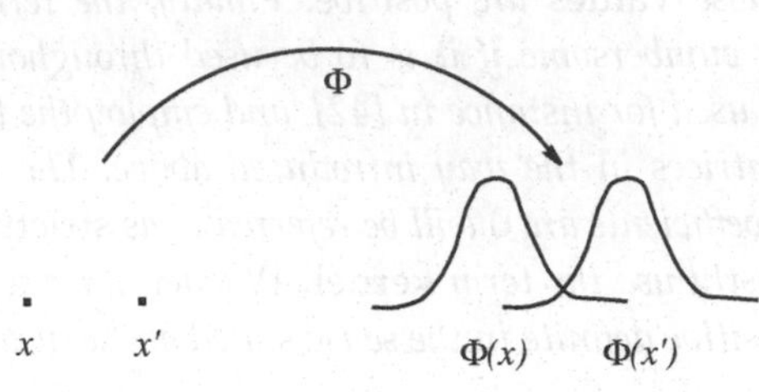

Figure 2.2 One instantiation of the feature map associated with a kernel is the map (2.21), which represents each pattern (in the picture, x or x') by a kernel-shaped *function* sitting on the pattern. In this sense, each pattern is represented by its similarity to *all* other patterns. In the picture, the kernel is assumed to be bell-shaped, e.g., a Gaussian $k(x, x') = \exp(-\|x - x'\|^2/(2\,\sigma^2))$. In the text, we describe the construction of a dot product $\langle .,. \rangle$ on the function space such that $k(x, x') = \langle \Phi(x), \Phi(x') \rangle$.

Substituting $k(x_i, x_j)$ for K_{ij}, we get the desired inequality. ∎

We now show how the feature spaces in question are defined by the choice of kernel function.

2.2.2 The Reproducing Kernel Map

Assume that k is a real-valued positive definite kernel, and $\mathcal{X}$ a nonempty set. We define a map from $\mathcal{X}$ into the space of functions mapping $\mathcal{X}$ into $\mathbb{R}$, denoted as $\mathbb{R}^{\mathcal{X}} := \{f : \mathcal{X} \to \mathbb{R}\}$, via

Feature Map

$$\Phi : \mathcal{X} \to \mathbb{R}^{\mathcal{X}}$$
$$x \mapsto k(., x). \tag{2.21}$$

Here, $\Phi(x)$ denotes the function that assigns the value $k(x', x)$ to $x' \in \mathcal{X}$, i.e., $\Phi(x)(.) = k(., x)$ (as shown in Figure 2.2).

We have thus turned each pattern into a function on the domain $\mathcal{X}$. In this sense, a pattern is now represented by its similarity to *all* other points in the input domain $\mathcal{X}$. This seems a very rich representation; nevertheless, it will turn out that the kernel allows the computation of the dot product in this representation. Below, we show how to construct a feature space associated with Φ, proceeding in the following steps:

1. Turn the image of Φ into a vector space,
2. define a dot product; that is, a strictly positive definite bilinear form, and
3. show that the dot product satisfies $k(x, x') = \langle \Phi(x), \Phi(x') \rangle$.

We begin by constructing a dot product space containing the images of the input patterns under Φ. To this end, we first need to define a vector space. This is done by taking linear combinations of the form

Vector Space

$$f(.) = \sum_{i=1}^{m} \alpha_i k(., x_i). \tag{2.22}$$

Here, $m \in \mathbb{N}$, $\alpha_i \in \mathbb{R}$ and $x_1, \ldots, x_m \in \mathcal{X}$ are arbitrary. Next, we define a dot product between f and another function

$$g(.) = \sum_{j=1}^{m'} \beta_j k(., x'_j), \tag{2.23}$$

Dot Product

where $m' \in \mathbb{N}$, $\beta_j \in \mathbb{R}$ and $x'_1, \ldots, x'_{m'} \in \mathcal{X}$, as

$$\langle f, g \rangle := \sum_{i=1}^{m} \sum_{j=1}^{m'} \alpha_i \beta_j k(x_i, x'_j). \tag{2.24}$$

This expression explicitly contains the expansion coefficients, which need not be unique. To see that it is nevertheless well-defined, note that

$$\langle f, g \rangle = \sum_{j=1}^{m'} \beta_j f(x'_j), \tag{2.25}$$

using $k(x'_j, x_i) = k(x_i, x'_j)$. The sum in (2.25), however, does not depend on the particular expansion of f. Similarly, for g, note that

$$\langle f, g \rangle = \sum_{i=1}^{m} \alpha_i g(x_i). \tag{2.26}$$

The last two equations also show that $\langle \cdot, \cdot \rangle$ is bilinear. It is symmetric, as $\langle f, g \rangle = \langle g, f \rangle$. Moreover, it is positive definite, since positive definiteness of k implies that for any function f, written as (2.22), we have

$$\langle f, f \rangle = \sum_{i,j=1}^{m} \alpha_i \alpha_j k(x_i, x_j) \geq 0. \tag{2.27}$$

The latter implies that $\langle \cdot, \cdot \rangle$ is actually itself a positive definite kernel, defined on our space of functions. To see this, note that given functions $f_1, \ldots, f_n$, and coefficients $\gamma_1, \ldots, \gamma_n \in \mathbb{R}$, we have

$$\sum_{i,j=1}^{n} \gamma_i \gamma_j \langle f_i, f_j \rangle = \left\langle \sum_{i=1}^{n} \gamma_i f_i, \sum_{j=1}^{n} \gamma_j f_j \right\rangle \geq 0. \tag{2.28}$$

Here, the left hand equality follows from the bilinearity of $\langle \cdot, \cdot \rangle$, and the right hand inequality from (2.27). For the last step in proving that it qualifies as a dot product, we will use the following interesting property of Φ, which follows directly from the definition: for all functions (2.22), we have

$$\langle k(., x), f \rangle = f(x) \tag{2.29}$$

— k is the *representer of evaluation*. In particular,

$$\langle k(., x), k(., x') \rangle = k(x, x'). \tag{2.30}$$

Reproducing Kernel

By virtue of these properties, positive definite kernels k are also called *reproducing kernels* [16, 42, 455, 578, 467, 202]. By (2.29) and Proposition 2.7, we have

$$|f(x)|^2 = |\langle k(., x), f \rangle|^2 \leq k(x, x) \cdot \langle f, f \rangle. \tag{2.31}$$

Therefore, $\langle f, f \rangle = 0$ directly implies $f = 0$, which is the last property that required proof in order to establish that $\langle \cdot, \cdot \rangle$ is a dot product (cf. Section B.2).

The case of complex-valued kernels can be dealt with using the same construction; in that case, we will end up with a complex dot product space [42].

The above reasoning has shown that any positive definite kernel can be thought of as a dot product in another space: in view of (2.21), the reproducing kernel property (2.30) amounts to

$$\langle \Phi(x), \Phi(x') \rangle = k(x, x'). \tag{2.32}$$

Therefore, the dot product space $\mathcal{H}$ constructed in this way is one possible instantiation of the feature space associated with a kernel.

Kernels from Feature Maps

Above, we have started with the kernel, and constructed a feature map. Let us now consider the opposite direction. Whenever we have a mapping Φ from $\mathcal{X}$ into a dot product space, we obtain a positive definite kernel via $k(x, x') := \langle \Phi(x), \Phi(x') \rangle$. This can be seen by noting that for all $c_i \in \mathbb{R}, x_i \in \mathcal{X}, i = 1, \ldots, m$, we have

$$\sum_{i,j} c_i c_j k(x_i, x_j) = \left\langle \sum_i c_i \Phi(x_i), \sum_j c_j \Phi(x_j) \right\rangle = \left\| \sum_i c_i \Phi(x_i) \right\|^2 \geq 0, \tag{2.33}$$

due to the nonnegativity of the norm.

Equivalent Definition of PD Kernels

This has two consequences. First, it allows us to give an equivalent definition of positive definite kernels as functions with the property that there exists a map Φ into a dot product space such that (2.32) holds true. Second, it allows us to construct kernels from feature maps. For instance, it is in this way that powerful linear representations of 3D heads proposed in computer graphics [575, 59] give rise to kernels. The identity (2.32) forms the basis for the kernel trick:

Kernel Trick

Remark 2.8 ("Kernel Trick") *Given an algorithm which is formulated in terms of a positive definite kernel k, one can construct an alternative algorithm by replacing k by another positive definite kernel $\tilde{k}$.*

In view of the material in the present section, the justification for this procedure is the following: effectively, the original algorithm can be thought of as a dot product based algorithm operating on vectorial data $\Phi(x_1), \ldots, \Phi(x_m)$. The algorithm obtained by replacing k by $\tilde{k}$ then is exactly the same dot product based algorithm, only that it operates on $\tilde{\Phi}(x_1), \ldots, \tilde{\Phi}(x_m)$.

The best known application of the kernel trick is in the case where k is the dot product in the input domain (cf. Problem 2.5). The trick is not limited to that case, however: k and $\tilde{k}$ can *both* be nonlinear kernels. In general, care must be exercised in determining whether the resulting algorithm will be useful: sometimes, an algorithm will only work subject to additional conditions on the input data, e.g., the data set might have to lie in the positive orthant. We shall later see that certain kernels induce feature maps which enforce such properties for the mapped data (cf. (2.73)), and that there are algorithms which take advantage of these aspects (e.g., in Chapter 8). In such cases, not every conceivable positive definite kernel will make sense.

Historical Remarks

Even though the kernel trick had been used in the literature for a fair amount of time [4, 62], it took until the mid 1990s before it was explicitly stated that *any* algorithm that only depends on dot products, i.e., any algorithm that is rotationally invariant, can be kernelized [479, 480]. Since then, a number of algorithms have benefitted from the kernel trick, such as the ones described in the present book, as well as methods for clustering in feature spaces [479, 215, 199].

Moreover, the machine learning community took time to comprehend that the definition of kernels on general sets (rather than dot product spaces) greatly extends the applicability of kernel methods [467], to data types such as texts and other sequences [234, 585, 23]. Indeed, this is now recognized as a crucial feature of kernels: they lead to an embedding of general data types in linear spaces.

Not surprisingly, the history of methods for representing kernels in linear spaces (in other words, the mathematical counterpart of the kernel trick) dates back significantly further than their use in machine learning. The methods appear to have first been studied in the 1940s by Kolmogorov [304] for countable $\mathcal{X}$ and Aronszajn [16] in the general case. Pioneering work on linear representations of a related class of kernels, to be described in Section 2.4, was done by Schoenberg [465]. Further bibliographical comments can be found in [42].

We thus see that the mathematical basis for kernel algorithms has been around for a long time. As is often the case, however, the practical importance of mathematical results was initially underestimated.[2]

2.2.3 Reproducing Kernel Hilbert Spaces

In the last section, we described how to define a space of functions which is a valid realization of the feature spaces associated with a given kernel. To do this, we had to make sure that the space is a vector space, and that it is endowed with a dot product. Such spaces are referred to as dot product spaces (cf. Appendix B), or equivalently as *pre-Hilbert* spaces. The reason for the latter is that one can turn them into Hilbert spaces (cf. Section B.3) by a fairly simple mathematical trick. This additional structure has some mathematical advantages. For instance, in Hilbert spaces it is always possible to define projections. Indeed, Hilbert spaces are one of the favorite concepts of functional analysis.

So let us again consider the pre-Hilbert space of functions (2.22), endowed with the dot product (2.24). To turn it into a Hilbert space (over $\mathbb{R}$), one *completes* it in the norm corresponding to the dot product, $\|f\| := \sqrt{\langle f, f\rangle}$. This is done by adding the limit points of sequences that are convergent in that norm (see Appendix B).

2. This is illustrated by the following quotation from an excellent machine learning textbook published in the seventies (p. 174 in [152]): *"The familiar functions of mathematical physics are eigenfunctions of symmetric kernels, and their use is often suggested for the construction of potential functions. However, these suggestions are more appealing for their mathematical beauty than their practical usefulness."*

RKHS

In view of the properties (2.29) and (2.30), this space is usually called a *reproducing kernel Hilbert space (RKHS)*.

In general, an RKHS can be defined as follows.

Definition 2.9 (Reproducing Kernel Hilbert Space) *Let $\mathcal{X}$ be a nonempty set (often called the index set) and by $\mathcal{H}$ a Hilbert space of functions $f : \mathcal{X} \to \mathbb{R}$. Then $\mathcal{H}$ is called a reproducing kernel Hilbert space endowed with the dot product $\langle \cdot, \cdot \rangle$ (and the norm $\|f\| := \sqrt{\langle f, f \rangle}$) if there exists a function $k : \mathcal{X} \times \mathcal{X} \to \mathbb{R}$ with the following properties.*

Reproducing Property

1. *k has the reproducing property*[3]

$$\langle f, k(x, \cdot) \rangle = f(x) \text{ for all } f \in \mathcal{H}; \tag{2.34}$$

in particular,

$$\langle k(x, \cdot), k(x', \cdot) \rangle = k(x, x'). \tag{2.35}$$

Closed Space

2. *k spans $\mathcal{H}$, i.e. $\mathcal{H} = \overline{\text{span}\{k(x, \cdot) | x \in \mathcal{X}\}}$ where $\overline{X}$ denotes the completion of the set X (cf. Appendix B).*

On a more abstract level, an RKHS can be defined as a Hilbert space of functions f on $\mathcal{X}$ such that all evaluation functionals (the maps $f \mapsto f(x')$, where $x' \in \mathcal{X}$) are continuous. In that case, by the Riesz representation theorem (e.g., [429]), for each $x' \in \mathcal{X}$ there exists a unique function of x, called $k(x, x')$, such that

$$f(x') = \langle f, k(., x') \rangle . \tag{2.36}$$

It follows directly from (2.35) that $k(x, x')$ is symmetric in its arguments (see Problem 2.28) and satisfies the conditions for positive definiteness.

Note that the RKHS uniquely determines k. This can be shown by contradiction: assume that there exist two kernels, say k and k', spanning the same RKHS $\mathcal{H}$.

Uniqueness of k

From Problem 2.28 we know that both k and k' must be symmetric. Moreover, from (2.34) we conclude that

$$\langle k(x, \cdot), k'(x', \cdot) \rangle_{\mathcal{H}} = k(x, x') = k'(x', x). \tag{2.37}$$

In the second equality we used the symmetry of the dot product. Finally, symmetry in the arguments of k yields $k(x, x') = k'(x, x')$ which proves our claim.

2.2.4 The Mercer Kernel Map

Section 2.2.2 has shown that any positive definite kernel can be represented as a dot product in a linear space. This was done by explicitly constructing a (Hilbert) space that does the job. The present section will construct another Hilbert space.

3. Note that this implies that each $f \in \mathcal{H}$ is actually a single function whose values at any $x \in \mathcal{X}$ are well-defined. In contrast, L_2 Hilbert spaces usually do not have this property. The elements of these spaces are equivalence classes of functions that disagree only on sets of measure 0; cf. footnote 15 in Section B.3.

One could argue that this is superfluous, given that any two separable Hilbert spaces are isometrically isomorphic, in other words, it is possible to define a one-to-one linear map between the spaces which preserves the dot product. However, the tool that we shall presently use, Mercer's theorem, has played a crucial role in the understanding of SVMs, and it provides valuable insight into the geometry of feature spaces, which more than justifies its detailed discussion. In the SVM literature, the kernel trick is usually introduced via Mercer's theorem.

We start by stating the version of Mercer's theorem given in [606]. We assume $(\mathcal{X}, \mu)$ to be a finite measure space.[4] The term *almost all* (cf. Appendix B) means *except for sets of measure zero*. For the commonly used Lebesgue-Borel measure, countable sets of individual points are examples of zero measure sets. Note that the integral with respect to a measure is explained in Appendix B. Readers who do not want to go into mathematical detail may simply want to think of the $d\mu(x')$ as a dx', and of $\mathcal{X}$ as a compact subset of $\mathbb{R}^N$. For further explanations of the terms involved in this theorem, cf. Appendix B, especially Section B.3.

Mercer's Theorem

Theorem 2.10 (Mercer [359, 307]) *Suppose $k \in L_\infty(\mathcal{X}^2)$ is a symmetric real-valued function such that the integral operator (cf. (2.16))*

$$\begin{aligned} T_k &: L_2(\mathcal{X}) \to L_2(\mathcal{X}) \\ (T_k f)(x) &:= \int_{\mathcal{X}} k(x, x') f(x')\, d\mu(x') \end{aligned} \tag{2.38}$$

is positive definite; that is, for all $f \in L_2(\mathcal{X})$, we have

$$\int_{\mathcal{X}^2} k(x, x') f(x) f(x')\, d\mu(x) d\mu(x') \geq 0. \tag{2.39}$$

Let $\psi_j \in L_2(\mathcal{X})$ be the normalized orthogonal eigenfunctions of T_k associated with the eigenvalues $\lambda_j > 0$, sorted in non-increasing order. Then

1. *$(\lambda_j)_j \in \ell_1$,*
2. *$k(x, x') = \sum_{j=1}^{N_{\mathcal{H}}} \lambda_j \psi_j(x) \psi_j(x')$ holds for almost all (x, x'). Either $N_{\mathcal{H}} \in \mathbb{N}$, or $N_{\mathcal{H}} = \infty$; in the latter case, the series converges absolutely and uniformly for almost all (x, x').*

For the converse of Theorem 2.10, see Problem 2.23. For a data-dependent approximation and its relationship to kernel PCA (Section 1.7), see Problem 2.26.

From statement 2 it follows that $k(x, x')$ corresponds to a dot product in $\ell_2^{N_{\mathcal{H}}}$, since $k(x, x') = \langle \Phi(x), \Phi(x') \rangle$ with

$$\begin{aligned} \Phi : \mathcal{X} &\to \ell_2^{N_{\mathcal{H}}} \\ x &\mapsto (\sqrt{\lambda_j} \psi_j(x))_{j=1,\ldots,N_{\mathcal{H}}}, \end{aligned} \tag{2.40}$$

for almost all $x \in \mathcal{X}$. Note that we use the same Φ as in (2.21) to denote the feature

4. A finite measure space is a set $\mathcal{X}$ with a σ-algebra (Definition B.1) defined on it, and a measure (Definition B.2) defined on the latter, satisfying $\mu(\mathcal{X}) < \infty$ (so that, up to a scaling factor, μ is a probability measure).

map, although the target spaces are different. However, this distinction is not important for the present purposes — we are interested in the existence of some Hilbert space in which the kernel corresponds to the dot product, and not in what particular representation of it we are using.

In fact, it has been noted [467] that the *uniform* convergence of the series implies that given any $\epsilon > 0$, there exists an $n \in \mathbb{N}$ such that even if $N_{\mathcal{H}} = \infty$, k can be approximated within accuracy ϵ as a dot product in $\mathbb{R}^n$: for almost all $x, x' \in \mathcal{X}$, $|k(x, x') - \langle \Phi^n(x), \Phi^n(x') \rangle| < \epsilon$, where $\Phi^n : x \mapsto (\sqrt{\lambda_1}\psi_1(x), \ldots, \sqrt{\lambda_n}\psi_n(x))$. The feature space can thus always be thought of as finite-dimensional within some accuracy ϵ. We summarize our findings in the following proposition.

Mercer Feature Map

Proposition 2.11 (Mercer Kernel Map) *If k is a kernel satisfying the conditions of Theorem 2.10, we can construct a mapping Φ into a space where k acts as a dot product,*

$$\langle \Phi(x), \Phi(x') \rangle = k(x, x'), \tag{2.41}$$

for almost all $x, x' \in \mathcal{X}$. Moreover, given any $\epsilon > 0$, there exists a map Φ_n into an n-dimensional dot product space (where $n \in \mathbb{N}$ depends on ϵ) such that

$$|k(x, x') - \langle \Phi^n(x), \Phi^n(x') \rangle| < \epsilon \tag{2.42}$$

for almost all $x, x' \in \mathcal{X}$.

Both Mercer kernels and positive definite kernels can thus be represented as dot products in Hilbert spaces. The following proposition, showing a case where the two types of kernels coincide, thus comes as no surprise.

Proposition 2.12 (Mercer Kernels are Positive Definite [359, 42]) *Let $\mathcal{X} = [a, b]$ be a compact interval and let $k : [a, b] \times [a, b] \to \mathbb{C}$ be continuous. Then k is a positive definite kernel if and only if*

$$\int_a^b \int_a^b k(x, x') f(x) f(x')\, dx\, dx' \geq 0 \tag{2.43}$$

for each continuous function $f : \mathcal{X} \to \mathbb{C}$.

Note that the conditions in this proposition are actually more restrictive than those of Theorem 2.10. Using the feature space representation (Proposition 2.11), however, it is easy to see that Mercer kernels are also positive definite (for almost all $x, x' \in \mathcal{X}$) in the more general case of Theorem 2.10: given any $\mathbf{c} \in \mathbb{R}^m$, we have

$$\sum_{i,j} c_i c_j k(x_i, x_j) = \sum_{i,j} c_i c_j \langle \Phi(x_i), \Phi(x_j) \rangle = \left\| \sum_i c_i \Phi(x_i) \right\|^2 \geq 0. \tag{2.44}$$

Being positive definite, Mercer kernels are thus also reproducing kernels.

We next show how the reproducing kernel map is related to the Mercer kernel map constructed from the eigenfunction decomposition [202, 467]. To this end, let us consider a kernel which satisfies the condition of Theorem 2.10, and construct a dot product $\langle \cdot, \cdot \rangle$ such that k becomes a reproducing kernel for the Hilbert space $\mathcal{H}$ containing the functions

$$f(x) = \sum_{i=1}^{\infty} \alpha_i k(x, x_i) = \sum_{i=1}^{\infty} \alpha_i \sum_{j=1}^{N_{\mathcal{H}}} \lambda_j \psi_j(x) \psi_j(x_i). \tag{2.45}$$

By linearity, which holds for any dot product, we have

$$\langle f, k(., x') \rangle = \sum_{i=1}^{\infty} \alpha_i \sum_{j,n=1}^{N_{\mathcal{H}}} \lambda_j \psi_j(x_i) \langle \psi_j, \psi_n \rangle \lambda_n \psi_n(x'). \tag{2.46}$$

Since k is a Mercer kernel, the ψ_i ($i = 1, \ldots, N_{\mathcal{H}}$) can be chosen to be orthogonal with respect to the dot product in $L_2(\mathcal{X})$. Hence it is straightforward to choose $\langle \cdot, \cdot \rangle$ such that

$$\langle \psi_j, \psi_n \rangle = \delta_{jn} / \lambda_j \tag{2.47}$$

(using the Kronecker symbol δ_{jn}, see (B.30)), in which case (2.46) reduces to the reproducing kernel property (2.36) (using (2.45)). For a coordinate representation in the RKHS, see Problem 2.29.

Equivalence of Feature Spaces

The above connection between the Mercer kernel map and the RKHS map is instructive, but we shall rarely make use of it. In fact, we will usually *identify* the different feature spaces. Thus, to avoid confusion in subsequent chapters, the following comments are necessary. As described above, there are different ways of constructing feature spaces for any given kernel. In fact, they can even differ in terms of their dimensionality (cf. Problem 2.22). The two feature spaces that we will mostly use in this book are the RKHS associated with k (Section 2.2.2) and the Mercer ℓ_2 feature space. We will mostly use the same symbol $\mathcal{H}$ for all feature spaces that are associated with a given kernel. This makes sense provided that everything we do, at the end of the day, reduces to dot products. For instance, let us assume that Φ_1, Φ_2 are maps into the feature spaces $\mathcal{H}_1, \mathcal{H}_2$ respectively, both associated with the kernel k; in other words,

$$k(x, x') = \langle \Phi_i(x), \Phi_i(x') \rangle_{\mathcal{H}_i}, \text{ for } i = 1, 2. \tag{2.48}$$

Then it will usually *not* be the case that $\Phi_1(x) = \Phi_2(x)$; due to (2.48), however, we always have $\langle \Phi_1(x), \Phi_1(x') \rangle_{\mathcal{H}_1} = \langle \Phi_2(x), \Phi_2(x') \rangle_{\mathcal{H}_2}$. Therefore, as long as we are only interested in dot products, the two spaces can be considered identical.

An example of this identity is the so-called large margin regularizer that is usually used in SVMs, as discussed in the introductory chapter (cf. also Chapters 4 and 7),

$$\langle \mathbf{w}, \mathbf{w} \rangle, \text{ where } \mathbf{w} = \sum_{i=1}^{m} \alpha_i \Phi(x_i). \tag{2.49}$$

No matter whether Φ is the RKHS map $\Phi(x_i) = k(., x_i)$ (2.21) or the Mercer map $\Phi(x_i) = (\sqrt{\lambda_j} \psi_j(x))_{j=1,\ldots,N_{\mathcal{H}}}$ (2.40), the value of $\|\mathbf{w}\|^2$ will not change.

This point is of great importance, and we hope that all readers are still with us.

It is fair to say, however, that Section 2.2.5 can be skipped at first reading.

2.2.5 The Shape of the Mapped Data in Feature Space

Using Mercer's theorem, we have shown that one can think of the feature map as a map into a high- or infinite-dimensional Hilbert space. The argument in the remainder of the section shows that this typically entails that the mapped data $\Phi(\mathcal{X})$ lie in some box with rapidly decaying side lengths [606]. By this we mean that the range of the data decreases as the dimension index j increases, with a rate that depends on the size of the eigenvalues.

Let us assume that for all $j \in \mathbb{N}$, we have $\sup_{x \in \mathcal{X}} \lambda_j |\psi_j(x)|^2 < \infty$. Define the sequence

$$l_j := \sup_{x \in \mathcal{X}} \lambda_j |\psi_j(x)|^2. \tag{2.50}$$

Note that if

$$C_k := \sup_j \sup_{x \in \mathcal{X}} |\psi_j(x)| \tag{2.51}$$

exists (see Problem 2.24), then we have $l_j \leq \lambda_j C_k^2$. However, if the λ_j decay rapidly, then (2.50) can be finite even if (2.51) is not.

By construction, $\Phi(\mathcal{X})$ is contained in an axis parallel parallelepiped in $\ell_2^{N_{\mathcal{H}}}$ with side lengths $2\sqrt{l_j}$ (cf. (2.40)).[5]

Consider an example of a common kernel, the Gaussian, and let μ (see Theorem 2.10) be the Lebesgue measure. In this case, the eigenvectors are sine and cosine functions (with supremum one), and thus the sequence of the l_j coincides with the sequence of the eigenvalues λ_j. Generally, whenever $\sup_{x \in \mathcal{X}} |\psi_j(x)|^2$ is finite, the l_j decay as fast as the λ_j. We shall see in Sections 4.4, 4.5 and Chapter 12 that for many common kernels, this decay is very rapid.

It will be useful to consider operators that map $\Phi(\mathcal{X})$ into balls of some radius R centered at the origin. The following proposition characterizes a class of such operators, determined by the sequence $(l_j)_{j \in \mathbb{N}}$. Recall that $\mathbb{R}^{\mathbb{N}}$ denotes the space of all real sequences.

Proposition 2.13 (Mapping $\Phi(\mathcal{X})$ into ℓ_2) *Let S be the diagonal map*

$$\begin{aligned} S: \mathbb{R}^{\mathbb{N}} &\to \mathbb{R}^{\mathbb{N}} \\ (x_j)_j &\mapsto S(x_j)_j = (s_j x_j)_j, \end{aligned} \tag{2.52}$$

where $(s_j)_j \in \mathbb{R}^{\mathbb{N}}$. If $\left(s_j\sqrt{l_j}\right)_j \in \ell_2$, then S maps $\Phi(\mathcal{X})$ into a ball centered at the origin whose radius is $R = \left\|\left(s_j\sqrt{l_j}\right)_j\right\|$.

5. In fact, it is sufficient to use the essential supremum in (2.50). In that case, subsequent statements also only hold true almost everywhere.

Proof Suppose $\left(s_j\sqrt{l_j}\right)_j \in \ell_2$. Using the Mercer map (2.40), we have

$$\|S\Phi(x)\|^2 = \sum_{j\in\mathbb{N}} s_j^2\lambda_j|\psi_j(x)|^2 \leq \sum_{j\in\mathbb{N}} s_j^2 l_j = R \tag{2.53}$$

for any $x \in \mathcal{X}$. Hence $S\Phi(\mathcal{X}) \subseteq \ell_2$. ■

The converse is not necessarily the case. To see this, note that if $\left(s_j\sqrt{l_j}\right)_j \notin \ell_2$, amounting to saying that

$$\sum_j s_j^2 \sup_{x\in\mathcal{X}} \lambda_j|\psi_j(x)|^2 \tag{2.54}$$

is not finite, then there need not always exist an $x \in \mathcal{X}$ such that $S\Phi(x) = \left(s_j\sqrt{\lambda_j}\psi_j(x)\right)_j \notin \ell_2$, i.e., that

$$\sum_j s_j^2\lambda_j|\psi_j(x)|^2 \tag{2.55}$$

is not finite.

To see how the freedom to rescale $\Phi(\mathcal{X})$ effectively restricts the class of functions we are using, we first note that everything in the feature space $\mathcal{H} = \ell_2^{N_{\mathcal{H}}}$ is done in terms of dot products. Therefore, we can compensate any invertible symmetric linear transformation of the data in $\mathcal{H}$ by the inverse transformation on the set of admissible weight vectors in $\mathcal{H}$. In other words, for any invertible symmetric operator S on $\mathcal{H}$, we have $\langle S^{-1}\mathbf{w}, S\Phi(x)\rangle = \langle \mathbf{w}, \Phi(x)\rangle$ for all $x \in \mathcal{X}$.

As we shall see below (cf. Theorem 5.5, Section 12.4, and Problem 7.5), there exists a class of generalization error bound that depends on the radius R of the smallest sphere containing the data. If the $(l_i)_i$ decay rapidly, we are not actually "making use" of the whole sphere. In this case, we may construct a diagonal scaling operator S which inflates the sides of the above parallelepiped as much as possible, while ensuring that it is still contained within a sphere of the original radius R in $\mathcal{H}$ (Figure 2.3). By effectively reducing the size of the function class, this will provide a way of strengthening the bounds. A similar idea, using kernel PCA (Section 14.2) to determine empirical scaling coefficients, has been successfully applied by [101].

We conclude this section with another useful insight that characterizes a property of the feature map Φ. Note that most of what was said so far applies to the case where the input domain $\mathcal{X}$ is a general set. In this case, it is not possible to make nontrivial statements about continuity properties of Φ. This changes if we assume $\mathcal{X}$ to be endowed with a notion of closeness, by turning it into a so-called topological space. Readers not familiar with this concept will be reassured to hear

Continuity of Φ

that Euclidean vector spaces are particular cases of topological spaces.

Proposition 2.14 (Continuity of the Feature Map [402]) *If $\mathcal{X}$ is a topological space and k is a continuous positive definite kernel on $\mathcal{X} \times \mathcal{X}$, then there exists a Hilbert space $\mathcal{H}$ and a continuous map $\Phi : \mathcal{X} \to \mathcal{H}$ such that for all $x, x' \in \mathcal{X}$, we have $k(x, x') = \langle \Phi(x), \Phi(x')\rangle$.*

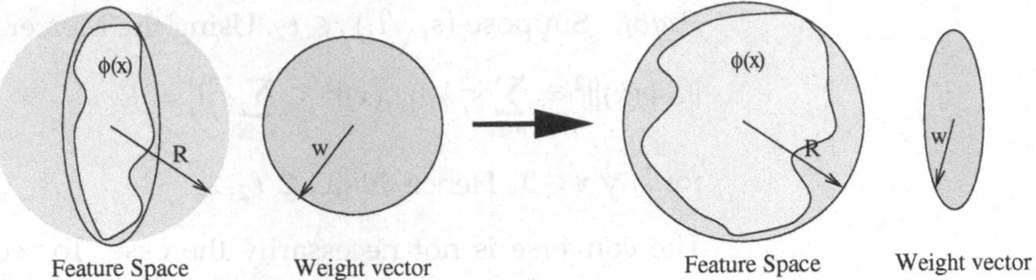

Figure 2.3 Since everything is done in terms of dot products, scaling up the data by an operator S can be compensated by scaling the weight vectors with S^{-1} (cf. text). By choosing S such that the data are still contained in a ball of the same radius R, we effectively reduce our function class (parametrized by the weight vector), which can lead to better generalization bounds, depending on the kernel inducing the map Φ.

2.2.6 The Empirical Kernel Map

The map Φ, defined in (2.21), transforms each input pattern into a function on $\mathcal{X}$, that is, into a potentially infinite-dimensional object. For any given set of points, however, it is possible to approximate Φ by only evaluating it on these points (cf. [232, 350, 361, 547, 474]):

Empirical Kernel Map

Definition 2.15 (Empirical Kernel Map) *For a given set $\{z_1, \ldots, z_n\} \subset \mathcal{X}$, $n \in \mathbb{N}$, we call*

$$\Phi_n : \mathbb{R}^N \to \mathbb{R}^n \text{ where } x \mapsto k(.,x)|_{\{z_1,\ldots,z_n\}} = (k(z_1,x), \ldots, k(z_n,x))^\top \tag{2.56}$$

the empirical kernel map *w.r.t.* $\{z_1, \ldots, z_n\}$.

As an example, consider first the case where k is a positive definite kernel, and $\{z_1, \ldots, z_n\} = \{x_1, \ldots, x_m\}$; we thus evaluate $k(.,x)$ on the training patterns. If we carry out a linear algorithm in feature space, then everything will take place in the linear span of the mapped training patterns. Therefore, we can represent the $k(.,x)$ of (2.21) as $\Phi_m(x)$ without losing information. The dot product to use in that representation, however, is not simply the canonical dot product in $\mathbb{R}^m$, since the $\Phi(x_i)$ will usually not form an orthonormal system. To turn Φ_m into a feature map associated with k, we need to endow $\mathbb{R}^m$ with a dot product $\langle \cdot, \cdot \rangle_m$ such that

$$k(x, x') = \langle \Phi_m(x), \Phi_m(x') \rangle_m . \tag{2.57}$$

To this end, we use the ansatz $\langle \cdot, \cdot \rangle_m = \langle \cdot, M \cdot \rangle$, with M being a positive definite matrix.[6] Enforcing (2.57) on the training patterns, this yields the self-consistency condition [478, 512]

$$K = KMK, \tag{2.58}$$

6. Every dot product in $\mathbb{R}^m$ can be written in this form. We do not require strict definiteness of M, as the null space can be projected out, leading to a lower-dimensional feature space.

where K is the Gram matrix. The condition (2.58) can be satisfied for instance by the (pseudo-)inverse $M = K^{-1}$. Equivalently, we could have incorporated this rescaling operation, which corresponds to a Kernel PCA "whitening" ([478, 547, 474], cf. Section 11.4), directly into the map, by whitening (2.56) to get

Kernel PCA Map

$$\Phi_m^w : x \mapsto K^{-\frac{1}{2}}(k(x_1, x), \ldots, k(x_m, x)). \tag{2.59}$$

This simply amounts to dividing the eigenvector basis vectors of K by $\sqrt{\lambda_i}$, where the λ_i are the eigenvalues of K.[7] This parallels the rescaling of the eigenfunctions of the integral operator belonging to the kernel, given by (2.47). It turns out that this map can equivalently be performed using kernel PCA feature extraction (see Problem 14.8), which is why we refer to this map as the *kernel PCA map*.

Note that we have thus constructed a data-dependent feature map into an m-dimensional space which satisfies $\langle \Phi_m^w(x), \Phi_m^w(x') \rangle = k(x, x')$, i.e., we have found an m-dimensional feature space associated with the given kernel. In the case where K is invertible, $\Phi_m^w(x)$ computes the coordinates of $\Phi(x)$ when represented in a basis of the m-dimensional subspace spanned by $\Phi(x_1), \ldots, \Phi(x_m)$.

For data sets where the number of examples is smaller than their dimension, it can actually be computationally attractive to carry out Φ_m^w explicitly, rather than using kernels in subsequent algorithms. Moreover, algorithms which are not readily "kernelized" may benefit from explicitly carrying out the kernel PCA map.

We end this section with two notes which illustrate why the use of (2.56) need not be restricted to the special case we just discussed.

- *More general kernels.* When using non-symmetric kernels k in (2.56), together with the canonical dot product, we effectively work with the positive definite matrix $K^\top K$. Note that each positive definite matrix can be written as $K^\top K$. Therefore, working with positive definite kernels leads to an equally rich set of nonlinearities as working with an empirical kernel map using general non-symmetric kernels. If we wanted to carry out the whitening step, we would have to use $(K^\top K)^{-1/4}$ (cf. footnote 7 concerning potential singularities).
- *Different evaluation sets.* Things can be sped up by using expansion sets of the form $\{z_1, \ldots, z_n\}$, mapping into an n-dimensional space, with $n < m$, as done in [100, 228]. In that case, one modifies (2.59) to

$$\Phi_n^w : x \mapsto K_n^{-\frac{1}{2}}(k(z_1, x), \ldots, k(z_n, x)), \tag{2.60}$$

where $(K_n)_{ij} := k(z_i, z_j)$. The expansion set can either be a subset of the training set,[8] or some other set of points. We will later return to the issue of how to choose

7. It is understood that if K is singular, we use the pseudo-inverse of $K^{1/2}$ in which case we get an even lower dimensional subspace.
8. In [228] it is recommended that the size n of the expansion set is chosen large enough to ensure that the smallest eigenvalue of K_n is larger than some predetermined $\epsilon > 0$. Alternatively, one can start off with a larger set, and use kernel PCA to *select* the most important components for the map, see Problem 14.8. In the kernel PCA case, the map (2.60) is com-

the best set (see Section 10.2 and Chapter 18). As an aside, note that in the case of Kernel PCA (see Section 1.7 and Chapter 14 below), one does not need to worry about the whitening step in (2.59) and (2.60): using the canonical dot product in $\mathbb{R}^m$ (rather than $\langle \cdot, \cdot \rangle$) will simply lead to diagonalizing K^2 instead of K, which yields the same eigenvectors with squared eigenvalues. This was pointed out by [350, 361]. The study [361] reports experiments where (2.56) was employed to speed up Kernel PCA by choosing $\{z_1, \ldots, z_n\}$ as a subset of $\{x_1, \ldots, x_m\}$.

2.2.7 A Kernel Map Defined from Pairwise Similarities

In practice, we are given a finite amount of data $x_1, \ldots, x_m$. The following simple observation shows that even if we do not want to (or are unable to) analyze a given kernel k analytically, we can still compute a map Φ such that k corresponds to a dot product in the linear span of the $\Phi(x_i)$:

Proposition 2.16 (Data-Dependent Kernel Map [467]) *Suppose the data $x_1, \ldots, x_m$ and the kernel k are such that the kernel Gram matrix $K_{ij} = k(x_i, x_j)$ is positive definite. Then it is possible to construct a map Φ into an m-dimensional feature space $\mathcal{H}$ such that*

$$k(x_i, x_j) = \langle \Phi(x_i), \Phi(x_j) \rangle . \tag{2.61}$$

Conversely, given an arbitrary map Φ into some feature space $\mathcal{H}$, the matrix $K_{ij} = \langle \Phi(x_i), \Phi(x_j) \rangle$ is positive definite.

Proof First assume that K is positive definite. In this case, it can be diagonalized as $K = SDS^\top$, with an orthogonal matrix S and a diagonal matrix D with nonnegative entries. Then

$$k(x_i, x_j) = (SDS^\top)_{ij} = \langle S_i, DS_j \rangle = \left\langle \sqrt{D} S_i, \sqrt{D} S_j \right\rangle , \tag{2.62}$$

where we have defined the S_i as the rows of S (note that the columns of S would be K's eigenvectors). Therefore, K is the Gram matrix of the vectors $\sqrt{D_{ii}} \cdot S_i$.[9] Hence the following map Φ, defined on $x_1, \ldots, x_m$ will satisfy (2.61)

$$\Phi : x_i \mapsto \sqrt{D_{ii}} \cdot S_i . \tag{2.63}$$

Thus far, Φ is only defined on a set of points, rather than on a vector space. Therefore, it makes no sense to ask whether it is linear. We can, however, ask whether it can be *extended* to a linear map, provided the x_i are elements of a vector space. The answer is that if the x_i are linearly dependent (which is often the case), then this will not be possible, since a linear map would then typically be over-

puted as $D_n^{-1/2} U_n^\top (k(z_1, x), \ldots, k(z_n, x))$, where $U_n D_n U_n^\top$ is the eigenvalue decomposition of K_n. Note that the columns of U_n are the eigenvectors of K_n. We discard all columns that correspond to zero eigenvalues, as well as the corresponding dimensions of D_n. To *approximate* the map, we may actually discard all eigenvalues smaller than some $\epsilon > 0$.

9. In fact, every positive definite matrix is the Gram matrix of some set of vectors [46].

determined by the m conditions (2.63).

For the converse, assume an arbitrary $\boldsymbol{\alpha} \in \mathbb{R}^m$, and compute

$$\sum_{i,j=1}^{m} \alpha_i \alpha_j K_{ij} = \left\langle \sum_{i=1}^{m} \alpha_i \Phi(x_i), \sum_{j=1}^{m} \alpha_j \Phi(x_j) \right\rangle = \left\| \sum_{i=1}^{m} \alpha_i \Phi(x_i) \right\|^2 \geq 0. \tag{2.64}$$

■

In particular, this result implies that given data $x_1, \ldots, x_m$, and a kernel k which gives rise to a positive definite matrix K, it is always possible to construct a feature space $\mathcal{H}$ of dimension at most m that we are implicitly working in when using kernels (cf. Problem 2.32 and Section 2.2.6).

If we perform an algorithm which requires k to correspond to a dot product in some other space (as for instance the SV algorithms described in this book), it is possible that even though k is not positive definite in general, it still gives rise to a positive definite Gram matrix K with respect to the training data at hand. In this case, Proposition 2.16 tells us that nothing will go wrong during training when we work with these data. Moreover, if k leads to a matrix with some small negative eigenvalues, we can add a small multiple of some strictly positive definite kernel k' (such as the identity $k'(x_i, x_j) = \delta_{ij}$) to obtain a positive definite matrix. To see this, suppose that $\lambda_{\min} < 0$ is the minimal eigenvalue of k's Gram matrix. Note that being strictly positive definite, the Gram matrix K' of k' satisfies

$$\min_{\|\boldsymbol{\alpha}\|=1} \langle \boldsymbol{\alpha}, K'\boldsymbol{\alpha} \rangle \geq \lambda'_{\min} > 0, \tag{2.65}$$

where $\lambda'_{\min}$ denotes its minimal eigenvalue, and the first inequality follows from Rayleigh's principle (B.57). Therefore, provided that $\lambda_{\min} + \lambda\lambda'_{\min} \geq 0$, we have

$$\langle \boldsymbol{\alpha}, (K + \lambda K')\boldsymbol{\alpha} \rangle = \langle \boldsymbol{\alpha}, K\boldsymbol{\alpha} \rangle + \lambda \langle \boldsymbol{\alpha}, K'\boldsymbol{\alpha} \rangle \geq \|\boldsymbol{\alpha}\|^2 (\lambda_{\min} + \lambda\lambda'_{\min}) \geq 0 \tag{2.66}$$

for all $\boldsymbol{\alpha} \in \mathbb{R}^m$, rendering $(K + \lambda K')$ positive definite.

2.3 Examples and Properties of Kernels

Polynomial

For the following examples, let us assume that $\mathcal{X} \subset \mathbb{R}^N$. Besides homogeneous polynomial kernels (cf. Proposition 2.1),

$$k(x, x') = \langle x, x' \rangle^d, \tag{2.67}$$

Gaussian

Boser, Guyon, and Vapnik [62, 223, 561] suggest the usage of Gaussian radial basis function kernels [26, 4],

$$k(x, x') = \exp\left(-\frac{\|x - x'\|^2}{2\,\sigma^2}\right), \tag{2.68}$$

Sigmoid

where $\sigma > 0$, and sigmoid kernels,

$$k(x, x') = \tanh(\kappa \langle x, x' \rangle + \vartheta), \tag{2.69}$$

where $\kappa > 0$ and $\vartheta < 0$. By applying Theorem 13.4 below, one can check that the latter kernel is not actually positive definite (see Section 4.6 and [85, 511] and the discussion in Example 4.25). Curiously, it has nevertheless successfully been used in practice. The reasons for this are discussed in [467].

Inhomogeneous Polynomial

Other useful kernels include the inhomogeneous polynomial,

$$k(x, x') = (\langle x, x' \rangle + c)^d, \tag{2.70}$$

($d \in \mathbb{N}, c \geq 0$) and the B_n-spline kernel [501, 572] (I_X denoting the indicator (or characteristic) function on the set X, and $\otimes$ the convolution operation, $(f \otimes g)(x) := \int f(x')g(x' - x)dx'$),

B_n-Spline of Odd Order

$$k(x, x') = B_{2p+1}(\|x - x'\|) \text{ with } B_n := \bigotimes_{i=1}^{n} I_{[-\frac{1}{2}, \frac{1}{2}]}. \tag{2.71}$$

The kernel computes B-splines of order $2p + 1$ ($p \in \mathbb{N}$), defined by the $(2p + 1)$-fold convolution of the unit interval $[-1/2, 1/2]$. See Section 4.4.1 for further details and a regularization theoretic analysis of this kernel.

Invariance of Kernels

Note that all these kernels have the convenient property of unitary invariance, $k(x, x') = k(Ux, Ux')$ if $U^\top = U^{-1}$, for instance if U is a rotation. If we consider complex numbers, then we have to use the adjoint $U^* := \overline{U}^\top$ instead of the transpose.

RBF Kernels

Radial basis function (RBF) kernels are kernels that can be written in the form

$$k(x, x') = f(d(x, x')), \tag{2.72}$$

where d is a metric on $\mathcal{X}$, and f is a function on $\mathbb{R}_0^+$. Examples thereof are the Gaussians and B-splines mentioned above. Usually, the metric arises from the dot product; $d(x, x') = \|x - x'\| = \sqrt{\langle x - x', x - x' \rangle}$. In this case, RBF kernels are unitary invariant, too. In addition, they are translation invariant; in other words, $k(x, x') = k(x + x_0, x' + x_0)$ for all $x_0 \in \mathcal{X}$.

In some cases, invariance properties alone can distinguish particular kernels: in Section 2.1, we explained how using polynomial kernels $\langle x, x' \rangle^d$ corresponds to mapping into a feature space whose dimensions are spanned by all possible dth order monomials in input coordinates. The different dimensions are scaled with the square root of the number of ordered products of the respective d entries (e.g., $\sqrt{2}$ in (2.13)). These scaling factors precisely ensure invariance under the group of all orthogonal transformations (rotations and mirroring operations). In many cases, this is a desirable property: it ensures that the results of a learning procedure do not depend on which orthonormal coordinate system (with fixed origin) we use for representing our input data.

Proposition 2.17 (Invariance of Polynomial Kernels [480]) *Up to a scaling factor, the kernel $k(x, x') = \langle x, x' \rangle^d$ is the only kernel inducing a map into a space of* all *monomials of degree d which is invariant under orthogonal transformations of $\mathbb{R}^N$.*

Properties of RBF Kernels

Some interesting additional structure exists in the case of a Gaussian RBF kernel k (2.68). As $k(x, x) = 1$ for all $x \in \mathcal{X}$, each mapped example has unit length, $\|\Phi(x)\| =$

1 (Problem 2.18 shows how to achieve this for general kernels). Moreover, as $k(x, x') > 0$ for all $x, x' \in \mathcal{X}$, all points lie inside the same orthant in feature space. To see this, recall that for unit length vectors, the dot product (1.3) equals the cosine of the enclosed angle. We obtain

$$\cos(\angle(\Phi(x), \Phi(x'))) = \langle \Phi(x), \Phi(x') \rangle = k(x, x') > 0, \tag{2.73}$$

which amounts to saying that the enclosed angle between any two mapped examples is smaller than $\pi/2$.

The above seems to indicate that in the Gaussian case, the mapped data lie in a fairly restricted area of feature space. However, in another sense, they occupy a space which is as large as possible:

Theorem 2.18 (Full Rank of Gaussian RBF Gram Matrices [360]) *Suppose that $x_1, \ldots, x_m \subset \mathcal{X}$ are distinct points, and $\sigma \neq 0$. The matrix K given by*

$$K_{ij} := \exp\left(-\frac{\|x_i - x_j\|^2}{2\sigma^2}\right) \tag{2.74}$$

has full rank.

Infinite-Dimensional Feature Space

In other words, the points $\Phi(x_1), \ldots, \Phi(x_m)$ are linearly independent (provided no two x_i are the same). They span an m-dimensional subspace of $\mathcal{H}$. Therefore a Gaussian kernel defined on a domain of infinite cardinality, with no a priori restriction on the number of training examples, produces a feature space of *infinite* dimension. Nevertheless, an analysis of the shape of the mapped data in feature space shows that capacity is distributed in a way that ensures smooth and simple estimates whenever possible (see Section 12.4).

The examples given above all apply to the case of vectorial data. Let us next give an example where $\mathcal{X}$ is *not* a vector space [42].

Proposition 2.19 (Similarity of Probabilistic Events) *If $(\mathcal{X}, \mathcal{C}, \mathrm{P})$ is a probability space with σ-algebra $\mathcal{C}$ and probability measure P, then*

$$k(A, B) = \mathrm{P}(A \cap B) - \mathrm{P}(A)\mathrm{P}(B) \tag{2.75}$$

is a positive definite kernel on $\mathcal{C} \times \mathcal{C}$.

Proof To see this, we define a feature map

$$\Phi : A \mapsto (I_A - \mathrm{P}(A)), \tag{2.76}$$

where I_A is the characteristic function on A. On the feature space, which consists of functions on $\mathcal{X}$ taking values in $[-1, 1]$, we use the dot product

$$\langle f, g \rangle := \int_{\mathcal{X}} f \cdot g \, d\mathrm{P}. \tag{2.77}$$

The result follows by noticing $\langle I_A, I_B \rangle = \mathrm{P}(A \cap B)$ and $\langle I_A, \mathrm{P}(B) \rangle = \mathrm{P}(A)\mathrm{P}(B)$. ∎

Further examples include kernels for string matching, as proposed by [585, 234, 23]. We shall describe these, and address the general problem of designing kernel functions, in Chapter 13.

The next section will return to the connection between kernels and feature spaces. Readers who are eager to move on to SV algorithms may want to skip this section, which is somewhat more technical.

2.4 The Representation of Dissimilarities in Linear Spaces

2.4.1 Conditionally Positive Definite Kernels

We now proceed to a larger class of kernels than that of the positive definite ones. This larger class is interesting in several regards. First, it will turn out that some kernel algorithms work with this class, rather than only with positive definite kernels. Second, its relationship to positive definite kernels is a rather interesting one, and a number of connections between the two classes provide understanding of kernels in general. Third, they are intimately related to a question which is a variation on the central aspect of positive definite kernels: the latter can be thought of as dot products in feature spaces; the former, on the other hand, can be embedded as *distance measures* arising from norms in feature spaces.

The present section thus attempts to extend the utility of the kernel trick by looking at the problem of which kernels can be used to compute distances in feature spaces. The underlying mathematical results have been known for quite a while [465]; some of them have already attracted interest in the kernel methods community in various contexts [515, 234].

Clearly, the squared distance $\|\Phi(x) - \Phi(x')\|^2$ in the feature space associated with a pd kernel k can be computed, using $k(x, x') = \langle\Phi(x), \Phi(x')\rangle$, as

$$\|\Phi(x) - \Phi(x')\|^2 = k(x, x) + k(x', x') - 2k(x, x'). \tag{2.78}$$

Positive definite kernels are, however, not the full story: there exists a *larger* class of kernels that can be used as generalized distances, and the present section will describe why and how [468].

Let us start by considering how a dot product and the corresponding distance measure are affected by a translation of the data, $x \mapsto x - x_0$. Clearly, $\|x - x'\|^2$ is translation invariant while $\langle x, x'\rangle$ is not. A short calculation shows that the effect of the translation can be expressed in terms of $\|. - .\|^2$ as

$$\langle (x - x_0), (x' - x_0)\rangle = \frac{1}{2}\left(-\|x - x'\|^2 + \|x - x_0\|^2 + \|x_0 - x'\|^2\right). \tag{2.79}$$

Note that this, just like $\langle x, x'\rangle$, is still a pd kernel: $\sum_{i,j} c_i c_j \langle (x_i - x_0), (x_j - x_0)\rangle = \|\sum_i c_i(x_i - x_0)\|^2 \geq 0$ holds true for any c_i. For any choice of $x_0 \in \mathcal{X}$, we thus get a similarity measure (2.79) associated with the dissimilarity measure $\|x - x'\|$.

This naturally leads to the question of whether (2.79) might suggest a connection that also holds true in more general cases: what kind of nonlinear dissimilarity measure do we have to substitute for $\|.-.\|^2$ on the right hand side of (2.79), to ensure that the left hand side becomes positive definite? To state the answer, we first need to define the appropriate class of kernels.

The following definition differs from Definition 2.4 only in the additional constraint on the sum of the c_i. Below, $\mathbb{K}$ is a shorthand for $\mathbb{C}$ or $\mathbb{R}$; the definitions are the same in both cases.

Definition 2.20 (Conditionally Positive Definite Matrix) *A symmetric $m \times m$ matrix K ($m \geq 2$) taking values in $\mathbb{K}$ and satisfying*

$$\sum_{i,j=1}^{m} c_i \bar{c}_j K_{ij} \geq 0 \text{ for all } c_i \in \mathbb{K}, \text{ with } \sum_{i=1}^{m} c_i = 0, \tag{2.80}$$

is called conditionally positive definite (cpd).

Definition 2.21 (Conditionally Positive Definite Kernel) *Let $\mathcal{X}$ be a nonempty set. A function $k : \mathcal{X} \times \mathcal{X} \to \mathbb{K}$ which for all $m \geq 2, x_1, \ldots, x_m \in \mathcal{X}$ gives rise to a conditionally positive definite Gram matrix is called a* conditionally positive definite (cpd) kernel.

Note that symmetry is also required in the complex case. Due to the additional constraint on the coefficients c_i, it does not follow automatically anymore, as it did in the case of complex positive definite matrices and kernels. In Chapter 4, we will revisit cpd kernels. There, we will actually introduce cpd kernels of different orders. The definition given in the current chapter covers the case of kernels which are cpd *of order* 1.

Connection PD — CPD

Proposition 2.22 (Constructing PD Kernels from CPD Kernels [42]) *Let $x_0 \in \mathcal{X}$, and let k be a symmetric kernel on $\mathcal{X} \times \mathcal{X}$. Then*

$$\tilde{k}(x, x') := \frac{1}{2}(k(x, x') - k(x, x_0) - k(x_0, x') + k(x_0, x_0))$$

is positive definite if and only if k is conditionally positive definite.

The proof follows directly from the definitions and can be found in [42]. This result does generalize (2.79): the negative squared distance kernel is indeed cpd, since $\sum_i c_i = 0$ implies $-\sum_{i,j} c_i c_j \|x_i - x_j\|^2 = -\sum_i c_i \sum_j c_j \|x_j\|^2 - \sum_j c_j \sum_i c_i \|x_i\|^2 + 2\sum_{i,j} c_i c_j \langle x_i, x_j \rangle = 2\sum_{i,j} c_i c_j \langle x_i, x_j \rangle = 2\|\sum_i c_i x_i\|^2 \geq 0$. In fact, this implies that all kernels of the form

$$k(x, x') = -\|x - x'\|^{\beta}, 0 \leq \beta \leq 2 \tag{2.81}$$

are cpd (they are not pd),[10] by application of the following result (note that the case $\beta = 0$ is trivial):

10. Moreover, they are not cpd if $\beta > 2$ [42].

Proposition 2.23 (Fractional Powers and Logs of CPD Kernels [42]) *If $k : \mathcal{X} \times \mathcal{X} \to (-\infty, 0]$ is cpd, then so are $-(-k)^\alpha$ $(0 < \alpha < 1)$ and $-\ln(1-k)$.*

To state another class of cpd kernels that are not pd, note first that as a trivial consequence of Definition 2.20, we know that (i) sums of cpd kernels are cpd, and (ii) any constant $b \in \mathbb{R}$ is a cpd kernel. Therefore, any kernel of the form $k + b$, where k is cpd and $b \in \mathbb{R}$, is also cpd. In particular, since pd kernels are cpd, we can take any pd kernel and offset it by b, and it will still be at least cpd. For further examples of cpd kernels, cf. [42, 578, 205, 515].

2.4.2 Hilbert Space Representation of CPD Kernels

We now return to the main flow of the argument. Proposition 2.22 allows us to construct the feature map for k from that of the pd kernel $\tilde{k}$. To this end, fix $x_0 \in \mathcal{X}$ and define $\tilde{k}$ according to Proposition 2.22. Due to Proposition 2.22, $\tilde{k}$ is positive definite. Therefore, we may employ the Hilbert space representation $\Phi : \mathcal{X} \to \mathcal{H}$ of $\tilde{k}$ (cf. (2.32)), satisfying $\langle \Phi(x), \Phi(x') \rangle = \tilde{k}(x, x')$; hence,

$$\|\Phi(x) - \Phi(x')\|^2 = \tilde{k}(x, x) + \tilde{k}(x', x') - 2\tilde{k}(x, x'). \tag{2.82}$$

Substituting Proposition 2.22 yields

$$\|\Phi(x) - \Phi(x')\|^2 = -k(x, x') + \frac{1}{2}\left(k(x, x) + k(x', x')\right). \tag{2.83}$$

This implies the following result [465, 42].

Feature Map for CPD Kernels

Proposition 2.24 (Hilbert Space Representation of CPD Kernels) *Let k be a real-valued CPD kernel on $\mathcal{X}$, satisfying $k(x, x) = 0$ for all $x \in \mathcal{X}$. Then there exists a Hilbert space $\mathcal{H}$ of real-valued functions on $\mathcal{X}$, and a mapping $\Phi : \mathcal{X} \to \mathcal{H}$, such that*

$$\|\Phi(x) - \Phi(x')\|^2 = -k(x, x'). \tag{2.84}$$

If we drop the assumption $k(x, x) = 0$, the Hilbert space representation reads

$$\|\Phi(x) - \Phi(x')\|^2 = -k(x, x') + \frac{1}{2}\left(k(x, x) + k(x', x')\right). \tag{2.85}$$

It can be shown that if $k(x, x) = 0$ for all $x \in \mathcal{X}$, then

$$d(x, x') := \sqrt{-k(x, x')} = \|\Phi(x) - \Phi(x')\| \tag{2.86}$$

is a semi-metric: clearly, it is nonnegative and symmetric; additionally, it satisfies the triangle inequality, as can be seen by computing $d(x, x') + d(x', x'') = \|\Phi(x) - \Phi(x')\| + \|\Phi(x') - \Phi(x'')\| \geq \|\Phi(x) - \Phi(x'')\| = d(x, x'')$ [42].

It is a metric if $k(x, x') \neq 0$ for $x \neq x'$. We thus see that we can rightly think of k as the negative of a distance measure.

We next show how to represent *general* symmetric kernels (thus in particular cpd kernels) as symmetric bilinear forms Q in feature spaces. This generalization of the previously known feature space representation for pd kernels comes at a cost: Q will no longer be a dot product. For our purposes, we can get away with this. The result will give us an intuitive understanding of Proposition 2.22: we can then write $\tilde{k}$ as $\tilde{k}(x,x') := Q(\Phi(x) - \Phi(x_0), \Phi(x') - \Phi(x_0))$. Proposition 2.22 thus essentially adds an origin in feature space which corresponds to the image $\Phi(x_0)$ of one point x_0 under the feature map.

Feature Map for General Symmetric Kernels

Proposition 2.25 (Vector Space Representation of Symmetric Kernels) *Let k be a real-valued symmetric kernel on $\mathcal{X}$. Then there exists a linear space $\mathcal{H}$ of real-valued functions on $\mathcal{X}$, endowed with a symmetric bilinear form $Q(.,.)$, and a mapping $\Phi : \mathcal{X} \to \mathcal{H}$, such that $k(x,x') = Q(\Phi(x), \Phi(x'))$.*

Proof The proof is a direct modification of the pd case. We use the map (2.21) and linearly complete the image as in (2.22). Define $Q(f,g) := \sum_{i=1}^{m}\sum_{j=1}^{m'} \alpha_i\beta_j k(x_i, x'_j)$. To see that it is well-defined, although it explicitly contains the expansion coefficients (which need not be unique), note that $Q(f,g) = \sum_{j=1}^{m'} \beta_j f(x'_j)$, independent of the α_i. Similarly, for g, note that $Q(f,g) = \sum_i \alpha_i g(x_i)$, hence it is independent of β_j. The last two equations also show that Q is bilinear; clearly, it is symmetric. ■

Note, moreover, that by definition of Q, k is a reproducing kernel for the feature space (which is not a Hilbert space): for all functions f (2.22), we have $Q(k(.,x), f) = f(x)$; in particular, $Q(k(.,x), k(.,x')) = k(x,x')$.

Rewriting $\tilde{k}$ as $\tilde{k}(x,x') := Q(\Phi(x) - \Phi(x_0), \Phi(x') - \Phi(x_0))$ suggests an immediate generalization of Proposition 2.22: in practice, we might want to choose other points as origins in feature space — points that do not have a pre-image x_0 in the input domain, such as the mean of a set of points (cf. [543]). This will be useful when considering kernel PCA. It is only crucial that the behavior of our reference point under translation is identical to that of individual points. This is taken care of by the constraint on the sum of the c_i in the following proposition.

Matrix Centering

Proposition 2.26 (Exercise 2.23 in [42]) *Let K be a symmetric matrix, $\mathbf{e} \in \mathbb{R}^m$ be the vector of all ones, $\mathbf{1}$ the $m \times m$ identity matrix, and let $\mathbf{c} \in \mathbb{C}^m$ satisfy $\mathbf{e}^*\mathbf{c} = 1$. Then*

$$\tilde{K} := (\mathbf{1} - \mathbf{e}\mathbf{c}^*)K(\mathbf{1} - \mathbf{c}\mathbf{e}^*) \tag{2.87}$$

is positive definite if and only if K is conditionally positive definite.[11]

Proof "$\Longrightarrow$": suppose $\tilde{K}$ is positive definite. Thus for any $\mathbf{a} \in \mathbb{C}^m$ which satisfies $\mathbf{a}^*\mathbf{e} = \mathbf{e}^*\mathbf{a} = 0$, we have $0 \leq \mathbf{a}^*\tilde{K}\mathbf{a} = \mathbf{a}^*K\mathbf{a} + \mathbf{a}^*\mathbf{e}\mathbf{c}^*K\mathbf{c}\mathbf{e}^*\mathbf{a} - \mathbf{a}^*K\mathbf{c}\mathbf{e}^*\mathbf{a} - \mathbf{a}^*\mathbf{e}\mathbf{c}^*K\mathbf{a} = \mathbf{a}^*K\mathbf{a}$. This means that $0 \leq \mathbf{a}^*K\mathbf{a}$, proving that K is conditionally positive definite.

"$\Longleftarrow$": suppose K is conditionally positive definite. This means that we have to show that $\mathbf{a}^*\tilde{K}\mathbf{a} \geq 0$ for all $\mathbf{a} \in \mathbb{C}^m$. We have

$$\mathbf{a}^*\tilde{K}\mathbf{a} = \mathbf{a}^*(\mathbf{1} - \mathbf{e}\mathbf{c}^*)K(\mathbf{1} - \mathbf{c}\mathbf{e}^*)\mathbf{a} = \mathbf{s}^*K\mathbf{s} \text{ for } \mathbf{s} = (\mathbf{1} - \mathbf{c}\mathbf{e}^*)\mathbf{a}. \tag{2.88}$$

---

11. $\mathbf{c}^*$ is the vector obtained by transposing and taking the complex conjugate of $\mathbf{c}$.

All we need to show is $\mathbf{e}^*\mathbf{s} = 0$, since then we can use the fact that K is cpd to obtain $\mathbf{s}^* K\mathbf{s} \geq 0$. This can be seen as follows $\mathbf{e}^*\mathbf{s} = \mathbf{e}^*(\mathbf{1} - \mathbf{c}\mathbf{e}^*)\mathbf{a} = (\mathbf{e}^* - (\mathbf{e}^*\mathbf{c})\mathbf{e}^*)\mathbf{a} = (\mathbf{e}^* - \mathbf{e}^*)\mathbf{a} = 0$. ■

This result directly implies a corresponding generalization of Proposition 2.22:

Kernel Centering

Proposition 2.27 (Adding a General Origin) *Let k be a symmetric kernel, $x_1, \ldots, x_m \in \mathcal{X}$, and let $c_i \in \mathbb{C}$ satisfy $\sum_{i=1}^m c_i = 1$. Then*

$$\tilde{k}(x, x') := \frac{1}{2}\left(k(x, x') - \sum_{i=1}^{m} c_i k(x, x_i) - \sum_{i=1}^{m} c_i k(x_i, x') + \sum_{i,j=1}^{m} c_i c_j k(x_i, x_j)\right)$$

is positive definite if and only if k is conditionally positive definite.

Proof Consider a set of $m' \in \mathbb{N}$ points $x'_1, \ldots, x'_{m'} \in \mathcal{X}$, and let K be the $(m + m') \times (m + m')$ Gram matrix based on $x_1, \ldots, x_m, x'_1, \ldots, x'_{m'}$. Apply Proposition 2.26 using $c_{m+1} = \ldots = c_{m+m'} = 0$. ■

Application to SVMs

The above results show that conditionally positive definite kernels are a natural choice whenever we are dealing with a translation invariant problem, such as the SVM: maximization of the margin of separation between two classes of data is independent of the position of the origin. Seen in this light, it is not surprising that the structure of the dual optimization problem (cf. [561]) allows cpd kernels: as noted in [515, 507], the constraint $\sum_{i=1}^m \alpha_i y_i = 0$ projects out the same subspace as (2.80) in the definition of conditionally positive definite matrices.

Application to Kernel PCA

Another example of a kernel algorithm that works with conditionally positive definite kernels is Kernel PCA (Chapter 14), where the data are centered, thus removing the dependence on the origin in feature space. Formally, this follows from Proposition 2.26 for $c_i = 1/m$.

Application to Parzen Windows Classifiers

Let us consider another example. One of the simplest distance-based classification algorithms proceeds as follows. Given m_+ points labelled with $+1$, m_- points labelled with -1, and a mapped test point $\Phi(x)$, we compute the mean squared distances between the latter and the two classes, and assign it to the one for which this mean is smaller;

$$y = \operatorname{sgn}\left(\frac{1}{m_-}\sum_{y_i=-1}\|\Phi(x) - \Phi(x_i)\|^2 - \frac{1}{m_+}\sum_{y_i=1}\|\Phi(x) - \Phi(x_i)\|^2\right). \tag{2.89}$$

We use the distance kernel trick (Proposition 2.24) to express the decision function as a kernel expansion in the input domain: a short calculation shows that

$$y = \operatorname{sgn}\left(\frac{1}{m_+}\sum_{y_i=1} k(x, x_i) - \frac{1}{m_-}\sum_{y_i=-1} k(x, x_i) + b\right), \tag{2.90}$$

with the constant offset

$$b = \frac{1}{2m_-}\sum_{y_i=-1} k(x_i, x_i) - \frac{1}{2m_+}\sum_{y_i=1} k(x_i, x_i). \tag{2.91}$$

Note that for some cpd kernels, such as (2.81), $k(x_i, x_i)$ is always 0, and thus $b = 0$. For others, such as the commonly used Gaussian kernel, $k(x_i, x_i)$ is a nonzero constant, in which case b vanishes provided that $m_+ = m_-$. For normalized Gaussians, the resulting decision boundary can be interpreted as the Bayes decision based on two Parzen window density estimates of the classes; for general cpd kernels, the analogy is merely a formal one; that is, the decision functions take the same form.

Properties of CPD Kernels

Many properties of positive definite kernels carry over to the more general case of conditionally positive definite kernels, such as Proposition 13.1.

Using Proposition 2.22, one can prove an interesting connection between the two classes of kernels:

Proposition 2.28 (Connection PD — CPD [465]) *A kernel k is conditionally positive definite if and only if* $\exp(tk)$ *is positive definite for all $t > 0$.*

Positive definite kernels of the form $\exp(tk)$ ($t > 0$) have the interesting property that their nth root ($n \in \mathbb{N}$) is again a positive definite kernel. Such kernels are called *infinitely divisible.* One can show that, disregarding some technicalities, the logarithm of an infinitely divisible positive definite kernel mapping into $\mathbb{R}_0^+$ is a conditionally positive definite kernel.

2.4.3 Higher Order CPD Kernels

For the sake of completeness, we now present some material which is of interest to one section later in the book (Section 4.8), but not central for the present chapter. We follow [341, 204].

Definition 2.29 (Conditionally Positive Definite Functions of Order q) *A continuous function h, defined on $[0, \infty)$, is called conditionally positive definite (cpd) of order q on $\mathbb{R}^N$ if for any distinct points $x_1, \ldots, x_m \in \mathbb{R}^N$, the quadratic form,*

$$\sum_{i,j=1}^{m} \alpha_i \alpha_j h(\|x_i - x_j\|^2), \tag{2.92}$$

is nonnegative, provided that the scalars $\alpha_1, \ldots, \alpha_m$ satisfy $\sum_{i=1}^{m} \alpha_i p(x_i) = 0$, for all polynomials $p(\cdot)$ on $\mathbb{R}^N$ of degree lower than q.

Let Π_q^N denote the space of polynomials of degree lower than q on $\mathbb{R}^N$. By definition, every cpd function h of order q generates a positive definite kernel for SV expansions in the space of functions orthogonal to Π_q^N, by setting $k(x, x') := h(\|x - x'\|^2)$.

There exists also an analogue to the positive definiteness of the integral operator in the conditions of Mercer's theorem. In [157, 341] it is shown that for cpd functions h of order q, we have

$$\int h(\|x - x'\|^2) f(x) f(x') dx dx' \geq 0, \tag{2.93}$$

provided that the projection of f onto Π_q^N is zero.

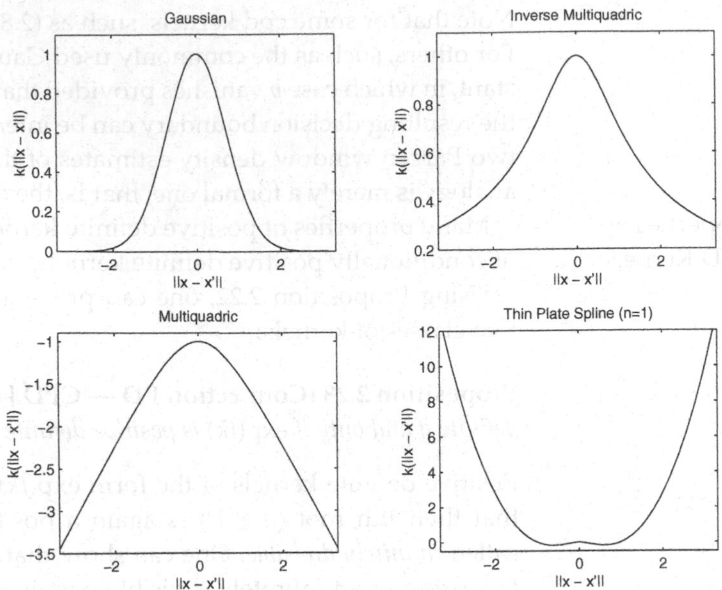

Figure 2.4 Conditionally positive definite functions, as described in Table 2.1. Where applicable, we set the free parameter c to 1; β is set to 2. Note that cpd kernels need not be positive anywhere (e.g., the Multiquadric kernel).

Table 2.1 Examples of Conditionally Positive Definite Kernels. The fact that the exponential kernel is pd (i.e., cpd of order 0) follows from (2.81) and Proposition 2.28.

Kernel	Order	
$e^{-c\|x-x'\|^\beta}, 0 \leq \beta \leq 2$	0	Exponential
$\frac{1}{\sqrt{\|x-x'\|^2+c^2}}$	0	Inverse Multiquadric
$-\sqrt{\|x-x'\|^2+c^2}$	1	Multiquadric
$\|x-x'\|^{2n} \ln \|x-x'\|$	n	Thin Plate Spline

Definition 2.30 (Completely Monotonic Functions) *A function $h(x)$ is called completely monotonic of order q if*

$$(-1)^n \frac{d^n}{dx^n} h(x) \geq 0 \text{ for all } x \in [0, \infty) \text{ and } n \geq q. \tag{2.94}$$

It can be shown [464, 465, 360] that a function $h(x^2)$ is conditionally positive definite if and only if $h(x)$ is completely monotonic of the same order. This gives a (sometimes simpler) criterion for checking whether a function is cpd or not.

If we use cpd kernels in learning algorithms, we must ensure orthogonality of the estimate with respect to Π_q^N. This is usually done via constraints $\sum_{i=1}^m \alpha_i p(x_i) = 0$ for all polynomials $p(\cdot)$ on $\mathbb{R}^N$ of degree lower than q (see Section 4.8).

2.5 Summary

The crucial ingredient of SVMs and other kernel methods is the so-called kernel trick (see (2.7) and Remark 2.8), which permits the computation of dot products in high-dimensional feature spaces, using simple functions defined on pairs of input patterns. This trick allows the formulation of nonlinear variants of any algorithm that can be cast in terms of dot products, SVMs being but the most prominent example. The mathematical result underlying the kernel trick is almost a century old [359]. Nevertheless, it was only much later that it was exploited by the machine learning community for the analysis [4] and construction of algorithms [62], and that it was described as a general method for constructing nonlinear generalizations of dot product algorithms [480].

The present chapter has reviewed the mathematical theory of kernels. We started with the class of polynomial kernels, which can be motivated as computing a combinatorially large number of monomial features rather efficiently. This led to the general question of which kernel can be used, or: which kernel can be represented as a dot product in a linear feature space. We defined this class and discussed some of its properties. We described several ways how, given such a kernel, one can construct a representation in a feature space. The most well-known representation employs Mercer's theorem, and represents the feature space as an ℓ_2 space defined in terms of the eigenfunctions of an integral operator associated with the kernel. An alternative representation uses elements of the theory of reproducing kernel Hilbert spaces, and yields additional insights, representing the linear space as a space of functions written as kernel expansions. We gave an in-depth discussion of the kernel trick in its general form, including the case where we are interested in dissimilarities rather than similarities; that is, when we want to come up with nonlinear generalizations of distance-based algorithms rather than dot-product-based algorithms.

In both cases, the underlying philosophy is the same: we are trying to express a complex nonlinear algorithm in terms of simple geometrical concepts, and we are then dealing with it in a linear space. This linear space may not always be readily available; in some cases, it may even be hard to construct explicitly. Nevertheless, for the sake of design and analysis of the algorithms, it is sufficient to know that the linear space exists, empowering us to use the full potential of geometry, linear algebra and functional analysis.

2.6 Problems

2.1 (Monomial Features in $\mathbb{R}^2$ •) *Verify the second equality in (2.9).*

2.2 (Multiplicity of Monomial Features in $\mathbb{R}^N$ [515] ••) *Consider the monomial kernel $k(x, x') = \langle x, x' \rangle^d$ (where $x, x' \in \mathbb{R}^N$), generating monomial features of order d. Prove* *that a valid feature map for this kernel can be defined coordinate-wise as*

$$\Phi_{\mathbf{m}}(x) = \sqrt{\frac{d!}{\prod_{i=1}^{n}[\mathbf{m}]_i!}} \prod_{i=1}^{n}[x]_i^{[\mathbf{m}]_i} \tag{2.95}$$

for every $\mathbf{m} \in \mathbb{N}^n$, $\sum_{i=1}^{n}[\mathbf{m}]_i = d$ (i.e., every such $\mathbf{m}$ corresponds to one dimension of $\mathcal{H}$).

2.3 (Inhomogeneous Polynomial Kernel ••) *Prove that the kernel (2.70) induces a feature map into the space of all monomials up to degree d. Discuss the role of c.*

2.4 (Eigenvalue Criterion of Positive Definiteness •) *Prove that a symmetric matrix is positive definite if and only if all its eigenvalues are nonnegative (see Appendix B).*

2.5 (Dot Products are Kernels •) *Prove that dot products (Definition B.7) are positive definite kernels.*

2.6 (Kernels on Finite Domains ••) *Prove that for finite $\mathcal{X}$, say $\mathcal{X} = \{x_1, \ldots, x_m\}$, k is a kernel if and only if the $m \times m$ matrix $(k(x_i, x_j))_{ij}$ is positive definite.*

2.7 (Positivity on the Diagonal •) *From Definition 2.5, prove that a kernel satisfies $k(x, x) \geq 0$ for all $x \in \mathcal{X}$.*

2.8 (Cauchy-Schwarz for Kernels ••) *Give an elementary proof of Proposition 2.7.*
Hint: start with the general form of a symmetric 2×2 matrix, and derive conditions for its coefficients that ensure that it is positive definite.

2.9 (PD Kernels Vanishing on the Diagonal •) *Use Proposition 2.7 to prove that a kernel satisfying $k(x, x) =$ for all $x \in \mathcal{X}$ is identically zero.*
How does the RKHS look in this case? Hint: use (2.31).

2.10 (Two Kinds of Positivity •) *Give an example of a kernel which is positive definite according to Definition 2.5, but not positive in the sense that $k(x, x') \geq 0$ for all x, x'.*
Give an example of a kernel where the contrary is the case.

2.11 (General Coordinate Transformations •) *Prove that if $\sigma : \mathcal{X} \to \mathcal{X}$ is a bijection, and $k(x, x')$ is a kernel, then $k(\sigma(x), \sigma(x'))$ is a kernel, too.*

2.12 (Positivity on the Diagonal •) *Prove that positive definite kernels are positive on the diagonal, $k(x, x) \geq 0$ for all $x \in \mathcal{X}$. Hint: use $m = 1$ in (2.15).*

2.13 (Symmetry of Complex Kernels ••) *Prove that complex-valued positive definite kernels are symmetric (2.18).*

2.14 (Real Kernels vs. Complex Kernels •) *Prove that a real matrix satisfies (2.15) for all $c_i \in \mathbb{C}$ if and only if it is symmetric and it satisfies (2.15) for* real *coefficients c_i.*
Hint: decompose each c_i in (2.15) into real and imaginary parts.

2.15 (Rank-One Kernels •) *Prove that if f is a real-valued function on $\mathfrak{X}$, then $k(x, x') := f(x)f(x')$ is a positive definite kernel.*

2.16 (Bayes Kernel ••) *Consider a binary pattern recognition problem. Specialize the last problem to the case where $f : \mathfrak{X} \to \{\pm 1\}$ equals the Bayes decision function $y(x)$, i.e., the classification with minimal risk subject to an underlying distribution $P(x, y)$ generating the data.*

Argue that this kernel is particularly suitable since it renders the problem linearly separable in a 1D feature space: State a decision function (cf. (1.35)) that solves the problem (hint: you just need one parameter α, and you may set it to 1; moreover, use $b = 0$) [124].

The final part of the problem requires knowledge of Chapter 16: Consider now the situation where some prior $P(f)$ over the target function class is given. What would the optimal kernel be in this case? Discuss the connection to Gaussian processes.

2.17 (Inhomogeneous Polynomials •) *Prove that the inhomogeneous polynomial (2.70) is a positive definite kernel, e.g., by showing that it is a linear combination of homogeneous polynomial kernels with positive coefficients. What kind of features does this kernel compute [561]?*

2.18 (Normalization in Feature Space •) *Given a kernel k, construct a corresponding normalized kernel $\tilde{k}$ by normalizing the feature map $\tilde{\Phi}$ such that for all $x \in \mathfrak{X}$, $\|\tilde{\Phi}(x)\| = 1$ (cf. also Definition 12.35). Discuss the relationship between normalization in input space and normalization in feature space for Gaussian kernels and homogeneous polynomial kernels.*

2.19 (Cosine Kernel •) *Suppose $\mathfrak{X}$ is a dot product space, and $x, x' \in \mathfrak{X}$. Prove that $k(x, x') = \cos(\angle(x, x))$ is a positive definite kernel. Hint: use Problem 2.18.*

2.20 (Alignment Kernel •) *Let $\langle K, K' \rangle_F := \sum_{ij} K_{ij} K'_{ij}$ be the Frobenius dot product of two matrices. Prove that the empirical alignment of two Gram matrices [124], $A(K, K') := \langle K, K' \rangle_F / \sqrt{\langle K, K \rangle_F \langle K', K' \rangle_F}$, is a positive definite kernel.*

Note that the alignment can be used for model selection, putting $K'_{ij} := y_i y_j$ (cf. Problem 2.16) and $K_{ij} := \operatorname{sgn}(k(x_i, x_j))$ or $K_{ij} := \operatorname{sgn}(k(x_i, x_j)) - b$ (cf. [124]).

2.21 (Equivalence Relations as Kernels •••) *Consider a similarity measure $k : \mathfrak{X} \to \{0, 1\}$ with*

$$k(x, x) = 1 \text{ for all } x \in \mathfrak{X}. \tag{2.96}$$

Prove that k is a positive definite kernel if and only if, for all $x, x', x'' \in \mathfrak{X}$,

$$k(x, x') = 1 \Longleftrightarrow k(x', x) = 1 \text{ and} \tag{2.97}$$

$$k(x, x') = k(x', x'') = 1 \Longrightarrow k(x, x'') = 1. \tag{2.98}$$

Equations (2.96) to (2.98) amount to saying that $k = I_T$, where $T \subset \mathfrak{X} \times \mathfrak{X}$ is an equivalence relation.

As a simple example, consider an undirected graph, and let $(x, x') \in T$ whenever x and x' are in the same connected component of the graph. Show that T is an equivalence relation.

Find examples of equivalence relations that lend themselves to an interpretation as similarity measures. Discuss whether there are other relations that one might want to use as similarity measures.

2.22 (Different Feature Spaces for the Same Kernel •) *Give an example of a kernel with two valid feature maps Φ_1, Φ_2, mapping into spaces $\mathcal{H}_1, \mathcal{H}_2$ of different dimensions.*

2.23 (Converse of Mercer's Theorem •) *Prove that if an integral operator kernel k admits a uniformly convergent dot product representation on some compact set $\mathcal{X} \times \mathcal{X}$,*

$$k(x, x') = \sum_{i=1}^{\infty} \psi_i(x)\psi_i(x'), \tag{2.99}$$

then it is positive definite. Hint: show that

$$\int_{\mathcal{X}\times\mathcal{X}} \left(\sum_{i=1}^{\infty} \psi_i(x)\psi_i(x') \right) f(x) f(x')\, dx\, dx' = \sum_{i=1}^{\infty} \left(\int_{\mathcal{X}} \psi_i(x) f(x)\, dx \right)^2 \geq 0.$$

Argue that in particular, polynomial kernels (2.67) satisfy Mercer's conditions.

2.24 (∞-Norm of Mercer Eigenfunctions ••) *Prove that under the conditions of Theorem 2.10, we have, up to sets of measure zero,*

$$\sup_j \left\| \sqrt{\lambda_j} \psi_j \right\|_\infty \leq \sqrt{\|k\|_\infty} < \infty. \tag{2.100}$$

Hint: note that $\|k\|_\infty \geq k(x, x)$ up to sets of measures zero, and use the series expansion given in Theorem 2.10. Show, moreover, that it is not generally the case that

$$\sup_j \|\psi_j\|_\infty < \infty. \tag{2.101}$$

Hint: consider the case where $\mathcal{X} = \mathbb{N}$, $\mu(\{n\}) := 2^{-n}$, and $k(i, j) := \delta_{ij}$. Show that

1. *$T_k((a_j)) = (a_j 2^{-j})$ for $(a_j) \in L_2(\mathcal{X}, \mu)$,*
2. *T_k satisfies $\langle (a_j), T_k(a_j) \rangle = \sum_j (a_j 2^{-j})^2 \geq 0$ and is thus positive definite,*
3. *$\lambda_j = 2^{-j}$ and $\psi_j = 2^{j/2} e_j$ form an orthonormal eigenvector decomposition of T_k (here, e_j is the jth canonical unit vector in ℓ_2), and*
4. *$\|\psi_j\|_\infty = 2^{j/2} = \lambda_j^{-1/2}$.*

Argue that the last statement shows that (2.101) is wrong and (2.100) is tight.[12]

2.25 (Generalized Feature Maps •••) *Via (2.38), Mercer kernels induce compact (integral) operators. Can you generalize the idea of defining a feature map associated with an*

12. Thanks to S. Smale and I. Steinwart for this exercise.

operator to more general bounded positive definite operators T? Hint: use the multiplication operator representation of T [467].

2.26 (Nyström Approximation (cf. [603]) •) *Consider the integral operator obtained by substituting the distribution P underlying the data into (2.38), i.e.,*

$$(T_k f)(x) = \int_{\mathcal{X}} k(x, x') f(x) \, d\mathrm{P}(x). \tag{2.102}$$

If the conditions of Mercer's theorem are satisfied, then k can be diagonalized as

$$k(x, x') = \sum_{j=1}^{N_{\mathcal{H}}} \lambda_j \psi_j(x) \psi_j(x'), \tag{2.103}$$

where λ_j and ψ_j satisfy the eigenvalue equation

$$\int_{\mathcal{X}} k(x, x') \psi_j(x) \, d\mathrm{P}(x) = \lambda_j \psi_j(x') \tag{2.104}$$

and the orthonormality conditions

$$\int_{\mathcal{X}} \psi_i(x) \psi_j(x) d\mathrm{P}(x) = \delta_{ij}. \tag{2.105}$$

Show that by replacing the integral by a summation over an iid sample $X = \{x_1, \ldots, x_m\}$ from $\mathrm{P}(x)$, one can recover the kernel PCA eigenvalue problem (Section 1.7). Hint: Start by evaluating (2.104) for $x' \in X$, to obtain m equations. Next, approximate the integral by a sum over the points in X, replacing $\int_{\mathcal{X}} k(x, x') \psi_j(x) \, d\mathrm{P}(x)$ by $\frac{1}{m} \sum_{n=1}^{m} k(x_n, x') \psi_j(x_n)$.

Derive the orthogonality condition for the eigenvectors $(\psi_j(x_n))_{n=1,\ldots,m}$ from (2.105).

2.27 (Lorentzian Feature Spaces ••) *If a finite number of eigenvalues is negative, the expansion in Theorem 2.10 is still valid. Show that in this case, k corresponds to a Lorentzian symmetric bilinear form in a space with indefinite signature [467].*

Discuss whether this causes problems for learning algorithms utilizing these kernels. In particular, consider the cases of SV machines (Chapter 7) and Kernel PCA (Chapter 14).

2.28 (Symmetry of Reproducing Kernels •) *Show that reproducing kernels (Definition 2.9) are symmetric. Hint: use (2.35) and exploit the symmetry of the dot product.*

2.29 (Coordinate Representation in the RKHS ••) *Write $\langle \cdot, \cdot \rangle$ as a dot product of coordinate vectors by expressing the functions of the RKHS in the basis $(\sqrt{\lambda_n}\psi_n)_{n=1,\ldots,N_{\mathcal{H}}}$, which is orthonormal with respect to $\langle \cdot, \cdot \rangle$, i.e.,*

$$f(x) = \sum_{n=1}^{N_{\mathcal{H}}} \alpha_n \sqrt{\lambda_n} \psi_n(x). \tag{2.106}$$

Obtain an expression for the coordinates α_n, using (2.47) and $\alpha_n = \langle f, \sqrt{\lambda_n}\psi_n \rangle$. Show that $\mathcal{H}$ has the structure of a RKHS in the sense that for f and g given by (2.106), and

$$g(x) = \sum_{j=1}^{N_{\mathcal{H}}} \beta_j \sqrt{\lambda_j} \psi_j(x), \tag{2.107}$$

we have $\langle \alpha, \beta \rangle = \langle f, g \rangle$. Show, moreover, that $f(x) = \langle \alpha, \Phi(x) \rangle$ in $\mathcal{H}$. In other words, $\Phi(x)$ is the coordinate representation of the kernel as a function of one argument.

2.30 (Equivalence of Regularization Terms •) *Using (2.36) and (2.41), prove that $\|\mathbf{w}\|^2$, where $\mathbf{w} = \sum_{i=1}^{m} \alpha_i \Phi(x_i)$, is the same no matter whether Φ denotes the RKHS feature map (2.21) or the Mercer feature map (2.40).*

2.31 (Approximate Inversion of Gram Matrices ••) *Use the kernel PCA map (2.59) to derive a method for approximately inverting a large Gram matrix.*

2.32 (Effective Dimension of Feature Space •) *Building on Section 2.2.7, argue that for a finite data set, we are always effectively working in a finite-dimensional feature space.*

2.33 (Translation of a Dot Product •) *Prove (2.79).*

2.34 (Example of a CPD Kernel ••) *Argue that the hyperbolic tangent kernel (2.69) is effectively conditionally positive definite, if the input values are suitably restricted, since it can be approximated by $k + b$, where k is a polynomial kernel (2.67) and $b \in \mathbb{R}$. Discuss how this explains that hyperbolic tangent kernels can be used for SVMs although, as pointed out in number of works (e.g., [86], cf. the remark following (2.69)), they are not positive definite.*

2.35 (Polarization Identity ••) *Prove the* polarization identity, *stating that for any symmetric bilinear form $\langle \cdot, \cdot \rangle : \mathcal{X} \times \mathcal{X} \to \mathbb{R}$, we have, for all $x, x' \in \mathcal{X}$,*

$$\langle x, x' \rangle = \frac{1}{4} \left(\langle x + x', x + x' \rangle - \langle x - x', x - x' \rangle \right). \tag{2.108}$$

Now consider the special case where $\langle \cdot, \cdot \rangle$ is a Euclidean dot product and $\langle x - x', x - x' \rangle$ is the squared Euclidean distance between x and x'. Discuss why the polarization identity does not imply that the value of the dot product can be recovered from the distances alone. What else does one need?

2.36 (Vector Space Representation of CPD Kernels •••) *Specialize the vector space representation of symmetric kernels (Proposition 2.25) to the case of cpd kernels. Can you identify a subspace on which a cpd kernel is actually pd?*

2.37 (Parzen Windows Classifiers in Feature Space ••) *Assume that k is a positive definite kernel. Compare the algorithm described in Section 1.2 with the one of (2.89). Construct situations where the two algorithms give different results. Hint: consider datasets where the class means coincide.*

2.38 (Canonical Distortion Kernel ∘∘∘) *Can you define a kernel based on Baxter's canonical distortion metric [28]?*

3 Risk and Loss Functions

One of the most immediate requirements in any learning problem is to specify what exactly we would like to achieve, minimize, bound, or approximate. In other words, we need to determine a criterion according to which we will assess the quality of an estimate $f : \mathcal{X} \to \mathcal{Y}$ obtained from data.

This question is far from trivial. Even in binary classification there exist ample choices. The selection criterion may be the fraction of patterns classified correctly, it could involve the confidence with which the classification is carried out, or it might take into account the fact that losses are not symmetric for the two classes, such as in health diagnosis problems. Furthermore, the loss for an error may be input-dependent (for instance, meteorological predictions may require a higher accuracy in urban regions), and finally, we might want to obtain probabilities rather than a binary prediction of the class labels -1 and 1. Multi class discrimination and regression add even further levels of complexity to the problem. Thus we need a means of encoding these criteria.

Overview

The chapter is structured as follows: in Section 3.1, we begin with a brief overview of common loss functions used in classification and regression algorithms. This is done without much mathematical rigor or statistical justification, in order to provide basic working knowledge for readers who want to get a quick idea of the default design choices in the area of kernel machines. Following this, Section 3.2 formalizes the idea of risk. The risk approach is the predominant technique used in this book, and most of the algorithms presented subsequently minimize some form of a risk functional. Section 3.3 treats the concept of loss functions from a statistical perspective, points out the connection to the estimation of densities and introduces the notion of efficiency. Readers interested in more detail should also consider Chapter 16, which discusses the problem of estimation from a Bayesian perspective. The later parts of this section are intended for readers interested in the more theoretical details of estimation. The concept of robustness is introduced in Section 3.4. Several commonly used loss functions, such as Huber's loss and the ε-insensitive loss, enjoy robustness properties with respect to rather general classes of distributions. Beyond the basic relations, will show how to adjust the ε-insensitive loss in such a way as to accommodate different amounts of variance automatically. This will later lead to the construction of so-called ν Support Vector Algorithms (see Chapters 7, 8, and 9).

While technical details and proofs can be omitted for most of the present chapter, we encourage the reader to review the practical implications of this section.

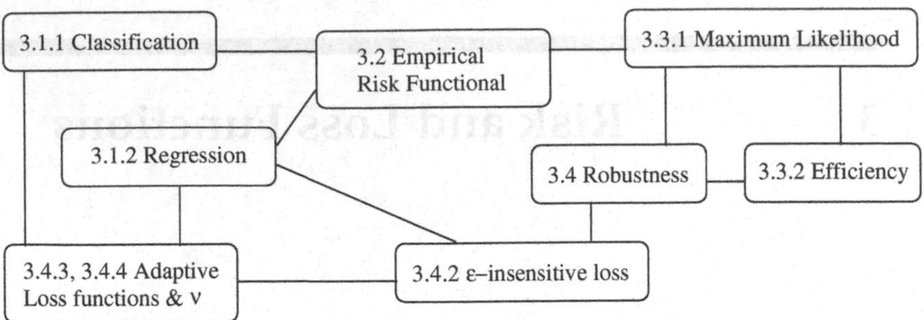

Prerequisites

As usual, exercises for all sections can be found at the end. The chapter requires knowledge of probability theory, as introduced in Section B.1.

3.1 Loss Functions

Let us begin with a formal definition of what we mean by the loss incurred by a function f at location x, given an observation y.

Definition 3.1 (Loss Function) *Denote by $(x, y, f(x)) \in \mathcal{X} \times \mathcal{Y} \times \mathcal{Y}$ the triplet consisting of a pattern x, an observation y and a prediction $f(x)$. Then the map $c : \mathcal{X} \times \mathcal{Y} \times \mathcal{Y} \to [0, \infty)$ with the property $c(x, y, y) = 0$ for all $x \in \mathcal{X}$ and $y \in \mathcal{Y}$ will be called a loss function.*

Note that we require c to be a nonnegative function. This means that we will never get a payoff from an extra good prediction. If the latter was the case, we could always recover non-negativity (provided the loss is bounded from below), by using a simple shift operation (possibly depending on x). Likewise we can always satisfy the condition that exact predictions ($f(x) = y$) never cause any loss. The advantage of these extra conditions on c is that we know that the minimum of the loss is 0 and that it is obtainable, at least for a given x, y.

Minimized Loss $\neq$ Incurred Loss

Next we will formalize different kinds of *loss*, as described informally in the introduction of the chapter. Note that the incurred loss is not always the quantity that we will attempt to minimize. For instance, for algorithmic reasons, some loss functions will prove to be infeasible (the binary loss, for instance, can lead to NP-hard optimization problems [367]). Furthermore, statistical considerations such as the desire to obtain confidence levels on the prediction (Section 3.3.1) will also influence our choice.

3.1.1 Binary Classification

Misclassification Error

The simplest case to consider involves counting the misclassification error if pattern x is classified wrongly we incur loss 1, otherwise there is no penalty.:

$$c(x, y, f(x)) = \begin{cases} 0 & \text{if } y = f(x) \\ 1 & \text{otherwise} \end{cases} \tag{3.1}$$

This definition of c does not distinguish between different classes and types of errors (false positive or negative).[1]

Asymmetric and Input-Dependent Loss

A slight extension takes the latter into account. For the sake of simplicity let us assume, as in (3.1), that we have a binary classification problem. This time, however, the loss may depend on a function $\tilde{c}(x)$ which accounts for input-dependence, i.e.

$$c(x, y, f(x)) = \begin{cases} 0 & \text{if } y = f(x) \\ \tilde{c}(x) & \text{otherwise} \end{cases} \tag{3.2}$$

A simple (albeit slightly contrived) example is the classification of objects into rocks and diamonds. Clearly, the incurred loss will depend largely on the weight of the object under consideration.

Analogously, we might distinguish between errors for $y = 1$ and $y = -1$ (see, e.g., [331] for details). For instance, in a fraud detection application, we would like to be really sure about the situation before taking any measures, rather than losing potential customers. On the other hand, a blood bank should consider even the slightest suspicion of disease before accepting a donor.

Confidence Level

Rather than predicting only whether a given object x belongs to a certain class y, we may also want to take a certain confidence level into account. In this case, $f(x)$ becomes a real-valued function, even though $y \in \{-1, 1\}$.

Soft Margin Loss

In this case, $\operatorname{sgn}(f(x))$ denotes the class label, and the absolute value $|f(x)|$ the confidence of the prediction. Corresponding loss functions will depend on the product $yf(x)$ to assess the quality of the estimate. The *soft margin* loss function, as introduced by Bennett and Mangasarian [40, 111], is defined as

$$c(x, y, f(x)) = \max(0, 1 - yf(x)) = \begin{cases} 0 & \text{if } yf(x) \geq 1, \\ 1 - yf(x) & \text{otherwise.} \end{cases} . \tag{3.3}$$

In some cases [348, 125] (see also Section 10.6.2) the squared version of (3.3) provides an expression that can be minimized more easily;

$$c(x, y, f(x)) = \max(0, 1 - yf(x))^2. \tag{3.4}$$

Logistic Loss

The soft margin loss closely resembles the so-called *logistic* loss function (cf. [251], as well as Problem 3.1 and Section 16.1.1);

$$c(x, y, f(x)) = \ln\left(1 + \exp\left(-yf(x)\right)\right). \tag{3.5}$$

We will derive this loss function in Section 3.3.1. It is used in order to associate a probabilistic meaning with $f(x)$.

Note that in both (3.3) and (3.5) (nearly) no penalty occurs if $yf(x)$ is sufficiently large, i.e. if the patterns are classified correctly with large confidence. In particular, in (3.3) a minimum confidence of 1 is required for zero loss. These loss functions

1. A *false positive* is a point which the classifier erroneously assigns to class 1, a *false negative* is erroneously assigned to class -1.

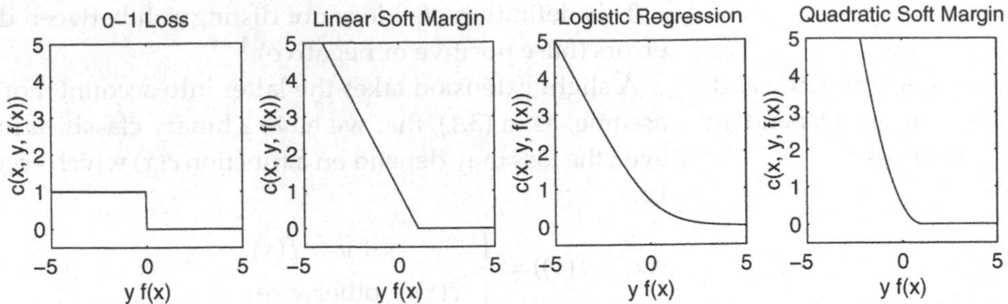

Figure 3.1 From left to right: 0-1 loss, linear soft margin loss, logistic regression, and quadratic soft margin loss. Note that both soft margin loss functions are upper bounds on the 0-1 loss.

led to the development of *large margin classifiers* (see [491, 460, 504] and Chapter 5 for further details). Figure 3.1 depicts various popular loss functions.[2]

Multi Class Discrimination

Matters are more complex when dealing with more than two classes. Each type of misclassification could potentially incur a different loss, leading to an $M \times M$ matrix (M being the number of classes) with positive off-diagonal and zero diagonal entries. It is still a matter of ongoing research in which way a confidence level should be included in such cases (cf. [41, 311, 593, 161, 119]).

3.1.2 Regression

When estimating real-valued quantities, it is usually the size of the difference $y - f(x)$, i.e. the amount of misprediction, rather than the product $yf(x)$, which is used to determine the quality of the estimate. For instance, this can be the actual loss incurred by mispredictions (e.g., the loss incurred by mispredicting the value of a financial instrument at the stock exchange), provided the latter is known and computationally tractable.[3] Assuming location independence, in most cases the loss function will be of the type

$$c(x, y, f(x)) = \tilde{c}(f(x) - y). \tag{3.7}$$

See Figure 3.2 below for several regression loss functions. Below we list the ones most common in kernel methods.

---

2. Other popular loss functions from the generalized linear model context include the inverse complementary log-log function. It is given by

$$c(x, y, f(x)) = 1 - \exp(-\exp(yf(x))). \tag{3.6}$$

This function, unfortunately, is not convex and therefore it will not lead to a convex optimization problem. However, it has nice robustness properties and therefore we think that it should be investigated in the present context.

3. As with classification, computational tractability is one of the primary concerns. This is not always satisfying from a statistician's point of view, yet it is crucial for any practical implementation of an estimation algorithm.

Squared Loss

The popular choice is to minimize the sum of squares of the residuals $f(x) - y$. As we shall see in Section 3.3.1, this corresponds to the assumption that we have additive normal noise corrupting the observations y_i. Consequently we minimize

$$c(x, y, f(x)) = (f(x) - y)^2 \text{ or equivalently } \tilde{c}(\xi) = \xi^2. \tag{3.8}$$

For convenience of subsequent notation, $\frac{1}{2}\xi^2$ rather than ξ^2 is often used.

ε-insensitive Loss and ℓ_1 Loss

An extension of the soft margin loss (3.3) to regression is the *ε-insensitive* loss function [561, 572, 562]. It is obtained by symmetrization of the "hinge" of (3.3),

$$\tilde{c}(\xi) = \max(|\xi| - \varepsilon, 0) =: |\xi|_\varepsilon. \tag{3.9}$$

The idea behind (3.9) is that deviations up to ε should not be penalized, and all further deviations should incur only a linear penalty. Setting $\varepsilon = 0$ leads to an ℓ_1 loss, i.e., to minimization of the sum of absolute deviations. This is written

$$\tilde{c}(\xi) = |\xi|. \tag{3.10}$$

We will study these functions in more detail in Section 3.4.2.

Practical Considerations

For efficient implementations of learning procedures, it is crucial that loss functions satisfy certain properties. In particular, they should be cheap to compute, have a small number of discontinuities (if any) in the first derivative, and be convex in order to ensure the uniqueness of the solution (see Chapter 6 and also Problem 3.6 for details). Moreover, we may want to obtain solutions that are computationally efficient, which may disregard a certain number of training points. This leads to conditions such as vanishing derivatives for a range of function values $f(x)$. Finally, requirements such as outlier resistance are also important for the construction of estimators.

3.2 Test Error and Expected Risk

Now that we have determined how errors should be penalized on specific instances $(x, y, f(x))$, we have to find a method to combine these (local) penalties. This will help us to assess a particular estimate f.

In the following, we will assume that there exists a probability distribution $\mathrm{P}(x, y)$ on $\mathcal{X} \times \mathcal{Y}$ which governs the data generation and underlying functional dependency. Moreover, we denote by $\mathrm{P}(y|x)$ the *conditional* distribution of y given x, and by $d\mathrm{P}(x, y)$ and $d\mathrm{P}(y|x)$ the integrals with respect to the distributions $\mathrm{P}(x, y)$ and $\mathrm{P}(y|x)$ respectively (cf. Section B.1.3).

3.2.1 Exact Quantities

Unless stated otherwise, we assume that the data (x, y) are drawn iid (independent and identically distributed, see Section B.1) from $\mathrm{P}(x, y)$. Whether or not we have knowledge of the test patterns at training time[4] makes a significant difference in the design of learning algorithms. In the latter case, we will want to minimize the *test error* on that *specific* test set; in the former case, the *expected* error over *all possible* test sets.

Transduction Problem

Definition 3.2 (Test Error) *Assume that we are not only given the* training *data* $\{x_1, \ldots, x_m\}$ *along with target values* $\{y_1, \ldots y_m\}$ *but also the* test *patterns* $\{x'_1, \ldots x'_{m'}\}$ *on which we would like to predict* y'_i $(i = 1, \ldots, m')$*. Since we already know* x'_i*, all we should care about is to minimize the* expected error *on the* test set*. We formalize this in the following definition*

$$R_{\text{test}}[f] := \frac{1}{m'} \sum_{i=1}^{m'} \int_{\mathcal{Y}} c(x'_i, y, f(x'_i)) dP(y|x'_i). \tag{3.11}$$

Unfortunately, this problem, referred to as *transduction*, is quite difficult to address, both computationally and conceptually, see [562, 267, 37, 211]. Instead, one typically considers the case where no knowledge about test patterns is available, as described in the following definition.

Definition 3.3 (Expected Risk) *If we have no knowledge about the test patterns (or decide to ignore them) we should minimize the expected error over all possible training patterns. Hence we have to minimize the expected loss with respect to* P *and* c

$$R[f] := \mathbf{E}\left[R_{\text{test}}[f]\right] = \mathbf{E}\left[c(x, y, f(x))\right] = \int_{\mathcal{X} \times \mathcal{Y}} c(x, y, f(x)) dP(x, y). \tag{3.12}$$

Here the integration is carried out with respect to the distribution $P(x, y)$. Again, just as (3.11), this problem is intractable, since we do not know $P(x, y)$ explicitly. Instead, we are only given the training patterns (x_i, y_i). The latter, however, allow us to replace the unknown distribution $P(x, y)$ by its empirical estimate.

To study connections between loss functions and density models, it will be convenient to assume that there exists a density $p(x, y)$ corresponding to $P(x, y)$. This means that we may replace $\int dP(x, y)$ by $\int p(x, y) dx dy$ and the appropriate measure on $\mathcal{X} \times \mathcal{Y}$. Such a density $p(x, y)$ need not always exist (see Section B.1 for more details) but we will not give further heed to these concerns at present.

3.2.2 Approximations

Unfortunately, this change in notation did not solve the problem. All we have at our disposal is the actual training data. What one usually does is replace $p(x, y)$ by the *empirical density*

Empirical Density

$$p_{\text{emp}}(x, y) := \frac{1}{m} \sum_{i=1}^{m} \delta_{x_i}(x) \delta_{y_i}(y). \tag{3.13}$$

4. The test *outputs*, however, are not available during training.

Here $\delta_{x'}(x)$ denotes the δ-distribution, satisfying $\int \delta_{x'}(x)f(x)dx = f(x')$. The hope is that replacing p by p_{emp} will lead to a quantity that is "reasonably close" to the expected risk. This will be the case if the class of possible solutions f is sufficiently limited [568, 571]. The issue of closeness with regard to different estimators will be discussed in further detail in Chapters 5 and 12. Substituting $p_{\mathrm{emp}}(x, y)$ into (3.12) leads to the empirical risk:

Definition 3.4 (Empirical Risk) *The empirical risk is defined as*

$$R_{\mathrm{emp}}[f] := \int_{\mathcal{X}\times\mathcal{Y}} c(x, y, f(x))p_{\mathrm{emp}}(x, y)dxdy = \frac{1}{m}\sum_{i=1}^{m} c(x_i, y_i, f(x_i)). \tag{3.14}$$

M-Estimator

This quantity has the advantage that, given the training data, we can readily compute and also minimize it. This constitutes a particular case of what is called an *M-estimator* in statistics. Estimators of this type are studied in detail in the field of empirical processes [554]. As pointed out in Section 3.1, it is crucial to understand that although our particular M-estimator is built from minimizing a loss, this need not always be the case. From a decision-theoretic point of view, the question of which loss to choose is a separate issue, which is dictated by the problem at hand as well as the goal of trying to evaluate the performance of estimation methods, rather than by the problem of trying to define a particular estimation method [582, 166, 43].

Ill-Posed Problems

These considerations aside, it may appear as if (3.14) is the answer to our problems, and all that remains to be done is to find a suitable class of functions $\mathcal{F} \ni f$ such that we can minimize $R_{\mathrm{emp}}[f]$ with respect to $\mathcal{F}$. Unfortunately, determining $\mathcal{F}$ is quite difficult (see Chapters 5 and 12 for details). Moreover, the minimization of $R_{\mathrm{emp}}[f]$ can lead to an ill-posed problem [538, 370]. We will show this with a simple example.

Example of an Ill-Posed Problem

Assume that we want to solve a regression problem using the quadratic loss function (3.8) given by $c(x, y, f(x) = (y - f(x))^2$. Moreover, assume that we are dealing with a linear class of functions,[5] say

$$\mathcal{F} := \left\{ f \,\middle|\, f(x) = \sum_{i=1}^{n} \alpha_i f_i(x) \text{ with } \alpha_i \in \mathbb{R} \right\}, \tag{3.15}$$

where the f_i are functions mapping $\mathcal{X}$ to $\mathbb{R}$.

We want to find the minimizer of R_{emp}, i.e.,

$$\underset{f\in\mathcal{F}}{\text{minimize}}\, R_{\mathrm{emp}}[f] = \underset{\alpha\in\mathbb{R}^n}{\text{minimize}}\, \frac{1}{m}\sum_{i=1}^{m}\left(y_i - \sum_{j=1}^{n}\alpha_j f_j(x_i)\right)^2. \tag{3.16}$$

5. In the simplest case, assuming $\mathcal{X}$ is contained in a vector space, these could be functions that extract coordinates of x; in other words, $\mathcal{F}$ would be the class of linear functions on $\mathcal{X}$.

Computing the derivative of $R_{\text{emp}}[f]$ with respect to $\boldsymbol{\alpha}$ and defining $F_{ij} := f_i(x_j)$, we can see that the minimum of (3.16) is achieved if

$$F^\top \mathbf{y} = F^\top F \boldsymbol{\alpha}. \tag{3.17}$$

A sufficient condition for (3.17) is $\boldsymbol{\alpha} = (F^\top F)^{-1} F^\top \mathbf{y}$ where $(F^\top F)^{-1}$ denotes the (pseudo-)inverse of the matrix.

Condition of a Matrix

If $F^\top F$ has a bad condition number (i.e. the quotient between the largest and the smallest eigenvalue of $F^\top F$ is large), it is numerically difficult [423, 530] to solve (3.17) for $\boldsymbol{\alpha}$. Furthermore, if $n > m$, i.e. if we have more basis functions f_i than training patterns x_i, there will exist a subspace of solutions with dimension at least $n - m$, satisfying (3.17). This is undesirable both practically (speed of computation) and theoretically (we would have to deal with a whole class of solutions rather than a single one).

One might also expect that if $\mathfrak{F}$ is too rich, the discrepancy between $R_{\text{emp}}[f]$ and $R[f]$ could be large. For instance, if F is an $m \times m$ matrix of full rank, $\mathfrak{F}$ contains an f that predicts all target values y_i correctly on the training data. Nevertheless, we cannot expect that we will also obtain zero prediction error on unseen points. Chapter 4 will show how these problems can be overcome by adding a so-called regularization term to $R_{\text{emp}}[f]$.

3.3 A Statistical Perspective

Given a particular pattern $\tilde{x}$, we may want to ask what risk we can expect for it, and with which *probability* the corresponding loss is going to occur. In other words, instead of (or in addition to) $\mathbf{E}\left[c(\tilde{x}, y, f(\tilde{x})\right]$ for a fixed $\tilde{x}$, we may want to know the distribution of y given $\tilde{x}$, i.e., $\mathrm{P}(y|\tilde{x})$.

(Bayesian) statistics (see [338, 432, 49, 43] and also Chapter 16) often attempt to estimate the density corresponding to the random variables (x, y), and in some cases, we may really *need* information about $p(x, y)$ to arrive at the desired conclusions given the training data (e.g., medical diagnosis). However, we always have to keep in mind that if we model the density p first, and subsequently, based on this approximation, compute a minimizer of the expected risk, we will have to make two approximations. This could lead to inferior or at least not easily predictable results. Therefore, wherever possible, we should avoid solving a more general problem, since additional approximation steps might only make the estimates worse [561].

3.3.1 Maximum Likelihood Estimation

All this said, we still may want to compute the conditional density $p(y|x)$. For this purpose we need to model how y is generated, based on some underlying dependency $f(x)$; thus, we specify the functional form of $p(y|x, f(x))$ and maximize the expression with respect to f. This will provide us with the function f that is *most likely* to have generated the data.

Definition 3.5 (Likelihood) *The likelihood of a sample $(x_1, y_1), \ldots (x_m, y_m)$ given an underlying functional dependency f is given by*

$$p(\{x_1, \ldots, x_m\}, \{y_1, \ldots, y_m\}|f) = \prod_{i=1}^{m} p(x_i, y_i|f) = \prod_{i=1}^{m} p(y_i|x_i, f)p(x_i) \tag{3.18}$$

Strictly speaking the likelihood only depends on the values $f(x_1), \ldots, f(x_m)$ rather than being a functional of f itself. To keep the notation simple, however, we write $p(\{x_1, \ldots, x_m\}, \{y_1, \ldots, y_m\}|f)$ instead of the more heavyweight expression $p(\{x_1, \ldots, x_m\}, \{y_1, \ldots, y_m\}|\{f(x_1), \ldots, f(x_m)\})$.

For practical reasons, we convert products into sums by taking the negative logarithm of $\mathrm{P}(\{x_1, \ldots, x_m\}, \{y_1, \ldots, y_m\}|f)$, an expression which is then conveniently minimized. Furthermore, we may drop the $p(x_i)$ from (3.18), since they do not depend on f. Thus maximization of (3.18) is equivalent to minimization of the *Log-Likelihood*

Log-Likelihood

$$\mathcal{L}[f] := \sum_{i=1}^{m} -\ln p(y_i|x_i, f). \tag{3.19}$$

Regression

Remark 3.6 (Regression Loss Functions) *Minimization of $\mathcal{L}[f]$ and of $R_{\mathrm{emp}}[f]$ coincide if the loss function c is chosen according to*

$$c(x, y, f(x)) = -\ln p(y|x, f). \tag{3.20}$$

Assuming that the target values y were generated by an underlying functional dependency f plus additive noise ξ with density p_ξ, i.e. $y_i = f_{\mathrm{true}}(x_i) + \xi_i$, we obtain

$$c(x, y, f(x)) = -\ln p_\xi(y - f(x)). \tag{3.21}$$

Things are slightly different in classification. Since all we are interested in is the probability that pattern x has label 1 or -1 (assuming binary classification), we can transform the problem into one of estimating the logarithm of the probability that a pattern assumes its correct label.

Classification

Remark 3.7 (Classification Loss Functions) *We have a finite set of labels, which allows us to model $\mathrm{P}(y|f(x))$ directly, instead of modelling a density. In the binary classification case (classes 1 and -1) this problem becomes particularly easy, since all we have to do is assume functional dependency underlying $\mathrm{P}(1|f(x))$: this immediately gives us $\mathrm{P}(-1|f(x)) = 1 - \mathrm{P}(1|f(x))$. The link to loss functions is established via*

$$c(x, y, f(x)) = -\ln \mathrm{P}(y|f(x)). \tag{3.22}$$

The same result can be obtained by minimizing the cross entropy[6] *between the classifica-*

6. In the case of discrete variables the cross entropy between two distributions P and Q is defined as $\sum_i \mathrm{P}(i) \ln \mathrm{Q}(i)$.

Table 3.1 Common loss functions and corresponding density models according to Remark 3.6. As a shorthand we use $\tilde{c}(f(x)-y) := c(x,y,f(x))$.

	loss function $\tilde{c}(\xi)$	density model $p(\xi)$
ε-insensitive	$\lvert\xi\rvert_\varepsilon$	$\frac{1}{2(1+\varepsilon)}\exp(-\lvert\xi\rvert_\varepsilon)$
Laplacian	$\lvert\xi\rvert$	$\frac{1}{2}\exp(-\lvert\xi\rvert)$
Gaussian	$\frac{1}{2}\xi^2$	$\frac{1}{\sqrt{2\pi}}\exp(-\frac{\xi^2}{2})$
Huber's robust loss	$\begin{cases} \frac{1}{2\sigma}(\xi)^2 & \text{if } \lvert\xi\rvert \leq \sigma \\ \lvert\xi\rvert - \frac{\sigma}{2} & \text{otherwise} \end{cases}$	$\propto \begin{cases} \exp(-\frac{\xi^2}{2\sigma}) & \text{if } \lvert\xi\rvert \leq \sigma \\ \exp(\frac{\sigma}{2} - \lvert\xi\rvert) & \text{otherwise} \end{cases}$
Polynomial	$\frac{1}{d}\lvert\xi\rvert^d$	$\frac{d}{2\Gamma(1/d)}\exp(-\lvert\xi\rvert^d)$
Piecewise polynomial	$\begin{cases} \frac{1}{d\sigma^{d-1}}\lvert\xi\rvert^d & \text{if } \lvert\xi\rvert \leq \sigma \\ \lvert\xi\rvert - \sigma\frac{d-1}{d} & \text{otherwise} \end{cases}$	$\propto \begin{cases} \exp(-\frac{\lvert\xi\rvert^d}{d\sigma^{d-1}}) & \text{if } \lvert\xi\rvert\sigma \\ \exp(\sigma\frac{d-1}{d} - \lvert\xi\rvert) & \text{otherwise} \end{cases}$

tion labels y_i and the probabilities $p(y|f(x))$, as is typically done in a generalized linear models context (see e.g., [355, 232, 163]). For binary classification (with $y \in \{\pm 1\}$) we obtain

$$c(x,y,f(x)) = \frac{1+y}{2}\ln \mathrm{P}(y=1|f(x)) + \frac{1-y}{2}\ln \mathrm{P}(y=-1|f(x)). \tag{3.23}$$

When substituting the actual values for y into (3.23), this reduces to (3.22).

At this point we have a choice in modelling $\mathrm{P}(y=1|f(x))$ to suit our needs. Possible models include the logistic transfer function, the probit model, the inverse complementary log-log model. See Section 16.3.5 for a more detailed discussion of the choice of such *link functions.* Below we explain connections in some more detail for the logistic link function.

For a logistic model, where $\mathrm{P}(y=\pm 1|x,f) \propto \exp(\pm\frac{1}{2}f(x))$, we obtain after normalization

$$\mathrm{P}(y=1|x,f) := \frac{\exp(f(x))}{1+\exp(f(x))} \tag{3.24}$$

and consequently $-\ln \mathrm{P}(y=1|x,f) = \ln(1+\exp(-f(x)))$. We thus recover (3.5) as the loss function for classification. Choices other than (3.24) for a map $\mathbb{R} \to [0,1]$ will lead to further loss functions for classification. See [579, 179, 596] and Section 16.1.1 for more details on this subject.

It is important to note that not every loss function used in classification corresponds to such a density model (recall that in this case, the probabilities have to add up to 1 for any value of $f(x)$). In fact, one of the most popular loss functions, the soft margin loss (3.3), does not enjoy this property. A discussion of these issues can be found in [521].

Examples

Table 3.1 summarizes common loss functions and the corresponding density models as defined by (3.21), some of which were already presented in Section 3.1. It is an exhaustive list of the loss functions that will be used in this book for regression. Figure 3.2 contains graphs of the functions.

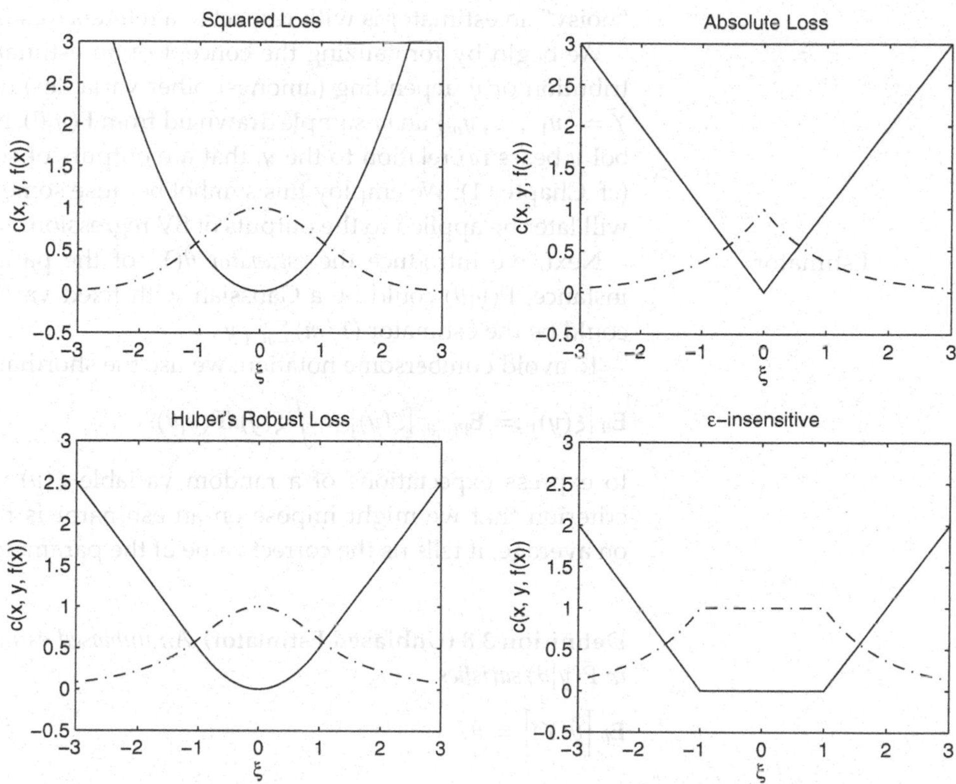

Figure 3.2 Graphs of loss functions and corresponding density models. upper left: Gaussian, upper right: Laplacian, lower left: Huber's robust, lower right: ε-insensitive.

Practical Considerations

We conclude with a few cautionary remarks. The loss function resulting from a maximum likelihood reasoning might be non-convex. This might spell trouble when we try to find an efficient solution of the corresponding minimization problem. Moreover, we made a very strong assumption by claiming to know $P(y|x, f)$ explicitly, which was necessary in order to evaluate (3.20).

Finally, the solution we obtain by minimizing the log-likelihood depends on the class of functions $\mathcal{F}$. So we are in no better situation than by minimizing $R_{\text{emp}}[f]$, albeit with the additional constraint, that the loss functions $c(x, y, f(x))$ must correspond to a probability density.

3.3.2 Efficiency

The above reasoning could mislead us into thinking that the choice of loss function is rather arbitrary, and that there exists no good means of assessing the performance of an estimator. In the present section we will develop tools which can be used to compare estimators that are derived from different loss functions. For this purpose we need to introduce additional statistical concepts which deal with the efficiency of an estimator. Roughly speaking, these give an indication of how "noisy" an estimator is with respect to a reference estimator.

We begin by formalizing the concept of an estimator. Denote by $P(y|\theta)$ a distribution of y depending (amongst other variables) on the parameters θ, and by $Y = \{y_1, \ldots, y_m\}$ an m-sample drawn iid from $P(y|\theta)$. Note that the use of the symbol y bears no relation to the y_i that are outputs of some functional dependency (cf. Chapter 1). We employ this symbol because some of the results to be derived will later be applied to the outputs of SV regression.

Estimator

Next, we introduce the *estimator* $\hat{\theta}(Y)$ of the parameters θ, based on Y. For instance, $P(y|\theta)$ could be a Gaussian with fixed variance and mean θ, and $\hat{\theta}(Y)$ could be the estimator $(1/m)\sum_{i=1}^{m} y_i$.

To avoid cumbersome notation, we use the shorthand

$$\mathbf{E}_\theta\left[\xi(y)\right] := \mathbf{E}_{P(y|\theta)}\left[\xi(y)\right] = \int \xi(y) dP(y|\theta), \tag{3.25}$$

to express expectations of a random variable $\xi(y)$ with respect to $P(y|\theta)$. One criterion that we might impose on an estimator is that it be unbiased, i.e., that on average, it tells us the correct value of the parameter it attempts to estimate.

Definition 3.8 (Unbiased Estimator) *An unbiased estimator $\hat{\theta}(Y)$ of the parameters θ in $P(y|\theta)$ satisfies*

$$\mathbf{E}_\theta\left[\hat{\theta}(Y)\right] = \theta. \tag{3.26}$$

In this section, we will focus on unbiased estimators. In general, however, the estimators we are dealing with in this book will not be unbiased. In fact, they will have a bias towards 'simple', low-complexity functions. Properties of such estimators are more difficult to deal with, which is why, for the sake of simplicity, we restrict ourselves to the unbiased case in this section. Note, however, that "biasedness" is not a bad property by itself. On the contrary, there exist cases as the one described by James and Stein [262] where biased estimators consistently outperform unbiased estimators in the finite sample size setting, both in terms of variance and prediction error.

A possible way to compare unbiased estimators is to compute their variance. Other quantities such as moments of higher order or maximum deviation properties would be valid criteria as well, yet for historical and practical reasons the variance has become a standard tool to benchmark estimators. The Fisher information matrix is crucial for this purpose since it will tell us via the Cramér-Rao bound (Theorem 3.11) the minimal possible variance for an unbiased estimator. The idea is that the smaller the variance, the lower (typically) the probability that $\hat{\theta}(Y)$ will deviate from θ by a large amount. Therefore, we can use the variance as a possible one number summary to compare different estimators.

Definition 3.9 (Score Function, Fisher Information, Covariance) *Assume there exists a density $p(y|\theta)$ for the distribution $P(y|\theta)$ such that $\ln p(y|\theta)$ is differentiable with*

Score Function

respect to θ. The score $V_\theta(Y)$ *of* $\mathrm{P}(y|\theta)$ *is a random variable defined by*[7]

$$V_\theta(Y) := \partial_\theta \ln p(Y|\theta) = \partial_\theta \sum_{i=1}^{m} \ln p(y_i|\theta) = \sum_{i=1}^{m} \frac{\partial_\theta p(y_i|\theta)}{p(y_i|\theta)}. \tag{3.27}$$

This score tells us how much the likelihood of the data depends on the different components of θ, and thus, in the maximum likelihood procedure, how much the data affect the choice of θ. The covariance of $V_\theta(Y)$ is called the Fisher information matrix I. *It is given by*

Fisher Information

$$I_{ij} := \mathbf{E}_\theta\left[\partial_{\theta_i} \ln p(Y|\theta) \cdot \partial_{\theta_j} \ln p(Y|\theta)\right]. \tag{3.28}$$

Covariance

and the covariance matrix B *of the estimator* $\hat{\theta}(Y)$ *is defined by*

$$B_{ij} := \mathbf{E}_\theta\left[\left(\hat{\theta}_i - \mathbf{E}_\theta\left[\hat{\theta}_i\right]\right)\left(\hat{\theta}_j - \mathbf{E}_\theta\left[\hat{\theta}_j\right]\right)\right]. \tag{3.29}$$

The covariance matrix B tells us the amount of variation of the estimator. It can therefore be used (e.g., by Chebychev's inequality) to bound the probability that $\hat{\theta}(Y)$ deviates from θ by more than a certain amount.

Remark 3.10 (Expected Value of Fisher Score) *One can check that the expected value of $V_\theta(Y)$ is 0 since*

$$\mathbf{E}_\theta\left[V_\theta(Y)\right] = \int p(Y|\theta)\partial_\theta \ln p(Y|\theta) dY = \partial_\theta \int p(Y|\theta) dY = \partial_\theta 1 = 0. \tag{3.30}$$

Average Fisher Score Vanishes

In other words, the contribution of Y to the adjustment of θ averages to 0 over all possible Y, drawn according to $\mathrm{P}(Y|\theta)$. Equivalently we could say that the average likelihood for Y drawn according to $\mathrm{P}(Y|\theta)$ is extremal, provided we choose θ: the derivative of the expected likelihood of the data $\mathbf{E}_\theta\left[\ln \mathrm{P}(Y|\theta)\right]$ with respect to θ vanishes. This is also what we expect, namely that the "proper" distribution is on average the one with the highest likelihood.

The following theorem gives a lower bound on the variance of an estimator, i.e. B is found in terms of the Fisher information I. This is useful to determine how well a given estimator performs with respect to the one with the lowest possible variance.

Theorem 3.11 (Cramér and Rao [425]) *Any unbiased estimator* $\hat{\theta}(Y)$ *satisfies*

$$\det IB \geq 1. \tag{3.31}$$

Proof We prove (3.31) for the scalar case. The extension to matrices is left as an exercise (see Problem 3.10). Using the Cauchy-Schwarz inequality, we obtain

$$\left(\mathbf{E}_\theta\left[\left(V_\theta(Y) - \mathbf{E}_\theta\left[V_\theta(Y)\right]\right)\left(\hat{\theta}(Y) - \mathbf{E}_\theta\left[\hat{\theta}(Y)\right]\right)\right]\right)^2 \tag{3.32}$$

$$\leq \mathbf{E}_\theta\left[\left(V_\theta(Y) - \mathbf{E}_\theta\left[V_\theta(Y)\right]\right)^2\right] \mathbf{E}_\theta\left[\left(\hat{\theta}(Y) - \mathbf{E}_\theta\left[\hat{\theta}(Y)\right]\right)^2\right] = IB. \tag{3.33}$$

7. Recall that $\partial_\theta p(Y|\theta)$ is the gradient of $p(Y|\theta)$ with respect to the parameters $\theta_1, \ldots, \theta_n$.

At the same time, $\mathbf{E}_\theta\left[V_\theta(Y)\right] = 0$ implies that

$$\left(\mathbf{E}_\theta\left[\left(V_\theta(Y) - \mathbf{E}_\theta\left[V_\theta(Y)\right]\right)\left(\hat{\theta}(Y) - \mathbf{E}_\theta\left[\hat{\theta}(Y)\right]\right)\right]\right)^2 \tag{3.34}$$

$$= \mathbf{E}_\theta\left[V_\theta(Y)\hat{\theta}(Y)\right]^2 \tag{3.35}$$

$$= \left(\int p(Y|\theta)V_\theta(Y)\hat{\theta}(Y)dY\right)^2$$

$$= \left(\partial_\theta \int p(Y|\theta)\hat{\theta}(Y)dY\right)^2 = (\partial_\theta\theta)^2 = 1, \tag{3.36}$$

since we may interchange integration by Y and ∂_θ. ■

Eq. (3.31) lends itself to the definition of a one-number summary of the properties of an estimator, namely how closely the inequality is met.

Definition 3.12 (Efficiency) *The statistical efficiency e of an estimator $\hat{\theta}(Y)$ is defined as*

$$e := 1/\det IB. \tag{3.37}$$

The closer e is to 1, the lower the variance of the corresponding estimator $\hat{\theta}(Y)$. For a special class of estimators minimizing loss functions, the following theorem allows us to compute B and e efficiently.

Asymptotic Variance

Theorem 3.13 (Murata, Yoshizawa, Amari [379, Lemma 3]) *Assume that $\hat{\theta}$ is defined by $\hat{\theta}(Y) := \operatorname{argmin}_\theta d(Y, \theta)$ and that d is a twice differentiable function in θ. Then asymptotically, for increasing sample size $m \to \infty$, the variance B is given by $B = Q^{-1}GQ^{-1}$. Here*

$$G_{ij} := \operatorname{cov}_\theta\left[\partial_{\theta_i} d(Y, \theta), \partial_{\theta_j} d(Y, \theta)\right] \text{ and} \tag{3.38}$$

$$Q_{ij} := \mathbf{E}_\theta\left[\partial^2_{\theta_i\theta_j} d(Y, \theta)\right], \tag{3.39}$$

and therefore $e = (\det Q)^2/(\det IG)$.

This means that for the class of estimators defined via d, the evaluation of their asymptotic efficiency can be conveniently achieved via (3.38) and (3.39). For scalar valued estimators $\theta(Y) \in \mathbb{R}$, these expressions can be greatly simplified to

$$I = \int \left(\partial_\theta \ln p(Y|\theta)\right)^2 dP(Y|\theta), \tag{3.40}$$

$$G = \int (\partial_\theta d(Y, \theta))^2 dP(Y|\theta), \tag{3.41}$$

$$Q = \int \partial^2_\theta d(Y, \theta) dP(Y|\theta). \tag{3.42}$$

Finally, in the case of continuous densities, Theorem 3.13 may be extended to piecewise twice differentiable continuous functions d, by convolving the latter with a twice differentiable smoothing kernel, and letting the width of the smoothing kernel converge to zero. We will make use of this observation in the next section when studying the efficiency of some estimators.

The current section concludes with the proof that the maximum likelihood estimator meets the Cramér-Rao bound.

Theorem 3.14 (Efficiency of Maximum Likelihood [118, 218, 43]) *The maximum likelihood estimator (cf. (3.18) and (3.19)) given by*

$$\hat{\theta}(Y) := \underset{\theta}{\operatorname{argmax}} \ln p(Y|\theta) = \underset{\theta}{\operatorname{argmin}} \mathcal{L}[\theta] \tag{3.43}$$

is asymptotically efficient ($e = 1$).

To keep things simple we will prove (3.43) only for the class of twice differentiable continuous densities by applying Theorem 3.13. For a more general proof see [118, 218, 43].

Proof By construction, G is equal to the Fisher information matrix, if we choose d according to (3.43). Hence a sufficient condition is that $Q = -I$, which is what we show below. To this end we expand the integrand of (3.42),

$$\partial_\theta^2 d(Y,\theta) = \partial_\theta^2 \ln p(Y|\theta) = \frac{\partial_\theta^2 p(Y|\theta)}{p(Y|\theta)} - \left(\frac{\partial_\theta p(Y|\theta)}{p(Y|\theta)}\right)^2 = \frac{\partial_\theta^2 p(Y|\theta)}{p(Y|\theta)} - V_\theta^2(Y). \tag{3.44}$$

The expectation of the second term in (3.44) equals $-I$. We now show that the expectation of the first term vanishes;

$$\int p(Y|\theta)\frac{\partial_\theta^2 p(Y|\theta)}{p(Y|\theta)}dY = \partial_\theta^2 \int p(Y|\theta)dY = \partial_\theta^2 1 = 0. \tag{3.45}$$

Hence $Q = -I$ and thus $e = Q^2/(IG) = 1$. This proves that the maximum likelihood estimator is asymptotically efficient. ∎

It appears as if the best thing we could do is to use the maximum likelihood (ML) estimator. Unfortunately, reality is not quite as simple as that. First, the above statement holds only asymptotically. This leads to the (justified) suspicion that for finite sample sizes we may be able to do better than ML estimation. Second, practical considerations such as the additional goal of sparse decomposition may lead to the choice of a non-optimal loss function.

Finally, we may not know the true density model, which is required for the definition of the maximum likelihood estimator. We can try to make an educated guess; bad guesses of the class of densities, however, can lead to large errors in the estimation (see, e.g., [251]). This prompted the development of robust estimators.

3.4 Robust Estimators

So far, in order to make any practical predictions, we had to *assume* a certain class of distributions from which P(Y) was chosen. Likewise, in the case of risk functionals, we also assumed that training and test data are identically distributed. This section provides tools to safeguard ourselves against cases where the above assumptions are not satisfied.

Outliers

More specifically, we would like to avoid a certain fraction ν of 'bad' observations (often also referred to as 'outliers') seriously affecting the quality of the estimate. This implies that the influence of individual patterns should be bounded from above. Huber [250] gives a detailed list of desirable properties of a robust estimator. We refrain from reproducing this list at present, or committing to a particular definition of robustness.

As usual for the estimation of location parameter context (i.e. estimation of the expected value of a random variable) we assume a specific parametric form of $p(Y|\theta)$, namely

$$p(Y|\theta) = \prod_{i=1}^{m} p(y_i|\theta) = \prod_{i=1}^{m} p(y_i - \theta). \tag{3.46}$$

Unless stated otherwise, this is the formulation we will use throughout this section.

3.4.1 Robustness via Loss Functions

Huber's idea [250] in constructing a robust estimator was to take a loss function as provided by the maximum likelihood framework, and modify it in such a way as to limit the influence of each individual pattern. This is done by providing an upper bound on the slope of $-\ln p(Y|\theta)$. We shall see that methods such as the trimmed mean or the median are special cases thereof. The ε-insensitive loss function can also be viewed as a trimmed estimator. This will lead to the development of adaptive loss functions in the subsequent sections. We begin with the main theorem of this section.

Mixture Densities

Theorem 3.15 (Robust Loss Functions (Huber [250])) *Let $\mathfrak{P}$ be a class of densities formed by*

$$\mathfrak{P} := \{p | p = (1-\varepsilon)p_0 + \varepsilon p_1\} \text{ where } \varepsilon \in (0,1) \text{ and } p_0 \text{ are known.} \tag{3.47}$$

Moreover assume that both p_0 and p_1 are symmetric with respect to the origin, their logarithms are twice continuously differentiable, $\ln p_0$ is convex and known, and p_1 is unknown. Then the density

$$\bar{p}(\theta) := (1-\varepsilon)\begin{cases} p_0(\theta) & \text{if } |\theta| \leq \theta_0 \\ p_0(\theta_0)e^{-k(|\theta|-\theta_0)} & \text{otherwise} \end{cases} \tag{3.48}$$

is robust in the sense that the maximum likelihood estimator corresponding to (3.48) has minimum variance with respect to the "worst" possible density $p_{\text{worst}} = (1-\varepsilon)p_0 + \varepsilon p_1$: it is a saddle point (located at p_{worst}) in terms of variance with respect to the true density $p \in \mathfrak{P}$ and the density $\bar{p} \in \mathfrak{P}$ used in estimating the location parameter. This means that no density p has larger variance than p_{worst} and that for $p = p_{\text{worst}}$ no estimator is better than the one where $\bar{p} = p_{\text{worst}}$, as used in the robust estimator.

The constants $k > 0$ and θ_0 are obtained by the normalization condition, that $\bar{p}$ be a *proper density and that the first derivative in* $\ln \bar{p}$ *be continuous.*

Proof To show that $\bar{p}$ is a saddle point in $\mathfrak{P}$ we have to prove that (a) no estimation procedure other than the one using $\ln \bar{p}$ as the loss function has lower variance for the density $\bar{p}$, and that (b) no density has higher variance than $\bar{p}$ if $\ln \bar{p}$ is used as loss function. Part (a) follows immediately from the Cramér-Rao theorem (Th. 3.11); part (b) can be proved as follows.

We use Theorem 3.13, and a proof technique pointed out in [559], to compute the variance of an estimator using $\ln \bar{p}$ as loss function;

$$B = \frac{\int \left(\partial_\theta \ln \bar{p}(y|\theta)\right)^2 \left((1-\varepsilon)p_0(y|\theta) + \varepsilon p'(y|\theta)\right) dy}{\int \partial_\theta^2 \ln \bar{p}(y|\theta) \left((1-\varepsilon)p_0(y|\theta) + \varepsilon p'(y|\theta)\right) dy}. \tag{3.49}$$

Here p' is an arbitrary density which we will choose such that B is maximized. By construction,

$$\left(\partial_\theta \ln \bar{p}(y|\theta)\right)^2 = \begin{cases} \left(\partial_\theta \ln p_0(y|\theta)\right)^2 \leq k^2 & \text{if } |y-\theta| \leq \theta_0, \\ k^2 & \text{otherwise,} \end{cases} \tag{3.50}$$

$$\partial_\theta^2 \ln \bar{p}(y|\theta) = \begin{cases} \partial_\theta^2 \ln p_0(y|\theta) \geq 0 & \text{if } |y-\theta| \leq \theta_0, \\ 0 & \text{otherwise.} \end{cases} \tag{3.51}$$

Thus any density p' which is 0 in $[-\theta_0, \theta_0]$ will minimize the denominator (the term depending on p' will be 0, which is the lowest obtainable value due to (3.51)), and maximize the numerator, since in the latter the contribution of p' is always limited to $k^2\varepsilon$. Now $\varepsilon^{-1}\left(\bar{p} - (1-\varepsilon)p_0\right)$ is exactly such a density. Hence the saddle point property holds. ■

Remark 3.16 (Robustness Classes) *If we have more knowledge about the class of densities* $\mathfrak{P}$*, a different loss function will have the saddle point property. For instance, using a similar argument as above, one can show that the normal distribution is robust in the class of all distributions with bounded variance. This implies that among all possible distributions with bounded variance, the estimator of the mean of a normal distribution has the highest variance.*

Likewise, the Laplacian distribution is robust in the class of all symmetric distributions with density $p(0) \geq c$ *for some fixed* $c > 0$ *(see [559, 251] for more details).*

Hence, even though a loss function defined according to Theorem 3.15 is generally desirable, we may be less cautious, and use a different loss function for improved performance, when we have additional knowledge of the distribution.

Remark 3.17 (Mean and Median) *Assume we are dealing with a mixture of a normal distribution with variance* σ^2 *and an additional unknown distribution with weight at most* ε*. It is easy to check that the application of Theorem 3.15 to normal distributions yields Huber's robust loss function from Table 3.1.*

The maximizer of the likelihood (see also Problem 3.17) is a trimmed mean estimator which discards ε *of the data: effectively all* θ_i *deviating from the mean by more than* σ *are ignored and the mean is computed from the remaining data. Hence Theorem 3.15 gives a formal justification for this popular type of estimator.*

If we let $\varepsilon \to 1$ we recover the median estimator which stems from a Laplacian distribution. Here, all patterns but the median one are discarded.

Trimmed Interval Estimator

Besides the classical examples of loss functions and density models, we might also consider a slightly unconventional estimation procedure: use the average between the k-smallest and the k-largest of all observations θ observations as the estimated mean of the underlying distribution (for sorted observations θ_i with $\theta_i \leq \theta_j$ for $1 \leq i \leq j \leq m$ the estimator computes $(\theta_k + \theta_{m-k+1})/2$). This procedure makes sense, for instance, when we are trying to infer the mean of a random variable generated by roundoff noise (i.e., noise whose density is constant within some bounded interval) plus an additional unknown amount of noise.

Support Patterns

Note that both the patterns strictly *inside* or *outside* an interval of size $[-\varepsilon, \varepsilon]$ around the estimate have no direct influence on the outcome. Only patterns *on* the boundary matter. This is a very similar situation to the behavior of Support Vector Machines in regression, and one can show that it corresponds to the minimizer of the ε-insensitive loss function (3.9). We will study the properties of the latter in more detail in the following section and thereafter show how it can be transformed into an adaptive risk functional.

3.4.2 Efficiency and the ε-Insensitive Loss Function

The tools of Section 3.3.2 allow us to analyze the ε-insensitive loss function in more detail. Even though the asymptotic estimation of a location parameter setting is a gross oversimplification of what is happening in a SV regression estimator (where we estimate a nonparametric function, and moreover have only a limited number of observations at our disposition), it will provide us with useful insights into this more complex case [510, 481].

In a first step, we compute the efficiency of an estimator, for several noise models and amounts of variance, using a density corresponding to the ε-insensitive loss function (cf. Table 3.1);

$$p_\varepsilon(y|\theta) = \frac{1}{2+2\varepsilon}\exp(-|y-\theta|_\varepsilon) = \frac{1}{2+2\varepsilon}\begin{cases} 1 & \text{if } |y-\theta| \leq \varepsilon, \\ \exp(\varepsilon - |y-\theta|) & \text{otherwise.} \end{cases} \tag{3.52}$$

For this purpose we have to evaluate the quantities G (3.41) and Q (3.42) of Theorem 3.13. We obtain

$$G = m\int \left(\partial_\theta \ln p(y|\theta)\right)^2 dP(y|\theta) = m\left(1 - \int_{-\varepsilon}^{\varepsilon} p(y|\theta)dy\right), \tag{3.53}$$

$$Q = m\int \partial_\theta^2 \ln p(y|\theta) dP(y|\theta) = m\left(p(-\varepsilon+\theta|\theta) + p(\varepsilon+\theta|\theta)\right). \tag{3.54}$$

The Fisher information I of m iid random variables distributed according to p_θ is m-times the value of a single random variable. Thus all dependencies on m in e cancel out and we can limit ourselves to the case of $m = 1$ for the analysis of the efficiency of estimators.

Now we may check what happens if we use the ε-insensitive loss function for different types of noise model. For the sake of simplicity we begin with Gaussian noise.

Example 3.18 (Gaussian Noise) *Assume that y is normally distributed with zero mean (i.e. $\theta = 0$) and variance σ. By construction, the minimum obtainable variance is $I^{-1} = \sigma^2$ (recall that $m = 1$). Moreover (3.53) and (3.54) yield*

$$\frac{G}{Q^2} = \sigma^2 \exp\left(\frac{\varepsilon^2}{\sigma^2}\right)\left(1 - \operatorname{erf}\frac{\varepsilon}{\sqrt{2}\sigma}\right). \tag{3.55}$$

The efficiency $e = \frac{Q^2}{GI}$ is maximized for $\varepsilon = 0.6120\sigma$. This means that if the underlying noise model is Gaussian with variance σ and we have to use an ε-insensitive loss function to estimate a location parameter, the most efficient estimator from this family is given by $\varepsilon = 0.6120\sigma$.

The consequence of (3.55) is that the optimal value of ε scales linearly with σ. Of course, we could just use squared loss in such a situation, but in general, we will not know the exact noise model, and squared loss does not lead to robust estimators. The following lemma (which will come handy in the next section) shows that this is a general property of the ε-insensitive loss.

Lemma 3.19 (Linear Dependency between ε-Tube Width and Variance) *Denote by p a symmetric density with variance $\sigma > 0$. Then the optimal value of ε (i.e. the value that achieves maximum asymptotic efficiency) for an estimator using the ε-insensitive loss is given by*

$$\varepsilon_{\mathrm{opt}} = \sigma \operatorname*{argmin}_{\tau} \frac{1}{(p_{\mathrm{std}}(-\tau) + p_{\mathrm{std}}(\tau))^2}\left(1 - \int_{-\tau}^{\tau} p_{\mathrm{std}}(\tau')d\tau'\right), \tag{3.56}$$

where $p_{\mathrm{std}}(\tau) := \sigma p(\sigma\tau + \theta|\theta)$ is the standardized version of $p(y|\theta)$, i.e. it is obtained by rescaling $p(y|\theta)$ to zero mean and unit variance.

Since p_{std} is independent of σ, we have a linear dependency between $\varepsilon_{\mathrm{opt}}$ and σ. The scaling factor depends on the noise model.

Proof We prove (3.56) by rewriting the efficiency $e(\varepsilon)$ in terms of p_{std} via $p(y|\theta) = \sigma^{-1}p_{\mathrm{std}}(\sigma^{-1}(y - \theta))$. This yields

$$e(\varepsilon) = \frac{Q^2}{IG} = \frac{(\sigma^{-1}p_{\mathrm{std}}(-\sigma^{-1}\varepsilon) + \sigma^{-1}p_{\mathrm{std}}(\sigma^{-1}\varepsilon))^2}{\sigma^{-2}\left(1 - \int_{-\varepsilon}^{\varepsilon}\sigma^{-1}p_{\mathrm{std}}(\sigma^{-1}\theta)d\theta\right)} = \frac{(p_{\mathrm{std}}(-\sigma^{-1}\varepsilon) + p_{\mathrm{std}}(\sigma^{-1}\varepsilon))^2}{\left(1 - \int_{-\sigma^{-1}\varepsilon}^{\sigma^{-1}\varepsilon} p_{\mathrm{std}}(\theta)d\theta\right)}$$

The maximum of $e(\varepsilon)$ does not depend directly on ε, but on $\sigma^{-1}\varepsilon$ (which is independent of σ). Hence we can find $\operatorname{argmax}_{\varepsilon} e(\varepsilon)$ by solving (3.56). ■

Lemma 3.19 made it apparent that in order to adjust ε we have to know σ beforehand. Unfortunately, the latter is usually unknown at the beginning of the estimation procedure.[8] The solution to this dilemma is to make ε adaptive.

3.4.3 Adaptive Loss Functions

We again consider the trimmed mean estimator, which discards a predefined fraction of largest and smallest samples. This method belongs to the more general class of quantile estimators, which base their estimates on the value of samples in a certain quantile. The latter methods do not require prior knowledge of the variance, and adapt to whatever scale is required. What we need is a technique which connects σ (in Huber's robust loss function) or ε (in the ε-insensitive loss case) with the deviations between the estimate $\hat{\theta}$ and the random variables y_i.

Let us analyze what happens to the negative log likelihood, if, in the ε-insensitive case, we change ε to $\varepsilon + \delta$ (with $\delta \in \mathbb{R}$) while keeping $\hat{\theta}$ fixed. In particular we assume that $|\delta|$ is chosen sufficiently small such that for all $i = 1, \ldots, m$,

$$|\hat{\theta} - y_i| \begin{cases} \leq \varepsilon + \delta & \text{if } |\hat{\theta} - y_i| < \varepsilon \\ \geq \varepsilon + \delta & \text{if } |\hat{\theta} - y_i| > \varepsilon \end{cases} \tag{3.57}$$

Moreover denote by $m_<, m_=, m_>$ the number of samples for which $|\hat{\theta} - y_i|$ is less than, equal to, or greater than ε, respectively. Then

$$\begin{aligned} \sum_{i=1}^{m} |\hat{\theta} - y_i|_{\varepsilon+\delta} &= \sum_{|\hat{\theta}-y_i|<\varepsilon} |\hat{\theta} - y_i|_{\varepsilon} + \sum_{|\hat{\theta}-y_i|>\varepsilon} |\hat{\theta} - y_i|_{\varepsilon} - m_>\delta + \sum_{|\hat{\theta}-y_i|=\varepsilon} |\hat{\theta} - y_i|_{\varepsilon+\delta} \\ &= \sum_{i=1}^{m} |\hat{\theta} - y_i|_{\varepsilon} - \begin{cases} m_>\delta & \text{if } \delta > 0, \\ (m_< + m_=)\delta & \text{otherwise.} \end{cases} \end{aligned} \tag{3.58}$$

In other words, the amount by which the loss changes depends only on the quantiles at ε. What happens if we make ε itself a variable of the optimization problem? By the scaling properties of (3.58) one can see that for $\nu \in [0, 1]$

$$\underset{\hat{\theta},\varepsilon}{\text{minimize}} \, \frac{1}{m} \sum_{i=1}^{m} |\hat{\theta} - y_i|_{\varepsilon} - \nu\varepsilon \tag{3.59}$$

ν-Property

is minimized if ε is chosen such that

$$\frac{m_>}{m} \leq \nu \leq \frac{m_> + m_=}{m}. \tag{3.60}$$

This relation holds since at the solution $(\hat{\theta}, \varepsilon)$ the solution also has to be optimal wrt. ε alone while keeping $\hat{\theta}$ fixed. In the latter case, however, the derivatives of

8. The obvious question is why one would ever like to choose an ε-insensitive loss in the presence of Gaussian noise in the first place. If the complexity of the function expansion is of no concern and the highest accuracy is required, squared loss is to be preferred. In most cases, however, it is not quite clear what *exactly* the type of the additive noise model is. This is when we would like to have a more conservative estimator. In practice, the ε-insensitive loss has been shown to work rather well on a variety of tasks (Chapter 9).

the log-likelihood (i.e. error) term wrt. ε at the solution are given by $\frac{m_>}{m}$ and $\frac{m_> + m_=}{m}$ on the left and right hand side respectively.[9] These have to cancel with ν which proves the claim. Furthermore, computing the derivative of (3.59) with respect to θ shows that the number of samples outside the interval $[\theta - \varepsilon, \theta + \varepsilon]$ has to be equal on both halves $(-\infty, \theta - \varepsilon)$ and $(\theta + \varepsilon, \infty)$. We have the following theorem:

Theorem 3.20 (Quantile Estimation as Optimization Problem [481]) *A quantile procedure to estimate the mean of a distribution by taking the average of the samples at the $\frac{\nu}{2}$th and $(1 - \frac{\nu}{2})$th quantile is equivalent to minimizing (3.59). In particular,*

1. *ν is an upper bound on the fraction of samples outside the interval $[\theta - \varepsilon, \theta + \varepsilon]$.*
2. *ν is a lower bound on the fraction of samples outside the interval $]\theta - \varepsilon, \theta + \varepsilon[$.*
3. *If the distribution $p(\theta)$ is continuous, for all $\nu \in [0, 1]$*

$$\lim_{m \to \infty} \mathrm{P}\left\{ \frac{m_=}{m} < \varepsilon \right\} = 1 \text{ for all } \varepsilon > 0. \tag{3.61}$$

One might question the practical advantage of this method over direct trimming of the sample Y. In fact, the use of (3.59) is not recommended if all we want is to estimate θ. That said, (3.59) does allow us to employ trimmed estimation in the nonparametric case, cf. Chapter 9.

Extension to General Robust Estimators

Unfortunately, we were unable to find a similar method for Huber's robust loss function, since in this case the change in the negative log-likelihood incurred by changing σ not only involves the (statistical) rank of y_i, but also the exact location of samples with $|y_i - \theta| < \sigma$.

One way to overcome this problem is re-estimate σ adaptively while minimizing a term similar to (3.59) (see [180] for details in the context of boosting, Section 10.6.3 for a discussion of online estimation techniques, or [251] for a general overview).

3.4.4 Optimal Choice of ν

Let us return to the ε-insensitive loss. A combination of Theorems 3.20, 3.13 and Lemma 3.19 allows us to compute optimal values of ν for various distributions, provided that an ε-insensitive loss function is to be used in the estimation procedure.[10]

The idea is to determine the optimal value of ε for a fixed density $p(y|\theta)$ via (3.56), and compute the corresponding fraction ν of patterns outside the interval $[-\varepsilon + \theta, \varepsilon + \theta]$.

---

9. Strictly speaking, the derivative is not defined at ε; the lhs and rhs values are defined, however, which is sufficient for our purpose.
10. This is not optimal in the sense of Theorem 3.15, which suggests the use of a more adapted loss function. However (as already stated in the introduction of this chapter), algorithmic or technical reasons such as computationally efficient solutions or limited memory may provide sufficient motivation to use such a loss function.

Table 3.2 Optimal ν and ε for various degrees of polynomial additive noise.

Polynomial Degree d	1	2	3	4	5
Optimal ν	1	0.5405	0.2909	0.1898	0.1384
Optimal ε for unit variance	0	0.6120	1.1180	1.3583	1.4844
Polynomial Degree d	6	7	8	9	10
Optimal ν	0.1080	0.0881	0.0743	0.0641	0.0563
Optimal ε for unit variance	1.5576	1.6035	1.6339	1.6551	1.6704

Theorem 3.21 (Optimal Choice of ν) *Denote by p a symmetric density with variance $\sigma > 0$ and by p_{std} the corresponding rescaled density with zero mean and unit variance. Then the optimal value of ν (i.e. the value that achieves maximum asymptotic efficiency) for an estimator using the ε-insensitive loss is given by*

$$\nu = 1 - \int_{-\varepsilon}^{\varepsilon} p_{\text{std}}(y)dy \tag{3.62}$$

where ε is chosen according to (3.56). This expression is independent of σ.

Proof The independence of σ follows from the fact that ν depends only on p_{std}. Next we show (3.62). For a given density p, the asymptotically optimal value of ε is given by Lemma 3.19. The average fraction of patterns outside the interval $[\theta - \varepsilon_{\text{opt}}, \theta + \varepsilon_{\text{opt}}]$ is

$$\nu = 1 - \int_{-\varepsilon_{\text{opt}}+\theta}^{\varepsilon_{\text{opt}}+\theta} p(y|\theta)dy = 1 - \int_{-\sigma^{-1}\varepsilon_{\text{opt}}}^{\sigma^{-1}\varepsilon_{\text{opt}}} p_{\text{std}}(y)dy, \tag{3.63}$$

which depends only on $\sigma^{-1}\varepsilon_{\text{opt}}$ and is thus independent of σ. Combining (3.63) with (3.56) yields the theorem. ■

This means that given the *type* of additive noise, we *can* determine the value of ν such that it yields the asymptotically most efficient estimator *independent* of the *level* of the noise. These theoretical predictions have since been confirmed rather accurately in a set of regression experiments [95].

Let us now look at some special cases.

Example 3.22 (Optimal ν for Polynomial Noise) *Arbitrary polynomial noise models ($\propto e^{-|\theta|^d}$) with unit variance can be written as*

$$p(y) = c_p \exp\left(-c'_p|y|^p\right) \text{ where } c_p = \frac{1}{2}\sqrt{\frac{\Gamma(3/d)}{\Gamma(1/d)}}\frac{d}{\Gamma(1/d)} \text{ and } c'_p = \left(\sqrt{\frac{\Gamma(3/d)}{\Gamma(1/d)}}\right)^d,$$

where $\Gamma(x)$ is the gamma function. Figure 3.3 shows ν_{opt} for polynomial degrees in the interval $[1, 10]$. For convenience, the explicit numerical values are repeated in Table 3.2.

Observe that as the distribution becomes "lighter-tailed", the optimal ν decreases; in other words, we may then use a larger amount of the data for the purpose of estimation. This is reasonable since it is only for very long tails of the distribution (data with many

Heavy Tails → Large ν

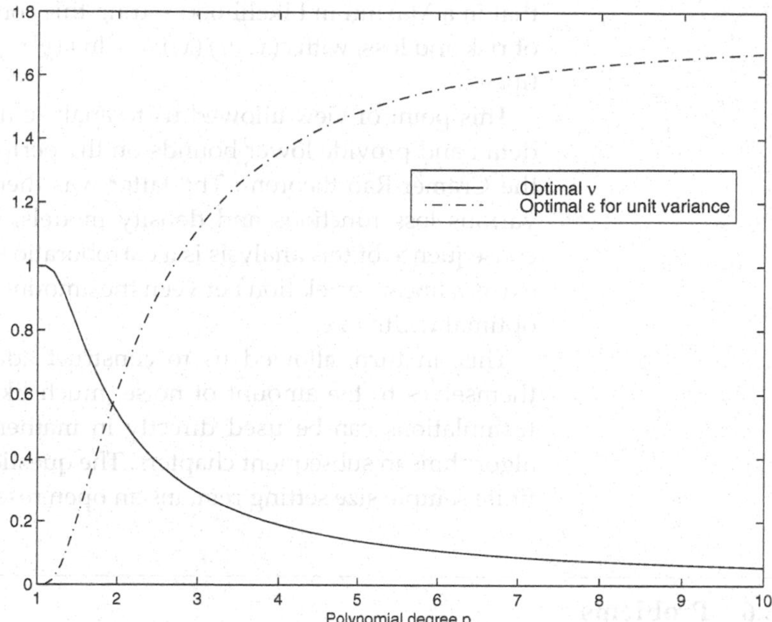

Figure 3.3 Optimal ν and ε for various degrees of polynomial additive noise.

outliers) that we have to be conservative and discard a large fraction of observations.

Even though we derived these relations solely for the case where a single number (θ) has to be estimated, experiments show that the same scaling properties hold for the nonparametric case. It is still an open research problem to establish this connection exactly.

As we shall see, in the nonparametric case, the effect of ν will be that it both determines the number of Support Vectors (i.e., the number of basis functions needed to expand the solution) and also the fraction of function values $f(x_i)$ with deviation larger than ε from the corresponding observations. Further information on this topic, both from the statistical and the algorithmic point of view, can be found in Section 9.3.

3.5 Summary

We saw in this chapter that there exist two complementary concepts as to how risk and loss functions should be designed. The first one is data driven and uses the incurred loss as its principal guideline, possibly modified in order to suit the need of numerical efficiency. This leads to loss functions and the definitions of empirical and expected risk.

A second method is based on the idea of estimating (or at least approximating) the distribution which may be responsible for generating the data. We showed that in a Maximum Likelihood setting this concept is rather similar to the notions of risk and loss, with $c(x, y, f(x)) = -\ln p(y|x, f(x))$ as the link between both quantities.

This point of view allowed us to analyze the properties of estimators in more detail and provide lower bounds on the performance of unbiased estimators, i.e. the Cramér-Rao theorem. The latter was then used as a benchmarking tool for various loss functions and density models, such as the ε-insensitive loss. The consequence of this analysis is a corroboration of experimental findings that there exists a linear correlation between the amount of noise in the observations and the optimal width of ε.

This, in turn, allowed us to construct adaptive loss functions which adjust themselves to the amount of noise, much like trimmed mean estimators. These formulations can be used directly in mathematical programs, leading to ν-SV algorithms in subsequent chapters. The question of which choices are optimal in a finite sample size setting remains an open research problem.

3.6 Problems

3.1 (Soft Margin and Logistic Regression •) *The soft margin loss function* c_{soft} *and the logistic loss* c_{logist} *are asymptotically almost the same; show that*

$$\lim_{f\to\infty} \left(c_{\text{soft}}(x,1,f) - c_{\text{logist}}(x,1,f)\right) = 1 \tag{3.64}$$

$$\lim_{f\to-\infty} \left(c_{\text{soft}}(x,1,f) - c_{\text{logist}}(x,1,f)\right) = 0. \tag{3.65}$$

3.2 (Multi-class Discrimination ••) *Assume you have to solve a classification problem with M different classes. Discuss how the number of functions used to solve this task affects the quality of the solution.*

- *How would the loss function look if you were to use only one real-valued function* $f: \mathcal{X} \to \mathbb{R}$. *Which symmetries are violated in this case (hint: what happens if you permute the classes)?*
- *How many functions do you need if each of them makes a binary decision* $f: \mathcal{X} \to \{0, 1\}$*?*
- *How many functions do you need in order to make the solution permutation symmetric with respect to the class labels?*
- *How should you assess the classification error? Is it a good idea to use the misclassification rate of one individual function as a performance criterion (hint: correlation of errors)? By how much can this error differ from the total misclassification error?*

3.3 (Mean and Median •) *Assume 8 people want to gather for a meeting; 5 of them live in Stuttgart and 3 in Munich. Where should they meet if (a) they want the total distance traveled by all people to be minimal, (b) they want the average distance traveled per person to be minimal, or (c) they want the average squared distance to be minimal? What happens* *to the meeting points if one of the 3 people moves from Munich to Sydney?*

3.4 (Locally Adaptive Loss Functions •••) *Assume that the loss function $c(x, y, f(x))$ varies with x. What does this mean for the expected loss? Can you give a bound on the latter even if you know $p(y|x)$ and f at every point but know c only on a finite sample (hint: construct a counterexample)? How will things change if c cannot vary much with x?*

3.5 (Transduction Error •••) *Assume that we want to minimize the test error of misclassification $R_{\text{test}}[f]$, given a training sample $\{(x_1, y_1), \ldots, (x_m, y_m)\}$, a test sample $\{x'_1, \ldots, x'_{m'}\}$ and a loss function $c(x, y, f(x))$.*

Show that any loss function $c'(x', f(x'))$ on the test sample has to be symmetric in f, i.e. $c'(x', f(x')) = c'(x', -f(x'))$. Prove that no non-constant convex function can satisfy this property. What does this mean for the practical solution of optimization problem? See [267, 37, 211, 103] for details.

3.6 (Convexity and Uniqueness ••) *Show that the problem of estimating a location parameter (a single scalar) has an interval $[a, b] \subset \mathbb{R}$ of equivalent global minima if the loss functions are convex. For non-convex loss functions construct an example where this is not the case.*

3.7 (Linearly Dependent Parameters ••) *Show that in a linear model $f = \sum_i \alpha_i f_i$ on $\mathcal{X}$ it is impossible to find a unique set of optimal parameters α_i if the functions f_i are not linearly independent. Does this have any effect on f itself?*

3.8 (Ill-posed Problems •••) *Assume you want to solve the problem $Ax = y$ where A is a symmetric positive definite matrix, i.e., a matrix with nonnegative eigenvalues. If you change y to y', how much will the solution x' of $Ax' = y'$ differ from x'. Give lower and upper bounds on this quantity. Hint: decompose y into the eigensystem of A.*

3.9 (Fisher Map [258] ••) *Show that the map*

$$U_\theta(x) := I^{-\frac{1}{2}} \partial_\theta \ln p(x|\theta) \tag{3.66}$$

maps x into vectors with zero mean and unit variance. Chapter 13 will use this map to design kernels.

3.10 (Cramér-Rao Inequality for Multivariate Estimators ••) *Prove equation (3.31). Hint: start by applying the Cauchy-Schwarz inequality to*

$$\left(\det E_{\bar{\theta}}[(\hat{\theta}(\theta) - E_{\bar{\theta}}\hat{\theta}(\theta))(T_\theta(\theta) - E_{\bar{\theta}}T_\theta(\theta))^\top]\right) \tag{3.67}$$

to obtain I and B and compute the expected value coefficient-wise.

3.11 (Soft Margin Loss and Conditional Probabilities [521] •••) *What is the conditional probability $p(y|x)$ corresponding to the soft margin loss function $c(x, y, f(x)) = \max(0, 1 - yf(x))$?*

- *How can you fix the problem that the probabilities $p(-1|x)$ and $p(1|x)$ have to sum up to 1?*
- *How does the introduction of a third class ("don't know") change the problem? What is the problem with this approach? Hint: What is the behavior for large $|f(x)|$?*

3.12 (Label Noise ••) *Denote by $\mathrm{P}(y = 1|f(x))$ and $\mathrm{P}(y = -1|f(x))$ the conditional probabilities of labels ± 1 for a classifier output $f(x)$. How will P change if we randomly flip labels with $\eta \in (0, 1)$ probability? How should you adapt your density model?*

3.13 (Unbiased Estimators ••) *Prove that the least mean square estimator is unbiased for arbitrary symmetric distributions. Can you extend the result to arbitrary symmetric losses?*

3.14 (Efficiency of Huber's Robust Estimator ••) *Compute the efficiency of Huber's Robust Estimator in the presence of pure Gaussian noise with unit variance.*

3.15 (Influence and Robustness •••) *Prove that for robust estimators using (3.48) as their density model, the maximum change in the minimizer of the empirical risk is bounded by $\frac{\delta k}{m}$ if a sample θ_i is changed to $\theta_i + \delta$. What happens in the case of Gaussian density models (i.e., squared loss)?*

3.16 (Robustness of Gaussian Distributions [559] •••) *Prove that the normal distribution with variance σ^2 is robust among the class of distributions with bounded variance (by σ^2). Hint: show that we have a saddle point analogous to Theorem 3.15 by exploiting Theorems 3.13 and Theorem 3.14.*

3.17 (Trimmed Mean ••) *Show that under the assumption of an unknown distribution contributing at most ε, Huber's robust loss function for normal distributions leads to a trimmed mean estimator which discards ε of the data.*

3.18 (Optimal ν for Gaussian Noise •) *Give an explicit solution for the optimal ν in the case of additive Gaussian noise.*

3.19 (Optimal ν for Discrete Distribution ••) *Assume that we have a noise model with a discrete distribution of θ, where $\mathrm{P}(\theta = \epsilon) = \mathrm{P}(\theta = -\epsilon) = p_1$, $\mathrm{P}(\theta = 2\epsilon) = \mathrm{P}(\theta = -2\epsilon) = p_2$, $2(p_1 + p_2) = 1$, and $p_1, p_2 \geq 0$. Compute the optimal value of ν.*

4 Regularization

Minimizing the empirical risk can lead to numerical instabilities and bad generalization performance. A possible way to avoid this problem is to restrict the class of admissible solutions, for instance to a compact set. This technique was introduced by Tikhonov and Arsenin [538] for solving inverse problems and has since been applied to learning problems with great success. In statistics, the corresponding estimators are often referred to as *shrinkage estimators* [262].

Kernel methods are best suited for two special types of regularization: a coefficient space constraint on the *expansion coefficients* of the weight vector in feature space [343, 591, 37, 517, 189], or, alternatively, a function space regularization *directly* penalizing the weight vector in feature space [573, 62, 561]. In this chapter we will discuss the connections between regularization, Reproducing Kernel Hilbert Spaces (RKHS), feature spaces, and regularization operators. The connection to Gaussian Processes will be explained in more detail in Section 16.3. These different viewpoints will help us to gain insight into the success of kernel methods.

Overview

We start by introducing regularized risk functionals (Section 4.1), followed by a discussion of the Representer Theorem describing the functional form of the minimizers of a certain class of such risk functionals (Section 4.2). Section 4.3 introduces regularization operators and details their connection to SV kernels. Sections 4.4 through 4.6 look at this connection for specific classes of kernels. Following that, we have several sections dealing with various regularization issues of interest for machine learning: vector-valued functions (Section 4.7), semiparametric regularization (Section 4.8), and finally, coefficient-based regularization (Section 4.9).

Prerequisites

This chapter may not be be easy to digest for some of our readers. We recommend that most readers should nevertheless consider going through Sections 4.1 and 4.2. Those two sections are accessible with the background given in Chapters 1 and Chapter 2. The following Section 4.3 is somewhat more technical, since it is using the concept of Green's functions and operators, but should nevertheless still be looked at. A background in functional analysis will be helpful.

Sections 4.4, 4.5, and 4.6 are more difficult, and require a solid knowledge of Fourier integrals and elements of the theory of special functions. To understand Section 4.7, some basic notions of group theory are beneficial. Finally, Sections 4.8 and Section 4.9 do not require additional knowledge beyond the basic concepts put forward in the introductory chapters. Yet, some readers may find it beneficial to read these two last sections after they gained a deeper insight into classification, regression and mathematical programming, as provided by Chapters 6, 7, and 9.

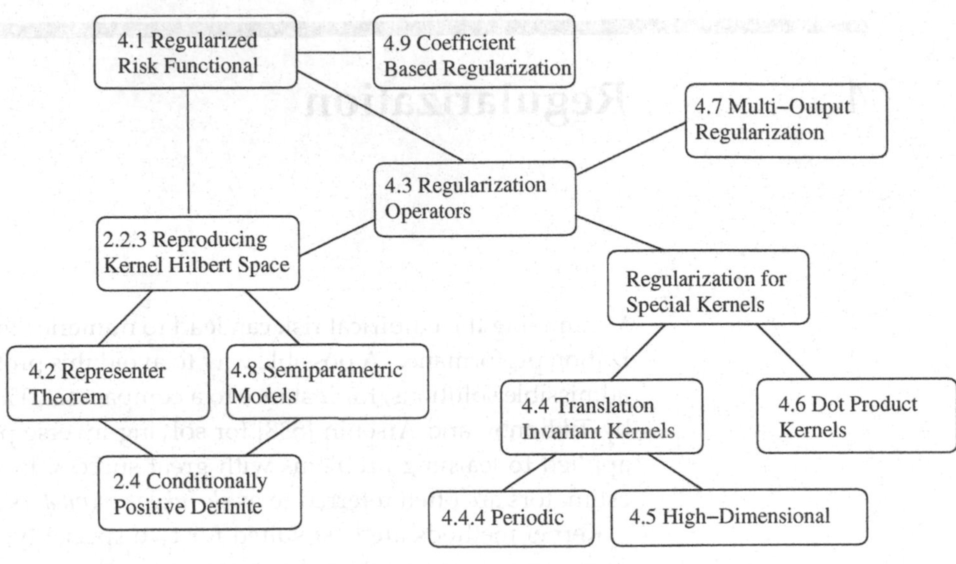

4.1 The Regularized Risk Functional

The key idea in regularization is to restrict the class of possible minimizers $\mathfrak{F}$ (with $f \in \mathfrak{F}$) of the empirical risk functional $R_{\text{emp}}[f]$ such that $\mathfrak{F}$ becomes a compact set. While there exist various characterizations for compact sets and we may define a large variety of such sets which will suit different assumptions on the type of estimates we get, the common key idea is compactness. In addition, we will assume that $R_{\text{emp}}[f]$ is continuous in f.

Continuity Assumption

Note that this is a stronger assumption than it may appear at first glance. It is easily satisfied for many regression problems, such as those using squared loss or the ε-insensitive loss. Yet binary valued loss functions, as are often used in classification (such as $c(x, y, f(x)) = \frac{1}{2}(1 - \operatorname{sgn} yf(x))$), do not meet the requirements. Since both the exact minimization of $R_{\text{emp}}[f]$ for classification problems [367], even with very restricted classes of functions, and also the approximate solution to this problem [20] have been proven to be NP-hard, we will not bother with this case any further, but rather attempt to minimize a continuous approximation of the $0 - 1$ loss, such as the one using a soft margin loss function (3.3).

We may now apply the operator inversion lemma to show that for compact $\mathfrak{F}$, the inverse map from the minimum of the empirical risk functional $R_{\text{emp}}[f] : \mathfrak{F} \to \mathbb{R}$ to its minimizer $\hat{f}$ is continuous and the optimization problem well-posed.

Theorem 4.1 (Operator Inversion Lemma (e.g., [431])) *Let X be a compact set and let the map $f : X \to Y$ be continuous. Then there exists an inverse map $f^{-1} : f(X) \to X$ that is also continuous.*

We do not directly specify a compact set $\mathfrak{F}$, since this leads to a constrained

Regularization Term

optimization problem, which can be cumbersome in practice. Instead, we add a stabilization (regularization) term $\Omega[f]$ to the original objective function; the latter could be $R_{\text{emp}}[f]$, for instance. This, too, leads to better conditioning of the problem. We consider the following class of regularized risk functionals (see also Problem 4.1)

$$R_{\text{reg}}[f] := R_{\text{emp}}[f] + \lambda\Omega[f]. \tag{4.1}$$

Here $\lambda > 0$ is the so-called regularization parameter which specifies the trade-off between minimization of $R_{\text{emp}}[f]$ and the smoothness or simplicity which is enforced by small $\Omega[f]$. Usually one chooses $\Omega[f]$ to be convex, since this ensures that there exists only one global minimum, provided $R_{\text{emp}}[f]$ is also convex (see Lemma 6.3 and Theorem 6.5).

Maximization of the margin of classification in feature space by using the regularizing term $\frac{1}{2}\|\mathbf{w}\|^2$, and thus minimizing

$$\Omega[f] := \frac{1}{2}\|\mathbf{w}\|^2, \text{ and therefore } R_{\text{reg}}[f] = R_{\text{emp}}[f] + \frac{\lambda}{2}\|\mathbf{w}\|^2, \tag{4.2}$$

Quadratic Regularizer

is the common choice in SV classification [573, 62]. In regression, the geometrical interpretation of minimizing $\frac{1}{2}\|\mathbf{w}\|^2$ is to find the *flattest* function with sufficient approximation qualities. Unless stated otherwise, we will limit ourselves to this type of regularizer in the present chapter. Other methods, e.g., minimizing the ℓ_p norm (where $\|\mathbf{x}\|_p^p = \sum_i x_i^p$) of the expansion coefficients for $\mathbf{w}$, will be discussed in Section 4.9.

Regularized Risk in RKHS

As described in Section 2.2.3, we can equivalently think of the feature space as a reproducing kernel Hilbert space. It is often useful, and indeed it will be one of the central themes of this chapter, to rewrite the risk functional (4.2) in terms of the RKHS representation of the feature space. In this case, we equivalently minimize

$$R_{\text{reg}}[f] := R_{\text{emp}}[f] + \frac{\lambda}{2}\|f\|^2_{\mathcal{H}} \tag{4.3}$$

over the whole space $\mathcal{H}$. The next section will study the properties of minimizers of (4.3), and similar regularizers that depend on $\|f\|_{\mathcal{H}}$.

4.2 The Representer Theorem

History of the Representer Theorem

The explicit form of a minimizer of $R_{\text{reg}}[f]$ is given by the celebrated representer theorem of Kimeldorf and Wahba [296] which plays a central role in solving practical problems of statistical estimation. It was first proven in the context of squared loss functions, and later extended to general pointwise loss functions [115]. For a machine learning point of view of the representer theorem, and variational proofs, see [205, 512]. The linear case has also been dealt with in [300]. We present a new and slightly more general version of the theorem with a simple proof [473]. As above, $\mathcal{H}$ is the RKHS associated to the kernel k.

Theorem 4.2 (Representer Theorem) *Denote by $\Omega : [0, \infty) \to \mathbb{R}$ a strictly monotonic increasing function, by $\mathcal{X}$ a set, and by $c : (\mathcal{X} \times \mathbb{R}^2)^m \to \mathbb{R} \cup \{\infty\}$ an arbitrary loss function. Then each minimizer $f \in \mathcal{H}$ of the regularized risk*

$$c\left((x_1, y_1, f(x_1)), \ldots, (x_m, y_m, f(x_m))\right) + \Omega\left(\|f\|_{\mathcal{H}}\right) \tag{4.4}$$

admits a representation of the form

$$f(x) = \sum_{i=1}^{m} \alpha_i k(x_i, x). \tag{4.5}$$

Note that this setting is slightly more general than Definition 3.1 since it allows *coupling* between the samples (x_i, y_i).

Before we proceed with the actual proof, let us make a few remarks. The original form, with pointwise mean squared loss

$$c((x_1, y_1, f(x_1)), \ldots, (x_m, y_m, f(x_m))) = \frac{1}{m} \sum_{i=1}^{m} (y_i - f(x_i))^2, \tag{4.6}$$

or hard constraints (i.e., hard limits on the maximally allowed error, incorporated formally by using a cost function that takes the value ∞), and $\Omega(\|f\|) = \frac{\lambda}{2}\|f\|_{\mathcal{H}}^2$ ($\lambda > 0$), is due to Kimeldorf and Wahba [296].

Requirements on $\Omega[f]$

Monotonicity of Ω is necessary to ensure that the theorem holds. It does not prevent the regularized risk functional (4.4) from having multiple local minima. To ensure a single minimum, we would need to require convexity. If we discard the strictness of the monotonicity, then it no longer follows that each minimizer of the regularized risk admits an expansion (4.5); it still follows, however, that there is always another solution that is as good, and that *does* admit the expansion.

Note that the freedom to use regularizers other than $\Omega(\|f\|) = \frac{\lambda}{2}\|f\|_{\mathcal{H}}^2$ allow us in principle to design algorithms that are more closely aligned with recommendations given by bounds derived from statistical learning theory, as described below (cf. Problem 5.7).

Significance

The significance of the Representer Theorem is that although we might be trying to solve an optimization problem in an infinite-dimensional space $\mathcal{H}$, containing linear combinations of kernels centered on *arbitrary* points of $\mathcal{X}$, it states that the solution lies in the span of m particular kernels — those centered on the training points. In the Support Vector community, (4.5) is called the *Support Vector expansion*. For suitable choices of loss functions, it has empirically been found that many of the α_i often equal 0 (see Problem 4.6 for more detail on the connection between sparsity and loss functions).

Sparsity and Loss Function

Proof For convenience we will assume that we are dealing with $\bar{\Omega}(\|f\|^2) := \Omega(\|f\|)$ rather than $\Omega(\|f\|)$. This is no restriction at all, since the quadratic function is strictly monotonic on $[0, \infty)$, and therefore $\bar{\Omega}$ is strictly monotonic on $[0, \infty)$ if and only if Ω also satisfies this requirement.

We may decompose any $f \in \mathcal{H}$ into a part contained in the span of the kernel functions $k(x_1, \cdot), \cdots, k(x_m, \cdot)$, and one in the orthogonal complement;

$$f(x) = f_{\|}(x) + f_{\perp}(x) = \sum_{i=1}^{m} \alpha_i k(x_i, x) + f_{\perp}(x). \tag{4.7}$$

Here $\alpha_i \in \mathbb{R}$ and $f_{\perp} \in \mathcal{H}$ with $\langle f_{\perp}, k(x_i, \cdot)\rangle_{\mathcal{H}} = 0$ for all $i \in [m] := \{1, \ldots, m\}$. By (2.34) we may write $f(x_j)$ (for all $j \in [m]$) as

$$f(x_j) = \langle f(\cdot), k(x_j, .)\rangle = \sum_{i=1}^{m} \alpha_i k(x_i, x_j) + \langle f_{\perp}(\cdot), k(x_j, .)\rangle_{\mathcal{H}} = \sum_{i=1}^{m} \alpha_i k(x_i, x_j). \tag{4.8}$$

Second, for all $f_{\perp}$,

$$\Omega(\|f\|_{\mathcal{H}}) = \bar{\Omega}\left(\left\|\sum_{i}^{m} \alpha_i k(x_i, \cdot)\right\|_{\mathcal{H}}^2 + \|f_{\perp}\|_{\mathcal{H}}^2\right) \geq \bar{\Omega}\left(\left\|\sum_{i}^{m} \alpha_i k(x_i, \cdot)\right\|_{\mathcal{H}}^2\right). \tag{4.9}$$

Thus for any fixed $\alpha_i \in \mathbb{R}$ the risk functional (4.4) is minimized for $f_{\perp} = 0$. Since this also has to hold for the solution, the theorem holds. ■

Let us state two immediate extensions of Theorem 4.2. The proof of the following theorem is left as an exercise (see Problem 4.3).

Prior Knowledge by Parametric Expansions

Theorem 4.3 (Semiparametric Representer Theorem) *Suppose that in addition to the assumptions of the previous theorem we are given a set of M real-valued functions* $\{\psi_p\}_{p=1}^{M} : \mathcal{X} \to \mathbb{R}$, *with the property that the* $m \times M$ *matrix* $(\psi_p(x_i))_{ip}$ *has rank M. Then any* $\tilde{f} := f + h$, *with* $f \in \mathcal{H}$ *and* $h \in \operatorname{span}\{\psi_p\}$, *minimizing the regularized risk*

$$c\left((x_1, y_1, \tilde{f}(x_1)), \ldots, (x_m, y_m, \tilde{f}(x_m))\right) + \Omega\left(\|f\|_{\mathcal{H}}\right) \tag{4.10}$$

admits a representation of the form

$$\tilde{f}(x) = \sum_{i=1}^{m} \alpha_i k(x_i, x) + \sum_{p=1}^{M} \beta_p \psi_p(x), \tag{4.11}$$

with $\beta_p \in \mathbb{R}$ *for all* $p \in [M]$.

We will discuss applications of the semiparametric extension in Section 4.8.

Bias

Remark 4.4 (Biased Regularization) *Another extension of the representer theorems can be obtained by including a term* $-\langle f_0, f\rangle$ *in (4.4) or (4.10), where* $f_0 \in \mathcal{H}$. *In this case, if a solution to the minimization problem exists, it admits an expansion which differs from those described above in that it additionally contains a multiple of* f_0. *To see this, decompose* $f_{\perp}(\cdot)$ *used in the proof of Theorem 4.2 into a part orthogonal to* f_0 *and the remainder.*

Biased regularization means that we do not assume that the function $f = 0$ is the most simple of all estimates. This is a convenient way of incorporating prior knowledge about the type of solution we expect from our estimation procedure.

After this rather abstract and formal treatment of regularization, let us consider some practical cases where the representer theorem can be applied. First consider the problem of regression, where the solution is chosen to be an element of a Reproducing Kernel Hilbert Space.

Application of Semiparametric Expansion

Example 4.5 (Support Vector Regression) *For Support Vector regression with the ε-insensitive loss (Section 1.6) we have*

$$c\left((x_i, y_i, f(x_i))_{i \in [m]}\right) = \frac{1}{m} \sum_{i=1}^{m} |y_i - f(x_i)|_\varepsilon \tag{4.12}$$

and $\Omega(\|f\|) = \frac{\lambda}{2}\|f\|^2$, where $\lambda > 0$ and $\varepsilon \geq 0$ are fixed parameters which determine the trade-off between regularization and fit to the training set. In addition, a single ($M = 1$) constant function $\psi_1(x) = 1$ is used as an offset, and is not regularized by the algorithm.

Section 4.8 and [507] contain details how the case of $M > 1$, for which more than one parametric function is used, can be dealt with algorithmically. Theorem 4.3 also applies in this case.

Example 4.6 (Support Vector Classification) *Here, the targets consist of $y_i \in \{\pm 1\}$, and we use the soft margin loss function (3.3) to obtain*

$$c\left((x_i, y_i, f(x_i))_i\right) = \frac{1}{m} \sum_{i}^{m} \max\left(0, 1 - y_i f(x_i)\right). \tag{4.13}$$

The regularizer is $\Omega(\|f\|) = \frac{\lambda}{2}\|f\|^2$, and $\psi_1(x) = 1$. For $\lambda \to 0$, we recover the hard margin SVM, for which the minimizer must correctly classify each training point (x_i, y_i). Note that after training, the actual classifier will be $\operatorname{sgn}(f(.))$.

Kernel Principal Component Analysis

Example 4.7 (Kernel PCA) *Principal Component Analysis (see Chapter 14 for details) in a kernel feature space can be shown to correspond to the case of*

$$c((x_i, y_i, f(x_i))_i) = \begin{cases} 0 & \text{if } \frac{1}{m}\sum_i \left(f(x_i) - \frac{1}{m}\sum_j f(x_j)\right)^2 = 1 \\ \infty & \text{otherwise} \end{cases} \tag{4.14}$$

with $\Omega(.)$ an arbitrary function that is strictly monotonically increasing [480]. The constraint ensures that we only consider linear feature extraction functionals that produce outputs of unit empirical variance. In other words, the task is to find the simplest function with unit variance. Note that in this case of unsupervised learning, there are no labels y_i to consider.

4.3 Regularization Operators

The RKHS framework proved useful in obtaining the explicit functional form of minimizers of the regularized risk functional. It still does not explain the good performance of kernel algorithms, however. In particular, it seems counter-intuitive that estimators using very high dimensional feature spaces (easily with some 10^{10} features as in optical character recognition with polynomial kernels, or even infinite dimensional spaces in the case of Gaussian RBF-kernels) should exhibit good

Curse of Dimensionality

performance. It seems as if kernel methods are defying the curse of dimensionality [29], which requires the number of samples to increase with the dimensionality of the space in which estimation is performed. However, the distribution of capacity in these spaces is not isotropic (cf. Section 2.2.5).

Regularization Operator Viewpoint

The basic idea of the viewpoint described in the present section is simple: rather than dealing with an abstract quantity such as an RKHS, which is defined by means of its corresponding kernel k, we take the converse approach of obtaining a kernel via the corresponding Hilbert space. Unless stated otherwise, we will use $L_2(\mathcal{X})$ as the Hilbert space (cf. Section B.3) on which the regularization operators will be defined. Note that $L_2(\mathcal{X})$ is *not* the feature space $\mathcal{H}$.

Recall that in Section 2.2.2, we showed that one way to think of the kernel mapping is as a map that takes a point $x \in \mathcal{X}$ to a function $k(x, .)$ living in an RKHS. To do this, we constructed a dot product $\langle ., . \rangle_{\mathcal{H}}$ satisfying

$$k(x, x') = \langle k(x, .), k(x, .)' \rangle_{\mathcal{H}}. \tag{4.15}$$

Physically, however, it is still unclear what the dot product $\langle f, g \rangle_{\mathcal{H}}$ actually does. Does it compute some kind of "overlap" of the functions, similar to the usual dot product between functions in $L_2(\mathcal{X})$? Recall that, assuming we can define an integral on $\mathcal{X}$, the latter is (cf. (B.60))

$$\langle f, g \rangle_{L_2(\mathcal{X})} = \int_{\mathcal{X}} f \cdot g. \tag{4.16}$$

Main Idea

In the present section, we will show that whilst our dot product in the RKHS is not quite a simple as (4.16), we can at least write it as

$$\langle f, g \rangle_{\mathcal{H}} = \langle \Upsilon f, \Upsilon g \rangle_{L_2} = \int_{\mathcal{X}} \Upsilon f(x) \Upsilon g(x) dx \tag{4.17}$$

in a suitable L_2 space of functions. This space contains transformed versions or the original functions, where the transformation Υ "extracts" those parts that should be affected by the regularization. This gives a much clearer physical understanding of the dot product in the RKHS (and thus of the similarity measure used by SVMs). It becomes particularly illuminating once one sees that for common kernels, the associated transformation Υ extracts properties like *derivatives* of functions. In other words, these kernels induce a form of regularization that penalizes non-smooth functions.

Definition 4.8 (Regularization Operator) *A regularization operator Υ is defined as a linear map from the space of functions $\mathcal{F} := \{f | f : \mathcal{X} \to \mathbb{R}\}$ into a space equipped with a dot product. The regularization term $\Omega[f]$ takes the form*

$$\Omega[f] := \frac{1}{2} \langle \Upsilon f, \Upsilon f \rangle. \tag{4.18}$$

Positive Definite Operator

Without loss of generality, we may assume that Υ is positive definite. This can be seen as follows: all that matters for the definition of $\Omega[f]$ is the positive definite operator $\Upsilon^* \Upsilon$ (since $\langle \Upsilon f, \Upsilon f \rangle = \langle f, \Upsilon^* \Upsilon f \rangle$). Hence we may always define a positive definite operator $\Upsilon_h := (\Upsilon^* \Upsilon)^{\frac{1}{2}}$ (cf. Section B.2.2) which has the same regularization properties as Υ. Next, we formally state the equivalence between RKHS and regularization operator view.

Theorem 4.9 (RKHS and Regularization Operators) *For every RKHS $\mathcal{H}$ with reproducing kernel k there exists a corresponding regularization operator $\Upsilon : \mathcal{H} \to \mathcal{D}$ such that for all $f \in \mathcal{H}$*

$$\langle \Upsilon k(x,\cdot), \Upsilon f(\cdot)\rangle_{\mathcal{D}} = f(x), \tag{4.19}$$

and in particular,

$$\langle \Upsilon k(x,\cdot), \Upsilon k(x',\cdot)\rangle_{\mathcal{D}} = k(x,x'). \tag{4.20}$$

Matching RKHS

Likewise, for every regularization operator $\Upsilon : \mathcal{F} \to \mathcal{D}$, where $\mathcal{F}$ is some function space equipped with a dot product, there exists a corresponding RKHS $\mathcal{H}$ with reproducing kernel k such that (4.19) and (4.20) are satisfied.

Equation (4.20) will become the central tool to analyze smoothness properties of kernels, in particular if we pick $\mathcal{D}$ to be $L_2(\mathcal{X})$. In this case we will obtain an explicit form of the dot product induced by the RKHS which will thereby clarify why kernel methods work.

From Section 2.2.4 we can see that minimization of $\|\mathbf{w}\|^2$ is equivalent to minimization of $\Omega[f]$ (4.18), due to the feature map $\Phi(x) := k(x,\cdot)$.

Proof We prove the first part by explicitly constructing an operator that takes care of the mapping. One can see immediately that $\Upsilon = \mathbf{1}$ and $\mathcal{D} = \mathcal{H}$ will satisfy all requirements.[1]

For the converse statement, we have to obtain k from $\Upsilon^*\Upsilon$ and show that this is, in fact, the kernel of an RKHS (note that this does not imply that $\mathcal{D} = \mathcal{H}$ since it may be equipped with a different dot product than $\mathcal{H}$).

A function $G_x(\cdot)$ satisfying the first equality in

$$f(x) = \langle \Upsilon^*\Upsilon G_x(\cdot), f\rangle_{\mathcal{F}} = \langle \Upsilon G_x, \Upsilon f\rangle_{\mathcal{F}} \tag{4.21}$$

for all $f \in \Upsilon^*\Upsilon\mathcal{F}$ is called *Green's function* of the operator $\Upsilon^*\Upsilon$ on $\mathcal{D}$. It is known that such functions exist [448]. Note that this amounts to our desired reproducing property (4.19), on the set $\Upsilon^*\Upsilon\mathcal{F}$. The second equality in (4.21) follows from the definition of the adjoint operator Υ^*.

By applying (4.21) to G_x it follows immediately that G is symmetric,

$$G_x(x') = \langle \Upsilon^*\Upsilon G_{x'}, G_x\rangle_{\mathcal{D}} = \langle \Upsilon G_{x'}, \Upsilon G_x\rangle_{\mathcal{D}} = \langle \Upsilon G_x, \Upsilon G_{x'}\rangle_{\mathcal{D}} = G_{x'}(x). \tag{4.22}$$

We will write it as $G(x,x')$. Observe that (4.22) actually tells us that $x \mapsto \Upsilon G_x$ is actually a valid feature map for G. Therefore, we may identify $G(x,x')$ with $k(x,x')$.

1. $\Upsilon = \mathbf{1}$ is not the most useful operator. Typically we will seek an operator Υ corresponding to a *specific* dot product space $\mathcal{D}$. Note that this need not always be possible if $\mathcal{D}$ is not suitably chosen, e.g., for $\mathcal{D} = \mathbb{R}$.

The corresponding RKHS is the closure of the set $\{f \in \Upsilon^*\Upsilon\mathcal{F} \,|\, \|\Upsilon f\|^2 < \infty\}$. ■

Kernel Function ≙ Regularization Operator

This means that $\mathcal{D}$ is an RKHS with inner product $\langle \Upsilon\cdot, \Upsilon\cdot\rangle_{\mathcal{D}}$. Furthermore, Theorem 4.9 means that fixing the regularization operator Υ determines the possible set of functions that we might obtain, independently[2] of the class of functions in which we expand the estimate f. Thus Support Vector Machines are simply a very convenient way of specifying the regularization and a matching class of basis functions via one kernel function. This is done mainly for algorithmic advantages when formulating the corresponding optimization problem (cf. Chapter 7). The case where the two do not match is discussed in detail in [512].

Given the eigenvector decomposition of a regularization operator we can define a class of kernels that satisfy the self consistency condition (4.20).

Proposition 4.10 (A Discrete Counterpart) *Given a regularization operator Υ with an expansion of $\Upsilon^*\Upsilon$ into a discrete eigenvector decomposition (λ_n, ψ_n), and a kernel k with*

$$k(x, x') := \sum_{n, \lambda_n \neq 0} \frac{d_n}{\lambda_n} \psi_n(x)\psi_n(x'), \tag{4.23}$$

where $d_n \in \{0, 1\}$ for all m, and $\sum_n \frac{d_n}{\lambda_n}$ convergent, then k satisfies (4.20). Moreover, the corresponding RKHS is given by span$\{\psi_i | d_i = 1 \text{ and } i \in \mathbb{N}\}$.

Proof We evaluate (4.21) and use the orthonormality of the system $(\frac{d_n}{\lambda_n}, \psi_n)$.

$$\begin{aligned} &\langle k(x_i, .), (\Upsilon^*\Upsilon k)(x_j, .)\rangle \\ &= \left\langle \sum_n \frac{d_n}{\lambda_n}\psi_n(x_i)\psi_n(.), \Upsilon^*\Upsilon\left(\sum_{n'} \frac{d_{n'}}{\lambda_{n'}}\psi_{n'}(x_j)\psi_{n'}(.)\right)\right\rangle \\ &= \sum_{n,n'} \frac{d_n}{\lambda_n}\frac{d_{n'}}{\lambda_{n'}}\psi_n(x_i)\psi_{n'}(x_j)\,\langle \psi_n(.), \Upsilon^*\Upsilon\psi_{n'}(.)\rangle \\ &= \sum_n \frac{d_n}{\lambda_n}\psi_n(x_i)\psi_n(x_j) = k(x_i, x_j). \end{aligned} \tag{4.24}$$

The statement about the span follows immediately from the construction of k. ■

The summation coefficients are permitted to be rearranged, since the eigenfunctions are orthonormal and the series $\sum_n \frac{d_n}{\lambda_n}$ converges absolutely. Consequently a large class of kernels can be associated with a given regularization operator (and vice versa), thereby restricting us to a subspace of the eigenvector decomposition of $\Upsilon^*\Upsilon$.

Null Space of $\Upsilon^*\Upsilon$

In other words, there exists a one to one correspondence between kernels and regularization operators only on the image of $\mathcal{H}$ under the integral operator

2. Provided that no $f \in \mathcal{D}$ contains directions of the null space of the regularization operator $\Upsilon^*\Upsilon$, and that the kernel functions k span the whole space $\mathcal{D}$. If this is not the case, simply define the space to be the span of $k(x, \cdot)$.

$(T_k f)(x) := \int k(x,x')f(x')dx$, namely that T_k and $\Upsilon^*\Upsilon$ are inverse to another. On the null space of T_k, however, the regularization operator $\Upsilon^*\Upsilon$ may take on an arbitrary form. In this case k still will fulfill the self consistency condition.

Excluding eigenfunctions of $\Upsilon^*\Upsilon$ from the kernel expansion effectively decreases the expressive power of the set of approximating functions, and limits the capacity of the system of functions. Removing low capacity (i.e. very flat) eigenfunctions from the expansion will have an adverse effect, though, as the data will then be approximated by the higher capacity functions.

We have now covered the main insights of the present chapter. The following sections are more technical and can be skipped if desired. Recall that at the beginning of the present section, we explained that regularization operators can be thought of as extracting those parts of the functions that should be affected by the regularization. In the next section, we show that for a specific class of kernels, this extraction coincides with the Fourier transform.

4.4 Translation Invariant Kernels

An important class of kernels $k(x,x')$, such as Gaussian RBF kernels or Laplacian kernels only depends on the difference between x and x'. For the sake of simplicity and with slight abuse of notation we will use the shorthand

$$k(x,x') = k(x - x') \tag{4.25}$$

or simply $k(x)$. Since such k are independent of the *absolute* position of x but depend only on $x - x'$ instead, we will refer to them as *translation invariant* kernels.

What we will show in the following is that for kernels defined via (4.25) there exists a simple recipe how to find a regularization operator $\Upsilon^*\Upsilon$ corresponding to k and vice versa. In particular, we will show that the Fourier transform of $k(x)$ will provide us with the representation of the regularization operator in the frequency domain.

Fourier Transformation For this purpose we need a few definitions. For the sake of simplicity we assume $\mathcal{X} \subset \mathbb{R}^N$. In this case the Fourier transformation of f is given by

$$F[f](\omega) := (2\pi)^{-\frac{N}{2}} \int_{\mathcal{X}} f(\mathbf{x}) \exp(-i \langle \mathbf{x}, \omega \rangle) d\mathbf{x}. \tag{4.26}$$

Note that here i is the imaginary unit and that, in general, $F[f](\omega) \in \mathbb{C}$ is a complex number. The inverse Fourier transformation is then given by

$$f(x) = F^{-1}[f](\omega) = (2\pi)^{-\frac{N}{2}} \int_{\mathcal{X}} F[f](\omega) \exp(i \langle \mathbf{x}, \omega \rangle) d\omega. \tag{4.27}$$

Regularization Operator in Fourier Domain We now specifically consider regularization operators Υ that may be written as multiplications in Fourier space (i.e. $\Upsilon^*\Upsilon$ is diagonalized in the Fourier basis).

Denote by $v(\omega)$ a nonnegative, symmetric function defined on $\mathfrak{X}$, i.e. $v(-\omega) = v(\omega) \geq 0$ which converges to 0 for $\|\omega\| \to \infty$. Moreover denote by Ω the support of $v(\omega)$ and by $\bar{x}$ the complex conjugate of x. Now we introduce a regularization operator by

$$\langle \Upsilon f, \Upsilon g \rangle_{\mathcal{D}} = (2\pi)^{\frac{N}{2}} \int_{\Omega} \frac{\overline{F[f](\omega)} F[g](\omega)}{v(\omega)} d\omega. \tag{4.28}$$

The goal of regularized risk minimization in RKHS is to find a function which minimizes $R_{\text{reg}}[f]$ while keeping $\langle \Upsilon f, \Upsilon f \rangle_{\mathcal{D}}$ reasonably small. In the context of (4.28) this means the following:

Small nonzero values of $v(\omega)$ correspond to a *strong* attenuation of the corresponding frequencies. Hence small values of $v(\omega)$ for large ω are desirable, since high frequency components of $F[f]$ correspond to rapid changes in f. It follows that $v(\omega)$ describes the filter properties of $\Upsilon^* \Upsilon$ — note that no attenuation takes place for $v(\omega) = 0$, since these frequencies have been excluded from the integration domain Ω.

Our next step is to construct kernels k corresponding to Υ as defined in (4.28).

Green's Functions and Fourier Transformations We show that

$$G(x, x') = (2\pi)^{-\frac{N}{2}} \int_{\Omega} e^{i\omega(x-x')} v(\omega) d\omega, \tag{4.29}$$

is a Green's function for $\Upsilon, \mathcal{D}$ and that it can be used as a kernel. For a function f, whose support of its Fourier transform is contained in Ω, we have

$$\langle G(x, \cdot), f \rangle_{\mathcal{D}} = (2\pi)^{-\frac{N}{2}} \int_{\Omega} \frac{\overline{F[G(x, \cdot)](\omega)} F[f](\omega)}{v(\omega)} d\omega \tag{4.30}$$

$$= (2\pi)^{-\frac{N}{2}} \int_{\Omega} \frac{\overline{v(\omega)} \exp(i \langle x, \omega \rangle) F[f](\omega)}{v(\omega)} d\omega \tag{4.31}$$

$$= (2\pi)^{-\frac{N}{2}} \int_{\Omega} \exp(i \langle x, \omega \rangle) F[f](\omega) d\omega = f(x). \tag{4.32}$$

From Theorem 4.9 it now follows that G is a Green's function and that it can be used as an RKHS kernel.

Eq. (4.29) provides us with an efficient tool for analyzing SV kernels and the types of capacity control they exhibit: we may also read (4.29) backwards and, in doing so, find the regularization operator for a given kernel, simply by applying the Fourier transform to $k(x)$. As expected, kernels with high frequency components will lead to less smooth estimates.

Note that (4.29) is a special case of Bochner's theorem [60], which states that the Fourier transform of a positive measure constitutes a positive definite kernel.

In the remainder of this section we will now apply our new insight to a wide range of popular kernels such as B_n-splines, Gaussian kernels, Laplacian kernels, and periodic kernels. A discussion of the multidimensional case which requires additional mathematical techniques is left to Section 4.5.

4.4.1 B_n-Splines

As was briefly mentioned in Section 2.3, splines are an important tool in interpolation and function estimation. They excel at problems of low dimensional interpolation. Computational problems become increasingly acute, however, as the dimensionality of the patterns (i.e. of x) increases; yet there exists a way to circumvent these difficulties. In [501, 572], a method is proposed for using B_n-splines (see Figure 4.1) as building blocks for kernels, i.e.,

$$k(x) = B_n(x). \tag{4.33}$$

Splines in $\mathbb{R}$

We start with $\mathcal{X} = \mathbb{R}$ (higher dimensional cases can also be obtained, for instance by taking products over the individual dimensions). Recall that B_n splines are defined as $n+1$ convolutions[3] of the centered unit interval (cf. (2.71) and [552]);

$$B_n = \bigotimes_{i=1}^{n+1} I_{[-0.5,0.5]}. \tag{4.34}$$

Given this kernel, we now use (4.29) in order to obtain the corresponding Fourier representation. In particular, we must compute the Fourier transform of $B_n(x)$. The following theorem allows us to do this conveniently for functions represented by convolutions.

Convolutions and Products

Theorem 4.11 (Fourier-Plancherel, e.g. [306, 112]) *Denote by f, g two functions in $L_2(\mathcal{X})$, by $F[f], F[g]$ their corresponding Fourier transforms, and by $\otimes$ the convolution operation. Then the following identities hold.*

$$F[f \otimes g] = F[f] \cdot F[g], \text{ and } F[f] \otimes F[g] = F[f \cdot g] \tag{4.35}$$

In other words, convolutions in the original space become products in the Fourier domain and vice versa. Hence we may jump from one representation to the other depending on which space is most convenient for our calculations.

Repeated application of Theorem 4.11 shows that in the case of B_n splines, the Fourier representation is conveniently given by the $n+1$st power of the Fourier transform of B_0. Since the Fourier transform of B_n equals $v(\omega)$, we obtain (up to a multiplicative constant)

$$v(\omega) = F[k](\omega) = \prod_{i=1}^{N} \operatorname{sinc}^{(n+1)}\left(\frac{\omega_i}{2}\right), \text{ where } \operatorname{sinc} x := \frac{\sin x}{x}. \tag{4.36}$$

---

3. A convolution $f \otimes g$ of two functions $f, g : \mathcal{X} \to \mathbb{R}$ is defined as

$$f \otimes g = (2\pi)^{-\frac{N}{2}} \int_{\mathcal{X}} f(x')g(x - x')dx'.$$

The normalization factor of $(2\pi)^{-\frac{N}{2}}$ serves to make the convolution compatible with the Fourier transform. We will need this property in Theorem 4.11. Note that $f \otimes g = g \otimes f$, as can be seen by exchange of variables.

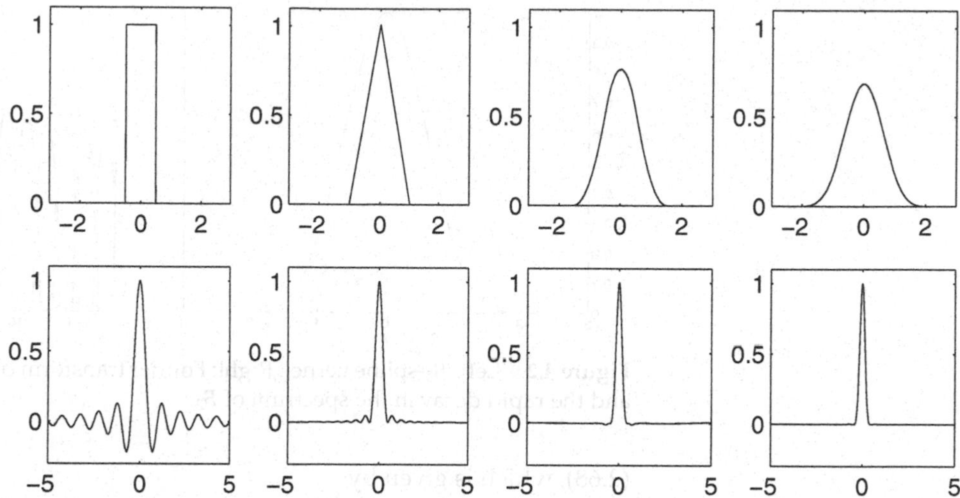

Figure 4.1 From left to right: B_n splines of order 0 to 3 (top row) and their Fourier transforms (bottom row). The length of the support of B_n is $n+1$, and the degree of continuous differentiability increases with $n-1$. Note that the higher the degree of B_n, the more peaked the Fourier transform (4.36) becomes. This is due to the increasing support of B_n. The frequency axis labels of the Fourier transform are multiples of 2π.

Only B_{2n+1} Splines Admissible

This illustrates why only B_n splines of odd order are positive definite kernels (cf. (2.71)):[4] The even ones have negative components in the Fourier spectrum (which would result in an amplification of the corresponding frequencies). The zeros in $F[k]$ stem from the fact that B_n has compact support; $[-\frac{n+1}{2}, \frac{n+1}{2}]$. See Figure 4.2 for details.

By using this kernel, we trade reduced computational complexity in calculating f (we need only take points into account whose distance $\|x_i - x_j\|$ is smaller than the support of B_n), for a potentially decreased performance of the regularization operator, since it completely removes (i.e., disregards) frequencies ω_p with $F[k](\omega_p) = 0$. Moreover, as we shall see below, in comparison to other kernels, such as the Gaussian kernel, $F[k](\omega)$ decays rather slowly.

4.4.2 Gaussian Kernels

Another class of kernels are Gaussian radial basis function kernels (Figure 4.3). These are widely popular in Neural Networks and approximation theory [80, 203, 201, 420]. We have already encountered $k(x, x') = \exp\left(-\frac{\|x-x'\|^2}{2\sigma^2}\right)$ in (2.68); we now investigate the regularization and smoothness properties of these kernels.

For a Fourier representation we need only compute the Fourier transform of

4. Although both even and odd order B_n splines converge to a Gaussian as $n \to \infty$ due to the law of large numbers.

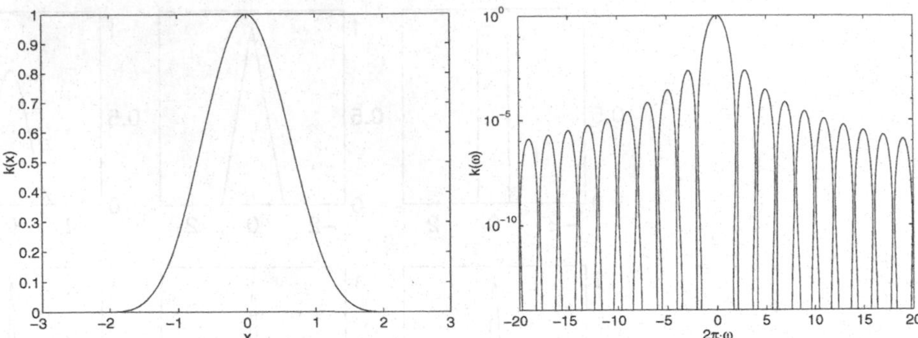

Figure 4.2 Left: B_3-spline kernel. Right: Fourier transform of k (in log-scale). Note the zeros and the rapid decay in the spectrum of B_3.

(2.68), which is given by

$$F[k](\omega) = v(\omega) = |\sigma| \exp\left(-\frac{\sigma^2\omega^2}{2}\right). \tag{4.37}$$

Uncertainty Relation

In other words, the smoother k is in pattern space, the more peaked its Fourier transform becomes. In particular, the product between the width of k and its Fourier transform is constant.[5] This phenomenon is also known as the uncertainty relation in physics and engineering.

Equation (4.37) also means that the contribution of high frequency components in estimates is relatively small, since $v(\omega)$ decays extremely rapidly. It also helps explain why Gaussian kernels produce full rank kernel matrices (Theorem 2.18).

We next determine an explicit representation of $\|\Upsilon f\|^2$ in terms of differential operators, rather than a pure Fourier space formalism. While this is not possible by using only "conventional" differential operators, we may achieve our goal by using *pseudo-differential* operators.

Pseudo-Differential Operators

Roughly speaking, a pseudo-differential operator differs from a differential operator in that it may contain an infinite sum of differential operators. The latter correspond to a Taylor expansion of the operator in the Fourier domain. There is an additional requirement that the arguments lie inside the radius of convergence, however.

Following the exposition of Yuille and Grzywacz [612] one can see that

$$\|\Upsilon f\|^2 = \int_{\mathcal{X}} \sum_n \frac{\sigma^{2n}}{n!\, 2^n} (O^n f(x))^2 dx, \tag{4.38}$$

with $O^{2n} = \Delta^n$ and $O^{2n+1} = \nabla\Delta^n$, Δ being the Laplacian and ∇ the Gradient operator, is equivalent to a regularization with $v(\omega)$ as in (4.37). The key observation in this context is that derivatives in $\mathcal{X}$ translate to multiplications in the frequency

5. The multidimensional case is completely analogous, since it can be decomposed into a product of one-dimensional Gaussians. See also Section 4.5 for more details.

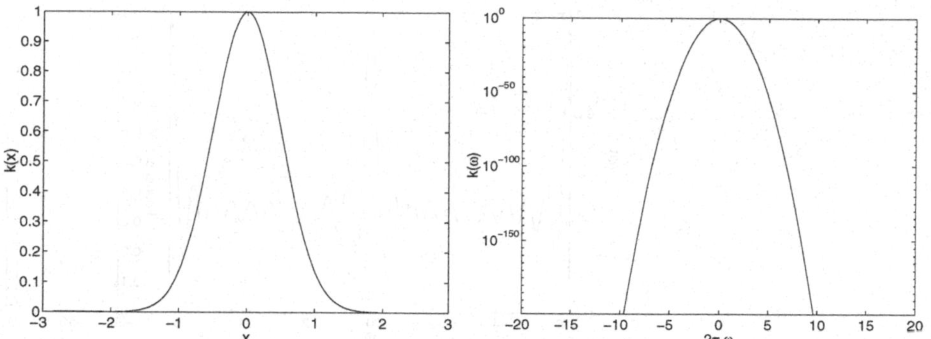

Figure 4.3 Left: Gaussian kernel with standard deviation 0.5. Right: Fourier transform of the kernel.

Taylor Expansion in Differential Operators

domain and vice versa.[6] Therefore a Taylor expansion of $v(\omega)$ in ω, can be rewritten as a Taylor expansion in $\mathcal{X}$ in terms of differential operators. See [612] and the references therein for more detail.

On the practical side, training an SVM with Gaussian RBF kernels [482] corresponds to minimizing the specific loss function with a regularization operator of type (4.38). Recall that (4.38) causes all derivatives of f to be penalized, to obtain a very smooth estimate. This also explains the good performance of SVMs in this case, since it is by no means obvious that choosing a flat function in *some* high dimensional space will correspond to a simple function in a low dimensional space (see Section 4.4.3 for a counterexample).

4.4.3 Dirichlet Kernels

Proposition 4.10 can also be used to generate practical kernels. In particular, [572] introduced a class of kernel based on Fourier expansions by

$$k(x) := 2\sum_{j=0}^{n} \cos jx = \frac{\sin(2n+1)\frac{x}{2}}{\sin\frac{x}{2}} \tag{4.39}$$

As in Section 4.4.1, we consider $x \in \mathbb{R}$ to avoid tedious notation. By construction, this kernel corresponds to $v(\omega) = \frac{1}{2}\sum_{i=-n}^{n} \delta_i(\omega)$, with δ_i being Dirac's delta function.

A regularization operator with these properties may not be desirable, however, as it only damps a finite number of frequencies (see Figure 4.4), and leaves all other frequencies unchanged, which can lead to overfitting (Figure 4.5).

6. Integrability considerations aside, one can see this by

$$\frac{d}{dx}f = \frac{d}{dx}\int_\Omega F[f](\omega)\exp(i\omega x)d\omega = \int_\Omega i\omega F[f](\omega)\exp(i\omega x)d\omega.$$

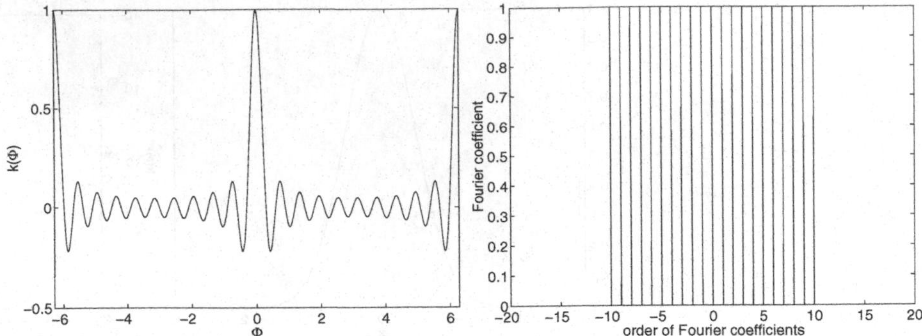

Figure 4.4 Left: Dirichlet kernel of order 10. Note that this kernel is periodic. Right: Fourier transform of the kernel.

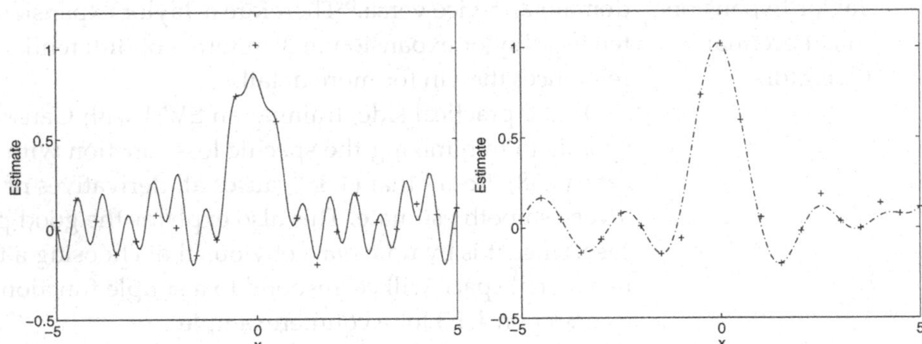

Figure 4.5 Left: Regression with a Dirichlet Kernel of order $N = 10$. One can clearly observe the overfitting (solid line: interpolation, '+': original data). Right: Regression based on the same data with a Gaussian Kernel of width $\sigma^2 = 1$ (dash dotted line: interpolation, '+': original data).

In other words, this kernel only describes band-limited periodic functions where no distinction is made between the different components of the frequency spectrum. Section 4.4.4 will present an example of a periodic kernel with a more suitable distribution of capacity over the frequency spectrum.

Types of Invariances

In some cases, it might be useful to approximate periodic functions, for instance functions defined on a circle. This leads to the second possible type of translation invariant kernel function, namely functions defined on factor spaces[7]. It is not reasonable to define translation invariant kernels on a bounded interval, since the data will lie beyond the boundaries of the specified interval when translated by a large amount. Therefore unbounded intervals and factor spaces are the only possible domains.

7. Factor spaces are vector spaces $\mathcal{X}$, with the additional property that for at least one nonzero element $\hat{x} \in \mathcal{X}$, we have $x + \hat{x} = x$ for all $x \in \mathcal{X}$. For instance, the modulo operation on $\mathbb{Z}$ forms such a space. We denote this space by $\mathbb{Z}/\hat{x}$.

We assume a period of 2π without loss of generality, and thus consider translation invariance on $\mathbb{R}/2\pi$. The next section shows how this setting affects the operator defined in section 4.4.2.

4.4.4 Periodic Kernels

Regularization Operator on $[0, 2\pi]$

One way of dealing with periodic invariances is to begin with a translation invariant regularization operator, defined similarly to (4.38), albeit on $L_2([0, 2\pi])$ (where the points 0 and π are identified) rather than on $L_2(\mathbb{R})$, and to find a matching kernel function. We start with the regularization operator;

$$\|\Upsilon f\|^2 := \pi^{-N} \int_{[0,2\pi]^N} \sum_n \frac{\sigma^{2n}}{n! 2^n} (O^n f(x))^2 dx, \tag{4.40}$$

with O defined as in Section 4.4.2. For the sake of simplicity, assume $\dim \mathcal{X} = 1$. A generalization to multidimensional kernels is straightforward.

To obtain the eigensystem of Υ we start with the Fourier basis, which is dense on $L_2([0, 2\pi])$ [69], the space of functions we are interested in. One can check that the Fourier basis $\{\frac{1}{2\pi}, \sin(nx), \cos(nx), n \in \mathbb{N}\}$ is an eigenvector decomposition of the operator defined in (4.40), with eigenvalues $\exp(\frac{n^2\sigma^2}{2})$, by substitution into (4.40). Due to the Fourier basis being dense in $L_2([0, 2\pi])$, we have thus identified all eigenfunctions of Υ. Next we apply Proposition 4.10, taking into account all eigenfunctions except the constant function with $n = 0$. This yields the following kernel,

Periodic Kernels via Fourier Coefficients

$$\begin{aligned} k(x, x') &= \sum_{n=1}^{\infty} e^{-\frac{n^2\sigma^2}{2}} (\sin(nx)\sin(nx') + \cos(nx)\cos(nx')) \\ &= \sum_{n=1}^{\infty} e^{-\frac{n^2\sigma^2}{2}} \cos(n(x - x')). \end{aligned} \tag{4.41}$$

For practical purposes, one may truncate the expansion after a finite number of terms. Since the expansion coefficients decay rapidly, this approximation is very good. If necessary, k can be rescaled to have a range of exactly $[0, 1]$.

While this is a convenient way of building kernels if the Fourier expansion is known, we would also like to be able to render arbitrary translation invariant kernels on $\mathbb{R}$ periodic. The method is rather straightforward, and works as follows. Given any translation invariant kernel k we obtain k_p by

Periodic Kernels via Translation

$$k_p(x, x') := \sum_{n \in \mathbb{Z}} k(x - x' + 2\pi n). \tag{4.42}$$

Again, we can approximate (4.42) by truncating the sum after a finite number of terms. The question is whether the definition of k_p leads to a positive definite kernel at all, and if so, which regularization properties it exhibits.

Proposition 4.12 (Spectrum of Periodized Kernels) *Denote by k a translation invariant kernel in $L_2(\mathcal{X})$, and by k_p its periodization according to (4.42). Moreover denote*

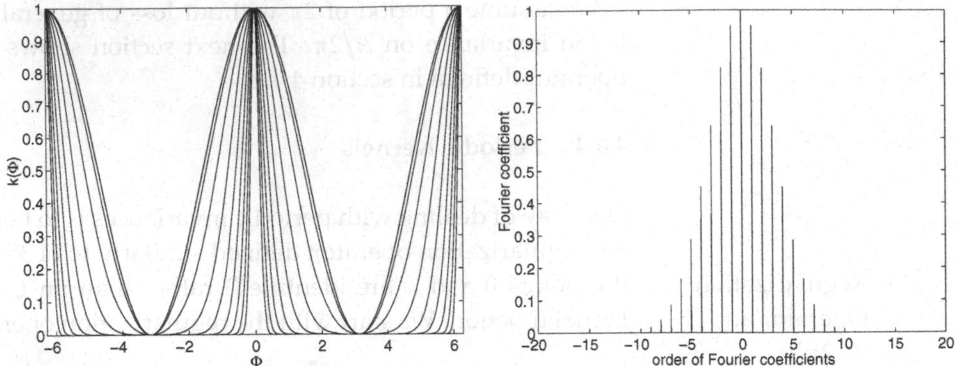

Figure 4.6 Left: Periodic Gaussian kernel for several values of σ (normalized to 1 as its maximum and 0 as its minimum value). Peaked functions correspond to small σ. Right: Fourier coefficients of the kernel for $\sigma^2 = 0.1$.

by $F[f]$ the Fourier transform of f. Then k_p can be expanded into the series

$$k_p(x, x') = (2\pi)^{-\frac{1}{2}} \left(F[f](0) + 2 \sum_{j=1}^{\infty} F[f](j) \cos(j(x - x')) \right). \tag{4.43}$$

Proof The proof makes use of the fact that for Lebesgue integrable functions k the integral over $\mathcal{X}$ can be split up into a sum over segments of size 2π. Specifically, we obtain

$$(2\pi)^{-\frac{1}{2}} \int_{\mathbb{R}} k(x) e^{-i\omega x} dx = (2\pi)^{-\frac{1}{2}} \sum_{j\in\mathbb{Z}} \int_{[0,2\pi]} k(x + 2\pi j) e^{-i\omega(x+2\pi j)} dx \tag{4.44}$$

$$= (2\pi)^{-\frac{1}{2}} \int_{[0,2\pi]} e^{-i\omega x} \sum_{j\in\mathbb{Z}} k(x + 2\pi j) dx \tag{4.45}$$

$$= (2\pi)^{-\frac{1}{2}} \int_{[0,2\pi]} e^{-i\omega x} k_p(x) dx. \tag{4.46}$$

The latter, however, is the Fourier transform of k_p over the interval $[0, 2\pi]$. Hence we have $F[k](j) = F[k_p](j)$ for $j \in \mathbb{Z}$, where $F[k_p](j)$ denotes the Fourier transform over the compact set $[0, 2\pi]$.

Now we may use the inverse Fourier transformation on $[0, 2\pi]$, to obtain a decomposition of k_p into a trigonometric series. Due to the symmetry of k, the imaginary part of $F[f]$ vanishes, and thus all contributions of $\sin jx$ cancel out. Moreover, we obtain (4.43) since $\cos x$ is a symmetric function. ■

In some cases, the full summation of k_p can be computed in closed form. See Problem 4.10 for an application of this reasoning to Laplacian kernels.

In the context of periodic functions, the difference between this kernel and the Dirichlet kernel of Section 4.4.3 is that the latter does not distinguish between the different frequency components in $\omega \in \{-n\pi, \dots, n\pi\}$.

4.4.5 Practical Implications

We are now able to draw some useful conclusions regarding the practical application of translation invariant kernels. Let us begin with two extreme situations.

- Suppose that the shape of the power spectrum $\text{Pow}[f](\omega)$ of the function we would like to estimate is known beforehand. In this case, we should choose k such that $F[k]$ matches the expected value of the power spectrum of f. The latter is given by the squared absolute value of the Fourier transformation of f, i.e.,

$$\text{Pow}[f](\omega) := |F[f](\omega)|^2. \tag{4.47}$$

Matched Filters

One may check, using the Fourier-Plancherel equality (Theorem 4.11) that $\text{Pow}[f]$ equals the Fourier transformation of the autocorrelation function of f, given by $f(x) \otimes f(-x)$. In signal processing this is commonly known as the problem of "matched filters" [581]. It has been shown that the optimal filter for the reconstruction of signals corrupted with white noise, has to match the frequency distribution of the signal which is to be reconstructed. (White noise has a uniform distribution over the frequency band occupied by the useful signal.)

- If we know very little about the given data, however, it is reasonable to make a general smoothness assumption. Thus a Gaussian kernel as in Section 4.4.2 or 4.4.4 is recommended. If computing time is important, we might instead consider kernels with compact support, such as the B_n-spline kernels of Section 4.4.1. This choice will cause many matrix elements $k_{ij} = k(x_i - x_j)$ to vanish.

Prior Knowledge

The usual scenario will be in between these two extremes, and we will have some limited prior knowledge available, which should be used in the choice of kernel. The goal of the present reasoning is to give a guide to selection of kernels through a deeper understanding of the regularization properties. For more information on using prior knowledge for choosing kernels, e.g. by explicit construction of kernels exhibiting only a limited amount of interaction, see Chapter 13.

Finally, note that the choice of the kernel width may be more important than the actual functional form of the kernel. For instance, there may be little difference in the relevant filter properties close to $\omega = 0$ between a B-spline and a Gaussian kernel (cf. Figure 4.7). This heuristic holds if we are interested only in uniform convergence results of a certain degree of precision, in which case only a small part of the power spectrum of k is relevant (see [604, 606] and also Section 12.4.1).

4.5 Translation Invariant Kernels in Higher Dimensions

Product Kernels

Things get more complicated in higher dimensions. There are basically two ways to construct kernels in $\mathbb{R}^N \times \mathbb{R}^N \to \mathbb{R}$ with $N > 1$, if no particular assumptions on the data are made. First, we could construct kernels $k : \mathbb{R}^N \times \mathbb{R}^N \to \mathbb{R}$, by

$$k(\mathbf{x} - \mathbf{x}') = k(x_1 - x'_1) \cdot \ldots \cdot k(x_N - x'_N). \tag{4.48}$$

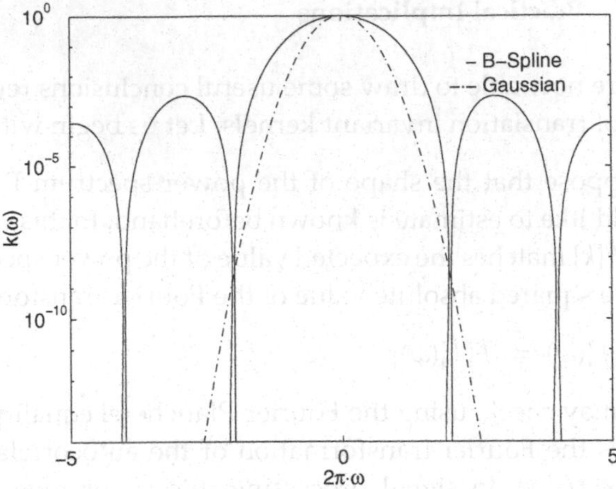

Figure 4.7 Comparison of regularization properties in the low frequency domain of the B_3-spline kernel and Gaussian kernel ($\sigma^2 = 20$). Down to an attenuation factor of $5 \cdot 10^{-3}$, i.e. in the interval $[-4\pi, 4\pi]$, both types of kernels exhibit somewhat similar filter characteristics.

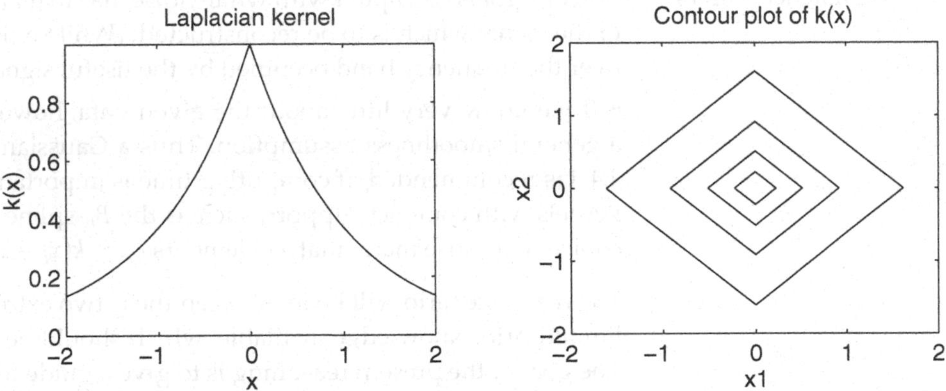

Figure 4.8 Laplacian product kernel in $\mathbb{R}$ and $\mathbb{R}^2$. Note the preferred directions in the two dimensional case.

Note that we have deviated from our usual notation in that in the present section, we use bold face letters to denote elements of the input space. This will help to simplify the notation, using $\mathbf{x} = (x_1, \ldots, x_N)$ and $\mathbf{w} = (w_1, \ldots, w_d)$ below.

The choice (4.48) usually leads to preferred directions in input space (see Figure 4.8), since the kernels are not generally rotation invariant, the exception being Gaussian kernels. This can also be seen from the corresponding regularization operator. Since k factorizes, we can apply the Fourier transform to k on a per-dimension basis, to obtain

$$F[k](\boldsymbol{\omega}) = F[k](\omega_1) \cdot \ldots \cdot F[k](\omega_N). \tag{4.49}$$

Kernels on Distance Matrices

The second approach is to assume $k(\mathbf{x} - \mathbf{x}') = k(\|\mathbf{x} - \mathbf{x}'\|_{\ell_2})$. This leads to kernels which are both translation invariant and rotation invariant. It is quite straightforward to generalize the exposition to the rotation asymmetric case, and norms other than the ℓ_2 norm. We now recall some basic results which will be useful later.

4.5.1 Basic Tools

Fourier Transform

The N-dimensional Fourier transform is defined as

$$F: L_2(\mathbb{R}^N) \to L_2(\mathbb{R}^N) \text{ with } F[f](\omega) := \frac{1}{(2\pi)^{N/2}} \int_{\mathbb{R}^N} e^{-i\langle \omega, \mathbf{x}\rangle} f(\mathbf{x}) d\mathbf{x}. \tag{4.50}$$

Its inverse transform is given by

$$F^{-1}: L_2(\mathbb{R}^N) \to L_2(\mathbb{R}^N) \text{ with } F^{-1}[f](x) = \frac{1}{(2\pi)^{N/2}} \int_{\mathbb{R}^N} e^{i\langle \omega, \mathbf{x}\rangle} f(\omega) d\omega. \tag{4.51}$$

For radially symmetric functions, i.e. $f(\mathbf{x}) = f(\|\mathbf{x}\|)$, we can explicitly carry out the integration on the sphere to obtain a Fourier transform which is also radially symmetric (cf. [520, 373]):

$$F[f](\|\omega\|) = \omega^{-\nu} H_\nu[r^\nu f(r)](\|\omega\|), \tag{4.52}$$

Hankel Transform

where $\nu := \frac{1}{2}d - 1$, and H_ν is the Hankel transform over the positive real line (we use the shorthand $\omega = \|\omega\|$). The latter is defined as

$$H_\nu[f](\omega) := \int_0^\infty r f(r) J_\nu(\omega r) dr. \tag{4.53}$$

Bessel Function

Here J_ν is the Bessel function of the first kind, which is given by

$$J_\nu(r) := r^\nu 2^{-\nu} \sum_{j=0}^{\infty} \frac{(-1)^j r^{2j}}{2^{2j} j! \Gamma(j+\nu+1)} \tag{4.54}$$

and $\Gamma(x)$ is the Gamma function, satisfying $\Gamma(n+1) = n!$ for $n \in \mathbb{N}$.

Note that $H_\nu = H_\nu^{-1}$, i.e. $f = H_\nu[H_\nu[f]]$ (in L_2) due to the Hankel inversion theorem [520] (see also Problem 4.11), which is just another way of writing the inverse Fourier transform in the rotation symmetric case. Based on the results above, we can now use (4.29) to compute the Green's functions in $\mathbb{R}^N$ directly from the regularization operators given in Fourier space.

4.5.2 Regularization Properties of Kernels in $\mathbb{R}^N$

We now give some examples of kernels typically used in SVMs, this time in $\mathbb{R}^N$. We must first compute the Fourier/Hankel transform of the kernels.

Gaussian → Gaussian

Example 4.13 (Gaussian RBFs) *For Gaussian RBFs in N dimensions, $k(r) = \sigma^{-N} e^{-\frac{r^2}{2\sigma^2}}$, and correspondingly (as before we use the shorthand $\omega := \|\omega\|$),*

$$F[k](\omega) = \omega^{-\nu}\sigma^{-N} H_\nu\left[r^\nu e^{-\frac{r^2}{2\sigma^2}}\right](\omega) = \omega^{-\nu}\sigma^{2(\nu+1)-N}\omega^\nu e^{-\frac{\omega^2\sigma^2}{2}} = e^{-\frac{\omega^2\sigma^2}{2}}.$$

In other words, the Fourier transform of a Gaussian is also a Gaussian, in higher dimensions.

Example 4.14 (Exponential RBFs) *In the case of* $k(r) = e^{-ar}$,

$$\begin{aligned} F[k](\omega) &= \omega^{-\nu} H_\nu \left[r^\nu e^{-ar}\right](\omega) \\ &= \omega^{-\nu} 2^{\nu+1} \omega^\nu a \pi^{-\frac{1}{2}} \Gamma\left(\nu + \tfrac{3}{2}\right) \left(a^2 + \omega^2\right)^{-\nu-\frac{3}{2}} \\ &= 2^{\frac{N}{2}} a \pi^{-\frac{1}{2}} \Gamma\left(\tfrac{N}{2} + 1\right) \left(a^2 + \omega^2\right)^{-\frac{N+1}{2}} \end{aligned} \tag{4.55}$$

Exponential → Inverse Polynomial

For $N = 1$ *we recover the damped harmonic oscillator in the frequency domain. In general, a decay in the Fourier spectrum approximately proportional to* $\omega^{-(N+1)}$ *can be observed. Moreover the Fourier transform of k, viewed itself as a kernel,* $k(r) = \left(1 + r^2\right)^{-\frac{N+1}{2}}$, *yields the initial kernel as its corresponding Fourier transform.*

Inverse Polynomial → Exponential

Example 4.15 (Damped Harmonic Oscillator) *Another way to generalize the harmonic oscillator, this time so that k does not depend on the dimensionality N, is to set* $k(r) = \frac{1}{a^2+r^2}$. *Following [586, Section 13.6],*

$$F[k](\omega) = \omega^{-\nu} H_\nu \left[\frac{r^\nu}{a^2 + r^2}\right](\omega) = \omega^{-\nu} a^\nu K_\nu(\omega a), \tag{4.56}$$

where K_ν *is the Bessel function of the second kind, defined by (see [520])*

$$K_\nu(x) = \int_0^\infty e^{-x \cosh t} \cosh(\nu t)\, dt. \tag{4.57}$$

It is possible to upper bound $F[k]$ *using*

$$K_\nu(x) = \sqrt{\frac{\pi}{2x}} e^{-x} \left[\sum_{j=0}^{p-1} (2x)^{-j} \frac{\Gamma\left(\nu + j + \frac{1}{2}\right)}{j!\Gamma\left(\nu - j + \frac{1}{2}\right)} + \theta \cdot (2x)^{-p} \frac{\Gamma\left(\nu + p + \frac{1}{2}\right)}{j!\Gamma\left(\nu - p + \frac{1}{2}\right)}\right], \tag{4.58}$$

with $p > \nu - \frac{1}{2}$ *and* $\theta \in [0, 1]$ *[209, eq. (8.451.6)]).The term in brackets* $[\cdot]$ *converges to 1 as* $x \to \infty$, *and thus results in an exponential decay of the Fourier spectrum.*

Example 4.16 (Modified Bessel Kernels) *In the previous example, we defined a kernel via* $k(r) = \frac{1}{a^2+r^2}$. *Since* $k(r)$ *is a nonnegative function with acceptable decay properties. Therefore we could also use this function to define a kernel in Fourier space via* $\upsilon(\omega) = \frac{1}{a^2+\|\omega\|^2}$. *The consequence thereof is that (4.56) will now be a kernel, i.e.,*

$$k(r) := r^{-\nu} a^\nu K_\nu(ra). \tag{4.59}$$

This is a popular kernel in Gaussian Process estimation [599] (see Section 16.3), since for $\nu > n$ *the corresponding Gaussian process is a mean-square differentiable stochastic processes. See [3] for more detail on this subject. For our purposes, it is sufficient to know that for* $\nu > n$, $k(\|\mathbf{x} - \mathbf{x}'\|)$ *is differentiable in* $\mathbb{R}^N$.

Example 4.17 (Generalized B_n Splines) *Finally, we generalize* B_n*-splines to N dimensions. One way is to define*

$$B_n^N := \bigotimes_{j=0}^{n} I_{U_N}, \tag{4.60}$$

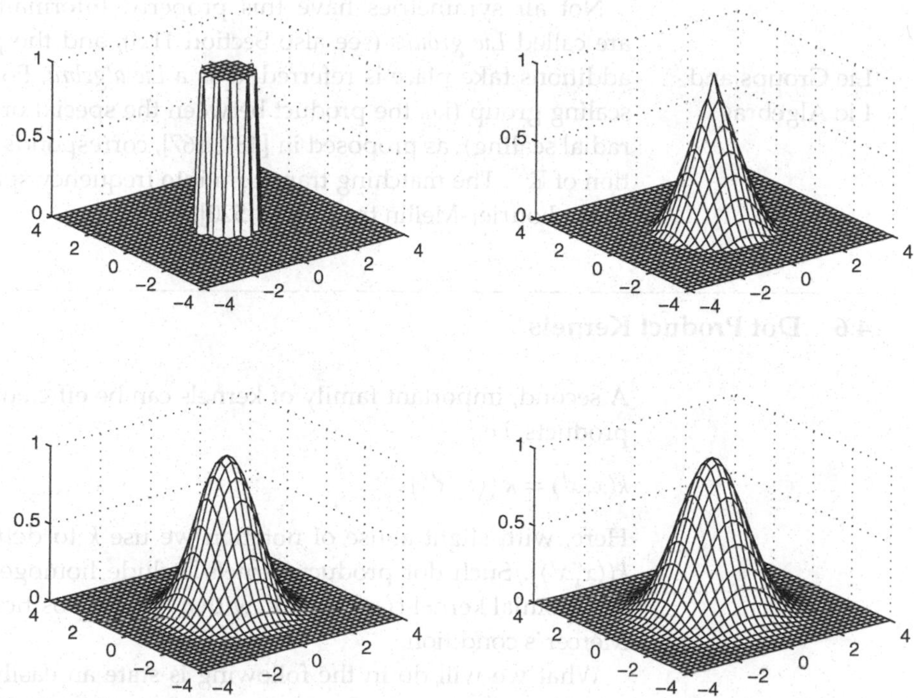

Figure 4.9 B_n splines in 2 dimensions. From left to right and top to bottom: Splines of order 0 to 3. Again, note the increasing degree of smoothness and differentiability with increasing order of the splines.

so that B_n^N is the $n+1$-times convolution of the indicator function of the unit ball U_N in N dimensions. See Figure 4.9 for examples of such functions. Employing the Fourier-Plancherel Theorem (Theorem 4.11), we find that its Fourier transform is the $(n+1)$st power of the Fourier transform of the unit ball,

B_n Splines → Bessel Functions

$$F[B_0^N](\omega) = \omega^{-(\nu+1)} J_{\nu+1}(\omega), \tag{4.61}$$

and therefore,

$$F[B_n^N](\omega) = \omega^{-(n+1)(\nu+1)} J_{\nu+1}^{n+1}(\omega). \tag{4.62}$$

Only odd n generate positive definite kernels, since it is only then that the kernel has a nonnegative Fourier transform.

4.5.3 A Note on Other Invariances

So far we have only been exploiting invariances with respect to the translation group in $\mathbb{R}^N$. The methods could also be applied to other symmetry transformations with corresponding canonical coordinate systems, however. This means that we use a coordinate system where invariance transformations can be represented as additions.

Not all symmetries have this property. Informally speaking, those that do are called *Lie groups* (see also Section 11.3), and the parameter space where the additions take place is referred to as a *Lie algebra*. For instance, the rotation and scaling group (i.e. the product between the special orthogonal group $SO(N)$ and radial scaling), as proposed in [487, 167], corresponds to a log-polar parametrization of $\mathbb{R}^N$. The matching transform into frequency space is commonly referred to as the Fourier-Mellin transform [520].

Lie Groups and Lie Algebras

4.6 Dot Product Kernels

A second, important family of kernels can be efficiently described in term of dot products, i.e.,

$$k(x, x') = k\left(\langle x, x'\rangle\right). \tag{4.63}$$

Here, with slight abuse of notation we use k to define dot product kernels via $k(\langle x, x'\rangle)$. Such dot product kernels include homogeneous and inhomogeneous polynomial kernel $\left(\langle x, x'\rangle + c\right)^p$ with $c \geq 0$. Proposition 2.1 shows that they satisfy Mercer's condition.

What we will do in the following is state an easily verifiable criterion, under which conditions a general kernel, as defined by (4.63), will satisfy Mercer's condition. A side-effect of this analysis will be a deeper insight into the regularization properties of the operator $\Upsilon^*\Upsilon$, when considered on the space $L_2(S_{N-1})$, where S_{N-1} is the unit sphere in $\mathbb{R}^N$. The choice of the domain S_{N-1} is made in order to exploit the symmetries inherent in k: $k(x, x')$ is rotation invariant in its arguments x, x'.

Regularization Properties via Mercer's Theorem

In a nutshell, we use Mercer's Theorem (Theorem 2.10) explicitly to obtain an expansion of k in terms of the eigenfunctions of the integral operator T_k (2.38) corresponding to k. For convenience, we briefly review the connection between T_k, the eigenvalues λ_i, and kernels k.

For a given kernel k, the integral operator $(T_k f)(x) := \int_{\mathcal{X}} k(x, x') f(x')\, d\mu(x')$ can be expanded into its eigenvector decomposition $(\lambda_i, \psi_i(x))$, such that

$$k(x, x') = \sum_j \lambda_j \psi_j(x) \psi_j(x') \tag{4.64}$$

holds. Furthermore, the eigensystem of the regularization operator $\Upsilon^*\Upsilon$ is given by $(\lambda_i^{-1}, \psi_i(x))$. The latter tells us the preference of a kernel expansion for specific types of functions (namely the eigenfunctions ψ_j), and the smoothness assumptions made via the size of the eigenvalues λ_i: for instance, large values of λ_i correspond to functions that are weakly penalized.

4.6.1 Conditions for Positivity and Eigenvector Decompositions

In the following we assume that $\mathcal{X}$ is the unit sphere $S_{N-1} \subset \mathbb{R}^N$ and that μ is the uniform measure on S_{N-1}. This takes advantage of the inherent invariances in dot product kernels and it simplifies the notation. We begin with a few definitions.

Legendre Polynomials Denote by $\mathcal{P}_n(\xi)$ the Legendre Polynomials of degree n and by $\mathcal{P}_n^N(\xi)$ the *associated* Legendre Polynomials (see [373] for more details and examples), where $\mathcal{P}_n = \mathcal{P}_n^3$. Without stating the explicit functional form we list some properties we will need:

Orthonormal Basis

1. The (associated) Legendre Polynomials form an orthogonal basis with

$$\int_{-1}^{1} \mathcal{P}_n^N(\xi)\mathcal{P}_m^N(\xi)(1-\xi^2)^{\frac{N-3}{2}}d\xi = \frac{|S_{N-1}|}{|S_{N-2}|}\frac{1}{M(N,n)}\delta_{m,n}. \tag{4.65}$$

Here $|S_{N-1}| = \frac{2\pi^{N/2}}{\Gamma(N/2)}$ denotes the surface of S_{N-1}, and $M(N,n)$ denotes the multiplicity of spherical harmonics of order n on S_{N-1}, which is given by $M(N,n) = \frac{2n+N-2}{n}\binom{n+N-3}{n-1}$.

Series Expansion

2. We can find an expansion for any analytic function $k(\xi)$ on $[-1,1]$ into orthogonal basis functions $\mathcal{P}_n^N$, by[8]

$$k(\xi) = \sum_{n=0}^{\infty} M(N,n)\frac{|S_{N-2}|}{|S_{N-1}|}\int_{-1}^{1} k(\xi)P_n^N(\xi)(1-\xi^2)^{\frac{N-3}{2}}d\xi. \tag{4.66}$$

3. The Legendre Polynomials may be expanded into an orthonormal basis of spherical harmonics $Y_{n,j}^N$ by the Funk-Hecke equation (see [373]), to obtain

$$\mathcal{P}_n^N(\langle x, x'\rangle) = \frac{|S_{N-1}|}{M(N,n)}\sum_{j=1}^{M(N,n)} Y_{n,j}^N(x)Y_{n,j}^N(x'). \tag{4.67}$$

The explicit functional form of $Y_{n,j}^N$ is not important for the further analysis.

Necessary and Sufficient Conditions Below we list conditions, as proven by Schoenberg [466], under which a function $k(\langle x, x'\rangle)$, defined on S_{N-1}, is positive definite. In particular, he proved the following two theorems:

Legendre Expansion

Theorem 4.18 (Dot Product Kernels in Finite Dimensions) *A kernel $k(\langle x, x'\rangle)$ defined on $S_{N-1} \times S_{N-1}$ is positive definite if and only if its expansion into Legendre polynomials $\mathcal{P}_n^N$ has only nonnegative coefficients, i.e.*

$$k(\xi) = \sum_{n=0}^{\infty} b_n \mathcal{P}_n^N(\xi) \text{ with } b_n \geq 0. \tag{4.68}$$

Taylor Series Expansion

Theorem 4.19 (Dot Product Kernels in Infinite Dimensions) *A kernel $k(\langle x, x'\rangle)$ defined on the unit sphere in a Hilbert space is positive definite if and only if its Tay-*

8. Typically, computer algebra programs can be used to find such expansions for given kernels k. This greatly reduces the problems in the analysis of such kernels.

lor series expansion has only nonnegative coefficients;

$$k(\xi) = \sum_{n=0}^{\infty} a_n \xi^n \text{ with } a_n \geq 0. \tag{4.69}$$

Therefore, all we have to do in order to check whether a particular kernel may satisfy Mercer's condition, is to look at its polynomial series expansion, and check the coefficients.

We note that (4.69) is a more stringent condition than (4.68). In other words, in order to prove positive definiteness for arbitrary dimensions it suffices to show that the Taylor expansion contains only positive coefficients. On the other hand, in order to prove that a candidate for a kernel function will never be positive definite, it is sufficient to show this for (4.68) where $\mathcal{P}_n^N = \mathcal{P}_n$, i.e. for the Legendre Polynomials.

Eigenvector Decomposition We conclude this section with an explicit representation of the eigensystem of $k(\langle x, x' \rangle)$. For a proof see [511].

Lemma 4.20 (Eigenvector Decomposition of Dot Product Kernels) *Denote by $k(\langle x, x' \rangle)$ a kernel on $S_{N-1} \times S_{N-1}$ satisfying condition (4.68) of Theorem 4.18. Then the eigenvectors of k are given by*

$$\psi_{n,j} = Y_{n,j}^N, \text{ with eigenvalues } \lambda_{n,j} = a_n \frac{|S_{N-1}|}{M(N,n)} \text{ of multiplicity } M(N,n). \tag{4.70}$$

In other words, $\frac{a_n}{M(N,n)}$ determines the regularization properties of $k(\langle x, x' \rangle)$.

4.6.2 Examples and Applications

In the following we will analyze a few kernels, and state under which conditions they may be used as SV kernels.

Example 4.21 (Homogeneous Polynomial Kernels $k(x, x') = \langle x, x' \rangle^p$) *As we showed Chapter 2, this kernel is positive definite for $p \in \mathbb{N}$. We will now show that for $p \notin \mathbb{N}$ this is never the case.*

We thus have to show that (4.68) cannot hold for an expansion in terms of Legendre Polynomials ($N = 3$). From [209, 7.126.1], we obtain for $k(\xi) = |\xi|^p$ (we need $|\xi|$ to make k well-defined),

$$\int_{-1}^{1} \mathcal{P}_n(\xi)|\xi|^p d\xi = \frac{\sqrt{\pi}\Gamma(p+1)}{2^p \Gamma\left(1 + \frac{p}{2} - \frac{n}{2}\right) \Gamma\left(\frac{3}{2} + \frac{p}{2} + \frac{n}{2}\right)} \text{ if } n \text{ even.} \tag{4.71}$$

For odd n, the integral vanishes, since $\mathcal{P}_n(-\xi) = (-1)^n \mathcal{P}_n(\xi)$. In order to satisfy (4.68), the integral has to be nonnegative for all n. One can see that $\Gamma\left(1 + \frac{p}{2} - \frac{n}{2}\right)$ is the only term in (4.71) that may change its sign. Since the sign of the Γ function alternates with period 1 for $x < 0$ (and has poles for negative integer arguments), we cannot find any p for which $n = 2\lfloor \frac{p}{2} + 1 \rfloor$ and $n = 2\lceil \frac{p}{2} + 1 \rceil$ correspond to positive values of the integral.

Example 4.22 (Inhomogeneous Polynomial Kernels $k(x, x') = (\langle x, x' \rangle + 1)^p$**)** *Likewise, let us analyze $k(\xi) = (1 + \xi)^p$ for $p > 0$. Again, we expand k in a series of Legendre Polynomials, to obtain [209, 7.127]*

$$\int_{-1}^{1} \mathcal{P}_n(\xi)(\xi + 1)^p d\xi = \frac{2^{p+1}\Gamma^2(p+1)}{\Gamma(p+2+n)\Gamma(p+1-n)}. \tag{4.72}$$

For $p \in \mathbb{N}$, all terms with $n > p$ vanish, and the remainder is positive. For non-integer p, however, (4.72) may change its sign. This is due to $\Gamma(p+1-n)$. In particular, for any $p \notin \mathbb{N}$ (with $p > 0$), we have $\Gamma(p+1-n) < 0$ for $n = \lceil p \rceil + 1$. This violates condition (4.68), hence such kernels cannot be used in SV machines unless $p \in \mathbb{N}$.

Example 4.23 (Vovk's Real Polynomial $k(x, y) = \frac{1-\langle x,y \rangle^p}{1-(\langle x,y \rangle)}$ *with $p \in \mathbb{N}$* **[459])** *This kernel can be written as $k(\xi) = \sum_{n=0}^{p-1} \xi^n$, hence all the coefficients $a_i = 1$, which means that the kernel can be used regardless of the dimensionality of the input space.*

Likewise we can analyze an infinite power series.

Example 4.24 (Vovk's Infinite Polynomial $k(x, x') = (1 - (\langle x, x' \rangle))^{-1}$ **[459])** *This kernel can be written as $k(\xi) = \sum_{n=0}^{\infty} \xi^n$, hence all the coefficients $a_i = 1$. The flat spectrum of the kernel suggests poor generalization properties.*

Example 4.25 (Neural Network Kernels $k(x, x') = \tanh(a + \langle x, x' \rangle)$**)** *We next show that $k(\xi) = \tanh(a + \xi)$ is never positive definite, no matter how we choose the parameters.*

The technique is identical to that of Examples 4.21 and 4.22: we have to show that the kernel does not satisfy the conditions of Theorem 4.18. Since this is very technical (and is best done using computer algebra programs such as Maple), we refer the reader to [401] for details, and explain how the method works in the simpler case of Theorem 4.19. Expanding $\tanh(a + \xi)$ into a Taylor series yields

$$\tanh a + \xi \frac{1}{\cosh^2 a} - \xi^2 \frac{\tanh a}{\cosh^2 a} - \frac{\xi^3}{3}(1 - \tanh^2 a)(1 - 3\tanh^2 a) + O(\xi^4). \tag{4.73}$$

We now analyze (4.73) coefficient-wise. Since the coefficients have to be nonnegative, we obtain $a \in [0, \infty)$ from the first term, $a \in (-\infty, 0]$ from the third term, and $|a| \in [\operatorname{arctanh} \frac{1}{3}, \operatorname{arctanh} 1]$ from the fourth term. This leaves us with $a \in \emptyset$, hence there are no parameters for which this kernel is positive definite.

4.7 Multi-Output Regularization

So far in this chapter we only considered scalar functions $f : \mathcal{X} \to \mathcal{Y}$. Below we will show that under rather mild assumptions on the symmetry properties of $\mathcal{Y}$, there exist no other vector valued extensions to $\Upsilon^*\Upsilon$ than the trivial extension, i.e., the application of a scalar regularization operator to each of the dimensions of $\mathcal{Y}$ separately. The reader not familiar with group theory may want to skip the more detailed discussion given below.

The type of regularization we study are quadratic functionals $\Omega[f]$. Ridge regression, RKHS regularizers and also Gaussian Processes are examples of such regularization. Our proofs rely on a result from [509] which is stated without proof.

Proposition 4.26 (Homogeneous Invariant Regularization [509]) *Any regularization term $\Omega[f]$ that is both homogeneous quadratic, and invariant under an irreducible orthogonal representation ρ of the group[9] $\mathcal{G}$ on $\mathcal{Y}$; i.e., that satisfies*

$$\Omega[f] \geq 0 \text{ for all } f \in \mathcal{F}, \tag{4.74}$$

$$\Omega[af] = |a|^2 \Omega[f] \text{ for all scalars } a, \tag{4.75}$$

$$\Omega[\rho(g)f] = \Omega[f] \text{ for all } g \in \mathcal{G}, \tag{4.76}$$

is of the form

$$\Omega[f] = \langle \Upsilon f, \Upsilon f \rangle, \text{ where } \Upsilon \text{ is a scalar operator.} \tag{4.77}$$

Positivity

The motivation for the requirements (4.74) to (4.76) can be seen as follows: the necessity that a regularization term be positive (4.74) is self evident — it must at least be bounded from below. Otherwise we could obtain arbitrarily "good" estimates by exploiting the pathological behavior of the regularization operator. Hence, via a positive offset, $\Omega[f]$ can be transformed such that it satisfies the positivity condition (4.74).

Homogeneity

Homogeneity (4.75) is a useful condition for efficient capacity control — it allows easy capacity control by noting that the entropy numbers (a quantity to be introduced in Chapter 12), which are a measure of the size of the set of possible solutions, scale in a linear (hence, homogeneous) fashion when the hypothesis class is rescaled by a constant. Practically speaking, this means that we do not need new capacity bounds for every scale the function f might assume. The requirement of being quadratic is merely algorithmic, as it allows to avoid taking absolute values in the linear or cubic case to ensure positivity, or when dealing with derivatives.

Invariance

Finally, the invariance must be chosen beforehand. If it happens to be sufficiently strong, it can rule out all operators but scalars. Permutation symmetry is such a case; in classification, for instance, this would mean that all class labels are treated equally.

No Vector Valued Regularizer

A consequence of the proposition is that there exists no vector valued regularization operator satisfying the invariance conditions. We now look at practical applications of Proposition 4.26, which will be stated in the form of corollaries.

Corollary 4.27 (Permutation and Rotation Symmetries) *Under the assumptions of Proposition 4.26, both the canonical representation of the permutation group (by permutation matrices) in a finite dimensional vector space $\mathcal{Y}$, and the group of orthogonal transformations on $\mathcal{Y}$, enforce scalar operators Υ.*

9. $\mathcal{G}$ also may be directly defined on $\mathcal{Y}$, i.e. it might be a matrix group like $SU(N)$.

This follows immediately from the fact that both rotations and permutations (or more precisely their representations on $\mathcal{Y}$), are unitary and irreducible on $\mathcal{Y}$ by construction. For instance if the permutation group was reducible on $\mathcal{Y}$, then there would exist subspaces on $\mathcal{Y}$ which do not change under any permutation on $\mathcal{Y}$. This is impossible, however, since we are considering the group of all possible permutations over $\mathcal{Y}$. Finally, permutations are a subgroup of the group of all possible orthogonal transformations.

Permutation and Rotation Symmetries are Irreducible

Let us now address the more practical side of such operators, namely how they translate into function expansions. We need only evaluate $\langle \Upsilon \alpha f, \alpha' f' \rangle$, where f, f' are scalar function and $\alpha, \alpha' \in \mathcal{Y}$. Since Υ is also scalar, this yields $\langle \alpha, \alpha' \rangle \langle \Upsilon f, \Upsilon f' \rangle$. It then remains to evaluate $\Omega[f]$ for a kernel expansion of f. We obtain:

Corollary 4.28 (Kernel Expansions) *Under the assumptions of proposition 4.26, the regularization functional $\Omega[f]$ for a kernel expansion*

$$f(x) = \sum_i \alpha_i k(x_i, x), \text{ with } \alpha_i \in \mathcal{Y}, \tag{4.78}$$

where $k(x_i, x)$ is a function mapping $\mathcal{X} \times \mathcal{X}$ to the space of scalars $\mathcal{S}$, compatible with the dot product space $\mathcal{Y}$ (we require that $\beta\alpha \in \mathcal{Y}$ for $\alpha \in \mathcal{Y}$ and $\beta \in \mathcal{S}$) can be stated

$$\Omega[f] = \sum_{i,j} \langle \alpha_i, \alpha_j \rangle \langle \Upsilon k(x_i, \cdot), \Upsilon k(x_j, \cdot) \rangle . \tag{4.79}$$

In particular, if k is the Green's function of $\Upsilon^* \Upsilon$, we get

$$\Omega[f] = \sum_{i,j} \langle \alpha_i, \alpha_j \rangle k(x_i, x_j). \tag{4.80}$$

For possible applications such as regularized principal manifolds, see Chapter 17.

4.8 Semiparametric Regularization

In some cases, we may have additional knowledge about the solution we are going to encounter. In particular, we may know that a specific *parametric* component is very likely going to be part of the solution. It would be unwise not to take advantage of this extra knowledge. For instance, it might be the case that the major properties of the data are described by a combination of a small set of linearly independent basis functions $\{\phi_1(\cdot), \ldots, \phi_n(\cdot)\}$. Or we might want to correct the data for some (e.g. linear) trends. Second, it may also be the case that the user wants to have an *understandable* model, without sacrificing accuracy. Many people in life sciences tend to have a preference for linear models. These reasons motivate the construction of *semiparametric* models, which are both easy to understand (due to the parametric part) and perform well (often thanks to the nonparametric term). For more advantages and advocacy on semiparametric models, see [47].

Preference for Parametric Part

Understandable Model

A common approach is to fit the data with the parametric model and train the nonparametric add-on using the errors of the parametric part; that is, we fit the nonparametric part to the errors. We will show that this is useful only in a very restricted situation. In general, this method does not permit us to find the best model amongst a given class for different loss functions. It is better instead to solve a convex optimization problem, as in standard SVMs, but with a different set of admissible functions;

Backfitting vs. Global Solution

$$f(x) = g(x) + \sum_{i=1}^{n} \beta_i \phi_i(x). \tag{4.81}$$

Here $g \in \mathcal{H}$, where $\mathcal{H}$ is a Reproducing Kernel Hilbert Space as used in Theorem 4.3. In particular, this theorem implies that there exists a mixed expansion in terms of kernel functions $k(x_i, x)$ *and* the parametric part ϕ_i.

Keeping the standard regularizer $\Omega[f] = \frac{1}{2}\|f\|^2_{\mathcal{H}}$, we can see that there exist functions $\phi_1(\cdot), \ldots, \phi_n(\cdot)$ whose contribution is not regularized at all. This need not be a major concern if n is sufficiently smaller than m, as the VC dimension (and thus the capacity) of this additional class of linear models is n, hence the overall capacity control will still work, provided the nonparametric part is sufficiently restricted.

Capacity Control

The Algorithm

We will show, in the case of SV regression, how the semiparametric setting translates into optimization problems. The application to classification is straightforward, and is left as an exercise (see Problem 4.8).

Formulating the optimization equations for the expansion (4.81), using the ε-insensitive loss function, and introducing kernels, we arrive at the following primal optimization problem:

Primal Objective Function

$$\text{maximize} \quad \frac{\lambda}{2}\|\mathbf{w}\|^2 + \sum_{i=1}^{m} \xi_i + \xi_i^*,$$

$$\text{subject to} \quad \begin{cases} \langle \mathbf{w}, \psi(x_i)\rangle + \sum_{j=1}^{n} \beta_j \phi_j(x_i) - y_i & \leq \quad \epsilon + \xi_i^*, \\ y_i - \langle \mathbf{w}, \psi(x_i)\rangle - \sum_{j=1}^{n} \beta_j \phi_j(x_i) & \leq \quad \epsilon + \xi_i, \\ \xi_i, \xi_i^* & \geq \quad 0. \end{cases} \tag{4.82}$$

Computing the Lagrangian (we introduce $\alpha_i, \alpha_i^*, \eta_i, \eta_i^*$ for the constraints) and solving for the Wolfe dual, yields[10]

Dual Objective Function

$$\text{maximize} \quad \begin{cases} -\frac{1}{2} \sum_{i,j=1}^{m} (\alpha_i - \alpha_i^*)(\alpha_j - \alpha_j^*) k(x_i, x_j), \\ -\varepsilon \sum_{i=1}^{m} (\alpha_i + \alpha_i^*) + \sum_{i=1}^{m} y_i(\alpha_i - \alpha_i^*), \end{cases}$$

$$\text{subject to} \quad \begin{cases} \sum_{i=1}^{m} (\alpha_i - \alpha_i^*)\phi_j(x_i) & = \quad 0 \text{ for all } 1 \leq j \leq n, \\ \alpha_i, \alpha_i^* & \in \quad [0, 1/\lambda]. \end{cases} \tag{4.83}$$

10. See also (1.26) for details how to formulate the Lagrangian.

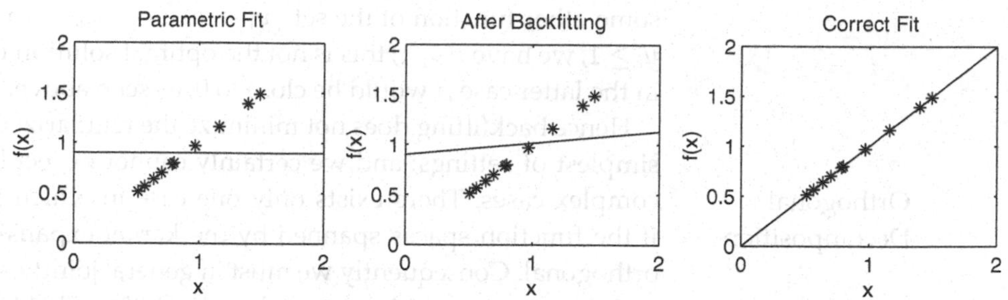

Figure 4.10 Backfitting of a model with two parameters, $f(x) = wx + \beta$. Data was generated by taking 10 samples from the uniform distribution on $[\frac{1}{2}, \frac{3}{2}]$. The target values were obtained by the dependency $y_i = x_i$. From left to right: (left) best fit with the parametric model of a constant function; (middle) after adaptation of the second parameter while keeping the first parameter fixed; (right) optimal fit with both parameters.

Note the similarity to the standard SV regression model. The objective function, and the box constraints on the Lagrange multipliers α_i, α_i^*, remain unchanged. The only modification comes from the additional un-regularized basis functions. Instead of a single (constant) function $\phi_1(x) = 1$ as in the standard SV case, we now have an expansion in the basis $\beta_i \phi_i(\cdot)$. This gives rise to n constraints instead of one. Finally, f can be found as

Semiparametric Kernel Expansion

$$f(x) = \sum_{i=1}^{m} (\alpha_i - \alpha_i^*) k(x_i, x) + \sum_{i=1}^{n} \beta_i \phi_i(x) \text{ since } \mathbf{w} = \sum_{i=1}^{m} (\alpha_i - \alpha_i^*) \psi(x_i). \tag{4.84}$$

The only difficulty remaining is how to determine β_i. This can be done by exploiting the Karush-Kuhn-Tucker optimality conditions in an analogous manner to (1.30), or more easily, by using an interior point algorithm (Section 6.4). In the latter case, the variables β_i can be obtained as the dual variables of the dual (dual dual = primal) optimization problem (4.83), as a by-product of the optimization process.

Why Backfitting Is Not Sufficient

It might seem that the approach presented above is quite unnecessary, and overly complicated for semiparametric modelling. In fact, we could try to fit the data to the parametric model first, and then fit the nonparametric part to the residuals; this approach is called backfitting. In most cases, however, this does not lead to the minimum of the regularized risk functional. We will show this using a simple example.

Backfitting for SVMs

Coordinate Descent

Consider a SV regression machine as defined in Section 1.6, with linear kernel (i.e. $k(x, x') = \langle x, x' \rangle$) in one dimension, and a constant term as parametric part (i.e. $f(x) = wx + \beta$). Now suppose the data was generated by $y_i = x_i$, where x_i is uniformly drawn from $[\frac{1}{2}, \frac{3}{2}]$ without noise. Clearly, $y_i \geq \frac{1}{2}$ also holds for all i. By construction, the best overall fit of the pair (β, w) will be arbitrarily close to $(0, 1)$ if the regularization parameter λ is chosen sufficiently small. For backfitting, we first carry out the parametric fit, to find a constant β minimizing the term $\sum_{i=1}^{m} c(y_i - \beta)$. Depending on the chosen loss function $c(\cdot)$, β will be the mean (L_2-error), the median (L_1-error), a trimmed mean (related to the ε-insensitive loss), or some other function of the set $\{y_1 - wx_1, \ldots, y_m - wx_m\}$ (cf. Section 3.4). Since all $y_i \geq 1$, we have $\beta \geq 1$; this is not the optimal solution of the overall problem, since in the latter case β would be close to 0, as seen above.

Orthogonal Decomposition

Hence backfitting does not minimize the regularized risk functional, even in the simplest of settings; and we certainly cannot expect backfitting to work in more complex cases. There exists only one case in which backfitting suffices, namely if the function spaces spanned by the kernel expansion $\{k(x_i, \cdot)\}$ and $\{\phi_i(\cdot)\}$ are orthogonal. Consequently we must in general jointly solve for both the parametric and the nonparametric part, as done in (4.82) and (4.83).

$\Omega[f]$ for Subspaces

Above, we effectively excluded a set of basis functions $\phi_1, \ldots, \phi_n$ from being regularized at all. This means that we could use regularization functionals $\Omega[f]$ that need not be positive definite on the whole Reproducing Kernel Hilbert Space $\mathcal{H}$ but only on the orthogonal complement to span $\{\phi_1, \ldots \phi_n\}$.

This brings us back to the notion of conditional positive definite kernels, as explained in Section 2.2. These exclude the space of linear functions from the space of admissible functions f, in order to achieve a positive definite regularization term $\Omega[f]$ on the orthogonal complement.

Connecting CPD Kernels and Semiparametric Models

In (4.83), this is precisely what happens with the functions ϕ_i, which are not supposed to be regularized. Consequently, if we choose ϕ_i to be the family of all linear functions, the semiparametric approach will allow us to use conditionally positive definite (cpd) kernels (see Definition 2.21 and below) without any further problems.

4.9 Coefficient Based Regularization

Most of the discussion in the current chapter was based on regularization in Reproducing Kernel Hilbert Spaces, and explicitly avoided any specific restrictions on the type of coefficient expansions used. This is useful insofar as it provides a powerful mathematical framework to assess the quality of the estimates obtained in this process.

Function Space vs. Coefficient Space

In some cases, however, we would rather use a regularization operator that acts *directly* on coefficient space, be it for theoretical reasons (see Section 16.5), or to satisfy the practical desire to obtain sparse expansions (Section 4.9.2); or simply by the heuristic that small coefficients generally translate into simple functions.

General Kernel Expansion

We will now consider the situation where $\Omega[f]$ can be written as a function of the coefficients α_i, where f will again be expanded as a linear combination of kernel functions,

$$f(x) = \sum_{i=1}^{n} \alpha_i k(x_i', x) \text{ and } \Omega[f] = \Omega[\alpha], \tag{4.85}$$

but with the possibility that x_i' and the training patterns x_i do not coincide, and that possibly $m \neq n$.

4.9.1 Ridge Regression

A popular choice to regularize linear combinations of basis functions is by a weight decay term (see [339, 49] and the references therein), which penalizes large weights. Thus we choose

Weight Decay

$$\Omega[f] := \frac{1}{2}\sum_{i=1}^{n} \alpha_i^2 = \frac{1}{2}\|\alpha\|^2. \tag{4.86}$$

This is also called Ridge Regression [245, 377], and is a very common method in the context of shrinkage estimators.

Similar to Section 4.3, we now investigate whether there exists a correspondence between Ridge Regression and SVMs. Although no strict equivalence holds, we will show that it is possible to obtain models generated by the same type of regularization operator. The requirement on an operator Υ for a strict equivalence would be

$$\Omega[f] = \frac{1}{2}\sum_{i,j=1}^{n} \langle (\Upsilon k)(x_i, .), (\Upsilon k)(x_j, .)\rangle \alpha_i \alpha_j = \frac{1}{2}\sum_{i=1}^{n} \alpha_i^2, \tag{4.87}$$

Equivalence Condition

and thus,

$$\langle (\Upsilon k)(x_i, .), (\Upsilon k)(x_j, .)\rangle = \delta_{ij}. \tag{4.88}$$

Unfortunately this requirement is not suitable for the case of the Kronecker δ, as (4.88) implies the functions $(\Upsilon k)(x_i, \cdot)$ to be elements of a non-separable Hilbert space. The solution is to change the finite Kronecker δ into the more appropriate δ-distribution, i.e. $\delta(x_i - x_j)$.

By reasoning similar to Theorem 4.9, we can see that (4.88) holds, with $k(x, x')$ the Green's function of Υ. Note that as a regularization operator, $(\Upsilon^*\Upsilon)^{\frac{1}{2}}$ is equivalent to Υ, as we can always replace the latter by the former without any difference in the regularization properties. Therefore, we assume without loss of generality that Υ is a positive definite operator. Formally, we require

Equivalent Operator

$$\langle (\Upsilon k)(x_i, .), (\Upsilon k)(x_j, .)\rangle = \langle \delta_{x_i}(.), \delta_{x_j}(.)\rangle = \delta_{x_i, x_j}. \tag{4.89}$$

Again, this allows us to connect regularization operators and kernels: the Green's function of Υ must be found in order to satisfy (4.89). For the special case of translation invariant operators represented in Fourier space, we can associate Υ with $\Upsilon_{\text{ridge}}(\omega)$ as with (4.28), leading to

$$\|\Upsilon f\|_2^2 = \int \left| \frac{F[f](\omega)}{\Upsilon_{\text{ridge}}(\omega)} \right|^2 d\omega. \tag{4.90}$$

This expansion is possible since the Fourier transform diagonalizes the corresponding regularization operator: repeated applications of Υ become multiplications in the Fourier domain. Comparing (4.90) with (4.28) leads to the conclusion that the following relation between kernels for Support Vector Machines and

Ridge Regression holds,

$$\Upsilon_{SV}(\omega) = |\Upsilon_{\text{ridge}}(\omega)|^2. \tag{4.91}$$

In other words, in Ridge Regression it is the *squared* Fourier transform of the kernels that determines the regularization properties. Later on in Chapter 16, Theorem 16.9 will give a similar result, derived under the assumption that the penalties on α_i are given by a prior probability over the distribution of expansion coefficients.

This connection also explains the performance of Ridge Regression Models in a smoothing regularizer context (the squared norm of the Fourier transform of the kernel function describes its regularization properties), and allows us to "transform" Support Vector Machines to Ridge Regression models and vice versa. Note, however, that the sparsity properties of Support Vectors are lost.

4.9.2 Linear Programming Regularization (ℓ_1^m)

A squared penalty on the coefficients α_i has the disadvantage that even though some kernel functions $k(x_i, x)$ may not contribute much to the overall solution, they still appear in the function expansion. This is due to the fact that the gradient of α_i^2 tends to 0 for $\alpha_i \to 0$ (this can easily be checked by looking at the partial derivative of $\Omega[f]$ wrt. α_i). On the other hand, a regularizer whose derivative does not vanish in the neighborhood of 0 will not exhibit such problems. This is why we choose

ℓ_1 for Sparsity

$$\Omega[f] = \sum_i |\alpha_i|. \tag{4.92}$$

The regularized risk minimization problem can then be rewritten as

$$\begin{aligned} &\text{minimize} \quad R_{\text{reg}}[f] = \lambda \sum_{i=1}^m |\alpha_i| + \sum_{i=1}^m (\xi_i + \xi_i^*), \\ &\text{subject to} \quad \begin{cases} y_i - \sum_{j=1}^m \alpha_j k(x_j, x_i) - \sum_{j=1}^n \phi_j(x_i) - b & \leq \varepsilon + \xi_i, \\ \sum_{j=1}^m \alpha_j k(x_j, x_i) + \sum_{j=1}^n \phi_j(x_i) + b - y_i & \leq \varepsilon + \xi_i^*, \\ \xi_i, \xi_i^* & \geq 0. \end{cases} \end{aligned} \tag{4.93}$$

Besides replacing α_i with $\alpha_i - \alpha_i^*$, $|\alpha_i|$ with $\alpha_i + \alpha_i^*$, and requiring $\alpha_i, \alpha_i^* \geq 0$, there is hardly anything that can be done to render the problem more computationally feasible — the constraints are already linear. Moreover most optimization software can deal efficiently with problems of this kind.

Soft Margin → Linear Program

4.9.3 Mixed Semiparametric Regularizers

We now investigate the use of mixed regularization functionals, with different penalties for distinct parts of the function expansion, as suggested by equations (4.92) and (4.81). Indeed, we can construct the following variant, which is a mixture of linear and quadratic regularizers,

$$\Omega[f] = \frac{1}{2}\|\mathbf{w}\|^2 + \sum_{i=1}^{n} |\beta_i|. \tag{4.94}$$

The equation above is essentially the SV estimation model, with an additional linear regularization term added for the parametric part. In this case, the constraints on the optimization problem (4.83) become

Mixed Dual Problem

$$\begin{aligned} -1 \;\leq\; \sum_{i=1}^{m} (\alpha_i - \alpha_i^*)\phi_j(x_i) \;&\leq\; 1 \qquad \text{for all } 1 \leq j \leq n, \\ \alpha_i, \alpha_i^* \;&\in\; [0, 1/\lambda], \end{aligned} \tag{4.95}$$

and the variables β_i are obtained as the dual variables of the constraints, as discussed previously in similar cases. Finally, we could reverse the setting to obtain a regularizer,

Semiparametric and Sparse

$$\Omega[f] = \sum_{i=1}^{m} |\alpha_i - \alpha_i^*| + \frac{1}{2} \sum_{i,j=1}^{n} \beta_i \beta_j M_{ij}, \tag{4.96}$$

for some positive definite matrix M. Note that (4.96) can be reduced to the case of (4.94) by renaming variables accordingly, given a suitable choice of M.

The proposed regularizers are a simple extension of existing methods such as Basis Pursuit [104], or Linear Programming for classification (e.g. [184]). The common idea is to have two different sets of basis functions which are regularized differently, or a subset that is not regularized at all. This is an efficient way of encoding prior knowledge or user preference, since the emphasis is on the functions with little or no regularization.

Finally, one could also use a regularization functional $\Omega[f] = \|\alpha\|_0$ which simply counts the number of nonzero terms in the vector $\alpha \in \mathbb{R}^m$, or alternatively, combine this regularizer with the ℓ_1 norm to obtain $\Omega[f] = \|\alpha\|_0 + \|\alpha\|_1$. This is a *concave* function in α, which, in combination with the soft-margin loss function, leads to an optimization problem which is, as a whole, concave. Therefore one may apply Rockafellar's theorem (Theorem 6.12) to obtain an optimal solution. See [189] for further details and an explicit algorithm.

4.10 Summary

A connection between Support Vector kernels and regularization operators has been established, which can provide one key to understanding why Support Vector Machines have been found to exhibit high generalization ability. In particular, for common choices of kernels, the mapping into feature space is not arbitrary, but corresponds to useful regularization operators (see Sections 4.4.1, 4.4.2 and 4.4.4). For kernels where this is not the case, Support Vector Machines may show poor performance (Section 4.4.3). This will become more obvious in Section 12, where, building on the results of the current chapter, the eigenspectrum of integral operators is connected with generalization bounds of the corresponding Support Vector Machines.

The link to regularization theory can be seen as a tool for determining the structure, consisting of sets of functions, in which Support Vector Machines and other kernel algorithms (approximately) perform structural risk minimization [561], possibly in a data dependent manner. In other words, it allows us to choose an appropriate kernel given the data and the problem specific knowledge.

Bayesian Methods

A simple consequence of this link is a Bayesian interpretation of Support Vector Machines. In this case, the choice of a special kernel can be regarded as a prior on the hypothesis space, with $P[f] \propto \exp(-\lambda \|\Upsilon f\|^2)$. See Chapter 16 for more detail on this matter.

Vector Valued Functions

It should be clear by now that the setting of Tikhonov and Arsenin [538], whilst very powerful, is certainly not the only conceivable one. A theorem on vector valued regularization operators showed, however, that under quite generic conditions on the isotropy of the space of target values, only scalar operators are possible; an extended version of their approach is thus the only possible option.

Finally a closer consideration of the null space of regularization functionals $\Omega[f]$ led us to formulate semiparametric models. The roots of such models lie in the representer theorem (Theorem 4.2), proposed and explored in the context of smoothing splines in [296]. In fact, the SV expansion is a direct consequence of the representer theorem.

Semiparametric Models

Moreover the semiparametric setting solves a problem created by the use of *conditionally* positive definite kernels of order q (see Section 2.4.3). Here, polynomials of order lower than q are excluded. Hence, to cope with this effect, we must add polynomials back in "manually." The semiparametric approach presents a way of doing that. Another application of semiparametric models, besides the conventional approach of treating the nonparametric part as *nuisance parameters* [47], is in the domain of hypothesis testing, for instance to test whether a parametric model fits the data sufficiently well. This can be achieved in the framework of structural risk minimization [561] — given the different models (nonparametric vs. semiparametric vs. parametric), we can evaluate the bounds on the expected risk, and then choose the model with the best bound.

4.11 Problems

4.1 (Equivalent Optimization Strategies •••) *Denote by S a metric space and by $R, \Omega : S \to \mathbb{R}$ two strictly convex continuous maps. Let $\lambda > 0$.*

- *Show that the map $f \mapsto R[f] + \lambda\Omega[f]$ has only one minimum and a unique minimizer. Hint: assume the contrary and consider a straight line between two minima.*
- *Show that for every $\lambda > 0$, there exists an Ω_λ such that minimization of $R[f] + \lambda\Omega[f]$, is equivalent to minimizing $R[f]$ subject to $\Omega[f] \leq \Omega_\lambda$. Show that an analogous statement holds with R and Ω exchanged. Hint: consider the minimizer of $R[f] + \lambda\Omega[f]$, and keep*

the second term fixed while minimizing over the first term.

- *Consider the parametrized curve* $(\Omega(\lambda), R(\lambda))$. *What is the shape of this curve? Show that (barring discontinuities)* $-\lambda$ *is the tangent on the curve.*
- *Consider the parametrized curve* $(\ln \Omega(\lambda), \ln R(\lambda))$ *as proposed by Hansen [225]. Show that a tangent criterion similar to that imposed above is scale insensitive wrt.* Ω *and* R. *Why is this useful? What are the numerical problems with such an ansatz?*

4.2 (Orthogonality and Span ••) *Show that the second condition of Definition 2.9 is equivalent to requiring*

$$\langle f, k(x,\cdot)\rangle_{\mathcal{H}} = 0 \text{ for all } x \in \mathcal{X} \Longrightarrow f = 0. \tag{4.97}$$

4.3 (Semiparametric Representer Theorem ••) *Prove Theorem 4.3. Hint: start with a decomposition of* $\tilde{f}$ *into a parametric part, a kernel part, and an orthogonal contribution and evaluate the loss and regularization terms independently.*

4.4 (Kernel Boosting •••) *Show that for* $f \in \mathcal{H}$ *and* $c(x, y, f(x)) = \exp(-yf(x))$, *you can develop a boosting algorithm by performing a coefficient-wise gradient descent on the coefficients* α_i *of the expansion* $f(x) = \sum_{i=1}^{m} \alpha_i k(x_i, x)$. *In particular, show that the expansion above is optimal.*

What changes if we drop the regularization term $\Omega[f] = \|f\|^2$? *See [498, 577, 221] for examples.*

4.5 (Monotonicity of the Regularizer ••) *Give an example where, due to the fact that* $\Omega[f]$ *is not strictly monotonic the kernel expansion (4.5) is not the only minimizer of the regularized risk functional (4.4).*

4.6 (Sparse Expansions ••) *Show that it is a sufficient requirement for the coefficients* α_i *of the kernel expansion of the minimizer of (4.4) to vanish, if for the corresponding loss functions* $c(x_i, y_i, f(x_i))$ *both the lhs and the rhs derivative with respect to* $f(x_i)$ *vanish. Hint: use the proof strategy of Theorem 4.2.*

Furthermore show that for loss functions $c(x, y, f(x))$ *this implies that we can obtain vanishing coefficients only if* $c(x_i, y_i, f(x_i)) = 0$.

4.7 (Biased Regularization ••) *Show that for biased regularization (Remark 4.4) with* $g(\|f\|_{\mathcal{H}}) = \frac{1}{2}\|f\|^2_{\mathcal{H}}$, *the effective overall regularizer is given by* $\frac{1}{2}\|f - f_0\|^2$.

4.8 (Semiparametric Classification ••) *Show that given a set of parametric basis functions* ϕ_i, *the optimization problem for SV classification has the same objective function as (1.31), however with the constraints [506]*

$$0 \le \alpha_i \le C \text{ for all } i \in [m] \text{ and } \sum_{i=1}^{m} \alpha_i y_i \phi_j(x_i) = 0 \text{ for all } j. \tag{4.98}$$

What happens if you combine semiparametric classification with adaptive margins (the ν*-trick)?*

4.9 (Regularization Properties of Kernels •) *Analyze the regularization properties of the Laplacian kernel $k(x, x') = e^{-|x-x'|}$. What is the rate of decay in its power spectrum? What is the kernel corresponding to the operator*

$$\|\Upsilon f\|^2 := \|f\|^2 + \|\partial_x f\|^2 + \|\partial_x^2 f\|^2? \tag{4.99}$$

Hint: rewrite Υ in the Fourier domain.

4.10 (Periodizing the Laplacian Kernel •) *Show that for the Laplacian kernel $k(x, x') = e^{-|x-x'|}$, the periodization with period a results in a kernel proportional to*

$$k_p(x, x') = e^{-\left[|x-x'| \bmod a\right]} + e^{-\left[|x-x'| \bmod a\right]+a}. \tag{4.100}$$

4.11 (Hankel Transform and Inversion •••) *Show that for radially symmetric functions, the Fourier transform is given by (4.52). Moreover use (4.51) to prove the Hankel inversion theorem, stating that H_ν is its own inverse.*

4.12 (Eigenvector Decompositions of Polynomial Kernels •••) *Compute the eigenvalues of polynomial kernels on U_N. Hint: use [511] and separate the radial from the angular part in the eigenvector decomposition of k, and solve the radial part empirically via numerical analysis. Possible kernels to consider are Vovk's kernel, (in)homogeneous polynomials and the hyperbolic tangent kernel.*

4.13 (Necessary Conditions for Kernels ••) *Burges [86] shows, by using differential geometric methods, that a necessary condition for a differentiable translation invariant kernel $k(x, x') = k(\|x - x'\|^2)$ to be positive definite is*

$$k(0) > 0 \text{ and } k'(0) < 0. \tag{4.101}$$

Prove this using functional analytic methods.

4.14 (Mixed Semiparametric Regularizers ••) *Derive (4.96). Hint: set up the primal optimization problem as described in Section 1.4, compute the Lagrangian, and eliminate the primal variables.*

Can you find an interpretation of (4.95)? What is the effect of $\sum_{i=1}^{m}(\alpha_i - \alpha_i^*)\phi_j(x_i)$?

5 Elements of Statistical Learning Theory

We now give a more complete exposition of the ideas of statistical learning theory, which we briefly touched on in Chapter 1. We mentioned previously that in order to learn from a small training set, we should try to *explain* the data with a model of *small* capacity; we have not yet justified *why* this is the case, however. This is the main goal of the present chapter.

Overview

We start by revisiting the difference between risk minimization and empirical risk minimization, and illustrating some common pitfalls in machine learning, such as overfitting and training on the test set (Section 5.1). We explain that the motivation for empirical risk minimization is the law of large numbers, but that the classical version of this law is not sufficient for our purposes (Section 5.2). Thus, we need to introduce the statistical notion of *consistency* (Section 5.3). It turns out that consistency of learning algorithms amounts to a law of large numbers, which holds uniformly over all functions that the learning machine can implement (Section 5.4). This crucial insight, due to Vapnik and Chervonenkis, focuses our attention on the set of attainable functions; this set must be restricted in order to have any hope of succeeding. Section 5.5 states probabilistic bounds on the risk of learning machines, and summarizes different ways of characterizing precisely how the set of functions can be restricted. This leads to the notion of *capacity concepts*, which gives us the main ingredients of the typical generalization error bound of statistical learning theory. We do not indulge in a complete treatment; rather, we try to give the main insights to provide the reader with some intuition as to how the different pieces of the puzzle fit together. We end with a section showing an example application of risk bounds for model selection (Section 5.6).

Prerequisites

The chapter attempts to present the material in a fairly non-technical manner, providing intuition wherever possible. Given the nature of the subject matter, however, a limited amount of mathematical background is required. The reader who is not familiar with basic probability theory should first read Section B.1.

5.1 Introduction

Let us start with an example. We consider a regression estimation problem. Suppose we are given empirical observations,

$$(x_1, y_1), \ldots, (x_m, y_m) \in \mathcal{X} \times \mathcal{Y}, \tag{5.1}$$

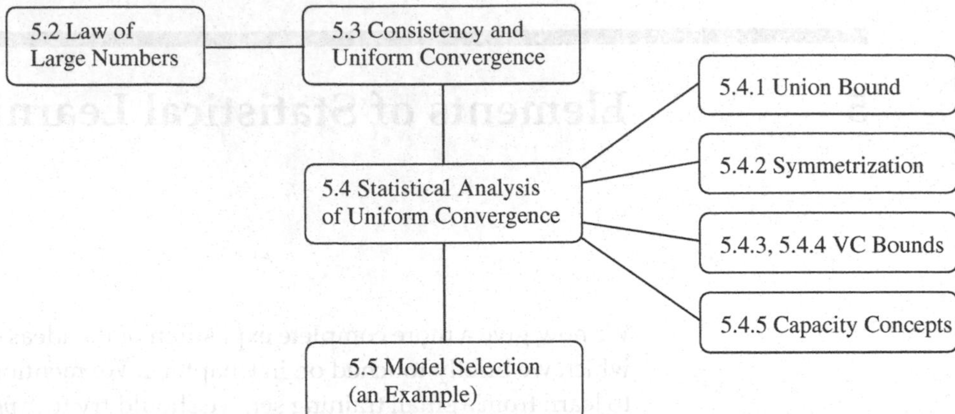

Regression Example

where for simplicity we take $\mathcal{X} = \mathcal{Y} = \mathbb{R}$. Figure 5.1 shows a plot of such a dataset, along with two possible functional dependencies that could underlie the data. The dashed line represents a fairly complex model, and fits the training data perfectly. The straight line, on the other hand, does not completely "explain" the data, in the sense that there are some residual errors; it is much "simpler," however. A physicist measuring these data points would argue that it cannot be by chance that the measurements almost lie on a straight line, and would much prefer to attribute the residuals to measurement error than to an erroneous model. But is it possible to *characterize* the way in which the straight line is simpler, and why this should imply that it is, in some sense, closer to an underlying true dependency?

Bias-Variance Dilemma

In one form or another, this issue has long occupied the minds of researchers studying the problem of learning. In classical statistics, it has been studied as the *bias-variance dilemma*. If we computed a linear fit for every data set that we ever encountered, then every functional dependency we would ever "discover" would be linear. But this would not come from the data; it would be a *bias* imposed by us. If, on the other hand, we fitted a polynomial of sufficiently high degree to any given data set, we would always be able to fit the data perfectly, but the exact model we came up with would be subject to large fluctuations, depending on

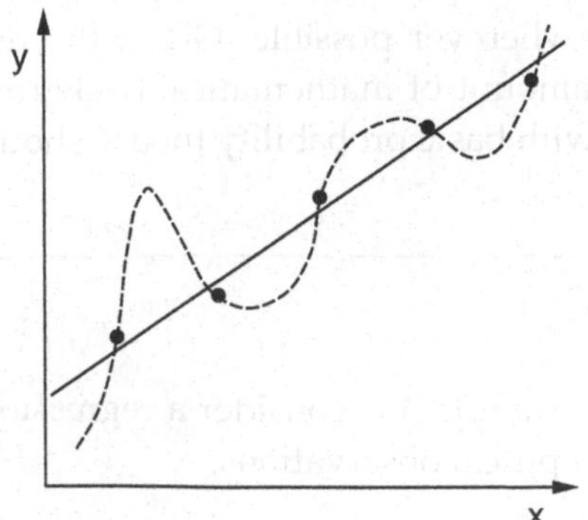

Figure 5.1 Suppose we want to estimate a functional dependence from a set of examples (black dots). Which model is preferable? The complex model perfectly fits all data points, whereas the straight line exhibits residual errors. Statistical learning theory formalizes the role of the *complexity* of the model class, and gives probabilistic guarantees for the validity of the inferred model.

how accurate our measurements were in the first place — the model would suffer from a large *variance*. A related dichotomy is the one between *estimation error* and *approximation error*. If we use a small class of functions, then even the best possible solution will poorly approximate the "true" dependency, while a large class of functions will lead to a large statistical estimation error.

Overfitting

In the terminology of applied machine learning and the design of neural networks, the complex explanation shows *overfitting*, while an overly simple explanation imposed by the learning machine design would lead to *underfitting*. A great deal of research has gone into clever engineering tricks and heuristics; these are used, for instance, to aid in the design of neural networks which will not overfit on a given data set [397]. In neural networks, overfitting can be avoided in a number of ways, such as by choosing a number of hidden units that is not too large, by *stopping* the training procedure early in order not to enforce a perfect explanation of the training set, or by using *weight decay* to limit the size of the weights, and thus of the function class implemented by the network.

Risk

Statistical learning theory provides a solid mathematical framework for studying these questions in depth. As mentioned in Chapters 1 and 3, it makes the assumption that the data are generated by sampling from an unknown underlying distribution $P(x, y)$. The learning problem then consists in minimizing the *risk* (or *expected loss* on the test data, see Definition 3.3),

$$R[f] = \int_{\mathcal{X}\times\mathcal{Y}} c(x, y, f(x))\, dP(x, y). \tag{5.2}$$

Here, c is a loss function. In the case of pattern recognition, where $\mathcal{Y} = \{\pm 1\}$, a common choice is the misclassification error, $c(x, y, f(x)) = \frac{1}{2}|f(x) - y|$.

The difficulty of the task stems from the fact that we are trying to minimize a quantity that we cannot actually evaluate: since we do not know P, we cannot compute the integral (5.2). What we *do* know, however, are the training data (5.1), which are sampled from P. We can thus try to infer a function f from the training sample that is, in some sense, *close* to the one minimizing (5.2). To this end, we need what is called an *induction principle*.

Empirical Risk

One way to proceed is to use the training sample to approximate the integral in (5.2) by a finite sum (see (B.18)). This leads to the empirical risk (Definition 3.4),

$$R_{\text{emp}}[f] = \frac{1}{m}\sum_{i=1}^{m} c(x_i, y_i, f(x_i)), \tag{5.3}$$

and the *empirical risk minimization (ERM) induction principle*, which recommends that we choose an f that minimizes (5.3).

Cast in these terms, the fundamental trade-off in learning can be stated as follows: if we allow f to be taken from a very large class of functions $\mathcal{F}$, we can always find an f that leads to a rather small value of (5.3). For instance, if we allow the use of *all* functions f mapping $\mathcal{X} \to \mathcal{Y}$ (in compact notation, $\mathcal{F} = \mathcal{Y}^{\mathcal{X}}$), then we can minimize (5.3) yet still be distant from the minimizer of (5.2). Considering a pattern recognition problem, we could set

$$f(x) = \begin{cases} y_i & \text{if } x = x_i \text{ for some } i = 1, \ldots, m \\ 1 & \text{otherwise.} \end{cases} \tag{5.4}$$

This does not amount to any form of learning, however: suppose we are now given a test point drawn from the same distribution, $(x, y) \sim P(x, y)$. If $\mathcal{X}$ is a continuous domain, and we are not in a degenerate situation, the new pattern x will almost never be exactly equal to any of the training inputs x_i. Therefore, the learning machine will almost always predict that $y = 1$. *If we allow* all *functions from $\mathcal{X}$ to $\mathcal{Y}$, then the values of the function at points $x_1, \ldots, x_m$ carry no information about the values at other points.* In this situation, a learning machine cannot do better than chance. This insight lies at the core of the so-called *No-Free-Lunch Theorem* popularized in [608]; see also [254, 48].

The message is clear: if we make no restrictions on the class of functions from which we choose our estimate f, we cannot hope to learn anything. Consequently, machine learning research has studied various ways to implement such restrictions. In statistical learning theory, these restrictions are enforced by taking into account the *complexity* or *capacity* (measured by VC dimension, covering numbers, entropy numbers, or other concepts) of the class of functions that the learning machine can implement.[1]

In the Bayesian approach, a similar effect is achieved by placing *prior distributions* $P(f)$ over the class of functions (Chapter 16). This may sound fundamentally different, but it leads to algorithms which are closely related; and on the theoretical side, recent progress has highlighted intriguing connections [92, 91, 353, 238].

5.2 The Law of Large Numbers

Let us step back and try to look at the problem from a slightly different angle. Consider the case of pattern recognition using the misclassification loss function. Given a fixed function f, then for each example, the loss $\xi_i := \frac{1}{2}|f(x_i) - y_i|$ is either

1. As an aside, note that the same problem applies to *training on the test set* (sometimes called *data snooping*): sometimes, people optimize tuning parameters of a learning machine by looking at how they change the results on an independent test set. Unfortunately, once one has adjusted the parameter in this way, the test set is not independent anymore. This is identical to the corresponding problem in training on the *training* set: once we have chosen the function to minimize the training error, the latter no longer provides an unbiased estimate of the test error. Overfitting occurs much faster on the training set, however, than it does on the test set. This is usually due to the fact that the number of tuning parameters of a learning machine is much smaller than the total number of parameters, and thus the capacity tends to be smaller. For instance, an SVM for pattern recognition typically has two tuning parameters, and optimizes m weight parameters (for a training set size of m). See also Problem 5.3 and [461].

0 or 1 (provided we have a ± 1-valued function f), and all examples are drawn independently. In the language of probability theory, we are faced with *Bernoulli trials*. The $\xi_1, \ldots, \xi_m$ are independently sampled from a random variable

$$\xi := \frac{1}{2}|f(x) - y|. \tag{5.5}$$

Chernoff Bound

A famous inequality due to Chernoff [107] characterizes how the empirical mean $\frac{1}{m}\sum_{i=1}^{m} \xi_i$ converges to the expected value (or expectation) of ξ, denoted by $\mathbf{E}(\xi)$:

$$\mathrm{P}\left\{\left|\frac{1}{m}\sum_{i=1}^{m} \xi_i - \mathbf{E}(\xi)\right| \geq \epsilon\right\} \leq 2\exp(-2m\epsilon^2) \tag{5.6}$$

Note that the P refers to the probability of getting a sample $\xi_1, \ldots, \xi_m$ with the property $\left|\frac{1}{m}\sum_{i=1}^{m} \xi_i - \mathbf{E}(\xi)\right| \geq \epsilon$. Mathematically speaking, P strictly refers to a so-called *product* measure (cf. (B.11)). We will presently avoid further mathematical detail; more information can be found in Appendix B.

In some instances, we will use a more general bound, due to Hoeffding (Theorem 5.1). Presently, we formulate and prove a special case of the Hoeffding bound, which implies (5.6). Note that in the following statement, the ξ_i are no longer restricted to take values in $\{0, 1\}$.

Hoeffding Bound

Theorem 5.1 (Hoeffding [244]) *Let $\xi_i, i \in [m]$ be m independent instances of a bounded random variable ξ, with values in $[a, b]$. Denote their average by $Q_m = \frac{1}{m}\sum_i \xi_i$. Then for any $\epsilon > 0$,*

$$\left.\begin{array}{l} \mathrm{P}\{Q_m - \mathbf{E}(\xi) \geq \epsilon\} \\ \mathrm{P}\{\mathbf{E}(\xi) - Q_m \geq \epsilon\} \end{array}\right\} \leq \exp\left(-\frac{2m\epsilon^2}{(b-a)^2}\right). \tag{5.7}$$

The proof is carried out by using a technique commonly known as Chernoff's bounding method [107]. The proof technique is widely applicable, and generates bounds such as Bernstein's inequality [44] (exponential bounds based on the variance of random variables), as well as concentration-of-measure inequalities (see, e.g., [356, 66]). Readers not interested in the technical details underlying laws of large numbers may want to skip the following discussion.

We start with an auxiliary inequality.

Lemma 5.2 (Markov's Inequality (e.g., [136])) *Denote by ξ a nonnegative random variable with distribution* P. *Then for all $\lambda > 0$, the following inequality holds:*

$$\mathrm{P}\{\xi \geq \lambda \mathbf{E}(\xi)\} \leq \frac{1}{\lambda}. \tag{5.8}$$

Proof Using the definition of $\mathbf{E}(\xi)$, we have

$$\mathbf{E}(\xi) = \int_0^\infty \xi dP(\xi) \geq \int_{\lambda\mathbf{E}(\xi)}^\infty \xi dP(\xi) \geq \lambda\mathbf{E}(\xi) \int_{\lambda\mathbf{E}(\xi)}^\infty dP(\xi) = \lambda\mathbf{E}(\xi)\mathrm{P}\{\xi \geq \lambda\mathbf{E}(\xi)\}.$$

■

Proof of Theorem 5.1. Without loss of generality, we assume that $\mathbf{E}(\xi) = 0$ (otherwise simply define a random variable $\bar{\xi} := \xi - \mathbf{E}(\xi)$ and use the latter in the proof). Chernoff's bounding method consists in transforming a random variable ξ into $\exp(s\xi)$ $(s > 0)$, and applying Markov's inequality to it. Depending on ξ, we can obtain different bounds. In our case, we use

$$\mathrm{P}\{\xi \geq \epsilon\} = \mathrm{P}\left\{\exp(s\xi) \geq \exp(s\epsilon)\right\} \leq e^{-s\epsilon}\mathbf{E}\left[\exp(s\xi)\right] \tag{5.9}$$

$$= e^{-s\epsilon}\mathbf{E}\left[\exp\left(\frac{s}{m}\sum_{i=1}^{m}\xi_i\right)\right] \leq e^{-s\epsilon}\prod_{i=1}^{m}\mathbf{E}\left[\exp\left(\frac{s}{m}\xi_i\right)\right]. \tag{5.10}$$

In (5.10), we exploited the fact that for positive random variables $\mathbf{E}\left[\prod_i \xi_i\right] \leq \prod_i \mathbf{E}\left[\xi_i\right]$. Since the inequality holds independent of the choice of s, we may minimize over s to obtain a bound that is as tight as possible. To this end, we transform the expectation over $\exp\left(\frac{s}{m}\xi_i\right)$ into something more amenable. The derivation is rather technical; thus we state without proof [244]: $\mathbf{E}\left[\exp(\frac{s}{m}\xi_i)\right] \leq \exp\left(\frac{s^2(b-a)^2}{8m^2}\right)$. From this, we conclude that the optimal value of s is given by $s = \frac{4m\epsilon}{(b-a)^2}$. Substituting this value into the right hand side of (5.10) proves the bound. ■

Let us now return to (5.6). Substituting (5.5) into (5.6), we have a bound which states how likely it is that for a given function f, the empirical risk is close to the actual risk,

$$\mathrm{P}\{|R_{\mathrm{emp}}[f] - R[f]| \geq \epsilon\} \leq 2\exp(-2m\epsilon^2). \tag{5.11}$$

Using Hoeffding's inequality, a similar bound can be given for the case of regression estimation, provided the loss $c(x, y, f(x))$ is bounded.

For any fixed function, the training error thus provides an unbiased estimate of the test error. Moreover, the convergence (in probability) $R_{\mathrm{emp}}[f] \to R[f]$ as $m \to \infty$ is exponentially fast in the number of training examples.[2] Although this sounds just about as good as we could possibly have hoped, there is one caveat: a crucial property of both the Chernoff and the Hoeffding bound is that they are probabilistic in nature. They state that the probability of a large deviation between test error and training error of f is small; the larger the sample size m, the smaller the probability. Granted, they do not rule out the presence of cases where the deviation is large, and our learning machine will have many functions that it can implement. Could there be a function for which things go wrong? It appears that

---

2. *Convergence in probability*, denoted as

$$|R_{\mathrm{emp}}[f] - R[f]| \xrightarrow{\mathrm{P}} 0 \text{ as } m \to \infty,$$

means that for all $\epsilon > 0$, we have

$$\lim_{m\to\infty} \mathrm{P}\{|R_{\mathrm{emp}}[f] - R[f]| > \epsilon\} = 0.$$

we would be very unlucky for this to occur *precisely* for the function f chosen by empirical risk minimization.

At first sight, it seems that empirical risk minimization should work — in contradiction to our lengthy explanation in the last section, arguing that we have to do more than that. What is the catch?

5.3 When Does Learning Work: the Question of Consistency

It turns out that in the last section, we were too sloppy. When we find a function f by choosing it to minimize the training error, we are no longer looking at independent Bernoulli trials. We are actually choosing f such that the mean of the ξ_i is as small as possible. In this sense, we are actively looking for the worst case, for a function which is very atypical, with respect to the average loss (i.e., the empirical risk) that it will produce.

Consistency

We should thus state more clearly what it is that we actually need for empirical risk minimization to work. This is best expressed in terms of a notion that statisticians call *consistency*. It amounts to saying that as the number of examples m tends to infinity, we want the function f^m that minimizes $R_{\text{emp}}[f]$ (note that f^m need not be unique), to lead to a test error which converges to the lowest achievable value. In other words, f^m is asymptotically as good as whatever we could have done if we were able to directly minimize $R[f]$ (which we cannot, as we do not even know it). In addition, consistency requires that asymptotically, the training and the test error of f^m be identical.[3]

It turns out that *without restricting the set of admissible functions*, empirical risk minimization is not consistent. The main insight of VC (Vapnik-Chervonenkis) theory is that actually, the *worst case* over all functions that the learning machine can implement determines the consistency of empirical risk minimization. In other words, we need a version of the law of large numbers which is *uniform* over all functions that the learning machine can implement.

5.4 Uniform Convergence and Consistency

The present section will explain how consistency can be characterized by a uniform convergence condition on the set of functions $\mathcal{F}$ that the learning machine can implement. Figure 5.2 gives a simplified depiction of the question of consistency. Both the empirical risk and the actual risk are drawn as functions of f. For

3. We refrain from giving a more formal definition of consistency, the reason being that there are some caveats to this classical definition of consistency; these would necessitate a discussion leading us away from the main thread of the argument. For the precise definition of the required notion of "nontrivial consistency," see [561].

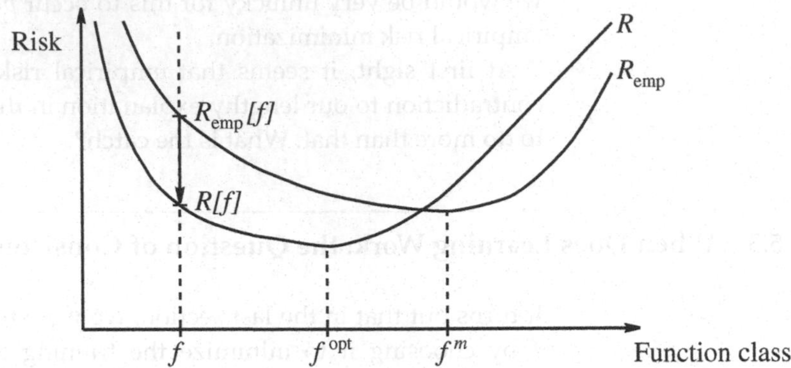

Figure 5.2 Simplified depiction of the convergence of empirical risk to actual risk. The x-axis gives a one-dimensional representation of the function class; the y axis denotes the risk (error). For each *fixed* function f, the law of large numbers tells us that as the sample size goes to infinity, the empirical risk $R_{emp}[f]$ converges towards the true risk $R[f]$ (indicated by the downward arrow). This does not imply, however, that in the limit of infinite sample sizes, the minimizer of the empirical risk, f^m, will lead to a value of the risk that is as good as the best attainable risk, $R[f^{opt}]$ (*consistency*). For the latter to be true, we require convergence of $R_{emp}[f]$ towards $R[f]$ to be uniform over all functions that the learning machines can implement (see text).

simplicity, we have summarized all possible functions f by a single axis of the plot. Empirical risk minimization consists in picking the f that yields the minimal value of R_{emp}. If it is consistent, then the minimum of R_{emp} converges to that of R in probability. Let us denote the minimizer of R by f^{opt}, satisfying

$$R[f] - R[f^{opt}] \geq 0 \tag{5.12}$$

for all $f \in \mathcal{F}$. This is the optimal choice that we could make, given complete knowledge of the distribution P.[4] Similarly, since f^m minimizes the empirical risk, we have

$$R_{emp}[f] - R_{emp}[f^m] \geq 0, \tag{5.13}$$

for all $f \in \mathcal{F}$. Being true for all $f \in \mathcal{F}$, (5.12) and (5.13) hold in particular for f^m and f^{opt}. If we substitute the former into (5.12) and the latter into (5.13), we obtain

$$R[f^m] - R[f^{opt}] \geq 0, \tag{5.14}$$

and

$$R_{emp}[f^{opt}] - R_{emp}[f^m] \geq 0. \tag{5.15}$$

4. As with f^m, f^{opt} need not be unique.

The sum of these two inequalities satisfies

$$\begin{aligned} 0 &\leq R[f^m] - R[f^{\text{opt}}] + R_{\text{emp}}[f^{\text{opt}}] - R_{\text{emp}}[f^m] \\ &= R[f^m] - R_{\text{emp}}[f^m] + R_{\text{emp}}[f^{\text{opt}}] - R[f^{\text{opt}}] \\ &\leq \sup_{f \in \mathcal{F}} (R[f] - R_{\text{emp}}[f]) + R_{\text{emp}}[f^{\text{opt}}] - R[f^{\text{opt}}]. \end{aligned} \tag{5.16}$$

Let us first consider the second half of the right hand side. Due to the law of large numbers, we have convergence in probability, i.e., for all $\epsilon > 0$,

$$|R_{\text{emp}}[f^{\text{opt}}] - R[f^{\text{opt}}]| \xrightarrow{P} 0 \text{ as } m \to \infty. \tag{5.17}$$

This holds true since f^{opt} is a fixed function, which is independent of the training sample (see (5.11)).

Uniform Convergence of Risk

The important conclusion is that if the empirical risk converges to the actual risk one-sided *uniformly*, over all functions that the learning machine can implement,

$$\sup_{f \in \mathcal{F}} (R[f] - R_{\text{emp}}[f]) \xrightarrow{P} 0 \text{ as } m \to \infty, \tag{5.18}$$

then the left hand sides of (5.14) and (5.15) will likewise converge to 0;

$$R[f^m] - R[f^{\text{opt}}] \xrightarrow{P} 0, \tag{5.19}$$

$$R_{\text{emp}}[f^{\text{opt}}] - R_{\text{emp}}[f^m] \xrightarrow{P} 0. \tag{5.20}$$

As argued above, (5.17) is not always true for f^m, since f^m is chosen to minimize R_{emp}, and thus depends on the sample. Assuming that (5.18) holds true, however, then (5.19) and (5.20) imply that in the limit, $R[f^m]$ cannot be larger than $R_{\text{emp}}[f^m]$. One-sided uniform convergence on $\mathcal{F}$ is thus a sufficient condition for consistency of the empirical risk minimization over $\mathcal{F}$.[5]

What about the other way round? Is one-sided uniform convergence also a *necessary* condition? Part of the mathematical beauty of VC theory lies in the fact that this is the case. We cannot go into the necessary details to prove this [571, 561, 562], and only state the main result. Note that this theorem uses the notion of nontrivial consistency that we already mentioned briefly in footnote 3. In a nutshell, this concept requires that the induction principle be consistent even after the "best" functions have been removed. Nontrivial consistency thus rules out, for instance, the case in which the problem is trivial, due to the existence of a function which uniformly does better than all other functions. To understand this, assume that there exists such a function. Since this function is uniformly better than all others, we can already select this function (using ERM) from *one* (arbitrary) data point. Hence the method would be trivially consistent, no matter what the

5. Note that the onesidedness of the convergence comes from the fact that we only require consistency of empirical risk *minimization*. If we required the same for empirical risk *maximization*, then we would end up with standard uniform convergence, and the parentheses in (5.18) would be replaced with modulus signs.

rest of the function class looks like. Having one function which gets picked as soon as we have seen one data point would essentially void the inherently *asymptotic* notion of consistency.

Theorem 5.3 (Vapnik & Chervonenkis (e.g., [562])) *One-sided uniform convergence in probability,*

$$\lim_{m\to\infty} \mathrm{P}\{\sup_{f\in\mathcal{F}}(R[f]-R_{\mathrm{emp}}[f]) > \epsilon\} = 0, \tag{5.21}$$

for all $\epsilon > 0$, *is a* necessary *and* sufficient *condition for nontrivial consistency of empirical risk minimization.*

As explained above, consistency, and thus learning, crucially depends on the set of functions. In Section 5.1, we gave an example where we considered the set of all possible functions, and showed that learning was impossible. The dependence of learning on the set of functions has now returned in a different guise: the condition of uniform convergence will crucially depend on the set of functions for which it must hold.

The abstract characterization in Theorem 5.3 of consistency as a uniform convergence property, whilst theoretically intriguing, is not all that useful in practice. We do not want to check some fairly abstract convergence property every time we want to use a learning machine. Therefore, we next address whether there are properties of learning machines, i.e., of sets of functions, which *ensure* uniform convergence of risks.

5.5 How to Derive a VC Bound

We now take a closer look at the subject of Theorem 5.3; the probability

$$\mathrm{P}\{\sup_{f\in\mathcal{F}}(R[f]-R_{\mathrm{emp}}[f]) > \epsilon\}. \tag{5.22}$$

We give a simplified account, drawing from the expositions of [561, 562, 415, 238]. We do not aim to describe or even develop the theory to the extent that would be necessary to give precise bounds for SVMs, say. Instead, our goal will be to convey central insights rather than technical details. For more complete treatments geared specifically towards SVMs, cf. [562, 491, 24]. We focus on the case of pattern recognition; that is, on functions taking values in $\{\pm 1\}$.

Two tricks are needed along the way: the *union bound* and the method of *symmetrization by a ghost sample.*

5.5.1 The Union Bound

Suppose the set $\mathcal{F}$ consists of two functions, f_1 and f_2. In this case, uniform convergence of risk trivially follows from the law of large numbers, which holds for each of the two. To see this, let

$$C_\epsilon^i := \{(x_1, y_1), \ldots, (x_m, y_m) | (R[f_i] - R_{\text{emp}}[f_i]) > \epsilon\} \quad (5.23)$$

denote the set of samples for which the risks of f_i differ by more than ϵ. Then, by definition, we have

$$\mathrm{P}\{\sup_{f \in \mathcal{F}} (R[f] - R_{\text{emp}}[f]) > \epsilon\} = \mathrm{P}(C_\epsilon^1 \cup C_\epsilon^2). \quad (5.24)$$

The latter, however, can be rewritten as

$$\mathrm{P}(C_\epsilon^1 \cup C_\epsilon^2) = \mathrm{P}(C_\epsilon^1) + \mathrm{P}(C_\epsilon^2) - \mathrm{P}(C_\epsilon^1 \cap C_\epsilon^2) \leq \mathrm{P}(C_\epsilon^1) + \mathrm{P}(C_\epsilon^2), \quad (5.25)$$

where the last inequality follows from the fact that P is nonnegative. Similarly, if $\mathcal{F} = \{f_1, \ldots, f_n\}$, we have

$$\mathrm{P}\{\sup_{f \in \mathcal{F}} (R[f] - R_{\text{emp}}[f]) > \epsilon\} = \mathrm{P}(C_\epsilon^1 \cup \ldots \cup C_\epsilon^n) \leq \sum_{i=1}^{n} \mathrm{P}(C_\epsilon^i). \quad (5.26)$$

Union Bound

This inequality is called the *union bound*. As it is a crucial step in the derivation of risk bounds, it is worthwhile to emphasize that it becomes an equality if and only if all the events involved are *disjoint*. In practice, this is rarely the case, and we therefore lose a lot when applying (5.26). It is a step with a large "slack."

Nevertheless, when $\mathcal{F}$ is finite, we may simply apply the law of large numbers (5.11) for each individual $\mathrm{P}(C_\epsilon^i)$, and the sum in (5.26) then leads to a constant factor n on the right hand side of the bound — it does not change the exponentially fast convergence of the empirical risk towards the actual risk. In the next section, we describe an ingenious trick used by Vapnik and Chervonenkis, to reduce the infinite case to the finite one. It consists of introducing what is sometimes called a *ghost sample*.

5.5.2 Symmetrization

The central observation in this section is that we can bound (5.22) in terms of a probability of an event referring to a *finite* function class. Note first that the empirical risk term in (5.22) effectively refers only to a finite function class: for any given training sample of m points $x_1, \ldots, x_m$, the functions of $\mathcal{F}$ can take at most 2^m different values $y_1, \ldots, y_m$ (recall that the y_i take values only in $\{\pm 1\}$). In addition, the probability that the empirical risk differs from the actual risk by more than ϵ, can be bounded by the twice the probability that it differs from the empirical risk on a *second* sample of size m by more than $\epsilon/2$.

Symmetrization

Lemma 5.4 (Symmetrization (Vapnik & Chervonenkis) (e.g. [559])) *For $m\epsilon^2 \geq 2$, we have*

$$\mathrm{P}\{\sup_{f \in \mathcal{F}} (R[f] - R_{\text{emp}}[f]) > \epsilon\} \leq 2\mathrm{P}\{\sup_{f \in \mathcal{F}} (R_{\text{emp}}[f] - R'_{\text{emp}}[f]) > \epsilon/2\}. \quad (5.27)$$

Here, the first P *refers to the distribution of iid samples of size m, while the second one* *refers to iid samples of size 2m. In the latter case,* R_{emp} *measures the loss on the first half of the sample, and* R'_{emp} *on the second half.*

Although we do not prove this result, it should be fairly plausible: if the empirical error rates on two independent m-samples are close to each other, then they should also be close to the true error rate.

5.5.3 The Shattering Coefficient

The main result of Lemma 5.4 is that it implies, for the purpose of bounding (5.22), that the function class $\mathcal{F}$ is effectively finite: restricted to the $2m$ points appearing on the right hand side of (5.27), it has *at most* 2^{2m} elements. This is because only the outputs of the functions on the patterns of the sample count, and there are $2m$ patterns with two possible outputs, ± 1. The number of effectively different functions can be smaller than 2^{2m}, however; and for our purposes, this is the case that will turn out to be interesting.

Let $Z_{2m} := ((x_1, y_1), \ldots, (x_{2m}, y_{2m}))$ be the given $2m$-sample. Denote by $\mathcal{N}(\mathcal{F}, Z_{2m})$ the cardinality of $\mathcal{F}$ when restricted to $\{x_1, \ldots, x_{2m}\}$, that is, the number of functions from $\mathcal{F}$ that can be distinguished from their values on $\{x_1, \ldots, x_{2m}\}$. Let us, moreover, denote the maximum (over all possible choices of a $2m$-sample) number of functions that can be distinguished in this way as $\mathcal{N}(\mathcal{F}, 2m)$.

Shattering Coefficient

The function $\mathcal{N}(\mathcal{F}, m)$ is referred to as the *shattering coefficient*, or in the more general case of regression estimation, the *covering number* of $\mathcal{F}$.[6] In the case of pattern recognition, which is what we are currently looking at, $\mathcal{N}(\mathcal{F}, m)$ has a particularly simple interpretation: it is the number of different outputs $(y_1, \ldots, y_m)$ that the functions in $\mathcal{F}$ can achieve on samples of a given size.[7] In other words, it simply measures the *number of ways that the function class can separate the patterns into two classes.* Whenever $\mathcal{N}(\mathcal{F}, m) = 2^m$, all possible separations can be implemented by functions of the class. In this case, the function class is said to *shatter m* points. Note that this means that there *exists* a set of m patterns which can be separated in all possible ways — it does not mean that this applies to *all* sets of m patterns.

Shattering

5.5.4 Uniform Convergence Bounds

Let us now take a closer look at the probability that for a $2m$-sample Z_{2m} drawn iid from P, we get a one-sided uniform deviation larger than $\epsilon/2$ (cf. (5.27)),

$$P\{\sup_{f \in \mathcal{F}}(R_{\text{emp}}[f] - R'_{\text{emp}}[f]) > \epsilon/2\}. \tag{5.28}$$

6. In regression estimation, the covering number also depends on the accuracy within which we are approximating the function class, and on the loss function used; see Section 12.4 for more details.

7. Using the zero-one loss $c(x, y, f(x)) = 1/2|f(x) - y| \in \{0, 1\}$, it also equals the number of different loss vectors $(c(x_1, y_1, f(x_1)), \ldots, c(x_m, y_m, f(x_m)))$.

The basic idea now is to pick a maximal set of functions $\{f_1, \ldots, f_{\mathcal{N}(\mathcal{F}, Z_{2m})}\}$ that can be distinguished based on their values on Z_{2m}, then use the union bound, and finally bound each term using the Chernoff inequality. However, the fact that the f_i depend on the sample Z_{2m} will make things somewhat more complicated. To deal with this, we have to introduce an auxiliary step of randomization, using a uniform distibution over permutations σ of the $2m$-sample Z_{2m}.

Let us denote the empirical risks on the two halves of the sample after the permutation σ by $R^{\sigma}_{\text{emp}}[f]$ and $R'^{\sigma}_{\text{emp}}[f]$, respectively. Since the $2m$-sample is iid, the permutation does not affect (5.28). We may thus instead consider

$$\mathrm{P}_{Z_{2m},\sigma}\{\sup_{f\in\mathcal{F}}(R^{\sigma}_{\text{emp}}[f] - R'^{\sigma}_{\text{emp}}[f]) > \epsilon/2\}, \tag{5.29}$$

where the subscripts of P were added to clarify what the distribution refers to. We next rewrite this as

$$\int_{(\mathcal{X}\times\{\pm 1\})^{2m}} \mathrm{P}_{\sigma|Z_{2m}}\{ \sup_{f\in\mathcal{F}|_{Z_{2m}}} (R^{\sigma}_{\text{emp}}[f] - R'^{\sigma}_{\text{emp}}[f]) > \epsilon/2 \mid Z_{2m}\}\, d\mathrm{P}(Z_{2m}). \tag{5.30}$$

We can now express the event $C_\epsilon := \{\sigma|\sup_{f\in\mathcal{F}|_{Z_{2m}}}(R^{\sigma}_{\text{emp}}[f] - R'^{\sigma}_{\text{emp}}[f]) > \epsilon/2\}$ as

$$C_\epsilon = \bigcup_{n=1}^{\mathcal{N}(\mathcal{F},Z_{2m})} C_\epsilon(f_n), \tag{5.31}$$

where the events $C_\epsilon(f_n) := \{\sigma|(R^{\sigma}_{\text{emp}}[f_n] - R'^{\sigma}_{\text{emp}}[f_n]) > \epsilon/2\}$ refer to individual functions f_n chosen such that $(\bigcup_n\{f_n\})\,|_{Z_{2m}} = \mathcal{F}|_{Z_{2m}}$. Note that the functions f_n may be considered as fixed, since we have conditioned on Z_{2m}.

We are now in a position to appeal to the classical law of large numbers. Our random experiment consists of drawing σ from the uniform distribution over all permutations of $2m$-samples. This turns our sequence of losses $\xi^{\sigma}_i = \frac{1}{2}|f(x^{\sigma}_i) - y^{\sigma}_i|$ $(i = 1, \ldots, 2m)$ into an iid sequence of independent Bernoulli trials. We then apply a modified Chernoff inequality to bound the probability of each event $C_\epsilon(f_n)$. It states that given a $2m$-sample of Bernoulli trials, we have (see Problem 5.4)

$$\mathrm{P}\left\{\frac{1}{m}\sum_{i=1}^{m}\xi_i - \frac{1}{m}\sum_{i=m+1}^{2m}\xi_i \geq \epsilon\right\} \leq 2\exp\left(-\frac{m\epsilon^2}{2}\right). \tag{5.32}$$

For our present problem, we thus obtain

$$\mathrm{P}_{\sigma|Z_{2m}}(C_\epsilon(f_n)) \leq 2\exp\left(-\frac{m\epsilon^2}{8}\right), \tag{5.33}$$

independent of f_n. We next use the union bound to get a bound on the probability of the event C_ϵ defined in (5.31). We obtain a sum over $\mathcal{N}(\mathcal{F}, Z_{2m})$ identical terms of the form (5.33). Hence (5.30) (and (5.29)) can be bounded from above by

$$\begin{aligned}&\int_{(\mathcal{X}\times\{\pm1\})^{2m}} \mathcal{N}(\mathcal{F}, Z_{2m})\, 2\exp\left(-\frac{m\epsilon^2}{8}\right) d\mathrm{P}(Z_{2m})\\ &= 2\,\mathbf{E}[\mathcal{N}(\mathcal{F}, Z_{2m})]\exp\left(-\frac{m\epsilon^2}{8}\right),\end{aligned} \tag{5.34}$$

where the expectation is taken over the random drawing of Z_{2m}. The last step is to combine this with Lemma 5.4, to obtain

$$\mathrm{P}\{\sup_{f\in\mathcal{F}}(R[f]-R_{\mathrm{emp}}[f])>\epsilon\}\leq 4\,\mathbf{E}\left[\mathcal{N}(\mathcal{F},Z_{2m})\right]\exp\left(-\frac{m\epsilon^2}{8}\right)$$
$$=4\exp\left(\ln\mathbf{E}\left[\mathcal{N}(\mathcal{F},Z_{2m})\right]-\frac{m\epsilon^2}{8}\right). \tag{5.35}$$

Inequality of Vapnik-Chervonenkis Type

We conclude that provided $\mathbf{E}\left[\mathcal{N}(\mathcal{F},Z_{2m})\right]$ does not grow exponentially in m (i.e., $\ln\mathbf{E}\left[\mathcal{N}(\mathcal{F},Z_{2m})\right]$ grows sublinearly), it is actually possible to make nontrivial statements about the *test* error of learning machines.

The above reasoning is essentially the VC style analysis. Similar bounds can be obtained using a strategy which is more common in the field of empirical processes, first proving that $\sup_f(R[f]-R_{\mathrm{emp}}[f])$ is concentrated around its mean [554, 14].

5.5.5 Confidence Intervals

It is sometimes useful to rewrite (5.35) such that we specify the probability with which we want the bound to hold, and then get the confidence interval, which tells us how close the risk should be to the empirical risk. This can be achieved by setting the right hand side of (5.35) equal to some $\delta>0$, and then solving for ϵ. As a result, we get the statement that with a probability at least $1-\delta$,

Risk Bound

$$R[f]\leq R_{\mathrm{emp}}[f]+\sqrt{\frac{8}{m}\left(\ln\mathbf{E}\left[\mathcal{N}(\mathcal{F},Z_{2m})\right]+\ln\frac{4}{\delta}\right)}. \tag{5.36}$$

Note that this bound holds independent of f; in particular, it holds for the function f^m minimizing the empirical risk. This is not only a strength, but also a weakness in the bound. It is a strength since many learning machines do not truly minimize the empirical risk, and the bound thus holds for them, too. It is a weakness since by taking into account more information on which function we are interested in, one could hope to get more accurate bounds. We will return to this issue in Section 12.1.

Bounds like (5.36) can be used to justify induction principles different from the empirical risk minimization principle. Vapnik and Chervonenkis [569, 559] proposed minimizing the right hand side of these bounds, rather than just the empirical risk. The confidence term, in the present case, $\sqrt{\frac{8}{m}\left(\ln\mathbf{E}\left[\mathcal{N}(\mathcal{F},Z_{2m})\right]+\ln\frac{4}{\delta}\right)}$, then ensures that the chosen function, denoted f_*, not only leads to a small risk, but also comes from a function class with small capacity.

The capacity term is a property of the function class $\mathcal{F}$, and not of any individual function f. Thus, the bound cannot simply be minimized over choices of f. Instead, we introduce a so-called *structure* on $\mathcal{F}$, and minimize over the choice of the structure. This leads to an induction principle called *structural risk minimization*. We leave out the technicalities involved [559, 136, 562]. The main idea is depicted in Figure 5.3.

Structural Risk Minimization

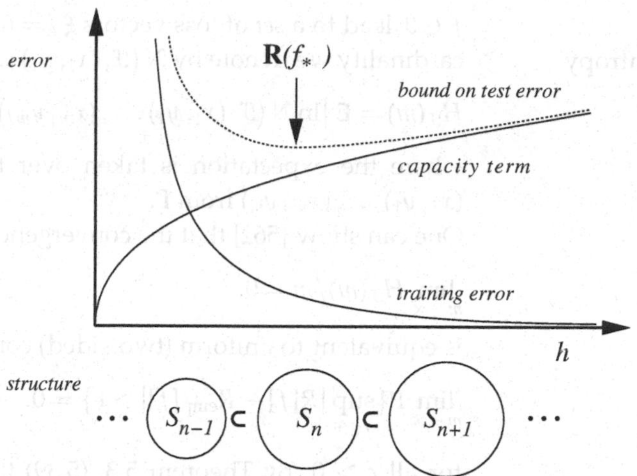

Figure 5.3 Graphical depiction of the structural risk minimization (SRM) induction principle. The function class is decomposed into a nested sequence of subsets of increasing size (and thus, of increasing capacity). The SRM principle picks a function f_* which has small training error, and comes from an element of the structure that has low capacity h, thus minimizing a risk bound of type (5.36).

For practical purposes, we usually employ bounds of the type (5.36) as a guideline for coming up with risk functionals (see Section 4.1). Often, the risk functionals form a compromise between quantities that *should* be minimized from a statistical point of view, and quantities that *can* be minimized efficiently (cf. Problem 5.7).

There exists a large number of bounds similar to (5.35) and its alternative form (5.36). Differences occur in the constants, both in front of the exponential and in its exponent. The bounds also differ in the exponent of ϵ — in some cases, by a factor greater than 2. For instance, if a training error of zero is achievable, we can use Bernstein's inequality instead of Chernoff's result, which leads to ϵ rather than ϵ^2. For further details, cf. [136, 562, 492, 238]. Finally, the bounds differ in the way they measure capacity. So far, we have used covering numbers, but this is not the only method.

5.5.6 The VC Dimension and Other Capacity Concepts

So far, we have formulated the bounds in terms of the so-called *annealed entropy* $\ln \mathbf{E}[\mathcal{N}(\mathcal{F}, Z_{2m})]$. This led to statements that depend on the distribution and thus can take into account characteristics of the problem at hand. The downside is that they are usually difficult to evaluate; moreover, in most problems, we do not have knowledge of the underlying distribution. However, a number of different capacity concepts, with different properties, can take the role of the term $\ln(\mathbf{E}[\mathcal{N}(\mathcal{F}, Z_{2m})])$ in (5.36).

- Given an example (x, y), $f \in \mathcal{F}$ causes a loss that we denote by $c(x, y, f(x)) := \frac{1}{2}|f(x) - y| \in \{0, 1\}$. For a larger sample $(x_1, y_1) \ldots, (x_m, y_m)$, the different functions

$f \in \mathcal{F}$ lead to a *set* of loss vectors $\boldsymbol{\xi}_f = (c(x_1, y_1, f(x_1)), \ldots, c(x_m, y_m, f(x_m)))$, whose cardinality we denote by $\mathcal{N}\left(\mathcal{F}, (x_1, y_1) \ldots, (x_m, y_m)\right)$. The *VC entropy* is defined as

VC Entropy

$$H_{\mathcal{F}}(m) = \mathbf{E}\left[\ln \mathcal{N}\left(\mathcal{F}, (x_1, y_1) \ldots, (x_m, y_m)\right)\right], \tag{5.37}$$

where the expectation is taken over the random generation of the m-sample $(x_1, y_1) \ldots, (x_m, y_m)$ from P.
One can show [562] that the convergence

$$\lim_{m \to \infty} H_{\mathcal{F}}(m)/m = 0, \tag{5.38}$$

is equivalent to uniform (two-sided) convergence of risk,

$$\lim_{m \to \infty} \mathrm{P}\{\sup_{f \in \mathcal{F}} |R[f] - R_{\mathrm{emp}}[f]| > \epsilon\} = 0, \tag{5.39}$$

for all $\epsilon > 0$. By Theorem 5.3, (5.39) thus implies consistency of empirical risk minimization.

▪ If we exchange the expectation $\mathbf{E}$ and the logarithm in (5.37), we obtain the annealed entropy used above,

Annealed Entropy

$$H^{\mathrm{ann}}_{\mathcal{F}}(m) = \ln \mathbf{E}\left[\mathcal{N}\left(\mathcal{F}, (x_1, y_1) \ldots, (x_m, y_m)\right)\right]. \tag{5.40}$$

Since the logarithm is a concave function, the annealed entropy is an upper bound on the VC entropy. Therefore, whenever the annealed entropy satisfies a condition of the form (5.38), the same automatically holds for the VC entropy.
One can show that the convergence

$$\lim_{m \to \infty} H^{\mathrm{ann}}_{\mathcal{F}}(m)/m = 0, \tag{5.41}$$

implies exponentially fast convergence [561],

$$P\{\sup_{f \in \mathcal{F}} |R[f] - R_{\mathrm{emp}}[f]| > \epsilon\} \leq 4\ \exp(((H^{\mathrm{ann}}_{\mathcal{F}}(2m)/m) - \epsilon^2) \cdot m). \tag{5.42}$$

It has recently been proven that in fact (5.41) is not only sufficient, but also necessary for this [66].

▪ We can obtain an upper bound on both entropies introduced so far, by taking a supremum over all possible samples, instead of the expectation. This leads to the *growth function*,

Growth Function

$$G_{\mathcal{F}}(m) = \max_{(x_1,y_1),\ldots,(x_m,y_m) \in \mathcal{X} \times \{\pm 1\}} \ln \mathcal{N}\left(\mathcal{F}, (x_1, y_1) \ldots, (x_m, y_m)\right). \tag{5.43}$$

Note that by definition, the growth function is the logarithm of the shattering coefficient, $G_{\mathcal{F}}(m) = \ln \mathcal{N}(\mathcal{F}, m)$.
The convergence

$$\lim_{m \to \infty} G_{\mathcal{F}}(m)/m = 0, \tag{5.44}$$

is necessary and sufficient for exponentially fast convergence of risk *for all underlying distributions* P.

■ The next step will be to summarize the main behavior of the growth function with a single number. If $\mathcal{F}$ is as rich as possible, so that for any sample of size m, the points can be chosen such that by using functions of the learning machine, they can be separated in all 2^m possible ways (i.e., they can be shattered), then

$$G_{\mathcal{F}}(m) = m \cdot \ln(2). \tag{5.45}$$

In this case, the convergence (5.44) does not take place, and learning will not generally be successful. What about the other case? Vapnik and Chervonenkis [567, 568] showed that either (5.45) holds true for all m, or there exists some *maximal* m for which (5.45) is satisfied. This number is called the *VC dimension* and is denoted by h. If the maximum does not exist, the VC dimension is said to be infinite.

VC Dimension

By construction, the VC dimension is thus the maximal number of points which can be shattered by functions in $\mathcal{F}$. It is possible to prove that for $m > h$ [568],

$$G_{\mathcal{F}}(m) \leq h\left(\ln\frac{m}{h}+1\right). \tag{5.46}$$

This means that up to $m = h$, the growth function increases linearly with the sample size. Thereafter, it only increases logarithmically, i.e., *much* more slowly. This is the regime where learning can succeed.

Although we do not make use of it in the present chapter, it is worthwhile to also introduce the *VC dimension of a class of real-valued functions* $\{f_{\mathbf{w}}|\mathbf{w} \in \Lambda\}$ at this stage. It is defined to equal the VC dimension of the class of indicator functions

$$\left\{\operatorname{sgn}(f_{\mathbf{w}} - \beta)|\mathbf{w} \in \Lambda, \beta \in \left(\inf_x f_{\mathbf{w}}(x), \sup_x f_{\mathbf{w}}(x)\right)\right\}. \tag{5.47}$$

VC Dimension for Real-Valued Functions

In summary, we get a succession of capacity concepts,

$$H_{\mathcal{F}}(m) \leq H_{\mathcal{F}}^{\text{ann}}(m) \leq G_{\mathcal{F}}(m) \leq h\left(\ln\frac{m}{h}+1\right). \tag{5.48}$$

From left to right, these become less precise. The entropies on the left are distribution-dependent, but rather difficult to evaluate (see, e.g., [430, 391]). The growth function and VC dimension are distribution-independent. This is less accurate, and does not always capture the essence of a given problem, which might have a much more benign distribution than the worst case; on the other hand, we want the learning machine to work for all distributions. If we knew the distribution beforehand, then we would not need a learning machine anymore.

VC Dimension Example

Let us look at a simple example of the VC dimension. As a function class, we consider hyperplanes in $\mathbb{R}^2$, i.e.,

$$f(x) = \operatorname{sgn}(a + b[x]_1 + c[x]_2), \text{ with parameters } a, b, c \in \mathbb{R}. \tag{5.49}$$

Suppose we are given three points x_1, x_2, x_3 which are not collinear. No matter how they are labelled (that is, independent of our choice of $y_1, y_2, y_3 \in \{\pm 1\}$), we can always find parameters $a, b, c \in \mathbb{R}$ such that $f(x_i) = y_i$ for all i (see Figure 1.4 in the introduction). In other words, there exist three points that we can shatter. This shows that the VC dimension of the set of hyperplanes in $\mathbb{R}^2$ satisfies $h \geq 3$. On the other hand, we can never shatter *four* points. It follows from simple geometry that given any four points, there is always a set of labels such that we cannot realize the corresponding classification. Therefore, the VC dimension is $h = 3$. More generally, for hyperplanes in $\mathbb{R}^N$, the VC dimension can be shown to be $h = N + 1$. For a formal derivation of this result, as well as of other examples, see [523].

VC Dimension of Hyperplanes

How does this fit together with the fact that SVMs can be shown to correspond to hyperplanes in feature spaces of possibly infinite dimension? The crucial point is that SVMs correspond to *large margin* hyperplanes. Once the margin enters, the capacity can be much smaller than the above general VC dimension of hyperplanes. For simplicity, we consider the case of hyperplanes containing the origin.

VC Dimension of Margin Hyperplanes

Theorem 5.5 (Vapnik [559]) *Consider hyperplanes $\langle \mathbf{w}, \mathbf{x} \rangle = 0$, where $\mathbf{w}$ is normalized such that they are in canonical form w.r.t. a set of points $X^* = \{\mathbf{x}_1, \ldots, \mathbf{x}_r\}$; i.e.,*

$$\min_{i=1,\ldots,r} |\langle \mathbf{w}, \mathbf{x}_i \rangle| = 1. \tag{5.50}$$

The set of decision functions $f_{\mathbf{w}}(\mathbf{x}) = \operatorname{sgn} \langle \mathbf{x}, \mathbf{w} \rangle$ defined on X^*, and satisfying the constraint $\|\mathbf{w}\| \leq \Lambda$, has a VC dimension satisfying

$$h \leq R^2 \Lambda^2. \tag{5.51}$$

Here, R is the radius of the smallest sphere centered at the origin and containing X^*.

Before we give a proof, several remarks are in order.

- The theorem states that we can control the VC dimension *irrespective of the dimension of the space* by controlling the length of the weight vector $\|\mathbf{w}\|$. Note, however, that this needs to be done a priori, by choosing a value for Λ. It therefore does not strictly motivate what we will later see in SVMs, where $\|\mathbf{w}\|$ is minimized in order to control the capacity. Detailed treatments can be found in the work of Shawe-Taylor et al. [491, 24, 125].
- There exists a similar result for the case where R is the radius of the smallest sphere (not necessarily centered at the origin) enclosing the data, and where we allow for the possibility that the hyperplanes have a nonzero offset b [562]. In this case, we give a simple visualization in figure Figure 5.4, which shows it is plausible that enforcing a large margin amounts to reducing the VC dimension.
- Note that the theorem talks about functions defined on X^*. To extend it to the case where the functions are defined on all of the input domain $\mathcal{X}$, it is best to state it for the *fat shattering dimension*. For details, see [24].

The proof [24, 222, 559] is somewhat technical, and can be skipped if desired.

Proof Let us assume that $\mathbf{x}_1, \ldots, \mathbf{x}_r$ are shattered by canonical hyperplanes with $\|\mathbf{w}\| \leq \Lambda$. Consequently, for all $y_1, \ldots, y_r \in \{\pm 1\}$, there exists a $\mathbf{w}$ with $\|\mathbf{w}\| \leq \Lambda$, such that

$$y_i \langle \mathbf{w}, \mathbf{x}_i \rangle \geq 1 \text{ for all } i = 1, \ldots, r. \tag{5.52}$$

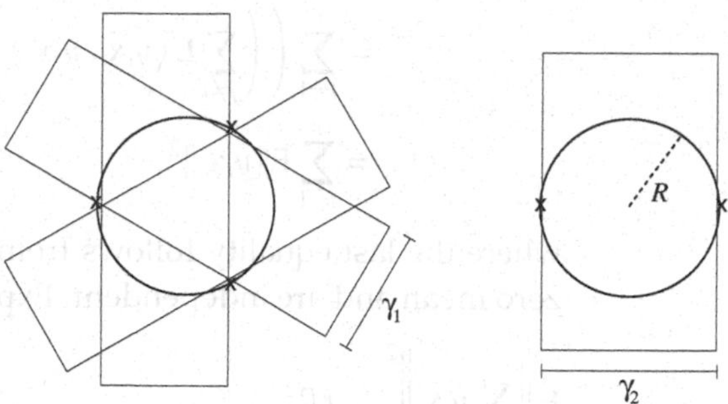

Figure 5.4 Simple visualization of the fact that enforcing a large margin of separation amounts to limiting the VC dimension. Assume that the data points are contained in a ball of radius R (cf. Theorem 5.5). Using hyperplanes with margin γ_1, it is possible to separate three points in all possible ways. Using hyperplanes with the larger margin γ_2, this is only possible for *two* points, hence the VC dimension in that case is two rather than three.

The proof proceeds in two steps. In the first part, we prove that the more points we want to shatter (5.52), the larger $\|\sum_{i=1}^r y_i \mathbf{x}_i\|$ must be. In the second part, we prove that we can upper bound the size of $\|\sum_{i=1}^r y_i \mathbf{x}_i\|$ in terms of R. Combining the two gives the desired condition, which tells us the maximum number of points we can shatter.

Summing (5.52) over $i = 1, \ldots, r$ yields

$$\left\langle \mathbf{w}, \left(\sum_{i=1}^r y_i \mathbf{x}_i \right) \right\rangle \geq r. \tag{5.53}$$

By the Cauchy-Schwarz inequality, on the other hand, we have

$$\left\langle \mathbf{w}, \left(\sum_{i=1}^r y_i \mathbf{x}_i \right) \right\rangle \leq \|\mathbf{w}\| \left\| \sum_{i=1}^r y_i \mathbf{x}_i \right\| \leq \Lambda \left\| \sum_{i=1}^r y_i \mathbf{x}_i \right\|. \tag{5.54}$$

Here, the second inequality follows from $\|\mathbf{w}\| \leq \Lambda$.

Combining (5.53) and (5.54), we get the desired lower bound,

$$\frac{r}{\Lambda} \leq \left\| \sum_{i=1}^r y_i \mathbf{x}_i \right\|. \tag{5.55}$$

We now move on to the second part. Let us consider independent random labels $y_i \in \{\pm 1\}$ which are uniformly distributed, sometimes called *Rademacher variables.* Let $\mathbf{E}$ denote the expectation over the choice of the labels. Exploiting the linearity of $\mathbf{E}$, we have

$$\begin{aligned}
\mathbf{E} \left\| \sum_{i=1}^r y_i \mathbf{x}_i \right\|^2 &= \sum_{i=1}^r \mathbf{E} \left\langle y_i \mathbf{x}_i, \sum_{j=1}^r y_j \mathbf{x}_j \right\rangle \\
&= \sum_{i=1}^r \mathbf{E} \left\langle y_i \mathbf{x}_i, \left(\left(\sum_{j \neq i} y_j \mathbf{x}_j \right) + y_i \mathbf{x}_i \right) \right\rangle
\end{aligned}$$

$$= \sum_{i=1}^{r} \left(\left(\sum_{j \neq i} \mathbf{E} \langle y_i \mathbf{x}_i, y_j \mathbf{x}_j \rangle \right) + \mathbf{E} \langle y_i \mathbf{x}_i, y_i \mathbf{x}_i \rangle \right)$$

$$= \sum_{i=1}^{r} \mathbf{E} \| y_i \mathbf{x}_i \|^2, \tag{5.56}$$

where the last equality follows from the fact that the Rademacher variables have zero mean and are independent. Exploiting the fact that $\|y_i \mathbf{x}_i\| = \|\mathbf{x}_i\| \leq R$, we get

$$\mathbf{E} \left\| \sum_{i=1}^{r} y_i \mathbf{x}_i \right\|^2 \leq r R^2. \tag{5.57}$$

Since this is true for the expectation over the random choice of the labels, there must be at least one set of labels for which it also holds true. We have so far made no restrictions on the labels, hence we may now use this specific set of labels. This leads to the desired upper bound,

$$\left\| \sum_{i=1}^{r} y_i \mathbf{x}_i \right\|^2 \leq r R^2. \tag{5.58}$$

Combining the upper bound with the lower bound (5.55), we get

$$\frac{r^2}{\Lambda^2} \leq r R^2; \tag{5.59}$$

hence,

$$r \leq R^2 \Lambda^2. \tag{5.60}$$

In other words, if the r points are shattered by a canonical hyperplane satisfying the assumptions we have made, then r is constrained by (5.60). The VC dimension h also satisfies (5.60), since it corresponds to the maximum number of points that can be shattered. ■

In the next section, we give an application of this theorem. Readers only interested in the theoretical background of learning theory may want to skip this section.

5.6 A Model Selection Example

In the following example, taken from [470], we use a bound of the form (5.36) to predict which kernel would perform best on a character recognition problem (USPS set, see Section A.1). Since the problem is essentially separable, we disregard the empirical risk term in the bound, and choose the parameters of a polynomial kernel by minimizing the second term. Note that the second term is a monotonic function of the capacity. As a capacity measure, we use the upper bound on the VC dimension described in Theorem 5.5, which in turn is an upper bound on the logarithm of the covering number that appears in (5.36) (by the arguments put forward in Section 5.5.6).

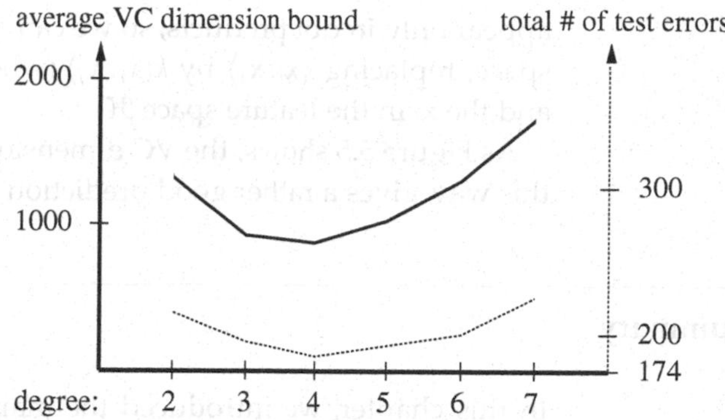

Figure 5.5 Average VC dimension (solid), and total number of test errors, of ten two-class-classifiers (dotted) with polynomial degrees 2 through 7, trained on the USPS set of handwritten digits. The baseline 174 on the error scale, corresponds to the total number of test errors of the ten *best* binary classifiers, chosen from degrees 2 through 7. The graph shows that for this problem, which can essentially be solved with zero training error for all degrees greater than 1, the VC dimension allows us to predict that degree 4 yields the best overall performance of the two-class-classifier on the test set (from [470, 467]).

We employ a version of Theorem 5.5, which uses the radius of the smallest sphere containing the data in a feature space $\mathcal{H}$ associated with the kernel k [561]. The radius was computed by solving a quadratic program [470, 85] (cf. Section 8.3). We formulate the problem as follows:

Computing the Enclosing Sphere in $\mathcal{H}$

$$\begin{aligned} &\underset{R\geq 0, \mathbf{x}^*\in\mathcal{H}}{\text{minimize}} \quad R^2 \\ &\text{subject to} \quad \|\mathbf{x}_i - \mathbf{x}^*\|^2 \leq R^2, \end{aligned} \tag{5.61}$$

where $\mathbf{x}^*$ is the center of the sphere, and is found in the course of the optimization. Employing the tools of constrained optimization, as briefly described in Chapter 1 (for details, see Chapter 6), we construct a Lagrangian,

$$R^2 - \sum_{i=1}^{m} \lambda_i (R^2 - (\mathbf{x}_i - \mathbf{x}^*)^2), \tag{5.62}$$

and compute the derivatives with respect to $\mathbf{x}^*$ and R, to get

$$\mathbf{x}^* = \sum_{i=1}^{m} \lambda_i \mathbf{x}_i, \tag{5.63}$$

and the Wolfe dual problem:

$$\underset{\boldsymbol{\lambda}\in\mathbb{R}^m}{\text{maximize}} \quad \sum_{i=1}^{m} \lambda_i \cdot \langle \mathbf{x}_i, \mathbf{x}_i \rangle - \sum_{i,j=1}^{m} \lambda_i \lambda_j \cdot \langle \mathbf{x}_i, \mathbf{x}_j \rangle, \tag{5.64}$$

$$\text{subject to} \quad \sum_{i=1}^{m} \lambda_i = 1, \; \lambda_i \geq 0, \tag{5.65}$$

where $\boldsymbol{\lambda}$ is the vector of all Lagrange multipliers $\lambda_i, i = 1, \ldots, m$.

As in the Support Vector algorithm, this problem has the property that the $\mathbf{x}_i$

appear only in dot products, so we can again compute the dot products in feature space, replacing $\langle \mathbf{x}_i, \mathbf{x}_j \rangle$ by $k(x_i, x_j)$ (where the x_i belong to the input domain $\mathcal{X}$, and the $\mathbf{x}_i$ in the feature space $\mathcal{H}$).

As Figure 5.5 shows, the VC dimension bound, using the radius R computed in this way, gives a rather good prediction of the error on an independent test set.

5.7 Summary

In this chapter, we introduced the main ideas of statistical learning theory. For learning processes utilizing empirical risk minimization to be successful, we need a version of the law of large numbers that holds uniformly over all functions the learning machine can implement. For this uniform law to hold true, the capacity of the set of functions that the learning machine can implement has to be "well-behaved." We gave several capacity measures, such as the VC dimension, and illustrated how to derive bounds on the test error of a learning machine, in terms of the training error and the capacity. We have, moreover, shown how to bound the capacity of margin classifiers, a result which will later be used to motivate the Support Vector algorithm. Finally, we described an application in which a uniform convergence bound was used for model selection.

Whilst this discussion of learning theory should be sufficient to understand most of the present book, we will revisit learning theory at a later stage. In Chapter 12, we will present some more advanced material, which applies to kernel learning machines. Specifically, we will introduce another class of generalization error bound, building on a concept of *stability* of algorithms minimizing regularized risk functionals. These bounds are proven using concentration-of-measure inequalities, which are themselves generalizations of Chernoff and Hoeffding type bounds. In addition, we will discuss *leave-one-out* and *PAC-Bayesian* bounds.

5.8 Problems

5.1 (No Free Lunch in Kernel Choice ••) *Discuss the relationship between the "no-free-lunch Theorem" and the statement that there is no free lunch in kernel choice.*

5.2 (Error Counting Estimate [136] •) *Suppose you are given a test set with n elements to assess the accuracy of a trained classifier. Use the Chernoff bound to quantify the probability that the mean error on the test set differs from the true risk by more than $\epsilon > 0$. Argue that the test set should be as large as possible, in order to get a reliable estimate of the performance of a classifier.*

5.3 (The Tainted Die ••) *A con-artist wants to taint a die such that it does not generate any '6' when cast. Yet he does not know exactly how. So he devises the following scheme:*

he makes some changes and subsequently rolls the die 20 times to check that no '6' occurs. Unless pleased with the outcome, he changes more things and repeats the experiment.

How long will it take on average, until, even with a perfect die, he will be convinced that he has a die that never generates a '6'? What is the probability that this already happens at the first trial? Can you improve the strategy such that he can be sure the die is 'well' tainted (hint: longer trials provide increased confidence)?

5.4 (Chernoff Bound for the Deviation of Empirical Means ••) *Use (5.6) and the triangle inequality to prove that*

$$\mathrm{P}\left\{\left|\frac{1}{m}\sum_{i=1}^{m}\xi_i - \frac{1}{m}\sum_{i=m+1}^{2m}\xi_i\right| \geq \epsilon\right\} \leq 4\exp\left(-\frac{m\epsilon^2}{2}\right). \tag{5.66}$$

Next, note that the bound (5.66) is symmetric in how it deals with the two halves of the sample. Therefore, since the two events

$$\left\{\frac{1}{m}\sum_{i=1}^{m}\xi_i - \frac{1}{m}\sum_{i=m+1}^{2m}\xi_i \geq \epsilon\right\} \tag{5.67}$$

and

$$\left\{\frac{1}{m}\sum_{i=1}^{m}\xi_i - \frac{1}{m}\sum_{i=m+1}^{2m}\xi_i \leq -\epsilon\right\} \tag{5.68}$$

are disjoint, argue that (5.32) holds true. See also Corollary 6.34 below.

5.5 (Consistency and Uniform Convergence ••) *Why can we not get a bound on the generalization error of a learning algorithm by applying (5.11) to the outcome of the algorithm? Argue that since we do not know in advance which function the learning algorithm returns, we need to consider the worst possible case, which leads to uniform convergence considerations.*

Speculate whether there could be restrictions on learning algorithms which imply that effectively, empirical risk minimization only leads to a subset of the set of all possible functions. Argue that this amounts to restricting the capacity. Consider as an example neural networks with back-propagation: if the training algorithm always returns a local minimum close to the starting point in weight space, then the network effectively does not explore the whole weight (i.e., function) space.

5.6 (Confidence Interval and Uniform Convergence •) *Derive (5.36) from (5.35).*

5.7 (Representer Algorithms for Minimizing VC Bounds ∘∘∘) *Construct kernel algorithms that are more closely aligned with VC bounds of the form (5.36). Hint: in the risk functional, replace the standard SV regularizer $\|\mathbf{w}\|^2$ with the second term of (5.36), bounding the shattering coefficient with the VC dimension bound (Theorem 5.5). Use the representer theorem (Section 4.2) to argue that the minimizer takes the form of a kernel expansion in terms of the training examples. Find the optimal expansion coefficients by minimizing the modified risk functional over the choice of expansion coefficients.*

5.8 (Bounds in Terms of the VC Dimension •) *From (5.35) and (5.36), derive bounds in terms of the growth function and the VC dimension, using the results of Section 5.5.6. Discuss the conditions under which they hold.*

5.9 (VC Theory and Decision Theory •••) *(i) Discuss the relationship between minimax estimation (cf. footnote 7 in Chapter 1) and VC theory. Argue that the VC bounds can be made "worst case" over distributions by picking suitable capacity measures. However, they only bound the difference between empirical risk and true risk, thus they are only "worst case" for the variance term, not for the bias (or empirical risk). The minimization of an upper bound on the risk of the form (5.36) as performed in SRM is done in order to construct an induction principle rather than to make a minimax statement. Finally, note that the minimization is done with respect to a structure on the set of functions, while in the minimax paradigm one takes the minimum directly over (all) functions.*

(ii) Discuss the following folklore statement: "VC statisticians do not care about doing the optimal thing, as long as they can guarantee how well they are doing. Bayesians do not care how well they are doing, as long as they are doing the optimal thing."

5.10 (Overfitting on the Test Set •••) *Consider a learning algorithm which has a free parameter C. Suppose you randomly pick n values $C_1, \ldots, C_n$, and for each n, you train your algorithm. At the end, you pick the value for C which did best on the test set. How would you expect your misjudgment of the true test error to scale with n?*

How does the situation change if the C_i are not picked randomly, but by some adaptive scheme which proposes new values of C by looking at how the previous ones did, and guessing which change of C would likely improve the performance on the test set?

5.11 (Overfitting the Leave-One-Out Error ••) *Explain how it is possible to overfit the leave-one-out error. I.e., consider a learning algorithm that minimizes the leave-one-out error, and argue that it is possible that this algorithm will overfit.*

5.12 (Learning Theory for Differential Equations ○○○) *Can you develop a statistical theory of estimating differential equations from data? How can one suitably restrict the "capacity" of differential equations?*

Note that without restrictions, already ordinary differential equations may exhibit behavior where the capacity is infinite, as exemplified by Rubel's universal differential equation [447]

$$\begin{aligned} 3y'^4y''y''''^2 - 4y'^4y'''^2y'''' + 6y'^3y''^2y'''y'''' + 24y'^2y''^4y'''' \\ -12y'^3y''y'''^3 - 29y'^2y''^3y'''^2 + 12y''^7 &= 0. \end{aligned} \tag{5.69}$$

Rubel proved that given any continuous function $f : \mathbb{R} \to \mathbb{R}$ and any positive continuous function $\varepsilon : \mathbb{R} \to \mathbb{R}^+$, there exists a C^∞ solution y of (5.69) such that $|y(t) - f(t)| < \varepsilon(t)$ for all $t \in \mathbb{R}$. Therefore, all continuous functions are uniform limits of sequences of solutions of (5.69). Moreover, y can be made to agree with f at a countable number of distinct points (t_i). Further references of interest to this problem include [61, 78, 63].

6 Optimization

This chapter provides a self-contained overview of some of the basic tools needed to solve the optimization problems used in kernel methods. In particular, we will cover topics such as minimization of functions in one variable, convex minimization and maximization problems, duality theory, and statistical methods to solve optimization problems approximately.

The focus is noticeably different from the topics covered in works on optimization for Neural Networks, such as Backpropagation [588, 452, 317, 7] and its variants. In these cases, it is necessary to deal with non-convex problems exhibiting a large number of local minima, whereas much of the research on Kernel Methods and Mathematical Programming is focused on problems with global exact solutions. These boundaries may become less clear-cut in the future, but at the present time, methods for the solution of problems with unique optima appear to be sufficient for our purposes.

Overview

In Section 6.1, we explain general properties of convex sets and functions, and how the extreme values of such functions can be found. Next, we discuss practical algorithms to best minimize convex functions on unconstrained domains (Section 6.2). In this context, we will present techniques like interval cutting methods, Newton's method, gradient descent and conjugate gradient descent. Section 6.3 then deals with constrained optimization problems, and gives characterization results for solutions. In this context, Lagrangians, primal and dual optimization problems, and the Karush-Kuhn-Tucker (KKT) conditions are introduced. These concepts set the stage for Section 6.4, which presents an interior point algorithm for the solution of constrained convex optimization problems. In a sense, the final section (Section 6.5) is a departure from the previous topics, since it introduces the notion of randomization into the optimization procedures. The basic idea is that unless the exact solution is required, statistical tools can speed up search maximization by orders of magnitude.

For a general overview, we recommend Section 6.1, and the first parts of Section 6.3, which explain the basic ideas underlying constrained optimization. The latter section is needed to understand the calculations which lead to the dual optimization problems in Support Vector Machines (Chapters 7–9). Section 6.4 is only intended for readers interested in practical implementations of optimization algorithms. In particular, Chapter 10 will require some knowledge of this section. Finally, Section 6.5 describes novel randomization techniques, which are needed in the sparse greedy methods of Section 10.2, 15.3, 16.4, and 18.4.3. Unconstrained

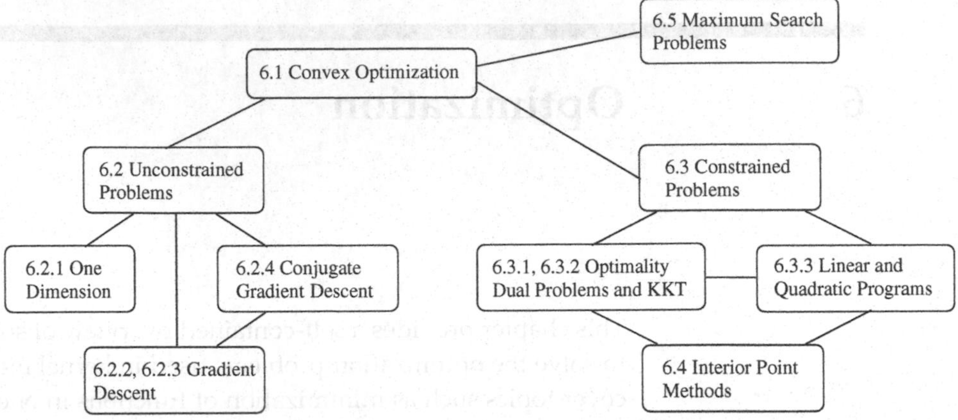

optimization problems (Section 6.2) are less common in this book and will only be required in the gradient descent methods of Section 10.6.1, and the Gaussian Process implementation methods of Section 16.4.

Prerequisites

The present chapter is intended as an introduction to the basic concepts of optimization. It is relatively self-contained, and requires only basic skills in linear algebra and multivariate calculus. Section 6.3 is somewhat more technical, Section 6.4 requires some additional knowledge of numerical analysis, and Section 6.5 assumes some knowledge of probability and statistics.

6.1 Convex Optimization

In the situations considered in this book, learning (or equivalently statistical estimation) implies the minimization of some risk functional such as $R_{\text{emp}}[f]$ or $R_{\text{reg}}[f]$ (cf. Chapter 4). While minimizing an arbitrary function on a (possibly not even compact) set of arguments can be a difficult task, and will most likely exhibit many local minima, minimization of a convex objective function on a convex set exhibits exactly one *global* minimum. We now prove this property.

Definition 6.1 (Convex Set) *A set X in a vector space is called convex if for any $x, x' \in X$ and any $\lambda \in [0,1]$, we have*

$$\lambda x + (1-\lambda)x' \in X. \tag{6.1}$$

Definition and Construction of Convex Sets and Functions

Definition 6.2 (Convex Function) *A function f defined on a set X (note that X need not be convex itself) is called convex if, for any $x, x' \in X$ and any $\lambda \in [0,1]$ such that $\lambda x + (1-\lambda)x' \in X$, we have*

$$f(\lambda x + (1-\lambda)x') \leq \lambda f(x) + (1-\lambda) f(x'). \tag{6.2}$$

A function f is called strictly *convex if for $x \neq x'$ and $\lambda \in (0,1)$ (6.2) is a strict inequality.*

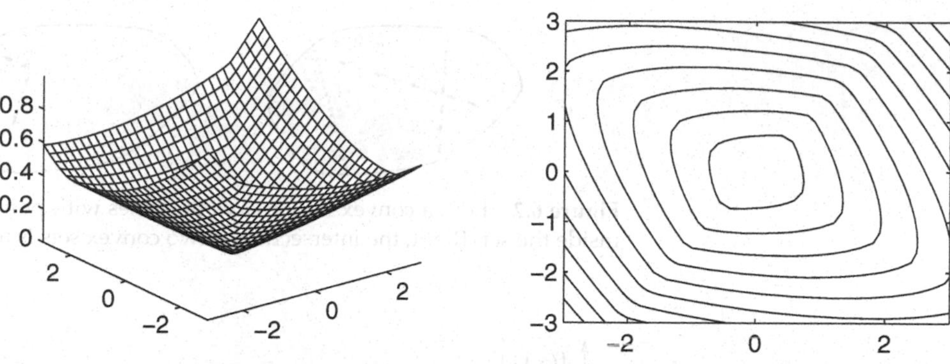

Figure 6.1 Left: Convex Function in two variables. Right: the corresponding convex level sets $\{x|f(x) \leq c\}$, for different values of c.

There exist several ways to define convex sets. A convenient method is to define them via *below sets* of convex functions, such as the sets for which $f(x) \leq c$, for instance.

Lemma 6.3 (Convex Sets as Below-Sets) *Denote by $f : \mathfrak{X} \to \mathbb{R}$ a convex function on a convex set $\mathfrak{X}$. Then the set*

$$X := \{x|x \in \mathfrak{X} \text{ and } f(x) \leq c\}, \text{ for all } c \in \mathbb{R}, \tag{6.3}$$

is convex.

Proof We must show condition (6.1). For any $x, x' \in \mathfrak{X}$, we have $f(x), f(x') \leq c$. Moreover, since f is convex, we also have

$$f(\lambda x + (1-\lambda)x') \leq \lambda f(x) + (1-\lambda) f(x') \leq c \text{ for all } \lambda \in [0,1]. \tag{6.4}$$

Hence, for all $\lambda \in [0,1]$, we have $(\lambda x + (1-\lambda)x') \in X$, which proves the claim. Figure 6.1 depicts this situation graphically. ■

Intersections

Lemma 6.4 (Intersection of Convex Sets) *Denote by $X, X' \subset \mathfrak{X}$ two convex sets. Then $X \cap X'$ is also a convex set.*

Proof Given any $x, x' \in X \cap X'$, then for any $\lambda \in [0,1]$, the point $x_\lambda := \lambda x + (1-\lambda)x'$ satisfies $x_\lambda \in X$ and $x_\lambda \in X'$, hence also $x_\lambda \in X \cap X'$. ■

See also Figure 6.2. Now we have the tools to prove the central theorem of this section.

Theorem 6.5 (Minima on Convex Sets) *If the convex function $f : \mathfrak{X} \to \mathbb{R}$ has a minimum on a convex set $X \subset \mathfrak{X}$, then its arguments $x \in \mathfrak{X}$, for which the minimum value is attained, form a convex set. Moreover, if f is strictly convex, then this set will contain only one element.*

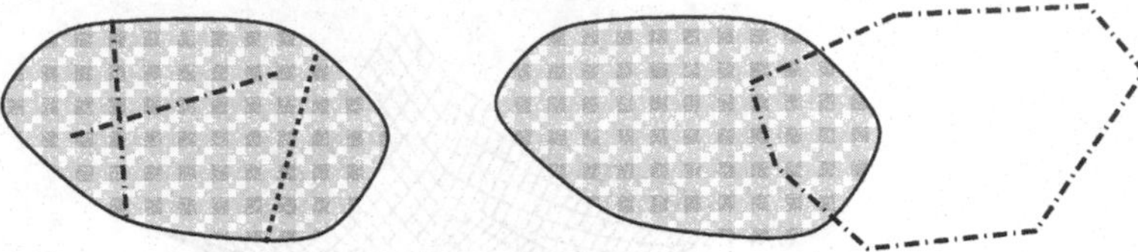

Figure 6.2 Left: a convex set; observe that lines with points in the set are fully contained inside the set. Right: the intersection of two convex sets is also a convex set.

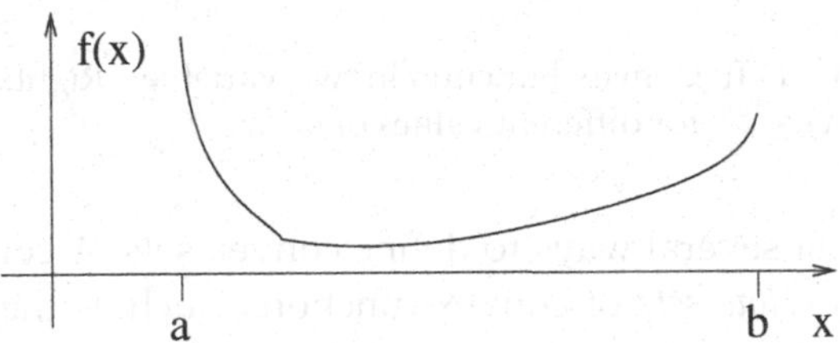

Figure 6.3 Note that the maximum of a convex function is obtained at the ends of the interval $[a, b]$.

Proof Denote by c the minimum of f on X. Then the set $X_m := \{x | x \in \mathcal{X} \text{ and } f(x) \leq c\}$ is clearly convex. In addition, $X_m \cap X$ is also convex, and $f(x) = c$ for all $x \in X_m \cap X$ (otherwise c would not be the minimum).

If f is strictly convex, then for any $x, x' \in X$, and in particular for any $x, x' \in X \cap X_m$, we have (for $x \neq x'$ and all $\lambda \in (0, 1)$),

$$f(\lambda x + (1 - \lambda)x') < \lambda f(x) + (1 - \lambda)f(x') = \lambda c + (1 - \lambda)c = c. \tag{6.5}$$

This contradicts the assumption that $X_m \cap X$ contains more then one element.

■

Global Minima

A simple application of this theorem is in constrained convex minimization. Recall that the notation $[n]$, used below, is a shorthand for $\{1, \ldots, n\}$.

Corollary 6.6 (Constrained Convex Minimization) *Given the set of convex functions $f, c_1, \ldots, c_n$ on the convex set $\mathcal{X}$, the problem*

$$\begin{aligned} &\underset{x}{\text{minimize}} && f(x), \\ &\textit{subject to} && c_i(x) \leq 0 \textit{ for all } i \in [n], \end{aligned} \tag{6.6}$$

has as its solution a convex set, if a solution exists. This solution is unique if f is strictly convex.

Many problems in Mathematical Programming or Support Vector Machines can be cast into this formulation. This means either that they all have unique solutions (if f is strictly convex), or that all solutions are equally good and form a convex set (if f is merely convex).

We might ask what can be said about convex *maximization*. Let us analyze a simple case first: convex maximization on an interval.

Lemma 6.7 (Convex Maximization on an Interval) *Denote by f a convex function on $[a, b] \in \mathbb{R}$. Then the problem of maximizing f on $[a, b]$ has $f(a)$ and $f(b)$ as solutions.*

Maxima on Extreme Points

Proof Any $x \in [a, b]$ can be written as $\frac{b-x}{b-a}a + (1 - \frac{b-x}{b-a})\, b$, and hence

$$f(x) \leq \frac{b-x}{b-a} f(a) + \left(1 - \frac{b-x}{b-a}\right) f(b) \leq \max(f(a), f(b)). \tag{6.7}$$

Therefore the maximum of f on $[a, b]$ is obtained on one of the points a, b. ■

We will next show that the problem of convex *maximization* on a convex set is typically a hard problem, in the sense that the maximum can only be found at one of the extreme points of the constraining set. We must first introduce the notion of vertices of a set.

Definition 6.8 (Vertex of a Set) *A point $x \in X$ is a vertex of X if, for all $x' \in X$ with $x' \neq x$, and for all $\lambda > 1$, the point $\lambda x + (1 - \lambda)x' \notin X$.*

This definition implies, for instance, that in the case of X being an ℓ_2 ball, the vertices of X make up its surface. In the case of an ℓ_∞ ball, we have 2^n vertices in n dimensions, and for an ℓ_1 ball, we have only $2n$ of them. These differences will guide us in the choice of admissible sets of parameters for optimization problems (see, e.g., Section 14.4). In particular, there exists a connection between suprema on sets and their convex hulls. To state this link, however, we need to define the latter.

Definition 6.9 (Convex Hull) *Denote by X a set in a vector space. Then the convex hull $\operatorname{co} X$ is defined as*

$$\operatorname{co} X := \left\{ \bar{x} \,\middle|\, \bar{x} = \sum_{i=1}^{n} \alpha_i x_i \text{ where } n \in \mathbb{N}, \alpha_i \geq 0 \text{ and } \sum_{i=1}^{n} \alpha_i = 1 \right\}. \tag{6.8}$$

Theorem 6.10 (Suprema on Sets and their Convex Hulls) *Denote by X a set and by $\operatorname{co} X$ its convex hull. Then for a convex function f*

$$\sup\{f(x) | x \in X\} = \sup\{f(x) | x \in \operatorname{co} X\}. \tag{6.9}$$

Evaluating Convex Sets on Extreme Points

Proof Recall that the below set of convex functions is convex (Lemma 6.3), and that the below set of f with respect to $c = \sup\{f(x) | x \in X\}$ is by definition a superset of X. Moreover, due to its convexity, it is also a superset of $\operatorname{co} X$. ■

This theorem can be used to replace search operations over sets X by subsets $X' \subset X$, which are considerably smaller, if the convex hull of the latter generates X. In particular, the vertices of convex sets are sufficient to reconstruct the whole set.

Theorem 6.11 (Vertices) *A compact convex set is the convex hull of its vertices.*

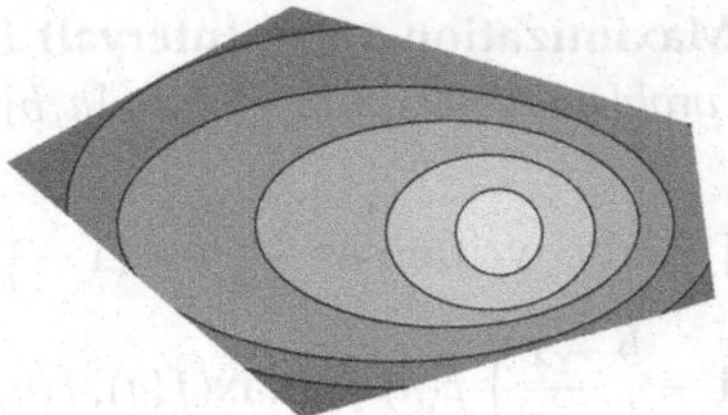

Figure 6.4 A convex function on a convex polyhedral set. Note that the minimum of this function is unique, and that the maximum can be found at one of the vertices of the constraining domain.

Reconstructing Convex Sets from Vertices

The proof is slightly technical, and not central to the understanding of kernel methods. See Rockafellar [435, Chapter 18] for details, along with further theorems on convex functions. We now proceed to the second key theorem in this section.

Theorem 6.12 (Maxima of Convex Functions on Convex Compact Sets) *Denote by X a compact convex set in $\mathcal{X}$, by $|X$ the vertices of X, and by f a convex function on X. Then*

$$\sup\{f(x)|x \in X\} = \sup\{f(x)|x \in |X\}. \tag{6.10}$$

Proof Application of Theorem 6.10 and Theorem 6.11 proves the claim, since under the assumptions made on X, we have $X = \text{co}(|X)$. Figure 6.4 depicts the situation graphically. ■

6.2 Unconstrained Problems

After the characterization and uniqueness results (Theorem 6.5, Corollary 6.6, and Lemma 6.7) of the previous section, we will now study numerical techniques to obtain minima (or maxima) of convex optimization problems. While the choice of algorithms is motivated by applicability to kernel methods, the presentation here is not problem specific. For details on implementation, and descriptions of applications to learning problems, see Chapter 10.

6.2.1 Functions of One Variable

We begin with the easiest case, in which f depends on only one variable. Some of the concepts explained here, such as the interval cutting algorithm and Newton's method, can be extended to the multivariate setting (see Problem 6.5). For the sake of simplicity, however, we limit ourselves to the univariate case.

Assume we want to minimize $f : \mathbb{R} \to \mathbb{R}$ on the interval $[a, b] \subset \mathbb{R}$. If we cannot make any further assumptions regarding f, then this problem, as simple as it may seem, cannot be solved numerically.

Continuous Differentiable Functions

If f is *differentiable*, the problem can be reduced to finding $f'(x) = 0$ (see Problem 6.4 for the general case). If in addition to the previous assumptions, f is convex, then f' is nondecreasing, and we can find a fast, simple algorithm (Algorithm

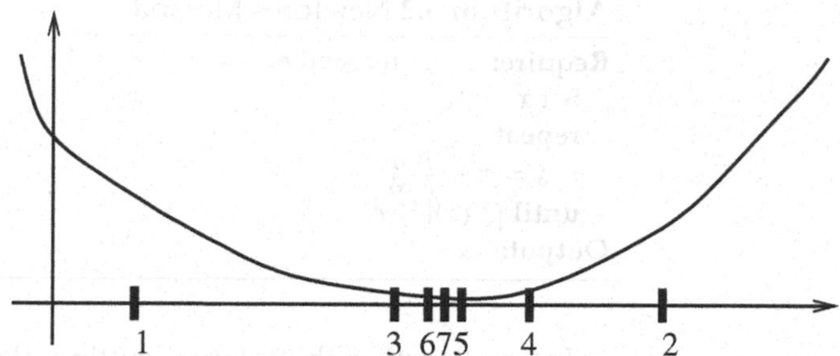

Figure 6.5 Interval Cutting Algorithm. The selection of points is ordered according to the numbers beneath (points 1 and 2 are the initial endpoints of the interval).

Algorithm 6.1 Interval Cutting

Require: a, b, Precision ϵ
  Set $A = a, B = b$
  repeat
    if $f'\left(\frac{A+B}{2}\right) > 0$ **then**
      $B = \frac{A+B}{2}$
    else
      $A = \frac{A+B}{2}$
    end if
  until $(B - A)\min(|f'(A)|, |f'(B)|) \leq \epsilon$
Output: $x = \frac{A+B}{2}$

Interval Cutting

6.1) to solve our problem (see Figure 6.5).

This technique works by halving the size of the interval that contains the minimum x^* of f, since it is always guaranteed by the selection criteria for B and A that $x^* \in [A, B]$. We use the following Taylor series expansion to determine the stopping criterion.

Theorem 6.13 (Taylor Series) *Denote by $f : \mathbb{R} \to \mathbb{R}$ a function that is d times differentiable. Then for any $x, x' \in \mathbb{R}$, there exists a ξ with $|\xi| \leq |x - x'|$, such that*

$$f(x') = \sum_{i=0}^{d-1} \frac{1}{i!} f^{(i)}(x)(x' - x)^i + \frac{\xi^d}{d!} f^{(d)}(x + \xi). \tag{6.11}$$

Now we may apply (6.11) to the stopping criterion of Algorithm 6.1. We denote by x^* the minimum of $f(x)$. Expanding f around $f(x^*)$, we obtain for some $\xi_A \in [A - x^*, 0]$ that $f(A) = f(x^*) + \xi_A f'(x^* + \xi_A)$, and therefore,

$$|f(A) - f(x^*)| = |\xi_A||f'(x^* + \xi_A)| \leq (B - A)|f'(A)|.$$

Proof of Linear Convergence

Taking the minimum over $\{A, B\}$ shows that Algorithm 6.1 stops once f is ϵ-close to its minimal value. The convergence of the algorithm is *linear* with constant 0.5, since the intervals $[A, B]$ for possible x^* are halved at each iteration.

Algorithm 6.2 Newton's Method

Require: x_0, Precision ϵ
Set $x = x_0$
repeat
$x = x - \frac{f'(x)}{f''(x)}$
until $|f'(x)| \leq \epsilon$
Output: x

In constructing the interval cutting algorithm, we in fact wasted most of the information obtained in evaluating f' at each point, by only making use of the sign of f. In particular, we could fit a parabola to f and thereby obtain a method that converges more rapidly. If we are only allowed to use f and f', this leads to the *Method of False Position* (see [334] or Problem 6.3).

Moreover, if we may compute the second derivative as well, we can use (6.11) to obtain a quadratic approximation of f and use the latter to find the minimum of f. This is commonly referred to as *Newton's method* (see Section 16.4.1 for a practical application of the latter to classification problems). We expand $f(x)$ around x_0;

Newton's Method

$$f(x) \approx f(x_0) + (x - x_0)f'(x_0) + \frac{(x - x_0)^2}{2} f''(x_0). \tag{6.12}$$

Minimization of the expansion (6.12) yields

$$x = x_0 - \frac{f'(x_0)}{f''(x_0)}. \tag{6.13}$$

Hence, we hope that if the approximation (6.12) is good, we will obtain an algorithm with fast convergence (Algorithm 6.2). Let us analyze the situation in more detail. For convenience, we state the result in terms of $g := f'$, since finding a zero of g is equivalent to finding a minimum of f.

Theorem 6.14 (Convergence of Newton Method) *Let $g : \mathbb{R} \to \mathbb{R}$ be a twice continuously differentiable function, and denote by $x^* \in \mathbb{R}$ a point with $g'(x^*) \neq 0$ and $g(x^*) = 0$. Then, provided x_0 is sufficiently close to x^*, the sequence generated by (6.13) will converge to x^* at least quadratically.*

Quadratic Convergence

Proof For convenience, denote by x_n the value of x at the nth iteration. As before, we apply Theorem 6.13. We now expand $g(x^*)$ around x_n. For some $\xi \in [0, x^* - x_n]$, we have

$$g(x_n) = g(x_n) - g(x^*) = g(x_n) - \left[g(x_n) + g'(x_n)(x^* - x_n) + \frac{\xi^2}{2} g''(x_n)\right], \tag{6.14}$$

and therefore by substituting (6.14) into (6.13),

$$x_{n+1} - x^* = x_n - x^* - \frac{g(x_n)}{g'(x_n)} = \xi^2 \frac{g''(x_n)}{2g'(x_n)}. \tag{6.15}$$

Since by construction $|\xi| \leq |x_n - x^*|$, we obtain a quadratically convergent algorithm in $|x_n - x^*|$, provided that $\left|(x_n - x^*)\frac{g''(x_n)}{2g'(x_n)}\right| < 1$. ■

Region of Convergence

In other words, if the Newton method converges, it converges more rapidly than interval cutting or similar methods. We cannot guarantee beforehand that we are really in the region of convergence of the algorithm. In practice, if we apply the Newton method and find that it converges, we know that the solution has converged to the minimizer of f. For more information on optimization algorithms for unconstrained problems see [173, 530, 334, 15, 159, 45].

Line Search

In some cases we will not know an upper bound on the size of the interval to be analyzed for the presence of minima. In this situation we may, for instance, start with an initial guess of an interval, and if no minimum can be found strictly *inside* the interval, enlarge it, say by doubling its size. See [334] for more information on this matter. Let us now proceed to a technique which is quite popular (albeit not always preferable) in machine learning.

6.2.2 Functions of Several Variables: Gradient Descent

Gradient descent is one of the simplest optimization techniques to implement for minimizing functions of the form $f : \mathcal{X} \to \mathbb{R}$, where $\mathcal{X}$ may be $\mathbb{R}^N$, or indeed any set on which a gradient may be defined and evaluated. In order to avoid further complications we assume that the gradient $f'(x)$ exists and that we are able to compute it.

Direction of Steepest Descent

The basic idea is as follows: given a location x_n at iteration n, compute the gradient $g_n := f'(x_n)$, and update

$$x_{n+1} = x_n - \gamma g_n \tag{6.16}$$

such that the decrease in f is maximal over all $\gamma > 0$. For the final step, one of the algorithms from Section 6.2.1 can be used. It is straightforward to show that $f(x_n)$ is a monotonically decreasing series, since at each step the line search updates x_{n+1} in such a way that $f(x_{n+1}) < f(x_n)$. Such a value of γ must exist, since (again by Theorem 6.13) we may expand $f(x_n + \gamma g_n)$ in terms of γ around x_n, to obtain[1]

$$f(x_n - \gamma g_n) = f(x_n) - \gamma \|g_n\|^2 + O(\gamma^2). \tag{6.17}$$

As usual $\|\cdot\|$ is the Euclidean norm. For small γ the linear contribution in the Taylor expansion will be dominant, hence for some $\gamma > 0$ we have $f(x_n - \gamma g_n) < f(x_n)$. It can be shown [334] that after a (possibly infinite) number of steps, gradient descent (see Algorithm 6.3) will converge.

Problems of Convergence

In spite of this, the performance of gradient descent is far from optimal. Depending on the shape of the landscape of values of f, gradient descent may take a long time to converge. Figure 6.6 shows two examples of possible convergence behavior of the gradient descent algorithm.

1. To see that Theorem 6.13 applies in (6.17), note that $f(x_n + \gamma g_n)$ is a mapping $\mathbb{R} \to \mathbb{R}$ when viewed as a function of γ.

Algorithm 6.3 Gradient Descent

Require: x_0, Precision ϵ
  $n = 0$
  repeat
    Compute $g = f'(x_n)$
    Perform line search on $f(x_n - \gamma g)$ for optimal γ.
    $x_{n+1} = x_n - \gamma g$
    $n = n + 1$
  until $\|f'(x_n)\| \leq \epsilon$
Output: x_n

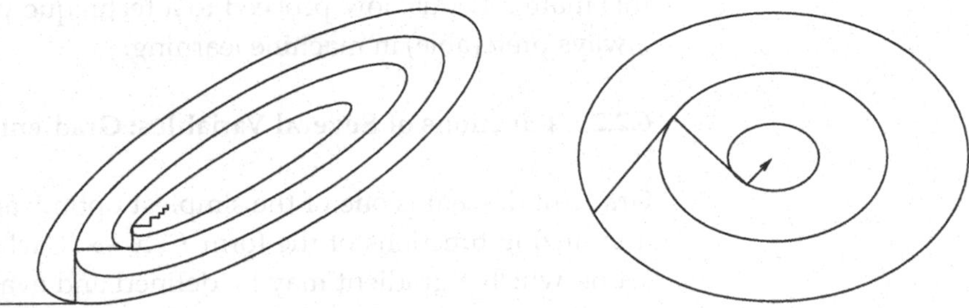

Figure 6.6 Left: Gradient descent takes a long time to converge, since the landscape of values of f forms a long and narrow valley, causing the algorithm to zig-zag along the walls of the valley. Right: due to the homogeneous structure of the minimum, the algorithm converges after very few iterations. Note that in both cases, the next direction of descent is *orthogonal* to the previous one, since line search provides the optimal step length.

6.2.3 Convergence Properties of Gradient Descent

Let us analyze the convergence properties of Algorithm 6.3 in more detail. To keep matters simple, we assume that f is a quadratic function, i.e.

$$f(x) = \frac{1}{2}(x - x^*)^\top K(x - x^*) + c_0, \tag{6.18}$$

where K is a positive definite symmetric matrix (cf. Definition 2.4) and c_0 is constant.[2] This is clearly a convex function with minimum at x^*, and $f(x^*) = c_0$. The gradient of f is given by

$$g := f'(x) = K(x - x^*). \tag{6.19}$$

To find the update of the steepest descent we have to minimize

$$f(x - \gamma g) = \frac{1}{2}(x - \gamma g - x^*)K(x - \gamma g - x^*) = \frac{1}{2}\gamma^2 g^\top K g - \gamma g^\top g. \tag{6.20}$$

2. Note that we may rewrite (up to a constant) any convex quadratic function $f(x) = x^\top Kx + c^\top x + d$ in the form (6.18), simply by expanding f around its minimum value x^*.

By minimizing (6.20) for γ, the update of steepest descent is given explicitly by

$$x_{n+1} = x_n - \frac{g^\top g}{g^\top K g} g. \tag{6.21}$$

Improvement per Step

Substituting (6.21) into (6.18) and subtracting the terms $f(x_n)$ and $f(x_{n+1})$ yields the following improvement after an update step

$$\begin{aligned} f(x_n) - f(x_{n+1}) &= (x_n - x^*)^\top K \frac{g^\top g}{g^\top K g} g - \frac{1}{2}\left(\frac{g^\top g}{g^\top K g}\right)^2 g^\top K g \\ &= \frac{1}{2}\frac{(g^\top g)^2}{g^\top K g} = f(x_n)\left[\frac{(g^\top g)^2}{(g^\top K g)(g^\top K^{-1} g)}\right]. \end{aligned} \tag{6.22}$$

Thus the relative improvement per iteration depends on the value of $t(g) := \frac{(g^\top g)^2}{(g^\top K g)(g^\top K^{-1} g)}$. In order to give performance guarantees we have to find a lower bound for $t(g)$. To this end we introduce the *condition* of a matrix.

Definition 6.15 (Condition of a Matrix) *Denote by K a matrix and by $\lambda_{\max}$ and $\lambda_{\min}$ its largest and smallest singular values (or eigenvalues if they exist) respectively. The condition of a matrix is defined as*

$$\operatorname{cond} K := \frac{\lambda_{\max}}{\lambda_{\min}}. \tag{6.23}$$

Clearly, as cond K decreases, different directions are treated in a more homogeneous manner by $x^\top K x$. In particular, note that smaller cond K correspond to less elliptic contours in Figure 6.6. Kantorovich proved the following inequality which allows us to connect the condition number with the convergence behavior of gradient descent algorithms.

Theorem 6.16 (Kantorovich Inequality [278]) *Denote by $K \in \mathbb{R}^{m \times m}$ (typically the kernel matrix) a strictly positive definite symmetric matrix with largest and smallest eigenvalues $\lambda_{\max}$ and $\lambda_{\min}$. Then the following inequality holds for any $g \in \mathbb{R}^m$:*

Lower Bound for Improvement

$$\frac{(g^\top g)^2}{(g^\top K g)(g^\top K^{-1} g)} \geq \frac{4\lambda_{\min}\lambda_{\max}}{(\lambda_{\min} + \lambda_{\max})^2} \geq \frac{1}{\operatorname{cond} K}. \tag{6.24}$$

We typically denote by g the gradient of f. The second inequality follows immediately from Definition 6.15; the proof of the first inequality is more technical, and is not essential to the understanding of the situation. See Problem 6.7 and [278, 334] for more detail.

A brief calculation gives us the correct order of magnitude. Note that for any x, the quadratic term $x^\top K x$ is bounded from above by $\lambda_{\max}\|x\|^2$, and likewise $x^\top K^{-1} x \leq \lambda_{\min}^{-1}\|x\|^2$. Hence we bound the relative improvement $t(g)$ (as defined below (6.22)) by $1/(\operatorname{cond} K)$ which is almost as good as the second term in (6.24) (the latter can be up to a factor of 4 better for $\lambda_{\min} \ll \lambda_{\max}$).

This means that gradient descent methods perform poorly if some of the eigenvalues of K are very small in comparison with the largest eigenvalue, as is usually the case with matrices generated by positive definite kernels (and as sometimes desired for learning theoretical reasons); see Chapter 4 for details. This is one of the reasons why many gradient descent algorithms for training Support Vector Machines, such as the Kernel AdaTron [183, 12] or AdaLine [185], exhibit poor convergence. Section 10.6.1 deals with these issues, and sets up the gradient descent directions both in the Reproducing Kernel Hilbert Space $\mathcal{H}$ and in coefficient space $\mathbb{R}^m$.

6.2.4 Functions of Several Variables: Conjugate Gradient Descent

Let us now look at methods that are better suited to minimizing convex functions. Again, we start with quadratic forms. The key problem with gradient descent is that the quotient between the smallest and the largest eigenvalue can be very large, which leads to slow convergence. Hence, one possible technique is to *rescale* $\mathcal{X}$ by some matrix M such that the condition of $K \in \mathbb{R}^{m \times m}$ in this rescaled space, which is to say the condition of $M^\top KM$, is much closer to 1 (in numerical analysis this is often referred to as *preconditioning* [247, 423, 530]). In addition, we would like to focus first on the largest eigenvectors of K.

A key tool is the concept of *conjugate directions*. The basic idea is that rather than using the metric of the normal dot product $x^\top x' = x^\top \mathbf{1} x'$ ($\mathbf{1}$ is the unit matrix) we use the metric imposed by K, i.e. $x^\top Kx'$, to guide our algorithm, and we introduce an equivalent notion of orthogonality with respect to the new metric.

Definition 6.17 (Conjugate Directions) *Given a symmetric matrix $K \in \mathbb{R}^{m \times m}$, any two vectors $v, v' \in \mathbb{R}^m$ are called K-orthogonal if $v^\top Kv' = 0$.*

Likewise, we can introduce notions of a basis and of linear independence with respect to K. The following theorem establishes the necessary identities.

Theorem 6.18 (Orthogonal Decompositions in K) *Denote by $K \in \mathbb{R}^{m \times m}$ a strictly positive definite symmetric matrix and by $v_1, \ldots, v_m$ a set of mutually K-orthogonal and nonzero vectors. Then the following properties hold:*

(i) The vectors $v_1, \ldots, v_m$ form a basis.

(ii) Any $x \in \mathbb{R}^m$ can be expanded in terms of v_i by

$$x = \sum_{i=1}^{m} v_i \frac{v_i^\top Kx}{v_i^\top Kv_i}. \tag{6.25}$$

In particular, for any $y = Kx$, we can find x by

$$x = \sum_{i=1}^{m} v_i \frac{v_i^\top y}{v_i^\top Kv_i}. \tag{6.26}$$

Linear Independence

Proof (i) Since we have m vectors in $\mathbb{R}^m$, all we have to show is that the vectors v_i are linearly independent. Assume that there exist some $\alpha_i \in \mathbb{R}$ such that $\sum_{i=1}^m \alpha_i v_i =$

0. Then due to K-orthogonality, we have

$$0 = v_j^\top K \left[\sum_{i=1}^{m} \alpha_i v_i\right] = \sum_{i=1}^{m} \alpha_i v_j^\top K v_i = \alpha_j v_j^\top K v_j \text{ for all } j. \tag{6.27}$$

Hence $\alpha_j = 0$ for all j. This means that all v_j are linearly independent.

(ii) The vectors $\{v_1, \ldots, v_m\}$ form a basis. Therefore we may expand any $x \in \mathbb{R}^m$ as a linear combination of v_j, i.e. $x = \sum_{i=1}^m \alpha_i v_i$. Consequently we can expand $v_j^\top K x$ in terms of $v_j^\top K v_i$, and we obtain

$$v_j^\top K x = v_j^\top K \left[\sum_{i=1}^{m} \alpha_i v_i\right] = \alpha_j v_j^\top K v_j. \tag{6.28}$$

Basis Expansion

Solving for α_j proves the claim.

(iii) Let $y = Kx$. Since the vectors v_i form a basis, we can expand x in terms of α_i. Substituting this definition into (6.28) proves (6.26). ■

The practical consequence of this theorem is that, provided we know a set of K-orthogonal vectors v_i, we can solve the linear equation $y = Kx$ via (6.26). Furthermore, we can also use it to minimize quadratic functions of the form $f(x) = \frac{1}{2}x^\top K x - c^\top x$. The following theorem tells us how.

Theorem 6.19 (Deflation Method) *Denote by $v_1, \ldots, v_m$ a set of mutually K-orthogonal vectors for a strictly positive definite symmetric matrix $K \in \mathbb{R}^{m\times m}$. Then for any $x_0 \in \mathbb{R}^m$ the following method finds x_i that minimize $f(x) = \frac{1}{2}x^\top K x - c^\top x$ in the linear manifold $\mathfrak{X}_i := x_0 + \operatorname{span}\{v_1, \ldots, v_i\}$.*

Optimality in Linear Space

$$x_i := x_{i-1} - v_i \frac{g_{i-1}^\top v_i}{v_i^\top K v_i} \text{ where } g_{i-1} = f'(x_{i-1}) \text{ for all } i > 0. \tag{6.29}$$

Proof We use induction. For $i = 0$ the statement is trivial, since the linear manifold consists of only one point.

Assume that the statement holds for i. Since f is convex, we only need prove that the gradient of $f(x_i)$ is orthogonal to $\operatorname{span}\{v_1, \ldots, v_i\}$. In that case no further improvement can be gained on the linear manifold $\mathfrak{X}_i$. It suffices to show that for all $j \leq i+1$,

$$0 = v_j^\top g_i. \tag{6.30}$$

Gradient Descent in Rescaled Space

Additionally, we may expand x_{i+1} to obtain

$$v_j^\top g_i = v_j^\top \left[Kx_{i-1} - c - Kv_i \frac{g_{i-1}^\top v_i}{v_i^\top K v_i}\right] = v_j^\top g_{i-1} - (g_{i-1}^\top v_i)\frac{v_j^\top K v_i}{v_i^\top K v_i}. \tag{6.31}$$

For $j = i$ both terms cancel out. For $j < i$ both terms vanish due to the induction assumption. Since the vectors v_j form a basis $\mathfrak{X}_m = \mathbb{R}^m$, x_m is a minimizer of f. ■

In a nutshell, Theorem 6.19 already contains the Conjugate Gradient descent al-

Algorithm 6.4 Conjugate Gradient Descent

Require: x_0
Set $i = 0$
$g_0 = f'(x_0)$
$v_0 = g_0$
repeat
$x_{i+1} = x_i + \alpha_i v_i$ where $\alpha_i = -\frac{g_i^\top v_i}{v_i^\top K v_i}$
$g_{i+1} = f'(x_{i+1})$
$v_{i+1} = -g_{i+1} + \beta_i v_i$ where $\beta_i = \frac{g_{i+1}^\top K v_i}{v_i^\top K v_i}$.
$i = i + 1$
until $g_i = 0$
Output: x_i

gorithm: in each step we perform gradient descent with respect to one of the K-orthogonal vectors v_i, which means that after n steps we will reach the minimum. We still lack a method to obtain such a K-orthogonal basis of vectors v_i. It turns out that we can get the latter directly from the gradients g_i. Algorithm 6.4 describes the procedure.

All we have to do is prove that Algorithm 6.4 actually does what it is required to do, namely generate a K-orthogonal set of vectors v_i, and perform deflation in the latter. To achieve this, the v_i are obtained by an orthogonalization procedure akin to Gram-Schmidt orthogonalization.

Theorem 6.20 (Conjugate Gradient) *Assume we are given a quadratic convex function $f(x) = \frac{1}{2} x^\top K x - c^\top x$, to which we apply conjugate gradient descent for minimization purposes. Then algorithm 6.4 is a deflation method, and unless $g_i = 0$, we have for every $0 \leq i \leq m$,*

(i) $\operatorname{span}\{g_0, \ldots, g_i\} = \operatorname{span}\{v_0, \ldots, v_i\} = \operatorname{span}\{g_0, Kg_0, \ldots, K^i g_0\}$.

(ii) The vectors v_i are K-orthogonal.

(iii) The equations in Algorithm 6.4 for α_i and β_i can be replaced by $\alpha_i = \frac{g_i^\top g_i}{v_i^\top K v_i}$ and $\beta_i = \frac{g_{i+1}^\top g_{i+1}}{g_i^\top g_i}$.

(iv) After i steps, x_i is the solution in the manifold $x_0 + \operatorname{span}\{g_0, Kg_0, \ldots, K^{i-1} g_0\}$.

Proof **(i) and (ii)** We use induction. For $i = 0$ the statements trivially hold since $v_0 = g_0$. For i note that by construction (see Algorithm 6.4) $g_{i+1} = Kx_{i+1} - c = g_i + \alpha_i K v_i$, hence $\operatorname{span}\{g_0, \ldots, g_{i+1}\} = \operatorname{span}\{g_0, Kg_0, \ldots, K^{i+1} g_0\}$. Since $v_{i+1} = -g_{i+1} + \beta_i v_i$ the same statement holds for $\operatorname{span}\{v_0, \ldots, v_{i+1}\}$. Moreover, the vectors g_i are linearly independent or 0 due to Theorem 6.19.
Finally $v_j^\top K v_{i+1} = -v_j^\top K g_{i+1} + \beta_i v_j^\top K v_i = 0$, since for $j = i$ both terms cancel out, and for $j < i$ both terms individually vanish (due to Theorem 6.19 and (i)).

(iii) We have $-g_i^\top v_i = g_i^\top g_i - \beta_{i-1} g_i^\top v_{i-1} = g_i^\top g_i$, since the second term vanishes due to Theorem 6.19. This proves the result for α_i.

Table 6.1 Non-quadratic modifications of conjugate gradient descent.

Generic Method	Compute Hessian $K_i := f''(x_i)$ and update α_i, β_i with $\alpha_i = -\frac{g_i^\top v_i}{v_i^\top K_i v_i}$ $\beta_i = \frac{g_{i+1}^\top K_i v_i}{v_i^\top K_i v_i}$ This requires calculation of the Hessian at each iteration.
Fletcher-Reeves [173]	Find α_i via a line search and use Theorem 6.20 (iii) for β_i $\alpha_i = \operatorname{argmin}_\alpha f(x_i + \alpha v_i)$ $\beta_i = \frac{g_{i+1}^\top g_{i+1}}{g_i^\top g_i}$
Polak-Ribiere [414]	Find α_i via a line search $\alpha_i = \operatorname{argmin}_\alpha f(x_i + \alpha v_i)$ $\beta_i = \frac{(g_{i+1} - g_i)^\top g_{i+1}}{g_i^\top g_i}$ Experimentally, Polak-Ribiere tends to be better than Fletcher-Reeves.

For β_i note that $g_{i+1}^\top K v_i = \alpha_i^{-1} g_{i+1}^\top (g_{i+1} - g_i) = \alpha_i^{-1} g_{i+1}^\top g_{i+1}$. Substitution of the value of α_i proves the claim.

(iv) Again, we use induction. At step $i = 1$ we compute the solution within the space spanned by g_0. ■

We conclude this section with some remarks on the optimality of conjugate gradient descent algorithms, and how they can be extended to arbitrary convex functions.

Space of Largest Eigenvalues

Due to Theorems 6.19 and 6.20, we can see that after i iterations, the conjugate gradient descent algorithm finds a solution on the linear manifold $x_0 + \operatorname{span}\{g_0, Kg_0, \ldots, K^{i-1}g_0\}$. This means that the solutions will be mostly aligned with the largest eigenvalues of K, since after multiple application of K to any arbitrary vector g_0, the largest eigenvectors dominate. Nonetheless, the algorithm here is significantly cheaper than computing the eigenvalues of K, and subsequently minimizing f in the subspace corresponding to the largest eigenvalues. For more detail see [334]

Nonlinear Extensions

In the case of general convex functions, the assumptions of Theorem 6.20 are no longer satisfied. In spite of this, conjugate gradient descent has proven to be effective even in these situations. Additionally, we have to account for some modifications. Basically, the update rules for g_i and v_i remain unchanged but the parameters α_i and β_i are computed differently. Table 6.1 gives an overview of different methods. See [173, 334, 530, 414] for details.

6.2.5 Predictor Corrector Methods

As we go to higher order Taylor expansions of the function f to be minimized (or set to zero), the corresponding numerical methods become increasingly complicated to implement, and require an ever increasing number of parameters to be estimated or computed. For instance, a quadratic expansion of a multivariate function $f : \mathbb{R}^m \to \mathbb{R}$ requires $m \times m$ terms for the quadratic part (the Hessian), whereas the linear part (the gradient) can be obtained by computing m terms. Since the quadratic expansion is only an approximation for most non-quadratic functions, this is wasteful (for interior point programs, see Section 6.4). We might instead be able to achieve roughly the same goal without computing the quadratic term explicitly, or more generally, obtain the performance of higher order methods without actually implementing them.

Increasing the Order

This can in fact be achieved using predictor-corrector methods. These work by computing a tentative update $x_i \to x_{i+1}^{\text{pred}}$ (predictor step), then using x_{i+1}^{pred} to account for higher order changes in the objective function, and finally obtaining a *corrected* value x_{i+1}^{corr} based on these changes. A simple example illustrates the method. Assume we want to find the solution to the equation

Predictor Corrector Methods for Quadratic Equations

$$f(x) = 0 \text{ where } f(x) = f_0 + ax + \frac{1}{2}bx^2. \tag{6.32}$$

We assume $a, b, f_0, x \in \mathbb{R}$. Exact solution of (6.32) requires taking a square root. Let us see whether we can find an approximate method that avoids this (in general b will be an $m \times m$ matrix, so this is a worthwhile goal). The predictor corrector approach works as follows: first solve

$$f_0 + ax = 0 \text{ and hence } x^{\text{pred}} = -\frac{f_0}{a}. \tag{6.33}$$

Second, substitute x^{pred} into the nonlinear parts of (6.32) to obtain

$$f_0 + ax^{\text{corr}} + \frac{1}{2}b\left(\frac{f_0}{a}\right)^2 = 0 \text{ and hence } x^{\text{corr}} = -\frac{f_0}{a}\left(1 + \frac{1}{2}\frac{bf_0}{a^2}\right). \tag{6.34}$$

Comparing x^{pred} and x^{corr}, we see that $\frac{1}{2}\frac{bf_0}{a^2}$ is the correction term that takes the effect of the changes in x into account.

No Quadratic Residuals

Since neither of the two values (x^{pred} or x^{corr}) will give us the exact solution to $f(x) = 0$ in just one step, it is worthwhile having a look at the errors of both approaches.

$$f(x^{\text{pred}}) = \frac{1}{2}\frac{bf_0^2}{a^2} \text{ and } f(x^{\text{corr}}) = 2\frac{f^2(x^{\text{pred}})}{f_0} + \frac{f^3(x^{\text{pred}})}{f_0^2}. \tag{6.35}$$

We can check that if $\frac{bf_0}{a^2} \leq 2 - 2\sqrt{2}$, the corrector estimate will be better than the predictor one. As our initial estimate f_0 decreases, this will be the case. Moreover, we can see that $f(x^{\text{corr}})$ only contains terms in x that are of higher order than quadratic. This means that even though we did not solve the quadratic form explicitly, we eliminated all corresponding terms.

The general scheme is described in Algorithm 6.5. It is based on the assumption that $f(x + \xi)$ can be split up into

$$f(x + \xi) = f(x) + f_{\text{simple}}(\xi, x) + T(\xi, x), \tag{6.36}$$

Algorithm 6.5 Predictor Corrector Method

Require: x_0, Precision ϵ
 Set $i = 0$
 repeat
  Expand f into $f(x_i) + f_{\text{simple}}(\xi, x_i) + T(\xi, x_i)$.
 Predictor Solve $f(x_i) + f_{\text{simple}}(\xi^{\text{pred}}, x_i) = 0$ for ξ^{pred}.
 Corrector Solve $f(x_i) + f_{\text{simple}}(\xi^{\text{corr}}, x_i) + T(\xi^{\text{pred}}, x_i) = 0$ for ξ^{corr}.
  $x_{i+1} = x_i + \xi^{\text{corr}}$.
  $i = i + 1$.
 until $|f(x_i)| \leq \epsilon$
Output: x_i

where $f_{\text{simple}}(\xi, x)$ contains the simple, possibly low order, part of f, and $T(\xi, x)$ the higher order terms, such that $f_{\text{simple}}(0, x) = T(0, x) = 0$. While in the previous example we introduced higher order terms into f that were not present before (f is only quadratic), usually such terms will already exist anyway. Hence the corrector step will just eliminate additional lower order terms without too much additional error in the approximation.
We will encounter such methods for instance in the context of interior point algorithms (Section 6.4), where we have to solve a set of quadratic equations.

6.3 Constrained Problems

After this digression on unconstrained optimization problems, let us return to constrained optimization, which makes up the main body of the problems we will have to deal with in learning (e.g., quadratic or general convex programs for Support Vector Machines). Typically, we have to deal with problems of type (6.6). For convenience we repeat the problem statement:

$$\begin{aligned} &\underset{x}{\text{minimize}} \quad f(x) \\ &\text{subject to} \quad c_i(x) \leq 0 \text{ for all } i \in [n]. \end{aligned} \tag{6.37}$$

Here f and c_i are convex functions and $n \in \mathbb{N}$. In some cases[3], we additionally have *equality* constraints $e_j(x) = 0$ for some $j \in [n']$. Then the optimization problem can be written as

$$\begin{aligned} &\underset{x}{\text{minimize}} \quad f(x), \\ &\text{subject to} \quad c_i(x) \leq 0 \text{ for all } i \in [n], \\ &\qquad\qquad\quad e_j(x) = 0 \text{ for all } j \in [n']. \end{aligned} \tag{6.38}$$

3. Note that it is common practice in Support Vector Machines to write c_i as positivity constraints by using concave functions. This can be fixed by a sign change, however.

Before we start minimizing f, we have to discuss what optimality means in this case. Clearly $f'(x) = 0$ is too restrictive a condition. For instance, f' could point into a direction which is forbidden by the constraints c_i and e_i. Then we could have optimality, even though $f' \neq 0$. Let us analyze the situation in more detail.

6.3.1 Optimality Conditions

We start with optimality conditions for optimization problems which are independent of their differentiability. While it is fairly straightforward to state *sufficient* optimality conditions for arbitrary functions f and c_i, we will need convexity and "reasonably nice" constraints (see Lemma 6.23) to state *necessary* conditions. This is not a major concern, since for practical applications, the constraint qualification criteria are almost always satisfied, and the functions themselves are usually convex and differentiable. Much of the reasoning in this section follows [345], which should also be consulted for further references and detail.

Some of the most important sufficient criteria are the Kuhn-Tucker[4] saddle point conditions [312]. As indicated previously, they are independent of assumptions on convexity or differentiability of the constraints c_i or objective function f.

Lagrangian

Theorem 6.21 (Kuhn-Tucker Saddle Point Condition [312, 345]) *Assume an optimization problem of the form (6.37), where $f : \mathbb{R}^m \to \mathbb{R}$ and $c_i : \mathbb{R}^m \to \mathbb{R}$ for $i \in [n]$ are arbitrary functions, and a Lagrangian*

$$L(x, \alpha) := f(x) + \sum_{i=1}^{n} \alpha_i c_i(x) \text{ where } \alpha_i \geq 0. \tag{6.39}$$

If a pair of variables $(\bar{x}, \bar{\alpha})$ with $\bar{x} \in \mathbb{R}^n$ and $\bar{\alpha}_i \geq 0$ for all $i \in [n]$ exists, such that for all $x \in \mathbb{R}^m$ and $\alpha \in [0, \infty)^n$,

$$L(\bar{x}, \alpha) \leq L(\bar{x}, \bar{\alpha}) \leq L(x, \bar{\alpha}) \text{ (Saddle Point)} \tag{6.40}$$

then $\bar{x}$ is a solution to (6.37).

The parameters α_i are called Lagrange multipliers. As described in the later chapters, they will become the coefficients in the kernel expansion in SVM.

Proof The proof follows [345]. Denote by $(\bar{x}, \bar{\alpha})$ a pair of variables satisfying (6.40). From the first inequality it follows that

$$\sum_{i=1}^{n} (\alpha_i - \bar{\alpha}_i) c_i(\bar{x}) \leq 0. \tag{6.41}$$

Since we are free to choose $\alpha_i \geq 0$, we can see (by setting all but one of the terms α_i to $\bar{\alpha}_i$ and the remaining one to $\alpha_i = \bar{\alpha}_i + 1$) that $c_i(x) \leq 0$ for all $i \in [n]$. This shows that $\bar{x}$ satisfies the constraints, i.e. it is feasible.

4. An earlier version is due to Karush [283]. This is why often one uses the abbreviation KKT (Karush-Kuhn-Tucker) rather than KT to denote the optimality conditions.

Additionally, by setting one of the α_i to 0, we see that $\bar{\alpha}_i c_i(\bar{x}) \geq 0$. The only way to satisfy this is by having

$$\bar{\alpha}_i c_i(\bar{x}) = 0 \text{ for all } i \in [n]. \tag{6.42}$$

Eq. (6.42) is often referred to as the KKT condition [283, 312]. Finally, combining (6.42) and $c_i(x) \leq 0$ with the second inequality in (6.40) yields $f(\bar{x}) \leq f(x)$ for all feasible x. This proves that $\bar{x}$ is optimal. ■

We can immediately extend Theorem 6.21 to accommodate equality constraints by splitting them into the conditions $e_i(x) \leq 0$ and $e_i(x) \geq 0$. We obtain:

Theorem 6.22 (Equality Constraints) *Assume an optimization problem of the form (6.38), where $f, c_i, e_j : \mathbb{R}^m \to \mathbb{R}$ for $i \in [n]$ and $j \in [n']$ are arbitrary functions, and a Lagrangian*

$$L(x, \alpha) := f(x) + \sum_{i=1}^{n} \alpha_i c_i(x) + \sum_{j=1}^{n'} \beta_j e_j(x) \text{ where } \alpha_i \geq 0 \text{ and } \beta_j \in \mathbb{R}. \tag{6.43}$$

If a set of variables $(\bar{x}, \bar{\alpha}, \bar{\beta})$ with $\bar{x} \in \mathbb{R}^m$, $\bar{\alpha} \in [0, \infty)$, and $\bar{\beta} \in \mathbb{R}^{n'}$ exists such that for all $x \in \mathbb{R}^m$, $\alpha \in [0, \infty)^n$, and $\beta \in \mathbb{R}^{n'}$,

$$L(\bar{x}, \alpha, \beta) \leq L(\bar{x}, \bar{\alpha}, \bar{\beta}) \leq L(x, \bar{\alpha}, \bar{\beta}), \tag{6.44}$$

then $\bar{x}$ is a solution to (6.38).

Now we determine when the conditions of Theorem 6.21 are necessary. We will see that convexity and sufficiently "nice" constraints are needed for (6.40) to become a necessary condition. The following lemma (see [345]) describes three *constraint qualifications*, which will turn out to be exactly what we need.

Feasible Region

Lemma 6.23 (Constraint Qualifications) *Denote by $\mathcal{X} \subset \mathbb{R}^m$ a convex set, and by $c_1, \ldots, c_n : \mathcal{X} \to \mathbb{R}$ n convex functions defining a feasible region by*

$$X := \{x | x \in \mathcal{X} \text{ and } c_i(x) \leq 0 \text{ for all } i \in [n]\}. \tag{6.45}$$

Then the following additional conditions on c_i are connected by (i) $\Longleftrightarrow$ (ii) and (iii) $\Longrightarrow$ (i).

Equivalence Between Constraint Qualifications

(i) There exists an $x \in \mathcal{X}$ such that for all $i \in [n]$ $c_i(x) < 0$ (Slater's condition [500]).

(ii) For all nonzero $\alpha \in [0, \infty)^n$ there exists an $x \in \mathcal{X}$ such that $\sum_{i=1}^n \alpha_i c_i(x) \leq 0$ (Karlin's condition [281]).

(iii) The feasible region X contains at least two distinct elements, and there exists an $x \in X$ such that all c_i are strictly convex at x wrt. X (Strict constraint qualification).

The connection (i) $\Longleftrightarrow$ (ii) is also known as the Generalized Gordan Theorem [164]. The proof can be skipped if necessary. We need an auxiliary lemma which we state without proof (see [345, 435] for details).

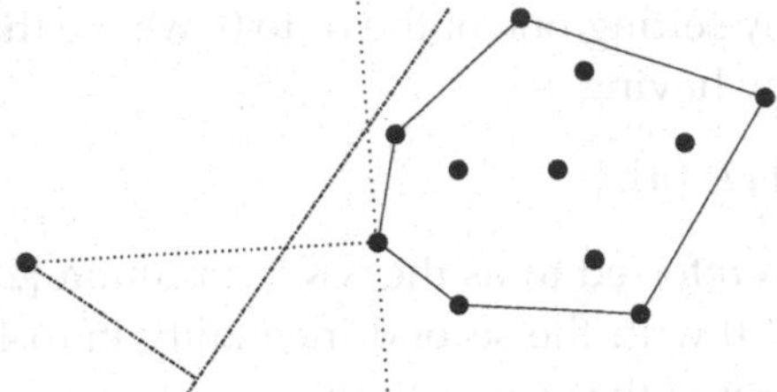

Figure 6.7 Two hyperplanes (and their normal vectors) separating the convex hull of a finite set of points from the origin.

Lemma 6.24 (Separating Hyperplane Theorem) *Denote by $X \in \mathbb{R}^m$ a convex set not containing the origin 0. Then there exists a hyperplane with normal vector $\alpha \in \mathbb{R}^m$ such that $\alpha^\top x > 0$ for all $x \in X$.*

See also Figure 6.7.

Proof of Lemma 6.23. We prove $\{(i) \Longleftrightarrow (ii)\}$ by showing $\{(i) \Longrightarrow (ii)\}$ and $\{$ not $(i) \Longrightarrow$ not $(ii)\}$.

$(i) \Longrightarrow (ii)$ For a point $x \in X$ with $c_i(x) < 0$, for all $i \in [n]$ we have that $\alpha_i c_i(x) \geq 0$ implies $\alpha_i = 0$.

$\overline{(i)} \Longrightarrow \overline{(ii)}$ Assume that there is no x with $c_i(x) < 0$ for all $i \in [n]$. Hence the set

$$\Gamma := \{\gamma | \gamma \in \mathbb{R}^n \text{ and there exists some } x \in X \text{ with } \gamma_i > c_i(x) \text{ for all } i \in [n]\} \tag{6.46}$$

is convex and does not contain the origin. The latter follows directly from the assumption. For the former take $\gamma, \gamma' \in \Gamma$ and $\lambda \in (0, 1)$ to obtain

$$\lambda\gamma_i + (1-\lambda)\gamma_i' > \lambda c_i(x) + (1-\lambda)c_i(x') \geq c_i(\lambda x + (1-\lambda)x'). \tag{6.47}$$

Now by Lemma 6.24, there exists some $\alpha \in \mathbb{R}^n$ such that $\alpha^\top \gamma \geq 0$ and $\|\alpha\|^2 = 1$ for all $\gamma \in \Gamma$. Since each of the γ_i for $\gamma \in \Gamma$ can be arbitrarily large (with respect to the other coordinates), we conclude $\alpha_i \geq 0$ for all $i \in [n]$.

Denote by $\delta := \inf_{x \in X} \sum_{i=1}^n \alpha_i c_i(x)$ and by $\delta' := \inf_{\gamma \in \Gamma} \alpha^\top \gamma$. One can see that by construction $\delta = \delta'$. By Lemma 6.24 α was chosen such that $\delta' \geq 0$, and hence $\delta \geq 0$. This contradicts *(ii)*, however, since it implies the existence of a suitable α with $\alpha_i c_i(x) \geq 0$ for all x.

$(iii) \Longrightarrow (i)$ Since X is convex we get for all c_i and for any $\lambda \in (0, 1)$:

$$\lambda x + (1-\lambda)x' \in X \text{ and } 0 \geq \lambda c_i(x) + (1-\lambda)c_i(x') > c_i(\lambda x + (1-\lambda)x'). \tag{6.48}$$

This shows that $\lambda x + (1-\lambda)x'$ satisfies (i) and we are done.

■

We proved Lemma 6.23 as it provides us with a set of constraint qualifications (conditions on the constraints) that allow us to determine cases where the KKT saddle point conditions are both *necessary* and sufficient. This is important, since we will use the KKT conditions to transform optimization problems into their duals, and solve the latter numerically. For this approach to be valid, however, we must ensure that we do not change the solvability of the optimization problem.

Theorem 6.25 (Necessary KKT Conditions [312, 553, 281]) *Under the assumptions and definitions of Theorem 6.21 with the additional assumption that f and c_i are convex on the convex set $X \subseteq \mathbb{R}^m$ (containing the set of feasible solutions as a subset) and that c_i satisfy one of the constraint qualifications of Lemma 6.23, the saddle point criterion (6.40) is necessary for optimality.*

Proof Denote by $\bar{x}$ the solution to (6.37), and by X' the set

$$X' := X \cap \{x | x \in \mathcal{X} \text{ with } f(x) - f(\bar{x}) \leq 0 \text{ and } c_i(x) \leq 0 \text{ for all } i \in [n]\}. \tag{6.49}$$

By construction $\bar{x} \in X'$. Furthermore, there exists no $x' \in X'$ such that all inequality constraints including $f(x) - f(\bar{x})$ are satisfied as *strict* inequalities (otherwise $\bar{x}$ would not be optimal). In other words, X' violates Slater's conditions (i) of Lemma 6.23 (where both $(f(x) - f(\bar{x}))$ and $c(x)$ *together* play the role of $c_i(x)$), and thus also Karlin's conditions (ii). This means that there exists a nonzero vector $(\bar{\alpha}_0, \bar{\alpha}) \in \mathbb{R}^{n+1}$ with nonnegative entries such that

$$\bar{\alpha}_0(f(x) - f(\bar{x})) + \sum_{i=1}^{n} \bar{\alpha}_i c_i(x) \geq 0 \text{ for all } x \in \mathcal{X}. \tag{6.50}$$

In particular, for $x = \bar{x}$ we get $\sum_{i=1}^{n} \bar{\alpha}_i c_i(\bar{x}) \geq 0$. In addition, since $\bar{x}$ is a solution to (6.37), we have $c_i(\bar{x}) \leq 0$. Hence $\sum_{i=1}^{n} \bar{\alpha}_i c_i(\bar{x}) = 0$. This allows us to rewrite (6.50) as

$$\bar{\alpha}_0 f(x) + \sum_{i=1}^{n} \bar{\alpha}_i c_i(x) \geq \bar{\alpha}_0 f(\bar{x}) + \sum_{i=1}^{n} \bar{\alpha}_i c_i(\bar{x}). \tag{6.51}$$

This looks almost like the first inequality of (6.40), except for the $\bar{\alpha}_0$ term (which we will return to later). But let us consider the second inequality first.

Again, since $c_i(\bar{x}) \leq 0$ we have $\sum_{i=1}^{n} \alpha_i c_i(\bar{x}) \leq 0$ for all $\alpha_i \geq 0$. Adding $\bar{\alpha}_0 f(\bar{x})$ on both sides of the inequality and $\sum_{i=1}^{n} \bar{\alpha}_i c_i(\bar{x})$ on the rhs yields

$$\bar{\alpha}_0 f(\bar{x}) + \sum_{i=1}^{n} \bar{\alpha}_i c_i(\bar{x}) \geq \bar{\alpha}_0 f(\bar{x}) + \sum_{i=1}^{n} \alpha_i c_i(\bar{x}). \tag{6.52}$$

This is almost all we need for the first inequality of (6.40).[5] If $\bar{\alpha}_0 > 0$ we can divide (6.51) and (6.52) by $\bar{\alpha}_0$ and we are done.

When $\bar{\alpha}_0 = 0$, then this implies the existence of $\bar{\alpha} \in \mathbb{R}^n$ with nonnegative entries satisfying $\sum_{i=1}^{n} \bar{\alpha}_i c_i(x) \geq 0$ for all $x \in X$. This contradicts Karlin's constraint qualification condition (ii), which allows us to rule out this case. ■

6.3.2 Duality and KKT-Gap

Now that we have formulated necessary and sufficient optimality conditions (Theorem 6.21 and 6.25) under quite general circumstances, let us put them to practical

5. The two inequalities (6.51) and (6.52) are also known as the Fritz-John saddle point necessary optimality conditions [269], which play a similar role as the saddle point conditions for the Lagrangian (6.39) of Theorem 6.21.

use for convex differentiable optimization problems. We first derive a more practically useful form of Theorem 6.21. Our reasoning is as follows: eq. (6.40) implies that $L(\bar{x}, \bar{\alpha})$ is a *saddle point* in terms of $(\bar{x}, \bar{\alpha})$. Hence, all we have to do is write the saddle point conditions in the form of derivatives.

Primal and Dual Feasibility

Theorem 6.26 (KKT for Differentiable Convex Problems [312]) *A solution to the optimization problem (6.37) with convex, differentiable f, c_i is given by $\bar{x}$, if there exists some $\bar{\alpha} \in \mathbb{R}^n$ with $\alpha_i \geq 0$ for all $i \in [n]$ such that the following conditions are satisfied:*

$$\partial_x L(\bar{x}, \bar{\alpha}) = \partial_x f(\bar{x}) + \sum_{i=1}^{n} \bar{\alpha}_i \partial_x c_i(\bar{x}) = 0 \text{ (Saddle Point in } \bar{x}\text{)}, \tag{6.53}$$

$$\partial_{\alpha_i} L(\bar{x}, \bar{\alpha}) = c_i(\bar{x}) \leq 0 \text{ (Saddle Point in } \bar{\alpha}\text{)}, \tag{6.54}$$

$$\sum_{i=1}^{n} \bar{\alpha}_i c_i(\bar{x}) = 0 \text{ (Vanishing KKT-Gap)}. \tag{6.55}$$

Proof The easiest way to prove Theorem 6.26 is to show that for any $x \in X$, we have $f(x) - f(\bar{x}) \geq 0$. Due to convexity we may linearize and obtain

$$f(x) - f(\bar{x}) \geq (\partial_x f(\bar{x}))^\top (x - \bar{x}) \tag{6.56}$$

$$= -\sum_{i=1}^{n} \bar{\alpha}_i (\partial_x c_i(\bar{x}))^\top (x - \bar{x}) \tag{6.57}$$

$$\geq -\sum_{i=1}^{n} \bar{\alpha}_i (c_i(x) - c_i(\bar{x})) \tag{6.58}$$

$$= -\sum_{i=1}^{n} \bar{\alpha}_i c_i(x) \geq 0. \tag{6.59}$$

Here we used the convexity and differentiability of f to arrive at the rhs of (6.56) and (6.58). To obtain (6.57) we exploited the fact that at the saddle point $\partial_x f(\bar{x})$ can be replaced by the corresponding expansion in $\partial_x c_i(\bar{x})$; thus we used (6.53). Finally, for (6.59) we used the fact that the KKT gap vanishes at the optimum (6.55) and that the constraints are satisfied (6.54). ■

Optimization by Constraint Satisfaction

In other words, we may solve a convex optimization problem by finding $(\bar{x}, \bar{\alpha})$ that satisfy the conditions of Theorem 6.26. Moreover, these conditions, together with the constraint qualifications of Lemma 6.23, ensure necessity.

Note that we transformed the problem of minimizing functions into one of solving a set of equations, for which several numerical tools are readily available. This is exactly how interior point methods work (see Section 6.4 for details on how to implement them). Necessary conditions on the constraints similar to those discussed previously can also be formulated (see [345] for a detailed discussion).

The other consequence of Theorem 6.26, or rather of the definition of the Lagrangian $L(x, \alpha)$, is that we may bound $f(\bar{x}) = L(\bar{x}, \bar{\alpha})$ from above and below *without* explicit knowledge of $f(\bar{x})$.

Theorem 6.27 (KKT-Gap) *Assume an optimization problem of type (6.37), where both f and c_i are convex and differentiable. Denote by $\bar{x}$ its solution. Then for any set of variables*

(x, α) with $\alpha_i \geq 0$, and for all $i \in [n]$ satisfying

$$\partial_x L(x, \alpha) = 0, \tag{6.60}$$

$$\partial_{\alpha_i} L(x, \alpha) \leq 0 \text{ for all } i \in [n], \tag{6.61}$$

Bounding the Error

we have

$$f(x) \geq f(\bar{x}) \geq f(x) + \sum_{i=1}^{m} \alpha_i c_i(x). \tag{6.62}$$

Strictly speaking, we only need differentiability of f and c_i at $\bar{x}$. However, since $\bar{x}$ is only known *after* the optimization problem has been solved, this is not a very useful condition.

Proof The first part of (6.62) follows from the fact that $x \in X$, so that x satisfies the constraints. Next note that $L(\bar{x}, \bar{\alpha}) = f(\bar{x})$ where $(\bar{x}, \bar{\alpha})$ denotes the saddle point of L. For the second part note that due to the saddle point condition (6.40), we have for any α with $\alpha_i \geq 0$,

$$f(\bar{x}) = L(\bar{x}, \bar{\alpha}) \geq L(\bar{x}, \alpha) \geq \inf_{x' \in X} L(x', \alpha). \tag{6.63}$$

The function $L(x', \alpha)$ is convex in x' since both f' and the constraints c_i are convex and all $\alpha_i \geq 0$. Therefore (6.60) implies that x minimizes $L(x', \alpha)$. This proves the second part of (6.63), which in turn proves the second inequality of (6.62). ■

Hence, no matter what algorithm we are using in order to solve (6.37), we may always use (6.62) to assess the proximity of the current set of parameters to the solution. Clearly, the relative size of $\sum_{i=1}^{n} \alpha_i c_i(x)$ provides a useful stopping criterion for convex optimization algorithms.

Finally, another concept that is useful when dealing with optimization problems is that of *duality*. This means that for the *primal* minimization problem considered so far, which is expressed in terms of x, we can find a *dual* maximization problem in terms of α by computing the saddle point of the Lagrangian $L(x, \alpha)$, and eliminating the primal variables x. We thus obtain the following dual maximization problem from (6.37):

$$\begin{aligned} &\text{maximize} \quad L(x, \alpha) = f(x) + \sum_{i=1}^{n} \alpha_i c_i(x), \\ &\text{where} \quad (x, \alpha) \in Y := \left\{ (x, \alpha) \,\middle|\, \begin{array}{l} x \in X, \alpha_i \geq 0 \text{ for all } i \in [n] \\ \text{and } \partial_x L(x, \alpha) = 0 \end{array} \right\}. \end{aligned} \tag{6.64}$$

We state without proof a theorem guaranteeing the existence of a solution to (6.64).

Existence of Dual Solution

Theorem 6.28 (Wolfe [607]) *Recall the definition of X (6.45) and of the optimization problem (6.37). Under the assumptions that $\mathcal{X}$ is an open set, X satisfies one of the constraint qualifications of Lemma 6.23, and f, c_i are all convex and differentiable, there exists an $\bar{\alpha} \in \mathbb{R}^n$ such that $(\bar{x}, \bar{\alpha})$ solves the dual optimization problem (6.64) and in addition $L(\bar{x}, \bar{\alpha}) = f(\bar{x})$.*

In order to prove Theorem 6.28 we first have to show that some $(\bar{x}, \bar{\alpha})$ exists satisfying the KKT conditions, and then use the fact that the KKT-Gap at the saddle point vanishes.

6.3.3 Linear and Quadratic Programs

Primal Linear Program

Let us analyze the notions of primal and dual objective functions in more detail by looking at linear and quadratic programs. We begin with a simple linear setting.[6]

$$\begin{aligned} &\underset{x}{\text{minimize}} && c^\top x \\ &\text{subject to} && Ax + d \leq 0 \end{aligned} \tag{6.65}$$

where $c, x \in \mathbb{R}^m$, $d \in \mathbb{R}^n$ and $A \in R^{n \times m}$, and where $Ax + d \leq 0$ is a shorthand for $\sum_{j=1}^m A_{ij}x_j + d_i \leq 0$ for all $i \in [n]$.

Unbounded and Infeasible Problems

It is far from clear that (6.65) always has a solution, or indeed a minimum. For instance, the set of x satisfying $Ax + d \leq 0$ might be empty, or it might contain rays going to infinity in directions where $c^\top x$ keeps increasing. Before we deal with this issue in more detail, let us compute the sufficient KKT conditions for optimality, and the dual of (6.65). We may use (6.26) since (6.65) is clearly differentiable and convex. In particular we obtain:

Theorem 6.29 (KKT Conditions for Linear Programs) *A sufficient condition for a solution to the linear program (6.65) to exist is that the following four conditions are satisfied for some $(x, \alpha) \in \mathbb{R}^{m+n}$ where $\alpha \geq 0$:*

$$\partial_x L(x, \alpha) = \partial_x \left[c^\top x + \alpha^\top (Ax + d)\right] = A^\top \alpha + c = 0, \tag{6.66}$$

$$\partial_\alpha L(x, \alpha) = Ax + d \leq 0, \tag{6.67}$$

$$\alpha^\top (Ax + d) = 0, \tag{6.68}$$

$$\alpha \geq 0. \tag{6.69}$$

Then the minimum is given by $c^\top x$.

Note that, depending on the choice of A and d, there may not always exist an x such that $Ax + d \leq 0$, in which case the constraint does not satisfy the conditions of Lemma 6.23. In this situation, no solution exists for (6.65). If a feasible x exists, however, then (projections onto lower dimensional subspaces aside) the constraint qualifications are satisfied on the feasible set, and the conditions above are necessary. See [334, 345, 555] for details.

6. Note that we encounter a small clash of notation in (6.65), since c is used as a symbol for the loss function in the remainder of the book. This inconvenience is outweighed, however, by the advantage of consistency with the standard literature (e.g., [345, 45, 555]) on optimization. The latter will allow the reader to read up on the subject without any need for cumbersome notational changes.

Next we may compute Wolfe's dual optimization problem by substituting (6.66) into $L(x, \alpha)$. Consequently, the primal variables x vanish, and we obtain a maximization problem in terms of α only:

Dual Linear Program

$$\begin{aligned} &\text{maximize} && d^\top \alpha, \\ &\text{subject to} && A^\top \alpha + c = 0 \text{ and } \alpha \geq 0. \end{aligned} \tag{6.70}$$

Note that the number of variables and constraints has changed: we started with m variables and n constraints. Now we have n variables together with m equality constraints and n inequality constraints. While it is not yet completely obvious in the linear case, dualization may render optimization problems more amenable to numerical solution (the contrary may be true as well, though).

Primal Solution ⇔ Dual Solution

What happens if a solution $\bar{x}$ to the primal problem (6.65) exists? In this case we know (since the KKT conditions of Theorem 6.29 are necessary and sufficient) that there must be an $\bar{\alpha}$ solving the dual problem, since $L(x, \alpha)$ has a saddle point at $(\bar{x}, \bar{\alpha})$.

If no feasible point of the primal problem exists, there must exist, by (a small modification of) Lemma 6.23, some $\alpha \in \mathbb{R}^n$ with $\alpha \geq 0$ and at least one $\alpha_i > 0$ such that $\alpha^\top(Ax + d) > 0$ for all x. This means that for all x, the Lagrangian $L(x, \alpha)$ is unbounded from above, since we can make $\alpha^\top(Ax + d)$ arbitrarily large. Hence the dual optimization problem is unbounded. Using analogous reasoning, if the primal problem is unbounded, the dual problem is infeasible.

Let us see what happens if we dualize (6.70) one more time. First we need more Lagrange multipliers, since we have two sets of constraints. The equality constraints can be taken care of by an unbounded variable x' (see Theorem 6.22 for how to deal with equalities). For the inequalities $\alpha \geq 0$, we introduce a second Lagrange multiplier $y \in \mathbb{R}^n$. After some calculations and resubstitution into the corresponding Lagrangian, we get

$$\begin{aligned} &\text{maximize} && c^\top x', \\ &\text{subject to} && Ax' + d + y = 0 \text{ and } y \geq 0. \end{aligned} \tag{6.71}$$

Dual Dual Linear Program → Primal

We can remove $y \geq 0$ from the set of variables by transforming $Ax' + d + y$ into $Ax + d \leq 0$; thus we recover the primal optimization problem (6.65).[7]

The following theorem gives an overview of the transformations and relations between primal and dual problems (see also Table 6.2). Although we only derived these relations for linear programs, they also hold for other convex differentiable settings [45].

Theorem 6.30 (Trichotomy) *For linear and convex quadratic programs exactly one of*

7. This finding is useful if we have to dualize twice in some optimization settings (see Chapter 10), since then we will be able to recover some of the primal variables without further calculations if the optimization algorithm provides us with both primal and dual variables.

Table 6.2 Connections between primal and dual linear and convex quadratic programs.

Primal Optimization Problem (in x)	Dual Optimization Problem (in α)
solution exists	solution exists and extrema are equal
no solution exists	maximization problem has unbounded objective from above or is infeasible
minimization problem has unbounded objective from below or is infeasible	no solution exists
inequality constraint	inequality constraint
equality constraint	free variable
free variable	equality constraint

the following three alternatives must hold:

1. *Both feasible regions are empty.*
2. *Exactly one feasible region is empty, in which case the objective function of the other problem is unbounded in the direction of optimization.*
3. *Both feasible regions are nonempty, in which case both problems have solutions and their extrema are equal.*

Primal Quadratic Program

We conclude this section by stating primal and dual optimization problems, and the sufficient KKT conditions for convex quadratic optimization problems. To keep matters simple we only consider the following type of optimization problem (other problems can be rewritten in the same form; see Problem 6.11 for details):

$$\begin{aligned} \underset{x}{\text{minimize}} \quad & \tfrac{1}{2}x^\top Kx + c^\top x, \\ \text{subject to} \quad & Ax + d \leq 0. \end{aligned} \tag{6.72}$$

Here K is a strictly positive definite matrix, $x, c \in \mathbb{R}^m$, $A \in \mathbb{R}^{n \times m}$, and $d \in \mathbb{R}^n$. Note that this is clearly a differentiable convex optimization problem. To introduce a Lagrangian we need corresponding multipliers $\alpha \in \mathbb{R}^n$ with $\alpha \geq 0$. We obtain

$$L(x, \alpha) = \frac{1}{2}x^\top Kx + c^\top x + \alpha^\top (Ax + d). \tag{6.73}$$

Next we may apply Theorem 6.26 to obtain the KKT conditions. They can be stated in analogy to (6.66)–(6.68) as

$$\partial_x L(x, \alpha) = \partial_x \left[c^\top x + \alpha^\top (Ax + d) + \frac{1}{2}x^\top Kx \right] = Kx + A^\top \alpha + c = 0, \tag{6.74}$$

$$\partial_\alpha L(x, \alpha) = Ax + d \leq 0, \tag{6.75}$$

$$\alpha^\top (Ax + d) = 0, \tag{6.76}$$

$$\alpha \geq 0. \tag{6.77}$$

In order to compute the dual of (6.72), we have to eliminate x from (6.73) and write it as a function of α. We obtain

$$L(x,\alpha) = -\frac{1}{2}x^\top Kx + \alpha^\top d \tag{6.78}$$

$$= -\frac{1}{2}\alpha^\top A^\top K^{-1}A\alpha + \left[d - c^\top K^{-1}A^\top\right]\alpha - \frac{1}{2}c^\top K^{-1}c. \tag{6.79}$$

In (6.78) we used (6.74) and (6.76) directly, whereas in order to eliminate x completely in (6.79) we solved (6.74) for $x = -K^{-1}(c + A^\top\alpha)$. Ignoring constant terms this leads to the dual quadratic optimization problem,

Dual Quadratic Program

$$\begin{aligned} &\underset{\alpha}{\text{minimize}} && -\frac{1}{2}\alpha^\top A^\top K^{-1}A\alpha + \left[d - c^\top K^{-1}A^\top\right]\alpha, \\ &\text{subject to} && \alpha \geq 0. \end{aligned} \tag{6.80}$$

The surprising fact about the dual problem (6.80) is that the constraints become significantly simpler than in the primal (6.72). Furthermore, if $n < m$, we also obtain a more compact representation of the quadratic term.

There is one aspect in which (6.80) differs from its linear counterpart (6.70): if we dualize (6.80) again, we do not recover (6.72) but rather a problem very similar in structure to (6.80). Dualizing (6.80) twice, however, we recover the dual itself (Problem 6.13 deals with this matter in more detail).

6.4 Interior Point Methods

Let us now have a look at simple, yet efficient optimization algorithms for constrained problems: interior point methods.

An interior point is a pair of variables (x, α) that satisfies both primal and dual constraints. As already mentioned before, finding a set of vectors $(\bar{x}, \bar{\alpha})$ that satisfy the KKT conditions is sufficient to obtain a solution in $\bar{x}$. Hence, all we have to do is devise an algorithm which solves (6.74)–(6.77), for instance, if we want to solve a quadratic program. We will focus on the quadratic case — the changes required for linear programs merely involve the removal of some variables, simplifying the equations. See Problem 6.14 and [555, 517] for details.

6.4.1 Sufficient Conditions for a Solution

We need a slight modification of (6.74)–(6.77) in order to achieve our goal: rather than the inequality (6.75), we are better off with an equality and a positivity constraint for an additional variable, i.e. we transform $Ax + d \leq 0$ into $Ax + d + \xi =$

0, where $\xi \geq 0$. Hence we arrive at the following system of equations:

$$\begin{aligned}
Kx + A^\top \alpha + c &= 0 \quad \text{(Dual Feasibility)}, \\
Ax + d + \xi &= 0 \quad \text{(Primal Feasibility)}, \\
\alpha^\top \xi &= 0, \\
\alpha, \xi &\geq 0.
\end{aligned} \tag{6.81}$$

Optimality as Constraint Satisfaction

Let us analyze the equations in more detail. We have three sets of variables: x, α, ξ. To determine the latter, we have an equal number of equations plus the positivity constraints on α, ξ. While the first two equations are linear and thus amenable to solution, e.g., by matrix inversion, the third equality $\alpha^\top \xi = 0$ has a small defect: given one variable, say α, we cannot solve it for ξ or vice versa. Furthermore, the last two constraints are not very informative either.

We use a primal-dual path-following algorithm, as proposed in [556], to solve this problem. Rather than requiring $\alpha^\top \xi = 0$ we modify it to become $\alpha_i \xi_i = \mu > 0$ for all $i \in [n]$, solve (6.81) for a given μ, and decrease μ to 0 as we go. The advantage of this strategy is that we may use a Newton-type predictor corrector algorithm (see Section 6.2.5) to update the parameters x, α, ξ, which exhibits the fast convergence of a second order method.

6.4.2 Solving the Equations

For the moment, assume that we have suitable initial values of x, α, ξ, and μ with $\alpha, \xi > 0$. Linearization of the first three equations of (6.81), together with the modification $\alpha_i \xi_i = \mu$, yields (we expand x into $x + \Delta x$, etc.):

Linearized Constraints

$$\begin{aligned}
K\Delta x + A^\top \Delta\alpha &= -Kx - A^\top \alpha - c &&=: \rho_p, \\
A\Delta x + \Delta\xi &= -Ax - d - \xi &&=: \rho_d, \\
\alpha_i^{-1}\xi_i \Delta\alpha_i + \Delta\xi_i &= \mu\alpha_i^{-1} - \xi_i - \alpha_i^{-1}\Delta\alpha_i\Delta\xi_i &&=: \rho_{\mathrm{KKT}_i} \text{ for all } i
\end{aligned} \tag{6.82}$$

Next we solve for $\Delta\xi_i$ to obtain what is commonly referred to as the *reduced* KKT system. For convenience we use $D := \mathrm{diag}(\alpha_1^{-1}\xi_1, \ldots, \alpha_n^{-1}\xi_n)$ as a shorthand;

$$\begin{bmatrix} K & A^\top \\ A & -D \end{bmatrix} \begin{bmatrix} \Delta x \\ \Delta\alpha \end{bmatrix} = \begin{bmatrix} \rho_p \\ \rho_d - \rho_{\mathrm{KKT}} \end{bmatrix}. \tag{6.83}$$

We apply a predictor-corrector method as in Section 6.2.5. The resulting matrix of the linear system in (6.83) is indefinite but of full rank, and we can solve (6.83) for $(\Delta x_{\mathrm{Pred}}, \Delta\alpha_{\mathrm{Pred}})$ by explicitly pivoting for individual entries (for instance, solve for Δx first and then substitute the result in to the second equality to obtain $\Delta\alpha$).

This gives us the *predictor* part of the solution. Next we have to correct for the linearization, which is conveniently achieved by updating ρ_{KKT} and solving (6.83) again to obtain the *corrector* values $(\Delta x_{\mathrm{Corr}}, \Delta\alpha_{\mathrm{Corr}})$. The value of $\Delta\xi$ is then obtained from (6.82).

Update in x, α

Next, we have to make sure that the updates in α, ξ do not cause the estimates to violate their positivity constraints. This is done by shrinking the length of $(\Delta x, \Delta\alpha, \Delta\xi)$ by some factor $\lambda \geq 0$, such that

$$\min\left(\frac{\alpha_1 + \lambda\Delta\alpha_1}{\alpha_1}, \ldots, \frac{\alpha_n + \lambda\Delta\alpha_n}{\alpha_n}, \frac{\xi_1 + \lambda\Delta\xi_1}{\xi_1}, \ldots, \frac{\xi_n + \lambda\Delta\xi_n}{\xi_n}\right) \geq \epsilon. \tag{6.84}$$

Of course, only the negative Δ terms pose a problem, since they lead the parameter values closer to 0, which may lead them into conflict with the positivity constraints. Typically [556, 502], we choose $\epsilon = 0.05$. In other words, the solution will not approach the boundaries in α, ξ by more than 95%. See Problem 6.15 for a formula to compute λ.

6.4.3 Updating μ

Next we have to update μ. Here we face the following dilemma: if we decrease μ too quickly, we will get bad convergence of our second order method, since the solution to the problem (which depends on the value of μ) moves too quickly away from our current set of parameters (x, α, ξ). On the other hand, we do not want to spend too much time solving an *approximation* of the unrelaxed ($\mu = 0$) KKT conditions *exactly*. A good indication is how much the positivity constraints would be violated by the current update. Vanderbei [556] proposes the following update of μ:

Tightening the KKT Conditions

$$\mu = \frac{\alpha^\top \xi}{n}\left(\frac{1-\lambda}{10+\lambda}\right)^2. \tag{6.85}$$

The first term gives the average value of satisfaction of the condition $\alpha_i\xi_i = \mu$ after an update step. The second term allows us to decrease μ rapidly if good progress was made (small $(1-\lambda)^2$). Experimental evidence shows that it pays to be slightly more conservative, and to use the *predictor* estimates of α, ξ for (6.85) rather than the corresponding corrector terms.[8] This imposes little overhead for the implementation.

6.4.4 Initial Conditions and Stopping Criterion

To provide a complete algorithm, we have to consider two more things: a stopping criterion and a suitable start value. For the latter, we simply solve a regularized version of the initial reduced KKT system (6.83). This means that we replace K by $K + \mathbf{1}$, use (x, α) in place of $\Delta x, \Delta\alpha$, and replace D by the identity matrix. Moreover, ρ_p and ρ_d are set to the values they would have if all variables had been set to 0 before, and finally ρ_{KKT} is set to 0. In other words, we obtain an initial guess of

Regularized KKT System

8. In practice it is often useful to replace $(1-\lambda)$ by $(1+\epsilon-\lambda)$ for some small $\epsilon > 0$, in order to avoid $\mu = 0$.

(x, α, ξ) by solving

$$\begin{bmatrix} K+\mathbf{1} & A^\top \\ A & -\mathbf{1} \end{bmatrix} \begin{bmatrix} x \\ \alpha \end{bmatrix} = \begin{bmatrix} -c \\ -d \end{bmatrix}, \tag{6.86}$$

and $\xi = -Ax - d$. Since we have to ensure positivity of α, ξ, we simply replace

$$\alpha_i = \max(\alpha_i, 1) \text{ and } \xi_i = \max(\xi_i, 1). \tag{6.87}$$

This heuristic solves the problem of a suitable initial condition.

Regarding the stopping criterion, we recall Theorem 6.27, and in particular (6.62). Rather than obtaining bounds on the precision of *parameters*, we want to make sure that $f(x)$ is close to its optimal value $f(\bar{x})$. From (6.64) we know, provided the feasibility constraints are all satisfied, that the value of the dual objective function is given by $f(x) + \sum_{i=1}^n \alpha_i c_i(x)$. We may use the latter to bound the *relative* size of the gap between primal and dual objective function by

$$\text{Gap}(x, \alpha) = \frac{2\left|f(x) - \left(f(x) + \sum\limits_{i=1}^n \alpha_i c_i(x)\right)\right|}{|f(x)| + \left|\left(f(x) + \sum\limits_{i=1}^n \alpha_i c_i(x)\right)\right|} \leq \frac{-\sum\limits_{i=1}^n \alpha_i c_i(x)}{\left|f(x) + \frac{1}{2}\sum\limits_{i=1}^n \alpha_i c_i(x)\right|}. \tag{6.88}$$

For the special case where $f(x) = \frac{1}{2}x^\top Kx + c^\top x$ as in (6.72), we know by virtue of (6.73) that the size of the feasibility gap is given by $\alpha^\top \xi$, and therefore

$$\text{Gap}(x, \alpha) = \frac{\alpha^\top \xi}{\left|\frac{1}{2}x^\top Kx + c^\top x + \frac{1}{2}\alpha^\top \xi\right|}. \tag{6.89}$$

In practice, a small number is usually added to the denominator of (6.89) in order to avoid divisions by 0 in the first iteration. The quality of the solution is typically measured on a logarithmic scale by $-\log_{10} \text{Gap}(x, \alpha)$, the number of significant figures.[9] We will come back to specific versions of such interior point algorithms in Chapter 10, and show how Support Vector Regression and Classification problems can be solved with them.

Number of Significant Figures

Primal-Dual path following methods are certainly not the only algorithms that can be employed for minimizing constrained quadratic problems. Other variants, for instance, are Barrier Methods [282, 45, 557], which minimize the unconstrained problem

$$f(x) + \mu \sum_{i=1}^n f \ln(-c_i(x)) \text{ for } \mu > 0. \tag{6.90}$$

Active set methods have also been used with success in machine learning [369, 284]. These select subsets of variables x for which the constraints c_i are not ac-

9. Interior point codes are very precise. They usually achieve up to 8 significant figures, whereas iterative approximation methods do not normally exceed more than 3 significant figures on large optimization problems.

tive, i.e., where the we have a strict inequality, and solve the resulting restricted quadratic program, for instance by conjugate gradient descent. We will encounter subset selection methods in Chapter 10.

6.5 Maximum Search Problems

Approximations

In several cases the task of finding an optimal function for estimation purposes means finding the best element from a finite set, or sometimes finding an optimal subset from a finite set of elements. These are discrete (sometimes combinatorial) optimization problems which are not so easily amenable to the techniques presented in the previous two sections. Furthermore, many commonly encountered problems are computationally expensive if solved exactly. Instead, by using probabilistic methods, it is possible to find *almost* optimal approximate solutions. These probabilistic methods are the topic of the present section.

6.5.1 Random Subset Selection

Consider the following problem: given a set of m functions, say $M := \{f_1, \ldots, f_m\}$, and some criterion $Q[f]$, find the function $\hat{f}$ that maximizes $Q[f]$. More formally,

$$\hat{f} := \operatorname*{argmax}_{f \in M} Q[f]. \tag{6.91}$$

Clearly, unless we have additional knowledge about the values $Q[f_i]$, we have to compute all terms $Q[f_i]$ if we want to solve (6.91) exactly. This will cost $O(m)$ operations. If m is large, which is often the case in practical applications, this operation is too expensive. In sparse greedy approximation problems (Section 10.2) or in Kernel Feature Analysis (Section 14.4), m can easily be of the order of 10^5 or larger (here, m is the number of training patterns). Hence we have to look for cheaper *approximate* solutions.

The key idea is to pick a random subset $M' \subset M$ that is sufficiently large, and take the maximum over M' as an approximation of the maximum over M. Provided the distribution of the values of $Q[f_i]$ is "well behaved", i.e., there exists not a small fraction of $Q[f_i]$ whose values are significantly smaller or larger than the average, we will obtain a solution that is close to the optimum with high probability. To formalize these ideas, we need the following result.

Lemma 6.31 (Maximum of Random Variables) *Denote by ξ, ξ' two independent random variables on $\mathbb{R}$ with corresponding distributions $P_\xi, P_{\xi'}$ and distribution functions $F_\xi, F_{\xi'}$. Then the random variable $\bar{\xi} := \max(\xi, \xi')$ has the distribution function $F_{\bar{\xi}} = F_\xi F_{\xi'}$.*

Proof Note that for a random variable, the distribution function $F(\xi_0)$ is given by the probability $P\{\xi \leq \xi_0\}$. Since ξ and ξ' are independent, we may write

$$F_{\bar{\xi}}(\bar{\xi}) = P\{\max(\xi, \xi') \leq \bar{\xi}\} = P\{\xi \leq \bar{\xi} \text{ and } \xi' \leq \bar{\xi}\} = P\{\xi \leq \bar{\xi}\}P\{\xi' \leq \bar{\xi}\} \\ = F_\xi(\bar{\xi})F_{\xi'}(\bar{\xi}), \tag{6.92}$$

which proves the claim. ■

Distribution Over $\bar{\xi}$ is More Peaked

Repeated application of Lemma 6.31 leads to the following corollary.

Corollary 6.32 (Maximum Over Identical Random Variables) *Let $\xi_1, \ldots, \xi_{\tilde{m}}$ be $\tilde{m}$ independent and identically distributed (iid) random variables, with corresponding distribution function F_ξ. Then the random variable $\bar{\xi} := \max(\xi_1, \ldots, \xi_{\tilde{m}})$ has the distribution function $F_{\bar{\xi}}(\bar{\xi}) = \left(F_\xi(\bar{\xi})\right)^{\tilde{m}}$.*

In practice, the random variables ξ_i will be the values of $Q[f_i]$, where the f_i are drawn from the set M. If we draw them without replacement (i.e. none of the functions f_i appears twice), however, the values after each draw are dependent and we cannot apply Corollary 6.32 directly. Nonetheless, we can see that the maximum over draws *without* replacement will be larger than the maximum *with* replacement, since recurring observations can be understood as reducing the effective size of the set to be considered. Thus Corollary 6.32 gives us a *lower bound* on the value of the distribution function for draws without replacement. Moreover, for large m the difference between draws with and without replacement is small.

If the distribution of $Q[f_i]$ is known, we may use the distribution directly to determine the size $\tilde{m}$ of a subset to be used to find some $Q[f_i]$ that is almost as good as the solution to (6.91). In all other cases, we have to resort to assessing the *relative* quality of maxima over subsets. The following theorem tells us how.

Best Element of a Subset

Theorem 6.33 (Ranks on Random Subsets) *Denote by $M := \{x_1, \ldots, x_m\} \subset \mathbb{R}$ a set of cardinality m, and by $\tilde{M} \subset M$ a random subset of size $\tilde{m}$. Then the probability that* $\max \tilde{M}$ *is greater equal than n elements of M is at least* $1 - \left(\frac{n}{m}\right)^{\tilde{m}}$.

Proof We prove this by assuming the converse, namely that $\max \tilde{M}$ is smaller than $(m - n)$ elements of M. For $\tilde{m} = 1$ we know that this probability is $\frac{n}{m}$, since there are n elements to choose from. For $\tilde{m} > 1$, the probability is the one of choosing $\tilde{m}$ elements out of a subset M_{low} of n elements, rather than all m elements. Therefore we have that

$$P(\tilde{M} \subset M_{\text{low}}) = \frac{\binom{n}{\tilde{m}}}{\binom{m}{\tilde{m}}} = \frac{n}{m} \cdot \frac{n-1}{m-1} \cdot \ldots \cdot \frac{n - \tilde{m} + 1}{m - \tilde{m} + 1} < \left(\frac{n}{m}\right)^{\tilde{m}}.$$

Consequently the probability that the maximum over $\tilde{M}$ will be larger than n elements of M is given by $1 - P(\tilde{M} \subset M_{\text{low}}) \geq 1 - \left(\frac{n}{m}\right)^{\tilde{m}}$. ■

The practical consequence is that we may use $1 - \left(\frac{n}{m}\right)^{\tilde{m}}$ to compute the required size of a random subset to achieve the desired degree of approximation. If we want to obtain results in the $\frac{n}{m}$ percentile range with $1 - \eta$ confidence, we must solve for $\tilde{m} = \frac{\log(1-\eta)}{\ln n/m}$. To give a numerical example, if we desire values that are better than 95% of all other estimates with $1 - 0.05$ probability, then $\kappa = 59$ samples are sufficient. This (95%, 95%, 59) rule is very useful in practice.[10] A similar method was used to speed up the process of boosting classifiers in the MadaBoost algorithm [143]. Furthermore, one could think whether it might not be useful to recycle old observations rather than computing all 59 values from scratch. If this can be done cheaply, and under some additional independence assumptions, subset selection methods can be improved further. For details see [424] who use the method in the context of memory management for operating systems.

6.5.2 Random Evaluation

Quite often, the evaluation of the term $Q[f]$ itself is rather time consuming, especially if $Q[f]$ is the sum of many (m, for instance) iid random variables. Again, we can speed up matters considerably by using probabilistic methods. The key idea is that averages over independent random variables are concentrated, which is to say that averages over subsets do not differ too much from averages over the whole set.

Approximating Sums by Partial Sums

Hoeffding's Theorem (Section 5.2) quantifies the size of the deviations between the expectation of a sum of random variables and their values at individual trials. We will use this to bound deviations between averages over sets and subsets. All we have to do is translate Theorem 5.1 into a statement regarding sample averages over different sample sizes. This can be readily constructed as follows:

Corollary 6.34 (Deviation Bounds for Empirical Means [508]) *Suppose $\xi_1, \ldots, \xi_m$ are iid bounded random variables, falling into the interval $[a, a+b]$ with probability one. Denote their average by $Q_m = \frac{1}{m}\sum_i \xi_i$. Furthermore, denote by $\xi_{s(1)}, \ldots, \xi_{s(\tilde{m})}$ with $\tilde{m} < m$ a subset of the same random variables (with $s : \{1, \ldots, \tilde{m}\} \to \{1, \ldots, m\}$ being an injective map, i.e. $s(i) = s(j)$ only if $i = j$), and $Q_{\tilde{m}} = \frac{1}{\tilde{m}}\sum_i \xi_{s(i)}$. Then for any $\varepsilon > 0$,*

Deviation of Subsets

$$\left.\begin{array}{l} \mathrm{P}\{Q_m - Q_{\tilde{m}} \geq \varepsilon\} \\ \mathrm{P}\{Q_{\tilde{m}} - Q_m \geq \varepsilon\} \end{array}\right\} \leq \exp\left(-\frac{2m\tilde{m}\varepsilon^2}{(m-\tilde{m})b^2}\right) = \exp\left(-2m\frac{\varepsilon^2}{b^2}\frac{\frac{\tilde{m}}{m}}{1-\frac{\tilde{m}}{m}}\right) \tag{6.93}$$

Proof By construction $\mathbf{E}[Q_m - Q_{\tilde{m}}] = 0$, since Q_m and $Q_{\tilde{m}}$ are both averages over sums of random variables drawn from the same distribution. Hence we only have to rewrite $Q_m - Q_{\tilde{m}}$ as an average over (different) random variables to apply Hoeffding's bound. Since all Q_i are identically distributed, we may pick the first $\tilde{m}$ random variables, without loss of generality. In other words, we assume that

10. During World War I tanks were often numbered in continuous increasing order. Unfortunately this "feature" allowed the enemy to estimate the number of tanks. How?

$s(i) = i$ for $i = 1, \ldots, \tilde{m}$. Then

$$Q_m - Q_{\tilde{m}} = \frac{1}{m}\sum_{i=1}^{m} \xi_i - \frac{1}{\tilde{m}}\sum_{i=1}^{\tilde{m}} \xi_i = \frac{1}{m}\sum_{i=1}^{\tilde{m}} (1 - \tfrac{m}{\tilde{m}})\xi_i + \frac{1}{m}\sum_{i=\tilde{m}+1}^{m} \xi_i. \tag{6.94}$$

Thus we may split up $Q_m - Q_{\tilde{m}}$ into a sum of $\tilde{m}$ random variables with range $b_i = (\frac{m}{\tilde{m}} - 1)b$, and $m - \tilde{m}$ random variables with range $b_i = b$. We obtain

$$\sum_{i=1}^{m} b_i^2 = b^2\tilde{m}\left(\frac{m}{\tilde{m}} - 1\right)^2 + (m - \tilde{m})b^2 = b^2(m - \tilde{m})\frac{m}{\tilde{m}}. \tag{6.95}$$

Substituting this into (5.7) and noting that $Q_m - Q_{\tilde{m}} - \mathbf{E}[Q_m - Q_{\tilde{m}}] = Q_m - Q_{\tilde{m}}$ completes the proof. ■

For small $\frac{\tilde{m}}{m}$ the rhs in (6.93) reduces to $\exp\left(-\frac{2\tilde{m}\varepsilon^2}{b^2}\right)$. In other words, deviations on the subsample $\tilde{m}$ dominate the overall deviation of $Q_m - Q_{\tilde{m}}$ from 0. This allows us to compute a cutoff criterion for evaluating Q_m by computing only a subset of its terms.

Cutoff Criterion

We need only solve (6.93) for $\frac{\tilde{m}}{m}$. Hence, in order to ensure that $Q_{\tilde{m}}$ is within ε of Q_m with probability $1 - \eta$, we have to take a fraction $\frac{\tilde{m}}{m}$ of samples that satisfies

$$\frac{\frac{\tilde{m}}{m}}{1 - \frac{\tilde{m}}{m}} = \frac{b^2(\ln 2 - \ln \eta)}{2m\varepsilon^2} =: c, \text{ and therefore } \frac{\tilde{m}}{m} = \frac{c}{1 + c}. \tag{6.96}$$

The fraction $\frac{\tilde{m}}{m}$ can be small for large m, which is exactly the case where we need methods to speed up evaluation.

6.5.3 Greedy Optimization Strategies

Quite often the overall goal is not necessarily to find the single best element x_i from a set X to solve a problem, but to find a good subset $\tilde{X} \subset X$ of size $\tilde{m}$ according to some quality criterion $Q[\tilde{X}]$. Problems of this type include approximating a matrix by a subset of its rows and columns (Section 10.2), finding approximate solutions to Kernel Fisher Discriminant Analysis (Chapter 15) and finding a sparse solution to the problem of Gaussian Process Regression (Section 16.3.4). These all have a common structure:

Applications

(i) Finding an optimal set $\tilde{X} \subset X$ is quite often a combinatorial problem, or it even may be NP-hard, since it means selecting $\tilde{m} = |\tilde{X}|$ elements from a set of $m = |X|$ elements. There are $\binom{m}{\tilde{m}}$ different choices, which clearly prevents an exhaustive search over all of them. Additionally, the size of $\tilde{m}$ is often not known beforehand. Hence we need a fast approximate algorithm.

(ii) The evaluation of $Q[\tilde{X} \cup \{x_i\}]$ is inexpensive, provided $Q[\tilde{X}]$ has been computed before. This indicates that an iterative algorithm can be useful.

(iii) The value of $Q[X]$, or equivalently how well we would do by taking the whole set X, can be bounded efficiently by using $Q[\tilde{X}]$ (or some by-products of the computation of $Q[\tilde{M}]$) without actually computing $Q[X]$.

Algorithm 6.6 Sparse Greedy Algorithm

Require: Set of functions X, Precision ϵ, Criterion $Q[\cdot]$
  Set $\tilde{X} = \emptyset$
  repeat
    Choose random subset X' of size m' from $X \backslash \tilde{X}$.
    Pick $\hat{x} = \operatorname{argmax}_{x \in X'} Q[X' \cup \{x\}]$
    $X' = X' \cup \{\hat{x}\}$
    If needed, (re)compute bound on $Q[X]$.
  until $Q[\tilde{X}] + \epsilon \geq$ Bound on $Q[X]$
Output: $\tilde{X}, Q[\tilde{X}]$

(iv) The set of functions X is typically very large (i.e. more than 10^5 elements), yet the individual improvements by f_i via $Q[\tilde{X} \cup \{x_i\}]$ do not differ too much, meaning that specific x_i for which $Q[\tilde{X} \cup \{x_i\}]$ deviate by a large amount from the rest of $Q[\tilde{X} \cup \{x_i\}]$ do not exist.

Iterative Enlargement of $\tilde{X}$

In this case we may use a sparse greedy algorithm to find near optimal solutions among the remaining $X \backslash \tilde{X}$ elements. This combines the idea of an iterative enlargement of $\tilde{X}$ by one more element at a time (which is feasible since we can compute $Q[\tilde{X} \cup \{f_i\}]$ cheaply) with the idea that we need not consider all f_i as possible candidates for the enlargement. This uses the reasoning in Section 6.5.1 combined with the fact that the distribution of the improvements is not too long tailed (cf. (iv)). The overall strategy is described in Algorithm 6.6.

Problems 6.9 and 6.10 contain more examples of sparse greedy algorithms.

6.6 Summary

This chapter gave an overview of different optimization methods, which form the basic toolbox for solving the problems arising in learning with kernels. The main focus was on convex and differentiable problems, hence the overview of properties of convex sets and functions defined on them.

The key insights in Section 6.1 are that *convex sets* can be defined by *level sets of convex functions* and that convex optimization problems have *one global minimum*. Furthermore, the fact that the solutions of convex maximization over polyhedral sets can be found on the vertices will prove useful in some unsupervised learning applications (Section 14.4).

Basic tools for unconstrained problems (Section 6.2) include interval cutting methods, the Newton method, Conjugate Gradient descent, and Predictor-Corrector methods. These techniques are often used as building blocks to solve more advanced constrained optimization problems.

Since constrained minimization is a fairly complex topic, we only presented a selection of fundamental results, such as necessary and sufficient conditions in the general case of nonlinear programming. The KKT conditions for differentiable convex functions then followed immediately from the previous reasoning. The main results are dualization, meaning the transformation of optimization problems via the Lagrangian mechanism into possibly simpler problems, and that optimality properties can be estimated via the KKT gap (Theorem 6.27).

Interior point algorithms are practical applications of the duality reasoning; these seek to find a solution to optimization problems by satisfying the KKT optimality conditions. Here we were able to employ some of the concepts introduced at an earlier stage, such as predictor corrector methods and numerical ways of finding roots of equations. These algorithms are robust tools to find solutions on moderately sized problems ($10^3 - 10^4$ examples). Larger problems require decomposition methods, to be discussed in Section 10.4, or randomized methods. The chapter concluded with an overview of randomized methods for maximizing functions or finding the best subset of elements. These techniques are useful once datasets are so large that we cannot reasonably hope to find exact solutions to optimization problems.

6.7 Problems

6.1 (Level Sets •) *Given the function $f : \mathbb{R}^2 \to \mathbb{R}$ with $f(x) := |x_1|^p + |x_2|^p$, for which p do we obtain a convex function?*

Now consider the sets $\{x | f(x) \leq c\}$ for some $c > 0$. Can you give an explicit parametrization of the boundary of the set? Is it easier to deal with this parametrization? Can you find other examples (see also [489] and Chapter 8 for details)?

6.2 (Convex Hulls •) *Show that for any set X, its convex hull $\operatorname{co} X$ is convex. Furthermore, show that $\operatorname{co} X = X$ if X is convex.*

6.3 (Method of False Position [334] •••) *Given a unimodal (possessing one minimum) differentiable function $f : \mathbb{R} \to \mathbb{R}$, develop a quadratic method for minimizing f.*

Hint: Recall the Newton method. There we used $f''(x)$ to make a quadratic approximation of f. Two values of $f'(x)$ are also sufficient to obtain this information, however.

What happens if we may only use f? What does the iteration scheme look like? See Figure 6.8 for a hint.

6.4 (Convex Minimization in one Variable ••) *Denote by f a convex function on $[a, b]$. Show that the algorithm below finds the minimum of f. What is the rate of convergence in x to $\operatorname{argmin}_x f(x)$? Can you obtain a bound in $f(x)$ wrt. $\min_x f(x)$?*

input a, b, f *and threshold* ε
  $x_1 = a, x_2 = \frac{a+b}{2}, x_3 = b$ *and compute* $f(x_1), f(x_2), f(x_3)$
  repeat
    if $x_3 - x_2 > x_2 - x_1$ **then**

$x_4 = \frac{x_2+x_3}{2}$ *and compute* $f(x_4)$
else
$x_4 = \frac{x_1+x_2}{2}$ *and compute* $f(x_4)$
end if
Keep the two points closest to the point with the minimum value of $f(x_i)$ *and rename them such that* $x_1 < x_2 < x_3$.
until $x_3 - x_1 \geq \varepsilon$

6.5 (Newton Method in $\mathbb{R}^d$ ••) *Extend the Newton method to functions on* $\mathbb{R}^d$. *What does the iteration rule look like? Under which conditions does the algorithm converge? Do you have to extend Theorem 6.13 to prove convergence?*

6.6 (Rewriting Quadratic Functionals •) *Given a function*

$$f(x) = x^\top Q x + c^\top x + d, \tag{6.97}$$

rewrite it into the form of (6.18). Give explicit expressions for $x^* = \operatorname{argmin}_x f(x)$ *and the difference in the additive constants.*

6.7 (Kantorovich Inequality [278] •••) *Prove Theorem 6.16. Hint: note that without loss of generality we may require* $\|x\|^2 = 1$. *Second, perform a transformation of coordinates into the eigensystem of K. Finally, note that in the new coordinate system we are dealing with convex combinations of eigenvalues* λ_i *and* $\frac{1}{\lambda_i}$. *First show (6.24) for only two eigenvalues. Then argue that only the largest and smallest eigenvalues matter.*

6.8 (Random Subsets •) *Generate m random numbers drawn uniformly from the interval* $[0,1]$. *Plot their distribution function. Plot the distribution of maxima of subsets of random numbers. What can you say about the distribution of the maxima? What happens if you draw randomly from the Laplace distribution, with density* $p(\xi) = e^{-\xi}$ *(for* $\xi \geq 0$*)?*

6.9 (Matching Pursuit [342] ••) *Denote by* $f_1, \ldots, f_M$ *a set of functions* $\mathcal{X} \to \mathbb{R}$, *by* $\{x_1, \ldots, x_m\} \subset \mathcal{X}$ *a set of locations and by* $\{y_1, \ldots, y_m\} \subset \mathcal{Y}$ *a set of corresponding observations.*

Design a sparse greedy algorithm that finds a linear combination of functions $f := \sum_i \alpha_i f_i$ *minimizing the squared loss between* $f(x_i)$ *and* y_i.

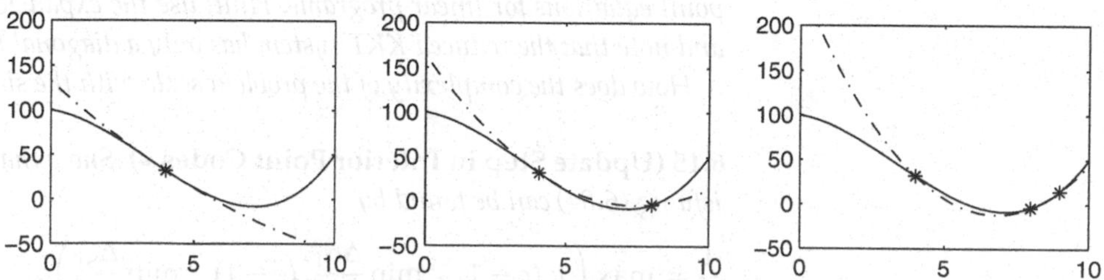

Figure 6.8 From left to right: Newton method, method of false position, quadratic interpolation through 3 points. Solid line: $f(x)$, dash-dotted line: interpolation.

6.10 (Reduced Set Approximation [474] ••) *Let $f(x) = \sum_{i=1}^{m} \alpha_i k(x_i, x)$ be a kernel expansion in a Reproducing Kernel Hilbert Space $\mathcal{H}_k$ (see Section 2.2.3). Give a sparse greedy algorithm that finds an approximation to f in $\mathcal{H}_k$ by using fewer terms. See also Chapter 18 for more detail.*

6.11 (Equality Constraints in LP and QP ••) *Find the dual optimization problem and the necessary KKT conditions for the following optimization problem:*

$$\begin{aligned} \underset{x}{\text{minimize}} \quad & c^\top x, \\ \textit{subject to} \quad & Ax + b \leq 0, \\ & Cx + d = 0, \end{aligned} \tag{6.98}$$

where $c, x \in \mathbb{R}^m$, $b \in \mathbb{R}^n$, $d \in \mathbb{R}^{n'}$, $A \in R^{n \times m}$ and $C \in \mathbb{R}^{n'}$. Hint: split up the equality constraints into two inequality constraints. Note that you may combine the two Lagrange multipliers again to obtain a free variable. Derive the corresponding conditions for

$$\begin{aligned} \underset{x}{\text{minimize}} \quad & \tfrac{1}{2} x^\top K x + c^\top x, \\ \textit{subject to} \quad & Ax + b \leq 0, \\ & Cx + d = 0, \end{aligned} \tag{6.99}$$

where K is a strictly positive definite matrix.

6.12 (Not Strictly Definite Quadratic Parts •••) *How do you have to change the dual of (6.99) if K does not have full rank? Is it better not to dualize in this case? Do the KKT conditions still hold?*

6.13 (Dual Problems of Quadratic Programs ••) *Denote by P a quadratic optimization problem of type (6.72) and by $(\cdot)^D$ the dualization operation. Prove that the following is true,*

$$((P^D)^D)^D = P^D \text{ and } (((P^D)^D)^D)^D = (P^D)^D, \tag{6.100}$$

where in general $(P^D)^D \neq P$. Hint: use (6.80). Caution: you have to check whether $KA^\top$ has full rank.

6.14 (Interior Point Equations for Linear Programs [336] •••) *Derive the interior point equations for linear programs. Hint: use the expansions for the quadratic programs and note that the reduced KKT system has only a diagonal term where we had K before.*

How does the complexity of the problem scale with the size of A?

6.15 (Update Step in Interior Point Codes •) *Show that the maximum value of λ satisfying (6.84) can be found by*

$$\frac{1}{\lambda} = \max\left(1, (\epsilon - 1)^{-1} \min_{i \in [n]} \frac{\Delta\alpha_i}{\alpha_i}, (\epsilon - 1)^{-1} \min_{i \in [n]} \frac{\Delta\xi_i}{\xi_i}\right). \tag{6.101}$$

II SUPPORT VECTOR MACHINES

The algorithms for constructing the separating hyperplane considered above will be utilized for developing a battery of programs for pattern recognition.

V. N. Vapnik [560, p. 364]

Now that we have the necessary concepts and tools, we move on to the class of Support Vector (SV) algorithms. SV algorithms are commonly considered the first practicable spin-off of statistical learning theory. We described the basic ideas of Support Vector machines (SVMs) in Chapter 1. It is now time for a much more detailed discussion and description of SVMs, starting with the case of *pattern recognition* (Chapter 7), which was historically the first to be developed.

Following this, we move on to a problem that can actually be considered as being even simpler than pattern recognition. In pattern recognition, we try to distinguish between patterns of at least two classes; in single-class classification (Chapter 8), however, there is only one class. In the latter case, which belongs to the realm of unsupervised learning, we try to learn a model of the data which describes, in a weak sense, what the training data looks like. This model can then be used to assess the "typicality" or novelty of previously unseen patterns, a task which is rather useful in a number of application domains.

Chapter 9 introduces SV algorithms for regression estimation. These retain most of the properties of the other SV algorithms, with the exception that in the regression case, the choice of the loss function, as described in Chapter 3, becomes a more interesting issue.

After this, we give details on how to implement the various types of SV algorithms (Chapter 10), and we describe some methods for incorporating prior knowledge about invariances of a given problem into SVMs (Chapter 11).

We conclude this part of the book by revisiting statistical learning theory, this time with a much stronger emphasis on elements that are specific to SVMs and kernel methods (Chapter 12).

7 Pattern Recognition

This chapter is devoted to a detailed description of SV classification (SVC) methods. We have already briefly visited the SVC algorithm in Chapter 1. There will be some overlap with that chapter, but here we give a more thorough treatment.

Overview

We start by describing the classifier that forms the basis for SVC, the separating hyperplane (Section 7.1). Separating hyperplanes can differ in how large a margin of separation they induce between the classes, with corresponding consequences on the generalization error, as discussed in Section 7.2. The "optimal" margin hyperplane is defined in Section 7.3, along with a description of how to compute it. Using the kernel trick of Chapter 2, we generalize to the case where the optimal margin hyperplane is not computed in input space, but in a feature space nonlinearly related to the latter (Section 7.4). This dramatically increases the applicability of the approach, as does the introduction of slack variables to deal with outliers and noise in the data (Section 7.5). Many practical problems require us to classify the data into more than just two classes. Section 7.6 describes how multi-class SV classification systems can be built. Following this, Section 7.7 describes some variations on standard SV classification algorithms, differing in the regularizers and constraints that are used. We conclude with a fairly detailed section on experiments and applications (Section 7.8).

Prerequisites

This chapter requires basic knowledge of kernels, as conveyed in the first half of Chapter 2. To understand details of the optimization problems, it is helpful (but not indispensable) to get some background from Chapter 6. To understand the connections to learning theory, in particular regarding the statistical basis of the regularizer used in SV classification, it would be useful to have read Chapter 5.

7.1 Separating Hyperplanes

Hyperplane

Suppose we are given a dot product space $\mathcal{H}$, and a set of pattern vectors $\mathbf{x}_1, \ldots, \mathbf{x}_m \in \mathcal{H}$. Any hyperplane in $\mathcal{H}$ can be written as

$$\{\mathbf{x} \in \mathcal{H} | \langle \mathbf{w}, \mathbf{x} \rangle + b = 0\}, \quad \mathbf{w} \in \mathcal{H}, b \in \mathbb{R}. \tag{7.1}$$

In this formulation, $\mathbf{w}$ is a vector orthogonal to the hyperplane: If $\mathbf{w}$ has unit length, then $\langle \mathbf{w}, \mathbf{x} \rangle$ is the length of $\mathbf{x}$ along the direction of $\mathbf{w}$ (Figure 7.1). For general $\mathbf{w}$, this number will be scaled by $\|\mathbf{w}\|$. In any case, the set (7.1) consists

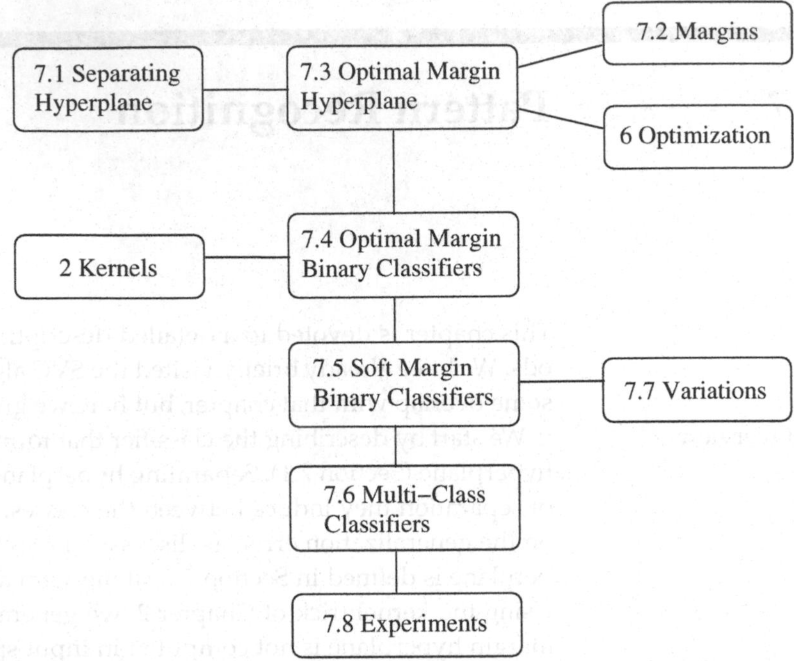

of vectors that all have the same length along $\mathbf{w}$. In other words, these are vectors that project onto the same point on the line spanned by $\mathbf{w}$.

In this formulation, we still have the freedom to multiply $\mathbf{w}$ and b by the same non-zero constant. This superfluous freedom — physicists would call it a "gauge" freedom — can be abolished as follows.

Definition 7.1 (Canonical Hyperplane) *The pair* $(\mathbf{w}, b) \in \mathcal{H} \times \mathbb{R}$ *is called a* canonical *form of the hyperplane (7.1) with respect to* $\mathbf{x}_1, \ldots, \mathbf{x}_m \in \mathcal{H}$*, if it is scaled such that*

$$\min_{i=1,\ldots,m} |\langle \mathbf{w}, \mathbf{x}_i \rangle + b| = 1, \tag{7.2}$$

which amounts to saying that the point closest to the hyperplane has a distance of $1/\|\mathbf{w}\|$ *(Figure 7.2).*

Note that the condition (7.2) still allows two such pairs: given a canonical hyperplane $(\mathbf{w}, b)$, another one satisfying (7.2) is given by $(-\mathbf{w}, -b)$. For the purpose of pattern recognition, these two hyperplanes turn out to be different, as they are oriented differently; they correspond to two *decision functions*,

Decision Function

$$f_{\mathbf{w},b} : \mathcal{H} \to \{\pm 1\}$$
$$\mathbf{x} \mapsto f_{\mathbf{w},b}(\mathbf{x}) = \operatorname{sgn}\left(\langle \mathbf{w}, \mathbf{x} \rangle + b\right), \tag{7.3}$$

which are the inverse of each other.

In the absence of class labels $y_i \in \{\pm 1\}$ associated with the $\mathbf{x}_i$, there is no way of distinguishing the two hyperplanes. For a *labelled* dataset, a distinction exists: The two hyperplanes make opposite class assignments. In pattern recognition,

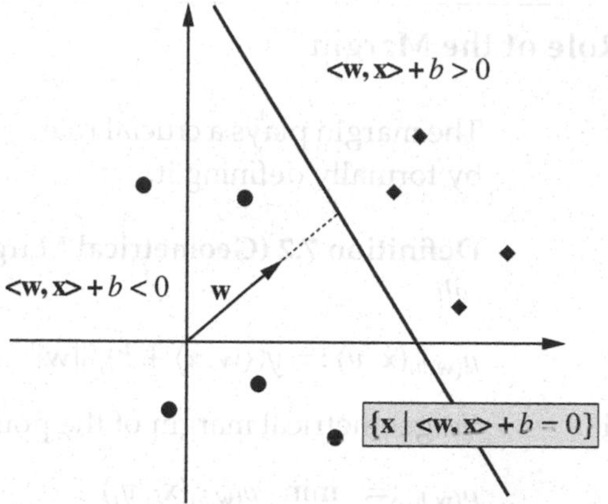

Figure 7.1 A separable classification problem, along with a separating hyperplane, written in terms of an orthogonal weight vector **w** and a threshold b. Note that by multiplying both **w** and b by the same non-zero constant, we obtain the same hyperplane, represented in terms of different parameters. Figure 7.2 shows how to eliminate this scaling freedom.

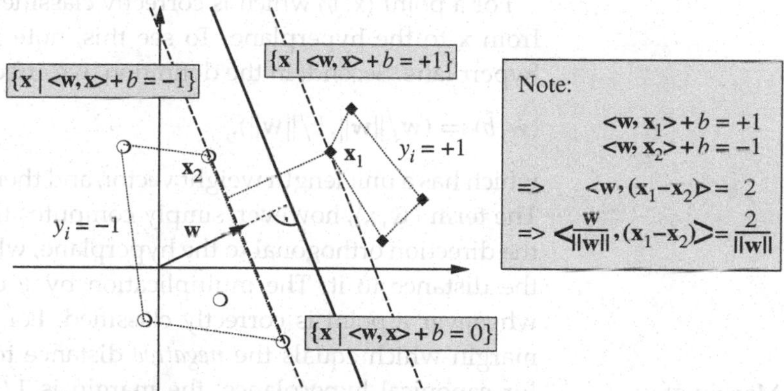

Figure 7.2 By requiring the scaling of **w** and b to be such that the point(s) closest to the hyperplane satisfy $|\langle \mathbf{w}, \mathbf{x}_i \rangle + b| = 1$, we obtain a *canonical* form $(\mathbf{w}, b)$ of a hyperplane. Note that in this case, the margin, measured perpendicularly to the hyperplane, equals $1/\|\mathbf{w}\|$. This can be seen by considering two opposite points which precisely satisfy $|\langle \mathbf{w}, \mathbf{x}_i \rangle + b| = 1$ (cf. Problem 7.4)

we attempt to find a solution $f_{\mathbf{w},b}$ which *correctly classifies* the labelled examples $(\mathbf{x}_i, y_i) \in \mathcal{H} \times \{\pm 1\}$; in other words, which satisfies $f_{\mathbf{w},b}(\mathbf{x}_i) = y_i$ for all i (in this case, the training set is said to be *separable*), or at least for a large fraction thereof.

The next section will introduce the term *margin*, to denote the distance to a separating hyperplane from the point closest to it. It will be argued that to generalize well, a large margin should be sought. In view of Figure 7.2, this can be achieved by keeping $\|\mathbf{w}\|$ small. Readers who are content with this level of detail may skip the next section and proceed directly to Section 7.3, where we describe how to construct the hyperplane with the largest margin.

7.2 The Role of the Margin

The margin plays a crucial role in the design of SV learning algorithms. Let us start by formally defining it.

Definition 7.2 (Geometrical Margin) *For a hyperplane* $\{\mathbf{x} \in \mathcal{H} | \langle \mathbf{w}, \mathbf{x} \rangle + b = 0\}$, *we call*

$$\rho_{(\mathbf{w},b)}(\mathbf{x}, y) := y(\langle \mathbf{w}, \mathbf{x} \rangle + b)/\|\mathbf{w}\| \tag{7.4}$$

Geometrical Margin

the geometrical margin of the point $(\mathbf{x}, y) \in \mathcal{H} \times \{\pm 1\}$. *The minimum value*

$$\rho_{(\mathbf{w},b)} := \min_{i=1,\dots,m} \rho_{(\mathbf{w},b)}(\mathbf{x}_i, y_i) \tag{7.5}$$

shall be called the geometrical margin of $(\mathbf{x}_1, y_1), \dots, (\mathbf{x}_m, y_m)$. *If the latter is omitted, it is understood that the training set is meant.*

Occasionally, we will omit the qualification *geometrical*, and simply refer to the *margin*.

For a point $(\mathbf{x}, y)$ which is correctly classified, the margin is simply the distance from $\mathbf{x}$ to the hyperplane. To see this, note first that the margin is zero *on* the hyperplane. Second, in the definition, we effectively consider a hyperplane

$$(\hat{\mathbf{w}}, \hat{b}) := (\mathbf{w}/\|\mathbf{w}\|, b/\|\mathbf{w}\|), \tag{7.6}$$

which has a unit length weight vector, and then compute the quantity $y(\langle \hat{\mathbf{w}}, \mathbf{x} \rangle + \hat{b})$. The term $\langle \hat{\mathbf{w}}, \mathbf{x} \rangle$, however, simply computes the length of the projection of $\mathbf{x}$ onto the direction orthogonal to the hyperplane, which, after adding the offset $\hat{b}$, equals the distance to it. The multiplication by y ensures that the margin is positive whenever a point is correctly classified. For misclassified points, we thus get a margin which equals the *negative* distance to the hyperplane. Finally, note that for canonical hyperplanes, the margin is $1/\|\mathbf{w}\|$ (Figure 7.2). The definition of the canonical hyperplane thus ensures that the length of $\mathbf{w}$ now corresponds to a meaningful geometrical quantity.

Margin of Canonical Hyperplanes

It turns out that the margin of a separating hyperplane, and thus the length of the weight vector $\mathbf{w}$, plays a fundamental role in support vector type algorithms. Loosely speaking, if we manage to separate the training data with a large margin, then we have reason to believe that we will do well on the test set. Not surprisingly, there exist a number of explanations for this intuition, ranging from the simple to the rather technical. We will now briefly sketch some of them.

Insensitivity to Pattern Noise

The simplest possible justification for large margins is as follows. Since the training and test data are assumed to have been generated by the same underlying dependence, it seems reasonable to assume that most of the test patterns will lie close (in $\mathcal{H}$) to at least one of the training patterns. For the sake of simplicity, let us consider the case where *all* test points are generated by adding bounded pattern noise (sometimes called input noise) to the training patterns. More precisely, given a training point $(\mathbf{x}, y)$, we will generate test points of the form $(\mathbf{x} + \Delta\mathbf{x}, y)$, where

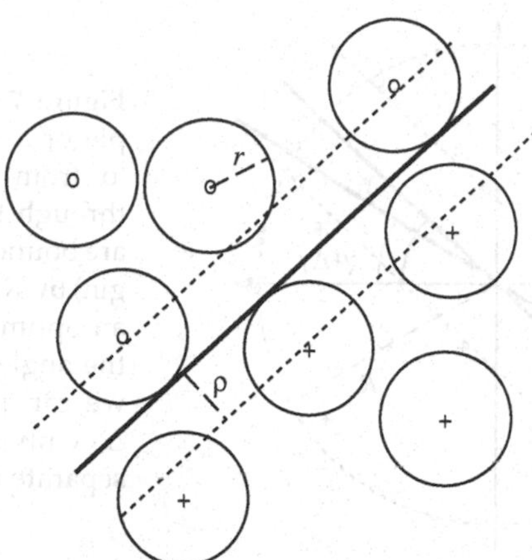

Figure 7.3 Two-dimensional toy example of a classification problem: Separate 'o' from '+' using a hyperplane. Suppose that we add bounded noise to each pattern. If the optimal margin hyperplane has margin ρ, and the noise is bounded by $r < \rho$, then the hyperplane will correctly separate even the noisy patterns. Conversely, if we ran the perceptron algorithm (which finds *some* separating hyperplane, but not necessarily the optimal one) on the noisy data, then we would recover the optimal hyperplane in the limit $r \to \rho$.

$\Delta\mathbf{x} \in \mathcal{H}$ is bounded in norm by some $r > 0$. Clearly, if we manage to separate the training set with a margin $\rho > r$, we will correctly classify *all* test points: Since all training points have a distance of at least ρ to the hyperplane, the test patterns will still be on the correct side (Figure 7.3, cf. also [152]).

If we knew ρ beforehand, then this could actually be turned into an optimal margin classifier training algorithm, as follows. If we use an r which is slightly smaller than ρ, then even the patterns with added noise will be separable with a nonzero margin. In this case, the standard perceptron algorithm can be shown to converge.[1]

Therefore, we can run the perceptron algorithm on the noisy patterns. If the algorithm finds a sufficient number of noisy versions of each pattern, with different perturbations $\Delta\mathbf{x}$, then the resulting hyperplane will not intersect any of the balls depicted in Figure 7.3. As r approaches ρ, the resulting hyperplane should better approximate the maximum margin solution (the figure depicts the limit $r = \rho$). This constitutes a connection between training with pattern noise and maximizing the margin. The latter, in turn, can be thought of as a regularizer, comparable to those discussed earlier (see Chapter 4 and (2.49)). Similar connections to training with noise, for other types of regularizers, have been pointed out before for neural networks [50].

1. Rosenblatt's perceptron algorithm [439] is one of the simplest conceivable iterative procedures for computing a separating hyperplane. In its simplest form, it proceeds as follows. We start with an arbitrary weight vector $\mathbf{w}_0$. At step $n \in \mathbb{N}$, we consider the training example $(\mathbf{x}_n, y_n)$. If it is classified correctly using the current weight vector (i.e., if $\operatorname{sgn}\langle \mathbf{x}_n, \mathbf{w}_{n-1}\rangle = y_n$), we set $\mathbf{w}_n := \mathbf{w}_{n-1}$; otherwise, we set $\mathbf{w}_n := \mathbf{w}_{n-1} + \eta y_i \mathbf{x}_i$ (here, $\eta > 0$ is a learning rate). We thus loop over all patterns repeatedly, until we can complete one full pass through the training set without a single error. The resulting weight vector will thus classify all points correctly. Novikoff [386] proved that this procedure terminates, provided that the training set is separable with a nonzero margin.

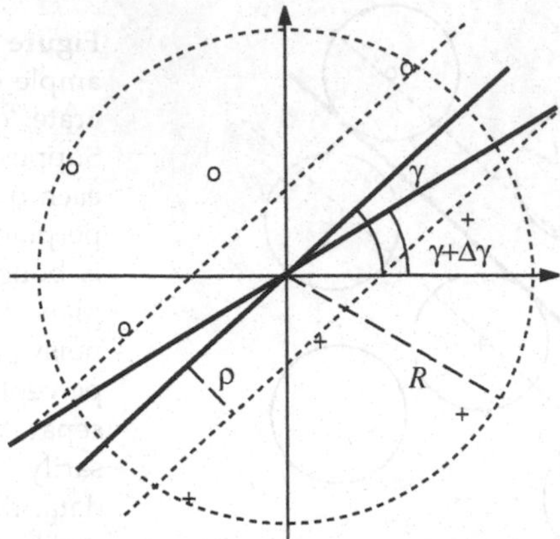

Figure 7.4 Two-dimensional toy example of a classification problem: Separate 'o' from '+' using a hyperplane passing through the origin. Suppose the patterns are bounded in length (distance to the origin) by R, and the classes are separated by an optimal hyperplane (parametrized by the angle γ) with margin ρ. In this case, we can perturb the parameter by some $\Delta\gamma$ with $|\Delta\gamma| < \arcsin \frac{\rho}{R}$, and still correctly separate the data.

Parameter Noise

A similar robustness argument can be made for the dependence of the hyperplane on the parameters $(\mathbf{w}, b)$ (cf. [504]). If all points lie at a distance of at least ρ from the hyperplane, and the patterns are bounded in length, then small perturbations to the hyperplane parameters will not change the classification of the training data (see Figure 7.4).[2] Being able to perturb the parameters of the hyperplane amounts to saying that to store the hyperplane, we need fewer bits than we would for a hyperplane whose *exact* parameter settings are crucial. Interestingly, this is related to what is called the Minimum Description Length principle ([583, 433, 485], cf. also [522, 305, 94]): The best description of the data, in terms of generalization error, should be the one that requires the fewest bits to store.

VC Margin Bound

We now move on to a more technical justification of large margin algorithms. For simplicity, we only deal with hyperplanes that have offset $b = 0$, leaving $f(\mathbf{x}) = \operatorname{sgn} \langle \mathbf{w}, \mathbf{x} \rangle$. The theorem below follows from a result in [24].

Margin Error

Theorem 7.3 (Margin Error Bound) *Consider the set of decision functions* $f(\mathbf{x}) = \operatorname{sgn} \langle \mathbf{w}, \mathbf{x} \rangle$ *with* $\|\mathbf{w}\| \leq \Lambda$ *and* $\|\mathbf{x}\| \leq R$, *for some* $R, \Lambda > 0$. *Moreover, let* $\rho > 0$, *and* ν *denote the fraction of training examples with margin smaller than* $\rho / \|\mathbf{w}\|$, *referred to as the* margin error.

For all distributions P *generating the data, with probability at least* $1 - \delta$ *over the drawing of the* m *training patterns, and for any* $\rho > 0$ *and* $\delta \in (0, 1)$, *the probability that a test pattern drawn from* P *will be misclassified is bounded from above, by*

$$\nu + \sqrt{\frac{c}{m}\left(\frac{R^2\Lambda^2}{\rho^2}\ln^2 m + \ln(1/\delta)\right)}. \tag{7.7}$$

Here, c *is a universal constant.*

2. Note that this would not hold true if we allowed patterns of arbitrary length — this type of restriction of the pattern lengths pops up in various places, such as Novikoff's theorem [386], Vapnik's VC dimension bound for margin classifiers (Theorem 5.5), and Theorem 7.3.

Let us try to understand this theorem. It makes a probabilistic statement about a probability, by giving an upper bound on the probability of test error, which *itself* only holds true with a certain probability, $1-\delta$. Where do these two probabilities come from? The first is due to the fact that the *test* examples are randomly drawn from P; the second is due to the *training* examples being drawn from P. Strictly speaking, the bound does not refer to a *single* classifier that has been trained on some fixed data set at hand, but to an ensemble of classifiers, trained on various instantiations of training sets generated by the same underlying regularity P.

It is beyond the scope of the present chapter to prove this result. The basic ingredients of bounds of this type, commonly referred to as *VC bounds*, are described in Chapter 5; for further details, see Chapter 12, and [562, 491, 504, 125]. Several aspects of the bound are noteworthy. The test error is bounded by a sum of the margin error ν, and a capacity term (the $\sqrt{\dots}$ term in (7.7)), with the latter tending to zero as the number of examples, m, tends to infinity. The capacity term can be kept small by keeping R and Λ small, and making ρ large. If we assume that R and Λ are fixed a priori, the main influence is ρ. As can be seen from (7.7), a large ρ leads to a small capacity term, but the margin error ν gets larger. A small ρ, on the other hand, will usually cause fewer points to have margins smaller than $\rho/\|\mathbf{w}\|$, leading to a smaller margin error; but the capacity penalty will increase correspondingly. The overall message: Try to find a hyperplane which is aligned such that even for a large ρ, there are few margin errors.

Maximizing ρ, however, is the same as minimizing the length of $\mathbf{w}$. Hence we might just as well keep ρ fixed, say, equal to 1 (which is the case for canonical hyperplanes), and search for a hyperplane which has a small $\|\mathbf{w}\|$ and few points with a margin smaller than $1/\|\mathbf{w}\|$; in other words (Definition 7.2), few points such that $y\langle\mathbf{w},\mathbf{x}\rangle < 1$.

It should be emphasized that dropping the condition $\|\mathbf{w}\| \leq \Lambda$ would prevent us from stating a bound of the kind shown above. We could give an alternative bound, where the capacity depends on the dimensionality of the space $\mathcal{H}$. The crucial advantage of the bound given above is that it is independent of that dimensionality, enabling us to work in very high dimensional spaces. This will become important when we make use of the kernel trick.

It has recently been pointed out that the margin also plays a crucial role in improving asymptotic rates in nonparametric estimation [551]. This topic, however, is beyond the scope of the present book.

Implementation in Hardware

To conclude this section, we note that large margin classifiers also have advantages of a practical nature: An algorithm that can separate a dataset with a certain margin will behave in a benign way when implemented in hardware. Real-world systems typically work only within certain accuracy bounds, and if the classifier is insensitive to small changes in the inputs, it will usually tolerate those inaccuracies.

We have thus accumulated a fair amount of evidence in favor of the following approach: Keep the margin training error small, and the margin large, in order to achieve high generalization ability. In other words, hyperplane decision functions should be constructed such that they maximize the margin, and at the same time separate the training data with as few exceptions as possible. Sections 7.3 and 7.5 respectively will deal with these two issues.

7.3 Optimal Margin Hyperplanes

Let us now derive the optimization problem to be solved for computing the optimal hyperplane. Suppose we are given a set of examples $(\mathbf{x}_1, y_1), \ldots, (\mathbf{x}_m, y_m)$, $\mathbf{x}_i \in \mathcal{H}$, $y_i \in \{\pm 1\}$. Here and below, the index i runs over $1, \ldots, m$ by default. We assume that there is at least one negative and one positive y_i. We want to find a decision function $f_{\mathbf{w},b}(\mathbf{x}) = \operatorname{sgn}(\langle \mathbf{w}, \mathbf{x}\rangle + b)$ satisfying

$$f_{\mathbf{w},b}(\mathbf{x}_i) = y_i. \tag{7.8}$$

If such a function exists (the non-separable case will be dealt with later), canonicality (7.2) implies

$$y_i(\langle \mathbf{x}_i, \mathbf{w}\rangle + b) \geq 1. \tag{7.9}$$

As an aside, note that out of the two canonical forms of the same hyperplane, $(\mathbf{w}, b)$ and $(-\mathbf{w}, -b)$, only one will satisfy equations (7.8) and (7.11). The existence of class labels thus allows to distinguish two orientations of a hyperplane.

Following the previous section, a separating hyperplane which generalizes well can thus be constructed by solving the following problem:

$$\underset{\mathbf{w}\in\mathcal{H}, b\in\mathbb{R}}{\text{minimize}} \quad \tau(\mathbf{w}) = \frac{1}{2}\|\mathbf{w}\|^2, \tag{7.10}$$

$$\text{subject to} \quad y_i(\langle \mathbf{x}_i, \mathbf{w}\rangle + b) \geq 1 \text{ for all } i = 1, \ldots, m. \tag{7.11}$$

This is called the *primal optimization problem.*

Problems like this one are the subject of optimization theory. For details on how to solve them, see Chapter 6; for a short intuitive explanation, cf. the remarks following (1.26) in the introductory chapter. We will now derive the so-called *dual problem*, which can be shown to have the same solutions as (7.10). In the present case, it will turn out that it is more convenient to deal with the dual. To derive it, we introduce the Lagrangian,

Lagrangian

$$L(\mathbf{w}, b, \boldsymbol{\alpha}) = \frac{1}{2}\|\mathbf{w}\|^2 - \sum_{i=1}^{m} \alpha_i \left(y_i(\langle \mathbf{x}_i, \mathbf{w}\rangle + b) - 1\right), \tag{7.12}$$

with Lagrange multipliers $\alpha_i \geq 0$. Recall that as in Chapter 1, we use bold face Greek variables to refer to the corresponding vectors of variables, for instance, $\boldsymbol{\alpha} = (\alpha_1, \ldots, \alpha_m)$.

The Lagrangian L must be maximized with respect to α_i, and minimized with respect to $\mathbf{w}$ and b (see Theorem 6.26). Consequently, at this saddle point, the derivatives of L with respect to the primal variables must vanish,

$$\frac{\partial}{\partial b}L(\mathbf{w}, b, \boldsymbol{\alpha}) = 0, \quad \frac{\partial}{\partial \mathbf{w}}L(\mathbf{w}, b, \boldsymbol{\alpha}) = 0, \tag{7.13}$$

which leads to

$$\sum_{i=1}^{m} \alpha_i y_i = 0, \tag{7.14}$$

and

$$\mathbf{w} = \sum_{i=1}^{m} \alpha_i y_i \mathbf{x}_i. \tag{7.15}$$

The solution vector thus has an expansion in terms of training examples. Note that although the solution $\mathbf{w}$ is unique (due to the strict convexity of (7.10), and the convexity of (7.11)), the coefficients α_i need not be.

According to the KKT theorem (Chapter 6), only the Lagrange multipliers α_i that are non-zero at the saddle point, correspond to constraints (7.11) which are precisely met. Formally, for all $i = 1, \ldots, m$, we have

$$\alpha_i[y_i(\langle \mathbf{x}_i, \mathbf{w}\rangle + b) - 1] = 0. \tag{7.16}$$

Support Vectors

The patterns $\mathbf{x}_i$ for which $\alpha_i > 0$ are called *Support Vectors*. This terminology is related to corresponding terms in the theory of convex sets, relevant to convex optimization (e.g., [334, 45]).[3] According to (7.16), they lie exactly on the margin.[4] All remaining examples in the training set are irrelevant: Their constraints (7.11) are satisfied automatically, and they do not appear in the expansion (7.15), since their multipliers satisfy $\alpha_i = 0$.[5]

This leads directly to an upper bound on the generalization ability of optimal margin hyperplanes. To this end, we consider the so-called leave-one-out method (for further details, see Section 12.2) to estimate the expected test error [335, 559]. This procedure is based on the idea that if we leave out one of the training

3. Given any boundary point of a convex set, there always exists a hyperplane separating the point from the interior of the set. This is called a *supporting hyperplane*.

SVs lie on the boundary of the convex hulls of the two classes, thus they possess supporting hyperplanes. The SV optimal hyperplane is the hyperplane which lies in the middle of the two parallel supporting hyperplanes (of the two classes) with maximum distance.

Conversely, from the optimal hyperplane, we can obtain supporting hyperplanes for all SVs of both classes, by shifting it by $1/\|\mathbf{w}\|$ in both directions.

4. Note that this implies the solution $(\mathbf{w}, b)$, where b is computed using $y_i(\langle \mathbf{w}, \mathbf{x}_i\rangle + b) = 1$ for SVs, *is* in canonical form with respect to the training data. (This makes use of the reasonable assumption that the training set contains both positive and negative examples.)

5. In a statistical mechanics framework, Anlauf and Biehl [12] have put forward a similar argument for the *optimal stability perceptron*, also computed using constrained optimization. There is a large body of work in the physics community on optimal margin classification. Some further references of interest are [310, 191, 192, 394, 449, 141]; other early works include [313].

examples, and train on the remaining ones, then the probability of error on the left out example gives us a fair indication of the true test error. Of course, doing this for a single training example leads to an error of either zero or one, so it does not yet give an estimate of the test error. The leave-one-out method *repeats* this procedure for each individual training example in turn, and averages the resulting errors.

Let us return to the present case. If we leave out a pattern $\mathbf{x}_{i^*}$, and construct the solution from the remaining patterns, the following outcomes are possible (cf. (7.11)):

1. $y_{i^*}(\langle \mathbf{x}_{i^*}, \mathbf{w}\rangle + b) > 1$. In this case, the pattern is classified correctly and does not lie on the margin. These are patterns that would not have become SVs anyway.
2. $y_{i^*}(\langle \mathbf{x}_{i^*}, \mathbf{w}\rangle + b) = 1$. In other words, $\mathbf{x}_{i^*}$ exactly meets the constraint (7.11). In this case, the solution $\mathbf{w}$ does not change, even though the coefficients α_i would change: Namely, if $\mathbf{x}_{i^*}$ might have become a Support Vector (i.e., $\alpha_{i^*} > 0$) had it been kept in the training set. In that case, the fact that the solution is the same, no matter whether $\mathbf{x}_{i^*}$ is in the training set or not, means that $\mathbf{x}_{i^*}$ can be written as $\sum_{\mathrm{SVs}} \beta_i y_i \mathbf{x}_i$ with, $\beta_i \geq 0$. Note that condition 2 is *not* equivalent to saying that $\mathbf{x}_{i^*}$ may be written as some linear combination of the remaining Support Vectors: Since the sign of the coefficients in the linear combination is determined by the class of the respective pattern, not any linear combination will do. Strictly speaking, $\mathbf{x}_{i^*}$ must lie in the cone spanned by the $y_i \mathbf{x}_i$, where the $\mathbf{x}_i$ are all Support Vectors.[6] For more detail, see [565] and Section 12.2.
3. $0 < y_{i^*}(\langle \mathbf{x}_{i^*}, \mathbf{w}\rangle + b) < 1$. In this case, $\mathbf{x}_{i^*}$ lies within the margin, but still on the correct side of the decision boundary. Thus, the solution looks different from the one obtained with $\mathbf{x}_{i^*}$ in the training set (in that case, $\mathbf{x}_{i^*}$ would satisfy (7.11) after training); classification is nevertheless correct.
4. $y_{i^*}(\langle \mathbf{x}_{i^*}, \mathbf{w}\rangle + b) > 0$. This means that $\mathbf{x}_{i^*}$ is classified incorrectly.

Note that cases 3 and 4 necessarily correspond to examples which would have become SVs if kept in the training set; case 2 potentially includes such situations. Only case 4, however, leads to an error in the leave-one-out procedure. Consequently, we have the following result on the generalization error of optimal margin classifiers [570]:[7]

Leave-One-Out Bound

Proposition 7.4 *The expectation of the number of Support Vectors obtained during training on a training set of size m, divided by m, is an* upper bound *on the expected probability of test error of the SVM trained on training sets of size* $m - 1$.[8]

6. Possible non-uniqueness of the solution's expansion in terms of SVs is related to zero Eigenvalues of $(y_i y_j k(x_i, x_j))_{ij}$, cf. Proposition 2.16. Note, however, the above caveat on the distinction between linear combinations, and linear combinations with coefficients of fixed sign.
7. It also holds for the generalized versions of optimal margin classifiers described in the following sections.
8. Note that the leave-one-out procedure performed with m training examples thus yields

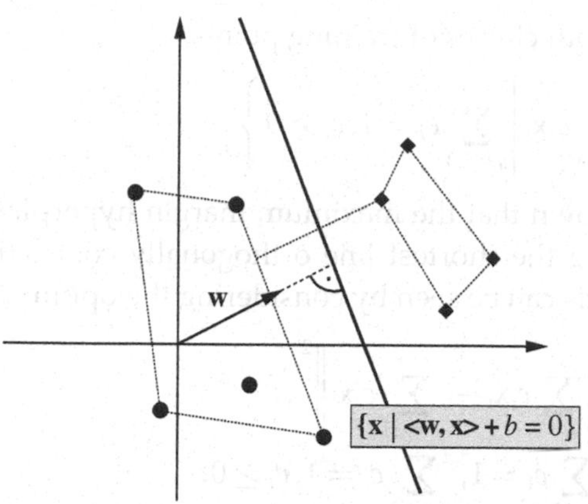

Figure 7.5 The optimal hyperplane (Figure 7.2) is the one bisecting the shortest connection between the convex hulls of the two classes.

A sharper bound can be formulated by making a further distinction in case 2, between SVs that must occur in the solution, and those that can be expressed in terms of the other SVs (see [570, 565, 268, 549] and Section 12.2).

We now return to the optimization problem to be solved. Substituting the conditions for the extremum, (7.14) and (7.15), into the Lagrangian (7.12), we arrive at the dual form of the optimization problem:

Quadratic Program of Optimal Margin Classifier

$$\underset{\alpha \in \mathbb{R}^m}{\text{maximize}} \; W(\alpha) = \sum_{i=1}^{m} \alpha_i - \frac{1}{2} \sum_{i,j=1}^{m} \alpha_i \alpha_j y_i y_j \langle \mathbf{x}_i, \mathbf{x}_j \rangle, \tag{7.17}$$

$$\text{subject to } \; \alpha_i \geq 0, \; i = 1, \ldots, m, \tag{7.18}$$

$$\text{and } \sum_{i=1}^{m} \alpha_i y_i = 0. \tag{7.19}$$

On substitution of the expansion (7.15) into the decision function (7.3), we obtain an expression which can be evaluated in terms of dot products, taken between the pattern to be classified and the Support Vectors,

$$f(\mathbf{x}) = \operatorname{sgn}\left(\sum_{i=1}^{m} \alpha_i y_i \langle \mathbf{x}, \mathbf{x}_i \rangle + b \right). \tag{7.20}$$

To conclude this section, we note that there is an alternative way to derive the dual optimization problem [38]. To describe it, we first form the convex hulls C_+

a bound valid for training sets of size $m-1$. This difference, however, does not usually mislead us too much. In statistical terms, the leave-one-out error is called *almost unbiased*. Note, moreover, that the statement talks about the *expected probability* of test error — there are thus *two* sources of randomness. One is the expectation over different training sets of size $m-1$, the other is the probability of test error when one of the SVMs is faced with a test example drawn from the underlying distribution generating the data. For a generalization, see Theorem 12.9.

and C_- of both classes of training points,

$$C_\pm := \left\{ \sum_{y_i=\pm 1} c_i \mathbf{x}_i \,\middle|\, \sum_{y_i=\pm 1} c_i = 1, c_i \geq 0 \right\}. \tag{7.21}$$

Convex Hull Separation

It can be shown that the maximum margin hyperplane as described above is the one bisecting the shortest line orthogonally connecting C_+ and C_- (Figure 7.5). Formally, this can be seen by considering the optimization problem

$$\begin{aligned} &\underset{\mathbf{c}\in\mathbb{R}^m}{\text{minimize}} \left\| \sum_{y_i=1} c_i \mathbf{x}_i - \sum_{y_i=-1} c_i \mathbf{x}_i \right\|^2, \\ &\text{subject to} \sum_{y_i=1} c_i = 1, \ \sum_{y_i=-1} c_i = 1, c_i \geq 0, \end{aligned} \tag{7.22}$$

and using the normal vector $\mathbf{w} = \sum_{y_i=1} c_i \mathbf{x}_i - \sum_{y_i=-1} c_i \mathbf{x}_i$, scaled to satisfy the canonicality condition (Definition 7.1). The threshold b is explicitly adjusted such that the hyperplane bisects the shortest connecting line (see also Problem 7.7).

7.4 Nonlinear Support Vector Classifiers

Thus far, we have shown why it is that a large margin hyperplane is good from a statistical point of view, and we have demonstrated how to compute it. Although these two points have worked out nicely, there is still a major drawback to the approach: Everything that we have done so far is linear in the data. To allow for much more general decision surfaces, we now use kernels to nonlinearly transform the input data $x_1, \ldots, x_m \in \mathcal{X}$ into a high-dimensional feature space, using a map $\Phi : x_i \mapsto \mathbf{x}_i$; we then do a linear separation there.

To justify this procedure, Cover's Theorem [113] is sometimes alluded to. This theorem characterizes the number of possible linear separations of m points in general position in an N-dimensional space. If $m \leq N+1$, then all 2^m separations are possible — the VC dimension of the function class is $n+1$ (Section 5.5.6). If $m > N+1$, then Cover's Theorem states that the number of linear separations equals

Cover's Theorem

$$2\sum_{i=0}^{N} \binom{m-1}{i}. \tag{7.23}$$

The more we increase N, the more terms there are in the sum, and thus the larger is the resulting number. This theorem formalizes the intuition that the number of separations increases with the dimensionality. It requires, however, that the points are in general position — therefore, it does not strictly make a statement about the separability of a given dataset in a given feature space. E.g., the feature map might be such that all points lie on a rather restrictive lower-dimensional manifold, which could prevent us from finding points in general position.

There is another way to intuitively understand why the kernel mapping in-

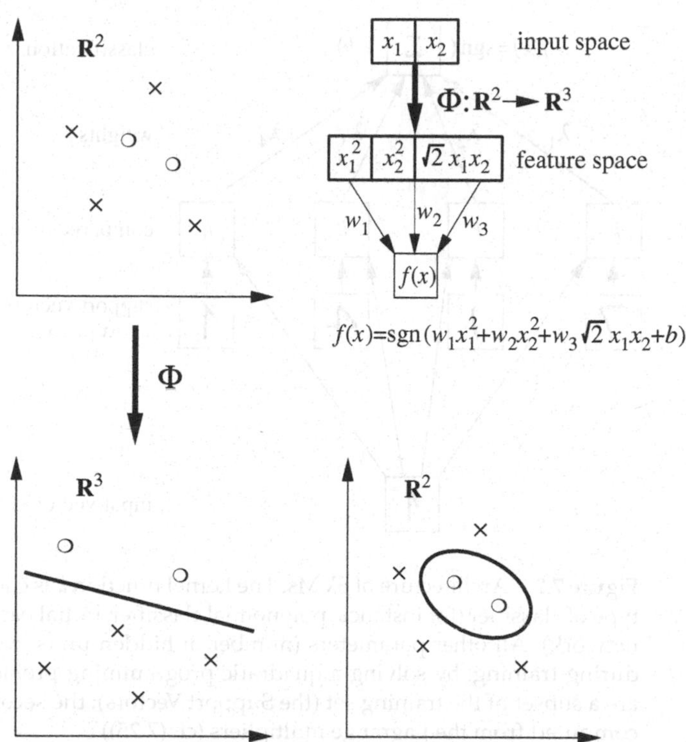

Figure 7.6 By mapping the input data *(top left)* nonlinearly (via Φ) into a higher-dimensional feature space $\mathcal{H}$ (here: $\mathcal{H} = \mathbb{R}^3$), and constructing a separating hyperplane there *(bottom left)*, an SVM *(top right)* corresponds to a nonlinear decision surface in input space (here: $\mathbb{R}^2$, *bottom right*). We use x_1, x_2 to denote the entries of the input vectors, and w_1, w_2, w_3 to denote the entries of the hyperplane normal vector in $\mathcal{H}$.

creases the chances of a separation, in terms of concepts of statistical learning theory. Using a kernel typically amounts to using a larger function class, thus increasing the capacity of the learning machine, and rendering problems separable that are not linearly separable to start with.

"Kernelizing" the Optimal Margin Hyperplane

On the practical level, the modification necessary to perform the algorithm in a high-dimensional feature space are minor. In the above sections, we made no assumptions on the dimensionality of $\mathcal{H}$, the space in which we assumed our patterns belong. We only required $\mathcal{H}$ to be equipped with a dot product. The patterns $\mathbf{x}_i$ that we talked about previously thus need not coincide with the input patterns. They can equally well be the results of mapping the original input patterns x_i into a high-dimensional feature space. Consequently, we take the stance that wherever we wrote $\mathbf{x}$, we actually meant $\Phi(x)$. Maximizing the target function (7.17), and evaluating the decision function (7.20), then requires the computation of dot products $\langle \Phi(x), \Phi(x_i) \rangle$ in a high-dimensional space. These expensive calculations are reduced significantly by using a positive definite kernel k (see Chapter 2), such that

Kernel Trick

$$\langle \Phi(x), \Phi(x_i) \rangle = k(x, x_i), \tag{7.24}$$

leading to decision functions of the form (cf. (7.20))

$$f(x) = \operatorname{sgn}\left(\sum_{i=1}^{m} y_i \alpha_i k(x, x_i) + b \right). \tag{7.25}$$

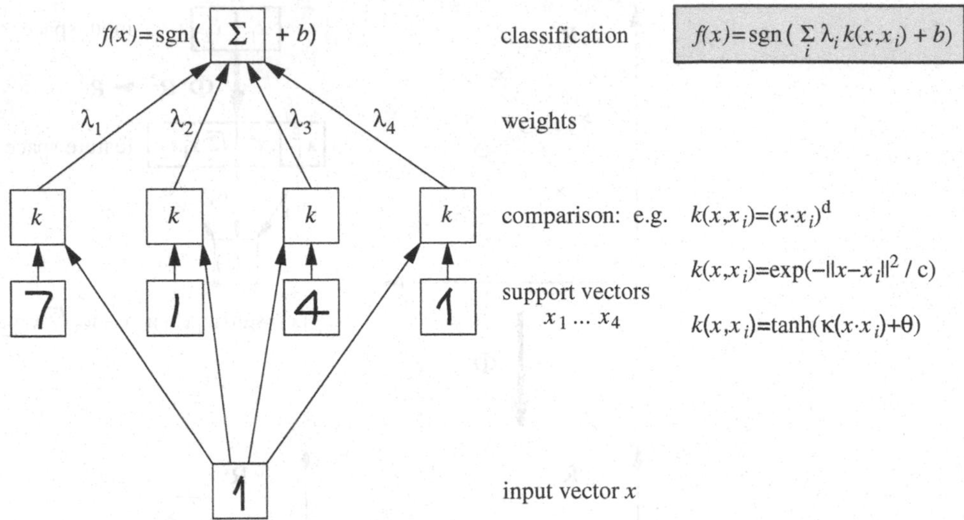

Figure 7.7 Architecture of SVMs. The kernel function k is chosen a priori; it determines the type of classifier (for instance, polynomial classifier, radial basis function classifier, or neural network). All other parameters (number of hidden units, weights, threshold b) are found during training, by solving a quadratic programming problem. The first layer weights x_i are a subset of the training set (the Support Vectors); the second layer weights $\lambda_i = y_i \alpha_i$ are computed from the Lagrange multipliers (cf. (7.25)).

At this point, a small aside regarding terminology is in order. As explained in Chapter 2, the input domain $\mathcal{X}$ need not be a vector space. Therefore, the Support Vectors in (7.25) (i.e., those x_i with $\alpha_i > 0$) are not necessarily vectors. One could choose to be on the safe side, and only refer to the corresponding $\Phi(x_i)$ as SVs. Common usage employs the term in a somewhat loose sense for both, however.

Consequently, everything that has been said about the linear case also applies to nonlinear cases, obtained using a suitable kernel k, instead of the Euclidean dot product (Figure 7.6). By using some of the kernel functions described in Chapter 2, the SV algorithm can construct a variety of learning machines (Figure 7.7), some of which coincide with classical architectures: *polynomial classifiers* of degree d,

Kernels

$$k(x, x_i) = \langle x, x_i \rangle^d, \tag{7.26}$$

radial basis function classifiers with Gaussian kernel of width $c > 0$,

$$k(x, x_i) = \exp\left(-\|x - x_i\|^2/c\right), \tag{7.27}$$

and *neural networks* (e.g., [49, 235]) with tanh activation function,

$$k(x, x_i) = \tanh(\kappa \langle x, x_i \rangle + \Theta). \tag{7.28}$$

The parameters $\kappa > 0$ and $\Theta \in \mathbb{R}$ are the gain and horizontal shift. As we shall see later, the tanh kernel can lead to very good results. Nevertheless, we should mention at this point that from a mathematical point of view, it has certain shortcomings, cf. the discussion following (2.69).

Quadratic Program

To find the decision function (7.25), we solve the following problem (cf. (7.17)):

$$\underset{\alpha}{\text{maximize}}\, W(\alpha) = \sum_{i=1}^{m} \alpha_i - \frac{1}{2} \sum_{i,j=1}^{m} \alpha_i \alpha_j y_i y_j k(x_i, x_j), \tag{7.29}$$

subject to the constraints (7.18) and (7.19).

If k is positive definite, $Q_{ij} := (y_i y_j k(x_i, x_j))_{ij}$ is a positive definite matrix (Problem 7.6), which provides us with a convex problem that can be solved efficiently (cf. Chapter 6). To see this, note that (cf. Proposition 2.16)

$$\sum_{i,j=1}^{m} \alpha_i \alpha_j y_i y_j k(x_i, x_j) = \left\langle \sum_{i=1}^{m} \alpha_i y_i \Phi(x_i), \sum_{j=1}^{m} \alpha_j y_j \Phi(x_j) \right\rangle \geq 0, \tag{7.30}$$

for all $\boldsymbol{\alpha} \in \mathbb{R}^m$.

As described in Chapter 2, we can actually use a larger class of kernels without destroying the convexity of the quadratic program. This is due to the fact that the constraint (7.19) excludes certain parts of the space of multipliers α_i. As a result, we only need the kernel to be positive definite on the remaining points. This is precisely guaranteed if we require k to be *conditionally* positive definite (see Definition 2.21). In this case, we have $\boldsymbol{\alpha}^\top Q \boldsymbol{\alpha} \geq 0$ for all coefficient vectors $\boldsymbol{\alpha}$ satisfying (7.19).

Threshold

To compute the threshold b, we take into account that due to the KKT conditions (7.16), $\alpha_j > 0$ implies (using (7.24))

$$\sum_{i=1}^{m} y_i \alpha_i k(x_j, x_i) + b = y_j. \tag{7.31}$$

Thus, the threshold can for instance be obtained by averaging

$$b = y_j - \sum_{i=1}^{m} y_i \alpha_i k(x_j, x_i), \tag{7.32}$$

over all points with $\alpha_j > 0$; in other words, all SVs. Alternatively, one can compute b from the value of the corresponding double dual variable; see Section 10.3 for details. Sometimes it is also useful not to use the "optimal" b, but to change it in order to adjust the number of false positives and false negatives.

Figure 1.7 shows how a simple binary toy problem is solved, using a Support Vector Machine with a radial basis function kernel (7.27). Note that the SVs are the patterns closest to the decision boundary — not only in the feature space, where by construction, the SVs are the patterns closest to the separating hyperplane, but also in the input space depicted in the figure. This feature differentiates SVMs from other types of classifiers. Figure 7.8 shows both the SVs and the centers extracted by k-means, which are the expansion patterns that a classical RBF network approach would employ.

Comparison to RBF Network

In a study comparing the two approaches on the USPS problem of handwritten character recognition, a SVM with a Gaussian kernel outperformed the classical RBF network using Gaussian kernels [482]. A hybrid approach, where the SVM

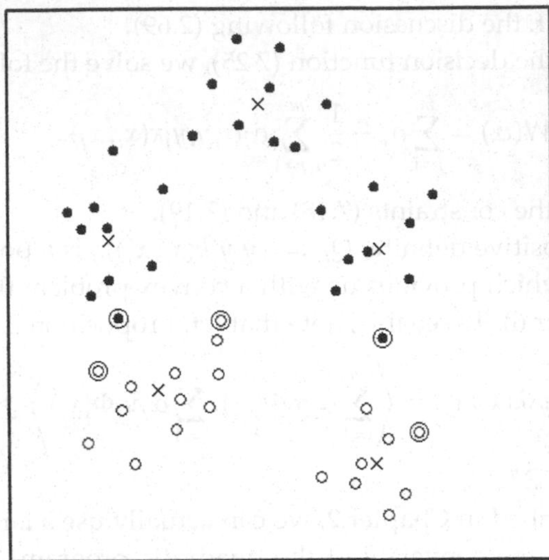

Figure 7.8 RBF centers automatically computed by the Support Vector algorithm (indicated by extra circles), using a Gaussian kernel. The number of SV centers accidentally coincides with the number of identifiable clusters (indicated by crosses found by k-means clustering, with $k = 2$ and $k = 3$ for balls and circles, respectively), but the naive correspondence between clusters and centers is lost; indeed, 3 of the SV centers are circles, and only 2 of them are balls. Note that the SV centers are chosen with respect to the classification task to be solved (from [482]).

algorithm was used to identify the centers (or hidden units) for the RBF network (that is, as a replacement for k-means), exhibited a performance which was in between the previous two. The study concluded that the SVM algorithm yielded two advantages. First, it better identified good expansion patterns, and second, its large margin regularizer led to second-layer weights that generalized better. We should add, however, that using clever engineering, the classical RBF algorithm can be improved to achieve a performance close to the one of SVMs [427].

7.5 Soft Margin Hyperplanes

So far, we have not said much about when the above will actually work. In practice, a separating hyperplane need not exist; and even if it does, it is not always the best solution to the classification problem. After all, an individual outlier in a data set, for instance a pattern which is mislabelled, can crucially affect the hyperplane. We would rather have an algorithm which can tolerate a certain fraction of outliers.

A natural idea might be to ask for the algorithm to return the hyperplane that leads to the *minimal* number of training errors. Unfortunately, it turns out that this is a combinatorial problem. Worse still, the problem is even hard to *approximate*: Ben-David and Simon [34] have recently shown that it is NP-hard to find a hyperplane whose training error is worse by some constant factor than the optimal one. Interestingly, they also show that this can be alleviated by taking into account the concept of the *margin*. By disregarding points that are within some fixed positive margin of the hyperplane, then the problem has polynomial complexity.

Cortes and Vapnik [111] chose a different approach for the SVM, following [40].

Slack Variables

To allow for the possibility of examples violating (7.11), they introduced so-called slack variables,

$$\xi_i \geq 0, \text{ where } i = 1, \ldots, m, \tag{7.33}$$

and use relaxed separation constraints (cf. (7.11)),

$$y_i(\langle \mathbf{x}_i, \mathbf{w} \rangle + b) \geq 1 - \xi_i, \quad i = 1, \ldots, m. \tag{7.34}$$

Clearly, by making ξ_i large enough, the constraint on $(\mathbf{x}_i, y_i)$ can always be met. In order not to obtain the trivial solution where all ξ_i take on large values, we thus need to penalize them in the objective function. To this end, a term $\sum_i \xi_i$ is included in (7.10).

C-SVC

In the simplest case, referred to as the C-SV classifier, this is done by solving, for some $C > 0$,

$$\underset{\mathbf{w} \in \mathcal{H}, \boldsymbol{\xi} \in \mathbb{R}^m}{\text{minimize}} \quad \tau(\mathbf{w}, \boldsymbol{\xi}) = \frac{1}{2}\|\mathbf{w}\|^2 + \frac{C}{m}\sum_{i=1}^{m} \xi_i, \tag{7.35}$$

subject to the constraints (7.33) and (7.34). It is instructive to compare this to Theorem 7.3, considering the case $\rho = 1$. Whenever the constraint (7.34) is met with $\xi_i = 0$, the corresponding point will not be a margin error. All non-zero slacks ξ correspond to margin errors; hence, roughly speaking, the fraction of margin errors in Theorem 7.3 increases with the second term in (7.35). The capacity term, on the other hand, increases with $\|\mathbf{w}\|$. Hence, for a suitable positive constant C, this approach approximately minimizes the right hand side of the bound.

Note, however, that if many of the ξ_i attain large values (in other words, if the classes to be separated strongly overlap, for instance due to noise), then $\sum_{i=1}^{m} \xi_i$ can be significantly larger than the fraction of margin errors. In that case, there is no guarantee that the hyperplane will generalize well.

As in the separable case (7.15), the solution can be shown to have an expansion

$$\mathbf{w} = \sum_{i=1}^{m} \alpha_i y_i \mathbf{x}_i, \tag{7.36}$$

where non-zero coefficients α_i can only occur if the corresponding example $(\mathbf{x}_i, y_i)$ precisely meets the constraint (7.34). Again, the problem only depends on dot products in $\mathcal{H}$, which can be computed by means of the kernel.

The coefficients α_i are found by solving the following quadratic programming problem:

$$\underset{\boldsymbol{\alpha} \in \mathbb{R}^m}{\text{maximize}} \quad W(\boldsymbol{\alpha}) = \sum_{i=1}^{m} \alpha_i - \frac{1}{2}\sum_{i,j=1}^{m} \alpha_i \alpha_j y_i y_j k(x_i, x_j), \tag{7.37}$$

$$\text{subject to } 0 \leq \alpha_i \leq \frac{C}{m} \text{ for all } i = 1, \ldots, m, \tag{7.38}$$

$$\text{and } \sum_{i=1}^{m} \alpha_i y_i = 0. \tag{7.39}$$

To compute the threshold b, we take into account that due to (7.34), for Support

Vectors x_j for which $\xi_j = 0$, we have (7.31). Thus, the threshold can be obtained by averaging (7.32) over all Support Vectors x_j (recall that they satisfy $\alpha_j > 0$) with $\alpha_j < C$.

In the above formulation, C is a constant determining the trade-off between two conflicting goals: minimizing the training error, and maximizing the margin. Unfortunately, C is a rather unintuitive parameter, and we have no a priori way to select it.[9] Therefore, a modification was proposed in [481], which replaces C by a parameter ν; the latter will turn out to control the number of margin errors and Support Vectors.

ν-SVC

As a primal problem for this approach, termed the ν-SV classifier, we consider

$$\underset{\mathbf{w}\in\mathcal{H},\boldsymbol{\xi}\in\mathbb{R}^m,\rho,b\in\mathbb{R}}{\text{minimize}} \quad \tau(\mathbf{w},\boldsymbol{\xi},\rho) = \frac{1}{2}\|\mathbf{w}\|^2 - \nu\rho + \frac{1}{m}\sum_{i=1}^{m}\xi_i \tag{7.40}$$

$$\text{subject to} \quad y_i(\langle \mathbf{x}_i, \mathbf{w}\rangle + b) \geq \rho - \xi_i \tag{7.41}$$

$$\text{and} \quad \xi_i \geq 0, \quad \rho \geq 0. \tag{7.42}$$

Note that no constant C appears in this formulation; instead, there is a parameter ν, and also an additional variable ρ to be optimized. To understand the role of ρ, note that for $\boldsymbol{\xi} = 0$, the constraint (7.41) simply states that the two classes are separated by the *margin* $2\rho/\|\mathbf{w}\|$ (cf. Problem 7.4).

Margin Error

To explain the significance of ν, let us first recall the term *margin error*: by this, we denote points with $\xi_i > 0$. These are points which are either errors, or lie within the margin. Formally, the fraction of margin errors is

$$R^{\rho}_{\text{emp}}[g] := \frac{1}{m}\left|\{i | y_i g(x_i) < \rho\}\right|. \tag{7.43}$$

Here, g is used to denote the argument of the sgn in the decision function (7.25): $f = \operatorname{sgn} \circ g$. We are now in a position to state a result that explains the significance of ν.

ν-Property

Proposition 7.5 ([481]) *Suppose we run ν-SVC with k on some data with the result that $\rho > 0$. Then*

(i) ν is an upper bound on the fraction of margin errors.

(ii) ν is a lower bound on the fraction of SVs.

(iii) Suppose the data $(x_1, y_1), \ldots, (x_m, y_m)$ were generated iid from a distribution $\mathrm{P}(x, y) = \mathrm{P}(x)\mathrm{P}(y|x)$, such that neither $\mathrm{P}(x, y = 1)$ nor $\mathrm{P}(x, y = -1)$ contains any discrete component. Suppose, moreover, that the kernel used is analytic and non-constant. With probability 1, asymptotically, ν equals both the fraction of SVs and the fraction of errors.

The proof can be found in Section A.2.

Before we get into the technical details of the dual derivation, let us take a look

9. As a default value, we use $C/m = 10$ unless stated otherwise.

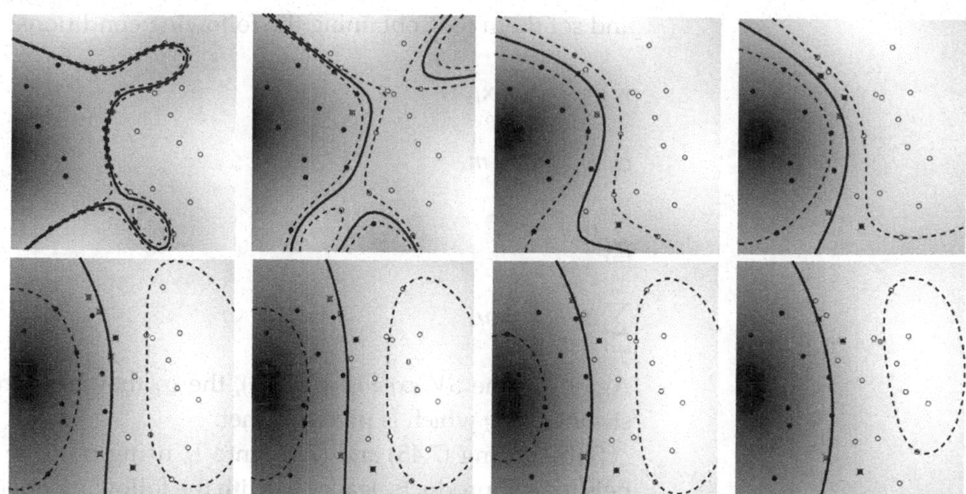

Figure 7.9 Toy problem (task: separate circles from disks) solved using ν-SV classification, with parameter values ranging from $\nu = 0.1$ (top left) to $\nu = 0.8$ (bottom right). The larger we make ν, the more points are allowed to lie inside the margin (depicted by dotted lines). Results are shown for a Gaussian kernel, $k(x, x') = \exp(-\|x - x'\|^2)$.

Table 7.1 Fractions of errors and SVs, along with the margins of class separation, for the toy example in Figure 7.9.
Note that ν upper bounds the fraction of errors and lower bounds the fraction of SVs, and that increasing ν, i.e., allowing more errors, increases the margin.

ν	0.1	0.2	0.3	0.4	0.5	0.6	0.7	0.8
fraction of errors	0.00	0.07	0.25	0.32	0.39	0.50	0.61	0.71
fraction of SVs	0.29	0.36	0.43	0.46	0.57	0.68	0.79	0.86
margin $\rho/\|\mathbf{w}\|$	0.005	0.018	0.115	0.156	0.364	0.419	0.461	0.546

at a toy example illustrating the influence of ν (Figure 7.9). The corresponding fractions of SVs and margin errors are listed in table 7.1.

Derivation of the Dual

The derivation of the ν-SVC dual is similar to the above SVC formulations, only slightly more complicated. We consider the Lagrangian

$$L(\mathbf{w}, \boldsymbol{\xi}, b, \rho, \boldsymbol{\alpha}, \boldsymbol{\beta}, \delta) = \frac{1}{2}\|\mathbf{w}\|^2 - \nu\rho + \frac{1}{m}\sum_{i=1}^{m}\xi_i - \sum_{i=1}^{m}(\alpha_i(y_i(\langle \mathbf{x}_i, \mathbf{w}\rangle + b) - \rho + \xi_i) + \beta_i\xi_i) - \delta\rho, \tag{7.44}$$

using multipliers $\alpha_i, \beta_i, \delta \geq 0$. This function has to be minimized with respect to the primal variables $\mathbf{w}, \boldsymbol{\xi}, b, \rho$, and maximized with respect to the dual variables $\boldsymbol{\alpha}, \boldsymbol{\beta}, \delta$. To eliminate the former, we compute the corresponding partial derivatives and set them to 0, obtaining the following conditions:

$$\mathbf{w} = \sum_{i=1}^{m} \alpha_i y_i \mathbf{x}_i, \tag{7.45}$$

$$\alpha_i + \beta_i = 1/m, \tag{7.46}$$

$$\sum_{i=1}^{m} \alpha_i y_i = 0, \tag{7.47}$$

$$\sum_{i=1}^{m} \alpha_i - \delta = \nu. \tag{7.48}$$

Again, in the *SV expansion* (7.45), the α_i that are non-zero correspond to a constraint (7.41) which is precisely met.

Substituting (7.45) and (7.46) into L, using $\alpha_i, \beta_i, \delta \geq 0$, and incorporating kernels for dot products, leaves us with the following quadratic optimization problem for ν-SV classification:

Quadratic Program for ν-SVC

$$\underset{\alpha \in \mathbb{R}^m}{\text{maximize}} \;\; W(\boldsymbol{\alpha}) = -\frac{1}{2} \sum_{i,j=1}^{m} \alpha_i \alpha_j y_i y_j k(x_i, x_j), \tag{7.49}$$

$$\text{subject to } \; 0 \leq \alpha_i \leq \frac{1}{m}, \tag{7.50}$$

$$\sum_{i=1}^{m} \alpha_i y_i = 0, \tag{7.51}$$

$$\sum_{i=1}^{m} \alpha_i \geq \nu. \tag{7.52}$$

As above, the resulting decision function can be shown to take the form

$$f(x) = \operatorname{sgn}\left(\sum_{i=1}^{m} \alpha_i y_i k(x, x_i) + b \right). \tag{7.53}$$

Compared with the C-SVC dual (7.37), there are two differences. First, there is an additional constraint (7.52).[10] Second, the linear term $\sum_{i=1}^{m} \alpha_i$ no longer appears in the objective function (7.49). This has an interesting consequence: (7.49) is now quadratically homogeneous in $\boldsymbol{\alpha}$. It is straightforward to verify that the same decision function is obtained if we start with the primal function

$$\tau(\mathbf{w}, \boldsymbol{\xi}, \rho) = \frac{1}{2}\|\mathbf{w}\|^2 + C\left(-\nu\rho + \frac{1}{m} \sum_{i=1}^{m} \xi_i \right), \tag{7.54}$$

10. The additional constraint makes it more challenging to come up with efficient training algorithms for large datasets. So far, two approaches have been proposed which work well. One of them slightly modifies the primal problem in order to avoid the *other* equality constraint (related to the offset b) [98]. The other one is a direct generalization of a corresponding algorithm for C-SVC, which reduces the problem for each chunk to a linear system, and which does not suffer any disadvantages from the additional constraint [407, 408]. See also Sections 10.3.2, 10.4.3, and 10.6.3 for further details.

i.e., if one does use C, cf. Problem 7.16.

To compute the threshold b and the margin parameter ρ, we consider two sets $S_\pm$, of identical size $s > 0$, containing SVs x_i with $0 < \alpha_i < 1$ and $y_i = \pm 1$, respectively. Then, due to the KKT conditions, (7.41) becomes an equality with $\xi_i = 0$. Hence, in terms of kernels,

$$b = -\frac{1}{2s} \sum_{x \in S_+ \cup S_-} \sum_{j=1}^{m} \alpha_j y_j k(x, x_j), \tag{7.55}$$

$$\rho = \frac{1}{2s} \left(\sum_{x \in S_+} \sum_{j=1}^{m} \alpha_j y_j k(x, x_j) - \sum_{x \in S_-} \sum_{j=1}^{m} \alpha_j y_j k(x, x_j) \right). \tag{7.56}$$

Note that for the decision function, only b is actually required.

Connection ν-SVC — C-SVC

A connection to standard SV classification, and a somewhat surprising interpretation of the regularization parameter C, is described by the following result:

Proposition 7.6 (Connection ν-SVC — C-SVC [481]) *If ν-SV classification leads to $\rho > 0$, then C-SV classification, with C set a priori to $1/\rho$, leads to the same decision function.*

Proof If we minimize (7.40), and then fix ρ to minimize only over the remaining variables, nothing will change. Hence the solution $\mathbf{w}_0, b_0, \boldsymbol{\xi}_0$ minimizes (7.35), for $C = 1$, subject to (7.41). To recover the constraint (7.34), we rescale to the set of variables $\mathbf{w}' = \mathbf{w}/\rho, b' = b/\rho, \boldsymbol{\xi}' = \boldsymbol{\xi}/\rho$. This leaves us with the objective function (7.35), up to a constant scaling factor ρ^2, using $C = 1/\rho$. ■

For further details on the connection between ν-SVMs and C-SVMs, see [122, 38]. A complete account has been given by Chang and Lin [98], who show that for a given problem and kernel, there is an interval $[\nu_{\min}, \nu_{\max}]$ of admissible values for ν, with $0 \leq \nu_{\min} \leq \nu_{\max} \leq 1$. The boundaries of the interval are computed by considering $\sum_i \alpha_i$ as returned by the C-SVM in the limits $C \to \infty$ and $C \to 0$, respectively.

It has been noted that ν-SVMs have an interesting interpretation in terms of *reduced convex hulls* [122, 38] (cf. (7.21)). If a problem is non-separable, the convex hulls will no longer be disjoint. Therefore, it no longer makes sense to search for the shortest line connecting them, and the approach of (7.22) will fail. In this situation, it seems natural to reduce the convex hulls in size, by limiting the size of the coefficients c_i in (7.21) to some value $\nu \in (0, 1)$. Intuitively, this amounts to limiting the influence of individual points — note that in the original problem (7.22), two single points can already determine the solution. It is possible to show that the ν-SVM formulation solves the problem of finding the hyperplane orthogonal to the closest line connecting the *reduced* convex hulls [122].

Robustness and Outliers

We now move on to another aspect of soft margin classification. When we introduced the slack variables, we did not attempt to justify the fact that in the objective function, we used a penalizer $\sum_{i=1}^{m} \xi_i$. Why not use another penalizer, such as $\sum_{i=1}^{m} \xi_i^p$, for some $p \geq 0$ [111]? For instance, $p = 0$ would yield a penalizer that exactly *counts* the number of margin errors. Unfortunately, however, it is also a penalizer that leads to a combinatorial optimization problem. Penalizers yielding optimization problems that are particularly convenient, on the other hand, are obtained for $p = 1$ and $p = 2$. By default, we use the former, as it possesses an additional property which is statistically attractive. As the following proposition shows, linearity of the target function in the slack variables ξ_i leads to a certain "outlier" resistance of the estimator. As above, we use the shorthand $\mathbf{x}_i$ for $\Phi(x_i)$.

Proposition 7.7 (Resistance of SV classification [481]) *Suppose* $\mathbf{w}$ *can be expressed in terms of the SVs which are not at bound,*

$$\mathbf{w} = \sum_{i=1}^{m} \gamma_i \mathbf{x}_i \tag{7.57}$$

with $\gamma_i \neq 0$ *only if* $\alpha_i \in (0, 1/m)$ *(where the* α_i *are the coefficients of the dual solution). Then local movements of any margin error* $\mathbf{x}_m$ *parallel to* $\mathbf{w}$ *do not change the hyperplane.*[11]

The proof can be found in Section A.2. For further results in support of the $p = 1$ case, see [527].

Note that the assumption (7.57) is not as restrictive as it may seem. Even though the SV expansion of the solution, $\mathbf{w} = \sum_{i=1}^{m} \alpha_i y_i \mathbf{x}_i$, often contains many multipliers α_i which are at bound, it is nevertheless quite conceivable, especially when discarding the requirement that the coefficients be bounded, that we can obtain an expansion (7.57) in terms of a subset of the original vectors.

For instance, if we have a 2-D problem that we solve directly in input space, i.e., with $k(x, x') = \langle x, x' \rangle$, then it suffices to have two linearly independent SVs which are not at bound, in order to express $\mathbf{w}$. This holds true regardless of whether or not the two classes overlap, even if there are many SVs which are at the upper bound. Further information on resistance and robustness of SVMs can be found in Sections 3.4 and 9.3.

We have introduced SVs as those training examples x_i for which $\alpha_i > 0$. In some cases, it is useful to further distinguish different types of SVs. For reference purposes, we give a list of different types of SVs (Table 7.2).

In Section 7.3, we used the KKT conditions to argue that in the hard margin case, the SVs lie exactly on the margin. Using an identical argument for the soft margin case, we see that in this instance, in-bound SVs lie on the margin (Problem 7.9).

Note that in the hard margin case, where $\alpha_{\max} = \infty$, every SV is an in-bound SV. Note, moreover, that for kernels that produce full-rank Gram matrices, such as the Gaussian (Theorem 2.18), in theory every SV is essential (provided there are no duplicate patterns in the training set).[12]

11. Note that the perturbation of the point is carried out in feature space. What it precisely corresponds to in input space therefore depends on the specific kernel chosen.
12. In practice, Gaussian Gram matrices usually have some eigenvalues that are close to 0.

Table 7.2 Overview of different types of SVs. In each case, the condition on the Lagrange multipliers α_i (corresponding to an SV x_i) is given. In the table, $\alpha_{\max}$ stands for the upper bound in the optimization problem; for instance, $\alpha_{\max} = \frac{C}{m}$ in (7.38) and $\alpha_{\max} = \frac{1}{m}$ in (7.50).

Type of SV	Definition	Properties
(standard) SV	$0 < \alpha_i$	lies on or in margin
in-bound SV	$0 < \alpha_i < \alpha_{\max}$	lies on margin
bound SV	$\alpha_i = \alpha_{\max}$	usually lies in margin ("margin error")
essential SV	appears in all possible expansions of solution	becomes margin error when left out (Section 7.3)

7.6 Multi-Class Classification

So far, we have talked about binary classification, where the class labels can only take two values: ± 1. Many real-world problems, however, have more than two classes — an example being the widely studied optical character recognition (OCR) problem. We will now review some methods for dealing with this issue.

7.6.1 One Versus the Rest

To get *M-class classifiers*, it is common to construct a set of binary classifiers $f^1, \ldots, f^M$, each trained to separate one class from the rest, and combine them by doing the multi-class classification according to the maximal output before applying the sgn function; that is, by taking

$$\operatorname*{argmax}_{j=1,\ldots,M} g^j(x), \text{ where } g^j(x) = \sum_{i=1}^{m} y_i \alpha_i^j k(x, x_i) + b^j \tag{7.58}$$

(note that $f^j(x) = \operatorname{sgn}(g^j(x))$, cf. (7.25)).

Reject Decisions

The values $g^j(x)$ can also be used for *reject decisions*. To see this, we consider the difference between the two largest $g^j(x)$ as a measure of confidence in the classification of x. If that measure falls short of a threshold θ, the classifier rejects the pattern and does not assign it to a class (it might instead be passed on to a human expert). This has the consequence that on the remaining patterns, a lower error rate can be achieved. Some benchmark comparisons report a quantity referred to as the *punt error*, which denotes the fraction of test patterns that must be rejected in order to achieve a certain accuracy (say 1% error) on the remaining test samples. To compute it, the value of θ is adjusted on the *test* set [64].

The main shortcoming of (7.58), sometimes called the *winner-takes-all* approach, is that it is somewhat heuristic. The binary classifiers used are obtained by training on different binary classification problems, and thus it is unclear whether their real-valued outputs (before thresholding) are on comparable scales.[13] This can be a problem, since situations often arise where *several* binary classifiers assign the pattern to their respective class (or where *none* does); in this case, *one* class must be chosen by comparing the real-valued outputs.

In addition, binary one-versus-the-rest classifiers have been criticized for dealing with rather asymmetric problems. For instance, in digit recognition, the classifier trained to recognize class '7' is usually trained on many more negative than positive examples. We can deal with these asymmetries by using values of the regularization constant C which differ for the respective classes (see Problem 7.10). It has nonetheless been argued that the following approach, which is more symmetric from the outset, can be advantageous.

7.6.2 Pairwise Classification

In pairwise classification, we train a classifier for each possible pair of classes [178, 463, 233, 311]. For M classes, this results in $(M-1)M/2$ binary classifiers. This number is usually larger than the number of one-versus-the-rest classifiers; for instance, if $M = 10$, we need to train 45 binary classifiers rather than 10 as in the method above. Although this suggests large training times, the individual problems that we need to train on are significantly smaller, and if the training algorithm scales superlinearly with the training set size, it is actually possible to save time.

Similar considerations apply to the runtime execution speed. When we try to classify a test pattern, we evaluate all 45 binary classifiers, and classify according to which of the classes gets the highest number of votes. A vote for a given class is defined as a classifier putting the pattern into that class.[14] The individual classifiers, however, are usually smaller in size (they have fewer SVs) than they would be in the one-versus-the-rest approach. This is for two reasons: First, the training sets are smaller, and second, the problems to be learned are usually easier, since the classes have less overlap.

Nevertheless, if M is large, and we evaluate the $(M-1)M/2$ classifiers, then the resulting system may be slower than the corresponding one-versus-the-rest SVM. To illustrate this weakness, consider the following hypothetical situation: Suppose, in a digit recognition task, that after evaluating the first few binary classifiers, both digit 7 and digit 8 seem extremely unlikely (they already "lost" on several classifiers). In that case, it would seem pointless to evaluate the 7-vs-8 classifier. This idea can be cast into a precise framework by embedding the binary classifiers into a directed acyclic graph. Each classification run then corresponds to a directed traversal of that graph, and classification can be much faster [411].

13. Note, however, that some effort has gone into developing methods for transforming the real-valued outputs into class probabilities [521, 486, 410].
14. Some care has to be exercised in tie-breaking. For further detail, see [311].

7.6.3 Error-Correcting Output Coding

The method of error-correcting output codes was developed in [142], and later adapted to the case of SVMs [5]. In a nutshell, the idea is as follows. Just as we can generate a binary problem from a multiclass problem by separating one class from the rest — digit 0 from digits 1 through 9, say — we can generate a large number of further binary problems by splitting the original set of classes into two subsets. For instance, we could separate the even digits from the odd ones, or we could separate digits 0 through 4 from 5 through 9. It is clear that if we design a set of binary classifiers $f^1, \ldots, f^L$ in the right way, then the binary responses will completely determine the class of a test patterns. Each class corresponds to a unique vector in $\{\pm 1\}^L$; for M classes, we thus get a so-called *decoding matrix* $M \in \{\pm 1\}^{M \times L}$. What happens if the binary responses are inconsistent with each other; if, for instance, the problem is noisy, or the training sample is too small to estimate the binary classifiers reliably? Formally, this means that we will obtain a vector of responses $f^1(x), \ldots, f^L(x)$ which does not occur in the matrix M. To deal with these cases, [142] proposed designing a clever set of binary problems, which yields robustness against some errors. Here, the closest match between the vector of responses and the rows of the matrix is determined using the Hamming distance (the number of entries where the two vectors differ; essentially, the L_∞ distance). Now imagine a situation where the code is such that the minimal Hamming distance is three. In this case, we can *guarantee* that we will correctly classify all test examples which lead to at most one error amongst the binary classifiers.

This method produces very good results in multi-class tasks; nevertheless, it has been pointed out that it does not make use of a crucial quantity in classifiers: the margin. Recently [5], a version was developed that replaces the Hamming-based decoding with a more sophisticated scheme that takes margins into account. Recommendations are also made regarding how to design good codes for margin classifiers, such as SVMs.

7.6.4 Multi-Class Objective Functions

Arguably the most elegant multi-class algorithm, and certainly the method most closely aligned with Vapnik's principle of always trying to solve problems *directly*, entails modifying the SVM objective function in such a way that it simultaneously allows the computation of a multi-class classifier. For instance [593, 58], we can modify (7.35) and use the following quadratic program:

$$\underset{\mathbf{w}_r \in \mathcal{H}, \boldsymbol{\xi}^r \in \mathbb{R}^m, b_r \in \mathbb{R}}{\text{minimize}} \quad \frac{1}{2}\sum_{r=1}^{M} \|\mathbf{w}_r\|^2 + \frac{C}{m}\sum_{i=1}^{m}\sum_{r \neq y_i} \xi_i^r, \tag{7.59}$$

$$\text{subject to } \langle \mathbf{w}_{y_i}, \mathbf{x}_i \rangle + b_{y_i} \geq \langle \mathbf{w}_r, \mathbf{x}_i \rangle + b_r + 2 - \xi_i^r,$$

$$\xi_i^r \geq 0, \tag{7.60}$$

where $m \in \{1, \ldots, M\} \setminus y_i$, and $y_i \in \{1, \ldots, M\}$ is the multi-class label of the pattern $\mathbf{x}_i$ (cf. Problem 7.17).

In terms of accuracy, the results obtained with this approach are comparable to those obtained with the widely used one-versus-the-rest approach. Unfortunately, the optimization problem is such that it has to deal with *all* SVs at the same time. In the other approaches, the individual binary classifiers usually have much smaller SV sets, with beneficial effects on the training time. For further multiclass approaches, see [160, 323]. Generalizations to *multi-label* problems, where patterns are allowed to belong to several classes at the same time, are discussed in [162].

Overall, it is fair to say that there is probably no multi-class approach that generally outperforms the others. For practical problems, the choice of approach will depend on constraints at hand. Relevant factors include the required accuracy, the time available for development and training, and the nature of the classification problem (e.g., for a problem with very many classes, it would not be wise to use (7.59)). That said, a simple one-against-the-rest approach often produces acceptable results.

7.7 Variations on a Theme

There are a number of variations of the standard SV classification algorithm, such as the elegant *leave-one-out machine* [589, 592] (see also Section 12.2.2 below), the idea of *Bayes point machines* [451, 239, 453, 545, 392], and extensions to *feature selection* [70, 224, 590]. Due to lack of space, we only describe one of the variations; namely, *linear programming machines*.

Linear Programming Machines

As we have seen above, the SVM approach automatically leads to a decision function of the form (7.25). Let us rewrite it as $f(x) = \operatorname{sgn}(g(x))$, with

$$g(x) = \sum_{i=1}^{m} \upsilon_i k(x, x_i) + b. \tag{7.61}$$

In Chapter 4, we showed that this form of the solution is essentially a consequence of the form of the regularizer $\|\mathbf{w}\|^2$ (Theorem 4.2). The idea of linear programming (LP) machines is to use the kernel expansion as an ansatz for the solution, but to use a different regularizer, namely the ℓ_1 norm of the coefficient vector [343, 344, 74, 184, 352, 37, 591, 593, 39]. The main motivation for this is that this regularizer is known to induce sparse expansions (see Chapter 4).

ℓ_1 Regularizer

This amounts to the objective function

$$R_{\text{reg}}[g] := \frac{1}{m}\|\boldsymbol{\upsilon}\|_1 + C\, R_{\text{emp}}[g], \tag{7.62}$$

where $\|\boldsymbol{\upsilon}\|_1 = \sum_{i=1}^{m} |\upsilon_i|$ denotes the ℓ_1 norm in coefficient space, using the soft margin empirical risk,

$$R_{\text{emp}}[g] = \frac{1}{m}\sum_i \xi_i, \tag{7.63}$$

with slack terms

$$\xi_i = \max\{1 - y_i g(x_i), 0\}. \tag{7.64}$$

We thus obtain a linear programming problem;

$$\begin{aligned} \underset{\alpha,\xi\in\mathbb{R}^m, b\in\mathbb{R}}{\text{minimize}} \quad & \frac{1}{m}\sum_{i=1}^{m}(\alpha_i + \alpha_i^*) + C\sum_{i=1}^{m}\xi_i, \\ \text{subject to} \quad & y_i g(x_i) \geq 1 - \xi_i, \\ & \alpha_i, \alpha_i^*, \xi_i \geq 0. \end{aligned} \tag{7.65}$$

Here, we have dealt with the ℓ_1-norm by splitting each component v_i into its positive and negative part: $v_i = \alpha_i - \alpha_i^*$ in (7.61). The solution differs from (7.25) in that it is no longer necessarily the case that each expansion pattern has a weight $\alpha_i y_i$, whose sign equals its class label. This property would have to be enforced separately (Problem 7.19). Moreover, it is also no longer the case that the expansion patterns lie on or beyond the margin — in LP machines, they can basically be anywhere.

ν-LPMs

LP machines can also benefit from the ν-trick. In this case, the programming problem can be shown to take the following form [212]:

$$\begin{aligned} \underset{\alpha,\xi\in\mathbb{R}^m, b,\rho\in\mathbb{R}}{\text{minimize}} \quad & \frac{1}{m}\sum_{i=1}^{m}\xi_i - \nu\rho, \\ \text{subject to} \quad & \frac{1}{m}\sum_{i=1}^{m}(\alpha_i + \alpha_i^*) = 1, \\ & y_i g(\mathbf{x}_i) \geq \rho - \xi_i, \\ & \alpha_i, \alpha_i^*, \xi_i, \rho \geq 0. \end{aligned} \tag{7.66}$$

We will not go into further detail at this point. Additional information on linear programming machines from a regularization point of view is given in Section 4.9.2.

7.8 Experiments

7.8.1 Digit Recognition Using Different Kernels

Handwritten digit recognition has long served as a test bed for evaluating and benchmarking classifiers [318, 64, 319]. Thus, it was imperative in the early days of SVM research to evaluate the SV method on widely used digit recognition tasks. In this section we report results on the US Postal Service (USPS) database (described in Section A.1). We shall return to the character recognition problem in Chapter 11, where we consider the larger MNIST database.

As described above, the difference between C-SVC and ν-SVC lies only in the fact that we have to select a different parameter a priori. If we are able to do this

Table 7.3 Performance on the USPS set, for three different types of classifier, constructed with the Support Vector algorithm by choosing different functions k in (7.25) and (7.29). Error rates on the test set are given; and for each of the ten-class-classifiers, we also show the average number of Support Vectors of the ten two-class-classifiers. The normalization factor of 256 is tailored to the dimensionality of the data, which is 16×16.

polynomial: $k(x, x') = (\langle x, x' \rangle / 256)^d$

d	1	2	3	4	5	6	7
raw error/%	8.9	4.7	4.0	4.2	4.5	4.5	4.7
av. # of SVs	282	237	274	321	374	422	491

RBF: $k(x, x') = \exp(-\|x - x'\|^2 / (256\, c))$

c	4.0	2.0	1.2	0.8	0.5	0.2	0.1
raw error/%	5.3	5.0	4.9	4.3	4.4	4.4	4.5
av. # of SVs	266	240	233	235	251	366	722

sigmoid: $k(x, x') = \tanh(2 \langle x, x' \rangle / 256 + \Theta)$

$-\Theta$	0.8	0.9	1.0	1.1	1.2	1.3	1.4
raw error/%	6.3	4.8	4.1	4.3	4.3	4.4	4.8
av. # of SVs	206	242	254	267	278	289	296

well, we obtain identical performance. The experiments reported were carried out before the development of ν-SVC, and thus all use C-SVC code.

In the present study, we put particular emphasis on comparing different types of SV classifiers obtained by choosing different kernels. We report results for polynomial kernels (7.26), Gaussian radial basis function kernels (7.27), and sigmoid kernels (7.28), summarized in Table 7.3. In all three cases, error rates around 4% can be achieved.

Kernel Scaling

Note that in practical applications, it is usually helpful to scale the argument of the kernel, such that the numerical values do not get extremely small or large as the dimension of the data increases. This helps avoid large roundoff errors, and prevents over- and underflow. In the present case, the scaling was done by including the factor 256 in Table 7.3.

The results show that the Support Vector algorithm allows the construction of a range of learning machines, all of which perform well. The similar performance for the three different functions k suggests that among these cases, the choice of the set of decision functions is less important than capacity control in the chosen type of structure. This phenomenon is well-known for the Parzen window density estimator in $\mathbb{R}^N$ (e.g., [226])

$$p(x) = \frac{1}{m} \sum_{i=1}^{m} \frac{1}{\omega^N} k\left(\frac{x - x_i}{\omega}\right). \tag{7.67}$$

It is of great importance in this case to choose an appropriate value of the band-

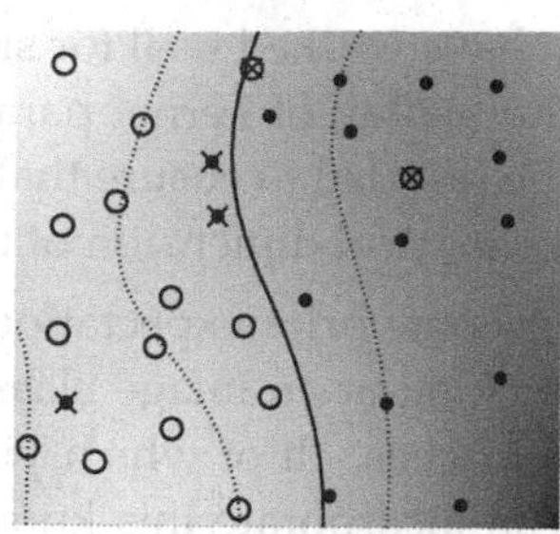
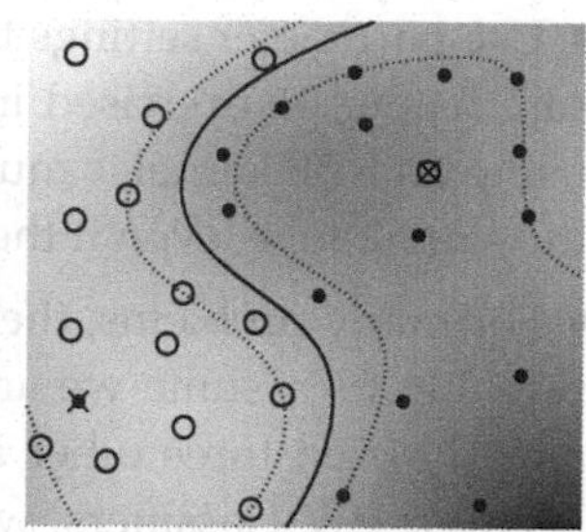
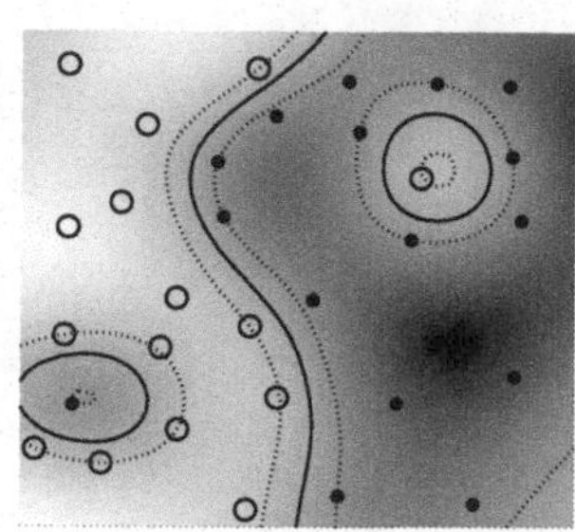

Figure 7.10 2D toy example of a binary classification problem solved using a soft margin SVC. In all cases, a Gaussian kernel (7.27) is used. From left to right, we decrease the kernel width. Note that for a large width, the decision boundary is almost linear, and the data set cannot be separated without error (see text). Solid lines represent decision boundaries; dotted lines depict the edge of the margin (where (7.34) becomes an equality with $\xi_i = 0$).

width parameter ω for a given amount of data. Similar parallels can be drawn to the solution of ill-posed problems; for a discussion, see [561].

Figure 7.10 shows a toy example using a Gaussian kernel (7.27), illustrating that it is crucial to pick the right kernel parameter. In all cases, the same value of C was used, but the kernel width c was varied. For large values of c, the classifier is almost linear, and it cannot separate the data set without errors. For a small width (right), the data set is practically *memorized*. For an intermediate width (middle), a trade-off is made between allowing *some* training errors and using a "simple" decision boundary.

Parameter Choice

In practice, both the kernel parameters and the value of C (or ν) are often chosen using *cross validation*. To this end, we first split the data set into p parts of equal size, say, $p = 10$. We then perform ten training runs. Each time, we leave out one of the ten parts and use it as an independent validation set for optimizing the parameters. In the simplest case, we choose the parameters which work best, on average over the ten runs. It is common practice, however, to then train on the full training set, using these average parameters. There are some problems with this. First, it amounts to optimizing the parameters on the same set as the one used for training, which can lead to overfitting. Second, the optimal parameter settings for data sets of size m and $\frac{9}{10}m$, respectively, do not usually coincide. Typically, the smaller set will require a slightly stronger regularization. This could mean a wider Gaussian kernel, a smaller polynomial degree, a smaller C, or a larger ν. Even worse, it is theoretically possible that there is a so-called phase transition (e.g., [393]) in the learning curve between the two sample sizes. This means that the generalization error as a function of the sample size could change dramatically between $\frac{9}{10}m$ and m. Having said all this, practitioners often do not care about these theoretical precautions, and use the unchanged parameters with excellent results. For further detail, see Section 12.2.

In some cases, one can try to avoid the whole procedure by using an educated guess. Below, we list several methods.

- Use parameter settings that have worked well for similar problems. Here, some care has to be exercised in the scaling of kernel parameters. For instance, when using an RBF kernel, c must be rescaled to ensure that $\|x_i - x_j\|^2/c$ roughly lies in the same range, even if the scaling and dimension of the data are different.
- For many problems, there is some prior expectation regarding the typical error rate. Let us assume we are looking at an image classification task, and we have already tried three other approaches, all of which yielded around 5% test error. Using ν−SV classifiers, we can incorporate this knowledge by choosing a value for ν which is in that range, say $\nu = 5\%$. The reason for this guess is that we know (Proposition 7.5) that the margin error is then below 5%, which in turn implies that the training error is below 5%. The training error will typically be smaller than the test error, thus it is consistent that it should be upper bounded by the 5% test error.
- In a slightly less elegant way, one can try to mimic this procedure for C-SV classifiers. To this end, we start off with a large value of C, and reduce it until the number of Lagrange multipliers that are at the upper bound (in other words, the number of margin errors) is in a suitable range (say, somewhat below 5%). Compared to the above procedure for choosing ν, the disadvantage is that this entails a number of training runs. We can also monitor the number of actual training errors during the training runs, but since not every margin error is a training error, this is often less sensitive. Indeed, the difference between training error and test error can often be quite substantial. For instance, on the USPS set, most of the results reported here were obtained with systems that had essentially zero training error.
- One can put forward scaling arguments which indicate that $C \propto 1/R^2$, where R is a measure for the range of the data in feature space that scales like the length of the points in $\mathcal{H}$. Examples thereof are the standard deviation of the distance of the points to their mean, the radius of the smallest sphere containing the data (cf. (5.61) and (8.17)), or, in some cases, the maximum (or mean) length $k(x_i, x_i)$ over all data points (see Problem 7.25).
- Finally, we can use theoretical tools such as VC bounds (see, for instance, Figure 5.5) or leave-one-out bounds (Section 12.2).

Having seen that different types of SVCs lead to similar performance, the question arises as to how these performances compare with other approaches. Table 7.4 gives a summary of a number of results on the USPS set. Note that the best SVM result is 3.0%; it uses additional techniques that we shall explain in chapters 11 and 13. It is known that the USPS test set is rather difficult — the human error rate is 2.5% [79]. For a discussion, see [496]. Note, moreover, that some of the results reported in the literature for the USPS set were obtained with an enhanced training set: For instance, the study of Drucker et al. [148] used an enlarged training set of size 9709, containing some additional machine-printed digits, and found that this improves the accuracy on the test set. Similarly, Bottou and Vapnik [65] used a training set of size 9840. Since there are no machine-printed digits in the com-

Table 7.4 Summary of error rates on the USPS set. Note that two variants of this database are used in the literature; one of them (denoted by USPS+) is enhanced by a set of machine-printed characters which have been found to improve the test error. Note that the virtual SV systems perform best out of all systems trained on the original USPS set.

Classifier	Training set	Test error	Reference
Linear SVM	USPS	8.9%	[470]
Relevance Vector Machine	USPS	5.1%	Chapter 16
Hard margin SVM	USPS	4.6%	[62]
SVM	USPS	4.0%	[470]
Hyperplane on KPCA features	USPS	4.0%	Chapter 14
KFD	USPS	3.7%	Chapter 15
Virtual SVM	USPS	3.2%	Chapter 11
Virtual SVM, local kernel	USPS	3.0%	Chapter 13
Nearest neighbor	USPS+	5.9%	[496]
LeNet1	USPS+	5.0%	[318]
Local learning Approach	USPS+	3.3%	[65]
Boosted Neural Net	USPS+	2.6%	[148]
Tangent distance	USPS+	2.6%	[496]
Human error rate	—	2.5%	[79]

monly used test set (size 2007), this addition distorts the original learning problem to a situation where results become somewhat hard to interpret. For our experiments, we only had the original 7291 training examples at our disposal. Of all the systems trained on this original set, the SVM system of Chapter 13 performs best.

7.8.2 Universality of the Support Vector Set

In the present section, we report empirical evidence that the SV set contains all the information necessary to solve a given classification task: Using the Support Vector algorithm to train three different types of handwritten digit classifiers, we observe that these types of classifiers construct their decision surface from small, strongly overlapping subsets of the database.

Overlap of SV Sets

To study the Support Vector sets for three different types of SV classifiers, we use the optimal kernel parameters on the USPS set according to Table 7.3. Table 7.5 shows that all three classifiers use around 250 Support Vectors per two-class-classifier (less than 4% of the training set), of which there are 10. The *total* number of different Support Vectors of the ten-class-classifiers is around 1600. It is less than 2500 (10 times the above 250), since for instance a particular vector that has been used as a positive SV (i.e., $y_i = +1$ in (7.25)) for digit 7, might at the same time be a negative SV ($y_i = -1$) for digit 1.

Table 7.6 shows that the SV sets of the different classifiers have about 90% overlap. This surprising result has been reproduced on the MNIST OCR set [467].

Table 7.5 First row: Total number of different SVs in three different ten-class-classifiers (i.e., number of elements of the union of the ten two-class-classifier SV sets), obtained by choosing different functions k in (7.25) and (7.29); Second row: Average number of SVs per two-class-classifier (USPS database size: 7291) (from [470]).

	Polynomial	RBF	Sigmoid
total # of SVs	1677	1498	1611
average # of SVs	274	235	254

Table 7.6 Percentage of the SV set of [column] contained in the SV set of [row]; for ten-class classifiers *(top)*, and binary recognizers for digit class 7 *(bottom)* (USPS set) (from [470]).

	Polynomial	RBF	Sigmoid
Polynomial	100	93	94
RBF	83	100	87
Sigmoid	90	93	100

	Polynomial	RBF	Sigmoid
Polynomial	100	84	93
RBF	89	100	92
Sigmoid	93	86	100

Using a leave-one-out procedure similar to Proposition 7.4, Vapnik and Watkins have put forward a theoretical argument for shared SVs. We state it in the following form: If the SV set of three SV classifiers had no overlap, we could obtain a fourth classifier which has zero test error.

Voting Argument for Shared SVs

To see why this is the case, note that if a pattern is left out of the training set, it will always be classified correctly by voting between the three SV classifiers trained on the remaining examples: Otherwise, it would have been an SV of at least two of them, if kept in the training set. The expectation of the number of patterns which are SVs of at least two of the three classifiers, divided by the training set size, thus forms an upper bound on the expected test error of the voting system. Regarding error rates, it would thus in fact be desirable to be able to construct classifiers with different SV sets. An alternative explanation, studying the effect of the input density on the kernel, was recently proposed by Williams [597]. Finally, we add that the result is also plausible in view of the similar regularization characteristics of the different kernels that were used (see Chapter 4).

Training on SV Sets

As described in Section 7.3, the Support Vector set contains all the information a given classifier needs for constructing the decision function. Due to the overlap in the Support Vector sets of different classifiers, we can even train classifiers on the Support Vector set of *another* classifier; the latter having a different kernel to the former. Table 7.7 shows that this leads to results comparable to those after training

Table 7.7 Training classifiers on the Support Vector sets of other classifiers, leads to performances on the test set (USPS problem) which are as good as the results for training on the full database (number of errors on the 2007-element test set are shown, for two-class classifiers separating digit 7 from the rest). Additionally, the results for training on a random subset of the database of size 200 are displayed.

kernel	trained on: *size:*	poly-SVs *178*	rbf-SVs *189*	tanh-SVs *177*	full db *7291*	rnd. subs. *200*
Poly		13	13	12	13	23
RBF		17	13	17	15	27
tanh		15	13	13	15	25

on the whole database. In Section 11.3, we will use this finding as a motivation for a method to make SVMs transformation invariant, to obtain *virtual SV* machines.

What do these results concerning the nature of Support Vectors tell us? Learning can be viewed as inferring regularities from a set of training examples. Much research has been devoted to the study of various learning algorithms, which allow the extraction of these underlying regularities. No matter how different the outward appearance of these algorithms is, they must all rely on intrinsic regularities of the data. If the learning has been successful, these intrinsic regularities are captured in the values of certain parameters of a learning machine; for a polynomial classifier, these parameters are the coefficients of a polynomial, for a neural network, they are weights, biases, and gains, and for a radial basis function classifier, they are weights, centers, and widths. This variety of different representations of the intrinsic regularities, however, conceals the fact that they all stem from a common root. This is why SVMs with different kernel functions identify the same subset of the training examples as crucial for the regularity to be learned.

7.8.3 Other Applications

SVMs have been successfully applied in other computer vision tasks, which relate to the OCR problems discussed above. Examples include object and face detection and recognition, as well as image retrieval [57, 467, 399, 419, 237, 438, 99, 75].

Another area where SVMs have been used with success is that of *text categorization*. Being a high-dimensional problem, text categorization has been found to be well suited for SVMs. A popular benchmark is the Reuters-22173 text corpus. The news agency Reuters collected 21450 news stories from 1997, and partitioned and indexed them into 135 different categories. The feature typically used to classify Reuters documents are 10^4-dimensional vectors containing word frequencies within a document (sometimes called the "bag-of-words" representation of texts, as it completely discards the information on word ordering). Using this coding, SVMs have led to excellent results, see [155, 265, 267, 150, 333, 542, 149, 326].

Since the use of classification techniques is ubiquitous throughout technology, we cannot give an exhaustive listing of all successful SVM applications. We thus conclude the list with some of the more exotic applications, such as in High-Energy-Physics [19, 558], in the monitoring of household appliances [390], in protein secondary structure prediction [249], and, with rather intriguing results, in the design of decision feedback equalizers (DFE) in telephony [105].

7.9 Summary

This chapter introduced SV pattern recognition algorithms. The crucial idea is to use kernels to reduce a complex classification task to one that can be solved with separating hyperplanes. We discussed what kind of hyperplane should be constructed in order to get good generalization performance, leading to the idea of large margins. It turns out that the concept of large margins can be justified in a number of different ways, including arguments based on statistical learning theory, and compression schemes. We described in detail how the optimal margin hyperplane can be obtained as the solution of a quadratic programming problem. We started with the linear case, where the hyperplane is constructed in the space of the inputs, and then moved on to the case where we use a kernel function to compute dot products, in order to compute the hyperplane in a feature space.

Two further extensions greatly increase the applicability of the approach. First, to deal with noisy data, we introduced so-called slack variables in the optimization problem. Second, for problems that have more than just two classes, we described a number of generalizations of the binary SV classifiers described initially.

Finally, we reported applications and benchmark comparisons for the widely used USPS handwritten digit task. SVMs turn out to work very well in this field, as well as in a variety of other domains mentioned briefly.

7.10 Problems

7.1 (Weight Vector Scaling •) *Show that instead of the "1" on the right hand side of the separation constraint (7.11), we can use any positive number $\gamma > 0$, without changing the optimal margin hyperplane solution. What changes in the soft margin case?*

7.2 (Dual Perceptron Algorithm [175] ••) *Kernelize the perceptron algorithm described in footnote 1. Which of the patterns will appear in the expansion of the solution?*

7.3 (Margin of Optimal Margin Hyperplanes [62] ••) *Prove that the geometric margin ρ of the optimal margin hyperplane can be computed from the solution $\boldsymbol{\alpha}$ via*

$$\rho^{-2} = \sum_{i=1}^{m} \alpha_i. \tag{7.68}$$

Also prove that

$$\rho^{-2} = 2W(\boldsymbol{\alpha}) = \|\mathbf{w}\|^2. \tag{7.69}$$

Note that for these relations to hold true, $\boldsymbol{\alpha}$ needs to be the solution of (7.29).

7.4 (Relationship Between $\|\mathbf{w}\|$ and the Geometrical Margin •) *(i) Consider a separating hyperplane in canonical form. Prove that the margin, measured perpendicularly to the hyperplane, equals $1/\|\mathbf{w}\|$, by considering two opposite points which precisely satisfy $|\langle \mathbf{w}, \mathbf{x}_i\rangle + b| = 1$.*

(ii) How does the corresponding statement look for the case of ν-SVC? Use the constraint (7.41), and assume that all slack variables are 0.

7.5 (Compression Bound for Large Margin Classification ∘∘∘) *Formalize the ideas stated in Section 7.2: Assuming that the data are separable and lie in a ball of radius R, how many bits are necessary to encode the labels of the data by encoding the parameters of a hyperplane? Formulate a generalization error bound in terms of the compression ratio by using the analysis of Vapnik [561, Section 4.6]. Compare the resulting bound with Theorem 7.3. Take into account the eigenvalues of the Gram matrix, using the ideas of from [604] (cf. Section 12.4).*

7.6 (Positive Definiteness of the SVC Hessian •) *From Definition 2.4, prove that the matrix $Q_{ij} := (y_i y_j k(x_i, x_j))_{ij}$ is positive definite.*

7.7 (Geometric Interpretation of Duality in SVC [38] ••) *Prove that the programming problem (7.10), (7.11) has the same solution as (7.22), provided the threshold b is adjusted such that the hyperplane bisects the shortest connection of the two convex hulls. Hint: Show that the latter is the dual of the former. Interpret the result geometrically.*

7.8 (Number of Points Required to Define a Hyperplane •) *From (7.22), argue that no matter what the dimensionality of the space, there can always be situations where two training points suffice to determine the optimal hyperplane.*

7.9 (In-Bound SVs in Soft Margin SVMs •) *Prove that in-bound SVs lie exactly on the margin. Hint: Use the KKT conditions, and proceed analogously to Section 7.3, where it was shown that in the hard margin case, all SVs lie exactly on the margin.*

Argue, moreover, that bound SVs can lie both on or in the margin, and that they will "usually" lie in the margin.

7.10 (Pattern-Dependent Regularization •) *Derive a version of the soft margin classification algorithm which uses different regularization constants C_i for each training example. Start from (7.35), replace the second term by $\frac{1}{m}\sum_{i=1}^m C_i\xi_i$, and derive the dual. Discuss both the mathematical form of the result, and possible applications (cf. [462]).*

7.11 (Uncertain Labels ••) *In this chapter, we have been concerned mainly with the case where the patterns are assigned to one of two classes, i.e., $y \in \{\pm 1\}$. Consider now the* *case where the assignment is not strict, i.e., $y \in [-1, 1]$. Modify the soft margin variants of the SV algorithm, (7.34), (7.35) and (7.41), (7.40), such that*

- *whenever $y = 0$, the corresponding pattern has effectively no influence*
- *if all labels are in $\{\pm 1\}$, the original algorithm is recovered*
- *if $|y| < 1$, then the corresponding pattern has less influence than it would have for $|y| = 1$.*

7.12 (SVMs vs. Parzen Windows ∘∘∘) *Develop algorithms that approximate the SVM (soft or hard margin) solution by starting from the Parzen Windows algorithm (Figure 1.1) and sparsifying the expansion of the solution.*

7.13 (Squared Error SVC [111] ••) *Derive a version of the soft margin classification algorithm which penalizes the errors quadratically. Start from (7.35), replace the second term by $\frac{1}{m}\sum_{i=1}^{m}\xi_i^2$, and derive the dual. Compare the result to the usual C-SVM, both in terms of algorithmic differences and in terms of robustness properties. Which algorithm would you expect to work better for Gaussian-like noise, which one for noise with longer tails (and thus more outliers) (cf. Chapter 3)?*

7.14 (C-SVC with Group Error Penalty ••) *Suppose the training data are partitioned into ℓ groups,*

$$\begin{array}{l}(\mathbf{x}_1^1, y_1^1), \ldots, (\mathbf{x}_1^{m_1}, y_1^{m_1}) \\ \quad \vdots \qquad\qquad \vdots \\ (\mathbf{x}_\ell^1, y_\ell^1), \ldots, (\mathbf{x}_\ell^{m_\ell}, y_\ell^{m_\ell}),\end{array} \tag{7.70}$$

where $\mathbf{x}_i^j \in \mathcal{H}$ and $y_i^j \in \{\pm 1\}$ (it is understood that the index i runs over $\{1, 2, \ldots, \ell\}$ and the index j runs over $\{1, 2, \ldots, m_i\}$).

Suppose, moreover, that we would like to count a point as misclassified already if one point belonging to the same group is misclassified.

Design an SV algorithm where each group's penalty equals the slack of the worst point in that group.

Hint: Use the objective function

$$\frac{1}{2}\|\mathbf{w}\|^2 + \sum_i C_i \xi_i, \tag{7.71}$$

and the constraints

$$y_i^j \cdot (\langle \mathbf{w}, \mathbf{x}_i^j \rangle + b) \geq 1 - \xi_i, \tag{7.72}$$

$$\xi_i \geq 0. \tag{7.73}$$

Show that the dual problem consists of maximizing

$$W(\boldsymbol{\alpha}) = \sum_{i,j} \alpha_i^j - \frac{1}{2} \sum_{i,j,i',j'} \alpha_i^j \alpha_{i'}^{j'} y_i^j y_{i'}^{j'} \left\langle \mathbf{x}_i^j, \mathbf{x}_{i'}^{j'} \right\rangle, \tag{7.74}$$

subject to

$$0 = \sum_{i,j} \alpha_i^j y_i^j, \; 0 \le \alpha_i^j, \text{ and } \sum_j \alpha_i^j \le C_i. \tag{7.75}$$

Argue that typically, only one point per group will become an SV.
Show that C-SVC is a special case of this algorithm.

7.15 (ν-SVC with Group Error Penalty •••) *Derive a ν-version of the algorithm in Problem 7.14.*

7.16 (C-SVC vs. ν-SVC ••) *As a modification of ν-SVC (Section 7.5), compute the dual of $\tau(\mathbf{w}, \boldsymbol{\xi}, \rho) = \|\mathbf{w}\|^2/2 + C(-\nu\rho + (1/m)\sum_{i=1}^m \xi_i)$ (note that in ν-SVC, $C = 1$ is used). Argue that due to the homogeneity of the objective function, the dual solution gets scaled by C, however, the decision function will not change. Hence we may set $C = 1$.*

7.17 (Multi-class vs. Binary SVC [593] ••) *(i) Prove that the multi-class SVC formulation of (7.59) specializes to the binary C-SVC (7.35) in the case $k = 2$, by using $\mathbf{w}_1 = -\mathbf{w}_2$, $b_1 = -b_2$, and $\xi_i = \frac{1}{2}\xi_i^r$ for pattern $\mathbf{x}_i$ in class r. (ii) Derive the dual of (7.59).*

7.18 (Multi-Class ν-SVC ∘∘∘) *Derive a ν-version of the approach described in Section 7.6.4.*

7.19 (LPM with Constrained Signs •) *Modify the LPM algorithm such that it is guaranteed that each expansion pattern will have a coefficient v_i whose sign equals the class label y_i. Hint: Do not introduce additional constraints, but eliminate the α_i^* variables and use a different ansatz for the solution.*

7.20 (Multi-Class LPM [593] ••) *In analogy to Section 7.6.4, develop a multi-class version of the LP machine (Section 7.7).*

7.21 (Version Space [368, 239, 451, 238] •••) *Consider hyperplanes passing through the origin, $\{\mathbf{x} | \langle \mathbf{w}, \mathbf{x} \rangle = 0\}$, with weight vectors $\mathbf{w} \in \mathcal{H}$, $\|\mathbf{w}\| = 1$. The set of all such hyperplanes forms a unit sphere in weight space. Each training example $(\mathbf{x}, y) \in \mathcal{H} \times \{\pm 1\}$ splits the sphere into two halves: one that correctly classifies $(\mathbf{x}, y)$, i.e., $\operatorname{sgn} \langle \mathbf{w}, \mathbf{x} \rangle = y$, and one that does not. Each training example thus corresponds to a hemisphere (or, equivalently, an oriented great circle) in weight space, and a training set $(\mathbf{x}_1, y_1), \ldots, (\mathbf{x}_m, y_m)$ corresponds to the intersection of m hemispheres, called the* version space.

1. *Discuss how the distances between the training example and the hyperplane in the two representations are related.*
2. *Discuss the relationship to the idea of the Hough transform [255]. The Hough transform is sometimes used in image processing to detect lines. In a nutshell, each point gets to cast votes in support for all potential lines that are consistent with it, and at the end, the lines can be read off the histogram of votes.*
3. *Prove that if all $\mathbf{x}_i$ have the same norm, the maximum margin weight vector corresponds to the center of the largest $m-1$-dimensional sphere that fits into version space.*

4. *Construct situations where the center of the above largest sphere will generalize poorly, and compare it to the center of mass of version space, called the* Bayes point.

5. *If you disregard the labels of the training examples, there is no longer a single area on the unit sphere which is distinguished from the others due to its corresponding to the correct labelling. Instead, the sphere is split into a number of cells. Argue that the expectation of the natural logarithm of this number equals the VC entropy (Section 5.5.6).*

7.22 (Kernels on Sets ○○○) *Use the construction of Proposition 2.19 to define a kernel that compares two points $\mathbf{x}, \mathbf{x}' \in \mathcal{H}$ by comparing the version spaces (see Problem 7.21) of the labelled examples $(\mathbf{x}, 1)$ and $(\mathbf{x}', 1)$. Define a prior distribution* P *on the unit sphere in $\mathcal{H}$, and discuss the implications of its choice for the induced kernel. What can you say about the connection between this kernel and the kernel $\langle \mathbf{x}, \mathbf{x}' \rangle$?*

7.23 (Training Algorithms for ν-SVC ○○○) *Try to come up with efficient training algorithms for ν-SVC, building on the material presented in Chapter 10.*

(i) Design a simple chunking algorithm that gradually removes all non-SVs.

(ii) Design a decomposition algorithm.

(iii) Is it possible to modify the SMO algorithm such that it deals with the additional equality constraint that ν-SVC comes with? What is the smallest set of patterns that you can optimize over without violating the two equality constraints? Can you design a generalized SMO algorithm for this case?

7.24 (Prior Class Probabilities ••) *Suppose that it is known a priori that π_+ and π_- are the probabilities that a pattern belongs to the class ± 1, respectively. Discuss ways of modifying the simple classification algorithm described in Section 1.2 to take this information into account.*

7.25 (Choosing C ••) *Suppose that R is a measure for the range of the data in feature space that scales like the length of the points in $\mathcal{H}$ (cf. Section 7.8.1). Argue that C should scale like $1/R^2$.*[15] *Hint: consider scaling the data by some $\gamma > 0$. How do you have to scale C such that $f(x) = \langle \mathbf{w}, \Phi(x_j) \rangle + b$ (where $\mathbf{w} = \sum_i \alpha_i y_i \Phi(x_i)$) remains invariant ($j \in [m]$)?*[16] *Discuss measures R that can be used. Why does $R := \max_j k(x_j, x_j)$ not make sense for the Gaussian RBF kernel?*

Moreover, argue that in the asymptotic regime, the upper bound on the α_j should scale with $1/m$, justifying the use of m in (7.38).

7.26 (Choosing C, Part II ○○○) *Problem 7.25 does not take into account the class labels, and hence also not the potential overlap of the two classes. Note that this is different in the ν-approach, which automatically scales the margin with the noise. Can you modify the recommendation in Problem 7.25 to get a selection criterion for C which takes into account the labels, e.g., in the form of prior information on the noise level?*

---

15. Thanks to Olivier Chapelle for this suggestion.
16. Note that in the ν-parametrization, this scale invariance comes for free.

8 Single-Class Problems: Quantile Estimation and Novelty Detection

This chapter describes an SV approach to the problem of *novelty detection* and high-dimensional *quantile estimation* [475]. This is an *unsupervised* problem, which can be described as follows. Suppose we are given some dataset drawn from an underlying probability distribution P, and we want to estimate a "simple" subset S of input space, such that the probability that a test point drawn from P lies outside of S equals some a priori specified value between 0 and 1.

We approach the problem by trying to estimate a function f which is positive on S and negative on the complement. The functional form of f is given by a kernel expansion in terms of SVs; it is regularized by controlling the length of the weight vector in an associated feature space (or, equivalently, by maximizing a margin). The expansion coefficients are found by solving a quadratic programming problem, which can be done by carrying out sequential optimization over pairs of input patterns. We also state theoretical results concerning the statistical performance. The algorithm is a natural extension of the Support Vector classification algorithm, as described in the previous chapter, to the case of unlabelled data.

Overview

The chapter is organized as follows. After a review of some previous work in Section 8.2, taken from [475], we describe SV algorithms for single class problems. Section 8.4 gives details of the implementation of the optimization procedure, specifically for the case of single-class SVMs. Following this, we report theoretical results characterizing the present approach (Section 8.5). In Section 8.7, we deal with the application of the algorithm to artificial and real-world data.

Prerequisites

The prerequisites of the chapter are almost identical to the previous chapter. Those who have read Chapter 7, should be fine with the current chapter. Section 8.2 requires some knowledge of probability theory, as explained in Section B.1; readers who are only interested in the algorithms, however, can skip this slightly more technical section. Likewise, there are some technical parts of Section 8.5 which would benefit from knowledge of Chapter 5, but these can be skipped if desired.

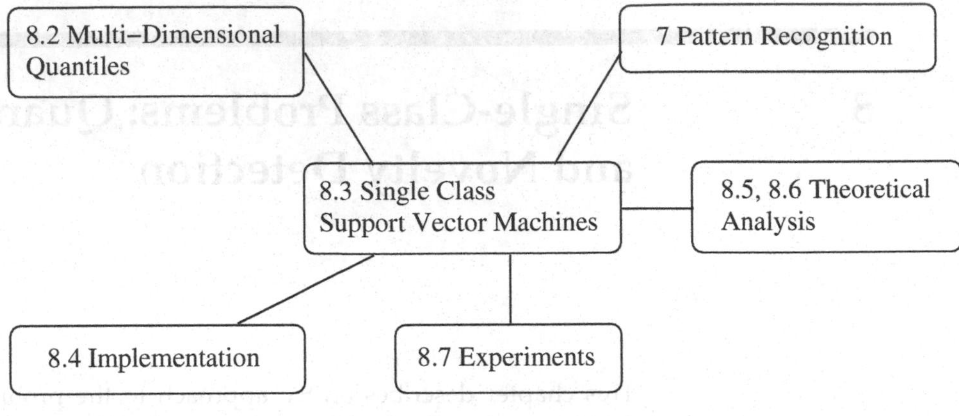

8.1 Introduction

There have been a number of attempts to transfer the idea of using kernels to compute dot products in feature spaces to the domain of unsupervised learning. The problems in this domain are, however, less precisely specified. Generally, they can be characterized as estimating *functions* of the data which tell you something interesting about the underlying distributions. For instance, kernel PCA (Chapter 14) can be described as computing functions which on the training data produce unit variance outputs while having minimum norm in feature space. Another kernel-based unsupervised learning technique, regularized principal manifolds (Chapter 17), computes functions which give a mapping onto a lower-dimensional manifold minimizing a regularized quantization error. Clustering algorithms are further examples of unsupervised learning techniques which can be kernelized [480].

An extreme point of view is that unsupervised learning is about estimating the density of the distribution P generating the data. Knowledge of the density would then allow us to solve whatever problem can be solved on the basis of data *sampled* from that density.

The present chapter addresses an easier problem: it proposes an algorithm that computes a binary function which is supposed to capture regions in input space where the probability density is in some sense large (its support, or, more generally, quantiles); that is, a function which is nonzero in a region where most of the data are located. In doing so, this method is in line with Vapnik's principle never to solve a problem which is more general than the one we actually need to solve [561]. Moreover, it is also applicable in cases where the density of the data's distribution is not even well-defined, as can be the case if the distribution has singular components.

8.2 A Distribution's Support and Quantiles

Quantile Function

In order to describe previous work, it is convenient to introduce the following definition of a (multi-dimensional) quantile function [158]. Let $x_1, \ldots, x_m$ be an iid sample of a random experiment in a set $\mathcal{X}$ with distribution P. Let $\mathfrak{C}$ be a class of measurable subsets of $\mathcal{X}$ and let λ be a real-valued function defined on $\mathfrak{C}$. The *quantile function* with respect to $(\mathrm{P}, \lambda, \mathfrak{C})$ is

$$U(\mu) = \inf\{\lambda(C) | \mathrm{P}(C) \geq \mu, C \in \mathfrak{C}\}, \quad 0 < \mu \leq 1. \tag{8.1}$$

Loosely speaking, the quantile function measures how large a set one needs in order to capture a certain amount of probability mass of P.

An interesting special case is the *empirical quantile function*, where P is the empirical distribution

$$\mathrm{P}^m_{\mathrm{emp}}(C) = \frac{1}{m} \sum_{i=1}^{m} I_C(x_i), \tag{8.2}$$

which is the fraction of observations that fall into C.

We denote by $C_\lambda(\mu)$ and $C^m_\lambda(\mu)$ the (not necessarily unique) $C \in \mathfrak{C}$ that attain the infimum (when it is achievable). Intuitively speaking, these are the smallest sets (where size is measured by λ) which contain a probability mass μ.

The most common choice of λ is Lebesgue measure (loosely speaking, the *volume* of the set C), in which case $C_\lambda(\mu)$ is the minimum volume set $C \in \mathfrak{C}$ that contains at least a fraction μ of the probability mass. Estimators of the form $C^m_\lambda(\mu)$ are called *minimum volume estimators*. Of course, it is not sufficient that the estimated set have a small volume and contain a fraction μ of the training examples. In machine learning applications, we want to find a set that contains a fraction of *test* examples that is close to μ. This is where the complexity trade-off enters (see Figure 8.1), as with the methodology that we have already described in a number of learning scenarios. On the one hand, we want to use a large class $\mathfrak{C}$, to ensure that it contains sets C which are very small yet can contain a fraction μ of training examples. On the other hand, if we allowed just *any* set, the chosen set C could consist of only the training points (we would then "memorize" the training points), and it would generalize poorly to test examples; in other words, it would not contain a large probability mass P(C). Therefore, we have to consider classes of sets which are suitably restricted. As we will see below, this can be achieved using an SVM regularizer.

Support of a Distribution

Observe that for $\mathfrak{C}$ being all measurable sets, and λ being the Lebesgue measure, $C_\lambda(1)$ is the *support* of the density p corresponding to P, assuming it exists (note that $C_\lambda(1)$ is well defined even when p does not exist). For smaller classes $\mathfrak{C}$, $C_\lambda(1)$ is the minimum volume $C \in \mathfrak{C}$ containing the support of p. In the case where $\mu < 1$, it seems the first work was reported in [454, 229], in which $\mathcal{X} = \mathbb{R}^2$, with $\mathfrak{C}$ being the class of closed convex sets in $\mathcal{X}$ (they actually considered density contour clusters; cf. [475] for a definition). Nolan [385] considered higher dimensions, with

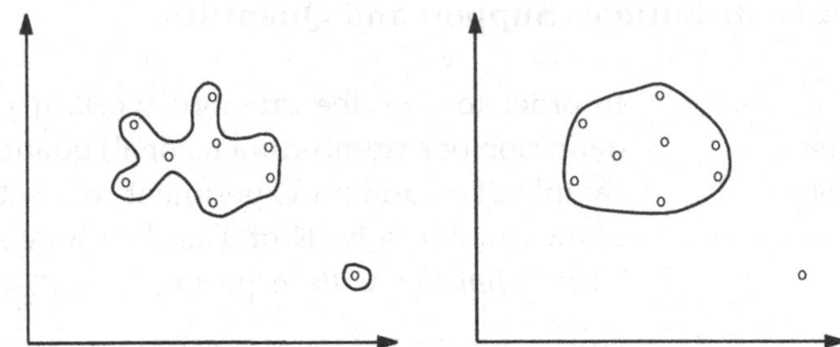

Figure 8.1 A single-class toy problem, with two different solutions. The left graph depicts a rather complex solution, which captures all training points (thus, P^m_{emp} of the estimated region equals 1, cf. (8.2)), while having small volume in $\mathbb{R}^2$. On the right, we show a solution which misses one training point (it does not capture all of P^m_{emp}), but since it is "simpler," it is conceivable that it will nevertheless capture more of the true underlying distribution P that is assumed to have generated the data. In the present context, a function λ is used to measure the simplicity of the estimated region. In the algorithm described below, λ is a SV style regularizer.

$\mathcal{C}$ being the class of ellipsoids. Tsybakov [550] studied an estimator based on piecewise polynomial approximation of $C_\lambda(\mu)$ and showed it attains the asymptotically minimax rate for certain classes of densities. Polonik [417] studied the estimation of $C_\lambda(\mu)$ by $C^m_\lambda(\mu)$. He derived asymptotic rates of convergence in terms of various measures of richness of $\mathcal{C}$. More information on minimum volume estimators can be found in that work, and in [475].

Let us conclude this section with a short discussion of how the present work relates to the above. The present chapter describes an algorithm which finds regions close to $C_\lambda(\mu)$. Our class $\mathcal{C}$ is defined implicitly via a kernel k as the set of half-spaces in a SV feature space. We do not try to minimize the volume of C in input space. Instead, we minimize a SV style regularizer which, using a kernel, controls the smoothness of the estimated function describing C. In terms of multi-dimensional quantiles, the present approach employs $\lambda(C_{\mathbf{w}}) = \|\mathbf{w}\|^2$, where $C_{\mathbf{w}} = \{x|f_{\mathbf{w}}(x) \geq \rho\}$, and $(\mathbf{w}, \rho)$ are respectively a weight vector and an offset parametrizing a hyperplane in the feature space associated with the kernel.

8.3 Algorithms

We consider unlabelled training data

$$X = \{x_1, \ldots, x_m\} \subset \mathcal{X}, \tag{8.3}$$

where $m \in \mathbb{N}$ is the number of observations, and $\mathcal{X}$ is some set. For simplicity, we think of it as a compact subset of $\mathbb{R}^N$. Let Φ be a feature map $\mathcal{X} \to \mathcal{H}$; in other words, a map into a dot product space $\mathcal{H}$ such that the dot product in the image of Φ can be computed by evaluating some simple kernel (Chapters 2 and 4),

$$k(x, x') = \langle \Phi(x), \Phi(x') \rangle, \tag{8.4}$$

such as the Gaussian,

$$k(x, x') = e^{-\|x-x'\|^2/c}. \tag{8.5}$$

Indices i and j are understood to range over $1, \ldots, m$ (in compact notation: $i, j \in [m]$). Bold face Greek letters denote m-dimensional vectors whose components are labelled using normal face type.

In the remainder of this section, we shall describe an algorithm which returns a function f that takes the value $+1$ in a "small" region capturing most of the data points, and -1 elsewhere. The strategy, inspired by the previous chapter, is to map the data into the feature space corresponding to the kernel, and to separate them from the origin with maximum margin. For a new point x, the value $f(x)$ is determined by evaluating which side of the hyperplane it falls on, in feature space. Due to the freedom to utilize different types of kernel functions, this simple geometric picture corresponds to a variety of nonlinear estimators in input space.

To separate the data set from the origin, we solve the following quadratic program:

$$\underset{\mathbf{w}\in\mathcal{H},\boldsymbol{\xi}\in\mathbb{R}^m,\rho\in\mathbb{R}}{\text{minimize}} \; \frac{1}{2}\|\mathbf{w}\|^2 + \frac{1}{\nu m}\sum_i \xi_i - \rho, \tag{8.6}$$

$$\text{subject to } \langle \mathbf{w}, \Phi(x_i) \rangle \geq \rho - \xi_i, \;\; \xi_i \geq 0. \tag{8.7}$$

Here, $\nu \in (0, 1]$ is a parameter which is introduced in close analogy to the ν-SV classification algorithm detailed in the previous chapter. Its meaning will become clear later.

Slack Variables

Since nonzero slack variables ξ_i are penalized in the objective function, we can expect that if $\mathbf{w}$ and ρ solve this problem, then the decision function,

$$f(x) = \operatorname{sgn}(\langle \mathbf{w}, \Phi(x) \rangle - \rho), \tag{8.8}$$

will equal 1 for most examples x_i contained in the training set,[1] while the regularization term $\|\mathbf{w}\|$ will still be small. For an illustration, see Figure 8.2. As in ν-SVC (Section 7.5), the trade-off between these two goals is controlled by a parameter ν.

Using multipliers $\alpha_i, \beta_i \geq 0$, we introduce a Lagrangian,

$$L(\mathbf{w}, \boldsymbol{\xi}, \rho, \boldsymbol{\alpha}, \boldsymbol{\beta}) = \frac{1}{2}\|\mathbf{w}\|^2 + \frac{1}{\nu m}\sum_i \xi_i - \rho - \sum_i \alpha_i(\langle \mathbf{w}, \Phi(x_i) \rangle - \rho + \xi_i) - \sum_i \beta_i \xi_i, \tag{8.9}$$

and set the derivatives with respect to the primal variables $\mathbf{w}, \boldsymbol{\xi}, \rho$ equal to zero, yielding

$$\mathbf{w} = \sum_i \alpha_i \Phi(x_i), \tag{8.10}$$

1. We use the convention that $\operatorname{sgn}(z)$ equals 1 for $z \geq 0$ and -1 otherwise.

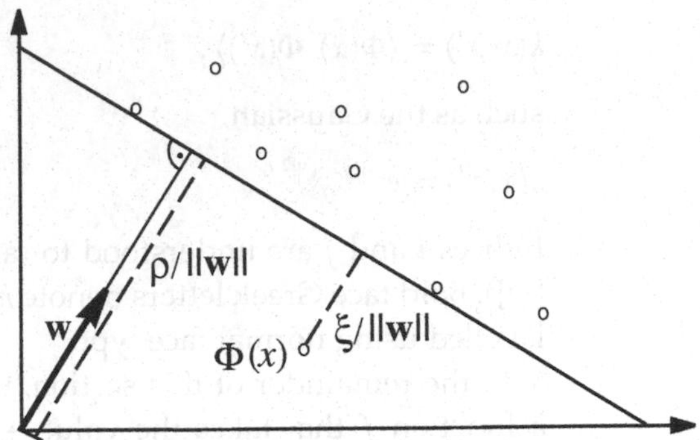

Figure 8.2 In the 2-D toy example depicted, the hyperplane $\langle \mathbf{w}, \Phi(x) \rangle = \rho$ (with normal vector $\mathbf{w}$ and offset ρ) separates all but one of the points from the origin. The outlier $\Phi(x)$ is associated with a slack variable ξ, which is penalized in the objective function (8.6). The distance from the outlier to the hyperplane is $\xi/\|\mathbf{w}\|$; the distance between hyperplane and origin is $\rho/\|\mathbf{w}\|$. The latter implies that a small $\|\mathbf{w}\|$ corresponds to a large margin of separation from the origin.

$$\alpha_i = \frac{1}{\nu m} - \beta_i \leq \frac{1}{\nu m}, \quad \sum_i \alpha_i = 1. \tag{8.11}$$

Eq. (8.10) is the familiar Support Vector expansion (cf. (7.15)). Together with (8.4), it transforms the decision function (8.8) into a kernel expansion,

$$f(x) = \operatorname{sgn}\left(\sum_i \alpha_i k(x_i, x) - \rho\right). \tag{8.12}$$

Single-Class Quadratic Program

Substituting (8.10)–(8.11) into L (8.9), and using (8.4), we obtain the dual problem:

$$\underset{\alpha \in \mathbb{R}^m}{\text{minimize}} \ \frac{1}{2} \sum_{ij} \alpha_i \alpha_j k(x_i, x_j), \tag{8.13}$$

$$\text{subject to } 0 \leq \alpha_i \leq \frac{1}{\nu m}, \tag{8.14}$$

$$\sum_i \alpha_i = 1. \tag{8.15}$$

We can show that at the optimum, the two inequality constraints (8.7) become equalities if α_i and β_i are nonzero, which implies $0 < \alpha_i < 1/(\nu m)$ (KKT conditions). Therefore, we can recover ρ by exploiting that for any such α_i, the corresponding pattern x_i satisfies

$$\rho = \langle \mathbf{w}, \Phi(x_i) \rangle = \sum_j \alpha_j k(x_j, x_i). \tag{8.16}$$

Note that if ν approaches 0, the upper bounds on the Lagrange multipliers tend to infinity and the second inequality constraint in (8.14) becomes void. We then have a *hard margin* problem, since the penalization of errors becomes infinite, as can be seen from the primal objective function (8.6). The problem is still feasible, since we have placed no restriction on the offset ρ, so ρ can become a large negative number in order to satisfy (8.7).

Parzen Windows

It is instructive to compare (8.13)–(8.15) to a Parzen windows estimator (cf. page 6). To this end, suppose we use a kernel which can be normalized as a density in input space, such as the Gaussian (8.5). If we use $\nu = 1$ in (8.14), then the two constraints only allow the solution $\alpha_1 = \ldots = \alpha_m = 1/m$. Thus the kernel expansion in (8.12) reduces to a Parzen windows estimate of the underlying density. For $\nu < 1$, the equality constraint (8.15) still ensures that the decision function is a thresholded density; in that case, however, the density will only be represented by a *subset* of training examples (the SVs) — those which are important for the decision (8.12) to be taken. Section 8.5 will explain the precise meaning of the parameter ν.

To conclude this section, we note that *balls* can also be used to describe the data in feature space, close in spirit to the algorithms described in [470], with hard boundaries, and [535], with "soft margins" (cf. also the algorithm described in Section 5.6). Again, we try to put *most of* the data into a small ball by solving

$$\begin{aligned} &\underset{R\in\mathbb{R},\xi\in\mathbb{R}^m,c\in\mathcal{H}}{\text{minimize}} \quad R^2 + \frac{1}{\nu m}\sum_i \xi_i \text{ for } 0 < \nu \leq 1 \\ &\text{subject to } \|\Phi(x_i) - c\|^2 \leq R^2 + \xi_i \text{ and } \xi_i \geq 0 \text{ for } i \in [m]. \end{aligned} \tag{8.17}$$

This leads to the dual,

$$\underset{\alpha}{\text{minimize}} \sum_{ij} \alpha_i\alpha_j k(x_i, x_j) - \sum_i \alpha_i k(x_i, x_i), \tag{8.18}$$

$$\text{subject to } 0 \leq \alpha_i \leq \frac{1}{\nu m} \text{ and } \sum_i \alpha_i = 1, \tag{8.19}$$

and the solution

$$c = \sum_i \alpha_i \Phi(x_i), \tag{8.20}$$

corresponding to a decision function of the form

$$f(x) = \operatorname{sgn}\left(R^2 - \sum_{ij} \alpha_i\alpha_j k(x_i, x_j) + 2\sum_i \alpha_i k(x_i, x) - k(x, x)\right). \tag{8.21}$$

As above, R^2 is computed such that for any x_i with $0 < \alpha_i < 1/(\nu m)$ the argument of the sgn is zero.

For kernels $k(x, x')$ which only depend on $x - x'$ (the translation invariant kernels, such as RBF kernels), $k(x, x)$ is constant. In this case, the equality constraint implies that the linear term in the dual target function (8.18) is constant, and the problem (8.18–8.19) turns out to be equivalent to (8.13–8.15). It can be shown that the same holds true for the decision function, hence the two algorithms coincide in this case. This is geometrically plausible: for constant $k(x, x)$, all mapped patterns lie on a sphere in feature space. Therefore, finding the smallest ball containing the

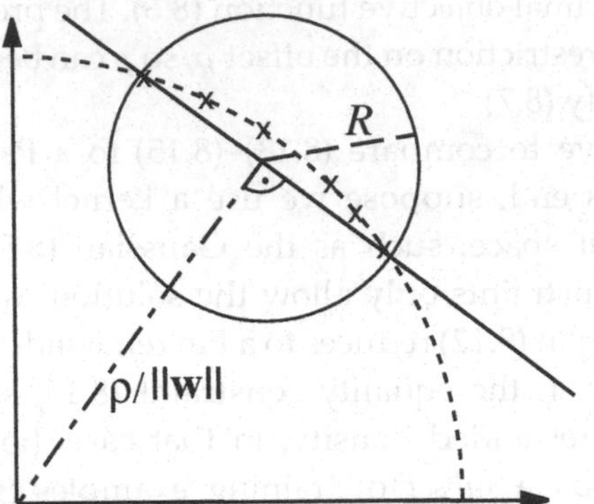

Figure 8.3 For RBF kernels, which depend only on $x - x'$, $k(x, x)$ is constant, and the mapped data points thus lie on a hypersphere in feature space. In this case, finding the smallest sphere enclosing the data is equivalent to maximizing the margin of separation from the origin (cf. Figure 8.2).

points amounts to finding the smallest segment of the sphere on which the data lie. This segment, however, can be found in a straightforward way by simply intersecting the data sphere with a hyperplane — the hyperplane with maximum margin of separation from the origin cuts off the smallest segment (Figure 8.3).

8.4 Optimization

The previous section formulated quadratic programs (QPs) for computing regions that capture a certain fraction of the data. These constrained optimization problems can be solved via an off-the-shelf QP package (cf. Chapter 6). In the present section, however, we describe an algorithm which takes advantage of the precise form of the QPs [475], which is an adaptation of the SMO (Sequential Minimal Optimization) algorithm [409]. Although most of the material on implementations is dealt with in Chapter 10, we will spend a few moments to describe the single class algorithm here. Further information on SMO in general can be found in Section 10.5; additional information on *single-class* SVM implementations, including variants which work in an online setting, can be found in Section 10.6.3.

The SMO algorithm has been reported to work well in C-SV classification. The latter has a structure resembling the present optimization problem: just as the dual of C-SV classification (7.37), the present dual also has only one equality constraint (8.15).[2]

The strategy of SMO is to break up the constrained minimization of (8.13) into the smallest optimization steps possible. Note that it is not possible to modify variables α_i *individually* without violating the sum constraint (8.15). We therefore resort to optimizing over pairs of variables.

2. The ν-SV classification algorithm (7.49), on the other hand, has two equality constraints. Therefore, it is not directly amenable to an SMO approach, unless we remove the equality constraint arising from the offset b, as done in [98].

Elementary SMO Optimization Step

Thus, consider optimizing over two variables α_i and α_j with all other variables fixed. Using the shorthand $K_{ij} := k(x_i, x_j)$, (8.13)–(8.15)) then reduce to (up to a constant)

$$\begin{aligned} \underset{\alpha_i,\alpha_j}{\text{minimize}} \quad & \frac{1}{2}\left[\alpha_i^2 K_{ii} + \alpha_j^2 K_{jj} + 2\alpha_i\alpha_j K_{ij}\right] + c_i\alpha_i + c_j\alpha_j \\ \text{subject to} \quad & \alpha_i + \alpha_j = \gamma \\ & 0 \le \alpha_i, \alpha_j \le \tfrac{1}{\nu m} \end{aligned} \tag{8.22}$$

in analogy to (10.63) below. Here the constants c_i, c_j, and γ are defined as follows;

$$c_i := \sum_{l\neq i,j}^{m} \alpha_l K_{il},\; c_j := \sum_{l\neq i,j}^{m} \alpha_l K_{jl}, \text{ and } \gamma = 1 - \sum_{l\neq i,j}^{m} \alpha_l. \tag{8.23}$$

To find the minimum, we use $\alpha_i + \alpha_j = \gamma$. This allows us to obtain a constrained optimization problem in α_i alone by elimination of α_j. For convenience we introduce $\chi := K_{ii} + K_{jj} - 2K_{ij}$.

$$\begin{aligned} \underset{\alpha_i}{\text{minimize}} \quad & \alpha_i^2\chi + \alpha_i\left(c_i - c_j + 2\gamma(K_{ij} - K_{jj})\right) \\ \text{subject to} \quad & L \le \alpha_i \le H, \text{ where } L = \max(0, \gamma - 1/(\nu m)) \text{ and } H = \min(1/(\nu m), \gamma). \end{aligned}$$

Without going into details (a similar calculation can be found in Section 10.5.1) the minimizer α_i of this optimization problem is given by

$$\alpha_i = \min(\max(L, \tilde{\alpha}_i), H). \tag{8.24}$$

where $\tilde{\alpha}_i$, the unconstrained solution, is given by

$$\tilde{\alpha}_i = \alpha_i^{\text{old}} + \chi^{-1}\left(c_j - c_i + K_{jj}\alpha_j^{\text{old}} + K_{ij}\left(\alpha_j^{\text{old}} - \alpha_i^{\text{old}}\right) - K_{ii}\alpha_i^{\text{old}}\right) \tag{8.25}$$

$$= \alpha_i^{\text{old}} + \chi^{-1}\left(f^{\text{old}}(x_j) - f^{\text{old}}(x_i)\right). \tag{8.26}$$

Finally, α_j can be obtained via $\alpha_j = \gamma - \alpha_i$. Eq. (8.26) tells us that the change in α_i will depend on the difference between the values $f(x_i)$ and $f(x_j)$. The less close these values are, i.e., the larger the difference in the distances to the hyperplane, the larger the possible change in the set of variables. Note, however, that there is no guarantee that the actual change in α_i will indeed be large, since α_i has to satisfy the constraint $L \le \alpha_i \le H$. Finally, the size of χ plays an important role, too (for the case of $\chi = 0$ see Lemma 10.3). The larger it is, the smaller the likely change in α_i.

We next briefly describe how to do the overall optimization.

Initialization of the Algorithm We start by setting a random fraction ν of all α_i to $1/(\nu m)$. If νm is not an integer, then one of the examples is set to a value in $(0, 1/(\nu m))$ to ensure that $\sum_i \alpha_i = 1$. Furthermore, we set the initial ρ to $\max\{f(x_i)|i \in [m],\ \alpha_i > 0\}$.

Optimization Algorithm We then select the first variable for the elementary optimization step in one of two following ways. Here, we use the shorthand SV_{nb} for the indices of variables which are not at bound (see also Section 10.5.5 for a more detailed description of such a strategy),

$$SV_{\text{nb}} := \{i | i \in [m], 0 < \alpha_i < 1/(\nu m)\}. \tag{8.27}$$

These correspond to points which will sit exactly on the hyperplane once optimization is complete, and which will therefore have a strong influence on its precise position.

(i) We scan over the entire data set[3] until we find a variable that violates a KKT condition (Section 6.3.1); in other words, a point such that $(O_i - \rho) \cdot \alpha_i > 0$ or $(\rho - O_i) \cdot (1/(\nu m) - \alpha_i) > 0$. Calling this variable α_i, we pick α_j according to

$$j = \operatorname*{argmax}_{n \in SV_{\text{nb}}} |O_i - O_n|. \tag{8.28}$$

(ii) Same as (i), but the scan is only performed over SV_{nb}.

In practice, one scan of type (i) is followed by multiple scans of type (ii), until there are no KKT violators in SV_{nb}, whereupon the optimization goes back to a single scan of type (i). If the type (i) scan finds no KKT violators, the optimization algorithm terminates.

In unusual circumstances, the choice heuristic (8.28) cannot make positive progress. Therefore, a hierarchy of other choice heuristics is applied to ensure positive progress. These other heuristics are the same as in the case of pattern recognition, cf. Chapter 10 and [409], and were found to work well in the experiments reported below.

Tolerance in the Margin

We conclude this section by stating a trick which is of importance in implementations. In practice, we must use a nonzero accuracy tolerance in tests for equality of numerical quantities. In particular, comparisons of this type are used in determining whether a point lies on the margin. Since we want the final decision function to return 1 for points which lie *on* the margin, we need to subtract this tolerance from ρ at the end.

In the next section, it will be argued that subtracting something from ρ is also advisable from a *statistical* point of view.

8.5 Theory

We now analyze the algorithm theoretically, starting with the uniqueness of the hyperplane (Proposition 8.1). We describe the connection to pattern recognition (Proposition 8.2), and show that the parameter ν characterizes the fractions of

Outlier

SVs and *outliers*. The latter term refers to points which are on the wrong side of

3. This scan can be accelerated by not checking patterns which are on the correct side of the hyperplane by a large margin, using the method of [266].

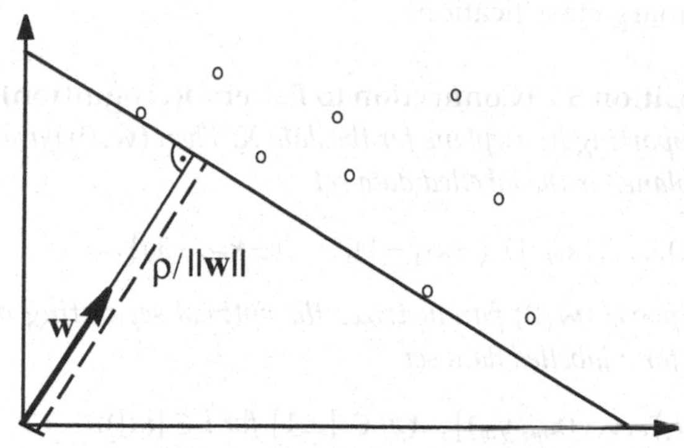

Figure 8.4 A separable data set, with the unique supporting hyperplane separating the data from the origin with maximum margin.

the hyperplane (Proposition 8.3). Following this, we give a robustness result for the soft margin (Proposition 8.4) and we present a theoretical result regarding the generalization error (Theorem 8.6).

As in some of the earlier chapters, we will use boldface letters to denote the feature space images of the corresponding patterns in input space,

$$\mathbf{x}_i := \Phi(x_i). \tag{8.29}$$

We will call a data set

$$\mathbf{X} := \{\mathbf{x}_1, \ldots, \mathbf{x}_m\} \tag{8.30}$$

Separable Dataset

separable if there exists some $\mathbf{w} \in \mathcal{H}$ such that $\langle \mathbf{w}, \mathbf{x}_i \rangle > 0$ for $i \in [m]$ (see also Lemma 6.24). If we use a Gaussian kernel (8.5), then any data set $x_1, \ldots, x_m$ is separable after it is mapped into feature space, since in this case, all patterns lie inside the same orthant and have unit length (Section 2.3).

The following proposition is illustrated in Figure 8.4.

Supporting Hyperplane

Proposition 8.1 (Supporting Hyperplane) *If the data set* $\mathbf{X}$ *is separable, then there exists a unique* supporting hyperplane *with the properties that (1) it separates all data from the origin, and (2) its distance to the origin is maximal among all such hyperplanes. For any* $\rho > 0$*, the supporting hyperplane is given by*

$$\underset{\mathbf{w} \in \mathcal{H}}{\text{minimize}} \ \frac{1}{2}\|\mathbf{w}\|^2 \ \text{subject to} \ \langle \mathbf{w}, \mathbf{x}_i \rangle \geq \rho, \ i \in [m]. \tag{8.31}$$

Proof Due to the separability, the convex hull of the data does not contain the origin. The existence and uniqueness of the hyperplane then follows from the supporting hyperplane theorem [45, e.g.].

In addition, separability implies that there actually exists some $\rho > 0$ and $\mathbf{w} \in \mathcal{H}$ such that $\langle \mathbf{w}, \mathbf{x}_i \rangle \geq \rho$ for $i \in [m]$ (by rescaling $\mathbf{w}$, this can be seen to work for arbitrarily large ρ). The distance from the hyperplane $\{\mathbf{z} \in \mathcal{H} : \langle \mathbf{w}, \mathbf{z} \rangle = \rho\}$ to the origin is $\rho/\|\mathbf{w}\|$. Therefore the optimal hyperplane is obtained by minimizing $\|\mathbf{w}\|$ subject to these constraints; that is, by the solution of (8.31). ■

The following result elucidates the relationship between single-class classification and binary classification.

Proposition 8.2 (Connection to Pattern Recognition) *(i) Suppose $(\mathbf{w}, \rho)$ parametrizes the supporting hyperplane for the data $\mathbf{X}$. Then $(\mathbf{w}, 0)$ parametrizes the optimal separating hyperplane for the labelled data set*

$$\{(\mathbf{x}_1, 1), \ldots, (\mathbf{x}_m, 1), (-\mathbf{x}_1, -1), \ldots, (-\mathbf{x}_m, -1)\}. \tag{8.32}$$

(ii) Suppose $(\mathbf{w}, 0)$ parametrizes the optimal separating hyperplane passing through the origin for a labelled data set

$$\{(\mathbf{x}_1, y_1), \ldots, (\mathbf{x}_m, y_m)\}, \quad (y_i \in \{\pm 1\} \text{ for } i \in [m]), \tag{8.33}$$

aligned such that $\langle \mathbf{w}, \mathbf{x}_i \rangle$ is positive for $y_i = 1$. Suppose, moreover, that $\rho/\|\mathbf{w}\|$ is the margin of the optimal hyperplane. Then $(\mathbf{w}, \rho)$ parametrizes the supporting hyperplane for the unlabelled data set $\mathbf{X}' = \{y_1\mathbf{x}_1, \ldots, y_m\mathbf{x}_m\}$.

Proof *Ad (i)*. By construction, the separation of $\mathbf{X}'$ is a point-symmetric problem. Hence, the optimal separating hyperplane passes through the origin, as if it did not, we could obtain another optimal separating hyperplane by reflecting the first one with respect to the origin — this would contradict the uniqueness of the optimal separating hyperplane.

Next, observe that $(-\mathbf{w}, \rho)$ parametrizes the supporting hyperplane for the data set reflected through the origin, and that it is parallel to that given by $(\mathbf{w}, \rho)$. This provides an optimal separation of the two sets, with distance $2\rho/\|\mathbf{w}\|$, and a separating hyperplane $(\mathbf{w}, 0)$.

Ad (ii). By assumption, $\mathbf{w}$ is the shortest vector satisfying $y_i \langle \mathbf{w}, \mathbf{x}_i \rangle \geq \rho$ (note that the offset is 0). Hence, equivalently, it is also the shortest vector satisfying $\langle \mathbf{w}, y_i\mathbf{x}_i \rangle \geq \rho$ for $i \in [m]$. ■

Note that the relationship is similar for nonseparable problems. In this case, *margin errors* in binary classification (points which are either on the wrong side of the separating hyperplane or which fall inside the margin) translate into *outliers* in single-class classification, which are points that fall on the wrong side of the hyperplane. Proposition 8.2 then holds, cum grano salis, for the training sets with margin errors and outliers, respectively, removed.

The utility of Proposition 8.2 lies in the fact that it allows us to recycle certain results from binary classification (Chapter 7) for use in the single-class scenario. The following property, which explains the significance of the parameter ν, is such a case.

ν-Property

Proposition 8.3 (ν-Property) *Assume the solution of (8.6),(8.7) satisfies $\rho \neq 0$. The following statements hold:*
(i) ν is an upper bound on the fraction of outliers.
(ii) ν is a lower bound on the fraction of SVs.
(iii) Suppose the data $\mathbf{X}$ were generated independently from a distribution $\mathrm{P}(x)$ which does not contain discrete components. Suppose, moreover, that the kernel is analytic and non-

ν, width c	0.5, 0.5	0.5, 0.5	0.1, 0.5	0.5, 0.1
frac. SVs/OLs	0.54, 0.43	0.59, 0.47	0.24, 0.03	0.65, 0.38
margin $\rho/\|\mathbf{w}\|$	0.84	0.70	0.62	0.48

Figure 8.5 *First two pictures:* A single-class SVM applied to two toy problems; $\nu = c = 0.5$, domain: $[-1, 1]^2$. Note how in both cases, at least a fraction $1 - \nu$ of all examples is in the estimated region (cf. table). The large value of ν causes the additional data points in the upper left corner to have almost no influence on the decision function. For smaller values of ν, such as 0.1 *(third picture)*, these points can no longer be ignored. Alternatively, we can force the algorithm to take these 'outliers' (OLs) into account by changing the kernel width (8.5): in the *fourth picture*, using $c = 0.1, \nu = 0.5$, the data are effectively analyzed on a different length scale, which leads the algorithm to consider the outliers as meaningful points.

constant. With probability 1, asymptotically, ν equals both the fraction of SVs and the fraction of outliers.

The proof can be found in [475]. The result also applies to the soft margin ball algorithm of [535], provided that it is stated in the ν-parametrization given in (8.17). Figure 8.5 displays a 2-D toy example, illustrating how the choice of ν and the kernel width influence the solution.

Resistance

Proposition 8.4 (Resistance) *Local movements of outliers parallel to* $\mathbf{w}$ *do not change the hyperplane.*

Proof **(Proposition 8.4)** Suppose $\mathbf{x}_o$ is an outlier, for which $\xi_o > 0$; hence by the KKT conditions (Chapter 6) $\alpha_o = 1/(\nu m)$. Transforming it into $\mathbf{x}'_o := \mathbf{x}_o + \delta \cdot \mathbf{w}$, where $|\delta| < \xi_o/\|\mathbf{w}\|$, leads to a slack which is still nonzero, $\xi'_o > 0$, hence we still have $\alpha_o = 1/(\nu m)$. Therefore, $\boldsymbol{\alpha}' = \boldsymbol{\alpha}$ is still feasible, as is the primal solution $(\mathbf{w}', \boldsymbol{\xi}', \rho')$. Here, we use $\xi'_i = (1 + \delta \cdot \alpha_o)\xi_i$ for $i \neq o$, $\mathbf{w}' = (1 + \delta \cdot \alpha_o)\mathbf{w}$, and ρ' as computed from (8.16). Finally, the KKT conditions are still satisfied, as $\alpha'_o = 1/(\nu m)$ still holds. Thus (Section 6.3), $\boldsymbol{\alpha}$ remains the solution. ■

Note that although the hyperplane does not change, its parametrization in $\mathbf{w}$ and ρ is different. In single-class SVMs, the hyperplane is not constrained to be in canonical form as it was in SV classifiers (Definition 7.1).

Generalization Error

We now move on to the subject of *generalization*. The goal is to bound the probability that a novel point drawn from the same underlying distribution lies outside of the estimated region. As in the case of pattern recognition, it turns out that the *margin* plays a central role. In the single-class case there is no margin between the two classes, for the simple reason that there is just one class. We can nevertheless introduce a "safety margin" and make a conservative statement about a slightly larger region than the one estimated. In a sense, this is not so different from pattern recognition: in Theorem 7.3, we try to separate the training data into two half-spaces separated by a margin, and then make a statement about the actual test error (rather than the margin test error); that is, about the probability that a new point will be misclassified, no matter whether it falls inside the margin or not. Just as in the single-class case, the statement regarding the test error thus refers to a region slightly larger than the one in which we try to put the training data.

Definition 8.5 *Let f be a real-valued function on a space $\mathcal{X}$. Fix $\theta \in \mathbb{R}$. For $x \in \mathcal{X}$ let $d(x, f, \theta) = \max\{0, \theta - f(x)\}$. Similarly, for a training sequence $X := (x_1, \ldots, x_m)$, we define*

$$\mathcal{D}(X, f, \theta) = \sum_{x \in X} d(x, f, \theta). \tag{8.34}$$

Theorem 8.6 (Generalization Error Bound) *Suppose we are given a set of m examples $X \in \mathcal{X}^m$, generated from an unknown distribution P that does not have discrete components. Suppose, moreover, that we solve the optimization problem (8.6),(8.7) (or equivalently (8.13)–(8.15)) and obtain a solution $f_{\mathbf{w},\rho}$ given explicitly by (8.12). Let $R_{\mathbf{w},\rho} := \{x | f_{\mathbf{w}}(x) \geq \rho\}$ denote the induced decision region. With probability $1 - \delta$ over the draw of the random sample $X \in \mathcal{X}^m$, for any $\gamma > 0$,*

$$\mathrm{P}\{x' | x' \notin R_{\mathbf{w},\rho-\gamma}\} \leq \frac{2}{m}\left(k + \log_2 \frac{m^2}{2\delta}\right), \tag{8.35}$$

where

$$k = \frac{c_1 \log_2(c_2 \hat{\gamma}^2 m)}{\hat{\gamma}^2} + \frac{2\mathcal{D}}{\hat{\gamma}} \log_2\left(e\left(\frac{(2m-1)\hat{\gamma}}{2\mathcal{D}} + 1\right)\right) + 2, \tag{8.36}$$

$c_1 = 16c^2$, $c_2 = \ln(2)/(4c^2)$, $c = 103$, $\hat{\gamma} = \gamma / \|\mathbf{w}\|$, $\mathcal{D} = \mathcal{D}(X, f_{\mathbf{w},0}, \rho) = \mathcal{D}(X, f_{\mathbf{w},\rho}, 0)$, and ρ is given by (8.16).

The proof can be found in [475].

The training sample X defines (via the algorithm) the decision region $R_{\mathbf{w},\rho}$. We expect that new points generated according to P will lie in $R_{\mathbf{w},\rho}$. The theorem gives a probabilistic guarantee that new points lie in the larger region $R_{\mathbf{w},\rho-\gamma}$.

The parameter ν can be adjusted when running the algorithm to trade off incorporating outliers against minimizing the "size" of $R_{\mathbf{w},\rho}$. Adjusting ν changes the value of $\mathcal{D}$. Note that since $\mathcal{D}$ is measured with respect to ρ while the bound applies to $\rho - \gamma$, any point which is outside of the region to which the bound applies will make a contribution to $\mathcal{D}$ that is bounded away from 0. Therefore, (8.35) does *not* imply that asymptotically, we will always estimate the complete support.

The parameter γ allows us to trade off the confidence with which we wish the assertion of the theorem to hold against the size of the predictive region $R_{\mathbf{w},\rho-\gamma}$:

we can see from (8.36) that k, and hence the rhs of (8.35), scales inversely with γ. In fact, it scales inversely with $\hat{\gamma}$; in other words, it increases with $\mathbf{w}$. This justifies measuring the complexity of the estimated region by the size of $\mathbf{w}$, and minimizing $\|\mathbf{w}\|^2$ in order to find a region that generalizes well. In addition, the theorem suggests not to use the offset ρ returned by the algorithm, which corresponds to $\gamma = 0$, but a smaller value $\rho - \gamma$ (with $\gamma > 0$).

In the present form, Theorem 8.6 is not a practical means to determine the parameters ν and γ explicitly. It is loose in several ways. The constant c used is far from its smallest possible value. Furthermore, no account is taken of the smoothness of the kernel. If that were done (by using refined bounds on the covering numbers of the induced class of functions, as in Chapter 12), then the first term in (8.36) would increase much more slowly when decreasing γ. The fact that the second term would not change indicates a different trade-off point. Nevertheless, the theorem provides some confidence that ν and γ are suitable parameters to adjust.

8.6 Discussion

Before we move on to experiments, it is worthwhile to discuss some aspects of the algorithm described. As mentioned in the introduction, we could view it as being in line with Vapnik's principle never to solve a problem which is more general than the one that we are actually interested in [561]. For instance, in situations where one is only interested in detecting *novelty*, it is not always necessary to estimate a full density model of the data. Indeed, density estimation is more difficult than what we are doing, in several respects.

Vapnik's Principle

Existence of a Density

Mathematically speaking, a density only exists if the underlying probability measure possesses an absolutely continuous distribution function. The general problem of estimating the measure for a large class of sets, say the sets measurable in Borel's sense, is not solvable, however (for a discussion, see [562]). Therefore we need to restrict ourselves to making a statement about the measure of *some* sets. Given a small class of sets, the simplest estimator which accomplishes this task is the empirical measure, which simply looks at how many training points fall into the region of interest. The present algorithm does the opposite. It starts with the number of training points that are supposed to fall into the region, and then estimates a region with the desired property. Often, there will be many such regions — the solution becomes unique only by applying a regularizer, which in the SV case enforces that the region be small in a feature space associated with the kernel.

Therefore, we must keep in mind that the measure of smallness in this sense depends on the kernel used, in a way that is no different to any other method that regularizes in a feature space. A similar problem, however, already appears in density estimation when done in input space. Let p denote a density on $\mathcal{X}$. If we perform a (nonlinear) coordinate transformation in the input domain $\mathcal{X}$, then the density values *change*; loosely speaking, what remains constant is $p(x)\,dx$, where dx is also transformed. When directly estimating the probability *measure* of regions, we are not faced with this problem, as the regions automatically change accordingly.

Regularization Interpretation

An attractive property of the measure of smallness that the present algorithm uses is that it can also be placed in the context of regularization theory, leading to an interpretation of the solution as maximally smooth in a sense which depends on the specific kernel used. More specifically, if k is a Green's function of $\Upsilon^*\Upsilon$ for an operator Υ mapping into some dot product space (cf. Section 4.3), then the dual objective function that we minimize equals

$$\sum_{i,j} \alpha_i \alpha_j k(x_i, x_j) = \|\Upsilon f\|^2, \tag{8.37}$$

using $f(x) = \sum_i \alpha_i k(x_i, x)$. In addition, we show in Chapter 4 that the regularization operators of common kernels can be shown to correspond to derivative operators — therefore, minimizing the dual objective function has the effect of maximizing the smoothness of the function f (which is, up to a thresholding operation, the function we estimate). This, in turn, is related to a prior with density $p(f) \propto e^{-\|\Upsilon f\|^2}$ on the function space (cf. Chapter 16).

Interestingly, as the minimization of the dual objective function also corresponds to a maximization of the margin in feature space, an equivalent interpretation is in terms of a prior on the distribution of the unknown other class (the "novel" class in a novelty detection problem) — trying to separate the data from the origin amounts to assuming that the novel examples lie around the origin.

Earlier Work

The main inspiration for the approach described stems from the earliest work of Vapnik and collaborators. In 1962, they proposed an algorithm for characterizing a set of unlabelled data points by separating it from the origin using a hyperplane [573, 570]. However, they quickly moved on to two-class classification problems, both in terms of algorithms and in terms of the theoretical development of statistical learning theory which originated in those days.

From an algorithmic point of view, we can identify two shortcomings of the original approach, which may have caused research in this direction to stop for more than three decades. First, the original algorithm [570] was limited to linear decision rules in input space; second, there was no way of dealing with outliers. In conjunction, these restrictions are indeed severe — a generic dataset need not be separable from the origin by a hyperplane in input space. The two modifications that the single-class SVM incorporates dispose of these shortcomings. First, the kernel trick allows for a much larger class of functions by nonlinearly mapping into a high-dimensional feature space, and thereby increases the chances of a separation from the origin being possible. In particular, using a Gaussian kernel (8.5), such a separation is always possible, as shown in Section 8.5. The second modification directly allows for the possibility of outliers. This 'softness' of the decision rule is incorporated using the ν-trick, which we have already seen in the classification case (Section 7.5), leading to a direct handle on the fraction of outliers.

Given $\nu \in (0,1]$, the resulting algorithm computes (8.6) subject to (8.7), and thereby constructs a region R such that for $OL = \{i : x_i \notin R\}$, we have $\frac{|OL|}{m} \leq \nu$. The "$\leq$" is *sharp* in the sense that if we multiply the solution $\mathbf{w}$ by $(1-\epsilon)$ (with $\epsilon > 0$), it becomes a "$>$." The algorithm does *not* solve the following *combinatorial* problem, however: given $\nu \in (0,1]$, compute

Combinatorial Problem

$$\underset{\mathbf{w}\in\mathcal{H}, OL\subset[m]}{\text{minimize}} \quad \frac{1}{2}\|\mathbf{w}\|^2,$$

$$\text{subject to} \quad \langle \mathbf{w}, \Phi(x_i)\rangle \geq 1 \text{ for } i \in [m] \setminus OL \text{ and } \frac{|OL|}{m} = \nu. \tag{8.38}$$

Ben-David et al. [31] analyze a problem related to (8.38): they consider a sphere (which for some feature spaces is equivalent to a half-space, as shown in Section 8.3), fix its radius, and attempt to find its center such that it encloses as many points as possible. They prove that it is already NP hard to approximate the maximal number to within a factor smaller than 3/418.

Kernel-Based Vector Quantization

We conclude this section by mentioning another kernel-based algorithm that has recently been proposed for the use on unlabelled data [541]. This algorithm applies to vector quantization, a standard process which finds a codebook such that the training set can be approximated by elements of the codebook with small error. Vector quantization is briefly described in Example 17.2 below; for further detail, see [195].

Given some metric d, the kernel-based approach of [541] uses a kernel that indicates whether two points lie within a distance $R \geq 0$ of each other,

$$k(x, x') = I_{\{(x,x')\in\mathcal{X}\times\mathcal{X}:d(x,x')\leq R\}}. \tag{8.39}$$

Let Φ_m be the empirical kernel map (2.56) with respect to the training set. The main idea is that if we can find a vector $\boldsymbol{\alpha} \in \mathbb{R}^m$ such that

$$\boldsymbol{\alpha}^\top \Phi_m(x_i) > 0 \tag{8.40}$$

holds true for all $i = 1, \ldots, m$, then each point x_i lies within a distance R of some point x_j which has a positive weight $w_j > 0$. To see this, note that otherwise all nonzero components of $\boldsymbol{\alpha}$ would get multiplied by components of Φ_m which are 0, and the dot product in (8.40) would equal 0.

To perform vector quantization, we can thus use optimization techniques, which produce a vector $\boldsymbol{\alpha}$ that satisfies (8.40) while being sparse. As in Section 7.7, this can be done using linear programming techniques. Once optimization is complete, the nonzero entries of $\boldsymbol{\alpha}$ indicate the codebook vectors.

8.7 Experiments

We apply the method to artificial and real-world data. Figure 8.6 shows a comparison with a Parzen windows estimator on a 2-D problem, along with a family of

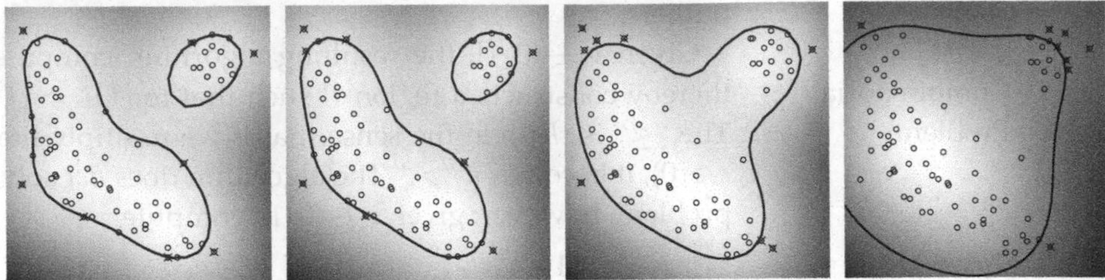

Figure 8.6 A single-class SVM applied to a toy problem; $c = 0.5$, domain: $[-1,1]^2$, for various settings of the offset ρ. As discussed in Section 8.3, $\nu = 1$ yields a Parzen windows expansion. However, to get a Parzen windows estimator of the distribution's support, we must not use the offset returned by the algorithm (which would allow *all* points to lie outside the estimated region). Therefore, in this experiment, we adjusted the offset such that a fraction $\nu' = 0.1$ of patterns lie outside. From left to right, we show the results for $\nu \in \{0.1, 0.2, 0.4, 1\}$. The rightmost picture corresponds to the Parzen estimator which utilizes all kernels; the other estimators use roughly a fraction ν of kernels. Note that as a result of the averaging over all kernels, the Parzen windows estimate does not model the shape of the distribution very well for the chosen parameters.

estimators which lie "in between" the present one and the Parzen one.

Figure 8.7 shows a plot of the outputs $\langle \mathbf{w}, \Phi(x) \rangle$ on training and test sets of the USPS database of handwritten digits (Section A.1). We used a Gaussian kernel (8.5), which has the advantage that the data are always separable from the origin in feature space (Section 2.3). For the kernel parameter c, we used $0.5 \cdot 256$. This value was chosen a priori, and is a common value for SVM classifiers on that data set, cf. Chapter 7.[4] The algorithm was given only the training instances of digit 0. Testing was done on both digit 0 and on all other digits. We present results for two values of ν, one large, one small; for values in between, the results are qualitatively similar. In the first experiment, we used $\nu = 50\%$, thus aiming for a description of "0-ness" which only captures half of all zeros in the training set. As shown in figure 8.7, this leads to *zero* false positives (i.e., even though the learning machine has not seen any non-0s during training, it correctly identifies all non-0s as such), while still recognizing 44% of the digits 0 in the *test* set. Higher recognition rates can be achieved using smaller values of ν. For $\nu = 5\%$, we get 91% correct recognition of digits 0 in the test set, with a fairly moderate false positive rate of 7%.

Although leading to encouraging results, this experiment does not really address the actual task the algorithm was designed for. Therefore, we next focus on a problem of *novelty detection*. Again, we utilized the USPS set; this time, however, we trained the algorithm on the test set and used it to identify outliers — it is well known that the USPS test set (Figure 8.8) contains a number of patterns which

4. In [236], the following procedure is used to determine a value of c. For small c, all training points become SVs — the algorithm just memorizes the data, and will not generalize well. As c increases, the number of SVs drops. As a simple heuristic, we can thus start with a small value of c and increase it until the number of SVs does not decrease any further.

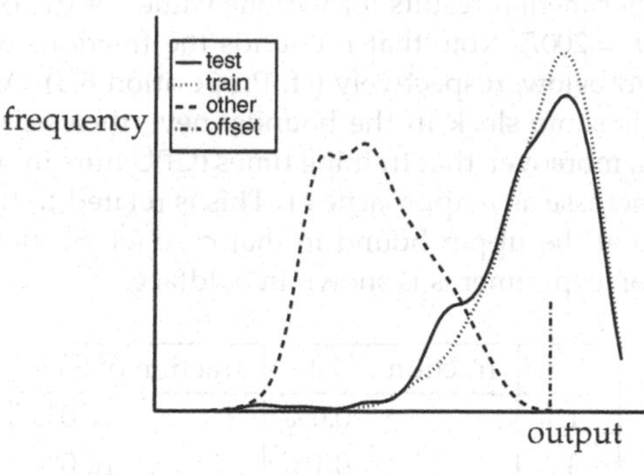

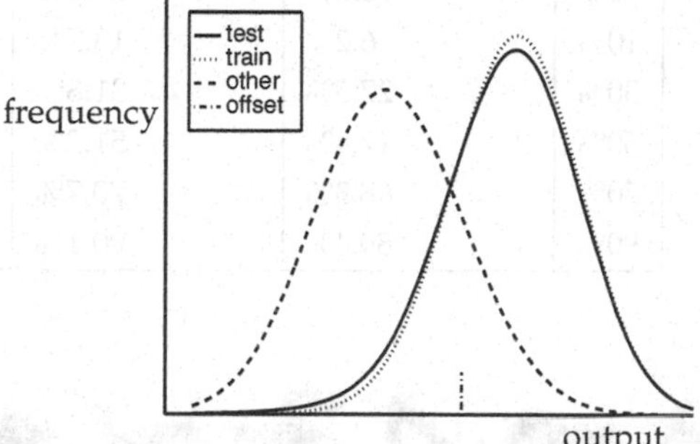

Figure 8.7 Experiments using the USPS OCR dataset. Recognizer for digit 0; output histogram for the exemplars of 0 in the training/test set, and on test exemplars of other digits. The x-axis gives the output values; in other words, the argument of the sgn function in (8.12). For $\nu = 50\%$ *(top)*, we get 50% SVs and 49% outliers (consistent with Proposition 8.3), 44% true positive test examples, and zero false positives from the "other" class. For $\nu = 5\%$ *(bottom)*, we get 6% and 4% for SVs and outliers, respectively. In that case, the true positive rate is improved to 91%, while the false positive rate increases to 7%. The offset ρ is marked in the graphs.
Note, finally, that the plots show a Parzen windows density estimate of the output histograms. In reality, many examples sit exactly at the offset value (the non-bound SVs). Since this peak is smoothed out by the estimator, the fractions of outliers in the training set appear slightly larger than they should be.

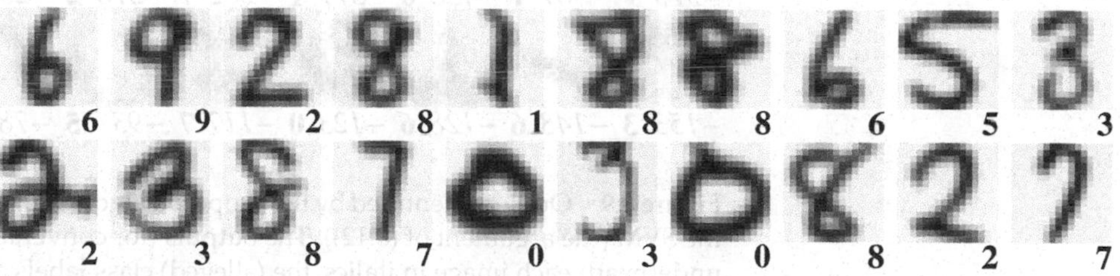

Figure 8.8 20 examples randomly drawn from the USPS test set, with class labels.

are hard or impossible to classify, due to segmentation errors or mislabelling. In this experiment, we augmented the input patterns by ten extra dimensions corresponding to the class labels of the digits. The rationale for this is that if we disregard the labels, there would be no hope of identifying *mislabelled* patterns as outliers. With the labels, the algorithm has the chance to identify both unusual patterns *and* usual patterns with unusual labels. Figure 8.9 shows the 20 worst outliers for the USPS test set, respectively. Note that the algorithm indeed extracts patterns which are very hard to assign to their respective classes. In the experiment, we used the same kernel width as above, and a ν value of 5%. The latter was chosen to roughly reflect the expectation as to how many "bad" patterns there are in the test set: most good learning algorithms achieve error rates of 3 - 5% on the USPS benchmark (for a list of results, cf. Table 7.4).

Table 8.1 Experimental results for various values of the outlier control constant ν, USPS test set, size $m = 2007$. Note that ν bounds the fractions of outliers and Support Vectors from above and below, respectively (cf. Proposition 8.3). As we are not in the asymptotic regime, there is some slack in the bounds; nevertheless, ν can be used to control these fractions. Note, moreover, that training times (CPU time in seconds on a Pentium II running at 450 MHz) increase as ν approaches 1. This is related to the fact that almost all Lagrange multipliers are at the upper bound in that case (cf. Section 8.4). The system used in the outlier detection experiments is shown in boldface.

ν	fraction of OLs	fraction of SVs	training time
1%	0.0%	10.0%	36
3%	0.1%	10.0%	31
5%	**1.4%**	**10.6%**	**36**
10%	6.2%	13.7%	65
30%	27.5%	31.8%	269
50%	47.4%	51.2%	1284
70%	68.3%	70.7%	1512
90%	89.4%	90.1%	2349

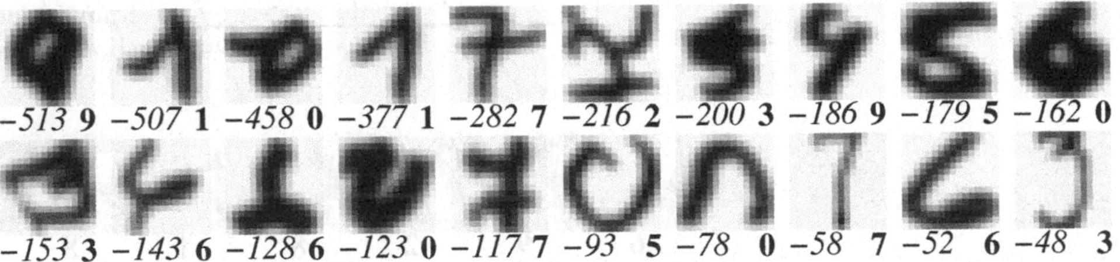

Figure 8.9 Outliers identified by the proposed algorithm, ranked by the negative output of the SVM (the argument of (8.12)). The outputs (for convenience in units of 10^{-5}) are written underneath each image in italics, the (alleged) class labels are given in bold face. Note that most of the examples are "difficult" in that they are either atypical or mislabelled.

In the last experiment, we tested the runtime scaling behavior of the SMO solver used for training (Figure 8.10). Performance was found to depend on ν. For the small values of ν which are typically used in outlier detection tasks, the algorithm scales very well to larger data sets, with a dependency of training times on the sample size which is at most quadratic.

In addition to the experiments reported above, the present algorithm has since been applied in several other domains, such as the modelling of parameter regimes for the control of walking robots [528], condition monitoring of jet engines [236], and hierarchical clustering problems [35].

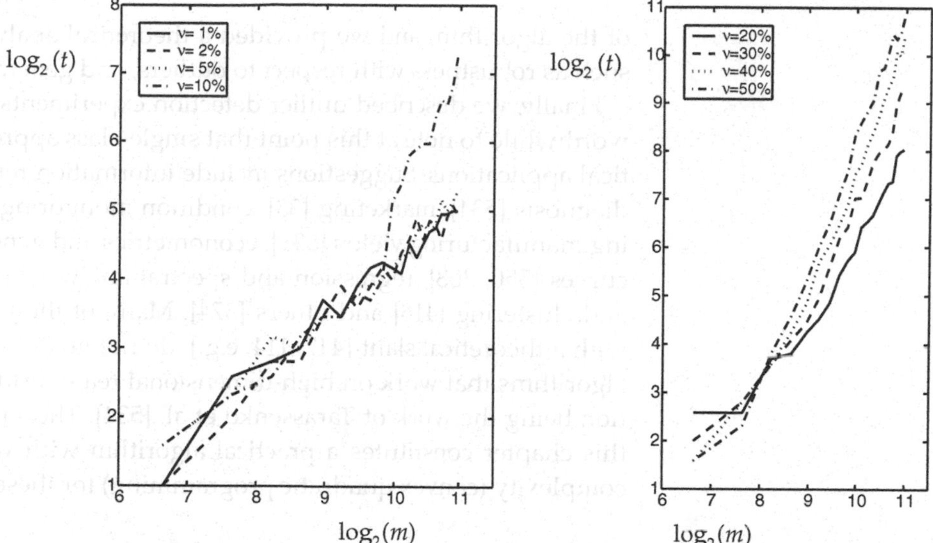

Figure 8.10 Training times t (in seconds) vs. data set sizes m (both axes depict logs at base 2; CPU time in seconds on a Pentium II running at 450 MHz, training on subsets of the USPS test set); $c = 0.5 \cdot 256$. As in Table 8.1, it can be seen that larger values of ν generally lead to longer training times (note that the plots use different y-axis ranges). Times also differ in their scaling with the sample size, however. The exponents can be directly read from the slope of the graphs, as they are plotted in log scale with equal axis spacing: for small values of ν ($\leq 5\%$), the training times are approximately linear in the training set size (left plot). The scaling gets worse as ν increases. For large values of ν, training times are roughly proportional to the sample size raised to the power of 2.5 (right plot). The results should be taken only as an indication of what is going on: they were obtained using fairly small training sets; the largest being 2007, the size of the USPS test set. As a consequence, they are fairly noisy, and strictly speaking, they refer only to the examined regime. Encouragingly, the scaling is better than the cubic scaling that we would expect when solving the optimization problem using all patterns at once, cf. Section 8.4. Moreover, for *small* values of ν, which are typically used in outlier detection (in Figure 8.9, we used $\nu = 5\%$), the algorithm is particularly efficient.

8.8 Summary

In the present chapter, we described SV algorithms that can be applied to unlabelled data. Statistically speaking, these are a solution to the problem of multidimensional quantile estimation. Practically speaking, they provide a "description" of the dataset that can thought of as a "single-class" classifier, which can tell whether a new point is likely to have been generated by the same regularity as the training data. This makes them applicable to problems such as novelty detection.

We began with a discussion of the quantile estimation problem, which led us to a quantile estimation algorithm, which is very similar to the SV classification algorithm in that it uses the same type of large margin regularizer. To deal with outliers in the data, we made use of the ν-trick introduced in the previous chapter. We described an SMO-style optimization problem to compute the unique solution of the algorithm, and we provided a theoretical analysis of a number of aspects, such as robustness with respect to outliers, and generalization to unseen data.

Finally, we described outlier detection experiments using real-world data. It is worthwhile to note at this point that single-class approaches have abundant practical applications. Suggestions include information retrieval, problems in medical diagnosis [534], marketing [33], condition monitoring of machines [138], estimating manufacturing yields [531], econometrics and generalized nonlinear principal curves [550, 308], regression and spectral analysis [417], tests for multimodality and clustering [416] and others [374]. Many of these papers, in particular those with a theoretical slant [417, 114, e.g.], do not go all the way in devising practical algorithms that work on high-dimensional real-world-problems, a notable exception being the work of Tarassenko et al. [534]. The single-class SVM described in this chapter constitutes a practical algorithm with well-behaved computational complexity (convex quadratic programming) for these problems.

8.9 Problems

8.1 (Uniqueness of the Supporting Hyperplane ••) *Using Lemma 6.24 (cf. Figure 6.7), prove that if the convex hull of the training data does not contain the origin, then there exists a unique hyperplane with the properties that (1) it separates all data from the origin, and (2) its distance to the origin is maximal among all such hyperplanes. (cf. Proposition 8.1).*

Hint: argue that you can limit yourself to finding the maximum margin of separation over all weight vectors of length $\|\mathbf{w}\| \leq 1$; that is, over a convex set.

8.2 (Soft Ball Algorithm [535] ••) *Extend the hard ball algorithm described in Section 5.6 to the soft margin case; in other words, derive (8.18) and (8.19) from (8.17).*

8.3 (Hard Margin Limit for Positive Offsets •) *Show that if we require $\rho \geq 0$ in the primal problem, we end up with the constraint $\sum_i \alpha_i \geq 1$ instead of $\sum_i \alpha_i = 1$ (see (8.15)). Consider the hard margin limit $\nu \to 0$ and argue that in this case, the problem can become infeasible, and the multipliers α_i can diverge during the optimization. Give a geometric interpretation of why this happens for $\rho \geq 0$, but not if ρ is free.*

8.4 (Positivity of ρ ••) *Prove that the solution of (8.6) satisfies $\rho \geq 0$.*

8.5 (Hard Margin Identities ••) *Consider the hard margin optimization problem, consisting of minimizing $\|\mathbf{w}\|^2$ subject to $\langle \mathbf{w}, \mathbf{x}_i \rangle \geq \rho$ for $i \in [m]$ (here, $\rho > 0$ is a constant). Prove that the following identities hold true for the solution $\boldsymbol{\alpha}$:*

$$\frac{\rho^2}{d^2} = \|\mathbf{w}\|^2 = 2W(\boldsymbol{\alpha}) \tag{8.41}$$

Here, $W(\boldsymbol{\alpha})$ denotes the value of the dual objective function, and d is the distance of the hyperplane to the origin. Hint: use the KKT conditions and the primal constraints.

8.6 (ν-Property for Single-Class SVMs [475] ••) *Prove Proposition 8.3, using the techniques from the proof of Proposition 7.5.*

8.7 (Graphical Proof of ν-Property •) *Give a graphical proof of the first two statements of Proposition 8.3 along the lines of Figure 9.5.*

8.8 (ν-Property for the Soft Ball Algorithm ••) *Prove Proposition 8.3 for the soft ball algorithm (8.18), (8.19).*

8.9 (Multi-class SV Classification ••) *Implement the single-class algorithm and use it to solve a multi-class classification problem by training a single-class recognizer on each class. Discuss how to best compare the outputs of the individual recognizers in order to get to a multi-class decision.*

8.10 (Negative Data [476] ••) *Derive a variant of the single-class algorithm that can handle negative data by reflecting the negative points at the origin in feature space, and then solving the usual one-class problem. Show that this leads to the following problem:*

$$\underset{\alpha \in \mathbb{R}^m}{\text{minimize}} \; \frac{1}{2}\sum_{ij} \alpha_i \alpha_j y_i y_j k(x_i, x_j), \tag{8.42}$$

$$\textit{subject to } \; 0 \leq \alpha_i \leq \frac{1}{\nu m}, \tag{8.43}$$

$$\sum_i \alpha_i = 1 \tag{8.44}$$

Argue, moreover, that the decision function takes the form

$$f(x) = \operatorname{sgn}\left(\sum_i \alpha_i y_i k(x_i, x) - \rho\right), \tag{8.45}$$

and that ρ can be computed by exploiting that for any x_i such that $\alpha_i \in (0, 1/(\nu m))$,

$$\rho = \langle \mathbf{w}, \Phi(x_i)\rangle = \sum_j \alpha_j y_j k(x_j, x_i). \tag{8.46}$$

Show that the algorithm (8.13) is a special case of the above one. Discuss the connection to the SVC algorithm (Chapter 7), in particular with regard to how the two algorithms deal with unbalanced data sets.

8.11 (Separation from General Points [476] ••) *Derive a variant of the single-class algorithm that, rather than separating the points from the origin in feature space, separates them from the mean of some other set of points $\Phi(z_1), \ldots, \Phi(z_t)$. Argue that this lets you take into account the unknown "other" class in a "weak" sense. Hint: modify the first constraint in (8.7) to*

$$\left\langle \mathbf{w}, \Phi(x_i) - \frac{1}{t}\sum_{n=1}^{t} \Phi(z_n) \right\rangle \geq \rho - \xi_i, \tag{8.47}$$

and the decision function to

$$f(x) = \operatorname{sgn}\left(\left\langle \mathbf{w}, \Phi(x) - \frac{1}{t}\sum_{n=1}^{t}\Phi(z_n)\right\rangle - \rho\right). \tag{8.48}$$

Prove that the dual problem takes the following form:

$$\underset{\alpha\in\mathbb{R}^m}{\text{minimize}}\ \frac{1}{2}\sum_{ij}\alpha_i\alpha_j\left(k(x_i, x_j) + q - q_j - q_i\right), \tag{8.49}$$

$$\text{subject to } 0 \leq \alpha_i \leq \frac{1}{\nu m}, \tag{8.50}$$

$$\sum_i \alpha_i = 1, \tag{8.51}$$

where $q = \frac{1}{t^2}\sum_{np} k(z_n, z_p)$ *and* $q_j = \frac{1}{t}\sum_n k(x_j, z_n)$.

Discuss the special case where you try to separate a data set from its own mean and argue that this provides a method for computing one-sided quantiles with large margin.

8.12 (Cross-Validation •) *Discuss the question of how to validate whether a single-class SVM generalizes well. What are the main differences with the problem of pattern recognition?*

8.13 (Leave-One-Out Bound ••) *Using Theorem 12.9, prove that the generalization error of single-class SVMs trained on samples of size* $m-1$ *is bounded by the number of SVs divided by* m.

Note that this bound makes a statement about the case where $\gamma = 0$ *(cf. Theorem 8.6). Argue that this can cause the bound to be loose. Compare the case of pattern recognition, and argue that the usual leave-one-out bound is also loose there, since it makes a statement about the probability of a test point being misclassified* or *lying inside the margin.*

8.14 (Kernel-Dependent Generalization Error Bounds ◦◦◦) *Modify Theorem 8.6 to take into account properties of the kernel along the lines of the entropy number methods described in Chapter 12.*

8.15 (Model Selection ◦◦◦) *Try to come up with principled model selection methods for single-class SVMs. How would you recommend to choose* ν *and the kernel parameter? How would you choose* γ *(Theorem 8.6)?*

9 Regression Estimation

Overview

In this chapter, we explain the ideas underlying Support Vector (SV) machines for function estimation. We start by giving a brief summary of the motivations and formulations of an SV approach for regression estimation (Section 9.1), followed by a derivation of the associated dual programming problems (Section 9.2). After some illustrative examples, we cover extensions to linear programming settings and a ν-variant that utilizes a more convenient parametrization. In Section 9.6, we discuss some applications, followed by a summary (Section 9.7) and a collection of problems for the reader.

Prerequisites

Although it is not strictly indispensable, we recommend that the reader first study the basics of the SVM classification algorithm, at least at the level of detail given in Chapter 1. The derivation of the dual (Section 9.2) is self-contained, but would benefit from some background in optimization (Chapter 6), especially in the case of the more advanced formulations given in Section 9.2.2. If desired, these can actually be skipped at first reading. Section 9.3 describes a modification of the standard SV regression algorithm, along with some considerations on issues such as robustness. The latter can be best understood within the context given in Section 3.4. Finally, Section 9.4 deals with linear programming regularizers, which were discussed in detail in Section 4.9.2.

9.1 Linear Regression with Insensitive Loss Function

SVMs were first developed for pattern recognition. As described in Chapter 7, they represent the decision boundary in terms of a typically small subset of all training examples — the Support Vectors. When the SV algorithm was generalized to the case of regression estimation (that is, to the estimation of *real-valued* functions, rather than just $\{\pm 1\}$-valued ones, as in the case in pattern recognition), it was crucial to find a way of retaining this feature. In order for the sparseness property to carry over to the case of SV Regression, Vapnik devised the so-called *ε-insensitive loss function* (Figure 1.8) [561],

ε-Insensitive Loss

$$|y - f(\mathbf{x})|_{\varepsilon} = \max\{0, |y - f(\mathbf{x})| - \varepsilon\}, \tag{9.1}$$

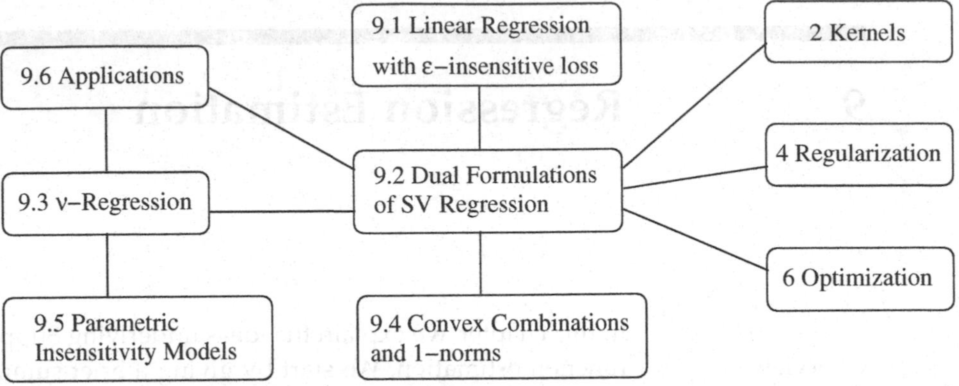

which does not penalize errors below some $\varepsilon \geq 0$, chosen a priori.[1] The rationale behind this choice is the following. In pattern recognition, when measuring the loss incurred for a particular pattern, there is a large area where we accrue zero loss: whenever a pattern is on the correct side of the decision surface, and does not touch the margin, it does not contribute any loss to the objective function (7.35). Correspondingly, it does not carry any information about the position of the decision surface — after all, the latter is computed by minimizing that very objective function. This is the underlying reason why the pattern does not appear in the SV expansion of the solution. A loss function for regression estimation must also have an insensitive zone; hence we use the ε-insensitive loss.

The regression algorithm is then developed in close analogy to the case of pattern recognition. Again, we estimate linear functions, use a $\|\mathbf{w}\|^2$ regularizer, and rewrite everything in terms of dot products to generalize to the nonlinear case. The basic SV regression algorithm, which we will henceforth call **ε-SVR**, seeks to estimate linear functions[2],

$$f(\mathbf{x}) = \langle \mathbf{w}, \mathbf{x} \rangle + b, \text{ where } \mathbf{w}, \mathbf{x} \in \mathcal{H}, b \in \mathbb{R}, \tag{9.2}$$

based on independent and identically distributed (iid) data,

$$(\mathbf{x}_1, y_1), \ldots, (\mathbf{x}_m, y_m) \in \mathcal{H} \times \mathbb{R}. \tag{9.3}$$

Here, $\mathcal{H}$ is a dot product space in which the (mapped) input patterns live (i.e., the feature space induced by a kernel). The goal of the learning process is to find a

1. The insensitive zone is sometimes referred to as the *ε-tube*. Actually, this term is lightly misleading, as in multi-dimensional problems, the insensitive zone has the shape of a *slab* rather than a tube; in other words, the region between two parallel hyperplanes, differing in their y offset.

2. Strictly speaking, these should be called *affine* functions. We will not indulge in these fine distinctions. The crucial bit is that the part to which we apply the kernel trick is linear.

function f with a small risk (or test error) (cf. Chapter 3),

$$R[f] = \int c(f, \mathbf{x}, y)\, dP(\mathbf{x}, y), \tag{9.4}$$

where P is the probability measure which is assumed to be responsible for the generation of the observations (9.3), and c is a loss function, such as $c(f, \mathbf{x}, y) = (f(\mathbf{x}) - y)^2$, or one of many other possible choices (Chapter 3). The particular loss function for which we would like to minimize (9.4) depends on the specific regression estimation problem at hand. Note that this does not necessarily have to coincide with the loss function used in our learning algorithm. First, there might be additional constraints that we would like our regression estimation to satisfy, for instance that it have a sparse representation in terms of the training data — in the SV case, this is achieved through the insensitive zone in (9.1). Second, we cannot minimize (9.4) directly in any case, since we do not know P. Instead, we are given the sample (9.3), and we try to obtain a small risk by minimizing the regularized risk functional,

$$\frac{1}{2}\|\mathbf{w}\|^2 + C \cdot R^{\varepsilon}_{\text{emp}}[f]. \tag{9.5}$$

Regularized Risk Functional

Here,

$$R^{\varepsilon}_{\text{emp}}[f] := \frac{1}{m}\sum_{i=1}^{m} |y_i - f(\mathbf{x}_i)|_{\varepsilon} \tag{9.6}$$

measures the ε-insensitive training error, and C is a constant determining the trade-off with the complexity penalizer $\|\mathbf{w}\|^2$. In short, minimizing (9.5) captures the main insight of statistical learning theory, stating that in order to obtain a small risk, we need to control both training error and model complexity, by explaining the data with a simple model (Chapter 5).

Flatness vs. Margin

A small $\|\mathbf{w}\|^2$ corresponds to a linear function (9.2) that is flat — in feature space. Note that in the case of pattern recognition, we use the same regularizer (cf. (7.35)); however, it corresponded to a large *margin* in this case. How does this difference arise? A related question, it turns out, is why SV regression requires an extra parameter ε, while SV pattern recognition does not.

Let us try to understand how these seemingly different problems are actually identical.

Definition 9.1 (ε-margin) *Let $(E, \|.\|_E)$, $(G, \|.\|_G)$ be normed spaces, and $\mathcal{X} \subset E$. We define the ε-margin of a function $f : \mathcal{X} \to G$ as*

$$m_{\varepsilon}(f) := \inf\{\|x - x'\|_E \mid x, x' \in \mathcal{X}, \|f(x) - f(x')\|_G \geq 2\varepsilon\}. \tag{9.7}$$

Let us look at a 1-D toy problem (Figure 9.1). In pattern recognition, we are looking for a function which exceeds some constant ε (using the canonical hyperplanes of Definition 7.1, this constant is $\varepsilon = 1$) on the positive patterns, and which is smaller than $-\varepsilon$ on the negative patterns. The points where the function takes the values $\pm\varepsilon$ define the ε-margin in the space of the patterns (the x-axis in

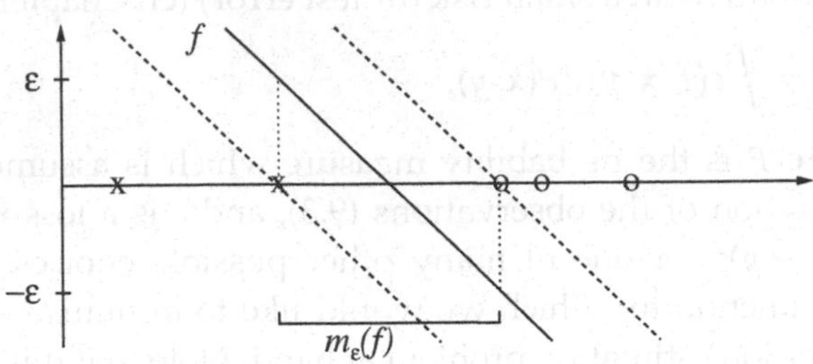

Figure 9.1 1D toy problem: separate 'x' from 'o'. The SV classification algorithm constructs a linear function $f(x) = \langle w, x\rangle + b$ satisfying the canonicality condition $\min\{|f(x)||x \in \mathcal{X}\} = 1$ (or equivalently, $\varepsilon = 1$). To maximize the margin $m_\varepsilon(f)$, we have to minimize $|w|$.

the plot). Therefore, the *flatter* the function f, the *larger* the classification margin. This illustrates why both SV regression and SV pattern recognition use the same regularizer $\|\mathbf{w}\|^2$, albeit with different effects. For more detail on these issues and on the ε-margin, cf. Section 9.8; cf. also [561, 418].

Primal Objective Function, ε-SVR

The minimization of (9.5) is equivalent to the following constrained optimization problem:

$$\underset{\mathbf{w}\in\mathcal{H},\boldsymbol{\xi}^{(*)}\in\mathbb{R}^m,b\in\mathbb{R}}{\text{minimize}} \quad \tau(\mathbf{w},\boldsymbol{\xi}^{(*)}) = \frac{1}{2}\|\mathbf{w}\|^2 + C\cdot\frac{1}{m}\sum_{i=1}^{m}(\xi_i+\xi_i^*), \tag{9.8}$$

$$\text{subject to } ((\langle \mathbf{w},\mathbf{x}_i\rangle + b) - y_i \le \varepsilon + \xi_i, \tag{9.9}$$

$$y_i - (\langle \mathbf{w},\mathbf{x}_i\rangle + b) \le \varepsilon + \xi_i^*, \tag{9.10}$$

$$\xi_i^{(*)} \ge 0. \tag{9.11}$$

Here and below, it is understood that $i = 1,\ldots,m$, and that bold face Greek letters denote m-dimensional vectors of the corresponding variables; $^{(*)}$ is a shorthand implying both the variables with and without asterisks.

9.2 Dual Problems

9.2.1 ε-Insensitive Loss

The key idea is to construct a Lagrangian from the objective function and the corresponding constraints, by introducing a dual set of variables. It can be shown that this function has a saddle point with respect to the primal and dual variables at the solution; for details see Chapter 6. We define a Lagrangian,

$$\begin{aligned} L := \frac{1}{2}\|\mathbf{w}\|^2 + \frac{C}{m}\sum_{i=1}^{m}(\xi_i+\xi_i^*) - \sum_{i=1}^{m}(\eta_i\xi_i + \eta_i^*\xi_i^*) \\ - \sum_{i=1}^{m}\alpha_i(\varepsilon + \xi_i + y_i - \langle \mathbf{w},\mathbf{x}_i\rangle - b) \\ - \sum_{i=1}^{m}\alpha_i^*(\varepsilon + \xi_i^* - y_i + \langle \mathbf{w},\mathbf{x}_i\rangle + b), \end{aligned} \tag{9.12}$$

where the dual variables (or Lagrange multipliers) in (9.12) have to satisfy positivity constraints,

$$\alpha_i^{(*)}, \eta_i^{(*)} \geq 0. \tag{9.13}$$

It follows from the saddle point condition (Chapter 6) that the partial derivatives of L with respect to the primal variables $(\mathbf{w}, b, \xi_i, \xi_i^*)$ have to vanish for optimality;

$$\partial_b L = \sum_{i=1}^m (\alpha_i - \alpha_i^*) = 0, \tag{9.14}$$

$$\partial_{\mathbf{w}} L = \mathbf{w} - \sum_{i=1}^m (\alpha_i^* - \alpha_i)\mathbf{x}_i = 0, \tag{9.15}$$

$$\partial_{\xi_i^{(*)}} L = \tfrac{C}{m} - \alpha_i^{(*)} - \eta_i^{(*)} = 0. \tag{9.16}$$

Substituting (9.14), (9.15), and (9.16) into (9.12) yields the dual optimization problem,

$$\begin{aligned} \underset{\alpha^{(*)} \in \mathbb{R}^m}{\text{maximize}} & \begin{cases} -\frac{1}{2} \sum_{i,j=1}^{m} (\alpha_i^* - \alpha_i)(\alpha_j^* - \alpha_j) \langle \mathbf{x}_i, \mathbf{x}_j \rangle \\ -\varepsilon \sum_{i=1}^{m} (\alpha_i^* + \alpha_i) + \sum_{i=1}^{m} y_i(\alpha_i^* - \alpha_i), \end{cases} \\ \text{subject to} & \sum_{i=1}^{m} (\alpha_i - \alpha_i^*) = 0 \text{ and } \alpha_i, \alpha_i^* \in [0, C/m]. \end{aligned} \tag{9.17}$$

In deriving (9.17), we eliminate the dual variables η_i, η_i^* through condition (9.16). Eq. (9.15) can be rewritten as

$$\mathbf{w} = \sum_{i=1}^{m} (\alpha_i^* - \alpha_i)\mathbf{x}_i, \text{ thus } f(\mathbf{x}) = \sum_{i=1}^{m} (\alpha_i^* - \alpha_i) \langle \mathbf{x}_i, \mathbf{x} \rangle + b. \tag{9.18}$$

SV Expansion

This is the familiar *SV expansion*, stating that $\mathbf{w}$ can be completely described as a linear combination of a subset of the training patterns $\mathbf{x}_i$.

Note that just as in the pattern recognition case, the complete algorithm can be described in terms of dot products between the data. Even when evaluating $f(\mathbf{x})$, we need not compute $\mathbf{w}$ explicitly. This will allow the formulation of a nonlinear extension using kernels.

Computing the Offset b

So far we have neglected the issue of computing b. The latter can be done by exploiting the Karush-Kuhn-Tucker (KKT) conditions (Chapter 6). These state that at the point of the solution, the product between dual variables and constraints has to vanish;

$$\begin{aligned} \alpha_i(\varepsilon + \xi_i - y_i + \langle \mathbf{w}, \mathbf{x}_i \rangle + b) &= 0, \\ \alpha_i^*(\varepsilon + \xi_i^* + y_i - \langle \mathbf{w}, \mathbf{x}_i \rangle - b) &= 0, \end{aligned} \tag{9.19}$$

and

$$\begin{aligned} (\tfrac{C}{m} - \alpha_i)\xi_i &= 0, \\ (\tfrac{C}{m} - \alpha_i^*)\xi_i^* &= 0. \end{aligned} \tag{9.20}$$

This allows us to draw several useful conclusions.

- First, only examples $(\mathbf{x}_i, y_i)$ with corresponding $\alpha_i^{(*)} = C/m$ can lie outside the

ε-insensitive tube (i.e., $\xi_i^{(*)} > 0$) around f.

- Second, we have $\alpha_i \alpha_i^* = 0$. In other words, there can never be a set of dual variables α_i, α_i^* which are both simultaneously nonzero (cf. Problem 9.1).

- Third, for $\alpha_i^{(*)} \in (0, C/m)$ we have $\xi_i^{(*)} = 0$, and furthermore the second factor in (9.19) must vanish. Hence b can be computed as follows:

$$\begin{aligned} b &= y_i - \langle \mathbf{w}, \mathbf{x}_i \rangle - \varepsilon \quad \text{for } \alpha_i \in (0, C/m), \\ b &= y_i - \langle \mathbf{w}, \mathbf{x}_i \rangle + \varepsilon \quad \text{for } \alpha_i^* \in (0, C/m). \end{aligned} \tag{9.21}$$

Theoretically, it suffices to use any Lagrange multiplier in $(0, C/m)$, If given the choice between several such multipliers (usually there are many multipliers which are not 'at bound,' meaning that they do not equal 0 or C/m), it is safest to use one that is not too close to 0 or C/m.
Another way of computing b will be discussed in the context of interior point optimization (cf. Chapter 10). There, b turns out to be a by-product of the optimization process. See also [291] for further methods to compute the constant offset.

- A final note must be made regarding the *sparsity* of the SV expansion. From (9.19) it follows that the Lagrange multipliers may be nonzero only for $|f(\mathbf{x}_i) - y_i| \geq \varepsilon$; in other words, for all examples inside the ε-tube (the shaded region in Figure 1.8) the α_i, α_i^* vanish. This is because when $|f(\mathbf{x}_i) - y_i| < \varepsilon$ the second factor in (9.19) is nonzero, hence α_i, α_i^* must be zero for the KKT conditions to be satisfied. Therefore we have a sparse expansion of $\mathbf{w}$ in terms of $\mathbf{x}_i$ (we do not need all $\mathbf{x}_i$ to describe $\mathbf{w}$). The examples that come with nonvanishing coefficients are called *Support Vectors*. It is geometrically plausible that the points inside the tube do not contribute to the solution: we could remove any one of them, and still obtain the same solution, therefore they cannot carry any information about it.

9.2.2 More General Loss Functions

We will now consider loss functions $c(\mathbf{x}, y, f(\mathbf{x}))$ which for fixed $\mathbf{x}$ and y are convex in $f(\mathbf{x})$. This requirement is chosen as we want to ensure the existence and uniqueness (for strict convexity) of a minimum of optimization problems (Chapter 6). Further detail on loss functions can be found in Chapter 3; for now, we will focus on how, given a loss function, the optimization problems are derived.

For the sake of simplicity, we will additionally assume c to be symmetric, to have (at most) two (for symmetry) discontinuities at $\pm\varepsilon, \varepsilon \geq 0$ in the first derivative, and to be zero in the interval $[-\varepsilon, \varepsilon]$. All loss functions from table 3.1 belong to this class. Hence c will take on the form

$$c(\mathbf{x}, y, f(\mathbf{x})) = \tilde{c}(|y - f(\mathbf{x})|_\varepsilon). \tag{9.22}$$

Note the similarity to Vapnik's ε-insensitive loss. It is rather straightforward to extend this special choice to more general convex loss functions: for nonzero loss functions in the interval $[-\varepsilon, \varepsilon]$, we use an additional pair of slack variables. Furthermore we might choose different loss functions $\tilde{c}_i$, $\tilde{c}_i^*$ and different values of ε_i, ε_i^* for each example. At the expense of additional Lagrange multipliers in the dual formulation, additional discontinuities can also be dealt with. In a manner analogous to (9.8), we arrive at a convex minimization problem [512] (note that for ease of notation, we have absorbed the sample size in C; cf. (9.8)):

$$\begin{aligned} &\underset{\mathbf{w}\in\mathcal{H},\xi^{(*)}\in\mathbb{R}^m,b\in\mathbb{R}}{\text{minimize}} && \tfrac{1}{2}\|\mathbf{w}\|^2 + C\sum_{i=1}^{m}(\tilde{c}(\xi_i)+\tilde{c}(\xi_i^*)), \\ &\text{subject to} && \begin{cases} \langle \mathbf{w},\mathbf{x}_i\rangle + b - y_i \le \varepsilon + \xi_i, \\ y_i - \langle \mathbf{w},\mathbf{x}_i\rangle - b \le \varepsilon + \xi_i^*, \\ \xi_i, \xi_i^* \ge 0. \end{cases} \end{aligned} \tag{9.23}$$

Again, by standard Lagrange multiplier techniques, using exactly the same reasoning as in the $|\cdot|_\varepsilon$ case, we can compute the dual optimization problem. In some places, we will omit the indices $_i$ and * to avoid tedious notation. This yields

$$\begin{aligned} &\underset{\alpha^{(*)}\in\mathbb{R}^m}{\text{maximize}} && \begin{cases} -\frac{1}{2}\sum_{i,j=1}^{m}(\alpha_i^*-\alpha_i)(\alpha_j^*-\alpha_j)\langle\mathbf{x}_i,\mathbf{x}_j\rangle \\ +\sum_{i=1}^{m}(y_i(\alpha_i^*-\alpha_i)-\varepsilon(\alpha_i^*+\alpha_i)) \\ +C\sum_{i=1}^{m}(T(\xi_i^*)+T(\xi_i)), \end{cases} \\ &\text{where} && \begin{cases} \mathbf{w} = \sum_{i=1}^{m}(\alpha_i^*-\alpha_i)\mathbf{x}_i, \\ T(\xi) := \tilde{c}(\xi) - \xi\partial_\xi\tilde{c}(\xi), \end{cases} \\ &\text{subject to} && \begin{cases} \sum_{i=1}^{m}(\alpha_i-\alpha_i^*) = 0, \\ \alpha \le C\partial_\xi\tilde{c}(\xi), \\ \xi = \inf\{\xi \,|\, C\partial_\xi\tilde{c} \ge \alpha\}, \\ \alpha, \xi \ge 0. \end{cases} \end{aligned} \tag{9.24}$$

Let us consider the examples of Table 3.1 as special cases. We will explicitly show for two examples how (9.24) can be further simplified to reduce it to a form that is practically useful. In the ε-insensitive case, where $\tilde{c}(\xi) = |\xi|$, we get

$$T(\xi) = \xi - \xi\cdot 1 = 0. \tag{9.25}$$

We can further conclude from $\partial_\xi\tilde{c}(\xi) = 1$ that

$$\xi = \inf\{\xi \,|\, C \ge \alpha\} = 0 \text{ and } \alpha \in [0, C]. \tag{9.26}$$

In the case of piecewise polynomial loss, we have to distinguish two different cases: $\xi \le \sigma$ and $\xi > \sigma$. In the first case we get

$$T(\xi) = \frac{1}{p\sigma^{p-1}}\xi^p - \frac{1}{\sigma^{p-1}}\xi^p = -\frac{p-1}{p}\sigma^{1-p}\xi^p, \tag{9.27}$$

and $\xi = \inf\{\xi \,|\, C\sigma^{1-p}\xi^{p-1} \ge \alpha\} = \sigma C^{-\frac{1}{p-1}}\alpha^{\frac{1}{p-1}}$; thus

$$T(\xi) = -\frac{p-1}{p}\sigma C^{-\frac{p}{p-1}}\alpha^{\frac{p}{p-1}}. \tag{9.28}$$

Table 9.1 Terms of the convex optimization problem depending on the choice of the loss function.

	ε	α	$CT(\alpha)$
ε-insensitive	$\varepsilon \neq 0$	$\alpha \in [0, C]$	0
Laplacian	$\varepsilon = 0$	$\alpha \in [0, C]$	0
Gaussian	$\varepsilon = 0$	$\alpha \in [0, \infty)$	$-\frac{1}{2}C^{-1}\alpha^2$
Huber's robust loss	$\varepsilon = 0$	$\alpha \in [0, C]$	$-\frac{1}{2}\sigma C^{-1}\alpha^2$
Polynomial	$\varepsilon = 0$	$\alpha \in [0, \infty)$	$-\frac{p-1}{p}C^{-\frac{1}{p-1}}\alpha^{\frac{p}{p-1}}$
Piecewise polynomial	$\varepsilon = 0$	$\alpha \in [0, C]$	$-\frac{p-1}{p}\sigma C^{-\frac{1}{p-1}}\alpha^{\frac{p}{p-1}}$

In the second case ($\xi \geq \sigma$) we have

$$T(\xi) = \xi - \sigma\frac{p-1}{p} - \xi = -\sigma\frac{p-1}{p}, \tag{9.29}$$

and $\xi = \inf\{\xi \,|\, C \geq \alpha\} = \sigma$; hence $\alpha \in [0, C]$. These two cases can be combined to yield

$$\alpha \in [0, C] \text{ and } T(\alpha) = -\frac{p-1}{p}\sigma C^{-\frac{p}{p-1}}\alpha^{\frac{p}{p-1}}. \tag{9.30}$$

Table 9.1 contains a summary of the various conditions on α, and formulas for $T(\alpha)$ for different loss functions.[3] Note that the maximum slope of $\tilde{c}$ determines the region of feasibility of α, meaning that $s := \sup_{\xi \in \mathbb{R}^+} \partial_\xi \tilde{c}(\xi) < \infty$ leads to compact intervals $[0, Cs]$ for α. This means that the influence of a single pattern is bounded, leading to robust estimators (cf. Chapter 3 and Proposition 9.4 below). We also observe experimentally that the performance of an SVM depends on the loss function used [376, 515, 95].

A cautionary remark is necessary regarding the use of loss functions other than the ε-insensitive loss. Unless $\varepsilon \neq 0$, we lose the advantage of a sparse decomposition. This may be acceptable in the case of few data, but will render the prediction step rather slow otherwise. Hence we have to trade off a potential loss in prediction accuracy with faster predictions. Note, however, that this issue could be addressed using reduced set algorithms like those described in Chapter 18, or sparse decomposition techniques [513]. In a Bayesian setting, Tipping [539] recently showed how the squared loss function can be used without sacrificing sparsity, cf. Section 16.6.

3. The table displays $CT(\alpha)$ instead of $T(\alpha)$, since the former can be plugged directly into the corresponding optimization equations.

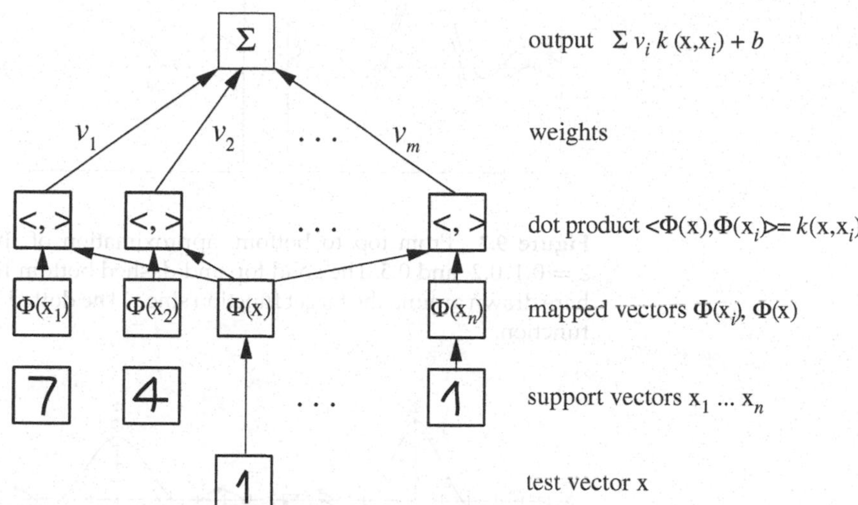

Figure 9.2 Architecture of a regression machine constructed using the SV algorithm. In typical regression applications, the inputs would not be visual patterns. Nevertheless, in this example, the inputs are depicted as handwritten digits.

9.2.3 The Bigger Picture

Let us briefly review the basic properties of the SV algorithm for regression, as described so far. Figure 9.2 contains a graphical overview of the different steps in the regression stage. The input pattern (for which a prediction is to be made) is mapped into feature space by a map Φ. Then dot products are computed with the images of the training patterns under the map Φ. This corresponds to evaluating kernel functions $k(x_i, x)$. Finally, the dot products are added up using the weights $\nu_i = \alpha_i^* - \alpha_i$. This, plus the constant term b, yields the final prediction output. The process described here is very similar to regression in a neural network, with the difference that in the SV case, the weights in the input layer are a subset of the training patterns.

The toy example in Figure 9.3 demonstrates how the SV algorithm chooses the flattest function among those approximating the original data with a given precision. Although requiring flatness only in *feature* space, we observe that the functions are also *smooth* in *input* space. This is due to the fact that kernels can be associated with smoothness properties via regularization operators, as explained in more detail in Chapter 4.

Finally, Figure 9.4 shows the relation between approximation quality and sparsity of representation in the SV case. The lower the precision required for approximating the original data, the fewer SVs are needed to encode this data. The non-SVs are redundant — even without these patterns in the training set, the SVM

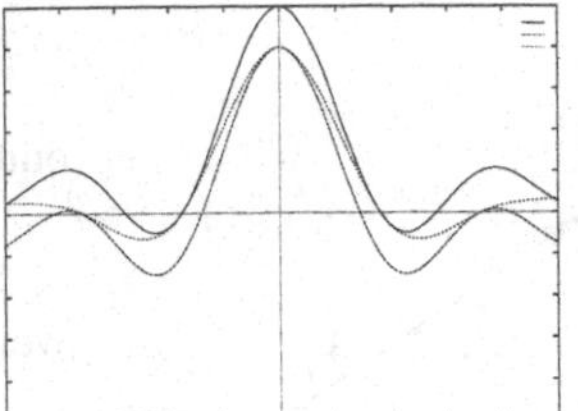
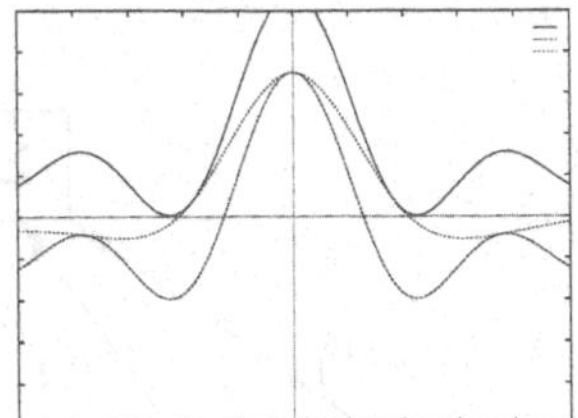
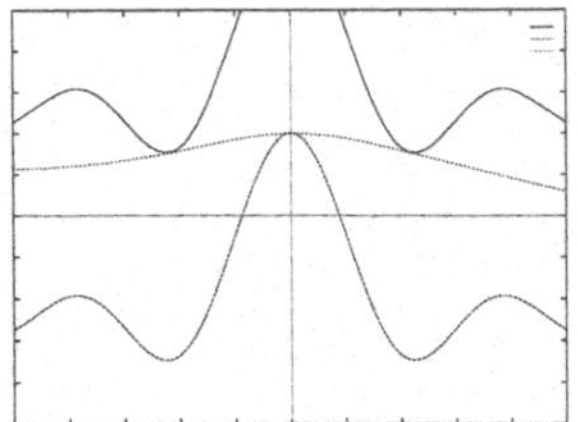

Figure 9.3 From top to bottom: approximation of the function sinc x with precisions $\varepsilon = 0.1, 0.2$, and 0.5. The solid top and dashed bottom lines indicate the size of the ε-tube, here drawn around the target function sinc x. The dotted line between them is the regression function.

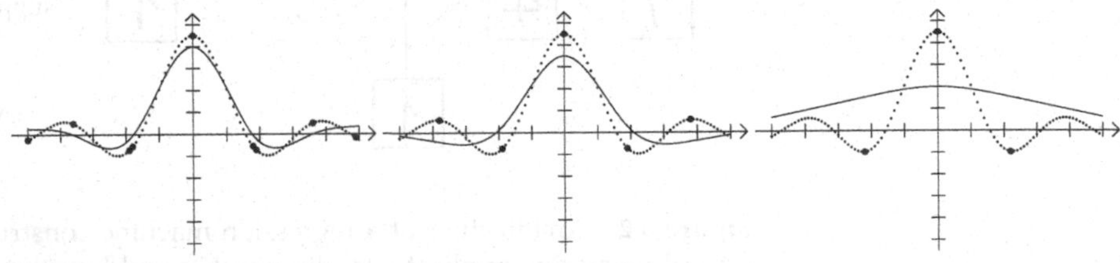

Figure 9.4 Left to right: regression (solid line), data points (small dots) and SVs (big dots) for an approximation of sinc x (dotted line) with $\varepsilon = 0.1, 0.2$, and 0.5. Note the decrease in the number of SVs.

would have constructed exactly the same function f. We might be tempted to use this property as an efficient means of data compression, namely by storing only the support patterns, from which the estimate can be reconstructed completely. Unfortunately, this approach turns out not to work well in the case of noisy high-dimensional data, since for moderate approximation quality, the number of SVs can be rather high [572].

9.3 ν-SV Regression

The parameter ε of the ε-insensitive loss is useful if the desired accuracy of the approximation can be specified beforehand. In some cases, however, we just want the estimate to be as accurate as possible, without having to commit ourselves to a specific level of accuracy a priori. We now describe a modification of the ε-SVR algorithm, called ν-SVR, which automatically computes ε [481].

To estimate functions (9.2) from empirical data (9.3) we proceed as follows. At each point $\mathbf{x}_i$, we allow an error ε. Everything above ε is captured in slack variables $\xi_i^{(*)}$, which are penalized in the objective function via a regularization constant C, chosen a priori. The size of ε is traded off against model complexity and slack variables via a constant $\nu \geq 0$:

$$\underset{\mathbf{w}\in\mathcal{H},\boldsymbol{\xi}^{(*)}\in\mathbb{R}^m,\varepsilon,b\in\mathbb{R}}{\text{minimize}} \quad \tau(\mathbf{w},\boldsymbol{\xi}^{(*)},\varepsilon) = \frac{1}{2}\|\mathbf{w}\|^2 + C\cdot\left(\nu\varepsilon + \frac{1}{m}\sum_{i=1}^{m}(\xi_i+\xi_i^*)\right), \tag{9.31}$$

$$\text{subject to } ((\langle\mathbf{w},\mathbf{x}_i\rangle + b) - y_i \leq \varepsilon + \xi_i, \tag{9.32}$$

$$y_i - (\langle\mathbf{w},\mathbf{x}_i\rangle + b) \leq \varepsilon + \xi_i^*, \tag{9.33}$$

$$\xi_i^{(*)} \geq 0, \;\; \varepsilon \geq 0. \tag{9.34}$$

Primal Problem ν-SVR

For the constraints, we introduce multipliers $\alpha_i^{(*)}, \eta_i^{(*)}, \beta \geq 0$, and obtain the Lagrangian,

$$L(\mathbf{w},b,\boldsymbol{\alpha}^{(*)},\beta,\boldsymbol{\xi}^{(*)},\varepsilon,\boldsymbol{\eta}^{(*)}) = \tag{9.35}$$

$$\frac{1}{2}\|\mathbf{w}\|^2 + C\nu\varepsilon + \frac{C}{m}\sum_{i=1}^{m}(\xi_i+\xi_i^*) - \beta\varepsilon - \sum_{i=1}^{m}(\eta_i\xi_i + \eta_i^*\xi_i^*)$$

$$-\sum_{i=1}^{m}\alpha_i(\xi_i + y_i - \langle\mathbf{w},\mathbf{x}_i\rangle - b + \varepsilon) - \sum_{i=1}^{m}\alpha_i^*(\xi_i^* + \langle\mathbf{w},\mathbf{x}_i\rangle + b - y_i + \varepsilon).$$

To minimize (9.31), we have to find the saddle point of L, meaning that we minimize over the primal variables $\mathbf{w}, \varepsilon, b, \xi_i^{(*)}$ and maximize over the dual variables $\alpha_i^{(*)}, \beta, \eta_i^{(*)}$. Setting the derivatives with respect to the primal variables equal to zero yields the four equations

$$\mathbf{w} = \sum_i(\alpha_i^* - \alpha_i)\mathbf{x}_i, \tag{9.36}$$

$$C\cdot\nu - \sum_i(\alpha_i + \alpha_i^*) - \beta = 0, \tag{9.37}$$

$$\sum_{i=1}^{m}(\alpha_i - \alpha_i^*) = 0, \tag{9.38}$$

$$\frac{C}{m} - \alpha_i^{(*)} - \eta_i^{(*)} = 0. \tag{9.39}$$

As in Section 9.2, the $\alpha_i^{(*)}$ are nonzero in the *SV expansion* (9.36) only when a constraint (9.32) or (9.33) is precisely met.

Substituting the above four conditions into L leads to the dual optimization problem (sometimes called the Wolfe dual). We will state it in the kernelized form: as usual, we substitute a kernel k for the dot product, corresponding to a dot product in some feature space related to input space via a nonlinear map Φ,

$$k(x,x') = \langle\Phi(x),\Phi(x')\rangle = \langle\mathbf{x},\mathbf{x}'\rangle\,. \tag{9.40}$$

ν-SVR Dual Program

Rewriting the constraints, and noting that $\beta, \eta_i^{(*)} \geq 0$ do not appear in the dual, we arrive at the ν-SVR Optimization Problem: for $\nu \geq 0, C > 0$,

$$\underset{\boldsymbol{\alpha}^{(*)}\in\mathbb{R}^m}{\text{maximize}}\; W(\boldsymbol{\alpha}^{(*)}) = \sum_{i=1}^{m}(\alpha_i^* - \alpha_i)y_i - \frac{1}{2}\sum_{i,j=1}^{m}(\alpha_i^* - \alpha_i)(\alpha_j^* - \alpha_j)k(x_i,x_j), \tag{9.41}$$

$$\text{subject to } \sum_{i=1}^{m}(\alpha_i - \alpha_i^*) = 0, \tag{9.42}$$

$$\alpha_i^{(*)} \in \left[0, \tfrac{C}{m}\right], \tag{9.43}$$

$$\sum_{i=1}^{m} (\alpha_i + \alpha_i^*) \leq C \cdot \nu. \tag{9.44}$$

The regression estimate then takes the form (cf. (9.2), (9.36), (9.40))

$$f(x) = \sum_{i=1}^{m} (\alpha_i^* - \alpha_i) k(x_i, x) + b, \tag{9.45}$$

where b (and ε) can be computed by taking into account that (9.32) and (9.33) become equalities with $\xi_i^{(*)} = 0$ for points with $0 < \alpha_i^{(*)} < C/m$, due to the KKT conditions. Here, substitution of $\sum_j (\alpha_j^* - \alpha_j) k(x_j, x)$ for $\langle \mathbf{w}, \mathbf{x} \rangle$ is understood, cf. (9.36), (9.40). Geometrically, this amounts to saying that we can compute the thickness and vertical position of the tube by considering some points that sit exactly on the edge of the tube.[4]

We now show that ν has an interpretation similar to the case of ν-SV pattern recognition (Section 7.5). This is not completely obvious: recall that in the case of pattern recognition, we introduced ν to replace C. In regression, on the other hand, we introduced it to replace ε.

Before we give the result, the following observation concerning ε is helpful. If $\nu > 1$, then necessarily $\varepsilon = 0$, since it does not pay to increase ε. This can be seen either from (9.31) — the slacks are "cheaper" — or by noting that for $\nu \geq 1$, (9.43) implies (9.44), since $\alpha_i \alpha_i^* = 0$ for all i (9.58). Therefore, (9.44) is redundant, and all values $\nu \geq 1$ are actually equivalent. Hence, we restrict ourselves to $0 \leq \nu \leq 1$.

If $\nu < 1$, we mostly find $\varepsilon > 0$. It is still possible that $\varepsilon = 0$, for instance if the data are noise-free and can be perfectly interpolated with a low capacity model. The case $\varepsilon = 0$ is not what we are interested in: it corresponds to plain L_1-loss regression.

Below, we will use the term *errors* to refer to training points lying outside the tube, and the term *fraction* of errors/SVs to denote the relative numbers of errors/SVs; that is, these respective quantities are divided by m. In this proposition, we define the *modulus of absolute continuity* of a function f as the function $\epsilon(\delta) := \sup \sum_i |f(b_i) - f(a_i)|$, where the supremum is taken over all disjoint intervals (a_i, b_i) with $a_i < b_i$ satisfying $\sum_i (b_i - a_i) < \delta$. Loosely speaking, the condition on the conditional density of y given x asks that it be absolutely continuous 'on average.'

ν-Property

Proposition 9.2 *Suppose ν-SVR is applied to some data set and the resulting ε is nonzero. The following statements hold:*

4. Should it occur, for instance due to numerical problems, that it is impossible to find two non-bound SVs at the two edges of the tube, then we can replace them by the SVs which are closest to the tube. The SV closest to the top of the tube can be found by minimizing $y_i - \langle \mathbf{w}, \mathbf{x}_i \rangle$ over all points with $\alpha_i^* > 0$; similarly, for the bottom SVs we minimize $\langle \mathbf{w}, \mathbf{x}_i \rangle - y_i$ over the points with $\alpha_i > 0$. We then proceed as we would with the non-bound SVs, cf. Problem 9.16.

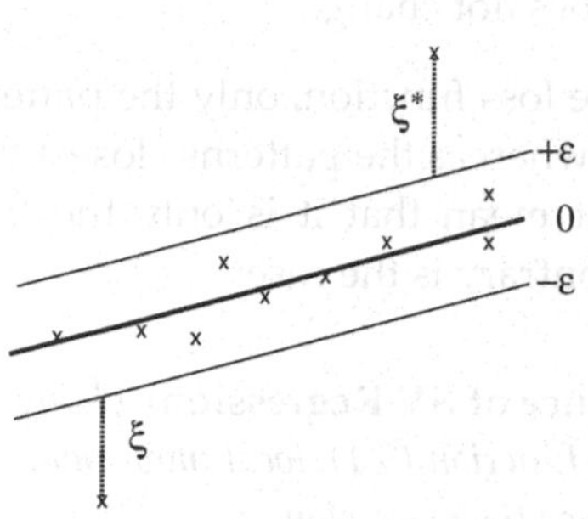

Figure 9.5 Graphical depiction of the ν-trick. Imagine increasing ε, starting from 0. The first term in $\nu\varepsilon + \frac{1}{m}\sum_{i=1}^{m}(\xi_i + \xi_i^*)$ (cf. (9.31)) increases proportionally to ν, while the second term decreases proportionally to the fraction of points outside of the tube. Hence, ε grows as long as the latter fraction is larger than ν. At the optimum, it must therefore be $\leq \nu$ (Proposition 9.2, (i)). Next, imagine decreasing ε, starting from some large value. Again, the change in the first term is proportional to ν, but this time, the change in the second term is proportional to the fraction of SVs (even points *on* the edge of the tube contribute). Hence, ε shrinks as long as the fraction of SVs is smaller than ν, leading eventually to Proposition 9.2, (ii).

(i) ν is an upper bound on the fraction of errors.

(ii) ν is a lower bound on the fraction of SVs.

(iii) Suppose the data (9.3) were generated iid from a distribution $P(x, y) = P(x)P(y|x)$, with $P(y|x)$ continuous and the expectation of the modulus of absolute continuity of its density satisfying $\lim_{\delta \to 0} \mathbf{E}_x[\epsilon(\delta)] = 0$. With probability 1, asymptotically, ν equals both the fraction of SVs and the fraction of errors.

The proposition shows that $0 \leq \nu \leq 1$ can be used to control the number of errors. Since the constraint (9.42) implies that (9.44) is equivalent to $\sum_i \alpha_i^{(*)} \leq C\nu/2$, we conclude that Proposition 9.2 actually holds separately for the upper and the lower edge of the tube, with $\nu/2$ each. As an aside, note that by the same argument, the number of SVs at the two edges of the standard ε-SVR tube asymptotically agree.

The proof of Proposition 9.2 can be found in Section A.2. In its stead, we use a graphical argument that should make the result plausible (Figure 9.5). For further information on the ν-trick in a more general setting, cf. Section 3.4.3.

Connection ν-SVR / ε-SVR

Let us briefly discuss how ν-SVR relates to ε-SVR (Section 9.1). Both algorithms use the ε-insensitive loss function, but ν-SVR *automatically* computes ε. From a Bayesian viewpoint, this automatic adaptation of the loss function can be interpreted as adapting the error model, controlled by the hyperparameter ν (cf. Chapter 3). Comparing (9.17) (substitution of a kernel for the dot product is understood) and (9.41), we note that ε-SVR requires an additional term $-\varepsilon\sum_{i=1}^{m}(\alpha_i^* + \alpha_i)$, which, for fixed $\varepsilon > 0$, encourages some of the $\alpha_i^{(*)}$ to be 0. Accordingly, the constraint (9.44), which appears in ν-SVR, is not needed. The primal problems (9.8) and (9.31) differ in the term $\nu\varepsilon$. If $\nu = 0$, then the optimization can grow ε arbitrarily large, hence zero empirical risk can be obtained even when all α are zero.

In the following sense, ν-SVR includes ε-SVR. Note that in the general case, using kernels, $\bar{\mathbf{w}}$ is a vector in feature space.

Proposition 9.3 *If ν-SVR leads to the solution $\bar{\varepsilon}, \bar{\mathbf{w}}, \bar{b}$, then ε-SVR with ε set a priori to $\bar{\varepsilon}$, and the same value of C, has the solution $\bar{\mathbf{w}}, \bar{b}$.*

Proof If we minimize (9.31), then fix ε and minimize only over the remaining variables, the solution does not change. ■

Connection to Robust Estimators

Using the ε-insensitive loss function, only the patterns outside the ε-tube enter the empirical risk term, whereas the patterns closest to the actual regression have zero loss. This does not mean that it is only the 'outliers' that determine the regression. In fact, the contrary is the case:

Proposition 9.4 (Resistance of SV Regression) *Using Support Vector Regression with the ε-insensitive loss function (9.1), local movements of target values of points outside the tube do not influence the regression.*

Proof Shifting y_i locally does not change the status of (x_i, y_i) as being a point outside the tube. The dual solution $\boldsymbol{\alpha}^{(*)}$ then remains feasible; which is to say it satisfies the constraints (the point still has $\alpha_i^{(*)} = C/m$). In addition, the primal solution, with ξ_i transformed according to the movement of x_i, is also feasible. Finally, the KKT conditions are still satisfied, as $\alpha_i^{(*)} = C/m$. Thus (Chapter 6), $\boldsymbol{\alpha}^{(*)}$ remains the solution. ■

The proof relies on the fact that everywhere outside the tube, the upper bound on the $\alpha_i^{(*)}$ is the same. This, in turn, is precisely the case if the loss function increases linearly outside the ε-tube (cf. Chapter 3 for requirements for robust loss functions). Inside, a range of functions is permissible, provided their first derivative is smaller than that of the linear part.

In the case of ν-SVR with ε-insensitive loss, the above proposition implies that essentially, the regression is a generalization of an estimator for the mean of a random variable which

(a) throws away the largest and smallest examples (a fraction $\nu/2$ of either category — in Section 9.3, it is shown that the sum constraint (9.42) implies that Proposition 9.2 can be applied separately for the two sides, using $\nu/2$); and

(b) estimates the mean by taking the average of the two extremal ones of the remaining examples.

Trimmed Mean

This resistance to outliers is close in spirit to robust estimators like the *trimmed mean*. In fact, we could get closer to the idea of the trimmed mean, which first throws away the largest and smallest points and then computes the mean of the remaining points, by using a quadratic loss inside the ε-tube. This would leave us with Huber's robust loss function (see Table 3.1).

Note, moreover, that the parameter ν is related to the breakdown point of the corresponding robust estimator [251]. As it specifies the fraction of points which may be arbitrarily bad outliers, ν is related to the fraction of some arbitrary distribution that may be added to a known noise model without leading to a failure of the estimator.

Finally, we add that by a simple modification of the loss function (cf. [594]), namely weighting the slack variables $\boldsymbol{\xi}^{(*)}$ above and below the tube in the target

Table 9.2 Asymptotic behavior of the fraction of errors and SVs.
The ε found by ν-SV regression is largely independent of the sample size m. The fraction of SVs and the fraction of errors approach $\nu = 0.2$ from above and below, respectively, as the number of training examples m increases (cf. Proposition 9.2).

m	10	50	100	200	500	1000	1500	2000
ε	0.27	0.22	0.23	0.25	0.26	0.26	0.26	0.26
fraction of errors	0.00	0.10	0.14	0.18	0.19	0.20	0.20	0.20
fraction of SVs	0.40	0.28	0.24	0.23	0.21	0.21	0.20	0.20

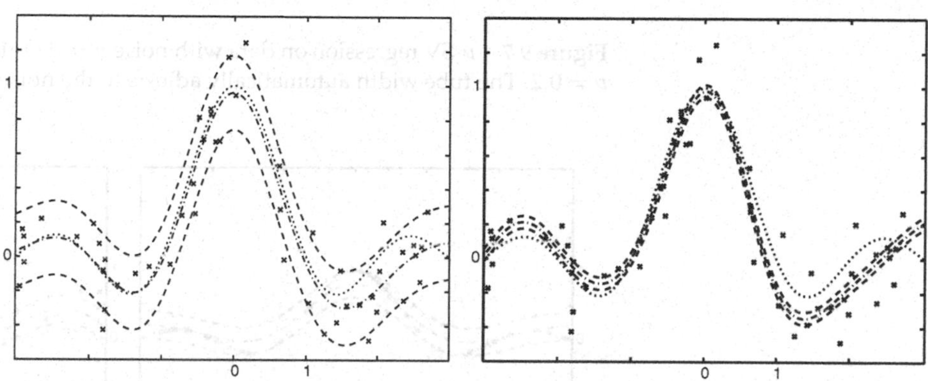

Figure 9.6 ν-SV regression with $\nu = 0.2$ (left) and $\nu = 0.8$ (right). The larger ν allows more points to lie outside the tube (see Section 9.3). The algorithm automatically adjusts ε to 0.22 (left) and 0.04 (right). Shown are the sinc function (dotted), the regression f and the tube $f \pm \varepsilon$.

function (9.31) by 2λ and $2(1-\lambda)$ respectively, with $\lambda \in [0, 1]$, we can estimate generalized *quantiles*. The argument proceeds as follows. Asymptotically, all patterns have multipliers at bound (cf. Proposition 9.2). The parameter λ, however, changes the upper bounds in the box constraints applying to the two different types of slack variables to $2C\lambda/m$ and $2C(1-\lambda)/m$, respectively. The equality constraint (9.38) then implies that $(1-\lambda)$ and λ give the fractions of points (of those which are outside the tube) which lie on the top and bottom of the tube, respectively.

Quantile

Experiments

Let us now look at some experiments. We start with a toy example, which involves estimating the regression of a noisy sinc function, given m examples (x_i, y_i), with x_i drawn uniformly from $[-3, 3]$, and $y_i = \sin(\pi x_i)/(\pi x_i) + v_i$. The v_i were drawn from a Gaussian with zero mean and variance σ^2, and we used the RBF kernel $k(x, x') = \exp(-|x - x'|^2)$, $m = 50, C = 100, \nu = 0.2$, and $\sigma = 0.2$. Standard deviation error bars were computed from 100 trials. Finally, the *risk* (or test error) of a regression estimate f was computed with respect to the sinc function without noise, as $\frac{1}{6}\int_{-3}^{3} |f(x) - \sin(\pi x)/(\pi x)|\, dx$. Results are given in Table 9.2 and Figures 9.6–9.12.

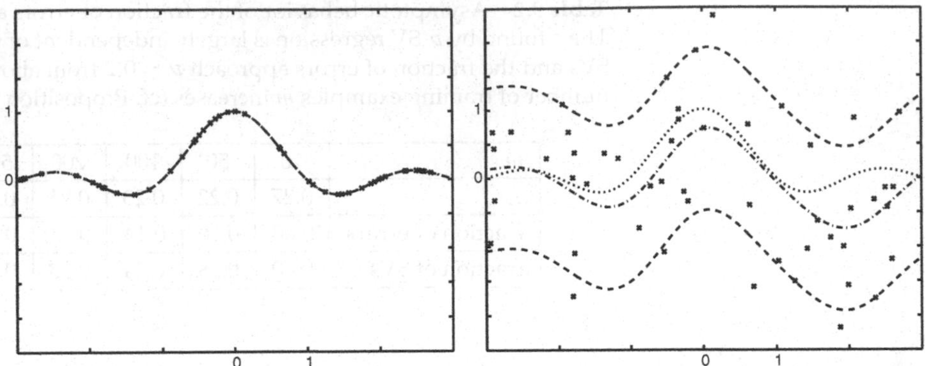

Figure 9.7 ν-SV regression on data with noise $\sigma = 0$ (left) and $\sigma = 1$ (right). In both cases, $\nu = 0.2$. The tube width automatically adjusts to the noise (top: $\varepsilon = 0$, bottom: $\varepsilon = 1.19$).

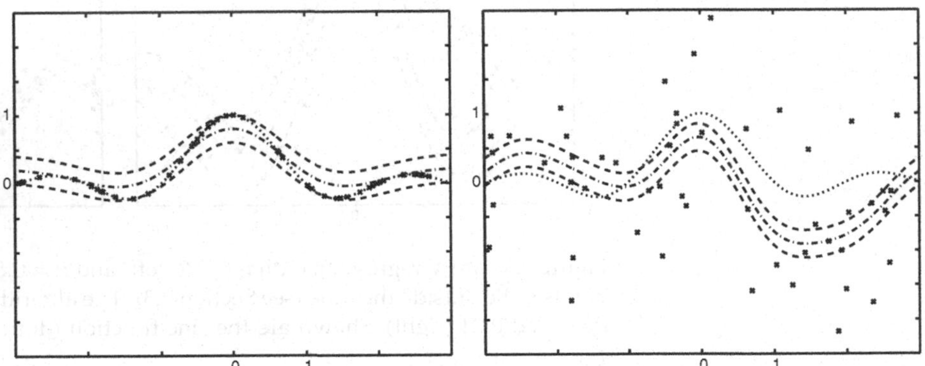

Figure 9.8 ε-SV regression (Section 9.2) on data with noise $\sigma = 0$ (left) and $\sigma = 1$ (right). In both cases, $\varepsilon = 0.2$ — this choice, which has to be specified a priori, is ideal for neither case: in the upper figure, the regression estimate is biased; in the lower figure, ε does not match the external noise [510].

9.4 Convex Combinations and ℓ_1-Norms

All the algorithms presented so far involve convex, and at best, quadratic programming. Yet we might think of reducing the problem to a case where linear programming techniques can be applied. This can be done in a straightforward fashion [591, 517] for both SV pattern recognition and regression. The key is to replace the original objective function by

$$R_{\text{reg}}[f] := \frac{1}{m}\|\alpha\|_1 + C \cdot R_{\text{emp}}[f] \tag{9.46}$$

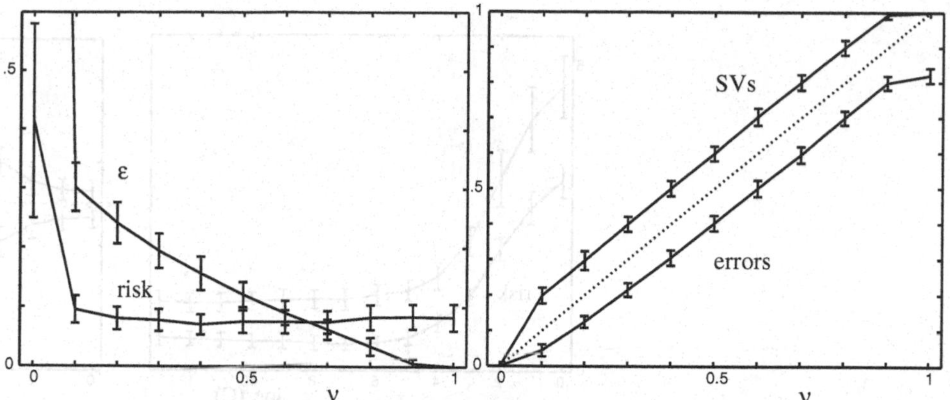

Figure 9.9 ν-SVR for different values of the error constant ν. Notice how ε decreases when more errors are allowed (large ν), and that over a large range of ν, the test error (risk) is insensitive to changes in ν.

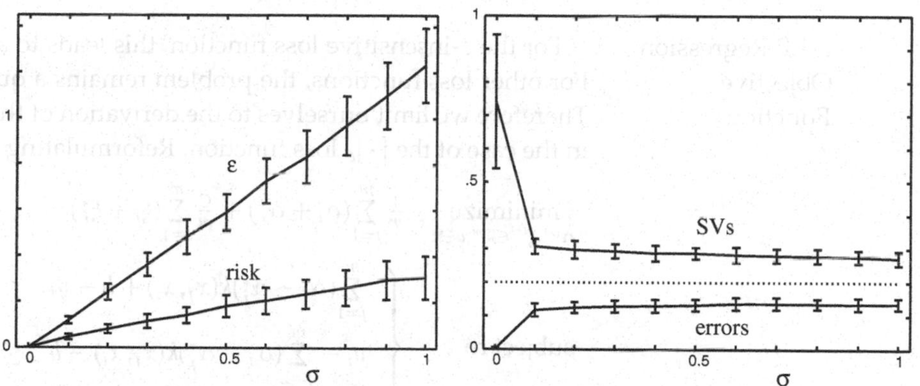

Figure 9.10 ν-SVR for different values of the noise σ. The tube radius ε increases linearly with σ (largely due to the fact that both ε and the $\xi_i^{(*)}$ enter the loss function linearly). Due to the automatic adaptation of ε, the number of SVs and of points outside the tube (errors) is largely independent of σ, except for the noise-free case $\sigma = 0$.

where $\|\alpha\|_1 = \sum_{i=1}^m |\alpha_i|$ denotes the ℓ_1 norm in coefficient space. Using the SV kernel expansion (9.18),

$$f(x) = \sum_{i=1}^{m} \alpha_i k(x_i, x) + b, \tag{9.47}$$

this translates to the objective function

$$R_{\text{reg}}[f] = \frac{1}{m} \sum_{i=1}^{m} |\alpha_i| + \frac{C}{m} \sum_{i=1}^{m} c(x_i, y_i, f(x_i)). \tag{9.48}$$

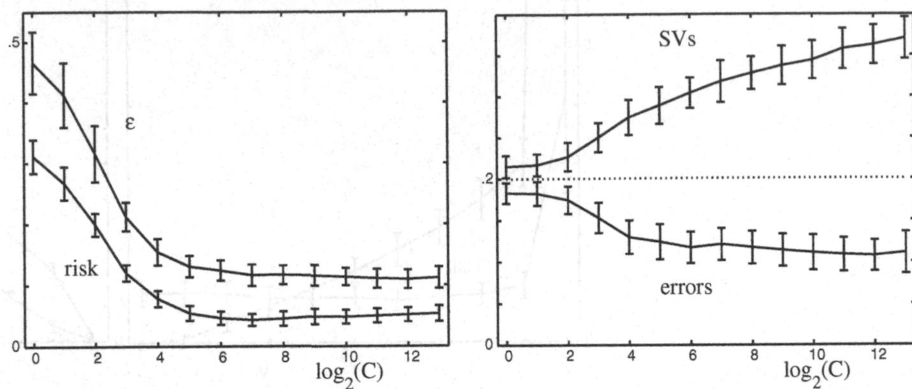

Figure 9.11 ν-SVR for different values of the constant C. The left graph shows that ε decreases when the regularization is decreased (large C). Only very little, if any, overfitting occurs. In the right graph, note that ν upper bounds the fraction of errors, and lower bounds the fraction of SVs (cf. Proposition 9.2). The bound gets looser as C increases — this corresponds to a smaller number of examples m relative to C (cf. Table 9.2).

ε-LP Regression Objective Function

For the ε-insensitive loss function, this leads to a linear programming problem. For other loss functions, the problem remains a quadratic or general convex one. Therefore we limit ourselves to the derivation of the linear programming problem in the case of the $|\cdot|_\varepsilon$ loss function. Reformulating (9.48) yields

$$\begin{aligned} \underset{\alpha^{(*)},\xi^{(*)}\in\mathbb{R}^m, b\in\mathbb{R}}{\text{minimize}} \quad & \tfrac{1}{m}\sum_{i=1}^{m}(\alpha_i+\alpha_i^*) + \tfrac{C}{m}\sum_{i=1}^{m}(\xi_i+\xi_i^*), \\ \text{subject to} \quad & \begin{cases} \sum_{j=1}^{m}(\alpha_j-\alpha_j^*)k(x_j,x_i)+b-y_i & \leq \ \varepsilon+\xi_i, \\ y_i-\sum_{j=1}^{m}(\alpha_j-\alpha_j^*)k(x_j,x_i)-b & \leq \ \varepsilon+\xi_i^*, \\ \alpha_i,\alpha_i^*,\xi_i,\xi_i^* & \geq \ 0. \end{cases} \end{aligned} \tag{9.49}$$

Unlike the SV case, the transformation into its dual does not give any improvement in the structure of the optimization problem. Hence it is best to minimize $R_{\text{reg}}[f]$ directly, which can be achieved using a linear optimizer (see [130, 336, 555]).

Weston et al. [591] use a similar LP approach to estimate densities on a line. We may even obtain bounds on the generalization error [505] which exhibit better rates than in the SV case [606]; cf. Chapter 12.

ν-LP Regression

We conclude this section by noting that we can combine these ideas with those presented in the previous section, and construct a ν-LP regression algorithm [517]. It differs from the previous ν-SV algorithm in that we now minimize

$$R_{\text{reg}} + C\nu\varepsilon = \frac{1}{m}\sum_{i=1}^{m}|\alpha_i| + CR^{\varepsilon}_{\text{emp}}[f] + C\nu\varepsilon. \tag{9.50}$$

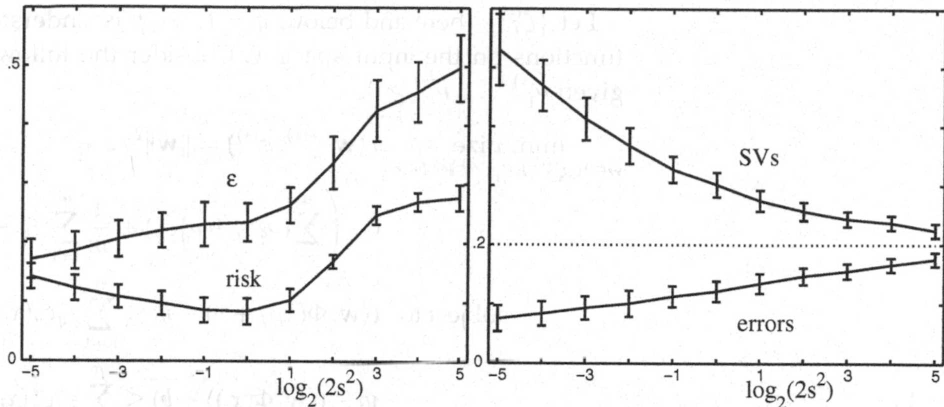

Figure 9.12 ν-SVR for different values of the Gaussian kernel width $2s^2$, using $k(x, x') = \exp(-|x - x'|^2/(2s^2))$. Using a kernel that is too wide results in underfitting; moreover, since the tube becomes too rigid as $2s^2$ gets larger than 1, the ε which is needed to accomodate a fraction $(1 - \nu)$ of points increases significantly. In the plot on the right, it can again be seen that the speed of the uniform convergence responsible for the asymptotic statement given in Proposition 9.2 depends on the capacity of the underlying model. Increasing the kernel width leads to smaller covering numbers (Chapter 12) and therefore faster convergence.

The goal here is not only to achieve a small training error (with respect to ε), but also to obtain a solution with a small ε. Rewriting (9.50) as a linear program yields

$$\begin{aligned} \underset{\alpha^{(*)}, \xi^{(*)} \in \mathbb{R}^m, b, \varepsilon \in \mathbb{R}}{\text{minimize}} \quad & \frac{1}{m} \sum_{i=1}^{m} (\alpha_i + \alpha_i^*) + \frac{C}{m} \sum_{i=1}^{m} (\xi_i + \xi_i^*) + C\nu\varepsilon, \\ \text{subject to} \quad & \begin{cases} \sum_{j=1}^{m} (\alpha_j - \alpha_j^*) k(x_j, x_i) + b - y_i \ \leq \ \varepsilon + \xi_i, \\ y_i - \sum_{j=1}^{m} (\alpha_j - \alpha_j^*) k(x_j, x_i) - b \ \leq \ \varepsilon + \xi_i^*, \\ \alpha_i, \alpha_i^*, \xi_i, \xi_i^*, \varepsilon \ \geq \ 0. \end{cases} \end{aligned} \tag{9.51}$$

The difference between (9.50) and (9.49) lies in the objective function, and the fact that ε has now become a variable of the optimization problem.

The ν-property (Proposition 9.2) also holds for ν-LP regression. The proof is analogous to the ν-SV case, and can be found in [517].

9.5 Parametric Insensitivity Models

In Section 9.3, we generalized ε-SVR by estimating the width of the tube rather than taking it as given a priori. What we retained, however, is the assumption that the ε-insensitive zone has a tube shape. We now go one step further and use parametric models of arbitrary shape [469]. This can be useful in situations where the noise depends on x (this is called heteroscedastic noise).

Let $\{\zeta_q^{(*)}\}$ (here and below, $q = 1, \ldots, p$ is understood) be a set of $2p$ positive functions on the input space $\mathcal{X}$. Consider the following quadratic program: for given $\nu_1^{(*)}, \ldots, \nu_p^{(*)} \geq 0$,

$$\underset{\mathbf{w}\in\mathcal{H},\boldsymbol{\xi}^{(*)}\in\mathbb{R}^m,\boldsymbol{\varepsilon}^{(*)}\in\mathbb{R}^p,b\in\mathbb{R}}{\text{minimize}} \quad \tau(\mathbf{w}, \boldsymbol{\xi}^{(*)}, \boldsymbol{\varepsilon}^{(*)}) = \|\mathbf{w}\|^2/2 +$$

$$C \cdot \left(\sum_{q=1}^{p} (\nu_q \varepsilon_q + \nu_q^* \varepsilon_q^*) + \frac{1}{m} \sum_{i=1}^{m} (\xi_i + \xi_i^*) \right), \tag{9.52}$$

$$\text{subject to} \quad ((\mathbf{w}, \Phi(x_i)) + b) - y_i \leq \sum_{q=1}^{p} \varepsilon_q \zeta_q(x_i) + \xi_i, \tag{9.53}$$

$$y_i - ((\mathbf{w}, \Phi(x_i)) + b) \leq \sum_{q=1}^{p} \varepsilon_q^* \zeta_q^*(x_i) + \xi_i^*, \tag{9.54}$$

$$\xi_i^{(*)} \geq 0, \;\; \varepsilon_q^{(*)} \geq 0. \tag{9.55}$$

A calculation analogous to that in Section 9.3 shows that the Wolfe dual consists of maximizing (9.41) subject to (9.42), (9.43), and, instead of (9.44), the modified constraints,

$$\sum_{i=1}^{m} \alpha_i^{(*)} \zeta_q^{(*)}(x_i) \leq C \cdot \nu_q^{(*)}. \tag{9.56}$$

which are still linear in $\boldsymbol{\alpha}^{(*)}$. In the toy experiment shown in Figure 9.13, we use a simplified version of this optimization problem, where we drop the term $\nu_q^* \varepsilon_q^*$ from the objective function (9.52), and use ε_q and ζ_q in (9.54). By this, we render the problem symmetric with respect to the two edges of the tube. In addition, we use $p = 1$. This leads to the same Wolfe dual, except for the last constraint, which becomes (cf. (9.44))

$$\sum_{i=1}^{m} (\alpha_i + \alpha_i^*) \zeta(x_i) \leq C \cdot \nu. \tag{9.57}$$

Note that the optimization problem of Section 9.3 can be recovered using the constant function $\zeta \equiv 1$.[5]

The advantage of this setting is that since the same ν is used for both sides of the tube, the computation of ε and b is straightforward: for instance, by solving a linear system, using two conditions such as those described following (9.45). Otherwise, general statements become cumbersome: the linear system can have a zero determinant, depending on whether the functions $\zeta_p^{(*)}$, evaluated on the x_i with $0 < \alpha_i^{(*)} < C/m$, are linearly dependent. The latter occurs, for instance, if we use constant functions $\zeta^{(*)} \equiv 1$. In this case, it is pointless to use two different

5. Observe the similarity to semiparametric SV models (Section 4.8) where a modification of the expansion of f leads to similar additional constraints. The important difference in the present setting is that the Lagrange multipliers α_i and α_i^* are treated equally, and not with different signs as in semiparametric modelling.

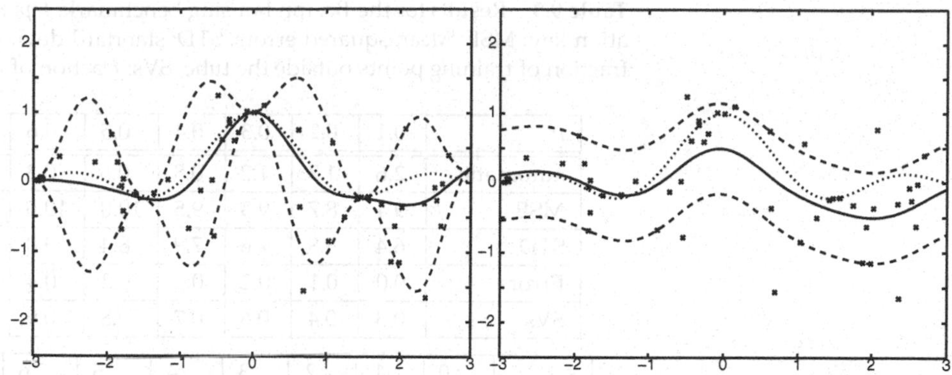

Figure 9.13 Toy example, using prior knowledge about an x-dependence of the noise. Additive noise ($\sigma = 1$) was multiplied by the function $\sin^2((2\pi/3)x)$. *Left:* the *same* function was used as ζ in the context of a parametric insensitivity tube (Section 9.5). *Right:* ν-SVR with standard tube.

values ν, ν^*, since the constraint (9.42) then implies that *both* sums $\sum_{i=1}^m \alpha_i^{(*)}$ are bounded by $C \cdot \min\{\nu, \nu^*\}$. We conclude this section by giving, without proof, a generalization of Proposition 9.2 to the optimization problem with constraint (9.57):

Proposition 9.5 *Suppose we run the above algorithm on a data set with the result that* $\varepsilon > 0$. *Then*

(i) $\frac{\nu m}{\sum_i \zeta(x_i)}$ *is an upper bound on the fraction of errors.*

(ii) $\frac{\nu m}{\sum_i \zeta(x_i)}$ *is an upper bound on the fraction of SVs.*

(iii) Suppose the data (9.3) were generated iid from a distribution $P(x, y) = P(x)P(y|x)$, *with* $P(y|x)$ *continuous and the expectation of its modulus of continuity satisfying* $\lim_{\delta \to 0} \mathbf{E}\epsilon(\delta) = 0$. *With probability 1, asymptotically, the fractions of SVs and errors equal* $\nu \cdot (\int \zeta(x)\, d\tilde{P}(x))^{-1}$, *where* $\tilde{P}$ *is the asymptotic distribution of SVs over* x.

Figure 9.13 gives an illustration of how we can make use of parametric insensitivity models. Using the proper model, the estimate gets much better. In the parametric case, we used $\nu = 0.1$ and $\zeta(x) = \sin^2((2\pi/3)x)$, which, due to $\int \zeta(x)\, dP(x) = 1/2$, corresponds to our standard choice $\nu = 0.2$ in ν-SVR (cf. Proposition 9.5). Although this relies on the assumption that the SVs are uniformly distributed, the experimental findings are consistent with the asymptotes predicted theoretically: for $m = 200$, we got 0.24 and 0.19 for the fraction of SVs and errors, respectively.

Table 9.3 Results for the Boston housing benchmark; *top:* ν-SVR, *bottom:* ε-SVR. Abbreviation key: MSE: Mean squared errors, STD: standard deviation thereof (100 trials), Errors: fraction of training points outside the tube, SVs: fraction of training points which are SVs.

ν	0.1	0.2	0.3	0.4	0.5	0.6	0.7	0.8	0.9	1.0
automatic ε	2.6	1.7	1.2	0.8	0.6	0.3	0.0	0.0	0.0	0.0
MSE	9.4	8.7	9.3	9.5	10.0	10.6	11.3	11.3	11.3	11.3
STD	6.4	6.8	7.6	7.9	8.4	9.0	9.6	9.5	9.5	9.5
Errors	0.0	0.1	0.2	0.2	0.3	0.4	0.5	0.5	0.5	0.5
SVs	0.3	0.4	0.6	0.7	0.8	0.9	1.0	1.0	1.0	1.0

ε	0	1	2	3	4	5	6	7	8	9	10
MSE	11.3	9.5	8.8	9.7	11.2	13.1	15.6	18.2	22.1	27.0	34.3
STD	9.5	7.7	6.8	6.2	6.3	6.0	6.1	6.2	6.6	7.3	8.4
Errors	0.5	0.2	0.1	0.0	0.0	0.0	0.0	0.0	0.0	0.0	0.0
SVs	1.0	0.6	0.4	0.3	0.2	0.1	0.1	0.1	0.1	0.1	0.1

9.6 Applications

Boston Housing Benchmark

Empirical studies using ε-SVR have shown excellent performance on the widely used Boston housing regression benchmark set [529]. Due to Proposition 9.3, the only difference between ν-SVR and standard ε-SVR lies in the fact that different parameters, ε vs. ν, have to be specified a priori. We now describe how the results obtained on this benchmark set change with the adjustment of parameters ε and *nu*. In our experiments, we kept all remaining parameters fixed, with C and the width $2s^2$ in $k(x, x') = \exp(-\|x - x'\|^2/(2s^2))$ chosen as in [482]: we used $2s^2 = 0.3 \cdot N$, where $N = 13$ is the input dimension, and $C/m = 10 \cdot 50$ (the original value of 10 was corrected since in the present case, the maximal y-value is 50 rather than 1). We performed 100 runs, where each time the overall set of 506 examples was randomly split into a training set of $m = 481$ examples and a test set of 25 examples (cf. [529]). Table 9.3 shows that over a wide range of ν (recall that only $0 \leq \nu \leq 1$ makes sense), we obtained performances which are close to the *best* performances that can be achieved using a value of ε selected a priori by looking at the test set.[6] Finally, note that although we did not use validation techniques to select the optimal values for C and $2s^2$, the performances are state of the art: Stitson et al. [529] report an MSE of 7.6 for ε-SVR using ANOVA kernels (cf. (13.13) in Section 13.6), and 11.7 for Bagging regression trees. Table 9.3 also shows that in this real-world application, ν can be used to control the fractions of SVs and errors.

Time Series Prediction

Time series prediction is a field that often uses regression techniques. The stan-

6. For a theoretical analysis of how to select the asymptotically optimal ν for a given noise model, cf. Section 3.4.4.

dard method for writing a time series prediction problem in a regression estimation framework is to consider the time series as a dynamical system and to try to learn an attractor. For many time series $z(t)$, it is the case that if $N \in \mathbb{N}$ and $\tau > 0$ are chosen appropriately, then $z(t)$ can be predicted rather well from $(z(t-\tau), \ldots, z(t-N\tau)) \in \mathbb{R}^N$. We can thus consider a regression problem where the training set consists of the inputs $(z(t-\tau), \ldots, z(t-N\tau))$ and outputs $z(t)$, for a number of different values of t. Several characteristics of time series prediction make the problem hard for this naive regression approach. First, time series are often nonstationary — the regularity underlying the data changes over time. As a consequence, training examples that are generated as described above become less useful if they are taken from the distant past. Second, the different training examples are not iid, which is one of the assumptions on which the statistical learning model underlying SV regression is based.

Nevertheless, excellent results have been obtained using SVR in time series problems [376, 351]. In [376], a record result was reported for a widely studied benchmark dataset from the Santa Fe Institute. The study combined an ε-SVR with a method for segmenting the data, which stem from a time series that switches between different dynamics. SVR using ε-insensitive loss or Huber loss was found to significantly outperform all other results on that benchmark. Another benchmark record, on a different problem, has recently been achieved by [97]. To conclude, we note that SV regression has also successfully been applied in black-box system identification [216].

9.7 Summary

In this chapter, we showed how to generalize the SV algorithm to regression estimation. The generalization retains the sparsity of the solution through use of a SV expansion, exploits the kernel trick, and uses the same regularizer as its pattern recognition and single-class counterparts. We demonstrated how to derive the dual problems for a variety of loss functions, and we described variants of the algorithm. The LP-variant uses a different regularizer, which leads to sparse expansions in terms of patterns which no longer need to lie on the edge of the ε-tube; the ν-variant uses the same regularizer, but makes the loss function adaptive. The latter method has the advantage that the number of outliers and SVs can be controlled by a parameter of the algorithm, and, serendipitously, that the ε-parameter, which can be hard to set, is abolished.

Several interesting topics were omitted from this chapter, such as Density Estimation with SVMs [591, 563]. In this case, we make use of the fact that distribution functions are monotonically increasing, and that their values can be predicted with variable confidence which is adjusted by selecting different values of ε in the loss function. We also omitted the topic of Dictionaries, as introduced in the context of wavelets by [104] to allow a large class of basis functions to be considered simultaneously, for instance kernels with different widths. In the standard SV case, this can only be achieved by defining new kernels as linear combinations of differently scaled kernels. This is due to the fact that once a regularization operator is chosen, the solution minimizing the regularized risk function has to expanded into the corresponding Green's functions of P^*P (Chapter 4). In these cases, a possible way out is to resort to the LP version (Section 9.4). A final area of research left out of this chapter is the problem of estimating the values of functions at given test points, sometimes referred to as transduction [103].

9.8 Problems

9.1 (Product of SVR Lagrange Multipliers [561] •) *Show that for $\varepsilon > 0$, the solution of the SVR dual problem satisfies*

$$\alpha_i \alpha_i^* = 0 \tag{9.58}$$

for all $i = 1, \ldots, m$. Prove it either directly from (9.17), or from the KKT conditions.

Show that for $\varepsilon = 0$, we can always find a solution which satisfies (9.58) and which is optimal, by subtracting $\min\{\alpha_i, \alpha_i^*\}$ from both multipliers.

Give a mechanical interpretation of this result, in terms of forces on the SVs (cf. Chapter 7).

9.2 (SV Regression with Fewer Slack Variables ••) *Prove geometrically that in SV regression, we always have $\xi_i \xi_i^* = 0$. Argue that it is therefore sufficient to just introduce slacks ξ_i and use them in both (9.9) and (9.10). Derive the dual problem and show that it is identical to (9.17) except for a modified constraint $0 \le \alpha_i + \alpha_i^* \le C$. Using the result of Problem 9.1, prove that this problem is equivalent to(9.10).*

Hint: although the number of slacks is half of the original quantity, you still need both α_i and α_i^* to deal with the constraints.

9.3 (ν-Property from the Primal Objective Function •) *Try to understand the ν-property from the primal objective function (9.31). Assume that at the point of the solution, $\varepsilon > 0$, and set $(\partial/\partial\varepsilon)\tau(\mathbf{w}, \varepsilon)$ equal to 0.*

9.4 (One-Sided Regression ••) *Consider a situation where you are seeking a flat function that lies above all of the data points; that is, a regression that only measures errors in one direction. Formulate an SV algorithm by starting with the linear case and later introducing kernels. Generalize to the soft margin case, using the ν-trick. Discuss the applicability of such an algorithm. Also discuss how this algorithm is related to ν-SVR using different values of ν for the two sides of the tube.*

9.5 (Basis Pursuit ••) *Formulate a basis pursuit variant of SV regression, where, starting from zero, SVs are added iteratively in a greedy way (cf. [577]).*

9.6 (SV Regression with Hard Constraints •) *Derive dual programming problems for variants of ε-SVR and ν-SVR where all points are required to lie inside the ε-tubes (in* *other words, without slack variables ξ_i). Discuss how they relate to the problems that can be obtained from the usual duals by letting the error penalization C tend to infinity.*

9.7 (Modulus of Continuity vs. Margin •) *Discuss how the ε-margin (Definition 9.1) is related (albeit not identical) to the* modulus of continuity *of a function: given $\delta > 0$, the latter measures the largest difference in function values which can be obtained using points within a distance δ in E.*

9.8 (Margin of Continuous Functions [481] •) *Give an example of a continuous function f for which $m_\varepsilon(f)$ is zero.*[7]

9.9 (Margin of Uniformly Continuous Functions [481] •) *Prove that $m_\varepsilon(f)$ (Definition 9.1) is positive for all $\varepsilon > 0$ if and only if f is uniformly continuous.*[8]

9.10 (Margin of Lipschitz-Continuous Functions [481] •) *Prove that if f is Lipschitz-continuous, meaning that if there exists some $L > 0$ such that for all $x, x' \in E$, $\|f(x) - f(x')\|_G \leq L \cdot \|x - x'\|_E$, then $m_\varepsilon \geq \frac{2\varepsilon}{L}$.*

9.11 (SVR as Margin Maximization [481] •) *Suppose that E (Definition 9.1) is endowed with a dot product $\langle .,. \rangle$ (generating the norm $\|.\|_E$). Prove that for linear functions (9.2), the margin takes the form $m_\varepsilon(f) = \frac{2\varepsilon}{\|\mathbf{w}\|}$. Argue that for fixed $\varepsilon > 0$, maximizing the margin thus amounts to minimizing $\|\mathbf{w}\|$, as done in SV regression with hard constraints.*

9.12 (ε-Margin and Canonical Hyperplanes [481] •) *Specialize the setting of Problem 9.11 to the case where $\mathcal{X} = \{x_1, \ldots, x_m\}$, and show that $m_1(f) = \frac{2}{\|\mathbf{w}\|}$ is equal to (twice) the margin defined for Vapnik's* canonical hyperplane *(Definition 7.1). Argue that the parameter ε is superfluous in pattern recognition.*

9.13 (SVR for Vector-Valued Functions [481] ∘∘∘) *Assume $E = \mathbb{R}^N$. Consider linear functions $f(x) = Wx + b$, with W being an $N \times N$ matrix, and $b \in \mathbb{R}^N$. Give a lower bound on $m_\varepsilon(f)$ in terms of a matrix norm* compatible *[247] with $\|.\|_E$, using the solution of Problem 9.10.*

Consider the case where the matrix norm is induced by $\|.\|_E$, which is to say there exists a unit vector $\mathbf{z} \in E$ such that $\|W\mathbf{z}\|_E = \|W\|$. Give an exact expression for $m_\varepsilon(f)$.

Show that for the Hilbert-Schmidt norm $\|W\|_2 = \sqrt{\sum_{i,j=1}^N W_{ij}^2}$, which is compatible with the vector norm $\|.\|_2$, the problem of minimizing $\|W\|$ subject to separate constraints for each output dimension separates into N regression problems.

---

7. A function $f : E \to G$ is called *continuous* if for every $\delta > 0$ and $x \in E$, there exists an $\epsilon > 0$ such that *for all* $x' \in E$ satisfying $\|x - x'\|_E < \epsilon$, we have $\|f(x) - f(x')\|_G < \delta$.
8. A function $f : E \to G$ is called *uniformly continuous* if for every $\delta > 0$ there exists an $\epsilon > 0$ such that *for all* $x, x' \in E$ satisfying $\|x - x'\|_E < \epsilon$, we have $\|f(x) - f(x')\|_G < \delta$.

Try to conceive more interesting cases where the regression problems are coupled.[9]

9.14 (Multi-Class Problems ○○○) *Try to generalize $m_\varepsilon(f)$ to multi-class classification problems, and use it to conceive useful margin maximization algorithms for this case.*

9.15 (SV Regression With Overall ε-Insensitive Loss ●●) *Instead of (9.5), consider the objective function*

$$\frac{1}{2}\|\mathbf{w}\|^2 + C \cdot \frac{1}{m}\left|\sum_{i=1}^{m}|y_i - f(\mathbf{x}_i)|\right|_\varepsilon . \tag{9.59}$$

Note that this allows for an overall ℓ_1 error of ε which is "for free." Therefore, poor performance on some of the points can, to some extent, be compensated for by high accuracies on other points (Figure 9.14). Show that this leads to the kernelized dual problem of maximizing

$$W(\boldsymbol{\alpha}^{(*)}, \beta) = \sum_{i=1}^{m}(\alpha_i^* - \alpha_i)y_i - \beta\varepsilon - \frac{1}{2}\sum_{i,j=1}^{m}(\alpha_i^* - \alpha_i)(\alpha_j^* - \alpha_j)k(\mathbf{x}_i, \mathbf{x}_j), \tag{9.60}$$

subject to

$$\sum_{i=1}^{m}(\alpha_i - \alpha_i^*) = 0, \ 0 \le \alpha_i^{(*)} \le \frac{\beta}{m}, \ 0 \le \beta \le C. \tag{9.61}$$

Hint: Introduce slacks $\eta_i^{(*)} \ge 0$ which measure the deviation at each point, and put an ε-insensitive constraint on their sum. Introduce another slack $\xi \ge 0$ for allowing violations of that constraint, and penalize $C\xi$ in the primal objective function.[10]

9.16 (Computation of ε and b in ν-SVR ●) *Suppose i and j are the indices of two points such that $0 < \alpha_i < C/m$ and $0 < \alpha_j^* < C/m$ ("in-bound SVs"). Compute ε and b by exploiting that the KKT conditions imply (9.32) and (9.33) become equalities with $\xi_i = 0$ and $\xi_j^* = 0$.*

9.17 (Parametric ν-SVR Dual ●●) *Derive the dual optimization problem of ν-SVR with parametric loss models (Section 9.5).*

9.18 (Parametric ν-Property ●●●) *Prove Proposition 9.5.*

9.19 (Heteroscedastic Noise ●●●) *Combine ν-SVR using parametric tubes with a variance (e.g., [488]) or quantile estimator (Section 9.3) to construct a SVR algorithm that can deal with heteroscedastic noise.*

---

9. Cf. also Chapter 4, where it is shown that under certain invariance conditions, the regularizer has to act on the output dimensions separately and identically (that is, in a scalar fashion). In particular it turns out that under the assumption of quadratic homogeneity and permutation symmetry, the Hilbert-Schmidt norm is the only admissible norm.
10. This problem builds on joint work with Bob Williamson.

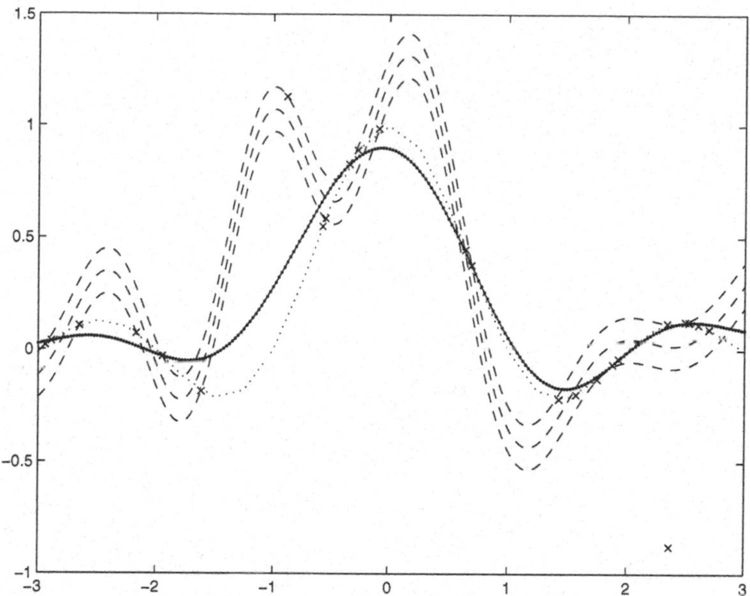

Figure 9.14 Solid line: SVR with overall ε-insensitive loss, dashed lines: standard ε-SVR, with $\pm\varepsilon$ tube. $m = 25$ data points were generated as follows: x-values drawn from uniform distribution over $[-3, 3]$, y-values computed from $y = \sin(\pi x)/(\pi x)$; to create two outliers, the y values of two random points were changed by ± 1. The SV machine parameters were $\varepsilon = 0.1, C = 10000$. For this value of C, which is essentially the hard margin case, the original SVM does a poor job as it tries to follow the outliers. The alternative approach, with a value of ε adjusted such that the overall ℓ_1 error is the same as before, does better, as it is willing to "spend" a large part of its ε on the outliers.

9.20 (SV Regression using ν and ε ∘∘∘) *Try to come up with a formulation of SV regression which uses ν and ε rather than C and ε (ε-SVR) or C and ν (ν-SVR).*

9.21 (ν-SV Regression with Huber's Loss Function ∘∘∘) *Try to generalize ν-SV regression to use loss functions other than the ε-insensitive one, such as the Huber loss, which is quadratic inside the ε-tube and linear outside (cf. Chapter 3).*

Study the relationship between ν and the breakdown point of the estimator [251].

9.22 (Relationship to "Almost Exact Interpolation" ∘∘∘) *Discuss the relationship between SVR and Powell's algorithm for interpolation with thin plate spline kernels [422]. Devise a variant of Powell's algorithm that uses the ε-insensitive loss.*

10 Implementation

This chapter gives an overview of methods for solving the optimization problems specific to Support Vector Machines. Algorithms specific to other settings, such as Kernel PCA and Kernel Feature Analysis (Chapter 14), Regularized Principal Manifolds (Chapter 17), estimation of the support of a distribution (Chapter 8), Kernel Discriminant Analysis (Chapter 15), or Relevance Vector Machines (Chapter 16) can be found in the corresponding chapters. The large amount of code and number of publications available, and the importance of the topic, warrants this separate chapter on Support Vector implementations. Moreover, many of the techniques presented here are prototypical of the solutions of optimization problems in other chapters of this book and can be easily adapted to particular settings.

Overview

Due to the sheer size of the optimization problems arising in the SV setting we must pay special attention to how these problems can be solved efficiently. In Section 10.1 we begin with a description of strategies which can benefit almost all currently available optimization methods, such as universal stopping criteria, caching strategies and restarting rules. Section 10.2 details low rank approximations of the kernel matrix, $K \in \mathbb{R}^{m \times m}$. These methods allow the replacement of K by the outer product $ZZ^\top$ of a "tall and skinny" matrix $Z \in \mathbb{R}^{m \times n}$ where $n \ll m$. The latter can be used directly in algorithms whose speed improves with linear Support Vector Machines (SMO, Interior Point codes, Lagrangian SVM, and Newton's method).

Subsequently we present four classes of algorithms; interior point codes, subset selection, sequential minimization, and iterative methods. Interior Point methods are explained in Section 10.3. They are some of the most reliable methods for moderate problem sizes, yet their implementation is not trivial. Subset selection methods, as in Section 10.4, act as meta-algorithms on top of a basic optimization algorithm by carving out sets of variables on which the actual optimization takes place. Sequential Minimal Optimization, presented in Section 10.5, is a special case thereof. Due to the choice of only two variables at a time the restricted optimization problem can be solved analytically which obviating the need for an underlying base optimizer. Finally, iterative methods such as online learning, gradient descent, and Lagrangian Support Vector Machines are described in Section 10.6. Figure 10.1 gives a rough overview describing under which conditions which optimization algorithm is recommended.

Prerequisites

This chapter is intended for readers interested in implementing an SVM themselves. Consequently we assume that the reader is familiar with the basic concepts of both optimization (Chapter 6) and SV estimation (Chapters 1, 7, and 9).

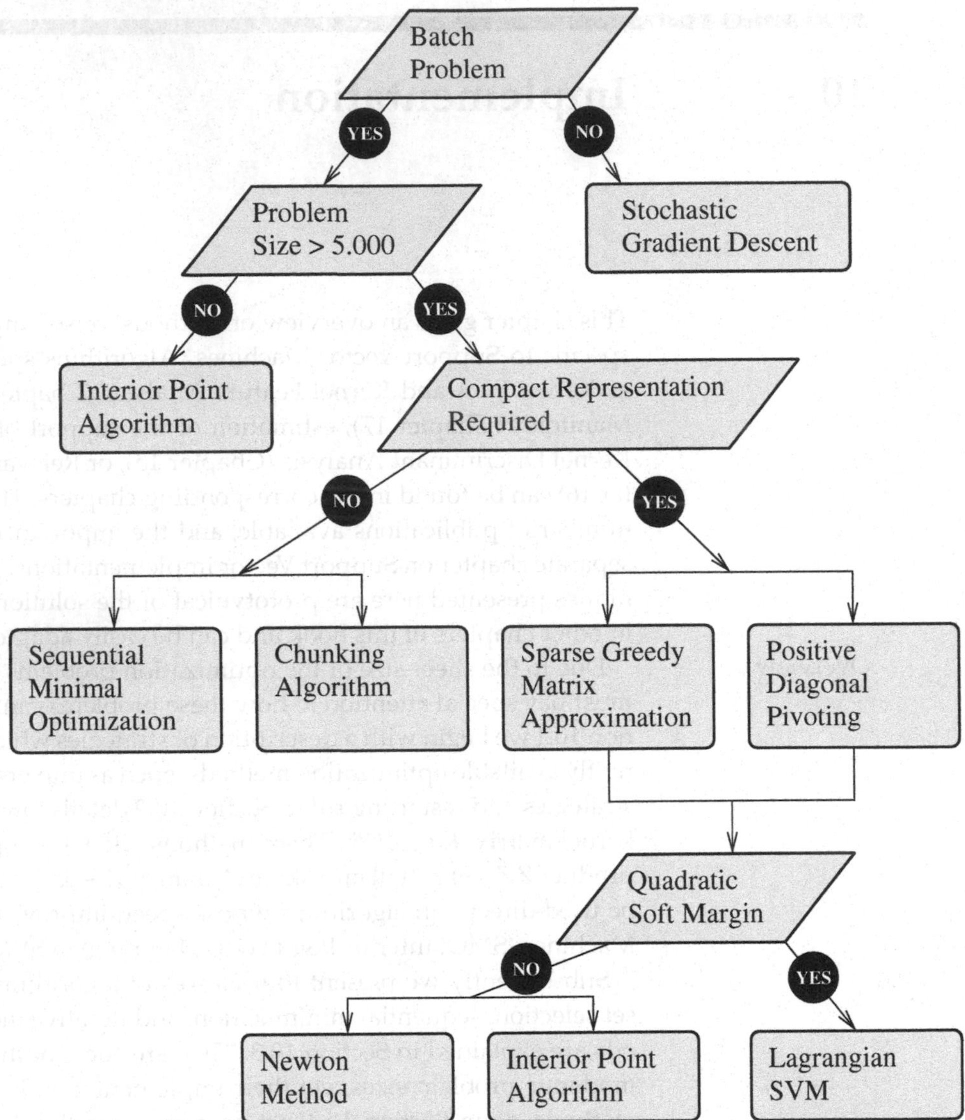

Figure 10.1 A decision tree for selecting suitable optimization algorithms. Most kernel learning problems will be batch ones (for the online setting see Section 10.6.3). For small and medium sized problems, that is as long as the kernel matrix fits into main memory, an interior point code is recommended, since it produces optima of very high quality. For larger problems approximations are required which leads to sparse greedy approximation schemes or other reduced set methods. An alternative strategy, which is particularly attractive if the size of the final kernel expansion is not important, can be found in subset selection methods such as chunking and SMO.

Knowledge of Lagrangians, duality, and optimality conditions (Section 6.3.1) is required to understand both the stopping rules in more detail and the section on interior point methods. Essentially, this chapter builds on the general exposition of Section 6.4. In addition, some of the methods from subset approximation rely on the randomized optimization concepts of Section 6.5. A basic understanding of fundamental concepts in numerical analysis, for example the notion of a Cholesky decomposition, will also prove useful, yet it is not an essential requirement. See textbooks [530, 247, 207, 46] for more on this topic.

Notation Issues

Note that in this chapter we will alternate between the ν and the C-formulation (see Section 7.5), for different algorithms. This is due to the fact that some algorithms are not capable of treating the ν-formulation efficiently. Furthermore, the C-formulation differs from the one of minimizing the regularized risk functional insofar as we minimize

$$C \sum_{i=1}^{m} c(x_i, y_i, f(x_i)) + \Omega[f] \tag{10.1}$$

rather than

$$\frac{1}{m} \sum_{i=1}^{m} c(x_i, y_i, f(x_i)) + \lambda\Omega[f]. \tag{10.2}$$

We can transform one setting into the other via $C = \frac{1}{\lambda m}$. The C notation is used in order to be consistent with the published literature on SV optimization algorithms.

10.1 Tricks of the Trade

We start with an overview of useful "tricks,"; modifications from which almost any algorithm will benefit. For instance, techniques which are useful for speeding up training significantly or which determine when the algorithm should be stopped.

This section is intended both for the practitioner who would like to improve an existing SV algorithm and also for readers new to SV optimization, since most of the tools developed prove useful in the optimization equations later. We present three tricks; a practical stopping criterion, a restart method, and an overview of caching strategies.

10.1.1 Stopping Criterion

It would be ideal if we always were able to obtain the solution by optimization methods (e.g., from Section 6.4). Unfortunately, due to the size of the problem, this is often not possible and we must limit ourselves to *approximating* the solution by an iterative strategy.

Several stopping criteria have been suggested regarding when to stop training a Support Vector Machine. Some of these focus mainly on the precision of the Lagrange multipliers α_i [266, 409, 494], whereas others [514, 459] use the proximity of the values of the primal and dual objective functions. Yet others stop simply when no further improvement is made [398].

Before we develop a stopping criterion recall that ultimately we want to find a solution $f(x) = \langle \mathbf{w}, \Phi(x) \rangle + b$ that minimizes one of the regularized risk functionals described below. In the case of classification,

$$\begin{array}{llcl} \underset{\mathbf{w},\xi}{\text{minimize}} & C\sum_{i=1}^{m} c(\xi_i) + \frac{1}{2}\|\mathbf{w}\|^2 & & \sum_{i=1}^{m} c(\xi_i) + \frac{1}{2}\|\mathbf{w}\|^2 - \nu\rho \\ \text{subject to} & y_i f(x_i) \geq 1 - \xi_i & \text{or} & y_i f(x_i) \geq \rho - \xi_i \\ & \xi_i \geq 0 & & \xi_i \geq 0, \rho \in \mathbb{R} \end{array} \tag{10.3}$$

(the right half of the equations describes the analogous setting with the ν-parameter), similarly, for regression,

$$\begin{array}{llcl} \underset{\mathbf{w},\xi}{\text{minimize}} & C\sum_{i=1}^{m} c(\xi_i) + c(\xi_i^*) + \frac{1}{2}\|\mathbf{w}\|^2 & & C\sum_{i=1}^{m} c(\xi_i) + c(\xi_i^*) + \frac{1}{2}\|\mathbf{w}\|^2 - \nu\epsilon \\ \text{subject to} & f(x_i) \geq y_i - \epsilon - \xi_i & \text{or} & f(x_i) \geq y_i - \epsilon - \xi_i \\ & f(x_i) \leq y_i + \epsilon + \xi_i^* & & f(x_i) \leq y_i + \epsilon + \xi_i^* \\ & \xi_i, \xi_i^* \geq 0 & & \xi_i, \xi_i^* \geq 0, \epsilon \in \mathbb{R} \end{array} \tag{10.4}$$

This means that ultimately not the Lagrange multipliers α_i but rather $\mathbf{w}$, or only the value of the primal objective function, matters. Thus, algorithms [266, 290, 291, 398] which rely on the assumption that proximity to the optimal parameters will ensure a good solution may not be using an optimal stopping criterion. In particular, such a criterion may sometimes be overly conservative, especially if the influence of individual parameters on the final estimate is negligible. For instance, assume that we have a linear dependency in the dual objective function. Then there exists a linear subspace of parameters which would all be suitable solutions, leading to identical vectors $\mathbf{w}$. Therefore, convergence within this subspace may not occur and, even if it does, it would not be relevant to the quality of the solution.

Proximity in Parameters $\neq$ Proximity in Solution

What we would prefer to have is a way of bounding the distance between the objective function at the current solution f and at f_{opt}. Since (10.3) and (10.4) are both constrained optimization problems we may make use of Theorem 6.27 and lower bound the values of (10.3) and (10.4) via the KKT Gap. The advantage is that we do not have to know the optimal value in order to assess the quality of the approximate solution. The following Proposition formalizes this connection.

Proposition 10.1 (KKT-Gap for Support Vector Machines) *Denote by f the (possibly not optimal) estimate obtained during a minimizing procedure of the optimization problem (10.3) or (10.4) derived from the regularized risk functional $R_{\text{reg}}[f]$. Further, denote by f_{opt} the minimizer of $R_{\text{reg}}[f]$. Then under the condition of dual feasible variables (namely that the equality and box constraints are satisfied), the following inequality holds:*

$$R_{\text{reg}}[f] \geq R_{\text{reg}}[f^*] \geq R_{\text{reg}}[f] - \frac{1}{Cm}\text{Gap}[f] \tag{10.5}$$

where Gap$[f]$ *is defined as follows:*

1. *In the case of classification with C-parametrization*

$$\begin{aligned}\text{Gap}[f] &= \sum_{j=1}^{m} \max(0, 1 - y_j f(x_j)) C \partial_{\xi_j} \tilde{c}(\max(0, 1 - y_j f(x_j))) + \alpha_j (y_j f(x_j) - 1) \\ &= \sum_{j=1}^{m} C \max(0, 1 - y_j f(x_j)) + \alpha_j (y_j f(x_j) - 1)\end{aligned} \tag{10.6}$$

2. *For classification in the ν-formulation*

$$\text{Gap}[f] = \sum_{j=1}^{m} \max(0, \rho - y_j f(x_j)) + \alpha_j (y_j f(x_j) - \rho) \tag{10.7}$$

3. *For ε-regression, where* $\xi_j = \max(0, y_i - f(x_i) - \varepsilon)$ *and* $\xi_j^* = \max(0, f(x_i) - y_i - \varepsilon)$,

$$\begin{aligned}\text{Gap}[f] &= \sum_{j=1}^{m} \xi_j C \partial_{\xi_j} \tilde{c}(\xi_j) + \xi_j^* C \partial_{\xi_j^*} \tilde{c}(\xi_j^*) + \alpha_j (\varepsilon + f(x_j) - y_j) + \alpha_j^* (\varepsilon - f(x_j) + y_j) \\ &= \sum_{j=1}^{m} C \xi_j + C \xi_j^* + \alpha_j (\varepsilon + f(x_j) - y_j) + \alpha_j^* (\varepsilon - f(x_j) + y_j)\end{aligned} \tag{10.8}$$

4. *In the ν-formulation the gap is identical to (10.8), with the only difference being that $C = 1$ and that ε is a variable of the optimization problem.*

Here $\rho = 1$ is a constant in the C-formulation and $C = 1$ is one in the ν-formulation. For regression we denote by $\tilde{c}(\xi)$ the nonzero branch of $c(x_i, y_i, f(x_i))$ which for the ε-insensitive regression setting becomes $\tilde{c}(\xi) = \xi$. Finally, note that in the ν-regression formulation, ε is a variable.

Stopping Criterion and Significant Number of Figures

Such a lower bound on the minimum of the objective function has the added benefit that it can be used to devise a stopping criterion. We simply use the same strategy as in interior point codes (Section 6.4.4) and stop when the relative size of the gap is below some threshold ϵ, that is, if

$$\text{Gap}[f] \leq \epsilon \frac{|R_{\text{reg}}[f]| + |R_{\text{reg}}[f] - \text{Gap}|}{2}. \tag{10.9}$$

Proof All we must do is apply Theorem 6.27 by rewriting (6.60) in terms of the currently used expressions and subsequently find good values for the variables that have not been specified explicitly. This will show that the size of the KKT-gap is given by (10.6), (10.7), and (10.8).

The first thing to note is that free variables do not contribute directly to the size of the KKT gap provided the corresponding equality constraints in the dual optimization problem are satisfied. Therefore it is sufficient to give the proof only for the C-parametrization — the ν-parametrization simply uses an additional equality constraint due to an extra free variable.

Rewriting (6.60) in terms of the SV optimization problem means that now $\mathbf{w}$ and ξ are the *variables* of the optimization problem and x_i, y_i are merely constants. We review the constraints,

$$0 \;\geq\; \rho - \xi_i - y_i f(x_i) \quad \text{and } 0 \;\geq\; -\xi_i \quad \text{(classification)} \tag{10.10}$$

$$\begin{aligned} 0 &\geq -f(x_i) + y_i - \epsilon - \xi_i \quad \text{and } 0 \geq -\xi_i \quad \text{(regression)} \\ 0 &\geq +f(x_i) - y_i - \epsilon - \xi_i^* \quad \text{and } 0 \geq -\xi_i^* \end{aligned} \tag{10.11}$$

Since the optimizations take place in dual space (the space of the corresponding Lagrange multipliers α_i, η_i), we can use the latter directly in our bound. What remains to be done is to find ξ_i, since f is determined by α_i. The constraint imposed on ξ_i is that f and the corresponding α_i satisfy the dual feasibility constraints (6.53). We obtain

$$\begin{aligned} \partial_{\xi_j} L(f, \xi, \alpha, \eta) &= \partial_{\xi_j} \left(C \sum_{i=1}^{m} \tilde{c}(\xi_i) + \frac{1}{2}\|\mathbf{w}\|^2 + \sum_{i=1}^{m} \alpha_i \left(1 - \xi_i - y_i f(x_i)\right) - \eta_i \xi_i \right) \\ &= C \partial_{\xi_j} \tilde{c}(\xi_j) - \alpha_j - \eta_j = 0 \end{aligned} \tag{10.12}$$

for classification. Now we have to choose η_j, ξ_j such that $C\partial_{\xi_j}\tilde{c}(\xi_j) = \alpha_j + \eta_j$ is satisfied. At the same time we would like to obtain good lower bounds. Hence we must choose the parameters in such a way that the KKT gap (6.53) is minimal, that is, all the terms

$$\mathrm{KKT}_j := \eta_j \xi_j + \alpha_j \left(y_j f(x_j) - 1 + \xi_j\right) \tag{10.13}$$

$$= \left(C \partial_{\xi_j} \tilde{c}\left(\xi_j\right) - \alpha_j\right) \xi_j + \alpha_j \left(y_j f(x_j) - 1 + \xi_j\right) \tag{10.14}$$

$$= \xi_j C \partial_{\xi_j} \tilde{c}(\xi_j) + \alpha_j \left(y_j f(x_j) - 1\right) \tag{10.15}$$

are minimized. The second term is independent of ξ_j and the first term is monotonically increasing with ξ_j (since $\tilde{c}$ is convex). The smallest value for ξ_j is given by (10.10). Combining of these two constraints gives

$$\xi_j = \max(0, 1 - y_j f(x_j)). \tag{10.16}$$

Together (10.16), (10.13), and (6.53) prove the bound for classification. Finally, substituting $\tilde{c}(\xi_j) = \xi_j$ (the soft-margin loss function [40, 111]) yields (10.6). For regression we proceed analogously. The optimality criteria for ξ_j, ξ_j^* and η_j, η_j^* are

$$C\partial_{\xi_j}\tilde{c}(\xi_j) - \alpha_j - \eta_j = 0 \text{ and } C\partial_{\xi_j^*}\tilde{c}(\xi_j^*) - \alpha_j^* - \eta_j^* = 0 \tag{10.17}$$

Explicit Optimization of Dual Variables

In addition, from (6.53), we obtain

$$\mathrm{KKT}_j := \eta_j \xi_j + \eta_j^* \xi_j^* + \alpha_j \left(\varepsilon + \xi_j + f(x_j) - y_j\right) + \alpha_j^* \left(\varepsilon + \xi_j^* - f(x_j) + y_j\right) \tag{10.18}$$

$$= \xi_j C \partial_{\xi_j} c(\xi_j) + \xi_j^* C \partial_{\xi_j^*} c(\xi_j) + \alpha_j(\varepsilon + f(x_j) - y_j) + \alpha_j(\varepsilon + y_j - f(x_j)). \tag{10.19}$$

By similar reasoning as before we can see that the optimal ξ_j is given by

$$\xi_j = \max(0, y_i - f(x_i) - \varepsilon) \text{ and } \xi_j^* = \max(0, f(x_i) - y_i - \varepsilon) \tag{10.20}$$

which completes the proof. ■

The advantage of (10.6) and (10.8) is that they can be computed in $O(m)$ time provided that the function values $f(x_i)$ are already known. This means that convergence checking can be done for almost no additional cost with respect to the overall cost of the training algorithm.

Non-monotonic Gap Size

An important thing to remember is that for algorithms which minimize only the dual or only the primal objective function the size of the gap may *grow* between optimization steps. This is since an improvement in the primal objective does not necessarily imply an improvement in the dual and vice versa. One way to overcome this problem (besides a redesign of the optimization algorithm which may be out of question in most cases) is to note that it immediately follows from (10.5) that

$$\min_i R_{\text{reg}}[f_i] \geq R_{\text{reg}}[f_{\text{opt}}] \geq \max_i \left[R_{\text{reg}}[f_i] - \text{Gap}[f_i]\right] \quad (10.21)$$

where f_i is the estimate at iteration i. In many algorithms such as SMO, where the dual gap can fluctuate considerably, this leads to much improved bounds on $R_{\text{reg}}[f_{\text{opt}}]$ compared to (10.5). In experiments a gap-optimal choice of b led to decreased, but still existing, fluctuations. See also [291, 494] for details how such an optimal value of b can be found.

10.1.2 Restarting with Different Parameters

Quite often we must train a Support Vector Machine for more than one specific parameter setting. In such cases it is beneficial to re-use the solution obtained for one specific parameter setting in finding the remaining ones. In particular, situations involving different choices of regularization parameter or different kernel widths benefit significantly from this parameter re-use as opposed to starting from $f = 0$. Let us analyze the situation in more detail.

Restarting for C: Denote by f_C the minimizer of the regularized risk functional (slightly modified to account for C rather than for λ)

$$R_{\text{reg}}[f, C] := C \sum_{i=1}^{m} c(x_i, y_i, f(x_i)) + \Omega[f]. \quad (10.22)$$

By construction

$$R_{\text{reg}}[f_C, C'] \geq R_{\text{reg}}[f_{C'}, C'] \geq R_{\text{reg}}[f_{C'}, C] \geq R_{\text{reg}}[f_C, C] \text{ for all } C' > C. \quad (10.23)$$

The first inequality follows from the fact that $f_{C'}$ is the minimizer of $R_{\text{reg}}[f, C']$. The second inequality is a direct consequence of $C' > C$, and, finally, the third inequality is due to the optimality of f_C. Additionally, we conclude from (10.22) that

$$R_{\text{reg}}[f_{C'}, C'] \leq R_{\text{reg}}[f_C, C] + (C' - C)mR_{\text{emp}}[f_C] \leq \frac{C'}{C} R_{\text{reg}}[f_C, C] \quad (10.24)$$

and thus

$$\frac{C}{C'} R_{\text{reg}}[f_{C'}, C'] \leq R_{\text{reg}}[f_C, C] \leq R_{\text{reg}}[f_{C'}, C']. \quad (10.25)$$

In other words, changes in the regularized risk functional $R_{\text{reg}}[f, C]$ are bounded by the changes in C. This has two implications; first, it does not make sense to use an overly fine grid in C when looking for minima of $R_{\text{reg}}[f]$. Second, (10.23) shows that for changes of C into C' which are not too large it is beneficial to re-use f_C rather than to restart from $f = 0$.

Decreasing C

In practice it is often advantageous to start with a solution for large C and keep on increasing the regularization (decrease C). This has the effect that initially most of the α_i, α_i^* will be unconstrained. Subsequently, all the variables that have been found to be constrained will typically tend to stay that way. This can dramatically speed up the training phase by up to a factor of 20, since the algorithm can focus on unconstrained variables only. See [502], among others, for experimental details. In order to satisfy the dual constraints it is convenient to rescale the Lagrange multipliers in accordance with the change in C. This means we rescale each coefficient by $\alpha_i' = \frac{C'}{C}\alpha_i$, where α_i' are the start values when training with C' instead of C. Such a modification leaves the summation constraints intact. See also [288] for further details on how to adjust parameters for changed values of C.

Restarting for σ: Gaussian RBF kernels (2.68) are popular choices for Support Vector Machines. Here one problem is to adapt the width σ of the kernel suitably. In [123] it is shown that for the soft-margin loss function the minimizer (and its RKHS norm) of the regularized risk is a smooth function of σ.

More generally, if the regularization operator only changes smoothly, we can employ similar reasoning to that above. Note that in the current case not only the regularizer but also f itself changes (since we only have a representation of f via α_i). Yet, unless the change in σ is too large, the value of the regularized risk functional will be smaller than for the default guess $f = 0$, hence it is advantageous to re-use the old parameters α_i, b.

10.1.3 Caching

A simple and useful trick is to store parts of the kernel matrix K_{ij}, or also $f(x_i)$, for future use when storage of the whole kernel matrix K is impossible due to memory constraints. We have to distinguish between different techniques.

Row Cache: This is one of the easiest techniques to implement. Usually we allocate as much space for an $m_c \times m$ matrix as memory is available. Simple caching strategies as LRU (least recently used — keep only the most recently used rows of K in the cache and update the oldest rows first) can provide an 80% – 90% hit rate (= fraction of elements found in the cache) with a cache size of 10% of the original matrix. See, for example, [266, 309, 494, 134] for details. Row cache strategies work best for sequential update and subset selection methods such as SMO (see Section 10.5). Moreover, we can expect significant improvement via row cache strategies if the number of non-bound Lagrange multipliers $\alpha_i \in (0, C)$ is small, since these are the parameters revisited many times.

Hit Rate

Element Cache: A more fine-grained caching strategy would store individual elements of K rather than entire rows or columns. This has the additional advantage that for sparse solutions, where many $\alpha_i = 0$, possibly all relevant entries K_{ij} can be cached [172]. The downside is that the organization of the cache, as, for example, a list, is considerably more complex and that this overhead[1] may easily outweigh the improvement in the hit rate in terms of kernel entries.

Function Cache: If only very few Lagrange Multipliers α_i change per iteration step, we may update $f(x_j)$ (which is useful for the KKT stopping criteria described in Section 10.1.1) cheaply.

Assume that a set $\alpha_1, \ldots, \alpha_n$ of Lagrange multipliers is changed (without loss of generality we pick the first n). Then $f(x_j)$ can be rewritten as

$$f^{\text{new}}(x_j) = \sum_{i=1}^{m} \alpha_i^{\text{new}} k(x_i, x_j) + b = f^{\text{old}}(x_j) + \left[\sum_{i=1}^{n} (\alpha_i^{\text{new}} - \alpha_i^{\text{old}}) k(x_i, x_j)\right]. \tag{10.26}$$

Numerical Precision

Note that in order to prevent numerical instabilities building up too quickly, it is advisable to update (10.26) in the way displayed rather than computing

$$f^{\text{old}}(x_j) + \sum_{i=1}^{n} \alpha_i^{\text{new}} k(x_i, x_j) - \sum_{i=1}^{n} \alpha_i^{\text{old}} k(x_i, x_j).$$

After several updates, depending on the machine precision, it is best to recalculate $f(x_j)$ from scratch.

10.1.4 Shrinking the Training Set

While it may not always be possible to carry out optimization on a subset of patterns right from the beginning, we may, as the optimization progresses, drop the patterns for which the corresponding Lagrange multipliers will end up being constrained to their upper or lower limits.

If we discard those patterns x_i with $\alpha_i = 0$ this amounts to effectively reducing the training set (see also Section 10.4.2 for details and equations). This is in agreement with the idea that only the Support Vectors will influence the decision functions. There exist several implementations which use such subset selection heuristics to improve training time [559, 111, 561, 463, 409, 172].

We describe another example of subset methods in Section 10.3 where we apply subset selection to interior point methods. In a nutshell the idea is that with decreasing KKT terms (10.13) either the constraint must be satisfied and the corresponding Lagrange multiplier vanishes or the constraint must be met exactly.

Sticky Patterns

Finally, assigning *sticky*-flags (cf. [85]) to variables at the boundaries also improves optimization. This means that once a variable is determined to be bound constrained it will remain fixed for the next few iterations. This heuristic avoids oscillatory behavior during the solution process.

1. Modern microprocessor architectures are largely limited by their memory bandwidth which means that an increased hardware cache miss rate due to non-contiguous storage of the matrix elements may affect performance quite dramatically. Furthermore such a strategy will also lead to paging operations of the operating system.

10.2 Sparse Greedy Matrix Approximation

In the following we describe what can be thought of as another useful trick. The practical significance warrants a more detailed description however. The reader only interested in the basic optimization algorithms may skip this section.

Low Dimensional Approximation is Sufficient

Sparse greedy approximation techniques are based on the observation that typically the matrix K has many small eigenvalues which could easily be removed without sacrificing too much precision.[2] This suggests that we could possibly find a subset of basis functions $k(x_i, x)$ which would minimize the regularized risk functional $R_{\text{reg}}[f]$ almost as well as the full expansion required by the Representer Theorem (Th. 4.2). This topic will be discussed in more detail in Chapter 18.

10.2.1 Sparse Approximations

In one way or another, most kernel algorithms have to deal with the kernel matrix K which is of size $m \times m$. Unfortunately the cost of computing or of storing the latter increases with $O(m^2)$ and the cost of evaluating the solution (sometimes referred to as the *prediction*) increases with $O(m)$. Hence, one idea is to pick some functions $k(x_1, \cdot), \ldots, k(x_n, \cdot)$ (for notational convenience we chose the first n, but this assumption will be dropped at a later stage) with $n \ll m$ such that we can approximate every single $k(x_i, \cdot)$ by a linear combination of $k(x_1, \cdot), \ldots, k(x_n, \cdot)$. Without loss of generality we assume that $x_1, \ldots, x_n$ are the first n patterns of the set $\{x_1, \ldots, x_m\}$. We approximate[3]

$$k(x_i, \cdot) \approx \tilde{k}_i(\cdot) := \sum_{j=1}^{n} \alpha_{ij} k(x_j, \cdot). \tag{10.27}$$

Approximation in Feature Space

As an approximation criterion we choose proximity in the Reproducing Kernel Hilbert Space $\mathcal{H}$, hence we choose α_{ij} such that the approximation error

$$\left\| k(x_i) - \sum_{j=1}^{n} \alpha_{ij} k(x_j, \cdot) \right\|_{\mathcal{H}}^2 = k(x_i, x_i) - 2 \sum_{j=1}^{n} \alpha_{ij} k(x_i, x_j) + \sum_{j,l=1}^{n} \alpha_{ij} \alpha_{il} k(x_j, x_l)$$

is minimized. An alternative would be to approximate the values of $k(x_i, \cdot)$ on X directly. The computational cost of doing the latter is much higher however (see Problem 10.4 and [514] for details). Since we wish to optimize the overall approximation quality we have to minimize the total approximation error for all i,

2. This can be seen from the results in Table 14.1.
3. Likewise we could formalize the problem as one of approximating patterns mapped into feature space; we approximate $\Phi(x_i)$ by $\tilde{\Phi}(x_i) := \sum_{i=1}^{m} \alpha_{ij} \Phi(x_j)$ and measure the goodness-of-fit via $\|\Phi(x_i) - \tilde{\Phi}(x_i)\|^2$. For a streamlined notation and to emphasize to fact that we are approximating a *function space* we will, however, use the RKHS notation.

giving

$$\mathrm{Err}(\alpha) := \sum_{i=1}^{m} \|k(x_i, \cdot) - \tilde{k}_i\|_{\mathcal{H}}^2 = \sum_{i=1}^{m} K_{ii} - 2\sum_{j=1}^{n} \alpha_{ij} K_{ij} + \sum_{j,j'=1}^{n} \alpha_{ij}\alpha_{ij'} K_{jj'}. \tag{10.28}$$

Here we use (as before) $K_{ij} := k(x_i, x_j)$. Since $\mathrm{Err}(\alpha)$ is a convex quadratic function in α, all we must do is set the first derivative of $\mathrm{Err}(\alpha)$ to zero in order to find the minimizer of $\mathrm{Err}(\alpha)$. Note that in the present case $\alpha \in \mathbb{R}^{m\times n}$ is a *matrix* and therefore, with some abuse of notation, we will use ∂_α to denote the derivative with respect to all matrix elements. The minimizer of (10.28) satisfies

$$\partial_\alpha \mathrm{Err}(\alpha) = -2K^{mn} + 2\alpha K^{nn} = 0. \tag{10.29}$$

Here K^{mn} is an $m \times n$ matrix with $K^{mn}_{ij} = K_{ij}$, so K^{mn} is the left sub-matrix of K. Likewise $K^{nn} \in \mathbb{R}^{n\times n}$ is the upper left sub-matrix of K. This leads to

$$\alpha_{\mathrm{opt}} = K^{mn}(K^{nn})^{-1} \tag{10.30}$$

We can exploit this property in order to determine the minimal approximation error $\mathrm{Err}(\alpha_{\mathrm{opt}})$ and properties of the matrix $\tilde{K}$ where $\tilde{K}_{ij} = \langle \tilde{k}_i, \tilde{k}_j \rangle$. The following theorem holds.

Theorem 10.2 (Properties of $\tilde{k}$ and $\tilde{K}$) *With the above definitions and (10.30), the matrices K, $\tilde{K}$, and $K - \tilde{K}$ are positive definite and*

$$\mathrm{Err}(\alpha_{\mathrm{opt}}) = \mathrm{tr}\, K - \mathrm{tr}\, \tilde{K}, \tag{10.31}$$

where $\tilde{K} = K^{mn}(K^{nn})^{-1}(K^{mn})^\top = \alpha(K^{mn})^\top = \alpha K^{nn}\alpha^\top$.

This means that we have an approximation of K in such a way that $\tilde{K}$ is strictly smaller than K (since $K - \tilde{K}$ is positive definite as well) and, furthermore, that the approximation error in terms of $\mathcal{H}$ can be computed cheaply by finding $\mathrm{tr}\, K - \mathrm{tr}\, \tilde{K}$, that is by looking at only m elements of the $m \times m$ matrix K and $\tilde{K}$.

Bounding Norms

Finally, we obtain a bound on the operator norm of $K - \tilde{K}$ by computing the trace of the difference, since the trace is the sum of all eigenvalues, and the latter are nonnegative for positive matrices. In particular, for positive definite matrices K (and their eigenvalues λ_i) we have

$$\|K\| = \max_i \lambda_i \leq \|K\|_{\mathrm{Frob}} = \mathrm{tr}\, KK^\top = \left(\sum_{i=1}^{m} \lambda_i^2\right)^{\frac{1}{2}} \leq \mathrm{tr}\, K = \sum_{i=1}^{m} \lambda_i. \tag{10.32}$$

Note that the Frobenius norm $\|K\|_{\mathrm{Frob}}$ is simply the 2-norm of all coefficients of K. (For symmetric matrices we may decompose K into its eigensystem via $K = U^\top \Lambda U$ where U is an orthogonal matrix and Λ is a diagonal matrix. This allows us to write $\mathrm{tr}\, KK^\top = \mathrm{tr}\, U^\top \Lambda U U^\top \Lambda U = \mathrm{tr}\, \Lambda^2$.)

Proof We prove the functional form of $\tilde{K}$ first. By construction we have

$$\tilde{K}_{ij} = \langle \tilde{k}_i, \tilde{k}_j \rangle = \sum_{l,l'=1}^{n} \alpha_{il}\alpha_{jl'} \langle k(x_l, \cdot), k(x_{l'}, \cdot) \rangle = \sum_{l,l'=1}^{n} \alpha_{il}\alpha_{jl'} K_{ll'} \tag{10.33}$$

and, therefore, by construction of α

$$\tilde{K} = \alpha K^{nn} \alpha^\top = K^{mn}(K^{nn})^{-1}K^{nn}(K^{nn})^{-1}(K^{mn})^\top = K^{mn}(K^{nn})^{-1}(K^{mn})^\top.$$

Next note that for optimal α we have (with $\mathbf{k}_i$ as a shorthand for the vector $(K_{i1}, \ldots, K_{in})$)

$$\|k(x_i, \cdot) - \tilde{k}_i\|^2_{\mathcal{H}} = K_{ii} - 2\mathbf{k}_i^\top (K^{nn})^{-1}\mathbf{k}_i + \mathbf{k}_i^\top (K^{nn})^{-1}K^{nn}(K^{nn})^{-1}\mathbf{k}_i \tag{10.34}$$

$$= K_{ii} - \mathbf{k}_i^\top (K^{nn})^{-1}\mathbf{k}_i = K_{ii} - \tilde{K}_{ii}. \tag{10.35}$$

Summation over i proves the first part of (10.31). What remains is to prove positive definiteness of $K, \tilde{K}$, and $K - \tilde{K}$. As Gram matrices both K and $\tilde{K}$ are positive definite. To prove that $K - \tilde{K}$ is also positive definite we show that

$$K - \tilde{K} = \bar{K} \text{ where } \bar{K}_{ij} := \langle k(x_i, \cdot) - \tilde{k}_i(\cdot), k(x_j, \cdot) - \tilde{k}_j(\cdot)\rangle \tag{10.36}$$

All we have to do is substitute the optimal value of α, i.e., $\alpha = K^{mn}(K^{nn})^{-1}$ into the definition of $\bar{K}$ to obtain

$$\bar{K} = K - 2K^{mn}\alpha + \alpha K^{nn}\alpha^\top = K - K^{mn}(K^{nn})^{-1}K^{mn\top} = K - \tilde{K}. \tag{10.37}$$

■

Note that (10.36) also means that $\langle k(x_i, \cdot) - \tilde{k}_i(\cdot), k(x_j, \cdot) - \tilde{k}_j(\cdot)\rangle = \langle k(x_i, \cdot), k(x_j, \cdot)\rangle - \langle \tilde{k}_i(\cdot), \tilde{k}_j(\cdot)\rangle$.

10.2.2 Iterative Methods and Random Sets

While (10.31) can tell us how well we are able to approximate a set of m kernel functions $k(x_i, \cdot)$ by a subset of size n, it cannot be used to *predict* how large n should be. Let us first assume that we choose to pick the subset of kernel functions $k(x_i, \cdot)$ at random to approximate the full set, as suggested in the context of Gaussian Processes [603]. We will present a more efficient method of choosing the kernel functions in the next section but, for the moment, assume that the selection process is completely random.

Rank-1 Update

Given that, for some n, we have already computed the values of $(K^{nn})^{-1}$ and $\alpha_{\text{opt}} = (K^{nn})^{-1}K^{mn}$. For an additional kernel function, say $k(x_{n+1}, \cdot)$ we need to find a way to compute the values of α_{opt} and $(K^{n+1,n+1})^{-1}$ efficiently (since the difference between K^{nn} and $K^{n+1,n+1}$ is only of rank 1 such a change is commonly referred to as a rank-1 update). We may either do this directly or use a Cholesky decomposition for increased numerical stability. For details on the latter strategy see [423, 530, 247] and Problem 10.5.

Denote by $\mathbf{k} \in \mathbb{R}^n$ the upper right vector $(K_{n+1,1}, \ldots, K_{n+1,n})$ of the matrix $K^{n+1,n+1} \in \mathbb{R}^{(n+1)\times(n+1)}$ to be inverted, and $\kappa := K_{n+1,n+1}$. Then we have

$$\left(K^{n+1,n+1}\right)^{-1} = \begin{bmatrix} K^{nn} & \mathbf{k}^\top \\ \mathbf{k} & \kappa \end{bmatrix}^{-1} = \begin{bmatrix} (K^{nn})^{-1} + \eta^{-1}\mathbf{v}\mathbf{v}^\top & -\eta^{-1}\mathbf{v} \\ -\eta^{-1}\mathbf{v}^\top & \eta^{-1} \end{bmatrix} \tag{10.38}$$

where $\eta = (\kappa - \mathbf{k}^\top (K^{nn})^{-1}\mathbf{k})$ and $\mathbf{v} = ((K^{nn})^{-1}\mathbf{k})$. This means that computing $(K^{n+1,n+1})^{-1}$ costs $O(n^2)$ operations once $(K^{nn})^{-1}$ is known. Next we must update α. Splitting $K^{m,n+1}$ into K^{mn} and $\bar{\mathbf{k}} = (K_{1,n+1}, \ldots K_{m,n+1})$ yields

$$\alpha = K^{m,n+1}\left(K^{n+1,n+1}\right)^{-1} \tag{10.39}$$

$$= \left[K^{mn}(K^{nn})^{-1} + \eta^{-1}\left[K^{mn}\mathbf{v} - \bar{\mathbf{k}}\right]\mathbf{v}^\top, -\eta^{-1}\left[K^{mn}\mathbf{v} - \bar{\mathbf{k}}\right]\right]. \tag{10.40}$$

Computing (10.39) involves $O(mn)$ operations since $K^{mn}(K^{nn})^{-1}$ is the old value of α for the case of n basis functions and the most expensive part of the procedure. Computing $K^{mn}\mathbf{v}$ requires only $O(mn)$ operations and the approximation error $\mathrm{Err}(\alpha)$ can be computed efficiently. It is given by

$$\mathrm{Err}(\alpha) = \mathrm{tr}\, K - \mathrm{tr}\, \alpha (K^{m,n+1})^\top = \mathrm{tr}\, K - \sum_{i=1}^{m}\sum_{j=1}^{n} \alpha_{ij} K_{ij}. \tag{10.41}$$

Since $\tilde{K} = K^{m,n+1}\alpha^\top$ we only have to account for the changes in α and the additional row due to $K^{m,n+1}$. Without going into further details one can check that (10.41) can be computed in $O(m)$ time, provided the previous value of n is already known.

Computational Cost

Overall, successive applications of a rank-1 update method to compute a sparse approximation using n kernel functions to approximate a set of m incurs a computational cost of $O\left(\sum_{n'=1}^{n} mn'\right) = O(mn^2)$. One can see that this is only a constant factor worse than a direct calculation. Besides that, the memory footprint of the algorithm is also only $O(mn)$ which can be significantly smaller than storage of the matrix K, namely $O(m^2)$.

Note the similarity in computational cost between this iterative method and Conjugate Gradient Descent methods (Section 6.2.4) where the inverse of K was effectively constructed by building up a n-dimensional subspace of conjugate directions. The difference is that we never actually need to compute the full matrix K.[4]

10.2.3 Optimal and Greedy Selections

We showed that the problem of finding good coefficients α can be solved efficiently once a set of basis functions $k(x_1, \cdot), \ldots, k(x_n, \cdot)$ is available. The problem of selecting a good subset is the more difficult issue. One can show that even relatively simple problems such as one-target optimal approximation are NP-hard [381]; we cannot expect to find a solution in polynomial time.

We can take a greedy approach in the spirit of [381, 474] (see Section 6.5.3), with the difference being that we are not approximating one single target function but a set of m basis functions. This means that, rather than picking the functions

4. Strictly speaking, it is also the case that conjugate gradient descent does not require computation of K but only of $K\alpha$ for $\alpha \in \mathbb{R}^m$.

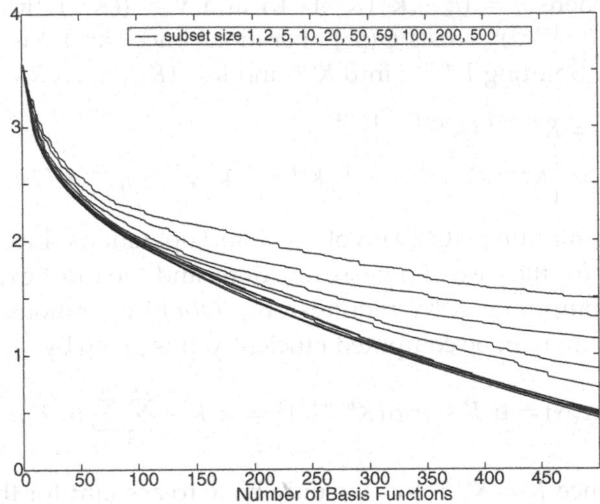

Figure 10.2 Size of the residuals $\log_{10} \operatorname{tr}(K - \tilde{K})$ for the **Abalone** dataset from the UCI repository [56]. From top to bottom: subsets of size 1, 2, 5, 10, 20, 50, 59, 100, 200. Note that, for subsets of size 50 or more, no noticeable difference in performance can be observed. After rescaling each input individually to zero mean and unit variance we used a Gaussian kernel (2.68) with $2\sigma^2 = N = 13$ where N is the dimension of the data. The size of the overall matrix was $m = 3000$.

at random, we choose one function at a time depending on which of them will decrease $\operatorname{Err}(\alpha)$ most and add this function to the set of kernels I chosen so far. Next we recompute the residual $\operatorname{Err}(\alpha)$ and continue iterating.

It would be wasteful to compute a full update for α and $(K^{n+1,n+1})^{-1}$ for every possible candidate since all we are interested in is the change in $\operatorname{Err}(\alpha)$. Simple (but tedious) algebra yields that, with the definitions $\mathbf{k}, \mathbf{v}$, and $\bar{\mathbf{k}}$ of Section 10.2.2,

$$\begin{aligned}
\operatorname{Err}(\alpha^{m,n+1}) &= \operatorname{tr} K - \operatorname{tr} \alpha^{m,n+1}(K^{m,n+1})^\top \\
&= \operatorname{tr} K - \operatorname{tr} \begin{bmatrix} K^{mn}(K^{nn})^{-1} + \eta^{-1}\left[K^{mn}\mathbf{v} - \bar{\mathbf{k}}\right]\mathbf{v}^\top \\ -\eta^{-1}\left[K^{mn}\mathbf{v} - \bar{\mathbf{k}}\right] \end{bmatrix} \begin{bmatrix} K^{mn} \\ \bar{\mathbf{k}} \end{bmatrix}^\top \\
&= \operatorname{Err}(\alpha^{mn}) - \eta^{-1}\left\|K^{mn}\mathbf{v} - \bar{\mathbf{k}}\right\|^2.
\end{aligned} \tag{10.42}$$

Hence, our selection criterion is to find that function $k(x_{\bar{\imath}}, \cdot)$ for which the decrease in the approximation error $\eta^{-1}\left\|K^{mn}\mathbf{v} - \bar{\mathbf{k}}\right\|^2$ is largest. This method still has a downside — at every step we would have to test for the $m - n$ different remaining kernel functions $k(x_i, \cdot)$ to find which would yield the largest improvement. With this the cost per iteration would be $O(mn(m-n))$ which is clearly infeasible.

Problems with Naive Greedy Methods

The key trick is not to analyze the complete set of $m - n$ functions but to pick a random subset instead. Section 6.5.1 and in particular Theorem 6.33 tell us that a random subset of size $N = 59$ is sufficiently large to yield a function $k(x_{\bar{\imath}}, \cdot)$ which is, with 95% confidence, better than 95% of all other kernel functions.

Random Subsets

Figure 10.2 shows that, in practice, subsets of 59 yield results almost as good as when a much larger set or even the complete dataset is used to find the next basis function. Note the rapid decay in $\ln \operatorname{Err}(\alpha) = \ln \operatorname{tr}(K - \tilde{K})$.

We conclude this section with the pseudocode (Algorithm 10.1) needed to find a sparse greedy approximation of K and $k(x_i, \cdot)$ in the Reproducing Kernel Hilbert Space $\mathcal{H}$. Note that the cost of the algorithm is now $O(Nmn^2)$, hence it is of the

Algorithm 10.1 Sparse Greedy Matrix Approximation (SGMA)

input basis functions k_i, bound on residuals ϵ
  $n = 0, I = \{\}, \alpha = [], K^{mn} = 0$
  repeat
    $n{+}{+}$
    Draw random subset M of size N from $[m]\backslash I$
    {**Select best basis function**}
    for all $j \in M$ **do**
      $\mathbf{v} = (K^{nn})^{-1}\mathbf{k}$
      $\eta = \kappa - \mathbf{v}^\top \mathbf{k}$
      $\mathrm{Err}(\alpha^{mn}) - \mathrm{Err}(\alpha^{m,n+1}) = \eta^{-1}\|K^{mn}\mathbf{v} - \bar{\mathbf{k}}\|^2$
    end for
    Select best $\hat{\imath} \in M$ and update $I = I \cup \{\hat{\imath}\}$.
    Update $(K^{n+1,n+1})^{-1}$ and $\alpha^{m,n+1}$ from (10.38) and (10.39).
    Update $\mathrm{Err}(\alpha^{m,n+1})$
  until $\mathrm{Err}(\alpha^{m,n+1}) < \epsilon$
output $n, \alpha, I, \mathrm{Err}(\alpha^{m,n+1})$

same order as an algorithm choosing kernel functions at random.[5]

10.2.4 Experiments

To illustrate the performance of Sparse Greedy Matrix Approximation (SGMA) we compare it with a conventional low-rank approximation method, namely PCA. The latter is optimal in terms of finite dimensional approximations (see Problem 10.7), however, it comes at the expense of requiring the full set of basis functions. We show in experiments that the approximation rates when SGMA is used are not much worse than those obtained with PCA. Experimental evidence also shows that the generalization performance of the two methods is very similar (see [513] for more details). Figure 10.3 shows that under various different choices of a Hilbert space (we varied the kernel width σ) the approximation quality obtained from SGMA closely resembles that of PCA.

Since SGMA picks individual basis functions $k(x_i, \cdot)$ with corresponding observations x_i we may ask whether the so-chosen x_i are special in some way. Figure 10.4 shows the first observations for the USPS dataset of handwritten digits (Gaussian RBF kernels with width $2\sigma^2 = 0.5 \cdot N$ where $N = 16 \times 16$ pixels). Note that among the first 15 observations (and corresponding basis functions) chosen on the USPS database, all 10 digits appear at least once. The pair of ones is due to a horizontal shift of the two images with respect to each other. This makes them almost

5. If the speed of prediction is not of utmost importance, random subset selection instead of the '59-trick' may just be good enough, since it is $N = 59$ times less expensive per basis function but will typically use only four times as many basis functions. With a run-time which is quadratic in the number n of basis functions this may lead to an effective speed up, at the expense of a larger memory footprint.

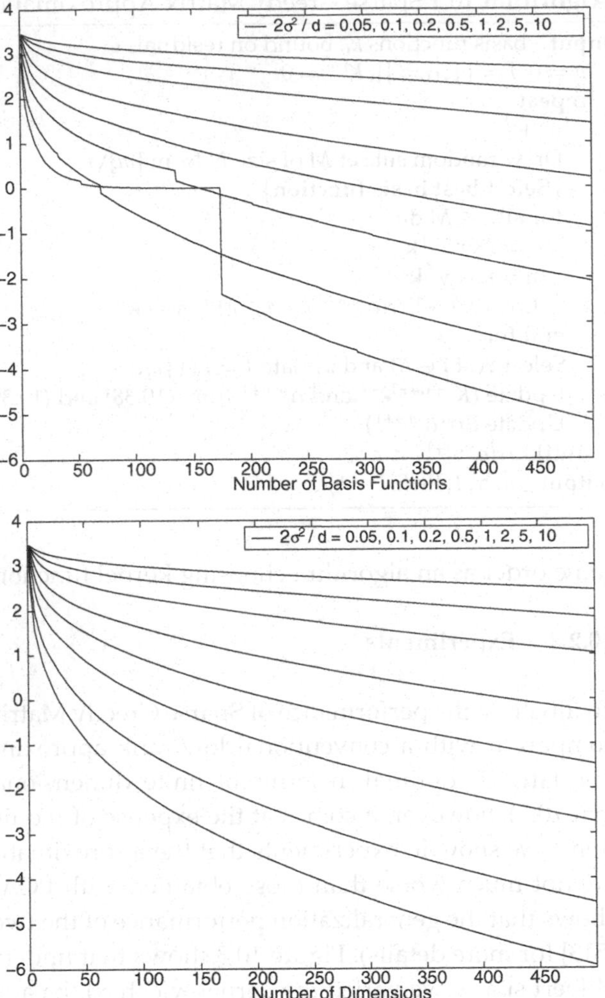

Figure 10.3 Size of the residuals for the `Abalone` dataset. Top: size of the residual trace ($\log_{10} \operatorname{tr}(K - \tilde{K})$) for projection on basis functions given by the greedy approximation scheme. Bottom: size of the residuals ($\log_{10} \sum_{j=i}^{m} \lambda_j$) for projection on subspaces given by principal component analysis. In both graphs, from top to bottom: $2\sigma^2/d = 0.05, 0.1, 0.2, 0.5, 1, 2, 5, 10$.

orthogonal to each other in feature space — their bitmaps hardly overlap at all.

Open Problem: Performance Guarantee

It is still an open question how and whether the good approximation qualities shown in Figures 10.3 can be guaranteed theoretically (3 orders of magnitude approximation with fewer than 10% of the basis functions). This need not be of any concern for the practitioner since he or she can always easily observe when the algorithm works (yet a theoretical guarantee would be nice to have).

In practice, generalization performance is more important than the question of whether the initial class of functions can be approximated well enough. As experimental evidence shows [514] the size of $\operatorname{tr}(K - \tilde{K})$, that is, the residual error, is conservative in determining the performance of a reduced rank estimator. For modest values of approximation, such as 2 orders of magnitude reduction in $\operatorname{tr}(K - \tilde{K})$, the performance is as good as the one of the estimator obtained without approximations. In some cases, such a sparse approximation may provide better

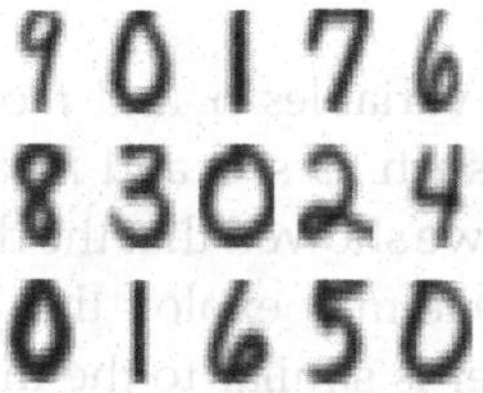

Figure 10.4 Left to Right, Top to Bottom. Patterns corresponding to the first basis functions. Note that 9 out of 10 digits are chosen among the first 10 patterns and that all patterns are sufficiently different (or shifted).

performance.

A practical use of SGMA lies in the fact that it allows us to find increasingly accurate, yet sparse approximations $\tilde{K}$ which can subsequently be used in optimization algorithms as replacements for K. It is also worth noting that the approximation and training algorithms can be coupled to obtain fast methods that do not require computation of K. Many methods find a dense expansion first and only subsequently employ a reduced set algorithm (Chapter 18) to find a more compact representation.

10.3 Interior Point Algorithms

Interior point algorithms are some of the most reliable and accurate optimization techniques and are the method of choice for small and moderately sized problems. We will discuss approximations applicable to large-scale problems in Sections 10.4, 10.5 and 10.6. We assume that the reader is familiar with the basic notions of interior point algorithms. Details can be found in Section 6.4 and references therein. In this section we focus on Support Vector specific details.

In order to deal with optimization problems which have both equality constraints and box constrained variables, we need to extend the notation of (6.72) slightly. The following optimization problem is general enough to cover classification, regression, and novelty detection:

$$\begin{aligned} \underset{\alpha,t}{\text{minimize}} \quad & \tfrac{1}{2}\alpha^\top Q\alpha + c^\top \alpha \\ \text{subject to} \quad & A\alpha = d \\ & \{0 \le \alpha \le u\} \text{ or } \{\alpha + t = u \text{ and } \alpha, t \ge 0\}. \end{aligned} \tag{10.43}$$

Here Q is a square matrix, typically of size $m \times m$ or $(2m) \times (2m)$, c, α, t, u are vectors of the same dimension, and A is a corresponding rectangular matrix. The dual can be found to be

$$\begin{aligned} \underset{\alpha,s,z,y}{\text{minimize}} \quad & -\tfrac{1}{2}\alpha^\top Q\alpha + d^\top h - u^\top s \\ \text{subject to} \quad & Q\alpha + c - A^\top h + s - z = 0 \\ & s, z \ge 0 \text{ and } h \text{ free} \end{aligned} \tag{10.44}$$

Furthermore, we have the Karush-Kuhn-Tucker (KKT) conditions

$$\alpha_i z_i = 0 \text{ and } s_i t_i = 0 \text{ for all } i \in [m] \tag{10.45}$$

which are satisfied at optimality.

Note that besides the primal variables α and t of the optimization problem (10.43), also the dual variables, such as s, z, and h carry information. Recall the reasoning of Section 6.3.3, where we showed that the dual-dual of a linear program is the original linear program. One may exploit this connection in the context of (10.43) and (10.44), since the latter is similar to the initial problem of minimizing regularized risks. In particular, the $A\alpha = d$ stems from the free variables (such as b or the semiparametric coefficients β_i). Consequently the dual variables h of (10.44) agree with b (or the semiparametric coefficients β_i). In practice this means that we need not perform any additional calculation in order to obtain b if we use an interior point code.

Dual-Dual Trick

10.3.1 Solving the Equations

As in Section 6.4.2 we solve the optimization problem by simultaneously satisfying primal and dual feasibility conditions and a relaxed version of (10.45). Linearization by analogy with (6.82) leads to

Linearization

$$\begin{array}{rclcl} A\Delta\alpha & = & d - A\alpha & = & \rho_{p1} \\ \Delta\alpha + \Delta t & = & u - \alpha - t & = & \rho_{p2} \\ Q\Delta\alpha - A^\top \Delta h + \Delta s - \Delta z & = & -Q\alpha - c + A^\top h - s + z & = & \rho_d \\ \alpha_i^{-1} z_i \Delta\alpha_i + \Delta z_i & = & \mu\alpha_i^{-1} - z_i - \alpha_i^{-1}\Delta\alpha_i \Delta z_i & =: & \rho_{\mathrm{KKT1}} \\ t_i^{-1} s_i \Delta t_i + \Delta s_i & = & \mu t_i^{-1} - s_i - t_i^{-1}\Delta t_i \Delta s_i & =: & \rho_{\mathrm{KKT2}} \end{array} \tag{10.46}$$

Solving for $\Delta t, \Delta z, \Delta s$ yields

$$\begin{array}{rcl} \Delta t & = & \rho_{p2} - \Delta\alpha \\ \Delta z_i & = & \rho_{\mathrm{KKT1}} - \alpha_i^{-1} z_i \Delta\alpha_i \\ \Delta s_i & = & \rho_{\mathrm{KKT2}} + t_i^{-1} s_i \Delta\alpha_i \end{array} \tag{10.47}$$

and the *reduced KKT system* (see (6.83))

$$\begin{bmatrix} (Q + \mathrm{diag}(t^{-1}s + \alpha^{-1}z)) & -A^\top \\ -A & 0 \end{bmatrix} \begin{bmatrix} \Delta\alpha \\ \Delta h \end{bmatrix} = \begin{bmatrix} \rho_d + \rho_{\mathrm{KKT1}} - \rho_{\mathrm{KKT2}} \\ \rho_{p1} \end{bmatrix}. \tag{10.48}$$

Eq. (10.48) is best solved by a standard Cholesky decomposition of the upper left submatrix and explicit solution for the remaining parts of the linear system.[6] For details of the predictor and corrector iteration strategies, the updates of μ,

Predictor Corrector Strategy

6. Pseudocode for a Cholesky decomposition can be found in most numerical analysis textbooks such as [423]. If $(Q + \mathrm{diag}(t^{-1}s + \alpha^{-1}z))$ should happen to be ill-conditioned, as may occur in rare cases during the iterations then it is recommended to use the pseudo-inverse or the Bunch-Kaufman decomposition [83] as a fall-back option. Linear algebra libraries such as LAPACK typically contain optimized versions of these algorithms.

convergence monitoring via the KKT gap and regarding initial conditions we refer the reader to Section 6.4.

10.3.2 Special Considerations for Classification

We now consider the particular case of SV classification and assign values to Q, c, A, and u. For standard SV classification we obtain

$$\begin{aligned} Q_{ij} &= y_i y_j k(x_i, x_j) && \text{where } Q \in \mathbb{R}^{m \times m} \\ c &= (1, \ldots, 1) && \text{where } c \in \mathbb{R}^m \\ u &= (C, \ldots, C) = (\tfrac{1}{m\lambda}, \ldots, \tfrac{1}{m\lambda}) && \text{where } u \in \mathbb{R}^m \\ A &= (y_1, \ldots, y_m) && \text{where } A \in \mathbb{R}^m \\ d &= 0 && \text{where } b \in \mathbb{R} \end{aligned} \tag{10.49}$$

For ν-classification (see Section 7.2), the parameters A and d are changed to

$$\begin{aligned} A &= \begin{bmatrix} y_1, \ldots, y_m \\ 1, \ldots, 1 \end{bmatrix} \\ d &= \begin{bmatrix} 0 \\ C\nu \end{bmatrix}. \end{aligned} \tag{10.50}$$

In addition, we now can give meaning to the variables t, z, and s. For each α_i there exists a dual variable z_i for which $\alpha_i z_i \to 0$ as the iteration advances, due to the KKT conditions. This means that either $z_i \to 0$ or $\alpha_i \to 0$. The practical consequence of this is that we can eliminate α_i before the algorithm converges completely. All we need do is look at the size of the entries $\alpha_i^{-1} z_i$. If they exceed a certain threshold, say c, we eliminate the corresponding set of variables $(t_i, z_i, s_i, \alpha_i)$ from the optimization process, since the point will not be a Support Vector (see also Section 10.4 for details on how the optimization problem changes).

Removing Patterns

The advantage is twofold; first, this reduces computational requirements since the size of the matrix to be inverted decreases. Second, the condition of the remaining reduced KKT system improves (large entries on the main diagonal can worsen the condition significantly) which allows for faster convergence. A similar reasoning can be applied to t_i and s_i. Again, if $t_i^{-1} s_i \to \infty$ this indicates that the corresponding patterns will be a Support Vector with, however, the coefficient α_i hitting the upper boundary u_i. Elimination of this variable is slightly more complicated since we have to account for it in the equality constraints $A\alpha = d$ and update d accordingly.

As far as computational efficiency is concerned, plain interior point codes without any further modifications, are a good choice for data sets of size up to $10^3 - 10^4$ since they are simple to implement, reliable in convergence, and very precise (the size of the KKT gap is several orders of magnitude smaller than what could be achieved by SMO or other chunking algorithms). Fast numerical mathematics packages such as BLAS [316, 145] and LAPACK [11] are crucial in this case though.

Beyond that, the memory footprint and the computational cost of performing a Cholesky decomposition of Q is too expensive. We will show in Section 10.3.4 how to overcome this restriction.

10.3.3 Special Considerations for SV Regression

In the generic case we have

$$\begin{aligned} Q &= \begin{bmatrix} K & -K \\ -K & K \end{bmatrix} && \text{where } K \in \mathbb{R}^{m\times m} \\ c &= (y_1-\varepsilon,\ldots,y_m-\varepsilon,-y_1-\varepsilon,\ldots,-y_m-\varepsilon) && \text{where } c \in \mathbb{R}^{2m} \\ u &= (C,\ldots,C) = (\tfrac{1}{m\lambda},\ldots,\tfrac{1}{m\lambda}) && \text{where } u \in \mathbb{R}^{2m} \\ A &= (1,\ldots,1,-1,\ldots,-1) && \text{where } A \in \mathbb{R}^{2m} \\ d &= 0 \end{aligned} \tag{10.51}$$

The constraint matrix A changes analogously to (10.49) if we use ν regression, that is, we have two constraints rather than one. Another minor modification allows us to also deal with Huber's robust regression. All we need do is define Q as $Q = \begin{bmatrix} K+D & -K \\ -K & K+D' \end{bmatrix}$, where D is a positive definite diagonal matrix. Since the reduced KKT system only modifies Q by adding diagonal terms, we can solve both Huber's robust regression and the generic case using identical code.

The key trick in inverting Q and the matrices derived from Q by addition to the main diagonal is to exploit the redundancy of its off-diagonal elements. By an orthogonal transform

Speedup via Orthogonal Transform

$$O := \frac{1}{\sqrt{2}} \begin{bmatrix} \mathbf{1} & \mathbf{1} \\ -\mathbf{1} & \mathbf{1} \end{bmatrix} \tag{10.52}$$

one obtains

$$O^\top Q O = \begin{bmatrix} 2K + \frac{D+D'}{2} & \frac{D-D'}{2} \\ \frac{D-D'}{2} & \frac{D+D'}{2} \end{bmatrix}. \tag{10.53}$$

Therefore, the $O^\top QO$ system can be inverted essentially by inverting an $m \times m$ matrix instead of a $2m \times 2m$ system. "Essentially," since in addition to the inversion of $2K + \frac{D+D'}{2}$ we must solve for the diagonal matrices $D \pm D'$. The latter is simply an operation of computational cost $O(m)$. Furthermore, $Q^{-1} = O(O^\top QO)^{-1}O^\top$.

All other considerations are identical to those for classification. Hence we can use the slightly more efficient matrix inversion with (10.53) as a drop-in replacement of a more pedestrian approach. This is the additional advantage we can gain from a direct implementation instead of using an off the shelf optimizer such as LOQO [556] or CPLEX [117]; in general the latter will not be able to exploit the special structure of Q.

Obtaining b,ε

Finally, note that by solving the primal and dual optimization problem simultaneously we also compute parameters corresponding to the initial SV optimization problem. This observation is useful as it allows us to obtain the constant term b directly, namely by setting $b = h$. See Problem 6.13 for details.

10.3.4 Large Scale Problems

The key stumbling block encountered in scaling interior point codes up to larger problems is that Q is of the size of m. Therefore, the cost of storing or of inverting Q (or any matrices derived from it) is prohibitively high. A possible solution to large problems is to use an efficient storage method for Q by low rank approximations.

Using Low Rank

Linear Systems Assume for a moment that we are using a linear SV kernel only, namely $k(x, x') = \langle x, x' \rangle$. In this case $K = XX^\top$ where $X \in \mathbb{R}^{m \times n}$ is (with slight abuse of notation) the matrix of all the training patterns, that is $X_{ij} = (x_i)_j$. Ferris and Munson [168] use this idea to find a more efficient solution for a linear SVM. They employ the Sherman-Woodbury-Morrison formula [207] (see also Section 16.4.1 for further applications) which gives

$$(V + RHR^\top)^{-1} = V^{-1} - V^{-1}R(H^{-1} + R^\top V^{-1}R)^{-1}R^\top V^{-1}, \tag{10.54}$$

Swapping Data to Disk

to invert $\left(Q + \operatorname{diag}(t^{-1}s + \alpha^{-1}z)\right)$ efficiently (see Problem 10.10). In particular they use out-of-core storage of the data (i.e. storage on the hard disk) in order to be able to deal with up to 10^8 samples.

Approximation by Low Rank Matrix

Nonlinear Systems For nonlinear SVMs, unfortunately, an application of the same technique is not directly feasible since storage requirements for K are enormous. But we can rely on the matrix approximation techniques of Section 10.2 and approximate K by $\tilde{K} = K^{mn}(K^{nn})^{-1}(K^{mn})^\top$. We only give the equations for SV classification where $Q = K$. The extension to regression is straightforward — all we must do is apply the orthogonal transform (10.53) beforehand. The problem is then solved in $O(mn^2)$ time since

$$\left(K^{mn}(K^{nn})^{-1}(K^{mn})^\top + D\right)^{-1} = \tag{10.55}$$
$$D^{-1} - D^{-1}K^{mn}\left(K^{nn} + (K^{mn})^\top D K^{mn}\right)^{-1}(K^{mn})^\top D^{-1}.$$

The expensive part is the matrix multiplications with K^{mn} and the storage of K^{mn}. As before, in the linear case, we resort to out-of-core storage (we write the matrix K^{mn} to disk once it has been computed). By this we obtain a preliminary solution using a subset consisting of only n basis functions.

Iterative Improvement If further precision is required we need to decrease the size of the problem by eliminating patterns for which the corresponding value of α can be reliably predicted. We can do this by dropping those patterns which have the largest distance from the boundary (either with $\alpha_i = 0$ or α_i at the upper constraint). These patterns are equivalent to those with the largest corresponding dual Lagrange multipliers, since these are least likely to change their value when we increase the precision of our method (see Section 10.3.2). The reduced size m of the training set then allows us to store matrices with larger n and to continue the optimization on the smaller dataset. This is done until no further minimization of the regularized risk functional $R_{\text{reg}}[f]$ is observed, or until the computational restrictions of the user are met (the maximum number of basis functions we are willing to use for the solution of the optimization problem is attained).

Dimension vs. Patterns Tradeoff

Parallelization Note that this formulation lends itself to a parallel implementation of a SV training algorithm since the matrix multiplications can readily be implemented on a cluster of workstations by using matrix manipulation libraries such as SCALAPACK [144] or BLACS [146].

Stopping Rule Finally, if desired, we could also use the value of the primal objective function (10.43), namely $\frac{1}{2}\alpha^\top Q\alpha + c^\top\alpha$, with K rather than $\tilde{K}$ as an upper bound for the minimum of (10.43). This is due to Theorem 10.2 which states that $\alpha^\top\tilde{K}\alpha \leq \alpha^\top K\alpha$. We may not always want to use this bound, since it requires computation of K which may be too costly (but given that it is provided only as a performance guarantee this may not be a major concern).

10.4 Subset Selection Methods

In many applications the precision of the solution (in terms of the Lagrange multipliers α_i) is not a prime objective. In other situations we can reasonably assume that a large number of patterns will either become SVs with α_i constrained to the boundary, or will not become SVs at all. In any of these cases we may break the optimization problem up into small manageable subproblems and solve these iteratively. This technique is commonly referred to as chunking, or subset selection.

10.4.1 Chunking

The simplest chunking idea, introduced in [559], relies on the observation that only the SVs contribute to the final form of the hypothesis. In other words — if we were given only the SVs, we would obtain *exactly* the same final hypothesis as if we had the full training set at our disposal (see Section 7.3). Hence, knowing the SV set beforehand and, further, being able to fit it (and the dot product matrix) into memory, one could directly solve the reduced problem and thereby deal with significantly larger datasets.

Training on SVs

The catch is, that we do *not* know the SV set before solving the problem. The heuristic is to start with an arbitrary subset; a first *chunk* that fits into memory. We then train the SV algorithm on it, keep the SVs, while discarding the non-SV data in the chunk, and replace it with data on which the current estimator would make errors (for instance, data lying outside the ε-tube of the current regression). The system is then retrained and we keep on iterating until the KKT-conditions are satisfied for all samples.

10.4.2 Working Set Algorithms

The problem with chunking is that the strategy will break down on datasets where the dot-product matrix built from SVs cannot be suitably kept in memory. A possible solution to this dilemma was given in [398]. The idea is to have only a subset of the variables as a working set, and optimize the problem with respect to them while *freezing* the other variables. In other words, to perform coordinate descent on subsets of variables. This method is described in detail in [398, 266] for the case of pattern recognition. Further information can be found in [459], for example.

In the following we describe the concept behind optimization problems of type (10.43). Subsequently we will adapt it to regression and classification. Let us assume that there exists a subset $S_w \subset [m]$, also referred to as the *working set*, which is an index set determining the variables α_i we will be using for optimization purposes. Next denote by $S_f = [m] \backslash S_w$ the *fixed set* of variables which will not be modified in the current iteration. Finally, we split up Q, c, A, and u accordingly into

Splitting up Q

$$Q = \begin{bmatrix} Q_{ww} & Q_{fw} \\ Q_{wf} & Q_{ff} \end{bmatrix} \tag{10.56}$$

and $c = (c_w, c_f)$, $A = \begin{bmatrix} A_w & A_f \end{bmatrix}$, $u = (u_w, u_f)$. In this case (10.43) reads as

$$\begin{aligned} \underset{\alpha_w}{\text{minimize}} \quad & \tfrac{1}{2}\alpha_w^\top Q_{ww}\alpha_w + \left[c_w + Q_{wf}\alpha_f\right]^\top \alpha + \\ & \left[\tfrac{1}{2}\alpha_f^\top Q_{ff}\alpha_f + c_f^\top \alpha_f\right] \\ \text{subject to} \quad & A_w\alpha_w = d - A_f\alpha_f \\ & \{0 \le \alpha_w \le u_w\} \text{ or } \{\alpha_w + t_w = u_w \text{ and } \alpha_w, t_w \ge 0\} \end{aligned} \tag{10.57}$$

This means that we recover a standard convex program in a subset of variables, with the only difference being that the linear constraints and the linear contribution have to be changed due to their dependency on α_f. For the sake of completeness we keep the constant offset produced by α_f but it need not be taken into account during the actual optimization process.

Progress on Subset = Progress on Full Set

Minimizing (10.57) with respect to α_w will also decrease (10.43). In particular, the amount of progress on the subset is identical to the progress on the whole[7]. For these subsets we may use any optimization algorithm we prefer; interior point codes for example. Algorithm 10.2 contains the details. The main difficulty in implementing subset selection strategies is how to choose S_w and S_f. We will address this issue in the next section.

Under certain technical assumptions (see [289, 96]) Algorithm 10.2 can be shown to converge to a global minimum. Several variants of such working set algorithms

7. Such a decrease will always occur when the optimality conditions in (10.57) are not satisfied and, of course, we choose working-sets with this property.

Algorithm 10.2 Subset Selection

input kernel k, data X, precision ϵ
Initialize $\alpha_i, \alpha_i^* = 0$
repeat
Compute coupling terms $Q_{wf}\alpha_f$ and $A_f\alpha_f$ for S_w.
Solve reduced optimization problem on S_w.
Choose new S_w from variables α_i, α_i^* not satisfying the KKT conditions.
Compute bound on the Error in computing the minimum (e.g. by the KKT Gap)
until Error $< \epsilon$ or $S_w = \emptyset$

have been proposed [284, 266, 398, 459, 108], most of them with slightly different selection strategies. In the following we focus on the common features among them and explain the basic ideas. For practical implementations we recommend the reader look for the most recent information since seemingly minor details in the selection strategy appear to have a significant impact on the performance. It is important to also be aware that the performance of these heuristics often depends on the dataset.

10.4.3 Selection Strategies

Recall Proposition 10.1, and in particular (10.6) and (10.8). For classification, the terms $\partial_{\xi_j} c(\max(0, 1 - y_j f(x_j)))$ and $\alpha_j(y_j f(x_j) - 1)$ give an upper bound on the deviation between the current solution and the optimal one. A similar relation applies for regression.

Contribution to KKT Gap

The central idea behind most selection strategies is to pick those patterns whose contribution to the size of the KKT Gap (10.13), (10.18) is largest. This is a reasonable strategy since, after optimization over the working set S_w, the corresponding terms of the KKT Gap will have vanished (see Problem 10.11). Unfortunately though this does not guarantee that the overall size of the KKT gap will diminish by the same amount, since the other terms KKT_i for $i \in S_f$ may increase. Still, we will have picked the set of variables for which the KKT gap size for the restricted optimization problem on S_w is largest. Note that in this context we also have to take the constraint $A\alpha = d$ into account. This means that we have to select the working set S_w such that

$$\Omega_w := \{\alpha_w | A_w \alpha_w = d - A_f \alpha_f\} \cap \{\alpha_w | 0 \le \alpha_w \le C\} \tag{10.58}$$

Lower Dimensional Subspace

is sufficiently large or, at least, does not only contain one element (see Figure 10.5 for the case of standard SV classification).

As before we focus on classification (the regression case is completely analogous), and in particular on soft margin loss functions (10.6).

KKT Selection Criterion Since $\xi = \max(\xi, 0) - \max(0, -\xi)$ we can rewrite KKT_i as

$$\mathrm{KKT}_i = (C - \alpha_i)\max(0, 1 - y_i f(x_i)) + \alpha_i \max(0, y_i f(x_i) - 1). \tag{10.59}$$

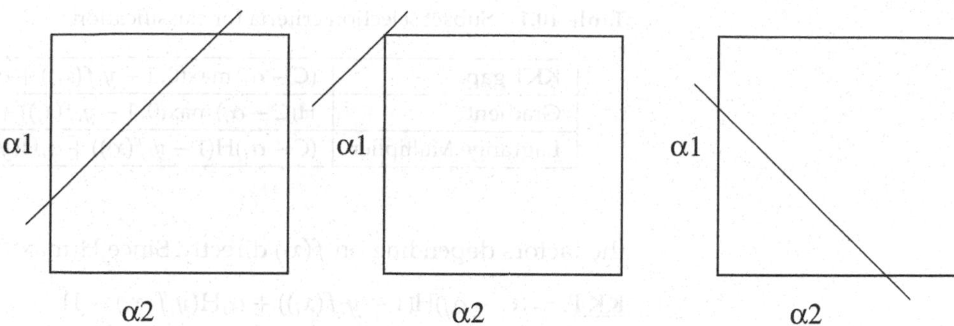

Figure 10.5 Constraints on the working set S_w in the case of classification. In all cases the box constraints $0 \leq \alpha_i \leq C$ apply. Left: two patterns of different classes result in $(+1)\alpha_1 + (-1)\alpha_2 = c$. Middle: the same case with $c = C$, thus the only feasible point is $(C, 0)$. Right: two patterns of the same class with $\alpha_1 + \alpha_2 < C$.

The size of KKT_i is used to select which variables to use for optimization purposes in the RHUL SV package [459].

Dual Constraint Satisfaction Other algorithms, such as SVMLight [266] or SVMTorch [108], see also [502], choose those patterns i in the working set for which

$$\overline{\mathrm{KKT}}_i = \mathrm{H}(C - \alpha_i)\max(0, 1 - y_i f(x_i)) + \mathrm{H}(\alpha_i)\max(0, y_i f(x_i) - 1) \tag{10.60}$$

is maximal[8], where H denotes the Heaviside function;

$$\mathrm{H}(\xi) = \begin{cases} 1 & \text{if } \xi > 0 \\ 0 & \text{otherwise} \end{cases} \tag{10.61}$$

Heaviside Function

As one can see, $C\overline{\mathrm{KKT}}_i$ is clearly an upper bound on KKT_i, and thus, if in the process of the optimization $\sum_i \overline{\mathrm{KKT}}_i$ vanishes, we can automatically ensure that the KKT gap will also decrease. The only problem with (10.60) is that it may be overly conservative in the stopping criterion and overestimate the influence of the constraint on $f(x_i)$, when the corresponding constraint on α_i is almost met.

A quite similar (albeit less popular) selection rule to (10.60) can be obtained from considering the gradient of the objective function of the optimization problem (10.43), namely $Q\alpha + c$. In this case we want to search in a direction d where $d^\top(Q\alpha + c)$ is large.

Primal Constraint Satisfaction Equations (10.59) and (10.60) suggest a third selection criterion, this time based only on the behavior of the Lagrange multipliers α_i. Rather than applying the Heaviside function to them we could also apply it to

8. This may not be immediately obvious from the derivations in [266] and [108], since their reasoning is based on the idea of [618] that we should select (feasible) directions where the gradient of the objective function is maximal. An explicit calculation of the gradient, however, reveals that both strategies lead to the same choice of a working set.

Table 10.1 Subset selection criteria for classification.

KKT gap	$(C-\alpha_i)\max(0, 1-y_i f(x_i)) + \alpha_i \max(0, y_i f(x_i) - 1)$
Gradient	$\mathrm{H}(C-\alpha_i)\max(0, 1-y_i f(x_i)) + \mathrm{H}(\alpha_i)\max(0, y_i f(x_i) - 1)$
Lagrange Multiplier	$(C-\alpha_i)\mathrm{H}(1-y_i f(x_i)) + \alpha_i \mathrm{H}(y_i f(x_i) - 1)$

the factors depending on $f(x_i)$ directly. Since $\mathrm{H}(\max(0,\xi)) = \mathrm{H}(\xi)$ we obtain

$$\underline{\mathrm{KKT}}_i = (C-\alpha_i)\mathrm{H}(1-y_i f(x_i)) + \alpha_i \mathrm{H}(y_i f(x_i) - 1). \tag{10.62}$$

In other words, only those patterns where the KKT conditions are violated *and* the Lagrange multipliers α_i differ from their optimal values by a large amount are chosen.

Selection Strategies

Summarizing, we may either select patterns (i) based on their contribution to the size of the KKT gap, (ii) based on the size of the gradient of the objective function at the particular location, or (iii) depending on the mismatch of the Lagrange multipliers. Table 10.1 summarizes the three strategies. Overall, strategy (i) is preferred, since it uses the tightest of all three bounds on the minimum of the objective function.

Feasible Directions In all cases we need to select a subset such that both the constraints $A\alpha = d$ and the box constraints on α are enforced. A direction e with $Ae = 0$ and $0 \leq \alpha + \delta e \leq C$ for some $\delta > 0$, that is a direction taking only points into account where the KKT conditions are violated, will surely do. In order to keep memory requirements low we will only choose a small subset $S_w \subset \{1, \ldots, m\}$ of size typically less than 100.

Balancing Samples

Balanced Sample To obtain a relatively large search space while satisfying $A\alpha = d$, we keep only coordinates d_i (and corresponding α_i) at which the gradient points away from the (possibly active) boundary constraints. Since A, in general, has a rather simple form (only entries 1 and -1) this requirement can be met by selecting a direction e where the signs of the corresponding entries in A alternate. This can mean, for example for classification, that an equal number of positive and negative samples need be selected. For ν-SVM we additionally have to balance between points on either side of the margin within each class. The case of regression is analogous, with the only difference being that we have two "margins" rather than one.

Summing up, a simple (and very much recommended) heuristic for subset selection is to pick directions where the gradient $Q\alpha + c$ is largest, the KKT conditions for the corresponding variables are violated, and where the number of samples of either class and relation to the margin is balanced. This is what is done in [266, 108]. A proof of convergence can be found in [330]. One can show that the patterns selected by the gradient rule are identical to that chosen by (10.60) according to $\overline{\mathrm{KKT}}_i$ (see Problem 10.13).

10.5 Sequential Minimal Optimization

SMO as Special Case of Subset Selection

One algorithm, Sequential Minimal Optimization (SMO), introduced by Platt [409], puts chunking to the extreme by iteratively selecting subsets of size 2 and optimizing the target function with respect to them. It has been reported to be several orders of magnitude faster on certain data sets (up to a factor of 1000) and to exhibit better scaling properties (typically up to one order better) than classical chunking (Section 10.4.1). The key point is that for a working set of 2 the optimization subproblem can be solved analytically without explicitly invoking a quadratic optimizer[9].

SMO is one of the most easily implementable algorithms and it has a very benign memory footprint, essentially only of the size of the number of samples. In Section 8.4, we considered the special case of single-class problems; we now develop the classification and regression cases. This development includes a treatment of pattern dependent regularization and details how the algorithm can be extended to more general convex loss functions.

The exposition proceeds as follows; first we solve the generic optimization problem in two variables (Section 10.5.1) and subsequently we determine the value of the placeholders of the generic problem in the special cases of classification and regression. Finally we discuss how to adjust b properly and we determine how patterns should be selected to ensure speedy convergence (Section 10.5.5).

10.5.1 Analytic Solutions

We begin with a generic convex constrained optimization problem in two variables (for regression we actually have to consider four variables — $\alpha_i, \alpha_i^*, \alpha_j, \alpha_j^*$, however, only two of them may be nonzero simultaneously). By analogy to (10.43) and (10.57) we have

Quadratic Program in Two Variables

$$\begin{aligned} \underset{\alpha_i,\alpha_j}{\text{minimize}} \quad & \tfrac{1}{2}\left[\alpha_i^2 Q_{ii} + \alpha_j^2 Q_{jj} + 2\alpha_i\alpha_j Q_{ij}\right] + c_i\alpha_i + c_j\alpha_j \\ \text{subject to} \quad & s\alpha_i + \alpha_j = \gamma \\ & 0 \le \alpha_i \le C_i \text{ and } 0 \le \alpha_j \le C_j. \end{aligned} \tag{10.63}$$

Here $c_i, c_j, \gamma \in \mathbb{R}$, $s \in \{\pm 1\}$, and $Q \in \mathbb{R}^{2\times 2}$ are chosen suitably to take the effect of the $m-2$ variables that are kept fixed into account. The constants C_i represent

9. Note that in the following we will only consider standard SV classification and regression, since most other settings (an exception being the single-class algorithm described in Section 8.4) have more than one equality constraint and would require at least (the number of equality constraints + 1) variables per iteration in order to make any progress. In such a case (a) the difficulty of selecting a suitable set of directions would increase significantly and (b) the computational cost incurred by performing an update in a one-dimensional space would increase linearly with the number of constraints rendering SMO less attractive. See also Problem 10.14.

pattern dependent regularization parameters (as proposed in [331], among others, for unbalanced observations). Recall that we consider only optimization problems with one equality constraint. The following auxiliary lemma states the solution of (10.63).

Lemma 10.3 (Analytic Solution of Constrained Optimization) *Assume we have an optimization problem of type (10.63). Further, denote by*

$$\zeta := sc_j - c_i + \gamma s Q_{jj} - \gamma Q_{ij} \tag{10.64}$$

$$\chi := Q_{ii} + Q_{jj} - 2sQ_{ij} \tag{10.65}$$

two auxiliary variables derived from (10.63). Then, for $\chi = 0$ we have

$$\alpha_i = \begin{cases} L & \text{if } \zeta > 0 \\ H & \text{otherwise} \end{cases} \tag{10.66}$$

and for $\chi > 0$ we obtain $\alpha_i = \min(\max(L, \chi^{-1}\zeta), H)$. The case of $\chi < 0$ never occurs. Furthermore $\alpha_j = \gamma - s\alpha_i$ and L, H are defined as

$$L = \begin{cases} \max(0, s^{-1}(\gamma - C_j)) & \text{if } s > 0 \\ \max(0, s^{-1}\gamma) & \text{otherwise} \end{cases} \tag{10.67}$$

$$H = \begin{cases} \min(C_i, s^{-1}\gamma) & \text{if } s > 0 \\ \max(C_i, s^{-1}(\gamma - C_j)) & \text{otherwise} \end{cases} \tag{10.68}$$

Proof The idea is to remove α_j and the corresponding constraint from the optimization problem and to solve for α_i. We begin with constraints on α_i and the connection between α_i and α_j. Due to the equality constraint in (10.63) we have

$$\alpha_j = \gamma - s\alpha_i \tag{10.69}$$

and additionally, due to the constraints on α_j,

$$s\alpha_i = \gamma - \alpha_j \text{ and thus } \gamma \geq s\alpha_i \geq \gamma - C_j. \tag{10.70}$$

Since $C_i \geq \alpha_i \geq 0$ we may combine the two constraints into the constraint $H \geq \alpha_i \geq L$ where H and L are given by (10.67) and (10.68). Now that we have determined the constraints we look for the minimum. Elimination of $\alpha_j = \gamma - s\alpha_i$ yields

Reduction to Optimization Problem in One Variable

$$\begin{aligned} \underset{\alpha_i}{\text{minimize}} \quad & \tfrac{1}{2}\alpha_i^2(Q_{ii} + Q_{jj} - 2sQ_{ij}) + \alpha_i(c_i - sc_j + \gamma Q_{ij} - \gamma s Q_{jj}) \\ \text{subject to} \quad & L \leq \alpha_i \leq H. \end{aligned} \tag{10.71}$$

We have ignored constant terms independent of α_i since they do not influence the location of the minimum. The unconstrained objective function, which can also be written as $\frac{\chi}{2}\alpha_i^2 - \zeta\alpha_i$, has its minimum at $\chi^{-1}\zeta$. In order to ensure that the solution is also optimal for the constraint $\alpha_i \in [L, H]$ we only have to "clip" the unconstrained solution $\chi^{-1}\zeta$ to the interval, i.e. $\alpha_i = \min(\max(\chi^{-1}\zeta, L), H)$. This concludes the proof. ■

During the optimization process it may happen, due to numerical instabilities, that the numerical value of χ is negative. In this situation we simply reset $\chi = 0$ and use (10.66). All that now remains is to find explicit values in the cases of classification and regression.

10.5.2 Classification

Proposition 10.4 (Optimal Values for Classification) *In classification the optimal values of α_i and α_j are given as follows. Denote by $\chi = K_{ii} + K_{jj} - 2y_iy_jK_{ij}$, $s = y_iy_j$, and let L, H be defined as in*

	$y_i = y_j$	$y_i \neq y_j$
α_i	$L = \max(0, \alpha_i^{\text{old}} + \alpha_j^{\text{old}} - C_j)$ $H = \min(C_i, \alpha_i^{\text{old}} + \alpha_j^{\text{old}})$	$L = \max(0, \alpha_i^{\text{old}} - \alpha_j^{\text{old}})$ $H = \min(C_i, C_j + \alpha_i^{\text{old}} - \alpha_j^{\text{old}})$

We have $\alpha_i = \min(\max(\bar{\alpha}, L, H))$ and $\alpha_j = s(\alpha_i^{\text{old}} - \alpha_i) - \alpha_j^{\text{old}}$. With the auxiliary definition $\delta := y_i((f(x_j) - y_j) - (f(x_i) - y_i))$, $\bar{\alpha}$ is given by

$$\bar{\alpha} = \begin{cases} \alpha_i^{\text{old}} + \chi^{-1}\delta & \text{if } \chi > 0 \\ -\infty & \text{if } \chi = 0 \text{ and } \delta > 0 \\ \infty & \text{if } \chi = 0 \text{ and } \delta < 0 \end{cases} \tag{10.72}$$

This means that the change in α_i and α_j depends on the difference between the approximation errors in i and j. Moreover, in the case that the unconstrained solution of the problem is identical to the constrained one ($\alpha_i = \bar{\alpha}$) the improvement in the objective function is given by $\chi^{-1}((f(x_j) - y_j) - (f(x_i) - y_i))^2$. Hence we should attempt to find pairs of patterns (i, j) where the difference in the classification errors is largest (and the constraints will still allow improvements in terms of the Lagrange multipliers).

Proof We begin with γ. In classification we have $\sum_{i=1}^m y_i\alpha_i = 0$ and thus $y_i\alpha_i + y_j\alpha_j = y_i\alpha_i^{\text{old}} + y_j\alpha_j^{\text{old}}$, or equivalently

$$y_iy_j\alpha_i + \alpha_j = y_iy_j\alpha_i^{\text{old}} + \alpha_j^{\text{old}} =: \gamma \text{ and } s = y_iy_j. \tag{10.73}$$

Now we turn our attention to Q. From (10.56) we conclude that $Q_{ii} = K_{ii}$, $Q_{jj} = K_{jj}$, and $Q_{ij} = Q_{ji} = sK_{ij}$. This leads to

$$\chi = K_{ii} + K_{jj} - 2K_{ij}. \tag{10.74}$$

Next we compute c_i and c_j. Eq. (10.57) leads to

$$c_i = -1 + y_i\left(\sum_{l \neq i,j}^{m} \alpha_l k(x_i, x_l)\right) = y_i(f(x_i) - b - y_i) - \alpha_i K_{ii} - \alpha_j s K_{ij} \tag{10.75}$$

and similarly for c_j. Using $y_i = y_j s$ we compute ζ as

$$\zeta = -y_i(f(x_i) - b - y_i) + \alpha_i K_{ii} + \alpha_j s K_{ij} + y_i(f(x_j) - b - y_j) \tag{10.76}$$

$$+\alpha_j s K_{jj} + \alpha_i K_{ij} + (\alpha_i + s\alpha_j)(K_{ij} - K_{jj})$$
$$= y_i((f(x_j) - y_j) - (f(x_i) - y_i)) + \alpha_i \chi \tag{10.77}$$

Substituting the values of γ, χ, and ζ into Lemma 10.3 concludes the proof. ■

10.5.3 Regression

We proceed as in classification. We have the additional difficulty, however, that for each pair of patterns x_i and x_j we have four Lagrange multipliers $\alpha_i, \alpha_i^*, \alpha_j$, and α_j^*. Hence we must possibly consider up to three different pairs of solutions[10]. Let us rewrite the restricted optimization problem in regression as follows

$$\begin{aligned}
\underset{\alpha_i,\alpha_i^*,\alpha_j,\alpha_j^*}{\text{minimize}} \quad & \frac{1}{2}\begin{bmatrix}\alpha_i - \alpha_i^* \\ \alpha_j - \alpha_j^*\end{bmatrix}^\top \begin{bmatrix}K_{ii} & K_{ij} \\ K_{ij} & K_{jj}\end{bmatrix}\begin{bmatrix}\alpha_i - \alpha_i^* \\ \alpha_j - \alpha_j^*\end{bmatrix} \\
& + \begin{bmatrix}c_i \\ c_j\end{bmatrix}^\top \begin{bmatrix}\alpha_i - \alpha_i^* \\ \alpha_j - \alpha_j^*\end{bmatrix} + \varepsilon(\alpha_i + \alpha_i^* + \alpha_j + \alpha_j^*) \\
\text{subject to} \quad & 0 \le \alpha_l \le C_l \text{ and } 0 \le \alpha_l^* \le C_l^* \text{ for all } l \in \{i, j\} \\
& (\alpha_i - \alpha_i^*) + (\alpha_j - \alpha_j^*) = (\alpha_i^{\text{old}} - \alpha_i^{*\text{old}}) + (\alpha_j^{\text{old}} - \alpha_j^{*\text{old}}) =: \gamma.
\end{aligned} \tag{10.78}$$

Here c_i, c_j are suitably chosen constants depending solely on the differences $\alpha_i - \alpha_i^*$ and $\alpha_j - \alpha_j^*$. One can check that

$$c_i = -y_i + (f(x_i) - b - K_{ii}(\alpha_i - \alpha_i^*) - K_{ij}(\alpha_j - \alpha_j^*)) \tag{10.79}$$

and c_j likewise. We deliberately keep the contribution due to ε separate since this is the only part where sums $\alpha_i + \alpha_i^*$ rather than differences enter the equations.

As in the classification case we begin with the constraints on α_i and α_i^*. Due to the summation constraint in the optimization problem we obtain $(\alpha_i - \alpha_i^*) = \gamma - (\alpha_j - \alpha_j^*)$. Using the additional box constraints on α_i, α_i^* of (10.78) leads to

Eliminating α_j, α_j^*

$$L := \max(\gamma - C_j, -C_i^*) \le \alpha_i - \alpha_i^* \le \min(\gamma + C_j^*, C_i) =: H. \tag{10.80}$$

This allows us to eliminate α_j, α_j^* and rewrite (10.78) in terms of $\beta := \alpha_i - \alpha_i^*$,

$$\begin{aligned}
\underset{\beta}{\text{minimize}} \quad & \tfrac{1}{2}\beta^2(K_{ii} + K_{jj} - 2K_{ij}) + \beta(\gamma(K_{ij} - K_{jj}) + c_i - c_j) \\
& + \varepsilon(|\beta| + |\gamma - \beta|) \\
= \quad & \tfrac{1}{2}\beta^2\chi + \beta((f(x_i) - y_i) - (f(x_j) - y_j) - \chi(\alpha_i^{\text{old}} - \alpha_i^{*\text{old}})) \\
& + \varepsilon(|\beta| + |\gamma - \beta|) \\
\text{subject to} \quad & L \le \beta \le H.
\end{aligned} \tag{10.81}$$

10. The number of solutions is restricted to four due to the restriction that α_i and α_i^* (or analogously α_j and α_j^*) may never both be nonzero at the same time. In addition, the constraint that $\alpha_i - \alpha_i^* + \alpha_j - \alpha_j^* = \gamma$ rules out one of these remaining four combinations.

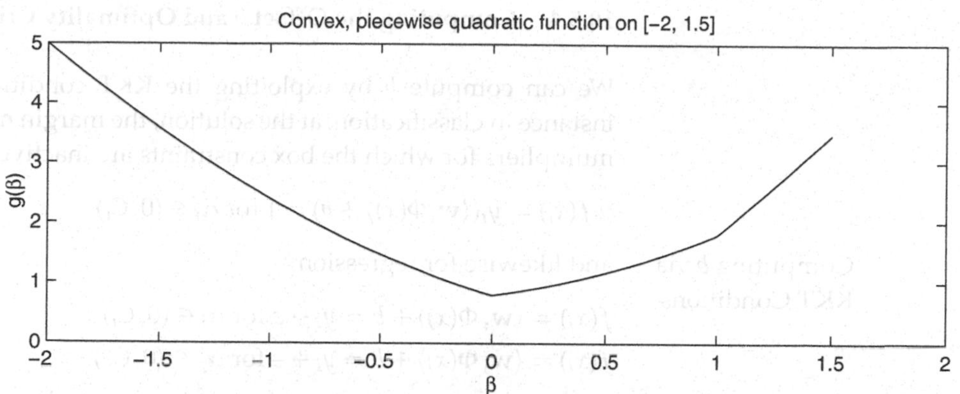

Figure 10.6 The minimum of this function occurs at $\beta = 0$ due to the change in $\varepsilon|\beta|$.

Here we used the $\chi = K_{ii} + K_{jj} - 2y_iy_jK_{ij}$, as in classification. The objective function is convex and piecewise quadratic on the three intervals

$$I_- := [L, \min(0,\gamma)],\ I_0 := [\min(0,\gamma), \max(0,\gamma)],\ I_+ := [\max(0,\gamma), H] \tag{10.82}$$

(for $\gamma = 0$ the interval I_2 vanishes). An example of such a function is given in Figure 10.6. One can check that the *unconstrained* minimum of the quadratic objective function (10.81), as defined on the intervals I_-, I_0, I_+, would be given by

Effect of Piecewise Convex Function

$$\left.\begin{array}{l}\beta_-\\ \beta_0\\ \beta_+\end{array}\right\} = (\alpha_i^{\text{old}} - \alpha_i^{*\text{old}}) + \frac{1}{\chi}((f(x_j) - y_j) - (f(x_i) - y_i)) + \frac{\varepsilon}{\chi}\left\{\begin{array}{rl} 2 & \text{if } \beta \in I_- \\ 0 & \text{if } \beta \in I_0 \\ -2 & \text{if } \beta \in I_+ \end{array}\right. \tag{10.83}$$

For $\chi = 0$ the same considerations as in classification apply; the optimum is found on one of the interval boundaries. Furthermore, since (10.78) is convex all we now have to do is match up the solutions β_i with the corresponding intervals I_i.

For convenience we start with β_0 and I_0. If $\beta_0 \in I_0$ we have found the optimum. Otherwise we must continue our search in the direction in which β_0 exceeds I_0. Without loss of generality assume that this is I_+. Again, if $\beta_+ \in I_+$ we may stop. Otherwise we simply "clip" β_+ to the interval boundaries of I_+. Now we have to reconstruct α from β. Due to the box constraints and the fact that $\sum_i(\alpha_i - \alpha_i^*) = 0$ we obtain

Update is Independent of b

$$\begin{aligned} \alpha_i &= \max(0,\beta), & \alpha_j &= \max(0,\gamma-\beta) \\ \alpha_i^* &= \max(0,-\beta), & \alpha_j^* &= \max(0,-\gamma+\beta). \end{aligned} \tag{10.84}$$

In order to arrive at a complete SV regression or classification algorithm, we still need a way of selecting the patterns x_i, x_j and a method specifying how to update the constant offset b efficiently. Since most pattern selection methods use b as additional information to select patterns we will start with b.

10.5.4 Computing the Offset b and Optimality Criteria

We can compute b by exploiting the KKT conditions (see Theorem 6.21). For instance in classification; at the solution, the margin must be exactly 1 for Lagrange multipliers for which the box constraints are inactive. We obtain

$$y_i f(x_i) = y_i(\langle \mathbf{w}, \Phi(x) \rangle + b) = 1 \text{ for } \alpha_i \in (0, C_i) \tag{10.85}$$

Computing b via KKT Conditions

and likewise for regression

$$f(x_i) = \langle \mathbf{w}, \Phi(x) \rangle + b = y_i - \varepsilon \text{ for } \alpha_i \in (0, C_i) \tag{10.86}$$

$$f(x_i) = \langle \mathbf{w}, \Phi(x) \rangle + b = y_i + \varepsilon \text{ for } \alpha_i^* \in (0, C_i^*). \tag{10.87}$$

Hence, if all the Lagrange multipliers α_i were optimal, we could easily find b by picking any of the unconstrained α_i or α_i^* and solving (10.85), (10.86), or (10.87).

Unfortunately, during training, not all Lagrange multipliers will be optimal, since, if they were, we would already have obtained the solution. Hence, obtaining b by the aforementioned procedure is not accurate. We resort to a technique suggested by Keerthi et al. [291, 289] in order to overcome this problem.

For the sake of simplicity we start with the classification setting; we first split the patterns X into the following five sets:

Sets of KKT Violation and Satisfaction

$$I_0 = \{i | \alpha_i \in (0, C_i)\} \quad I_{+,0} = \{i | \alpha_i = 0, y_i = +1\} \quad I_{+,C} = \{i | \alpha_i = C_i, y_i = +1\}$$
$$I_{-,0} = \{i | \alpha_i = 0, y_i = -1\} \quad I_{-,C} = \{i | \alpha_i = C_i, y_i = -1\}$$

Moreover we define

$$\begin{aligned} e_{\text{hi}} &:= \min_{i \in I_0 \cup I_{+,0} \cup I_{-,C}} f(x_i) - y_i \\ e_{\text{lo}} &:= \max_{i \in I_0 \cup I_{-,0} \cup I_{+,C}} f(x_i) - y_i. \end{aligned} \tag{10.88}$$

Since the KKT conditions have to hold for a solution we can check that this corresponds to $e_{\text{hi}} \geq 0 \geq e_{\text{lo}}$. For I_0 we have already exploited this fact in (10.85). Formally we can always satisfy the conditions for e_{hi} and e_{lo} by introducing two thresholds: $b_{\text{hi}} = b - e_{\text{hi}}$ and $b_{\text{lo}} = b - e_{\text{lo}}$. Optimality in this case corresponds to $b_{\text{hi}} \leq b_{\text{lo}}$. Additionally, we may use $\frac{1}{2}(b_{\text{up}} + b_{\text{lo}})$ as an improved estimate of b.

The real benefit, however, comes from the fact that we may use e_{hi} and e_{lo} to choose patterns to focus on. The largest contribution to the discrepancy between e_{hi} and e_{lo} stems from that pair of patterns (i, j) for which

Choose Large Discrepancy with Large Possible Updates

$$\text{discrepancy}(i, j) := (f(x_i) - y_i) - (f(x_j) - y_j) \text{ where } \begin{array}{l} i \in I_0 \cup I_{-,0} \cup I_{+,C} \\ j \in I_0 \cup I_{+,0} \cup I_{-,C} \end{array} \tag{10.89}$$

is largest. This is a reasonable strategy for the following reason: from Proposition 10.4 we conclude that the potential change in the variables α_i, α_j is largest if the discrepancy $(f(x_i) - y_i) - (f(x_j) - y_j)$ is largest. The only modification is that i and j are not chosen arbitrarily any more.

Finally, we obtain another stopping criterion. Instead of requiring that the violation of the KKT condition is smaller than some tolerance Tol we may require that $e_{lo} \leq e_{hi}$ holds with some tolerance; $e_{lo} \leq e_{hi} - 2$ Tol. In addition, we will not consider patterns where discrepancy$(i, j) < 2$ Tol. See [290] for more details and pseudocode of their implementation.

To adapt these ideas to regression we have to modify the sets I slightly. The change is needed since we have to add or subtract ε in a way that is very similar to our treatment of the classification case, where $y_i \in \{\pm 1\}$.

1. If $\alpha_i = 0$ at optimality we must have $f(x_i) - (y_i - \varepsilon) \geq 0$.
2. For $\alpha_i \in (0, C_i)$ we must have $f(x_i) - (y_i - \varepsilon) = 0$.
3. For $\alpha_i = C_i$ we get $f(x_i) - (y_i - \varepsilon) \leq 0$.

Analogous inequalities hold for α_i^*. As before we split the patterns X into several sets according to

$$I_0 = \{i|\alpha_i \in (0, C_i)\} \quad I_{+,0} = \{i|\alpha_i = 0\} \quad I_{+,C} = \{i|\alpha_i = C_i\}$$
$$I_0^* = \{i|\alpha_i^* \in (0, C_i^*)\} \quad I_{-,0} = \{i|\alpha_i^* = 0\} \quad I_{-,C} = \{i|\alpha_i^* = C_i^*\}$$

Computing b for Regression

and introduce e_{hi}, e_{lo} by

$$e_{hi} := \min\left(\min_{i \in I_0 \cup I_{+,0}} f(x_i) - (y_i - \varepsilon), \min_{i \in I_0^* \cup I_{-,C}} f(x_i) - (y_i + \varepsilon)\right) \tag{10.90}$$

$$e_{lo} := \max\left(\max_{i \in I_0 \cup I_{+,C}} f(x_i) - (y_i - \varepsilon), \max_{i \in I_0^* \cup I_{-,0}} f(x_i) - (y_i + \varepsilon)\right). \tag{10.91}$$

The equations for computing a more robust estimate of b are identical to the ones in the classification case. Note that (10.90) and (10.91) are equivalent to the ansatz in [494], the only difference being that we sacrifice a small amount of numerical efficiency for a somewhat simpler definition of the sets I (some of them are slightly larger than in [494]) and the rules regarding which e_{hi} and e_{lo} are obtained (the cases $\alpha_i = 0, \alpha_i^* = C_i^*$ and $\alpha_i^* = 0, \alpha_i = C_i$ are counted twice).

Without going into further details, we may use a definition of a discrepancy like (10.89) and then choose patterns (i, j) for optimization where this discrepancy is largest. See the original work [494] for more details. Below we give a simpler (and slightly less powerful) reasoning.

10.5.5 Selection Rules

The previous section already indicated some ways to pick the indices (i, j) such that the decrease in the objective function is maximized. We largely follow the reasoning of Platt [409, Section 12.2.2]. See also the pseudocode (Algorithms 10.3 and 10.4).

We choose a two loop approach to maximizing the objective function. The outer loop iterates over all patterns violating the KKT conditions, or possibly over those where the threshold condition of the previous section (using e_{hi} and e_{lo}) is violated.

Usually we first loop only over those with Lagrange multipliers neither on the upper nor lower boundary. Once all of these are satisfied we loop over all patterns violating the KKT conditions, to ensure self consistency on the complete dataset. This solves the problem of choosing the index i.

Full Sweep for Noisy Data

It is sometimes useful, especially when dealing with noisy data, to iterate over the complete KKT violating dataset before complete self consistency on the subset has been achieved. Otherwise considerable computational resources are spent making subsets self consistent that are not globally self consistent. The trick is to perform a full sweep through the data once only less than, say, 10% of the non bound variables change[11].

Now to select j: To make a large step towards the minimum, one looks for large steps in α_i. Since it is computationally expensive to compute χ for all possible pairs (i, j) one chooses a heuristic to maximize the change in the Lagrange multipliers α_i and thus to maximize the absolute value of the numerator in the expressions (10.72) and (10.83). This means that we are looking for patterns with large differences in their relative errors $f(x_i) - y_i$ and $f(x_j) - y_j$. The index j corresponding to the maximum absolute value is chosen for this purpose.

Second Choice Hierarchy

If this heuristic happens to fail, in other words if little progress is made by this choice, all other indices j are looked at (this is what is called "second choice hierarchy" in [409]) in the following way.

1. All indices j corresponding to non-bound examples are looked at, searching for an example to make progress on.
2. In the case that the first heuristic was unsuccessful, all other samples are analyzed until an example is found where progress can be made.
3. If both previous steps fail, SMO proceeds to the next index i.

For a more detailed discussion and further modifications of these heuristics see [409] and [494, 291].

10.6 Iterative Methods

Many training algorithms for SVMs or similar estimators can be understood as iterative methods. Their main advantage lies in the simplicity with which they can be implemented. While not all of them provide the best performance (plain gradient descent in Section 10.6.1) and some may come with restrictions on the scope of applications (Lagrangian SVM in Section 10.6.2 can be used only for quadratic soft-margin loss), the algorithms presented in this section will allow practitioners to obtain first results in a very short time. Finally, Section 10.6.3 indicates how Support Vector algorithms can be extended to online learning problems.

11. This modification is not contained in the pseudocodes, however, its implementation should not pose any further problems. See also [494, 291] for further pseudocodes.

Algorithm 10.3 Pseudocode for SMO Classification

```
function TakeStep(i, j)
  if i = j then return 0
  s = y_i y_j
  if s = 1 then
    L = max(0, α_i + α_j − C_j)
    H = min(C_i, α_i + α_j)
  else
    L = max(0, α_i − α_j)
    H = min(C_i, C_j + α_i − α_j)
  end if
  if L = H then return 0
  χ = K_ii + K_jj − 2K_ij
  if χ > 0 then
    ᾱ = α_i + χ^{-1} y_i((f(x_j) − y_j) − (f(x_i) − y_i))
    ᾱ = min(max(ᾱ, L), H)
  else if y_i((f(x_j) − y_j) − (f(x_i) − y_i)) < 0 then
    ᾱ = H
  else
    ᾱ = L
  end if
  if |α_i − ᾱ| < ε(ε + ᾱ + α_i) then return 0
  α_j += s(α_i − ᾱ) and α_i = ᾱ (note: x += y means x = x + y)
  Update b
  Update f(x_1), ..., f(x_m)
  return 1
end function

function ExamineExample(i)
  \overline{KKT}_i = H(α_i) max(0, y_i f(x_i) − 1) + H(1 − α_i) max(0, 1 − y_i f(x_i))
  if \overline{KKT}_i > Tol then
    if Number of nonzero and non bound α_i > 1 then
      Find j with second choice heuristic
      if TakeStep(i, j) = 1 then return 1
    end if
    for all α_j > 0 and α_j < C_j (start at random point) do
      if TakeStep(i, j) = 1 then return 1
    end for
    for all remaining α_j do
      if TakeStep(i, j) = 1 then return 1
    end for
  end if
  return 0
end function

main SMO Classification(k, X, Y, ε)
  Initialize α_i, α_i^* = 0 and b = 0, make X, Y, α global variables
  ExamineAll = 1
  while NumChanged > 0 or ExamineAll = 1 do
    NumChanged = 0
    if ExamineAll = 1 then
      for all α_i do  NumChanged += ExamineExample(i)
    else
      for all α_i > 0 and α_i < C_i do  NumChanged += ExamineExample(i)
    end if
    if ExamineAll = 1 then
      ExamineAll = 0
    else if NumChanged = 0 then
      ExamineAll = 1
    end if
  end while
end main
```

Algorithm 10.4 Pseudocode for SMO Regression

```
function TakeStep(i, j)
  if i = j then return 0
  γ = (α_i − α_i^*) + (α_j − α_j^*)
  L = max(γ − C_j, −C_i^*) and H = min(γ + C_j^*, C_i)
  if L = H then return 0
  l = min(γ, 0) and h = max(γ, 0)
  χ = K_ii + K_jj − 2K_ij
  if χ > 0 then
    β_0 = (α_i − α_i^*) + χ^{−1}((f(x_i) − y_i) − (f(x_j) − y_j))
    β_+ = β_0 − 2 ε/χ and β_− = β_0 + 2 ε/χ.
    β = max(min(β_0, h), l) (clip β_0 to I_0)
    if β = h then β = max(min(β_+, H), h)
    if β = l then β = max(min(β_−, l), L)
  else if (f(x_i) − y_i) − (f(x_j) − y_j) < 0 then
    β = h
    if (f(x_i) − y_i) − (f(x_j) − y_j) + 2ε < 0 then β = H
  else
    β = l
    if (f(x_i) − y_i) − (f(x_j) − y_j) − 2ε > 0 then β = L
  end if
  if |β − (α_i − α_i^*)| < ε(ε + |β| + α_i + α_i^*) then return 0
  α_i = max(β, 0), α_i^* = max(−β, 0), and α_j = max(0, γ − β), max(0, −γ + β)
  Update b
  Update f(x_1), ..., f(x_m)
  return 1
end function

function ExamineExample(i)
  KKT_i  =  H(α_i) max(0, f(x_i) − (y_i − ε)) + H(α_i^*) max(0, (y_i + ε) − f(x_i))+
            H(C_i − α_i) max(0, (y_i − ε) − f(x_i)) + H(C_i^* − α_i^*) max(0, f(x_i) − (y_i + ε))
  if KKT_i > Tol then
    if Number of nonzero and non bound α_i > 1 then
      Find j with second choice heuristic
      if TakeStep(i, j) = 1 then return 1
    end if
    for all α_j > 0 and α_j < C_j (start at random point) do
      if TakeStep(i, j) = 1 then return 1
    end for
    for all remaining α_j do
      if TakeStep(i, j) = 1 then return 1
    end for
  end if
  return 0
end function

main SMO Regression(k, X, Y, ε)
  Initialize α_i, α_i^* = 0 and b = 0
  ExamineAll = 1
  while NumChanged > 0 or ExamineAll = 1 do
    NumChanged = 0
    if ExamineAll = 1 then
      for all α_i do NumChanged += ExamineExample(i)
    else
      for all α_i > 0 and α_i < C_i do NumChanged += ExamineExample(i)
    end if
    if ExamineAll = 1 then
      ExamineAll = 0
    else if NumChanged = 0 then
      ExamineAll = 1
    end if
  end while
end main
```

(In the printed listing, $\overline{\mathrm{KKT}}_i$ carries an overline.)

10.6.1 Gradient Descent

Most of the methods in this chapter are concerned with the *dual* optimization problem of the regularized risk functional. It is, however, perfectly legitimate to ask whether or not a primal optimization approach would also lead to good solutions. The maximum margin perceptron of Kowalczyk [309] for instance follows such an approach. Another method which can be understood as gradient descent is Boosting (see [349, 179]).

It is important to keep in mind that the choice of parametrization will have a significant impact on the performance of the algorithm (see [9] for a discussion of these issues in the context of Neural Networks). We could either choose to compute the gradient in the function space (thus the Reproducing Kernel Hilbert Space $\mathcal{H}$) of f, namely $\partial_f R_{\text{reg}}[f]$, or choose a particular parametrization $f(x) = \sum_i \alpha_i k(x_i, x)$ and compute the gradient with respect to the parameters α_i. Depending on the formulation we obtain different (and variably efficient) algorithms. We also briefly mention how the kernel AdaTron [183] fits into this context. For convenience of notation we choose the λ formulation of the regularized risk functional.

Gradient in Function Space

Let us start with gradients in function space. We use the standard RKHS regularization ([349] and, later, [221] use gradients in the space ℓ_2^m induced by the values of f on the training set) terms $\Omega[f] = \frac{1}{2}\|f\|^2_{\mathcal{H}}$. With the definitions of (4.1) this yields:

$$R_{\text{reg}}[f] = \frac{1}{m}\sum_{i=1}^{m} c(x_i, y_i, f(x_i)) + \frac{\lambda}{2}\|f\|^2_{\mathcal{H}} \tag{10.92}$$

$$\partial_f R_{\text{reg}}[f] = \frac{1}{m}\sum_{i=1}^{m} c'(x_i, y_i, f(x_i))k(x_i, \cdot) + \lambda f. \tag{10.93}$$

Consequently, we obtain the following update rules for f, given a learning rate Λ,

$$f \longleftarrow f - \Lambda \partial_f R_{\text{reg}}[f] = (1 - \Lambda\lambda) f - \Lambda \sum_{i=1}^{m} c'(x_i, y_i, f(x_i))k(x_i, \cdot). \tag{10.94}$$

Here the symbol '$\longleftarrow$' means 'is updated to'. For computational reasons we have to *represent* f as a linear combination of functions in a finite dimensional space (the Representer Theorem of Section 4.2 tells us that m basis functions $k(x_i, x)$ are sufficient for this). With the usual expansion $f(\cdot) = \sum_i \alpha_i k(x_i, \cdot)$ the update rule for the coefficients becomes

$$\alpha \longleftarrow (1 - \Lambda\lambda)\alpha - \Lambda\gamma = \alpha - \Lambda(\lambda\alpha + \gamma), \text{ where } \gamma_i = c'(x_i, y_i, f(x_i)). \tag{10.95}$$

Distinguishing between the different cases of regression, classification, and classification with a Boosting cost function [498, 221] we obtain the derivatives as described in Table 10.2.

Note that we can obtain update rules similar to the Kernel AdaTron [183] if we

Table 10.2 Cost functions and their derivatives for ε-Regression, Soft-Margin Classification, and Boosting with an exponential cost function.

$c(x, y, f(x))$	$c'(x, y, f(x))$
Regression $c = \begin{cases} f(x) - y - \varepsilon & \text{if } f(x) - y > \varepsilon \\ y - f(x) - \varepsilon & \text{if } y - f(x) > \varepsilon \\ 0 & \text{otherwise} \end{cases}$	$c' = \begin{cases} 1 & \text{if } f(x) - y > \varepsilon \\ -1 & \text{if } y - f(x) > \varepsilon \\ 0 & \text{otherwise} \end{cases}$
Classification $c = \begin{cases} 1 - yf(x) & \text{if } yf(x) < 1 \\ 0 & \text{otherwise} \end{cases}$	$c' = \begin{cases} -y & \text{if } yf(x) < 1 \\ 0 & \text{otherwise} \end{cases}$
Boosting $c = \exp(-yf(x))$	$c' = -y\exp(-yf(x))$

modify the loss function c to become

$$c(x, y, f(x)) = \begin{cases} \frac{1}{2}(1 - yf(x))^2 & \text{if } yf(x) < 1 \\ 0 & \text{otherwise.} \end{cases} \tag{10.96}$$

AdaTron

On a per-pattern basis, this leads to update rules identical to the ones of the AdaTron. In particular, if we combine (10.96) with the online extensions of Section 10.6.3, we fully recover the update rule of the Kernel AdaTron. This means that the AdaTron uses squared soft margin loss functions as opposed to the standard soft margin loss of SVMs.[12]

Gradient in Coefficient Space

Rather than a parametrization in function space $\mathcal{H}$ we may also choose to start immediately with a parametrization in coefficient space [577, 221]. It is straightforward to see that, in the case of RKHS regularization as above (here $\|f\|^2 = \alpha^\top K\alpha$), we obtain, with the definitions of γ as in (10.94),

$$\partial_\alpha R_{\text{reg}}[f] = \frac{1}{m}K\gamma + \lambda K\alpha \tag{10.97}$$

$$\alpha \longleftarrow \alpha - \Lambda\lambda K\alpha - \Lambda K\gamma = \alpha - \Lambda K(\lambda\alpha + \gamma). \tag{10.98}$$

In other words the updates from (10.95) are multiplied by the kernel matrix K to obtain the update rules in the coefficient space. This means that we are performing gradient descent in a space with respect to the metric given by K rather than the Euclidean metric. The other difference to (10.93) is that it allows us to deal with regularization operators other than those based on the RKHS norm of f; $\Omega[f] = \sum_i |\alpha_i|$ for example, (see Section 4.9.2 and [498]). Table 10.3 gives an overview of different regularization operators and their gradients.

12. The strategy for computing b is different though. Since $\partial_b R_{\text{reg}}[f] = \frac{1}{m}\sum_{i=1}^m y_i c'(x_i, y_i, f(x_i))$ we may also update b iteratively if desired, whereas in the AdaTron we must add a constant offset to the kernel function in order to obtain an update rule.

Table 10.3 Gradients of the regularization term.

$\Omega[f]$	Regularization	Gradient wrt. α
$\frac{1}{2}\|f\|_{\mathcal{H}}^2$	standard SV regularizer	$K\alpha$
$\frac{1}{2}\|f\|_{\mathcal{H}}$	renormalized SV regularizer	$(\alpha^\top K\alpha)^{\frac{1}{2}} K\alpha$
$\sum_{i=1}^m \|\alpha_i\|$	sparsity regularizer	$(\operatorname{sgn}(\alpha_1), \ldots, \operatorname{sgn}(\alpha_m))$
$\sum_{i=1}^m \|f(x_i)\|^2$	ℓ_2 norm on data	$K^\top K\alpha$

Line Search

Since a unit step in the direction of the negative gradient of $R_{\text{reg}}[f]$ does not necessarily guarantee that $R_{\text{reg}}[f]$ will decrease, it is advantageous in many cases to perform a line-search in the direction of $\partial_\alpha R_{\text{reg}}[f]$, specifically, to seek γ such that $R_{\text{reg}}\left[f - \gamma\partial_\alpha R_{\text{reg}}[f]\right]$ is minimized. Details of how this can be achieved are in Section 6.2.1, and Algorithm 6.5. Moreover, Section 10.6.3 describes how the gradient descent approach may be adapted to online learning, that is, stochastic gradient descent.

We conclude the discussion of gradient descent algorithms by stating a lower bound on the minimum value of the regularized risk functional [221], which depends on the size of the gradient in function space.

Theorem 10.5 (Lower Bound on Primal Objective Function) *Denote by $R_{\text{emp}}[f]$ a convex and differentiable functional on a Hilbert space $\mathcal{H}$ and consider the regularized risk functional*

$$R_{\text{reg}}[f] = R_{\text{emp}}[f] + \lambda\|f\|_{\mathcal{H}}^2, \text{ where } \lambda > 0 \tag{10.99}$$

Then, for any $f, \Delta f \in \mathcal{H}$

$$R_{\text{reg}}[f] - R_{\text{reg}}[f - \Delta f] \leq \frac{1}{2}\|\nabla R_{\text{reg}}[f]\|^2. \tag{10.100}$$

Proof We assume that $f - \Delta f$ is the minimizer of $R_{\text{reg}}[f]$, since proving the inequality for the minimizer is sufficient. Since R_{emp} is convex and differentiable we know that

$$R_{\text{emp}}[f] - R_{\text{emp}}[f - \Delta f] \leq \langle \Delta f, \nabla R_{\text{emp}}[f]\rangle. \tag{10.101}$$

Therefore we may bound $\rho(f, \Delta f) := R_{\text{reg}}[f] - R_{\text{reg}}[f - \Delta f]$ by

$$\rho(f, \Delta f) \leq \langle \Delta f, \nabla R_{\text{emp}}[f]\rangle + \lambda\omega(\|f\|) - \lambda\omega(\|f - \Delta f\|). \tag{10.102}$$

It is easy to check that if $\omega(\|f\|) = \frac{1}{2}\|f\|^2$, (10.102) is minimized by

$$\lambda\Delta f = \nabla R_{\text{emp}}[f] + \lambda f = \nabla R_{\text{reg}}[f]. \tag{10.103}$$

Substituting this back into $\rho(f, \Delta f)$ proves (10.100). ∎

Eq. (10.100) shows that a stopping criterion based on the size of the gradient is a feasible strategy when minimizing regularized risk functionals.

Gradient descent algorithms are relatively simple to implement but we should keep in mind that they often do not enjoy the convergence guarantees of more sophisticated algorithms. They are useful tools for a first implementation if no other optimization code is available, however.

10.6.2 Lagrangian Support Vector Machines

Mangasarian and Musicant [348] present a particularly fast and simple algorithm which deals with classification problems involving squared slacks (this is the same problem that the AdaTron algorithm also attempts to minimize). Below we show a version thereof extended to the nonlinear case. We begin with the basic definitions

$$c(x, y, f(x)) = \begin{cases} 0 & \text{if } yf(x) \geq 1 \\ (1 - yf(x))^2 & \text{otherwise.} \end{cases} \quad (10.104)$$

The second modification needed for the algorithm is that we also regularize the constant offset b in the function expansion, i.e. $\Omega[f] = \|\mathbf{w}\|^2 + b^2$ where $f(x) = \langle \mathbf{w}, \phi(x) \rangle + b$. This reduces the number of constraints in the optimization problem at the expense of losing translation invariance in feature space. It is still an open question whether this modification is detrimental to generalization performance. In short, we have the following optimization problem;

Primal Optimization Problem

$$\begin{aligned} &\underset{\mathbf{w}, b, \xi}{\text{minimize}} \quad \frac{1}{m} \sum_{i=1}^{m} \xi_i^2 + \frac{\lambda}{2} \left(\|\mathbf{w}\|^2 + b^2 \right) \\ &\text{subject to} \quad y_i(\langle \mathbf{w}, \phi(x_i) \rangle + b) \geq 1 - \xi_i \text{ where } \xi_i \geq 0. \end{aligned} \quad (10.105)$$

By using the tools from Chapter 6 (see also [345, 348]) one can show that the dual optimization problem of (10.105) is given by

Dual Optimization Problem

$$\begin{aligned} &\underset{\alpha}{\text{minimize}} \quad \frac{1}{2} \sum_{i,j=1}^{m} \alpha_i \alpha_j y_i y_j (K_{ij} + 1 + \lambda m \delta_{ij}) - \sum_{i=1}^{m} \alpha_i \\ &\text{subject to} \quad \alpha_i \geq 0 \text{ for all } i \in [m] \end{aligned} \quad (10.106)$$

where $\mathbf{w} = \sum_{i=1}^{m} y_i \alpha_i \Phi(x_i)$, $b = \sum_{i=1}^{m} \alpha_i$, and $\xi_i = \lambda m \alpha_i$.

In the following we develop a recursion relation to determine a solution of (10.105). For convenience we use a slightly more compact representation of the quadratic matrix in (10.106). We define

$$Q := \text{diag}(y)(K + \lambda m \mathbf{1} + \vec{1}^\top \vec{1})\text{diag}(y) \quad (10.107)$$

where diag(y) denotes the matrix with diagonal entries y_i and $\mathbf{1}$ is the unit matrix. Since α_i are Lagrange multipliers, it follows from the KKT conditions (see Theorem 6.21) that only if the constraints $y_i(\langle \mathbf{w}, \phi(x_i) \rangle + b) \geq 1 - \xi_i$ of (10.105) are active may the Lagrange multipliers α_i be nonzero. With the definition of Q we can write these conditions as $\alpha_i > 0$ only if $(Q\alpha)_i = 1$. Summing over all indices i we have

$$\alpha^\top (Q\alpha - \vec{1}) = 0. \quad (10.108)$$

Now, if we can find some α which are both feasible (they satisfy the constraints imposed on them) and which also satisfy $\alpha^\top(Q\alpha - \vec{1}) = 0$, then we have found a solution. The key optimization algorithm trick lies in the following lemma [348].

Lemma 10.6 (Orthogonality and Clipping) *Denote by $a, b \in \mathbb{R}^m$ two arbitrary vectors. Then the following two conditions are equivalent*

$$\left\{a, b \geq 0 \text{ and } a^\top b = 0\right\} \Longleftrightarrow \{a = (a - \gamma b)_+ \text{ for all } \gamma > 0\} \tag{10.109}$$

See Problem 10.15 for a proof.

Rewriting the KKT Conditions

Consequently it is a condition on α that, for all $\gamma > 0$,

$$Q\alpha - \vec{1} = ((Q\alpha - \vec{1}) - \gamma\alpha)_+ \tag{10.110}$$

must hold. As previously mentioned [348] a solution α satisfying (10.108) is the minimizer of the constrained optimization problem (10.106). Furthermore, Lemma 10.6 implies that (10.108) is equivalent to (10.110) for all $\gamma > 0$. This suggests an iteration scheme for obtaining α whereby

$$\alpha^{i+1} = Q^{-1}(((Q\alpha^i - \vec{1}) - \gamma\alpha^i)_+ + \vec{1}). \tag{10.111}$$

The theorem below shows that (10.111) is indeed a convergent algorithm and that it converges linearly.

Theorem 10.7 (Global Convergence of Lagrangian SVM [348]) *For any symmetric positive matrix K and Q given by (10.107) under the condition that $0 < \gamma < 2\lambda m$, the iteration scheme (10.111) will converge at a linear rate to the solution $\bar{\alpha}$ and*

$$\|Q\alpha^{i+1} - Q\bar{\alpha}\| \leq \|\mathbf{1} - \gamma Q^{-1}\| \cdot \|Q\alpha^i - Q\bar{\alpha}\|. \tag{10.112}$$

Proof By construction $\bar{\alpha}$ is a fixed point of (10.111). Therefore we have

$$\|Q\alpha^{i+1} - Q\bar{\alpha}\| = \|(Q\alpha^i - \vec{1} - \gamma\alpha^i)_+ - (Q\bar{\alpha} - \vec{1} - \gamma\bar{\alpha})_+\| \tag{10.113}$$

$$\leq \|(Q - \gamma\mathbf{1})(\alpha^i - \bar{\alpha})\| \tag{10.114}$$

$$\leq \|\mathbf{1} - \gamma Q^{-1}\| \cdot \|Q\alpha^i - Q\bar{\alpha}\|. \tag{10.115}$$

Next we bound the norm of $\|\mathbf{1} - \gamma Q^{-1}\|$ and, in particular, we show under which conditions it is less than 1. By construction we know that the smallest eigenvalue of Q is at least λm and, moreover, Q is a positive matrix. Hence Q^{-1} is also positive and its largest eigenvalue is bounded from above by $\frac{1}{\lambda m}$. Therefore the largest eigenvalue of $\|\mathbf{1} - \gamma Q^{-1}\|$ is bounded from above by $|1 - \gamma\frac{1}{\lambda m}|$ and, consequently, for all $0 < \gamma < 2\lambda m$ the algorithm will converge. ■

Sherman Morrison Woodbury

To make practical use of (10.111) on large amounts of data we need to find a way to invert Q cheaply. Recall Section 10.3.4 where we dealt with a similar problem in the context of interior point optimization codes. Assuming that we can find a low rank approximation of K, by $\tilde{K} = K^{mn}(K^{nn})^{-1}(K^{mn})^\top$ for example, we may replace K by $\tilde{K}$ throughout the algorithm, apply the Sherman-Woodbury-Morrison formula (10.54) and invert Q approximately.

The additional benefit is that we get a compact representation of the solution of the classification problem in a small number of basis functions, n. Thus the evaluation of the solution is much faster than if the full matrix K had been used. The approximation in this setting ignores the smallest eigenvalues of K, which will be dominated by the addition of the regularization term $\lambda m \mathbf{1}$ in the definition (10.110) of Q anyway. In analogy to (10.55) we obtain

$$\left(\tilde{K} + \lambda m \mathbf{1} + \vec{1}^\top \vec{1}\right)^{-1} \tag{10.116}$$

$$= \left(K^{mn}(K^{nn})^{-1}(K^{mn})^\top + \lambda m \mathbf{1} + \vec{1}^\top \vec{1}\right)^{-1} \tag{10.117}$$

$$= (\lambda m)^{-1}\mathbf{1} - (\lambda m)^{-2} \left[\begin{array}{cc} K^{mn} & \vec{1} \end{array} \right] Q_{\text{red}}^{-1} \left[\begin{array}{cc} K^{mn} & \vec{1} \end{array} \right]^\top \tag{10.118}$$

Speedup for Low Rank Approximations

where

$$Q_{\text{red}} = \left(\left[\begin{array}{cc} K^{nn} & 0 \\ 0 & 1 \end{array} \right] + \lambda m \left[\begin{array}{cc} K^{mn} & \vec{1} \end{array} \right]^\top \left[\begin{array}{cc} K^{mn} & \vec{1} \end{array} \right] \right). \tag{10.119}$$

Likewise, the matrix multiplications by Q can be sped up by the low rank decomposition of K. Overall, the cost of one update step is $O(n^2 m)$; significantly less than $O(m^3)$, which would be incurred if we had to invert Q exactly. The same methods that can be used to implement any interior point method (out-of-core storage of the matrix K^{mn} for example) can also be applied to Lagrangian SVM.

Linear Kernels

For the special case that we have only linear kernels $k(x, x') = \langle x, x' \rangle$, the update rule becomes particularly simple. Here we can represent K as $K = X^\top X$ where X denotes the matrix of all patterns x_i. The MATLAB code (courtesy of Mangasarian and Musicant) is given in Algorithm 10.5 (in the nonlinear case, we can adapt the algorithm easily by replacing X with $K^{mn}(K^{nn})^{-\frac{1}{2}}$, where K^{mn} and K^{nn} are defined as in Section 10.2.1).

10.6.3 Online Extensions

Online learning differs from the settings in the other chapters of this book, which study *batch* learning, insofar as it assumes that we have a (possibly infinite) stream of incoming data $(x_i, y_i) \in \mathcal{X} \times \mathcal{Y}$. The goal is to predict y_i and incur as little loss as possible during the iterations. This goal is quite different from that of minimizing the expected risk since the distribution from which the data (x_i, y_i) is drawn may change over time and thus no single estimate $f : \mathcal{X} \to \mathcal{Y}$ may be optimal over the total time (see [32, 54, 378]).

Increasing Number of Kernels

At every step t we could attempt to perform an optimal prediction based on the minimizer of the regularized risk functional $R_{\text{reg}}[f]$ where our training set consists of $(x_1, y_1), \ldots (x_{t-1}, y_{t-1})$. Unfortunately this task is completely computationally infeasible since it would require that we solve an ever-increasing optimization problem in t variables at every instance. Hence the time required to perform the

Algorithm 10.5 Linear Lagrangian Support Vector Machines

```
function [it, opt, w, gamma] = lsvm(X,Y,lambdam,itmax,tol)

[m,n]=size(X);
gamma=1.9 * nu;
e=ones(m,1);
H=Y*[X -e];
it=0;
S=H*inv((speye(n+1)*lambdam+H'*H));
alpha=(1-S*(H'*e)) / lambdam;
oldalpha=alpha+1;
while it<itmax & norm(oldalpha-alpha)>tol
        z=(1+pl(((speye(m)*lambdam*alpha+H*(H'*alpha))-gamma*alpha)-1));
        oldalpha=alpha;
        alpha=(z-S*(H'*z))/lambdam;
        it=it+1;
end;
opt=norm(alpha-oldalpha);w=X'*Y*alpha;b=-e'*Y*alpha;

function pl = pl(x); pl = (abs(x)+x)/2;
```

prediction would increase polynomially over time due to the increasing sample size. This is clearly not desirable.

Another problem arises from the Representer Theorem (Th. 4.2). It states that the solution is a linear combination of kernel functions $k(x_t, \cdot)$ centered at the training points. Assuming that the probability of whether a point will become a kernel function does not depend on t this shows that, at best, the selection of basis functions will change while, typically, the number of basis functions selected will grow without bound (see Problem 10.18). This means that prediction will also become increasingly expensive and the computational effort is likely to grow polynomially.

From these two problems we conclude that if we want to use an online setting we should perform some sort of approximation rather than trying to solve the learning problem exactly.

Fixed Dimensional Setting

One possibility is to project every new basis function $k(x_t, \cdot)$ onto a set of existing basis functions, say $k(x_{n_1}, \cdot), \ldots k(x_{n_N}, \cdot)$ and find a solution in the so-chosen subspace. This is very similar to online learning with a neural network with fixed architecture. We thus perform learning with respect to the functional

$$R_{\text{reg}}[f] := \frac{1}{m}\sum_{i=1}^{m} c\left(x_i, y_i, \sum_{j=1}^{N} \alpha_j k(x_{n_j}, x_i)\right) + \frac{\lambda}{2}\sum_{j,j'=1}^{N} k(x_{n_j}, x_{n'_j})\alpha_j\alpha_{j'}, \tag{10.120}$$

Computational Cost

where $f = \sum_{i=1}^{N} \alpha_j k(x_{n_j}, \cdot)$. Unfortunately the computational cost is at least $O(N^2)$ per iteration since computing the gradient of (10.120) with respect to α already requires a matrix-vector multiplication, no matter how simple we manage to keep the sample dependent term $\frac{1}{m}\sum_{i=1}^{m} c\left(x_i, y_i, f(x_i)\right)$[13]. This shows that any gradient descent algorithm in a lower dimensional fixed space will exhibit this problem. Hence, projection algorithms do not appear to be a promising strategy.

Likewise, incremental update algorithms [93] claim to overcome this problem but cannot guarantee a bound on the number of operations required per iteration. Hence, we must resort to different methods.

Recently proposed algorithms [194, 242, 214, 329] perform perceptron-like updates for classification at each step. Some algorithms work only in the noise free case, others do not work for moving targets, and still others assume an upper bound on the complexity of the estimators. Below we present a simple method which allows the use of kernel estimators for classification, regression, and novelty detection and which copes with a large number of kernel functions efficiently.

Direct Online Algorithm

Stochastic Approximation The following method [299] addresses the problem by formulating it in the Reproducing Kernel Hilbert Space $\mathcal{H}$ directly and then by carrying out approximations during the update process. We will minimize the ordinary regularized risk functional (4.2); $R_{\text{reg}}[f] = R_{\text{emp}}[f] + \frac{\lambda}{2}\|f\|^2_{\mathcal{H}}$. Since we want to perform *stochastic* gradient descent, the empirical error term $R_{\text{emp}}[f]$ is replaced by the empirical error *estimate at instance* (x_t, y_t), namely $c(x_t, y_t, f(x_t))$. This means that at time t we have to compute the gradient of

$$R_{\text{stoch}}[f, t] := c(x_t, y_t, f(x_t)) + \frac{\lambda}{2}\|f\|^2_{\mathcal{H}} \tag{10.121}$$

and then perform gradient descent with respect to $R_{\text{stoch}}[f, t]$. Here t is either randomly chosen from $\{1, \ldots m\}$ or it is the new training instance observed at time t. Consequently the gradient of $R_{\text{stoch}}[f, t]$ with respect to f is

$$\partial_f R_{\text{stoch}}[f, t] = c'(x_t, y_t, f(x_t))k(x_t, \cdot) + \lambda f. \tag{10.122}$$

The update equations are thus straightforward,

$$f \longleftarrow f - \Lambda \partial_f R_{\text{stoch}}[f, t], \tag{10.123}$$

where $\Lambda \in \mathbb{R}^+$ is the learning rate controlling the size of updates undertaken at each iteration. We will return to the issue of adjusting (λ, Λ) at a later stage.

Descent Algorithm Substituting the definition of $R_{\text{stoch}}[f, t]$ into (10.123) we obtain

$$f \longleftarrow f - \Lambda\left(c'(x_t, y_t, f(x_t))k(x_t, \cdot) + \lambda f\right) \tag{10.124}$$

$$= (1 - \lambda\Lambda)f - \Lambda c'(x_t, y_t, f(x_t))k(x_t, \cdot). \tag{10.125}$$

While (10.124) is convenient in a theoretical analysis, it is not directly amenable to

13. If we decide to use the gradient in function space instead then the gradient itself will be cheap to compute, but projection of the gradient onto the N dimensional subspace will cost us $O(N^2)$ operations.

computation. For this purpose we have to express f as a kernel expansion

$$f(x) = \sum_i \alpha_i k(x_i, x) \tag{10.126}$$

where the x_i are (previously seen) training patterns. Then (10.126) becomes

$$\alpha_t \longleftarrow (1 - \lambda\Lambda)\alpha_t - \Lambda c'(x_t, y_t, f(x_t)) \tag{10.127}$$

$$= -\Lambda c'(x_t, y_t, f(x_t)) \quad \text{for } \alpha_t = 0 \tag{10.128}$$

$$\alpha_i \longleftarrow (1 - \lambda\Lambda)\alpha_i \quad \text{for } i \neq t. \tag{10.129}$$

Eq. (10.127) means that, at each iteration, the kernel expansion may grow by one term. Further, the cost of training at each step is not larger than the prediction cost. Once we have computed $f(x_t)$, α_t is obtained by the value of the derivative of c at $(x_t, y_t, f(x_t))$.

Instead of updating all coefficients α_i we may simply cache the power series $1, (1 - \lambda\Lambda), (1 - \lambda\Lambda)^2, (1 - \lambda\Lambda)^3, \ldots$ and pick suitable terms as needed. This is particularly useful if the derivatives of the loss function c only assume discrete values, say $\{-1, 0, 1\}$ as is the case when using the soft-margin type loss functions.

Truncation The problem with (10.127) and (10.129) is that, without any further measures, the number of basis functions n will grow without bound. This is not desirable since n determines the amount of computation needed for prediction. The regularization term helps us here. At each iteration the coefficients α_i with $i \neq t$ are shrunk by $(1 - \lambda\Lambda)$. Thus, after τ iterations, the coefficient α_i will be reduced to $(1 - \lambda\Lambda)^\tau \alpha_i$.

Proposition 10.8 (Truncation Error) *For a loss function $c(x, y, f(x))$ with its first derivative bounded by C and a kernel k with bounded norm $\|k(x, \cdot)\| \leq X$, the truncation error in f incurred by dropping terms α_i from the kernel expansion of f after τ update steps is bounded by $\Lambda(1 - \lambda\Lambda)^\tau CX$. In addition, the total truncation error due to dropping all terms which are at least τ steps old is bounded by*

$$\|f - f_{\text{trunc}}\|_{\mathcal{H}} \leq \sum_{i=1}^{t-\tau} \Lambda(1 - \lambda\Lambda)^{t-i} CX < \lambda^{-1}(1 - \lambda\Lambda)^\tau CX \tag{10.130}$$

Here $f_{\text{trunc}} = \sum_{i=t-\tau+1}^{t} \alpha_i k(x_i, \cdot)$. Obviously the approximation quality increases exponentially with the number of terms retained.

The regularization parameter λ can thus be used to control the storage requirements for the expansion. Moreover, it naturally allows for distributions $P(x, y)$ that change over time in which case it is desirable to *forget* instances (x_i, y_i) that are much older than the average time scale of the distribution change [298].

We now proceed to applications of (10.127) and (10.129) in specific learning situations. We utilize the standard addition of the constant offset b to the function expansion, $g(x) = f(x) + b$ where $f \in \mathcal{H}$ and $b \in \mathbb{R}$. Hence we also update b into $b - \Lambda\partial_b R_{\text{stoch}}[g]$.

Classification We begin with the soft margin loss (3.3), given by $c(x, y, g(x)) =$

$\max(0, 1 - yg(x))$. In this situation the update equations become

$$(\alpha_i, \alpha_t, b) \longleftarrow \begin{cases} ((1-\Lambda\lambda)\alpha_i, y_i\Lambda, b + \Lambda y_i) & \text{if } yg(x_t) < 1 \\ ((1-\Lambda\lambda)\alpha_i, 0, b) & \text{otherwise.} \end{cases} \tag{10.131}$$

For **classification with the ν-trick**, as defined in (7.40), we also have to take care of the margin ρ, since there $c(x, y, g(x)) = \max(0, \rho - yg(x)) - \nu\rho$. On the other hand, one can show [481] (see also Problem 7.16) that the specific choice of λ has no influence on the estimate in ν-SV classification. Therefore, we may set $\lambda = 1$ and obtain

$$(\alpha_i, \alpha_t, b, \rho) \longleftarrow \begin{cases} ((1-\Lambda)\alpha_i, y_i\Lambda, b + \Lambda y_i, \rho + \Lambda(1-\nu)) & \text{if } yg(x_t) < \rho \\ ((1-\Lambda)\alpha_i, 0, b, \rho - \Lambda\nu) & \text{otherwise.} \end{cases} \tag{10.132}$$

By analogy to Propositions 8.3 and 7.5, only a fraction of ν points will be used for updates. Finally, if we choose the **hinge-loss**, $c(x, y, g(x)) = \max(0, -yg(x))$,

$$(\alpha_i, \alpha_t, b) \longleftarrow \begin{cases} ((1-\Lambda\lambda)\alpha_i, y_i\Lambda, b + \Lambda y_i) & \text{if } yg(x_t) < 0 \\ ((1-\Lambda\lambda)\alpha_i, 0, b) & \text{otherwise.} \end{cases} \tag{10.133}$$

Setting $\lambda = 0$ recovers the kernel-perceptron algorithm. For nonzero λ we obtain the kernel-perceptron with regularization.

Novelty Detection Results for novelty detection (see Chapter 8 and [475]) are similar in spirit. The **ν-setting** is most useful here, particularly where the estimator acts as a warning device (network intrusion detection for example) or when we would like to specify an upper limit on the frequency of alerts $f(x) < \rho$. The relevant loss function, as introduced in (8.6), is $c(x, y, f(x)) = \max(0, \rho - f(x)) - \nu\rho$ and usually [475] one uses $f \in \mathcal{H}$ rather than $f + b$, where $b \in \mathbb{R}$, in order to avoid trivial solutions. The update equations are

$$(\alpha_i, \alpha_t, \rho) \longleftarrow \begin{cases} ((1-\Lambda)\alpha_i, \Lambda, \rho + \Lambda(1-\nu)) & \text{if } f(x) < \rho \\ ((1-\Lambda)\alpha_i, 0, \rho - \Lambda\nu) & \text{otherwise.} \end{cases} \tag{10.134}$$

Adjusting Λ

Considering the update of ρ we can see that, on average, only a fraction of ν observations will be considered for updates. Thus we only have to store a small fraction of the x_i. We can see that the learning rate Λ provides us with a handle to trade off the cost of the expansion (in terms of the number of basis functions needed) with the time horizon of the prediction; the smaller Λ, the more patterns are included since the coefficients α_i will decay only very slowly. Beyond this point, further research needs to be done to show how Λ is best adjusted (a rule of thumb is to let it decay as $\frac{1}{\sqrt{m}}$). Figure 10.7 contains initial results of the online novelty detection algorithm.

Algorithm 10.6 describes the learning procedure for novelty detection in detail.

Regression We consider the following four settings: squared loss, the ε-insensitive loss using the ν-trick, Huber's robust loss function, and trimmed mean estimators. For convenience we only use estimates $f \in \mathcal{H}$ rather than $g = f + b$ where $b \in \mathbb{R}$. The extension to the latter case is straightforward.

Figure 10.7 Online novelty detection on the USPS dataset (dimension $N = 256$). We use Gaussian RBF kernels with width $2\sigma^2 = 0.5N = 128$. The learning rate was adjusted to $\frac{1}{\sqrt{m}}$ where m is the number of iterations. The left column contains results after one pass through the database, the right column results after 10 random passes. From top to bottom: (top) the first 50 patterns which incurred a margin error, (middle) the 50 worst patterns according to $f(x) - \rho$ on the training set, (bottom) the 50 worst patterns on an unseen test set.

- We begin with **squared loss** (3.8) where c is given by $c(x, y, f(x)) = \frac{1}{2}(y - f(x))^2$. Consequently the update equation is

$$(\alpha_i, \alpha_t) \longleftarrow ((1 - \lambda\Lambda)\alpha_i, \Lambda(y_t - f(x_t))). \tag{10.135}$$

This means that we have to store *every* observation we make or, more precisely, the prediction error we make on every observation.

- The ε**-insensitive loss** (see (3.9)) $c(x, y, f(x)) = \max(0, |y - f(x)| - \varepsilon)$ avoids this problem but introduces a new parameter — the width of the insensitivity zone ε. By making ε a variable of the optimization problem, as shown in Section 9.3, we have

$$c(x, y, f(x)) = \max(0, |y - f(x)| - \varepsilon) + \nu\varepsilon. \tag{10.136}$$

Algorithm 10.6 Online SV Learning

input kernel k, input stream of data X, Λ, ν. time horizon T
Initialize "time" $t = 0$,
repeat
$t = t + 1$
Draw new pattern x_t and compute $f(x_t)$

$$\text{Update} \quad \begin{aligned} \alpha_i &\longleftarrow (1-\Lambda)\alpha_i \\ \alpha_t &= \Lambda \mathrm{H}(\rho - f(x)) \\ \rho &\longleftarrow \rho + \Lambda(\nu - \mathrm{H}(\rho - f(x))) \end{aligned}$$

Truncate the expansion to T terms.
until no more data arrives

The update equations now have to be stated in terms of α_i, α_t, and ε, which is allowed to change during the optimization process. This leads to

$$(\alpha_i, \alpha_t, \varepsilon) \longleftarrow \begin{cases} ((1-\lambda\Lambda)\alpha_i, \Lambda \operatorname{sgn}(y_t - f(x_t)), \varepsilon + (1-\nu)\Lambda) & \text{if } |y_t - f(x_t)| > \varepsilon \\ ((1-\lambda\Lambda)\alpha_i, 0, \varepsilon - \Lambda\nu) & \text{otherwise.} \end{cases} \tag{10.137}$$

Meaning that every time the prediction error exceeds ε we increase the insensitivity zone by $\Lambda\nu$. Likewise, if it is smaller than ε, the insensitive zone is decreased by $\Lambda(1-\nu)$.

▪ Finally, we analyze the case of regression with **Huber's robust loss.** The loss (see Table 3.1) is given by

$$c(x, y, f(x)) = \begin{cases} |y - f(x)| - \frac{1}{2}\sigma & \text{if } |y - f(x)| \geq \sigma \\ \frac{1}{2\sigma}(y - f(x))^2 & \text{otherwise.} \end{cases} \tag{10.138}$$

As before, we obtain update equations by computing the derivative of c with respect to $f(x)$.

$$(\alpha_i, \alpha_t) \longleftarrow \begin{cases} ((1-\Lambda)\alpha_i, \Lambda \operatorname{sgn}(y_t - f(x_t))) & \text{if } |y_t - f(x_t)| > \sigma \\ ((1-\Lambda)\alpha_i, \sigma^{-1}(y_t - f(x_t))) & \text{otherwise.} \end{cases} \tag{10.139}$$

▪ Comparing (10.139) and (10.137) leads to the question of whether σ might not also be **adjusted adaptively**. This is a desirable goal since we may not know the amount of noise present in the data. While the ν-setting allows us to form such adaptive estimators for batch learning with the ε-insensitive loss, this goal has proven elusive for other estimators in the standard batch setting. In the online situation, however, such an extension is quite natural (see also [180]). All we need do is make σ a variable of the optimization problem and set

$$(\alpha_i, \alpha_t, \sigma) \longleftarrow \begin{cases} ((1-\Lambda)\alpha_i, \Lambda \operatorname{sgn}(y_t - f(x_t)), \sigma + \Lambda(1-\nu)) & \text{if } |y_t - f(x_t)| > \sigma \\ ((1-\Lambda)\alpha_i, \sigma^{-1}(y_t - f(x_t)), \sigma - \Lambda\nu) & \text{otherwise.} \end{cases} \tag{10.140}$$

The theoretical analysis of such online algorithms is still an area of ongoing research and we expect significant new results within the next couple of years. For first results see [175, 242, 299, 298, 194, 329]. For instance, one may show [298] that the estimate obtained by an online algorithm converges to the minimizer of the batch setting. Likewise, [242] gives performance guarantees under the assumption of bounded RKHS norms.

For practitioners, however, currently online algorithms offer an alternative to (sometimes rather tricky) batch settings and extend the domain of application available to kernel machines. It will be interesting to see whether the integration of Bayesian techniques [546, 128] leads to other novel online methods.

10.7 Summary

10.7.1 Topics We Did Not Cover

While it is impossible to cover all algorithms currently used for Kernel Machines we give an (incomplete) list of some other important methods.

Kernel Billiard This algorithm was initially proposed in [450] and subsequently modified to accommodate kernel functions in [451]. It works by simulating an ergodic dynamical system of a billiard ball bouncing off the boundaries of the version space (the version space is the set of all $\mathbf{w}$ for which the training data is classified correctly). The estimate is then obtained by averaging over the trajectories.

Bayes Point Machine The algorithm [239, 453] is somewhat similar in spirit to the Kernel Billiard. The main idea is that, by sampling from the posterior distribution of possible estimates (see Chapter 16 for a definition of these quantities), we obtain a solution close to the mean of the posterior.

Iterative Re-weighted Least Squares SVM The main idea is to use clever working set selection strategies to identify the subset of SVs that are likely to sit exactly on the margin. For those SVs, the separation inequality constraints become equalities, and, for these, the reduced QP for the working set can be solved via a linear system (by quadratically penalizing deviations from the exact equality constraints) [407]. This approach can handle additional equality constraints without significant extra effort. Accordingly, it has been generalized to situations with further equality constraints, such as the ν-SVM [408].

Maximum Margin Perceptron This algorithm works in primal space and relies on the idea that the weight vector $\mathbf{w}$ is a linear combination between vectors contained in the convex hull of patterns with $y_i = 1$ and the convex hull of patterns with $y_i = -1$. That convergence requires a finite number of steps can be proven. Moreover, the constant threshold b can be determined rather elegantly. See [309] for a variety of versions of the MMP algorithm.

AdaTron Originally introduced in [12], the kernel version of the AdaTron appeared in [183]. It is, essentially, an extension of the perceptron algorithm to the maximum margin case. As we saw in Section 10.6, similar update rules can be derived with a quadratic soft-margin loss function.

More Mathematical Programming Methods Once one is willing to go beyond the standard setting of regularization in a Reproducing Kernel Hilbert Space, one is offered a host of further Support-Vector like methods derived from optimization theory. The papers of Mangasarian and coworkers [324, 325, 188, 189] present such techniques.

10.7.2 Topics We Covered

Several algorithms can be used to solve the quadratic programming problem arising in SV regression. Most of them can be shown to share a common strategy that can be understood well through duality theory. In particular, this viewpoint leads to useful optimization and stopping criteria for many different classes of algorithm, since the Lagrange multipliers α_i are less interesting quantities than the value of the objective function itself.

Interior Point Codes A class of algorithms to exploit these properties explicitly are interior point primal-dual path following algorithms (see Section 10.3). They are relatively fast and achieve high solution precision in the case of moderately sized problems (up to approximately 3000 samples). Moreover, these algorithms can be modified easily for general convex loss functions without additional computational cost. They require computation and inversion of the kernel matrix K however, and are thus overly expensive for large problems.

Greedy Approximation We presented a way to extend this method to large scale problems which makes use of sparse greedy approximation techniques. The latter are particularly well suited to this type of algorithm since they find a low rank approximation of the dense and excessively large kernel matrix K directly, without ever requiring full computation of the latter. Moreover, we obtain sparse (however approximate) solutions, independent of the number of Support Vectors.

Chunking in its different variants is another modification to make large scale problems solvable by classical optimization methods. It requires the breaking up of the initial problem into subproblems which are then, in turn, solved separately. This is guaranteed to decrease the objective function, thus approaching the global optimum. Selection rules, in view of duality theory, are given in section 10.4.3.

Sequential Minimal Optimization (SMO) is probably one of the easiest algorithms to implement for SV optimization. It might thus be the method of choice for a first attempt to implement an SVM. It exhibits good performance, and proofs of convergence have been obtained. Recent research has pointed out several ways of improving the basic algorithm. We briefly sketched one technique which improves the estimation of the constant threshold b and thus also helps select good subsets more easily. Pseudocode for regression and classification conclude this section.

Iterative Methods Finally, another class of algorithms can be summarized as iterative methods, such as gradient descent, Lagrangian SVM which are extremely simple but which are only applicable for a specific choice of cost function, and online support vector methods. These have the potential to make the area of large scale problems accessible to kernel methods and we expect good progress in the future. While it is far from clear what the optimal strategy might be, it is our hope that the reasoning of Section 10.6.3 will help to propel research in this area.

10.7.3 Future Developments and Code

We anticipate that future research will focus on efficient *approximate* and sparse solutions. This means that, quite often, it is not necessary to find a kernel expansion $f = \sum_{i=1}^{m} \alpha_i k(x_i, \cdot)$, where the α_i are the Lagrange multipliers of the corresponding optimization problem and, instead, a much more compact function representation can be used.

Second, we expect that both lightweight optimizers, which can be deployed on small consumer hardware, and large-scale optimizers, which take advantage of large clusters of workstations, will become available. It is our hope that, in a few years, kernel methods will be readily accessible as plug-ins and toolboxes for many statistical analysis packages.

Finally, the choice of parameters is still a problem which requires further attention. While there exist several promising approaches (see [288, 102, 268]) for assessing the generalization performance, mainly involving leave-one-out estimates or their approximation, the problem is far from solved. In particular, every new bound on the generalization performance of kernel machines will inevitably prompt the need for an improved training algorithm which can take advantage of the bound.

Some readers will miss pointers to readily available code for SVM in this book. We deliberately decided not to include such information since such information is likely to become obsolete rather quickly. Instead, we refer the reader to the kernel-machines website (http://www.kernel-machines.org) for up-to-date information on the topic.

10.8 Problems

10.1 (KKT Gap for Linear Programming Regularizers ••)
Compute the explicit functional form of the KKT gap for Linear Programming Regularizers. Why can't you simply use the expansion coefficients α_i as in Proposition 10.1?

10.2 (KKT Gap for Sub-Optimal Offsets ••)
Compute the functional form of the KKT gap for non-optimal parametric parts in the expansion of f, e.g., if $f(x) = \langle \Phi(x), \mathbf{w} \rangle + b$ where b is not optimal. Hint: consider

Theorem 6.22 and prove a variant of Theorem 6.27.

10.3 (Restarting for λ •)
Prove an analogous inequality for $R_{\text{reg}}[f]$ as (10.22) for λ rather than C, i.e. prove

$$R_{\text{reg}}[f_\lambda, \lambda'] \geq R_{\text{reg}}[f_{\lambda'}, \lambda'] \geq R_{\text{reg}}[f_\lambda, \lambda] \text{ for all } \lambda' > \lambda. \tag{10.141}$$

10.4 (Sparse Approximation in the Function Values ••)
State the optimal expansion for approximations of $k(x_i, \cdot)$ by $\tilde{k}_i(\cdot)$ in the space of function values on $X = \{x_1, \ldots, x_m\}$. How many operations does it cost to compute the expansion?

10.5 (Rank-1 Updates for Cholesky Decompositions ••)
Given a positive definite matrix $K \in \mathbb{R}^{n\times n}$, its Cholesky decomposition $TT^\top = K$ into triangular matrices $T \in \mathbb{R}^{n\times n}$, a vector $\mathbf{k} \in \mathbb{R}^n$, and a real number κ such that the matrix $\begin{bmatrix} K & \mathbf{k} \\ \mathbf{k}^\top & \kappa \end{bmatrix}$ is positive definite, show that the Cholesky decomposition of the larger matrix is given by

$$\begin{bmatrix} K & \mathbf{k} \\ \mathbf{k}^\top & \kappa \end{bmatrix} = \begin{bmatrix} T & 0 \\ \mathbf{t} & \tau \end{bmatrix} \begin{bmatrix} T^\top & \mathbf{t}^\top \\ 0 & \tau \end{bmatrix} \tag{10.142}$$

where

$$\mathbf{t} = T^{-1}\mathbf{k} \text{ and } \tau = \left(\kappa - \mathbf{t}^\top \mathbf{t}\right)^{\frac{1}{2}}. \tag{10.143}$$

Why would we replace the equation for τ by $\tau = \max\left(0, (\kappa - \mathbf{t}^\top\mathbf{t})^{\frac{1}{2}}\right)$ for numerical stability? How can you compute (10.143) in $O(n^2)$ time?

10.6 (Smaller Memory Footprint for SGMA •••)
Show that rather than caching K^{mn}, $(K^{nn})^{-1}$ and $\alpha = (K^{nn})^{-1}K^{mn}$ (and updating the three matrices accordingly) we can reformulate the sparse greedy matrix approximation algorithm to use only T_n and $T_n^{-1}K^{mn}$ where T_n is the Cholesky decomposition (see Problem 10.5) of K^{nn} into a product of triangular matrices, that is $T_n T_n^\top = K^{nn}$.

In particular, show that the update for $T_n^{-1}K^{mn}$ is given by

$$T_{n+1}^{-1}K^{m,n+1} = \begin{bmatrix} T_n^{-1}K^{mn} \\ \tau^{-1}\left(\bar{k} - \mathbf{t}\left(T_n^{-1}K^{mn}\right)\right) \end{bmatrix} \tag{10.144}$$

where $\mathbf{t}$ and τ are defined as in (10.143).

10.7 (Optimality of PCA •••)
Show that for the problem of approximating a positive definite matrix K by a matrix $\tilde{K}$ of rank n such that both $\tilde{K}$ and $K - \tilde{K}$ are positive definite the solution is given by projecting onto the largest n principal components of K, i.e., by PCA. Here we consider an approximation to be optimal if the residual trace of $K - \tilde{K}$ is minimized. Show that PCA is also optimal if we consider the largest eigenvalue of $K - \tilde{K}$ as the quantity to be minimized. Hint: recall that K is a Gram matrix for some x_i, i.e., $K_{ij} = \langle x_i, x_j \rangle$.

10.8 (General Convex Cost Functions [516] ••)
Show that for a convex optimization problem

$$\begin{aligned} \underset{\alpha}{\text{minimize}} \quad & \tfrac{1}{2}q(\alpha) + \langle c, \alpha \rangle \\ \text{subject to} \quad & A\alpha = d \\ & l \leq \alpha \leq u \end{aligned} \tag{10.145}$$

with $c, \alpha, l, u \in \mathbb{R}^m$, $A \in \mathbb{R}^{n \cdot m}$, *and* $d \in \mathbb{R}^n$, *the inequalities between vectors holding component-wise, and* $q(\alpha)$ *being a convex function of* α, *the dual optimization problem is given by*

$$\begin{aligned} \text{maximize} \quad & \tfrac{1}{2}\left(q(\alpha) - \langle \partial_\alpha q(\alpha), \alpha \rangle\right) + \langle d, h \rangle + \langle l, z \rangle - \langle u, s \rangle \\ \text{subject to} \quad & \tfrac{1}{2}\partial_\alpha q(\alpha) + c - (Ay)^\top + s = z \\ & s, z \geq 0, \ h \text{ free} \end{aligned} \tag{10.146}$$

Moreover, the KKT conditions read

$$g_i z_i = s_i t_i = 0 \text{ for all } i \in [m]. \tag{10.147}$$

10.9 (Interior Point Algorithm for (10.145) [516] ••)
Derive an interior point algorithm for the optimization problem given in (10.145). Hint: use a quadratic approximation of $q(\alpha)$ *for each iteration and apply an interior point code to this modification. Which cost functions does this allow you to use in an SVM?*

10.10 (Sherman-Woodbury-Morrison for Linear SVM [168] ••)
Show that for linear SVMs the cost per interior point iteration is $O(mn^2)$. *Hint: use (10.54) to solve (10.48).*

10.11 (KKT Gap and Optimality on Subsets ••)
Prove that after optimization over a subset S_w *(and adjusting b in accordance to the subset) the corresponding contributions to the KKT gap, i.e. the terms* KKT_i *for* $i \in S_w$ *will vanish.*

10.12 (SVMTorch Selection Criteria [502, 108] •)
Derive the SVMTorch optimality criteria for SV regression; derive the equations analogous to (10.60) for the regression setting.

10.13 (Gradient Selection and KKT Conditions •)
Show that for regression and classification the patterns selected according to (10.60) are identical to those chosen by the gradient selection rule, i.e. according to $Q\alpha + c$. *Hint: show that gradient and* $\overline{\mathrm{KKT}}_i$ *differ only in the constant offset b, hence taking the maxima of both sets yields identical results.*

10.14 (SMO and Number of Constraints •)
Show that for SMO to make any progress we need at least $n+1$ *variables where n is the number of equality constraints in* $A\alpha = d$. *What does this mean in terms of speed of optimization?*

Find a reformulation of the optimization problem which can do without any equality constraints. Hint: drop the constant offset b from the expansion. State the explicit solution to the constrained optimization problem in one variable.

Which selection criteria would you use in this case to find good patterns? Can you adapt KKT_i, $\overline{\mathrm{KKT}}_i$, *and* $\underline{\mathrm{KKT}}_i$ *accordingly? Can you bound the improvement explicitly?*

10.15 (Orthogonality and Clipping •)
Prove Lemma 10.6. Hint: first prove that for $a, b \in \mathbb{R}$ *(10.109) holds. The lemma then follows by summation over the coordinates.*

10.16 (Lagrangian Support Vector Machines for Regression ••) *Derive a variant of the Lagrangian Support Vector Algorithm for regression. Hint: begin with a regularized risk functional where b is regularized and the squared ε-insensitive loss function* $c(x, y, f(x)) = \max(|f(x) - y| - \varepsilon, 0)^2$. *Next derive an equation analogous to (10.110).*

For the iteration scheme you may want to take advantage of orthogonal transformations such as the one given in (10.52). What is the condition on γ *in this case?*

10.17 (Laplace Approximation ••)
Use Newton's method as described in (6.12) to find an iterative minimization scheme for the regularized risk functional. See also Section 16.4.1 for details. For which cost functions is it suitable (Hint: Newton's method is a second order approach)? Can you apply the Sherman-Morrison-Woodbury formula to find quick approximate minimizers? Compare the algorithm to the Lagrangian Support Vector Machines.

10.18 (Online Learning and Number of Support Vectors ••)
Show that for a classification problem with nonzero minimal risk the number of Support Vectors increases linearly with the number of patterns, provided one chooses a regularization parameter that avoids overfitting. Hint: first show that all misclassified patterns on the training set will become Support Vectors, then show that the fraction of misclassified patterns is non-vanishing.

10.19 (Online Learning with ν-SVM •••)
Derive an online version of the ν-SVM classification algorithm. For this purpose begin with the modified regularized risk functional as given by

$$R_{\mathrm{reg}}[f] = \frac{1}{m}\sum_{i=1}^{m} c_\rho(x_i, y_i, f(x_i)) - \rho\nu + \frac{1}{2}\|f\|^2_{\mathcal{H}}. \tag{10.148}$$

Next replace $\frac{1}{m}\sum_{i=1}^{m} c_\rho(x_i, y_i, f(x_i))$ *by the stochastic estimate* $c_\rho(x_t, y_t, f(x_t))$. *Note that you have to perform updates not only in f but also in the margin* ρ.

What happens if you change ρ *rather than letting* α_i *decay in the cases where no margin error occurs? Why don't you need* λ *any more? Hint: consider the analogous case of Chapter 9.*

11 Incorporating Invariances

Practical experience has shown that in order to obtain the best possible performance, prior knowledge about a problem at hand ought to be incorporated into the training procedure. We describe and review methods for incorporating prior knowledge on invariances in Support Vector Machines, provide experimental results, and discuss their respective merits, gathering material from various sources [471, 467, 478, 134, 562].

Overview

The chapter is organized as follows. The first section introduces the concept of prior knowledge, and discusses what types of prior knowledge are used in pattern recognition. Following this, we will deal specifically with transformation invariances (Section 11.2), discussing two rather different approaches to make SVMs invariant: by generating virtual examples from the SVs (Section 11.3) or by modifying the kernel function (Section 11.4). Finally, in Section 11.5, we combine ideas from both approaches by effectively making the virtual examples part of the kernel definition.

Prerequisites

The prerequisites for the chapter are largely limited to basics of the SV classification algorithm (Chapter 7) and some knowledge of linear algebra (Appendix B). Section 11.4.2 uses Kernel PCA, as described in Section 1.7 and Chapter 14.

11.1 Prior Knowledge

In 1995, LeCun et al. [320] published a pattern recognition performance comparison noting the following:

"The optimal margin classifier has excellent accuracy, which is most remarkable, because unlike the other high performance classifiers, it does not include *a priori* knowledge about the problem. In fact, this classifier would do just as well if the image pixels were permuted by a fixed mapping. [...] However, improvements are expected as the technique is relatively new."

Two things have changed in the five years since this statement was made. First, optimal margin classifiers, or Support Vector Machines, as they are now known, have become a mainstream method which is part of the standard machine learning toolkit. Second, methods for incorporating prior knowledge into optimal margin classifiers are now part of the standard SV methodology.

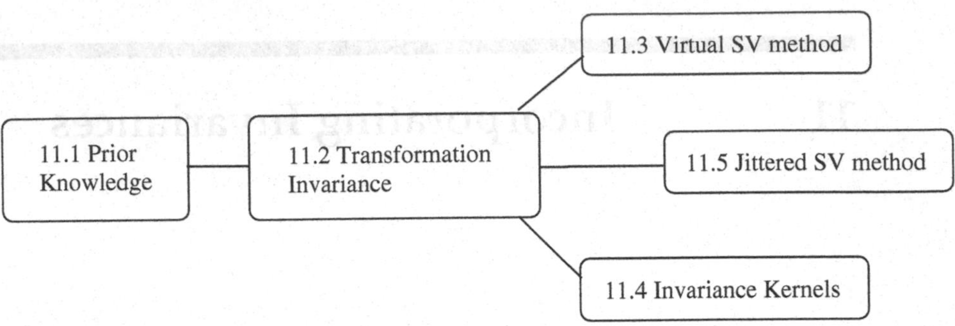

These two developments are actually closely related. Initially, SVMs had been considered a theoretically elegant spin-off of the general, but apparently largely useless, VC-theory of statistical learning. In 1995, using the first methods for incorporating prior knowledge, SVMs became competitive with the state of the art, in the handwritten digit classification benchmarks that were popularized by AT&T Bell Labs [471]. At that point, application engineers who were not interested in theory, but in results, could no longer ignore SVMs. In this sense, the methods described below actually helped pave the way to make the SVM a widely used machine learning tool.

Prior Knowledge

By *prior knowledge* we refer to all information about the learning task which is available in addition to the training examples. In this most general form, only prior knowledge makes it *possible* to generalize from the training examples to novel test examples.

For instance, many classifiers incorporate general *smoothness assumptions* about the problem. A test pattern which is similar to one of the training examples thus tends to be assigned to the same class. For SVMs, using a kernel function k amounts to enforcing smoothness with a regularizer $\|\Upsilon f\|^2$, where f is the estimated function, and k is a Green's function of the regularization operator Υ (Chapter 4). In a Bayesian maximum-a-posteriori setting, this corresponds to a smoothness prior of $\exp(-\|\Upsilon f\|^2)$ ([295], see Section 16.2.3).

A second method for incorporating prior knowledge, which is somewhat more specific, consists of *selecting features* which are thought to be particularly informative or reliable for the task at hand. For instance, in handwritten character recognition, correlations between image pixels that are nearby tend to be more reliable than those between distant pixels. The intuitive reason for this is that variations in writing style tends to leave the local structure of a handwritten digit fairly unchanged, while the global structure is usually quite variable. In the case of SVMs, this type of prior knowledge is readily incorporated by designing polynomial kernels which mainly compute products of nearby pixels (Section 13.3).

One way to look at feature selection is that it changes the representation of the data, in which respect it resembles another method for incorporating prior knowledge in SVMs that has recently attracted attention. In the latter case, it is assumed that we have knowledge about probabilistic models generating the data.

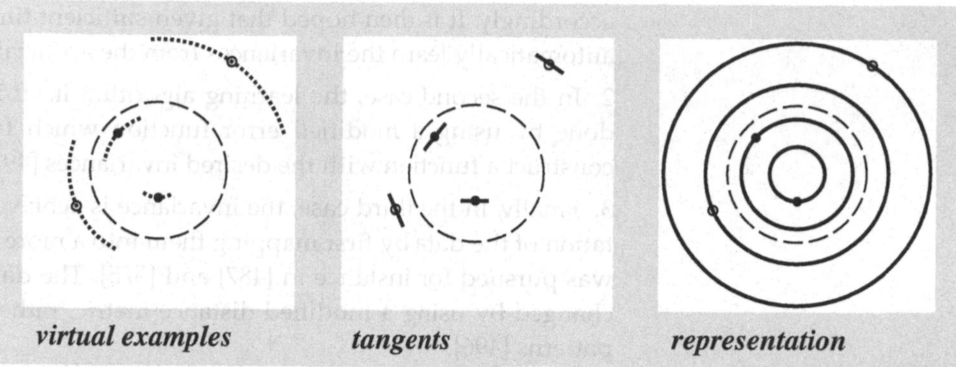

Figure 11.1 Different ways of incorporating invariances in a decision function. The dashed line marks the "true" boundary, disks and circles are the training examples. We assume that prior information tells us that the classification function only depends on the norm of the input vector (the origin being in the center of each picture). Lines through the examples indicate the type of information conveyed by the different methods for incorporating prior information. *Left:* virtual examples are generated in a localized region around each training example; *middle:* a regularizer is incorporated to learn tangent values (cf. [497]); *right:* the representation of the data is changed by first mapping each example to its norm. If feasible, the latter method yields the most information. However, if the necessary nonlinear transformation cannot be found, or if the desired invariances are of a localized nature, we have to resort to one of the former techniques. Finally, note that examples close to the boundary allow us to exploit prior knowledge very effectively: given a method to get a first approximation of the true boundary, the examples closest to the approximate boundary allow good estimation of the true boundary. A similar two-step approach is pursued in Section 11.3. (From [471].)

Specifically, let $p(x|\Theta)$ be a generative model that characterizes the probability of a pattern x, given the underlying parameter Θ. It is possible to construct a class of kernels which are invariant with respect to reparametrizations of Θ, and which, loosely speaking, have the property that $k(x, x')$ is the similarity of x and x', subject to the assumption that they both stem from the generative model. These kernels are called Fisher kernels ([258], cf. Chapter 13). A different approach to designing kernels based on probabilistic models is presented in [585, 333].

Finally, we get to the type of prior knowledge that we shall start with: prior knowledge about *invariances*.

11.2 Transformation Invariance

In many applications of learning procedures, certain transformations of the input are known to leave function values unchanged. At least three different ways of exploiting this knowledge have been used (illustrated in Figure 11.1):

1. In the first case, the knowledge is used to generate artificial training examples, termed "virtual examples," [18, 413, 2] by transforming the training examples

accordingly. It is then hoped that given sufficient time, the learning machine will automatically learn the invariances from the artificially enlarged training data.

2. In the second case, the learning algorithm itself is modified. This is typically done by using a modified error function which forces a learning machine to construct a function with the desired invariances [497].

3. Finally, in the third case, the invariance is achieved by changing the representation of the data by first mapping them into a more suitable space; this approach was pursued for instance in [487] and [575]. The data representation can also be changed by using a modified distance metric, rather than actually changing the patterns [496].

Simard et al. [497] compare the first two techniques and find that for the problem considered — learning a function with three plateaus, where function values are locally invariant — training on the artificially enlarged data set is significantly slower, due both to correlations in the artificial data, and the increase in training set size. Moving to real-world applications, the latter factor becomes even more important. If the size of a training set is multiplied by a number of desired invariances (by generating a corresponding number of artificial examples for each training pattern), the resulting training sets can get rather large, such as those used in [148]. However, the method of generating virtual examples has the advantage of being readily implemented for all kinds of learning machines and symmetries. If instead of continuous groups of symmetry transformations we are dealing with discrete symmetries, such as the bilateral symmetries of [576], derivative-based methods such as those of [497] are not applicable. It is thus desirable to have an intermediate method which has the advantages of the virtual examples approach without its computational cost.

The methods described in this chapter try to combine merits of all the approaches mentioned above. The *Virtual SV method* (Section 11.3) retains the flexibility and simplicity of virtual examples approaches, while cutting down on their computational cost significantly. The Invariant Hyperplane method (Section 11.4), on the other hand, is comparable to the method of [497] in that it is applicable to all differentiable local 1-parameter groups of local invariance transformations, comprising a fairly general class of invariances. In addition, it has an equivalent interpretation as a preprocessing operation applied to the data before learning. In this sense, it can also be viewed as changing the representation of the data to be more invariant, in a task-dependent way. Another way to interpret this method is as a way to construct kernels that respect local image structures; this will be discussed further in a later chapter (Section 13.3). The latter interpretation gives rise to a resemblance to the last technique that we discuss, the *Jittered SV method* (Section 11.5), which combines the flexibility of the VSV method with the elegance of an approach that directly modifies the kernel and does not need to enlarge the training set.

11.3 The Virtual SV Method

In Section 7.8.2, it has been argued that the SV set contains all information necessary to solve a given classification task. It particular, it is possible to train any one of three different types of SVMs solely on the Support Vector set extracted by another machine, with a test performance no worse than after training on the full database. Using this finding as a starting point, we now investigate whether it might be sufficient to generate virtual examples from the Support Vectors only. After all, we might hope that it does not add much information to generate virtual examples from patterns which are not close to the boundary. In high-dimensional cases, however, care has to be exercised regarding the validity of this intuitive picture. Thus, an experimental test on a high-dimensional real-world problem is imperative. In our experiments, we proceeded as follows (cf. Figure 11.2):

1. Train a Support Vector Machine to extract the Support Vector set.

2. Generate artificial examples by applying the desired invariance transformations to the Support Vectors. In the following, we will refer to these examples as *Virtual Support Vectors (VSVs)*.

3. Train another Support Vector Machine on the examples generated.

Clearly, the scheme can be iterated; care must be exercised, however, since the iteration of local invariances can lead to global invariances which are not always desirable — consider the example of a '6' rotating into a '9' [496].

If the desired invariances are incorporated, the curves obtained by applying Lie group transformations to points on the decision surface should have tangents parallel to the latter (cf. [497]).[1] If we use small Lie group transformations (e.g., translations) to generate the virtual examples, this implies that the Virtual Support Vectors should be approximately as close to the decision surface as the original Support Vectors. Hence, they are fairly likely to become Support Vectors after the second training run. Vice versa, if a substantial fraction of the Virtual Support Vectors turn out to become Support Vectors in the second run, we have reason to expect that the decision surface does have the desired shape.

USPS Digit Recognition

Let us now look at some experiments validating the above intuition. The first set of experiments was conducted on the USPS database of handwritten digits (Section A.1). This database has been used extensively in the literature, with a LeNet1 Convolutional Network achieving a test error rate of 5.0% [318]. As in

1. The reader who is not familiar with the concept of a Lie group may think of it as a group of transformations where each element is labelled by a set of continuously variable parameters. Such a group may be considered also to be a manifold, where the parameters are the coordinates. For Lie groups, it is required that all group operations are smooth maps. It follows that we can, for instance, compute derivatives with respect to the parameters. Examples of Lie groups are the translation group, the rotation group, and the Lorentz group; further details can be found in textbooks on differential geometry, e.g., [120].

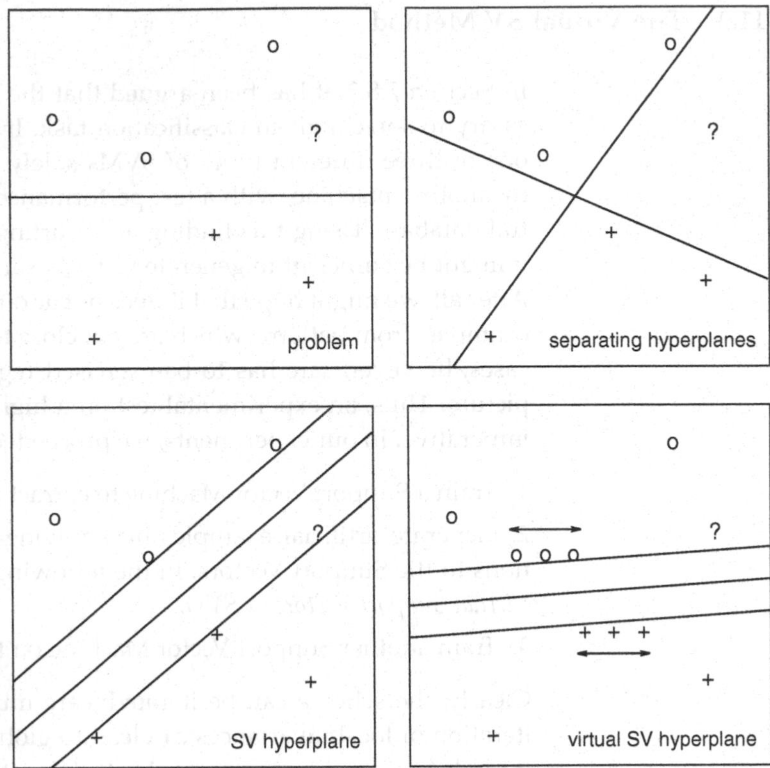

Figure 11.2 Suppose we have prior knowledge indicating that the decision function should be invariant with respect to horizontal translations. The true decision boundary is drawn as a horizontal line (*top left*); as we are just given a limited training sample, however, different separating hyperplanes are conceivable (*top right*). The SV algorithm finds the unique separating hyperplane with maximal margin (*bottom left*), which in this case is quite different from the true boundary. For instance, it leads to incorrect classification of the ambiguous point indicated by the question mark. Making use of the prior knowledge by generating Virtual Support Vectors from the Support Vectors found in a first training run, and retraining on these, yields a more accurate decision boundary (*bottom right*). Furthermore, note that for the example considered, it is sufficient to train the SVM *only* on virtual examples generated from the Support Vectors.

Section 7.8.1, we used $C = 10$.

Table 11.1 shows that incorporating only translational invariance already improves performance significantly, from an error rate of 4.0% to 3.2%.[2] For other types of invariances (Figure 11.3), we also found improvements, albeit smaller ones: generating Virtual Support Vectors by rotations or by line thickness transformations,[3] we constructed polynomial classifiers with a 3.7% error rate (in both

2. For a number of reference results, cf. Table 7.4.
3. Briefly, the idea of the line thickness transformation of an image is to add some multiple of its gradient. As the original outline of the image is the area of highest gradient, this

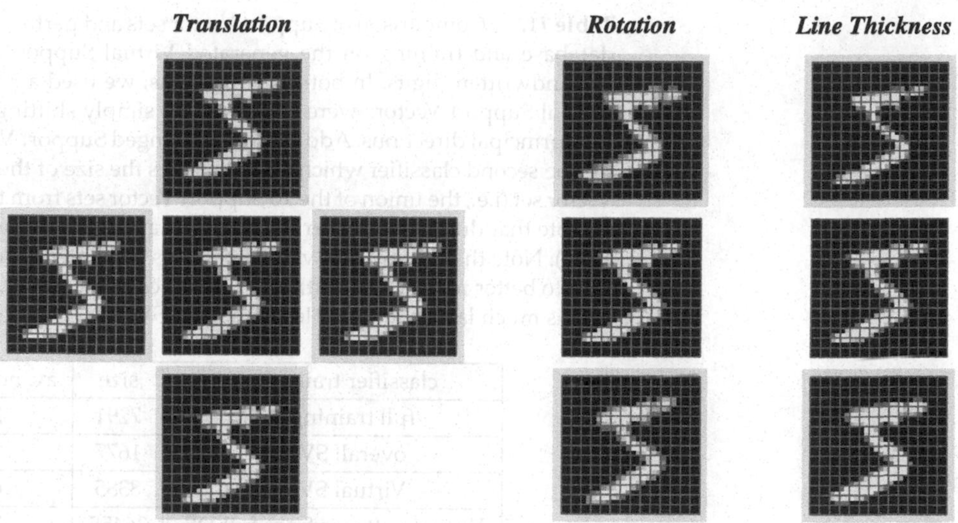

Figure 11.3 Different invariance transformations in the case of handwritten digit recognition (MNIST database). In all three cases, the central pattern is the original which is transformed into "virtual examples" (marked by gray frames) with the same class membership, by applying small transformations.

cases). For details, see [467].

Note, moreover, that generating Virtual examples from the full database rather than just from the SV sets did not improve the accuracy, nor did it substantially enlarge the SV set of the final classifier. This finding was reproduced for a Virtual SV system with a Gaussian RBF kernel [482]: in that case, as in Table 11.1, generating Virtual examples from the full database led to identical performance, and only slightly increased the SV set size (861 instead of 806). We conclude that for this recognition task, it is sufficient to generate Virtual examples only from the SVs — Virtual examples generated from the other patterns do not add much useful information.

MNIST Digit Recognition

The larger a database, the more information about invariances of the decision function is already contained in the differences between patterns of the same class. To show that it is nonetheless possible to improve classification accuracy using our technique, we applied the method to the MNIST database (Section A.1) of 60000 handwritten digits. This database has become the standard for performance comparisons at AT&T Bell Labs; the error rate record of 0.7% was held until recently by a boosted LeNet4 [64, 321], which represents an ensemble of learning machines; the best single machine performance was achieved at this time by a LeNet5 convolutional neural network (0.9%). Other high performance systems include a Tangent Distance nearest neighbor classifier (1.1%).

procedure tends to make lines thicker [148].

Table 11.1 Comparison of Support Vector sets and performance for training on the original database and training on the generated Virtual Support Vectors, for the USPS database of handwritten digits. In both training runs, we used a polynomial classifier of degree 3. Virtual Support Vectors were generated by simply shifting the images by one pixel in the four principal directions. Adding the unchanged Support Vectors, this leads to a training set for the second classifier which has five times the size of the first classifier's overall Support Vector set (i.e., the union of the 10 Support Vector sets from the binary classifiers, of size 1677 — note that due to some overlap, this is smaller than the sum of the ten Support Vector set sizes). Note that training on virtual patterns generated from *all* training examples does not lead to better results than in the Virtual SV case; moreover, although the training set in this case is much larger, it barely leads to more SVs.

classifier trained on	size	av. no. of SVs	test error
full training set	7291	274	4.0%
overall SV set	1677	268	4.1%
Virtual SV set	8385	686	3.2%
Virtual patterns from full DB	36455	719	3.4%

Using Virtual Support Vectors generated by 1-pixel translations into the four principal directions, we improved a degree 5 polynomial SV classifier from an error rate of 1.4% to 1.0% on the 10000 element test set. We applied our technique separately for all ten Support Vector sets of the binary classifiers (rather than for their union) in order to avoid having to deal with large training sets in the retraining stage. In addition, note that for the MNIST database, we did not attempt to generate Virtual examples from the whole database, as this would have required training on a very large training set.[4]

After retraining, the number of SVs more than doubles [467] Thus, although the training sets for the second set of binary classifiers are substantially smaller than the original database (for four Virtual SVs per SV, four times the size of the original SV sets, in our case amounting to around 10^4), we conclude that the amount of data in the region of interest, close to the decision boundary, more than doubles. Therefore, it should be possible to use a more complex decision function in the second stage (note that the typical risk bounds (Chapter 5) depend on the *ratio* of VC-dimension and training set size). Indeed, using a degree 9 polynomial leads to an error rate of 0.8%, very close to the boosted LeNet4 (0.7%).

Recently, several systems have been designed which are on par with or better than the boosted LeNet4 [536, 134, 30]. The new record is now held by a virtual SV classifier which used more virtual examples, leading to results which are

4. We did, however, compute such a solution for the *small* MNIST database (Section A.1). In this case, a degree 5 polynomial classifier was improved from an error of 3.8% to 2.5% using the Virtual SV method, with an increase of the average SV set sizes from 324 to 823. By generating Virtual examples from the full training set, and retraining on these, we obtained a system which had slightly more SVs (939), but an unchanged error rate.

Table 11.2 Summary of error rates on the MNIST handwritten digit set, using the 10,000 element test set (cf. Section A.1). At 0.6% (0.56% before rounding), the VSV system using 12 translated virtual examples per SV (described in the text) performs best.

Classifier	test error	reference
linear classifier	8.4%	[319]
3-nearest-neighbor	2.4%	[319]
LeNet1	1.7%	[319]
Neural Net with one hidden layer	1.6%	[319]
SVM	1.4%	[87]
SVM, deslanted data	1.2%	[134]
Local learning Approach	1.1%	[65]
Tangent distance	1.1%	[496]
LeNet4	1.1%	[319]
Virtual SVM with 4 VSVs per SV	0.8%	*present chapter*, [467]
LeNet5	0.8%	[319]
Boosted LeNet4	0.7%	[64, 319]
Virtual SVM with 8 VSVs per SV	0.7%	*present chapter*, [134]
Virtual SVM with 12 VSVs per SV	0.6%	*present chapter*, [134]

actually superior to the boosted LeNet4. Since this dataset is considered the "gold standard" of classifier benchmarks, it is worth reporting some details of this study. Table 11.3 summarizes the results, giving the lowest published test error for this data set (0.56%, [134]). Figure 11.4 shows the 56 misclassified test examples. For reference purposes, Table 11.2 gives a summary of error rates on the MNIST set.

As above, a polynomial kernel of degree 9 was used. Patterns were deslanted and normalized so that dot-products giving values within $[0,1]$ yielded kernel values within $[0,1]$; specifically,

$$k(x, x') = \frac{1}{512}(\langle x, x'\rangle + 1)^9. \tag{11.1}$$

This ensures that the kernel value 1 has the same meaning that holds for other kernels, such as radial-basis function (RBF) kernels. Namely, a kernel value of 1 corresponds to the minimum distance (between identical examples) in the feature space. It was ensured that any dot-product was within [0,1] by normalizing each example by its 2-norm scalar value (such that the dot product of each example with itself gave a value of 1).

The value of the regularization constant C (the upper bound on the α_i) was determined as follows. By trying a large value when training a binary recognizer for digit "8", it was determined that no training example reached an α_i value above 7, and only a handful of examples in each of the 10 digit classes had alpha values above 2. Under the assumption that only a few training examples in each class are particularly noisy and that digit "8" is one of the harder digits to recognize,

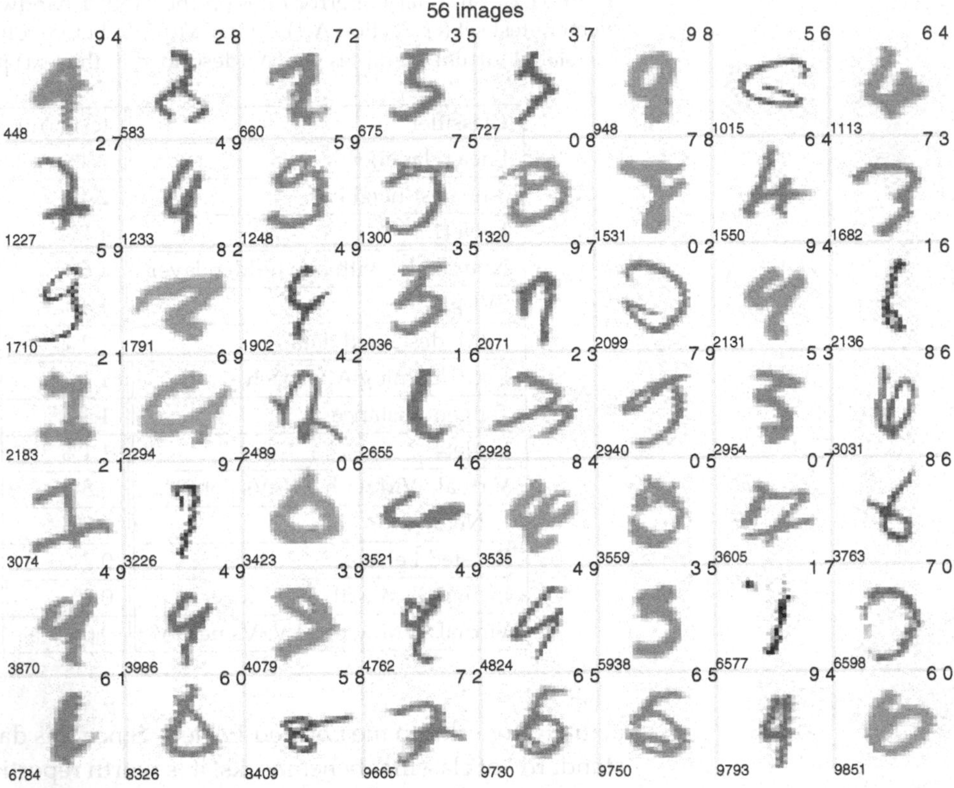

Figure 11.4 The 56 test errors of the record VSV system for MNIST. The number in the lower left corner of each image box indicates the test example number (1 through 10000). The first number in the upper right corner represents the predicted digit label, and the second denotes the true label (from [134]).

we chose $C = 2$. This simplistic choice is likely suboptimal, and could possibly be improved by (time-consuming) experiments on validation sets.

The experiments employed new SMO-based methods (see Chapter 10 for a description of SMO), as described in [134], including a technique called *digestion*, which switches SMO from "full" to "inbounds" iteration every time the working set of SVs grows by a large amount. The resulting faster training times can be put to good use by trying the VSV method with more invariance than was practical in previous experiments. In our case, it was possible to generate VSVs by translation of each SV by a distance of one pixel in any of the 8 directions (horizontal, vertical, or both), plus two-pixel translations horizontally and vertically. Total training time, for obtaining 10 binary recognizers for each of the base SV and the VSV stages, was about 2 days (50 hours) on a Sun Ultra60 workstation with a 450MHz processor and 2 Gigabytes of RAM (allowing an 800Mb kernel cache). The VSV stage was more expensive that the base SV stage (averaging about 4 hours versus 1 hour) — a majority of examples used in VSV training typically ended up being Support Vectors.

Table 11.3 Results for the MNIST benchmark (10000 test examples), using an inhomogeneous polynomial kernel of degree 9 and deslanted data. The *VSV* system was trained using 12 virtual examples per SV. *First table:* test error rates of the multi-class systems; *second table:* error rates of the individual binary recognizers that were trained for each digit class, *third table:* numbers of SVs (from [134]).

Misclassifications

	digit misclassifications										10-class
digit	0	1	2	3	4	5	6	7	8	9	test error rate
SV	5	5	14	12	13	10	13	13	12	25	1.22%
VSV	3	3	5	3	6	7	7	6	5	11	**0.56%**

Errors for each binary recognizer

SVM for digit	0	1	2	3	4	5	6	7	8	9
SV										
false negatives	9	11	21	22	15	21	22	24	21	47
false positives	7	6	7	5	8	6	9	9	10	8
VSV										
false negatives	5	5	12	11	4	9	13	12	11	18
false positives	4	5	9	4	9	4	11	9	3	7

Number of Support Vectors for each binary recognizer

digit	0	1	2	3	4	5	6	7	8	9
SV	1859	1057	3186	3315	2989	3311	2039	2674	3614	3565
$0<\alpha_i<C$	1758	927	3023	3090	2830	3124	1934	2475	3301	3202
$\alpha_i=C$	101	130	163	225	159	187	105	199	313	363
VSV	11305	6298	18549	18680	16800	18550	11910	16489	21826	23003
$0<\alpha_i<C$	10650	5117	17539	17141	15329	17294	11084	14645	19382	19898
$\alpha_i=C$	655	1181	1010	1539	1471	1256	826	1844	2444	3105

We conclude this section by noting that the same technique has also been applied in the domains of face classification and object recognition. In these areas, where we are dealing with bilaterally symmetric objects, useful virtual SVs can also be generated by reflection with respect to a vertical axis. This kind of discrete transformation does not arise from a continuous group of transformations, but this does not present a problem with the VSV approach [467].

11.4 Constructing Invariance Kernels

In this section, we describe a self-consistency argument for obtaining invariant SVMs. Interestingly, it will turn out that the criterion we end up with can be viewed as a meaningful modification of the kernel function.

11.4.1 Invariance in Input Space

We need a self-consistency argument because we face the following problem: to express the condition of invariance of the decision function, we already need to know its coefficients α_i, which are found only during the optimization; this in turn should already take into account the desired invariances. As a way out of this circle, we use the following ansatz: consider the linear decision functions $f = \text{sgn} \circ g$,[5] where g is defined as

$$g(x_j) := \sum_{i=1}^{m} \alpha_i y_i \langle Bx_j, Bx_i \rangle + b, \tag{11.2}$$

with a matrix B to be determined below. This follows a suggestion of [561], using the conjecture that we could incorporate invariances by modifying the dot product used. Any nonsingular B defines a dot product, which can equivalently be written in the form $\langle x_j, Ax_i \rangle$, with a positive definite matrix $A = B^\top B$.

Clearly, if g is invariant under a class of transformations of the x_j, then the same holds true for $f = \text{sgn} \circ g$, which is what we are aiming for. Strictly speaking, however, invariance of g is not *necessary* at points which are not Support Vectors, since these lie in a region where $(\text{sgn} \circ g)$ is constant.

The above notion of invariance refers to invariance when evaluating the decision function. A different notion could relate to whether the separating hyperplane, including its margin, changes if the training examples are transformed. It turns out that when discussing the invariance of g rather than f, these two concepts are closely related. In the following argument, we restrict ourselves to the separable case ($\xi_i = 0$ for all $i = 1, \ldots, m$). As the separating hyperplane and its margin are expressed in terms of Support Vectors, *locally* transforming a Support Vector x_i changes the hyperplane or the margin if $g(x_i)$ changes: if $|g|$ gets smaller than 1, the transformed pattern lies in the margin, and the recomputed margin is smaller; if $|g|$ gets larger than 1, the margin might become larger, depending on whether the pattern can be expressed in terms of the other SVs (cf. the remarks preceding Proposition 7.4). In terms of the mechanical analogy of Section 7.3: moving Support Vectors changes the mechanical equilibrium for the sheet separating the classes. Conversely, a *local* transformation of a non-Support Vector x_i never changes f, even if the value $g(x_i)$ changes, as the solution of the problem is expressed in terms of the Support Vectors only.

In this sense, invariance of f under local transformations of the given data corresponds to invariance of (11.2) for the Support Vectors. Note, however, that this criterion is not readily applicable: before finding the Support Vectors in the optimization, we already need to know how to enforce invariance. Thus the above observation cannot be used directly, however it could serve as a starting point for

5. As usual, $\text{sgn} \circ g$ denotes composition of the functions sgn and g; in other words, the application of sgn to the result of g.

constructing heuristics or iterative solutions. In the Virtual SV method described in Section 11.3, a first run of the standard SV algorithm is carried out to obtain an initial SV set; similar heuristics could be applied in the present case.

Local invariance of g for each pattern x_j under transformations of a differentiable local 1-parameter Lie group of local transformations $\mathcal{L}_t$,

$$\frac{\partial}{\partial t}\bigg|_{t=0} g(\mathcal{L}_t x_j) = 0, \tag{11.3}$$

can be approximately enforced by minimizing the regularizer

$$\frac{1}{m}\sum_{j=1}^{m}\left(\frac{\partial}{\partial t}\bigg|_{t=0} g(\mathcal{L}_t x_j)\right)^2. \tag{11.4}$$

Note that the sum may run over labelled as well as unlabelled data, so in principle we could also require the decision function to be invariant with respect to transformations of elements of a *test* set, without looking at the test labels. In addition, we could use different transformations for different patterns.

For (11.2), the local invariance term (11.3) becomes

$$\begin{aligned}
\frac{\partial}{\partial t}\bigg|_{t=0} g(\mathcal{L}_t x_j) &= \frac{\partial}{\partial t}\bigg|_{t=0}\left(\sum_{i=1}^{m}\alpha_i y_i \langle B\mathcal{L}_t x_j, Bx_i\rangle + b\right) \\
&= \sum_{i=1}^{m}\alpha_i y_i \frac{\partial}{\partial t}\bigg|_{t=0}\langle B\mathcal{L}_t x_j, Bx_i\rangle \\
&= \sum_{i=1}^{m}\alpha_i y_i \partial_1 \langle B\mathcal{L}_0 x_j, Bx_i\rangle \cdot B\frac{\partial}{\partial t}\bigg|_{t=0}\mathcal{L}_t x_j,
\end{aligned} \tag{11.5}$$

using the chain rule. Here, $\partial_1 \langle B\mathcal{L}_0 x_j, Bx_i\rangle$ denotes the gradient of $\langle x, x'\rangle$ with respect to x, evaluated at the point $\langle x, x'\rangle = \langle B\mathcal{L}_0 x_j, Bx_i\rangle$.

As an aside, note that a sufficient, albeit rather strict condition for invariance is thus that $\frac{\partial}{\partial t}\big|_{t=0}\langle B\mathcal{L}_t x_j, Bx_i\rangle$ vanish for all i, j [86]; we will proceed in our derivation, however, with the goal to impose weaker conditions which apply for one specific decision function, rather than simultaneously for all decision functions expressible through different choices of the coefficients $\alpha_i y_i$.

Substituting (11.5) into (11.4), and using the relations $\mathcal{L}_0 = \mathbf{1}$ (the identity) and $\partial_1 \langle x, x'\rangle = x'^{\top}$, yields the regularizer

$$\begin{aligned}
&\frac{1}{m}\sum_{j=1}^{m}\left(\sum_{i=1}^{m}\alpha_i y_i (Bx_i)^{\top} B\frac{\partial}{\partial t}\bigg|_{t=0}\mathcal{L}_t x_j\right)^2 \\
&= \frac{1}{m}\sum_{j=1}^{m}\left(\sum_{i=1}^{m}\alpha_i y_i (Bx_i)^{\top} B\frac{\partial}{\partial t}\bigg|_{t=0}\mathcal{L}_t x_j\right)\left(\sum_{k=1}^{m}\alpha_k y_k \left(B\frac{\partial}{\partial t}\bigg|_{t=0}\mathcal{L}_t x_j\right)^{\top}(Bx_k)\right) \\
&= \sum_{i,k=1}^{m}\alpha_i y_i \alpha_k y_k \left\langle Bx_i, BTB^{\top}Bx_k\right\rangle,
\end{aligned} \tag{11.6}$$

where

$$T := \frac{1}{m}\sum_{j=1}^{m}\left(\frac{\partial}{\partial t}\Big|_{t=0}\mathfrak{L}_t x_j\right)\left(\frac{\partial}{\partial t}\Big|_{t=0}\mathfrak{L}_t x_j\right)^{\top}. \tag{11.7}$$

Self-consistency Argument

We now choose B such that (11.6) reduces to the standard SV target function (7.10), in the form obtained following the substitution of (7.15) (cf. the quadratic term of (7.17)), where we utilize the dot product chosen in (11.2) so that

$$\left\langle Bx_i, BTB^{\top}Bx_k\right\rangle = \langle Bx_i, Bx_k\rangle. \tag{11.8}$$

A sufficient condition for this to hold is

$$B^{\top}BTB^{\top}B = B^{\top}B, \tag{11.9}$$

or, by requiring B to be nonsingular (meaning that no information get lost during the preprocessing), $BTB^{\top} = \mathbf{1}$. This can be satisfied by a preprocessing matrix

$$B = T^{-\frac{1}{2}}, \tag{11.10}$$

the positive definite square root of the inverse of the positive definite matrix T defined in (11.7). We have thus transformed the standard SV programming problem into one which uses an invariance regularizer instead of the standard maximum margin regularizers, simply by choosing a different dot product, or equivalently, by making use of a linear preprocessing operation.

In practice, we usually want something in between. In other words, we want some invariance, but still a reasonably large margin. To this end, we use a matrix

$$T_\lambda := (1-\lambda)T + \lambda\mathbf{1}, \tag{11.11}$$

with $0 < \lambda \leq 1$, instead of T. As T is positive definite, T_λ is strictly positive definite, and thus invertible. For $\lambda = 1$, we recover the standard SV optimal hyperplane algorithm; other values of λ determine the trade-off between invariance and model complexity control.

Reduction to Standard SVM Formulation

By choosing the preprocessing matrix B according to (11.10), we obtain a formulation of the problem in which the standard SV quadratic optimization technique minimizes the tangent regularizer (11.4): the maximum of (7.17) subject to (7.18) and (7.19), using the modified dot product as in (11.2), coincides with the minimum of (11.4) subject to the separation conditions $y_i \cdot g(x_i) \geq 1$, where g is defined as in (11.2).

Note that preprocessing with B does not affect classification speed: since $\langle Bx_j, Bx_i\rangle = \langle x_j, B^{\top}Bx_i\rangle$, we can precompute $B^{\top}Bx_i$ for all SVs x_i, and thus obtain a machine (with modified SVs) which is as fast as a standard SVM.

Tangent Covariance Matrix

Let us now provide some interpretation of (11.10) and (11.7). The tangent vectors $\pm\frac{\partial}{\partial t}|_{t=0}\mathfrak{L}_t x_j$ have zero mean, thus T is a sample estimate of the covariance matrix of the random vector $\pm\frac{\partial}{\partial t}|_{t=0}\mathfrak{L}_t x$. Based on this observation, we call T the *Tangent Covariance Matrix* of the data set $\{x_i | i = 1, \ldots, m\}$ with respect to the transformations $\mathfrak{L}_t$.

Being strictly positive definite,[6] T can be diagonalized as $T = UDU^\top$, where the columns of the unitary matrix U are the eigenvectors of T, and the diagonal matrix D contains the corresponding positive eigenvalues. Then we can compute

$$B = T^{-\frac{1}{2}} = UD^{-\frac{1}{2}}U^\top, \tag{11.12}$$

where $D^{-\frac{1}{2}}$ is the diagonal matrix obtained from D by taking the inverse square roots of the diagonal elements. Since the dot product is unitarily invariant (see Section B.2.2), we may drop the leading U, and (11.2) becomes

$$g(x_j) = \sum_{i=1}^{m} \alpha_i y_i \left\langle D^{-\frac{1}{2}}U^\top x_j, D^{-\frac{1}{2}}U^\top x_i \right\rangle + b. \tag{11.13}$$

A given pattern is thus first transformed by projecting it onto the eigenvectors of the tangent covariance matrix T, which are the rows of $U^\top$. The resulting feature vector is then rescaled by dividing by the square roots of the eigenvalues of T.[7] In other words, the directions of main variance of the random vector $\frac{\partial}{\partial t}|_{t=0}\mathfrak{L}_t x$ are scaled back, thus more emphasis is put on features which are less variant under $\mathfrak{L}_t$. This can be thought of as a whitening operation.

For example, in image analysis, if the $\mathfrak{L}_t$ represent translations, more emphasis is put on the relative proportions of ink in the image rather than the positions of lines. The PCA interpretation of our preprocessing matrix suggests the possibility of regularizing and reducing dimensionality by discarding some of the features, as is common when doing PCA. As an aside, note that the resulting matrix will still satisfy (11.9).[8]

Combining the PCA interpretation with the considerations following (11.2) leads to an interesting observation: the tangent covariance matrix could be rendered a task-dependent covariance matrix by computing it entirely from the SVs, rather than from the full data set. Although the summation in (11.7) does not take into account class labels y_i, it then implicitly depends on the task to be solved, via the SV set. Thus, it allows the extraction of features which are invariant in a task-

6. It is understood that we use T_λ if T is not *strictly* positive definite (cf. (11.11)) (for the concept of strict positive definiteness, cf. Definition 2.4 and the remarks thereafter).

7. As an aside, note that our goal to build invariant SVMs has thus serendipitously provided us with an approach for another intriguing problem, namely that of scaling: in SVMs, there is no obvious way of automatically assigning different weight to different directions in input space (see [102]) — in a trained SVM, the weights of the first layer (the SVs) form a subset of the training set. Choosing these Support Vectors from the training set only gives rather limited possibilities for appropriately dealing with different scales in different directions of input space.

8. To see this, first note that if B solves $B^\top BTB^\top B = B^\top B$, and the polar decomposition of B is $B = UB_s$, with $UU^\top = 1$ and $B_s = B_s^\top$, then B_s also solves this expression. Thus, we may restrict ourselves to symmetrical solutions. For our choice $B = T^{-\frac{1}{2}}$, B commutes with T, hence they can be diagonalized simultaneously. In this case, $B^2TB^2 = B^2$ can also be satisfied by any matrix which is obtained from B by setting an arbitrary selection of eigenvalues to 0 (in the diagonal representation).

dependent way: it does not matter whether features for "easy" patterns change with transformations; it is more important that the "hard" patterns, close to the decision boundary, lead to invariant features.

11.4.2 Invariance in Feature Space

Let us now move on to the nonlinear case. We now enforce invariance in a slightly less direct way, by requiring that the action of the invariance transformations move the patterns parallel to the separating hyperplane; in other words, orthogonal to the weight vector normal to the hyperplane [467, 562]. This approach may seem specific to hyperplanes; similar methods can be used for kernel Fisher discriminant analysis (Chapter 15), however. In the latter case, invariances are enforced by performing *oriented PCA* [364, 140].

Let us now modify the analysis of the SV classification algorithm as described in Chapter 7. There, we had to minimize (7.10) subject to (7.11). When we want to construct invariant hyperplanes, the situation is slightly different. We do not only want to separate the training data, but we want to separate it in such a way that submitting a pattern to a transformation of an a priori specified Lie group (with elements $\mathfrak{L}_t, t \in \mathbb{R}$) does not alter its class assignment. This can be achieved by enforcing that the classification boundary be such that group actions move patterns parallel to the decision boundary, rather than across it. A local statement of this property is the requirement that the Lie derivatives $\frac{\partial}{\partial t}\big|_{t=0} \mathfrak{L}_t \mathbf{x}_i$ be orthogonal to the normal vector $\mathbf{w}$ which determines the separating hyperplane in feature space. Thus we modify (7.10) by adding a second term to enforce invariance;

Invariant Hyperplane Objective Function

$$\tau(\mathbf{w}) = \frac{1}{2}\left((1-\lambda)\frac{1}{m}\sum_{i=1}^{m}\left\langle \mathbf{w}, \frac{\partial}{\partial t}\bigg|_{t=0} \mathfrak{L}_t \mathbf{x}_i \right\rangle^2 + \lambda\|\mathbf{w}\|^2\right). \tag{11.14}$$

For $\lambda = 1$, we recover the original objective function; for values $1 > \lambda \geq 0$, different amounts of importance are assigned to invariance with respect to the Lie group of transformations $\mathfrak{L}_t$.

The above sum can be rewritten as

$$\begin{aligned}\frac{1}{m}\sum_{i=1}^{m}\left\langle \mathbf{w}, \frac{\partial}{\partial t}\bigg|_{t=0} \mathfrak{L}_t \mathbf{x}_i \right\rangle^2 &= \frac{1}{m}\sum_{i=1}^{m}\left\langle \mathbf{w}, \frac{\partial}{\partial t}\bigg|_{t=0} \mathfrak{L}_t \mathbf{x}_i \right\rangle \left\langle \frac{\partial}{\partial t}\bigg|_{t=0} \mathfrak{L}_t \mathbf{x}_i, \mathbf{w} \right\rangle \\ &= \langle \mathbf{w}, T\mathbf{w} \rangle,\end{aligned} \tag{11.15}$$

where the matrix T is defined as in (11.7),

$$T := \frac{1}{m}\sum_{i=1}^{m}\left(\frac{\partial}{\partial t}\bigg|_{t=0} \mathfrak{L}_t \mathbf{x}_i\right)\left(\frac{\partial}{\partial t}\bigg|_{t=0} \mathfrak{L}_t \mathbf{x}_i\right)^\top \tag{11.16}$$

(if we want to use more than one derivative operator, we also sum over these; normalization may then be required). To solve the optimization problem, we introduce a Lagrangian,

$$L(\mathbf{w}, b, \boldsymbol{\alpha}) = \frac{1}{2}\left((1-\lambda)\langle \mathbf{w}, T\mathbf{w}\rangle + \lambda\|\mathbf{w}\|^2\right) - \sum_{i=1}^{m} \alpha_i \left(y_i(\langle \mathbf{x}_i, \mathbf{w}\rangle + b) - 1\right), \quad (11.17)$$

with Lagrange multipliers α_i. At the solution, the gradient of L with respect to $\mathbf{w}$ must vanish,

$$(1-\lambda)T\mathbf{w} + \lambda\mathbf{w} - \sum_{i=1}^{m} \alpha_i y_i \mathbf{x}_i = 0. \quad (11.18)$$

As the left hand side of (11.15) is non-negative for any $\mathbf{w}$, T is a positive definite (though not necessarily strictly definite) matrix. It follows that for

$$T_\lambda := (1-\lambda)T + \lambda\mathbf{1} \quad (11.19)$$

to be invertible, $\lambda > 0$ is a sufficient condition. In this case, we get the following expansion for the solution vector;

$$\mathbf{w} = \sum_{i=1}^{m} \alpha_i y_i T_\lambda^{-1} \mathbf{x}_i. \quad (11.20)$$

Decision Function

Together with (7.3), (11.20) yields the decision function

$$f(\mathbf{x}) = \operatorname{sgn}\left(\sum_{i=1}^{m} \alpha_i y_i \langle \mathbf{x}, T_\lambda^{-1}\mathbf{x}_i\rangle + b\right). \quad (11.21)$$

Substituting (11.20) into the Lagrangian (11.17), and given the fact that at the point of the solution, the partial derivative of L with respect to b must vanish ($\sum_{i=1}^{m} \alpha_i y_i = 0$), we get

$$W(\boldsymbol{\alpha}) = \frac{1}{2}\sum_{i=1}^{m} \alpha_i y_i \left\langle T_\lambda^{-1}\mathbf{x}_i, (T_\lambda T_\lambda^{-1}) \sum_{j=1}^{m} \alpha_j y_j \mathbf{x}_j \right\rangle - \left\langle \sum_{i=1}^{m} \alpha_i y_i \mathbf{x}_i, T_\lambda^{-1} \sum_{j=1}^{m} \alpha_j y_j \mathbf{x}_j \right\rangle + \sum_{i=1}^{m} \alpha_i. \quad (11.22)$$

By virtue of the fact that T_λ, and thus also T_λ^{-1}, is symmetric, the dual form of the optimization problem takes the form

$$\begin{aligned} &\underset{\boldsymbol{\alpha}\in\mathbb{R}^m}{\text{maximize}} && W(\boldsymbol{\alpha}) = \textstyle\sum_{i=1}^{m} \alpha_i - \frac{1}{2}\sum_{i,j=1}^{m} \alpha_i\alpha_j y_i y_j \langle \mathbf{x}_i, T_\lambda^{-1}\mathbf{x}_j\rangle, \\ &\text{subject to} && \alpha_i \geq 0, \ i = 1, \ldots, m, \\ &\text{and} && \textstyle\sum_{i=1}^{m} \alpha_i y_i = 0 \end{aligned} \quad (11.23)$$

— we have thus arrived at the result of Section 11.4.1, using a rather different approach. The same derivation can be carried out for the nonseparable case, leading to the corresponding result with the soft margin constraints (7.38) and (7.39).

We are now in a position to take the step into feature space. As in Section 7.4, we now think of the patterns $\mathbf{x}_i$ as belonging in some dot product space $\mathcal{H}$ related to input space by a map

$$\Phi : \mathcal{X} \to \mathcal{H} \tag{11.24}$$

$$x_i \mapsto \mathbf{x}_i = \Phi(x_i). \tag{11.25}$$

Here $\mathcal{X}$ could be $\mathbb{R}^N$, or some other space that allows us to compute Lie derivatives.

Unfortunately, (11.21) and (11.23) are not expressed in terms of dot products between images of input patterns under Φ. Hence, substituting kernel functions for dot products will not do. In addition, note that T_λ now becomes an operator in a possibly infinite-dimensional space, and is written $\mathbf{T}_\lambda$. In this case, we can no longer easily compute the derivatives of patterns with respect to the transformations. We thus resort to finite differences with some small $t > 0$, and define the tangent covariance matrix C as

Tangent Covariance Matrix in Feature Space

$$\mathbf{T} := \frac{1}{mt^2} \sum_{j=1}^{m} \left(\Phi(\mathcal{L}_t \mathbf{x}_j) - \Phi(\mathbf{x}_j)\right) \left(\Phi(\mathcal{L}_t \mathbf{x}_j) - \Phi(\mathbf{x}_j)\right)^\top. \tag{11.26}$$

For the sake of brevity, we omit the summands corresponding to derivatives in the opposite direction, which ensure that the data set is centered. For the final tangent covariance matrix $\mathbf{T}$, these do not make a difference, as the two negative signs cancel out.

We cannot compute $\mathbf{T}$ explicitly, but we can nevertheless compute (11.21) and (11.23). First note that for all $x, x' \in \mathbb{R}^N$,

$$\langle \Phi(x), \mathbf{T}_\lambda^{-1} \Phi(x') \rangle = \left\langle \mathbf{T}_\lambda^{-\frac{1}{2}} \Phi(x), \mathbf{T}_\lambda^{-\frac{1}{2}} \Phi(x') \right\rangle, \tag{11.27}$$

with $\mathbf{T}_\lambda^{-\frac{1}{2}}$ being the positive definite square root of $\mathbf{T}_\lambda^{-1}$. At this point, Kernel PCA (Section 1.7) comes to our rescue. As $\mathbf{T}_\lambda$ is symmetric, we may diagonalize it as

$$\mathbf{T}_\lambda = UDU^\top, \tag{11.28}$$

where U is a unitary matrix ($U^\top U = \mathbf{1}$); hence,

$$\mathbf{T}_\lambda^{-\frac{1}{2}} = UD^{-\frac{1}{2}} U^\top. \tag{11.29}$$

Substituting (11.29) into (11.27), and using the fact that U is unitary, we obtain

$$\langle \Phi(x), \mathbf{T}_\lambda^{-1} \Phi(x') \rangle = \left\langle UD^{-\frac{1}{2}} U^\top \Phi(x), UD^{-\frac{1}{2}} U^\top \Phi(x') \right\rangle \tag{11.30}$$

$$= \left\langle D^{-\frac{1}{2}} U^\top \Phi(x), D^{-\frac{1}{2}} U^\top \Phi(x') \right\rangle. \tag{11.31}$$

This, however, is simply a dot product between Kernel PCA feature vectors: $U^\top \Phi(x)$ computes projections onto eigenvectors of $\mathbf{T}_\lambda$ (i.e., features), and $D^{-\frac{1}{2}}$ rescales them. To get the eigenvectors, we carry out Kernel PCA on $\mathbf{T}_\lambda$. Essentially, we have to go through the analysis of Kernel PCA using $\mathbf{T}_\lambda$ instead of the covariance matrix of the mapped data in $\mathcal{H}$. We expand the eigenvectors as

$$\mathbf{v} = \sum_{i=1}^{m} \alpha_i (\Phi(\mathcal{L}_t x_i) - \Phi(x_i)), \tag{11.32}$$

and look for solutions of the eigenvalue equation $\mu \mathbf{v} = \mathbf{T}_\lambda \mathbf{v}$, with $\mu > \lambda$ (let us assume that $\lambda < 1$; for $\lambda = 1$, all eigenvalues are identical to λ, the minimal eigenvalue). Note that if $\mathcal{H}$ is infinite-dimensional, then there are infinitely many eigenvectors with eigenvalue $\mu = \lambda$. We cannot find all of these via Kernel PCA, hence we impose the restriction $\mu > \lambda$. We shall return to this point below.

These associated eigenvectors lie in the span of the tangent vectors. By analogy to (1.59), we then obtain

$$m\mu\boldsymbol{\alpha} = ((1-\lambda)K_t + \lambda\mathbf{1})\boldsymbol{\alpha}, \tag{11.33}$$

where K_t is the Gram matrix of the tangent vectors, computed using the same finite difference approximation for the tangent vectors as in (11.26) (see [467]);

$$(K_t)_{ij} = \langle \Phi(\mathcal{L}_t x_i) - \Phi(x_i), \Phi(\mathcal{L}_t x_j) - \Phi(x_j) \rangle \tag{11.34}$$

(for a different way of expressing K_t, see Problem 11.4). To ensure that the eigenvectors $\mathbf{v}^k$ (11.32) are normalized, the corresponding expansion coefficient vectors $\boldsymbol{\alpha}^k$ have to satisfy

$$1 = \frac{\mu_k - \lambda}{1-\lambda} \left\langle \boldsymbol{\alpha}^k, \boldsymbol{\alpha}^k \right\rangle, \tag{11.35}$$

where the μ_k are those eigenvalues of $(1-\lambda)K_t + \lambda\mathbf{1}$ that are larger than λ (Problem 11.6). Feature extraction is carried out by computing the projection of $\Phi(x)$ onto eigenvectors $\mathbf{v}$;

$$\begin{aligned}\langle \mathbf{v}, \Phi(x) \rangle &= \sum_{k=1}^{m} \alpha_k \langle (\Phi(\mathcal{L}_t x_k) - \Phi(x_k)), \Phi(x) \rangle \\ &= \sum_{k=1}^{m} \alpha_k (k(\mathcal{L}_t x_k, x) - k(x_k, x)).\end{aligned} \tag{11.36}$$

What happens to all the eigenvectors of $\mathbf{T}_\lambda$ with eigenvalue λ? To take these into account, we decompose $\mathbf{T}_\lambda$ into a part $\frac{1}{\lambda}\mathbf{1} - \mathbf{T}_\lambda$ that has a rank of at most m, and another part $\frac{1}{\lambda}\mathbf{1}$ that is a multiple of the identity.[9] We thus find that the invariant kernel (11.27) can be written as

$$\langle \Phi(x), \mathbf{T}_\lambda^{-1} \Phi(x') \rangle = \frac{1}{\lambda} \langle \Phi(x), \Phi(x') \rangle - \left\langle \Phi(x), \left(\frac{1}{\lambda}\mathbf{1} - \mathbf{T}_\lambda^{-1} \right) \Phi(x') \right\rangle. \tag{11.37}$$

For the first term, we can immediately substitute the original kernel to get $\frac{1}{\lambda}k(x, x')$. For the second term, we employ the eigenvector decomposition (11.28), $\mathbf{T}_\lambda = UDU^\top$. The diagonal elements of D are the eigenvalues of $\mathbf{T}_\lambda$, and satisfy $D_{ii} \geq \lambda$ for all i. Using the same eigenvectors, we can decompose $\frac{1}{\lambda}\mathbf{1} - \mathbf{T}_\lambda^{-1}$ as

$$\frac{1}{\lambda}\mathbf{1} - \mathbf{T}_\lambda^{-1} = U \left(\frac{1}{\lambda}\mathbf{1} - D^{-1} \right) U^\top. \tag{11.38}$$

The rank of this operator being at most m, it suffices to compute the columns of

9. Thanks to Olivier Chapelle for useful suggestions.

U which correspond to the part of the space where the operator is nonzero. These columns are the normalized eigenvectors $\mathbf{v}^1, \ldots, \mathbf{v}^q$ ($q \leq m$) of $\mathbf{T}_\lambda$ that have eigenvalues $\mu > \lambda$, as described above. Let us denote the corresponding eigenvalues by $\mu_1, \ldots, \mu_q$.

We can thus evaluate the invariant kernel (11.37) as

$$\langle \Phi(x), \mathbf{T}_\lambda^{-1} \Phi(x') \rangle = \frac{1}{\lambda} k(x, x') - \sum_{i=1}^{q} \langle \mathbf{v}^i, \Phi(x) \rangle \left(\frac{1}{\lambda} - \frac{1}{\mu_i} \right) \langle \mathbf{v}^i, \Phi(x') \rangle , \tag{11.39}$$

where the dot product terms are computed using (11.36).

As in the linear case, we can interpret the second part of this kernel as a preprocessing operation. Since $\frac{1}{\lambda} - \frac{1}{\mu_i} > 0$ for all $i = 1, \ldots, q$, we can take square roots, ending up with the preprocessing operation

$$\begin{bmatrix} \sqrt{\lambda^{-1} - \mu_1^{-1}} & 0 & \cdots \\ 0 & \ddots & 0 \\ \vdots & 0 & \sqrt{\lambda^{-1} - \mu_p^{-1}} \end{bmatrix} U^\top . \tag{11.40}$$

As above, $U^\top$ computes q eigenvector projections of the form (11.36).

We conclude the theoretical part of this section by noting an essential difference between the approach described and that of Section 11.4.1, which we believe is an advantage of the present method: in Section 11.4.1, the pattern preprocessing is assumed to be linear. In the present method, the goal to get invariant hyperplanes in feature space leads to a nonlinear preprocessing operation.

11.4.3 Experiments

Let us now consider some experimental results, for the linear case. The nonlinear case has only recently been explored experimentally on real-world data, with promising initial results [100]. We used the small MNIST database described in Section A.1. We start by giving some baseline classification results.

Using a standard linear SVM (that is, a separating hyperplane, Section 7.5), we observe a test error rate of 9.8%; by using a polynomial kernel of degree 4, this drops to 4.0%. In all of the following experiments, we used degree 4 kernels of various types. In a series of reference experiments with a homogeneous polynomial kernel $k(x, x') = \langle x, x' \rangle^4$, using preprocessing with Gaussian smoothing kernels of standard deviation in the range $0.1, 0.2, \ldots, 1.0$, we obtained error rates which gradually increase from 4.0% to 4.3%. We conclude that no improvement of the original 4.0% performance is possible by a simple smoothing operation. Therefore, if our linear preprocessing ends up doing better, it is not due to a simple smoothing effect.

Smoothing Results

Table 11.4 reports results obtained by preprocessing all patterns with B (cf. (11.10)), with various values of λ (cf. (11.11)). In the experiments, the patterns were scaled to have entries in $[0, 1]$, then B was computed, using horizontal and

Table 11.4 Classification error rates, when the kernel $k(x, x') = \langle x, x' \rangle^4$ is modified with the invariant hyperplane preprocessing matrix $B_\lambda = C_\lambda^{-\frac{1}{2}}$; cf. Eqs. (11.10)–(11.11). Enforcing invariance with $\lambda = 0.2, 0.3, \ldots, 0.9$ leads to improvements over the original performance ($\lambda = 1$).

λ	0.1	0.2	0.3	0.4	0.5	0.6	0.7	0.8	0.9	1.0
error rate in %	4.2	3.8	3.6	3.6	3.7	3.8	3.8	3.9	3.9	4.0

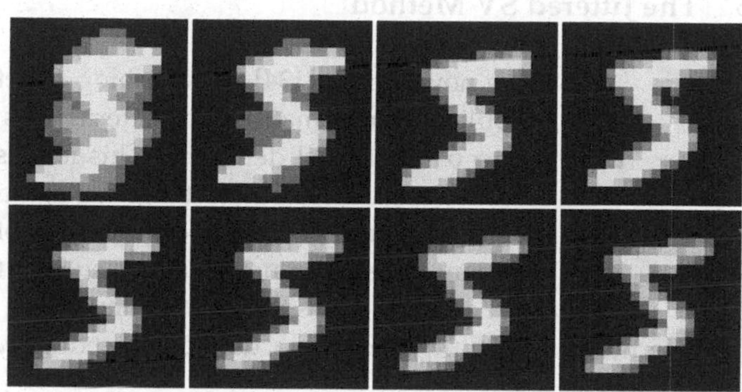

Figure 11.5 The first pattern in the small MNIST database, preprocessed with $B_\lambda = C_\lambda^{-\frac{1}{2}}$ (cf. equations (11.10)–(11.11)), with various amounts of invariance enforced. *Top row:* $\lambda = 0.1, 0.2, 0.3, 0.4$; *bottom row:* $\lambda = 0.5, 0.6, 0.7, 0.8$. For some values of λ, the preprocessing resembles a smoothing operation; preprocessing leads to somewhat higher classification accuracies (see text) than the latter, however.

Invariant Hyperplanes Results

vertical translations (this was our choice of $\mathfrak{L}_t$), and preprocessing was carried out; finally, the resulting patterns were scaled back again (for snapshots of the resulting patterns, see Figure 11.5). The scaling was done to ensure that patterns and derivatives lay in comparable regions of $\mathbb{R}^N$: the most common value of the derivative is 0, corresponding to the constant pattern background; this value should thus also be the most common value in the original patterns. The results show that even though (11.7) is derived for the linear case, it leads to slight improvements in the nonlinear case (for a degree 4 polynomial).

Dimensionality Reduction Results

The above [0, 1] scaling operation is affine rather than linear, hence the argument leading to (11.13) does not hold for this case. We thus only report results on dimensionality reduction for the case where the data are kept in [0, 1] scaling during the whole procedure.

We used a translation invariant radial basis function kernel (7.27) with $c = 0.5$. On the $[-1, 1]$ data, for $\lambda = 0.4$, this leads to the same performance as the degree 4 polynomial; that is, 3.6% (without invariance preprocessing, meaning that for $\lambda = 1$, the performance is 3.9%). To get the identical system on [0, 1] data, the RBF width was rescaled accordingly, to $c = 0.125$. Table 11.5 shows that discarding principal components can further improve performance, up to 3.3%.

Table 11.5 Results obtained through dropping directions corresponding to small eigenvalues of C, or in other words, dropping less important principal components (cf. (11.13)), for the translation invariant RBF kernel (see text). All results given are for the case $\lambda = 0.4$ (cf. Table 11.4).

PCs discarded	0	50	100	150	200	250	300	350
error rate in %	3.6	3.6	3.6	3.5	3.5	3.4	3.3	3.6

11.5 The Jittered SV Method

We now follow [134] in describing a method which, like the virtual SV method, applies transformations to patterns; this time, however, the transformations are part of the kernel definition. This idea is called *kernel jittering* [134]; it is closely related to a concept called tangent distance [496]. Loosely speaking, kernel jittering consists of moving around the inputs of the kernel (or, in [496], of a two-norm distance), using transformations such as translations, until the match is best.

Jittered Kernel

For any admissible SVM Gram matrix $K_{ij} = k(x_i, x_j)$, consider a jittering kernel form $K^J_{ij} = k^J(x_i, x_j)$, defined procedurally as follows:

1. Consider all jittered forms of example x_i (including itself) in turn, and select the one (x_q) "closest" to x_j; specifically, select x_q to minimize the metric distance between x_q and x_j in the space induced by the kernel. This distance is given by [10]

$$K_{qq} - 2K_{qj} + K_{jj} \tag{11.41}$$

2. Let $K^J_{ij} = K_{qj}$.

For some kernels, such as radial-basis functions (RBFs), simply selecting the maximum K_{qj} value to be the value for K^J_{ij} suffices, since the K_{qq} and K_{jj} terms are constant in this case. This similarly holds for translation jitters, as long as sufficient padding exists so that no image pixels fall off the image after translations. In general, a jittering kernel may have to consider jittering one or both examples. For symmetric invariances such as translation, however, it suffices to jitter just one example.

The use of jittering kernels is referred to as the *JSV* approach. A major motivation for considering this approach is that VSV approaches scale at least quadratically in the number (J) of jitters considered. This is because SVM training scales at least quadratically in the number of training examples, and VSV essentially ex-

10. This corresponds to Euclidean distance in the feature space defined by the kernel, using the definition of the two-norm,

$$\|\mathbf{x}_i - \mathbf{x}_j\|^2 = \langle \mathbf{x}_i, \mathbf{x}_i \rangle - 2\langle \mathbf{x}_i, \mathbf{x}_j \rangle + \langle \mathbf{x}_j, \mathbf{x}_j \rangle .$$

pands the training set by a factor of J. Jittering kernels are J times more expensive to compute, since each K^J_{ij} computation involves finding a minimum over J computations of K_{ij}. The potential benefit, however, is that the training set is J times smaller than methods such as VSV. Thus, the potential net gain is that JSV training may only scale linearly in J, instead of quadratically as in VSV. Furthermore, through comprehensive use of kernel caching, as is common in modern practical SVM implementations, even that factor of J may be largely amortized away.

As mentioned above, the kernel values induce a set of distances between the points (cf. footnote 10). For positive definite kernels, we know that the feature space has the structure of a dot product space, thus we obtain a valid metric in that space (see Section B.2.2). For jittering kernels, this is not necessarily the case; in particular, the triangle inequality can be violated.

For example, imagine three simple images A, B, and C consisting of a single row of three binary pixels, with A =(1,0,0), B=(0,1,0), and C=(0,0,1). The minimal jittered distances (under 1-pixel translation) between A and B and between B and C are 0. However, the distance between A and C is positive (e.g., 1-2*0+1 = 2 for a linear kernel). Thus, the triangle inequality requirement of $d(A,B) + d(B,C) \geq d(A,C)$ is violated in this example (cf. also [496]). Note that with a sufficiently large jittering set (such as the one including both 1-pixel and 2-pixel translations in the above example), the triangle inequality is not violated.

In practice, violations tend to be rare, and are unlikely to present difficulties in training convergence (the SMO algorithm usually handles such cases; see [134]). Based on experiments with kernel jittering to date, it is still unclear how much impact any such violations typically have on generalization performance in practice.

Jittering kernels have one other potential disadvantage compared with VSV approaches: the kernels must continue to jitter at test time. In contrast, the VSV approach effectively compiles the relevant jittering into the final set of SVs it produces. Nonetheless, in cases where the final JSV SV set size is much smaller than the final VSV SV set size, the JSV approach can still be faster at test time.

In [134], some experiments are reported which compare VSV and JSV methods on a small subset of the MNIST training set. These experiments illustrate typical relative behaviors, such as the JSV test time often being almost as fast or faster than VSV (even though JSV must jitter at test time), due to JSV having many fewer final SVs. Furthermore, both JSV and VSV typically beat standard SVMs (which do not incorporate invariance). They also both typically beat *query jitter* as well, in which the test examples are jittered inside the kernels during SVM output computations. Query jitter effectively uses jittering kernels at test time, even though the SVM is not specifically trained for a jittering kernel. This case was tested simply as a control in such experiments, to verify that training the SVM with the actual jittering kernel used at test time is indeed important.

While relative test errors between VSV and JSV vary, it does seem that VSV methods are substantially more robust than JSV methods, in terms of the generalization error variance.

11.6 Summary

Invariances can readily be incorporated in Support Vector learning machines, by generating virtual examples from the Support Vectors, rather than from the whole training set. The method yields a significant gain in classification accuracy for a moderate cost in time: it requires two training runs (rather than one), and it constructs classification rules utilizing more Support Vectors, thus slowing down classification speed (cf. (7.25)). Given that Support Vector Machines are known to exhibit fairly short training times (as indicated by the benchmark comparison of [64], cf. also Chapter 10), the first point is usually not critical. Certainly, training on virtual examples generated from the whole database would be significantly slower. To compensate for the second point, we can use reduced set methods (Chapter 18).

As an alternative approach, we can build known invariances directly into the SVM objective function via the choice of kernel. With its rather general class of admissible kernel functions, the SV algorithm provides ample possibilities for constructing task-specific kernels. The method described for constructing kernels for *transformation invariant* SVMs (invariant hyperplanes) has so far only been applied to real world problems in the linear case (for encouraging toy results on nonlinear data, cf. [100]), which probably explains why it is only seen to lead to moderate improvements, especially when compared with the large gains achieved by the Virtual SV method. The transformation invariant kernel method is applicable to differentiable transformations — other types, such as those for mirror symmetry, have to be dealt with using other techniques, such as the Virtual Support Vector method or jittered kernels. Its main advantages compared with the latter techniques are that in the linear case, it does not slow down testing speed, and that using more invariances leaves training time almost unchanged. In addition, it is rather attractive from a theoretical point of view, as it establishes a surprising connection to invariant feature extraction, preprocessing, and principal component analysis.

Although partly heuristic, the techniques in this chapter have led to the record result on the MNIST database. In addition, SVMs present clear opportunities for further improvement. More invariances (in the pattern recognition case, for instance, small rotations, or varying ink thickness) could be incorporated. Further, we might use only those Virtual Support Vectors which provide new information about the decision boundary, or use a measure of such information to keep only the most important vectors. Finally, if locality-improved kernels, to be described in Section 13.3, prove to be as useful on the full MNIST database as they are on subsets of it, accuracies could be substantially increased — admittedly at a cost in classification speed.

We conclude this chapter by noting that all three techniques described should be directly applicable to other kernel-based methods, such as SV regression [561] and Kernel PCA (Chapter 14). Note, finally, that this chapter only covers some aspects of incorporating prior knowledge, namely about *invariances*. Further facets are treated elsewhere, such as semiparametric modelling (Section 4.8), and methods for dealing with heteroscedastic noise (Section 9.5).

11.7 Problems

11.1 (VSVs in Regression •) *Apply the VSV method to a regression problem.*

11.2 (Examples of Pattern Invariance Transformations •) *Try to think of other pattern transformations that leave class membership invariant; for instance, in the case of image processing: translations, brightness transformations, contrast transformations, ...*

11.3 (Task-Dependent Tangent Covariance Matrix ••) *Experiment with tangent covariance matrices computed from the SVs only. Compare with the method of [364].*

11.4 (Alternative Expression of the Tangent Vector Gram Matrix [100] ••) *Prove that under suitable differentiability conditions, the elements (11.34) of the tangent vector Gram matrix can be written as a quadratic form in terms of the kernel Hessian,*

$$(K_t)_{ij} = \lim_{t \to 0} \left(((\mathfrak{L}_t x_i) - x_i)^\top \frac{\partial^2 k(x_i, x_j)}{\partial x_i \partial x_j} ((\mathfrak{L}_t x_j) - x_j) \right). \tag{11.42}$$

Hint: note that the Hessian can be written as

$$\frac{\partial^2 k(x_i, x_j)}{\partial x_i \partial x_j} = \left\langle \frac{\partial}{\partial x_i} \Phi(x_i), \frac{\partial}{\partial x_j} \Phi(x_j) \right\rangle. \tag{11.43}$$

11.5 (Regularizing the Tangent Covariance Matrix ••) *Discuss the difference between adding $\lambda \mathbf{1}$ to the tangent covariance matrix in the linear case, and in the nonlinear case (Section 11.4). Note that in the nonlinear case, $\lambda \mathbf{1}$ only has an effect in the span of the training patterns.*

Rather than using the decomposition (11.37), try to deal with this problem by including other patterns in the expansion. Perform experiments to test your approach.

11.6 (Eigenvectors of the Regularized Tangent Covariance Matrix •) *Suppose $\mathbf{v}^k$ is an eigenvector of $(1 - \lambda)K_t + \lambda \mathbf{1}$ with eigenvalue $\mu_k > \lambda$. Prove that to ensure $\langle \mathbf{v}^k, \mathbf{v}^k \rangle = 1$ in $\mathcal{H}$, the coefficient vector $\boldsymbol{\alpha}^k$ has to satisfy (11.35).*

11.7 (Nonlinear Invariant Kernels ••) *Implement the kernel (11.39) for a visual pattern recognition problem, using small image translations to compute the approximate tangent vectors (cf. (11.26)). Apply it and study the effect of λ and of the size of the image translations.*

11.8 (Scaling of Input Dimensions •••) *Consider kernels of the form $k_D(x, x') = k(Dx, Dx')$, where D is a diagonal scaling matrix. How can you use prior knowledge* *to choose D? Can you devise a method which will drive a large fraction of the diagonal entries of D to 0 ("input feature selection")? Discuss the relationship to Automatic Relevance Determination and Relevance Vector Machines (Chapter 16).*

12 Learning Theory Revisited

Chapter 5 mainly dealt with the fundamental problem of uniform convergence and under which conditions it occurs, based on a VC perspective. The present chapter takes a slightly more practical approach by proving that certain estimation methods such as the minimization of a regularized risk functional or the leave-one-out error are, indeed, reliable estimators of the expected risk. Furthermore, it shows alternative means of determining the reliability of estimators, based on entropy numbers of compact operators associated with function classes, and the Kullback-Leibler divergence between prior and posterior distributions.

Overview

The chapter is organized as follows. In Section 12.1 we will introduce the notion of a concentrated random variable and state a concentration of measure inequality of McDiarmid. This notion will become useful to prove that for minimizers of the regularized risk functional the empirical risk is a not too unreliable estimator of the expected loss. A similar fact holds also for the leave-one-out estimator, discussed in Section 12.2. This estimator also enjoys other good properties, such as being unbiased, its computation, however, is rather expensive. For this reason, we give three methods of approximating this estimator, ranging from an $O(d)$ to an $O(d^4)$ method, where d is the number of nonzero expansion coefficients.

Further ways of assessing the generalization performance of an estimator are explained in Sections 12.3 and 12.4. The first of these methods is based on the concept of a distribution over classifiers much akin to a Bayesian estimator. The second, in turn, takes an operator theoretic approach to measure the capacity of the function class described by a kernel estimator explicitly. In short, it derives a more fine grained measure of capacity than the VC dimension.

Prerequisites

It is useful if the reader has some familiarity with the contents of Chapter 5, however it is not essential for an understanding of the Sections 12.1, 12.2, 12.3. Only Section 12.4 assumes familiarity with the techniques underlying the derivation of a VC Bound, as described in Section 5.5.

Knowledge of the theory of Reproducing Kernel Hilbert Spaces (Section 2.2.2) is required for some of the proofs of Section 12.1 and 12.2. A good working knowledge of matrix algebra is useful in Section 12.2, and before reading Section 12.3 we recommend that the reader become familiar with the basics of Bayesian inference, as described in Section 16.1. Finally, Section 12.4 will most likely be difficult for readers not familiar with notions of functional analysis.

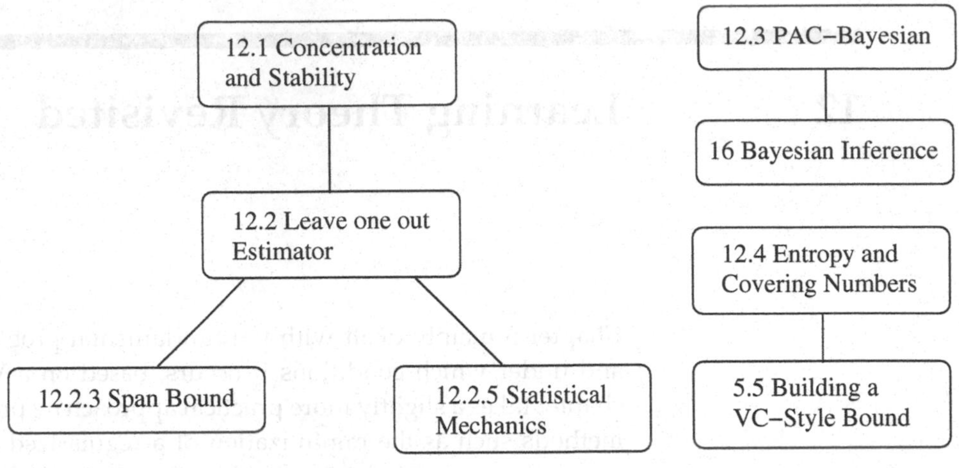

12.1 Concentration of Measure Inequalities

Most of the reasoning presented in this book is concerned with minimizing a regularized risk functional $R_{\mathrm{reg}}[f]$. This generates a very specific type of statistical estimator and it may be expected that we could find some uniform convergence bounds that take advantage of the fact that it is not an arbitrary estimator we are dealing with. In what follows we use a slight extension of an idea by Bousquet and Elisseeff [67], originally described in [160], to provide such a bound. It is based on the concentration of measure inequalities.

These are a family of theorems which state that certain random variables ξ are concentrated, which means that, with high probability, the values of random draws of ξ are very close to their expected values $\mathbf{E}[\xi]$. In this case we say that the distribution is *concentrated* around its mean. We have already encountered one of these cases in Theorem 5.1, where we saw that the average over a set of bounded random variables is, with high probability, close to the expected average.

The concept of concentration is, however, much more general than just that. It deals with classes of functions $g(\xi_1, \ldots, \xi_m)$ of random variables $(\xi_1, \ldots, \xi_m)$ which have the property of being concentrated. For instance, if the influence of each ξ_i on g is limited, g is not likely to vary much. What we show in the following is that the minimizers of the regularized risk functional enjoy this property.

12.1.1 McDiarmid's Bound

Roughly speaking, McDiarmid's bound states that if arbitrary replacements of random variables ξ_i do not affect the value of g excessively, then the random variable $g(\xi_1, \ldots, \xi_m)$ is concentrated.

McDiarmid's Bound

Theorem 12.1 (McDiarmid [356]) *Denote by $\xi_1, \ldots, \xi_m$ iid random variables and assume that there exists a function $g : \xi^m \to \mathbb{R}$ with the property that for all $i \in [m]$ (we use* *the shorthand* $[m] := \{1, \ldots, m\}$*), and* $c_i > 0$,

$$\sup_{\xi_1,\ldots,\xi_m,\xi_i' \in \xi} |g(\xi_1, \ldots, \xi_m) - g(\xi_1, \ldots, \xi_{i-1}, \xi_i', \xi_{i+1}, \ldots, \xi_m)| \leq c_i \tag{12.1}$$

where ξ_i' *is drawn from the same distribution as* ξ_i*. Then*

$$\mathrm{P}\{|g(\xi_1, \ldots, \xi_m) - \mathbf{E}(g(\xi_1, \ldots, \xi_m))| > \varepsilon\} \leq 2\exp\left(-\frac{2\varepsilon^2}{\sum_{i=1}^m c_i^2}\right). \tag{12.2}$$

This means that a bound similar to the law of large numbers can be applied to any function g which does not overly depend on individual samples ξ_i. Returning to the example from the introduction, if we define

$$g(\xi_1, \ldots, \xi_m) := \frac{1}{m}\sum_{i=1}^m \xi_i \tag{12.3}$$

where $\xi_i \in [a, b]$, then, clearly, $c_i = \frac{1}{m}(b-a)$ since f can only change by this amount if one particular sample is replaced by another. This means that the rhs of (12.2) becomes $2\exp\left(-\frac{2m\varepsilon^2}{(b-a)^2}\right)$, in other words, we recover Hoeffding's bound (Theorem 5.1) as a special case. See also [137] for details.

12.1.2 Uniform Stability and Convergence

In order to apply these bounds to learning algorithms we must introduce the notion of *uniform stability*. This is to determine the amount by which an estimate $f : \mathcal{X} \to \mathcal{Y}$ based on the training data $Z := \{(x_1, y_1), \ldots, (x_m, y_m)\} \subset \mathcal{X} \times \mathcal{Y}$ changes if we change one of the training patterns.

Uniform Stability

Definition 12.2 (Uniform Stability) *Denote a training sample of size m by Z. Moreover, denote by* $Z^i := (Z \setminus \{z_i\}) \cup \{z\}$ *(where* $z := (x, y)$*) the training sample where the ith observation is replaced by z. Finally, denote by* f_Z *the estimate produced by our learning algorithm of choice (and likewise by* f_{Z^i} *the estimate based on* Z^i*). We call this mapping* $Z \to f_Z$ *uniformly* β*-stable with respect to a loss function c if*

$$\left|c\left(x, y, f_Z(x)\right) - c\left(x, y, f_{Z^i}(x)\right)\right| \leq \beta \text{ for all } (x, y) \in \mathcal{X} \times \mathcal{Y}, \text{ all } Z, \text{ and all } i. \tag{12.4}$$

This means that the loss due to the estimates generated from Z, where an arbitrary pattern of the sample has been replaced, will not differ anywhere by more than β*.*

As we shall see, the notion of uniform stability is satisfied for regularization networks of different types, provided that the loss function c is Lipschitz continuous (provided that c has bounded slope). The following theorem uses Theorem 12.1 to prove that β-stable algorithms exhibit uniform convergence of the empirical risk $R_{\mathrm{emp}}[f]$ to the expected risk $R[f]$.

Theorem 12.3 (Bousquet and Elisseeff [67]) *Assume that we have a β-stable algorithm with the additional requirement that $f_Z(x) \leq M$ for all $x \in \mathcal{X}$ and for all training samples $Z \subset \mathcal{X} \times \mathcal{Y}$. Then, for $m \geq \frac{8M^2}{\varepsilon^2}$, we have,*

$$\mathrm{P}\left\{\left|R_{\mathrm{emp}}[f_Z] - R[f_Z]\right| > \varepsilon\right\} \leq \frac{64Mm\beta + 8M^2}{m\varepsilon^2} \tag{12.5}$$

and for any $m \geq 1$

$$\mathrm{P}\left\{\left|R_{\mathrm{emp}}[f_Z] - R[f_Z]\right| > \varepsilon + \beta\right\} \leq 2\exp\left(-\frac{m\varepsilon^2}{2(m\beta + M)^2}\right). \tag{12.6}$$

This means that if β decreases with increasing m, or, in particular, if $\beta = O(m^{-1})$, then we obtain bounds that are optimal in their rate of convergence, specifically, bounds which have the same convergence rate as Hoeffding's bound (5.7).

To keep matters simple, we only prove (12.6). The details for the proof of (12.5), which is rather technical, can be found in [160].

Proof We first give a bound on the expected difference between $R_{\mathrm{emp}}[f_Z]$ and $R[f_Z]$ (hence the bias term) and subsequently will bound the variance. This leads to

$$\left|\mathbf{E}_Z\left[R_{\mathrm{emp}}[f_Z] - R[f_Z]\right]\right| = \left|\mathbf{E}_{Z,z}\left[\frac{1}{m}\sum_{i=1}^{m} c(x_i, y_i, f_Z(x_i)) - c(x, y, f_Z(x))\right]\right| \tag{12.7}$$

$$= \left|\mathbf{E}_Z\left[\frac{1}{m}\sum_{i=1}^{m} c(x, y, f_{Z^i}(x)) - c(x, y, f_Z(x))\right]\right| \leq \beta \tag{12.8}$$

The last equality (12.8) followed from the fact that, since we are taking the expectation over Z, z, we may as well replace z_i by z in the terms stemming from the empirical error. The bound then follows from the assumption that we have a uniformly β-stable algorithm.

Now that we have a bound on the expectation, we deal with the variance. Since we want to apply Theorem 12.1, we have to analyze the deviations of $(R_{\mathrm{emp}}[f_Z] - R[f_Z])$ from $(R_{\mathrm{emp}}[f_{Z^i}] - R[f_{Z^i}])$.

$$\left|\left(R_{\mathrm{emp}}\left[f_Z\right] - R\left[f_Z\right]\right) - \left(R_{\mathrm{emp}}\left[f_{Z^i}\right] - R\left[f_{Z^i}\right]\right)\right| \leq \tag{12.9}$$

$$\left|R\left[f_Z\right] - R\left[f_{Z^i}\right]\right| + \left|R_{\mathrm{emp}}\left[f_Z\right] - R_{\mathrm{emp}}\left[f_{Z^i}\right]\right| \leq \tag{12.10}$$

$$\beta + \frac{1}{m}\left|c\left(x_i, y_i, f_Z(x_i)\right) - c\left(x, y, f_{Z^i}(x)\right)\right|$$

$$+ \frac{1}{m}\sum_{j \neq i}^{m}\left|c\left(x_j, y_j, f_Z(x_j)\right) - c\left(x_j, y_j, f_{Z^i}(x_j)\right)\right| \leq \beta + \tfrac{2M}{m} + \beta \tag{12.11}$$

Here (12.10) follows from the triangle inequality and the fact that the learning algorithm is β-stable. Finally, we split the empirical risks into their common parts depending on Z^i and the remainder. From (12.11) it follows that $c_i = 2\frac{\beta m + M}{m}$, as required by Theorem 12.1. This, in combination with (12.8), completes the proof. ∎

12.1.3 Uniform Stability of Regularization Networks

We next show that the learning algorithms we have been studying so far actually satisfy Definition 12.2 and compute the corresponding value of β.

Theorem 12.4 (Algorithmic Stability of Risk Minimizers) *The algorithm minimizing the regularized risk functional R_{reg}*

$$R_{\text{reg}}[f] := R_{\text{emp}}[f] + \frac{\lambda}{2}\|f\|^2 = \frac{1}{m}\sum_{i=1}^{m} c(x_i, y_i, f(x_i)) + \frac{\lambda}{2}\|f\|^2 \tag{12.12}$$

has stability $\beta = \frac{2C^2\kappa^2}{m\lambda}$, where κ is a bound on $\|k(x,\cdot)\| = \sqrt{k(x,x)}$, c is a convex loss function, $\|\cdot\|$ is the RKHS norm induced by k, and C is a bound on the Lipschitz constant of the loss function $c(x, y, f(x))$, viewed as a function of $f(x)$.

Since the proof is somewhat technical we relegate it to Section 12.1.4. Let us now discuss the implications of the theorem.

We can see that the stability of the algorithm depends on the regularization constant via $\frac{1}{\lambda m}$, hence we may be able to afford to choose weaker regularization if the sample size increases. For many estimators, such as Support Vector Machines, we use a constant value of $C = \frac{1}{\lambda m}$. In the context of algorithmic stability this means that we effectively use algorithms with the same stability, regardless of the sample size.

The next step is to substitute the values of β into (12.6) to obtain practically useful uniform convergence bounds (to keep matters simple we will only use (12.6) of Theorem 12.3). It is straightforward to obtain corresponding statements for (12.5) (see Problem 12.1). The following theorem is a direct consequence of Theorems 12.3 and 12.4.

Theorem 12.5 (Uniform Convergence Bounds for RKHS) *Given an algorithm minimizing the regularized risk functional, as in (12.12), with the assumptions of Theorem 12.4 we obtain*

$$\mathrm{P}\left\{\left|R_{\text{emp}}[f_Z] - R[f_Z]\right| > \varepsilon + \beta\right\} \leq 2\exp\left(-\frac{m}{2}\left(\frac{\varepsilon}{M}\right)^2\left(1 + \frac{2}{\lambda M}(C\kappa)^2\right)^{-2}\right) \tag{12.13}$$

where $\beta = \frac{2C^2\kappa^2}{m\lambda}$. The $\frac{\varepsilon^2}{M^2}$ term in the exponent stems from the fact that, in order to make a statement concerning a certain precision ε, we have to take the total scale M of the function values and loss functions into account. The $(C\kappa)^2$ term determines the effective dynamic range of the function class, namely by how much the functions may change. λM specifies the effective regularization strength; how much simple functions are preferred with respect to the full range M of the loss function c.

Finally, we can see that for fixed λ the rate of convergence of the empirical risk $R_{\text{emp}}[f_Z]$ to $R[f_Z]$ is given by $\exp(-c_0 m)$, which is identical to the rates given by Hoeffding's bound (5.7). Note, however, that in (5.7) the constant is 2, whereas in the present case c_0 may be significantly smaller. Thus, it seems as if the current bounds are much worse than the classical VC-type bounds (see Section 5.5) which essentially scale with $\mathcal{N}(\mathfrak{F}, m, \varepsilon) \exp(-2m\varepsilon^2 M^{-2})$ [574]. Yet this is not true in general; usually the covering number $\mathcal{N}(\mathfrak{F}, m, \varepsilon)$ (see Section 12.4 for more details) grows with the sample size m which counteracts the effect of the exponential term, $\exp(-2m\varepsilon^2 M^{-2})$.

Furthermore, for practical considerations, (12.13) may be very useful, even if the rates are not optimal, since the bound is predictive even for small sample sizes and moderate regularization strength. Still, we expect that the constants could be improved. In particular, instead of $\frac{m}{2}$, we suspect that $2m$ would be more appropriate.

In addition, note that the current bound uses a result concerning worst case stability. For most observations such as non-Support Vectors, however, changing a single pattern is unlikely to change the estimate at all. We suspect that the *average* stability of the estimator is much higher than what has been shown so far. It is (still) an open problem how this goal can be achieved. Finally, the bound does not take the specific form of the RKHS $\mathcal{H}$ into account, but instead assumes that the space is completely spherical. This leaves room for further theoretical improvement of the bound. Let us proceed to a practical example.

Corollary 12.6 (Gaussian Kernel SV Regression with ε-loss) *In the case of SV Regression with Gaussian RBF kernels and the ε-insensitive loss (1.44) the risk of deviation between empirical and expected risk is given by*

$$\mathrm{P}\left\{\left|R_{\mathrm{emp}}[f_Z] - R[f_Z]\right| > \bar{\varepsilon} + \beta\right\} \leq 2\exp\left(-\frac{m}{2}\left(\frac{\bar{\varepsilon}}{M}\right)^2\left(1 + \frac{2}{\lambda M}\right)^{-2}\right) \tag{12.14}$$

where M denotes an upper bound on the loss and λ is a regularization parameter.

This is since $\kappa = 1$ for Gaussian RBF kernels (here $k(x, x) = 1$) and, further, the loss function (1.44) has bounded slope 1, thus also $C = 1$.

12.1.4 Proof of Theorem 12.4

We require an auxiliary lemma.

Lemma 12.7 (Convex Functions and Derivatives) *For any differentiable convex function $f : \mathbb{R} \to \mathbb{R}$ and any $a, b \in \mathbb{R}$ we have*

$$(f'(a) - f'(b))(a - b) \geq 0. \tag{12.15}$$

Proof Due to the convexity of f we know that $f(a) + (b - a)f'(a) \leq f(b)$ and, likewise, $f(b) + (a - b)f'(b) \leq f(a)$. Summing up both inequalities and subtracting the terms in $f(a)$ and $f(b)$ proves (12.15). ■

Proof of Theorem 12.4. We must extend the notation slightly insofar as we will explicitly introduce the dependency on the data in the empirical risk functional.

This simply means that, instead of writing $R_{\text{reg}}[f]$, we will use $R_{\text{reg}}[f,Z]$ and $R_{\text{reg}}[f,Z^i]$ (and likewise $R_{\text{emp}}[f,Z]$) for the remainder of the proof in order to distinguish between different training sets.

Recall that f_Z minimizes $R_{\text{reg}}[f,Z]$, that is, the functional derivative of $R_{\text{reg}}[f,Z]$ at f_Z vanishes,

$$\partial_f R_{\text{reg}}[f_Z, Z] = \partial_f R_{\text{emp}}[f_Z, Z] + \lambda f_Z = 0, \tag{12.16}$$

$$\partial_f R_{\text{reg}}[f_{Z^i}, Z^i] = \partial_f R_{\text{emp}}[f_{Z^i}, Z^i] + \lambda f_{Z^i} = 0. \tag{12.17}$$

Next, we construct an auxiliary risk function $\tilde{R}[f]$ by

$$\tilde{R}[f] := \left\langle \partial_f R_{\text{emp}}[f_Z, Z] - \partial_f R_{\text{emp}}\left[f_{Z^i}, Z^i\right], f - f_{Z^i} \right\rangle + \frac{\lambda}{2} \|f - f_{Z^i}\|^2. \tag{12.18}$$

Clearly $\tilde{R}[f]$ is a convex function in f (the first term is linear, the second quadratic). Additionally, by construction

$$\tilde{R}[f_{Z^i}] = 0. \tag{12.19}$$

Furthermore, the minimum of $\tilde{R}[f]$ is obtained for $f = f_Z$. One can see this by taking the functional derivative of $\tilde{R}[f]$ to find

$$\partial_f \tilde{R}[f] = \partial_f R_{\text{emp}}[f_Z, Z] - \partial_f R_{\text{emp}}\left[f_{Z^i}, Z^i\right] + \lambda\left(f - f_{Z^i}\right) = \partial_f R_{\text{emp}}[f_Z, Z] - \lambda f. \tag{12.20}$$

Eq. (12.20) vanishes for $f = f_Z$ due to (12.16). From (12.19) we therefore conclude that $\tilde{R}[f_Z] \leq 0$. In order to obtain bounds on $\|f_Z - f_{Z^i}\|$, we have to get rid of some of the first terms in $\tilde{R}[f]$. We observe

$$m \left\langle \partial_f R_{\text{emp}}[f_Z, Z] - \partial_f R_{\text{emp}}\left[f_{Z^i}, Z^i\right], f_Z - f_{Z^i} \right\rangle \tag{12.21}$$

$$\begin{aligned} &= \sum_{j \neq i} \left(c'\left(x_j, y_j, f_Z\left(x_j\right)\right) - c'\left(x_j, y_j, f_{Z^i}\left(x_j\right)\right)\right)\left(f_Z(x_j) - f_{Z^i}(x_j)\right) \\ &\quad + c'\left(x_i, y_i, f_Z\left(x_i\right)\right)\left(f_Z(x_i) - f_{Z^i}(x_i)\right) - c'\left(x, y, f_{Z^i}(x)\right)\left(f_Z(x) - f_{Z^i}(x)\right) \end{aligned} \tag{12.22}$$

$$\geq c'\left(x_i, y_i, f_Z\left(x_i\right)\right)\left(f_Z(x_i) - f_{Z^i}(x_i)\right) - c'\left(x, y, f_{Z^i}(x)\right)\left(f_Z(x) - f_{Z^i}(x)\right). \tag{12.23}$$

In order to obtain (12.22) we use the same techniques as exploited in the proof of Theorem 4.2, in particular that $\partial_f c(x,y,f(x)) = c'(x,y,f(x))k(x,\cdot)$. Collecting common terms between $R_{\text{emp}}[f,Z]$ and $R_{\text{emp}}[f,Z^i]$ leads to the result. For (12.23) we use Lemma 12.7 applied to the loss function $c(x,y,f(x))$ which is a convex function of $f(x)$. Combining (12.23) with $\tilde{R}[f_Z] \leq 0$ gives

$$\begin{aligned} 0 \geq\, & c'\left(x_i, y_i, f_Z\left(x_i\right)\right)\left(f_Z(x_i) - f_{Z^i}(x_i)\right) - c'\left(x, y, f_{Z^i}(x)\right)\left(f_Z(x) - f_{Z^i}(x)\right) \\ & + \frac{m\lambda}{2}\|f_Z - f_{Z^i}\|^2. \end{aligned} \tag{12.24}$$

Since the norm of the derivative of the loss function $|c'(x,y,f(x))|$ is bound by C and $|f_Z(x)|, |f_{Z^i}| \leq M$ we have

$$\begin{aligned} & \frac{m\lambda}{2}\|f_Z - f_{Z^i}\|^2 \\ & \leq c'\left(x, y, f_{Z^i}(x)\right)\left(f_Z(x) - f_{Z^i}(x)\right) - c'\left(x_i, y_i, f_Z\left(x_i\right)\right)\left(f_Z(x_i) - f_{Z^i}(x_i)\right) \end{aligned} \tag{12.25}$$

Finally, we must convert our result regarding the proximity of f_Z and f_{Z^i} in $\mathcal{H}$ to a statement regarding the corresponding values of the loss functions. By the Cauchy-Schwarz inequality we can see that, for any $f, f' \in \mathcal{H}$ and any $x \in \mathcal{X}$

$$|f(x) - f'(x)| = |\langle f - f', k(x, \cdot)\rangle| \leq \|f - f'\| \, \|k(x, \cdot)\| \leq \kappa \|f - f'\|. \tag{12.26}$$

Since c is Lipschitz continuous this leads to

$$|c(x, y, f_Z) - c(x, y, f_{Z^i})| \leq C|f_Z(x) - f_{Z^i}(x)| \leq C\kappa \|f_Z - f_{Z^i}\| \leq C\kappa \sqrt{\frac{8CM}{m\lambda}}. \tag{12.27}$$

Using (12.27) in (12.25) yields

$$\frac{m\lambda}{2} \|f_Z - f_{Z^i}\|^2 \leq C\kappa \|f_Z - f_{Z^i}\| \tag{12.28}$$

and, thus, $\|f_Z - f_{Z^i}\| \leq \frac{2C\kappa}{m\lambda}$. Substituting this into (12.27) proves the claim by

$$|c(x, y, f_Z) - c(x, y, f_{Z^i})| \leq \frac{2C^2\kappa^2}{m\lambda}.$$ ■

An extension to piecewise convex loss functions can be achieved by replacing the derivatives by subdifferentials. Most equalities for optimality conditions become statements about memberships in sets. The auxiliary lemma can be analogously extended, and the overall theorem stated in terms of an upper bound on the values of the subdifferentials of the loss function. Since this would clutter the notation even further, we have refrained from that. A second way of proving the theorem for arbitrary convex loss functions uses Legendre transformations of the empirical risk term. See [615] among others, for details.

12.2 Leave-One-Out Estimates

Rather than betting on the proximity between the empirical risk and the expected risk we may make further use of the training data and compute what is commonly referred to as the *leave-one-out error* of a sample. The basic idea is that we find an estimate f^i from a sample consisting of $m - 1$ patterns by leaving the ith pattern out and, subsequently, compute the error of misprediction on (x_i, y_i). The error is then averaged over all m possible patterns. The hope is that such a procedure will provide us with a quantity that is very closely related to the real expected error.

12.2.1 Theoretical Background

Before we delve into the practical details of estimating the leave-one-out error, we need a formal definition and have to prove that the leave-one-out estimator is a useful quantity.

Leave-One-Out Error

Definition 12.8 (Leave-One-Out Error) *Denote by f_Z the estimate obtained by a learning algorithm, given the sample Z, by $Z^i := Z \backslash \{(x_i, y_i)\}$ the sample obtained by removing the ith pattern, and by f_{Z^i} the corresponding estimate, obtained by the same learning algorithm (note that we changed the definition of Z^i from that in the previous section). Then the leave-one-out error is defined as*

$$R_{\mathrm{LOO}}(Z) := \frac{1}{m} \sum_{i=1}^{m} c(x_i, y_i, f_{Z^i}(x_i)). \tag{12.29}$$

The following theorem by Luntz and Brailovsky [335] shows that $R_{\mathrm{LOO}}(Z)$ is an almost unbiased estimator.[1]

Unbiasedness of Leave-One-Out

Theorem 12.9 (Leave-One-Out Error is Almost Unbiased [335]) *Denote by P a distribution over $\mathcal{X} \times \mathcal{Y}$, and by Z_m and Z_{m-1} samples of size m and $m-1$ respectively, drawn iid from P. Moreover, denote by $R[f_{Z_{m-1}}]$ the expected risk of an estimator derived from the sample Z_{m-1}. Then, for any learning algorithm, the leave-one-out error is almost unbiased,*

$$\mathbf{E}_{Z_{m-1}}\left[R[f_{Z_{m-1}}]\right] = \mathbf{E}_{Z_m}\left[R_{\mathrm{LOO}}(Z_m)\right]. \tag{12.30}$$

Proof We begin by rewriting $\mathbf{E}_{Z_{m-1}}\left[R[f_{Z_{m-1}}]\right]$ in terms of expected values only. By definition (see (3.12)) $R[f] := \mathbf{E}\left[c(x, y, f(x))\right]$ and, therefore, the lhs of (12.30) can be written as

$$\mathbf{E}_{Z_{m-1}}\left[R[f_{Z_{m-1}}]\right] = \mathbf{E}_{Z_{m-1} \cup \{(x,y)\}}\left[c(x, y, f_{Z_{m-1}}(x))\right]. \tag{12.31}$$

The leave-one-out error, on the other hand, can be restated as

$$\begin{aligned} \mathbf{E}_{Z_m}\left[R_{\mathrm{LOO}}(Z_m)\right] &= \frac{1}{m} \sum_{i=1}^{m} \mathbf{E}_{Z_m}\left[c(x_i, y_i, f_{Z_m^i}(x_i))\right] \\ &= \mathbf{E}_{Z_{m-1} \cup \{(x_m, y_m)\}}\left[c(x_m, y_m, f_{Z_{m-1}}(x_m))\right] \end{aligned} \tag{12.32}$$

Here we use the fact that expectation and summation can be interchanged. In addition, a permutation argument shows that all terms under the sum have to be equal, hence we can replace the average by one of the terms. Finally, if we rename (x_m, y_m) by (x, y), then (12.32) becomes identical to the rhs of (12.31) which proves the theorem. ∎

This demonstrates that the leave-one-out error is a sensible quantity to use. We are short, however, of another key ingredient required in the use of this method when bounding the error of an estimator; we need a bound on the variance of $R_{\mathrm{LOO}}(Z)$. While general results exist, which show that the leave-one-out estimator is not a *worse* estimate than the estimate based on the empirical error (see Kearns [285] for example, who shows that at least the *rate* is not worse), we would expect that, on the contrary, the leave-one-out error is much *more* reliable than the empirical risk.

1. The term "almost" refers to the fact that the leave-one-out error provides an estimate for training on sets of size $m-1$ rather than m, cf. Proposition 7.4.

We are not aware of any such result in the context of minimizers of the regularized risk functional (see [136] for an overview of bounds on the leave-one-out error). In the following we state a result which is a slight improvement on Theorem 12.3 and which uses the same concentration of measure techniques as in Section 12.1 (see also [68]).

Tail Bound for LOO

Theorem 12.10 (Tail Bound for Leave-One-Out Estimators) *Denote by A a β-stable algorithm (for training set of size $m-1$) with the additional requirement that $0 \leq A(Z) \leq M$ for all $z \in \mathcal{X} \times \mathcal{Y}$ and for all training samples $Z \subset \mathcal{X} \times \mathcal{Y}$. Then we have;*

$$\mathrm{P}\left\{\left|R_{\mathrm{LOO}}(Z) - \mathbf{E}_Z\left[R_{\mathrm{LOO}}(Z)\right]\right| > \varepsilon\right\} \leq 2\exp\left(-\frac{2m\varepsilon^2}{(m\beta+M)^2}\right). \tag{12.33}$$

Proof The proof is very similar to that of Theorem 12.3 and uses Theorem 12.1. All we must do is show that $R_{\mathrm{LOO}}(Z)$ does not change by too much if we replace one of the patterns in Z by a different pattern. This means that, for $Z^i := Z \backslash z_i \cup \{z\}$ (where $z := (x, y)$), we have to determine a constant c_0 such that

$$\left|R_{\mathrm{LOO}}(Z) - R_{\mathrm{LOO}}(Z^i)\right| \leq c_0 \text{ for all } i. \tag{12.34}$$

In the following we denote by f_Z^j (and $f_{Z^i}^j$ respectively) the estimate obtained when leaving out the jth pattern. We may now expand (12.34) as follows.

$$\begin{aligned}\left|R_{\mathrm{LOO}}(Z) - R_{\mathrm{LOO}}(Z^i)\right| &\leq \left[\frac{1}{m}\sum_{j\neq i}\left|c\left(x_j, y_j, f_Z^j(x_j)\right) - c\left(x_j, y_j, f_{Z^i}^j(x_j)\right)\right|\right] + \\ &\quad \frac{1}{m}\left|c\left(x_i, y_i, f_Z^i(x_i)\right) - c\left(x, y, f_{Z^i}^i(x)\right)\right| && (12.35)\\ &\leq \frac{1}{m}\sum_{j\neq i}\beta + \frac{M}{m} < \beta + \frac{M}{m}. && (12.36)\end{aligned}$$

In (12.36) we use the fact that we have a β-stable algorithm, hence the individual summands are bounded by β. In addition, the loss at arbitrary locations is bounded from above by M (and by 0 from below), hence two losses may not differ by more than M overall. This shows that $c_o \leq \beta + \frac{M}{m}$. Substituting this into (12.2) proves the bound. ∎

We may use the values of β computed for minimizers of the regularized risk functional (Theorem 12.4 and Corollary 12.6) in order to obtain practical bounds. The current result is an improvement on the confidence bounds available for minimizers of the regularized risk functional (there is no dependency on β in the confidence bound and the constants in the exponential term are slightly better). One would, however, suspect that much better bounds should be possible.

In particular, rather than bounding each individual term in (12.35) by $\frac{\beta}{m}$, it should be possible to take advantage of averaging effects and, thus, replace the overall bound β by $\frac{\beta}{\sqrt{m}}$ for example. It is an open question whether such a bound can be obtained.

Also note that Theorem 12.10 only applies to Lipschitz continuous, convex loss functions. This means that we cannot use the bound in the case of classification, since the loss function is discontinuous (we have 0-1 loss). Still, the leave-one-out error turns out to be currently the most reliable estimator of the expected error available. Hence, despite some lack of theoretical justification, one should consider it a method of choice when performing model selection for kernel methods.

This brings us to another problem; how should we compute the leave-one-out error efficiently, without running a training algorithm m times? We must find approximations or good upper bounds for $R_{\text{LOO}}(Z)$ which are cheap to compute.

12.2.2 Lagrange Multiplier Estimates

One of the most intuitive and simplest bounds on the leave-one-out error to compute is one based on the values of the Lagrange multipliers [259]. In its original form it was proven for regularized risk functionals without constant threshold b, so, for $f \in \mathcal{H}$. It can be stated as follows.

Theorem 12.11 (Jaakkola and Haussler [259]) *Denote by $Z \subset \mathcal{X} \times \mathcal{Y}$ a training set for classification, and by $f(x) = \sum_{i=1}^m \alpha_i y_i k(x_i, x)$ the minimizer of the regularized risk functional (7.35). Then an upper bound on the leave-one-out error is*

$$R_{\text{LOO}}(Z) \leq \frac{1}{m} \sum_{i=1}^{m} \theta\left(y_i\left(f(x_i) - \alpha_i k(x_i, x_i)\right)\right), \tag{12.37}$$

where θ is the step function.

Proof Recall (7.37). This is the special case of a convex optimization problem of the following form;

$$\begin{aligned} &\text{minimize} \quad D(\alpha) := -\sum_{i=1}^{m} \gamma(\alpha_i) + \frac{1}{2}\sum_{i,j=1}^{m} \alpha_i \alpha_j y_i y_j k(x_i, x_j) \\ &\text{subject to} \quad 0 \leq \alpha_i \leq C \text{ for all } i \in [m] \end{aligned} \tag{12.38}$$

Here $\gamma(\alpha_i)$ is the term stemming from the loss function (in SV classification $\gamma(\alpha_i) = \alpha_i$). Moreover, denote the restriction of D into the set $Z \backslash \{(x_i, y_i)\}$ by $D^i(\alpha)$. Denote by $\alpha^* \in \mathbb{R}^m$ the minimizer of (12.38) and by $\alpha^i \in \mathbb{R}^{m-1}$ the minimizer of the corresponding problem in D^i. Finally, denote the restriction of α^* onto $\mathbb{R}^m$ obtained by removing the ith component by $\bar{\alpha}^*$ (and likewise $\bar{f}^*, f^i, \bar{f}^i$).

By construction $D^i(\alpha^i) \leq D^i(\bar{\alpha}^*)$. We modify D^i slightly such that the changed version has $\bar{\alpha}^*$ as its minimum. One may check that

$$\bar{D}^i(\alpha) := D^i(\alpha) + y_i \alpha_i^* \sum_{j=1, j\neq i}^{m} y_j \alpha_j k(x_i, x_j) = D^i(\alpha) + y_i \alpha_i^* (f(x_i) - \alpha_i y_i k(x_i, x_i)) \tag{12.39}$$

satisfies this property. Thus, we have $\bar{D}^i(\alpha^i) \geq \bar{D}^i(\bar{\alpha}^*)$. Expanding terms we obtain

$$\bar{D}^i(\bar{\alpha}^*) - D^i(\bar{\alpha}^*) \leq \bar{D}^i(\alpha^i) - D^i(\alpha^i) = y_i \alpha_i^* \sum_{j=1, j\neq i}^{m} y_j \alpha_j^i k(x_i, x_j) = y_i \alpha_i^* f^i(x_i). \tag{12.40}$$

Since $\alpha_i^* \geq 0$ for all $i \in [m]$ this implies

$$y_i(f(x_i) - \alpha_i^* k(x_i, x_i)) \leq y_i f^i(x_i). \tag{12.41}$$

As a leave-one-out error occurs exactly if $y_i f^i(x_i) < 0$ this means that $y_i(f(x_i) - \alpha_i^* k(x_i, x_i)) < 0$ is a necessary condition for a leave-one-out error and, thus, can be used as an upper bound on it. ■

Note that we cannot directly apply this bound to the classical SV setting since there $f(x) = \langle \mathbf{w}, \Phi(x) \rangle + b$, specifically, there exists a parametric constant term b which is not regularized at all. Joachims [268] shows that Theorem 12.11 can be modified in such a way to accommodate for this setting, namely replacing $f(x_i) - \alpha_i k(x_i, x_i)$ by $f(x_i) - 2\alpha_i k(x_i, x_i)$. Practical experiments show that this bound is overly conservative [268]. In fact, for all practical purposes, Theorem 12.11 seems to be predictive enough, even in the case of a constant threshold.

Leave-One-Out Machine

Additionally, (12.37) motivates a modified SV training algorithm [592] by directly minimizing the bound of Theorem 12.11,

$$\begin{aligned} \text{minimize} \quad & \sum_{i=1}^{m} \xi_i \\ \text{subject to} \quad & y_i \sum_{j \neq i} \alpha_j y_j k(x_i, x_j) \geq 1 - \xi_i \text{ for all } i \in [m] \\ & \alpha_i, \xi_i \geq 0 \text{ for all } i \in [m]. \end{aligned} \tag{12.42}$$

Here we choose a fixed constant for the margin to ensure non-zero solutions. It appears that an algorithm which minimizes (12.42) does not have any free parameters. Unfortunately this is not quite true. Weston and Herbrich [592] modify (12.42) to regularize the setting by replacing the inequality constraint by

$$y_i \sum_{j \neq i} \alpha_j y_j k(x_i, x_j) + \lambda \alpha_i y_i k(x_i, x_i) \geq 1 - \xi_i \text{ for all } i \in [m] \tag{12.43}$$

where $\lambda \in [0, 1]$. Unfortunately the effect of λ is not so easily understood. See the original work [592] for more details, or Problem 12.2 for an alternative approach to fixing the parametrization problem via the ν-trick. Let us now proceed to a more accurate bound on the leave-one-out error, this time computed by using the distribution of the Support Vectors.

12.2.3 The Span Bound for Classification

Vapnik and Chapelle [565] use a quantity, called the *span* of the Support Vectors, in order to provide an upper bound on the number of errors incurred by a SVM. The proof technique is quite similar to the one in the previous section. The main difference is that the Lagrange multipliers are adapted in such a way as to accomodate the constant threshold and the fact that only a subset of patterns are chosen as Support Vectors. Consequently, we obtain a more complicated (and possibly more precise) bound on the leave-one-out error.

In what follows, we state the main theorems from [565] without proof (see the original publication for details). In addition, we adapt the results to quantile estimation and novelty detection (see Chapter 8 for the description of the algorithm) and prove the latter (the proofs being similar, one can easily infer the original from the modification). Before we proceed, we recall the notion of *in-bound* Support Vectors. As introduced in Table 7.2, these are the SVs x_i whose Lagrange multipliers lie in the interior of the box constraints; using the present notation, $0 < \alpha_i < C$.

In-Bound SVs

Span

Definition 12.12 (Span of a SV Classification Solution) *Denote by* X, Y *the training sample and by* $\alpha_1, \ldots, \alpha_m, b$ *the solution obtained by solving the corresponding SV soft-margin classification problem with upper bound C on the Lagrange multipliers (see Section 1.5 and Chapter 7). Furthermore, denote by* $\alpha_1, \ldots, \alpha_n$ *the* in-bound *SVs (without loss of generality we assume that they are the first n patterns of the sample). Then the span* $S_{\text{class}}(l)$ *of an SV classification solution with respect to the pattern l is defined by*

$$S^2_{\text{class}}(l) := \min_{\beta \in \bar{\beta}_l} \sum_{i,j=1}^{n} \beta_i \beta_j k(x_i, x_j), \tag{12.44}$$

where

$$\bar{\beta}_l = \{\beta \mid \beta_l = -1, \sum_{i=1}^{n} \beta_i = 0, \text{ and } 0 \leq \alpha_i + y_i y_l \alpha_l \beta_i \leq C\}. \tag{12.45}$$

Note that $\sum_{i,j=1}^{n} \beta_i \beta_j k(x_i, x_j) = \|\sum_{i=1}^{n} \beta_i \Phi(x_i)\|^2$ and, in particular, that $S^2_{\text{class}}(l)$ is the minimum distance between the patterns $\Phi(x_l)$ and a linear combination of the remaining in-bound Support Vectors which leaves the box and inequality constraints intact.[2] This is a measure for how well $\Phi(x_l)$ can be replaced by the remaining in-bound SVs.

The first thing to show is that (12.44) is actually well defined, that is, the set $\bar{\beta}_l$ is nonempty. The following lemma tells us this and gives an upper bound on $S^2_{\text{class}}(l)$.

Lemma 12.13 (The Span is Well Defined [565]) *The quantity* $S^2_{\text{class}}(l)$ *is well defined, in particular, the set* $\bar{\beta}_l$ *is nonempty and, further,*

$$S_{\text{class}}(l) \leq D_{\text{SV}} \tag{12.46}$$

where D_{SV} *is the diameter of the smallest sphere containing the in-bound Support Vectors.*

After these definitions we have to put our results to practical use. The two key relevant bounds are now given.

Theorem 12.14 (Misclassification Bound via the Span [565]) *If in the leave-one-out procedure an in-bound Support Vector* x_l *is recognized incorrectly, then the following inequality holds:*

$$\alpha_l S_{\text{class}}(l) \max\left(D, C^{-\frac{1}{2}}\right) \geq 1. \tag{12.47}$$

---

2. Vapnik and Chapelle [565] actually define a geometrical object which they call the span of a set of Support Vectors and then compute its distance to a pattern $\Phi(x_l)$.

Additionally, if the sets of SVs, and of in-bound SVs, remain the same during the leave-one-out procedure, then, for any SV x_l, the following equality holds,

$$y_l(f(x_l) - f^l(x_l)) = \alpha_l S_{\text{class}}(l)^2. \tag{12.48}$$

Here f^l is the minimizer of the SV classification problem in which x_l has been removed.

This means that we may use (12.47) as an upper bound on the size of the misclassification error. Furthermore, (12.48) can be employed as an *approximation* of the leave-one-out error, simply by counting the number of instances where $y_l f(x_l) \leq \alpha_l S_{\text{class}}(l)^2$. This is, of course, not a bound on the leave-one-out error any more, since we can, in general, not expect that the remaining Support Vectors will not change if the pattern x_l is removed. Yet it may be a more reliable estimate in practice. Note the similarity to the result of Jaakkola and Haussler [259] of the previous section; there, $S_{\text{class}}(l)^2$ is replaced by $k(x_l, x_l)$. We conclude this section by noting that the span bound for the ν-SVM has been studied in detail in [217].

12.2.4 The Span Bound for Quantile Estimation

Let us briefly review the approach of Chapter 8. A key feature was the integration of a single class SVM with the ν-trick, namely the fact that we may specify a certain fraction of patterns to lie beyond the hyperplane beforehand. In particular recall (8.6) and, subsequently, the dual problem (8.13) with constraints (8.14) and (8.15).

In this case the constraints on the Lagrange multipliers are given by $0 \leq \alpha_i \leq \frac{1}{\nu m}$. This setting, however, creates a problem in the case of a leave-one-out procedure; should we adjust $\frac{1}{\nu m}$ to $\frac{1}{\nu(m-1)}$ or keep the original upper constraint and simply remove the variable corresponding to the pattern x_l? The first case is more faithful to the concept of leave-one-out error testing. The second, as we shall see, is much more amenable to the proof of practical bounds. In addition, keeping the original constraints can be seen as a replacement of ν by $\nu' = \nu(1 + \frac{1}{m})$. This means that the threshold ν is slightly increased for leave-one-out training. Therefore we can expect that the number of leave-one-out errors committed in the case of an estimator trained with ν' will be larger than for one trained with ν. Further, for large m, this change is negligible. We begin with a definition of the span.

Definition 12.15 (Span/Swap of an SV Quantile Estimation Solution) *Denote by* X *the training sample and by $\alpha_1, \ldots, \alpha_m$, ρ the solution obtained by solving the corresponding quantile estimation problem with corresponding parameter ν. Moreover, denote by $\alpha_1, \ldots, \alpha_n$ the* in-bound *SVs. Then the span $S_{\text{support}}(l)$ with respect to the pattern l is defined as follows.*

- *If the number of SVs (in-bound or not) n^* is bounded from below by $n^* - 1 \geq \nu m$ we define the span as*

$$S^2_{\text{support}}(l) := \min_{\beta \in \mathcal{B}_l} \sum_{i,j=1}^{n} \beta_i \beta_j k(x_i, x_j), \tag{12.49}$$

where

$$\bar{\beta}_l = \{\beta \mid \beta_l = -1, \sum_{i=1}^{n} \beta_i = 0, \text{ and } 0 \le \alpha_i + \alpha_l \beta_i \le 1/(\nu m)\}. \tag{12.50}$$

- *If the number of SVs is given by* $n^* = \lceil \nu m \rceil$ *we define the* swap *of a Support Vector by*

$$\mathrm{Swap}^2(l) := \min_{j \notin \mathrm{SV}} \left[\alpha_l \left(\sum_{i=1}^{n^*} \alpha_i K_{ij} - \rho \right) + \alpha_l^2 \left(K_{ll} + K_{jj} - 2K_{jl} \right) \right] \tag{12.51}$$

where as usual we use the kernel matrix $K_{ij} := k(x_i, x_j)$.

We do not have to consider the case $n^* < \lceil \nu m \rceil$ since, according to Proposition 8.3, $n^* \ge \nu m$. We next show that $S_{\mathrm{support}}(l)$ is well defined and compute a bound on it.

Lemma 12.16 (The Span is Well Defined) *The quantity* $S^2_{\mathrm{support}}(l)$ *is well defined; the set* $\bar{\beta}_l$ *is nonempty and, moreover,*

$$S_{\mathrm{support}}(l) \le D_{\mathrm{SV}} \tag{12.52}$$

where D_{SV} *is the diameter of the smallest sphere containing the in-bound Support Vectors.*

Proof For $n^* = \lceil \nu m \rceil$ it is clear that Swap(l) is well defined. For $n^* - 1 > \nu m$ we have to show that a set of β_i (with $i \ne l$) exists such that

$$\sum_{i=1, i \ne l}^{n} \beta_i = 1 \text{ where } 0 \le \alpha_i + \alpha_l \beta_i \le \frac{1}{\nu m} \text{ and } \beta_i \ge 0 \tag{12.53}$$

since in this case $S^2_{\mathrm{support}}(l) = \alpha_l^2 \|\Phi(x_l) - \bar{\Phi}\|^2$ where $\bar{\Phi} = \sum_{i=1, i \ne l}^{n} \beta_i \Phi(x_i)$ is an element of the convex hull of the in-bound Support Vectors, and thus the diameter of the corresponding sphere D_{SV} is an upper bound.

Note that the maximum value for each β_i (with $i \ne l$) is given by $\alpha_l \beta_i^* = \frac{1}{\nu m} - \alpha_i$ and, thus,

$$\alpha_l \sum_{i=1, i \ne l}^{n} \beta_i^* = \sum_{i=1, i \ne l}^{n} \left[\frac{1}{\nu m} - \alpha_i \right] = \sum_{i=1, i \ne l}^{n^*} \left[\frac{1}{\nu m} - \alpha_i \right] = \frac{n^*}{m\nu} - 1 + \alpha_l \ge \alpha_l. \tag{12.54}$$

By rescaling each β_i^* with a constant factor $0 < \mu \le 1$ we obtain suitable $\beta_i = \mu \beta_i^*$ which satisfy the conditions imposed in the definition of $S^2_{\mathrm{support}}(l)$. ■

Next we have to state an analog of Theorem 12.14. In this context we must define more specifically what we consider an error, and, thus, a leave-one-out error for the problem of quantile estimating.

Rather than using the threshold ρ obtained by minimizing the adaptive regularized risk functional (see Chapter 8) we should introduce an additional[3] "margin" $\Delta\rho$. A pattern is only classified as atypical if $f(x) < \rho - \Delta\rho$. Otherwise all SVs, whether in-bound or not, would be classified as leave-one-out errors.

3. This additional margin $\Delta\rho$ is also needed in order to prove uniform convergence-type results.

Theorem 12.17 (Misclassification Bound via the Span) *If, in the leave-one-out procedure, an in-bound Support Vector x_l is recognized incorrectly, then (with the additional margin $\Delta\rho$ as described above) the following inequality holds,*

$$\alpha_l S_{\text{support}}(l) \max\left(\frac{D}{\Delta\rho}, \frac{\nu m}{D}\right) \geq 1 \tag{12.55}$$

if $n^* - 1 \geq \nu m$. Otherwise

$$\alpha_l \Delta\rho \operatorname{Swap}(l) \max\left(D, C^{-\frac{1}{2}}\right) \geq 1 \tag{12.56}$$

is applicable. Furthermore, if the sets of Support Vectors and of in-bound Support Vectors remain the same during the leave-one-out procedure, then for any Support Vector x_l the following equality holds;

$$(\rho^l - f^l(x_l)) = \alpha_l S_{\text{support}}(l)^2. \tag{12.57}$$

Here f^l is the minimizer of the SV classification problem where x^l has been removed.

Proof As in [565], denote by α^0 the solution obtained by minimizing the regularized risk functional depending on m samples, and by α^l the solution obtained through leaving out sample l (analogously denote by ρ^l the margin obtained by such an estimator). Further, denote the value of the dual objective function derived from the regularized risk functional by

$$D(\alpha) := \min_{\alpha} -\frac{1}{2}\alpha^\top K\alpha \text{ subject to } \sum_{i=1}^{m} \alpha_i = 1 \text{ and } 0 \leq \alpha_i \leq \frac{1}{\nu m}. \tag{12.58}$$

By construction $D(\alpha^0) \leq D(\alpha^0 - \delta)$ for all $\delta \in \mathbb{R}^m$ such that the constraints of (12.58) are satisfied, and, in particular, for $\delta_l = \alpha_l$. Similarly, for α^l we have $D(\alpha^l) \leq D(\alpha^l + \gamma)$ for all $\gamma \in \mathbb{R}^m$ satisfying the constraints of (12.58) and $\gamma_l = 0$. Hence we obtain

$$D_1 := D(\alpha^0) - D(\alpha^0 - \delta) \leq D(\alpha^0) - D(\alpha^l) \leq D(\alpha^l + \gamma) - D(\alpha^l) =: D_2. \tag{12.59}$$

Next we have to compute or bound D_1 and D_2. For $n^* - 1 \geq \nu m$ we choose δ to be the minimizer of (12.49); $\delta_i = -\alpha_l \beta_i$. This gives,

$$D_1 = -\frac{1}{2}(\alpha^0)^\top K\alpha^0 + \frac{1}{2}(\alpha^0 - \delta)^\top K(\alpha^0 - \delta) \tag{12.60}$$

$$= \frac{1}{2}\delta^\top K\delta - \delta^\top K\alpha^0 \tag{12.61}$$

$$= \frac{1}{2}\alpha_l^2 \beta^\top K\beta - \delta^\top\left(K\alpha^0 - \rho\right) \tag{12.62}$$

$$= \frac{\alpha_l^2}{2} S^2_{\text{support}}(l). \tag{12.63}$$

Here (12.62) follows from the choice of δ and the fact that $\sum_i \delta_i = 0$ (note also that $\sum_i \delta_i \rho = 0$). Finally, (12.63) is due to the fact that $\delta_l \neq 0$ for in-bound SVs only and thus the second term in (12.62) vanishes.

For $n^* = \lceil \nu m \rceil$ we cannot find a suitable δ based solely on in-bound SVs and therefore we must add an additional pattern, say with index j, which was not previously a Support Vector. All we do is swap α_l and α_j, giving $\delta_l = \alpha_l$ and $\delta_j = -\alpha_l$. In particular, we pick j to minimize (12.51). For D_1 we thus obtain

$$D_1 = \frac{1}{2}\delta^\top K\delta - \delta^\top K\alpha^0 \tag{12.64}$$
$$= \alpha_l^2(K_{ll} + K_{jj} - 2K_{lj}) + \delta^\top(\rho - K\alpha^0) \tag{12.65}$$
$$= \alpha_l^2(K_{ll} + K_{jj} - 2K_{lj}) + \alpha_l\left(\sum_{i=1}^{n^*}\alpha_i K_{ij} - \rho\right) = \text{Swap}^2(l). \tag{12.66}$$

Next we have to compute D_2. We choose a particular value of γ, namely $\gamma_j = a = -\gamma_l$ for some j, within the set of in-bound SVs obtained from leave-one-out training and set all other coefficients to 0. Expanding D_2 leads to

$$D_2 = -\frac{1}{2}\gamma^\top K\gamma - \gamma^\top K\alpha^l = -\frac{1}{2}\gamma^\top K\gamma - \gamma^\top\left[K\alpha^l - \rho^l\right] \tag{12.67}$$
$$= -\frac{a^2}{2}\left(K_{ll} + K_{jj} - 2K_{lj}\right) - a\left(\sum_{i=1}\alpha_i^l K_{il} - \rho^l\right). \tag{12.68}$$

If x_l generates a leave-one-out error we know that $\left(\rho^l - \sum_{i=1}\alpha_i^l K_{il}\right) \geq \Delta\rho$. In addition, $\left(K_{ll} + K_{jj} - 2K_{lj}\right)$ is the squared distance between two SVs obtained by leaving x_l out. This, of course, can be bounded by D^2, where D^2 is the radius of the data (in feature space). Therefore

$$D_2 \geq -\frac{a^2}{2}D^2 + a\Delta\rho \tag{12.69}$$

and, after unconstrained maximization over a, we obtain $D_2 \geq \frac{(\Delta\rho)^2}{2D^2}$ for $a_{\min} = \frac{\Delta\rho}{D^2}$. We have to take into account, however, that $a \leq \frac{1}{\nu m}$ and thus, for $a_{\min} > \frac{1}{\nu m}$, we obtain

$$D_2 \geq -\frac{D^2}{2(\nu m)^2} + \frac{\Delta\rho}{\nu m} \geq -\frac{D^2}{2(\nu m)^2} + \frac{D^2}{(\nu m)^2} = \frac{D^2}{2(\nu m)^2}. \tag{12.70}$$

Here we exploit the assumption that $a_{\min} = \frac{\Delta\rho}{D^2} > \frac{1}{\nu m}$. Taking the minimum of the two lower bounds leads to the following inequality for D_2;

$$D_2 \geq \frac{1}{2}\min\left(\frac{(\Delta\rho)^2}{D^2}, \frac{D^2}{(\nu m)^2}\right). \tag{12.71}$$

Finally, since $D_1 \leq D_2$, then (12.71) in combination with (12.63) proves the bound.

To prove (12.57) note that, for the case where no additional point becomes a Support Vector, then, by construction $\min_\delta D(\alpha^0 - \delta) = D(\alpha^l)$ and, furthermore, $\min_\gamma D(\alpha^l + \gamma) = D(\alpha^0)$. Moreover, note that in this case $n^* - 1 \geq \nu m$ since, otherwise, the ν-property would not be satisfied for the leave-one-out estimate. We next show that $\delta = -\alpha_l\lambda$ where λ is the minimizer of $S^2_{\text{support}}(l)$. To see this note that, for any $\delta \in \mathbb{R}^m$ with $\sum_i \delta_i = 0$ and $\delta_l = \alpha_l$, it follows from (12.60) that

$$D_1 = -\frac{1}{2}\delta^\top K\delta + \delta^\top K\alpha^0 = -\frac{1}{2}\delta^\top K\delta + \delta^\top(K\alpha^0 - \rho) = -\frac{1}{2}\delta^\top K\delta. \tag{12.72}$$

The latter is maximized ($D(\alpha - \delta)$ is minimized) for $\delta = -\alpha_l \lambda$ and, thus, $D_1 = -\frac{1}{2}\alpha_l^2 S_{\text{support}}^2$. Finally, note that

$$D(\alpha^l + \gamma) - D(\alpha^l) = -\frac{1}{2}\gamma^\top K \gamma - \gamma^\top K \alpha^l \tag{12.73}$$

$$= -\frac{1}{2}\gamma^\top K \gamma - \gamma^\top (K\alpha^l - \rho^l) \tag{12.74}$$

$$= -\frac{1}{2}\alpha_l^2 S_{\text{support}}^2(l) - \gamma^\top (K\alpha^l - \rho^l) \tag{12.75}$$

$$= -\frac{1}{2}\alpha_l^2 S_{\text{support}}^2(l) - \alpha_l (f^l(x_l) - \rho^l) \tag{12.76}$$

where (12.74) follows from $\sum_i \delta_i = 0$, (12.75) is a consequence of the optimality of $\alpha_l \lambda$ for γ, and in (12.76) all but one term in the dot product vanish since $f^l(x_i) - \rho^l = 0$ for all in-bound Support Vectors. Exploiting the equality between D_1 and the minimum value of $D(\alpha^l + \gamma) - D(\alpha^l)$ proves (12.57). ■

Even though the assumption that led to (12.57) is rarely satisfied in practice, it provides a good *approximation* of the leave-one-out error and therefore may be preferrable to the more conservative estimate obtained from Theorem 12.17.

12.2.5 Methods from Statistical Physics

Opper and Winther [396] use a reasoning similar to the above that leading to provide an *estimator* of the leave-one-out bound. As in (12.48) and (12.57), the following assumptions are made:

- In-Bound Support Vectors x_i will remain so even after removing a pattern x_l and the corresponding function values $f(x_i)$ will not change under the leave-one-out procedure.
- Margin errors will remain margin errors.
- Correctly classified patterns with a margin will remain correctly classified.

These assumptions are typically not satisfied, yet in practice the leave-one out approximation that follows from them is still fairly accurate (in the experiments of [396] the accuracy was to within 1 ± 10^{-3}).[4] The practical appeal of the methods in this section is their computational simplicity when compared to the span bound and similar methods, which require the solution of a quadratic program.[5]

For the sake of simplicity we assume that the first n patterns are in-bound SVs, and that patterns $n+1$ to n^* are bound SVs. We begin with a simple example —

4. Other studies, such as the one by Dawson [131] found lower but still relatively high accuracies of the estimate at a very favorable computational cost of the method.
5. In fact, the span bound almost attempts to solve the quadratic program resulting from leaving one sample out exactly, under the assumption that the SVs remain unchanged.

SV classification without a constant threshold. Here

$$f(x) = \sum_{j=1}^{n^*} \alpha_j k(x_j, x) \tag{12.77}$$

$$f^l(x) = \sum_{j=1, j \neq l}^{n^*} \alpha_j^l k(x_j, x) \tag{12.78}$$

Using the notation $\delta\alpha_j := \alpha_j^l - \alpha_j$, we obtain

$$f^l(x) - f(x) = \sum_{j=1, j \neq l}^{n^*} \delta\alpha_j k(x_j, x) - \alpha_l k(x_l, x). \tag{12.79}$$

For an in-bound SV x_i (where $i \neq l$) to remain so after the leave-one out procedure we need $f(x_i) = f^l(x_i)$ or, more specifically,

$$\alpha_l k(x_l, x_i) = \sum_{j=1, j \neq l}^{n^*} \delta\alpha_j k(x_j, x_i). \tag{12.80}$$

This leads to a system of n variables with n linear constraints if x_i is a bound constrained SV (and $n - 1$ variables and constraints if x_i is an in-bound SVs). The obvious search is for a method to solve this linear system efficiently for all n^* SVs. We will show that, in a slightly more general setting of semiparametric models (and/or additional adaptive margins), we may compute the leave-one-out approximation with $O((n+N)^2 n^*)$ cost. This is considerably cheaper than the n linear programs in n variables that must be solved in the case of the span bound. Additionally, the estimates may be even more precise than those when using the span bound; margin errors are not necessarily real errors, nor does the fact that a pattern is a margin error automatically imply that it will be misclassified by a classifier which ignored it during training.

Rather than deriving equations for the simple case of a pure kernel expansion, we consider the situation that we have a semiparametric model, in particular a kernel expansion plus a small, fixed number of terms (see Section 4.8), and we derive a closed form expression for it. This includes the addition of a constant offset b, as a special case. Without going into details (which can be found in Chapter 4) we have the following kernel expansion

$$f(x) = \sum_{i=1}^{N} \beta_i \psi_i(x) + \sum_{i=1}^{m} \alpha_i k(x_i, x) \tag{12.81}$$

$$\text{subject to} \quad \sum_{i=1}^{m} \alpha_i \psi_j(x_i) = 0 \text{ for all } j \in [N]. \tag{12.82}$$

Here ψ_i, with $i \in [N]$, are additional parametric functions (setting $\psi_1(x) = 1$ and $N = 1$ would lead the case of a constant offset, b). The following proposition gives an approximation of the changes due to leave-one-out training. As before, only the Support Vectors matter in the calculations. To give a more concise representation, we state the equations in matrix notation.

Mean Field Leave-One-Out Approximation

Proposition 12.18 (Mean Field Leave-One-Out Approximation) *Denote by $K^n \in \mathbb{R}^{n \times n}$ the submatrix of kernel functions between in-bound SVs and by $K^{n^*} \in \mathbb{R}^{(n^*-n) \times n}$ the submatrix of kernel functions between in-bound and bound SVs. Likewise, denote by $\Psi^n \in \mathbb{R}^{n \times N}$ the matrix consisting of the function values $\psi_j(x_i)$, where x_i are in-bound SVs, and by $\Psi^{n^*} \in \mathbb{R}^{(n^*-n) \times N}$ the matrix of function values $\psi_j(x_i)$ where x_i are bound SVs. Then, if x_l is an in-bound SV, the following approximation holds;*

$$f(x_l) - f^l(x_l) \approx \alpha_l \left[\begin{bmatrix} K^n & (\Psi^n)^\top \\ \Psi^n & 0 \end{bmatrix}_{ll}^{-1} \right]^{-1} \tag{12.83}$$

and, for bound constrained SVs,

$$f(x_l) - f^l(x_l) \approx \alpha_l \left[K_{ll} - \left[\begin{bmatrix} K^{n^*} \\ \Psi^{n^*} \end{bmatrix} \begin{bmatrix} K^n & (\Psi^n)^\top \\ \Psi^n & 0 \end{bmatrix}^{-1} \begin{bmatrix} K^{n^*} \\ \Psi^{n^*} \end{bmatrix}^\top \right]_{ll} \right] \tag{12.84}$$

Here we use K_{ll} as shorthand for $k(x_l, x_l)$.

Proof We begin with the case that x_l is a bound constrained Support Vector. Since we have to enforce $f(x_i) = f^l(x_i)$ for all in-bound SVs, while maintaining the constraints (12.82), we have a system of $n + N$ variables (α_i and β_i) together with $n + N$ constraints. In matrix notation the above condition translates into

$$\begin{bmatrix} K^n & (\Psi^n)^\top \\ \Psi^n & 0 \end{bmatrix} \begin{bmatrix} \delta\alpha_1 \\ \vdots \\ \delta\alpha_n \\ \delta\beta_1 \\ \vdots \\ \delta\beta_N \end{bmatrix} = \alpha_l \begin{bmatrix} k(x_1, x_l) \\ \vdots \\ k(x_n, x_l) \\ \psi_1(x_l) \\ \vdots \\ \psi_N(x_l) \end{bmatrix} \tag{12.85}$$

Solving (12.85) for $\delta\alpha_i$ and $\delta\beta_i$ and substituting into the approximation for $f^l(x_l)$ leads to

$$f(x_l) - f^l(x_l) \approx \alpha_l k(x_l, x_l) - \sum_{i=1}^{n} \delta\alpha_i k(x_i, x_l) - \sum_{i=1}^{N} \delta\beta_i \psi_i(x_l) \tag{12.86}$$

$$= \alpha_l K_{ll} - \alpha_l \begin{bmatrix} k(x_1, x_l) \\ \vdots \\ k(x_n, x_l) \\ \psi_1(x_l) \\ \vdots \\ \psi_N(x_l) \end{bmatrix}^\top \begin{bmatrix} K^n & (\Psi^n)^\top \\ \Psi^n & 0 \end{bmatrix}^{-1} \begin{bmatrix} k(x_1, x_l) \\ \vdots \\ k(x_n, x_l) \\ \psi_1(x_l) \\ \vdots \\ \psi_N(x_l) \end{bmatrix} \tag{12.87}$$

Rewriting (12.87) leads to (12.84). To compute this expression efficiently we may use an indefinite symmetric (e.g. triangular) factorization of the inverse matrix into $T^\top DT$. Often it will be necessary to compute the pseudoinverse [131], since K^n tends to be rank degenerate for many practical kernels. Overall, the calculation costs $O((n+N)^2(n^*+N))$ operations.

In the case that x_l is an in-bound Support Vector we obtain a similar expression, the only difference being that the row and columns corresponding to x_l were removed from (12.87) in both K^n and Ψ^n. Recall that (see [337], 9.11.3.2a)

$$\begin{bmatrix} A & C \\ C^\top & D \end{bmatrix}^{-1} = \begin{bmatrix} A^{-1} + A^{-1}C(D - C^\top A^{-1}C)^{-1}C^\top A^{-1} & -A^{-1}C(D - C^\top A^{-1}C)^{-1} \\ -(D - C^\top A^{-1}C)^{-1}C^\top A^{-1} & (D - C^\top A^{-1}C)^{-1} \end{bmatrix} \tag{12.88}$$

By setting A equal to the square matrix in (12.87), with the contributions of x_l removed, and, further, identifying C with the remaining column vector (which contains the contribution of x_l) we see that (12.87) can be rewritten as in (12.83). ■

Remark 12.19 (Modifications for Classification) *In the case of classification, the function expansions are usually given by sums of $y_i\alpha_i k(x_i, x)$. Simply replace α_i by $y_i\alpha_i$ throughout to apply Proposition 12.18.*

Since the assumptions regarding the stability of the types of SVs that led to this result are the same as the ones that led to (12.48) and (12.57), it comes as no surprise that the trick (12.88) can also be applied to compute (12.44) under those assumptions. This is due to the fact that in this case, the box constraints in 12.45 can be dropped. These issues are discussed in detail in [102].

In order to apply a similar reasoning to ν-SVM a slightly modified approach is needed. We only state the result for classification. The proof and extensions to regression and novelty detection are left as an exercise (see Problem 12.4).

Proposition 12.20 (Mean Field Leave-One-Out for ν-Classification) *Let K^n denote the $n \times n$ submatrix of kernel functions between in-bound SVs, and K^{n^*} the $(n^* - n) \times n$ submatrix of kernel functions between in-bound and bound SVs. Moreover, denote by $y^n \in \mathbb{R}^n$ the vector of labels (± 1) of the in-bound SVs, likewise by $y^{n^*} \in \mathbb{R}^{n^*-n}$ the vector of labels of bound SVs, and by $1^n \in \mathbb{R}^n$ and $1^{n^*} \in \mathbb{R}^{n^*-n}$ the corresponding vectors with all entries set to 1. Then, if x_l is an in-bound SV, the following approximation holds;*

$$(y_l f(x_l) - \rho) - (y_l f^l(x_l) - \rho^l) \approx \alpha_l y_l \left[\begin{bmatrix} K^n & y^n & 1^n \\ y^{n\top} & 0 & 0 \\ 1^{n\top} & 0 & 0 \end{bmatrix}^{-1}_{ll} \right]^{-1} \tag{12.89}$$

and, for bound SVs;

$$(y_l f(x_l) - \rho) - (y_l f^l(x_l) - \rho^l) \approx$$
$$\alpha_l y_l \left[K_{ll} - \left[\begin{bmatrix} K^{n^*} \\ y^{n^*} \\ 1^{n^*} \end{bmatrix} \begin{bmatrix} K^n & y^n & 1^n \\ y^{n\top} & 0 & 0 \\ 1^{n\top} & 0 & 0 \end{bmatrix}^{-1} \begin{bmatrix} K^{n^*} \\ y^{n^*} \\ 1^{n^*} \end{bmatrix}^\top \right]_{ll} \right] \tag{12.90}$$

Again, we use K_{ll} as a shorthand for $k(x_l, x_l)$.

Remark 12.21 (Absolute Differences in Classification) *Often it will appear more useful to compute $y_l(f(x_l) - f^l(x_l))$ only, rather than the relative distance from the margin. In this case we have to compensate for the changes in ρ^l; we should compute only the changes in $\delta\alpha_i$ and δb (for the constant offset). One can see that, for boundary constrained SVs,*

$$\begin{bmatrix} \delta\alpha_1 \\ \vdots \\ \delta\alpha_n \\ \delta b \\ \delta\rho \end{bmatrix} = \begin{bmatrix} K^n & y^n & 1^n \\ y^{n\top} & 0 & 0 \\ 1^{n\top} & 0 & 0 \end{bmatrix}^{-1} \begin{bmatrix} K^{n^*} \\ y^{n^*} \\ 1^{n^*} \end{bmatrix}^\top \tag{12.91}$$

and, therefore, the correction term in $\delta\rho$ can be easily ignored in the expansion. We obtain

$$y_l(f(x_l) - f^l(x_l)) = y_l \left[\sum_{i=1}^{n} \delta\alpha_i y_i k(x_i, x_l) + \delta b \right]. \tag{12.92}$$

As far as in-bound SVs are concerned, this is not so easily achieved, since the matrix to be inverted is different for each pattern x_l. Luckily it is obtained by removing one row and one column from the full $(n+2) \times (n+2)$ system (see the proof of Proposition 12.18 and (12.91)). This allows us to compute its inverse by performing the converse operation to a rank-1 update. To do this we use (12.88) in the opposite direction. One can easily check by substitution that for $\begin{bmatrix} A & C \\ C^\top & D \end{bmatrix}^{-1} = \begin{bmatrix} \Upsilon & \Gamma \\ \Gamma^\top & \Delta \end{bmatrix}$ we have $A^{-1} = \Upsilon - \Gamma^\top \Delta^{-1} \Gamma$. Computing A^{-1} costs only $O(n^2)$ operations per in-bound Support Vector, which is acceptable, in particular, when compared to the cost of inverting the $(n+2) \times (n+2)$ system itself. This means that we can perform prediction as cheaply as in the standard SVM case.

Extensions to the situation where we have loss functions other than the ε-insensitive or the soft margin will require further investigation. It is not yet clear what the equivalent of in-bound and bound SVs should be, since it is a very rare case that the slope of the loss function $c(x, y, f(x))$ changes at only a small number of locations (for example, only once in the soft margin case, or twice in the ε-insensitive case, etc.). This is needed, however, for cheap computation of the leave-one-out approximation.

12.3 PAC-Bayesian Bounds

This section requires some basic knowledge of ideas common to Bayesian estimation (see Chapter 16). In particular, we suggest that the reader be familiar with the content of Section 16.1 before going further in this section. The reasoning below focuses on the case of classification, primarily in the noise-free case. The first work in this context is by McAllester [353, 354] with further applications by Herbrich and coworkers [240, 213, 238].

The proof strategy works as follows; after definitions of quantities such as the Gibbs and the Bayes classifier, needed in the context, we prove a set of theorems, commonly referred to as PAC-Bayesian theorems. These relate the posterior probability of sets of hypotheses to uniform convergence bounds. Finally, we show how large margins and large posterior probabilities are connected through the concept of version spaces.

12.3.1 Gibbs and Bayes Classifiers

In a departure from the concepts of the previous chapters we will extend our view from single classifiers to *distributions* over classifiers. This means that, instead of a deterministic prediction, say $f(x) = y$, we may obtain predictions f according to some $\mathrm{P}(y|x)$. This additionally means that we have to extend the notion of empirical or expected loss of a function f to the empirical or expected loss with respect to a *distribution*.

In the following denote by $\mathfrak{F}$ such a set of classifier, by $\mathrm{P}(f)$ a *prior* probability distribution over mappings $f: \mathfrak{X} \to \mathfrak{Y}$ and by $\mathrm{P}(f|Z)$ a *posterior* probability distribution (see Section 16.1), based on $\mathrm{P}(f)$ and the data Z. We now proceed with the definitions of risk and loss wrt. $\mathrm{P}(f)$ and $\mathrm{P}(f|Z)$.

Definition 12.22 (Risk with Respect to Distributions) *Denote by* $\mathrm{P}(f)$ *a distribution over* $\mathfrak{F}$. *Then the risk functional, with respect to a distribution, is defined as*

$$R[\mathrm{P}(f)] := \mathbf{E}_{f \sim \mathrm{P}(f)} [R[f]] \tag{12.93}$$

and, in particular,

$$R_{\mathrm{emp}}[\mathrm{P}(f)] := \mathbf{E}_{f \sim \mathrm{P}(f)} [R_{\mathrm{emp}}[f]] \tag{12.94}$$

$$R_{\mathrm{reg}}[\mathrm{P}(f)] := \mathbf{E}_{f \sim \mathrm{P}(f)} [R_{\mathrm{emp}}[f] + \lambda\Omega[f]]. \tag{12.95}$$

Taking a sampling point of view, by considering the classifiers f directly, we arrive at the Gibbs classifier.

Gibbs Classifier

Definition 12.23 (Gibbs Classifier) *The Gibbs Classifier is defined by the following random variable,*

$$f_{\mathrm{Gibbs}}(x) = f(x) \text{ where } f \sim \mathrm{P}(f|Z). \tag{12.96}$$

In other words, $f_{\text{Gibbs}}(x)$ is given by $f(x)$ where f is drawn randomly from $\mathrm{P}(f|Z)$ for fixed Z. Note that, by definition, $R[f_{\text{Gibbs}}] \equiv R[\mathrm{P}(f|Z)]$.

Another way to construct a predictor from a distribution $p(f|Z)$ is to predict according to the majority values of $f(x)$ where $f \sim \mathrm{P}(f|Z)$. We obtain the Bayes Classifier:

Definition 12.24 (Bayes Classifier) *Denote by $\mathrm{P}(f|Z)$ a distribution over mappings $f : \mathcal{X} \to \mathcal{Y}$ where $x \in \mathcal{X}$ and $Z \in (\mathcal{X} \times \mathcal{Y})^m$. Then the Bayes optimal classifier is given by*

$$f_{\text{Bayes}}(x) := \operatorname*{argmax}_y \mathrm{P}(f(x) = y|Z). \tag{12.97}$$

In other words, the Bayes optimal estimator chooses the class y with the largest posterior probability.

Note that for regression (12.97) will lead to an estimator based on the *mode* of the posterior distribution $p(f(x)|Z)$. While in many cases the mode and the mean of a distribution may be reasonably close (this is one of the practical justifications of the maximum a posterior estimates, see (16.22)) the mean need not necessarily be anywhere close to the optimal estimate. For instance, for the exponential distribution $e^{-\xi}$ on $[0, \infty)$, the mode of the distribution is 0, the mean, however, is 1.

Despite their different definitions, the Bayes classifier and the Gibbs classifier are not completely unrelated. In fact, the following lemma, due to Herbrich, holds:

Lemma 12.25 (Gibbs-Bayes Lemma [238]) *Denote by $\mathrm{P}(f|Z)$ a distribution over mappings $f : \mathcal{X} \to \mathcal{Y}$, where $x \in \mathcal{X}$ and $Z \in (\mathcal{X} \times \mathcal{Y})^m$, and by $R[f]$ the loss due to f under the $0-1$ loss, namely the loss function $c(x, y, f(x)) = (1 - \delta_y(f(x)))$. Further, denote by $|\mathcal{Y}|$ the cardinality of $\mathcal{Y}$. Then the following inequalities hold;*

$$R[f_{\text{Bayes}}] \leq |\mathcal{Y}| R[f_{\text{Gibbs}}] = |\mathcal{Y}| R[\mathrm{P}(f|Z)]. \tag{12.98}$$

Proof To prove (12.98) we must consider the set ΔZ, where the Bayes classifier commits an error. It is given by

$$\Delta Z := \{(x, y) | (x, y) \in \mathcal{X} \times \mathcal{Y} \text{ and } c(x, y, f_{\text{Bayes}}(x)) = 1\}. \tag{12.99}$$

Then, for any given distribution $\tilde{\mathrm{P}}(x, y)$, the error of the Bayes estimator is given by $R[f_{\text{Bayes}}] = \tilde{\mathrm{P}}(\Delta Z)$. On ΔZ, however, the conditional probability $\mathrm{P}(y = f_{\text{Bayes}}(x)|Z, x)$ is bounded from below by $\frac{1}{|\mathcal{Y}|}$ since $f_{\text{Bayes}}(x)$ is chosen according to (12.97). This means that the error of the Gibbs classifier f_{Gibbs} on ΔZ is at least $\frac{1}{|\mathcal{Y}|} R[f_{\text{Bayes}}]$ which is a lower bound for $R[f_{\text{Gibbs}}]$ on $\mathcal{X} \times \mathcal{Y}$. ■

Note that a converse statement for bounding $R[f_{\text{Gibbs}}]$ in terms of $R[f_{\text{Bayes}}]$ is not true. In particular, one can find cases where $R[f_{\text{Bayes}}] = 0$ and $R[f_{\text{Gibbs}}] \geq \frac{1}{2} + \varepsilon$ for any $\varepsilon > 0$ (see also Problem 12.5). The practical use of Lemma 12.25 is in the ability to extend bounds on $R[f_{\text{Gibbs}}]$ to bounds on $R[f_{\text{Bayes}}]$.

In many cases it is necessary to relate the behavior of f_{Bayes} or f_{Gibbs} to the behavior of a single hypothesis f obtained by a (possibly) different learning algorithm. The following characterization for sets of hypotheses (due to Herbrich [238]) is useful.

Definition 12.26 (Bayes Admissible Hypotheses) *Denote by $\mathcal{F}$ a space of hypotheses and by $\mathrm{P}(f)$ a probability (measure) over $\mathcal{F}$. Then a subset $\mathcal{F}_B \subseteq \mathcal{F}$ is called Bayes admissible with respect to $\mathrm{P}(f)$ and some function $f \in \mathcal{F}$ if, for all $(x, y) \in \mathcal{X} \times \mathcal{Y}$,*

$$c(x, y, f(x)) = c(x, y, f_{\text{Bayes}}(x)). \tag{12.100}$$

Here c is the $0-1$ loss function and f_{Bayes} is the Bayes estimator with respect to $\mathrm{P}(f|f \in \mathcal{F}_B)$, that is, with respect to f restricted to $\mathcal{F}_B$.

Simply put, the loss of the single hypothesis $f \in \mathcal{F}$ has to agree with the Bayes estimator f_{Bayes} based on $\mathrm{P}(f|f \in \mathcal{F}_B)$. This criterion is not always easily verified, in the case of kernels, however, the following lemma holds.

Lemma 12.27 (Balls in RKHS are Bayes Admissible) *Denote by $\mathrm{P}(f)$ the uniform measure over a subset $\mathcal{F}' \subset \mathcal{H}$ of the RKHS $\mathcal{H}$. Then, for any additive offset b, any ball $B_r(f) \subseteq \mathcal{F}_B$ with radius r and center f is Bayes admissible with respect to $f + b$.*

Proof Simply note that, for any cut through the ball, the center of the ball always lies in the bigger of the two parts (the offset b determines the amount by which the cutting hyperplane misses the center). Thus the estimator at the center of the ball $f + b$ will agree with f_{Bayes}. ■

We use this lemma to connect the concept of maximum margin classifiers with the notion of Bayes estimators derived from a large posterior probability.

12.3.2 PAC-Bayesian Bounds for Single Classifiers

Our aim in this section is to bound the expected error of f_{Bayes} and f_{Gibbs} based on the posterior distribution $\mathrm{P}(f|Z)$ of the hypotheses on which zero, or low, training error is obtained. We begin with a simple binomial tail bound on a single hypothesis which achieves zero classification error on a sample of size m. Essentially it plays an analogous role to Hoeffding's bound (5.7) in the nonzero loss classification and regression cases.

Lemma 12.28 (Binomial Tail Bound) *Denote by $\xi \sim \mathrm{P}$ a random variable with values $\{0, 1\}$ and by $\xi_1, \ldots, \xi_m$ m instances of ξ, as drawn independently from P. Then, for*

$$R_{\text{emp}} := \frac{1}{m} \sum_{i=1}^{m} \xi_i \text{ and } R := \mathbf{E}[\xi] \tag{12.101}$$

the following inequality holds

$$\mathrm{P}(R_{\text{emp}} = 0 \text{ and } R > \varepsilon) < e^{-m\varepsilon} \text{ for all } m \in \mathbb{N} \text{ and } \varepsilon > 0. \tag{12.102}$$

Proof We prove the lemma by computing a bound on the probability of $R_{\text{emp}} = 0$ under the assumption that $R > \varepsilon$. For any $R = p > \varepsilon$

$$\mathrm{P}(\xi_1 = \ldots = \xi_m = 0 | R = p) = (1-p)^m < (1-\varepsilon)^m < \exp(-m\varepsilon) \tag{12.103}$$

since, for all $\varepsilon \in (0,1)$, we have $(1-\varepsilon) \leq e^{-\varepsilon}$. ■

This bound implies that, for a single hypothesis, achieving zero training error over a sample of size m (equivalently the probability for the expected error to differ from 0) decays exponentially as m increases. In all realistic cases, however, we have more than one hypothesis to choose from.

While, given a set of possible hypotheses f to choose from, we could assign equal weight to all of them, there is absolutely no need to do so. In fact, we could "bet" beforehand, that is, before any data arrives, on the hypotheses we think will obtain a low error. Qualitatively, our goal is to obtain better bounds in the case where our bet is lucky, at the expense of obtaining slightly worse bounds for unlucky guesses. This concept was formalized by Shawe-Taylor et al. [491] and is commonly referred to as the *Luckiness Framework* (see also [241] for an extension of the framework to algorithms rather than classes of functions). We give a simple version [238], which can be used to combine bounds for individual hypotheses.

Theorem 12.29 (Combining Hypotheses) *Denote by* P *a probability measure on* $\mathcal{X}$ *and by* $\psi_i(x, \delta) : \mathcal{X} \times \mathbb{R} \to \{\text{TRUE}, \text{FALSE}\}$ *with* $i \in \mathbb{N}$*, parametrized logical formulas for which*

$$\mathrm{P}_x(\psi_i(x,\delta) = \text{TRUE}) \geq 1 - \delta \text{ for all } 0 < \delta < 1. \tag{12.104}$$

Then, for all $\delta_i \geq 0$ *with* $\sum_i \delta_i = \delta \leq 1$*, the following inequality holds*

$$\mathrm{P}_x\left(\prod_i \psi_i(x, \delta_i) = \text{TRUE}\right) \geq 1 - \delta. \tag{12.105}$$

Here we used $\prod$ to denote a logical AND, and $\sum$ to denote a logical OR.

Proof To prove (12.105) we replace the lhs by its complementary event and then use a simple union bound argument on the individual terms. We obtain

$$\mathrm{P}_x\left(\prod_i \psi_i(x, \delta_i) = \text{TRUE}\right) = 1 - \mathrm{P}_x\left(\sum_i \psi_i(x,\delta_i) = \text{FALSE}\right) \tag{12.106}$$

$$\geq 1 - \sum_i \mathrm{P}_x\left(\psi_i(x,\delta_i) = \text{FALSE}\right) \tag{12.107}$$

$$\geq 1 - \sum_i \delta_i = 1 - \delta. \tag{12.108}$$

Here the last inequality follows from (12.104). ■

Note that typically the logical formulas $\psi_i(x, \delta)$ will be expressions as to whether a certain bound holds and, moreover, P_x will be the probability measure over all m-samples. Next we combine Lemmas 12.28 and 12.29 to obtain McAllester's first PAC-Bayesian theorem [353], namely bounds on the generalization performance of classifiers with zero training error. Furthermore, by using Hoeffding's bound (Theorem 5.1), we may obtain a counterpart for the case of $R_{\text{emp}}[f] > 0$.

Zero Loss Case

Theorem 12.30 (Single Classifiers with Zero Loss [353]) *For any probability distribution* $\mathrm{P}(\mathfrak{X}, \mathfrak{Y})$ *from which the training sample Z is drawn in an iid fashion, for any (prior) probability distribution* $\mathrm{P}(f)$ *on the space of hypotheses* $\mathfrak{F}$*, for any* $\delta \in (0,1)$*, and for any f for which* $R_{\text{emp}}[f] = 0$ *and which has nonzero* $\mathrm{P}(f)$*, the following bound on the expected risk holds;*

$$\mathrm{P}\left(R[f] > \varepsilon\right) \leq \delta \text{ for } \varepsilon = \frac{-\ln \mathrm{P}(f) - \ln \delta}{m}. \tag{12.109}$$

This means that the bound becomes better if we manage to "guess" f as well as possible by a suitable prior distribution $\mathrm{P}(f)$. Additionally, it justifies the maximum a posteriori estimation procedure (see also Section 16.2.1) since for identical likelihoods (zero error) the prior probability is the only quantity to distinguish between different hypotheses f. We prove this by a combination of Lemma 12.28 and Theorem 12.29.

Proof A sufficient condition for (12.109) is to show that, *simultaneously* for all f (and not only, say, for the maximizer of $\mathrm{P}(f)$) the bound holds. All we must do is set $\delta_i = \delta \mathrm{P}(f)$ and consider the logical formulas $\psi_i(Z, \delta)$ (here Z is the training sample) where the binomial tail-bound (12.103) is violated;

$$\psi_i(Z, \delta) := \left\{ R_{\text{emp}}[f_i] \neq 0 \text{ or } R[f_i] \geq -\frac{1}{m} \ln \delta \right\}. \tag{12.110}$$

Since $\sum_i \delta_i = \delta \sum_i \mathrm{P}(f_i) = \delta$ we satisfy all conditions of Theorem 12.29, which proves (12.109). ■

It is straightforward to obtain an analogous version for nonzero loss. The only difference is that we have to use Hoeffding's theorem 5.1 instead of the binomial tail bound.

Nonzero Loss Case

Corollary 12.31 (Single Classifiers with Nonzero Loss [353]) *For any probability distribution* $\mathrm{P}(\mathfrak{X}, \mathfrak{Y})$ *from which the training sample Z is drawn in an iid fashion, for any (prior) probability distribution* $\mathrm{P}(f)$ *on the space of hypotheses* $\mathfrak{F}$*, for any* $\delta \in (0,1)$*, and for any f with nonzero* $\mathrm{P}(f)$ *the following bound on the expected risk holds;*

$$\mathrm{P}\left(R[f] > \varepsilon\right) \leq \delta \text{ for } \varepsilon = R_{\text{emp}}[f] + \sqrt{\frac{-\ln \mathrm{P}(f) - \ln \delta}{2m}}. \tag{12.111}$$

Proof Using (5.7) define the logical formulas $\psi_i(Z, \delta)$ with

$$\psi_i(Z, \delta) := \left\{ R[f_i] \geq R_{\text{emp}}[f_i] + \sqrt{\frac{-\ln \delta}{2m}} \right\}. \tag{12.112}$$

By construction we have $\mathrm{P}_Z(\psi_i(Z, \delta)) \leq \delta$. Setting $\delta_i := \delta \mathrm{P}(f_i)$ and using $\cap_i X_i$ we obtain (12.111). ■

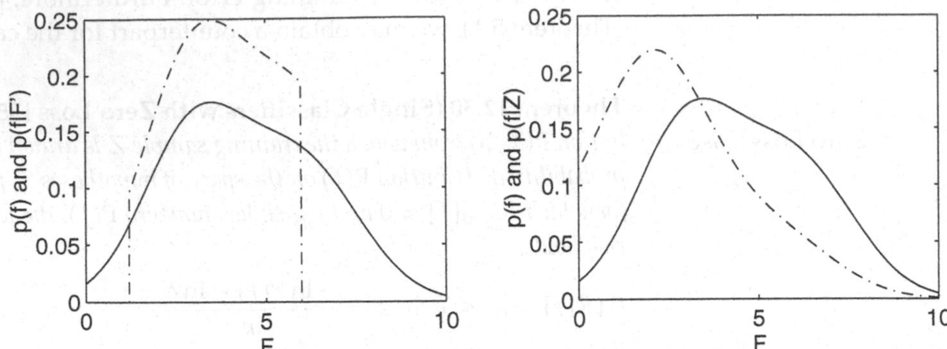

Figure 12.1 Left: prior probability distribution $\mathrm{P}(f)$ (solid line) on $\mathfrak{F}$ and restriction of $\mathrm{P}(f|\mathfrak{F}')$ to $\mathfrak{F}'$ (dotted line). Right: $\mathrm{P}(f)$ (solid line) and reweighted posterior distribution $\mathrm{P}(f|Z)$ (dotted line).

Comparing (12.111) with (12.109) we note the difference in the dependency on m. It appears that (12.111) with $\frac{1}{\sqrt{m}}$ in the denominator is much less tight than (12.109), where the bound depends on $\frac{1}{m}$.

This is, however, an artifact of Hoeffding's bound in the sense that the factor of $2m$ in the denominator increases with decreasing $R[f]$ and, thus, allows for a tighter bound (for $R[f] \to 0$ we recover the behavior of the binomial tail bound). Unfortunately, the latter is rather technical, which is why we omit a detailed description of the improvement. See [574], among others, for details on how to obtain tighter bounds.

12.3.3 PAC-Bayesian Bounds for Combinations of Classifiers

More interesting than single classifiers, however, is the question of whether and how bounds on combinations of such classifiers can be obtained. Two possible strategies come to mind; we could combine from a subset $\mathfrak{F}' \subset \mathfrak{F}$ of the space of hypotheses and weigh them according to the *prior* distribution $\mathrm{P}(f)$ which we fix *before* finding a good set of estimates [353]. Alternatively, we could use the *posterior* distribution $\mathrm{P}(f|Z)$, influenced by the performance of estimates on the data, as a weighting scheme [354]. See Figure 12.1 for an illustration of the two cases. The following two theorems give uniform convergence bounds for these.

Theorem 12.32 (Combination with Prior Weighting [353]) *As before, denote by $\mathfrak{F}$ a hypothesis class and by $\mathrm{P}(f)$ a probability measure on $\mathfrak{F}$, denote by $\mathfrak{F}' \subset \mathfrak{F}$ a measurable subset, and by $\mathrm{P}(f|\mathfrak{F}')$ the probability distribution obtained from $\mathrm{P}(f)$ by restricting f to $\mathfrak{F}'$ and with normalization by $\mathrm{P}(\mathfrak{F}')$. Then the following bounds hold with probability $1-\delta$:*

$$R[\mathrm{P}(f|\mathfrak{F}')] \leq R_{\mathrm{emp}}[\mathrm{P}(f|\mathfrak{F}')] + \sqrt{\frac{-\ln\delta - \ln \mathrm{P}(\mathfrak{F}') + 2\ln m}{2m}} + \frac{1}{m} \tag{12.113}$$

$$R[P(f|\mathcal{F}')] \leq \frac{-\ln\delta - \ln P(\mathcal{F}') + 2\ln m + 1}{m} \text{ if } R_{\text{emp}}[P(f|\mathcal{F}')] = 0 \tag{12.114}$$

We will give a proof of (12.114) at the end of this section, after we stated the "Quantifier Reversal Lemma" (Lemma 12.34), which is needed in the proof. Eq. (12.113) can be proven analogously and its proof is therefore omitted. Before we do so, however, we give the related result for a *posterior* distribution $P(f|Z)$ rather than only a restriction of $P(f)$ onto $\mathcal{F}'$.

Theorem 12.33 (Combination with Posterior Weighting [354]) *Again denote by $\mathcal{F}$ a hypothesis class and by $P(f)$ and $P(f|Z)$ two probability measure on $\mathcal{F}$, where $P(f|Z)$ depends on the data Z. Then the following bound holds with probability $1-\delta$;*

$$R[P(f|Z)] \leq R_{\text{emp}}[P(f|Z)] + \sqrt{\frac{d(P(f|Z)\|P(f)) - \ln\delta + \ln m + 2}{2m-1}}. \tag{12.115}$$

Here $d(P(f|Z)\|P(f))$ is the Kullback-Leibler divergence between $P(f|Z)$ and $P(f)$. It is given by

$$d(P(f|Z)\|P(f)) := \mathbf{E}_{P(f|Z)}\left[\ln\frac{dP(f|Z)}{dP(f)}\right]. \tag{12.116}$$

The proof of Theorem 12.33 is rather technical and we refer the reader to [354] for details. Note that (12.115) depends on the Kullback-Leibler divergence between the prior and posterior distributions. This is an (asymmetric) distance measure between the two distributions and vanishes only if they coincide. Consequently, the bound improves with our ability to guess (represented by the prior probability distribution $P(f)$) the likely outcome of the estimation procedure.

On the other hand, it means that unless we make a lucky guess, the alternative being to remain cautious and choose a flat (= constant) prior $P(f)$ over $\mathcal{F}$, we will not obtain a bound that is much tighter than the logarithm of the number of significantly distinct functions in $\mathcal{F}$. We obtain a bound similar to (5.36), the only benefit being the automatic adaptation of the scale, determined by the spread of $P(f|Z)$, to the learning problem at hand. This "lucky guess" will allow us to take advantage of favorable data. However, we have to keep in mind, that the performance guarantees can also be significantly worse, if we are "unlucky" in the specification of the prior. The remaining terms such as $\ln\delta$ or the $m^{-\frac{1}{2}}$ dependency are standard.

Finally, note that for a restriction of $\mathcal{F}$ onto a subset $\mathcal{F}'$ the Kullback-Leibler divergence between $P(f|\mathcal{F}')$ and $P(f)$ becomes $-\ln P(\mathcal{F}')$ since in this case $dP(f|\mathcal{F}') = P(\mathcal{F}')dP(f)$ if $f \in \mathcal{F}$. This means that, up to constant terms, (12.113) is a special case of (12.113).

As promised we conclude this section with a proof of (12.114). For this purpose we need a key lemma; the so-called "Quantifier Reversal Lemma".

Quantifier Reversal Lemma

Lemma 12.34 (Quantifier Reversal [353]) *Denote by x, y random variables and let $\delta \in (0,1]$. Furthermore, let $\psi(x, y, \delta)$ be a measurable formula such that, for any x, y, we have $\{\delta \in (0,1] : \psi(x, y, \delta) = \text{TRUE}\} = (0, \delta_{\max}]$ for some $\delta_{\max}$. If, for all x, and $\delta > 0$,*

$$\mathrm{P}_y\{\psi(x, y, \delta) = \text{TRUE}\} \geq 1 - \delta \tag{12.117}$$

then, for all $\delta > 0$, and $\beta \in (0,1)$,

$$\mathrm{P}_y\left\{\textit{for all } \alpha > 0 : \mathrm{P}_x\left\{\psi\left(x, y, (\alpha\beta\delta)^{\frac{1}{1-\beta}}\right) = \text{TRUE}\right\} \geq 1 - \alpha\right\} \geq 1 - \delta. \tag{12.118}$$

This means that, if a logical formula holds for all x and δ with high probability for all y, then, with high probability for all y, x, and for a fixed δ, the formula is also true. We transferred the uncertainty, initially encoded by δ, into one, jointly encoded by δ and α. Now we are ready to prove (12.114). For the purpose of the proof below, f will play the role of x and Z the role of y.

Proof of (12.114). We will use the Binomial tail-bound of Lemma 12.28. By analogy to (12.110) we define

$$\psi(Z, f, \delta) := \left\{R_{\text{emp}}[f] = 0 \text{ implies } R[f] \leq -\frac{1}{m}\ln\delta\right\}. \tag{12.119}$$

By construction (and via Lemma 12.28) we have that, for all f, and all $\delta > 0$, $\mathrm{P}_Z\{\psi(Z, f, \delta) = \text{TRUE}\} \leq 1 - \delta$. This expression has the same form as the one needed in (12.117). Therefore, for all $\delta > 0$, and $\beta \in (0,1)$,

$$\mathrm{P}_Z\left\{\text{for all } \alpha > 0 : \mathrm{P}_f\left\{\psi\left(f, Z, (\alpha\beta\delta)^{\frac{1}{1-\beta}}\right) = \text{TRUE}\right\} \geq 1 - \alpha\right\} \geq 1 - \delta. \tag{12.120}$$

The goal is to contract the two nested probability statements on Z and f into one on Z alone. This is done by replacing the inner (probabilistic) statement by a (deterministic) superset. Consider the argument of the first probability statement. Here, with probability $1 - \delta$,

$$\mathrm{P}_f\left\{\psi\left(f, Z, (\alpha\beta\delta)^{\frac{1}{1-\beta}}\right) = \text{TRUE}\right\} \geq 1 - \alpha \tag{12.121}$$

Now we substitute values for α and β. Denote by $\mathcal{F}' \subset \mathcal{F}$ a set for which $R_{\text{emp}}[\mathrm{P}(f|\mathcal{F}')] = 0$ and, moreover, let $\alpha = \frac{\mathrm{P}(\mathcal{F}')}{m}$ and $\beta = \frac{1}{m}$. We obtain

$$\mathrm{P}_f\left\{R_{\text{emp}}[f] = 0 \text{ implies } R[f] \leq -\frac{\ln \mathrm{P}(\mathcal{F}') - \ln\delta + 2\ln m}{(1 - \frac{1}{m})m}\right\} \geq 1 - \frac{\mathrm{P}(\mathcal{F}')}{m} \tag{12.122}$$

This means that on $\mathcal{F}'$ the bound holds at least with $(1 - \frac{1}{m})$ probability (recall that $\mathcal{F}' \subseteq \{f | R_{\text{emp}}[f] = 0\}$). In all other cases, the loss is bounded by 1 (we are dealing with a classification problem). Averaging over all $f \in \mathcal{F}'$ adds a $\frac{1}{m}$ term to the inequality of the lhs of (12.122). This replaces the probabilistic statement over f by a deterministic bound and we obtain that with probability $1 - \delta$,

$$R_{\text{emp}}[\mathrm{P}(f|\mathcal{F}')] = 0 \text{ implies } R[\mathrm{P}(f|\mathcal{F}')] \leq -\frac{\ln \mathrm{P}(\mathcal{F}') - \ln\delta + 2\ln m + 1}{m}. \tag{12.123}$$

The proof of (12.113) is similar and is left as an exercise (see Problem 12.7). ■

12.3.4 Applications to Large Margin Classifiers

We conclude this section with applications of the PAC-Bayesian theorems to the domain of large margin classifiers. The central idea is that a classifier achieving a large *margin* (or, equivalently, a small value of $\|w\|$) corresponds to the summary of a large *set* of classifiers, which all have desirable generalization performance properties. This is so since, for a large margin classifier, there exist many similar classifiers which (albeit with a smaller margin) achieve the same (or similar) training error.

To keep matters simple we show the basic idea using classifiers that achieve zero training error and where, further, all points lie on the surface of a hypersphere. The latter is a technical restriction that renders the computation of the volume of version spaces, the space $\mathcal{F}'$ of hypotheses with $R_{\text{emp}}[f] = 0$, much easier. We begin with the definition of a normalized margin.

Definition 12.35 (Normalized Margin) *Denote by $f(x) := \langle \mathbf{w}, \Phi(x)\rangle$ a classifier with $\|\mathbf{w}\| = 1$. Here the normalized margin $\rho_{\text{norm}}(f)$ is defined as*

$$\rho_{\text{norm}}(f) := \min_{i\in[m]} \frac{y_i f(x_i)}{\|\Phi(x_i)\|}. \tag{12.124}$$

In other words, this margin is normalized with respect to the length of the feature vectors of the training sample. The following bound on the generalization performance holds.

Theorem 12.36 (PAC-Bayesian Margin Bound [238]) *For a feature space with dimension $n \in \mathbb{N} \cup \{\infty\}$ and a linear classifier $\langle \mathbf{w}, \Phi(x)\rangle$ achieving zero empirical risk $R_{\text{emp}}[f] = 0$ the following bound holds with probability $1-\delta$;*

$$R[f] \le \frac{2}{m}\left(-d \ln\left(1-\sqrt{1-\rho_{\text{norm}}^2(f)}\right) + 2\ln m - \ln\delta + 2\right). \tag{12.125}$$

Here $d := \min(m, n)$.

Proof In a first step we must translate the size of $\rho_{\text{norm}}(f)$ into a corresponding size of the version space. For this purpose we give a lower bound on the maximum angle. Any other $\mathbf{w}'$ may be such that a corresponding $f'(x) := \langle \mathbf{w}', \Phi(x)\rangle$ will still achieve $R_{\text{emp}}[f'] = 0$.

The latter is equivalent to requiring that the angle $\angle(\mathbf{w}', \Phi(x_i))$ between $\mathbf{w}'$ and $\Phi(x_i)$ must not exceed $\frac{\pi}{2}$. By the triangle inequality we have

$$|\angle(\mathbf{w}', \Phi(x_i))| \le |\angle(\mathbf{w}', \mathbf{w})| + |\angle(\mathbf{w}, \Phi(x_i))| \le |\angle(\mathbf{w}', \mathbf{w})| + \max_j |\angle(\mathbf{w}, \Phi(x_j))|.$$

A sufficient condition for this inequality to hold is

$$|\angle(\mathbf{w}, \mathbf{w}')| \le \frac{\pi}{2} - \max_j |\angle(\mathbf{w}, \Phi(x_j))|. \tag{12.126}$$

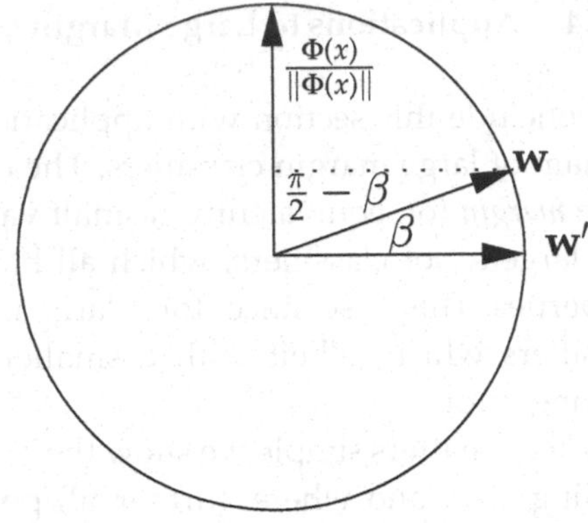

Figure 12.2 A geometric interpretation of $\langle \mathbf{w}, \mathbf{w}' \rangle \leq \sqrt{1 - \rho^2_{\text{norm}}(f)}$.

Taking the cosine on both sides (this is admissible since all angles involved are smaller than $\frac{\pi}{2}$) yields

$$|\langle w, w' \rangle| \geq \sqrt{1 - \min_j \left| \left\langle w, \frac{\Phi(x_j)}{\|\Phi(x_j)\|} \right\rangle \right|^2} = \sqrt{1 - \rho^2_{\text{norm}}(f)}. \tag{12.127}$$

Figure 12.2 depicts this situation graphically.

We assume a uniform prior distribution over all functions on the unit sphere, thus $P(f) = \text{const.}$ in addition, previous results mean that the set given by $\mathcal{F}' := \{w' | \langle w, w' \rangle \geq \sqrt{1 - \rho^2_{\text{norm}}(f)}$ is consistent with the observations Z, hence $R_{\text{emp}}[P(f|\mathcal{F}')] = 0$. Therefore, $P(\mathcal{F}')$ is given by the volume ratio between $\mathcal{F}'$ (the cap of the cone spanned between w and w') and the unit sphere in N dimensions. After tedious calculations involving spherical harmonics and a binomial tail bound (see [238] and [209, 373]) we find that

$$\ln P(\mathcal{F}') = \ln \frac{\text{Vol}(\mathcal{F}')}{\text{Vol}(\mathcal{F})} \leq d \ln \left(1 - \sqrt{1 - \rho^2_{\text{norm}}(f)} \right). \tag{12.128}$$

This means that, for f drawn from $P(f|\mathcal{F}')$, we may apply (12.113) of Theorem 12.32. Therefore, with probability $1 - \delta$, the following bound holds;

$$R[P(f|\mathcal{F}')] \leq m^{-1} \left(-\ln \delta - \ln d \ln \left(1 - \sqrt{1 - \rho^2_{\text{norm}}(f)} \right) + 2 \ln m + 1 \right). \tag{12.129}$$

The final step is to translate the statement about a distribution of functions into one about a single classifier, namely the one given by w. This is achieved by appealing to the Gibbs-Bayes Lemma (Lemma 12.25) which allows the conversion from a Gibbs classifier to a Bayes-optimal classifier, and Lemma 12.27, which shows that, in fact, w is the Bayes-optimal classifier corresponding to $\mathcal{F}'$.

The net effect is that the rhs of (12.129) increases by a factor of 2 (we have $y = 1$ and $y = -1$ as possible outcomes of the classification).[6] ■

6. See also [314] for an improved version which does not depend on the cardinality of $\mathcal{Y}$.

12.4 Operator-Theoretic Methods in Learning Theory

In the previous section we considered distributions over the space of hypotheses $\mathcal{F}$ which correspond to a weighting scheme over all possible functions. One could, however, also use an explicit covering of $\mathcal{F}$ with a set of "representative" functions in order to approximate a (possibly) infinite number of hypotheses by a finite number $\mathcal{N}$. This is advantageous since there exist many uniform convergence bounds for finite hypothesis classes. Further, there exist tools from the theory of Banach spaces which allow us to bound the number of functions needed to approximate $\mathcal{F}$ with sufficiently high precision.

The concepts presented in this section build largely on [606, 605, 518]. It is impossible to convey the results in complete detail and to point out further extensions, many of which are due to Mendelson [358, 357], Kolchinskiĭ [303], and coworkers. For another application of entropy numbers in mathematical learning theory, see [129].

We limit ourselves to the basic ideas underlying scale sensitive capacity measures such as covering and entropy numbers, and the fat shattering VC dimension (Section 12.4.1). In this context we show how these capacity measures can be used to formulate bounds on the generalization performance of estimators and present analogues of Theorems 12.32 and 12.33, based on the number of functions needed to approximate $\mathcal{F}$. The rest of the section is then devoted to methods for efficiently computing such capacity measures. Examples of translation invariant kernels (cf. Section 4.4) conclude the presentation.

The material below builds on the mathematical prerequisites of functional analaysis and entropy numbers summarized in Section B.3.1.

12.4.1 Scale-Sensitivity and the Fat Shattering Dimension

In Section 5.5.6 we introduced the notion of the VC dimension of a class of indicator functions $\mathcal{F}$ as the maximum number of points which $\mathcal{F}$ is able to shatter in any arbitrary way. Note that this notion was scale insensitive — changes of the sign of f were considered relevant regardless of the *amount* of change in f. This is not always the best way of measuring the capacity of functions, in particular when considering regression problems or large margin classifiers, where the scale of the solution matters. The following remark sheds some light on this problem:

Remark 12.37 (Gaussian RBF Networks with Infinite VC Dimension) *Denote by r an arbitrary positive number and $\mathcal{X} \in \mathbb{R}^N$ a compact set. Consider the class of functions*

$$\mathcal{F} := \left\{ f \,\middle|\, f = \sum_i \alpha_i k(x_i, \cdot) \text{ with } x_i \in \mathcal{X}, \sum_{i,j} \alpha_i \alpha_j k(x_i, x_j) \leq r \right\}, \tag{12.130}$$

where k is the Gaussian kernel. We show that $\mathcal{F}$ has infinite VC dimension by demonstrating that any arbitrary set $X = \{x_1, \ldots, x_m\} \subset \mathcal{X}$ of size m can be shattered by thresh-

olded functions from $\mathfrak{F}$. According to Theorem 2.18, the matrix $(k(x_i, x_j))_{ij}$ has full rank. Hence, for arbitrary $\{y_1, \ldots y_m\} \in \{-1, 1\}$, there exists a function $f(\cdot) = \sum_i \alpha_i k(x_i, \cdot)$ with $f(x_j) = y_j$ for all j. Rescaling f to satisfy the inequality in (12.130) yields an $\tilde{f} \in \mathfrak{F}$ which still shatters the set, proving the statement.

The term $\sum_{i,j} \alpha_i \alpha_j k(x_i, x_j)$ in (12.130) equals the $\|\mathbf{w}\|^2$ regularizer in $\mathcal{H}$, as used in SVMs (see (2.49)). The VC dimension is thus infinite even if $\|\mathbf{w}\|$ is small, and it can thus not directly be used to justify the large margin regularizer in SV regression. Things are slightly different in pattern recognition. There, our final scaling operation (obtaining $\tilde{f}$ from f) would leave us with a hyperplane which is no longer in canonical form with respect to $(x_1, y_1), \ldots, (x_m, y_m)$, cf. Definition 7.1. Nevertheless, there are some problems in using the VC dimension also in that case, see [491].[7]

The construction described in Remark 12.37 was possible since we were allowed to *rescale* f without sacrificing any of its discriminatory power. With a large margin classifier, on the other hand, we seek to find a solution which is the least scale sensitive possible.

A first step towards better bounds is to introduce a *scale sensitive* counterpart of the VC dimension, dubbed the (level) fat shattering VC dimension. It was introduced to statistical learning theory by [286]. According to [537], however, the idea of fat shattering itself had been proposed by Kolmogorov already in the late 1950s in the context of approximation theory.

Fat Shattering Dimension

The *fat shattering dimension* of a function class $\mathfrak{F}$ is a straightforward extension of the VC dimension. It is defined for real valued functions as the maximum number of points that can be γ-shattered. Here a set $\{x_1, \ldots, x_m\}$ is γ-shattered, if there exist some $b_i \in \mathbb{R}$ such that for all sets $y_i\{\pm 1\}$ there is an $f \in \mathfrak{F}$ with $y_i(f(x_i) - b_i) \geq \gamma$. A slightly more restrictive definition is the *level fat shattering dimension*, where a set is γ shattered if $y_i(f(x_i) - b) \geq \gamma$ for one common value of b. For applications to classification see [491, 460]. [22, 6] discuss the estimation of real valued functions.

12.4.2 Entropy and Covering Numbers

Despite its improvement over the original definition, the fat shattering dimension is still a fairly crude summary of the capacity of the class of functions under consideration. Covering and entropy numbers can be used to derived more finely grained capacity measures. We begin with some definitions.

---

7. Note that in Theorem 5.5, the hyperplane decision functions are only defined on a finite set of points. When defined on the whole space, the notion of canonicality cannot be employed anymore. Canonicality, however, is the notion that introduces scale sensitivity into the VC dimension analysis of margin classifiers. To work around this problem, we either have to use the notion of fat shattering dimension described below, or we have to define decision functions taking values in $\{\pm 1, 0\}$, with the value 0 referring to the margin [85, 564].

Recall that an ϵ-cover of a set M in E is a set of points in E such that the union of all ϵ-balls around these points contains M.

The *ϵ-covering number of $\mathcal{F}$ with respect to the metric d*, denoted $\mathcal{N}(\epsilon, \mathcal{F}, d)$, is the smallest number of elements of an ϵ-cover for $\mathcal{F}$ using the metric d. Typically, $\mathcal{F}$ will be the class of functions under consideration. Moreover, d will be the metric induced by the values of $f \in \mathcal{F}$ on some data $X = \{x_1, \ldots, x_m\}$, such as the ℓ_∞^m metric. We denote this quantity by $\ell_\infty^m(X)$. For $\epsilon = 1$ we recover the (scale less) definition of the covering number (Section 5.5.3).

To avoid some of the technical difficulties, that come with this dependency on X, one usually takes the supremum of $\mathcal{N}(\epsilon, \mathcal{F}, \ell_\infty^m(X))$ with respect to X. This quantity will be called the *ϵ-growth function* of the function class $\mathcal{F}$. Formally we have

$$\mathcal{N}^m(\epsilon, \mathcal{F}) := \sup_{x_1, \ldots, x_m \in \mathcal{X}} \mathcal{N}(\epsilon, \mathcal{F}, \ell_\infty^X), \tag{12.131}$$

where $\mathcal{N}(\epsilon, \mathcal{F}, \ell_\infty^X)$ is the ϵ-covering number of $\mathcal{F}$ with respect to ℓ_∞^X. Most generalization error bounds can be expressed in terms of $\mathcal{N}^m(\epsilon, \mathcal{F})$. An example (Theorem 12.38) is given in the following section.

Entropy Numbers

Covering numbers and the growth function are inherently discrete quantities. The functional inverse of $\mathcal{N}^m(\epsilon, \mathcal{F})$, referred to as the entropy number, however, is more amenable to our analysis. The nth*entropy number of a set $M \subset E$*, for $n \in \mathbb{N}$, is given by

$$\epsilon_n(M) := \inf \left\{ \epsilon > 0 \;\middle|\; \begin{array}{l} \text{there exists an } \epsilon\text{-cover for } M \text{ in } E \\ \text{containing } n \text{ or fewer points} \end{array} \right\} \tag{12.132}$$

Since we are dealing with linear function classes, we will introduce the notion of entropy numbers of operators and represent the possible function values that these linear function classes can assume on the data as images of linear operators.

For this purpose we need to introduce the notion of entropy numbers of operators. Denote by E, G Banach spaces and by $\mathfrak{L}(E, G)$ the space of linear operators from E into G. The *entropy numbers of an operator $T \in \mathfrak{L}(E, G)$* are defined as

$$\epsilon_n(T) := \epsilon_n(T(U_E)). \tag{12.133}$$

Note that $\epsilon_1(T) = \|T\|$, and that $\epsilon_n(T)$ is well-defined for all $n \in \mathbb{N}$ precisely if T is bounded (see Section B.3.1). Moreover, $\lim_{n \to \infty} \epsilon_n(T) = 0$ if and only if T is *compact*; that is, if $T(U_E)$ is precompact.

Compact and Precompact

A set is called *precompact* if its closure is compact. A set is called *compact* if every sequence in S has a subsequence that converges to an element also contained in S.[8]

8. Strictly speaking, we should be considering the notion of *relative compactness*; however, for Banach spaces, this coincides with precompactness, and we can disregard these ramifications.

The *dyadic entropy numbers of an operator* are defined as

$$e_n(T) := \epsilon_{2^{n-1}}(T), \quad n \in \mathbb{N}; \tag{12.134}$$

similarly, the dyadic entropy numbers of a set are defined from its entropy numbers. A beautiful introduction to entropy numbers of operators is given in a book by Carl and Stephani [90].

12.4.3 Generalization Bounds via Uniform Convergence

Recall the reasoning of Section 5.5. There we explained how uniform convergence bounds in terms of the covering number could be obtained. For the sake of concreteness, we quote a result suitable for regression, which was proved in [6]. Let $\mathbf{E}_m[f] := \frac{1}{m}\sum_{i=1}^m f(x_i)$ denote the *empirical mean* of f on the sample $x_1, \ldots, x_m$.

Uniform Convergence Bounds

Lemma 12.38 (Alon, Ben-David, Cesa-Bianchi, and Haussler, 1997) *Let $\mathcal{F}$ be a class of functions from $\mathcal{X}$ into $[0,1]$. For all $\epsilon > 0$, and all $m \geq \frac{2}{\epsilon^2}$,*

$$\mathrm{P}\left\{\sup_{f\in\mathcal{F}} |\mathbf{E}_m[f] - \mathbf{E}[f]| > \epsilon\right\} \leq 12m \cdot \mathbf{E}\left[\mathcal{N}\left(\tfrac{\epsilon}{6}, \mathcal{F}, \ell_\infty^{\bar{X}}\right)\right] \exp\left(-\frac{\epsilon^2 m}{36}\right), \tag{12.135}$$

where the P *on the left hand side denotes the probability w.r.t. the sample $x_1, \ldots, x_m$ drawn iid from the underlying distribution, and* **E** *the expectation w.r.t. a second sample $\bar{X} = (\bar{x}_1^\top, \ldots, \bar{x}_{2m}^\top)$, also drawn iid from the underlying distribution.*

In order to use this lemma one usually makes use of the fact that, for any P,

$$\mathbf{E}_{\bar{X}}\left[\mathcal{N}(\epsilon, \mathcal{F}, \ell_\infty^m(\bar{X}))\right] \leq \mathcal{N}^m(\epsilon, \mathcal{F}). \tag{12.136}$$

An alternative is to exploit the fact that $\mathcal{N}(\epsilon, \mathcal{F}, \ell_\infty^m(\bar{X}))$ is a concentrated random variable and measure $\mathcal{N}$ on the actual training set. See [66, 293] for further details on this subject. Theorem 12.38 in conjunction with (12.136) can be used to give a generalization error result by applying it to the loss-function induced class. The connection is made by the following lemma:

Lemma 12.39 (Lipschitz-Continuous Loss [606, 14]) *Denote by $\mathcal{F}$ a set of functions from $\mathcal{X}$ to $[a,b]$, with $a < b$, $a, b \in \mathbb{R} \cup \pm\infty$ and by $l : \mathbb{R} \to \mathbb{R}_0^+$ a loss function satisfying a Lipschitz-condition*

Loss Functions

$$l(\xi) - l(\xi') \leq C|\xi - \xi'| \text{ for all } \xi, \xi' \in [a-b, b-a]. \tag{12.137}$$

Moreover, let $Z := (x_i, y_i)_{j=1}^m$, $l_f|_{Z_j} := l(f(x_j) - y_j)$, $l_f|_Z := (l_f|_{Z_j})_{j=1}^m$, $l_{\mathcal{F}}|_Z := \{l_f|_Z : f \in \mathcal{F}\}$ and $\mathcal{N}(\epsilon, l|_Z) := \mathcal{N}(\epsilon, l_{\mathcal{F}}|_Z, \ell_\infty^Z)$. Then the following equation holds;

$$\max_{Z \in (\mathcal{X}\times[a,b])^m} \mathcal{N}(\epsilon, l|_Z) \leq \max_{X\in\mathcal{X}^m} \mathcal{N}\left(\frac{\epsilon}{C}, \mathcal{F}|_X\right) \tag{12.138}$$

The proof works by explicitly exploiting the Lipschitz property of the loss. Applying this result to polynomial loss leads to the following corollary.

Corollary 12.40 (Polynomial Loss) *Let the assumptions be as in Lemma 12.39. Then, for loss functions of type*

$$l(\eta) = p^{-1}\eta^p \text{ with } p > 1, \tag{12.139}$$

we have $C = (b-a)^{(p-1)}$, *in particular* $C = (b-a)$ *for* $p = 2$ *and, therefore,*

$$\max_{Z \in (\mathcal{X}\times[a,b])^m} \mathcal{N}(\epsilon, l|_Z) \le \max_{x\in\mathcal{X}^m} \mathcal{N}\left(\frac{\epsilon}{(b-a)^{p-1}}, \mathcal{F}|_x\right) \tag{12.140}$$

We can readily combine the uniform convergence results with the above results to get overall bounds on generalization performance. We do not explicitly state such a result here, since the particular uniform convergence result needed depends on the exact setup of the learning problem. In summary, a typical uniform convergence result (see for instance (5.35) or (12.135)) takes the form

$$P\{\sup_f |R_{\text{emp}}(f) - R(f)| > \epsilon\} \le c_1(m)\mathcal{N}^m(\epsilon, \mathcal{F})e^{-\epsilon^\beta m/c_2}. \tag{12.141}$$

Even the exponent in (12.141) depends on the setting.[9] Since our primary interest is in determining $\mathcal{N}^m(\epsilon, \mathcal{F})$ we will not try to summarize the large body of work now done on uniform convergence results and generalization error.

Learning Curves

These generalization bounds are typically used by setting the right hand side equal to δ and solving for $m = m(\epsilon, \delta)$ (which is called the *sample complexity*). Another way to use these results is as a learning curve bound $\bar{\epsilon}(\delta, m)$, where

$$P\{\sup_f |R_{\text{emp}}(f) - R(f)| > \bar{\epsilon}(\delta, m)\} \le \delta. \tag{12.142}$$

We note here that the determination of $\bar{\epsilon}(\delta, m)$ is quite convenient in terms of e_n, the dyadic entropy number associated with the covering number $\mathcal{N}^m(\epsilon, \mathcal{F})$ in (12.141). Setting the right hand side of (12.141) equal to δ, we have

$$\begin{aligned} \delta &= c_1(m)\mathcal{N}^m(\epsilon, \mathcal{F})e^{-\epsilon^\beta m/c_2} \\ \Leftrightarrow \log_2\left(\tfrac{\delta}{c_1(m)}\right) + \tfrac{\epsilon^\beta m}{c_2 \ln 2} &= \log_2 \mathcal{N}^m(\epsilon, \mathcal{F}). \end{aligned} \tag{12.143}$$

Eq. (12.143) is satisfied if we can find some ϵ such that

$$e_{\left\lfloor \log_2\left(\frac{\delta}{c_1(m)}\right) + \frac{\epsilon^\beta m}{c_2 \ln 2} + 1\right\rfloor} \le \epsilon \tag{12.144}$$

holds. Clearly we want the minimal ϵ that satisfies (12.144), since ϵ determines the tightness of the bound (12.141). Therefore we define

$$\bar{\epsilon}(\delta, m) = \min\{\epsilon | (12.144) \text{ holds}\}. \tag{12.145}$$

Hence the use of ϵ_n or e_n (which will arise naturally from our techniques) is, in fact, a convenient thing to do to find learning curves.

9. In regression β can be set to 1, however, in agnostic learning Kearns et al. [287] show that, in general, $\beta = 2$, except if the class is convex, in which case it can be set to 1 [322].

The key idea in the present section concerns the manner in which the covering numbers are computed. Traditionally, appeal has been made to the Sauer-Shelah-Vapnik-Chervonenkis Lemma (originally due to [567] and rediscovered in [493, 458]). In the case of function learning, a generalization due to Pollard (called the pseudo-dimension), or Vapnik and Chervonenkis (called the VC dimension of real valued functions, see Section 5.5.6), or a scale-sensitive generalization of that (the fat-shattering dimension) is used to bound the covering numbers. These results reduce the computation of $\mathcal{N}^m(\epsilon, \mathcal{F})$ to the computation of a single "dimension-like" quantity. An overview of various dimensions, some details of their history, and some examples of their computation can be found in [13].

12.4.4 Entropy Numbers for Kernel Machines

The derivation of bounds on the covering number (and entropy number) of $\mathcal{F}$ proceeds by making statements about the shape of the image of the input space $\mathcal{X}$ under the feature map Φ. We make use of Mercer's theorem (Theorem 2.10) and of the scaling operator constructed in Section 2.2.5.

Recall that in Proposition 2.13, where we described valid scaling operators that map $\Phi(\mathcal{X})$ into ℓ_2, the numbers l_i are related to the eigenvalues according to (2.50). Following (2.50), it was pointed out that for some common kernels, it is not necessary to distinguish between l_i and λ_i. In the present section, we will formulate the results for the l_i; however, the reader may bear in mind that these are essentially determined by the λ_i.

In the following (without loss of generality) we assume the sequence of $(l_j)_j$ (cf. (2.50)) is sorted in nonincreasing order.

As discussed in Section 2.2.5, the rate of decay of the eigenvalues has implications for the area occupied by the data in feature space.

As a consequence of Proposition 2.13, we can construct a mapping A from the unit ball in ℓ_2 to an ellipsoid $\mathcal{E}$ such that $\Phi(\mathcal{X}) \subset \mathcal{E}$, as in the following diagram:

$$\begin{array}{ccccc} \mathcal{X} & \xrightarrow{\quad\Phi\quad} & \Phi(\mathcal{X}) & \xrightarrow{\quad A^{-1}\quad} & U_{\ell_2} \\ & & \cap & \swarrow_{A} & \\ & & \mathcal{E} & & \end{array} \tag{12.146}$$

Shrinkage Operator

The operator A will be useful for computing the entropy numbers of concatenations of operators. (Knowing the inverse will allow us to compute the forward operator, and that can be used to bound the covering numbers of the class of functions, as shown in the next subsection.)

Define

$$R := \left\| \left(s_j \sqrt{l_j} \right)_j \right\|_{\ell_2}. \tag{12.147}$$

From Proposition 2.13 it is clear that we may use

$$A = RS^{-1} = \left\| \left(s_j\sqrt{l_j}\right)_j \right\|_{\ell_2} S^{-1}. \tag{12.148}$$

We call such scaling (inverse) operators *admissible*. The next step is to compute the entropy numbers of the operator A and use this to obtain bounds on the entropy numbers for kernel machines such as SVMs. We make use of the following theorem (see [208, p. 226], stated in the given form in [90, p. 17]).

Theorem 12.41 (Diagonal Scaling Operators) *Let $\sigma_1 \geq \sigma_2 \geq \cdots \geq \sigma_j \geq \cdots \geq 0$ be a non-increasing sequence of non-negative numbers and let*

$$D\mathbf{x} = (\sigma_1 x_1, \sigma_2 x_2, \ldots, \sigma_j x_j, \ldots) \tag{12.149}$$

for $\mathbf{x} = (x_1, x_2, \ldots, x_j, \ldots) \in \ell_p$ be the diagonal operator from ℓ_p into itself, generated by the sequence $(\sigma_j)_j$, where $1 \leq p \leq \infty$. Then, for all $n \in \mathbb{N}$,

$$\sup_{j\in\mathbb{N}} n^{-\frac{1}{j}}(\sigma_1\sigma_2\cdots\sigma_j)^{\frac{1}{j}} \leq \epsilon_n(D) \leq 6 \cdot \sup_{j\in\mathbb{N}} n^{-\frac{1}{j}}(\sigma_1\sigma_2\cdots\sigma_j)^{\frac{1}{j}}. \tag{12.150}$$

We can exploit the freedom in choosing A to minimize an entropy number as the following corollary shows. This is a key ingredient in our calculation of the covering numbers for SV classes, as shown below.

Application to $\Phi(\mathcal{X})$

Corollary 12.42 (Entropy Numbers for Admissible Scaling Operators) *Let $k: \mathcal{X} \times \mathcal{X} \to \mathbb{R}$ be a Mercer kernel and let the scaling operator A be defined by (12.148) and R by (12.147), with $\left(\sqrt{l_i}s_i\right)_i \in \ell_2$. Then*

$$\epsilon_n(A: \ell_2 \to \ell_2) \leq \sup_{j\in\mathbb{N}} 6R\left(n \cdot a_1 a_2 \cdots a_j\right)^{-\frac{1}{j}}. \tag{12.151}$$

This result follows immediately from the identification of D and A. We can optimize (12.151) by exploiting the freedom that we still have in choosing a particular operator A among the class of admissible ones. This leads to the following result (the infimum is in fact attainable [220]).

Corollary 12.43 (Entropy Numbers for Optimal Scaling) *There exists an A defined by (12.148) and R defined in (12.147) that satisfies*

$$\epsilon_n(A: \ell_2 \to \ell_2) \leq \inf_{(s_i)_i: \left(\sqrt{l_i}s_i\right)_i \in \ell_2} \sup_{j\in\mathbb{N}} 6R\left(n \cdot a_1 a_2 \cdots a_j\right)^{-\frac{1}{j}}. \tag{12.152}$$

The functions that an SV machine generates can be expressed as $x \mapsto \langle \mathbf{w}, \Phi(x)\rangle + b$, where $\mathbf{w}, \Phi(x) \in \mathcal{H}$ and $b \in \mathbb{R}$. The "$+b$" term is dealt with in [606]; for now we consider the simplified class

$$\mathcal{F}_\Lambda := \{x \mapsto \langle \mathbf{w}, \Phi(x)\rangle | x \in \mathcal{X}, \|\mathbf{w}\| \leq \Lambda\} \subseteq \mathbb{R}^{\mathcal{H}}. \tag{12.153}$$

What we seek are the ℓ_∞^m covering numbers for the class $\mathcal{F}_\Lambda$ induced by the kernel in terms of the parameter Λ. As described in Chapter 7, this is the inverse

SV Classes

of the size of the margin in feature space, or, equivalently, the size of the weight vector in feature space as defined by the dot product in $\mathcal{H}$. We call such hypothesis classes with a length constraint on the weight vectors in feature space *SV classes*. Let T be the operator $T = S_{\Phi(X)}\Lambda$ where $\Lambda \in \mathbb{R}^+$, and define the operator $S_{\Phi(X)}$ by

$$\begin{aligned} S_{\Phi(X)} : \ell_2 &\to \ell_\infty^m \\ S_{\Phi(X)} : \mathbf{w} &\mapsto (\langle \Phi(x_1), \mathbf{w}\rangle, \ldots, \langle \Phi(x_m), \mathbf{w}\rangle). \end{aligned} \tag{12.154}$$

The following theorem is useful in computing entropy numbers in terms of T and A. Originally due to Maurey, it was extended in [89]. See [605] for further extensions and historical remarks.

Maurey's Theorem

Theorem 12.44 (Maurey's Bound [90]) *Let $m \in \mathbb{N}$ and $S \in \mathfrak{L}(H, \ell_\infty^m)$, where H is a Hilbert space. Then there exists a constant $c > 0$ such that, for all $m, n \in \mathbb{N}$,*

$$e_n(S) \leq c\|S\| \left(n^{-1} \log_2 \left(1 + \frac{m}{n}\right)\right)^{1/2}. \tag{12.155}$$

An alternative proof of this result (given in [605]) provides a small explicit value for the constant; $c \leq 103$.

The restatement of Theorem 12.44 in terms of $\epsilon_{2^{n-1}} = e_n$ will be useful in the following. Under the assumptions given we have

$$\epsilon_n(S) \leq c\|S\| \left((\log_2 n)^{-1} \log_2 \left(1 + \frac{m}{\log_2 n}\right)\right)^{1/2} \quad \text{for } n > 1. \tag{12.156}$$

Now we can combine the bounds on entropy numbers of A and $S_{\Phi(X)}$ to obtain bounds for SV classes. First we need the following lemma.

Product Bounds

Lemma 12.45 (Product Bound [90]) *Let E, F, G be Banach spaces, $R \in \mathfrak{L}(F, G)$, and $S \in \mathfrak{L}(E, F)$. Then, for $n, t \in \mathbb{N}$,*

$$\epsilon_{nt}(RS) \leq \epsilon_n(R)\epsilon_t(S) \tag{12.157}$$

$$\epsilon_n(RS) \leq \epsilon_n(R)\|S\| \tag{12.158}$$

$$\epsilon_n(RS) \leq \epsilon_n(S)\|R\|. \tag{12.159}$$

Note that the latter two inequalities follow directly from (12.157) and the fact that $\epsilon_1(R) = \|R\|$ for all $R \in \mathfrak{L}(F, G)$.

Theorem 12.46 (Bounds for SV classes) *Let k be a Mercer kernel, let Φ be induced via (2.40) and let $T := S_{\Phi(X)}\Lambda$ where $S_{\Phi(X)}$ is given by (12.154) and $\Lambda \in \mathbb{R}^+$. Let A be defined by (12.148). Then the entropy numbers of T satisfy the following inequalities, for $n > 1$;*

$$\epsilon_n(T) \leq c\|A\|\Lambda \log_2^{-1/2} n \log_2^{1/2} \left(1 + \tfrac{m}{\log_2 n}\right) \tag{12.160}$$

$$\epsilon_n(T) \leq 6\Lambda\epsilon_n(A) \tag{12.161}$$

$$\epsilon_{nt}(T) \leq 6c\Lambda \log_2^{-1/2} n \log_2^{1/2} \left(1 + \tfrac{m}{\log_2 n}\right) \epsilon_t(A) \tag{12.162}$$

where c is defined as in Lemma 12.44.

This result gives several options for bounding $\epsilon_n(T)$. We shall see in examples later that the best inequality to use depends on the rate of decay of the eigenvalues of k. The result gives effective bounds on $\mathcal{N}^m(\epsilon, \mathcal{F}_\Lambda)$ since

$$\epsilon_n(T: \ell_2 \to \ell_\infty^m) \le \epsilon_0 \Rightarrow \mathcal{N}^m(\epsilon_0, \mathcal{F}_\Lambda) \le n. \tag{12.163}$$

Factorization

Proof We use the following factorization of T to upper bound $\epsilon_n(T)$.

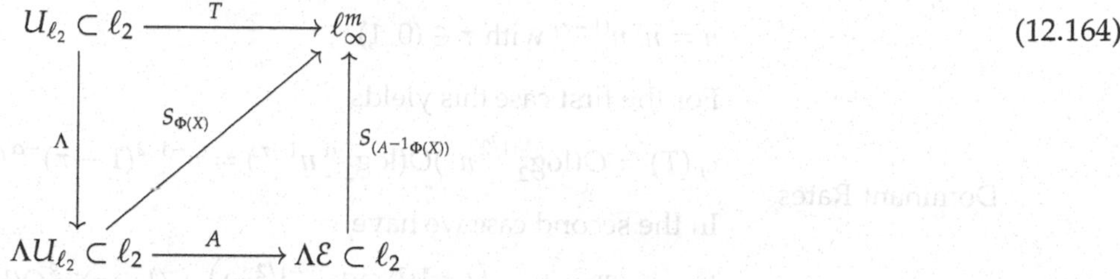

$$\tag{12.164}$$

The top left part of the diagram follows from the definition of T. The fact that the diagram commutes stems from the fact that, since A is diagonal, it is self-adjoint and hence for any $x \in \mathcal{X}$,

$$\langle \mathbf{w}, \Phi(x) \rangle = \langle \mathbf{w}, AA^{-1}\Phi(x) \rangle = \langle A\mathbf{w}, A^{-1}\Phi(x) \rangle. \tag{12.165}$$

Instead of computing the covering number of $T = S_{\Phi(X)}\Lambda$ directly, which is difficult or wasteful, as the bound on $S_{\Phi(X)}$ does not take into account that $\Phi(x) \in \mathcal{E}$ but just makes the assumption of $\Phi(x) \in \rho U_{\ell_2}$ for some $\rho > 0$, we will represent T as $S_{(A^{-1}\Phi(X))}A\Lambda$. This is more efficient as we construct A such that $\Phi(\mathcal{X})A^{-1} \in U_{\ell_2}$ fills a larger proportion of it than just $\frac{1}{\rho}\Phi(\mathcal{X})$.

By construction of A, and due to the Cauchy-Schwarz inequality, we know that $\|S_{A^{-1}\Phi(X)}\| = 1$. Thus, applying Lemma 12.45 to the factorization of T, and using Theorem 12.44 proves the theorem. ∎

As we see below, we can give asymptotic rates of decay for $\epsilon_n(A)$. (In fact we give non-asymptotic results with explicitly evaluable constants.) It is thus of some interest to give overall asymptotic rates of decay of $\epsilon_n(T)$ in terms of the order of $\epsilon_n(A)$. By "asymptotic" here we mean asymptotic in n; this corresponds to asking how $\mathcal{N}(\epsilon, \mathcal{F})$ scales as $\epsilon \to 0$ for fixed m.

Overall Asymptotic Rates

Lemma 12.47 (Rate bounds on ϵ_n) *Let k be a Mercer kernel and suppose A is the scaling operator associated with it, as defined by (12.148).*

1. *If $\epsilon_n(A) = O(\log_2^{-\alpha} n)$ for some $\alpha > 0$ then for fixed m*

$$\epsilon_n(T) = O(\log_2^{-(\alpha+1/2)} n). \tag{12.166}$$

2. *If $\log_2 \epsilon_n(A) = O(\log_2^{-\beta} n)$ for some $\beta > 0$ then for fixed m*

$$\log_2 \epsilon_n(T) = O(\log_2^{-\beta} n). \tag{12.167}$$

This lemma shows that, in the first case, Maurey's result (Theorem 12.44) allows an improvement in the exponent of the entropy number of T, whereas in the second, it affords none (since the entropy numbers decay so fast anyway). The Maurey result may still help in that case for nonasymptotic n. Note that for simplicity of notation we dropped to mention the dependency of the bounds on m. See e.g., [526, 606] for further details.

Proof From Theorem 12.44 we know that $\epsilon_n(S) = O(\log_2^{-1/2} n)$. Now use (12.157), splitting the index n in the following way;

$$n = n^{\tau} n^{(1-\tau)} \text{ with } \tau \in (0,1). \tag{12.168}$$

For the first case this yields

Dominant Rates

$$\epsilon_n(T) = O(\log_2^{-1/2} n^{\tau}) O(\log_2^{-\alpha} n^{1-\tau}) = \tau^{-1/2}(1-\tau)^{-\alpha} O(\log_2^{-(\alpha+1/2)} n). \tag{12.169}$$

In the second case we have

$$\log_2 \epsilon_n(T) = \log_2 \left((\tau^{-1/2}) O(\log_2^{-1/2} n) \right) + (1-\tau)^{-\beta} O(\log_2^{-\beta} n) = O(\log_2^{-\beta} n). \tag{12.170}$$

■

In a nutshell we can always obtain rates of convergence better than those due to Maurey's theorem, because we are not dealing with *arbitrary* mappings into infinite dimensional spaces. In fact, for logarithmic dependency of $\epsilon_n(T)$ on n, the effect of the kernel is so strong that it completely dominates the $n^{-1/2}$ behavior for arbitrary Hilbert spaces. An example of such a kernel is $k(x, y) = \exp(-(x-y)^2)$; see Proposition 12.51 and also Section 12.4.5 for the discretization question.

12.4.5 Discrete Spectra of Convolution Operators

The results presented above show that if we know the eigenvalue sequence of a compact operator, we can bound its entropy numbers. Whilst it is always possible to assume that the *data* fed into a SV machine has bounded support, the same can not be said of the kernel $k(\cdot, \cdot)$. A commonly used kernel is $k(x, y) = \exp(-(x-y)^2)$ which has noncompact support. The induced integral operator

Integral Operator

$$(T_k f)(x) = \int_{-\infty}^{\infty} k(x, y) f(y)\, dy \tag{12.171}$$

then has a continuous spectrum and is not compact [17, p.267]. The question arises as to whether we make use of such kernels in SVMs and still obtain generalization error bounds of the form developed above? A further motivation stems from the fact that, by a theorem of Widom [595], the eigenvalue decay of any convolution operator defined on a a compact set via a kernel having compact support can be no faster than $\lambda_j = O(e^{-j^2})$. Thus, if we seek very rapid decay of eigenvalues (with concomitantly small entropy numbers), we must use convolution kernels with noncompact support.

We will resolve these issues in this section. Before doing so, let us first consider the case that $\operatorname{supp} k \subseteq [-a, a]$ for some $a < \infty$. Suppose, further, that the data points x_j satisfy $x_j \in [-b, b]$ for all j. If $k(\cdot, \cdot)$ is a convolution kernel ($k(x, y) = k(x - y)$), then the SV hypothesis $h_k(\cdot)$ can be written

$$h_k(x) := \sum_{j=1}^{m} \alpha_j k(x, x_j) = \sum_{j=1}^{m} \tilde{\alpha}_j k_p(x, x_j) =: h_{k_p}(x) \tag{12.172}$$

for $p \geq 2(a+b)$, where $k_p(\cdot)$ is the p-periodic extension of $k(\cdot)$, as given by (4.42);

$$k_p(x, x') := \sum_{j=-\infty}^{\infty} k(x - jp, x'). \tag{12.173}$$

Here we used $k(x, x') = k(x - x')$. We now relate the eigenvalues of T_{k_p} to the Fourier transform of $k(\cdot)$. The following lemma is a direct consequence of Proposition 4.12 (all we need to do is replace 2π by the new period p).

Connection between Spectrum and Fourier Transform

Lemma 12.48 (Discrete Spectrum of Periodic Kernels) *Let $k\colon \mathbb{R} \to \mathbb{R}$ be a symmetric convolution kernel, let $K(\omega) = F[k(x)](\omega)$ denote the Fourier transform of $k(\cdot)$ and k_v denote the p-periodical kernel derived from k (assume also that k_p exists). Then k_p has a representation as a Fourier series with $\omega_0 := \frac{2\pi}{p}$ and*

$$\begin{aligned} k_p(x - y) &= \sum_{j=-\infty}^{\infty} \frac{\sqrt{2\pi}}{p} K(j\omega_0) e^{ij\omega_0 x} \\ &= \frac{\sqrt{2\pi}}{p} K(0) + \sum_{j=1}^{\infty} \frac{2}{p} \sqrt{2\pi} K(j\omega_0) \cos(j\omega_0 (x - y)). \end{aligned} \tag{12.174}$$

Moreover, $\lambda_j = \sqrt{2\pi} K(j\omega_0)$ for $j \in \mathbb{Z}$ and $C_k = \sqrt{\frac{2}{p}}$ (see (2.51) for the definition of C_k). Finally, for $k : \mathbb{R}^N \to \mathbb{R}^N$ and a p-periodic kernel k_p in each direction ($\mathbf{x} = (x_1, \ldots, x_N)$) (derived from k), we get the following spectrum $\lambda_{\mathbf{j}}$ of k_p

$$\lambda_{\mathbf{j}} = (2\pi)^{N/2} K(\omega_0 \mathbf{j}) = (2\pi)^{N/2} K(\omega_0 \|\mathbf{j}\|) \text{ where } C_k = (2/p)^{N/2}. \tag{12.175}$$

Thus, even though T_k may not be compact, T_{k_p} may be (if $(K(j\omega_0))_{j\in\mathbb{N}} \subset \ell_2$ for example). The above lemma can be applied whenever we can form $k_p(\cdot)$ from $k(\cdot)$. Clearly $k(x) = O(x^{-(1+\epsilon)})$ for some $\epsilon > 0$ suffices to ensure the sum in (12.173) converges.

Let us now consider how to choose p. Note that the Riemann-Lebesgue lemma tells us that, for integrable $k(\cdot)$ of bounded variation (surely any kernel we would use would satisfy that assumption), one has $K(\omega) = O(1/\omega)$. There is an trade-off in choosing p in that, for large enough ω, $K(\omega)$ is a decreasing function of ω (at least as fast as $1/\omega$) and thus, by Lemma 12.48, $\lambda_j = \sqrt{2\pi} K(2\pi j/p)$ is an increasing function of p. This suggests one should choose a small value of p. But a small p will lead to high empirical error (as the kernel "wraps around" and its localization properties are lost) and large C_k. There are several approaches to picking a value of p. One obvious one is to *a priori* pick some $\tilde{\epsilon} > 0$ and choose the smallest p such that $|k(x) - k_p(x)| \leq \tilde{\epsilon}$ for all $x \in [-p/2, p/2]$. Thus one would obtain a hypothesis $h_{k_p}(x)$ uniformly within $C\tilde{\epsilon}$ of $h_k(x)$, where $\sum_{j=1}^{m} |\alpha_j| \leq C$.

Influence of Bandwidth

Finally, it is worth to note how the choice of a different bandwidth of the kernel, namely letting $k^{(\sigma)}(x) := \sigma k(\sigma x)$, affects the spectrum of the corresponding operator. We have $K^{(\sigma)}(\omega) = K(\omega/\sigma)$, hence scaling a kernel by σ means more densely spaced eigenvalues in the spectrum of the integral operator $T_{k^{(\sigma)}}$.

In conclusion: in order to obtain a discrete spectrum, we need to use a periodic kernel. For a problem at hand, one can always periodize a nonperiodic kernel in a way that changes the estimated function in an arbitrarily small way, hence the above results can be applied.

12.4.6 Covering Numbers for Given Decay Rates

In this section we will show how the asymptotic behavior of $\epsilon_n(A\colon \ell_2 \to \ell_2)$, where A is the scaling operator introduced before, depends on the eigenvalues of T_k.

Note that we need to sort the l_i in a nonincreasing manner because of the requirements in Corollary 12.43. Many one-dimensional kernels have nondegenerate systems of eigenvalues. In this case it is straightforward to explicitly compute the geometrical means of the eigenvalues, as will be shown below. Note that whilst all of the examples which follow are for convolution kernels ($k(x, y) = k(x - y)$), there is nothing in the formulations of the propositions themselves that requires this. When we consider the N-dimensional case we shall see that, with rotationally invariant kernels, degenerate systems of eigenvalues are generic. This can be dealt with by a slight modification of theorem 12.41 — see [606] for details.

Let us consider the special case in which $(l_j)_j$ decays asymptotically with some polynomial or exponential degree. In this case we can choose a sequence $(a_j)_j$ for which we can evaluate (12.152) explicitly. By the eigenvalues of a kernel k we mean the eigenvalues of the induced integral operator T_k.

Laplacian Kernel

Proposition 12.49 (Polynomial Decay [606]) *Let k be a Mercer kernel with $l_j = \beta^2 j^{-(\alpha+1)}$ for some $\alpha > 0$. Then for any $\delta \in (0, \alpha/2)$ we have*

$$\epsilon_n(A\colon \ell_2 \to \ell_2) = O(\ln^{-\frac{\alpha}{2}+\delta} n). \tag{12.176}$$

An example of such a kernel is $k(x) = e^{-x}$.

Proposition 12.50 (Exponential Decay [606]) *Suppose k is a Mercer kernel with $l_j = \beta^2 e^{-\alpha(j-1)}$ for some $\alpha, \beta > 0$. Then*

$$\ln \epsilon_n^{-1}(A\colon \ell_2 \to \ell_2) = O(\ln^{\frac{1}{2}} n) \tag{12.177}$$

An example of such a kernel is $k(x) = \frac{1}{1+x^2}$.

Gaussian Kernel

Proposition 12.51 (Exponential Quadratic Decay) *Suppose k is a Mercer kernel with $l_j = \beta^2 e^{-\alpha(j-1)^2}$ for some $\alpha, \beta > 0$. Then*

$$\ln \epsilon_n(A\colon \ell_2 \to \ell_2) = O(\ln^{\frac{2}{3}} n). \tag{12.178}$$

An example of such a kernel is the Gaussian $k(x) = e^{-x^2}$.

We conclude this section with a general relation between exponential-polynomial decay rates and orders of bounds on $\epsilon_n(A)$.

Proposition 12.52 (Exponential-Polynomial decay) *Suppose k is a Mercer kernel with $l_j = \beta^2 e^{-\alpha j^p}$ for some $\alpha, \beta, p > 0$. Then*

$$\ln \epsilon_n(A\colon \ell_2 \to \ell_2) = O(\ln^{\frac{p}{p+1}} n) \quad (12.179)$$

In [606], it is shown that the rates given in Propositions 12.49, 12.50, 12.51, and 12.52 are tight. These results give the guarantees on the learning rates of estimators using such types of kernels, which is theoretically satisfying and leads to desirable sample complexity rates. In practice, however, it is often better to take advantage of estimates based on an analysis of the distribution of the training data since the rates obtained by the latter can be superior [604].

12.5 Summary

In this chapter we studied four alternative ways of assessing the quality of an estimator, none of which relies on the VC dimension as the basic mechanism.

The first method was based on the concept of *algorithmic stability*, i.e., on the fact that the estimates we obtain by minimizing the regularized risk functional do not depend to a large extent on individual instances. This facilitated the application of concentration of measure inequalities and ultimately the proof of uniform convergence bounds.

A second strategy relied on leave-one-out estimators, which provide an (almost) unbiased, yet somewhat noisy estimate of the expected error of the estimation algorithm. In some cases, however, such as the minimization of regularized risk functionals, it is possible to derive upper bounds on the variance of the leave-one-out estimate. In this context we presented three means of computing such estimates, based on ideas from statistical mechanics and optimization theory.

Thirdly, also Bayesian-like concepts can be employed in the assessment of an estimator. In this context, we introduced the notion of the risk of a distribution over hypotheses rather than a single function. Using a connection between the width of the margin and the posterior weight we established bounds which are readily predictive already for small sample sizes but which are oblivious of the shape of the data mapped into feature space.

Finally, we gave a brief overview over a capacity concept based on the metric entropy of function spaces which crucially relies on the shape of the data in feature space. This enabled us to give significantly improved bounds on the capacity of function classes derived from specific kernels, by combining concepts from the theory of Banach spaces and functional analysis.

Only time and future research will tell, whether we may be able to establish a master concept which encompasses all these different facets of bounds on the generalization performance of estimators. It seems to be a rewarding and promising avenue for future work.

12.6 Problems

12.1 (Uniform Convergence Bounds for SVM •) *Prove a uniform convergence statement for Support Vector Machines using (12.5) and Theorem 12.4.*

12.2 (Adaptive Margin SVM with the ν-Property ••) *An alternative to (12.43) is to use the ν-trick (see Section 3.4.3) to modify the optimization problem (12.42). Prove that*

$$\begin{aligned} &\text{minimize} && \frac{1}{m}\sum_{i=1}^{m}\xi_i - \nu\rho \\ &\text{subject to} && y_i\sum_{j\neq i}\alpha_j y_j k(x_i,x_j) \geq \rho - \xi_i \text{ for all } i\in[m] \\ &&& \alpha_i,\xi_i,\rho \geq 0 \text{ for all } i\in[m] \end{aligned} \tag{12.180}$$

has the ν-property, that is, that at most a fraction of $1-\nu$ patterns are classified correctly with margin larger than ρ and that at most a fraction of ν patterns are margin errors.

12.3 (Span Bound for ν-Classification ∘∘∘) *Prove an analog to the Span Bound (Theorem 12.14) in the case of ν-Classification. Hint: you will have to distinguish between the case of $n^* = \lceil \nu m \rceil$ and $n^* > \lceil \nu m \rceil$ which will lead to the introduction of Span and Swap of a SV solution as in the case of quantile estimation (see Section 12.2.4).*

12.4 (Leave-One-Out Approximation for ν-SVM ∘∘∘) *Using the techniques from Section 12.2.5 derive an approximation of the leave-one-out error in the case of ν-SVM. As opposed to the standard SV setting you also have to take possible changes in the width of the margin into account. Hint: assume that in-bound SVs will remain so and adapt the Lagrange multipliers α_i accordingly such that $\sum_{i\neq l}\alpha_i = 1$ is satisfied (note: do not rescale the bound constrained multipliers from $\frac{1}{\nu m}$ to $\frac{1}{\nu(m-1)}$). Simultaneously adapt the margin ρ such that the in-bound SVs still remain in-bound SVs. In other words choose $\delta\rho$ and $\delta\alpha_i$ such that, for all in-bound SVs, $\sum_{i\neq l}\delta\alpha_i k(x_i,x_j) = \alpha_j k(x_j,x_j) + \delta\rho$.*

12.5 (Counterexample for $R[f_{\text{Gibbs}}] \leq CR[f_{\text{Bayes}}]$ ••) *Show that there exist cases where $R[f_{\text{Bayes}}] = 0$ and $R[f_{\text{Gibbs}}] \geq \frac{1}{2}+\varepsilon$ for any $\varepsilon > 0$. Hint: consider a posterior distribution $p(f|Z)$ where $\frac{1}{2} > p(f(x)=1|Z,x) \geq \frac{1}{2}-\varepsilon$.*

12.6 (Error of the Gibbs Classifier •) *Assume that we know the distribution* $\mathrm{P}(x,y)$ *according to which data are generated. What is the error that the Gibbs classifier f_{Gibbs} will achieve? Prove that it is always greater or equal to the error of the Bayes classifier.*

Can you construct a case where the Gibbs classifier has smaller error than the Bayes classifier (in the case where posterior distribution and true distribution disagree)?

12.7 (PAC-Bayesian Bound for Nonzero Loss [353]•••) *Prove (12.113) by following the steps of the proof of (12.114). Step 1: derive a suitable $\psi(f,Z,\delta)$ by using Hoeffding's bound. Step 2: apply the Quantifier Reversal Lemma with $\alpha = \frac{\mathrm{P}(\mathcal{F}')}{m}$ and $\beta = \frac{1}{m}$ and recall that the loss incurred by classification is bounded by 1.*

III KERNEL METHODS

Nur droben, wo die Sterne,
Gibt's Kirschen ohne Kerne.

H. Heine[1]

We have previously argued that one of the merits of SV algorithms is that they draw the attention of the machine learning community to the practical usefulness of statistical learning theory. Whilst the mathematical formalization that this has brought about is certainly beneficial to the field of statistical machine learning, it is by no means the only merit. The second advantage, potentially even more far-reaching, is that SV methods popularize the use of positive definite kernels for learning. The use of such kernels is not limited to SVMs, and a number of interesting and useful algorithms also benefit from the "kernel trick."

The third and final part of the present book therefore focuses on kernels. This is done in two ways. First, by presenting some non-SV algorithms utilizing kernel functions, starting with *Kernel PCA* (historically the first such algorithm), and efficient modifications thereof (Chapter 14). We then move on to a supervised variant, the *kernel Fisher discriminant* (Chapter 15), and describe a kernel algorithm for modelling unlabelled data using nonlinear *regularized principal manifolds* (Chapter 17). We also discuss *Bayesian* variants and insights into kernel algorithms (Chapter 16). Finally, we describe some rather useful techniques for reducing the complexity

1. From *Nachgelesene Gedichte 1845 - 1856*.

of the kernel expansion returned by the above algorithms, and by SVMs (Chapter 18). It turns out that these techniques also have the potential to develop into other algorithms, in areas such as denoising and nonlinear modelling of data.

13 Designing Kernels

In general, the choice of a kernel corresponds to

- choosing a similarity measure for the data — Section 1.1 introduces kernels as a mathematical formalization of a notion of similarity;
- choosing a linear representation of the data — given a kernel, Section 2.2 constructs a linear space endowed with a dot product that corresponds to the kernel;
- choosing a function space for learning — the representer theorem (Section 4.2) states that the solutions of a large class of kernel algorithms, among them SVMs, are precisely given by kernel expansions; thus, the kernel determines the functional form of all possible solutions;
- choosing a regularization functional — given a kernel, Theorem 4.9 characterizes a regularization term with the property that an SVM using that kernel can be thought of as penalizing that term; for instance, Gaussian kernels penalize derivatives of all orders, and thus enforce smoothness of the solution;
- choosing a covariance function for correlated observations; in other words, encoding prior knowledge about how observations at different points of the input domain relate to each other — this interpretation is explained in Section 16.3;
- choosing a prior over the set of functions — as explained in Section 4.10 and 16.3, each kernel induces a distribution encoding how likely different functions are considered a priori.

Therefore, the choice of the kernel should reflect prior knowledge about the problem at hand. Specifically, the kernel *is* the prior knowledge we have about a problem and its solution. Accordingly, just as there is no "free lunch" in learning (Section 5.1), there is also no free lunch in kernel choice.

This chapter gathers a number of methods and results concerning the design of kernel functions. We start with a somewhat anecdotal collection of general methods for the construction of kernels that are positive definite (Section 13.1). We then consider some interesting classes of kernels engineered for particular tasks. Specifically, we look at string kernels for the processing of sequence data (Section 13.2), and locality-improved kernels that take into account local structure in data, such as spatial vicinity in images (Section 13.3). Following this, we summarize the key features of a class of kernels that take into account underlying probabilistic models, and can thus be thought of as defining a similarity measure which respects the

Overview

process that generated the patterns (Section 13.4).

Prerequisites

The chapter strongly relies on background from Chapter 2; in particular, on Sections 2.1 through 2.3. Some background from Section 4.4 is useful to understand the Fourier space representation of translation invariant kernels. The material in Section 13.3 requires basic knowledge of the SVM classification algorithm, as described in Section 1.5 and Chapter 7. Finally, the section on natural kernels, builds on concepts introduced in Section 3.3.

13.1 Tricks for Constructing Kernels

We now gather a number of results useful for designing positive definite kernels (referred to as *kernels* for brevity) [42, 121, 1, 85, 340, 480, 125]. Many of these techniques concern manipulations that preserve the positive definiteness of Definition 2.5; which is to say, closure properties of the set of admissible kernels.

Linear Combination of Kernels

Proposition 13.1 (Sums and Limits of Kernels) *The set of kernels forms a convex cone, closed under pointwise convergence. In other words,*

- *if k_1 and k_2 are kernels, and $\alpha_1, \alpha_2 \geq 0$, then $\alpha_1 k_1 + \alpha_2 k_2$ is a kernel;*
- *if $k_1, k_2, \ldots$ are kernels, and $k(x, x') := \lim_{n\to\infty} k_n(x, x')$ exists for all x, x', then k is a kernel.*

Whilst the above statements are fairly obvious, the next one is rather surprising and often useful for verifying that a given kernel is positive definite.

Product of Kernels

Proposition 13.2 (Pointwise Products [483]) *If k_1 and k_2 are kernels, then $k_1 k_2$, defined by $(k_1 k_2)(x, x') := k_1(x, x') k_2(x, x')$, is a kernel.*

Note that the corresponding result for positive definite matrices concerns the positivity of the matrix that is obtained by element-wise products of two positive definite matrices. The original proof of Schur [483] is somewhat technical. Instead, we briefly reproduce the proof of [402], which should be enlightening to readers with a basic knowledge of multivariate statistics.

Proof Let $(V_1, \ldots, V_m)$ and $(W_1, \ldots, W_m)$ be two independent normally distributed random vectors, with mean zero, and respective covariance matrices K_1 and K_2. Then the matrix K, whose elements are the products of the corresponding elements of K_1 and K_2, is the covariance matrix of the random vector $(V_1 W_1, \ldots, V_m W_m)$, hence it is positive definite. ■

Conformal Transformation

A special case of the above are *conformal transformations* [10],

$$k_f(x, x') = f(x) k(x, x') f(x'), \tag{13.1}$$

obtained by multiplying a kernel k with a rank-one kernel (cf. Problem 2.15) $k'(x, x') = f(x)f(x')$, where f is a positive function. Since

$$\cos\left(\angle\left(\Phi_f(x), \Phi_f(x')\right)\right) = \frac{f(x)k(x,x')f(x')}{\sqrt{f(x)k(x,x)f(x)}\sqrt{f(x')k(x',x')f(x')}} = \frac{k(x,x')}{\sqrt{k(x,x)}\sqrt{k(x',x')}} = \cos\left(\angle\left(\Phi(x), \Phi(x')\right)\right),$$

this transformation does not affect *angles* in the feature space.

Dot Product Kernels

For kernels of the dot product type, written $k(x, x') = k(\langle x, x'\rangle)$, the following conditions apply.

Theorem 13.3 (Necessary Conditions for Dot Product Kernels [86]) *A differentiable function of the dot product $k(x, x') = k(\langle x, x'\rangle)$ has to satisfy*

$$k(t) \geq 0,\ k'(t) \geq 0 \text{ and } k'(t) + tk''(t) \geq 0 \tag{13.2}$$

for any $t \geq 0$, in order to be a positive definite kernel.

Note that the conditions in Theorem 13.3 are only *necessary* but not *sufficient*. The general case is given by the following theorem (see also Section 4.6.1 for the finite dimensional counterpart).

Theorem 13.4 (Power Series of Dot Product Kernels [466]) *A function $k(x, x') = k(\langle x, x'\rangle)$ defined on an infinite dimensional Hilbert space, with a power series expansion*

$$k(t) = \sum_{n=0}^{\infty} a_n t^n, \tag{13.3}$$

is a positive definite kernel if and only if for all n, we have $a_n \geq 0$.

A slightly weaker condition applies for finite dimensional spaces. For further details and examples see Section 4.6 and [42, 511].

We next state a condition for translation invariant kernels, meaning kernels of the form $k(x, x') = k(x - x')$.

Theorem 13.5 (Fourier Criterion [516]) *Suppose $\mathcal{X} \subset \mathbb{R}^N$. A translation invariant function $k(x, x') = k(x - x')$ is a positive definite kernel if the Fourier transform*

$$F[k](\omega) = (2\pi)^{-\frac{N}{2}} \int_{\mathcal{X}} e^{-i\langle\omega, x\rangle}\, k(x)\, dx \tag{13.4}$$

is nonnegative.

This theorem is proved, and further discussed, in Section 4.4.

Kernels Constructed from Mappings

As discussed in Chapter 2, we typically do not worry about the exact map Φ to which the kernel corresponds, once we have a suitable kernel. For the purpose of constructing kernels, however, it can be useful to compute the kernels from mappings into some dot product space $\mathcal{H}$, $\Phi : \mathcal{X} \to \mathcal{H}$. Ideally, we would like to choose Φ such that we can obtain an expression for $\langle \Phi(x), \Phi(x') \rangle$ that can be computed efficiently. Consider now mappings into function spaces,

$$x \mapsto f_x, \tag{13.5}$$

with f_x being a real-valued function. We further assume that these spaces are equipped with a dot product,

$$\langle f_x, f_{x'} \rangle = \int f_x(u) f_{x'}(u)\, du. \tag{13.6}$$

We can then define kernels of the form

$$k(x, x') := \langle f_x, f_{x'} \rangle^d, \tag{13.7}$$

for instance. As an example, suppose the input patterns x_i are $q \times q$ images. Then we can map these patterns to two-dimensional image intensity distributions f_{x_i} (for instance, splines on $[0,1]^2$). The dot product between the f_{x_i} then approximately equals the original dot product between the images represented as pixel vectors, which can be seen by considering the finite sum approximation to the integral,

$$\int_0^1 \int_0^1 f_x(u) f_{x'}(u)\, d^2u \approx \frac{1}{q^2} \sum_{i=1}^{q} \sum_{j=1}^{q} f_x\left(\frac{i-\frac{1}{2}}{q}, \frac{j-\frac{1}{2}}{q}\right) f_{x'}\left(\frac{i-\frac{1}{2}}{q}, \frac{j-\frac{1}{2}}{q}\right).$$

Note that in the function representation, it is possible, for instance, to define kernels that can compare images in different resolutions.

Iterating Kernels

Given a function $k(x, x')$, we can construct iterated kernels (e.g., [112]) using

$$k^{(2)}(x, x') := \int k(x, x'') k(x', x'')\, dx''. \tag{13.8}$$

Note that $k^{(2)}$ is a positive definite kernel even if k is not, as can be seen by verifying the condition of Mercer's theorem,

$$\begin{aligned} \int k^{(2)}(x, x') f(x) f(x')\, dx dx' &= \int \int k(x, x'') k(x', x'') f(x) f(x')\, dx'' dx dx' \\ &= \int \left(\int k(x, x'') f(x)\, dx \right)^2 dx''. \end{aligned} \tag{13.9}$$

A similar construction can be accomplished in the discrete case, cf. Problem 13.3.

According to Proposition 13.2, the *product* of kernels is also a kernel. Let us now consider a different form of product, the *tensor product*, which also works if the two kernels are defined on different domains.

Tensor Product Kernel

Proposition 13.6 (Tensor Products) *If k_1 and k_2 are kernels defined respectively on $\mathcal{X}_1 \times \mathcal{X}_1$ and $\mathcal{X}_2 \times \mathcal{X}_2$, then their tensor product,*

$$(k_1 \otimes k_2)(x_1, x_2, x_1', x_2') = k_1(x_1, x_1') k_2(x_2, x_2'), \tag{13.10}$$

is a kernel on $(\mathcal{X}_1 \times \mathcal{X}_2) \times (\mathcal{X}_1 \times \mathcal{X}_2)$. Here, $x_1, x_1' \in \mathcal{X}_1$ and $x_2, x_2' \in \mathcal{X}_2$.

This result follows from the fact that the (usual) product of kernels is a kernel (see Proposition 13.2 and Problem 13.4).

There is a corresponding generalization from the sum of kernels to their *direct sum* [234, 480].

Proposition 13.7 (Direct Sums) *If k_1 and k_2 are kernels defined respectively on $\mathcal{X}_1 \times \mathcal{X}_1$ and $\mathcal{X}_2 \times \mathcal{X}_2$, then their direct sum,*

$$(k_1 \oplus k_2)(x_1, x_2, x_1', x_2') = k_1(x_1, x_1') + k_2(x_2, x_2'), \tag{13.11}$$

is a kernel on $(\mathcal{X}_1 \times \mathcal{X}_2) \times (\mathcal{X}_1 \times \mathcal{X}_2)$. Here, $x_1, x_1' \in \mathcal{X}_1$ and $x_2, x_2' \in \mathcal{X}_2$.

This construction can be useful if the different parts of the input have different meanings, and should be dealt with differently. In this case, we can split the inputs into two parts x_1 and x_2, and use two different kernels for these parts [480].

Kernels on Structured Objects

This observation naturally leads to the general problem of defining kernels on structured objects [234, 585]. Suppose the object $x \in \mathcal{X}$ is composed of $x_d \in \mathcal{X}_d$, where $d = 1, \ldots, D$ (note that the sets $\mathcal{X}_d$ need not be equal). For instance, consider the string $x = ATG$, and $D = 2$. It is composed of the parts $x_1 = AT$ and $x_2 = G$, or alternatively, of $x_1 = A$ and $x_2 = TG$. Mathematically speaking, the set of "allowed" decompositions can be thought of as a *relation* $R(x_1, \ldots, x_D, x)$, to be read as "$x_1, \ldots, x_D$ constitute the composite object x."

R-Convolution Kernel

Haussler [234] investigated how to define a kernel between composite objects by building on similarity measures that assess their respective *parts*; in other words, kernels k_d defined on $\mathcal{X}_d \times \mathcal{X}_d$. Define the *R-convolution* of $k_1, \ldots, k_D$ as

$$(k_1 \star \ldots \star k_D)(x, x') := \sum_R \prod_{d=1}^{D} k_d(x_d, x_d'), \tag{13.12}$$

where the sum runs over all possible ways (allowed by R) in which we can decompose x into $x_1, \ldots, x_D$ and x' into $x_1', \ldots, x_D'$; that is, all $(x_1, \ldots, x_D, x_1', \ldots, x_D')$ such that $R(x_1, \ldots, x_D, x)$ and $R(x_1', \ldots, x_D', x')$.[1] If there is only a finite number of ways, the relation R is called finite. In this case, it can be shown that the R-convolution is a valid kernel [234].

ANOVA Kernel

Specific examples of convolution kernels are Gaussians (Problem 13.7) and ANOVA kernels [578, 88, 562, 529]. ANOVA stands for analysis of variance, and denotes a statistical technique to analyze interactions between attributes of the data. To construct an ANOVA kernel, we consider $\mathcal{X} = S^N$ for some set S, and kernels $k^{(i)}$ on $S \times S$, where $i = 1, \ldots, N$. For $D = 1, \ldots, N$, the *ANOVA kernel of order D* is defined as

$$k_D(x, x') := \sum_{1 \le i_1 < \ldots < i_D \le N} \prod_{d=1}^{D} k^{(i_d)}(x_{i_d}, x_{i_d}'). \tag{13.13}$$

1. Note that we use the convention that an empty sum equals zero, hence if either x or x' cannot be decomposed, then $(k_1 \star \ldots \star k_D)(x, x') = 0$.

Note that if $D = N$, the sum consists only of the term for which $(i_1, \ldots, i_D) = (1, \ldots, N)$, and k equals the tensor product $k^{(1)} \otimes \ldots \otimes k^{(N)}$. At the other extreme, if $D = 1$, then the products collapse to one factor each, and k equals the direct sum $k^{(1)} \oplus \ldots \oplus k^{(N)}$. For intermediate values of D, we get kernels that lie in between tensor products and direct sums. It is also possible to use ANOVA kernels to interpolate between (ordinary) products and sums of kernels, cf. Problem 13.6.

ANOVA kernels typically use some moderate value of D, which specifies the order of the interactions between attributes x_{i_d} that we are interested in. The sum then runs over the numerous terms that take into account interactions of order D; fortunately, the computational cost can be reduced by utilizing recurrent procedures for the kernel evaluation [88, 529]. ANOVA kernels have been shown to work rather well in multi-dimensional SV regression problems (cf. Chapter 9 and [529]). In this case, the inputs were N-dimensional vectors, and all $k^{(n)}$ where chosen identically as one-dimensional linear spline kernels with an infinite number of nodes: for $x, x' \in \mathbb{R}_0^+$,

$$k^{(n)}(x, x') = \frac{\min(x, x')^3}{3} + \frac{\min(x, x')^2 |x - x'|}{2} + 1 + xx', \quad n = 1, \ldots, N. \tag{13.14}$$

Note that it is advisable to use a kernel for $k^{(n)}$ which never or rarely takes the value zero, since a single zero term would eliminate the product in (13.13). Finally, it is possible to prove that ANOVA kernels are special cases of R-convolutions ([234], cf. Problem 13.8).

13.2 String Kernels

One way in which SVMs have been used for text categorization [265] is the *bag-of-words* representation, as briefly mentioned in Chapter 7. This maps a given text to a sparse vector, where each component corresponds to a word, and a component is set to one (or some other number) whenever the related word occurs in the text. Using an efficient sparse representation, the dot product between two such vectors can be computed quickly. Furthermore, this dot product is by construction a valid kernel, referred to as a *sparse vector kernel*. One of its shortcomings, however, is that it does not take into account the word ordering of a document. Other sparse vector kernels are also conceivable, such as one that maps a text to the set of pairs of words that are in the same sentence [265, 585], or those which look only at pairs of words within a certain vicinity with respect to each other [495].

Sparse Vector Kernel

A more sophisticated way of dealing with string data was recently proposed [585, 234]. The basic idea is as described above for general structured objects (13.12): Compare the strings by means of the substrings they contain. The more substrings two strings have in common, the more similar they are. The substrings need not always be contiguous; that said, the further apart the first and last element of a substring are, the less weight should be given to the similarity.

Remarkably, it is possible to define an efficient kernel which computes the dot product in the feature space spanned by *all* substrings of documents, with a computational complexity that is linear in the lengths of the documents being compared, and the length of the substrings. We now describe this kernel, following [333].

Consider a finite alphabet Σ, the set of all strings of length n, Σ^n, and the set of all finite strings,

$$\Sigma^* := \bigcup_{n=0}^{\infty} \Sigma^n. \tag{13.15}$$

The length of a string $s \in \Sigma^*$ is denoted by $|s|$, and its elements by $s(1)\dots s(|s|)$; the concatenation of s and $t \in \Sigma^*$ is written st. Let us now form subsequences u of strings. Given an index sequence $\mathbf{i} := (i_1, \dots, i_{|u|})$ with $1 \le i_1 < \dots < i_{|u|} \le |s|$, we define $u := s(\mathbf{i}) := s(i_1)\dots s(i_{|u|})$. We call $l(\mathbf{i}) := i_{|u|} - i_1 + 1$ *the length of the subsequence in* s. Note that if $\mathbf{i}$ is not contiguous, then $l(\mathbf{i})$ is longer than u.

The feature space built from strings of length n is defined to be $\mathcal{H}_n := \mathbb{R}^{(\Sigma^n)}$. This notation means that the space has one dimension (or coordinate) for each element of Σ^n, labelled by that element (equivalently, we can think of it as the space of all real-valued functions on Σ^n). We can thus describe the feature map coordinate-wise for each $u \in \Sigma^n$ via

$$[\Phi_n(s)]_u := \sum_{\mathbf{i}:s(\mathbf{i})=u} \lambda^{l(\mathbf{i})}. \tag{13.16}$$

Here, $0 < \lambda \le 1$ is a decay parameter: The larger the length of the subsequence in s, the smaller the respective contribution to $[\Phi_n(s)]_u$. The sum runs over all subsequences of s which equal u.

For instance, consider a dimension of $\mathcal{H}_3$ spanned (that is, labelled) by the string `asd`. In this case, we have $[\Phi_3(\texttt{Nasdaq})]_{\texttt{asd}} = \lambda^3$, while $[\Phi_3(\texttt{lass das})]_{\texttt{asd}} = 2\lambda^5$.[2]

String Kernel

The kernel induced by the map Φ_n takes the form

$$k_n(s,t) = \sum_{u\in\Sigma^n} [\Phi_n(s)]_u [\Phi_n(t)]_u = \sum_{u\in\Sigma^n} \sum_{(\mathbf{i},\mathbf{j}):s(\mathbf{i})=t(\mathbf{j})=u} \lambda^{l(\mathbf{i})}\lambda^{l(\mathbf{j})}. \tag{13.17}$$

To take into account strings of different lengths n, we can use linear combinations,

$$k := \sum_n c_n k_n, \tag{13.18}$$

with $c_n \ge 0$. Let us denote the corresponding feature map by Φ. Clearly, the number and size of the terms in the above sum strongly depend on the lengths of s and t. Normalization of the feature map, using $\Phi(t)/\|\Phi(t)\|$, is therefore recommended [333]. For the kernel, this implies that we should use $k(s,t)/\sqrt{k(s,s)k(t,t)}$.

2. In the first string, `asd` is a contiguous substring. In the second string, it appears twice as a non-contiguous substring of length 5 in `lass das`, the two occurrences are `lass das` and `lass das`.

To describe the actual computation of k_n, define

$$k'_i(s,t) := \sum_{u \in \Sigma^i} \sum_{(\mathbf{i},\mathbf{j}):s(\mathbf{i})=t(\mathbf{j})=u} \lambda^{|s|+|t|-i_1-j_1+2}, \text{ for } i = 1, \ldots, n-1. \tag{13.19}$$

Using $x \in \Sigma^1$, we then have the following recursions, which allow the computation of $k_n(s,t)$ for all $n = 1, 2, \ldots$ (note that the kernels are symmetric):

$$\begin{aligned}
k'_0(s,t) &= 1 \text{ for all } s, t\\
k'_i(s,t) &= 0 \text{ if } \min(|s|,|t|) < i\\
k_i(s,t) &= 0 \text{ if } \min(|s|,|t|) < i\\
k'_i(sx,t) &= \lambda k'_i(s,t) + \sum_{j:t_j=x} k'_{i-1}(s, t[1,\ldots,j-1])\lambda^{|t|-j+2}, \; i = 1,\ldots,n-1\\
k_n(sx,t) &= k_n(s,t) + \sum_{j:t_j=x} k'_{n-1}(s, t[1,\ldots,j-1])\lambda^2
\end{aligned} \tag{13.20}$$

For further detail, see [585, 333, 156].

13.3 Locality-Improved Kernels

13.3.1 Image Processing

As described in Chapter 2, using a kernel $k(x,x') = \langle x, x'\rangle^d$ in an SVM classifier implicitly leads to a decision boundary in the space of all possible products of d pixels. Using *all* such products, however, may not be desirable, since in real-world images, correlations over short distances are much more reliable features than are long-range correlations. To take this into account, we give the following procedural definition of the kernel $k_p^{d_1,d_2}$ (cf. Figure 13.1 and [478]):

Local Image Kernel

1. Compute a third image $(x. * x')$, defined as the pixel-wise product of x and x'
2. Sample $(x. * x')$ with pyramidal receptive fields of diameter p, centered at all locations (i,j), to obtain the values

$$z_{ij} := \sum_{i'j'} w\left(\max(|i-i'|, |j-j'|)\right) (x. * x')_{i'j'}. \tag{13.21}$$

A possible choice for the weighting function $w : \mathbb{N}_0 \to \mathbb{R}$ is $w(n) = \max(q-n, 0)$, where $q \in \mathbb{N}_0$. In this case, $p = 2q+1$ is the *width* of the pyramidal receptive field.

3. Raise each z_{ij} to the power d_1, to take into account local correlations within the range of the pyramid
4. Sum $z_{ij}^{d_1}$ over the whole image, and raise the result to the power d_2 to allow for long-range correlations of order d_2

The resulting kernel is of order $d_1 \cdot d_2$, however it does *not* contain *all* possible correlations of $d_1 \cdot d_2$ pixels unless $d_1 = 1$. In the latter case, we recover the standard complete polynomial kernel of degree d_2.

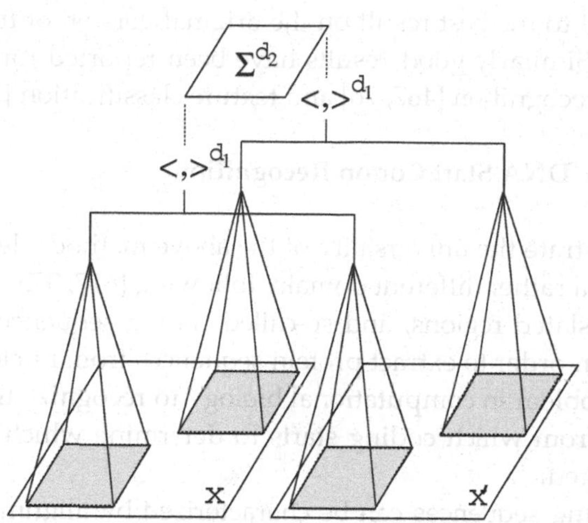

Figure 13.1 Kernel utilizing local correlations in images. To compute $k(x, x')$ for two images x and x', we sum over products between corresponding pixels of the two images, in localized regions (in the figure, this is denoted by dot products $\langle .,. \rangle$), weighed by pyramidal receptive fields. A first nonlinearity in form of an exponent d_1 is applied to the outputs. The resulting numbers for all patches (only two are displayed) are summed, and the d_2th power of the result is taken as the value $k(x, x')$. This kernel corresponds to a dot product in a polynomial space which is spanned mainly by localized correlations between pixels (see Section 13.3).

Table 13.1 Summary: Error rates on the small MNIST database (Section A.1), for various methods of incorporating prior knowledge. In all cases, degree 4 polynomial kernels were used, either of the local type, or (by default) of the complete polynomial type.

Classifier	Test Error in %
SV (complete polynomial kernel of degree 4)	4.0
semi-local kernel $k_9^{2,2}$ (Section 13.3.1)	3.1
purely local kernel $k_9^{4,1}$ (Section 13.3.1)	3.4
Virtual SV (Section 11.3), with translations	2.8
Virtual SV with $k_9^{2,2}$	2.0

Character Recognition Results

We now report experimental results. As in Section 11.4, we used the small MNIST database (Section A.1). As a reference, we employ the degree 4 polynomial SVM, performing at 4.0% error (Table 11.4). To exploit locality in images, we used the pyramidal receptive field kernel $k_p^{d_1,d_2}$ with diameter $p = 9$ and $d_1 \cdot d_2 = 4$; these are degree 4 polynomials kernels that do not use *all* products of 4 pixels. For $d_1 = d_2 = 2$, we observe an improved error rate of 3.1%; a different degree 4 kernel with *only* local correlations ($d_1 = 4, d_2 = 1$) leads to an error rate of 3.4% (Table 13.1, [467]).

Although better than the 4.0% error rate for the degree 4 homogeneous polynomial, this is still worse than the Virtual SV result: Using image translations to generate a set of Virtual SVs leads to an error rate of 2.8%. As the two methods exploit different types of prior knowledge, however, we expect that combining them will lead to still better performance; and indeed, this yields the best performance of all (2.0%), halving the error rate of the original system. Similar results were obtained on the USPS database, where the combination of VSVs and locality-improved kernels led to the best result on the original version of the dataset (see Table 7.4 and [478]). Similarly good results have been reported for other applications, such as object recognition [467, 76] and texture classification [25].

13.3.2 DNA Start Codon Recognition

To illustrate the universality of the above methods, let us now look at an application in a rather different domain, following [617, 375]. Genomic sequences contain untranslated regions, and so-called coding sequences (CDS) which encode proteins. In order to extract protein sequences from nucleotide sequences, it is a central problem in computational biology to recognize the translation initiation sites (TIS), from which coding starts to determine which parts of a sequence will be translated.

Coding sequences can be characterized by alignment methods using homologous proteins (e.g., [405]), or intrinsic properties of the nucleotide sequence which are learned for instance with Hidden Markov models (HMMs, e.g., [256]). A different approach, which has turned out to be more successful, is to model the task of finding TIS as a classification problem (see [406, 617]). Out of the four letter DNA alphabet $\{A, C, G, T\}$, a potential start codon is typically an ATG triplet. The classification task is therefore to decide whether a symmetrical sequence window around the ATG indicates a true TIS, or a so called pseudo site. Each nucleotide in the window is represented using a sparse four-number encoding scheme. For known nucleotides $\{A, C, G, T\}$, the corresponding entry is set to 1; unknown nucleotides are represented by distributions over the four entries, determined by their respective frequencies in the sequences. The SVM gets a training set consisting of an input of encoded nucleotides in windows of length 200 around the ATG, together with a label indicating true/false TIS. In the TIS recognition task, it turns out to be rather useful to include biological knowledge, by engineering an appropriate kernel function. We now give three examples of kernel modifications that are particularly useful for start codon recognition.

While certain local correlations are typical for TIS, dependencies between distant positions are of minor importance, or do not even exist. Just as in the image processing task described in Section 13.3.1, we want the feature space to reflect this. We therefore modify the kernel as follows: At each sequence position, we compare the two sequences locally, within a small window of length $2l + 1$ around that position. We sum matching nucleotides, multiplied by weights v_j, which increase from the boundaries to the center of the window. The resulting weighted counts are raised to the d_1^{th} power. As above, d_1 reflects the order of local correlations (within the window) that we expect to be of importance;

Locality-Improved DNA Kernel

$$\text{win}_p(x, x') = \left(\sum_{j=-l}^{+l} v_j \, \text{match}_{p+j}(x, x') \right)^{d_1} . \tag{13.22}$$

Table 13.2 Comparison of start codon classification errors (measured on the test set) achieved with different learning algorithms. All results are averages over the six data partitions. SVMs were trained on 8000 data points. An optimal set of parameters was selected according to the overall error on the remaining training data ($\approx$ 3300 points); only these results are presented. Note that the windows consist of $2l+1$ nucleotides. The neural net results were achieved by Pedersen and Nielsen ([406], personal communication). In the latter study, model selection seems to have involved test data, which might lead to slightly over-optimistic performance estimates. Positional conditional preference scores were calculated in a manner analogous to Salzberg [456], but extended to the same amount of input data supplied to the other methods. Note that all performance measures shown depend on the value of the classification function threshold. For SVMs, the thresholds are by-products of the training process; for the Salzberg method, 'natural' thresholds are derived from prior probabilities by Bayesian reasoning. Error rates denote the ratio of false predictions to total predictions.

algorithm	kernel parameters	error
neural network		15.4%
Salzberg method		13.8%
SVM, simple polynomial	d=1	13.2%
SVM, locality-improved kernel	d_1=4,l=4	11.9%
SVM, codon-improved kernel	d_1=2,l=3	12.2%
SVM, Salzberg kernel	d_1=3,l=1	11.4%

Here, $\text{match}_{p+j}(x, x')$ is defined to be 1 for matching nucleotides at position $p+j$, and 0 otherwise. The window scores computed with win_p are summed over the whole length of the sequence. Correlations between windows of order up to d_2 are taken into account by raising the resulting sum to the power of d_2; that is,

$$k(x, x') = \left(\sum_{p=1}^{l} \text{win}_p(x, x') \right)^{d_2} \tag{13.23}$$

We call this kernel *locality-improved*, as it emphasizes local correlations.

In an attempt to further improve performance, we incorporate another form of biological knowledge into the kernel, this time concerning the codon-structure of the coding sequence. A codon is a triplet of adjacent nucleotides that codes for one amino acid. By definition, the difference between a true TIS and a pseudo site is that downstream of a TIS, there are CDS (which shows codon structure), while upstream there are not. CDS and non-coding sequences show statistically different compositions. It is likely that the SVM exploits this difference for classification.

We also hope to improve the kernel by reflecting the fact that CDS shifted by three nucleotides still look like CDS. Therefore, we further modify the locality-improved kernel function to account for this translation-invariance. In addition to counting matching nucleotides on corresponding positions, we also count matches that are shifted by three positions. We call this kernel *codon-improved*. It can be shown to be an admissible kernel function by explicitly deriving the monomial features.

Codon-Improved Kernel

A third modification to the kernel function is obtained by the Salzberg method, where we essentially represent each data point by a sequence of log odd scores, corresponding to two probabilities for each position: First, the likelihood that the observed nucleotide at that position derives from a true TIS; and second, the likelihood that the nucleotide occurs at the given position relative to any ATG triplet, either centered around true translation initiation sites, or around pseudo sites. We then proceed in a manner analogous to the locality-improved kernel, replacing the sparse representation by the sequence of these scores. As expected, this leads to a further improvement in classification performance.

Local Kernel Using Salzberg Score

All three engineered kernel functions outperform both a neural net and the original Salzberg method, reducing the overall number of misclassifications by up to 25% compared with the neural network (see Table 13.2). These SVM results are encouraging, especially since they apply to a problem domain whose importance is increasing. Further successful applications of SVMs in bioinformatics have been reported for microarray gene expression data and other problems [81, 224, 190, 372, 403, 584, 611].

13.4 Natural Kernels

Generative model techniques such as Hidden Markov Models (HMMs), dynamic graphical models, or mixtures of experts, can provide a principled framework for dealing with missing and incomplete data, uncertainty, or variable length sequences. On the other hand, discriminative models like SVMs and other kernel methods have become standard tools of applied machine learning, leading to record benchmark results in a variety of domains. A promising approach to combine the strengths of both methods, by designing kernels inspired by generative models, was made in the work of Jaakkola and Haussler [259, 258]. They propose the use of a construction called the *Fisher kernel*, to give a "natural" similarity measure that takes into account an underlying probability distribution. Since defining a kernel function automatically implies assumptions about metric relations between the examples, they argue that these relations should be defined directly from a generative probability model $p(x|\theta)$, where θ are the parameters of the model. Below, we follow [388].

13.4.1 Natural Kernels

To define a class of kernels derived from generative models, we need to introduce some basic concepts of information geometry. Consider a family of generative models $p(x|\theta)$ (in other words, density functions), smoothly parametrized by $\theta = (\theta^1, \ldots, \theta^r)$. These models form a manifold (called the statistical manifold) in the space of all probability density functions. The key idea introduced by [259] is to exploit the geometric structure on this manifold to obtain an induced metric for the training patterns x_i.

Rather than dealing with $p(x|\theta)$ directly, we use the log-likelihood instead; $l(x, \theta) := \ln p(x|\theta)$. For convenience, we repeat a few concepts from Chapter 3, in particular Section 3.3.2:

Score Map

- The derivative map of $l(x|\theta)$ is called the *score* (cf. (3.27)) $V_\theta : \mathcal{X} \to \mathbb{R}^r$,

$$V_\theta(x) := (\partial_{\theta^1} l(x, \theta), \ldots, \partial_{\theta^r} l(x, \theta)) = \nabla_\theta l(x, \theta) = \nabla_\theta \ln p(x|\theta), \tag{13.24}$$

the coordinates of which are taken as a 'natural' basis of tangent vectors. For example, if $p(x|\theta)$ is a normal distribution, one possible parametrization is $\theta = (\mu, \sigma)$, where μ is the mean vector and σ is the covariance matrix of the Gaussian. The magnitude of the components of $V_\theta(x)$ specifies the extent to which a change in a particular component of θ (thus, a particular model parameter) changes the probability of generating the object x. The relationship of these components to *sufficient statistics* is discussed in [257].

- Since the manifold of $\ln p(x|\theta)$ is Riemannian (e.g., [8]), there is a metric defined on its tangent space (the space of the scores), with metric tensor given by the inverse of the *Fisher information matrix* (cf. (3.28)),

Fisher Information Matrix

$$I := E_p\left[V_\theta(x) V_\theta(x)^\top\right], \text{ i.e., } I_{ij} = E_p\left[\partial_{\theta^i} \ln p(x|\theta) \partial_{\theta^j} \ln p(x|\theta)\right]. \tag{13.25}$$

Here, E_p denotes the expectation with respect to the density p.
This metric is called the *Fisher information metric*, and induces a 'natural' distance in the manifold. As we will show below, it can be used to measure the difference in the generative process between a pair of examples x_i and x_j via the score map $V_\theta(x)$ and I^{-1}.

Natural Matrix

Definition 13.8 (Natural Kernel) *Denote by M a strictly positive definite matrix, to be referred to subsequently as the* natural matrix. *The corresponding* natural kernel *is given by*

$$k_M^{nat}(x, x') := V_\theta(x)^\top M^{-1} V_\theta(x') = \nabla_\theta \ln p(x|\theta)^\top M^{-1} \nabla_\theta \ln p(x'|\theta). \tag{13.26}$$

For $M = I$, we obtain the Fisher kernel; *for $M = \mathbf{1}$ we obtain a kernel which we will call the* plain kernel[3]. *The latter is often used for convenience if I is too difficult to compute.*[4]

In the next section, we give a regularization theoretic analysis of the class of natural kernels, and in particular of k_I^{nat} and $k_{\mathbf{1}}^{nat}$.

3. In [257], kernels of the form $k_M^{nat}(x, x') = \exp(-\|V_\theta(x) - V_\theta(x')\|^2/c)$ are also considered.
4. Strictly speaking, we should write $k_{M,p(x,\cdot)}^{nat}$ rather than k_M^{nat}, since k also depends on the generative model, and on the parameter θ chosen by some other procedure such as density estimation. In addition, note that rather than requiring M to be strictly positive definite, definiteness would be sufficient. We would then have to replace M^{-1} by the pseudo-inverse, however, and the subsequent reasoning would be more cumbersome.

13.4.2 The Natural Regularization Operator

Let us briefly recall Section 4.3. In SVMs, we minimize a regularized risk functional, where the complexity term can be written as $\|\mathbf{w}\|^2$ in feature space notation, or as $\|\Upsilon f\|^2$ when considering the functions in input space. The connection between kernels k and regularization operators Υ is given by

$$k(x_i, x_j) = \langle (\Upsilon k)(x_i, .), (\Upsilon k)(x_j, .) \rangle . \tag{13.27}$$

This relation states that if k is a *Green's* function of $\Upsilon^*\Upsilon$, minimizing $\|\mathbf{w}\|^2$ in feature space is equivalent to minimizing the regularization term $\|\Upsilon f\|^2$.

To analyze the properties of natural kernels k_I^{nat}, we exploit this connection between kernels and regularization operators by finding an associated operator Υ_M^{nat} such that (13.27) holds. To this end, we need to specify a dot product in (13.27). Note that this is one aspect of the choice of the class of regularization operators that we are looking at — in particular, we are choosing the dot product space into which Υ maps. We opt for the dot product in the $L_2(p)$ space of real-valued functions,

$$\langle f, g \rangle := \int f(x) g(x) p(x|\theta) dx, \tag{13.28}$$

since this leads to a simple form for the corresponding regularization operators. Measures different from $p(x|\theta)dx$ are also possible, leading to different forms of Υ.

Proposition 13.9 (Regularization Operators for Natural Kernels) *Given a strictly positive definite matrix M, a generative model $p(x|\theta)$, and a corresponding natural kernel $k_M^{nat}(x, x')$, Υ_M^{nat} is an equivalent regularization operator if it satisfies*

$$M = \int \left[\Upsilon_M^{nat} \nabla_\theta \ln p(x|\theta)\right] \left[\Upsilon_M^{nat} \nabla_\theta \ln p(x|\theta)\right]^\top p(x|\theta) dx. \tag{13.29}$$

Proof Substituting (13.26) into (13.27) yields

$$k_M^{nat}(x, x') \overset{\text{by def}}{=} \nabla_\theta \ln p(x|\theta)^\top M^{-1} \nabla_\theta \ln p(x'|\theta) \tag{13.30}$$

$$\overset{(13.27)}{=} \langle \Upsilon_M^{nat} k_M^{nat}(x, .), \Upsilon_M^{nat} k_M^{nat}(x', .) \rangle \tag{13.31}$$

$$= \int \nabla_\theta \ln p(x|\theta)^\top M^{-1} \left[\Upsilon_M^{nat} \nabla_\theta \ln p(x''|\theta)\right] \times \left[\Upsilon_M^{nat} \nabla_\theta \ln p(x''|\theta)^\top\right] M^{-1} \nabla_\theta \ln p(x'|\theta) p(x''|\theta) dx''. \tag{13.32}$$

Note that Υ_M^{nat} acts on p as a function of x'' only — the terms in x and x' are not affected, which is why we may collect them outside. Thus the necessary condition (13.29) ensures that the right hand side in (13.31) equals (13.32), which completes the proof. ■

Let us consider the two special cases proposed in [259].

Corollary 13.10 (Fisher Kernel) *The Fisher Kernel ($M = I$) induced by a generative probability model with density p corresponds to a regularizer equal to the squared $L_2(p)$-*

Fisher Regularization Operator

norm of the estimated function,

$$\|\Upsilon f\|^2 = \|f\|^2_{L_2(p)}. \tag{13.33}$$

This can be seen by substituting in $\Upsilon_I^{\text{nat}} = \mathbf{1}$ into the rhs of (13.29), which yields the definition of the Fisher information matrix.

We now explicitly describe the behavior of this regularizer. The solution of SV regression using the Fisher kernel has the form $f(x) = \sum_{i=1}^{m} \alpha_i k_I^{\text{nat}}(x, x_i)$, where the x_i are the SVs, and $\boldsymbol{\alpha}$ is the solution of the SV programming problem. By substitution, we obtain

$$\begin{aligned}\|f(\theta)\|^2_{L_2(p)} &= \int |f(x)|^2 p(x|\theta) dx \\ &= \int \left(\textstyle\sum_i \alpha_i \nabla_\theta \ln p(x|\theta) I^{-1} \nabla_\theta \ln p(x_i|\theta)\right)^2 p(x|\theta) dx.\end{aligned} \tag{13.34}$$

To understand this term, first recall that what we actually minimize is the regularized risk $R_{\text{reg}}[f]$; in other words, the sum of (13.34) and the empirical risk given by the normalized negative log likelihood. The regularization term (13.34) prevents overfitting by favoring solutions with smaller $\nabla_\theta \ln p(x|\theta)$. Consequently, the regularizer favors the solution which is more stable (flat). See [388] for further details. Note, however, that the validity of this intuitive explanation is somewhat limited: some effects can compensate each other, as the α_i come with different signs.

Finally, we remark that the regularization operator of the conformal transformation of the Fisher kernel k_I^{nat} into $\sqrt{p(x|\theta)}\sqrt{p(x'|\theta)} k_I^{\text{nat}}(x, x')$ is the identity.

In practice, $M = \mathbf{1}$ is often used [259]. In this case, Proposition 13.9 specializes to the following result. The proof is straightforward, and can be found in [388].

Corollary 13.11 (Plain Kernel) *The regularization operator associated with the plain kernel k_1^{nat} is the gradient operator ∇_x in the case where $p(x|\theta)$ belongs to the exponential family of densities; that is, $\ln p(x|\theta) = \langle \theta, x \rangle - \pi(x) + c_0$ with an arbitrary function $\pi(x)$ and a normalization constant c_0.*

This means that the regularization term can be written as

$$\|\Upsilon f\|^2 = \|\nabla_x f(x)\|^2_p = \int \|\nabla_x f(x)\|^2 p(x|\theta) dx, \tag{13.35}$$

thus favoring smooth functions via flatness in the first derivative.

13.4.3 The Feature Map of Natural Kernels

Recall Proposition 4.10, in which we constructed kernels from a discrete set of basis functions via (4.23),

$$k(x_i, x_j) := \sum_n \frac{d_n}{\lambda_n} \psi_n(x_i) \psi_n(x_j), \tag{13.36}$$

where $d_n \in \{0, 1\}$ for all m, and $\sum_n \frac{d_n}{\lambda_n}$ converges. Setting all $d_n = 1$ simply means that we chose to keep the full space spanned by ψ_n. Knowledge of ψ_n and λ_n

helps us to understand the regularization properties of the kernel. In particular, such information tells us which functions are considered simpler than others and how much emphasis is placed on the individual functions ψ_n. We can explicitly construct such an expansion using linear algebra.

Proposition 13.12 (Feature Map of Natural Kernels) *Denote by I the Fisher information matrix, by M the natural matrix, and by s_i, Λ_i the eigensystem of $M^{-\frac{1}{2}}IM^{-\frac{1}{2}}$. The kernel $k_M^{\text{nat}}(x, x')$ can be decomposed into an eigensystem*

$$\psi_i(x) = \frac{1}{\sqrt{\Lambda_i}} s_i^\top M^{-\frac{1}{2}} \nabla_\theta \ln p(x|\theta) \text{ and } \lambda_i = \Lambda_i. \tag{13.37}$$

Note that if $M = I$, we have $\lambda_i = \Lambda_i = 1$.

Proof It can be seen immediately that (13.36) is satisfied. This follows from the fact that s_i is an orthonormal basis, $\mathbf{1} = \sum_i s_i s_i^\top$, and the definition of k_M^{nat}; the terms depending on Λ_i cancel each other. The ψ_i are orthonormal, since

$$\begin{aligned}\langle \psi_i, \psi_j \rangle &= \int \left(\frac{1}{\sqrt{\Lambda_i}} s_i^\top M^{-\frac{1}{2}} \nabla_\theta \ln p(x|\theta) \right) \left(\frac{1}{\sqrt{\Lambda_j}} \nabla_\theta^\top \ln p(x|\theta) M^{-\frac{1}{2}} s_j \right) p(x|\theta)\, dx \\ &= \frac{1}{\sqrt{\Lambda_i \Lambda_j}} s_i^\top M^{-\frac{1}{2}} I M^{-\frac{1}{2}} s_j = \delta_{ij},\end{aligned} \tag{13.38}$$

which completes the proof.[5] ■

Unit Eigenvalues

The eigenvalues λ_i^I of k_I^{nat} are all 1, reflecting the fact that the matrix I whitens the scores $\nabla_\theta \ln(p(x|\theta))$. It can also be seen from $\Upsilon_I = \mathbf{1}$ that (13.37) becomes $\psi_i(x) = \frac{1}{\sqrt{\lambda_i^I}} s_i \cdot \nabla_\theta \ln(p(x|\theta)), 1 \leq i \leq r$.

What are the consequences of all eigenvalues being equal? Standard VC dimension bounds (e.g., Theorem 5.5) state that the capacity of a linear class of functions is bounded by $R^2\Lambda^2$. Here, R is the radius of the smallest sphere containing the data (in feature space), and Λ is the maximum allowed length of the weight vector. Recently, it has been shown that both the spectrum of an associated integral operator (Section 12.4.1) and the spectrum of the Gram matrix $k((x_i, x_j))_{ij}$ [606, 477] can be used to formulate tighter generalization error bounds, exploiting the fact that for standard kernels, such as Gaussians, the distribution of the data in feature space is rather non-isotropic, and the sphere bound is wasteful.

For the Fisher kernel, the non-isotropy does not occur, since the Fisher matrix whitens the scores. This suggests that the standard isotropic VC bounds should be fairly precise in this case. Moreover, the flat spectrum of the Fisher kernel suggests a way of comparing different models: if we compute the Gram matrix for a set of models $p(x|\theta^j)$, then we expect for the true model that $\lambda_i = 1$ for all i. In [388], it is shown experimentally that this can be used for model selection.

5. This result may be extended to generic kernels of the form $k(x, x') = U^\top(x)MU$ [597].

13.5 Summary

In this chapter, we collected a fair amount of material concerning the design of kernels. We started with generic recipes for constructing kernels, and then moved on to more specific methods which take into account features of a given problem domain. As examples, we considered sequence processing, where we discussed string kernels, and image recognition, where we introduced kernels that respect local structure in images. Similar techniques also prove useful in DNA start codon recognition. In both cases, these locality-improved kernels lead to substantial improvements in performance. They are applicable in all cases where the relative importance of subsets of products between features can be specified appropriately. They do, however, slow down both training and testing by a constant factor, which depends on the cost of evaluating the specific kernel used. Finally, we described and analyzed the Fisher kernel method, which designs a kernel respecting an underlying generative model. Further methods for constructing kernels had to be omitted due to lack of space; examples being the fairly well developed theory of kernels on groups (see Problem 13.11) and a recent modification of the Fisher kernel [548].

As explained at the outset, the choice of kernel function is crucial in all kernel algorithms. The kernel constitutes prior knowledge that is available about a task, and its proper choice is thus crucial for success. Although the question of how to choose the best kernel for a given dataset is often posed, it has no good answer. Indeed, it is impossible to come up with the best kernel *on the basis of the dataset* — the kernel reflects prior knowledge, and the latter is, by definition, knowledge that is available *in addition* to the empirical observations.

13.6 Problems

13.1 (Powers of Kernels •) *Using Proposition 13.2, prove that if k is a kernel and $d \in \mathbb{N}$, then k^d is a kernel.*

13.2 (Power Series of Dot Products •) *Prove that the kernel defined in (13.3) is positive definite if for all n, we have $a_n \geq 0$ (cf. Theorem 13.4).*

13.3 (Iterating Kernels •) *Let $z_1, \ldots, z_n \in \mathcal{X}$, and $k(x, x')$ be a function on $\mathcal{X}$. Prove that*

$$k^{(2)}(x, x') := \sum_{j=1}^{n} k(x, z_j) k(x', z_j) \tag{13.39}$$

is positive definite in the sense of Definition 2.5.

13.4 (Tensor Products ••) *Prove Proposition 13.6. Hint: represent the tensor product kernel as the product of two simpler kernels, and use Proposition 13.2.*

13.5 (Direct Sums •) *Prove Proposition 13.7.*

13.6 (Diagonal Projection ••) *If $k(x_1, x_2, x_1', x_2')$ is a kernel on $\mathfrak{X}^2 \times \mathfrak{X}^2$, then the diagonal projection is defined as (e.g., [234])*

$$k^{\Delta}(x, x') := k(x, x, x', x'). \tag{13.40}$$

Prove that if k_1 and k_2 are kernels on $\mathfrak{X} \times \mathfrak{X}$, we have $(k_1 \otimes k_2)^{\Delta} = k_1 k_2$ and $(k_1 \oplus k_2)^{\Delta} = k_1 + k_2$. Consider as a special case the ANOVA kernel (13.13), and compute its diagonal projections when $D = N$ and $D = 1$.

13.7 (Gaussian Kernels as R-Convolutions [234] •) *Consider (13.12) for $\mathfrak{X} = \mathfrak{X}_1 \times \ldots \times \mathfrak{X}_D$. In this case, each composite object x is simply a D-tuple consisting of the components $x_1, \ldots, x_D$. Show that $k_1 \star \ldots \star k_D(x, x') = \prod_{d=1}^{D} k_d(x_d, x_d')$. Next, specialize this result to the case where for $d = 1, \ldots, D$, $\mathfrak{X}_d = \mathbb{R}$, considering the one-dimensional Gaussian kernel $k_d(x_d, x_d') = \exp(-(x_d - x_d')^2 / c_d)$ with $c_d > 0$. Show that the convolution of $k_1, \ldots, k_D$ is a multi-dimensional Gaussian kernel (cf. Chapter 2).*

13.8 (ANOVA Kernels ••) *Prove that ANOVA kernels (13.13) are positive definite, either directly from the definition, or by showing that they are special cases of R-convolutions.*

13.9 (Kernels of Sets [234] •) *Let $\tilde{\mathfrak{X}}$ denote the set of all finite subsets of $\mathfrak{X}$. Prove that if k is a kernel on $\mathfrak{X} \times \mathfrak{X}$, then*

$$\tilde{k}(A, B) := \sum_{x \in A, x' \in B} k(x, x') \tag{13.41}$$

is a kernel on $\tilde{\mathfrak{X}} \times \tilde{\mathfrak{X}}$. Hint: consider the feature map $\tilde{\Phi}(A) := \sum_{x \in A} \Phi(x)$, where Φ is the feature map induced by k.

13.10 (Weighted Kernels of Sets ••) *Generalize the construction of the previous problem to allow for*

$$\tilde{\Phi}(A) = \sum_{x \in A} w(x) \Phi(x), \tag{13.42}$$

where w is some nonnegative function on $\mathfrak{X}$. Consider the case where w takes values in $\{0, 1\}$ only, and discuss the connection to the R-convolution kernel [234].

13.11 (Kernels on Groups ••) *Let G be a group, and $g, g' \in G$. Consider a kernel of the form $k(g, g') = h((g')^{-1} g)$ where the function $h : G \to \mathbb{C}$ is chosen such that k is positive definite [219]. Such functions are called* positive definite *(cf. also Definition 2.29).*

1. *Prove that h is* Hermitian, *that is, $h(g^{-1}) = \overline{h(g)}$*
2. *Prove that $|h(g)| \leq h(e)$, where e is the neutral element of the group*
3. *Prove that finite products of positive definite functions are again positive definite*

4. *Consider the special case where the group is* $(\mathbb{R}^N, +)$. *Construct a positive definite kernel on* $\mathbb{R}^N$ *via* $k(g, g') = h((g')^{-1}g)$, *where* h *is some positive definite function (e.g., one of the cpd functions of order 0 in Table 2.1).*

13.12 (The Kernel Map as a GNS Representation ••) *Let* $\mathcal{H}$ *be a complex Hilbert space. Using the notation of Problem 13.11, consider complex-valued functions of the form*

$$h(g) = \langle U(g)\mathbf{v}, \mathbf{v}\rangle, \tag{13.43}$$

where $\mathbf{v} \in \mathcal{H}$, *and* $U : G \to \mathfrak{L}(\mathcal{H})$ *is a unitary representation of* G. *Verify that* $k(g, g') := h((g')^{-1}g)$ *is a positive definite kernel on* $G \times G$. *Show that* $\Phi : g \mapsto U(g)\mathbf{v}$ *is a valid feature map for* k, *i.e., that* $k(g, g') = \langle \Phi(g), \Phi(g')\rangle$.

Next, consider the converse. Show that given any positive definite function h *on* G, *we can associate a complex Hilbert space* $\mathcal{H}_h$, *a unitary representation* U_h *of* G *in* $\mathcal{H}_h$, *and a (cyclic) unit vector* $\mathbf{v}_h$ *such that*

$$h(g) = \langle U_h(g)\mathbf{v}_h, \mathbf{v}_h\rangle \tag{13.44}$$

holds true. Proceed as follows: as the Hilbert space, use the RKHS associated with k; *as* $\mathbf{v}_h$, *use the function* $k(., e) = h(e^{-1}\cdot) = h(.)$ *(recall that* e *is* G*'s neutral element); finally, for* $f \in \mathcal{H}_h$, *define the representation* U_h *as*

$$(U_h(g)f)(g') := f(g^{-1}g'). \tag{13.45}$$

Using these definitions, verify (13.44).

This representation is called the Gelfand-Naimark-Segal (GNS) construction.

13.13 (Conditional Symmetric Independence Kernels [585] ••) *Consider the feature map*

$$\Phi(x) := \left[p(x|c_i)\sqrt{p(c_i)}\right]_{i=1,2,\ldots}, \tag{13.46}$$

where $p(x|c_i)$ *is the probability that some discrete random variable* X *takes the value* x, *conditional on* C *having taken the value* c_i. *Compute the kernel induced by this feature map, and interpret it as a probability distribution. What kind of distributions can be expressed in this way? A potentially rather useful class of such distributions arises from pair hidden Markov models [585].*

13.14 (String Kernel Recursion [585, 333] •••) *Prove that the recursion (13.20) allows the computation of (13.17).*

13.15 (Local String Kernels ∘∘∘) *Construct local string kernels by transferring the idea described in Section 13.3 to the kernels described in Section 13.2. How does this relate to the locality induced by the decay parameter* λ?

13.16 (String Kernels Penalizing Excess Length ••) *Note that the longer a matching sequence is, the less it contributes to the comparison, if* $\lambda < 1$. *Design a string kernel that does not suffer from this drawback, by choosing the* c_i *in (13.18) such that the overall kernel only penalizes 'excess' length.*

13.17 (Two-Dimensional Sequence Kernels ∘∘∘) *Can you generalize the ideas put forward for sequences in Section 13.2 to two-dimensional structures, such as images? Can you, for instance, construct a kernel that assesses the similarity of two images according to the number and contiguity of common sub-images?*

13.18 (Regularization for Composite Kernels ∘∘∘) *Denote by $\Phi : \mathcal{X} \to \mathcal{H}$ a feature map with known regularization operator Υ, i.e., there exists some Υ and a space with dot product $\langle \cdot, \cdot \rangle$ such that*

$$\langle \Upsilon k(x, \cdot), \Upsilon k(x', \cdot) \rangle = k(x, x').$$

Furthermore denote by $\Phi' : \mathcal{H} \to \mathcal{H}'$ a second feature map, also with known regularization operator Υ'.

Can you construct the composite regularization operator $\tilde{\Upsilon}$ corresponding to

$$\tilde{k}(x, x') := \langle \Phi'(\Phi(x)), \Phi'(\Phi(x')) \rangle$$

from this information?

As a special case, let Φ be the score map of Section 13.4.1, Φ' the map obtained by applying a Gaussian kernel to $\Phi(x), \Phi(x')$.

13.19 (Tracy-Widom Law for the Fisher Kernel Matrix ∘∘∘) *If the distribution in feature space is spherical and Gaussian, the Tracy-Widom law describes the average and standard deviation of the largest Eigenvalue in the Covariance matrix [544, 524, 270]. Noting that the distribution in the Fisher kernel feature space is spherical (but not necessarily Gaussian), study how accurately the Tracy-Widom law holds in this case.*

14 Kernel Feature Extraction

The idea of implicitly mapping the data into a high-dimensional feature space has been very fruitful in the context of SV machines. Indeed, as described in Chapter 1, it is this feature which distinguishes them from the Generalized Portrait algorithm, which has been around since the sixties [573, 570], and which makes SVMs applicable to complex real-world problems that are not linearly separable. Thus, it is natural to ask whether the same idea might prove useful in other domains of learning.

The present chapter describes a kernel-based method for performing a nonlinear form of Principal Component Analysis, called Kernel PCA. We show that through the use of positive definite kernels, we can efficiently compute principal components in high-dimensional feature spaces, which are related to input space by some nonlinear map. Furthermore, the chapter details how this method can be embedded in a general feature extraction framework, comprising classical algorithms such as projection pursuit, as well as sparse kernel feature analysis (KFA), a kernel algorithm for efficient feature extraction.

Overview

After a short introduction to classical PCA in Section 14.1, we describe how to transfer the algorithm to a feature space setting (Section 14.2). In Section 14.3, we describe experiments using Kernel PCA for feature extraction. Following this, we introduce a general framework for feature extraction (Section 14.4), for which Kernel PCA is a special case. Another special case, sparse KFA, is discussed in more detail in Section 14.5, with particular focus on efficient implementation. Section 14.6 presents toy experiments for sparse KFA.

Prerequisites

Most of the present chapter only requires knowledge of linear algebra, including matrix diagonalization, and some basics in statistics, such as the concept of variance. In addition, knowledge of positive definite kernels is required, as described in Chapter 1, and, in more detail, in Chapter 2. Section 14.5 requires slightly more background information, and builds on material explained in Chapters 4 and 6.

14.1 Introduction

Principal Component Analysis (PCA) is a powerful technique for extracting structure from possibly high-dimensional data sets. It is readily performed by solving an eigenvalue problem, or by using iterative algorithms which estimate princi-

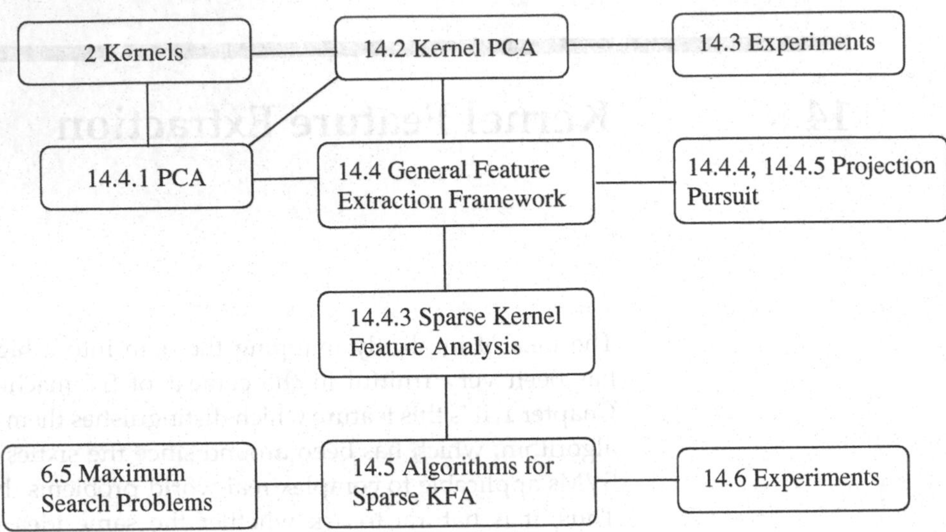

pal components. For reviews of the existing literature, see [271, 140]; some of the classical papers are [404, 248, 280]. PCA is an orthogonal transformation of the coordinate system in which we describe our data. The new coordinate system is obtained by projection onto the so-called *principal axes* of the data. The latter are called *principal components* or *features*. A small number of principal components is often sufficient to account for most of the structure in the data. These are sometimes called *factors* or *latent variables* of the data.

Let us begin by reviewing the standard PCA algorithm. In order to be able to generalize it to the nonlinear case, we formulate it in a way which uses dot products exclusively.

Covariance Matrix

Given a set of observations $x_i \in \mathbb{R}^N, i = 1, \ldots, m$, which are centered, $\sum_{i=1}^m x_i = 0$, PCA finds the principal axes by diagonalizing the covariance matrix[1],

$$C = \frac{1}{m} \sum_{j=1}^{m} x_j x_j^\top. \tag{14.1}$$

Note that C is positive definite, and can thus be diagonalized with nonnegative eigenvalues (Problem 14.1). To do this, we solve the eigenvalue equation,

$$\lambda v = Cv, \tag{14.2}$$

for eigenvalues $\lambda \geq 0$ and nonzero eigenvectors $v \in \mathbb{R}^N \setminus \{0\}$. Substituting (14.1)

1. More precisely, the covariance matrix is defined as the expectation of $xx^\top$; for convenience, we use the same term to refer to the estimate (14.1) of the covariance matrix from a finite sample.

into this expression,

$$\lambda v = Cv = \frac{1}{m}\sum_{j=1}^{m} \langle x_j, v\rangle\, x_j, \tag{14.3}$$

we see that all solutions v with $\lambda \neq 0$ lie in the span of $x_1 \ldots x_m$, hence for these solutions (14.2) is equivalent to

$$\lambda \langle x_i, v\rangle = \langle x_i, Cv\rangle \text{ for all } i = 1, \ldots, m. \tag{14.4}$$

14.2 Kernel PCA

We now study PCA in the case where we are not interested in principal components in input space, but rather principal components of variables, or features, which are nonlinearly related to the input variables. These include variables obtained by taking arbitrary higher-order correlations between input variables, for instance. In the case of image analysis, this amounts to finding principal components in the space of products of pixels.

As described in Chapter 2, the kernel trick enables us to construct different nonlinear versions of any algorithm which can be expressed solely in terms of dot products (thus, without explicit usage of the variables themselves).

14.2.1 Nonlinear PCA as an Eigenvalue Problem

Let us consider a feature space $\mathcal{H}$ (Chapter 2), related to the input domain (for instance, $\mathbb{R}^N$) by a map

$$\Phi : \mathcal{X} \rightarrow \mathcal{H}, \quad x \mapsto \Phi(x), \tag{14.5}$$

Feature Space

which is possibly nonlinear. The feature space $\mathcal{H}$ could have an arbitrarily large, and possibly infinite, dimension. Again, we assume that we are dealing with centered data, $\sum_{i=1}^{m} \Phi(x_i) = 0$ — we shall return to this point later. In $\mathcal{H}$, the covariance matrix takes the form

$$\mathbf{C} = \frac{1}{m}\sum_{j=1}^{m} \Phi(x_j)\Phi(x_j)^\top. \tag{14.6}$$

If $\mathcal{H}$ is infinite-dimensional, we think of $\Phi(x_j)\Phi(x_j)^\top$ as a linear operator on $\mathcal{H}$, mapping $\mathbf{x} \mapsto \Phi(x_j)\langle\Phi(x_j), \mathbf{x}\rangle$.

Eigenvalue Problem in $\mathcal{H}$

We now have to find eigenvalues $\lambda \geq 0$ and nonzero eigenvectors $\mathbf{v} \in \mathcal{H} \setminus \{0\}$ satisfying

$$\lambda \mathbf{v} = \mathbf{C}\mathbf{v}. \tag{14.7}$$

Again, all solutions $\mathbf{v}$ with $\lambda \neq 0$ lie in the span of $\Phi(x_1), \ldots, \Phi(x_m)$. For us, this has two useful consequences: first, we may instead consider the set of equations

$$\lambda \langle \Phi(x_n), \mathbf{v} \rangle = \langle \Phi(x_n), \mathbf{C}\mathbf{v} \rangle \text{ for all } n = 1, \ldots, m, \tag{14.8}$$

Dual Eigenvector Representation

and second, there exist coefficients α_i $(i = 1, \ldots, m)$ such that

$$\mathbf{v} = \sum_{i=1}^{m} \alpha_i \Phi(x_i). \tag{14.9}$$

Combining (14.8) and (14.9), we get

$$\lambda \sum_{i=1}^{m} \alpha_i \langle \Phi(x_n), \Phi(x_i) \rangle = \frac{1}{m} \sum_{i=1}^{m} \alpha_i \left\langle \Phi(x_n), \sum_{j=1}^{m} \Phi(x_j) \langle \Phi(x_j), \Phi(x_i) \rangle \right\rangle \tag{14.10}$$

Gram Matrix

for all $n = 1, \ldots, m$. In terms of the $m \times m$ Gram matrix $K_{ij} := \langle \Phi(x_i), \Phi(x_j) \rangle$, this reads

$$m\lambda K\boldsymbol{\alpha} = K^2\boldsymbol{\alpha}, \tag{14.11}$$

where $\boldsymbol{\alpha}$ denotes the column vector with entries $\alpha_1, \ldots, \alpha_m$. To find solutions of (14.11), we solve the dual eigenvalue problem,

Eigenvalue Problem for the Expansion Coefficients

$$m\lambda\boldsymbol{\alpha} = K\boldsymbol{\alpha}, \tag{14.12}$$

for nonzero eigenvalues. It can be shown that this yields all solutions of (14.11) that are of interest for us (Problem 14.14).

Eigenvalues

Let $\lambda_1 \geq \lambda_2 \geq \ldots \geq \lambda_m$ denote the eigenvalues of K (in other words, the solutions $m\lambda$ of (14.12)), and $\boldsymbol{\alpha}^1, \ldots, \boldsymbol{\alpha}^m$ the corresponding complete set of eigenvectors, with λ_p being the last nonzero eigenvalue (assuming that Φ is not identically 0). We normalize $\boldsymbol{\alpha}^1, \ldots, \boldsymbol{\alpha}^p$ by requiring that the corresponding vectors in $\mathcal{H}$ (see (14.9)) be normalized,

$$\langle \mathbf{v}^n, \mathbf{v}^n \rangle = 1 \text{ for all } n = 1, \ldots, p. \tag{14.13}$$

By virtue of (14.9) and (14.12), this translates to a normalization condition for $\boldsymbol{\alpha}^1, \ldots, \boldsymbol{\alpha}^p$,

Normalization in $\mathcal{H}$

$$\begin{aligned} 1 &= \sum_{i,j=1}^{m} \alpha_i^n \alpha_j^n \langle \Phi(x_i), \Phi(x_j) \rangle = \sum_{i,j=1}^{m} \alpha_i^n \alpha_j^n K_{ij} \\ &= \langle \boldsymbol{\alpha}^n, K\boldsymbol{\alpha}^n \rangle = \lambda_n \langle \boldsymbol{\alpha}^n, \boldsymbol{\alpha}^n \rangle. \end{aligned} \tag{14.14}$$

For the purpose of principal component extraction, we need to compute projections onto the eigenvectors $\mathbf{v}^n$ in $\mathcal{H}$ $(n = 1, \ldots, p)$. Let x be a test point, with an image $\Phi(x)$ in $\mathcal{H}$. Then

$$\langle \mathbf{v}^n, \Phi(x) \rangle = \sum_{i=1}^{m} \alpha_i^n \langle \Phi(x_i), \Phi(x) \rangle \tag{14.15}$$

are the nonlinear principal components (or features) corresponding to Φ.[2]

Summary of the Algorithm

Let us summarize the algorithm. To perform kernel-based PCA (Figure 14.1), henceforth referred to as *Kernel PCA*, the following steps are carried out. First, we compute the Gram matrix $K_{ij} = k(x_i, x_j)_{ij}$. Next, we diagonalize K, and normalize the eigenvector expansion coefficients α^n by requiring $\lambda_n \langle \alpha^n, \alpha^n \rangle = 1$. Finally, to extract the principal components (corresponding to the kernel k) of a test point x, we then compute projections onto the eigenvectors by

Feature Extraction

$$\langle \mathbf{v}^n, \Phi(x) \rangle = \sum_{i=1}^{m} \alpha_i^n k(x_i, x), \quad n = 1, \ldots, p; \tag{14.16}$$

see (14.15) and Figure 14.2.

For the sake of simplicity, we have so far made the assumption that the observations are centered. This is easy to achieve in input space, but more difficult in $\mathcal{H}$, as we cannot explicitly compute the mean of the mapped observations in $\mathcal{H}$. There is a way to do it, however, and this leads to slightly modified equations for kernel PCA. It turns out (Problem 14.5) that we then need to diagonalize

Centering

$$\tilde{K}_{ij} = (K - 1_m K - K 1_m + 1_m K 1_m)_{ij}, \tag{14.17}$$

using the notation $(1_m)_{ij} := 1/m$ for all i, j.

Kernel PCA based on the centered matrix $\tilde{K}$ can also be performed with the larger class of conditionally positive definite matrices. This is due to the fact that when we center the data, we make the problem translation invariant (cf. Proposition 2.26).

14.2.2 Properties of Kernel PCA

We know that Kernel PCA corresponds to standard PCA in some high-dimensional feature space. Consequently, all mathematical and statistical properties of PCA (cf. [271, 140]) carry over to Kernel PCA, with the modification that they become statements about a set of points $\Phi(x_i), i = 1, \ldots, m$, in $\mathcal{H}$, rather than in $\mathbb{R}^N$.

Proposition 14.1 (Optimality Properties of Kernel PCA) *Kernel PCA is the orthogonal basis transformation in $\mathcal{H}$ with the following properties (assuming that the eigenvectors are sorted in descending order of eigenvalue size):*

- *The first q ($q \in \{1, \ldots, m\}$) principal components, or projections on eigenvectors, carry more variance than any other q orthogonal directions*
- *The mean-squared approximation error in representing the observations in $\mathcal{H}$ by the first q principal components is minimal (over all possible q directions)*

2. Note that in our derivation, we could have used the known result (e.g., [297]) that PCA can be carried out on the dot product matrix $\langle x_i, x_j \rangle_{ij}$ instead of (14.1). For the sake of clarity and ease of extendability (regarding centering the data in $\mathcal{H}$), however, we gave a detailed derivation.

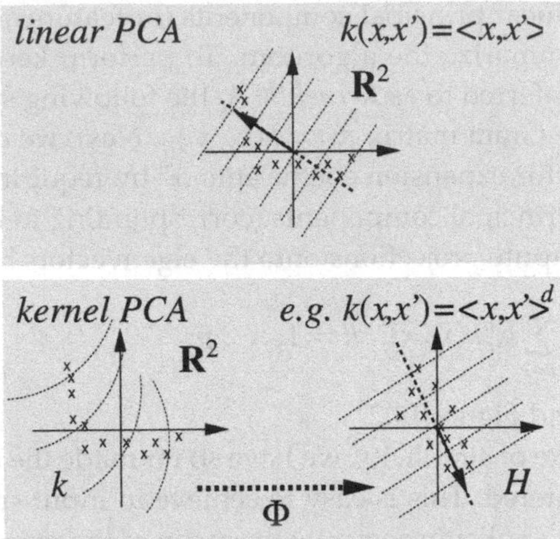

Figure 14.1 The basic idea of Kernel PCA. In some high-dimensional feature space $\mathcal{H}$ (bottom right), we perform linear PCA, as with classical PCA in input space (top). Since $\mathcal{H}$ is nonlinearly related to input space (via Φ), the contour lines of constant projections onto the principal eigenvector (drawn as an arrow) are *nonlinear* in input space. We cannot draw a pre-image of the eigenvector in input space, as it may not even exist. Crucial to Kernel PCA is the fact that there is no need to perform the map into $\mathcal{H}$: all necessary computations are carried out using a kernel function k in input space (here: $\mathbb{R}^2$).

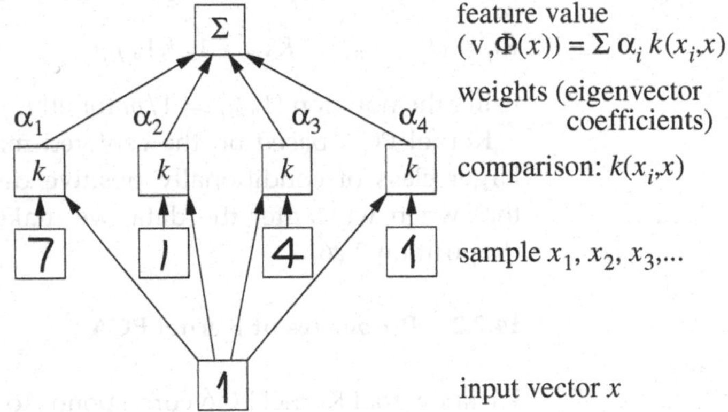

Figure 14.2 Feature extractor constructed using Kernel PCA (cf. (14.16)). In the first layer, the input vector is compared to the sample via a kernel function, chosen a priori (e.g. polynomial, Gaussian, or sigmoid). The outputs are then linearly combined using weights, which are found by solving an eigenvector problem. As shown in the text, the function of the network can be thought of as the projection onto an eigenvector of a covariance matrix in a high-dimensional feature space. As a function on input space, it is nonlinear.

- *The principal components are uncorrelated*
- *The first q principal components have maximal mutual information (see [140, 132]) with respect to the inputs (this holds under Gaussianity assumptions in $\mathcal{H}$, and thus strongly depends on the particular kernel chosen and on the data)*

Proof All these statements are completely analogous to the case of standard PCA. As an example, we prove the second property, in the simple case where the data $\mathbf{x}_1, \ldots, \mathbf{x}_m$ in feature space are centered. We consider an orthogonal basis transformation W, and use the notation P_q for the projector on the first q canonical basis vectors $\{\mathbf{e}_1, \ldots, \mathbf{e}_q\}$. Then the mean squared reconstruction error using q

vectors is

$$\frac{1}{m}\sum_i \|\mathbf{x}_i - W^\top P_q W\mathbf{x}_i\|^2 = \frac{1}{m}\sum_i \|W\mathbf{x}_i - P_q W\mathbf{x}_i\|^2$$
$$= \frac{1}{m}\sum_i \sum_{j>q} \langle W\mathbf{x}_i, \mathbf{e}_j\rangle^2$$
$$= \frac{1}{m}\sum_i \sum_{j>q} \left\langle \mathbf{x}_i, W^\top \mathbf{e}_j\right\rangle^2$$
$$= \frac{1}{m}\sum_i \sum_{j>q} \left\langle W^\top \mathbf{e}_j, \mathbf{x}_i\right\rangle \left\langle \mathbf{x}_i, W^\top \mathbf{e}_j\right\rangle$$
$$= \sum_{j>q} \left\langle W^\top \mathbf{e}_j, CW^\top \mathbf{e}_j\right\rangle. \tag{14.18}$$

It can easily be seen that the values of this quadratic form (which gives the variances in the directions $W^\top \mathbf{e}_j$) are minimal if the $W^\top \mathbf{e}_j$ are chosen as its (orthogonal) eigenvectors with smallest eigenvalues. ■

To translate these properties of PCA in $\mathcal{H}$ into statements about the data in input space, we must consider specific choices of kernel. One such input space characteristic is the invariance property of kernels depending only on $\langle x, x'\rangle$ (cf. Section 2.3).

Can we guarantee that this algorithm works well, particularly in high-dimensional spaces (cf. Problem 14.9)? It is possible to draw some simple analogies to the standard SV reasoning. The feature extractors (14.16) are linear functions in the feature space $\mathcal{H}$, with regularization properties characterized by the length of their weight vector $\mathbf{v}$, as in the SV case. When applied to the training data, the nth feature extractor generates a set of outputs with variance λ_n. Dividing each coefficient vector $\boldsymbol{\alpha}^n$ by $\sqrt{\lambda_n}$, we obtain a set of nonlinear feature extractors with unit variance output, and the following interesting property:

Connection to SVMs

Proposition 14.2 (Connection KPCA — SVM [480]) *For all $n \in \{1, \ldots, p\}$, the nth Kernel PCA feature extractor, scaled by $1/\lambda_n$, is optimal among all feature extractors of the form $f(\mathbf{x}) = \sum_i \alpha_i k(\mathbf{x}_i, \mathbf{x})$ (cf. (14.16)), in the sense that it has minimal weight vector norm in the RKHS $\mathcal{H}$,*

$$\|\mathbf{v}\|^2 = \sum_{i,j=1}^{m} \alpha_i \alpha_j k(\mathbf{x}_i, \mathbf{x}_j), \tag{14.19}$$

subject to the conditions that
(1) it is orthogonal to the first $n-1$ Kernel PCA feature extractors (in feature space), and
(2) it leads to a unit variance set of outputs when applied to the training set $\mathbf{x}_1, \ldots, \mathbf{x}_m$.

Therefore, Kernel PCA can be considered a method for extracting potentially interesting functions that have low capacity. Here, "interestingness" is ensured by the unit variance, and capacity is measured by the length of the weight vector. As discussed in Section 16.3, this capacity measure is identical to that used in Gaussian processes, hence it could be interpreted as a Bayesian prior on the space of functions by setting $p(f) \propto \exp(-\frac{1}{2}\|\Upsilon f\|^2)$, where Υ is the regularization operator corresponding to k (see Theorem 4.9 for details). From this perspective, the first extractor (cf. (14.16)) $f(x) = \sum_{i=1}^{m} \alpha_i k(x_i, x)$ is given by

$$f = \underset{\mathrm{Var}(f)=1}{\operatorname{argmax}} \exp\left(-\frac{1}{2}\|\Upsilon f\|^2\right), \tag{14.20}$$

where $\mathrm{Var}(f)$ denotes the (estimate of the) variance of $f(x)$ for x drawn from the underlying distribution. We return to this topic in Section 14.4, where we use Proposition 14.2 as the basis of a general feature extraction framework.

Number of Features

Unlike linear PCA, the method proposed allows the extraction of a number of principal components which *can* exceed the input dimensionality. Suppose that the number of observations m exceeds the input dimensionality N. Linear PCA, even when it is based on the $m \times m$ dot product matrix, can find at most N nonzero eigenvalues — the latter are identical to the nonzero eigenvalues of the $N \times N$ covariance matrix. By contrast, Kernel PCA can find up to m nonzero eigenvalues — a fact that illustrates that it is impossible to perform kernel PCA directly on an $N \times N$ covariance matrix.

Reconstruction from Principal Components

Being just a basis transformation, standard PCA allows the reconstruction of the original patterns $x_i, i = 1, \ldots, m$, from a complete set of extracted principal components $\langle \mathbf{x}_i, \mathbf{v}_j \rangle, j = 1, \ldots, m$, by expansion in the eigenvector basis. Even using an incomplete set of components, good reconstruction is often possible. In Kernel PCA, this is more difficult: we can reconstruct the image of a pattern in $\mathcal{H}$ from its nonlinear components; if we only have an approximate reconstruction, however, there is no guarantee that we can find an exact *pre*-image of the reconstruction in input space. In this case, we have to resort to approximations (cf. Chapter 18).

14.2.3 Comparison to Other Methods

Starting from some of the properties characterizing PCA, it is possible to develop a number of generalizations of linear PCA to the nonlinear case. Alternatively, we may choose an iterative algorithm which adaptively estimates principal components, and make some of its parts nonlinear to extract nonlinear features. Rather than giving a full review of this field here, we briefly describe four approaches, and refer the reader to [140] for more detail.

Hebbian Networks

Beginning with the pioneering work of Oja [387], a number of unsupervised neural-network type algorithms to compute principal components have been proposed (for instance, [457]). Compared with the standard approach of diagonalizing the covariance matrix, they have advantages in cases where the data are nonstationary. Nonlinear variants of these algorithms are obtained using nonlinear neurons. The algorithms then extract features, referred to by the authors as nonlinear principal components. These approaches, however, do not have the geometrical interpretation of Kernel PCA as being standard PCA in a feature space nonlinearly related to input space, and it is thus more difficult to understand what exactly they are extracting. For a discussion of some approaches, see [279].

Next, consider a linear perceptron with one hidden layer, which is smaller than the input (that is, the dimension of the data). If we train it to reproduce the input values as outputs (in other words, we use it in autoassociative mode), then the hidden unit activations form a lower-dimensional representation of the data, closely related to PCA (see for instance [140]). To generalize to a nonlinear setting, we use nonlinear neurons and additional layers.[3] While this can of course be considered a form of nonlinear PCA, it should be stressed that the resulting network training consists of solving a hard nonlinear optimization problem, with the possibility of getting trapped in local minima. Additionally, neural network implementations often pose a risk of overfitting. Another drawback of neural approaches to nonlinear PCA is that the number of components to be extracted has to be specified in advance. As an aside, note that hyperbolic tangent kernels can be used to extract neural network type nonlinear features using Kernel PCA (Figure 14.6). As in Figure 14.2, the principal components of a test point x in this case take the form $\sum_i \alpha_i^n \tanh(\kappa(x_i, x) + \Theta)$.

Autoassociative Multi-Layer Perceptrons

An approach with a clear geometric interpretation in input space is the method of principal curves [231], which iteratively estimates a curve (or surface) that captures the structure of the data. The data are projected onto a curve, determined by the algorithm, with the property that each point on the curve is the average of all data points projecting onto it. It can be shown that the only straight lines with the latter property are principal components, so principal curves are indeed a generalization of standard PCA. To compute principal curves, a nonlinear optimization problem must be solved. The dimensionality of the surface, and thus the number of features to extract, is specified in advance. Some authors [434] discuss parallels between the Principal Curve algorithm and self-organizing feature maps [302] for dimensionality reduction. For further information, and a kernel-based variant of the principal curves algorithm, cf. Chapter 17.

Principal Curves

Kernel PCA is a nonlinear generalization of PCA in the sense that (a) it performs PCA in feature spaces of arbitrarily large (possibly infinite) dimensionality, and (b) if we use the kernel $k(x, x') = \langle x, x' \rangle$, we recover the original PCA algorithm. Compared with the above approaches, the main advantage of Kernel PCA is that no nonlinear optimization is involved — it is essentially linear algebra, as with standard PCA. In addition, we need not specify the number of components that we want to extract in advance. Compared with principal curves, Kernel PCA is harder to interpret in input space; however, for polynomial kernels at least, it has a very clear interpretation in terms of higher-order features. Compared with neural approaches, Kernel PCA can be disadvantageous if we need to process a very large number of observations, as this results in a large matrix K. It is possible, however, to use sparse greedy methods to perform Kernel PCA approximately (Section 10.2).

Kernel PCA

3. Simply using nonlinear activation functions in the hidden layer does not suffice: the linear activation functions already lead to the best approximation of the data (given the number of hidden nodes), so for the nonlinearities to have an effect on the components, the architecture needs to be changed (see [140]).

All these techniques provide nonlinear feature extractors defined on the whole input space. In other words, they can be evaluated on patterns regardless of whether these are elements of the training set or not. Some other methods, such as the *LLE* algorithm [445] and *multidimensional scaling (MDS)* [116], are *restricted* to the training data. They aim to only provide a lower-dimensional representation of the training data, which is useful for instance for data visualization.

MDS

Williams [598] recently pointed out that when considering the special case where we only extract features from the training data, Kernel PCA is actually closely connected to MDS. In a nutshell, MDS is a method for embedding data into $\mathbb{R}^q$, based on pairwise dissimilarities. Consider a situation where the dissimilarities are actually Euclidean distances in $\mathbb{R}^N$ $(N > q)$. In the simplest variant of MDS ("classical scaling"), we attempt to embed the training data into $\mathbb{R}^q$ such that the squared distances $\Delta_{ij}^2 := \|x_i - x_j\|^2$ between all pairs of points are (on average) preserved as well as possible. It can be shown from Proposition 14.1 that this is readily achieved by projecting onto the first q principal components.

In *metric MDS*, the dissimilarities Δ_{ij} are transformed by a (nonlinear) function ϕ before the embedding is computed. In this case, the computation of the embedding involves the minimization of a nonlinear "stress" function, which consists of the sum over all mismatches. Usually, this stress function is minimized using nonlinear optimization methods. This can be avoided for a large class of nonlinearities ϕ, however. Williams [598] showed that the metric MDS solution is a by-product of performing kernel PCA with RBF kernels, $k(x_i, x_j) = \phi(\|x_i - x_j\|) = \phi(\Delta_{ij})$.[4] In this case, we thus get away with solving an eigenvalue problem.

Locally Linear Embedding

The second of the aforementioned dimensionality reduction algorithms, LLE, can also be related to kernel PCA. One can show that one obtains the solution of LLE by performing kernel PCA on the Gram matrix computed from what we might call the *locally linear embedding kernel*. This kernel assesses similarity of two patterns based on the similarity of the coefficients required to represent the two patterns in terms of neighboring patterns. For details, see Problem 14.16.

Orthogonal Series Density Estimation

We conclude this section by noting that it has recently been pointed out that one can also connect kernel PCA to *orthogonal series density estimation* [200]. The kernel PCA eigenvalue decomposition provides the coefficients for a truncated density estimator expansion taking the form $p_q(x) = \sum_{n=1}^{q} \lambda_n \left(\frac{1}{m} \sum_{i=1}^{m} \alpha_i^n \langle \mathbf{v}^n, \Phi(x)\rangle\right)$, where q is the number of components taken into account, and α_i^n and $\mathbf{v}$ are defined (and

4. One way of performing metric MDS is to first apply ϕ, and then run classical MDS on the resulting dissimilarity matrix. An interesting class of nonlinearities is the power transformation $\phi(\Delta_{ij}) = \Delta_{ij}^{\mu}$, where $\mu > 0$ ([127], cited after [598]). Provided the original dissimilarities Δ_{ij} arise from Euclidean distances, the power transformation generally leads to a conditionally positive definite matrix $(-\frac{1}{2}\phi(\Delta_{ij})^2)_{ij}$ if and only if $\mu \leq 1$ (cf. (2.81)). The *centered* version of this matrix, which is used in MDS, is thus positive definite if and only if $\mu \leq 1$ (cf. Proposition 2.26). Therefore, it is exactly in these cases that we can run classical MDS after applying ϕ without running into problems. This answers a problem posed by [127], for the case of Euclidean dissimilarities.

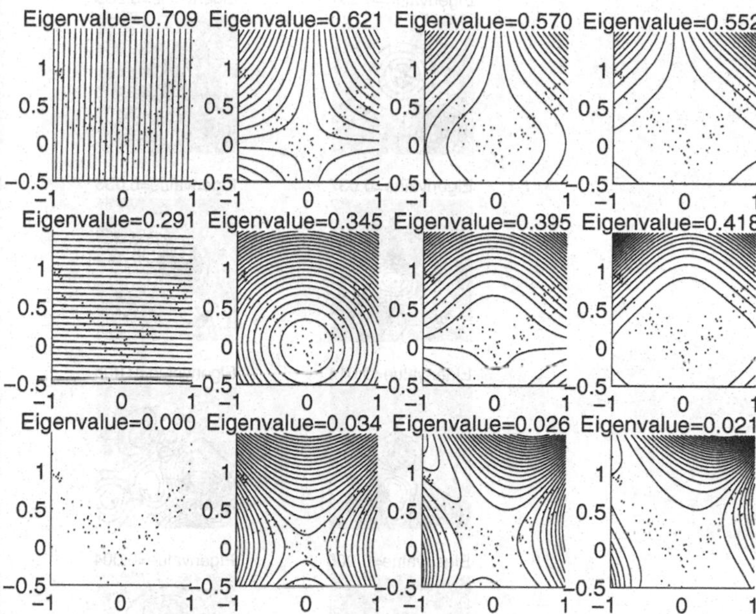

Figure 14.3 Two-dimensional toy example, with data generated as follows: x-values have uniform distribution in $[-1, 1]$, y-values are generated from $y_i = x_i^2 + v$, where v is normal noise with standard deviation 0.2. From left to right, the polynomial degree in the kernel (14.21) increases from 1 to 4; from top to bottom, the first 3 eigenvectors are shown, in order of decreasing eigenvalue size (eigenvalues are normalized to sum to 1). The figures contain lines of constant principal component value (contour lines); in the linear case ($d = 1$), these are orthogonal to the eigenvectors. We did not draw the eigenvectors, as in the general case, they belong to a higher-dimensional feature space. Note, finally, that for $d = 1$, there are only 2 nonzero eigenvectors, this number being equal to the dimension of the input space.

normalized) as in Section 14.2.1. This work builds on the connection between the eigenfunctions of the integral operator T_k associated with the kernel k and the eigenvectors of the Gram matrix (see Problem 2.26).

14.3 Kernel PCA Experiments

In this section, we present a set of experiments in which Kernel PCA is used (in the form taking into account centering in $\mathcal{H}$) to extract principal components. First, we take a look at a simple toy example; following this, we describe real-world experiments where we assess the utility of the extracted principal components in classification tasks.

Toy Examples

To provide insight into how PCA in $\mathcal{H}$ behaves in input space, we describe a set of experiments with an artificial 2-D data set, using polynomial kernels,

$$k(x, x') = \langle x, x' \rangle^d, \tag{14.21}$$

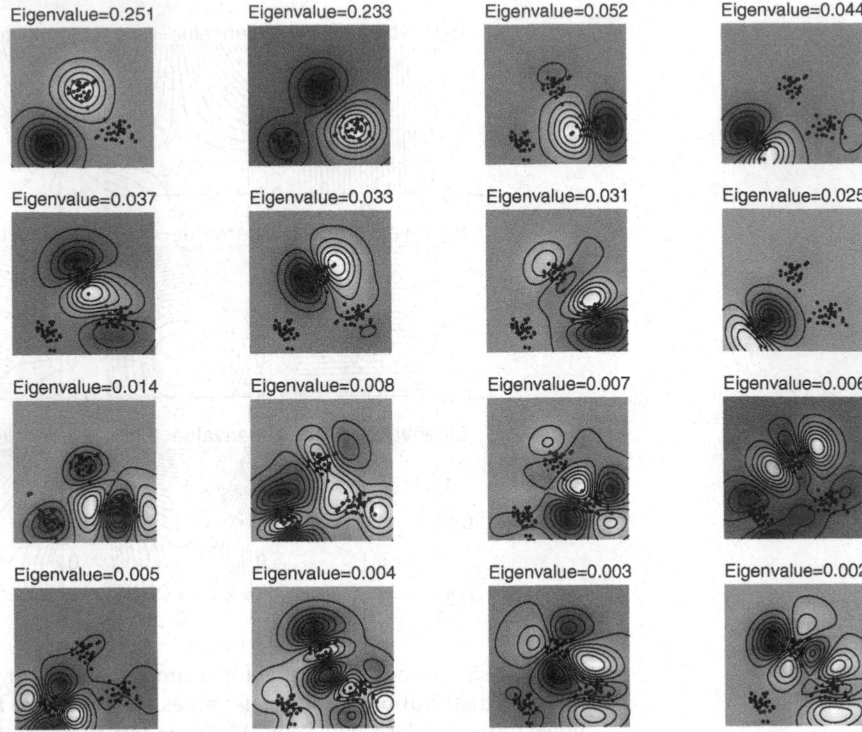

Figure 14.4 Two-dimensional toy example with three data clusters (Gaussians with standard deviation 0.1; depicted region, $[-1,1] \times [-0.5,1]$): first 16 nonlinear principal components extracted with $k(x,x') = \exp\left(-\|x-x'\|^2/0.1\right)$. Note that the first 2 principal component (top left), which possess the largest eigenvalues, nicely separate the three clusters. The components 3–5 split the clusters into halves. Similarly, components 6–8 split them again, in a manner orthogonal to the above splits. The higher components are more difficult to describe. They look for finer structure in the data set, identifying higher-order moments.

of degree $d = 1,\ldots,4$ (see Figure 14.3). Linear PCA (on the left) leads to just 2 nonzero eigenvalues, as the input dimensionality is 2. By contrast, nonlinear PCA allows the extraction of further components. In the figure, note that nonlinear PCA produces contour lines of constant feature value, which reflect the structure in the data better than in linear PCA. In all cases, the first principal component varies monotonically along the parabola that underlies the data. In the nonlinear cases, the second and the third components also show behavior which is similar across different polynomial degrees. The third component, which comes with small eigenvalues (rescaled to sum to 1), seems to pick up the variance caused by the noise, as can be seen in the case of degree 2. Dropping this component would thus amount to noise reduction.

Further toy examples, using radial basis function kernels (2.68) and neural network type sigmoid kernels (2.69), are shown in Figures 14.4–14.6.

In Figure 14.7, we illustrate the fact that Kernel PCA can also be carried out

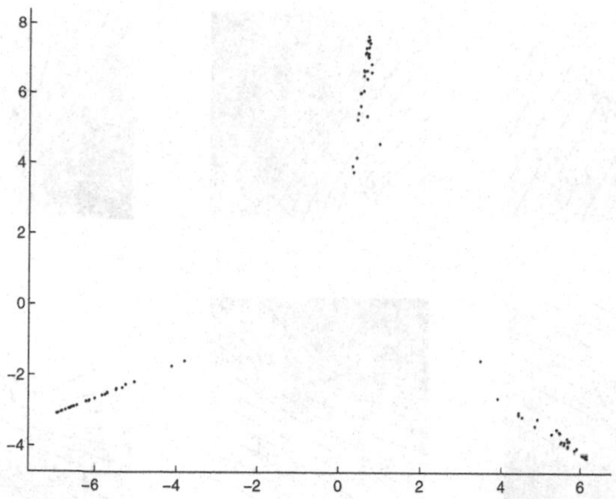

Figure 14.5 A plot of the data representation given by the first two principal components of Figure 14.4. The clusters of Figure 14.4 end up roughly on separate lines (the left, right, and top regions correspond to the clusters left, top, and right, respectively). Note that the first component (the horizontal axis) already separates the clusters — this cannot be done using linear PCA.

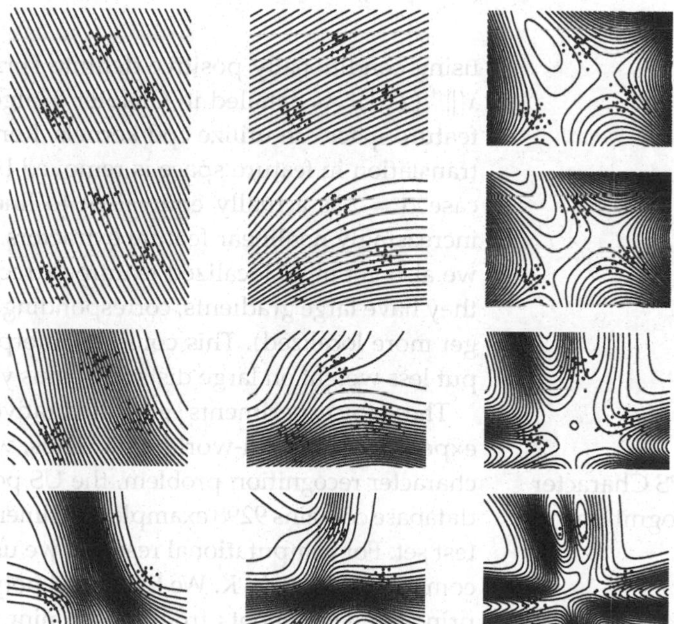

Figure 14.6 A smooth transition from linear PCA to nonlinear PCA is obtained using hyperbolic tangent kernels $k(x, x') = \tanh(\kappa \langle x, x' \rangle + 1)$ with varying gain κ: from top to bottom, $\kappa = 0.1, 1, 5, 10$ (data as in the previous figures). For $\kappa = 0.1$, the first two features look like linear PCA features. For large κ, the nonlinear region of the tanh function comes into play. In this case, kernel PCA can exploit the nonlinearity to allocate the highest feature gradients to regions where there are data points, as can be seen in the case $\kappa = 10$.

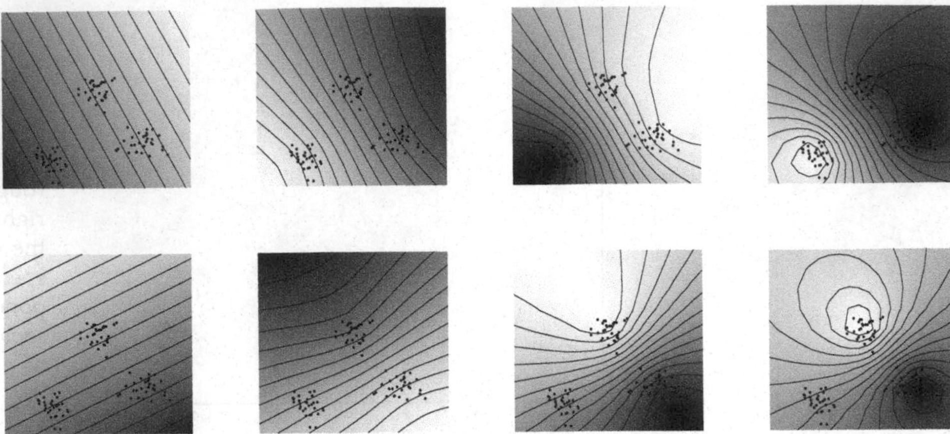

Figure 14.7 Kernel PCA on a toy dataset using the cpd kernel (2.81); contour plots of the feature extractors corresponding to projections onto the first two principal axes in feature space. From left to right: $\beta = 2, 1.5, 1, 0.5$. Notice how smaller values of β make the feature extractors increasingly nonlinear, which allows the identification of the cluster structure (from [468]).

using conditionally positive definite kernels. We use the kernel $k(x, x') = -\|x - x'\|^{\beta}$ (2.81). As detailed in Chapter 2, algorithms that are translation-invariant in feature space can utilize cpd kernels. Kernel PCA is such an algorithm, since any translation in feature space is removed by the centering operation. Note that the case $\beta = 2$ is actually equivalent to linear PCA. As we decrease β, we obtain increasingly nonlinear feature extractors. As the kernel parameter β gets smaller, we also get more localized feature extractors (in the sense that the regions where they have large gradients, corresponding to dense sets of contour lines in the plot, get more localized). This could be interpreted as saying that smaller values of β put less weight on large distances, thus yielding more robust distance measures.

USPS Character Recognition

These toy experiments serve illustrative purposes, but they are no substitute for experiments on real-world data. Thus, we next report a study on a handwritten character recognition problem, the US postal service database (Section A.1). This database contains 9298 examples of dimensionality 256, of which 2007 make up the test set. For computational reasons, we used a subset of 3000 training examples to compute the matrix K. We then used polynomial Kernel PCA to extract nonlinear principal components from the training and test set. To assess the utility of the components (or features), we trained a soft margin hyperplane classifier on the classification task.

Table 14.1 illustrates two advantages of using nonlinear kernels: first, performance of a linear classifier trained on nonlinear principal components is better than for the same number of linear components; second, the performance for nonlinear components can be further improved by using more components than possible in the linear case. The latter is related to the fact that there are many more higher-order features than there are pixels in an image. Regarding the first point,

Table 14.1 Test error rates on the USPS handwritten digit database, for linear Support Vector Machines trained on nonlinear principal components extracted by PCA with kernel (14.21), for degrees 1 through 7. The case of degree 1 corresponds to standard PCA, with the number of nonzero eigenvalues being at most the dimensionality of the space (256). Clearly, nonlinear principal components afford test error rates which are lower than in the linear case (degree 1).

	Test Error Rate for degree						
# of components	1	2	3	4	5	6	7
32	9.6	8.8	8.1	8.5	9.1	9.3	10.8
64	8.8	7.3	6.8	6.7	6.7	7.2	7.5
128	8.6	5.8	5.9	6.1	5.8	6.0	6.8
256	8.7	5.5	5.3	5.2	5.2	5.4	5.4
512	n.a.	4.9	4.6	4.4	5.1	4.6	4.9
1024	n.a.	4.9	4.3	4.4	4.6	4.8	4.6
2048	n.a.	4.9	4.2	4.1	4.0	4.3	4.4

note that extracting a certain number of features in a 10^{10}-dimensional space constitutes a much greater reduction of dimensionality than extracting the same number of features in 256-dimensional input space.

For all numbers of features, the optimal kernel degree to use is around 4, which is consistent with Support Vector Machine results on the same data set. Additionally, with only one exception, the nonlinear features are superior to their linear counterparts. The resulting error rate for the best of our classifiers (4.0%) is much better than that obtained using linear classifiers operating directly on the image data (a linear Support Vector Machine achieves 8.9%; [470]); performance is identical to that of nonlinear Support Vector classifiers [470]. This makes sense — recall from Section 2.2.6 that using *all* principal components is equivalent to running a nonlinear SVM with the same kernel. After all, if we consider *all* eigenvectors, Kernel PCA is just an orthogonal basis transformation, leaving the dot product invariant (cf. Section B.2). For a comprehensive list of results obtained on the USPS set, cf. Chapter 7. Note that the present results were obtained without using any prior knowledge about invariances of the problem at hand, which is why the performance is inferior to Virtual Support Vector classifiers (3.2%, Chapter 11). Adding local translation invariance, be it by generating "virtual" translated examples or by choosing a suitable kernel incorporating locality (such as those in Section 13.3, which led to an error rate of 3.0%), could further improve the results.

Similarly good results have been obtained for other visual processing tasks, such as object recognition [467] and texture classification [294]. Kernel PCA has also been successfully applied to other problems, such as processing of biological event-related potentials [440], nonlinear regression [441], and document retrieval [126], as well as face detection and pose estimation [328, 436]. Yet another application, in image denoising, is described later (Chapter 18). One of the more surprising applications, with impressive success, is model selection [101].

14.4 A Framework for Feature Extraction

Whilst it is encouraging that Kernel PCA leads to very good results, there are nevertheless some issues that need to be addressed. First, the computational complexity of the standard version of Kernel PCA, as described above, scales as $O(m^3)$ in the sample size m. Second, the resulting feature extractors are given as dense expansions in terms of the training patterns. Thus, for each test point, the feature extraction requires m kernel evaluations. Both issues can be dealt with using approximations. As mentioned above, Kernel PCA can be approximated in a sparse greedy way (Section 10.2); moreover, the feature extractors can be approximated in a sparse way using reduced set techniques, such as those described in Chapter 18. Alternatively, Tipping recently suggested a way of sparsifying Kernel PCA [540].

There is a second way of approaching the problem, however. Rather than sticking to the original algorithm, and trying to approximate its solution, we instead modify the algorithm to make it more efficient, and so that it automatically produces sparse feature extractors. In order to design the modified algorithm, called sparse kernel feature analysis (KFA), it is useful to first describe a general feature extraction framework, which will contain Kernel PCA and sparse KFA as special cases.

To this end, denote by $X := \{x_1, \ldots x_m\} \subset \mathcal{X}$ our set of patterns drawn independently and identically distributed from an underlying probability distribution $P(x)$. Our goal is to compute feature extractors that satisfy certain criteria of simplicity (such as small RKHS norm [578, 512] or ℓ_1 norm [343, 104, 37, 502, 72, 347]) and optimality (maximum variance [248, 280], for instance).

14.4.1 Principal Component Analysis

Let us start with PCA, assuming that $\mathcal{X} \subset \mathbb{R}^N$. The first principal component of a sample is given by the direction of projection with maximum variance. For centered data,

$$\tilde{X} := \left\{ \tilde{x}_i \,\middle|\, \tilde{x}_i = x_i - \frac{1}{m}\sum_{i=1}^{m} x_i,\ i = 1, \ldots, m \right\}, \tag{14.22}$$

Maximum Variance Under Constraints

the first eigenvector v^1 can be obtained as

$$v^1 = \underset{\|v\|^2 \leq 1}{\operatorname{argmax}} \frac{1}{m} \sum_{i=1}^{m} |\langle v, \tilde{x}_i \rangle|^2. \tag{14.23}$$

The successive eigenvectors $v^2, \ldots v^N$ are chosen to be orthogonal to those preceding, where each eigenvector v^i satisfies a property similar to (14.23) with respect to the remaining $(N - i + 1)$-dimensional subspace.

The solution of this optimization problem is normally obtained by computing the largest principal component of the covariance matrix of $\tilde{X}$ (14.1). We shall show below that there exist situations where finding the solution of problems like

(14.23) can be much easier than that. This simplification is achieved by replacing the constraint on v by one that lends itself to faster evaluation and optimization. We shall return to this point below, in a more general setting.

14.4.2 Kernel PCA

We denote by $\tilde{\Phi}(x_i) = \Phi(x_i) - \frac{1}{m}\sum_{i=1}^{m}\Phi(x_i)$ the centered version of the data in feature space, and define

Set of Projections

$$F_{\mathcal{H}} := \{\mathbf{w} \,|\, \mathbf{w} \in \mathcal{H},\ \|\mathbf{w}\|^2 \leq 1\} \tag{14.24}$$

to be the set of candidate vectors to project on. The problem of finding the first Kernel PCA eigenvector can then be stated as

$$\mathbf{v}^1 = \operatorname*{argmax}_{\mathbf{v}\in F_{\mathcal{H}}} \frac{1}{m}\sum_{i=1}^{m}\langle \mathbf{v}, \tilde{\Phi}(x_i)\rangle^2 = \operatorname*{argmax}_{\mathbf{v}\in F_{\mathcal{H}}} \operatorname{Var}\{\langle \mathbf{v}, \Phi(x_i)\rangle\}. \tag{14.25}$$

This modification, building on Proposition 14.2, may seem innocuous. Nevertheless, it allows us to modify the feature extraction problem in interesting ways, by replacing $F_{\mathcal{H}}$ with other sets that are more suitable for optimization. Before moving on, let us recall the function space interpretation of Kernel PCA, already mentioned in Section 14.2.2.

As explained in Section 2.2, we may think of the feature space $\mathcal{H}$ in different representations. One such representation, discussed in Chapter 4, uses functions f expanded in terms of kernels. Therefore, rather than using the abstract feature space element $\mathbf{w}$, the regularizer can be thought of in terms of functions f, and $\Omega[f] = \|f\|^2_{\mathcal{H}}$. In this case, the constraint (14.24) becomes a constraint in this function space. This means that we are looking for the function f with the largest *empirical* variance under the constraint $\Omega[f] \leq 1$; in other words, we would like f not to be overly complex. Depending on the specific RKHS $\mathcal{H}$ (and thus, depending on the kernel), this can mean a function with small first derivative, or a small sum of derivatives, or a particular frequency spectrum (cf. (4.28)). The criterion of large variance under constraints can thus be interpreted as the requirement to seek a simple yet "interesting" function of the current observations. In the next section, we replace $\Omega[f]$ by another regularization functional, which turns out to be better suited to optimization.

Maximum Variance Problem

14.4.3 Sparse Kernel Feature Analysis

Compact Functional Representation

Sparse solutions are often achieved in supervised learning settings by using an ℓ_1 penalty on the expansion coefficients (see Section 4.9.2 and [343, 104, 184, 459, 37, 502, 71, 347]). We now use the same approach in feature extraction, deriving an algorithm which requires only n basis functions to compute the first n features. This algorithm is computationally simple, and scales approximately one order of

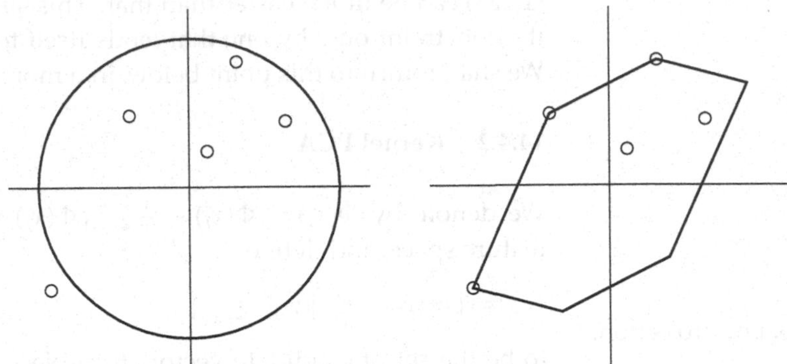

Figure 14.8 Left: the circle denotes the set $F_{\mathcal{H}}$ of possible $\mathbf{v}$ to be used to find the projection of maximum variance. Right: the absolute convex hull F_{LP} determines the set of possible directions of projection under the constraint $\sum_i |\alpha_i| \leq 1$. In both cases, the small circles represent observations.

magnitude better on large datasets than standard Kernel PCA. First, we choose

$$\Omega[f] = \sum_{i=1}^{m} |\alpha_i|, \tag{14.26}$$

as suggested in Section 4.9.2. This yields

$$F_{\text{LP}} := \left\{ \mathbf{w} \,\middle|\, \mathbf{w} = \sum_{i=1}^{m} \alpha_i \Phi(x_i) \text{ with } \sum_{i=1}^{m} |\alpha_i| \leq 1 \right\}, \tag{14.27}$$

Convexity Constraint

where the 'LP' in the name derives from the use of similar constructions in linear programming (see for instance Section 7.7). Figure 14.8 gives a depiction of F_{LP}.

This setting leads to the first "principal vector" in the ℓ_1 context,

$$\mathbf{v}^1 = \operatorname*{argmax}_{\mathbf{v} \in F_{\text{LP}}} \frac{1}{m} \sum_{i=1}^{m} \left\langle \mathbf{v}, \Phi(x_i) - \frac{1}{m} \sum_{j=1}^{m} \Phi(x_j) \right\rangle^2. \tag{14.28}$$

Again, subsequent "principal vectors" can be defined by enforcing optimality with respect to the remaining orthogonal subspaces. Due to the ℓ_1 constraint, the solution of (14.28) has the favorable property of being sparse in terms of the coefficients α_i (the coefficients are chosen from the "hyper-diamond-shaped" ℓ_1 ball).[5] In fact, as we shall show in Section 14.5, the optimal solution is found by picking the direction $\Phi(x_i)$ corresponding to a single pattern, meaning that the solution lies on one of the vertices of the ℓ_1 ball. We shall return to this point below.

5. Note that the requirement of $\|\mathbf{v}\|^2 = 1$, or the corresponding ℓ_1 constraint, are necessary — the value of the target function could otherwise increase without bound, simply by rescaling $\mathbf{v}$.

p-Convex Hulls

For the sake of completeness, note that rather than using ℓ_1 constraints, we could instead seek optimal solutions with respect to ℓ_p balls,

$$F_p := \left\{ \mathbf{w} \,\middle|\, \mathbf{w} = \sum_{i=1}^{m} \alpha_i \Phi(x_i) \text{ with } \sum_{i}^{m} |\alpha_i|^p \leq 1 \right\}. \tag{14.29}$$

In a nutshell, we have obtained sparse KFA by sticking with the variance criterion, and modifying the constraint. By contrast, in the next section, we revisit the standard ℓ_2 ball constraint that we know from (kernel) PCA, and instead change the objective function to be maximized subject to the constraint.

14.4.4 Projection Pursuit

Projection Pursuit [182, 252, 272, 176, 181, 139] differs from Principal Component Analysis (Section 14.4.1) in that it replaces the criterion of maximum variance by different criteria, such as non-Gaussianity. The first principal direction in Projection Pursuit is given by

$$v^1 = \operatorname*{argmax}_{\|v\|^2 \leq 1} \frac{1}{m} \sum_{i=1}^{m} q\left(\langle v, \tilde{x}_i \rangle\right), \tag{14.30}$$

Contrast Function

where $q : \mathbb{R} \to \mathbb{R}$ is a function such that $\sum_{i=1}^{m} q\left(\langle v, \tilde{x}_i \rangle\right)$ is large whenever the distribution of $\langle v, \tilde{x}_i \rangle$ is non-Gaussian. More generally, if some coupling between the different projections occurs, we can write Projection Pursuit as

$$v^1 = \operatorname*{argmax}_{\|v\|^2 \leq 1} Q\left(\langle v, \tilde{x}_1 \rangle, \ldots \langle v, \tilde{x}_m \rangle\right). \tag{14.31}$$

A possible function q is for instance $q(\xi) = \xi^4$. Apart from non-Gaussianity, contrast functions are sometimes designed to capture other properties, such as whether the distribution of features has multiple modes, the Fisher Information (so as to maximize it), the negative Shannon entropy, or other quantities of interest. For a detailed account of these issues see [182, 181, 252, 272, 176, 227].

To evaluate these contrast functions, it is often necessary to first compute a density estimate for the distribution of $\langle v, x_i \rangle$, for instance using the Parzen windows method. A final issue to note is that the determination of interesting directions is often quite computationally expensive [109, 301], since (14.31) may exhibit many local minima unless Q is convex. Practical projection pursuit tools (such as XGobi [533]) use gradient descent for optimization purposes, sometimes with additional (interactive) user input.

Cost of Projection Pursuit

14.4.5 Kernel Projection Pursuit

With slight abuse of notation, F is used below to denote both the set of possible weight vectors $\mathbf{w}$, and the set of functions f that satisfy a corresponding constraint on f (e.g., $f(x) = \langle \mathbf{w}, \Phi(x) \rangle$ where $\|\mathbf{w}\| \leq 1$).

We are now ready to state a general feature extraction framework that contains

General Feature Extractors

PCA, Projection Pursuit, and Kernel PCA as special cases, by combining the modifications of Sections 14.4.3 and 14.4.4. We obtain

$$f^1 = \operatorname*{argmax}_{f \in F} \frac{1}{m} \sum_{i=1}^{m} q(f(x_i)), \tag{14.32}$$

or more generally,

$$f^1 = \operatorname*{argmax}_{f \in F} Q\left(f(x_1), \ldots, f(x_m)\right), \tag{14.33}$$

where $q(\cdot)$ and $Q(\cdot)$ are functions which are maximized for a given property of the resulting function $f^1(x)$, and

$$F := \{f | f : \mathcal{X} \to \mathbb{R} \text{ and } \Omega[f] \leq 1\}. \tag{14.34}$$

Note that if F is the class of linear functions in input space (that is, if $\{f | f(x) = \langle w, x \rangle \text{ and } \|w\|^2 \leq 1\}$, where the projections are restricted to the unit ball), we recover Projection Pursuit.

14.4.6 Connections to Supervised Learning

The setting described above bears some resemblance to the problem of minimizing a regularized risk functional in supervised learning (Chapter 4). In the latter case, we try to *minimize* a function (the empirical risk $R_{\text{emp}}[f]$) that depends on the observed data, with the constraint $\Omega[f] \leq c$. In the feature extraction setting, we try to *maximize* a function $Q[f] = Q(f(x_1), \ldots, f(x_m))$ under the same constraint.

Risk Minimization		**Feature Extraction**	
minimize	$R_{\text{emp}}[f]$	maximize	$Q[f]$
subject to	$\Omega[f] \leq c$	subject to	$\Omega[f] \leq c$

(14.35)

This means that many of the theoretical guarantees from supervised learning, such as bounds on the difference between $Q[f]$ and the expectation $E[Q[f]]$, can be obtained directly from their analogues in classification and regression.

Properties of Q

A cautionary remark is necessary, however: since the class of possible feature extractors is now significantly larger than in projection pursuit, we have to be very careful not to pick a feature extractor f^i that renders *any* dataset "interesting" if viewed as $\{f^i(x_1), \ldots, f^i(x_m)\}$. This means that not all Q should be used, and in particular not the scale invariant versions of Q, since the latter render the constraint $\Omega[f] \leq c$ ineffective.

Finally, if Q is not convex, the maximum search over the extreme points does not provide us with the best solution. Although we may still apply the algorithm, we lose some of its good theoretical properties.

14.5 Algorithms for Sparse KFA

We now return to sparse KFA; that is, the feature extraction algorithm that maximizes variance subject to an ℓ_1 constraint (Section 14.4.3). We focus on how to actually solve the optimization problem. Despite the superficial similarity between the two settings in (14.35), the resulting algorithms for supervised and unsupervised learning are quite different. This is due to the fact that one problem (the supervised one) is usually a *convex minimization* problem, whereas the unsupervised problem requires *convex maximization*.

14.5.1 Solution by Maximum Search

Solution on Extreme Points

Recalling Theorem 6.10, the feasibility of the convex maximization problem depends largely on the *extreme points* of the set F, as defined by (14.34). In other words, the optimization problem can be solved efficiently only if the set of extreme points of F is small and can be computed easily. Otherwise, only a brute force search over the extreme points of F (which can be NP hard) yields the maximum. This effectively limits the choice of practically useful constraint sets F to F_{LP} and F_p (where $p \leq 1$). The extreme points in both sets coincide, and equal

$$\text{Extreme Points } (F_{\mathrm{LP}}) = \{\pm k(x_i, x) | i \in [m]\}. \tag{14.36}$$

Thus, we obtain the following corollary of Theorem 6.10.

Vertices Coincide

Corollary 14.3 (Vertex Solutions for Kernel Feature Analysis) *If the functions f and $-f$ generally yield the same Q value, and $p \leq 1$, we have*

$$f^1 = \operatorname*{argmax}_{f \in F_p} Q\left(f(x_1), \ldots, f(x_m)\right) \tag{14.37}$$

$$= \operatorname*{argmax}_{f \in F_{\mathrm{LP}}} Q\left(f(x_1), \ldots, f(x_m)\right) \tag{14.38}$$

$$= \operatorname*{argmax}_{f \in \{k(x_1,\cdot),\ldots,k(x_m,\cdot)\}} Q(f(x_1), \ldots, f(x_m)). \tag{14.39}$$

Under the above symmetry assumption, we can limit ourselves to analyzing the positive orthant only. See Figure 14.9 for a pictorial representation of the shapes of unit balls corresponding to different norms.

Eq. (14.37) provides us with a simple algorithm to solve the feature extraction problems introduced in Sections 14.4.3 and 14.4.5: simply seek the kernel function $k(x_i, \cdot)$ with the largest value of $Q(k(x_i, x_1), \ldots, k(x_i, x_m))$.

14.5.2 Sequential Decompositions

We now address how to proceed once the first direction of interest (or function) has been found. In the following, we denote by F^i the space of directions to select from in the ith round; in particular, $F^1 := F$. To keep matters simple, we limit ourselves

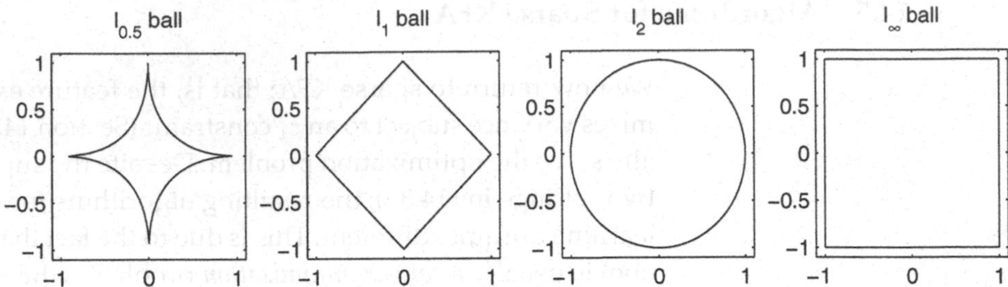

Figure 14.9 Several unit balls in $\mathbb{R}^2$. From left to right: $\ell_{0.5}, \ell_1, \ell_2$, and ℓ_∞. Note that the $\ell_{0.5}$ and ℓ_1 balls have identical extreme points.

to the dot product representation of the basis functions, $f(x) = \langle \mathbf{v}, \Phi(x) \rangle$. The vectors spanning this space are denoted by Φ_j^i. We start with $\Phi_j^1 = \Phi(x_j)$. Unless stated otherwise, we focus on F_{LP}, for which a 1-norm is taken on the coefficients.[6] Hence we have

ℓ_p Ball from Remaining Patterns

$$F^i := \left\{ \mathbf{w} \,\middle|\, \mathbf{w} = \sum_{j=1}^m \alpha_j^i \Phi_{ij} \text{ with } \sum_{j=1}^m |\alpha_j^i| \leq 1 \right\}. \tag{14.40}$$

We discuss the following three possible choices:

Similar Directions

Removal: We might, for instance, simply remove the corresponding vector $\Phi_j^i = \Phi(x_j)$ from the set of possible directions (and keep all other directions unchanged), so that $\Phi_j^{i+1} = \Phi_j^i$, and repeat the proposed procedure to find the next vector v_{i+1}. This may lead to many very similar 'principal' directions (each of which might be interesting on its own), however, which implies that many such directions add little additional information (cf. Figure 14.10). This is definitely not desirable, even though the computational cost for subsequent calculations is very low (a simple sorting operation), once all Q values are computed.

Unnormalized Projection: A second alternative is to require that each direction $\mathbf{v}^i$ be orthogonal to all previous directions, $\langle \mathbf{v}^i, \mathbf{v}^j \rangle = 0$ for all $i > j$. The easiest way to achieve this is by orthogonalizing all the vectors spanning F^{i+1} with respect to $\mathbf{v}^i$,

$$\Phi_j^{i+1} := \Phi_j^i - \frac{\mathbf{v}_i}{\|\mathbf{v}^i\|^2} \langle \Phi_j^i, \mathbf{v}^i \rangle. \tag{14.41}$$

Not a True Subset of F^{i-1}

As in the previous case, this approach also reduces the set of vectors spanning F^{i+1} by one, since $\mathbf{v}^i$ is chosen among Φ_j^i. Computation of the first p principal features involves only p kernel functions. This is because Φ_j^i is a linear combination of i images of patterns, of which $i - 1$ are already used in the computation of the

6. Recall that p-norms with $0 < p < 1$ lead to identical solutions on the corresponding set F_p^1.

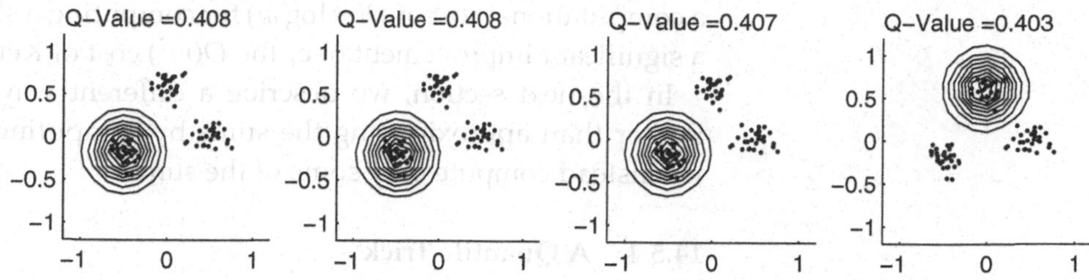

Figure 14.10 Contour plots of the first 4 feature extractors of sparse Kernel Feature Analysis, given that patterns are removed after being selected as interesting directions of projection. We used Gaussian RBF Kernels ($\sigma^2 = 0.05$) for a dataset of 120 samples. The small dots represent the data points. Note that the first three feature extractors are almost identical.

previous $i-1$ features.

Since Φ_j^i is not necessarily in F^1 (the sum of the expansion coefficients α is no longer contained inside the ℓ_p unit ball), we call this approach *Unnormalized* Kernel Feature Analysis.

Normalized Projection: We can obtain another version of the algorithm by normalizing the expansion coefficients of Φ_j^i to have unit p-norm. Since we do not use this version presently, we refer to [508] for details.

Henceforth, we consider only unnormalized projection. We thus obtain an algorithm for sparse KFA which requires just $O(p \cdot m)$ operations for the computation of p features for new data. For further detail, see [508].

Extraction of the principal directions themselves, however, is an $O(m^2)$ operation per feature extractor, as in the case of kernel PCA.[7] This cost arises since finding the direction with maximum Q value still requires computation of all dot products between all possible directions of projection and the actual patterns to be analyzed.

14.5.3 A Probabilistic Speedup

It is wasteful to compute all possible Q values for all directions, given that we only choose one of these directions. This suggests that we should terminate before completion the calculation of those directions that do not seem to be promising in the first place. When doing this, however, we must ensure a low likelihood that important directions are lost. In [508], Corollary 6.34 is used to derive probabilistic bounds on the error incurred. This leads to a method for approximating calculations by only summing over half of the terms. Applying the method in a divide and conquer fashion, similar to the Fast Fourier Transform [110]), we end up with

7. The constants, however, are significantly smaller than when computing eigenvectors of a matrix (the latter requires several passes over the matrix K_{ij}).

a computational cost of $O(m \log m)$ for computing a single function; this represents a significant improvement over the $O(m^2)$ cost of Kernel PCA.

In the next section, we describe a different way of speeding the algorithm. Rather than approximating the sums by computing only a subset of the terms, we instead compute only some of the sums.

14.5.4 A Quantile Trick

Relative Performance Guarantee

Rather than attempting to find the *best n* feature extractors, we may be content with feature extractors that are *among the best* obtainable. This is a reasonable simplification, given that $\mathbf{v}^2$ and related quantities are themselves obtained by approximation.

For instance, it might be sufficient for preprocessing purposes if each feature were among the best 5% obtainable. This leads to another approach for avoiding a search over all m possible directions: compute a subsample of $\tilde{m}$ directions, and choose the largest Q-value among them. We can show (see Corollary 6.32) that such a sub-sampling approach leads on average to values in the $\frac{\tilde{m}}{\tilde{m}+1}$ quantile range. Moreover, Theorem 6.33 shows that a subset of size 59 is already sufficient to obtain results in the 95% quantile range with 95% probability.

Distribution of Ranks

Overall, computational complexity for the extraction of a single feature is reduced to $O(cm)$ rather than $O(m^2)$. The same applies to memory requirements, since we no longer have to compute the whole matrix K beforehand. Thus unless the *best* feature extractors are needed, this should be the method of choice.

14.5.5 Theoretical Analysis

Due to lack of space, we do not give a statistical analysis of the algorithm. Suffice to say that [508] contains a brief analysis in terms of capacity concepts, such as covering numbers (cf. Chapters 5 and 12). The basic idea is that due to the use of regularizers such as the $\|\mathbf{w}\|^2$ term, uniform convergence bounds can be given on the reliability of the feature extractors; in other words, bounds can be derived on how much the variance of (say) a feature extractor differs between training and test sets.

14.6 KFA Experiments

Let us again consider the toy example of three artificial Gaussian data clusters, which we used in Figure 14.4 in the case of Kernel PCA. The randomized quantile version of KFA, shown in Figure 14.11, leads to rather similar feature extractors, although it is significantly faster to compute.

The main difference lies in the first few features. For instance, KFA uses only one basis function for the first feature (due to the built-in sparsity), which enforces a feature extractor that resides on one of the three clusters. Kernel PCA, on the other

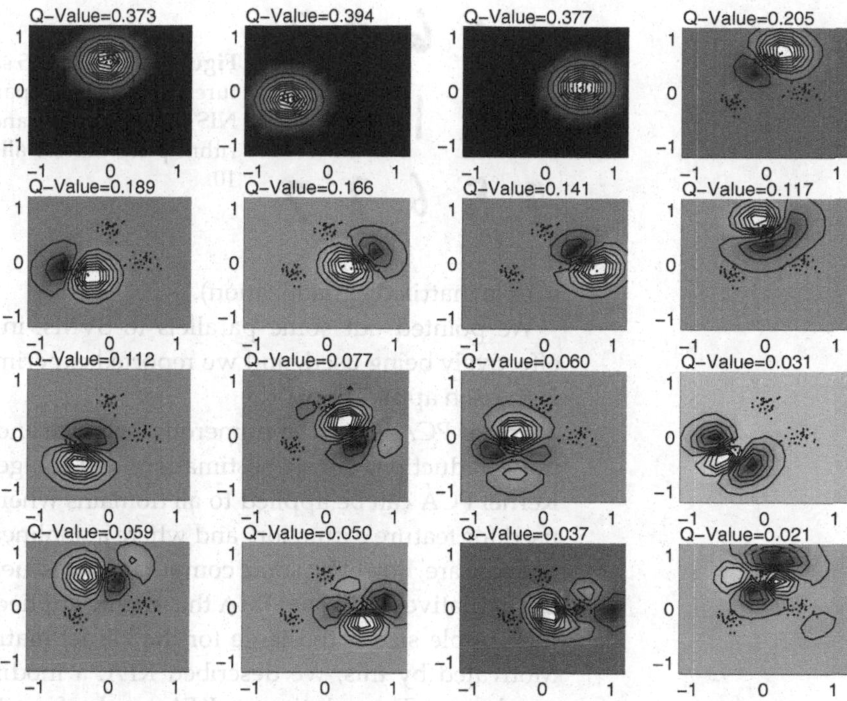

Figure 14.11 The first $p = 16$ features of sparse Kernel Feature Analysis, using the same kernel as in Figure 14.4. Note that every additional feature only needs one more kernel function to be computed. We used the randomized version of the algorithm, for which only a subset of 10 features per iteration is used (leading to an average quantile of over 95%). Note the similarity to Figure 14.4, which is an $O(m^2)$ rather than $O(pm)$ algorithm (per feature extractor).

hand, already has contributions from all basis functions for the first feature.

In all cases, it can be seen that the features are meaningful, in that they reveal nontrivial structure. The first features identify the cluster structure in the data set, while the higher order features analyze the individual clusters in more detail.

KFA and Clustering

To see the effect of Sparse KFA on real data, we carried out a small experiment on the MNIST dataset of handwritten digits (Figure 14.12). We observe that almost all digits appear among the first 10 basis kernels, and that the various copies of digit '1' do not overlap much and are therefore approximately orthogonal when compared with the Gaussian RBF kernel.

14.7 Summary

This chapter introduced the kernel generalization of the classical PCA algorithm. Known as Kernel PCA, it represents an elegant way of performing PCA in high dimensional feature spaces and getting rather good results in finite time (via a

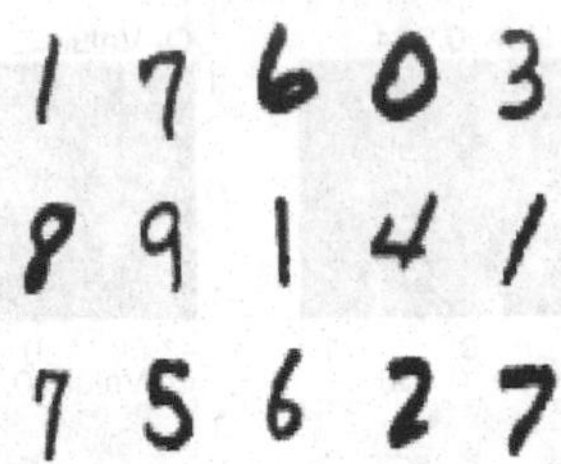

Figure 14.12 The 15 samples corresponding to the first features extracted by Sparse Kernel Feature Analysis from the NIST database of handwritten digits. Note how the algorithm picks almost all digits at least once among the first 10.

simple matrix diagonalization).

We pointed out some parallels to SVMs, in terms of the regularizer that is effectively being used, and we reported experimental results in nonlinear feature extraction applications.

Linear PCA is used in numerous technical and scientific applications, including noise reduction, density estimation, and image indexing and retrieval systems. Kernel PCA can be applied to all domains where traditional PCA has so far been used for feature extraction, and where a nonlinear extension would make sense.

There are, however, some computational issues, which make it desirable to think of alternatives to Kernel PCA that can be applied in situations where, for instance, the sample size is too large for the kernel matrix diagonalization to be feasible. Motivated by this, we described KFA, a modification which utilizes a sparsity regularizer. The solution of KFA can be found on the set of extreme points of the constraints, provided the contrast function itself is convex. In particular, if the constraints form a polyhedron, the extreme points can be found on the vertices. This reduces a potentially complex optimization problem to a maximum search over a finite set of size m. Randomized subset selection methods help to speed up the algorithm to linear cost and constant memory requirement per feature extractor.

We explained how both algorithms, along with classical approaches such as projection pursuit, can be understood as special cases of a general feature extraction framework, where we maximize a contrast function under a capacity constraint. This may be a sparsity constraint, a feature space vector length constraint, or some other restriction, such as the size of the derivatives.

14.8 Problems

14.1 (Positive Definiteness of the Covariance Matrix •) *Prove that the covariance matrix (14.1) is positive definite, by verifying the conditions of Definition 2.4. This implies that all its eigenvalues are nonnegative (Problem 2.4).*

14.2 (Toy Examples •) *Download the Kernel PCA Matlab code from http://www.kernel-machines.org. Run it on two toy datasets which are related to each other by a translation in input space. Why are the results identical?*

14.3 (Pre-Image Problem •) *Unlike PCA in input space, Kernel PCA only allows the computation of the feature values, but not explicitly the eigenvectors themselves. Discuss the reason for this difference, and the implied differences in the applicability of the techniques.*

14.4 (Null Space of Kernel PCA ••) *How many eigenvectors with eigenvalue 0 can Kernel PCA have in $\mathcal{H}$? Discuss the difference with respect to PCA in input space.*

14.5 (Centering [480] ••) *Derive the equations for Kernel PCA with data that does not have zero mean in $\mathcal{H}$.*

Hints: Given any Φ and any set of observations $x_1, \ldots, x_m$, the points

$$\tilde{\Phi}(x_i) := \Phi(x_i) - \frac{1}{m}\sum_{i=1}^{m}\Phi(x_i) \tag{14.42}$$

are centered.

1. *Expand the eigenvectors in term of the $\tilde{\Phi}(x_i)$, and derive the modified eigenvalue problem in the space of the expansion coefficients.*
2. *Derive the normalization condition for the coefficients to ensure the eigenvectors have unit norm.*
3. *For a set of test points $t_1, \ldots, t_n \in \mathcal{X}$, derive a matrix equation to evaluate the n feature values corresponding to the kth centered principal component.*

14.6 (Expansion of KPCA Solutions ••) *Argue that each solution of the eigenvalue problem for centered data could also be expanded in terms of the original mapped patterns. Derive the corresponding dual eigenvalue problem. How does it compare to the other one?*

14.7 (Explicit PCA in Feature Space •) *Consider an algorithm for nonlinear PCA which would explicitly map all data points into a feature space $\mathcal{H}$ via a nonlinear map Φ, such as the mapping induced by a kernel. Discuss under which conditions on the feature space this would be preferable to the kernel approach. Argue that Kernel PCA always effectively works in a finite dimensional subspace of $\mathcal{H}$, even when the dimensionality of $\mathcal{H}$ is infinite.*

14.8 (The Kernel PCA Feature Map ••) *Suppose that $\lambda_i > 0$ for all i. Prove that the feature map (2.59) satisfies*

$$\langle \Phi_m^w(x), \Phi_m^w(x') \rangle = \langle \Phi_{\text{KPCA}}(x), \Phi_{\text{KPCA}}(x') \rangle \tag{14.43}$$

for all $x, x' \in \mathcal{X}$, where (cf. (14.16))

$\Phi_{\text{KPCA}} : \mathcal{X} \to \mathbb{R}^m$

$$x \mapsto \left(\sum_{i=1}^{m} \alpha_i^n k(x_i, x) \right)_{i=1,\ldots,m}. \tag{14.44}$$

Hint: note that if $K = UDU^\top$ is K's diagonalization, with the columns of U being the eigenvectors of K, then $K^{-1/2} = UD^{-1/2}U^\top$. Use this to rewrite (2.59). Argue that as *in (11.12), the leading U can be dropped, since U is unitary. The entries of the diagonal matrix* $D^{-1/2}$ *equal* $\lambda_i^{-1/2}$*, thus performing the kernel PCA normalization (14.14).*

Next, argue that more generally, if $\lambda_i > 0$ *is not the case for all i, the above construction leads to a p-dimensional feature map (as in Section 14.2.1, we assume that the first p eigenvalues are the nonzero ones)*

$$\Phi_{\mathrm{KPCA}}(x) = \left(\sum_{i=1}^{m} \alpha_i^n k(x_i, x)\right)_{i=1,\ldots,p} \tag{14.45}$$

satisfying

$$\langle \Phi_{\mathrm{KPCA}}(x_i), \Phi_{\mathrm{KPCA}}(x_j) \rangle = k(x_i, x_j) \tag{14.46}$$

for all $i, j \in [m]$.

Finally, argue that the last equation may be approximately *satisfied by a feature map which is even lower dimensional, by discarding all eigenvalues which are smaller than some* $\epsilon > 0$.

14.9 (VC Bounds for Kernel PCA ∘∘∘) *Construct a VC theory of Kernel PCA; in other words, give bounds on the variance of a Kernel PCA feature extractor on the test set in terms of the variance on the training set, the size of the corresponding eigenvalue, and the covering numbers of the kernel-induced function class (see Section 14.4.6).*

14.10 (Connection KPCA — SVM ••) *From the known properties of PCA (cf. Proposition 14.1), prove Proposition 14.2.*

14.11 (Transformation Invariances ••) *Consider a transformation* $\mathfrak{L}_t$*, parametrized by t, such as translation along the x-axis. To first order, the effect of a small transformation (small t) can be studied by considering the* tangent vectors $\Phi(\mathfrak{L}_t x_i) - \Phi(x_i)$*. Mathematically derive invariant feature extractors by performing PCA on the covariance matrix of the tangent vectors (the* tangent covariance matrix*). Note the following problem:* invariant *feature extractors should have* small *eigenvalues, but eigenvectors with eigenvalue 0 do not necessarily lie in the span of the mapped examples (cf. (14.3)).*

14.12 (Transformation Invariances, Part II •••) *Extend the previous approach by simultaneously aiming for invariance under* $\mathfrak{L}_t$ *and for variance in the original Kernel PCA directions (cf. [364]).*

Hint: formulate a problem of simultaneous diagonalization.

14.13 (Singularity of the Centered Covariance Matrix •) *Prove that if* $\boldsymbol{\alpha}^k$ *is an eigenvector, with nonzero eigenvalue, of the centered covariance matrix, then* $\sum_i \alpha_i^k = 0$*. Why does this imply that the centered covariance matrix is singular?*

14.14 (Primal and Dual Eigenvalue Problems [480] ••) *Prove that (14.12) yields all solutions of (14.7).*

Hint: show that any solution of (14.11) which does not solve (14.12) differs from a solution of (14.12) only by a vector $\boldsymbol{\alpha}$ *with the property* $\sum_i \alpha_i \Phi(x_i) = 0$.

14.15 (Multi-Layer Support Vector Machines •) *By first extracting nonlinear principal components according to (14.16), and then training a Support Vector Machine, we can construct Support Vector type machines with additional layers. Discuss the architecture, and the different ways of training the different layers.*

14.16 (Mechanical Analogy ∘∘∘) *Try to generalize the mechanical PCA algorithm described in [443], which interprets PCA as an iterative spring energy minimization procedure, to a feature space setting. Try to come up with mechanically inspired ways of taking into account negative data in PCA (cf.* oriented PCA, *[140]).*

14.17 (Kernel PCA and Locally Linear Embedding ••) *Suppose we approximately represent each point of the dataset as a linear combination of its n nearest neighbors. Let $(W_n)_{ij}$, where $i, j \in [m]$, be the weight of point x_j in the expansion of x_i minimizing the squared representation error.*

1. *Prove that $k_n(x_i, x_j) := \left((\mathbf{1}-W_n)^\top(\mathbf{1}-W_n)\right)_{ij}$ is a positive definite kernel on the domain $\mathcal{X} = \{x_1, \ldots, x_m\}$.*

2. *Let λ be the largest eigenvalue of $(\mathbf{1} - W_n)^\top(\mathbf{1} - W_n)$. Prove that the* LLE *kernel $k_n^{\mathrm{LLE}}(x_i, x_j) := \left((\lambda - 1)\mathbf{1} + W_n^\top + W_n - W_n^\top W_n\right)_{ij}$ is positive definite on $\{x_1, \ldots, x_m\}$.*

3. *Prove that kernel PCA using the LLE kernel provides the LLE embedding coefficients [445] for a d-dimensional embedding as the first d coefficient eigenvectors $\boldsymbol{\alpha}^1, \ldots, \boldsymbol{\alpha}_d$. Note that if the eigenvectors are normalized in $\mathcal{H}$, then dimension i will be scaled by $\lambda_i^{-1/2}$, $i = 1, \ldots, d$.*

4. *Discuss the variant of LLE obtained using the centered Gram matrix*

$$(\mathbf{1} - \mathbf{1}_m)\left((\lambda - 1)\mathbf{1} + W_n^\top + W_n - W_n^\top W_n\right)(\mathbf{1} - \mathbf{1}_m) \tag{14.47}$$

(cf. (14.17)). Which space does the centering apply to?

5. *Interpret the LLE kernel as a similarity measure based on the similarity of the coefficients required to represent two patterns in terms of n neighboring patterns.*

14.18 (Optimal Approximation Property of PCA •) *Discuss whether the solutions of KFA satisfy the optimal approximation property of Proposition 14.1.*

14.19 (Scale Invariance ••) *Show that the problems of Kernel PCA and Sparse Kernel Feature Analysis are scale invariant; meaning that the solutions for $\Omega[f] \leq c$ and $\Omega[f] \leq c'$ for $c, c' > 0$ are identical up to a scaling factor.*

Show that this also applies for a rescaling of the data in Feature Space. What happens if we rescale in input space? Analyze specific kernels such as $k(x, x') = \langle x, x' \rangle^d$ and $k(x, x') = \exp(-\frac{\|x-x'\|^2}{2\sigma^2})$.

14.20 (Contrast Functions for Projection Pursuit •••) *Compute for $q(\xi) = \xi^4$ the expectations under a normal distribution of unit variance. What happens if you use a different distribution with the same variance?*

Can you find an optimal function $q(\xi)$ provided that we are only dealing with densities of zero mean and unit variance? Hint: use a Lagrangian and variational derivatives; in other words, set up a constrained optimization problem as in (6.39), but with integrals rather than sums in the individual constraints (see [206] for details on variational derivatives). You need three constraints: $\int p(\xi) = 1$, $\int \xi p(\xi) = 0$, and $\int \xi^2 p(\xi) = 1$.

14.21 (Cutting Planes and F_p •••) *Compute the vertices of the polyhedral set obtained by orthogonally cutting F_1 with one of the vectors $\Phi(x_i)$. Can you still compute them if we replace F_1 by F_p?*

Show that the number of $\Phi(x_j)$ required per vertex may double per cut (until it involves all m of the $\Phi(x_j)$).

14.22 (Pre-Image Problem ••) *Devise a denoising algorithm for Sparse Kernel Feature Analysis, using the methods of Chapter 18.*

14.23 (Comparison Between Kernel PCA and Sparse KFA •) *Plot the variances obtained from the sets of the Kernel PCA and Sparse KFA projections. Discuss similarities and differences. Why do the variances decay more slowly (with the index of the projection) for Sparse KFA?*

14.24 (Extension to General Kernels ○○○) *Can you extend the sparse feature extraction algorithm to kernels which are not positive definite? Hint: begin with a modification of V_1. Which criterion replaces orthogonality in feature space (e.g., ℓ_2^M on X)? Does the algorithm retain its favorable numerical properties (such as cheap diagonalization)? What happens if you use arbitrary functions f_j and $\langle \Upsilon f_i, \Upsilon f_j \rangle$ as the corresponding dot product?*

14.25 (Uniform Convergence Bounds •••) *Prove a bound for the deviation between the expected value of $Q[f]$ and its empirical estimate, $\mathrm{P}\{|\mathbf{E}[Q[f]] - Q[f]|\}$. Hint: use uniform convergence bounds for regression.*

15 Kernel Fisher Discriminant

In the previous chapter, we reported experiments in which kernel PCA feature extraction was applied to solve classification problems. This was done by following a two-step approach: first, extract the features, irrespective of the classification task; second, train a simple linear discriminative classifier on the features.

It is possible to combine both steps by constructing a so-called Kernel Fisher Discriminant (KFD) (e.g. [363, 364, 442, 27], cf. also [490]). The idea is to solve the problem of Fisher's linear discriminant [171, 186] in a feature space $\mathcal{H}$, thereby yielding a nonlinear discriminant in the input space.

Overview

The chapter is organized as follows. After a short introduction of the standard Fisher discriminant, we review its kernelized version, the KFD algorithm (Section 15.2). In Section 15.3, we describe an efficient implementation using sparse approximation techniques. Following this, we give details on how the outputs of the KFD algorithm can be converted into conditional probabilities of class membership (Section 15.4). We conclude with some experiments.

Prerequisites

Most of the chapter only requires knowledge of the kernel trick, as described in Chapter 1, and, in more detail, Chapter 2). To understand the connection to SVMs, it would be helpful to have read Chapter 7. The details of the training procedure described in Section 15.3 are relatively self-contained, but are easier to understand after reading the background material in Section 6.5, and (optionally) Section 16.4. Finally, Section 15.4 requires some basic knowledge of Bayesian methods, as provided for instance in Section 16.1.

15.1 Introduction

Let us start by giving a concise summary of the Fisher discriminant algorithm, following the treatment of [375]. For further detail, see [363].

Rayleigh Coefficient

In the linear case, Fisher's discriminant is computed by maximizing the so-called *Rayleigh coefficient* with respect to $\mathbf{w}$,

$$J(\mathbf{w}) = \frac{(\mathbf{w}^\top S_B \mathbf{w})}{(\mathbf{w}^\top S_W \mathbf{w})}, \tag{15.1}$$

depending on the between- and within-class variances,

$$S_B = (\mathbf{m}_- - \mathbf{m}_+)(\mathbf{m}_- - \mathbf{m}_+)^\top \tag{15.2}$$

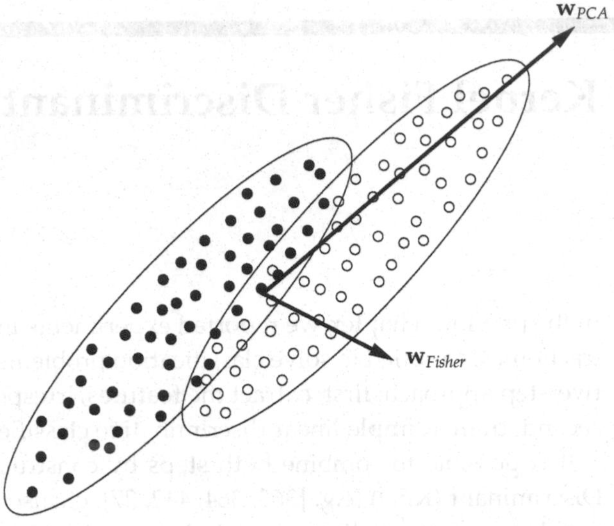

Figure 15.1 Illustration of the main projections of PCA and Fisher's Discriminant for a toy data set. PCA does not consider the labels (indicated by solid and open symbols, respectively) and simply returns the direction of overall maximum variance as the first eigenvector. Fisher's discriminant, on the other hand, returns a projection that yields a much better separation between the two classes (from [375]).

and

$$S_W = \sum_{q=\pm} \sum_{i \in \mathcal{I}_q} (\mathbf{x}_i - \mathbf{m}_q)(\mathbf{x}_i - \mathbf{m}_q)^\top. \tag{15.3}$$

Here, $\mathbf{m}_q$ and $\mathcal{I}_q$ denote the sample mean and the index set for class q, respectively. The idea is to look for a direction such that when the patterns are projected onto it, the class centers are far apart while the spread within each class is small — this should cause the overlap of the two classes to be small.

Figure 15.1 gives a sketch of the projection $\mathbf{w}$ found by Fisher's Discriminant. Unlike PCA, this projection takes the class labels into account. We can show that the Fisher discriminant finds the optimal discriminating direction between the classes (in the sense of having minimal expected misclassification error), subject to the assumption that the class distributions are (identical) Gaussians.

15.2 Fisher's Discriminant in Feature Space

To formulate the problem in a feature space $\mathcal{H}$, we can expand $\mathbf{w} \in \mathcal{H}$ as

$$\mathbf{w} = \sum_i \alpha_i \Phi(x_i), \tag{15.4}$$

as in the case of Kernel PCA (14.9). Below, we use the notation $\mathbf{1}_q$ to denote the m-dimensional vector with components $[\mathbf{1}_q]_i$ equal to 1 if the pattern x_i belongs to class q, and 0 otherwise. Additionally, let $m_\pm := |\mathcal{I}_q|$ be the class sizes, and $\mu_q := \frac{1}{m_q} K\mathbf{1}_q$,

$$N = KK^\top - \sum_{q=\pm} m_q \mu_q \mu_q^\top, \tag{15.5}$$

$\mu = \mu_- - \mu_+$, $M = \mu\mu^\top$, and $K_{ij} = \langle \Phi(x_i), \Phi(x_j) \rangle = k(x_i, x_j)$. A short calculation shows that the optimization problem consists of maximizing [364]

Rayleigh Coefficient in $\mathcal{H}$

$$J(\boldsymbol{\alpha}) = \frac{\boldsymbol{\alpha}^\top M \boldsymbol{\alpha}}{\boldsymbol{\alpha}^\top N \boldsymbol{\alpha}} = \frac{(\boldsymbol{\alpha}^\top \mu)^2}{\boldsymbol{\alpha}^\top N \boldsymbol{\alpha}}. \tag{15.6}$$

The projection of a test point onto the discriminant is computed by

$$\langle \mathbf{w}, \Phi(x) \rangle = \sum_{i=1}^{m} \alpha_i k(x_i, x). \tag{15.7}$$

As the dimensionality of the feature space is usually much higher than the number of training samples m, it is advisable to use regularization. In [363], the addition of a multiple of the identity or of the kernel matrix K to N was proposed, penalizing $\|\boldsymbol{\alpha}\|^2$ or $\|\mathbf{w}\|^2$ respectively (see also [177, 230]).

There are several equivalent ways of maximizing (15.6). We could solve the generalized eigenvalue problem,

Eigenvalue Formulation

$$M\boldsymbol{\alpha} = \lambda N \boldsymbol{\alpha}, \tag{15.8}$$

selecting the eigenvector $\boldsymbol{\alpha}$ with maximal eigenvalue λ, or compute

$$\boldsymbol{\alpha} \propto N^{-1}(\mu_- - \mu_+) \text{ (Problem 15.2).} \tag{15.9}$$

Although there exist many efficient off-the-shelf eigenvalue problem solvers or Cholesky packages which could be used to optimize (15.6), two problems remain: for a large sample size m, the matrices N and M become large, and the solutions $\boldsymbol{\alpha}$ are non-sparse. One way of dealing with this issue is to transform KFD into a convex quadratic programming problem [362]. Apart from algorithmic advantages, this formulation also allows for a more transparent view of the mathematical properties of KFD, and in particular its connection to SV classifiers (Chapter 7) and the Relevance Vector Machine ([539, 362], see Chapter 16).

Recalling that Fisher's Discriminant tries to minimize the variance of the data along the projection whilst maximizing the distance between the average outputs for each class, we can state the following quadratic program:

QP Formulation

$$\begin{aligned} &\underset{\boldsymbol{\alpha},\boldsymbol{\xi},b}{\text{minimize}}\ \|\boldsymbol{\xi}\|^2 + C\Omega(\boldsymbol{\alpha}), && (15.10)\\ &\text{subject to } K\boldsymbol{\alpha} + \mathbf{1}b = \mathbf{y} + \boldsymbol{\xi}, \\ &\qquad\qquad \mathbf{1}_q^\top \boldsymbol{\xi} = 0 \text{ for } q = \pm. \end{aligned}$$

Here, $\boldsymbol{\alpha}, \boldsymbol{\xi} \in \mathbb{R}^m$, $b, C \in \mathbb{R}$, $\mathbf{y}$ is the vector of class labels ± 1, and $\Omega(\boldsymbol{\alpha})$ is one of the regularizers mentioned above; that is, $\Omega(\boldsymbol{\alpha}) = \|\boldsymbol{\alpha}\|^2$ or $\Omega(\boldsymbol{\alpha}) = \boldsymbol{\alpha}^\top K \boldsymbol{\alpha}$. It can be shown that this program is equivalent to (15.6). The first constraint, which can be read as

$$\langle \mathbf{w}, \mathbf{x}_i \rangle + b = y_i + \xi_i \text{ for all } i = 1, \ldots, m, \tag{15.11}$$

pulls the output for each sample towards its class label. The term $\|\boldsymbol{\xi}\|^2$ minimizes the variance of the error committed, while the constraints $\mathbf{1}_q^\top \boldsymbol{\xi} = 0$ ensure that the average output for each class equals the label; in other words, for ±1 labels, the average distance of the projections is 2. The formulation in (15.10) has the additional benefit that it lends itself to the incorporation of more general noise models, which may be more robust than the Gaussian model [362].

Besides providing additional understanding, (15.10) allows the derivation of more efficient algorithms. Choosing an ℓ_1-norm regularizer, $\Omega(\alpha) = \|\boldsymbol{\alpha}\|_1$, we obtain sparse solutions: as discussed in Chapter 4, the ℓ_1-norm regularizer is a reasonable approximation to an ℓ_0 regularizer, which simply counts the number of nonzero elements in $\boldsymbol{\alpha}$.

Sparse Version

For large datasets, solving (15.10) is not practical. It is possible, however, to *approximate* the solution in a greedy way. In the next section, we iteratively approximate the solution to (15.10) with as few non-zero α_i as possible, following [366].

15.3 Efficient Training of Kernel Fisher Discriminants

To proceed, let us rewrite (15.10), using $\Omega(\boldsymbol{\alpha}) = \|\boldsymbol{\alpha}\|^2$. We define

$$\mathbf{a} = \begin{bmatrix} b \\ \boldsymbol{\alpha} \end{bmatrix} \quad \mathbf{c} = \begin{bmatrix} m_+ - m_- \\ K^\top \mathbf{y} \end{bmatrix} \quad A_\pm = \begin{bmatrix} m_\pm \\ K^\top \mathbf{1}_\pm \end{bmatrix} \quad H = \begin{bmatrix} m & \mathbf{1}^\top K \\ K^\top \mathbf{1} & K^\top K + C\mathbf{1} \end{bmatrix} \tag{15.12}$$

Here, $m_\pm$ denotes the number of samples in class ±1. Then (15.10) can be rewritten using the equivalent

$$\underset{\mathbf{a}}{\text{minimize}} \quad \frac{1}{2}\mathbf{a}^\top H\mathbf{a} - \mathbf{c}^\top\mathbf{a} + \frac{m}{2} \tag{15.13}$$

$$\text{subject to} \quad A_+^\top\mathbf{a} - m_+ = 0, \tag{15.14}$$

$$A_-^\top\mathbf{a} + m_- = 0. \tag{15.15}$$

Forming the Lagrangian of (15.13) with multipliers $\lambda_\pm$,

$$L(\mathbf{a}, \lambda_+, \lambda_-) = \frac{1}{2}\mathbf{a}^\top H\mathbf{a} - \mathbf{c}^\top\mathbf{a} + \lambda_+(A_+^\top\mathbf{a} - m_+) + \lambda_-(A_-{}^\top\mathbf{a} + m_-) + \frac{m}{2}, \tag{15.16}$$

and taking derivatives with respect to the primal variables $\mathbf{a}$, we obtain the dual

$$\underset{\mathbf{a},\lambda_+,\lambda_-}{\text{maximize}} \quad -\frac{1}{2}\mathbf{a}^\top H\mathbf{a} - \lambda_+ m_+ + \lambda_- m_- + \frac{m}{2}, \tag{15.17}$$

$$\text{subject to} \quad H\mathbf{a} - \mathbf{c} + (\lambda_+ A_+ + \lambda_- A_-) = 0. \tag{15.18}$$

We now use the dual constraint (15.18) to solve for $\mathbf{a}$,

$$\mathbf{a} = H^{-1}(\mathbf{c} - (\lambda_+ A_+ + \lambda_- A_-)). \tag{15.19}$$

This equation is well defined if K has full rank (see (15.12)). If not, we can still perform this step, as we approximate H^{-1} instead of computing it directly. Resubstituting (15.19) into the dual problem (which has no constraints left) yields the following problem in two variables λ_+ and λ_-:

$$\underset{\lambda_+,\lambda_-}{\text{maximize}} - \frac{1}{2}\begin{bmatrix} \lambda_+ \\ \lambda_- \end{bmatrix}^\top \begin{bmatrix} A_+^\top H^{-1} A_+ & A_+^\top H^{-1} A_- \\ A_-^\top H^{-1} A_+ & A_-^\top H^{-1} A_- \end{bmatrix} \begin{bmatrix} \lambda_+ \\ \lambda_- \end{bmatrix} + \begin{bmatrix} -m_+ + \mathbf{c}^\top H^{-1} A_+ \\ m_- + \mathbf{c}^\top H^{-1} A_- \end{bmatrix} \begin{bmatrix} \lambda_+ \\ \lambda_- \end{bmatrix} + -\frac{1}{2}\mathbf{c}^\top H^{-1}\mathbf{c} + \frac{m}{2}. \tag{15.20}$$

This problem can be solved analytically, yielding values for λ_+ and λ_-. Substituting these into (15.19) give values for $\mathbf{a}$ or $\boldsymbol{\alpha}$ and b, respectively.

Sparse Greedy Approximation

Of course, this problem is no easier to solve, nor does it yield a sparse solution: H^{-1} is an $(m+1) \times (m+1)$ matrix, and for large datasets its inversion is not feasible, due to the requisite time and memory costs.

The following greedy approximation scheme can be used (cf. Chapter 6), however. Instead of trying to find a full set of m coefficients α_i for the solution (15.4), we approximate the solution by a shorter expansion, containing only $n \ll m$ terms. Starting with an empty solution $n = 0$, we select at each iteration a new sample x_i (or an index i), and resolve the problem for the expansion (15.4) containing this new index and all previously picked indices; we stop as soon as a suitable criterion is satisfied. This approach would still be infeasible in terms of computational cost if we had to solve the full quadratic program (15.13) anew at each iteration, or invert H in (15.19) and (15.20). But with the derivation given above, it is possible to find a close approximation to the solution at each iteration with a cost of $O(\kappa m n^2)$, where κ is a user defined value (see below).

Writing down the quadratic program (15.10) for KFD, where the expansion for the solution is restricted to an n element subset $\mathcal{I} \subset [m]$ of the training patterns, and thus

$$\mathbf{w}_{\mathcal{I}} = \sum_{i \in \mathcal{I}} \alpha_i \Phi(x_i), \tag{15.21}$$

amounts to replacing the $m \times m$ matrix K by an $m \times n$ matrix K^n, where $K_{ij}^n = k(x_i, x_j)$, $i = 1, \ldots, m$ and $j \in \mathcal{I}$. We can derive the formulation (15.13) in an analogous manner using the matrix K^n in (15.12). The problem is then of size $n \times n$. Assume we already know the solution (and inverse of H) using n kernel functions. Then H^{-1} for $n+1$ samples can be obtained by a rank one update of the previous H^{-1} using only n basis functions: Eq. (10.38) tells us how. For convenience, we repeat the statement below.

To this end, denote by H^n the matrix obtained from n basis functions, and by H^{n+1} that obtained by adding one basis function to these n functions. Note that H^n and H^{n+1} differ by only one row/column; we denote this difference by B, for the n-vector, and C, for the diagonal entry $H^{n+1}_{n+1,n+1}$. We may now apply

$$(H^{n+1})^{-1} = \begin{bmatrix} H^n & B \\ B^\top & C \end{bmatrix}^{-1}$$

Algorithm 15.1 The Sparse Greedy Kernel Fisher Algorithm

arguments:
    Sample $X = \{x_1, \ldots, x_m\}, \mathbf{y} = \{y_1, \ldots, y_m\}$
    Maximum number of coefficients
    or parameters of other stopping criterion: $OPTS$
    Regularization constant C
    κ and kernel k
returns:
    Set of indices I and corresponding α-s.
function SG-KFD($X, \mathbf{y}, C, \kappa, k, OPTS$)
  Set $n = 0$
    $I = \{\}$
  while termination criterion not satisfied **do**
    Choose κ elements from $[m] \setminus I$
    for each chosen index **do**
      Compute column of kernel matrix
      Update inverse, compute optimal a
      Compute new dual objective
      if this objective is smaller than the ones before **do**
        remember this index
      endif
    end
    Update inverse H and solution a with the best index chosen
    Add this index to I
    Check termination criterion
  endwhile

$$= \begin{bmatrix} (H^n)^{-1} + ((H^n)^{-1}B)\gamma((H^n)^{-1}B)^\top & -\gamma((H^n)^{-1}B) \\ -(\gamma((H^n)^{-1}B))^\top & \gamma \end{bmatrix}, \tag{15.22}$$

where $\gamma = (C - B^\top H^{-1} B)^{-1}$. This means that we may compute the inverse of H^{n+1} by multiplying a vector with the inverse of H^n, and inverting a scalar. This is an operation of cost $O(n^2)$. The last major problem is to pick an index i at each iteration. Ideally we would choose the i for which we get the biggest decrease in the primal-objective (or equivalently the dual-objective, since they are identical for the optimal coefficients α). We would then need to compute the update H^{-1} for all $m - n$ indices which are unused so far, however — again, this is too expensive. One possible solution lies in a second approximation. Instead of choosing the *best* possible index, it is usually sufficient to find an index for which, with high probability, we achieve something close to the optimal choice. It turns out (Chapter 6) that it can be enough to consider a small subset of indices, chosen randomly from those remaining. According to Corollary 6.32 and the discussion following it, a random sample of size 59 is enough to obtain an estimate that is with probability 0.95 among the best 0.05 of all estimates.

The complete algorithm for a sparse greedy solution to the KFD problem is schematized in Figure 15.1. It is easy to implement using a linear algebra package

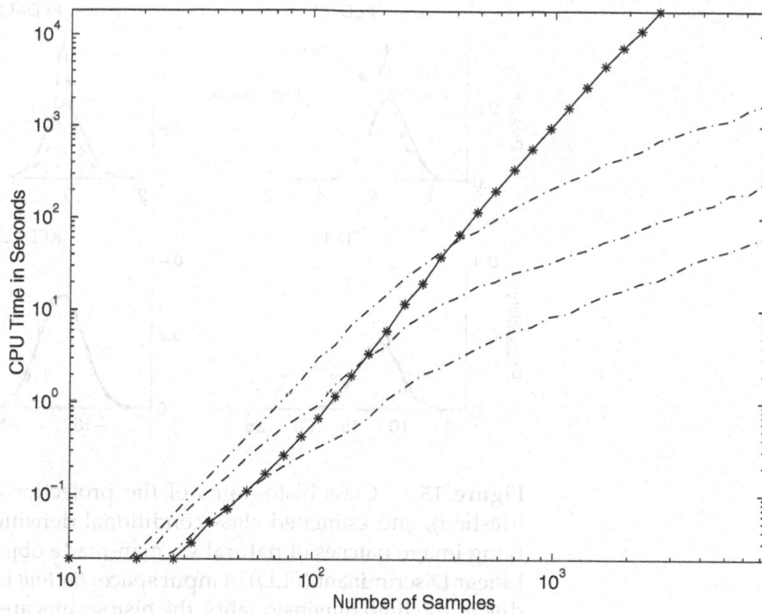

Figure 15.2 Runtime of sparse greedy KFD training. The number of samples in the training set versus the CPU time of the sparse greedy algorithm (dash dotted lines) and the QP formulation (15.10) (solid line) are depicted. The estimates are averages over ten trials, one for each of the ten one-against-the-rest problems in the USPS database. The three lines for the sparse greedy KFD are generated by requiring different accuracies for the dual error function, namely $10^{-a}, a = 1, \ldots, 3$, relative to the function value (the curves are plotted in this order from bottom to top). There is a speed-accuracy trade-off in that for large a, the algorithm converges more slowly. As a sanity check, the $a = 3$ system was evaluated on the USPS test set. Although the parameters used (kernel and regularization constant) were those found to be optimal for the QP algorithm, the performance of the sparse greedy algorithm is only slightly worse. In the log-log plot it can be seen that the QP algorithm roughly scales in a cubic manner with the number of samples, while for large sample sizes, the approximate algorithm scales with an exponent of about $\frac{3}{2}$.

like BLAS [316, 145], and has the potential to be easily parallelized (the matrix update) and distributed.

Training Time Experiment

In a first evaluation, we used a one-against-the-rest task constructed from the USPS handwritten digit data set to test the runtime behavior of our new algorithm. The data are $N = 256$ dimensional and the set contains 7291 samples. All experiments were done with a Gaussian kernel, $\exp(\|x - x'\|^2/(0.3\, N))$, and using a regularization constant $C = 1$. We compare the performance with the program given by (15.10) with the regularizer $\Omega(\alpha) = \|\alpha\|^2$. The results are given in Figure 15.2. It is important to keep in mind that the sparse greedy approach only needs to store at most an $n \times n$ matrix, where n is the maximal number of kernel functions chosen before termination. In contrast, previous approaches needed to store $m \times m$ matrices.

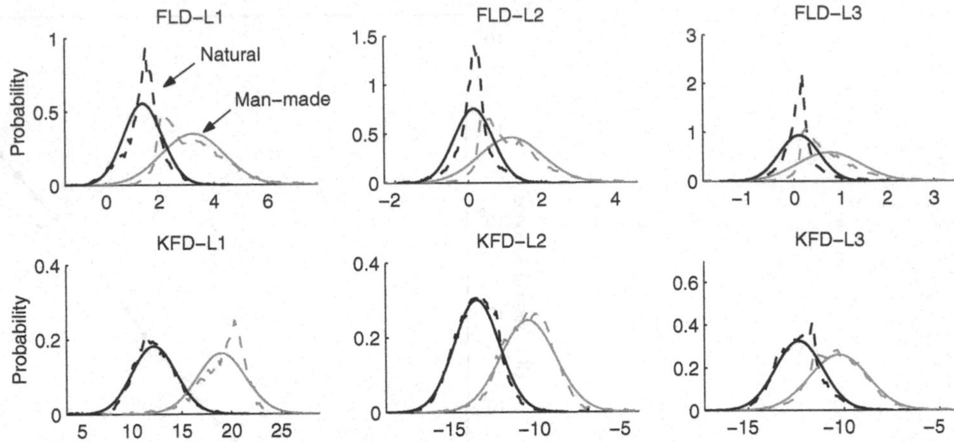

Figure 15.3 Class histograms of the projections onto the Fisher discriminant direction (dashed), and estimated class-conditional densities (solid), for a task consisting of classifying image patches of natural vs. man-made objects. *Top row:* three systems using a Fisher Linear Discriminant (FLD) in input space. *Bottom row:* plots for the KFD approach. Note that due to the high dimensionality, the histograms are more Gaussian in the KFD case, making it easier to estimate class probabilities accurately (from [75]).

15.4 Probabilistic Outputs

We conclude this section by noting that while generalization error performance of the KFD is comparable to an SVM (cf. Table 15.1), a crucial advantage of the Fisher discriminant algorithm over standard SV classification[1] is that the outputs of the former can easily be transformed into conditional probabilities of the classes; in other words, numbers that state not only whether a given test pattern belongs to a certain class, but also the *probability* of this event. This is due to the empirical observation (Figure 15.3) that in the high-dimensional feature space, the histogram of each class of training examples as projected onto the discriminant can be closely approximated by a Gaussian.

To obtain class probabilities, we proceed as follows. We first estimate two one-dimensional Gaussian densities for the projections of the training points onto the direction of discrimination. We then use Bayes' rule to derive the conditional probability that a test point x belongs to a given class $+$ or $-$.

Let m_+ and m_- denote the number of positive and negative examples respectively, such that $m = m_+ + m_-$. From the projections of the training points (cf. (15.7)),

$$q_j := q(x_j) := \langle \mathbf{w}, \Phi(x_j) \rangle = \sum_{i=1}^{m} \alpha_i k(x_i, x_j), \tag{15.23}$$

1. For extensions of the SVM that produce probabilistic outputs, see [521, 486, 410].

we can readily estimate the mean of each Gaussian,

$$\mu_\pm := \frac{1}{m_\pm} \sum_{y_i=\pm 1} q_i, \tag{15.24}$$

and the respective variances

$$\sigma_\pm^2 = \frac{1}{m_\pm - 1} \sum_{y_i=\pm 1} (q_i - \mu_\pm)^2. \tag{15.25}$$

Note that the -1 in the denominator renders the variance estimator unbiased (cf. Chapter 3, and for instance [49]). The class-conditional densities take the form

$$p(q|y = \pm 1) = (2\pi\sigma_\pm^2)^{-\frac{1}{2}} \exp\left(-\frac{(q-\mu_\pm)^2}{2\sigma_\pm^2}\right). \tag{15.26}$$

In order to apply Bayes' rule (Section 16.1.3), we need to determine prior probabilities of the two classes. These could either be known for the problem at hand (from some large set of previous observations, for example), or estimated from the current dataset. The latter approach only makes sense if the sample composition is representative of the problem at hand; it then amounts to setting

$$P(y = \pm 1) = \frac{m_\pm}{m}. \tag{15.27}$$

Conditional Probabilities

To obtain the *conditional probabilities* of class membership $y = \pm 1$ given the pattern x (sometimes called *posterior probabilities*), we use Bayes' rule,

$$P(y = \pm 1|x) = P(y = \pm 1|q) = \frac{p(q|y = \pm 1)P(y = \pm 1)}{p(q|y = 1)P(y = 1) + p(q|y = -1)P(y = -1)}, \tag{15.28}$$

where $q = q(x)$ is defined as above.

Being able to estimate the conditional probabilities can be useful, for instance, in applications where the output of a classifier needs to be merged with further sources of information. Another recent application is to classification in the presence of noisy class labels [315]. In this case, we formulate a probabilistic model for the label noise. During learning, an EM procedure is applied to optimize the parameters of the noise model and of the KFD, as well as the conditional probabilities for the training patterns. The procedure alternates between the estimation of the conditional probabilities, as detailed above, and a modified estimation of the KFD which takes into account the conditional probabilities.

In this way, a point that has been recognized as being very noisy has a smaller influence on the final solution. In [315], this approach was applied to the segmentation of images into sky and non-sky areas. A standard classification approach would require the hand-labelling of a large number of image patches, in order to get a sufficiently large training set. The new "noisy label" algorithm, on the other hand, is able to learn the task from images that are merely globally labelled according to whether they contain any sky at all. Images without sky are then used to produce training examples (image patches) of one class, while images with sky are used to produce *noisy* training examples of the second class.

15.5 Experiments

Toy Example

Let us first use a toy example to illustrate the KFD algorithm (Figure 15.4). The three panels show the same toy data set, with the KFD algorithm run three times, using Gaussian kernels

$$k(x, x') = \exp\left(-\frac{\|x - x'\|^2}{c}\right) \tag{15.29}$$

with different values of c. For large c, the induced feature space geometry resembles that of the input space, and the algorithm computes an almost linear discriminant function. For the problem at hand, which is not linearly separable, this is clearly not appropriate. For a very small c, on the other hand, the kernel becomes so local that the algorithm starts memorizing the data. For an intermediate kernel width, a good nonlinear separation can be computed. Note that in KFD, there is no geometrical notion of Support Vectors lying on the margin; indeed, the algorithm does not make use of a margin.

Benchmark Results

Applications of KFD to real world data are currently rather rare. Extensive benchmark comparisons were performed in [364], however, for a selection of binary classification problems available from [36]. As shown in Table 15.1, KFD performs very well, even when compared to state-of-the-art classifiers such as AdaBoost [174] and SVMs (Chapter 7). Performance comparisons on the USPS handwritten digit recognition task can be found in Table 7.4.

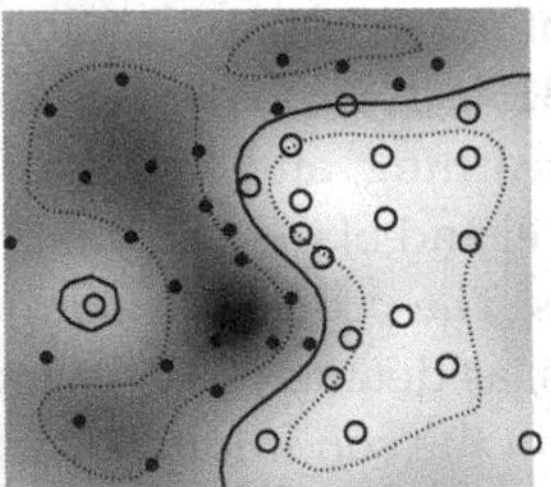
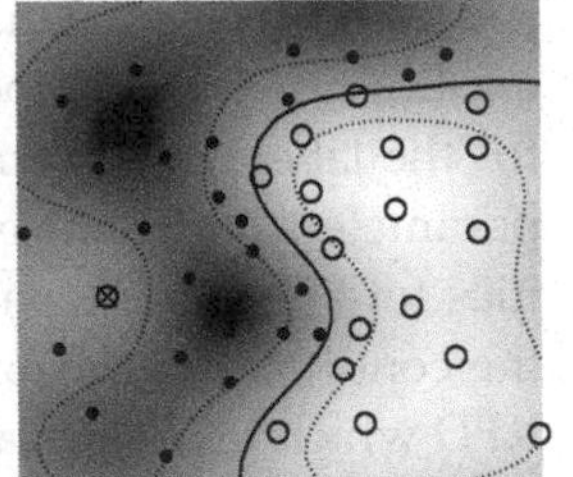
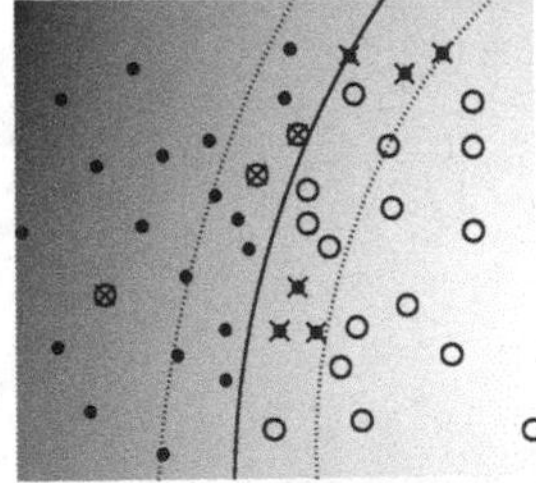

Figure 15.4 KFD toy example. In all three cases, a linear Fisher discriminant was computed based on the data points mapped into the feature space induced by a kernel. We used a Gaussian kernel (see text) in all cases, with different values of the kernel width. On the left, a rather small width was used, leading to data memorization. On the right, a wide kernel was used, with the effect that the decision boundary is almost linear; again, this is not appropriate for the given task. For an intermediate kernel size (middle), a good nonlinear separation is obtained. In all panels, the solid black line gives the actual decision boundary, while the dashed lines depict the areas corresponding to the two hyperplanes in feature space that, when projected on the direction of discrimination, fall on the means of the two classes.

Table 15.1 Comparison [364] between Support Vector Machines (Chapter 7), the Kernel Fisher Discriminant (KFD), a single radial basis function classifier (RBF), AdaBoost (AB, [174]), and regularized AdaBoost (AB_R, [428]) on 13 different benchmark datasets (see text). The best result in boldface, the second best in italics.

	SVM	KFD	RBF	AB	AB_R
Banana	11.5±0.07	**10.8±0.05**	**10.8±0.06**	12.3±0.07	*10.9±0.04*
Breast Cancer	*26.0±0.47*	**25.8±0.46**	27.6±0.47	30.4±0.47	26.5±0.45
Diabetes	*23.5±0.17*	**23.2±0.16**	24.3±0.19	26.5±0.23	23.8±0.18
German	**23.6±0.21**	*23.7±0.22*	24.7±0.24	27.5±0.25	24.3±0.21
Heart	**16.0±0.33**	*16.1±0.34*	17.6±0.33	20.3±0.34	16.5±0.35
Image	*3.0±0.06*	3.3±0.06	3.3±0.06	**2.7±0.07**	**2.7±0.06**
Ringnorm	1.7±0.01	**1.5±0.01**	1.7±0.02	1.9±0.03	*1.6±0.01*
F. Sonar	**32.4±0.18**	*33.2±0.17*	34.4±0.20	35.7±0.18	34.2±0.22
Splice	10.9±0.07	10.5±0.06	*10.0±0.10*	10.1±0.05	**9.5±0.07**
Thyroid	4.8±0.22	**4.2±0.21**	4.5±0.21	*4.4±0.22*	4.6±0.22
Titanic	**22.4±0.10**	23.2±0.20	23.3±0.13	*22.6±0.12*	*22.6±0.12*
Twonorm	3.0±0.02	**2.6±0.02**	2.9±0.03	3.0±0.03	*2.7±0.02*
Waveform	*9.9±0.04*	*9.9±0.04*	10.7±0.11	10.8±0.06	**9.8±0.08**

15.6 Summary

Kernel Fisher Discriminant (KFD) analysis can be considered a merge of SVM classifiers and Kernel PCA. As with any classifier, it takes into account the labels y_i of the data; as in PCA, it finds an "interesting" direction in a dataset by maximizing a criterion involving variances. Finally, KFD analysis resembles both SVMs and Kernel PCA by operating in a feature space induced by a kernel function.

The result is an algorithm which performs just as well as SVM classifiers; on some problems, it is actually slightly better, but it would be premature to draw any far-reaching conclusions from this. Its largest disadvantage compared with SVMs is that training procedures for KFD are not yet as well developed as those for SVMs. Until recently, KFD was only applicable to fairly small problems, as it required $m \times m$ matrices to be stored. In Section 15.3, we described new techniques which go some way in closing the gap between SVM training and KFD training; for very large datasets, however, it is an open question whether KFD analysis is competitive with sophisticated SVM training methods (Chapter 10).

On the other hand, KFD has the advantage that it lends itself to a probabilistic interpretation, since its outputs can readily be transformed into conditional probabilities of class membership. If we care only about the final classification, this may not be of interest; however, there are applications where we are interested not only in a class assignment, but also in a probability to go with it. Judging from present day training methodologies, KFD should excel in medium sized problems of this type ($m < 25000$, say), which are large enough that Bayesian techniques such as the Relevance Vector Machine (Section 16.6) are too expensive to train.

15.7 Problems

15.1 (Dual Eigenvalue Problem for KFD •) *Derive (15.6) from the Rayleigh coefficient.*

15.2 (Fisher Direction of Discriminination ••) *Prove that the solution* α *of the dual Fisher problem satisfies* $\alpha \propto N^{-1}(\mu_- - \mu_+)$.

15.3 (Quadratic Program for KFD [364, 362] ••) *Derive (15.10).*

15.4 (Fisher Loss Function ••) *Discuss the differences between the Fisher loss function and the SVM loss function, comparing the quadratic programs (7.35) and (15.10). Also compare to the loss employed in [532].*

15.5 (Relationship between KFD and SVM ••) *Study the SVM training algorithm of Pérez-Cruz et al. [407], and show that within the working set, it computes the KFD solution. Argue that the difference between SVM and KFD thus lies in the working set selection.*

15.6 (Optimality of Fisher Discriminant ••) *Prove that the KFD algorithm gives a decision boundary with the lowest possible error rate if the two classes are normally distributed with equal covariance matrices in feature space and the sample estimates of the covariance matrices are perfect.*

15.7 (Scale Invariance ••) *Prove that the KFD decision boundary does not change if some direction of feature space is scaled by* $c \neq 0$. *Hint: you do not need to worry about kernels. Just prove that the statement is true in a vector space. Note that it is sufficient to consider finite-dimensional vector spaces, as the data lie in a finite-dimensional subset of feature space.*

Argue that this invariance property does not hold true for (kernel) PCA.

15.8 (KFD performs Regularized Regression on the Class Labels •••) *Prove that a least-mean-squares regression (in feature space) on the class labels yields the same direction of discrimination as KFD (for the case of standard Fisher Discriminant Analysis, cf. [49], for example; see also [609]).*

Discuss the role of regularization as described in Section 15.2. To what kind of regularization does regression on the labels correspond?

15.9 (Conditional Class Probabilities vs. Probit ••) *Discuss the connections between probit (see (16.5)) and the method for estimating conditional probabilities described in Section 15.4.*

15.10 (Multi-Class KFD [171, 186, 442] ••) *Generalize the KFD algorithm to deal with M classes of patterns. In that case, there is no longer a one-dimensional direction of discrimination. Instead, the algorithm provides a projection on a* $M-1$*-dimensional subspace of* $\mathcal{H}$.

16 Bayesian Kernel Methods

The Bayesian approach to learning exhibits some fundamental differences with respect to the framework of risk minimization, which was the leitmotif of this book. The key distinction is that the former allows for a very intuitive incorporation of prior knowledge into the process of estimation. Moreover, it is possible, within the Bayesian framework, to obtain estimates of the confidence and reliability of the estimation process itself. These estimates can be computed easily, unlike the uniform convergence type bounds we encountered in Chapters 5 and 12.

Surprisingly enough, the Bayesian approach leads to algorithms much akin to those developed within the framework of risk minimization. This allows us to provide new insight into kernel algorithms, such as SV classification and regression. In addition, these similarities help us design Bayesian counterparts for risk minimization algorithms (such as Laplacian Processes (Section 16.5)), or vice versa (Section 16.6). In other words, we can tap into the knowledge from both worlds and combine it to create better algorithms.

Overview

We begin in Section 16.1 with an overview of the basic assumptions underlying Bayesian estimation. We explain the notion of prior distributions, which encode our prior belief concerning the likelihood of obtaining a certain estimate, and the concept of the posterior probability, which quantifies how plausible functions appear after we observe some data. Section 16.2 then shows how inference is performed, and how certain numerical problems that arise can be alleviated by various types of Maximum-a-Posteriori (MAP) estimation.

Once the basic tools are introduced, we analyze the specific properties of Bayesian estimators for three different types of prior probabilities: Gaussian Processes (Section 16.3 describes the theory and Section 16.4 the implementation), which rely on the assumption that adjacent coefficients are correlated, Laplacian Processes (Section 16.5), which assume that estimates can be expanded into a sparse linear combination of kernel functions, and therefore favor such hypotheses, and Relevance Vector Machines (Section 16.6), which assume that the contribution of each kernel function is governed by a normal distribution with its own variance.

Readers interested in a quick overview of the principles underlying Bayesian statistics will find the introduction sufficient. We recommend that the reader focus first on Sections 16.1 and 16.3. The subsequent sections are ordered in increasing technical difficulty, and decreasing bearing on the core issues of Bayesian estimation with kernels.

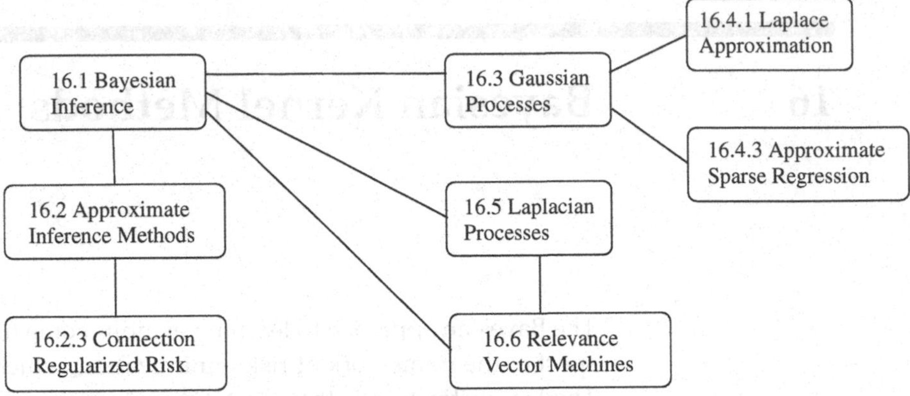

Prerequisites

This chapter is intended for readers who are already familiar with the basic concepts of classification and regression, as explained in the introduction (Chapter 1), and with the ideas underlying regularization (Chapter 4); in particular, the regularized risk functional in Section 4.1. Knowledge of Maximum Likelihood (as in Section 3.3.1) is also required. The treatment of Gaussian Processes assumes knowledge of regularization operators and Reproducing Kernel Hilbert Spaces (Section 2.2.2). Details of the implementation of Gaussian Processes require knowledge of optimization (Chapter 6), especially Newton's method (Section 6.2) and sparse greedy methods (Section 6.5).

16.1 Bayesics

The central characteristic of Bayesian estimation is that we assume certain prior knowledge or beliefs about the data generating process, and the functional dependencies we might encounter. Let us begin with the data generation process. The discussion following is closely connected to the reasoning we put forward in Section 3.3.1 to explain maximum likelihood estimation. Unless stated otherwise, we observe an m-sample $X := \{x_1, \ldots, x_m\}$ and $Y := \{y_1, \ldots, y_m\}$, based on which we will carry out inference. For notational convenience we sometimes use $Z := \{(x_1, y_1), \ldots, (x_m, y_m)\}$ instead of X, Y. We begin with an overview over the fundamental ideas (see also [49, 338, 383, 486, 432] for more details).

16.1.1 Likelihood

Assume that we are given a hypothesis f and information about the process that maps x into y. We can formalize the latter via the distribution $\mathrm{P}(y|x, f(x))$, and if a density exists, via $p(y|x, f(x))$. The key difference to the reasoning so far is that we assume the distribution $\mathrm{P}(y|x, f(x))$ is *known* (in Section 16.1.4, we relax this assumption to the knowledge of a parametric family through the use of hyperparameters).

- For instance, $f(x)$ could be the *true* wind speed at a location x, and y the *observed* speed, where the observation is corrupted by errors in the measurement process (imprecision of instruments, improper handling, etc.). In other words, we do not observe $f(x)$ but rather $f(x) + \xi$, where ξ with corresponding $P(\xi)$ is a random variable modelling the noise process. In this case, we obtain

$$y = f(x) + \xi \text{ and } P(y|x, f(x)) = P(y - f(x)) \tag{16.1}$$

- Likewise, y and $f(x)$ could be binary variables, such as black and white pixels on an image. Thus, consider the case where $f(x)$ is the color of the pixel at location x, and y the color of this pixel on a copy of the image received by a (noisy) fax transmission. In this case, we need only consider the probabilities

$$P(y|f(x)) \text{ where } y, f(x) \in \{\pm 1\}, \text{i.e., } P(1,1), P(1,-1), P(-1,1), P(-1,-1) \tag{16.2}$$

- We might want to model the *probability* that a patient develops cancer, $P(y = \text{cancer}|x)$, based on a set of medical observations x. We observe only the outcomes $y =$ "cancer" or $y =$ "no cancer", however. One way of solving this problem is to use a functional dependency $f(x)$ which can be transformed into $P(y|x)$ via a transfer function

We give three examples of such transfer functions below.

Logistic Transfer Function: this is given by

$$P(y = 1|x, f(x)) := \frac{\exp(f(x))}{1 + \exp(f(x))}. \tag{16.3}$$

Note that logistic regression with (16.3) is equivalent to modelling

$$f(x) = \ln \frac{p(y = 1|f(x))}{p(y = -1|f(x))}, \tag{16.4}$$

since $p(y = -1|f(x)) = 1 - p(y = 1|f(x))$. Solving (16.4) for $p(y = 1|f(x))$ yields (16.3).

Probit: we might also assume that y is given by the sign of f, but corrupted by Gaussian noise (see for instance [395, 396, 486]); thus, $y = \operatorname{sgn}(f(x) + \xi)$ where $\xi \sim \mathcal{N}(0, \sigma)$. In this case, we have

$$p(y|f(x)) = \int \frac{\operatorname{sgn}(yf(x) + \xi) + 1}{2} p(\xi) d\xi \tag{16.5}$$

$$= \frac{1}{\sqrt{2\pi\sigma^2}} \int_{-yf(x)}^{\infty} \exp\left(-\frac{\xi^2}{2\sigma^2}\right) d\xi = \Phi\left(\frac{yf(x)}{\sigma}\right). \tag{16.6}$$

Here Φ is the distribution function of the normal distribution.

Label Noise: finally, we might want to do classification in the presence of random label noise (possibly in addition to the noise model $p_0(y|t)$ discussed previously). In this case, a label is randomly *assigned* to observations with probability 2η (note that this is the same as randomly *flipping* with probability η). We then write

$$p(y|f(x)) = \eta + (1 - 2\eta)p_0(y|f(x)). \tag{16.7}$$

Factorizing Likelihood

Recall that in the (important) special case of iid generated data, the likelihood factorizes (3.18), and we obtain

$$\mathrm{P}(Y|X, f) = \prod_{i=1}^{m} \mathrm{P}(y_i|x_i, f(x_i)). \tag{16.8}$$

As long as $\mathrm{P}(y_i|x_i, f(x_i))$ is indeed the underlying distribution, $\mathrm{P}(Y|X, f)$ tells us how likely it is that the sample X, Y was generated by f. In the following discussion, we use Bayes' rule to turn this connection around, and consider how likely it is that f *explains* the data X, Y. Before we address this issue, however, we have to specify our assumptions about the hypotheses f that can be used.

16.1.2 Prior Distributions

When solving a practical estimation problem, we usually have some prior knowledge about the outcome we expect, be it a desire for smooth estimates, preference for a specific parametric form, or preferred correlations between certain dimensions of the inputs x_i or between the predictions at different locations. In short, we may have a (possibly vague) idea of the distribution of hypotheses f, $\mathrm{P}(f)$, that we expect to observe. Before we proceed with the technical details, let us review some examples.

Parametric Prior

- We may know that f is a linear combination of $\sin x, \cos x, \sin 2x$, and $\cos 2x$, and that the coefficients are chosen from the interval $[-1, 1]$. In this case, we can write the density $p(f)$ as

$$p(f) = \begin{cases} \frac{1}{16} & \text{if } f = \alpha_1 \sin x + \alpha_2 \cos x + \alpha_3 \sin 2x + \alpha_4 \cos 2x \text{ with } \alpha_i \in [-1, 1] \\ 0 & \text{otherwise} \end{cases}$$

This is a *parametric* prior on f

Prior on Function Values

- We may not know much more about f than that its values $f(x_i)$ are correlated and are distributed according to a Gaussian distribution with zero mean and covariance matrix K. For three values (we use f_i as a shorthand), this leads to

$$p(f_1, f_2, f_3) = \frac{1}{\sqrt{(2\pi)^3 \det K}} \exp\left(-\frac{1}{2}(f_1, f_2, f_3)^\top K^{-1}(f_1, f_2, f_3)\right). \tag{16.9}$$

The larger the off diagonal elements K_{ij}, the more the corresponding function values $f(x_i)$ and $f(x_j)$ are correlated. The main diagonal elements K_{ii} provide the variance of f_i, and the off diagonal elements the covariance between pairs f_i and f_j. Note that in this case we do not specify a prior assumption about the *function* f, but only about *its values* $f(x_i)$ at some previously specified locations.

The choice of K as a name for the covariance is deliberate. As we will see in Section 16.3, K is identical to the kernel matrix used in Reproducing Kernel Hilbert Spaces and regularization theory. The idea is that observations are generated by a stochastic process with a given covariance structure.

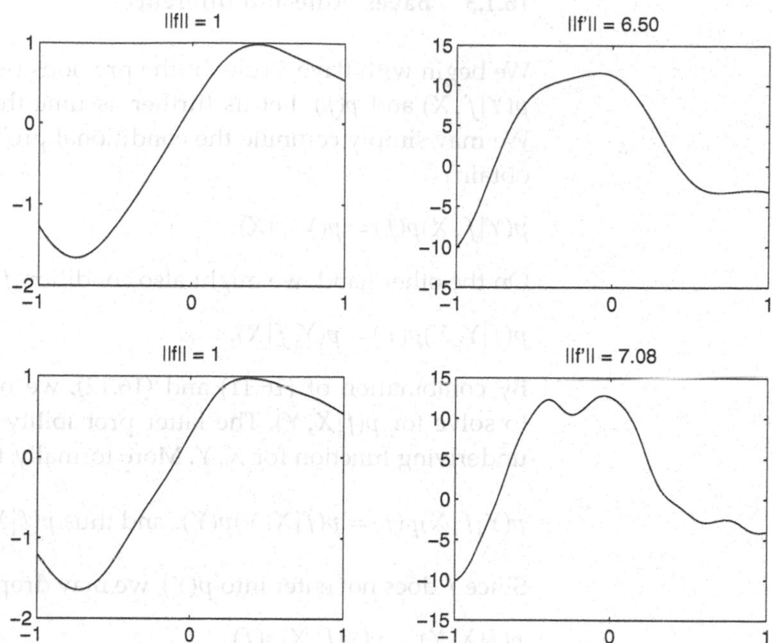

Figure 16.1 Two functions (left) on $[-1,1] \to \mathbb{R}$ and their derivatives (right). Even though the top and bottom functions closely resemble each other, the top function has a higher prior probability of occurrence according to (16.10), since its value of $\|f'\|$ is smaller.

- Finally, we may only have the abstract knowledge that smooth functions with small values are more likely to occur. Figure 16.1 is a pictorial example of such an assumption. One possible way of quantifying such a relation is to posit that the prior probability of a function occurring depends only on its L_2 norm and the L_2 norm of its first derivative. This leads to expressions of the form

Nonparametric Prior

$$-\ln p(f) = c + \|f\|^2 + \|\partial_x f\|^2. \tag{16.10}$$

In other words, non-smooth functions with large values of $\|\partial_x f\|^2$ and large functions are less likely to occur.

Eq. (16.10) is an example of a nonparametric prior on f. As in the previous example, we will see that (16.10) leads to Gaussian Processes (Section 16.3). Furthermore, we will point out the connection to regularization operators.[1]

Now that we have stated our assumptions as to the probability of certain hypotheses occurring, we will study the likelihood that a given hypothesis is responsible for a particular sample X, Y.

1. As we shall see, the connection with regularization is that $\ln p(f) = \Omega[f] + c$.

16.1.3 Bayes' Rule and Inference

We begin with Bayes' rule. In the previous two sections, we gave expressions for $p(Y|f,X)$ and $p(f)$. Let us further assume that $p(f)$ and $p(X)$ are independent.[2] We may simply combine the conditional probability with the prior probability to obtain

$$p(Y|f,X)p(f) = p(Y,f|X). \tag{16.11}$$

On the other hand, we might also condition f on Y, and decompose $p(Y,f|X)$ into

$$p(f|Y,X)p(Y) = p(Y,f|X). \tag{16.12}$$

By combination of (16.11) and (16.12), we obtain Bayes' rule, which allows us to solve for $p(f|X,Y)$. The latter probability quantifies the *evidence* that f is the underlying function for X, Y. More formally, this reads as follows:

$$p(Y|f,X)p(f) = p(f|X,Y)p(Y), \text{ and thus } p(f|X,Y) = \frac{p(Y|f,X)p(f)}{p(Y)}. \tag{16.13}$$

Since f does not enter into $p(Y)$, we may drop the latter from (16.13), leading to

$$p(f|X,Y) \propto p(Y|f,X)p(f). \tag{16.14}$$

Consequently, in order to assess which hypothesis f is more likely to occur, it is sufficient to analyze $p(Y|f,X)p(f)$. Furthermore, we may recover $p(Y)$ by computing the normalization factor on the right hand side of (16.14). Finally, $p(f|X,Y)$ also enables us to predict y at a new location x, using

$$p(y|X,Y,x) = \int p(y|f,x)p(f|X,Y)df. \tag{16.15}$$

The quantity $p(y|X,Y,x)$ tells us what observation we are likely to make at location x, given the previous observations X, Y. For instance, we could compute the expected value of the observation $y(x)$ via

$$\hat{y}(x) := \mathbf{E}\left[y(x)|Z\right], \tag{16.16}$$

and specify the confidence in the estimate. One way of computing the latter is via tail-bounds on the probability of large deviations from the expectation,

$$\mathrm{P}\left(|y(x) - E[y(x)|Z]| > \epsilon|Z\right) < \delta. \tag{16.17}$$

Unfortunately, evaluation of (16.17) can be expensive, and cannot be carried out analytically in most cases. Instead, we use approximation methods, which will be described in Section 16.2.

In some cases, it is more natural for inference purposes to analyze $p(y,Y)$ (in particular, if the dependency on x can be absorbed in a corresponding prior probabil-

2. In the absence of this assumption, we would have to find expressions for $p(X,Y|f)$, which would lead to an analogous result.

ity over (y, Y)). Since $p(y, Y) = p(y|Y)p(Y)$, however, we may easily obtain $p(y|Y)$ once we know the normalizing factor $p(Y)$. The latter is obtained by integration over y,

$$p(Y) = \int p(y, Y)dy \text{ and thus } p(y|Y) = \frac{p(y, Y)}{p(Y)} = \frac{p(y, Y)}{\int p(y, Y)dy}. \tag{16.18}$$

This process is called marginalization.

16.1.4 Hyperparameters

Consider (16.10). We might question whether the trade-off between $\|f\|^2$ and $\|\partial_x f\|^2$ is correct. Thus, rather than (16.10), we might instead write $-\ln p(f) = c + \|f\|^2 + \omega\|\partial_x f\|^2$ for some $\omega > 0$, effectively changing the *scale* of our flatness assumption. Likewise, we may not always know the exact form of the likelihood function, but we might instead have a rough idea about the amount of additive noise involved in the process of obtaining y from $f(x)$. Consequently, we need a device to encode our uncertainty about the *hyper*parameters used in the specification of the likelihood and prior probabilities.

It is only natural to extend the Bayesian reasoning to these parameters by assuming a prior distribution on the hyperparameters themselves, and making the latter variables of the inference procedure. Generalizing from the previous example, we denote by $\boldsymbol{\omega}$ the vector of *all* hyperparameters needed in a particular situation. We obtain

$$p(f, \boldsymbol{\omega}) = p(f|\boldsymbol{\omega})p(\boldsymbol{\omega}) \text{ and thus } p(f) = \int p(f, \boldsymbol{\omega})d\boldsymbol{\omega} = \int p(f|\boldsymbol{\omega})p(\boldsymbol{\omega})d\boldsymbol{\omega}. \tag{16.19}$$

Hyperprior

We call $p(\boldsymbol{\omega})$ a hyperprior, since it is a prior assumption on the prior $p(f)$ (or $p(Y|f, X)$) itself. In theory, we could integrate out the hypotheses f to obtain the posterior distribution over the hyperparameters $\boldsymbol{\omega}$,

$$p(\boldsymbol{\omega}|Z) \propto p(Z|\boldsymbol{\omega})p(\boldsymbol{\omega}) = p(\boldsymbol{\omega}) \int p(Z|f)p(f|\boldsymbol{\omega})df, \tag{16.20}$$

and use the latter to obtain

$$p(f|Z) = \int p(f|\boldsymbol{\omega}, Z)p(\boldsymbol{\omega}|Z)d\boldsymbol{\omega}. \tag{16.21}$$

Again, as in (16.15), an analytic solution of the integral is unlikely to be feasible, and we must resort to approximations (see Section 16.2.2).

16.2 Inference Methods

In this section we describe techniques useful for inference with Bayesian kernel methods, and relate these to algorithms used in the risk minimization framework. Readers interested in the connection with statistical learning theory are encouraged to read Section 12.3 on PAC-Bayesian bounds.

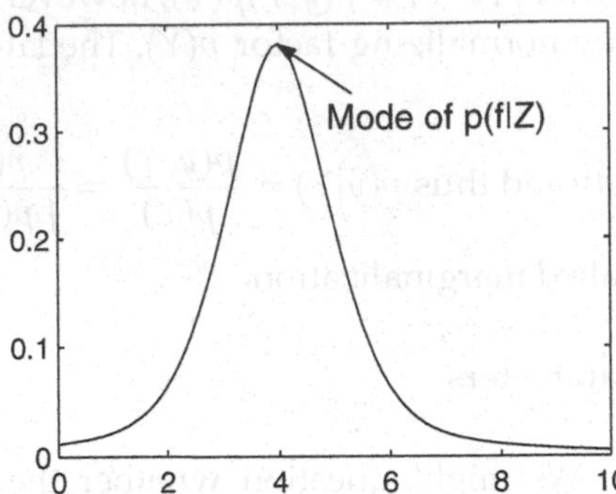

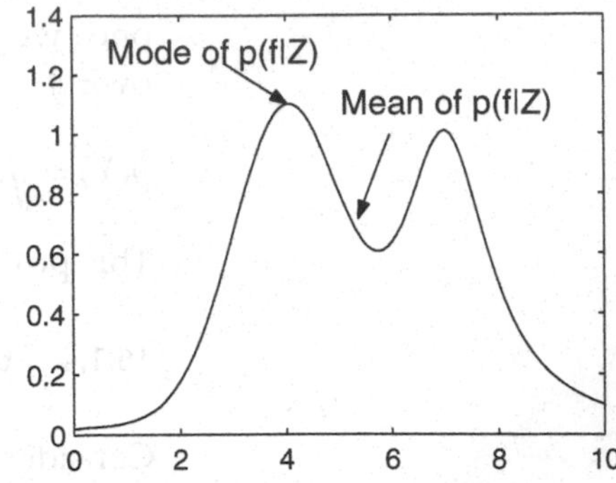

Figure 16.2 Left: The mode and mean of the distribution coincide, hence the MAP approximation is satisfied. Right: For multimodal distributions, the MAP approximation can be arbitrarily bad.

Methods other than those described below may also be suitable for this task; for the sake of brevity, however, we focus on techniques currently in common use. Other important techniques not covered here include Markov Chain Monte Carlo (MCMC) [426, 383, 384], and the Expectation Maximization (EM) algorithm [135, 275, 610, 193, 260].

16.2.1 Maximum a Posteriori Approximation

In most cases, integrals over $p(f|X, Y)$, such as the expectation of f in (16.15), are computationally intractable. This means that we have to use approximate techniques to make predictions. A popular approximation is to replace the integral over $p(f|X, Y)$ by the value of the integrand at the mode of the posterior distribution, where $p(f|X, Y)$ is maximal. The hope is that $p(f|X, Y)$ is concentrated around its mode, and that mode and mean will approximately coincide. We thus approximate (16.15) by

$$p(y|X, Y, x) \approx p(y|f_{\text{MAP}}, x) \text{ where } f_{\text{MAP}} = \operatorname*{argmax}_f p(f|X, Y). \tag{16.22}$$

We call f_{MAP} the maximum a posteriori (MAP) estimate since it maximizes the posterior distribution $p(f|X, Y)$ over the hypotheses f. In practice we obtain f_{MAP} by minimizing the negative log posterior,

Maximum a Posteriori Estimate

$$f_{\text{MAP}} = \operatorname*{argmin}_f \left[-\ln p(f|Z)\right] = \operatorname*{argmin}_f \left[-\ln p(Z|f) - \ln p(f)\right]. \tag{16.23}$$

The additional advantage of this method is that we completely avoid the issue of normalization, since (16.23) does not depend on $p(Z)$. This approximation is justified, for instance, if all distributions involved happen to be Gaussian, since mean and mode then coincide. See Figure 16.2 for an example where this assumption holds, and also for a counterexample.

We may also require an approximation in the integral over the hyperparameter ω due to the hyperprior $p(\omega)$. This situation occurs more frequently than the need to compute a MAP estimate, since a complicated prior distribution $p(f)$ stemming from an integration over ω will probably render any subsequent steps of integration intractable. Thus, we pick ω according to

MAP2 Estimate

$$\omega_{\text{MAP}} = \operatorname*{argmax}_{\omega} p(\omega|Z). \tag{16.24}$$

In order to compute $p(\omega|Z)$, we apply Bayes' rule. We then obtain

$$\omega_{\text{MAP}} = \operatorname*{argmax}_{\omega} \frac{p(Z|\omega)p(\omega)}{p(Z)} = \operatorname*{argmin}_{\omega} \left[-\ln p(Z|\omega) - \ln p(\omega)\right]. \tag{16.25}$$

This procedure is sometimes referred to as the MAP2 estimate. A practical example of the use of hyperparameters is automatic relevance determination [383]. This addresses the proper scaling of observations, and the removal of inputs that prove to be irrelevant to the problem at hand.

Remark 16.1 (Automatic Relevance Determination) *Denote by n the dimensionality of x, by $\omega := \operatorname{diag}(\omega_1, \ldots, \omega_n)$ a diagonal scaling matrix, and by*

$$p(\omega) = \prod_{i=1}^{n} p(\omega_i) \tag{16.26}$$

a factorizing prior on the hyperparameters $\omega_i \geq 0$, possibly with $p(\omega) > p(\omega')$ if $\omega > \omega'$ (this facilitates the elimination of irrelevant parameters). Assume moreover that we already have a prior $p(f)$ over hypotheses f. We can then form a prior distribution conditioned on a hyperprior by letting

$$p(f|\omega) := p(f(\omega^{-1} \cdot)). \tag{16.27}$$

In other words, functions $f(\omega \cdot\ )$ have the same prior distribution conditioned on the hyperparameter ω as their un-scaled counterparts $f(\cdot)$, with respect to the prior $p(f)$. This scaling is particularly useful to weed out unwanted inputs and to find the right scaling parameters for the remainder. See [338, 383] for more detail.

Another advantage (beyond the computational aspect) of the MAP2 approximation is that it obviates any problems with unnormalized or improper priors $p(\omega)$ on ω; in other words, functions $p(\omega)$ with integrals that do not amount to 1, or which are not integrable at all (see [539] or Section 16.6 for an example of a (log-scale) *flat* prior over a hyperparameter, where $p(\ln \omega) = \text{const.}$).

Improper Priors

This convenience comes at a price, however: Estimates obtained using improper priors no longer derive from true probability distributions, and much of the motivation for Bayesian techniques cannot then be justified. Nonetheless, these techniques work well in practice. We give an example of such a situation in Section 16.6.

16.2.2 Parametric Approximation of the Posterior Distribution

Instead of replacing $p(f|Z)$ by its mode, we may want to resort to slightly more sophisticated approximations. A first improvement is to use a normal distribution $\mathcal{N}(\mu, \sigma)$, with a mean μ coincides with the mode of $p(f|Z)$, and to use the second derivative of $-\ln p(f_{\mathrm{MAP}}|Z)$ for the variance σ. This is often referred to as the *Gaussian Approximation*. In practice, we set (see for instance [338])

Gaussian Approximation

$$f|Z \sim \mathcal{N}(E[f|Z], \Sigma^{-1}) \text{ where } \Sigma = -\partial_f^2 \left[\ln p(f|Z)\right]\big|_{E[f|Z]}. \tag{16.28}$$

The advantage of such a procedure is that the integrals remain tractable. This is also one of the reasons why normal distributions enjoy a high degree of popularity in Bayesian methods. Besides, the normal distribution is the least informative distribution (largest entropy) among all distributions with bounded variance.

As Figure 16.2 indicates, a single Gaussian may not always be sufficient to capture the important properties of $p(y|X, Y, x)$. A more elaborate *parametric* model $q_\theta(f)$ of $p(f|X, Y)$, such as a mixture of Gaussian densities, can then be used to improve the approximation of (16.15). A common strategy is to resort to variational methods. The details are rather technical and go beyond the scope of this section. The interested reader is referred to [274] for an overview, and to [53] for an application to the Relevance Vector Machine of Section 16.6. The following theorem describes the basic idea.

Variational Approximation

Theorem 16.2 (Variational Approximation of Densities) *Denote by f, y random variables with corresponding densities $p(f, y)$, $p(f|y)$, and $p(f)$. Then for any density $q(f)$, the following bound holds;*

$$\ln p(y) = \int_f \ln \frac{p(f, y)}{q(f)} q(f) df - \int_f \ln \frac{p(f|y)}{q(f)} q(f) df \leq \int_f \ln \frac{p(f, y)}{q(f)} q(f) df. \tag{16.29}$$

Proof We begin with the first equality of (16.29). Since $p(f, y) = p(f|y)p(y)$, we may decompose

$$\frac{p(f, y)}{q(f)} = \ln p(y) + \ln \frac{p(f|y)}{q(f)}. \tag{16.30}$$

Additionally, $\int_f \ln \frac{p(f|y)}{q(f)} q(f) df = \mathrm{KL}(p(f|y) \| q(f))$ is the Kullback-Leibler divergence between $p(f|y)$ and $q(f)$ [114]. The latter is a nonnegative quantity which proves the second part of (16.29). ∎

The true posterior distribution is usually $p(f|y)$, and $q(f)$ an approximation of it. The practical advantage of (16.29) is that $L := \ln \frac{p(f,y)}{q(f)} q(f) df$ can often be computed more easily, at least for simple enough $q(f)$. Furthermore, by maximizing L via a suitable choice of q, we maximize a lower bound on $\ln p(y)$.

16.2.3 Connection to Regularized Risk Functionals

A second glance at (16.23) reveals similarities between the log posterior $-\ln p(f|Z)$ and the regularized risk functional $R_{\text{reg}}[f]$ of (4.1). Both expressions are sums of two terms: One depending on f and Z ($R_{\text{emp}}[f]$ and $-\ln p(Z|f)$), and the other independent of Z ($\lambda\Omega[f]$ and $-\ln p(f)$). In particular, if we formally set

Bayesian Interpretation of Regularized Risk

$$mR_{\text{emp}}[f] = \sum_{i=1}^{m} c(x_i, y_i, f(x_i)) \equiv -\ln p(Z|f), \tag{16.31}$$

$$\lambda\Omega[f] \equiv -\ln p(f), \tag{16.32}$$

we may obtain a Bayesian interpretation of regularized risk minimization as MAP estimation, and vice versa. We next discuss the interpretation of (16.31) and (16.32).

- In the case of (16.31), recall that in Section 3.3.1 we assume that we are dealing with iid (independent and identically distributed) data, and that we *know* the dependency between the hypothesis f and the observations (x_i, y_i). As a consequence, we can write $p(Z|f)$ as a product involving one pair of observations (x_i, y_i) at a time. Finally, Remark 3.6 shows that if we set $c(x, y, f(x)) = -\ln p(y_i|x_i, f)$, we obtain direct correspondence in the data dependent part.

Likelihood and Loss Function

As described in Chapter 3, this means that the loss function in the regularized risk functional is the equivalent of the negative log likelihood in the probabilistic setting. For instance, squared loss corresponds to the assumption that normal noise is added to the data. Similar conclusions can be drawn for classification, with certain known caveats due to non-normalizability of some of the loss functions commonly used in the risk functional context [521].

- The correspondence $\lambda\Omega[f] \equiv -\ln p(f)$ in (16.32) shows that the choice of the regularizer influences the choice of the final estimate to the same extent as a prior over a function class. For instance, the choice of a particular feature space when using kernel methods acts in the same way as a prior over the class of possible functions in Bayesian estimation. This is an important fact to keep in mind when dealing with "distribution free" and "nonparametric" estimators. In effect, through a particular choice of regularization, and the consequent imposition of a partial order (roughly speaking, a ranking) on the set of possible solutions, we are selecting a particular prior. The only difference is that we do not use the probabilistic part of $-\ln p(f)$ when dealing with $\Omega[f]$ but merely compare different f, f' by the corresponding size of $\Omega[f]$.

Prior and Regularizer

Bear in mind that the correspondence between regularized risk minimization and Bayesian methods only works for algorithms maximizing the log posterior to obtain a MAP solution. The reasoning does not go beyond this point, and in particular the risk functional approach has no equivalent of the averaging process involved in obtaining the mean, rather than the mode, of a distribution.

Risk Functionals		Bayesian Methods	
Empirical Risk	$\sum_{i=1}^{m} c(x_i, y_i, f(x_i))$	neg. log-likelihood	$-\sum_{i=1}^{m} \ln p(y_i \mid f(x_i))$
Regularization	$\Omega[f]$	neg. log-prior	$-\ln p(f)$
Regularized Risk	$R_{\text{emp}}[f] + \lambda\Omega[f]$	neg. log-posterior	$-\ln p(Z\mid f) - \ln p(f)$
Risk Minimizer		MAP Estimate	

16.2.4 Translating Notations

For the sake of clarity, we present a table which puts corresponding quantities from Bayesian estimation and the risk functional approach side by side. Needless to say, the table is a gross oversimplification of the deeper connections, but it still may be useful for "decoding" scientific literature using a different framework.

16.3 Gaussian Processes

Gaussian Processes are based on the "prior" assumption that adjacent observations should convey information about each other. In particular, it is assumed that the observed variables are normal, and that the coupling between them takes place by means of the covariance matrix of a normal distribution. Eq. (16.9) is an example of such a coupling; the entries of the matrix K_{ij} tell us the correlation between the observations f_i and f_j.

It turns out that this is a convenient way of extending Bayesian modelling of linear estimators to nonlinear situations (cf. [601, 596, 486]). Furthermore, it represents the counterpart of the "kernel trick" in methods minimizing the regularized risk. We now present the basic ideas, and relegate details on efficient implementation of the optimization procedure required for inference to Section 16.4.

16.3.1 Correlated Observations

Assume we are observing function values $f(x_i)$ at locations x_i, as in (16.9). It is only natural to assume that these values are correlated, depending on their location x_i. Indeed, if this were not the case, we would not be able to perform inference, since by definition, independent random variables $f(x_i)$ do not depend on other observations $f(x_j)$.

In fact, we make a stringent assumption regarding the distribution of the $f(x_i)$, namely that they form a normal distribution with mean μ and covariance matrix K. We could of course assume *any* arbitrary distribution; most other settings, however, result in inference problems that are rather expensive to compute. Furthermore, as Theorem 16.9 will show, there exists a large class of assumptions on the distribution of $f(x_i)$ that have a normal distribution as their limit.

We begin with two observations, $f(x_1)$ and $f(x_2)$, for which we assume zero mean $\mu = (0,0)$ and covariance $K = \begin{bmatrix} 1 & 3/4 \\ 3/4 & 3/4 \end{bmatrix}$. Figure 16.3 shows the corresponding density of the random variables $f(x_1)$ and $f(x_2)$. Now assume that we observe $f(x_1)$. This gives us further information about $f(x_2)$, which allows us to state the conditional density[3]

$$p(f(x_2)|f(x_1)) = \frac{p(f(x_1), f(x_2))}{p(f(x_1))}. \tag{16.33}$$

Once the conditional density is known, the mean of $f(x_2)$ need no longer be 0, and the variance of $f(x_2)$ is decreased. In the example above, the latter becomes $\frac{3}{16}$ instead of $\frac{3}{4}$ — we have performed *inference* from the observation $f(x_1)$ to obtain possible values of $f(x_2)$.

In a similar fashion, we may infer the distribution of $f(x_i)$ based on more than two variables, provided we know the corresponding mean μ and covariance matrix K. This means that K determines how closely the prediction relates to the previous observations $f(x_i)$. In the following section, we formalize the concepts presented here and show how such matrices K can be generated efficiently.

16.3.2 Definitions and Basic Notions

Assume we are given a distribution over observations t_i at the points $x_1, \ldots, x_m$. Rather than directly specifying that the observations t_i are generated from an underlying functional dependency, we simply assume that they are generated by a Gaussian Process.[4] Loosely speaking, Gaussian processes allow us to extend the notion of a set of random variables to random functions. More formally, we have the following definition:

Definition 16.3 (Gaussian Process) *Denote by $t(x)$ a stochastic process parametrized by $x \in \mathcal{X}$ ($\mathcal{X}$ is an arbitrary index set). Then $t(x)$ is a Gaussian process if for any $m \in \mathbb{N}$ and $\{x_1, \ldots, x_m\} \subset \mathcal{X}$, the random variables $(t(x_1), \ldots, t(x_m))$ are normally distributed.*

We denote by $k(x, x')$ the function generating the covariance matrix

$$K := \operatorname{cov}\{t(x_1), \ldots, t(x_m)\}, \tag{16.34}$$

Covariance Function

and by μ the mean of the distribution. We also write $K_{ij} = k(x_i, x_j)$. This leads to

$$(t(x_1), \ldots, t(x_m)) \sim \mathcal{N}(\mu, K) \text{ where } \mu \in \mathbb{R}^m. \tag{16.35}$$

3. A convenient trick to obtain $p(f(x_2)|f(x_1))$ for normal distributions is to consider $p(f(x_1), f(x_2))$ as a function only of $f(x_2)$, while keeping $f(x_1)$ fixed at its observed value. The linear and quadratic terms then completely determine the normal distribution in $f(x_2)$.
4. We use t_i for the random variables of the Gaussian process, since they are not the labels or target values y_i that we observe at locations x_i. Instead, t_i are corrupted by noise ξ_i to yield the observed random variables y_i.

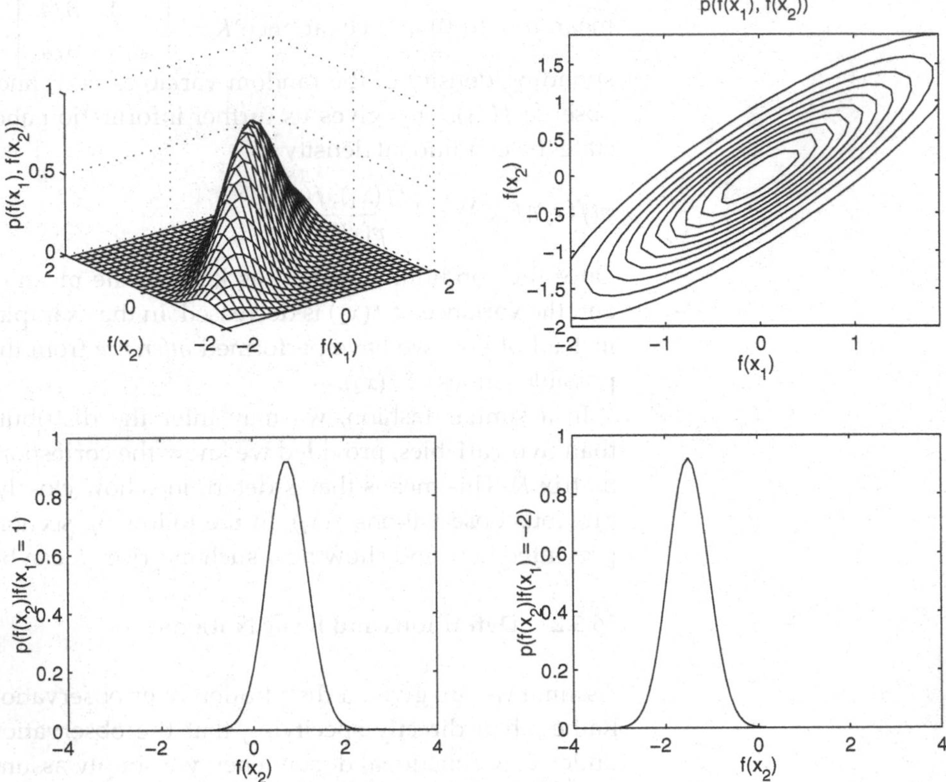

Figure 16.3 Normal distribution with two variables. Top left: normal density $p(f(x_1), f(x_2))$ with zero mean and covariance K; Top right: contour plot of $p(f(x_1), f(x_2))$; Bottom left: Conditional density of $f(x_2)$ when $f(x_1) = 1$; Bottom left: Conditional density of $f(x_2)$ when $f(x_1) = -2$. Note that in the last two plots, $f(x_2)$ is normally distributed, but with nonzero mean.

Remark 16.4 (Gaussian Processes and Positive Definite Matrices) *The function $k(x, x')$ is well defined, symmetric, and the matrix K is positive definite (cf. Definition 2.4).*

Proof We first show that $k(x, x')$ is well defined. By definition,

$$[\operatorname{cov}\{t(x_1), \ldots, t(x_m)\}]_{ij} = \operatorname{cov}\{t(x_i), t(x_j)\}. \tag{16.36}$$

Consequently, K_{ij} is only a function of *two* arguments (x_i and x_j), which shows that $k(x, x')$ is well defined.

Gaussian Processes and Mercer Kernels

It follows directly from the definition of the covariance that k is symmetric. Finally, to show that K is positive definite, we have to prove for any $\alpha \in \mathbb{R}^m$ that the inequality $\alpha^\top K \alpha \geq 0$ holds. This follows from

$$0 \leq \operatorname{Var}\left(\sum_{i=1}^{m} \alpha_i t(x_i)\right) = \alpha^\top [\operatorname{cov}\{t(x_i), t(x_j)\}]\, \alpha = \alpha^\top K \alpha. \tag{16.37}$$

Thus K is positive definite and the function k is an admissible kernel. ■

Note that even if k happens to be a smooth function (this turns out to be a reasonable assumption), the actual realizations $t(x)$, as drawn from the Gaussian process, need not be smooth at all. In fact, they may be even pointwise discontinuous.

Let us have a closer look at the prior distribution resulting from these assumptions. The standard setting is $\mu = 0$, which implies that we have no prior knowledge about the particular value of the estimate, but assume that small values are preferred. Then, for a given set of $(t(x_1), \ldots, t(x_m)) =: \mathbf{t}$, the prior density function $p(\mathbf{t})$ is given by

$$p(\mathbf{t}) = (2\pi)^{-\frac{m}{2}} (\det K)^{-\frac{1}{2}} \exp\left(-\frac{1}{2}\mathbf{t}^\top K^{-1}\mathbf{t}\right). \tag{16.38}$$

In most cases, we try to avoid inverting K. By a simple substitution,

$$\mathbf{t} = K\boldsymbol{\alpha}, \tag{16.39}$$

RKHS Regularization

we have $\boldsymbol{\alpha} \sim \mathcal{N}(0, K^{-1})$, and consequently

$$p(\boldsymbol{\alpha}) = (2\pi)^{-\frac{m}{2}} (\det K)^{-\frac{1}{2}} \exp\left(-\frac{1}{2}\boldsymbol{\alpha}^\top K\boldsymbol{\alpha}\right). \tag{16.40}$$

Taking logs, we see that this term is identical to $\Omega[f]$ from the regularization framework (4.80). This result thus connects Gaussian process priors and estimators using the Reproducing Kernel Hilbert Space framework: Kernels favoring smooth functions, as described in Chapters 2, 4, 11, and 13, translate immediately into covariance kernels with similar properties in a Bayesian context.

16.3.3 Simple Hypotheses

Let us analyze in more detail which functions are considered simple by a Gaussian process prior. As we know, hypotheses of low complexity correspond to vectors $\mathbf{y}$ for which $\mathbf{y}^\top K^{-1}\mathbf{y}$ is small. This is in particular the case for the (normalized) eigenvectors v_i of K with large eigenvalues λ_i, since

$$Kv_i = \lambda_i v_i \text{ yields } v_i^\top K^{-1} v_i = \lambda_i^{-1}. \tag{16.41}$$

In other words, the estimator is biased towards solutions with small λ_i^{-1}. This means that the spectrum and eigensystem of K represent a practical means of actually *viewing* the effect a certain prior has on the degree of smoothness of the estimates.

Let us consider a practical example: For a Gaussian covariance kernel (see also (2.68)),

$$k(x, x') = \exp\left(-\frac{\|x - x'\|^2}{2\omega^2}\right), \tag{16.42}$$

where $\omega = 1$, and under the assumption of a uniform distribution on $[-5, 5]$, we obtain the functions depicted in Figure 16.4 as simple base hypotheses for our estimator. Note the similarity to a Fourier decomposition: This means that the kernel has a strong preference for slowly oscillating functions.

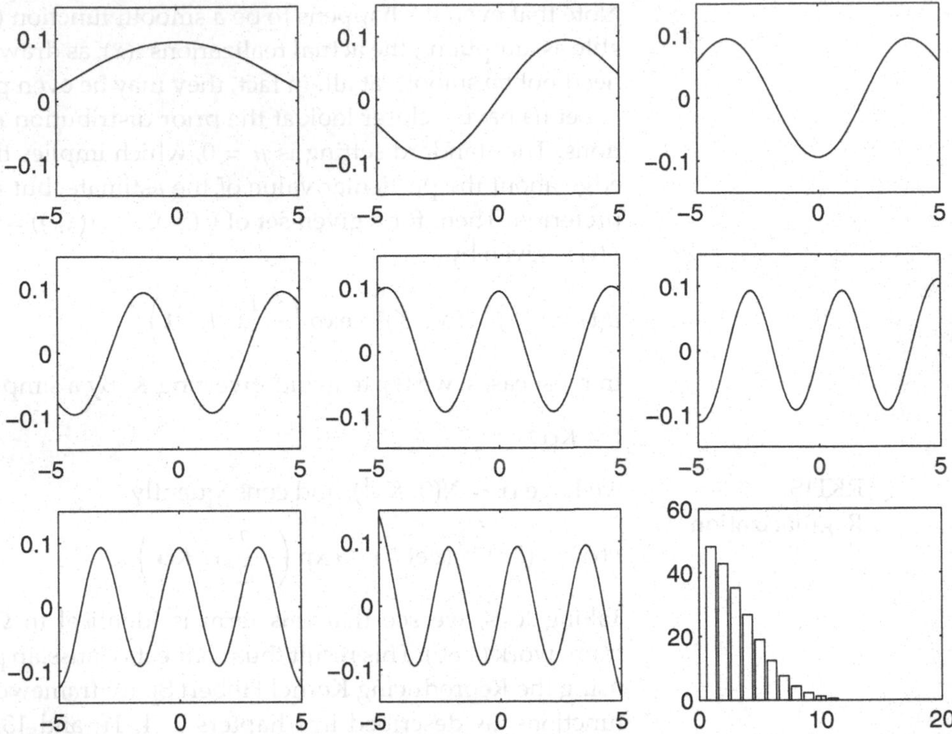

Figure 16.4 Hypotheses corresponding to the first eigenvectors of a Gaussian kernel of width 1 over a uniform distribution on the interval $[-5,5]$. From top to bottom and from left to right: The functions corresponding to the first eight eigenvectors of K. Lower right: the first 20 eigenvalues of K. Note that most of the information about K is contained in the first 10 eigenvalues. The plots were obtained by computing K for an equidistant grid of 200 points on $[-5,5]$. We then computed the eigenvectors $\mathbf{e}$ of K, and plotted them as the corresponding function values (this is possible since for $\boldsymbol{\alpha} = \mathbf{e}$ we have $K\boldsymbol{\alpha} = \lambda\boldsymbol{\alpha}$).

16.3.4 Regression

Let us put the previous discussion to practical use. For the sake of simplicity, we begin with regression (we analyze classification in Section 16.3.5). For regression estimation, we usually assume additive noise on top of the process generating $t(x_i)$; that is, rather than observing $t(x_i)$ directly, we observe $t(x_i)$ corrupted by noise,

$$y_i := t(x_i) + \xi_i \text{ and thus } \xi_i = y_i - t(x_i), \tag{16.43}$$

Additive Noise

where ξ_i are independent random variables with zero mean. In order to keep our notation simple, however, we assume that all ξ_i are drawn from the same distribution[5], $\xi \sim p(\xi)$. This allows us to state the likelihood $p(y|t(x))$ as

$$p(y_i|t(x_i)) = p(y_i - t(x_i)). \tag{16.44}$$

In other words, we eliminate the random variable ξ_i via (16.43). The posterior distribution is then given by

$$\begin{aligned} p(\mathbf{t}|\mathbf{y}) &\propto p(\mathbf{y}|\mathbf{t})p(\mathbf{t}) \\ &= \left[\prod_i p(y_i - t(x_i))\right] \frac{1}{\sqrt{(2\pi)^m \det K}} \exp\left(-\frac{1}{2}\mathbf{t}^\top K^{-1}\mathbf{t}\right). \end{aligned} \tag{16.45}$$

To perform inference, we have to specify the distribution connecting $\mathbf{t}$ and $\mathbf{y}$. We could use any possible distribution, such as those in Table 3.1.

A popular choice in Gaussian Process regression is to assume additive normal noise, $\xi_i \sim \mathcal{N}(0, \sigma)$. This has several advantages. First, all the distributions involved in the process of inference remain normal, which allows us to compute exact solutions. Second, as we will show below, we may find the mode of the distribution by a simple matrix inversion. After substituting $\mathbf{t} = K\boldsymbol{\alpha}$, taking logarithms, and ignoring terms independent of $\boldsymbol{\alpha}$, we obtain

$$\ln p(\boldsymbol{\alpha}|\mathbf{y}) = -\frac{1}{2\sigma^2}\|\mathbf{y} - K\boldsymbol{\alpha}\|^2 - \frac{1}{2}\boldsymbol{\alpha}^\top K\boldsymbol{\alpha} + c. \tag{16.46}$$

This is clearly a normal distribution, thus the mode and mean coincide, and the MAP approximation (16.22) becomes exact. The latter is obtained by maximizing (16.46) for $\boldsymbol{\alpha}$, which yields

$$\boldsymbol{\alpha} = (K + \sigma^2\mathbf{1})^{-1}\mathbf{y}. \tag{16.47}$$

Knowing $\boldsymbol{\alpha}$ allows us to predict y at a new location x. The Bayesian reasoning, however, also allows us to associate a level of confidence with the estimate. For normal distributions it suffices to know the variance.

One way to obtain this information is to write (16.45) for an $m + 1$ dimensional system where y_{m+1} is unknown and compute the variance of y_{m+1}. There exists a more elegant way of obtaining the variance Var y_{m+1} for additive Gaussian noise, however. Since $\mathbf{y}$ is a sum of two Gaussian random variables, its covariance is given by $(K + \sigma^2\mathbf{1})$, and thus

Conditioning on observed $\mathbf{y}$

$$\begin{aligned} &p(\mathbf{y}, y_{m+1}) \\ &\propto \exp\left(-\frac{1}{2}\begin{bmatrix}\mathbf{y} \\ y_{m+1}\end{bmatrix}\begin{bmatrix}K + \sigma^2\mathbf{1} & \mathbf{k} \\ \mathbf{k}^\top & k(x_{m+1}, x_{m+1}) + \sigma^2\end{bmatrix}^{-1}\begin{bmatrix}\mathbf{y} \\ y_{m+1}\end{bmatrix}^\top\right). \end{aligned} \tag{16.48}$$

Here K is an $m \times m$ matrix and $\mathbf{k} = [k(x_1, x_{m+1}), \ldots, k(x_m, x_{m+1})]$. Since we already know $\mathbf{y}$, we can obtain the variance of y_{m+1} in $p(y|\mathbf{y})$ by computing the lower right

5. This assumption is made for computational convenience only. We would otherwise have to consider different $p_i(\xi_i)$ for $1 \leq i \leq m$. The likelihood still factorizes in this case, but the observations can no longer be treated equally.

entry of the square matrix in (16.48). We can check (see for instance [337]) that this is given by

$$\operatorname{Var} y_{m+1} = k(x_{m+1}, x_{m+1}) + \sigma^2 - \mathbf{k}^\top (K + \sigma^2 \mathbf{1})^{-1} \mathbf{k}. \tag{16.49}$$

From (16.49) and (16.47), we conclude that $y(x_{m+1})$ is normally distributed with

$$y(x_{m+1}) \sim \mathcal{N}(K(K + \sigma^2 \mathbf{1})^{-1} \mathbf{y}, k(x_{m+1}, x_{m+1}) + \sigma^2 - \mathbf{k}^\top (K + \sigma^2 \mathbf{1})^{-1} \mathbf{k}). \tag{16.50}$$

In most other cases, such as for round-off noise, Laplacian noise, etc. , an exact solution for the posterior probability is not possible, and we have to make do with approximations. While we do not discuss this subject further in the current section (see [486] for more detail), we return to the issue of approximating a posterior distribution in Sections 16.5 and 16.6, where the form of the prior distribution makes an *exact* computation of $p(f|X, Y)$ difficult.

16.3.5 Classification

For the sake of simplicity we limit ourselves to the case of two classes; that is, to binary classification (see for instance [486, 600] for details on multi-class discrimination). Rather than attempting to predict the labels $y_i \in \{\pm 1\}$ directly, we use logistic regression. Hence we try to model the conditional probabilities $\mathrm{P}(y = 1|x)$ and $\mathrm{P}(y = -1|x)$ alike. A popular choice is to posit a functional form for the link between $f(x)$ and y, such as (16.3), (16.5), or (16.7).

Matters are slightly easier for classification than for regression: provided we are able to find a hypothesis f (or a distribution over such hypotheses), we *immediately* know the confidence of the estimate. Thus, $\mathrm{P}(y = 1|x)$ not only tells us whether the estimator classifies x as $+1$ or -1, but also the probability of obtaining these labels. Therefore, calculations regarding the variation of f are not as important as they were in Section 16.3.4 (16.49).

Let us proceed with a formal statement of a Gaussian process classification model. The posterior density is given by

$$p(f|Z) \propto p(Y|X, \mathbf{t}) \tag{16.51}$$

$$= \prod_{i=1}^{m} p(y_i|t(x_i)) \exp\left(-\frac{1}{2}\mathbf{t}^\top K^{-1}\mathbf{t}\right), \tag{16.52}$$

where $\mathbf{t} := (t(x_1), \ldots, t(x_m))$. With the transformation $\mathbf{t} = K\boldsymbol{\alpha}$, and thus

$$t(x) = \sum_{j=1}^{m} \alpha_j k(x_j, x), \tag{16.53}$$

Log-Posterior

the negative logarithm of the posterior density becomes

$$-\ln p(f|X, Y) = \sum_{i=1}^{m} -\ln p(y_i|t(x_i)) + \frac{1}{2}\boldsymbol{\alpha}^\top K \boldsymbol{\alpha}. \tag{16.54}$$

If we adopt the MAP (maximum a posterior) methodology of Section 16.2.1, inference is carried out by searching the mode of the density $p(f|X, Y)$. Therefore, the estimation problem can be reduced to a nonlinear function minimization problem, as in the regression case 16.3.4. We give examples of such techniques in Section 16.4.

16.3.6 Adjusting Hyperparameters for Gaussian Processes

More often than not, we will not know beforehand the exact amount of additive noise, or the specific form of the covariance kernel. To address this problem, the hyperparameter formalism of Section 16.1.4 is needed. To avoid technicalities, we only discuss the application of the MAP2 estimate (16.24) for the special case of regression with additive Gaussian noise, and refer the reader to [600, 193, 151, 426] and the references therein for integration methods based on Markov Chain Monte Carlo approximations (see also [486] for a more recent overview).

We denote by ω the set of hyperparameters we would like to adjust. In more compact notation, (16.48) becomes (now conditioned on ω)

$$p(\mathbf{y}|\omega) = \frac{1}{\sqrt{(2\pi)^m \det(K + \sigma^2 \mathbf{1})}} \exp\left(-\frac{1}{2}\mathbf{y}^\top (K + \sigma^2)^{-1}\mathbf{y}\right) \tag{16.55}$$

where K, σ are functions of ω. In other words, (16.55) tells us how likely it is that we observe $\mathbf{y}$, if we know ω.

Recall that the basic idea of the MAP2 estimate (16.24) is to maximize $p(\omega|\mathbf{y})$ by maximizing $p(\mathbf{y}|\omega)p(\omega)$. In practice, this is achieved by gradient ascent (see Section 6.2.2) or second order methods (see Section 6.2.1 for Newton's method) on $p(\mathbf{y}|\omega)p(\omega)$. Both cases require information about the gradient of (16.55) with respect to ω. We give an explicit expression for the gradient below.

Gradient wrt. Hyperparameters

Since the logarithm is monotonic, we can equivalently minimize the negative log posterior, $\ln p(\mathbf{y}|\omega)p(\omega)$. With the shorthand $Q := K + \sigma^2\mathbf{1}$, we obtain

$$\partial_\omega\left[-\ln p(\mathbf{y}|\omega)p(\omega)\right]$$

$$= \frac{1}{2}\partial_\omega(\ln\det Q) - \frac{1}{2}\partial_\omega\left[\mathbf{y}^\top Q^{-1}\mathbf{y}\right] - \partial_\omega \ln p(\omega) \tag{16.56}$$

$$= -\frac{1}{2}\operatorname{tr}\left(Q^{-1}\partial_\omega Q\right) + \frac{1}{2}\mathbf{y}^\top Q^{-1}\left(\partial_\omega Q\right)Q^{-1}\mathbf{y} - \partial_\omega \ln p(\omega). \tag{16.57}$$

Here (16.57) follows from (16.56) via standard matrix algebra [337]. Likewise, we could compute the Hessian of $\ln p(\mathbf{y}|\omega)p(\omega)$ with respect to ω and use a second order optimization method.[6]

Flat Hyperprior

If we assume a flat hyperprior ($p(\omega) = \text{const.}$), optimization over ω simply becomes gradient descent in $-\ln p(\mathbf{y}|\omega)$; in other words, the term depending on $p(\omega)$ vanishes. Computing (16.57) is still very expensive numerically since it involves the inversion of Q, which is an $m \times m$ matrix.

There exist numerous techniques, such as sparse greedy approximation meth-

6. This is rather technical, and the reader is encouraged to consult the literature for further detail [339, 426, 383, 197].

ods, to alleviate this problem. We present a selection of these techniques in the following section. Further detail on the topic of hyperparameter optimization can be found in Section 16.6, where hyperparameters play a crucial role in determining the sparsity of an estimate.

16.4 Implementation of Gaussian Processes

In this section, we discuss various methods to perform inference in the case of Gaussian process classification or regression. We begin with a general purpose technique, the *Laplace approximation*, which is essentially an application of Newton's method (Section 6.2.1) to the problem of minimizing the negative log-posterior density. Since it is a second order method, it is applicable as long as the log-densities have second order derivatives. Readers interested only in the basic ideas of Gaussian process estimation may skip the present section.

For classification with the logistic transfer function we present a variational method (Section 16.4.2), due to Jaakkola and Jordan [260], and Gibbs and MacKay [197, 198], a linear system of equations for optimization purposes.

Finally, the special case of regression in the presence of normal noise admits very efficient optimization algorithms based on the approximate minimization of quadratic forms (Section 16.4.3). We subsequently discuss the scaling behavior and approximation bounds for these algorithms.

16.4.1 Laplace Approximation

In general the negative log posterior (16.54), which is minimized to obtain the MAP estimate, is not quadratic, hence the minimum cannot be found analytically (compare with (16.47), where the minimizer *can* be stated explicitly). A possible solution is to make successive quadratic approximations of the negative log posterior, and minimize the latter iteratively. This strategy is referred to as the Laplace approximation[7] [525, 600, 486]; the Newton-Raphson method, in numerical analysis (see [530, 423]); or the Fisher scoring method, in statistics.

A necessary condition for the minimum of a differentiable function g is that its first derivative be 0. For convex functions, this requirement is also sufficient. We approximate g' linearly by

$$g'(x+\Delta x) \sim g'(x) + \Delta x g''(x), \text{ and hence } \Delta x = -\frac{g'(x)}{g''(x)}. \tag{16.58}$$

7. Strictly speaking, the Laplace approximation refers only to the fact that we approximate the mode of the posterior by a Gaussian distribution. We already use the Gaussian approximation in the second order method, however, in order to maximize the posterior. Hence, for all practical purposes, the two approximations just represent two different points of view on the same subject.

Taylor Expansion

Substituting $\ln p(f|X,Y)$ into (16.58) and using the definitions

$$c := \left(-\partial_{t(x_1)} \ln p(y_1|t(x_1)), \ldots, -\partial_{t(x_m)} \ln p(y_m|t(x_m))\right), \tag{16.59}$$

$$C := \operatorname{diag}\left(-\partial^2_{t(x_1)} \ln p(y_1|t(x_1)), \ldots, -\partial^2_{t(x_m)} \ln p(y_m|t(x_m))\right), \tag{16.60}$$

we obtain the following update rule for $\boldsymbol{\alpha}$ (see also Problem 16.12),

$$\boldsymbol{\alpha}_{\text{new}} = (KC + \mathbf{1})^{-1}(KC\boldsymbol{\alpha}_{\text{old}} - c). \tag{16.61}$$

While (16.61) is usually an efficient way of finding a maximizer of the log posterior, it is far from clear that this update rule is always convergent (to prove the latter, we would need to show that the initial guess of $\boldsymbol{\alpha}$ lies within the radius of attraction; see Problem 16.11). Nonetheless, this approximation turns out to work in practice, and the implementation of the update rule is relatively simple.

The major stumbling block if we want to apply (16.61) to large problems is that the update rule requires the inversion of an $m \times m$ matrix. This is costly, and effectively precludes efficient exact solutions for problems of size 5000 and beyond, due to memory and computational requirements. If we are able to provide a low rank approximation of K by

$$\tilde{K} = U^\top K_{\text{sub}} U \text{ where } U \in \mathbb{R}^{n \times m} \text{ and } K_{\text{sub}} \in \mathbb{R}^{n \times n} \tag{16.62}$$

with $n \ll m$, however, we may compute (16.61) much more efficiently. Problem 16.15 covers the computation of U given K_{sub}. It follows immediately from the Sherman-Woodbury-Morrison formula [207],

Sherman Woodbury Morrison Formula

$$(V + RHR^\top)^{-1} = V^{-1} - V^{-1}R(H^{-1} + R^\top V^{-1}R)^{-1}R^\top V^{-1}, \tag{16.63}$$

that we obtain the following update rule for $\tilde{K}$,

$$\boldsymbol{\alpha}_{\text{new}} = \left(\mathbf{1} - U^\top \left(K_{\text{sub}}^{-1} + UCU^\top\right)^{-1} UC\right)(U^\top K_{\text{sub}} UC\boldsymbol{\alpha}_{\text{old}} - c). \tag{16.64}$$

In particular, the number of operations required to solve (16.61) is $O(mn^2 + n^3)$ rather than $O(m^3)$.

There are several ways to obtain a good approximation of (16.62). One way is to project $k(x_i, x)$ on a random subset of dimensions, and express the missing terms as a linear combination of the resulting sub-matrix (this is the Nyström method proposed by Seeger and Williams [603]). We might also construct a randomized sparse greedy algorithm to select the dimensions (see Section 10.2 for more details), or resort to a positive diagonal pivoting strategy [169].

An approximation of K by its leading principal components, as often done in machine learning, is usually undesirable, since the computation of the eigensystem would still be costly, and the time required for prediction would still rise with the number of observations (since we cannot expect the leading eigenvectors of K to contain a significant number of zero coefficients).

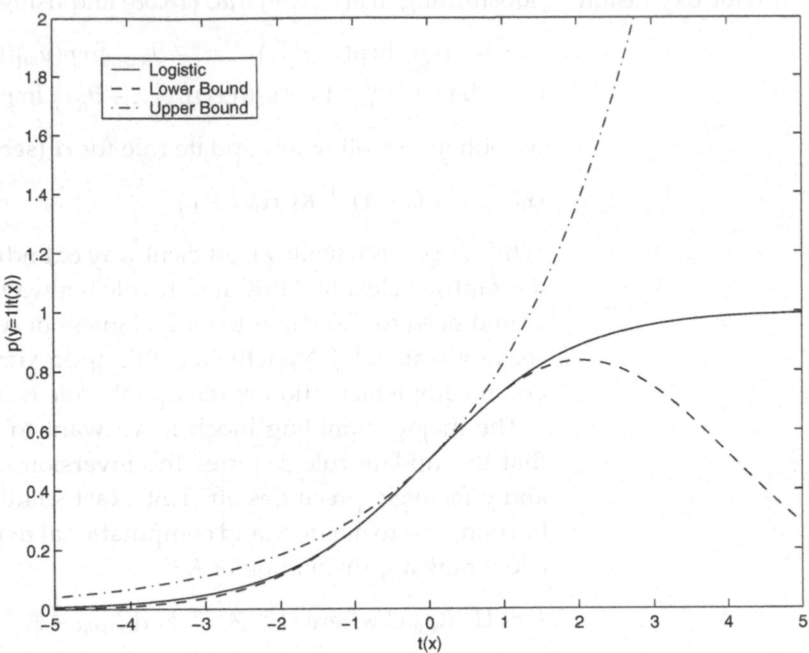

Figure 16.5 Variational Approximation for $\mu = \nu = 0.5$. Note that the quality of the approximation varies widely, depending on the value of $f(x)$.

16.4.2 Variational Methods

In the case of logistic regression, Jaakkola and Jordan [260] compute upper and lower bounds on the logistic $(1+e^{-t})^{-1}$, by exploiting the log-concavity of (3.5): A convex function can be bounded from below by its tangent at any point, and from above by a quadratic with sufficiently large curvature (provided the maximum curvature of the original function is bounded). These bounds are (see also exercise 16.13)

$$p(y=1|t) \geq \frac{1}{1+e^{-\nu}} \exp\left(\frac{(t-\nu)}{2} - \lambda(\nu)(t^2-\nu^2)\right), \quad (16.65)$$

$$p(y=1|t) \leq \exp\left(\mu t - H(\mu)\right), \quad (16.66)$$

Quadratic Approximation

where $\mu, \nu \in [0,1]$ and $\lambda(\nu) = \frac{(1+e^{-\nu})^{-1}-1/2}{2\nu}$. Furthermore, $H(\mu)$ is the binary entropy function,

$$H(\mu) = -\mu \ln \mu - (1-\mu)\ln(1-\mu). \quad (16.67)$$

Likewise, bounds for $p(y=-1|t)$ follow directly from $p(y=-1|t) = 1 - p(y=1|t)$. Equations (16.66) and (16.65) can be calculated quite easily, since they are linear or quadratic functions in t. This means that for *fixed* parameters μ and ν, we can optimize an upper and a lower bound on the log posterior using the same techniques as in Gaussian process regression (Section 16.3).

Validity of Approximation

Approximations (16.66) and (16.65) are only tight, however, if ν, μ are chosen suitably. Therefore we have to adapt these parameters at every iteration (or after each exact solution), for instance by gradient descent. See [198, 196] for details. As in the previous section, we could use the Sherman-Woodbury-Morrison formula to invert the quadratic terms more efficiently. The implementation is analogous to the application of this result in the previous section, hence we will not go into further detail.

16.4.3 Approximate Solutions for Gaussian Process Regression

The approximations of Section 16.4.1 indicate that one of the more efficient ways of implementing Gaussian process estimation on large amounts of data is to find a low rank approximation[8] of the matrix K. Such an approximation is very much needed in practice, since (16.45) and (16.51) show that exact solutions of Gaussian Processes can be hard to come by. Even if α is computed beforehand (see Table 16.1 for the scaling behavior), prediction of the mean at a new location still requires $O(m)$ operations. In particular, memory requirements are $O(m^2)$ to store K, and CPU time for matrix inversions, as are typically required for second order methods, scales with $O(m^3)$.

Proximity in $p(f|X,Y) \neq$ Proximity in f

Let us limit ourselves to an approximation of the MAP solution. One of the criteria to impose is that the posterior probability at the approximate solution be close to the maximum of the posterior probability. Note that this requirement is different from the requirement of closeness in the approximation itself, as represented for instance by the expansion coefficients (the latter requirement was used by Gibbs and Mackay [197]). Proximity in the coefficients, however, is not what we want, since it does not take into account the importance of the individual variables. For instance, it is not invariant under transformations of scale in the parameters.

For the remainder of the current section, we consider only additive normal noise. Here, the log posterior takes a quadratic form, given by (16.46). The following theorem, which uses an idea from [197], gives a bound on the approximation quality of minima of quadratic forms and is thus applicable to (16.46).

Theorem 16.5 (Approximation Bounds for Quadratic Forms [503]) *Denote by $K \in \mathbb{R}^{m\times m}$ a symmetric positive definite matrix, $\mathbf{y}, \boldsymbol{\alpha} \in \mathbb{R}^m$, and define the two quadratic forms*

$$Q(\boldsymbol{\alpha}) := -\mathbf{y}^\top K\boldsymbol{\alpha} + \frac{1}{2}\boldsymbol{\alpha}^\top(\sigma^2 K + K^\top K)\boldsymbol{\alpha}, \tag{16.68}$$

$$Q^*(\boldsymbol{\alpha}) := -\mathbf{y}^\top \boldsymbol{\alpha} + \frac{1}{2}\boldsymbol{\alpha}^\top(\sigma^2 \mathbf{1} + K)\boldsymbol{\alpha}. \tag{16.69}$$

8. Tresp [546] devised an efficient way of estimating $f(x)$ if the test set is known at the time of training. He proceeds by projecting the estimators on the subspace spanned by the functions $k(\tilde{x}_i, \cdot)$, where $\tilde{x}_i$ are the training data. Likewise, Csató and Opper [128] design an iterative algorithm that performs gradient descent on partial posterior distributions and simultaneously projects the estimates onto a subspace.

Suppose Q and Q^* have minima $Q_{\min}$ and $Q^*_{\min}$. Then for all $\boldsymbol{\alpha}, \boldsymbol{\alpha}^* \in \mathbb{R}^m$ we have

$$Q(\boldsymbol{\alpha}) \geq Q_{\min} \geq -\frac{1}{2}\|\mathbf{y}\|^2 - \sigma^2 Q^*(\boldsymbol{\alpha}^*), \tag{16.70}$$

$$Q^*(\boldsymbol{\alpha}^*) \geq Q^*_{\min} \geq \sigma^{-2}\left(-\frac{1}{2}\|\mathbf{y}\|^2 - Q(\boldsymbol{\alpha})\right), \tag{16.71}$$

with equalities throughout when $Q(\boldsymbol{\alpha}) = Q_{\min}$ and $Q^*(\boldsymbol{\alpha}^*) = Q^*_{\min}$.

Hence, by minimizing Q^* in addition to Q, we can bound Q's closeness to the optimum and vice versa.

Proof The minimum of $Q(\boldsymbol{\alpha})$ is obtained for $\boldsymbol{\alpha}_{\text{opt}} = (K + \sigma^2\mathbf{1})^{-1}\mathbf{y}$ (which also minimizes Q^*),[9] hence

$$Q_{\min} = -\frac{1}{2}\mathbf{y}^\top K(K+\sigma^2\mathbf{1})^{-1}\mathbf{y} \text{ and } Q^*_{\min} = -\frac{1}{2}\mathbf{y}^\top(K+\sigma^2\mathbf{1})^{-1}\mathbf{y}. \tag{16.72}$$

This allows us to combine $Q_{\min}$ and $Q^*_{\min}$ to $Q_{\min} + \sigma^2 Q^*_{\min} = -\frac{1}{2}\|\mathbf{y}\|^2$. Since by definition $Q(\boldsymbol{\alpha}) \geq Q_{\min}$ for all $\boldsymbol{\alpha}$ (and likewise $Q^*(\boldsymbol{\alpha}^*) \geq Q^*_{\min}$ for all $\boldsymbol{\alpha}^*$), we may solve $Q_{\min} + \sigma^2 Q^*_{\min}$ for either Q or Q^* to obtain lower bounds for each of the two quantities. This proves (16.70) and (16.71). ■

Equation (16.70) is useful for computing an approximation to the MAP solution (the objective function is identical to $Q(\boldsymbol{\alpha})$, ignoring constant terms independent of $\boldsymbol{\alpha}$), whereas (16.71) can be used to obtain error bars on the estimate. To see this, note that in calculating the variance (16.49), the expensive quantity to compute is $-\mathbf{k}^\top(K+\sigma^2\mathbf{1})^{-1}\mathbf{k}$. This can be found as

$$-\mathbf{k}^\top(K+\sigma^2\mathbf{1})^{-1}\mathbf{k} = 2\min_{\boldsymbol{\alpha}\in\mathbb{R}^m}\left[-\mathbf{k}^\top\boldsymbol{\alpha} + \tfrac{1}{2}\boldsymbol{\alpha}^\top\left(\sigma^2\mathbf{1} + K\right)\boldsymbol{\alpha}\right], \tag{16.73}$$

however. A close look reveals that the expression inside the parentheses is $Q^*(\boldsymbol{\alpha})$ with $\mathbf{y} = \mathbf{k}$ (see (16.69)). Consequently, an approximate minimizer of (16.73) gives an *upper bound* on the error bars, and lower bounds can be obtained from (16.71). In practice, we use the relative discrepancy between the upper and lower bounds,

Relative Gap Size between Upper and Lower Bound

$$\text{gap}(\boldsymbol{\alpha}, \boldsymbol{\alpha}^*) := \frac{2(Q(\boldsymbol{\alpha}) + \sigma^2 Q^*(\boldsymbol{\alpha}^*) + \frac{1}{2}\|\mathbf{y}\|^2)}{-Q(\boldsymbol{\alpha}) + \sigma^2 Q^*(\boldsymbol{\alpha}^*) + \frac{1}{2}\|\mathbf{y}\|^2}, \tag{16.74}$$

to determine how much further the approximation has to proceed.

16.4.4 Solutions on Subspaces

The central idea of the algorithm below is that improvements in speed can be achieved by a reduction in the number of free variables. Denote by $P \in \mathbb{R}^{m\times n}$ with $m \geq n$ and $m, n \in \mathbb{N}$ an extension matrix (in other words, $P^\top$ is a projection), with

9. If K does not have full rank, $Q(\boldsymbol{\alpha})$ still attains its minimum value for $\boldsymbol{\alpha}_{\text{opt}}$. There will then be additional $\boldsymbol{\alpha}'$ that minimize $Q(\boldsymbol{\alpha})$, however.

Table 16.1 Computational Cost of Various Optimization Methods. Note that $n \ll m$, and that different values of n are used in Conjugate Gradient, Sparse Decomposition, and Sparse Greedy Approximation methods: $n_{CG} \le n_{SD} \le n_{SGA}$, since the search spaces are progressively more restricted. Near-optimal results are obtained when $\kappa = 60$.

	Exact Solution	Conjugate Gradient [197]	Sparse Decomposition	Sparse Greedy Approximation
Memory	$O(m^2)$	$O(m^2)$	$O(nm)$	$O(nm)$
Initialization (= Training)	$O(m^3)$	$O(nm^2)$	$O(n^2m)$	$O(\kappa n^2 m)$
Prediction:				
Mean	$O(m)$	$O(m)$	$O(n)$	$O(n)$
Error Bars	$O(m^2)$	$O(nm^2)$	$O(n^2m)$ or $O(n^2)$	$O(\kappa n^2 m)$ or $O(n^2)$

$P^\top P = \mathbf{1}$. We make the ansatz

$$\boldsymbol{\alpha}_P := P\boldsymbol{\beta} \text{ where } \boldsymbol{\beta} \in \mathbb{R}^n, \tag{16.75}$$

Restricted Solution

and find solutions $\boldsymbol{\beta}$ such that $Q(\boldsymbol{\alpha}_P)$ (or $Q^*(\boldsymbol{\alpha}_P)$) is minimized. The solution is

$$\boldsymbol{\beta}_{\text{opt}} = \left(P^\top \left(\sigma^2 K + K^\top K\right) P\right)^{-1} P^\top K^\top \mathbf{y}. \tag{16.76}$$

If P is of rank m, this is also the solution of (16.46) (the minimum negative log posterior for all $\boldsymbol{\alpha} \in \mathbb{R}^m$). In all other cases, however, it is an approximation.

For a given $P \in \mathbb{R}^{m\times n}$, let us analyze the computational cost involved in computing (16.76). We need $O(nm)$ operations to evaluate $P^\top K\mathbf{y}$, $O(n^2m)$ operations for $(KP)^\top(KP)$, and $O(n^3)$ operations for the inversion of an $n \times n$ matrix. This brings the total cost to $O(n^2m)$. Predictions require $\mathbf{k}^\top\boldsymbol{\alpha}$, which entails $O(n)$ operations. Likewise, we may use P to minimize $Q^*(P\boldsymbol{\beta}^*)$, which is needed to upper-bound the log posterior. The latter costs no more than $O(n^3)$.

Approximation of Posterior Variance

To compute the posterior variance, we have to approximately minimize (16.73), which can done for $\boldsymbol{\alpha} = P\boldsymbol{\beta}$ at cost $O(n^3)$. If we compute $(PKP^\top)^{-1}$ beforehand, the cost becomes $O(n^2)$, and likewise for upper bounds. In addition to this, we have to minimize $-\mathbf{k}^\top KP\boldsymbol{\beta} + \frac{1}{2}\boldsymbol{\beta}^\top P^\top(\sigma^2 K + K^\top K)P\boldsymbol{\beta}$, which again costs $O(n^2m)$ (once the inverse matrices have been computed, however, we may also use them to compute error bars at different locations, thus limiting the cost to $O(n^2)$). Accurate lower bounds on the error bars are not especially crucial, since a bad estimate leads at worst to overly conservative confidence intervals, and has no further negative effect. Finally, note that we need only compute and store KP — that is, the $m \times n$ sub-matrix of K — and not K itself. Table 16.1 summarizes the scaling behavior of several optimization algorithms.

Choosing P

This leads us to the question of how to choose P for optimum efficiency. Possibilities include using the principal components of K [602], performing conjugate gradient descent to minimize Q [197], performing symmetric diagonal pivoting [169], or applying a sparse greedy approximation to K directly [513]. Yet these methods have the disadvantage that they either do not take the specific form of $\mathbf{y}$ into account [602, 513, 169], or lead to expansions that cost $O(m)$ for prediction, and require computation *and storage* of the full matrix [602, 197].

By contrast to these methods, we use a *data adaptive* version of a sparse greedy approximation algorithm. We may then only consider matrices P that are a collection of unit vectors $\mathbf{e}_i$ (here $(\mathbf{e}_i)_j = \delta_{ij}$), since these only select a number of rows of K equal to the rank of P. The details follow the algorithmic template described in Section 6.5.3.

Greedy Selection Strategy

- First, for $n = 1$, we choose $P = e_i$ such that $Q(P\boldsymbol{\beta})$ is minimal. In this case we could permit ourselves to consider *all possible* indices $i \in \{1, \ldots m\}$ and find the best one by trying all of them.
- Next, assume that we found a good solution $P\boldsymbol{\beta}$, where P contains n columns. In order to improve this solution, we expand P into the matrix $P_{\text{new}} := [P_{\text{old}}, \mathbf{e}_i] \in \mathbb{R}^{m\times(n+1)}$ and seek the best $\mathbf{e}_i$ such that P_{new} minimizes $\min_\beta Q(P_{\text{new}}\boldsymbol{\beta})$.

Note that this method is very similar to Matching Pursuit [342] and to iterative reduced set Support Vector algorithms (see Section 18.5 and [474]), with the difference that the target to be approximated (the full solution $\boldsymbol{\alpha}$) is only given implicitly via $Q(\boldsymbol{\alpha})$.

Recently Zhang [613] proved lower bounds on the rate of sparse approximation schemes. In particular, he shows that most subspace projection algorithms enjoy at least an $O(n^{-1})$ rate of convergence. See also [614] for details on further greedy approximation methods.

16.4.5 Implementation Issues

Performing a full search over all possible $n+1$ of m indices is excessively costly. Even a full search over all $m - n$ remaining indices to select the next basis function can be prohibitively expensive. Here Theorem 6.33 comes to our aid — it states that with high probability, a small subset of size $\kappa = 59$, chosen at random, guarantees near optimal performance. Hence, if we are satisfied with finding a *relatively good* index rather than the *best* index, we may resort to selecting only a random subset. It is now crucial to obtain the values of $Q(P\boldsymbol{\beta}_{\text{opt}})$ cheaply (with $P = [P_{\text{old}}, \mathbf{e}_i]$), assuming that we found P_{old} previously. From (16.76) we can see that we need only do a rank-1 update on the inverse. We now show that this can be obtained in $O(mn)$ operations, provided the inverse of the smaller subsystem is known. Expressing the relevant terms using P_{old} and $\mathbf{k}_i$, we obtain

Random Subset Selection

Rank-1 update

$$P^\top K^\top \mathbf{y} = [P_{\text{old}}, \mathbf{e}_i]^\top K^\top \mathbf{y} = (P_{\text{old}}^\top K^\top \mathbf{y}, \mathbf{k}_i^\top \mathbf{y}), \tag{16.77}$$

$$P^\top \left(K^\top K + \sigma^2 K\right) P = \begin{bmatrix} P_{\text{old}}^\top \left(K^\top K + \sigma^2 K\right) P_{\text{old}} & P_{\text{old}}^\top \left(K^\top + \sigma^2 \mathbf{1}\right) \mathbf{k}_i \\ \mathbf{k}_i^\top (K + \sigma^2 \mathbf{1}) P_{\text{old}} & \mathbf{k}_i^\top \mathbf{k}_i + \sigma^2 K_{ii} \end{bmatrix}. \tag{16.78}$$

Algorithm 16.1 Sparse Greedy Quadratic Minimization.

Require: Training data $X = \{x_1, \ldots, x_m\}$, Targets $\mathbf{y}$, Noise σ^2, Precision ϵ, corresponding quadratic forms Q and Q^*.
Initialize index sets $I, I^* = \{1, \ldots, m\}$; $S, S^* = \emptyset$.
repeat
Choose $M \subseteq I$, $M^* \subseteq I^*$.
Find $\operatorname{argmin}_{i \in M} Q\left([P, e_i]\beta_{\text{opt}}\right)$, $\operatorname{argmin}_{i^* \in M^*} Q^*\left([P^*, e_{i^*}]\beta^*_{\text{opt}}\right)$.
Move i from I to S, i^* from I^* to S^*.
Set $P := [P, e_i]$, $P^* := [P^*, e_{i^*}]$.
until $Q(P\beta_{\text{opt}}) + \sigma^2 Q^*(P\beta^*_{\text{opt}}) + \frac{1}{2}\|\mathbf{y}\|^2 \leq \frac{\epsilon}{2}(|Q(P\beta_{\text{opt}})| + |\sigma^2 Q^*(P\beta^*_{\text{opt}}) + \frac{1}{2}\|\mathbf{y}\|^2|$
Output: Set of indices S, β_{opt}, $(P^\top K P)^{-1}$, and $(P^\top(K^\top K + \sigma^2 K)P)^{-1}$.

Thus computation of the terms costs only $O(nm)$ once we know P_{old}. Furthermore, we can write the inverse of a strictly positive definite matrix as

$$\begin{bmatrix} A & B \\ B^\top & C \end{bmatrix}^{-1} = \begin{bmatrix} A^{-1} + (A^{-1}B)^\top \gamma (A^{-1}B) & -\gamma(A^{-1}B) \\ -(\gamma(A^{-1}B))^\top & \gamma \end{bmatrix}, \tag{16.79}$$

where $\gamma := (C - B^\top A^{-1} B)^{-1}$. Hence, inversion of $P^\top\left(K^\top K + \sigma^2 K\right) P$ costs only $O(n^2)$. Thus, to find the matrix P of size $m \times n$ takes $O(\kappa n^2 m)$ time. For the error bars, $(P^\top K P)^{-1}$ is generally a good starting value for the minimization of (16.73), so the typical cost for (16.73) is $O(\tau m n)$ for some $\tau < n$, rather than $O(mn^2)$.

Stability

If additional numerical stability is required, we might want to replace (16.79) by a rank-1 update rule for Cholesky decompositions of the corresponding positive definite matrix. Furthermore, we may want to add the kernel function chosen by positive diagonal pivoting [169] to the selected subset, in order to ensure that the $n \times n$ submatrix remains invertible. See numerical mathematics textbooks, such as [247], for more detail on update rules.

16.4.6 Hardness and Approximation Results

It is worthwhile to study the theoretical guarantees on the performance of the algorithm (as described in Algorithm 16.1). It turns out that our technique closely resembles a Sparse Linear Approximation problem studied by Natarajan [381]:

Given $A \in \mathbb{R}^{m \times n}$, $b \in \mathbb{R}^m$, and $\epsilon > 0$, find $x \in \mathbb{R}^n$ with minimal number of nonzero entries such that $\|Ax - b\|_2 \leq \epsilon$. If we define

$$A = \left(\sigma^2 K + K^\top K\right)^{\frac{1}{2}} \text{ and } b := A^{-1} K \mathbf{y}, \tag{16.80}$$

we may write

$$Q(\alpha) = \frac{1}{2}\|b - A\alpha\|^2 + c, \tag{16.81}$$

where c is a constant independent of α. Thus the problem of sparse approximate minimization of $Q(\alpha)$ is a special case of Natarajan's problem (where the matrix A is square, and strictly positive definite). In addition, the algorithm considered

Sparse Solution of Linear Systems

in [381] involves sequentially choosing columns of A to maximally decrease $\|Ax - b\|$. This is equivalent to the algorithm described above and we may apply the following result to our sparse greedy Gaussian process algorithm.

Theorem 16.6 (Natarajan, 1995 [381]) *A sparse greedy algorithm to approximately solve the problem*

$$\text{minimize } \|y - Ax\| \tag{16.82}$$

needs at most

$$n \leq 18n^*(\epsilon)\|A^+\|_2^2 \ln \frac{\|y\|}{2\epsilon} \tag{16.83}$$

non-zero components, where $n^*(\epsilon)$ is the minimum number of nonzero components in vectors $\boldsymbol{\alpha}$ for which $\|y - Ax\| \leq \epsilon$, and A^+ is the matrix obtained from A by normalizing its columns to unit length.

Corollary 16.7 (Approximation Rate for Gaussian Processes) *Algorithm 16.1 satisfies $Q(\boldsymbol{\alpha}) \leq Q(\boldsymbol{\alpha}_{\text{opt}}) + \epsilon^2$ when $\boldsymbol{\alpha}$ has*

$$n \leq \frac{18n^*(\epsilon)}{\lambda^2} \ln \frac{\|A^{-1}Ky\|}{2\epsilon} \tag{16.84}$$

non-zero components, where $n^*(\epsilon)$ is the minimum number of nonzero components in vectors $\boldsymbol{\alpha}$ for which $Q(\boldsymbol{\alpha}) \leq Q(\boldsymbol{\alpha}_{\text{opt}}) + \epsilon^2$, $A = (\sigma^2 K + K^\top K)^{1/2}$, and λ is the smallest magnitude of the singular values of $\mathbf{A}$, the matrix obtained by normalizing the columns of A.

Moreover, we can also show NP-hardness of sparse approximation of Gaussian process regression. The following theorem holds:

Theorem 16.8 (NP-Hardness of Approximate GP Regression) *There exist kernels K and labels $\mathbf{y}$ such that the problem of finding the minimal set of indices to minimize a corresponding quadratic function $Q(\boldsymbol{\alpha})$ with precision ε is NP-hard.*

Proof We use the hardness result [381, Theorem 1] for Natarajan's quadratic approximation problem in terms of A and b. More specifically, we have to proceed in the opposite direction to (16.80) and (16.81) and show that for every A and b, there exist K and $\mathbf{y}$ for an equivalent optimization problem.

Since $\|Ax - b\|^2 = x^\top(A^\top A)x - 2(b^\top A)x + \|b\|^2$, the value of A enters only via $A^\top A$, which means that we have to find K in (16.68) such that

$$A^\top A = K^\top K + \sigma^2 K. \tag{16.85}$$

We can check that it is possible to find a suitable positive definite K for any A, by using identical eigensystems for $A^\top A$ and K, and subsequently solving the equations $a_i = \lambda_i^2 + \sigma^2\lambda_i$ for the respective eigenvalues a_i and λ_i of $A^\top A$ and K. Furthermore, we have to satisfy

$$\mathbf{y}^\top K = bA. \tag{16.86}$$

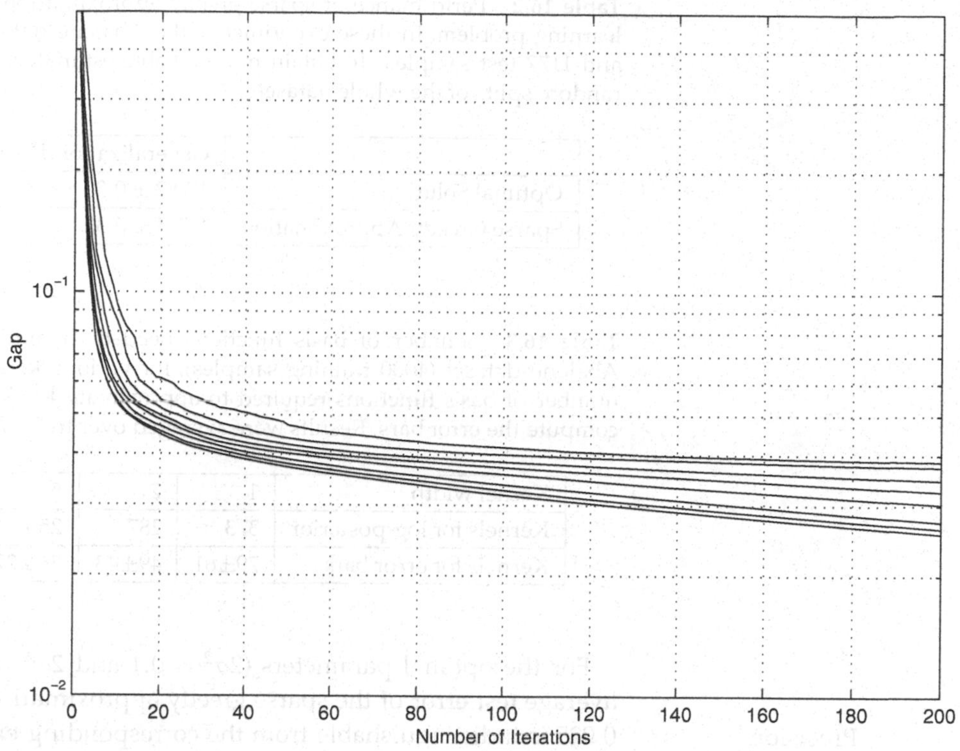

Figure 16.6 Speed of Convergence. We plot the size of the gap between upper and lower bound of the log posterior ($\text{gap}(\boldsymbol{\alpha}, \boldsymbol{\alpha}^*)$), for the first 4000 samples from the Abalone dataset ($\sigma^2 = 0.1$ and $2\omega^2 = 10$). From top to bottom: Subsets of size 1, 2, 5, 10, 20, 50, 100, 200. The results were averaged over 10 runs. The relative variance of the gap size is less than 10%. We can see that subsets of size 50 and above ensure rapid convergence.

To see this, recall that bA is a linear combination of the nonzero eigenvectors of $A^\top A$; and since K has the same rank and image as $A^\top A$, the vector bA can also be represented by $\mathbf{y}^\top K$. Thus for every A, b there exists an equivalent Q, which proves NP-hardness by reduction. ■

This shows that the sparse greedy algorithm is an efficient approximate solution of an NP-hard problem.

16.4.7 Experimental Evidence

We conclude this section with a brief experimental demonstration of the efficiency of sparse greedy approximation methods, using the Abalone dataset. Specifically, we used Gaussian covariance kernels, and we split the data into 4000 training and 177 test examples to assess training speed (to assess generalization performance, a 3000 training and 1177 test set split was used).

Table 16.2 Performance of sparse greedy approximation vs. explicit solution of the full learning problem. In these experiments, the Abalone dataset was split into 3000 training and 1177 test samples. To obtain more reliable estimates, the algorithm was run over 10 random splits of the whole dataset.

	Generalization Error	Log Posterior
Optimal Solution	1.782 ± 0.33	$-1.571 \cdot 10^5(1 \pm 0.005)$
Sparse Greedy Approximation	1.785 ± 0.32	$-1.572 \cdot 10^5(1 \pm 0.005)$

Table 16.3 Number of basis functions needed to minimize the log posterior on the Abalone dataset (4000 training samples), for various kernel widths ω. Also given is the number of basis functions required to approximate $\mathbf{k}^\top(K + \sigma^2\mathbf{1})^{-1}\mathbf{k}$, which is needed to compute the error bars. Results were averaged over the 177 test samples.

Kernel width	1	2	5	10	20	50
Kernels for log-posterior	373	287	255	257	251	270
Kernels for error bars	79±61	49±43	26±27	17±16	12±9	8±5

For the optimal parameters ($2\sigma^2 = 0.1$ and $2\omega^2 = 10$, chosen after [513]), the average test error of the sparse greedy approximation trained until $\text{gap}(\boldsymbol{\alpha}, \boldsymbol{\alpha}^*) < 0.025$ is indistinguishable from the corresponding error obtained by an exact solution of the full system. The same applies for the log posterior. See Table 16.2 for details. Consequently for all practical purposes, full inversion of the covariance matrix and the sparse greedy approximation have comparable generalization performance.

Precision Requirements

A more important quantity in practice is the number basis functions needed to minimize the log posterior to a sufficiently high precision. Table 16.3 shows this number for a precision of $\text{gap}(\boldsymbol{\alpha}, \boldsymbol{\alpha}^*) < 0.025$, and its variation as a function of the kernel width σ; the latter dependency is observed since the number of kernels determines time and memory needed for prediction and training. In all cases, less than 10% of the kernel functions suffice to find a good minimizer of the log posterior; less than 2% are sufficient to compute the error bars. This is a significant improvement over a direct minimization approach.

A similar result can be obtained on larger datasets. To illustrate, we generated a synthetic data set of size 10.000 in $\mathbb{R}^{20}$ by adding normal noise with variance $\sigma^2 = 0.1$ to a function consisting of 200 randomly chosen Gaussians of width $2\omega^2 = 40$ and with normally distributed expansion coefficients and centers.

To avoid trivial sparse expansions, we deliberately used an *inadequate* Gaussian process prior (but correct noise level) consisting of Gaussians with width $2\sigma^2 = 10$. After 500 iterations (thus, after using 5% of all basis functions), the size of $\text{gap}(\boldsymbol{\alpha}, \boldsymbol{\alpha}^*)$ was less than 0.023. This demonstrates the feasibility of the sparse greedy approach on larger datasets.

16.5 Laplacian Processes

All the prior distributions considered so far are *data independent* priors; in other words, $p(f)$ does not depend on X at all. This may not always be the most desirable choice, thus we now consider *data dependent* priors distributions, $p(f|X)$. This goes slightly beyond the commonly used concepts in Bayesian estimation.

Before we go into the technical details, let us give some motivation as to why the complexity of an estimate can depend on the locations where data occurs, since we are effectively updating our prior assumptions about f after observing the data placement. Note that we do not modify our prior assumptions based on the targets y_i, but rather as a result of the distribution of patterns x_i: Different input distribution densities might for instance correspond to different assumptions regarding the smoothness of the function class to be estimated. For example, it might be be advisable to favor smooth functions in areas where data are scarce, and allow more complicated functions where observations abound. We might not care about smoothness at all in regions where there is little or no chance of patterns occurring: In the problem of handwritten digit recognition, we do not (and should not) care about the behavior of the estimator on inputs x looking like faces.

Finally, we might assume a specific distribution of the *coefficients* of a function via a data-dependent function expansion; in other words, an expansion of f into the span of $\Phi := \{\phi_1, \ldots, \phi_M\}$, where ϕ_i are functions of the observed data X and of x. We focus henceforth on the case where $M = m$ and $\phi_i(x) := k(x_i, x)$.

The specific benefit of this strategy is that it provides us with a correspondence between linear programming regularization (Section 4.9.2) and weight decay regularizers (Section 4.9.1), and Bayesian priors over function spaces, by analogy to regularization in Reproducing Kernel Hilbert Spaces and Gaussian Processes.[10]

16.5.1 Data Dependent Priors

Recall the reasoning of Section 16.1.3. We obtained (16.11) under the assumption that X and f are independent random variables. In the following, we repeat the derivation without this restriction, and obtain

$$p(Y|f, X)p(f|X) = p(Y, f|X), \tag{16.87}$$

and likewise,

$$p(f|Y, X)p(Y|X) = p(Y, f|X). \tag{16.88}$$

Combining these two equations provides us with a modified version of Bayes' rule, which after solving for $p(f|Y, X)$, reads

$$p(Y|f, X)p(f|X) = p(f|X, Y)p(Y|X), \tag{16.89}$$

10. We thank Carl Magnus Rasmussen for discussions and suggestions.

and thus,

$$p(f|X,Y) = \frac{p(Y|f,X)p(f|X)}{p(Y|X)}. \tag{16.90}$$

Since $p(Y|X)$ is independent of f, we may treat $p(Y|X)$ as a mere normalization factor, and focus on $p(Y|f,X)p(f|X)$ for inference purposes. Let us now study a specific class of such priors, which are best formulated in coefficient space. We have

$$p(f|X) \propto \frac{1}{Z}\exp\left(-\sum_{i=1}^{m}\gamma(\alpha_i)\right), \text{ where } f(x) = \sum_{i=1}^{m}\alpha_i k(x_i, x). \tag{16.91}$$

Prior on Coefficients

Here Z is the corresponding normalization term and $x_i \in X$. Examples of priors that depend on the locations x_i include

Coding of Coefficients

$$\gamma(\alpha) = 1 - e^{p|\alpha|} \text{ with } p > 0 \text{ (feature selection prior)}, \tag{16.92}$$

$$\gamma(\alpha) = \alpha^2 \text{ (weight decay prior)}, \tag{16.93}$$

$$\gamma(\alpha) = |\alpha| \text{ (Laplacian prior)}. \tag{16.94}$$

The prior given by (16.92) was introduced in [70, 187] and is concave. While the latter characteristic is unfavorable in general, since the corresponding optimization problem exhibits many local minima, the regularized risk functional becomes strictly concave if we choose linear loss functions (such as the L_1 loss or the soft margin). According to Theorem 6.12, this means that the optimum occurs at one of the extreme points, which makes optimization more feasible.

Eq. (16.93) describes the popular *weight decay* prior used in Bayesian Neural Networks [338, 382, 383]. It assumes that the coefficients are independently normally distributed. We relax the assumption of a common normal distribution in Section 16.6 and introduce individual (hyper)parameters s_i. The resulting prior,

Relevance Vector Machines Prior

$$p(f|X,s) = (2\pi)^{-\frac{m}{2}}\left(\prod_{i=1}^{m}s_i\right)^{\frac{1}{2}}\exp\left(-\frac{1}{2}\sum_{i=1}^{m}s_i\alpha_i^2\right), \tag{16.95}$$

leads to the construction of the Relevance Vector Machine [539] and very sparse function expansions.

Finally, the assumption underlying the Laplacian prior (16.94) is that only very few basis functions will be nonzero. The specific form of the prior is why we will call such estimators *Laplacian Processes*. This prior has two significant advantages over (16.92): It leads to convex optimization problems, and the integral $\int p(\alpha)d\alpha$ is finite and thus allows normalization (this is not the case for (16.92), which is why we call the latter an *improper* prior).

Sparse Coding

The Laplacian prior corresponds to the regularization functional employed in sparse coding approaches, such as wavelet dictionaries [104], coding of natural images [389], independent component analysis [327], and linear programming regression [502, 517].

In the following, we focus on (16.94). It is straightforward to see that the MAP estimate can be obtained by minimizing the negative log posterior, which is given (up to constant terms) by

$$-\sum_{i=1}^{m} \ln p(y_i|f(x_i), x_i) + \sum_{i=1}^{m} |\alpha_i|. \tag{16.96}$$

Laplacian Prior

Depending on $\ln p(y_i|f(x_i), x_i)$, we may formulate (16.96) as a linear or quadratic program.

16.5.2 Samples from the Prior

In order to illustrate our reasoning, and to show that such priors correspond to useful classes of functions, we generate samples from the prior distribution. As in Gaussian processes, smooth kernels k correspond to smooth priors. This is not surprising: As we show in the next section (Theorem 16.9), there exists a corresponding Gaussian process for every kernel k and every distribution $p(x)$.

The obvious advantage, however, is that we do not have to worry about Mercer's condition for k but can take any arbitrary function $k(x, x')$ to generate a Laplacian process. We draw samples from the following three kernels,

$$k(x, x') = e^{-\frac{\|x-x'\|^2}{2\sigma^2}} \quad \text{Gaussian RBF kernel,} \tag{16.97}$$

$$k(x, x') = e^{-\frac{\|x-x'\|}{\sigma}} \quad \text{Laplacian RBF kernel,} \tag{16.98}$$

$$k(x, x') = \tanh(\theta\langle x, x'\rangle + \vartheta) \quad \text{Neural Networks kernel.} \tag{16.99}$$

Wide Class of Kernels

While (16.97) and (16.98) are also valid kernels for Gaussian Process estimation, (16.99) does not satisfy Mercer's condition (see Section 4.6 for details) and thus cannot be used in Gaussian processes[11]. Figure 16.7 gives sample realizations from the corresponding process. The use of (16.99) is impossible for GP priors, unless we diagonalize the matrix K explicitly and render it positive definite by replacing λ_i with $|\lambda_i|$. This is a very costly procedure (see also [480, 210]) as it involves computing the eigensystem of K.

16.5.3 Prediction

Since one of the aims of using a Laplacian prior on the coefficients α_i is to achieve sparsity of the expansion, it does not appear sensible to use a Bayesian averaging scheme (as in Section 16.1.3) to compute the mean of the posterior distribution, since such a scheme leads to mostly nonzero coefficients. Instead we seek to obtain the *mode* of the distribution (the MAP estimate), as described in Section 16.2.1.

MAP Approximation

11. The covariance matrix K has to be positive definite at all times. An analogous application of the theory of conditionally positive definite kernels would be possible as well, as pointed out in Section 2.4. We would simply assume a Gaussian Process prior on a linear subspace of the y_i.

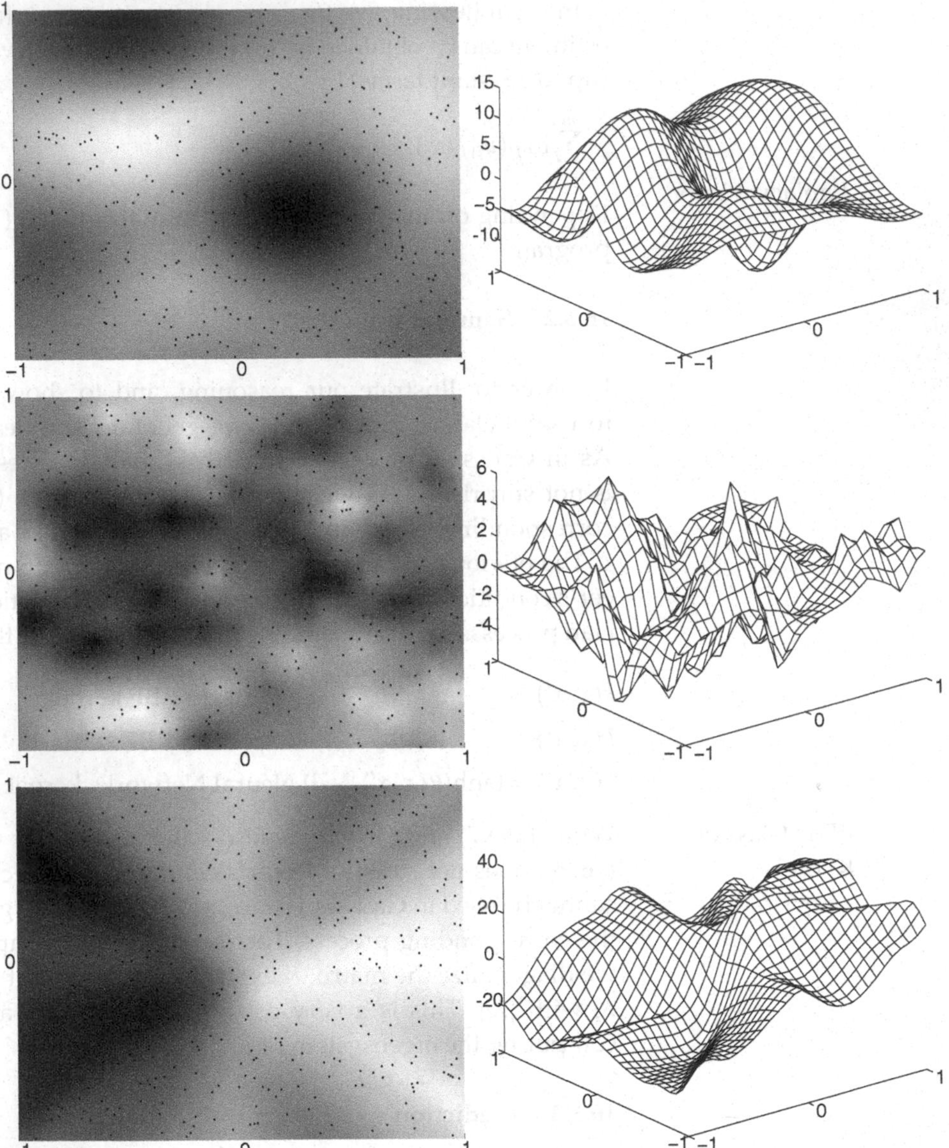

Figure 16.7 Left Column: Grayscale plots of the realizations of several Laplacian Processes. The black dots represent data points. Right Column: 3D plots of the same samples of the process. We used 400 data points sampled at random from $[0,1]^2$ using a uniform distribution. Top to bottom: Gaussian kernel (16.97) ($\sigma^2 = 0.1$), Laplacian kernel (16.98) ($\sigma = 0.1$), and Neural Networks kernel (16.99) ($\theta = 10, \vartheta = 1$). Note that the Laplacian kernel is significantly less smooth than the Gaussian kernel, as with a Gaussian Process with Laplacian kernels. Moreover, observe that the Neural Networks kernel corresponds to a nonstationary process; that is, its covariance properties are not translation invariant.

Unlike in Gaussian Process regression, this does not give an exact solution of the problem of finding the mean, since mode and mean do not coincide for Laplacian regularization (recall Figure 16.2). Nonetheless, the MAP estimate is computationally attractive, since if both $-\ln p(\xi_i)$ and $\gamma(\alpha_i)$ are convex, the optimization problem has a unique minimum.

The method closely follows our reasoning in the case of Gaussian Processes. Recall that the posterior probability of a hypothesis (16.23) is proportional to

$$p(f|X,Y) \propto p(Y|f,X)p(f|X) \tag{16.100}$$

$$= \left[\prod_{i=1}^{m} p(y_i - f(x_i))\right] p(f|X) \tag{16.101}$$

$$= \left[\prod_{i=1}^{m} p\left(y_i - \sum_{j=1}^{m} \alpha_j k(x_j, x_i)\right) e^{-\gamma(\alpha_i)}\right]. \tag{16.102}$$

To obtain (16.101), we exploit the deterministic dependency $t_i = f(x_i)$. The latter allows us to state $p(Y|f,X)$ explicitly by integrating out the random variables $\xi_i = y_i - t_i$.[12] To carry out inference we write the problem of finding the MAP estimate of (16.100) as an optimization problem and obtain

Constrained Optimization Problem

$$\begin{aligned} \text{minimize} \quad & \sum_{i=1}^{m} -\ln p(\xi_i) + \sum_{i=1}^{m} \gamma(\alpha_i), \\ \text{subject to} \quad & K\boldsymbol{\alpha} = y + \boldsymbol{\xi}, \end{aligned} \tag{16.103}$$

where $\boldsymbol{\alpha}, \boldsymbol{\xi} \in \mathbb{R}^m$ and $K_{ij} = k(x_i, x_j)$ as usual. For $p(\xi_i) = |\xi_i|$ and $\gamma(\alpha_i) = |\alpha_i|$, this leads to a linear program (see Section 4.9.2), and the solution can be readily used as a MAP estimate for Laplacian processes (a similar reasoning holds for soft margin loss functions). Likewise for Gaussian noise, we obtain a quadratic program with a simple objective function but a dense set of constraints, by analogy to Basis Pursuit [104]. The derivation is straightforward; see also Problem 16.17 for details.

16.5.4 Confidence Intervals for Gaussian Noise

One of the key advantages of Bayesian modelling is that we can obtain explicit confidence intervals for the predictions, provided the assumptions made regarding the priors and distribution are satisfied. Even for Gaussian noise, however, no explicit meaningful expansion using the MAP estimate $\boldsymbol{\alpha}_{\mathrm{MAP}}$ is possible, since $\gamma(\alpha_i) = |\alpha_i|$ is non-differentiable at 0 (otherwise we could make a quadratic approximation at $\alpha_i = 0$). Nonetheless, a slight modification permits computationally efficient approximation of such error bounds.

Ignoring all $\alpha_i = 0$

The modification consists of dropping all variables α_i for which $\alpha_{\mathrm{MAP},i} = 0$ from the expansion (this renders the distribution *flatter* and thereby overestimates the

12. For the purpose of minimizing (16.100), it is sometimes convenient to keep the ξ_i, which then serve as slack variables in the convex optimization problem.

error), and replacing all remaining variables by linear approximations (we replace $|\alpha_i|$ by $\operatorname{sgn}(\alpha_{\mathrm{MAP},i})\,\alpha_i$).

In other words, we assume that variables with zero coefficients do not influence the expansion, and that the signs of the remaining variables do not change. This is a sensible approximation since for large sample sizes, which Laplacian processes are designed to address, the posterior is strongly peaked around its mode [519]. Thus the contribution of $\|\boldsymbol{\alpha}\|_1$ around $\boldsymbol{\alpha}_{\mathrm{MAP}}$ can be considered to be approximately linear.

Laplace Approximation in $\alpha_i \neq 0$

Denote by $\boldsymbol{\alpha}_M$ the vector of nonzero variables, obtained by deleting all entries where $\alpha_{\mathrm{MAP},i} = 0$, by s the vector with elements ± 1 such that $\|\boldsymbol{\alpha}_{\mathrm{MAP}}\|_1 = s^\top \boldsymbol{\alpha}_M$, and by K_M the matrix generated from K by removing the columns corresponding to $\alpha_{\mathrm{MAP},i} = 0$. Then the posterior (now written in terms of $\boldsymbol{\alpha}$ for convenience) can be approximated as

$$p(\boldsymbol{\alpha}_M|Z) \propto \exp\left(-\frac{1}{2\sigma^2}\sum_{i=1}^{m}(y_i - K_M\boldsymbol{\alpha}_M)^2\right)\exp\left(-s^\top\boldsymbol{\alpha}_M\right). \tag{16.104}$$

Collecting linear and quadratic terms, we see that

$$\boldsymbol{\alpha}_M \sim \mathcal{N}(\boldsymbol{\alpha}_{\mathrm{MAP}}, (K_M^\top K_M)^{-1}), \text{ where } \boldsymbol{\alpha}_{\mathrm{MAP}} = (K_M^\top K_M)^{-1}(K_M^\top y + \sigma^2 s). \tag{16.105}$$

The equation for $\boldsymbol{\alpha}_{\mathrm{MAP}}$ follows from the conditions on the optimal solution of the quadratic programming problem (16.103), or directly from maximizing (16.100) (after s is fixed). Hence predictions at a new point x are approximately normally distributed, with

$$y(x) = \mathcal{N}\left(\mathbf{k}_M^\top\boldsymbol{\alpha}_M, \left(\sigma^2 + \mathbf{k}_M^\top\left(K_M^\top K_M\right)^{-1}\mathbf{k}_M\right)\right), \tag{16.106}$$

where $\mathbf{k}_M := (k(x_1, x), \ldots, k(x_M, x))$ and only x_i with nonzero $\alpha_{\mathrm{MAP},i}$ are considered (thus $M \leq m$). The additional σ^2 stems from the fact that we have additive Gaussian noise of variance σ^2 in addition to the Laplacian process. Equation (16.106) is still expensive to compute, but it is much cheaper to invert $\Sigma_M^\top\Sigma_M$ than a dense square matrix Σ (since $\boldsymbol{\alpha}_{\mathrm{MAP}}$ may be very sparse). In addition, greedy approximation methods (as described for instance in Section 16.4.4) or column generation techniques [39] could be used to render the computation of (16.106) numerically more efficient.

16.5.5 Data Independent Formulation

While (16.91) gives a very natural description of the behavior of the estimator, it is possible in the case of (16.91) to find an equivalent, albeit much less elegant, data independent formulation. Denote by K the standard kernel matrix ($K_{ij} = k(x_i, x_j)$) and by $[K^{-1}\mathbf{y}]_i$ the ith entry of the vector $K^{-1}\mathbf{y}$. Then we may write $p(f|X)$ as

Sparse Coding via Norms

$$p(\mathbf{y}) = \frac{1}{Z}\exp\left(-\sum_{i=1}^{m}\gamma\left([K^{-1}\mathbf{y}]_i\right)\right). \tag{16.107}$$

This can be seen as follows: if K has full rank, setting $\mathbf{y} = K\boldsymbol{\alpha}$ yields $K^{-1}\mathbf{y} = K^{-1}K\boldsymbol{\alpha} = \boldsymbol{\alpha}$.

As an aside, note that some priors, such as (16.94) and (16.93), can also be interpreted as changes in the metric given by Gaussian processes. Recall that the latter can be stated as

$$p(\mathbf{y}) \propto \exp\left(-\frac{1}{2}\|K^{-\frac{1}{2}}\mathbf{y}\|_2^2\right). \tag{16.108}$$

By changing the metric tensor from $K^{-\frac{1}{2}}$ to K^{-1}, we recover (16.93). Replacing the $\|\cdot\|_2$ norm by $\|\cdot\|_1$ yields (16.94). This formulation no longer depends explicitly on x. Nonetheless, the data dependent notation is much more natural and provides more insight into the inner workings of the estimator.

Changing Norms

16.5.6 An Equivalent Gaussian Process

We conclude this section with a proof that in the large sample size limit, there exists a Gaussian Process for each kernel expansion with a prior on the coefficients α_i. For the purpose of the proof, we have to slightly modify the normalization condition on f: That is, we assume

$$y(x) = 1/\sqrt{m}\sum_{i=1}^{m}\alpha_i k(x_i, x), \tag{16.109}$$

where $\alpha_i \sim \exp(-\gamma(\boldsymbol{\alpha}))$. In the limit $m \to \infty$, the following theorem holds.

Theorem 16.9 (Convergence to Gaussian Process) *Denote by α_i independent random variables (we do not require identical distributions on α_i) with unit variance and zero mean. Furthermore, assume that there exists a distribution $p(x)$ on $\mathcal{X}$ according to which a sample $\{x_1, \ldots, x_m\}$ is drawn, and that $k(x, x')$ is bounded on $\mathcal{X} \times \mathcal{X}$. Then the random variable $y(x)$ given by (16.109) converges for $m \to \infty$ to a Gaussian process with zero mean and covariance function*

Distribution Dependent Kernel

$$\tilde{k}(x, x') = \int_{\mathcal{X}} k(x, \bar{x})k(x', \bar{x})p(\bar{x})d\bar{x}. \tag{16.110}$$

This means that instead of a Laplacian process prior, we could use any other factorizing prior on the expansion coefficients α_i and in the limit still obtain an equivalent stochastic process.

Proof To prove the first part, we need only check is that $y(x)$ and any linear combination $\sum_j y(x_j)$ (for arbitrary $x'_j \in \mathcal{X}$) converge to a normal distribution. By application of a theorem of Cramér [118], this is sufficient to prove that $y(x)$ is distributed according to a Gaussian Process.

The random variable $y(x)$ is a sum of m independent random variables with bounded variance (since $k(x, x')$ is bounded on $\mathcal{X} \times \mathcal{X}$). Therefore in the limit $m \to \infty$, by virtue of the Central Limit Theorem (e.g., [118]), we have $y(x) \sim \mathcal{N}(0, \sigma^2(x))$ for some $\sigma^2(x) \in \mathbb{R}$. For arbitrary $x'_j \in \mathcal{X}$, linear combinations of $y(x'_j)$ also have

Central Limit Theorem

Gaussian distributions since

$$\sum_{j=1}^{n} \beta_i y(x_j') = \frac{1}{\sqrt{m}} \sum_{i=1}^{m} \alpha_i \sum_{j=1}^{n} \beta_j k(x_i, x_j'), \quad (16.111)$$

which allows the application of the Central Limit Theorem to the sum since the inner sum $\sum_{j=1}^{n} \beta_j k(x_i, x_j')$ is bounded for any x_i. This theorem also implies $\sum_{j=1}^{n} \beta_j y(x_j') \sim \mathcal{N}(0, \sigma^2)$ for $m \to \infty$ and some $\sigma^2 \in \mathbb{R}$, which proves that $y(x)$ is distributed according to a Gaussian Process.

To show (16.110), first note that $y(x)$ has zero mean. Thus the covariance function for finite m can be found as expectation with respect to the random variables α_i,

$$E[y(x)y(x')] = E\left[\frac{1}{m} \sum_{i,j=1}^{m} \alpha_i \alpha_j k(x_i, x) k(x_j, x')\right] = \frac{1}{m} \sum_{i=1}^{m} k(x_i, x) k(x_j, x'), \quad (16.112)$$

since the α_i are independent and have zero mean. This expression, however, converges to the Riemann integral over $\mathcal{X}$ with the density $p(x)$ as $m \to \infty$. Thus

$$E[y(x)y(x')] \underset{m\to\infty}{\longrightarrow} \int_{\mathcal{X}} k(x, \bar{x}) k(x', \bar{x}) p(\bar{x}) d\bar{x}, \quad (16.113)$$

which completes the proof. ■

16.6 Relevance Vector Machines

Recently, Tipping [539] proposed a method to obtain sparse solutions for regression and classification while maintaining their Bayesian interpretability. The basic idea is to make extensive use of hyperparameters in determining the priors $p(\alpha_i)$ on the individual expansion coefficients α_i.

In particular, we assume a normal distribution over α_i with adjustable variance. The latter is then determined with a hyperparameter that has its most likely value at 0; this leads to a concentration of the distribution of α_i around 0. This prior is expressed analytically as

$$p(\alpha_i|s_i) = \sqrt{\frac{s_i}{2\pi}} \exp\left(-\frac{1}{2} s_i \alpha_i^2\right), \quad (16.114)$$

where $s_i > 0$ plays the role of a hyperparameter with corresponding hyperprior

$$p(s_i) = \frac{1}{s_i} \text{ (this is a flat hyperprior on a log scale: } p(\ln s_i) = \text{const.), or} \quad (16.115)$$

$$p(s_i) = \Gamma(s_i|a, b). \quad (16.116)$$

Gamma Distribution

The Gamma distribution is given by

$$\Gamma(s_i|a, b) := \frac{s_i^{a-1} b^a exp(-s_i b)}{\Gamma(a)} \text{ for } s_i > 0. \quad (16.117)$$

For non-informative (flat) priors, we typically choose $a = b = 10^{-4}$ (see [539]). Note that (16.117) is heavily peaked for $s_i \to 0$. For regression, a similar assumption is made concerning the amount of additive Gaussian noise σ^2; thus $p(\bar{\sigma}^2) = 1/\bar{\sigma}^2$ or $p(\bar{\sigma}^2) = \Gamma(\bar{\sigma}^2|c, d)$ where typically $c = d = 10^{-4}$. Note that the priors are imposed on the *inverse* of σ and $\bar{\sigma}$.

To explain the method in more detail, we begin with a description of the steps required for regression estimation. The corresponding reasoning for classification is relegated to Section 16.6.4, since it uses methods similar to those already described in previous sections.

16.6.1 Regression with Hyperparameters

Additive Gaussian Noise

For the sake of simplicity, we assume additive Gaussian noise. Hence, given a kernel expansion $t = K\boldsymbol{\alpha}$, we have

$$p(\mathbf{y}|\boldsymbol{\alpha}, \sigma^2) = (2\pi\sigma^2)^{-\frac{m}{2}} \exp\left(-\frac{1}{2\sigma^2}\|\mathbf{y} - K\boldsymbol{\alpha}\|^2\right). \tag{16.118}$$

Normal Distribution of α_i

With the definition $S := \operatorname{diag}(s_1, \ldots s_m)$, we obtain

$$p(\boldsymbol{\alpha}|\mathbf{s}) = (2\pi)^{-\frac{m}{2}}|S|^{\frac{1}{2}} \exp\left(-\frac{1}{2}\boldsymbol{\alpha}^\top S\boldsymbol{\alpha}\right) \tag{16.119}$$

from (16.114). Since $p(\mathbf{y}|\boldsymbol{\alpha}, \sigma^2)$ and $p(\boldsymbol{\alpha}|\mathbf{s})$ are both Gaussian, we may integrate out $\boldsymbol{\alpha}$ to $\mathbf{s}$ (for proper normalizations) and obtain explicit expressions for the conditional distributions of $\boldsymbol{\alpha}$ and $\mathbf{s}$. In particular, since $p(\boldsymbol{\alpha}|\mathbf{t}, \mathbf{s}, \sigma^2) \propto p(\mathbf{t}|\boldsymbol{\alpha}, \sigma^2)p(\boldsymbol{\alpha}|\mathbf{s})$, then using (16.119) we get

$$p(\boldsymbol{\alpha}|\mathbf{y}, \mathbf{s}, \sigma^2) = (2\pi)^{-\frac{m}{2}}|\Sigma|^{-\frac{1}{2}} \exp\left(-\frac{1}{2}(\boldsymbol{\alpha} - \mu)^\top \Sigma^{-1}(\boldsymbol{\alpha} - \mu)\right), \tag{16.120}$$

Conditional Distributions

where

$$\Sigma = (\sigma^{-2}K^\top K + S)^{-1} \text{ and } \mu = \sigma^{-2}\Sigma K\mathbf{y}. \tag{16.121}$$

Additionally, note that $p(\mathbf{y}|\mathbf{s}, \sigma^2)$ is a convolution of two normal distributions, namely $p(\mathbf{y}|\boldsymbol{\alpha}, \sigma^2)$ and $p(\boldsymbol{\alpha}|\mathbf{s})$, hence the corresponding variances add up and we obtain

$$p(\mathbf{y}|\mathbf{s}, \sigma^2) = \int p(\mathbf{y}|\boldsymbol{\alpha}, \sigma^2)p(\boldsymbol{\alpha}|\mathbf{s})d\boldsymbol{\alpha} \tag{16.122}$$

$$= (2\pi)^{-\frac{m}{2}}|\boldsymbol{\Sigma}|^{-\frac{1}{2}} \exp\left(-\frac{1}{2}\mathbf{y}^\top \boldsymbol{\Sigma}^{-1}\mathbf{y}\right), \tag{16.123}$$

where $\boldsymbol{\Sigma} = \sigma^2\mathbf{1} + KS^{-1}K^\top$. Eq. (16.123) is useful since it allows us to maximize the posterior probability of $\mathbf{s}$ provided we know $\mathbf{y}$ and σ^2. This leads to

$$p(\mathbf{s}|\mathbf{y}, \sigma^2) \propto p(\mathbf{y}|\mathbf{s}, \sigma^2)p(\mathbf{s}). \tag{16.124}$$

In order to carry out Bayesian inference, we would have to compute

$$p(y|\mathbf{y}) = \int p(y|\boldsymbol{\alpha}, \mathbf{s}, \sigma^2)p(\boldsymbol{\alpha}, \mathbf{s}, \sigma^2|\mathbf{y})d\boldsymbol{\alpha}d\mathbf{s}d\sigma^2. \tag{16.125}$$

In most cases, however, this integral is intractable. Under the assumption that $p(\mathbf{y}|\mathbf{s},\sigma^2)p(\mathbf{s})p(\sigma^2)$ is peaked around its mode, we may use the MAP2 approximation (16.24) and obtain

MAP2 Approximation

$$p(y|\mathbf{y}) \approx \int p(y|\boldsymbol{\alpha}, \mathbf{s}_{\mathrm{MAP}}, \sigma^2_{\mathrm{MAP}}) p(\boldsymbol{\alpha}|\mathbf{y}, \mathbf{s}_{\mathrm{MAP}}, \sigma^2_{\mathrm{MAP}}) d\boldsymbol{\alpha}. \tag{16.126}$$

We cover the issue of finding optimal hyperparameters in the next section. For the moment, however, let us assume that we know the values of $\mathbf{s}_{\mathrm{MAP}}$ and σ^2_{MAP}.

Since the integral in (16.126) can be seen as the convolution of two normal distributions, we may solve the equations explicitly to obtain

$$p(y|\mathbf{y}, \mathbf{s}_{\mathrm{MAP}}, \sigma^2_{\mathrm{MAP}}) \sim \mathcal{N}(y_*, \sigma^2_*), \tag{16.127}$$

where, using the definition of Σ (16.121),

$$y_* = \sigma^{-2}_{\mathrm{MAP}} \mathbf{k}^\top \Sigma K \mathbf{y} \text{ and } \sigma^2_* = \sigma^2_{\mathrm{MAP}} + \mathbf{k}^\top \Sigma \mathbf{k}. \tag{16.128}$$

Note the similarity of (16.128) to (16.49) for Gaussian Processes.

16.6.2 Finding Optimal Hyperparameters

According to [539], the optimal parameters $\mathbf{s}$ and σ^2 cannot be obtained in closed form from

$$(\mathbf{s}_{\mathrm{MAP}}, \sigma^2_{\mathrm{MAP}}) = \operatorname*{argmin}_{(\mathbf{s},\sigma^2)} \left[-\ln p(\mathbf{y}|\mathbf{s},\sigma^2) - \ln p(\mathbf{s}) - \ln p(\sigma^2) \right]. \tag{16.129}$$

A possible solution, however, is to perform gradient descent on the objective function (16.129). Taking logs of the Gamma distribution (16.117) and substituting the explicit terms for $p(\mathbf{y}|\mathbf{s},\sigma^2)$ yields the following expression for the argument of (16.129);

$$\mathcal{P} = -\ln p(\mathbf{y}|\mathbf{s},\sigma^2) - \ln p(\mathbf{s}) - \ln p(\sigma^2) \tag{16.130}$$

$$= \frac{1}{2}\left[\ln \left| \sigma^{-2}\mathbf{1} + KSK^\top \right| + \mathbf{y}^\top \left(\sigma^{-2}\mathbf{1} + KSK^\top \right)^{-1} \mathbf{y} \right]$$

$$- \sum_{i=1}^{m} (a \ln s_i - b s_i) - c \ln \sigma^2 + d\sigma^2. \tag{16.131}$$

Of course, if we set $a = b = c = d = 0$ (flat prior) the terms in (16.131) vanish. Note the similarity to logarithmic barrier methods in constrained optimization, for which constrained minimization problems are transformed into unconstrained problems by adding logarithms of the constraints to the initial objective function (see Chapter 6, and in particular (6.90), for more detail). In other words, the Gamma distribution can be viewed as a positivity constraint on the hyperparameters s_i and σ^2.

Barrier Methods

Differentiating (16.131) and setting the corresponding terms to 0 leads to the update rules (see [539] and Problem 16.20 for more details)

$$s_i = \frac{1 - s_i \Sigma_{ii}}{\mu_i^2}, \tag{16.132}$$

where we use the definitions in (16.121). The quantity $1 - s_i\Sigma_{ii}$ is a measure of the degree to which the corresponding parameter α_i is "determined" by the data [338]. Likewise we obtain

$$\sigma^2 = \frac{\|\mathbf{y} - K\mu\|^2}{\sum_{i=1}^{m} s_i \Sigma_{ii}}. \tag{16.133}$$

Handling Divergences

It turns out that many of the parameters s_i tend to infinity during the optimization process. This means that the corresponding distribution of α_i is strongly peaked around 0, and we may drop these variables from the optimization process. This speeds up the process as the minimization progresses.

It seems wasteful to first consider the full set of possible functions $k(x_i, x)$, and only then weed out the functions not needed for prediction. We could instead use a greedy method for building up predictors, similar to the greedy strategy employed in Gaussian Processes (Section 16.4.4). This is the approach in [539], which proposes the following algorithm. After initializing the predictor with a single basis function (the bias, for example), we test whether each new basis function yields an improvement. This is done by guessing a large initial value s_i, and performing one update step. If (16.132) leads to an increase of s_i, we reject the corresponding basis function, otherwise we retain it in the optimization process.

Greedy Updates

16.6.3 Explicit Priors by Integration

A second way to perform inference while circumventing the MAP2 estimate is to integrate out the hyperparameters s_i and then deal with $p(\alpha_i)$ in a standard fashion. In the present case, integration can be carried out in closed form over the hyperprior. We obtain

Explicit Prior

$$p(\alpha_i) = \int p(\alpha_i|s_i)p(s_i|a,b)ds_i \propto \left(b + \frac{\alpha_i^2}{2}\right)^{-a-\frac{1}{2}}, \tag{16.134}$$

which is a Student-t distribution over α_i. In other words, the effective prior on α_i is given by (16.91) with

$$\gamma(\alpha_i) = \left(a + \frac{1}{2}\right)\ln\left(b + \frac{\alpha_i^2}{2}\right), \tag{16.135}$$

or after reparametrization $\gamma(\alpha_i) = a'\ln(1 + b'\alpha_i^2)$ for suitably chosen $a', b' > 0$. This connects the Relevance Vector Machine to other methods that encode priors directly in coefficient space without the aid of a hyperparameter. We can see that (16.135) is heavily peaked at $\alpha_i = 0$, which explains why most of the parameters are 0.

Connection to Gaussian Processes

Unfortunately (16.135) proves to be unsuited to implementation, since the posterior probability exhibits "horribly" [539] many local minima. Hence, estimates derived from the optimization of the log posterior are not particularly meaningful. Nonetheless, this alternative representation demonstrates a connection between Gaussian Processes and Relevance Vector Machines, based on Theorem 16.9: In the large sample size limit, Relevance Vector Machines converge to a Gaussian Process with kernel given by (16.110).

16.6.4 Classification

For classification, we follow a scheme similar to that in Section 16.3.5. In order to keep matters simple, we only consider the binary classification case. Specifically, we carry out logistic regression by using (16.3) as a model for the distribution of labels $y_i \in \{\pm 1\}$. As in regression, we use a kernel expansion, this time for the latent variables $\mathbf{t} = K\boldsymbol{\alpha}$. The negative log posterior is given by

$$-\ln p(\boldsymbol{\alpha}|\mathbf{y},\mathbf{s}) = \sum_{i=1}^{m} -\ln p(y_i|t(x_i)) - \sum_{i=1}^{m} \ln p(\alpha_i|s_i) + \text{const.} \tag{16.136}$$

Laplace Approximation

Unlike in regression, however, we cannot minimize (16.136) explicitly and have to resort to approximate methods, such as the Laplace approximation (see Section 16.4.1). Computing the first and second derivatives of (16.136) and using the definitions (16.59) and (16.60) yields

$$\partial_{\boldsymbol{\alpha}} \left[-\ln p(\boldsymbol{\alpha}|\mathbf{y},\mathbf{s})\right] = Kc + S\boldsymbol{\alpha}, \tag{16.137}$$

$$\partial^2_{\boldsymbol{\alpha}} \left[-\ln p(\boldsymbol{\alpha}|\mathbf{y},\mathbf{s})\right] = K^\top C K + S. \tag{16.138}$$

This allows us to obtain a MAP estimate of $p(\boldsymbol{\alpha}|\mathbf{y},\mathbf{s})$ by iterative application of (16.58), and we obtain an update rule for $\boldsymbol{\alpha}$ in a manner analogous to (16.61);

$$\boldsymbol{\alpha}_{\text{new}} = \boldsymbol{\alpha}_{\text{old}} - (K^\top CK + S)^{-1}(Kc + S\boldsymbol{\alpha}_{\text{old}}) = (K^\top CK + S)^{-1}K(CK\boldsymbol{\alpha}_{\text{old}} - c). \tag{16.139}$$

Adjusting Hyperparameters

If the iteration scheme converges, it will converge to the minimum of the negative log posterior. We next have to provide an iterative method for updating the hyperparameters $\mathbf{s}$ (note that we do not need σ^2). Since we cannot integrate out $\boldsymbol{\alpha}$ explicitly (we had to resort to an iterative method even to obtain the mode of the distribution), it is best to use the Gaussian approximation obtained from (16.138). This gives an approximation of the value of the posterior distribution $p(\mathbf{s}|\mathbf{y})$ and allows us to apply the update rules developed for regression in classification. Setting $\mu = \boldsymbol{\alpha}_{\text{MAP}}$ and $\Sigma = (K^\top CK + S)^{-1}$, we can use (16.132) to optimize s_i. See [539] for further detail and motivation.

16.6.5 Toy Example and Discussion

We conclude this brief description of RVMs with a toy example (Figure 16.8), taken from [539], in which regression is performed on a noisy sinc function (cf.

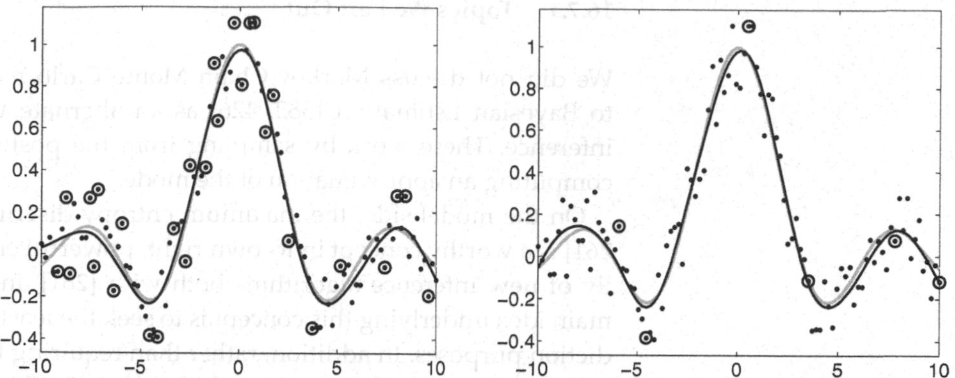

Figure 16.8 Support (left) and Relevance (right) Vector approximations to sinc (x), based on 100 noisy samples. The estimated functions are drawn as solid lines, the true function in gray, and Support/Relevance Vectors are circled.

Chapter 9) using RV and SV estimators. In both cases, a linear spline kernel [572],

$$K(x,x') = xx' + xx' \min\{x,x'\} - \frac{x+x'}{2}(\min\{x,x'\})^2 + \frac{(\min\{x,x'\})^3}{3}, \tag{16.140}$$

was used. The noise, added to the y-values, was uniformly distributed over $[-0.2, 0.2]$.

In the SV case, all points with a distance $\geq \varepsilon$ (not shown) become SVs; this leads to an expansion that is not particularly sparse. The RVM, on the other hand, constructs a solution which is not constrained to use these points, and delivers a much sparser solution.

It should be noted that similarly sparse solutions can be obtained for SVMs by using "reduced set" post-processing (Chapter 18). Although this step adds to the training time, SVMs train far more quickly than RVMs on large data sets (of the order of thousands of examples), and the added post-processing time is then often negligible. Nevertheless, it is fair to say that the RVM is an elegant and principled Bayesian alternative to SVMs.

16.7 Summary

In this chapter, we presented an overview over some of the more common techniques of Bayesian estimation, namely Gaussian Processes and the Relevance Vector Machine, and a novel method: Laplacian Processes. Due to the wealth of existing concepts and algorithms developed in Bayesian statistics, it is impossible to give a comprehensive treatment in a single chapter. Such a treatise would easily fill a whole book in its own right.

16.7.1 Topics We Left Out

We did not discuss Markov-Chain Monte Carlo methods and their application to Bayesian Estimation [382, 426] as an alternate way of performing Bayesian inference. These work by sampling from the posterior distribution rather than computing an approximation of the mode.

On the model side, the maximum entropy discrimination paradigm [499, 114, 261] is a worthy concept in its own right, powerful enough to spawn a whole family of new inference algorithms both with [261] and without [263] kernels. The main idea underlying this concept is to seek the least informative estimate for prediction purposes. In addition, rather than requiring that a specific function satisfy certain constraints, we require only that the distribution satisfy the constraints *on average*.

Methods such as the Bayes-Point machine [239] and Kernel Billiard [450, 451] can also be used for estimation purposes. The idea behind these methods is to "play billiard" in version space (see Problem 7.21) and average over the existing trajectories. The version space is the set of all w for which the empirical risk $R_{\text{emp}}[w]$ vanishes or is bounded by some previously chosen constant. Proponents of this strategy claim rapid convergence due to the good mixing properties of the dynamical system.

Finally, we left the field of graphical models (see for instance [525, 260, 274, 273] and the references therein) completely untouched. These algorithms model the dependency structure between different random variables in a rather explicit fashion and use efficient approximate inference techniques to solve the optimization problems. To date it is not clear how such methods can be combined with kernels.

16.7.2 Key Issues

Topics covered in the chapter include deterministic and approximate methods for Bayesian inference, with an emphasis on the Maximum a Posteriori (MAP) estimate and the treatment of hyperparameters. As a side-effect, we observe that the minimization of regularized risk is closely related to approximate Bayesian estimation.

One of the first consequences of this link is the connection between Gaussian Processes and Support Vector Machines. While the former are defined in terms of correlations between random variables, the latter are derived from smoothness assumptions regarding the estimate and feature space considerations. This connection also allows us to exchange uniform convergence statements and Bayesian error bounds between both types of reasoning.

As a side effect, this connection also gives rise to a new class of prior, namely those corresponding to ℓ_1 regularization and linear programming machines. Since the coefficients α_i then follow a Laplacian distribution, we name the corresponding stochastic process a *Laplacian Process*. This new point of view allows the derivation of error bars for the estimates in a way that is not easily possible in a statistical learning theory framework. It turns out that this leads to a data dependent prior on the function space.

Finally, the Relevance Vector Machine introduces individual hyperparameters for the distributions of the coefficients α_i. This makes certain optimization problems tractable (matrix inversion) that otherwise would have remained infeasible (MAP estimate with the Student-t distribution as a prior). We expect that the technique of representing complex distributions by a normal distribution *cum* hyperprior is also a promising approach for other estimation problems.

Taking a more abstract view, we expect a convergence between different estimation algorithms and inference principles derived from risk minimization, Bayesian estimation, and Minimum Description Length concepts. Laplacian Processes and the Relevance Vector Machine are two examples of such convergence. We hope that more such methods will follow in the next few years.

16.8 Problems

16.1 (Prior Distributions •) *Compute the log prior probability according to (16.10) for the following functions:* $\sin x$, $\sin x + 0.1 \sin 10x$, $\sin x + 0.01 \sin 100x$, *and more generally,* $f_n(x) := \sin x + \frac{1}{n} \sin nx$ *on* $[-\pi, \pi]$. *Show that the series* f_n *converges to* $\sin x$, *yet that* $f'_n(x)$ *does not converge to* $\cos x$. *Interpret this result in terms of prior distributions (Hint: What can you say about functions where the prior probability also converges).*

16.2 (Hypothesis Testing and Tail Bounds ••) *Assume we want to test whether a coin produces equal numbers of heads and tails. Compute the likelihood that among* m *trials we observe* m_h *heads and* $m_t = m - m_h$ *tails, given a probability* π_h *that a head is observed (Hint: Use the binomial distribution and, if necessary, its approximation with a normal distribution).*

Next, compute the posterior probability for the following two prior assumptions on the possible values of π_h:

$$p(\pi_h) = 1 \text{ (flat prior)}, \tag{16.141}$$

$$p(\pi_h) = 12\pi_h(1 - \pi_h). \tag{16.142}$$

Give an interpretation of (16.141) and (16.142). What is the minimum number of coins we need to toss (assuming that we get an equal number of heads and tails) in order to state that the probability of heads equals that of tails within precision ε *with* $1 - \eta$ *probability?*

How many tosses do you need on average to detect a faulty coin that generates heads with probability π_h?

16.3 (Label Noise •) *Assume that we have a random variable* y *with* $P(y = 1) = p$, *and consequently* $P(y = -1) = 1 - p$. *What is the probability of observing* $y = 1$ *if we flip each label with probability* η? *What is* $P(y = 1)$ *if we randomly* assign *a label for all* y *with probability* η?

16.4 (Projected Normal Distributions ••) *Assume that we have two clouds of points, one belonging to class 1 and a second belonging to class −1, and both normally distributed with unit variance.*

Show that for any projection onto a line, the distributions of the points on the line is a mixture of two normal distributions. What happens to the means and the variances? Formulate the likelihood that an arbitrary point on the line belongs to class 1 or −1.

16.5 (Entropic Priors •) *Assume we have an experiment with n possible outcomes where we would like to estimate the probabilities $\pi_1, \ldots, \pi_n$ with which these outcomes occur. We use the following prior distribution $p(\pi_1, \ldots, \pi_n)$,*

$$-\ln p(\pi_1, \ldots, \pi_n) = -H(\pi_1, \ldots, \pi_n) + c = \sum_{i=1}^{n} \pi_i \ln \pi_i + c, \tag{16.143}$$

where c is a normalization constant and H denotes the entropy of the probabilities $\pi_1, \ldots, \pi_n$.

Show that (16.143) describes a proper prior distribution. Compute the likelihood of observing the outcomes $1, \ldots, n$ at times $m_1, \ldots, m_n$ (see Problem 16.2). Derive the value of the log posterior distribution (use Gaussian approximation). Does the normalization constant c matter? What happens if we rescale (16.143) by a constant s? How does the log posterior change? Give examples of how s can be adjusted automatically (automatic relevance determination) and formulate the MAP2 estimate (•••).

16.6 (Inference and Variance •) *For a normal distribution in two variables with*

$$K = \begin{bmatrix} 1 & 0.75 \\ 0.75 & 0.75 \end{bmatrix} \tag{16.144}$$

as covariance and zero mean, compute the variance in terms of the first variable if the second one is observed, and vice versa.

16.7 (Samples from a Gaussian Process Prior •) *Draw a sample X at random from the uniform distribution on $[0,1]^2$ and compute the corresponding covariance matrix K. Use for instance the linear kernel $k(x, x') = \langle x, x' \rangle$ and the Gaussian RBF kernel $k(x, x') = \exp(-\frac{1}{2\sigma^2}\|x - x'\|^2)$.*

Write a program which draws samples uniformly from the normal distribution $\mathcal{N}(0, K)$ (Hint: Compute the eigenvectors of K first). What difference do you observe when using different kernels?

16.8 (Time Series and Autocorrelation •) *Assume a time series of normally distributed random variables ξ_t drawn from a stationary distribution. Why is the autocorrelation function independent of time? Show that the random variables ξ_t follow a Gaussian Process. What is the covariance kernel?*

16.9 (Gaussian Processes with Roundoff Noise •) *Give an expression for the posterior probability of a Gaussian Process with covariance function $k(x, x')$ in the presence of roundoff noise (see (16.45)).*

16.10 (Hyperparameter Updates •••) *Assume that $k(x, x')$ also depends on a parameter ω. Compute the derivative of the log posterior for GP regression with respect to ω (see [197, 198] for details).*

Can you adapt the sparse greedy approximation scheme (Section 16.4.4) to maximize the log posterior with respect to the hyperparameters (○○○)?

16.11 (Convergence of Laplace Approximation ○○○) *Find a lower bound on the radius of convergence of the Laplace Approximation (Section 16.4.1). Hint: show that the iteration step of the Laplace approximation is a contraction.*

16.12 (Laplace Approximation in Function Space ○○○) *Instead of formulating the Newton approximation steps in coefficient space, as done in (16.61), we may also derive the update rule in function space, which promises better convergence properties and a numerically less expensive implementation (see Section 10.6.1).*

Hint: Compute the gradient and the Hessian (Note: This is an operator in the present case) for the log posterior $p(f|X, Y)$ of a Gaussian Process. Show that we can still invert the Hessian efficiently since it is simply a projection operator on the subspace spanned by $k(x_i, \cdot)$. State the update rule.

16.13 (Upper and Lower Bounds on Convex Functionals •••) *Prove (16.65) and (16.66). Hint: For the lower bound, exploit convexity of the logistic function and construct a tangent. For the upper bound, construct a quadratic function with curvature larger than the logistic.*

Show that (16.65) and (16.66) are tight. What can you say in more general quadratic cases? See [264] for a detailed derivation.

16.14 (Eigenfunctions of k ••)

- *How do the eigenfunctions of Figure 16.4 change if ω changes? What happens to the eigenvalues? Confirm this behavior using numerical simulations.*
- *What do you expect if the dimensionality of x increases? What if it increases significantly? What happens if we replace the Gaussian kernel by a Laplacian kernel?*
- *Design an approximate training algorithm for Gaussian Processes using the fact that you can approximately represent K by a lower rank system (•••).*
- *How do these findings relate to Kernel Principal Component Analysis (Chapter 14)?*

16.15 (Low-rank approximations of K ••) *Denote by $\mathcal{H}$ an RKHS with kernel k. Given a set of basis functions $\tilde{S} := \{k(\tilde{x}_1, \cdot), \ldots, k(\tilde{x}_n, \cdot)\}$, compute the optimal approximation of $k(x, \cdot)$ in terms of $\tilde{S}$ with respect to the norm induced by $\mathcal{H}$.*

Now assume that we want to approximate functions from a larger set, say $S := \{k(x_1, \cdot), \ldots, k(x_m, \cdot)\}$. Show that this leads to the approximation of the matrix K with $K_{ij} := k(x_i, x_j)$ by a low rank matrix $\tilde{K}$.

16.16 (Sparse Greedy [503] and Random Approximation [602] ••) *Experimentally compare the settings where basis functions are selected purely at random (Nyström method) with the case where they are selected in a sparse greedy fashion.*

16.17 (Optimization Problems for Laplacian Process ••) *Derive the optimization problem for regression with a Laplacian process prior under the assumption of additive Gaussian noise. Hint: What is the posterior probability of an estimator f under the current assumptions? Compute the dual optimization problem. Is the latter easier to deal with?*

Now assume additive Laplacian noise. How does the optimization problem change?

16.18 (Confidence Intervals for Laplacian Noise •••) *Derive confidence intervals for Laplacian Noise and a Gaussian Process or Laplacian regularizer. Is there a closed-form expansion? Can you find an efficient sampling scheme (∘∘∘)?*

16.19 (Efficient Computation of Confidence Terms ••) *Using sparse greedy approximation, devise an algorithm for computing (16.106), and in particular $\mathbf{k}_M^\top (K_M^\top K_M)^{-1} \mathbf{k}_M$, more efficiently. Hint: Use a variant of Theorem 16.5 and a rank-one update method.*

16.20 (Hyperparameter Updates for Relevance Vector Machines •••) *Derive the update rules for the hyperparameters (16.132) and (16.133). Hint: See [338] for details.*

16.21 (Parameter Coding for Relevance Vector Machines ∘∘∘) *Denote by $p(\alpha_i)$ a prior on the coefficients α_i of a kernel expansion. Can you find a deconvolution function $p(s_i)$ such that*

$$p(\alpha_i) = \int (2\pi s_i)^{\frac{1}{2}} e^{-\frac{1}{2} s_i \alpha_i^2} p(s_i) ds_i? \tag{16.145}$$

Hint: Use the Fourier transformation. What does this mean when encoding sparse priors such as $p(\alpha_i) = \frac{1}{2} e^{-|\alpha_i|}$? Can you construct alternative training algorithms for Laplacian Processes?

16.22 (RVM and Generative Topographic Mapping ∘∘∘) *Apply the RVM method as a prior to the Generative Topographic Mapping described in Section 17.4.2; in other words, instead of using $\sum_i \alpha_i^2$ as the negative log prior probability on the weights of the individual nodes.*

Can you find an incremental approach? (Hint: Use the method described in [539])

17 Regularized Principal Manifolds

In Chapter 14, which covered Kernel Principal Component Analysis and Kernel Feature Analysis, we viewed the problem of unsupervised learning as a problem of finding good *feature extractors*. This is not the only possible way of extracting information from data, however.

For instance, we could determine the properties that best describe the data; in other words, that represent the data in an optimal compact fashion. This is useful for the purpose of data visualization, and to test whether new data is generated using the same distribution as the training set. Inevitably, this leads to a (possibly quite crude) model of the underlying probability distribution. Generative models such as Principal Curves [231], the Generative Topographic Mapping [52], several linear Gaussian models [444], and vector quantizers [21] are examples thereof.

Outline

The present chapter covers data descriptive models. We first introduce the quantization functional [509] (see Section 17.1), which plays the role of the risk $R[f]$ commonly used in supervised learning (see Chapter 3). This allows us to use techniques from regularization theory in unsupervised learning. In particular, it leads to a natural generalization (to higher dimensionality and different criteria of regularity) of the principal curves algorithm with a length constraint [292], which is presented in Section 17.2, together with an efficient algorithm (Section 17.3).

In addition, we show that regularized quantization functionals can be seen in the context of robust coding; that is, optimal coding in the presence of a noisy channel. The regularized quantization error approach also lends itself to a comparison with Bayesian techniques based on generative models. Connections to other algorithms are pointed out in Section 17.4. The regularization framework allows us to present a modified version of the Generative Topographic Mapping (GTM) [52] (Section 17.4.2), using recent developments in Gaussian Processes (Section 16.3).

Finally, the quantization functional approach also provides a versatile tool to find uniform convergence bounds. In Section 17.5, we derive bounds on the quantization error and on the rate of convergence that subsume several existing results as special cases. This is possible due to the use of functional analytic tools.

Priorities and Prerequisites

Readers mainly interested in the core algorithm are best served by reading the first three sections and possibly the experimental part (Section 17.6). Chapters 3 and 4 are useful to understand the formulation of regularized quantization functionals. Section 17.4 is mainly relevant to readers interested in Bayesian alternatives, such as the Generative Topographic Mapping. Clearly, knowledge of the basic Bayesian concepts presented in Section 16.1 will be useful. Finally, Section 17.5

requires an understanding of uniform convergence bounds and operator theoretic methods in learning theory (Section 12.4).

17.1 A Coding Framework

The basic idea of the quantization error approach is that we should be able to learn something about data by learning how to efficiently *compress* or *encode* it as a simpler yet still meaningful object. The quality of the encoding is assessed by the reconstruction error (the quantization error) it causes (in other words, how close the reconstructions come to the initial data), and the simplicity of the device that generates the code. The latter is important, since the coding device then contains the information we seek to extract.

Learning by Compression

Unlike most engineering applications,[1] we also allow for *continuous* codes. Practical encoding schemes, on the other hand, concern themselves with the number of bits needed to code an object. This reflects our emphasis on information extraction by learning the coding device itself. As we will see in Section 17.4.3, however, constraints on the simplicity of the coding device are crucial to avoid overfitting for real valued continuous codes.

17.1.1 Quantization Error

Let us begin with the usual definitions: denote by $\mathcal{X}$ a (possibly compact subset of a) vector space, and by $X := \{x_1, \ldots, x_m\} \subset \mathcal{X}$ a dataset drawn iid from an unknown underlying probability distribution $\mathrm{P}(x)$. The observations are members of $\mathcal{X}$. Additionally, we define the index sets $\mathcal{Z}$, maps $f : \mathcal{Z} \to \mathcal{X}$, and classes $\mathcal{F}$ of such maps (with $f \in \mathcal{F}$). Here $\mathcal{Z}$ is the domain of our code, and the map f is intended to describe certain basic properties of $\mathrm{P}(x)$. In particular, we seek f such that the so-called quantization error,

Expected Quantization Error

$$R[f] := \int_{\mathcal{X}} \min_{z \in \mathcal{Z}} c(x, f(z)) d\mathrm{P}(x), \tag{17.1}$$

is minimized. In this setting, $c(x, f(z))$ is the loss function determining the error of reconstruction. We very often set $c(x, f(z)) = \|x - f(z)\|^2$, where $\|\cdot\|$ denotes the Euclidean distance. Unfortunately, the problem of minimizing $R[f]$ is insolvable,

1. Consider the task of displaying an image with 24 bit color depth on an 8 bit display with color lookup table (CLUT), meaning that the 256 possible colors may be chosen from a 24 bit color-space. Simply keeping the most significant bits of each color is not a promising strategy: images of a forest benefit from an allocation of many colors in the green color-space, whereas images of the sky typically benefit from a dominance of white and blue colors in the CLUT. Consequently, the colors chosen in the CLUT provide us with information about the image.

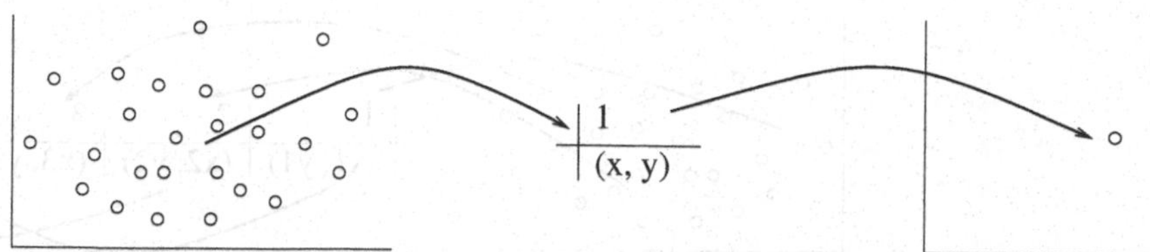

Figure 17.1 Sample Mean in $\mathbb{R}^2$. The observations are mapped to one codebook vector, denoted by the triplet $(1, x, y)$. Decoding is done by mapping the codebook vector back to (x, y). Obviously, the coding error is given by the average deviations between the sample mean and the data.

as P is generally unknown. Hence we replace P using the empirical density

$$P_m(x) := \frac{1}{m} \sum_{i=1}^{m} \delta(x - x_i), \tag{17.2}$$

Empirical Quantization Error

and instead of (17.1) we analyze the empirical quantization error

$$R_{\text{emp}}[f] := \int_{\mathcal{X}} \min_{z \in \mathcal{Z}} c(x, f(z)) dP_m(x) = \frac{1}{m} \sum_{i=1}^{m} \min_{z \in \mathcal{Z}} c(x_i, f(z)). \tag{17.3}$$

The general problem of minimizing (17.3) is ill posed [538, 370]. Even worse, with no further restrictions on $\mathcal{F}$, small values of $R_{\text{emp}}[f]$ fail to guarantee small values of $R[f]$.

Many problems in unsupervised learning can be cast in the form of finding a minimizer of (17.1) or (17.3). Let us consider some practical examples.

17.1.2 Examples with Finite Codes

We begin with cases where $\mathcal{Z}$ is a finite set; we can then encode f by a table of all its possible values.

Example 17.1 (Sample Mean) *Define $\mathcal{Z} := \{1\}$, $\mathcal{F}$ to be the set of all constant functions, and $f(1) \in \mathcal{X}$. In addition, set $c(x, f(z)) = \|x - f(z)\|^2$. Then the minimum of*

$$R[f] := \int_{\mathcal{X}} \|x - f\|^2 dP(x) \text{ and } R_{\text{emp}}[f] = \frac{1}{m} \sum_{i=1}^{m} \|f(1) - x_i\|^2 \tag{17.4}$$

yields the variance of the data. The minimizers of the quantization functionals can in this case be determined analytically,

$$\operatorname*{argmin}_{f \in \mathcal{F}} R[f] = \int_{\mathcal{X}} x dP(x) \text{ and } \operatorname*{argmin}_{f \in \mathcal{F}} R_{\text{emp}}[f] = \frac{1}{m} \sum_{i=1}^{m} x_i. \tag{17.5}$$

Variance as Quantization Error

This is the (empirical) sample mean (see also Figure 17.1).

Example 17.2 (k-means Vector Quantization) *Define $\mathcal{Z} := [k]$ and $f : i \to f_i$ with $f_i \in \mathcal{X}$, and denote by $\mathcal{F}$ the set of all such functions. If we again use $c(x, f(z)) = \|x - f(z)\|^2$,*

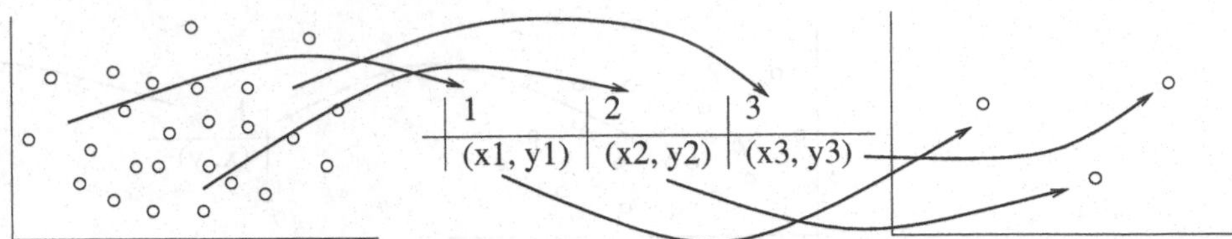

Figure 17.2 k-means clustering in $\mathbb{R}^2$ (in this figure, $k = 3$). The observations are mapped to one of the codebook vectors, denoted by the triplet (i, x_i, y_i). Decoding is done by mapping the codebook vectors back to (x_i, y_i).

then

$$R[f] := \int_{\mathcal{X}} \min_{z \in [k]} \|x - f_z\|^2 dP(x) \tag{17.6}$$

Intra-Cluster Variance as Quantization Error

denotes the canonical distortion error of a vector quantizer. In practice, we can use the k-means algorithm [332] to find a set of vectors $\{f_1, \ldots, f_k\}$ minimizing $R_{\text{emp}}[f]$ (see Figure 17.2). Furthermore there exist proofs of the convergence properties of the minimizer of $R_{\text{emp}}[f]$ to one of the minimizer(s) of $R[f]$ (see [21]).

Note that in this case, minimization of the empirical quantization error leads to local minima, a problem quite common in this type of setting. A different choice of loss functions c leads to a clustering algorithm proposed in [73].

Robust Clustering

Example 17.3 (k-median and Robust Vector Quantization) *Beginning with the definitions of the previous example, and choosing $c(x, f(z)) := \|x - f(z)\|_1$ we obtain the k-median problem. Recall that $\|\cdot\|_1$ is the city-block metric. In this case,*

$$R[f] := \int_{\mathcal{X}} \min_{z \in [k]} \|x - f_z\|_1 dP(x). \tag{17.7}$$

This setting is robust against outliers, since the maximum influence of each pattern is bounded. An intermediate setting can be derived from Huber's robust loss function [251] (see also Table 3.1). Here, we define

$$c(x, f(z)) := \begin{cases} \frac{1}{2\sigma}\|x - f(z)\|^2 & \text{for } \|x - f(z)\| \leq \sigma, \\ \|x - f(z)\| - \frac{\sigma}{2} & \text{otherwise,} \end{cases} \tag{17.8}$$

for suitably chosen σ. Eq. (17.8) behaves like a k-means vector quantizer for small x_i, but with the built-in safeguard of a limit on the influence of each individual pattern.

17.1.3 Examples with Infinite Codes

Instead of discrete quantization, we can also consider a mapping onto a manifold of dimensionality lower than that of the input space. PCA (see also Sections 14.1 and 14.4.1) can be viewed in the following way [231]:

Proximity to a Line Segment

Example 17.4 (Principal Components) *Define $\mathcal{Z} := \mathbb{R}$, $f : z \to f_0 + z \cdot f_1$ with $f_0, f_1 \in \mathcal{X}$, $\|f_1\| = 1$, and $\mathfrak{F}$ to be the set of all such line segments. Moreover, let $c(x, f(z)) := \|x - f(z)\|^2$. Then the minimizer of*

$$R[f] := \int_{\mathcal{X}} \min_{z \in [0,1]} \|x - f_0 - z \cdot f_1\|^2 dP(x) \tag{17.9}$$

over $f \in \mathfrak{F}$ yields a line parallel to the direction of largest variance in P(*x*) *(see [231] and Section 14.1).*

A slight modification results in simultaneous diagonalization of the covariance matrix with respect to an additional metric tensor.

Simultaneous Diagonalization

Example 17.5 (Transformed Loss Metrics) *Denote by D a strictly positive definite matrix. With the definitions above and the loss function*

$$c(x, f(z)) := (x - f(z))^\top D^{-1}(x - f(z)), \tag{17.10}$$

the minimizer of the empirical quantization can be found by simultaneous diagonalization of D and the covariance matrix cov(x).

This can be seen as follows: We replace x by $\tilde{x} := D^{-\frac{1}{2}}x$ and f by $\tilde{f} := D^{-\frac{1}{2}}f$. Now $c(x, f(z)) = \|\tilde{x} - \tilde{f}(z)\|^2$, hence we have reduced the problem to one of finding principal components for the covariance matrix $D^{-\frac{1}{2}}\text{cov}(x)D^{-\frac{1}{2}}$. This, however, is equivalent to simultaneous diagonalization of D and $\text{cov}(x)$, which completes the proof.

Further choices of c, such as the $\|\cdot\|_1$ metric or Huber's robust loss function, lead to algorithms that are less prone to instabilities caused by outliers than standard PCA.

k-Planes Clustering

A combination of k-means clustering and principal components leads to the k-planes clustering algorithm proposed in [72] (also known as *Local PCA* by Kambhatla & Leen [276, 277]).[2] Here, clustering is carried out with respect to k planes instead of k cluster points. After assigning the data points to the planes, the latter are re-estimated using PCA (thus, the directions with smallest variance are eliminated). Both Kambhatla & Leen [277] and Bradley & Mangasarian [72] show that this can improve results on certain datasets.

Hastie & Stuetzle [231] extended PCA in a different direction by allowing $f(z)$ to be other than a linear function.

2. While [277] introduces the problem by considering local linear versions of Principal Component Analysis and takes a Neural Networks perspective, [73] treats the task mainly as an optimization problem for which convergence to a local minimum in a finite number of steps is proven. While the resulting algorithm is identical, the motivation in the two cases differs significantly. In particular, the ansatz in [73] makes it easier for us to formulate the problem as one of minimizing a quantization functional.
The original local linear Vector Quantization formulation put forward in [276] also allows us to give a quantization formulation for local PCA. To achieve this, we simply consider linear subspaces together with their enclosing Voronoi cells.

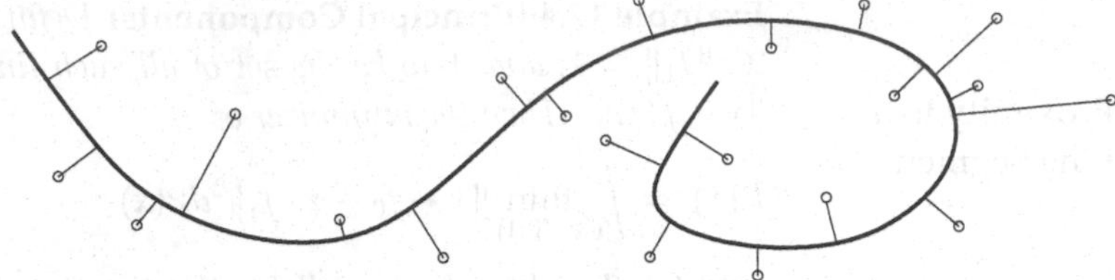

Figure 17.3 Projection of points x onto a manifold $f(\mathcal{Z})$, in this case with minimum Euclidean distance.

Projection on Manifolds

Example 17.6 (Principal Curves and Surfaces) *We define* $\mathcal{Z} := [0,1]^d$ *(with* $d \in \mathbb{N}$ *and* $d > 1$ *for principal surfaces),* $f : z \to f(z)$, *with* $f \in \mathfrak{F}$ *a class of continuous* $\mathbb{R}^d$-*valued continuous functions (possibly with further restrictions), and again* $c(x, f(z)) := \|x - f(z)\|^2$. *The minimizer of*

$$R[f] := \int_{\mathcal{X}} \min_{z \in [0,1]^d} \|x - f(z)\|^2 dP(x) \tag{17.11}$$

is not well defined, unless $\mathfrak{F}$ *is a compact set. Moreover, even the minimizer of* $R_{\text{emp}}[f]$ *is generally not well defined either. In fact, it is an ill posed problem in the sense of Arsenin and Tikhonov [538]. Until recently [292], no uniform convergence properties of* $R_{\text{emp}}[f]$ *to* $R[f]$ *could be stated.*

Principal Curves with a Length Constraint

Kégl et al. [292] modified the original principal curves algorithm in order to prove bounds on $R[f]$ in terms of $R_{\text{emp}}[f]$ and to show that the resulting estimate is well defined. The changes imply a restriction of $\mathfrak{F}$ to polygonal lines with a fixed number of knots, and most importantly, *fixed* length L.[3]

This is essentially equivalent to using a regularization operator. Instead of a length constraint, which as we will show in section 17.2.2, corresponds to a particular regularization operator, we now consider more general smoothness constraints on the estimated curve $f(x)$.

17.2 A Regularized Quantization Functional

What we would essentially like to have are estimates that not only yield small expected quantization error but are smooth curves (or manifolds) as well. The latter property is independent of the parametrization of the curve. It is difficult to compute such a quantity in practice, however. An easier task is to provide a measure of the smoothness of f *depending* on the *parametrization* of $f(z)$. A wide range of regularizers from supervised learning can readily be used for this purpose. As a side effect, we also obtain a smooth parametrization.

3. In practice, Kégl et al. use a constraint on the angles of the polygonal curves, rather than the actual length constraint, to achieve sample complexity rates on the training time of the algorithm. For the uniform convergence part, however, the length constraint is used.

Table 17.1 Comparison of the three basic learning problems considered in this book: supervised learning, quantization, and feature extraction. Note that the optimization problems for supervised learning and quantization can also be transformed into the problem of maximizing $R_{\text{emp}}[f]$ subject to the constraint $\Omega[f] \leq \Lambda$.

	Supervised Learning	Quantization	Feature Extraction
Data	$X = \{x_1, \ldots, x_m\} \subset \mathfrak{X}$ $Y = \{y_1, \ldots, y_m\} \subset \mathcal{Y}$	$X = \{x_1, \ldots, x_m\} \subset \mathfrak{X}$	$X = \{x_1, \ldots, x_m\} \subset \mathfrak{X}$
Objective	minimize Test Error $R[f] = \mathbf{E}\left[c(x, y, f(x))\right]$	minimize Coding Error $R[f] = \mathbf{E}\left[\min_{z \in \mathcal{Z}} c(x, f(z))\right]$	max. Interestingness $R[f] = \mathbf{E}\left[q(f(x))\right]$
Typical Examples	$c(x, y, f(x)) = (y - f(x))^2$ $c(x, y, f(x)) = \lvert y - f(x) \rvert_\varepsilon$	$c(x, f(z)) = \lVert x - f(z) \rVert_2^2$ $c(x, f(z)) = \lVert x - f(z) \rVert_1$	$q(f(x)) = f(x)^2$ $q(f(x)) = f(x)^4$
Loss	Mismatch between $f(x)$ and y	Approximation of x by $f(z(x))$	Anomality of $f(x)$ via $q(f(x))$
Empirical Quantity	Training Error $R_{\text{emp}}[f] = \sum_{i=1}^{m} c(x_i, y_i, f(x_i))$	Approximation Error $R_{\text{emp}}[f] = \sum_{i=1}^{m} \min_{z \in \mathcal{Z}} c(x_i, f(z))$	Contrast $Q[f] = \sum_{i=1}^{m} q(f(x_i))$
Regularizer	$\Omega[f]$		
Problem	minimize $R_{\text{emp}}[f] + \lambda\Omega[f]$	minimize $R_{\text{emp}}[f] + \lambda\Omega[f]$	maximize $Q[f]$ subj. to $\Omega[f] \leq \Lambda$

We now propose a variant to minimizing the empirical quantization functional, which seeks hypotheses from certain classes of smooth curves, leads to an algorithm that is readily implemented, and is amenable to the analysis of sample complexity via uniform convergence techniques. We will make use of a regularized version of the empirical quantization functional. Let

$$R_{\text{reg}}[f] := R_{\text{emp}}[f] + \lambda\Omega[f], \tag{17.12}$$

where $\Omega[f]$ is a convex nonnegative regularization term, and $\lambda > 0$ is a trade-off constant determining how much *simple* functions f should be favored over functions with low empirical quantization error. We now consider some possible choices of Q. This setting is very similar to those of supervised learning (4.1) and the feature extraction framework (14.35). Table 17.1 gives an overview. In all three cases we have the following three step procedure:

General Regularization Strategy

(i) Start with a measure of optimality (expected risk, quantization error, criterion of interestingness of the estimate f on the data) with respect to a distribution $\mathrm{P}(x)$
(ii) Replace the integration over $\mathrm{P}(x)$ by a sum over samples drawn iid from $\mathrm{P}(x)$
(iii) To ensure numerical stability and guarantee smooth estimates, add a regularization term (usually quadratic or linear)

17.2.1 Quadratic Regularizers

As we have seen several times (see Chapter 4), quadratic functionals [538] are a very popular choice of regularizer, and in the present case we can make use of the whole toolbox of regularization functionals, regularization operators, and Reproducing Kernel Hilbert Spaces. This illustrates how the simple transformation of a problem into a known framework can make life much easier, and it allows us to assemble new algorithms from readily available building blocks.

In the present case, $\Omega[f] = \|f\|^2_{\mathcal{H}}$, these building blocks are kernels, and we may expand f as

$$f(z) = f_0 + \sum_{i=1}^{M} \alpha_i k(z_i, z), \text{ with } z_i \in \mathcal{Z},\ \alpha_i \in \mathcal{X}, \text{ and } k: \mathcal{Z}^2 \to \mathbb{R}, \tag{17.13}$$

given previously chosen nodes $z_1, \ldots, z_M$ (of which we take as many as we can afford in terms of computational loss). It can be shown (see Problem 17.2) that the back-projections of the observations x_i onto f are in fact the most suitable expansion points.[4] Consequently, the regularization term can be written as

Kernel Expansion

$$\|f\|^2_{\mathcal{H}} = \sum_{i,j=1}^{M} \langle \alpha_i, \alpha_j \rangle k(z_i, z_j). \tag{17.14}$$

This is the functional form of $\|f\|^2_{\mathcal{H}}$ needed to to derive efficient algorithms.

17.2.2 Examples of Regularization Operators

In our first example, we consider the equivalence between principal curves with a length constraint and minimizing the regularized quantization functional.

Example 17.7 (Regularizers with a Length Constraint) *By choosing the differentiation operator $\Upsilon := \partial_z$, $\|\Upsilon f\|^2$ becomes an integral over the squared "speed" of the curve. Re-parametrizing f to constant speed leaves the empirical quantization error unchanged, whereas the regularization term is minimized. This can be seen as follows: By construction, $\int_{[0,1]} \|\partial_z f(z)\| dz$ does not depend on the (re-)parametrization. The variance, however, is minimal for a constant function, hence $\|\partial_z f(z)\|$ has to be constant over the interval $[0, 1]$. Thus, $\|\Upsilon f\|^2$ equals the squared length L^2 of the curve at the solution.*

Minimizing the sum of the empirical quantization error and a regularizer, however, is equivalent to minimizing the empirical quantization error for a fixed value of the regularization term (when λ is suitably adjusted).[5] Hence the proposed algo-

4. In practice, however, such expansions tend to become unstable during the optimization procedure. Hence, a set of z_i chosen a priori, for instance on a grid, is the default choice.
5. The reasoning is not completely true for the case of a finite number of basis functions — f *cannot* then be completely re-parametrized to constant speed. The basic properties still hold, however, provided the number of kernels is sufficiently high.

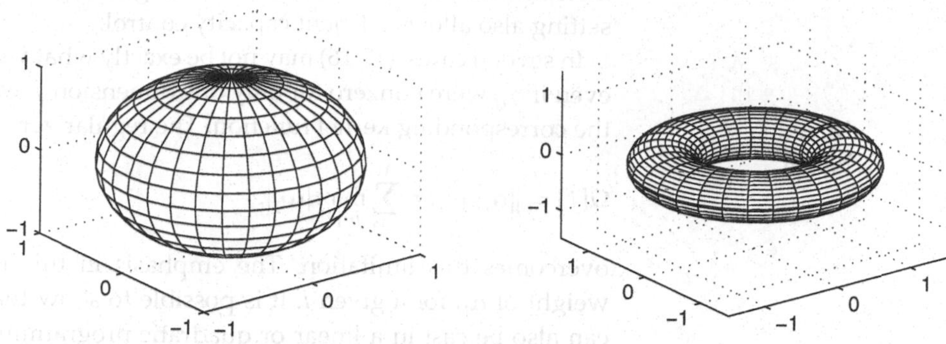

Figure 17.4 Two-dimensional periodic structures in $\mathbb{R}^3$. Left: unit sphere, which can be mapped to $[0, \pi] \times \mathbb{R}/2\pi$; right: toroid, which is generated from $[0, 2\pi]^2$.

rithm is equivalent to finding the optimal curve with a length constraint; in other words, it is equivalent to the algorithm proposed in [292].

As experimental and theoretical evidence from regression indicates, it may be beneficial to choose a kernel that also enforces higher degrees of smoothness in higher derivatives of the estimate. Hence, we could just as well use Gaussian RBF kernels (2.68),

$$k(x, x') = \exp\left(-\frac{\|x-x'\|^2}{2\sigma^2}\right). \tag{17.15}$$

This corresponds to a regularizer penalizing all derivatives simultaneously (see Section 4.4.2 for details, and Section 17.6 for experimental results with this kernel).

Periodical Kernels

The use of periodical kernels (see Section 4.4.4) has interesting consequences in the context of describing manifolds. Such kernels allow us to model circular structures in $\mathcal{X}$, hence we can find good approximations to objects such as the surface of balls or "donut"-shaped distributions (see Figure 17.4). Nonetheless, we have to keep in mind that this requires the spatial connectivity structure to be known (which we may not always assume).

The appealing property of this formulation is that it is completely independent of the dimensionality and of any particular structure of $\mathcal{Z}$.

17.2.3 Linear Programming Regularizers

It may not always be desirable to find expansions of $f = \sum_{i=1}^{M} \alpha_i k(z_i, \cdot)$ in terms of *many* basis functions $k(x_i, x)$. Instead, it is often better to obtain an estimate of f with just a few basis functions (but usually of almost equal quality). This can be achieved via a regularizer that enforces sparsity (see Section 4.9.2), for example by setting $\Omega[f] := \sum_{i=1}^{M} |\alpha_i|$. For $\alpha_i \in \mathbb{R}^d$, we use

Homogeneous ℓ_1 Norm

$$\Omega[f] = \sum_{i=1}^{M} \|\alpha_i\|_1 = \sum_{i=1}^{M} \sum_{j=1}^{d} |\alpha_{ij}| \tag{17.16}$$

instead. It is shown in [509] that by using an argument similar to that in [505], this setting also allows efficient capacity control.

In several cases, (17.16) may not be exactly what we are looking for. In particular, even if α_{ij} were nonzero for only one dimension j, we would still have to evaluate the corresponding kernel function. The regularizer

Mixed ℓ_1–ℓ_∞ Norm

$$\Omega[f] = \|\alpha_i\|_{1,\infty} = \sum_{i=1}^{M} \max_{j \in [d]} |\alpha_{ij}|. \tag{17.17}$$

overcomes this limitation. The emphasis in this instance is on the maximum weight of α_{ij} for a given i. It is possible to show that regularizers of type (17.17) can also be cast in a linear or quadratic programming setting, provided the loss function c is only linear or quadratic (see Problem 17.4).

17.3 An Algorithm for Minimizing $R_{\text{reg}}[f]$

In this section, we present an algorithm that approximately minimizes $R_{\text{reg}}[f]$ via coordinate descent.[6] We certainly do not claim it is the best algorithm for this task — our goal is simply to find an algorithm consistent with our framework (which is amenable to sample complexity theory), and which works in practice. Furthermore, commonly known training algorithms for the special cases in Section 17.1.2, such as k-means algorithms and the k-planes algorithm of Section 17.1.3, are special cases of the algorithm we propose.

Finite Term Expansion

In the following, we assume the data to be centered and therefore drop the term f_0 in the kernel expansion (17.13) of f. This greatly simplifies the notation (the extension is straightforward). We further assume, for the sake of practicability, that the ansatz for f can be written in terms of a finite number of parameters $\alpha_1, \ldots \alpha_M$ (see the representer theorem for regularized principal manifolds in Problem 17.2), and that likewise the regularizer $\Omega[f]$ can also be expressed as a function of $\alpha_1, \ldots, \alpha_M$. This allows us to rephrase the problem of minimizing the regularized quantization functional as

$$\min_{\substack{\{\alpha_1,\ldots,\alpha_M\} \subset \mathcal{X} \\ \{\zeta_1,\ldots,\zeta_m\} \subset \mathcal{Z}}} \left[\frac{1}{m} \sum_{i=1}^{m} c(x_i, f_{\{\alpha_1,\ldots,\alpha_M\}}(\zeta_i)) + \lambda Q(\alpha_1, \ldots, \alpha_M) \right]. \tag{17.18}$$

Coordinate Descent and EM

This minimization is achieved in an iterative fashion by coordinate descent over $\boldsymbol{\zeta}$ and $\boldsymbol{\alpha}$, in a manner analogous to the EM (expectation maximization) algorithm [135]. Recall that the aim of the latter procedure is to find the distribution $\mathrm{P}(x)$, or at least the parameters θ of a distribution $\mathrm{P}_\theta(x, l)$, where x are observations and l are latent variables. Keeping θ fixed, we first accomplish the E-step by maximizing

6. Coordinate descent means that to minimize a function $f(x_1, \ldots, x_n)$ of several (possibly vector valued) variables $x_1, \ldots, x_n$, we minimize f only with respect to one variable at a time while keeping the others fixed.

$P_\theta(x,l)$ with respect to l; the M-step then consists of maximizing $P_\theta(x,l)$ with respect to θ. These two steps are repeated until no further improvement can be achieved.

Likewise, to solve (17.18), we alternate between minimizing with respect to $\{\zeta_1,\ldots,\zeta_m\}$, which is equivalent to the E-step (projection), and with respect to $\{\alpha_1,\ldots,\alpha_M\}$, corresponding to the M-step (adaptation). This procedure is repeated until convergence; or, in practice, until the regularized quantization functional stops decreasing significantly. Let us now have a closer look at the individual phases of the algorithm.

17.3.1 Projection

For each $i \in [m]$, choose $\zeta_i := \underset{\zeta\in\mathcal{Z}}{\operatorname{argmin}}\, c(x_i, f(\zeta))$; thus for squared loss, $\zeta_i := \operatorname{argmin}_{\zeta\in\mathcal{Z}} \|x_i - f(\zeta)\|^2$. Clearly, for fixed α_i, the resulting ζ_i minimize the loss term in (17.18), which itself is equal to $R_{\text{reg}}[f]$ for given α_i and X. Hence $R_{\text{reg}}[f]$ is decreased while keeping $\Omega[f]$ fixed (since the variables α_i do not change). In practice we use standard low dimensional nonlinear function minimization algorithms (see Section 6.2 and [423] for details and references) to achieve this goal.

Projecting onto the Manifold

The computational complexity is $O(m \cdot M)$ since the minimization step has to be carried out for each sample separately. In addition, each function evaluation (the number of which we assume to be approximately constant per minimization) scales linearly with the number of basis functions M.

17.3.2 Adaptation

Next, the parameters ζ_i are fixed, and α_i is adapted such that $R_{\text{reg}}[f]$ decreases further. The design of practical algorithms to decrease $R_{\text{reg}}[f]$ is closely connected with the particular forms taken by the loss function $c(x, f(z))$ and the regularizer $\Omega[f]$. We restrict ourselves to squared loss in this section ($c(x, f(z)) = \|x - f(z)\|^2$), and to the quadratic or linear regularization terms described in section 17.2. We thus assume that $f(z) = \sum_{i=1}^M \alpha_i k(x_i, x)$ for some kernel k, which matches the regularization operator Υ in the quadratic case.

Quadratic Regularizers The problem to be solved in this case is to minimize

$$\frac{1}{m}\sum_{i=1}^{m}\left\| x_i - \sum_{j=1}^{M}\alpha_j k(z_j,\zeta_i)\right\|^2 + \frac{\lambda}{2}\sum_{i,j=1}^{M}\langle\alpha_i,\alpha_j\rangle k(z_i,z_j) \tag{17.19}$$

Adaptation Step as Regression Problem

with respect to $\boldsymbol{\alpha}$. This is equivalent to a multivariate regression problem where ζ_i are the *patterns* and x_i the *target* values. Differentiation of (17.19) with respect to α_i yields

$$\left(\frac{\lambda m}{2}K_z + K_\zeta^\top K_\zeta\right)\boldsymbol{\alpha} = K_\zeta^\top X, \text{ and hence } \boldsymbol{\alpha} = \left(\frac{\lambda m}{2}K_z + K_\zeta^\top K_\zeta\right)^{-1} K_\zeta^\top X, \tag{17.20}$$

where $(K_z)_{ij} := k(z_i, z_j)$ is an $M \times M$ matrix and $(K_\zeta)_{ij} := k(\zeta_i, z_j)$ is $m \times M$. Moreover, with slight abuse of notation, $\boldsymbol{\alpha}$, and X denote the *matrices* of all parameters and samples, respectively.

The computational complexity of the adaptation step is $O(M^2 \cdot m)$ for the matrix computation, and $O(M^3)$ for the computation of the parameters α_i. Assuming termination of the overall algorithm in a finite number of steps, the overall complexity of the proposed algorithm is $O(M^3) + O(M^2 \cdot m)$; thus, it scales linearly in the number of samples (but cubic in the number of parameters).[7]

Linear Regularizers In this case, the adaptation step can be solved via a quadratic optimization problem. The trick is to break up the ℓ_1 norms (that is, the city-block metric) of the coefficient vectors α_i into pairs of nonnegative variables $\alpha_i - \alpha_i^*$, thus replacing $\|\alpha_i\|_1$ by $\langle \alpha_i, \vec{1} \rangle + \langle \alpha_i^*, \vec{1} \rangle$. Consequently we have to minimize

$$\frac{1}{m} \sum_{i=1}^{m} \left\| x_i - \sum_{j=1}^{M} (\alpha_j - \alpha_j^*) k(z_j, \zeta_i) \right\|^2 + \lambda \sum_{i=1}^{M} \langle \alpha_i + \alpha_i^*, \vec{1} \rangle, \tag{17.21}$$

with the constraint that α_i, α_i^* belong to the positive orthant in $\mathcal{X}$. Here $\vec{1}$ denotes the vector of ones in $\mathbb{R}^d$. Optimization is carried out using standard quadratic programming codes (see Chapters 6 and 10, and [380, 253, 556]). Depending on the particular implementation of the algorithm, this has an order of complexity similar to a matrix inversion, this is the same number of calculations needed to solve the unconstrained quadratic optimization problem described previously.

An algorithm alternating between the projection and adaptation step, as described above, generally decreases the regularized risk term and eventually converges to a local minimum of the optimization problem (see Problem 17.6). What remains is to find good starting values.

17.3.3 Initialization

The idea is to choose the coefficients α_i such that the initial guess of f approximately points in the directions of the first D principal components given by the matrix $V := (v_1, \ldots, v_D)$. This is done in a manner analogous to the initialization in the generative topographic mapping (eq. (2.20) of [52]);

Initialization as Principal Hyperplane

$$\min_{\{\alpha_1, \ldots, \alpha_M\} \subset \mathcal{X}} \frac{1}{M} \sum_{i=1}^{M} c\left(V(z_i - z_0) - f_{\alpha_1, \ldots, \alpha_M}(z_i)\right) + \lambda \Omega[f]. \tag{17.22}$$

Hence for squared loss and quadratic regularizers, $\boldsymbol{\alpha}$ is given by the solution of $\left(\frac{\lambda}{2}\mathbf{1} + K_z\right) \boldsymbol{\alpha} = V(Z - Z_0)$, where Z denotes the matrix of z_i, z_0 the mean of z_i, and Z_0 the matrix of m identical copies of z_0. If we are not dealing with centered data as assumed, f_0 is set to the sample mean, $f_0 = \frac{1}{m} \sum_{i=1}^{m} x_i$.

7. Note that the memory requirements are also at least $O(M \cdot m)$, and that for optimal performance M should increase with increasing m.

17.4 Connections to Other Algorithms

There exists a strong connection between Regularized Principal Manifolds (RPM) and Generative Models, and in particular to the Generative Topographic Map (GTM). The main difference is that the latter attempts to estimate the *density* of the data, whereas the quantization functional is mainly concerned with approximating the observations X. In a nutshell, the relation to Generative Models is similar to the connection between classification or regression estimates and Maximum a Posteriori estimates (see Chapter 16) in supervised learning: the prior probability over different generative models, in our case decoders such as manifolds and finite sets, plays the role of a regularization term.

17.4.1 Generative Models

Let us begin with the basic setting of a generative model[8] in Bayesian estimation (for the basic properties see Chapter 16). We present a simplified version here. Denote by P_α a distribution parametrized by $\boldsymbol{\alpha}$, and by $P(\boldsymbol{\alpha})$ a prior probability distribution over all possible values of $\boldsymbol{\alpha}$, which encodes our prior beliefs as to which distributions P_α are more likely to occur. Then, by Bayes' rule (Section 16.1.3), the posterior probability of a distribution P_α given the observations $X = \{x_1, \ldots, x_m\} \subset \mathcal{X}$ is given by

Posterior Probability

$$P(\boldsymbol{\alpha}|X) = \frac{P(X|\boldsymbol{\alpha})P(\boldsymbol{\alpha})}{P(X)}. \tag{17.23}$$

Since we cannot compute $P(X)$, it is usually ignored, and later reintroduced as a normalization factor. We exploit the iid assumption on X to obtain

$$P(X|\boldsymbol{\alpha}) = \prod_{i=1}^{m} P_\alpha(x_i). \tag{17.24}$$

Taking the log (17.23) and substituting in (17.24) yields the log posterior probability,

$$\ln P(\boldsymbol{\alpha}|X) = \sum_{i=1}^{m} \ln P_\alpha(x_i) + \ln P(\boldsymbol{\alpha}) + c. \tag{17.25}$$

Formal Connection to Quantization Functionals

Here c is the obligatory additive constant we got by ignoring $P(X)$. As with supervised learning, (17.23) is very similar to the regularized quantization functional, if we formally identify $P_\alpha(x_i)$ with the negative quantization error incurred by encoding x_i and $-\ln P(\boldsymbol{\alpha})$ with the regularizer.

8. The term *generative model* is just a synonym for *density model*. The generative part comes from the fact that, given a density model, we can draw (=generate) data from this model, which will then be distributed similarly to the original data.

The difference lies in the form of $P_\alpha(x_i)$. Whereas the quantization functional approach assumes optimal encoding via (17.1), the generative model approach essentially assumes stochastic encoding via latent variables. For convenience, we denote the latter by ζ. In general, $P(x_i|\alpha, \zeta)$ takes on a relatively simple form, such as a normal distribution around some $f_\alpha(\zeta)$ with variance σ^2. In this case, we set

$$P(x|\alpha, \zeta) = (2\pi\sigma^2)^{-\frac{n}{2}} \exp\left(-\frac{\|f_\alpha(\zeta) - x\|^2}{2\sigma^2}\right). \tag{17.26}$$

Integration over $P(\zeta)$ yields

$$P(x|\alpha) = \int P(x|\alpha, \zeta) dP(\zeta). \tag{17.27}$$

EM Algorithm

The problem is that $P(\zeta)$ itself is unknown and must be estimated as well. Furthermore, we would like to find a $P(\zeta)$ such that $P(X|\alpha)$ is maximized. In fact, there exists an algorithm to iteratively improve $P(X|\alpha)$ — the EM algorithm [135] (we already encountered a similar method in Section 17.3).

Without going into further detail (for the special case of the GTM, see [52, 51]), the algorithm works by iteratively estimating $Pr(\zeta)$ via Bayes' rule,

$$P(\zeta|x, \alpha) = \frac{P(x|\zeta, \alpha)}{\sum_{x'} P(x'|\zeta, \alpha)}, \tag{17.28}$$

and subsequently maximizing the log posterior under the assumption that $P(\zeta)$ is fixed. This process is repeated until convergence occurs. The latent variables ζ play a role similar to the projections back onto the manifold in the RPM algorithm. Let us now have a closer look at an example: Generative Topographic Mappings.

17.4.2 The Generative Topographic Mapping

The specific form of $P(\alpha)$, f, and $P(x|\alpha)$ in the GTM is as follows: $P(x|\alpha, \zeta)$ is taken from (17.26), and ζ is assumed to belong to a low dimensional *grid*; for instance, $\zeta \in [1, p]^d$, where d is the dimensionality of the manifold. Hence, a finite number of "nodes" ζ_i may be "responsible" for having generated a particular data-point x_i. This is done in order to render the integral over $d\zeta$ and the computation of $P(\zeta|x, \alpha)$ practically feasible (see Figure 17.5). Moreover, $f_\alpha(\zeta)$ is the usual kernel expansion; in other words, for some ζ_i' we have

Finite Number of Nodes

$$f_\alpha(\zeta) = \sum_i \alpha_i k(\zeta_i', \zeta). \tag{17.29}$$

Bishop et al. [52] choose Gaussian RBF kernels (17.15) for (17.29).

Finally, we need a prior over the class of mappings f. In the initial version [52], a Gaussian prior over the weights α_i was chosen,

Spherical Normal Distribution

$$P(\alpha) = \prod_i (2\pi\omega^2)^{-\frac{n}{2}} \exp\left(-\frac{\|\alpha_i\|^2}{2\omega^2}\right). \tag{17.30}$$

Here ω denotes the variance of the coefficients and n is the dimensionality of $\mathcal{X}$ and α_i. Unfortunately, this setting depends heavily on the number of basis functions

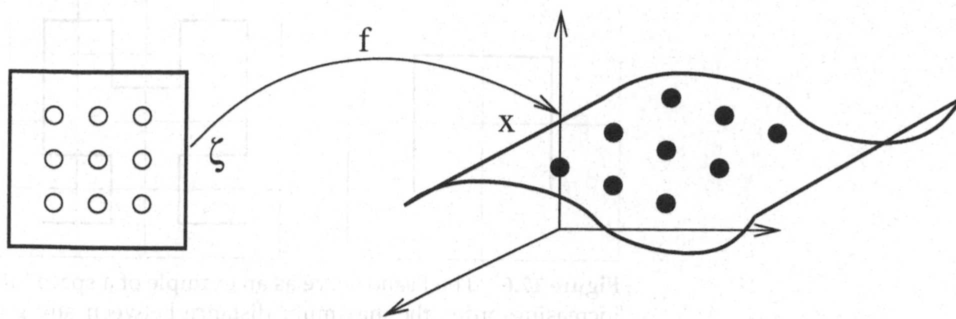

Figure 17.5 The function $f_\alpha(\zeta)$ describes the mapping from the space of latent variables ζ into $\mathcal{X}$. Around each $f(\zeta_i)$ we have a normal distribution with variance σ^2 (after [52]).

$k(\zeta_i', \zeta)$. Hence, in order to overcome this problem, [51] introduced a Gaussian Process prior (see Section 16.3); thus

Gaussian Process Prior

$$P(\boldsymbol{\alpha}) = (2\pi)^{-\frac{n}{2}}|K|^{\frac{1}{2}} \exp\left(-\sum_{i,j}\langle \alpha_i, \alpha_j\rangle K(\zeta_i', \zeta_j')\right). \tag{17.31}$$

Due to the Representer Theorem (Th. 4.2), we only need as many basis functions as we have ζ_i, and in particular, the centers may coincide (see Problem 17.9).

Many of the existing extensions in the regularization framework (e.g., semiparametric settings) and recent developments in Bayesian methods (Relevance Vector Priors and Laplacian Priors) could also be applied to the GTM (see Chapter 4, Sections 16.5 and 16.6, and Problems 17.10 and 17.11 for more details).

17.4.3 Robust Coding and Regularized Quantization

From a mere coding point of view, it might not seem too obvious at first glance that we need very smooth curves. In fact, one could construct a space-filling curve (see Figure 17.6). This would allow us to achieve zero empirical and expected quantization error, by exploiting the fact that codewords may be specified to arbitrary precision. The codebook in this setting would have to be *exact*, however, and the resulting estimate f would be quite useless for any practical purpose.

Peano Curve

The subsequent reasoning explains why such a solution f is also undesirable from a learning theory point of view. Let us modify the situation slightly and introduce a noisy channel; that is, the reconstruction does not occur for

Noisy Reconstruction

$$\zeta(x) = \operatorname*{argmin}_{\zeta \in \mathcal{Z}} c(x, f(\zeta)), \tag{17.32}$$

but for the random variable $\hat{\zeta}(x)$ with

$$\hat{\zeta}(x) := \operatorname*{argmin}_{\zeta \in \mathcal{Z}} c(x, f(\zeta)) + \xi. \tag{17.33}$$

Here ξ is a symmetrically distributed random variable drawn according to $P(\xi)$,

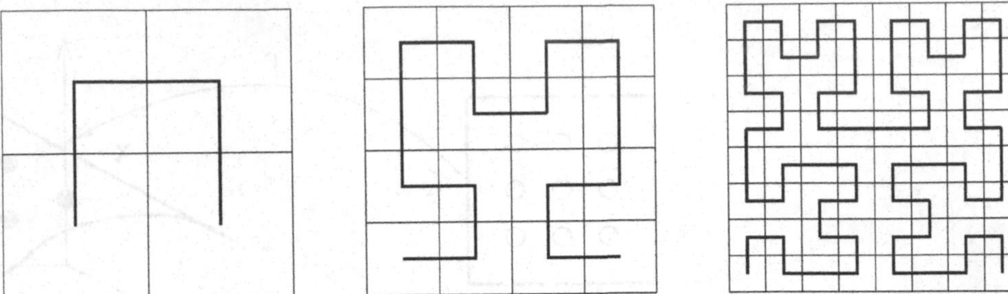

Figure 17.6 The Peano curve as an example of a space filling curve. We observe that with increasing order, the maximum distance between any point and the curve decreases as $2^{-(n+1)}$.

with zero mean and variance σ^2. In this case, we have to minimize a slightly different risk functional given by

Quantization with Noise

$$R_{\text{noise}}[f] := \int_{\mathcal{X}\times\mathbb{R}} c\left(x, f\left(\operatorname*{argmin}_{z\in\mathcal{Z}} c(x, f(z)) + \xi\right)\right) dP(x)dP(\xi). \tag{17.34}$$

This modified setting rules out space-filling curves such as the Peano curve, since the deviation in the encoding could then vary significantly. Eq. (17.34) is inspired by the problem of robust vector quantization [195], and Bishop's proof [50] that in supervised learning training with noise is equivalent to Tikhonov regularization. We use an adaptation of the techniques of [50] to derive a similar result in unsupervised learning.

Assume now that $c(x, f(\zeta))$ is the squared loss $(x - f(\zeta))^2$. If the overall influence of ξ is small, the moments of order higher than two are essentially negligible, and if f is twice differentiable, we may expand f as a Taylor expansion with $f(\zeta+\xi) \approx f(\zeta) + \xi f'(\zeta) + \frac{\xi^2}{2} f''(\zeta)$. Using the reasoning in [50], we arrive at

Taylor Expansion in the Noise ξ

$$\begin{aligned} R_{\text{noise}}[f] &\approx R[f] + 2\int_{\mathbb{R}} \xi^2 dP(\xi) \int_{\mathcal{X}} \|f'(\zeta)\|^2 + \frac{1}{2}\langle f(\zeta) - x, f''(\zeta)\rangle dP(x) \\ &= R[f] + 2\sigma^2 \int_{\mathcal{X}} \|f'(\zeta)\|^2 + \frac{1}{2}\langle f(\zeta) - x, f''(\zeta)\rangle dP(x), \end{aligned} \tag{17.35}$$

where ζ is defined as in (17.32). Finally we expand f at the unbiased solution f_0 (for which $\sigma = 0$) in terms of σ^2. Since the second term in (17.35) inside the integral is $O(\sigma^2)$, its overall contribution is only $O(\sigma^4)$, and thus it can be neglected. What remains is

$$R_{\text{noise}}[f] \approx R[f] + 2\sigma^2 \int_{\mathcal{X}} \|f'(\zeta)\|^2 dP(x) \text{ with } \zeta = \zeta(x) = \operatorname*{argmin}_{\zeta\in\mathcal{Z}} \|x - f(\zeta)\|^2. \tag{17.36}$$

Except for fact that the integral is with respect to x (and hence with respect to some complicated measure with respect to ζ), the second term is a regularizer enforcing smoothness by penalizing the first derivative, as discussed in section 4.4. Hence we recover Principal Curves with a length constraint as a by-product of robust coding.

We chose not to use the discrete sample size setting as in [50], since it appears not to be very practicable to use a training-with-input-noise scheme as in supervised learning for the problem of principal manifolds. The discretization of $R[f]$, meaning its approximation by the empirical risk functional, is independent of this reasoning, however. It might be of practical interest, though, to use a probabilistic projection of samples onto the curve for algorithmic stability (as done for instance in simulated annealing for the k-means algorithm).

Training with Noise and Annealing

17.5 Uniform Convergence Bounds

We next need a bound on the sample size sufficient to ensure that the above algorithm finds an f close to the best possible; or, less ambitiously, to bring the empirical quantization error $R_{\text{emp}}[f]$ close to the expected quantization error $R[f]$. This is achieved by methods which are very similar to those in [292], and are based on uniform (over a class of functions) convergence of empirical risk functionals to their expected value. The basic probabilistic tools we need are given in section 17.5.2. In section 17.5.3, we state bounds on the relevant covering numbers for the classes of functions induced by our regularization operators,

Bounding the Deviation Between $R_{\text{emp}}[f]$ and $R[f]$

$$\mathcal{F}_\Lambda := \{f : \mathcal{Z} \to \mathcal{X} \mid \Omega[f] \leq \Lambda\}. \tag{17.37}$$

Recall that $\Omega[f] = \frac{1}{2}\|\Upsilon f\|^2$, where $\|\Upsilon f\|^2$ is given by (17.14). Since bounding covering numbers can be technically intricate, we only state the results and basic techniques in the main body and relegate the proofs and more detailed considerations to the appendix. Section 17.5.4 gives overall sample complexity rates.

In order to avoid several technical requirements arising from unbounded loss functions (like boundedness of some moments of the distribution $P(x)$ [559]), we assume that there exists some $r > 0$ such that the probability measure of a ball of radius r is 1; that is, $P(U_r) = 1$. Kégl et al. [292] showed that under these assumptions, the principal manifold f is also contained in U_r, hence the quantization error is no larger than $e_c := \max_{x,x' \in U_r} c(x, x')$ for all x. For squared loss we have $e_c = 4r^2$.

17.5.1 Metrics and Covering Numbers

In order to derive bounds on the deviation between the empirical quantization error $R_{\text{emp}}[f]$ and the expected quantization error $R[f]$ (in other words, to derive uniform convergence bounds), let us introduce the notion of a (bracket) ε-cover [415] of the loss function induced class

$$\mathcal{F}_c := \{(x, z) \mapsto c(x, f(z)) | f \in \mathcal{F}\} \tag{17.38}$$

on U_r. A metric on $\mathfrak{F}_c$ is defined by letting

$$d(f_c, f_c') := \sup_{z \in \mathcal{Z}, x \in U_r} |c(x, f(z)) - c(x, f'(z))|, \tag{17.39}$$

where $f, f' \in \mathfrak{F}$. Whilst d is the metric we are interested in, it is quite hard to directly compute covering numbers with respect to it. By an argument from [606, 14], however, it is possible to upper bound these quantities in terms of corresponding entropy numbers of the class of functions $\mathfrak{F}$ itself if c is Lipschitz continuous. Denote by $l_c > 0$ a constant for which $|c(x, x') - c(x, x'')| \leq l_c \|x' - x''\|_2$ for all $x, x', x'' \in U_r$. In this case,

Lipschitz Continuous c

$$d(f_c, f_c') \leq l_c \sup_{z \in \mathcal{Z}} \|f(z) - f'(z)\|_2, \tag{17.40}$$

hence all we have to do is compute the $L_\infty(\ell_2^d)$ covering numbers of $\mathfrak{F}$ to obtain the corresponding covering numbers of $\mathfrak{F}_c$, with the norm on $\mathfrak{F}$ defined as

$$\|f\|_{L_\infty(\ell_2^d)} := \sup_{z \in \mathcal{Z}} \|f(z)\|_{\ell_2^d}. \tag{17.41}$$

The metric is induced by the norm in the usual fashion. For the polynomial loss $c(x, f(z)) := \|x - f(z)\|_2^p$, we obtain $l_c = p(2r)^{p-1}$. Given a metric ρ and a set $\mathfrak{F}$, the ϵ covering number of $\mathfrak{F}$, written $\mathcal{N}(\epsilon, \mathfrak{F}, \rho)$ (also $\mathcal{N}_\epsilon$ wherever the dependency is obvious), is the smallest number of ρ-balls of radius ε of which the union contains $\mathfrak{F}$. With the above definitions, we can see immediately that $\mathcal{N}(\epsilon, \mathfrak{F}_c, d) \leq \mathcal{N}\left(\frac{\epsilon}{l_c}, \mathfrak{F}, \|\cdot\|_{L_\infty(\ell_2^d)}\right)$.

Equivalent Covering Number

17.5.2 Upper and Lower Bounds

The next two results are similar in their flavor to the bounds obtained in [292]. They are slightly streamlined since they are independent of certain technical conditions on $\mathfrak{F}$ used in [292].

Proposition 17.8 ($L_\infty(\ell_2^d)$ bounds for Principal Manifolds) *Denote by $\mathfrak{F}$ a class of continuous functions from $\mathcal{Z}$ into $\mathcal{X} \subseteq U_r$, and let $\mathrm{P}(x)$ be a distribution over $\mathcal{X}$. If m points are drawn iid from $\mathrm{P}(x)$, then for all $\eta > 0, \epsilon \in (0, \eta/2)$,*

$$\mathrm{P}\left\{\sup_{f \in \mathfrak{F}} \left|R_{\text{emp}}^m[f] - R[f]\right| > \eta\right\} \leq 2\mathcal{N}\left(\tfrac{\epsilon}{2l_c}, \mathfrak{F}, L_\infty(\ell_2^d)\right) e^{-2m(\eta-\epsilon)^2/e_c}. \tag{17.42}$$

Proof By the definition of $R_{\text{emp}}^m[f] = \frac{1}{m}\sum_{i=1}^m \min_z \|f(z) - x_i\|^2$, the empirical quantization functional is an average over m iid random variables that are each bounded by e_c. Hence we may apply Hoeffding's inequality (Theorem 5.1) to obtain

Bracket Covers on f

$$\mathrm{P}\left\{\left|R_{\text{emp}}^m[f] - R[f]\right| > \eta\right\} \leq 2e^{-2m\eta^2/e_c}. \tag{17.43}$$

The next step is to discretize $\mathfrak{F}_c$ by a $\frac{\epsilon}{2}$ cover (that is, $\mathfrak{F}$ by a $\frac{\epsilon}{2l_c}$ cover) with respect to the metric d: for every $f_c \in \mathfrak{F}_c$ there exists some f_i in the cover such that $|R[f]-R[f_i]| \leq \frac{\epsilon}{2}$ and $|R_{\text{emp}}[f]-R_{\text{emp}}[f_i]| \leq \frac{\epsilon}{2}$. Consequently,

$$\mathrm{P}\left\{\left|R^m_{\text{emp}}[f]-R[f]\right| > \eta\right\} \leq \mathrm{P}\left\{\left|R^m_{\text{emp}}[f_i]-R[f_i]\right| > \eta-\epsilon\right\}. \tag{17.44}$$

Substituting (17.44) into (17.43) and taking the union bound over the $\frac{\epsilon}{2}$ cover of $\mathcal{F}_c$ gives the desired result. ■

This result is useful to assess the quality of an *empirically* found manifold. In order to obtain rates of convergence, we also need a result connecting the expected quantization error of the principal manifold f^*_{emp} minimizing $R^m_{\text{emp}}[f]$ and the manifold f^* with minimal quantization error $R[f^*]$.

Proposition 17.9 (Rates of Convergence for Optimal Estimates) *Suppose $\mathcal{F}$ is compact (thus f^*_{emp} and f^* exist as defined). With the definitions of Proposition 17.8,*

$$\mathrm{P}\left\{\sup_{f\in\mathcal{F}}\left|R[f^*_{\text{emp}}]-R[f^*]\right| > \eta\right\} \leq 2\left(\mathcal{N}\left(\tfrac{\epsilon}{l_c},\mathcal{F},L_\infty(\ell_2^d)\right)+1\right)e^{-\frac{m(\eta-\epsilon)^2}{2e_c}}. \tag{17.45}$$

The proof is similar to that of proposition 17.8, and can be found in Section A.2

17.5.3 Bounding Covering Numbers

Following propositions 17.8 and 17.9, the missing ingredient in the uniform convergence bounds is a bound on the covering number $\mathcal{N}(\epsilon,\mathcal{F})$.

Before going into detail, let us briefly review what already exists in terms of bounds on the covering number $\mathcal{N}$ for $L_\infty(\ell_2^d)$ metrics. Kégl et al. [292] essentially show that

$$\ln \mathcal{N}(\varepsilon,\mathcal{F}) = O(\tfrac{1}{\varepsilon}) \tag{17.46}$$

Covering Numbers for Polygonal Curves

under the following assumptions: They consider polygonal curves $f(\cdot)$ of length L in the ball $U_r \subset \mathcal{X}$. The distance measure (no metric!) for $\mathcal{N}(\varepsilon)$ is defined as $\sup_{x\in U_r}|\Delta(x,f)-\Delta(x,f')| \leq \varepsilon$. Here $\Delta(x,f)$ is the minimum distance between a curve $f(\cdot)$ and $x \in U_r$.

By using functional analytic tools developed in [606] (see Chapter 12) we can obtain results for more general regularization operators, which can then be used in place of (17.46) to obtain bounds on the expected quantization error.

While it is not essential to the understanding of the main results to introduce entropy numbers directly (they are essentially the functional inverse of the covering numbers $\mathcal{N}(\varepsilon,\mathcal{F})$, and are dealt with in more detail in Chapter 12 and [509]), we need to define ways of characterizing the simplicity of the class of functions via the regularization term under consideration.

From Mercer's Theorem (Theorem 2.10), we know that every kernel may be written as a dot product in some feature space,

$$k(x,x') = \sum_i \lambda_i \phi_i(x)\phi_i(x'). \tag{17.47}$$

The eigenvalues λ_i determine the *shape* of the data mapped into feature space (cf. Figure 2.3). Roughly speaking, if the λ_i decay rapidly, the possibly infinite expansion in (17.47) can be approximated with high precision by a low-dimensional space which means that we are effectively dealing only with simple functions.

Recall that in Section 12.4, and specifically in Section 12.4.6, we stated that for a Mercer kernel with $\lambda_j = O(e^{-\alpha j^p})$ for some $\alpha, p > 0$,

$$\ln \mathcal{N}(\mathcal{F}, \epsilon) = O\left(\log^{-\frac{p+1}{p}} \epsilon^{-1}\right) \tag{17.48}$$

Almost Finite Dimensional Spaces

Moreover if k is a Mercer kernel with $\lambda_j = O(j^{-\alpha-1})$ for some $\alpha > 0$, then

$$\ln \mathcal{N}(\mathcal{F}, \epsilon) = O\left(\epsilon^{-\frac{\alpha}{2}+\delta}\right) \tag{17.49}$$

for any $\delta \in (0, \alpha/2)$. The rates obtained in (17.48) and (17.49) are quite strong. In particular, recall that for compact sets in finite dimensional spaces of dimension d, the covering number is $\mathcal{N}(\epsilon, \mathcal{F}) = O(\epsilon^{-d})$ (see Problem 17.7 and [90]). In view of (17.48), this means that even though we are dealing with a nonparametric estimator, it behaves almost as if it were a finite dimensional estimator.

All that is left is to substitute (17.48) and (17.49) into the uniform convergence results to obtain bounds on the performance of our learning algorithm. Due to the slow growth in $\mathcal{N}(\epsilon, \mathcal{F})$, we are able to prove good rates of convergence below.

17.5.4 Rates of Convergence

Another property of interest is the sample complexity of learning Principal Manifolds. Kégl et al. [292] showed a $O(m^{-1/3})$ rate of convergence for principal curves ($d = 1$) with a length constraint regularizer. We prove that by utilizing a more powerful regularizer (as is possible using our algorithm), we may obtain a bound of the form $O(m^{-\frac{\alpha}{2(\alpha+1)}})$ for polynomial rates of decay of the eigenvalues of k ($\alpha + 1$ is the rate of decay), or $O(m^{-1/2+\beta})$ for exponential rates of decay (β is an arbitrary positive constant). It would be surprising if we could do any better, given that supervised learning rates are typically no better than $O(m^{-1/2})$. In the following, we assume that $\mathcal{F}_\Lambda$ is compact; this is true of all the specific $\mathcal{F}_\Lambda$ considered above.

Almost Optimal Rates

Proposition 17.10 (Learning Rates for Principal Manifolds) *Suppose $\mathcal{F}_\Lambda$ is compact. Define $f^*_{\text{emp}}, f^* \in \mathcal{F}_\Lambda$ as in Proposition 17.9.*

1. *If $\ln \mathcal{N}(\varepsilon, \mathcal{F}_c, d) = O(\ln^\alpha \frac{1}{\varepsilon})$ for some $\alpha > 0$, then*

$$R[f^*_{\text{emp}}] - R[f^*] = O(m^{-1/2} \ln^{\alpha/2} m) = O(m^{-1/2+\beta}) \tag{17.50}$$

for any $\beta > 0$

2. *If $\ln \mathcal{N}(\varepsilon, \mathcal{F}_c, d) = O(\varepsilon^{-\alpha})$ for some $\alpha > 0$, then*

$$R[f^*_{\text{emp}}] - R[f^*] \leq O(m^{-\frac{1}{\alpha+2}}) \tag{17.51}$$

The proof can be found in Section A.2. A restatement of the optimal learning rates in terms of the spectrum of the kernel leads to the following corollary:

Rates are Kernel Dependent

Corollary 17.11 (Learning Rates for given Spectra) *Suppose that $\mathfrak{F}_\Lambda$ is compact, $f^*_{\mathrm{emp}}, f^* \in \mathfrak{F}_\Lambda$ are as before, and λ_j are the eigenvalues of the kernel k inducing $\mathfrak{F}_\Lambda$ (sorted in decreasing order). If $\lambda_j \leq e^{-cj^\alpha}$, then*

$$R[f^*_{\mathrm{emp}}] - R[f^*] \leq O\left(m^{-1/2} \ln^{\frac{\alpha+1}{2\alpha}} m\right). \tag{17.52}$$

If $\lambda_j = O(j^{-\alpha})$ for quadratic regularizers, or $\lambda_j = O(j^{-\alpha/2})$ for linear regularizers, then

$$R[f^*_{\mathrm{emp}}] - R[f^*] \leq O\left(m^{-\frac{\alpha-1}{2\alpha}}\right). \tag{17.53}$$

Tightness of Bounds

Interestingly, the above result is slightly weaker than the result in [292] for the case of length constraints, as the latter corresponds to the differentiation operator, thus to polynomial eigenvalue decay of order 2, and therefore to a rate of $\frac{1}{4}$ (Kégl et al. [292] obtain $\frac{1}{3}$). For a linear regularizer, though, we obtain a rate of $\frac{3}{8}$. It is unclear whether this is due to our bound on the entropy numbers induced by k (possibly) not being optimal, or the fact that our results are stated in terms of the (stronger) $L_\infty(\ell_2^d)$ metric. This weakness, yet to be fully understood, should not detract from the fact that we *can* get better rates by using stronger regularizers, and our algorithm can utilize such regularizers.

17.6 Experiments

Robust Parameterization

In order to show that the algorithm proposed in section 17.3 is sound, we ran several experiments (cf. Figure 17.7, 17.9). In all cases, Gaussian RBF kernels (2.68) were used. First, we generated different data sets in 2 and 3 dimensions from 1 or 2 dimensional parametrizations. We then applied our algorithm, using the prior knowledge about the original parametrization dimension of the data set in choosing the size of the latent variable space. For almost any parameter setting (comprising our choice of λ, M, and the width of the basis functions) we obtained good results, which means that the parametrization is well behaved.
We found that for a suitable choice of the regularization factor λ, a very close match to the original distribution can be achieved. Although the number and width of the basis functions also affect the solution, their influence on its basic characteristics is quite small. Figure 17.8 shows the convergence properties of the algorithm. We observe that the overall regularized quantization error clearly decreases for each step, while both the regularization term and the quantization error term are free to vary. This empirically demonstrates that the algorithm strictly decreases $R_{\mathrm{reg}}[f]$ at every step, and eventually converges to a (local) minimum.[9]

9. $R_{\mathrm{reg}}[f]$ is bounded from below by 0, hence any decreasing series of $R_{\mathrm{reg}}[f_i]$, where f_i denotes the estimate at step i, has a limit that is either a global or (more likely) a local minimum. Note that this does not guarantee we will reach the minimum in a *finite* number of steps.

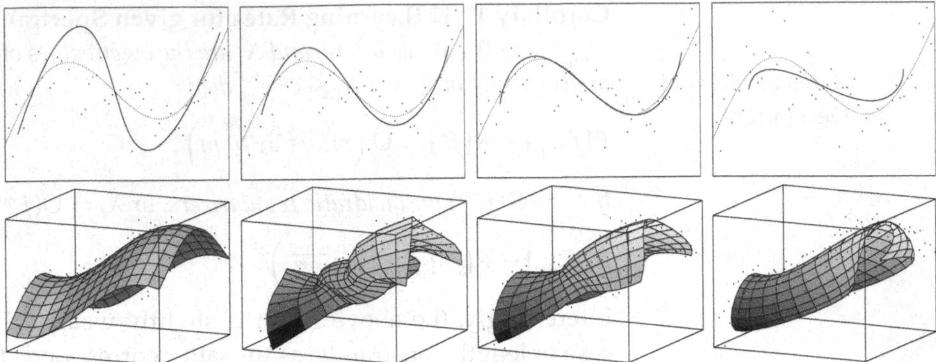

Figure 17.7 Upper 4 images: We generated a dataset (small dots) by adding noise to a distribution depicted by the dotted line. The resulting manifold generated by our approach is given by the solid line (over a parameter range of $\mathcal{Z} = [-1, 1]$). From left to right, the results are plotted for the regularization parameter values $\lambda = 0.1, 0.5, 1, 4$. The width and number of basis functions were held constant at 1 and 10, respectively. Lower 4 images: We generated a dataset by sampling (with noise) from a distribution depicted in the leftmost image (the small dots are the sampled data). The remaining three images show the manifold obtained by our approach, for $\lambda = 0.001, 0.1, 1$, plotted over the parameter space $\mathcal{Z} = [-1, 1]^2$. The width and number of basis functions were again constant (at 1 and 36, respectively).

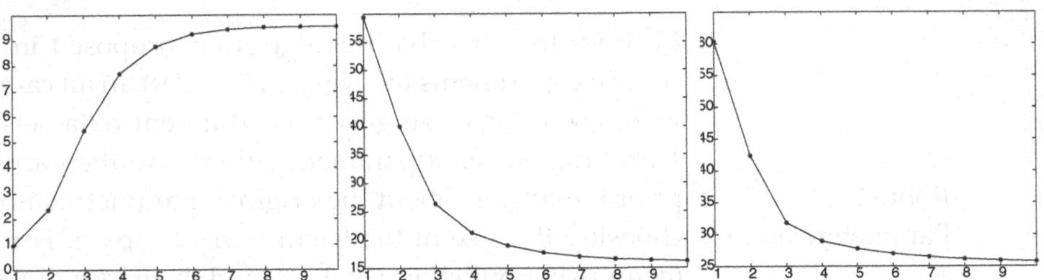

Figure 17.8 Left: regularization term, middle: empirical quantization error, right: regularized quantization error vs. number of iterations.

Given the close relationship to the GTM, we also applied Regularized Principal Manifolds to the oil flow data set used in [52]. This data set consists of 1000 samples from $\mathbb{R}^{12}$, organized into 3 classes. The goal is to visualize these samples, so we chose the latent space to be $\mathcal{Z} = [-1, 1]^2$ (with the exception of Figure 17.10, where we embedded the data in 3 dimensions). We then generated the principal manifold and plotted the distribution of the latent variables for each sample (see Figure 17.9). For comparison purposes, the same strategy was applied to principal component analysis (PCA). The result achieved using principal manifolds reveals much more of the structure intrinsic to the data set than a simple search for directions with high variance. The algorithm output is competitive with [52].

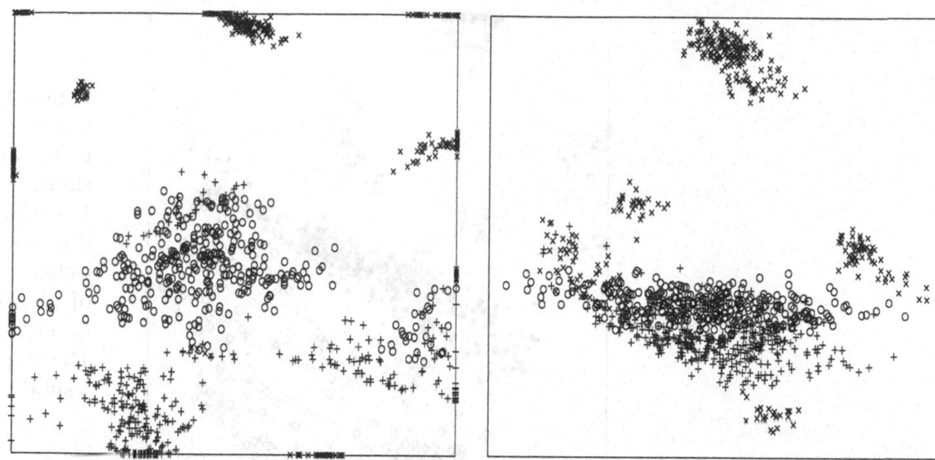

Figure 17.9 Organization of the latent variable space for the oil flow data set. The left hand plot depicts the result obtained using using principal manifolds, with 49 nodes, kernel width 1, and regularization 0.01. The right hand plot represents the output of principal component analysis. The lower dimensional representation found by principal manifolds nicely reveals the class structure, to a degree comparable to the GTM. Linear PCA fails completely.

17.7 Summary

Many data descriptive algorithms, such as k-means clustering, PCA, and principal curves, can be seen as special instances of a quantization framework. Learning is then perceived in terms of being able to represent (in our case, this means to compress) data by a simple code, be it discrete or not.

Quantization Framework

In deriving a feasible kernel based algorithm for this task, we first showed that minimizing the quantization error is an ill-posed problem, and thus requires additional regularization. This led to the introduction of regularized quantization functionals that can be solved efficiently in practice. Through the use of manifolds as a means of encoding, we obtained a new estimator: regularized principal manifolds.

The expansion in terms of kernel functions and the treatment by regularization operators made it easier to decouple the algorithmic part (finding a suitable manifold) from the specification of a class of manifolds with desirable properties. In particular, the algorithm does not crucially depend on the number of nodes used.

Bounds on the sample complexity of learning principal manifolds were given. Their proofs made use of concepts from regularization theory and supervised learning. More details on bounds involving entropy and covering numbers can be found in Chapter 12 and [509].

There are several directions for future work using the quantization functional approach; we mention the most obvious three.

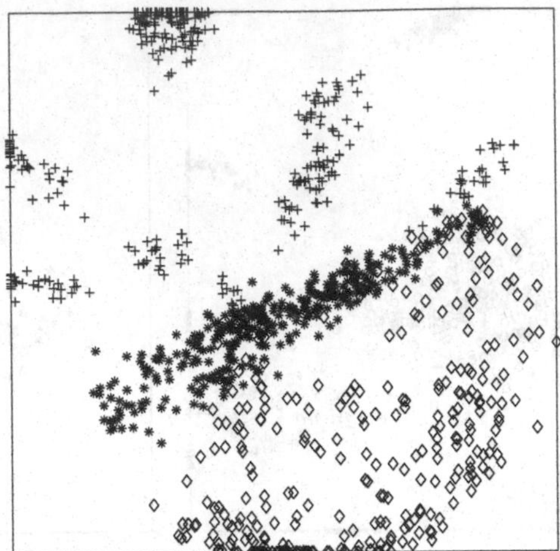

Figure 17.10 Organization of the latent variable space for the oil flow data set using principal manifolds in 3 dimensions, with $6^3 = 216$ nodes, kernel width 1, and regularization $\lambda = 0.01$. The 3-dimensional latent variable space is projected onto 2 dimensions for the purpose of visualization. Note the good separation between the different flow regimes. The map further suggests that there exist 5 subdivisions of the regime labelled +.

Open Problems

- The algorithm could be improved. In contrast to successful kernel algorithms, such as SVMs, the algorithm presented is not guaranteed to find a global minimum. Is it possible to develop an efficient algorithm that does?
- The algorithm is related to methods that carry out a probabilistic assignment of the observed data to the manifold (see Section 17.4.2). Such a strategy often exhibits improved numerical properties, and the assignments themselves can be interpreted statistically. It would be interesting to exploit this fact with RPMs.
- Finally, the theoretical bounds could be improved — hopefully achieving the same rate as in [292] for the special case addressed therein, while still keeping the better rates for more powerful regularizers.

17.8 Problems

17.1 (Sample Mean •) *Show that the sample mean is indeed the minimizer of empirical quantization function as defined in Example 17.1.*

17.2 (Representer Theorem for RPMs ••) *Prove that for a regularized quantization functional of the form*

$$R_{\text{reg}}[f] = \sum_{i=1}^{m} c(x_i, f(z_i)) + \frac{\lambda}{2}\|f\|^2_{\mathcal{H}} \tag{17.54}$$

with $z_i := \operatorname{argmin}_{z \in \mathcal{Z}} c(x_i, f(z))$, *the function at the minimum of (17.54) is given by*

$$f(z) = \sum_{i=1}^{m} \alpha_i k(z_i, z) \text{ where } \alpha_i \in \mathcal{X}. \tag{17.55}$$

Hint: consider the proof of Theorem 4.2. Now assume that there exists an optimal expansion that is different from (17.55). Decompose f *into* $f_\perp$ *and* $f_\parallel$, *and show that* $f_\perp = 0$.

17.3 (Estimating $R[f]$ •••) *Denote by $R_{\text{LOO}}[f]$ the leave-one-out error (see also Section 12.2) obtained for regularized quantization functionals. Show that this is an unbiased estimator (see Definition 3.8) for $R[f]$.*

Discuss the computational problems in obtaining $R_{\text{LOO}}[f]$. Can you find a cheap approximation for $R_{\text{LOO}}[f]$? Hint: remove one pattern at a time, keep the assignment ζ_i for the other observations fixed, and modify the encoding.

Can you find a sufficient statistic for k-means clustering with squared loss error? Hint: express the leave-one-out approximation in closed form and compare it to the inter-cluster variance. What do you have to change for absolute deviations rather than squared errors?

17.4 (Mixed Linear Programming Regularizers ••) *Show that minimizing the regularized risk functional $R_{\text{reg}}[f]$ with $\Omega[f]$ chosen according to (17.17) can be written as a quadratic program. Hint: use a standard trick from optimization: replace $\max(\xi_1, \ldots, \xi_n)$ by the set of inequalities $\bar{\xi} \geq \xi_i$ for $i \in [n]$, and use $\bar{\xi}$ in the objective function.*

How does the regularized quantization functional look in the case of regularized principal manifolds?

17.5 (Pearls on a Chain ••) *Denote by $f : [k] \to \mathcal{X}$ a mapping from k numbers to "cluster centers" in $\mathcal{X}$, where the ith cluster is given by $f(i) = \sum_{j=1}^{n} \alpha_j k(j, i)$ and $z_j \in \mathbb{R}$. Can you find a regularized quantization functional for clustering? Hint: use a quadratic regularizer.*

How would you find a suitable algorithm to minimize $R_{\text{reg}}[f]$? What is the assumption made about f when using such a regularizer? Can you find analogous settings for "nets" rather than "chains"? Can you modify the regularizer such that the chain becomes more and more "stiff" towards the end, thus effectively controlling the capacity?

17.6 (Coordinate Descent •) *Denote by $f : \mathbb{R}^N \to \mathbb{R}$ a multivariate function. Prove that coordinate descent strictly decreases f at each step. Find a case where this strategy can be very slow. Find cases where it converges only to a local minimum. Under what circumstances is coordinate descent fast (hint: use a quadratic function in two variables as a toy example)?*

17.7 (Covering Numbers in Compact Sets of $\mathbb{R}^d$ [90] ••) *Prove that in d-dimensional compact sets S for any metric, the covering number $\mathcal{N}(\epsilon, S)$ is bounded by $O(\epsilon^{-d})$. Hint: compute the volume of the unit ball under the metric, and divide* vol *S by the volume of the unit ball. Exploit scaling properties of volumes.*

17.8 (Convergence Bounds without Bracket Covers ○○○) *Prove uniform convergence bounds that do not require bracket covers, but instead make use of the fact that we are only comparing manifolds at a finite number of points.*

17.9 (Nodes for the GTM with GP Prior ••) *Assume we use the Generative Topographic Mapping algorithm with a Gaussian Process Prior on f and a discrete set for the possible values of ζ_i. Show that the minimum of a Maximum a Posteriori estimate is achieved if $\zeta(x_i) = \zeta_i$. Hint: apply the representer theorem of Problem 17.2.*

17.10 (Semiparametric Manifolds ••) *Derive optimization equations for a semiparametric regularization functional $\Omega[f]$ (Section 4.8) in the case of Regularized Principal Manifolds. Can you construct an estimator that smoothly blends over from Principal Component Analysis to nonlinear settings, i.e., that depends smoothly on a parameter such that for one value, one recovers PCA and for another one RPM. Hint: use hyperplanes in $\mathcal{X}$ as the parametric part.*

Can you apply the same reasoning to the GTM? Caution: you may obtain improper (that is, not normalizable) priors (•••).

17.11 (Laplacian Priors in the GTM •••) *Formulate the posterior probability for a Generative Topographic Map, where we use $\exp(-\|\alpha\|_1)$ as the prior probability rather than a Gaussian Process prior on the weights. Can you derive the EM equations?*

18 Pre-Images and Reduced Set Methods

Using a kernel k instead of a dot product in the input space $\mathcal{X}$ corresponds to mapping the data into a dot product space $\mathcal{H}$ with a map $\Phi : \mathcal{X} \to \mathcal{H}$, and taking the dot product there (cf. Chapter 2);

$$k(x, x') = \langle \Phi(x), \Phi(x') \rangle . \tag{18.1}$$

This way, all computations in $\mathcal{H}$ are done *implicitly*. The price paid for this elegance, however, is that the solutions to kernel algorithms are only obtained as *expansions* in terms of input patterns mapped into feature space. For instance, the normal vector of an SV hyperplane is expanded in terms of Support Vectors, just as the Kernel PCA feature extractors are expressed in terms of training examples;

$$\Psi = \sum_{i=1}^{m} \alpha_i \Phi(x_i). \tag{18.2}$$

When evaluating an SV decision function or a Kernel PCA feature extractor, this is normally not a problem: thanks to (18.1), taking the dot product between Ψ and some mapped test point $\Phi(x)$ transforms (18.2) into a kernel expansion $\sum_i \alpha_i k(x_i, x)$, which can be evaluated even if Ψ lives in an infinite-dimensional space. In some cases, however, a more comprehensive understanding is required of the exact connection between patterns in input space and elements of feature space, given as expansions such as (18.2). This field is far from being understood, and the current chapter, which partly follows [474], attempts to gather some ideas elucidating the problem, and describes algorithms for situations where the above connection is important.

Overview

We start by stating the pre-image problem. By this we refer to the problem of finding patterns in input space that map to specific vectors in feature space (Section 18.1). This has applications for instance in denoising by Kernel PCA (Section 18.2). In Section 18.3, we build on the methods for computing single pre-images and construct so-called *reduced set expansions*, which approximate feature space vectors. We distinguish between methods that construct the expansions by selecting from the training set (Section 18.4), and methods that come up with synthetic expansion patterns (Section 18.5). When applied to the solution vector of an SVM, these methods can lead to significant increases in speed, which are crucial for making SVMs competitive in tasks where speed on the test sets is a major concern, such as face detection (Section 18.6).

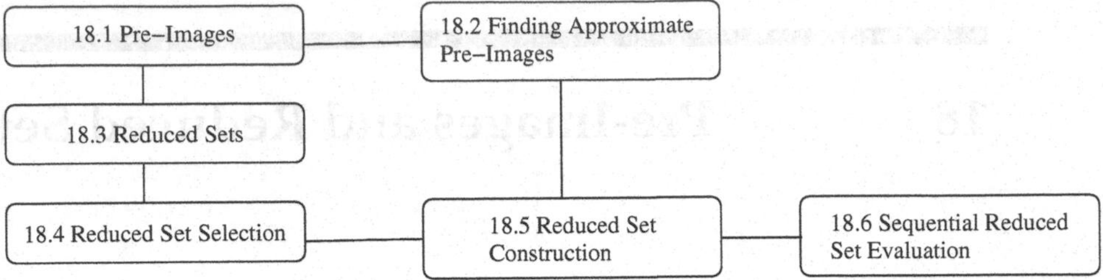

Prerequisites

The present chapter provides methods that are used in a number of kernel algorithms; background knowledge on the latter is therefore of benefit. Specifically, knowledge of SV classification is required in Sections 18.4 and 18.6, and parts of Section 18.4 additionally require knowledge of SV regression and of the basics of quadratic programming (cf. Chapter 6). The reader should also be familiar with the Kernel PCA algorithm (Section 14.2), which is used both as a tool and a subject of study in this chapter: on one hand, it is used for constructing approximation methods; on the other hand, it forms the basis of denoising methods, in which it is combined it with pre-image construction methods.

18.1 The Pre-Image Problem

In Chapter 2, we introduced kernels and described several ways to construct the feature map associated with a given kernel; the latter represent ways to get from input space to feature space. We now study maps that work in the *opposite* direction.

There has been a fair amount of work on aspects of this problem in the context of reduced set (RS) methods [84, 87, 184, 400, 474]. For pedagogical reasons, we postpone RS methods to Section 18.3, as they focus on a problem that is more complex than the one we would like to start with.

18.1.1 Exact Pre-Images

Kernel algorithms express their solutions as expansions in terms of mapped input points (18.2). Since the map Φ into the feature space $\mathcal{H}$ is nonlinear, however, we cannot generally assert that each such expansion has a pre-image under Φ; namely a point $z \in \mathcal{X}$ such that $\Phi(z) = \Psi$ (Figure 18.1). If the pre-image *exists*, then it will be easy to compute, as shown by the following result:

Proposition 18.1 (Exact Pre-Images [467]) *Consider a feature space expansion* $\Psi = \sum_{j=1}^{m} \alpha_j \Phi(x_j)$*, where* $x_j \in \mathcal{X}$*. We assume that* $\mathcal{X}$ *is a subset of* $\mathbb{R}^N$*. If there exists* $z \in \mathbb{R}^N$ *such that*

$$\Phi(z) = \Psi, \tag{18.3}$$

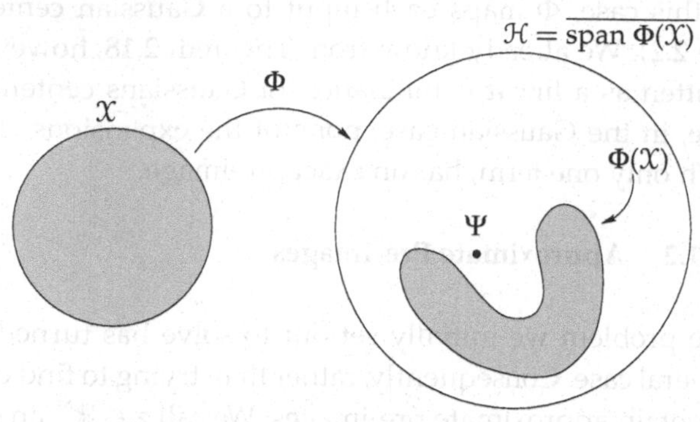

Figure 18.1 The pre-image problem: points in the span of the mapped input data are not all necessarily images of corresponding input patterns. Therefore, points that can be written as expansions in terms of mapped input patterns (such as a Kernel PCA eigenvector or a SVM hyperplane normal vector) cannot necessarily be expressed as images of single input patterns.

and an invertible function f_k such that $k(x, x') = f_k(\langle x, x' \rangle)$, then we can compute z as

$$z = \sum_{i=1}^{N} f_k^{-1}\left(\sum_{j=1}^{m} \alpha_j k(x_j, e_i)\right) e_i, \tag{18.4}$$

where $\{e_1, \ldots, e_N\}$ is any orthonormal basis of input space.

Proof We expand z as

$$z = \sum_{i=1}^{N} \langle z, e_i \rangle e_i = \sum_{i=1}^{N} f_k^{-1}(k(z, e_i)) e_i = \sum_{i=1}^{N} f_k^{-1}\left(\sum_{j=1}^{m} \alpha_j k(x_j, e_i)\right) e_i. \tag{18.5}$$

■

This proposition gives rise to a number of observations. First, examples of kernels that are invertible functions of $\langle x, x' \rangle$ include polynomial kernels,

$$k(x, x') = (\langle x, x' \rangle + c)^d, \text{ where } c \geq 0,\ d \text{ odd}, \tag{18.6}$$

and sigmoid kernels,

$$k(x, x') = \sigma(\kappa \cdot \langle x, x' \rangle + \Theta), \text{ where } \kappa, \Theta \in \mathbb{R}. \tag{18.7}$$

A similar result holds for RBF kernels (using the polarization identity) — we only require that the kernel allow the reconstruction of $\langle x, x' \rangle$ from k, evaluated on certain input points, which we are allowed to choose (for details, cf. [467]).

Existence of Pre-Images

The crucial assumption of the Proposition is the *existence* of the pre-image. Unfortunately, there are many situations for which there are no pre-images. To illustrate, we consider the feature map Φ in the form given by (2.21): $\Phi : \mathcal{X} \to \mathbb{R}^{\mathcal{X}}, x \mapsto k(., x)$. Clearly, only points in feature space that can be written as $k(., x)$ have a pre-image under this map. To characterize this set of points in a specific example, consider the Gaussian kernels,

$$k(x, x') = \exp\left(-\frac{\|x - x'\|^2}{2\,\sigma^2}\right). \tag{18.8}$$

In this case, Φ maps each input to a Gaussian centered on this point (see Figure 2.2). We already know from Theorem 2.18, however, that no Gaussian can be written as a linear combination of Gaussians centered at *different* points. Therefore, in the Gaussian case, none of the expansions (18.2), excluding trivial cases with only one term, has an exact pre-image.

18.1.2 Approximate Pre-Images

The problem we initially set out to solve has turned out to be insolvable in the general case. Consequently, rather than trying to find exact pre-images, we attempt to obtain approximate pre-images. We call $z \in \mathbb{R}^N$ an *approximate pre-image* of Ψ if

$$\rho(z) = \|\Psi - \Phi(z)\|^2 \tag{18.9}$$

is small.[1]

Are there vectors Ψ for which good approximate pre-images exist? As we shall see, this is indeed the case. As described in Chapter 14, for $n = 1, 2, \ldots, p$, Kernel PCA provides projections

$$P_n\Phi(x) := \sum_{j=1}^{n} \langle \Phi(x), \mathbf{v}^j \rangle \, \mathbf{v}^j \tag{18.10}$$

with the following optimal approximation property (Proposition 14.1): Assume that the $\mathbf{v}^j$ are sorted according to nonincreasing eigenvalues λ_j, with λ_p being the smallest nonzero eigenvalue. Then P_n is the n-dimensional projection minimizing

$$\sum_{i=1}^{m} \|P_n\Phi(x_i) - \Phi(x_i)\|^2. \tag{18.11}$$

Therefore, $P_n\Phi(x)$ can be expected to have a good approximate pre-image, provided that x is drawn from the same distribution as the x_i; to give a trivial example, x itself is already a good approximate pre-image. As we shall see in experiments, however, even better pre-images can be found, which makes some interesting applications possible [474, 365]:

Applications of Pre-Images

Denoising. Given a noisy x, map it to $\Phi(x)$, discard components corresponding to the eigenvalues $\lambda_{n+1}, \ldots, \lambda_m$ to obtain $P_n\Phi(x)$, and then compute a pre-image z. The hope here is that the main structure in the data set is captured in the first n directions in feature space, and the remaining components mainly pick up the noise — in this sense, z can be thought of as a denoised version of x.

Compression. Given the Kernel PCA eigenvectors and a small number of features $P_n\Phi(x)$ (cf. (18.10)) of $\Phi(x)$, but not x, compute a pre-image as an approximate reconstruction of x. This is useful if n is smaller than the dimensionality of the input data.

1. Just how small it needs to be in order to form a satisfactory approximation depends on the problem at hand. Therefore, we have refrained from giving a formal definition.

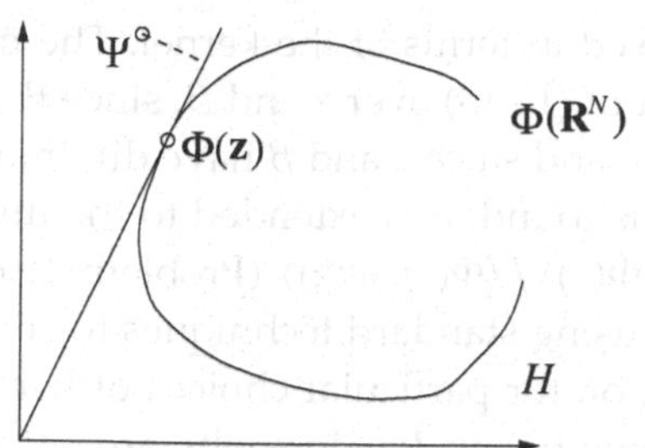

Figure 18.2 Given a vector $\Psi \in \mathcal{H}$, we try to approximate it by a multiple of a vector $\Phi(z)$ in the image of the input space ($\mathbb{R}^N$) under the nonlinear map Φ, by finding z such that the projection distance of Ψ onto span($\Phi(z)$), depicted by the straight line, is minimized.

Interpretation. Visualize a nonlinear feature extractor $\mathbf{v}^j$ by computing a pre-image.

In the present chapter, we mainly focus on the first application. In the next section, we develop a method for minimizing (18.9), which we later apply to the case where $\Psi = P_n\Phi(x)$.

18.2 Finding Approximate Pre-Images

18.2.1 Minimizing the Projection Distance

We start by considering a problem slightly more general than the pre-image problem. We are given a kernel expansion with $N_x \in \mathbb{N}$ terms,

$$\Psi = \sum_{i=1}^{N_x} \alpha_i \Phi(x_i), \tag{18.12}$$

and seek to approximate it by $\Psi' = \beta\Phi(z)$. For $\beta = 1$, this reduces to the pre-image problem. Allowing the freedom that $\beta \neq 1$ makes sense, since the length of Ψ is usually not crucial: in SV classification, for instance, it can be rescaled (along with the threshold b) without changing the decision function, cf. Chapter 7.

First observe that rather than minimizing

$$\|\Psi - \Psi'\|^2 = \sum_{i,j=1}^{N_x} \alpha_i\alpha_j k(x_i, x_j) + \beta^2 k(z, z) - 2\sum_{i=1}^{N_x} \alpha_i \beta k(x_i, z), \tag{18.13}$$

we can minimize the distance between Ψ and the orthogonal projection of Ψ onto span($\Phi(z)$) (Figure 18.2),

$$\left\| \frac{\langle \Psi, \Phi(z)\rangle}{\langle \Phi(z), \Phi(z)\rangle}\Phi(z) - \Psi \right\|^2 = \|\Psi\|^2 - \frac{\langle \Psi, \Phi(z)\rangle^2}{\langle \Phi(z), \Phi(z)\rangle}. \tag{18.14}$$

To this end, we maximize

$$\frac{\langle \Psi, \Phi(z)\rangle^2}{\langle \Phi(z), \Phi(z)\rangle}, \tag{18.15}$$

which can be expressed in terms of the kernel. The maximization of (18.15) over z is preferable to that of (18.13) over z and β, since the former comprises a lower-dimensional problem, and since z and β have different scaling behavior. Once the maximum of (18.15) is found, it is extended to the minimum of (18.13) by setting (cf. (18.14)) $\beta = \langle \Psi, \Phi(z) \rangle / \langle \Phi(z), \Phi(z) \rangle$ (Problem 18.6). The function (18.15) can either be minimized using standard techniques for unconstrained nonlinear optimization (as in [84]), or, for particular choices of kernels, using fixed-point iteration methods, as shown below. Readers who are not interested in the algorithmic details may want to skip Section 18.2.2, which shows that for a certain class of kernels, the pre-image problem can be solved approximately using an algorithm that resembles clustering methods.

18.2.2 Fixed Point Iteration Approach for RBF Kernels

For kernels that satisfy $k(z, z) = 1$ for all $z \in \mathcal{X}$ (such as Gaussian kernels and other normalized RBF kernels), (18.15) reduces to

$$\langle \Psi, \Phi(z) \rangle^2 . \tag{18.16}$$

Below, we assume that $\mathcal{X} \subset \mathbb{R}^N$. For the extremum, we have

$$0 = \nabla_z \langle \Psi, \Phi(z) \rangle^2 = 2 \langle \Psi, \Phi(z) \rangle \nabla_z \langle \Psi, \Phi(z) \rangle . \tag{18.17}$$

To evaluate the gradient in terms of k, we substitute (18.12) to get

$$0 = \sum_{i=1}^{N_x} \alpha_i \nabla_z k(x_i, z), \tag{18.18}$$

which is sufficient for (18.17) to hold.

For $k(x_i, z) = k(\|x_i - z\|^2)$ (Gaussians, for instance), we obtain

$$0 = \sum_{i=1}^{N_x} \alpha_i k'(\|x_i - z\|^2)(x_i - z), \tag{18.19}$$

k' being the derivative of k, leading to

$$z = \frac{\sum_{i=1}^{N_x} \alpha_i k'(\|x_i - z\|^2) x_i}{\sum_{i=1}^{N_x} \alpha_i k'(\|x_i - z\|^2)} . \tag{18.20}$$

For the Gaussian kernel $k(x_i, z) = \exp(-\|x_i - z\|^2/(2\sigma^2))$, we get

$$z = \frac{\sum_{i=1}^{N_x} \alpha_i \exp(-\|x_i - z\|^2/(2\sigma^2)) x_i}{\sum_{i=1}^{N_x} \alpha_i \exp(-\|x_i - z\|^2/(2\sigma^2))} \tag{18.21}$$

Fixed Point Iteration

(note that for $k(t) = \exp(\alpha t)$, we have $k'(t) = \alpha \exp(\alpha t)$), and devise an iteration

$$z_{n+1} = \frac{\sum_{i=1}^{N_x} \alpha_i \exp(-\|x_i - z_n\|^2/(2\sigma^2)) x_i}{\sum_{i=1}^{N_x} \alpha_i \exp(-\|x_i - z_n\|^2/(2\sigma^2))} . \tag{18.22}$$

The denominator equals $\langle \Psi, \Phi(z_n) \rangle$, and is thus nonzero in the neighborhood of the extremum of (18.16), unless the extremum itself is zero. The latter only occurs if the projection of Ψ on the linear span of $\Phi(\mathbb{R}^N)$ is zero, in which case it is pointless to try to approximate Ψ. Numerical instabilities related to $\langle \Psi, \Phi(z) \rangle$ being small can thus be approached by restarting the iteration with different starting values.

Connection to Clustering

Interestingly, (18.22) can be interpreted in the context of clustering (e.g., [82]). Iteration of this expression determines the center of a single Gaussian cluster, trying to capture as many of the x_i with positive α_i as possible, and simultaneously avoids those x_i with negative α_i. For SV classifiers, the sign of the α_i equals the label of the pattern x_i. It is this sign which distinguishes (18.22) from plain clustering or parametric density estimation. The occurrence of negative signs is related to the fact that we are not trying to estimate a parametric density but the *difference* between two densities (neglecting normalization constants).

To see this, we define the sets $pos = \{i : \alpha_i > 0\}$ and $neg = \{i : \alpha_i < 0\}$, and the shorthands

$$p_{pos}(z) = \sum_{pos} \alpha_i \exp(-\|x_i - z\|^2/(2\sigma^2)) \tag{18.23}$$

and

$$p_{neg}(z) = \sum_{neg} |\alpha_i| \exp(-\|x_i - z\|^2/(2\sigma^2)). \tag{18.24}$$

The target (18.16) then reads $(p_{pos}(z) - p_{neg}(z))^2$; in other words, we are trying to find a point z for which the difference between the (unnormalized) "probabilities" of the two classes is maximized, and to estimate the approximation of (18.12) by a Gaussian centered at z. Furthermore, note that we can rewrite (18.21) as

$$z = \frac{p_{pos}(z)}{p_{pos}(z) - p_{neg}(z)} x_{pos} + \frac{p_{neg}(z)}{p_{neg}(z) - p_{pos}(z)} x_{neg}, \tag{18.25}$$

where

$$x_{pos/neg} = \frac{\sum_{pos/neg} \alpha_i \exp(-\|x_i - z\|^2/(2\sigma^2)) x_i}{\sum_{pos/neg} \alpha_i \exp(-\|x_i - z\|^2/(2\sigma^2))}. \tag{18.26}$$

18.2.3 Toy Examples

Let us look at some experiments, for which we used an artificial data set generated from three Gaussians (standard deviation $\sigma = 0.1$). Figure 18.3 shows the results of performing kernel PCA on this data. Using the resulting eigenvectors, nonlinear principal components were extracted from a set of test points generated from the same model, and the points were reconstructed from varying numbers of principal components. Figure 18.4 shows that discarding higher-order components leads to removal of the noise — the points move towards their respective sources.

To obtain further intuitive understanding in a low-dimensional case, Figure 18.6 depicts the results of denoising a half circle and a square in the plane, using Kernel

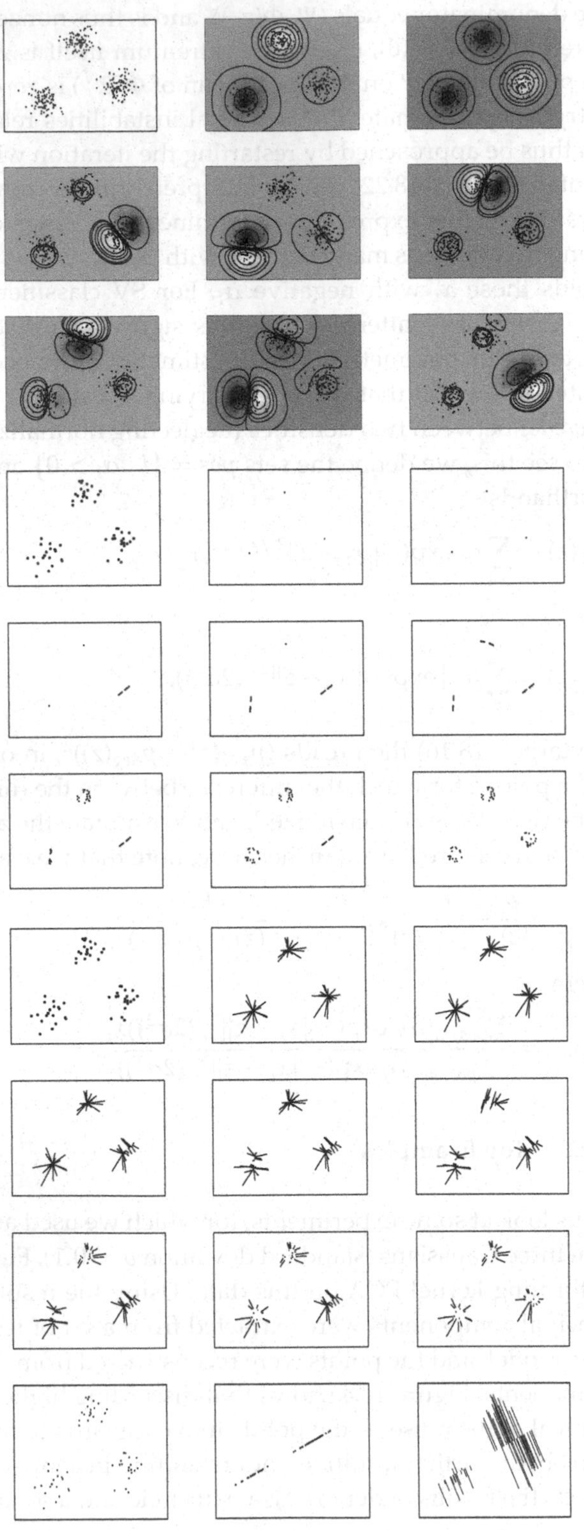

Figure 18.3 Kernel PCA toy example with a Gaussian kernel (see text). We plot lines of constant feature value for the first 8 nonlinear principal components extracted with $k(x, x') = \exp(-\|x - x'\|^2/0.1)$. The first 2 principal components (top middle/right) separate the three clusters, components 3–5 split the clusters, and components 6–8 split them again, orthogonal to the above splits [474].

Figure 18.4 Kernel PCA denoising by reconstruction from projections onto the eigenvectors of Figure 18.3. We generated 20 new points from each Gaussian, represented them in feature space by their first $n = 1, 2, \ldots, 8$ nonlinear principal components, and computed approximate pre-images, shown in the upper 9 pictures (top left: original data, top middle: $n = 1$, top right: $n = 2$, etc.). Note that by discarding higher order principal components (through using a small n), we removed the noise inherent in the nonzero variance σ^2 of the Gaussians. The lower 9 pictures show how the original points "moved" in the denoising. Unlike the corresponding case in linear PCA, where where we obtain lines (see Figure 18.5), clusters shrink to points in Kernel PCA [474].

Figure 18.5 Reconstructions and point movements for linear PCA, based on the first principal component [474].

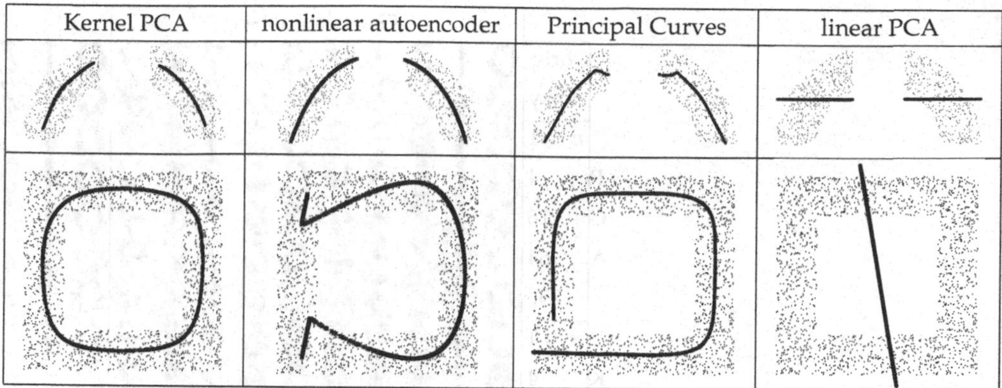

Figure 18.6 Denoising in 2-d (see text). The data set (small points) and its denoised version (solid lines) are depicted. For linear PCA, we used one component for reconstruction, since two components yield a perfect reconstruction, and thus do not denoise. Note that all algorithms except for the KPCA pre-image approach have problems in capturing the circular structure in the bottom example (from [365]).

PCA (with Gaussian kernel), a nonlinear autoencoder (see Section 14.2.3), principal curves (Example 17.6), and linear PCA. In all algorithms, parameter values were selected such that the best possible denoising result was obtained. The figure shows that on the closed square problem, Kernel PCA does best (subjectively), followed by principal curves and the nonlinear autoencoder; linear PCA fails completely. Note however that all algorithms other than Kernel PCA provide an explicit one-dimensional parametrization of the data, whereas Kernel PCA only provides us with a means of mapping points to their denoised versions (in this case, we used four Kernel PCA features, and hence obtained a four-dimensional parametrization).

18.2.4 Handwritten Digit Denoising

The approach has also been tested on real-world data, using the USPS database of handwritten digits (Section A.1). For each of the ten digits, 300 training examples and 50 test examples were chosen at random. Results are shown in Figures 18.7 and 18.8. In the experiments, linear and Kernel PCA (with Gaussian kernels) were performed on the original data. Two types of noise were added to the test patterns:

(i) Additive Gaussian noise with zero mean and standard deviation $\sigma = 0.5$

(ii) 'Speckle' noise, where each pixel is flipped to black or white with probability $p = 0.2$

For the noisy test sets, the projections onto the first n linear and nonlinear components were computed, and reconstruction was carried out in each case (using a basis expansion in the linear case, and the pre-image method in the kernel case).

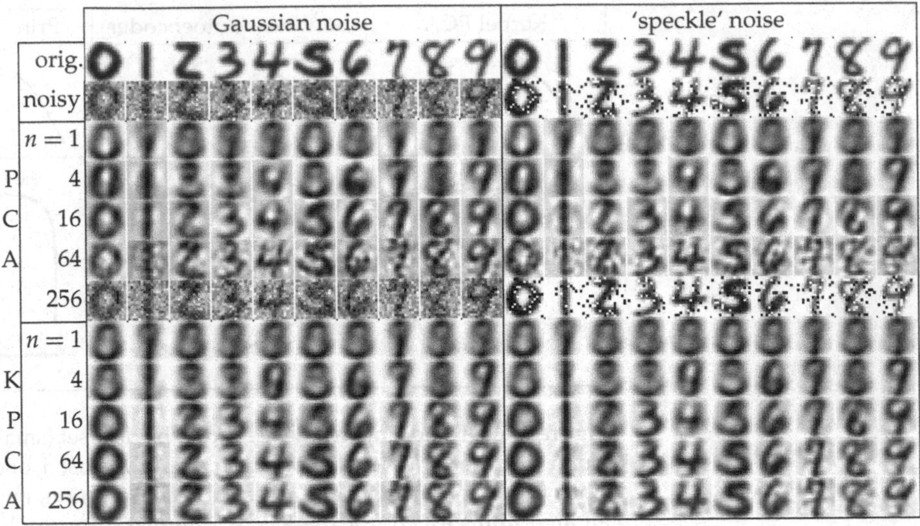

Figure 18.7 Denoising of USPS data (see text). We first describe the left hand plot. *Top:* the first occurrence of each digit in the test set. *Second row:* the digit above, but with added Gaussian noise. *Following five rows:* the reconstruction achieved with linear PCA using $n = 1, 4, 16, 64, 256$ components. *Last five rows:* the results of the Kernel PCA approach using the same number of components. In the right hand plot, the same approaches are illustrated for 'speckle' noise (from [365]).

When the optimal number of components was used in both linear and Kernel PCA, the Kernel PCA approach did significantly better. This can be interpreted as follows: Linear PCA can extract at most N components, where N is the dimensionality of the data. Being a basis transform, all N components together fully describe the data. If the data are noisy, a certain fraction of the components are devoted to the extraction of noise. Kernel PCA, on the other hand, allows the extraction of up to m features, where m is the number of training examples. Accordingly, Kernel PCA can provide a larger number of features carrying information about the structure in the data (in our experiments, $m > N$). In addition, if the structure to be extracted is nonlinear, then linear PCA must necessarily fail, as demonstrated in the toy examples.

18.3 Reduced Set Methods

18.3.1 The Problem

In the MNIST benchmark data set of 60000 handwritten digits, SVMs have achieved record accuracies (Chapter 11); they are inferior to neural nets in run-time classification speed, however [87]. In applications for which the latter is an issue, it is thus desirable to come up with methods to increase the speed by making

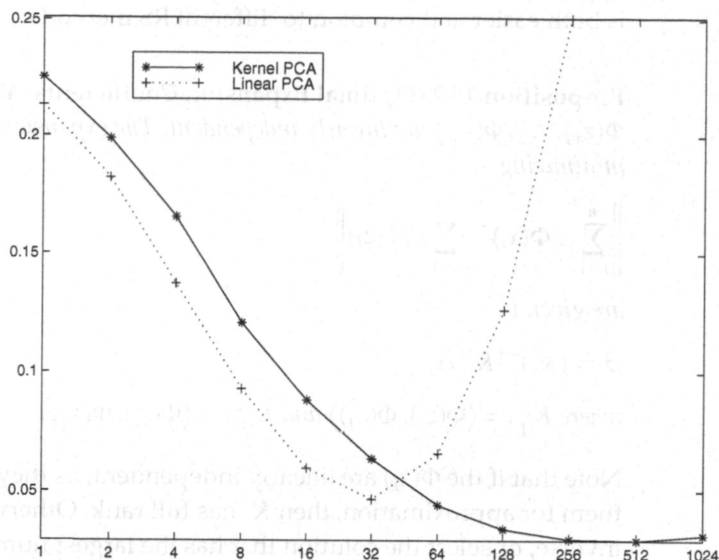

Figure 18.8 Mean squared error of the denoised images vs. # of features used, for Kernel PCA and linear PCA. Kernel PCA exploits nonlinearities and has the potential to utilize more features to code structure, rather than noise. Therefore, it outperforms linear PCA denoising if a sufficiently large number of features is used.

the SV expansion more sparse (cf. Chapter 10). This constitutes a problem slightly more general than the pre-image problem studied above: we no longer just look for single pre-images, but for expansions in terms of several input vectors [84]. It turns out that we can build on the methods developed in the previous section to design an algorithm for this more general case (see Section 18.5).

Assume we are given a vector $\Psi \in \mathcal{H}$, expanded in terms of the images of input patterns $x_i \in \mathcal{X}$,

$$\Psi = \sum_{i=1}^{N_x} \alpha_i \Phi(x_i), \tag{18.27}$$

with expansion coefficients $\alpha_i \in \mathbb{R}$. Rather than looking for a single pre-image, we try to approximate Ψ by a *reduced set* expansion [84],

$$\Psi' = \sum_{i=1}^{N_z} \beta_i \Phi(z_i), \tag{18.28}$$

with $N_z < N_x$, $\beta_i \in \mathbb{R}$, and points $z_i \in \mathcal{X}$. To this end, it was suggested in [84] that

$$\|\Psi - \Psi'\|^2 = \sum_{i,j=1}^{N_x} \alpha_i\alpha_j k(x_i, x_j) + \sum_{i,j=1}^{N_z} \beta_i\beta_j k(z_i, z_j) - 2\sum_{i=1}^{N_x}\sum_{j=1}^{N_z} \alpha_i\beta_j k(x_i, z_j) \tag{18.29}$$

be minimized. The crucial point is that even if Φ is not given explicitly, (18.29) can be computed (and minimized) in terms of the kernel.

18.3.2 Finding the Coefficients

Evidently, the RS problem consists of two parts: the determination the RS vectors z_i, and the computation the expansion coefficients β_i. We start with the latter, as it is both easier and common to different RS methods.

Proposition 18.2 (Optimal Expansion Coefficients [474]) *Suppose that the vectors $\Phi(z_1), \ldots, \Phi(z_{m'})$ are linearly independent. The expansion coefficients $\boldsymbol{\beta} = (\beta_1, \ldots, \beta_{m'})$ minimizing*

$$\left\| \sum_{i=1}^{m} \alpha_i \Phi(x_i) - \sum_{i=1}^{m'} \beta_i \Phi(z_i) \right\| \tag{18.30}$$

are given by

$$\boldsymbol{\beta} = (K^z)^{-1} K^{zx} \boldsymbol{\alpha}, \tag{18.31}$$

where $K^z_{ij} := \langle \Phi(z_i), \Phi(z_j) \rangle$ and $K^{zx}_{ij} := \langle \Phi(z_i), \Phi(x_j) \rangle$.

Note that if the $\Phi(z_i)$ are linearly independent, as they should be if we want to use them for approximation, then K^z has full rank. Otherwise, we can use the pseudo-inverse, or select the solution that has the largest number of zero components.

Proof We evaluate the derivative of the distance in $\mathcal{H}$,

$$\frac{\partial}{\partial \beta_j} \| \Psi - \sum_{i=1}^{m'} \beta_i \Phi(z_i) \|^2 = -2\Phi(z_j)(\Psi - \sum_{i=1}^{m'} \beta_i \Phi(z_i)), \tag{18.32}$$

and set it to 0. Substituting $\Psi = \sum_{i=1}^{m} \alpha_i \Phi(x_i)$, we obtain (using $\boldsymbol{\alpha} = (\alpha_1, \ldots, \alpha_m)$)

$$K^{zx} \boldsymbol{\alpha} = K^z \boldsymbol{\beta}, \tag{18.33}$$

hence

$$\boldsymbol{\beta} = (K^z)^{-1} K^{zx} \boldsymbol{\alpha}. \tag{18.34}$$

■

No RS algorithm using the feature space norm as an optimality criterion can improve on this result (cf. also Section 10.2.1). For instance, suppose we are given an algorithm that computes the β_i and z_i simultaneously. Proposition 18.2 can then be used to recompute the optimal coefficients $\boldsymbol{\beta}$, which must yield a solution at least as good. Algorithms may still be differentiated, however, by the way in which they determine the vectors z_i in the first place. In the next section, we describe algorithms that simply *select* subsets of the x_i, whereas methods detailed in Section 18.5 use vectors that can be different to the original x_i.

18.4 Reduced Set Selection Methods

Why should we expect to gain anything by *selecting* a subset of the expansion vectors in order to get a sparser expansion? Indeed, doesn't the SVM algorithm already find the sparsest solution? Unfortunately, this is not the case. Since the coefficients in an SVM expansion satisfy $\alpha_i \in [-C, C]$ (cf. Chapter 7) for some positive value of the regularization constant C, there is reason to believe that the SV expansion can be made sparser by removing this constraint on α_j [400].[2]

18.4.1 RS Selection via Kernel PCA

The idea for the first algorithm we describe arises from our observation that the null space of the Gram matrix $K_{ij} = \langle \Phi(x_i), \Phi(x_j) \rangle$ tells us precisely how many vectors can be removed from an expansion while incurring zero approximation error (assuming we correctly adjust the coefficients). In other words, it tell us how sparse we can make a kernel expansion without changing it in the least [467, 184].[3] Interestingly, it turns out that this problem is closely related to Kernel PCA (Chapter 14).

Let us start with the simplest case. Assume there exists an eigenvector $\alpha \neq 0$ of K with eigenvalue 0, hence $K\alpha = 0$. Using $K_{ij} = \langle \Phi(x_i), \Phi(x_j) \rangle$, this reads

$$\sum_{j=1}^{m} \langle \Phi(x_i), \Phi(x_j) \rangle \alpha_j = 0 \text{ for all } i = 1, \ldots, m, \tag{18.35}$$

hence

$$\sum_{j=1}^{m} \alpha_j \Phi(x_j) = 0. \tag{18.36}$$

Since $\alpha \neq 0$, the $\Phi(x_j)$ are linearly dependent, and therefore any of the $\Phi(x_j)$ with nonzero α_j can be expressed in terms of the others. Hence we may use the eigenvectors with eigenvalue 0 to eliminate certain terms from any expansion in the $\Phi(x_j)$.

What happens if we do not have vanishing eigenvalues, as in the case of Gaussian kernels (Theorem 2.18)? Intuitively, we anticipate that even though the above reasoning is no longer holds precisely true, it should give a good approximation. The crucial difference, however, is that in order to get the best possible approximation, we need to take into account the coefficients of the expansion $\Psi = \sum_{j=1}^{m} \alpha_j \Phi(x_j)$: if we incur an error by removing $\Phi(x_n)$, for example, then this error also depends on α_n. How do we then select the optimal n?

Clearly, we would like to find coefficients β_j that minimize the error we commit by replacing $\alpha_n \Phi(x_n)$ with $\sum_{j \neq n} \beta_j \Phi(x_j)$;

$$\rho(\beta, n) = \left\| \alpha_n \Phi(x_n) - \sum_{j \neq n} \beta_j \Phi(x_j) \right\|^2. \tag{18.37}$$

To establish a connection to Kernel PCA, we make a change of variables. First,

2. For instance, a certain pattern might appear twice in the training set, yet the SV expansion must utilize both copies since the upper bound constraint limits the coefficient of each to C.

3. The Gram matrix can either be computed using only those examples that have a nonzero α_j, or from a larger set containing further candidate expansion vectors.

define $\eta_j = 1$ for $j = n$ and $\eta_j = -\beta_j/\alpha_n$ for $j \neq n$. Hence the error (18.37) equals $|\alpha_n|^2 \|\sum_{j=1}^m \eta_j \Phi(x_j)\|^2$. Normalizing $\boldsymbol{\eta}$ to obtain $\boldsymbol{\gamma} := \boldsymbol{\eta}/\|\boldsymbol{\eta}\|$, and thus $\gamma_n = 1/\|\boldsymbol{\eta}\|$, leads to the problem of minimizing

$$\rho(\boldsymbol{\gamma}, n) = \left|\frac{\alpha_n}{\gamma_n}\right|^2 \langle \boldsymbol{\gamma}, K\boldsymbol{\gamma} \rangle \tag{18.38}$$

with respect to $\boldsymbol{\gamma}$, where $\|\boldsymbol{\gamma}\| = 1$ (note that ρ is invariant when $\boldsymbol{\gamma}$ is rescaled). A straightforward calculation shows that we can recover the approximation coefficients for $\alpha_n \Phi(x_n)$ (namely, the values that are added to the α_j $(j \neq n)$ when $\alpha_n \Phi(x_n)$ is left out): these are $\beta_j = -\frac{\alpha_n \gamma_j}{\gamma_n}$, $j \neq n$.

Rather than minimizing the nonlinear function (18.38), we now devise a computationally attractive approximate solution. This approximation is motivated by the observation that $\langle \boldsymbol{\gamma}, K\boldsymbol{\gamma} \rangle$ alone is minimized for the eigenvector with minimal eigenvalue, consistent with the special case discussed above (cf. (18.36)). In this case, $\langle \boldsymbol{\gamma}, K\boldsymbol{\gamma} \rangle = \lambda_{min}$. More generally, if $\boldsymbol{\gamma}^i$ is a normalized eigenvector of K with eigenvalue λ_i, then

$$\rho(i, n) = \left|\frac{\alpha_n}{\gamma_n^i}\right|^2 \lambda_i. \tag{18.39}$$

This can be minimized in $O(m^3)$ operations by performing kernel PCA and scanning through the matrix $(\rho(i,n))_{in}$. The complexity can be reduced to $O(m'm^2)$ by only considering the smallest m' eigenvalues, with $m' < m$ chosen a priori. Hence, we can eliminate $\Phi(x_n)$, where n is chosen in a principled yet efficient way.

Setting all computational considerations aside, the *optimal* greedy solution to the above selection problem, equivalent to (18.38), can also be obtained using Proposition 18.2: we compute the optimal solution for all possible patterns that could be left out (that is, we use subsets of $\{x_1, \ldots, x_m\}$ of size $m-1$ as $\{z_1, \ldots, z_{m'}\}$) and evaluate (18.32) in each case.

The same applies to subsets of any size. If we have the resources to exhaustively scan through all subsets of size m' $(1 \leq m' \leq m-1)$, then Proposition 18.2 provides the *optimal* way of selecting the best expansion of a given size. Better expansions can only be obtained if we drop the restriction that the approximation be written in terms of the original patterns, as done in Section 18.5.

No matter how we end up choosing n, we approximate Ψ by

$$\Psi = \sum_{j \neq n} \alpha_j \Phi(x_j) + \alpha_n \Phi(x_n) \approx \sum_{j \neq n} \left(\alpha_j - \frac{\alpha_n \gamma_j}{\gamma_n}\right) \Phi(x_j). \tag{18.40}$$

The whole scheme can be iterated until the expansion of Ψ is sufficiently sparse. If we want to avoid having to find the smallest eigenvalue of K anew at each step, then approximate schemes using heuristics can be conceived.

Experiments

We now describe experiments conducted to demonstrate this set reduction method. We determined the eigenvectors at each step using the Gram matrix computed from the SVs, and n was selected according to (18.39). For the USPS handwritten digit database, approximations were found to the SV expansions (7.25) of

Table 18.1 Number of test errors for each binary recognizer and test error rates for 10-class classification, using the RS method that selects patterns via Kernel PCA (Section 18.4.1). Top: number of SVs in the original SV RBF-system. Bottom, first row: original SV system, with 254 SVs on average; following rows: systems with varying average numbers of RS patterns. In the system RSS-n, equal fractions of SVs were removed from each recognizer such that on average, n RS patterns were left.

digit	0	1	2	3	4	5	6	7	8	9	ave.
#SVs	219	91	316	309	288	340	213	206	304	250	254

	0	1	2	3	4	5	6	7	8	9	10-class
SV-254	16	13	30	17	32	22	11	12	26	17	4.4%
RSS-50	47	18	70	52	192	95	54	38	97	157	17.6%
RSS-75	23	15	36	30	65	47	21	29	56	41	7.0%
RSS-100	19	15	42	22	40	29	14	18	37	27	5.5%
RSS-150	18	12	28	21	35	32	9	15	23	14	4.5%
RSS-200	14	13	27	25	27	26	11	13	26	21	4.5%
RSS-250	15	13	27	24	32	28	11	14	25	18	4.3%

ten binary classifiers, each trained to separate one digit from the rest. A Gaussian kernel $k(x, x') = \exp(-\|x - x'\|^2/(0.5 \cdot 16^2))$ was used. The original SV system has on average 254 SVs per classifier. Table 18.1 shows the classification error results for varying numbers of RS patterns (RSS-n means that for each binary classifier, SVs were removed until on average n were left). On each line, the number of misclassified digits for each single classifier is shown, as is the error of the combined 10-class machine. The optimal SV threshold b was re-computed on the training set after the RS approximation was found.

18.4.2 RS Selection via ℓ_1 Penalization

We next consider a method for enforcing sparseness inspired by ℓ_1 shrinkage penalizers (cf. Chapter 3), following the discussion in [474]. In a way, this allows us to benefit from the effect of ℓ_1 penalizers even if we do not want to use an ℓ_1 term as a *regularizer*, as was the case in LP-machines (Section 7.7).

Given an expansion $\sum_i \alpha_i \Phi(x_i)$, we approximate it by $\sum_i \beta_i \Phi(x_i)$ through the minimization of

$$\left\| \sum_{i=1}^{m} \alpha_i \Phi(x_i) - \sum_{i=1}^{m} \beta_i \Phi(x_i) \right\|^2 + \lambda \sum_{i=1}^{m} c_i |\beta_i| \tag{18.41}$$

over all β_i. Here, $\lambda > 0$ is a constant determining the trade-off between sparseness and the quality of approximation. The constants c_i can for instance be set to 1 or $\alpha/|\alpha_i|$ (where α is the mean of all $|\alpha_i|$). In the latter case, we hope for a sparser decomposition, since more emphasis is put on shrinking terms that are already small. This reflects the intuition that it is less promising to try to shrink very large terms. Ideally, we would like to *count* the number of nonzero coefficients, rather than sum their moduli; the former approach does not lead to an efficiently solvable optimization problem, however.

To dispose of the modulus, we rewrite β_i as

$$\beta_i := \beta_i^+ - \beta_i^-, \tag{18.42}$$

where $\beta_i^\pm \geq 0$. In terms of the new variables, we end up with the quadratic programming problem

$$\underset{\beta^+,\beta^-}{\text{minimize}} \quad \sum_{ij}(\beta_i^+ - \beta_i^-)(\beta_j^+ - \beta_j^-)K_{ij} \tag{18.43}$$

$$+\sum_j \left(\beta_j^+ \left(\lambda c_j - 2\sum_i K_{ij}\alpha_i\right) + \beta_j^- \left(\lambda c_j + 2\sum_i K_{ij}\alpha_i\right)\right)$$

subject to

$$\beta_j^+, \beta_j^- \geq 0. \tag{18.44}$$

This problem can be solved using standard quadratic programming tools. The solution (18.42) could be used directly as expansion coefficients. For optimal precision, however, we merely use it to select which patterns to use in the expansion (those with nonzero coefficients), and re-compute the optimal coefficients according to Proposition 18.2.

Multi-Class Case

In many applications, we face the problem of *simultaneously* approximating a set of M feature space expansions. For instance, in digit classification, a common approach is to train $M = 10$ binary recognizers, one for each digit. To this end, the quadratic programming formulation (18.43) can be modified to find all M expansions simultaneously, encouraging the use of the same expansion patterns in more than one binary classifier [474].

Experiments

These algorithms were evaluated on the same problem considered in the previous section. As with the results in Table 18.1, Table 18.2 shows that the accuracy of the original system can be closely approached by selecting sufficiently many RS patterns. The removal of about 40% of the Support Vectors leaves the test error practically unchanged.

18.4.3 RS Selection by Sparse Greedy Methods

Another set of methods were recently proposed to select patterns from the training set ([603, 514, 503], cf. also [580]). The basic idea, described in Section 10.2, is to start with an empty expansion, and greedily select the patterns that lead to the smallest error in approximating the remaining patterns. The resulting algorithms are very computationally efficient and have led to fine results.

It bears mentioning, however, that in many cases, with Gaussian Process regression being the exception (see Section 16.4 for more details), they do not take into account the expansion coefficients α_i of the original feature space vector, and

Table 18.2 Number of test errors for each binary recognizer and test error rates for 10-class classification, using the RS method employing ℓ_1 penalization (Section 18.4.2) (where $c_i = \alpha/|\alpha_i|$). First row: original SV system, with 254 SVs on average; following rows: systems with varying average numbers of RS patterns. In the system RSS$_2$-n, λ was adjusted such that the average number of RS patterns left was n (the constant λ, given in parentheses, was chosen such that the numbers n were comparable to Table 18.1). The results can be further improved using the multi-class method cited in Section 18.4.2. For instance, using about 570 expansion patterns (which is the same number that we get when taking the union of all SVs in the RSS$_2$ − 74 system) led to an improved error rate of 5.5%.

digit		0	1	2	3	4	5	6	7	8	9	10-cl.
SV-254		16	13	30	17	32	22	11	12	26	17	4.4%
RSS$_2$-50	(3.34)	225	24	171	146	149	124	94	147	100	101	28.5%
RSS$_2$-74	(2.55)	113	25	100	100	120	95	40	147	83	50	10.8%
RSS$_2$-101	(1.73)	38	21	46	64	81	54	23	143	49	37	5.9%
RSS$_2$-151	(0.62)	19	20	30	24	31	30	10	27	33	18	4.5%
RSS$_2$-200	(0.13)	17	15	25	27	34	27	11	14	26	22	4.3%
RSS$_2$-234	(0.02)	16	14	26	24	32	28	11	14	26	19	4.3%

thus do not always produce optimal results when the task is to approximate *one* given vector. Indeed, they do not even *start* from an original solution vector, as they compute everything in one pass. Therefore, they are not strictly speaking *reduced set post-processing* methods; we might equally well consider them to be *sparse training algorithms*. These algorithms are dealt with in Section 10.2.

On the other hand, if the effective dimensionality of the feature space is low, as is manifest in a rapid decay of the eigenvalues of the kernel matrix K, a sparse approximation of just about any function with small RKHS norm will be possible. In this case, which is rather frequent in practice, sparse approximation schemes which find a reduced set of expansion kernels *a priori* will perform well. See Section 10.2 for examples.

18.4.4 The Primal Reformulation

As discussed in Section 18.4, one of the reasons that SV expansions are not usually as sparse as they should be is the restriction of their coefficients to the interval $[-C, C]$. This problem derives directly from the structure of the quadratic program (QP) used to train an SVM. It is not the only problem caused by the QP, however.

A more fundamental reason for the SVM solution not being the sparsest possible is that *the set of SVs contains all the information necessary to solve the classification task*, as discussed in Section 7.8.2. This is a rather severe constraint, and is not enforced in other kernel-based classifiers such as Relevance Vector Machines (Chapter 16). It is partly this constraint that prevents SVMs from returning sparser solutions in the first place.

In an attempt to address this problem, Osuna and Girosi [400] proposed what they call the *primal reformulation* of the original SVC training problem (7.35). In their modification, they substitute the SV expansion $\mathbf{w} = \sum_i \alpha_i y_i \Phi(x_i)$ into (7.35) to obtain:

$$\underset{\alpha,\xi\geq 0, b\in\mathbb{R}}{\text{minimize}} \frac{1}{2}\sum_{i,j=1}^{m} \alpha_i\alpha_j y_i y_j k(x_i, x_j) + \frac{C}{m}\sum_{i=1}^{m}\xi_i, \tag{18.45}$$

$$\text{subject to } y_i\left(\sum_{i=1}^{m}\alpha_j y_j k(x_i, x_j) + b\right) \geq 1 - \xi_i \text{ for } i = 1, \ldots, m. \tag{18.46}$$

This formulation uses positivity constraints on α_i and ξ_i — the inequalities in (18.45) are to be read component-wise. We observe, however, that this formulation no longer requires that $\alpha_i \leq C$.

Note, moreover, that the optimization runs over $\boldsymbol{\alpha}, \boldsymbol{\xi}$, and b, and that the constraints (18.46) are linear in these variables; thus, we are still dealing with a QP. Its structure is not as appealing as that of the original form from an implementation viewpoint, however. The more complicated constraints make it harder to come up with algorithms that can solve large problems.

Although there is no a priori guarantee that this formulation will give sparser expansions; the method was nonetheless successfully applied to several small real-world problems [400]. The recommended starting point for the optimization is $\boldsymbol{\alpha} = 0$; other tricks for encouraging sparseness include the use of an ℓ_1 penalty term as in (18.4.2).

18.4.5 RS Selection via SV Regression

A second approach proposed by [400], which is particularly appealing in terms of its simplicity, uses SV regression to find RS vectors for SV classifiers. The idea is to apply ε-SV regression to the data set generated by evaluating the real-valued argument of the decision function,

$$g(x) = \sum_i \alpha_i y_i k(x_i, x) + b, \tag{18.47}$$

on the SVs; in other words, to

$$\{(x_i, g(x_i)) | \alpha_i > 0, i = 1, \ldots, m\}. \tag{18.48}$$

If the SVR training uses a large value of C (cf. Chapter 9), then (almost) all data points should be approximated within the accuracy ε set by the user. Therefore, the solution of the SVR algorithm has the same form as g (18.47) and can be used as a drop-in replacement for g. Since the SVR solution does not typically use all training examples (18.48), it is usually sparser than g. Note that when combined with the ν-SV regression algorithm (Section 9.3), this approach allows a rather more direct control of the size of the RS expansion (cf. Proposition 9.2).

18.5 Reduced Set Construction Methods

So far, we have considered the problem of how to *select* a reduced set of expansion vectors from the original set. We now return to the problem posed initially, which includes the *construction* of new vectors to reach high set size reduction rates.

18.5.1 Iterated Pre-Images

Suppose we want to approximate a vector

$$\Psi_1 = \sum_{i=1}^{m} \alpha_i \Phi(x_i) \tag{18.49}$$

with an expansion of type (18.28) with $N_z > 1$ and $z_i \in \mathbb{R}^N$.[4] To this end, we iterate a procedure for finding approximate pre-images (in the case of Gaussian kernels, for instance, this procedure is described in Section 18.2.2). This means that in step m', we need to find a pre-image z_m of

$$\Psi_{m'} = \sum_{i=1}^{m} \alpha_i \Phi(x_i) - \sum_{i=1}^{m'-1} \beta_i \Phi(z_i). \tag{18.50}$$

The coefficients are updated after each step according to Proposition 18.2 (if the discrepancy $\Psi_{m'+1}$ has not yet reached zero, then K^z is invertible).

The iteration is stopped after N_z steps; a number either specified in advance, or obtained by checking if $\|\Psi_{m'+1}\|$ (which equals $\|\Psi_1 - \sum_{i=1}^{m'} \beta_i \Phi(z_i)\|$) has fallen below a specified threshold. The solution vector takes the form (18.28). A toy example, using the Gaussian kernel, is shown in Figure 18.9.

For other kernel types, such as the polynomial kernels, we need to use a different procedure for computing approximate pre-images. One way of dealing with the problem is to minimize (18.15) directly. To achieve this, we can use unconstrained nonlinear optimization techniques, as proposed by Burges [84].

Finally, note that in many cases, such as multiclass SVMs and multiple Kernel PCA feature extractors, we may actually want to approximate several vectors simultaneously. This leads to rather more complex equations; cf. [474] for a discussion.

18.5.2 Phase II: Simultaneous Optimization of RS Vectors

Once all individual pre-images have been computed in this way, we could go ahead and *apply* the resulting RS expansion. It turns out, however, that it is still possible to improve things using a second phase, in which we *simultaneously*

4. Note that reduced set selection methods can work on general inputs. The present reduced set *construction* method, on the other hand, needs vectorial data, as it relies on forming linear combinations of patterns.

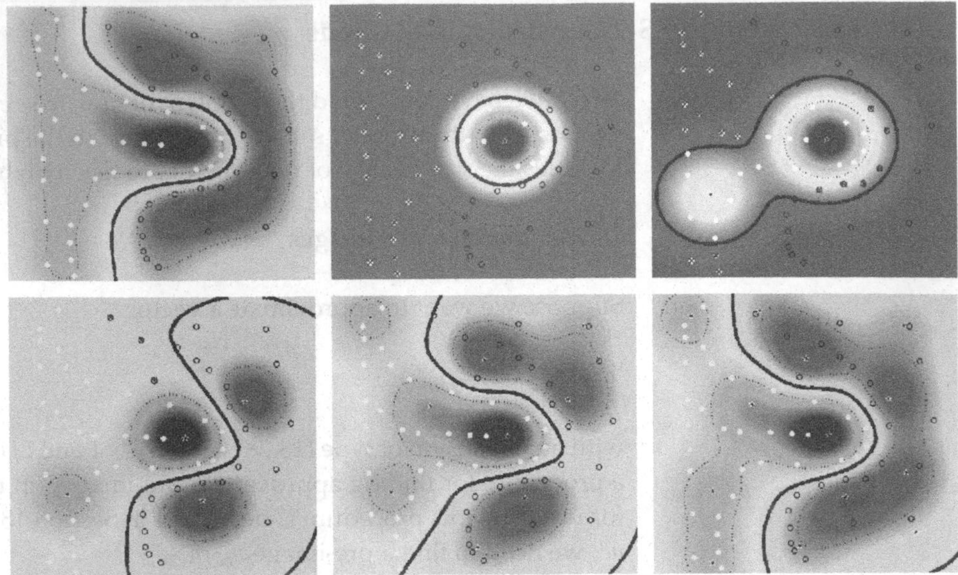

Figure 18.9 Toy example of the reduced set construction approach obtained by iterating the fixed-point algorithm of Section 18.2.2. The first image *(top left)* shows the SVM decision boundary that we are trying to approximate. The following images show the approximations using $N_z = 1, 2, 4, 9, 13$ RS vectors. Note that already the approximation with $N_z = 9$ *(bottom middle)* is almost identical to the original SVM, which has 31 expansion vectors (SVs) (from [437]).

optimize over all (z_i, β_i). Empirical observations have shown that this part of the optimization is more computationally expensive than the first phase, by about two orders of magnitude [84, 87]. In addition to this high computational cost, it is numerically difficult to handle: the optimization needs to be restarted several times to avoid getting trapped in local minima. At the end of phase II, it is advisable to recompute the β_i using Proposition 18.2. Let us now take a look at some experiments to see how well these methods do in practice.

18.5.3 Experiments

Table 18.3 shows that the RS construction method performs better than the RS selection methods described above (Tables 18.1 and 18.2). This is because it is able to utilize vectors different from the original support patterns in the expansion. To speed up the process by a factor of 10, we have to use a system with 25 RS vectors (RSC-25). We observe in Table 18.3 that the classification accuracy only drops moderately as a result, from 4.4% to 5.1%, which is still competitive with convolutional neural networks on this database (Table 7.4). In addition, we can further improve the system by adding the second phase described in Section 18.5.2, in which a global gradient descent is performed in the space of all

Table 18.3 Number of test errors for each binary recognizer and test error rates for 10-class classification, using the RS construction method of Section 18.5. First row: original SV system, with 254 SVs on average (see also Tables 18.1 and 18.2); following rows: systems with varying numbers of RS vectors (RSC-n stands for n vectors constructed) per binary recognizer, computed by iterating one-term RBF approximations (Section 18.5.1) separately for each recognizer. Last row: a subsequent global gradient descent (Section 18.5.2) further improves the results, as shown here for the RSC-25 system (see text).

digit	0	1	2	3	4	5	6	7	8	9	10-class
SV-254	16	13	30	17	32	22	11	12	26	17	4.4%
RSC-10	26	13	45	49	35	54	22	24	39	24	7.1%
RSC-20	27	11	38	30	35	43	12	16	30	25	5.6%
RSC-25	21	12	38	32	31	22	12	18	33	28	5.1%
RSC-50	18	10	33	28	32	23	12	15	35	27	5.0%
RSC-100	14	13	26	22	30	26	11	14	28	23	4.8%
RSC-150	13	14	28	32	27	24	12	14	29	26	4.7%
RSC-200	14	13	28	28	29	24	10	15	26	26	4.9%
RSC-250	12	13	26	26	32	25	11	14	26	24	4.6%
RSC$_2$-25	14	14	31	22	30	23	11	14	26	17	4.7%

(z_i, β_i); this leads to an error rate of 4.7%. For the kernel considered, this is almost identical to phases I + II of Burges's RS method, which yield 5.0% (for polynomial kernels, the latter method leads to an error of 4.3% with the same increase in speed [84]). Finally, Figure 18.10 shows the RSC-20 vectors of the 10 binary classifiers. As an aside, note that unlike Burges's method, which directly tackles the nonlinear optimization problem, the present algorithm produces images that look like digits.

As in [87], good RS construction results were obtained even though the objective function did not decrease to zero (in the RS construction experiments, it was reduced by a factor of 2 to 20 in the first phase, depending on how many RS vectors were computed; the global gradient descent yielded another factor of 2–3). We conjecture that this is due to the following: In classification, we are not interested in $\|\Psi - \Psi'\|$, but in $\int |\operatorname{sgn}(\sum_{i=1}^{N_x} \alpha_i k(x, x_i) + b) - \operatorname{sgn}(\sum_{j=1}^{N_z} \beta_i k(x, z_i) + \tilde{b})| dP(x)$, where P is the underlying probability distribution of the patterns (cf. [55]). This is consistent with the fact that the performance of an RS SV classifier can be improved by re-computing an optimal threshold b.

The RS selection methods lead to worse results than RS construction; they are simpler and computationally faster, however. Of the two RS selection methods described (Tables 18.1 and 18.2), that using Kernel PCA is slightly superior at higher reductions. The ℓ_1 penalization approach is computationally cheaper, however, since unlike the Kernel PCA based algorithm, it does not remove the SVs one at a time, and need not be iterated.

MNIST Experiments

We conclude this section by briefly describing another study, which combines the virtual SV method (Chapter 11) with Burges's RS algorithm [87]. Virtual SV systems have yielded the most accurate results on the widely used MNIST hand-

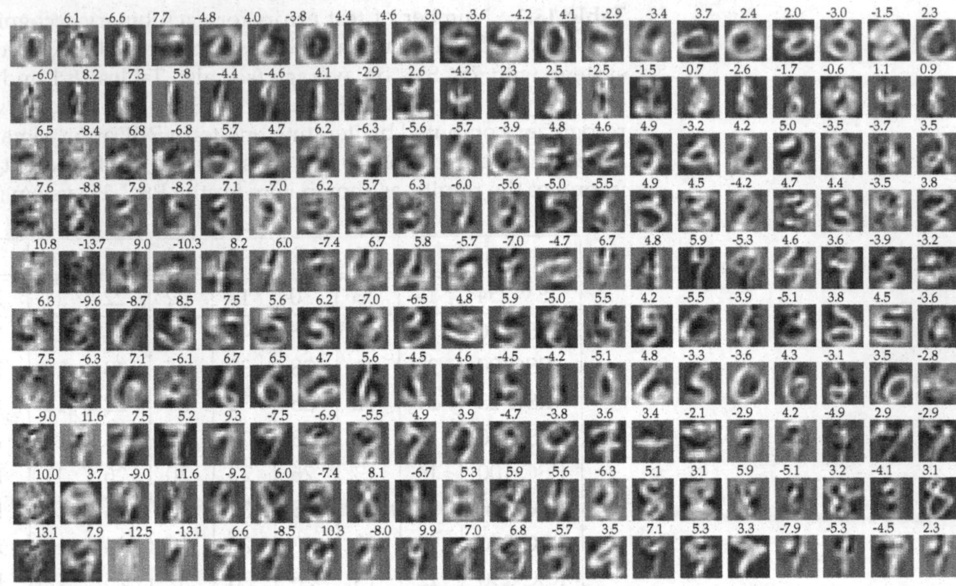

Figure 18.10 Illustration of all the reduced set vectors constructed by the iterative approach of Section 18.5.1 for $n = 20$. The associated coefficients are listed above the images. Top: recognizer of digit 0,..., bottom: recognizer of digit 9. Note that positive coefficients (roughly) correspond to positive examples in the classification problem.

written character benchmark (Section A.1). They come with a computational cost, however: the resulting classifiers tend to have more SVs than an ordinary SVM. They are thus an ideal target for RS methods. Combining both procedures, an increase in speed of order 50 was achieved over the Virtual SVM in the test phase, with only a small decrease in performance (the test error increased from 1.0% to 1.1%, cf. [87]), leading to a system that is approximately as fast as convolutional neural nets [320].

18.6 Sequential Evaluation of Reduced Set Expansions

As described above, RS algorithms typically work by finding RS vectors sequentially. This implies that we can stop calculating additional RS vectors once the approximation is satisfactory. There is, however, another implication that was recently pointed out [437]: even if we choose to compute a comprehensive RS expansion, we might not always want to *evaluate* it in full for a given problem. For instance, if after evaluating the first three RS vectors of a SV classifier we can already see the classification outcome is very likely 'class 1,' then it is not necessary to evaluate the remaining RS vectors. Romdhani et al. [437] applied this idea, together with the reduced set construction approach of Section 18.5.1, to the problem

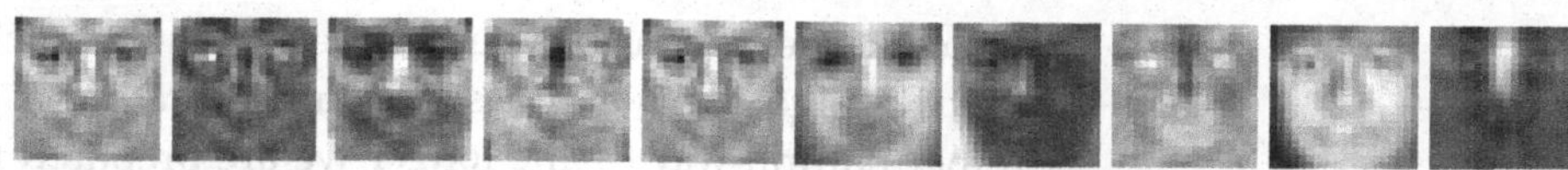

Figure 18.11 First 10 reduced set vectors. Note that all vectors can be interpreted as either faces (such as the first one) or anti-faces (the second one) [437].

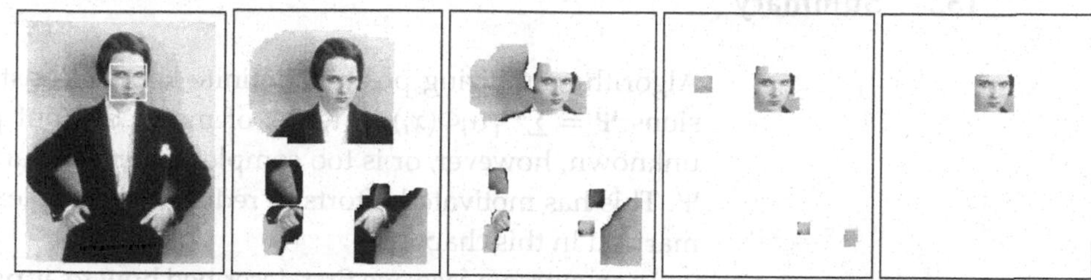

Figure 18.12 From left to right: input image, followed by patches that remain after the evaluation of 1 *(13.3% patches remaining)*, 10 *(2.6%)*, 20 *(0.01%)*, and 30 *(0.002%)* filters. Note that in these images, the pixels representing the full patch are displayed when it yields a positive classification *at its center*. This explains the apparent discrepancy between the above percentages and the visual impression [437].

of face detection.

In face detection, run time classification speed is a major requirement. This is due to the fact that we essentially need to look at *all* locations in a given test image in order to detect all faces that are present. The standard approach is to scan a binary classifier (trained on the task of distinguishing faces from non-faces) over the entire image, looking at one image patch at a time [446, 399]. To make things worse, we must usually consider the possibility that faces occur at widely different scales, which necessitates several such scans.

In their experimental investigation of this problem, Romdhani et al. obtain an initial SVM with 1742 SVs. Using the method of Section 18.5.1, these were reduced to 60 RS vectors. The first ten reduced set vectors are shown in Figure 18.11.

For each possible cut-off $n = 1, \ldots, 60$, a threshold was computed which ensured the false negative[5] rate of the classifier, when run with only the first n RS vectors, was sufficiently small. At the nth step, an RS expansion with n vectors was scanned over the image. Note that this only entailed computation of one additional kernel per image location, since the first $n-1$ evaluations were cached. Furthermore, the nth scan only had to cover those areas of the image that were not yet discarded as clear non-faces. For the data set considered, most of the image parts could typically be discarded with a *single* RS vector (cf. Figure 18.12); on average, each image location was "looked at" by 2.8 RS vectors.

This method is not limited to face detection. It could be used in any task for

5. By *false negatives*, we refer to faces that are erroneously classified as non-faces.

which kernel expansions need to be evaluated quickly. The method demonstrates that RS algorithms can assist in incorporating a speed-accuracy trade-off in a rather natural way — the longer we are prepared to wait, the more accurate the result we get (be it classification or function value estimation).

18.7 Summary

Algorithms utilizing positive definite kernels construct their solutions as expansions $\Psi = \sum_{i=1}^{m} \alpha_i \Phi(x_i)$ in terms of mapped input patterns. The map Φ is often unknown, however, or is too complex to provide any intuition about the solution Ψ. This has motivated efforts to reduce the complexity of the expansion, as summarized in this chapter.

As an extreme case, we first described how to approximate Ψ by a single $\Phi(z)$ (in other words, how to find an approximate pre-image of Ψ) and gave a fixed-point iteration algorithm to perform this task. The procedure was successfully applied to the problem of statistical denoising via Kernel PCA reconstruction.

In situations where no good approximate pre-image exists, we can still reduce the complexity of $\Psi = \sum_{i=1}^{N_x} \alpha_i \Phi(x_i)$ by expressing it as a sparser expansion, $\sum_{i=1}^{N_z} \beta_i \Phi(z_i)$ $(N_z < N_x)$. We described methods for computing the optimal coefficients β_i, and for obtaining suitable patterns z_i, either by selecting among the x_i or by iterating the above pre-image algorithm to construct synthetic patterns z_i. This led to rather useful algorithms for speeding up the evaluation of kernel expansions, such as SV decision functions. We reviewed applications of these algorithms in OCR and face detection. Comparing the RS construction and RS selection methods, we observe that the greatest speed gains are usually achieved using construction methods. These are computationally more expensive, however, and require the input data to lie to $\mathbb{R}^N$.

In the case of face detection, we described a sequential approach that requires on average less than 3 kernel evaluations per image patch, making it competitive with the fastest available systems.

Both the pre-image and the reduced set procedures are thus not only of theoretical interest for feature space methods, but also lead to practical applications. The proposed methods are applicable to a variety of feature space algorithms based on positive definite kernels. For instance, we could also speed up SV regression machines and Kernel PCA feature extractors. We expect further possibilities to open up in future, as kernel methods are applied in an increasing range of learning and signal processing problems.

18.8 Problems

18.1 (Exact Pre-Images for RBF Kernels [467] ••) *Generalize Proposition 18.1 to kernels which are functions of* $\|x - x'\|$.

18.2 (Exact Pre-Images for Gaussian Kernels ••) *Use the reasoning following (18.8) to argue that a greedy approach, such as the iterated pre-image method from Section 18.5.1, does not necessarily find the optimal reduced set solution. Argue that this supports the use of a "phase II" approach (Section 18.5.2; cf. Section 18.2).*

18.3 (Justification of Approximate Pre-Images •) *Use the Cauchy-Schwarz inequality to show that if* $\|\Psi - \Phi(z)\|^2$ *(cf. (18.9)) is small, then for any* $\mathbf{v} \in \mathcal{H}$*, the dot product* $\langle \Psi, \mathbf{v} \rangle$ *can be approximated by* $\langle \Phi(z), \mathbf{v} \rangle$*. Argue that this is all that is needed for a kernel algorithm.*
Specialize to the case where $\mathbf{v}$ *has a pre-image* x*.*

18.4 (Approximate Single Pre-Images •) *Consider the normal vector of a SV hyperplane in feature space. Using your favorite kernel, argue that it is usually impossible to find a single pre-image for the normal, as otherwise, the resulting class of decision function would only have one term in the kernel expansion, which is not adequate for most complex problems.*

18.5 (Reconstruction from Principal Components ••) *Devise an alternative to the suggested method for computing approximate pre-images from examples expressed in terms of their first principal components in feature space. For instance, use a suitable multi-output regression method for estimating the reconstruction mapping from the first* q $(q < m)$ *kernel-based principal components to the inputs. Use the method for denoising.*

18.6 (Optimal Coefficient in the 1-Pattern Case •) *Prove that the maximum of (18.15) can be extended to the minimum of (18.13) by setting*

$$\beta = \langle \Psi, \Phi(z) \rangle \, / \, \langle \Phi(z), \Phi(z) \rangle \,. \tag{18.51}$$

Discuss the relationship to Proposition 18.2.

18.7 (Data-Dependent RS Formulations ∘∘∘) *Change the RS objective function* $\|\Psi - \Psi'\|^2$ *to* $\sum_i \langle (\Psi - \Psi'), \Phi(x_i) \rangle^2$*. Argue that this takes into account the distribution of the data points* x_i *in a sensible way. Which of the algorithms in the present chapter can be generalized to use this objective function? Try to devise efficient algorithms to minimize it.*

18.8 (Speedup via Faster Evaluation of the Full Expansion ∘∘∘) *In [421], a method was considered which speeds up the evaluation of an* m*-term kernel expansion to* $\log m$ *by using tree structures.*

(i) Apply this method, and compare the performance to the RS methods described in the present chapter.

(ii) Can you combine this approach with those taken in the present chapter by designing RS algorithms which produce expansions that lend themselves well to the approach of [421]?

18.9 (Minimum Support Solutions ○○○) *Can you use the minimum support methods of Mangasarian [346] to devise reduced set methods?*

18.10 (Reduced Sets via Clustering ○○○) *Discuss how you could speed up SVMs by clustering the input data, for instance using the k-means algorithm [152]. Would you use the cluster centers as training examples? If yes, how would you label them? Can you think of modifications to clustering algorithms that would make them particularly suited to a reduced set approach?*

18.11 (ℓ_1 Penalization for Multi-Class RS Expansions [474] ••) *Generalize the approach of Section 18.4.2 to the case where you are trying to simultaneously approximate several feature space expansions with few RS vectors (overall).*

18.12 (RS Construction for Degree 2 Monomial Kernels [84] •••) *Consider the kernel $k(x, x') = \langle x, x' \rangle^2$ on $\mathbb{R}^N \times \mathbb{R}^N$. Denote by S the symmetric matrix with elements*

$$S_{jn} := \sum_{i=1}^{N_x} \alpha_i [x_i]_j [x_i]_n. \tag{18.52}$$

Prove that $\rho(\beta, z) := \| \sum_{i=1}^{N_x} \alpha_i \Phi(x_i) - \beta \Phi(z) \|^2$ is minimized for (β, z) satisfying

$$Sz = \beta \langle z, z \rangle z. \tag{18.53}$$

Prove, moreover, that with this choice of (β, z),

$$\rho(\beta, z) = \sum_{jn} S_{jn} - \beta^2 \langle z, z \rangle^2. \tag{18.54}$$

Therefore, one should choose the first pre-image z to be the eigenvector of S for which the eigenvalue λ is largest in absolute value, scaled such that $\langle z, z \rangle = |\lambda|$. In this case (cf. (18.53)), $|\beta| = 1$.

Generalize this argument to $N_z > 1$, showing that the RS vectors that follow should be the next eigenvectors (in terms of the absolute size of the eigenvalues) of S. Argue that this shows that using at most N terms, the RS expansion can be made exact.

18.13 (Direct Approximation of SVC Decision Functions ○○○) *The RS algorithms described approximate a SVC decision function by approximating the weight vector normal to the hyperplane and then recomputing the threshold. Can you come up with an RS approach that addresses the problem in a rather more direct way, using a cost function which looks at the approximation of the resulting decision boundary (cf. [55])?*

A Addenda

Das also war des Pudels Kern!
Ein fahrender Skolast? Der Kasus macht mich lachen.

J. W. Goethe's Faust

A.1 Data Sets

In the present section, we describe three of the datasets used. They are available from http://www.kernel-machines.org/data.html.

USPS Set

The *US Postal Service (USPS)* database (see Figure A.1) contains 9298 handwritten digits (7291 for training, 2007 for testing), collected from mail envelopes in Buffalo [318]. Each digit is a 16×16 image, represented as a 256-dimensional vector with entries in the range -1 to 1. Preprocessing consisted of smoothing with a Gaussian kernel of width $\sigma = 0.75$.

It is known that the USPS test set is rather difficult — the human error rate is 2.5% [79]. For a discussion, see [496]. Note, moreover, that some of the results reported in the literature for the USPS set were obtained with an enhanced training set. For instance, [148] used an enlarged training set of size 9709 containing some additional machine-printed digits. The authors note that this improves the accuracy on the *test* set. Similarly, [65] used a training set of size 9840. Since there are no machine-printed digits in the commonly used test set (size 2007), this addition distorts the original learning problem to a situation where results become somewhat hard to interpret. In our experiments, we only used the original 7291 training examples. Results on the USPS problem can be found in Table 7.4.

MNIST Set

The *MNIST* database (Figure A.2) contains 120000 handwritten digits, divided equally into training and test sets. The database is a modified version of *NIST Special Database 3* and *NIST Test Data 1*. Both training and test set consist of patterns generated by different writers. The images are first size normalized to fit into a 20×20 pixel box, and then centered in a 28×28 image [319].

Most of the test results on the MNIST database given in the literature [e.g. 320, 319] for do not use the full MNIST test set of 60000 characters. Instead, a subset of 10000 characters is used, consisting of the test set patterns from 24476 to 34475. To obtain results that can be compared to the literature, we also use this test

Figure A.1 The first 100 USPS training images, with class labels (from [467]).

Figure A.2 The first 100 MNIST training images, with class labels (from [467]).

Figure A.3 The first 100 small-MNIST training images, with class labels (from [467]).

set, although the larger one would be preferable from the point of view of obtaining more accurate estimates of the true risk. The error rates on the 10000 element test set are estimated to be reliable within about 0.1% [64]. The MNIST benchmark dataset is available from http://www.research.att.com/~yann/ocr/mnist/. MNIST results are listed in Table 11.2.

The USPS database has been criticized (Burges, LeCun, private communication; [64]) as not providing the most adequate classifier benchmark. First, it only comes with a small test set; and second, the test set contains a number of corrupted patterns, which not even humans can classify correctly. The MNIST database, which is the classifier benchmark currently used in the AT&T and Bell Labs learning research groups, does not have these drawbacks; moreover, its training set is much larger. In some cases, however, it is useful to be able to study an algorithm on a smaller database. First, this can save computation time, and second, this allows the study of learning from smaller sample sizes. We thus generated a smaller version of the MNIST database which we used in some experiments. It is smaller in two respects: First, the patterns have a resolution of 20×20, obtained from the 28×28 patterns by downsampling (combined with a Gaussian smoothing of standard deviation 0.75 pixels, to avoid aliasing effects). Second, it only comprises a subset of the training set, namely the first 5000 patterns. We define the same 10000 test examples as above as our test set. We refer to this database as the *small MNIST* database (Figure A.3).

Small MNIST Set

Abalone

The *Abalone* database from the UCI repository [56] contains 4177 patterns. It is an integer regression problem, the labels are the different ages of Abalones. For most practical purposes, it is treated as a generic regression problem in the examples of this book. The data is rescaled to zero mean and unit variance coordinate-wise, and the gender encoding (male/female/infant) is mapped into $\{(1,0,0),(0,1,0),(0,0,1)\}$.

A.2 Proofs

Proposition 7.5

Proof **Ad (i):** By the KKT conditions, $\rho > 0$ implies $\delta = 0$, hence (7.52) becomes an equality (cf. (7.46)). Thus, at most a fraction ν of all examples can have $\alpha_i = 1/m$. All examples with $\xi_i > 0$ satisfy $\alpha_i = 1/m$ (if not, α_i could grow further to reduce ξ_i).

Ad (ii): SVs can contribute at most $1/m$ to (7.52), hence there must be at least νm of them.

Ad (iii): This part of the proof is somewhat technical. Readers who prefer to skip it may instead consider the following sloppy argument: The difference between (i) and (ii) lies only in the points that sit exactly *on* the edge of the margin, since these are SVs with zero slack variables. As the training set size tends to infinity, however, only a negligible fraction of points can sit exactly on the margin, provided the distribution is well-behaved.

For the formal proof, note that it follows from the condition on $P(x, y)$ that apart from some set of measure zero (arising from possible singular components), the two class distributions are absolutely continuous and can be written as integrals over distribution functions. As the kernel is analytic and non-constant, it cannot be constant in any open set, otherwise it would be constant everywhere. Therefore, the class of functions f constituting the argument of the sgn in the SV decision function ((7.53); essentially, functions in the class of SV regression functions) transforms the distribution over x into distributions such that for all f and all $t \in \mathbb{R}$, $\lim_{\gamma \to 0} P(|f(x) + t| < \gamma) = 0$. At the same time, we know that the class of these functions has well-behaved covering numbers, hence we get uniform convergence: for all $\gamma > 0$, $\sup_f |P(|f(x)+t| < \gamma) - \hat{P}_m(|f(x)+t| < \gamma)|$ converges to zero in probability, where $\hat{P}_m$ is the sample-based estimate of P (that is, the proportion of points that satisfy $|f(x) + t| < \gamma$). But then for all $\alpha > 0$, $\lim_{\gamma \to 0} \lim_{m \to \infty} P(\sup_f \hat{P}_m(|f(x) + t| < \gamma) > \alpha) = 0$. Hence, $\sup_f \hat{P}_m(|f(x) + t| = 0)$ converges to zero in probability. Using $t = \pm\rho$ thus shows that the fraction of points exactly on the margin almost surely tends to zero, hence the fraction of SVs equals that of margin errors. Combining (i) and (ii) then shows that both fractions converge almost surely to ν. ■

Additionally, since (7.51) means that the sums over the coefficients of positive and negative SVs respectively are equal, we conclude that Proposition 7.5 actually holds for both classes separately, with $\nu/2$. As an aside, note that by the same argument, the number of SVs on each side of the margin asymptotically agree.

Proposition 7.7

Proof Since the slack variable of $\mathbf{x}_m$ satisfies $\xi_m > 0$, the KKT conditions (Chapter 6) imply $\alpha_m = 1/m$. If δ is sufficiently small, then transforming the point into $\mathbf{x}'_m := \mathbf{x}_m + \delta\mathbf{w}$ results in a slack that is still nonzero, $\xi'_m > 0$, hence we have $\alpha'_m = 1/m = \alpha_m$. Updating the ξ_m, and keeping all other primal variables unchanged, we obtain a modified set of primal variables that is still feasible.

We next show how to obtain a corresponding set of feasible dual variables. To keep $\mathbf{w}$ unchanged, we need to satisfy

$$\sum_{i=1}^{m} \alpha_i y_i \mathbf{x}_i = \sum_{i \neq m} \alpha'_i y_i \mathbf{x}_i + \alpha_m y_m \mathbf{x}'_m. \tag{A.1}$$

Substituting $\mathbf{x}'_m = \mathbf{x}_m + \delta\mathbf{w}$ and (7.57), we note that a sufficient condition for this to hold is that for all $i \neq m$, $\alpha'_i = \alpha_i - \delta\gamma_i y_i \alpha_m y_m$.

Since by assumption γ_i is only nonzero if $\alpha_i \in (0, 1/m)$, then α'_i will be in $(0, 1/m)$ if $\alpha_i \in (0, 1/m)$, provided δ is sufficiently small, and it will equal $1/m$ if $\alpha_i = 1/m$. In both cases, we end up with a feasible solution $\boldsymbol{\alpha}'$, and the KKT conditions are still satisfied. Thus (cf. Chapter 6), $(\mathbf{w}, b)$ are still the hyperplane parameters of the solution. ■

Proposition 9.2

Proof **Ad (i):** The constraints (9.43) and (9.44) imply that at most a fraction ν of all examples can have $\alpha_i^{(*)} = C/m$. All examples with $\xi_i^{(*)} > 0$ (in other words, those outside the tube) certainly satisfy $\alpha_i^{(*)} = C/m$ (if not, $\alpha_i^{(*)}$ could grow further to reduce $\xi_i^{(*)}$).

Ad (ii): By the KKT conditions, $\varepsilon > 0$ implies $\beta = 0$. Hence, (9.44) becomes an equality (cf. (9.37)).[1] Since SVs are those examples for which $0 < \alpha_i^{(*)} \leq C/m$, the result follows (using $\alpha_i \alpha_i^* = 0$ for all i, (9.58)).

Ad (iii): The strategy of proof is to show that asymptotically, the probability of a point lying *on* the edge of the tube vanishes. The condition on $P(y|x)$ means that

$$\sup_{f,t} \mathbf{E}_{x,y}\left[\mathrm{P}\left(|f(x) + t - y| < \gamma | x\right)\right] < \delta(\gamma) \tag{A.2}$$

for some function $\delta(\gamma)$ that approaches zero as $\gamma \to 0$. Since the class of SV regression estimates f has well-behaved covering numbers, we have [14, Chapter 21] that for all t,

$$\mathrm{P}\left(\sup_f \left(\hat{P}_m(|f(x) + t - y| < \gamma/2) - P(|f(x) + t - y| < \gamma)\right) > \alpha\right) < c_1 c_2^{-m}, \tag{A.3}$$

where $\hat{P}_m$ is the sample-based estimate of P (that is, the proportion of points that satisfy $|f(x) - y + t| < \gamma$), and c_1, c_2 may depend on γ and α. Discretizing the

1. In practice, we can alternatively work with (9.44) as an equality constraint, provided that ν is chosen small enough ($\nu < 1$) to ensure that it does not pay to make ε negative.

values of t, taking the union bound (Chapter 5), and applying (A.2) shows that the supremum over f and t of $\hat{P}_m(f(x) - y + t = 0)$ converges to zero in probability. Thus, the fraction of points on the edge of the tube almost surely converges to 0. Consequently the fraction of SVs equals that of errors. Combining (i) and (ii) then shows that both fractions converge almost surely to ν. ■

Proposition 17.9 ***Proof*** We proceed in a manner similar to the proof of proposition 17.8, but use $\mathcal{N}(\epsilon, \mathfrak{F}_c, d)$ and $\frac{\eta}{2}$ to bound $R[f^*_{\text{emp}}]$

$$R[f^*_{\text{emp}}] - R[f^*] = R[f^*_{\text{emp}}] - R_{\text{emp}}[f^*_{\text{emp}}] + R_{\text{emp}}[f^*_{\text{emp}}] - R[f^*] \tag{A.4}$$

$$\leq \epsilon + R[f_i] - R_{\text{emp}}[f_i] + R_{\text{emp}}[f^*_{\text{emp}}] - R[f^*] \tag{A.5}$$

$$\leq \epsilon + 2 \max_{f \in V_\epsilon \cup \{f^*\}} |R[f] - R_{\text{emp}}[f]| \tag{A.6}$$

where V_ϵ is the ε-cover of $\mathfrak{F}$ of size $\mathcal{N}(\varepsilon, \mathfrak{F}, L_\infty(\ell_2^d))$, $f_i \in V_\varepsilon$, and clearly $R_{\text{emp}}[f^*_{\text{emp}}] \leq R_{\text{emp}}[f^*]$. The application of Hoeffding's inequality and the union bound, and the change of $\eta + \varepsilon$ to η, then prove the claim. ■

Proposition 17.10 ***Proof*** The proof uses a clever trick from [292], however without the difficulty of also having to bound the approximation error. Since by hypothesis $\mathfrak{F}_\Lambda$ is compact, we can use Proposition 17.9. We have

$$R[f^*_{\text{emp}}] - R[f^*] = \int_0^\infty \mathrm{P}\left\{R[f^*_{\text{emp}}] - R[f^*] > \eta\right\} d\eta$$

$$\leq u + \epsilon + 2(\mathcal{N}(\epsilon, \mathfrak{F}_c, d) + 1) \int_{u+\epsilon}^\infty e^{-\frac{m(\eta-\epsilon)^2}{2e_c}} d\eta$$

$$\leq u + \epsilon + \frac{2e_c}{um}(\mathcal{N}(\epsilon, \mathfrak{F}_c, d) + 1) e^{-\frac{mu^2}{2e_c}}$$

$$\leq \sqrt{\frac{2e_c \ln(\mathcal{N}(\epsilon, \mathfrak{F}_c, d)+1)}{m}} + \epsilon + \sqrt{\frac{2e_c}{m \ln(\mathcal{N}(\epsilon, \mathfrak{F}_c, d)+1)}}. \tag{A.7}$$

Here we use $\int_x^\infty \exp(-t^2/2)dt \leq \exp(-x^2/2)/x$ in the second step. The third inequality is derived by substituting

$$u = \sqrt{\frac{2e_c}{m} \ln(\mathcal{N}(\epsilon, \mathfrak{F}_c, d) + 1)}. \tag{A.8}$$

For part **1**, we set $\epsilon = m^{-1/2}$ and obtain

$$R[f^*_{\text{emp}}] - R[f^*] = O\left(m^{-1/2} \ln^{\alpha/2} m\right). \tag{A.9}$$

For part **2**, (A.7) implies (for some constants $c, c' > 0$)

$$R[f^*_{\text{emp}}] - R[f^*] \leq c\varepsilon^{-\alpha/2} m^{-1/2} + \epsilon + c' \varepsilon^{\alpha/2} m^{-1/2}. \tag{A.10}$$

The minimum is obtained for $\epsilon = c'' m^{-1/(\alpha+2)}$ for some $c'' > 0$. Hence the overall term is of order $O(m^{-\frac{1}{\alpha+2}})$, as required. ■

B Mathematical Prerequisites

The beginner... should not be discouraged if... he finds that he does not have the prerequisites for reading the prerequisites.

P. Halmos[1]

In this chapter, we introduce mathematical results that might not be known to all readers, but which are sufficiently standard that they not be put into the actual chapters.

This exposition is almost certainly incomplete, and some readers will inevitably happen upon terms in the book that are unknown to them, yet not explained here. Consequently, we also give some further references.

B.1 Probability

B.1.1 Probability Spaces

Let us start with some basic notions of probability theory. For further detail, we refer to [77, 165, 561]. We do not try to be rigorous; instead, we endeavor to give some intuition and explain how these concepts are related to our present interests.

Domain

Assume we are given a nonempty set $\mathcal{X}$, called the *domain* or *universe*. We refer to the elements x of $\mathcal{X}$ as *patterns*. The patterns are generated by a stochastic source. For instance, they could be handwritten digits, which are subject to fluctuations in their generation best modelled probabilistically. In the terms of probability theory, each pattern x is considered the outcome of a *random experiment*.

We would next like to assign probabilities to the patterns. We naively think of a probability as being the limiting frequency of a pattern; in other words, how often, relative to the number of trials, a certain pattern x comes up in a random experiment, if we repeat this experiment infinitely often?

Event
Probability

It turns out to be convenient to be slightly more general, and to talk about the probability of *sets* of possible outcomes; that is, subsets C of $\mathcal{X}$ called *events*. We denote the *probability* that the outcome of the experiment lies in C by

1. Quoted after [429].

$$P\{x \in C\}. \tag{B.1}$$

If Υ is a logical formula in terms of x, meaning a mapping from $\mathcal{X}$ to { true, false}, then it is sometimes convenient to talk about the probability of Υ being true. We will use the same symbol P in this case, and define its usage as

$$P\{\Upsilon(x)\} := P\{x \in C\} \text{ where } C = \{x \in \mathcal{X} | \Upsilon(x) = \text{true}\}. \tag{B.2}$$

Let us also introduce the shorthand

$$P(C) := P\{x \in C\}, \tag{B.3}$$

Distribution of x

to be read as "the probability of the event C." If P satisfies some fairly natural conditions, it is called a *probability measure*. It is also referred to as the *(probability) distribution of x*.

In the case where $\mathcal{X} \subset \mathbb{R}^N$, the patterns are usually referred to as *random variables* ($N = 1$) or *random vectors* ($N > 1$). A generic term we shall sometimes use is *random quantity*.[2]

To emphasize the fact that P is the distribution of x, we sometimes denote it as P_x or $P(x)$.[3] To give the precise definition of a probability measure, we first need to be a bit more formal about which sets C we are going to allow. Certainly,

$$C = \mathcal{X} \tag{B.4}$$

should be a possibility, corresponding to the event that necessarily occurs ("sure thing"). If C is allowed, then its complement,

$$\overline{C} := \mathcal{X} \setminus C, \tag{B.5}$$

should also be allowed. This corresponds to the event "not C." Finally, if $C_1, C_2, \ldots$ are events, then we would like to be able to talk about the probability of the event "C_1 or C_2 or ...", hence

$$\bigcup_{i=1}^{\infty} C_i \tag{B.6}$$

should be an allowed event.

σ-Algebra

Definition B.1 (σ-Algebra) *A collection $\mathcal{C}$ of subsets of $\mathcal{X}$ is called a* σ-algebra on $\mathcal{X}$ *if*

(i) *$\mathcal{X} \in \mathcal{C}$; in other words, (B.4) is one of its elements;*

(ii) *it is closed under complementation, meaning if $C \in \mathcal{C}$, then also (B.5); and*

(iii) *it is closed under countable[4] unions: if $C_1, C_2, \ldots \in \mathcal{C}$, then also (B.6).*

---

2. For simplicity, we are somewhat sloppy in not distinguishing between a random variable and the values it takes. Likewise, we deviate from standard usage in not having introduced random variables as functions on underlying universes of events.
3. The latter is somewhat sloppy, as it suggests that P takes *elements* of $\mathcal{X}$ as inputs, which it does not: P is defined for *subsets* of $\mathcal{X}$.
4. *Countable* means with a number of elements not larger than that of $\mathbb{N}$. Formally, a set

The elements of a σ-algebra are sometimes referred to as measurable sets.

We are now in a position to formalize our intuitions about the probability measure.

Definition B.2 (Probability Measure) *Let $\mathcal{C}$ be a σ-algebra on the domain $\mathcal{X}$. A function*

$$P: \mathcal{C} \to [0,1] \tag{B.7}$$

Probability Measure

is called a probability measure *if it is normalized,*

$$P(\mathcal{X}) = 1, \tag{B.8}$$

and σ-additive, meaning that for sets $C_1, C_2, \ldots \in \mathcal{C}$ that are mutually disjoint ($C_i \cap C_j = \emptyset$ if $i \neq j$), we have

$$P\left(\bigcup_{i=1}^{\infty} C_i\right) = \sum_{i=1}^{\infty} P(C_i). \tag{B.9}$$

As an aside, note that if we drop the normalization condition, we are left with what is called a *measure*.

Measure

Probability Space

Taken together, $(\mathcal{X}, \mathcal{C}, P)$ are called a *probability space*. This is the mathematical description of the probabilistic experiment.

B.1.2 IID Samples

Nevertheless, we are not quite there yet, since most of the probabilistic statements in this book do not talk about the outcomes of the experiment described by $(\mathcal{X}, \mathcal{C}, P)$. For instance, when we are trying to learn something about a regularity (that is, about some aspects of P) based on a collection of patterns $x_1, \ldots, x_m \in \mathcal{X}$ (usually called a *sample*), we actually perform the random experiment m times, under identical conditions. This is referred to as *drawing an iid (independent and identically distributed) sample* from P.

Sample

IID Sample

Formally, drawing an iid sample can be described by the probability space $(\mathcal{X}^m, \mathcal{C}^m, P^m)$. Here, $\mathcal{X}^m$ denotes the m-fold Cartesian product of $\mathcal{X}$ with itself (thus, each element of $\mathcal{X}^m$ is an m-tuple of elements of $\mathcal{X}$), and $\mathcal{C}^m$ denotes the smallest σ-algebra that contains the elements of the m-fold Cartesian product of $\mathcal{C}$ with itself. Likewise, the product measure P^m is determined uniquely by

$$P^m((C_1, \ldots, C_m)) := \prod_{i=1}^{m} P(C_i). \tag{B.10}$$

Note that the independence of the "iid" is encoded in (B.10) being a product of measures on $\mathcal{C}$, while the identicality lies in the fact that all the measures on $\mathcal{C}$ are one and the same.

---

is countable if there is a surjective map from $\mathbb{N}$ onto this set; that is, a map with range encompassing the whole set.

By analogy to (B.2), we sometimes talk about the probability of a logical formula involving an m-sample,[5]

$$P\{\Upsilon(x_1, \ldots, x_m)\} := P^m(\{(x_1, \ldots, x_m) \in \mathcal{X}^m | \Upsilon(x_1, \ldots, x_m) = \text{true}\}). \tag{B.11}$$

So far, we have denoted the outcomes of the random experiments as x for simplicity, and have referred to them as patterns. In many cases studied in this book, however, we will not only observe patterns $x \in \mathcal{X}$ but also *targets* $y \in \mathcal{Y}$. For instance, in binary pattern recognition, we have $\mathcal{Y} = \{\pm 1\}$. The underlying regularity is now assumed to generate *examples* (x, y). All of the above applies to this case, with the difference that we now end up with a probability measure on $\mathcal{X} \times \mathcal{Y}$, called the (joint) distribution of (x, y).

B.1.3 Densities and Integrals

We now move on to the concept of a *density*, often confused with the distribution. For simplicity, we restrict ourselves to the case where $\mathcal{X} = \mathbb{R}^N$; in this instance, $\mathcal{C}$ is usually taken to be the *Borel σ-algebra*.[6]

Definition B.3 (Density) *We say that the nonnegative function p is the* density *of the distribution* P *if for all* $C \in \mathcal{C}$,

$$P(C) = \int_C p(x) dx. \tag{B.12}$$

If such a p exists, it is uniquely determined.[7]

Not all distributions actually *have* a density. To see this, let us consider a distribution that does. If we plug a set of the form $C = \{x\}$ into (B.12), we see that $P(\{x\}) = 0$; that is, the distribution assigns zero probability to any set of the form $\{x\}$. We infer that only distributions that assign zero probability to individual points can have densities.[8]

It is important to understand the difference between distributions and densities. The distribution takes *sets* of patterns as inputs, and assigns them a probability between 0 and 1. The density takes an individual pattern as its input, and assigns a nonnegative number (possibly larger than 1) to it. Using (B.12), the density can be used to compute the probability of a set C. If the density is a continuous function, and we use a small neighborhood of point x as the set C, then P is approximately

5. Note that there is some sloppiness in the notation: strictly speaking, we should denote this quantity as P^m — usually, however, it can be inferred from the context that we actually mean the m-fold product measure.
6. Readers not familiar with this concept may simply think of it as a collection that contains all "reasonable" subsets of $\mathbb{R}^N$.
7. *Almost everywhere*; in other words, up to a set N with $P(N) = 0$.
8. In our case, we can show that the distribution P has a density if and only if it is *absolutely continuous* with respect to the Lebesgue measure on $\mathbb{R}^N$, meaning that every set of Lebesgue-measure zero also has P-measure zero.

the size (i.e. , the measure) of the neighborhood times the value of p; in this case, and in this sense, the two quantities are proportional.

Distribution Function

A more fundamental concept, which exists for *every* distribution of a random quantity taking values in $\mathbb{R}^N$, is the *distribution function*,[9]

$$\mathrm{F}: \mathbb{R}^N \to [0, 1] \tag{B.13}$$

$$z \mapsto \mathrm{F}(z) = \mathrm{P}\{[x]_1 < [z]_1 \wedge \ldots \wedge [x]_N < [z]_N\}. \tag{B.14}$$

Finally, we need to introduce the notion of an integral with respect to a measure. Consider a function $f : \mathbb{R}^N \to \mathbb{R}$. We denote by

$$\int_C f(x) d\mathrm{P}(x) \tag{B.15}$$

the integral of a function with respect to the distribution (or measure) P, provided that f is *measurable*. For our purposes, the latter means that for every interval $[a, b] \subset \mathbb{R}$, $f^{-1}([a, b])$ (the set of all points in $\mathbb{R}^N$ that get mapped to $[a, b]$) is an element of $\mathfrak{C}$. Component-wise extension to vector-valued functions is straightforward.

In the case where P has a density p, (B.15) equals

$$\int_C f(x) p(x) dx, \tag{B.16}$$

which is a standard integral in $\mathbb{R}^N$, weighted by the density function p.

If P does not have a density, we can define the integral by decomposing the range of f into disjoint half-open intervals $[a_i, b_i)$, and computing the measure of each set $f^{-1}([a_i, b_i))$ using P. The contribution of each such set to the integral is determined by multiplying this measure with the function value (on the set), which by construction is in $[a_i, b_i)$. The exact value of the integral is obtained by taking the limit at infinitely small intervals. This construction, which is the basic idea of the Lebesgue integral, does not rely on f being defined on $\mathbb{R}$; it works for general sets $\mathcal{X}$ as long as they are suitably endowed with a measure.

Empirical Measure

Let us consider a special case. If P is the *empirical measure* with respect to $x_1, \ldots, x_m$,[10]

$$\mathrm{P}^m_{\mathrm{emp}}(C) := \frac{|C \cap \{x_1, \ldots, x_m\}|}{m}, \tag{B.17}$$

which represents the fraction of points that lie in C, then the integral takes the form

$$\int_C f(x) d\mathrm{P}^m_{\mathrm{emp}}(x) = \frac{1}{m} \sum_{i=1}^{m} f(x_i). \tag{B.18}$$

As an aside, note that this shows the empirical risk term (1.17) can actually be thought of as an integral, just like the actual risk (1.18).

9. We use $\wedge$ to denote the logical "and" operation, and $[z]_i$ to denote the i^{th}component of z.
10. By $|.|$ we denote the number of elements in a set.

Expectation, Variance, Covariance

If P is a probability distribution (rather than a general measure), then two more special cases of interest are obtained for particular choices of functions f in (B.15). If f is the identity on $\mathbb{R}^N$, we get the *expectation* $\mathbf{E}[x]$. If $f(x) = (x - \mathbf{E}[x])^2$ (on $\mathbb{R}$), we obtain the *variance* of x, denoted by $\text{var}(x)$. In the N-dimensional case, the functions $f_{ij}(x) = (x_i - \mathbf{E}[x_i])(x_j - \mathbf{E}[x_j])$ lead to the *covariance* $\text{cov}(x_i, x_j)$. For a data set $\{x_1, \ldots, x_m\}$, the matrix $(\text{cov}(x_i, x_j))_{ij}$ is called the *covariance matrix*.

B.1.4 Stochastic Processes

A *stochastic process* y on a set $\mathcal{X}$ is a random quantity indexed by $x \in \mathcal{X}$. This means that for every x, we get a random quantity $y(x)$ taking values in $\mathbb{R}$, or more generally, in a *set* $\mathcal{R}$. A stochastic process is characterized by the joint probability distributions of y on arbitrary finite subsets of $\mathcal{X}$; in other words, of $(y(x_1), \ldots, y(x_m))$.[11]

A *Gaussian process* is a stochastic process with the property that for any $\{x_1, \ldots, x_m\} \subset \mathcal{X}$, the random quantities $(y(x_1), \ldots, y(x_m))$ have a joint Gaussian distribution with mean μ and covariance matrix K. The matrix elements K_{ij} are given by a covariance kernel $k(x_i, x_j)$.

When a Gaussian process is used for learning, the *covariance function* $k(x_i, x_j) := \text{cov}(y(x_i), y(x_j))$ essentially plays the same role as the kernel in a SVM. See Section 16.3 and [587, 596] for further information.

B.2 Linear Algebra

B.2.1 Vector Spaces

We move on to basic concepts of linear algebra, which is to say the study of vector spaces. Additional detail can be found in any textbook on linear algebra (e.g., [170]). The feature spaces studied in this book have a rich mathematical structure, which arises from the fact that they allow a number of useful operations to be carried out on their elements: addition, multiplication with scalars, and the product between the elements themselves, called the dot product.

What's so special about these operations? Let us, for a moment, go back to our earlier example (Chapter 1), where we classify sheep. Surely, nobody would come up with the idea of trying to add two sheep, let alone compute their dot product. The set of sheep does not form a vector space; mathematically speaking, it could be argued that it does not have a very rich structure. However, as discussed in Chapter 1 (cf. also Chapter 2), it is possible to *embed* the set of all sheep into a dot product space such that we can think of the dot product as a measure of

11. Note that knowledge of the finite-dimensional distributions (fdds) does not yield complete information on the properties of the sample paths of the stochastic process; two different processes which have the same fdds are known as *versions* of one another.

the similarity of two sheep. In this space, we can perform the addition of two sheep, multiply sheep with numbers, compute hyperplanes spanned by sheep, and achieve many other things that mathematicians like.

Vector Space

Definition B.4 (Real Vector Space) *A set $\mathcal{H}$ is called a* vector space *(or* linear space*) over $\mathbb{R}$ if addition and scalar multiplication are defined, and satisfy (for all $\mathbf{x}, \mathbf{x}', \mathbf{x}'' \in \mathcal{H}$, and $\lambda, \lambda' \in \mathbb{R}$)*

$$\mathbf{x} + (\mathbf{x}' + \mathbf{x}'') = (\mathbf{x} + \mathbf{x}') + \mathbf{x}'', \tag{B.19}$$

$$\mathbf{x} + \mathbf{x}' = \mathbf{x}' + \mathbf{x} \in \mathcal{H}, \tag{B.20}$$

$$0 \in \mathcal{H}, \ \mathbf{x} + 0 = \mathbf{x}, \tag{B.21}$$

$$-\mathbf{x} \in \mathcal{H}, \ -\mathbf{x} + \mathbf{x} = 0, \tag{B.22}$$

$$\lambda \mathbf{x} \in \mathcal{H}, \tag{B.23}$$

$$1\mathbf{x} = \mathbf{x}, \tag{B.24}$$

$$\lambda(\lambda' \mathbf{x}) = (\lambda \lambda')\mathbf{x}, \tag{B.25}$$

$$\lambda(\mathbf{x} + \mathbf{x}') = \lambda \mathbf{x} + \lambda \mathbf{x}', \tag{B.26}$$

$$(\lambda + \lambda')\mathbf{x} = \lambda \mathbf{x} + \lambda' \mathbf{x}. \tag{B.27}$$

The first four conditions amount to saying that $(\mathcal{H}, +)$ is a commutative group.[12]

We have restricted ourselves to vector spaces over $\mathbb{R}$. The definition in the complex case is analogous, both here and in most of what follows. Any non-empty subset of $\mathcal{H}$ that is itself a vector space is called a *subspace* of $\mathcal{H}$.

Linear Combination

Among the things we can do in a vector space are *linear combinations*,

$$\sum_{i=1}^{m} \lambda_i \mathbf{x}_i, \text{ where } \lambda_i \in \mathbb{R}, \mathbf{x}_i \in \mathcal{H}, \tag{B.28}$$

Convex Combination

and *convex combinations*,

$$\sum_{i=1}^{m} \lambda_i \mathbf{x}_i, \text{ where } \lambda_i \geq 0, \sum_i \lambda_i = 1, \mathbf{x}_i \in \mathcal{H}. \tag{B.29}$$

Span

The set $\{\sum_{i=1}^{m} \lambda_i \mathbf{x}_i | \lambda_i \in \mathbb{R}\}$ is referred to as the *span* of the vectors $\mathbf{x}_1, \ldots, \mathbf{x}_m$.

A set of vectors $\mathbf{x}_i$, chosen such that none of the $\mathbf{x}_i$ can be written as a linear combination of the others, is called *linearly independent*. A set of vectors $\mathbf{x}_i$ that allows us to uniquely write each element of $\mathcal{H}$ as a linear combination is called a *basis* of $\mathcal{H}$. For the uniqueness to hold, the vectors have to be linearly independent. All bases of a vector space $\mathcal{H}$ have the same number of elements, called the *dimension* of $\mathcal{H}$.

Basis

Dimension

$\mathbb{R}^N$

The standard example of a finite-dimensional vector space is $\mathbb{R}^N$, the space of column vectors $([\mathbf{x}]_1, \ldots, [\mathbf{x}]_N)^\top$, where the $^\top$ denotes the transpose. In $\mathbb{R}^N$,

12. Note that (B.21) and (B.22) should be read as existence statements. For instance, (B.21) states that there exists an element, denoted by 0, with the required property.

addition and scalar multiplication are defined element-wise. The canonical basis of $\mathbb{R}^N$ is $\{\mathbf{e}_1, \ldots, \mathbf{e}_N\}$, where for $j = 1, \ldots, N$, $[\mathbf{e}_j]_i = \delta_{ij}$. Here δ_{ij} is the Kronecker symbol;

Kronecker δ_{ij}

$$\delta_{ij} = \begin{cases} 1 & \text{if } i = j, \\ 0 & \text{otherwise.} \end{cases} \tag{B.30}$$

A somewhat more abstract example of a vector space is the space of all real-valued functions on a domain $\mathcal{X}$, denoted by $\mathbb{R}^{\mathcal{X}}$. Here, addition and scalar multiplication are defined by

$$(f+g)(x) := f(x) + g(x), \tag{B.31}$$

$$(\lambda f)(x) := \lambda f(x). \tag{B.32}$$

We shall return to this example below.

Linear Map

Linear algebra is the study of vector spaces and *linear maps* (sometimes called *operators*) between vector spaces. Given two real vector spaces $\mathcal{H}_1$ and $\mathcal{H}_2$, the latter are maps

$$L : \mathcal{H}_1 \to \mathcal{H}_2 \tag{B.33}$$

that for all $\mathbf{x}, \mathbf{x}' \in \mathcal{H}$, $\lambda, \lambda' \in \mathbb{R}$ satisfy

$$L(\lambda \mathbf{x} + \lambda' \mathbf{x}') = \lambda L(\mathbf{x}) + \lambda' L(\mathbf{x}'). \tag{B.34}$$

It is customary to omit the parentheses for linear maps; thus we normally write $L\mathbf{x}$ rather than $L(\mathbf{x})$.

Let us go into more detail, using (for simplicity) the case where $\mathcal{H}_1$ and $\mathcal{H}_2$ are identical, have dimension N, and are written $\mathcal{H}$. Due to (B.34), a linear map L is completely determined by the values it takes on a basis of $\mathcal{H}$. This can be seen by writing an arbitrary input as a linear combination in terms of the basis vectors $\mathbf{e}_j$, and then applying L;

$$L \sum_{j=1}^{N} \lambda_j \mathbf{e}_j = \sum_{j=1}^{N} \lambda_j L \mathbf{e}_j. \tag{B.35}$$

The image of each basis vector, $L\mathbf{e}_j$, is in turn completely determined by its expansion coefficients A_{ij}, $i = 1, \ldots, N$;

$$L\mathbf{e}_j = \sum_{i=1}^{N} A_{ij} \mathbf{e}_i. \tag{B.36}$$

Matrix

The coefficients (A_{ij}) form the *matrix* A of L with respect to the basis $\{\mathbf{e}_1, \ldots, \mathbf{e}_N\}$. We often think of linear maps as matrices in the first place, and use the same symbol to denote them. The *unit* (or *identity*) matrix is denoted by $\mathbf{1}$. Occasionally, we also use the symbol $\mathbf{1}$ as the identity map on arbitrary sets (rather than vector spaces).

Matrix Product

In this book, we assume elementary knowledge of matrix algebra, including the *matrix product*, corresponding to the composition of two linear maps,

$$(AB)_{ij} = \sum_{n=1}^{N} A_{in} B_{nj}, \tag{B.37}$$

Transpose

and the *transpose* $(A^\top)_{ij} := A_{ji}$.

Inverse and Pseudo-Inverse

The *inverse* of a matrix A is written A^{-1} and satisfies $AA^{-1} = A^{-1}A = \mathbf{1}$. The *pseudo-inverse* $A^\dagger$ satisfies $AA^\dagger A = A$. While every matrix has a pseudo-inverse, not all have an inverse. Those which do are called *invertible* or *nonsingular*, and their inverse coincides with the pseudo-inverse. Sometimes, we simply use the notation A^{-1}, and it is understood that we mean the pseudo-inverse whenever A is not invertible.

B.2.2 Norms and Dot Products

Thus far, we have explained the linear structure of spaces such as the feature space induced by a kernel. We now move on to the *metric* structure. To this end, we introduce concepts of length and angles.

Definition B.5 (Norm) *A function* $\|\cdot\| : \mathcal{H} \to \mathbb{R}_0^+$ *that for all* $\mathbf{x}, \mathbf{x}' \in \mathcal{H}$ *and* $\lambda \in \mathbb{R}$ *satisfies*

$$\|\mathbf{x} + \mathbf{x}'\| \leq \|\mathbf{x}\| + \|\mathbf{x}'\|, \tag{B.38}$$

$$\|\lambda \mathbf{x}\| = |\lambda| \|\mathbf{x}\|, \tag{B.39}$$

$$\|\mathbf{x}\| > 0 \text{ if } \mathbf{x} \neq 0, \tag{B.40}$$

Norm

is called a norm *on* $\mathcal{H}$. *If we replace the "$>$" in (B.40) by "$\geq$," we are left with what is called a* semi-norm.

Metric

Any norm defines a *metric* d via

$$d(\mathbf{x}, \mathbf{x}') := \|\mathbf{x} - \mathbf{x}'\|; \tag{B.41}$$

likewise, any semi-norm defines a *semi-metric*. The (semi-)metric inherits certain properties from the (semi-)norm, in particular the triangle inequality (B.39) and positivity (B.40).

While every norm gives rise to a metric, the converse is not the case. In this sense, the concept of the norm is stronger. Similarly, every *dot product* (to be introduced next) gives rise to a norm, but not vice versa.

Before describing the dot product, we start with a more general concept.

Definition B.6 (Bilinear Form) *A* bilinear form *on a vector space* $\mathcal{H}$ *is a function*

$$Q : \mathcal{H} \times \mathcal{H} \to \mathbb{R}$$

$$(\mathbf{x}, \mathbf{x}') \to Q(\mathbf{x}, \mathbf{x}') \tag{B.42}$$

with the property that for all $\mathbf{x}, \mathbf{x}', \mathbf{x}'' \in \mathcal{H}$ *and all* $\lambda, \lambda' \in \mathbb{R}$, *we have*

$$Q((\lambda\mathbf{x} + \lambda'\mathbf{x}'), \mathbf{x}'') = \lambda Q(\mathbf{x}, \mathbf{x}'') + \lambda' Q(\mathbf{x}', \mathbf{x}''), \tag{B.43}$$

$$Q(\mathbf{x}'', (\lambda\mathbf{x} + \lambda'\mathbf{x}')) = \lambda Q(\mathbf{x}'', \mathbf{x}) + \lambda' Q(\mathbf{x}'', \mathbf{x}'). \tag{B.44}$$

If the bilinear form also satisfies

$$Q(\mathbf{x}, \mathbf{x}') = Q(\mathbf{x}', \mathbf{x}) \tag{B.45}$$

for all $\mathbf{x}, \mathbf{x}' \in \mathcal{H}$, *it is called* symmetric.

Dot Product

Definition B.7 (Dot Product) *A* dot product *on a vector space* $\mathcal{H}$ *is a symmetric bilinear form,*

$$\begin{aligned} \langle .,. \rangle : \mathcal{H} \times \mathcal{H} &\to \mathbb{R} \\ (\mathbf{x}, \mathbf{x}') &\mapsto \langle \mathbf{x}, \mathbf{x}' \rangle , \end{aligned} \tag{B.46}$$

that is strictly positive definite; *in other words, it has the property that for all* $\mathbf{x} \in \mathcal{H}$,

$$\langle \mathbf{x}, \mathbf{x} \rangle \geq 0 \text{ with equality only for } \mathbf{x} = 0. \tag{B.47}$$

Definition B.8 (Normed Space and Dot Product Space) *A* normed space *is a vector space endowed with a norm; a* dot product space *(sometimes called* pre-Hilbert space*) is a vector space endowed with a dot product.*

Any dot product defines a corresponding norm via

$$\|\mathbf{x}\| := \sqrt{\langle \mathbf{x}, \mathbf{x} \rangle}. \tag{B.48}$$

Cauchy-Schwarz

We now describe the *Cauchy-Schwarz inequality*: For all $\mathbf{x}, \mathbf{x}' \in \mathcal{H}$,

$$|\langle \mathbf{x}, \mathbf{x}' \rangle| \leq \|\mathbf{x}\| \|\mathbf{x}'\|, \tag{B.49}$$

with equality occurring only if $\mathbf{x}$ and $\mathbf{x}'$ are linearly dependent. In some instances, the left hand side can be much smaller than the right hand side. An extreme case is when $\mathbf{x}$ and $\mathbf{x}'$ are *orthogonal*, and $\langle \mathbf{x}, \mathbf{x}' \rangle = 0$.

Orthogonality

Basis Expansion

One of the most useful constructions possible in dot product spaces are *orthonormal basis expansions*. Suppose $\mathbf{e}_1, \ldots, \mathbf{e}_N$, where $N \in \mathbb{N}$, form an *orthonormal set*; that is, they are mutually orthogonal and have norm 1. If they also form a basis of $\mathcal{H}$, they are called an *orthonormal basis (ONB)*. In this case, any $\mathbf{x} \in \mathcal{H}$ can be written as a linear combination,

$$\mathbf{x} = \sum_{j=1}^{N} \langle \mathbf{x}, \mathbf{e}_j \rangle \, \mathbf{e}_j. \tag{B.50}$$

The standard example of a dot product space is again $\mathbb{R}^N$. We usually employ the canonical dot product,

$$\langle \mathbf{x}, \mathbf{x}' \rangle := \sum_{i=1}^{N} [\mathbf{x}]_i [\mathbf{x}']_i = \mathbf{x}^\top \mathbf{x}', \tag{B.51}$$

and refer to $\mathbb{R}^N$ as the *Euclidean space of dimension N*. Using this dot product and the canonical basis of $\mathbb{R}^N$, each coefficient $\langle \mathbf{x}, \mathbf{e}_j \rangle$ in (B.50) just picks out one entry from the column vector $\mathbf{x}$, thus $\mathbf{x} = \sum_{j=1}^{N} [\mathbf{x}]_j \mathbf{e}_j$.

Pythagorean Theorem

A rather useful result concerning norms arising from dot products is the *Pythagorean Theorem*. In its general form, it reads as follows:

Theorem B.9 (Pythagoras) *If* $\mathbf{e}_1, \ldots, \mathbf{e}_q$ *are orthonormal (they need not form a basis), then*

$$\|\mathbf{x}\|^2 = \sum_{i=1}^{q} \langle \mathbf{x}, \mathbf{e}_i \rangle^2 + \left\| \mathbf{x} - \sum_{i=1}^{q} \langle \mathbf{x}, \mathbf{e}_i \rangle \mathbf{e}_i \right\|^2 . \tag{B.52}$$

Now that we have a dot product, we are in a position to summarize a number of useful facts about matrices.

- It can readily be verified that for the canonical dot product, we have

$$\langle \mathbf{x}, A\mathbf{x}' \rangle = \left\langle A^\top \mathbf{x}, \mathbf{x}' \right\rangle \tag{B.53}$$

for all $\mathbf{x}, \mathbf{x}' \in \mathcal{H}$.

Symmetric Matrices

- Matrices A such that $A = A^\top$ are called *symmetric*. Due to (B.53), they can be swapped between the two arguments of the canonical dot product without changing its value

- Symmetric matrices A that satisfy

$$\langle \mathbf{x}, A\mathbf{x} \rangle \geq 0 \tag{B.54}$$

for all $\mathbf{x} \in \mathcal{H}$ are called *positive definite* (cf. Remark 2.16 for a note on this terminology)

- Another interesting class of matrices are the *unitary* (or *orthogonal*) matrices. A unitary matrix U is characterized by an inverse U^{-1} that equals its transpose $U^\top$. Unitary matrices thus satisfy

$$\langle U\mathbf{x}, U\mathbf{x}' \rangle = \left\langle U^\top U\mathbf{x}, \mathbf{x}' \right\rangle = \langle U^{-1}U\mathbf{x}, \mathbf{x}' \rangle = \langle \mathbf{x}, \mathbf{x}' \rangle \tag{B.55}$$

for all $\mathbf{x}, \mathbf{x}' \in \mathcal{H}$; in other words, they leave the canonical dot product invariant

- A final aspect of matrix theory of interest in machine learning is matrix diagonalization. Suppose A is a linear operator. If there exists a basis $\mathbf{v}_1, \ldots, \mathbf{v}_N$ of $\mathcal{H}$ such that for all $i = 1, \ldots, N$,

$$A\mathbf{v}_i = \lambda_i \mathbf{v}_i, \tag{B.56}$$

Eigenvalue and Eigenvector

with $\lambda_i \in \mathbb{R}$, then A can be *diagonalized*: written in the basis $\mathbf{v}_1, \ldots, \mathbf{v}_N$, we have $A_{ij} = 0$ for all $i \neq j$ and $A_{ii} = \lambda_i$ for all i. The coefficients λ_i are called *eigenvalues*, and the $\mathbf{v}_i$ *eigenvectors*, of A

Let us now consider the special case of symmetric matrices. These can always be diagonalized, and their eigenvectors can be chosen to form an orthonormal basis with respect to the canonical dot product. If we form a matrix V with these eigenvectors as columns, then we obtain the diagonal matrix as $VAV^\top$.

Rayleigh's principle states that the smallest eigenvalue $\lambda_{\min}$ coincides with the minimum of

$$R(\mathbf{v}) := \frac{\langle \mathbf{v}, A\mathbf{v} \rangle}{\langle \mathbf{v}, \mathbf{v} \rangle}. \tag{B.57}$$

The minimizer of R is an eigenvector with eigenvalue $\lambda_{\min}$. Likewise, the largest eigenvalue and its corresponding eigenvector can be found by maximizing R.
Functions $f : I \to \mathbb{R}$, where $I \subset \mathbb{R}$, can be defined on symmetric matrices A with eigenvalues in I. To this end, we diagonalize A and apply f to all diagonal elements (the eigenvalues).
Since a symmetric matrix is positive definite if and only if all its eigenvalues are nonnegative, we may choose $f(x) = \sqrt{x}$ to obtain the unique *square root* $\sqrt{A}$ of a positive definite matrix A.

Many statements about matrices generalize in some form to operators on spaces of arbitrary dimension; for instance, Mercer's theorem (Theorem 2.10) can be viewed as a generalized version of a matrix diagonalization, with eigenvectors (or eigenfunctions) ψ_j satisfying $\int_{\mathcal{X}} k(x, x')\psi_j(x')\, d\mu(x') = \lambda_j \psi_j(x)$.

B.3 Functional Analysis

Functional analysis combines concepts from linear algebra and analysis. Consequently, it is also concerned with questions of convergence and continuity. For a detailed treatment, cf. [429, 306, 112].

Cauchy Sequence

Definition B.10 (Cauchy Sequence) *A sequence* $(\mathbf{x}_i)_i := (\mathbf{x}_i)_{i \in \mathbb{N}} = (\mathbf{x}_1, \mathbf{x}_2, \ldots)$ *in a normed space* $\mathcal{H}$ *is said to be a* Cauchy sequence *if for every* $\epsilon > 0$, *there exists an* $n \in \mathbb{N}$ *such that for all* $n', n'' > n$, *we have* $\|\mathbf{x}_{n'} - \mathbf{x}_{n''}\| < \epsilon$.

A Cauchy sequence is said to converge to a point $\mathbf{x} \in \mathcal{H}$ *if* $\|\mathbf{x}_n - \mathbf{x}\| \to 0$ *as* $n \to \infty$.

Banach / Hilbert Space

Definition B.11 (Completeness, Banach Space, Hilbert Space) *A space* $\mathcal{H}$ *is called* complete *if all Cauchy sequences in the space converge.*

A Banach space *is a complete normed space; a* Hilbert space *is a complete dot product space.*

The simplest example of a Hilbert space (and thus also of a Banach space) is again $\mathbb{R}^N$. More interesting Hilbert spaces, however, have *infinite* dimensionality. A number of surprising things can happen in this case. To prevent the nasty ones, we generally assume that the Hilbert spaces we deal with are *separable*,[13] which means that there exists a countable dense subset. A *dense subset* is a set S such that each element of $\mathcal{H}$ is the limit of a sequence in S. Equivalently, the completion of

13. One of the positive side effects of this is that we essentially only have to deal with one Hilbert space: all separable Hilbert spaces are equivalent, in a sense that we won't define presently.

S equals $\mathcal{H}$. Here, the *completion* $\overline{S}$ is obtained by adding all limit points of Cauchy sequences to the set.[14]

Example B.12 (Hilbert Space of Functions) *Let $C[a,b]$ denote the real-valued continuous functions on the interval $[a,b]$. For $f,g \in C[a,b]$,*

$$\langle f,g\rangle := \int_a^b f(x)g(x)\,dx \tag{B.58}$$

L2[a, b]

defines a dot product. The completion of $C[a,b]$ in the corresponding norm is the Hilbert space $L_2[a,b]$ of measurable functions[15] that are square integrable;

$$\int_a^b f(x)^2\,dx < \infty. \tag{B.59}$$

This notion can be generalized to $L_2(\mathbb{R}^N, P)$. Here, P is a Borel measure on $\mathbb{R}^N$, and the dot product is given by

$$\langle f,g\rangle := \int_{\mathbb{R}^N} f(x)g(x)\,dP(x). \tag{B.60}$$

One of the most useful properties of Hilbert spaces is that as in the case of finite-dimensional vector spaces, it is possible to compute projections. Before stating the theorem, recall that a subset M of $\mathcal{H}$ is called *closed* if every convergent sequence in $\mathcal{H}$ with elements that lie in M also has its limit in M. Any closed subspace of a Hilbert space is itself a Hilbert space.

Projections

Theorem B.13 (Projections in Hilbert Spaces) *Let $\mathcal{H}$ be a Hilbert space and M be a closed subspace. Then every $\mathbf{x} \in \mathcal{H}$ can be written uniquely as $\mathbf{x} = \mathbf{z} + \mathbf{z}^\perp$, where $\mathbf{z} \in M$ and $\langle \mathbf{z}^\perp, \mathbf{t}\rangle = 0$ for all $\mathbf{t} \in M$. The vector $\mathbf{z}$ is the unique element of M minimizing $\|\mathbf{x}-\mathbf{z}\|$; it is called the* projection $P\mathbf{x} := \mathbf{z}$ of $\mathbf{x}$ onto M. *The projection operator P is a linear map.*

Another feature of Hilbert spaces is that they come with a useful generalization of the concept of a basis. Recall that a basis is a set of vectors that allows us to uniquely write each $\mathbf{x}$ as a linear combination. In the context of infinite-dimensional Hilbert spaces, this is quite restrictive (note that linear combinations (B.28) always involve *finitely* many terms) and leads to bases that are not countable. Therefore, we usually work with what is called a *complete orthonormal system* or an *orthonormal basis (ONB)*.[16] Formally, this is defined as an orthonormal set S in a Hilbert space $\mathcal{H}$ with the property that no other nonzero vector in $\mathcal{H}$ is orthogonal to all elements of S.

Orthonormal Basis

14. Note that the completion is denoted by the same symbol as the set complement. Mathematics is full of this kind of symbol overloading, which adds to the challenge.
15. These are not strictly speaking individual functions, but equivalence classes of functions that are allowed to differ on sets of measure zero.
16. These systems are often referred to as *bases* in the context of Hilbert spaces. This is slightly misleading, since they are not bases in the vector space sense.

Gram-Schmidt Orthonormalization

Separable Hilbert spaces possess countable ONBs, which can be constructed using the *Gram-Schmidt* procedure. Suppose $\{\mathbf{v}_i\}_{i\in\Lambda}$ is a linearly independent set of vectors with a span dense in $\mathcal{H}$, with Λ being a countable index set. A countable ONB $\mathbf{e}_1, \mathbf{e}_2, \ldots$ can then be constructed as follows:

$$\begin{aligned}
\mathbf{e}_1 &:= \mathbf{v}_1/\|\mathbf{v}_1\|,\\
\mathbf{e}_2 &:= (\mathbf{v}_2 - P_1\mathbf{v}_2)/\|\mathbf{v}_2 - P_1\mathbf{v}_2\|,\\
\mathbf{e}_3 &:= (\mathbf{v}_3 - P_2\mathbf{v}_3)/\|\mathbf{v}_3 - P_2\mathbf{v}_3\|,\\
&\vdots \quad \vdots
\end{aligned} \tag{B.61}$$

Here, we use the shorthand P_n for the operator

$$P_n\mathbf{x} := \sum_{i=1}^{n} \langle \mathbf{e}_i, \mathbf{x}\rangle\, \mathbf{e}_i. \tag{B.62}$$

It is easy to show that P_n projects onto the subspace spanned by $\mathbf{e}_1, \ldots, \mathbf{e}_n$.

If the $\mathbf{v}_1, \mathbf{v}_2, \ldots$ are not linearly independent, then it is possible that $\mathbf{v}_{n+1} - P_n\mathbf{v}_{n+1} = 0$, which means $\mathbf{v}_{n+1}$ can be expressed as a linear combination of $\mathbf{v}_1, \ldots, \mathbf{v}_n$. In this case, we simply leave out $\mathbf{v}_{n+1}$ and proceed with $\mathbf{v}_{n+2}$, shifting all subsequent indices by 1.

ONB Expansion

Using an ONB, we can give basis expansions in infinite-dimensional Hilbert spaces, which look just like basis expansions in the finite-dimensional case. For separable Hilbert spaces, the index set Λ is countable.

Theorem B.14 (ONB Expansions & Parseval's Relation) *Let $\{\mathbf{e}_i\}_{i\in\Lambda}$ be an ONB of the Hilbert space $\mathcal{H}$. Then for each $\mathbf{x} \in \mathcal{H}$,*

$$\mathbf{x} = \sum_{i\in\Lambda} \langle \mathbf{e}_i, \mathbf{x}\rangle\, \mathbf{e}_i \tag{B.63}$$

and

$$\|\mathbf{x}\|^2 = \sum_{i\in\Lambda} \langle \mathbf{e}_i, \mathbf{x}\rangle^2 . \tag{B.64}$$

Note that this generalizes the Pythagorean Theorem to the infinite-dimensional case.

Kernel PCA

Let us describe an application of this result, with the dual purpose of demonstrating a standard trick from functional analysis, and mathematically justifying a crucial step in the "kernelization" of many algorithms. In Kernel PCA, we need to solve an eigenvalue problem of the form (cf. (14.7))

$$\lambda\mathbf{v} = \mathbf{C}\mathbf{v}, \tag{B.65}$$

and we know a priori that all solutions $\mathbf{v}$ lie in the span of $\mathbf{x}_1, \ldots, \mathbf{x}_m \in \mathcal{H}$. In Chapter 14, we argued that this means we may instead consider the set of equations

$$\langle \mathbf{x}_n, \mathbf{v}_1\rangle = \langle \mathbf{x}_n, \mathbf{v}_2\rangle \text{ for all } n = 1, \ldots, m, \tag{B.66}$$

where we use the shorthand $\mathbf{v}_1 = \lambda\mathbf{v}$ and $\mathbf{v}_2 = \mathbf{C}\mathbf{v}$.

We are now in a position to prove this formally. It suffices to consider the case where the $\{\mathbf{x}_1, \ldots, \mathbf{x}_m\}$ are orthonormal. If they are not, we first apply the Gram-Schmidt procedure to construct an orthonormal set $\{\mathbf{e}_1, \ldots, \mathbf{e}_n\}$. The latter is a basis for the span of the $\mathbf{x}_i$, hence each $\mathbf{x}_i$ can be written as a linear combination of the $\mathbf{e}_i$. Conversely, each $\mathbf{e}_i$ can be written as a linear combination of the $\mathbf{x}_i$ by construction (cf. (B.61)). Therefore, (B.66) is actually equivalent to the corresponding statement for the orthonormal set $\{\mathbf{e}_1, \ldots, \mathbf{e}_n\}$.

In the orthonormal case, the Parseval relation (B.64), applied to the completion of the span of the $\mathbf{x}_i$ (which is a Hilbert space), implies that (we replace $x = \mathbf{v}_1 - \mathbf{v}_2$)

$$\|\mathbf{v}_1 - \mathbf{v}_2\|^2 = \sum_{i=1}^{m} (\langle \mathbf{x}_i, \mathbf{v}_1 \rangle - \langle \mathbf{x}_i, \mathbf{v}_2 \rangle)^2. \tag{B.67}$$

Therefore $\mathbf{v}_1 = \mathbf{v}_2$ if and only if (14.8) holds true. In a nutshell, the ONB expansion coefficients are unique and completely characterize each vector in a Hilbert space.

We next revisit the L_2 space. Since we will be using the complex exponential, we consider for a moment the case where $\mathcal{H}$ is a Hilbert space over $\mathbb{C}$ rather than $\mathbb{R}$.

Fourier Series

Example B.15 (Fourier Series) *The collection of functions*[17]

$$\left\{ \frac{e^{ix}}{\sqrt{2\pi}}, \frac{e^{-ix}}{\sqrt{2\pi}}, \frac{e^{2ix}}{\sqrt{2\pi}}, \frac{e^{-2ix}}{\sqrt{2\pi}}, \ldots \right\} \tag{B.68}$$

is an ONB for $L_2[0, 2\pi]$. *As a consequence of Theorem B.14, we can thus expand any* $f \in L_2[0, 2\pi]$ *as*

$$\lim_{M \to \infty} \frac{1}{\sqrt{2\pi}} \sum_{n=-M}^{M} c_n e^{inx}, \tag{B.69}$$

where the Fourier coefficients c_n *are given by*[18]

$$c_n = \frac{1}{\sqrt{2\pi}} \int_0^{2\pi} e^{-inx} f(x)\, dx. \tag{B.70}$$

B.3.1 Advanced Topics

ℓ_p^N Spaces

We now move on to concepts that are only used in a few of the chapters; these mainly comprise results that build on [606]. We define normed spaces ℓ_p^N as follows: As vector spaces, they are identical to $\mathbb{R}^N$, but are endowed in addition with p-norms. For $1 \leq p < \infty$, these p-norms are defined as

$$\|x\|_{\ell_p^N} := \|x\|_p = \left(\sum_{j=1}^{N} |x_j|^p \right)^{1/p}; \tag{B.71}$$

17. Here i is the imaginary unit $\sqrt{-1}$.
18. Comparing this to (B.60), we note that there is an unexpected minus sign in e^{-inx}. This is due to the fact that in the complex case, the dot product (B.60) includes a complex conjugation in the first argument.

for $p = \infty$, as

$$\|x\|_{\ell_\infty^N} := \|x\|_\infty = \max_{j=1,\dots,N} |x_j|. \tag{B.72}$$

We use the shorthand ℓ_p to denote the case where $N = \infty$. In this case, it is understood that ℓ_p contains all sequences with finite p-norm. For $N = \infty$, the max in (B.72) is replaced by a sup.

Often the above notations are also used in the case where $0 < p < 1$. In that case, however, we are no longer dealing with norms.

Suppose $\mathcal{F}$ is a class of functions $f : \mathcal{X} \to \mathbb{R}$. The ℓ_∞^N norm of $f \in \mathcal{F}$ *with respect to a sample* $X = (x_1, \dots, x_m)$ is defined as

$$\|f\|_{\ell_\infty^X} := \max_{i=1,\dots,m} |f(x_i)|. \tag{B.73}$$

Likewise,

$$\|f\|_{\ell_p^X} = \|(f(x_1), \dots, f(x_m))\|_{\ell_p^m}. \tag{B.74}$$

L_p Spaces

Given some set $\mathcal{X}$ with a σ-algebra, a measure μ on $\mathcal{X}$, some p in the range $1 \leq p < \infty$, and a function $f : \mathcal{X} \to \mathbb{R}$, we define

$$\|f\|_{L_p(\mathcal{X})} := \|f\|_p := \left(\int |f(x)|^p d\mu(x) \right)^{1/p} \tag{B.75}$$

if the integral exists, and

$$\|f\|_{L_\infty(\mathcal{X})} := \|f\|_\infty := \operatorname*{ess\,sup}_{x \in \mathcal{X}} |f(x)|. \tag{B.76}$$

Here, ess sup denotes the essential supremum; that is, the smallest number that upper bounds $|f(x)|$ almost everywhere.

For $1 \leq p \leq \infty$, we define

$$L_p(\mathcal{X}) := \{ f : \mathcal{X} \to \mathbb{R} \mid \|f\|_{L_p(\mathcal{X})} < \infty \}. \tag{B.77}$$

Here, we have glossed over some details: in fact, these spaces do not consist of functions, but of equivalence classes of functions differing on sets of measure zero. An interesting exception to this rule are reproducing kernel Hilbert spaces (Section 2.2.3). For these, we know that point evaluation of all functions in the space is well-defined: it is determined by the reproducing kernel, see (2.29).

Let $\mathfrak{L}(E, G)$ be the set of all bounded linear operators T between the normed spaces $(E, \|\cdot\|_E)$ and $(G, \|\cdot\|_G)$; in other words, operators such that the image of the (closed) unit ball,

$$U_E := \{ x \in E \mid \|x\|_E \leq 1 \}, \tag{B.78}$$

is bounded. The smallest such bound is called the *operator norm*,

$$\|T\| := \sup_{x \in U_E} \|Tx\|_G. \tag{B.79}$$

References

[1] P. Abrahamsen. A review of Gaussian random fields and correlation functions. Rapport 917, Norwegian Computing Center, Oslo, 1992. www.nr.no/publications/917_Rapport.ps.

[2] Y. S. Abu-Mostafa. Hints. *Neural Computation*, 7(4):639–671, 1995.

[3] R. J. Adler. *The Geometry of Random Fields*. Wiley Series in Probability and Mathematical Statistics. Wiley, New York, 1981.

[4] M. A. Aizerman, É. M. Braverman, and L. I. Rozonoér. Theoretical foundations of the potential function method in pattern recognition learning. *Automation and Remote Control*, 25:821–837, 1964.

[5] E. L. Allwein, R. E. Schapire, and Y. Singer. Reducing multiclass to binary: a unifying approach for margin classifiers. *Journal of Machine Learning Research*, pages 113–141, 2000. http://www.jmlr.org.

[6] N. Alon, S. Ben-David, N. Cesa-Bianchi, and D. Haussler. Scale-sensitive dimensions, uniform convergence, and learnability. *Journal of the ACM*, 44(4):615–631, 1997.

[7] S.-I. Amari. A theory of adaptive pattern classifiers. *IEEE Transactions on Electronic Computers*, 16:299–307, 1967.

[8] S.-I. Amari. Mathematical foundations of neurocomputing. *Proceedings of the IEEE*, 78(9):1443–1463, 1990.

[9] S.-I. Amari. Natural gradient works efficiently in learning. *Neural Computation*, 10(2):251–276, 1998.

[10] S.-I. Amari and S. Wu. Improving support vector machines by modifying kernel functions. Technical report, RIKEN, 1999.

[11] E. Anderson, Z. Bai, C. Bischof, J. Demmel, J. Dongarra, J. Du Croz, A. Greenbaum, S. Hammarling, A. McKenney, S. Ostrouchov, and D. Sorensen. *LAPACK Users' Guide*. SIAM, Philadelphia, second edition, 1995.

[12] J. K. Anlauf and M. Biehl. The AdaTron: an adaptive perceptron algorithm. *Europhysics Letters*, 10:687–692, 1989.

[13] M. Anthony. Probabilistic analysis of learning in artificial neural networks: The PAC model and its variants. *Neural Computing Surveys*, 1:1–47, 1997. http://www.icsi.berkeley.edu/~jagota/NCS.

[14] M. Anthony and P. L. Bartlett. *Neural Network Learning: Theoretical Foundations*. Cambridge University Press, 1999.

[15] M. Aoki. *Introduction to Optimization Techniques*. MacMillan, Inc., New York, 1970.

[16] N. Aronszajn. Theory of reproducing kernels. *Transactions of the American Mathematical Society*, 68:337–404, 1950.

[17] R. Ash. *Information Theory*. Interscience Publishers, New York, 1965.

[18] H. Baird. Document image defect models. In *Proceedings, IAPR Workshop on Syntactic and Structural Pattern Recognition*, pages 38–46, Murray Hill, NJ, 1990.

[19] N. Barabino, M. Pallavicini, A. Petrolini, M. Pontil, and A. Verri. Support vector machines vs multi-layer perceptrons in particle identification. In M. Verleysen, editor, *Proceedings ESANN*, pages 257–262, Brussels, 1999. D Facto.

[20] P. L. Bartlett and S. Ben-David. Hardness results for neural network approximation problems. In P. Fischer and H. U. Simon, editors, *Proceedings of the 4th European Conference on Computational Learning Theory*, volume 1572 of *LNAI*, pages 50–62, Berlin, 1999. Springer.

[21] P. L. Bartlett, T. Linder, and G. Lugosi. The minimax distortion redundancy in empirical

quantizer design. *IEEE Transactions on Information Theory*, 44(5):1802–1813, 1998.

[22] P. L. Bartlett, P. Long, and R. Williamson. Fat-shattering and the learnability of real-valued functions. *Journal of Computer and System Sciences*, 52(3):434–452, 1996.

[23] P. L. Bartlett and B. Schölkopf. Some kernels for structured data. Technical report, Biowulf Technologies, 2001.

[24] P. L. Bartlett and J. Shawe-Taylor. Generalization performance of support vector machines and other pattern classifiers. In B. Schölkopf, C. J. C. Burges, and A. J. Smola, editors, *Advances in Kernel Methods — Support Vector Learning*, pages 43–54, Cambridge, MA, 1999. MIT Press.

[25] O. Barzilay and V. L. Brailovsky. On domain knowledge and feature selection using a support vector machine. *Pattern Recognition Letters*, 20:475–484, 1999.

[26] O. A. Bashkirov, É. M. Braverman, and I. B. Muchnik. Theoretical foundations of the potential function method in pattern recognition learning. *Automation and Remote Control*, 25:629–631, 1964.

[27] G. Baudat and F. Anouar. Generalized discriminant analysis using a kernel approach. *Neural Computation*, 12:2385–2404, 2000.

[28] J. Baxter. The canonical distortion measure for vector quantization and function approximation. In *Proceedings of the 14th International Conference on Machine Learning*, 1997.

[29] R. E. Bellman. *Adaptive Control Processes*. Princeton University Press, Princeton, NJ, 1961.

[30] S. Belongie, J. Malik, and J. Puzicha. Matching shapes. In *Eighth IEEE International Conference on Computer Vision*, Vancouver, Canada, 2001. To appear.

[31] S. Ben-David, N. Eiron, and H. U. Simon. The computational complexity of densest region detection. In N. Cesa-Bianchi and S. Goldman, editors, *Proceedings of the 13th Annual Conference on Computational Learning Theory*, pages 255–265, San Francisco, 2000. Morgan Kaufman.

[32] S. Ben-David, E. Kushilevitz, and Y. Mansour. Online learning versus offline learning. *Machine Learning*, 29:45–63, 1997.

[33] S. Ben-David and M. Lindenbaum. Learning distributions by their density levels: A paradigm for learning without a teacher. *Journal of Computer and System Sciences*, 55:171–182, 1997.

[34] S. Ben-David and H. Simon. Efficient learning of linear perceptrons. In T. K. Leen, T. G. Dietterich, and V. Tresp, editors, *Advances in Neural Information Processing Systems 13*. MIT Press, 2001.

[35] A. Ben-Hur, D. Horn, H. Siegelmann, and V. Vapnik. A support vector method for hierarchical clustering. In T. K. Leen, T. G. Dietterich, and V. Tresp, editors, *Advances in Neural Information Processing Systems 13*. MIT Press, 2001.

[36] http://ida.first.gmd.de/~raetsch/data/benchmarks.htm. Benchmark repository used in several Boosting, KFD and SVM papers.

[37] K. P. Bennett. Combining support vector and mathematical programming methods for induction. In B. Schölkopf, C. J. C. Burges, and A. J. Smola, editors, *Advances in Kernel Methods - SV Learning*, pages 307–326, Cambridge, MA, 1999. MIT Press.

[38] K. P. Bennett and E. J. Bredensteiner. Duality and geometry in SVM classifiers. In P. Langley, editor, *Proceedings of the 17th International Conference on Machine Learning*, pages 57–64, San Francisco, California, 2000. Morgan Kaufmann.

[39] K. P. Bennett, A. Demiriz, and J. Shawe-Taylor. A column generation algorithm for boosting. In P. Langley, editor, *Proceedings of the 17th International Conference on Machine Learning*, San Francisco, 2000. Morgan Kaufman.

[40] K. P. Bennett and O. L. Mangasarian. Robust linear programming discrimination of two linearly inseparable sets. *Optimization Methods and Software*, 1:23–34, 1992.

[41] K. P. Bennett and O. L. Mangasarian. Multicategory separation via linear programming. *Optimization Methods and Software*, 3:27–39, 1993.

[42] C. Berg, J. P. R. Christensen, and P. Ressel. *Harmonic Analysis on Semigroups*. Springer-Verlag, New York, 1984.

[43] J. O. Berger. *Statistical Decision theory and Bayesian Analysis*. Springer Verlag, New York, 1985.

[44] S. Bernstein. Sur les fonctions absolument monotones. *Acta Mathematica*, 52:1–66, 1929.

[45] D. P. Bertsekas. *Nonlinear Programming*. Athena Scientific, Belmont, MA, 1995.

[46] R. Bhatia. *Matrix Analysis*. Springer Verlag, New York, 1997.

[47] P. J. Bickel, C. A. J. Klaassen, Y. Ritov, and J. A. Wellner. *Efficient and adaptive estimation for semiparametric models*. J. Hopkins Press, Baltimore, ML, 1994.

[48] L. Birgé. On estimating a density using Hellinger distance and some other strange facts. *Probability Theory and Related Fields*, 71:271–291, 1986.

[49] C. M. Bishop. *Neural Networks for Pattern Recognition*. Clarendon Press, Oxford, 1995.

[50] C. M. Bishop. Training with noise is equivalent to Tikhonov regularization. *Neural Computation*, 7:108–116, 1995.

[51] C. M. Bishop, M. Svensén, and C. K. I. Williams. Developments of the generative topographic mapping. *Neurocomputing*, 21:203–224, 1998.

[52] C. M. Bishop, M. Svensén, and C. K. I. Williams. GTM: The generative topographic mapping. *Neural Computation*, 10(1):215–234, 1998.

[53] C. M. Bishop and M. E. Tipping. Variational relevance vector machines. In *Proceedings of 16th Conference on Uncertainty in Artificial Intelligence UAI'2000*, 2000.

[54] K. L. Blackmore, R. C. Williamson, I. M. Mareels, and W. A. Sethares. Online learning via congregational gradient descent. In *Proceedings of the 8th Annual Conference on Computational Learning Theory (COLT'95)*, pages 265–272, New York, NY, USA, 1995. ACM Press.

[55] K. L. Blackmore, R. C. Williamson, and I. M. Y. Mareels. Decision region approximation by polynomials or neural networks. *IEEE Transactions on Information Theory*, 43:903–907, 1997.

[56] C. L. Blake and C. J. Merz. UCI repository of machine learning databases, 1998. http://www.ics.uci.edu/~mlearn/MLRepository.html.

[57] V. Blanz, B. Schölkopf, H. Bülthoff, C. Burges, V. Vapnik, and T. Vetter. Comparison of view-based object recognition algorithms using realistic 3D models. In C. von der Malsburg, W. von Seelen, J. C. Vorbrüggen, and B. Sendhoff, editors, *Artificial Neural Networks — ICANN'96*, pages 251–256, Berlin, 1996. Springer Lecture Notes in Computer Science, Vol. 1112.

[58] V. Blanz, V. Vapnik, and C. Burges. Multiclass discrimination with an extended support vector machine. Talk given at AT&T Bell Labs, 1995.

[59] V. Blanz and T. Vetter. A morphable model for the synthesis of 3d faces. In *SIGGRAPH'99 Conference Proceedings*, pages 187–194, Los Angeles, 1999. ACM Press.

[60] S. Bochner. *Lectures on Fourier integral*. Princeton Univ. Press, Princeton, New Jersey, 1959.

[61] H. G. Bock. Randwertproblemmethoden zur Parameteridentifizierung in Systemen nichtlinearer Differentialgleichungen. *Bonner Mathematische Schriften*, 183, 1987.

[62] B. E. Boser, I. M. Guyon, and V. Vapnik. A training algorithm for optimal margin classifiers. In D. Haussler, editor, *Proceedings of the 5th Annual ACM Workshop on Computational Learning Theory*, pages 144–152, Pittsburgh, PA, July 1992. ACM Press.

[63] M. Boshernitzan. An extension of Hardy's class L of orders of infinity. *Journal d'Analyse Mathematique*, 39:235–255, 1981.

[64] L. Bottou, C. Cortes, J. S. Denker, H. Drucker, I. Guyon, L. D. Jackel, Y. LeCun, U. A. Müller, E. Säckinger, P. Simard, and V. Vapnik. Comparison of classifier methods: a case study in handwritten digit recognition. In *Proceedings of the 12th International Conference on Pattern Recognition and Neural Networks, Jerusalem*, pages 77–87. IEEE Computer Society Press, 1994.

[65] L. Bottou and V. Vapnik. Local learning algorithms. *Neural Computation*, 4(6):888–900, 1992.

[66] S. Boucheron, G. Lugosi, and S. Massart. A sharp concentration inequality with applications. *Random Structures and Algorithms*, 16:277–292, 2000.

[67] O. Bousquet and A. Elisseeff. Algorithmic stability and generalization performance. In T. K. Leen, T. G. Dietterich, and V. Tresp, editors, *Advances in Neural Information Processing Systems 13*. MIT Press, 2001.

[68] O. Bousquet and A. Elisseeff. Stability and generalization. *Journal of Machine Learning Research*, 2001. Submitted.

[69] R. N. Bracewell. *The Fourier transform and its applications*. McGraw-Hill, New York, 1978.

[70] P. S. Bradley and O. L. Mangasarian. Feature selection via concave minimization and support vector machines. In J. Shavlik, editor, *Machine Learning Proceedings of the Fifteenth International Conference(ICML '98)*, pages 82–90, San Francisco, California, 1998. Morgan Kaufmann. ftp://ftp.cs.wisc.edu/math-prog/tech-reports/98-03.ps.Z.

[71] P. S. Bradley and O. L. Mangasarian. *k*-plane clustering. Mathematical Programming Technical Report 98-08, University of Wisconsin Madison, 1998.

[72] P. S. Bradley and O. L. Mangasarian. Massive data discrimination via linear support vector machines. Mathematical Programming Technical Report 98-05, University of Wisconsin Madison, 1998.

[73] P. S. Bradley, O. L. Mangasarian, and W. N. Street. Clustering via concave minimization. In *Advances in Neural Information Processing Systems*, volume 9, pages 368–374, Cambridge, MA, 1997. MIT Press.

[74] P. S. Bradley, O. L. Mangasarian, and W. N. Street. Feature selection via mathematical programming. *INFORMS Journal on Computing*, 10(2):209–217, 1998. ftp://ftp.cs.wisc.edu/math-prog/tech-reports/95-21.ps.Z.

[75] B. Bradshaw, B. Schölkopf, and J. Platt. Kernel methods for extracting local image semantics. Preprint, 2001.

[76] V. L. Brailovsky, O. Barzilay, and R. Shahave. On global, local, mixed and neighborhood kernels for support vector machines. *Pattern Recognition Letters*, 20:1183–1190, 1999.

[77] L. Breiman. *Probability*. Addison-Wesley, Reading, MA, 1968.

[78] K. Briggs. Another universal differential equation. Submitted to *Electronic Journal of Differential Equations*, 2000.

[79] J. Bromley and E. Säckinger. Neural-network and k-nearest-neighbor classifiers. Technical Report 11359–910819–16TM, AT&T, 1991.

[80] D. S. Broomhead and D. Lowe. Multivariable functional interpolation and adaptive networks. *Complex Systems*, 2:321–355, 1988.

[81] M. P. S. Brown, W. N. Grundy, D. Lin, N. Cristianini, C. Sugnet, T. S. Furey, M. Ares, and D. Haussler. Knowledge-based analysis of microarray gene expression data using support vector machines. *Proceedings of the National Academy of Sciences*, 97(1):262–267, 2000.

[82] J. M. Buhmann. Data clustering and learning. In M. A. Arbib, editor, *The Handbook of Brain Theory and Neural Networks*, pages 278–281. MIT Press, 1995.

[83] J. R. Bunch and L. Kaufman. Some stable methods for calculating inertia and solving symmetric linear systems. *Mathematics of Computation*, 31:163–179, 1977.

[84] C. J. C. Burges. Simplified support vector decision rules. In L. Saitta, editor, *Proceedings of the 13th International Conference on Machine Learning*, pages 71–77, San Mateo, CA, 1996. Morgan Kaufmann.

[85] C. J. C. Burges. A tutorial on support vector machines for pattern recognition. *Data Mining and Knowledge Discovery*, 2(2):121–167, 1998.

[86] C. J. C. Burges. Geometry and invariance in kernel based methods. In B. Schölkopf, C. J. C. Burges, and A. J. Smola, editors, *Advances in Kernel Methods — Support Vector Learning*, pages 89–116, Cambridge, MA, 1999. MIT Press.

[87] C. J. C. Burges and B. Schölkopf. Improving the accuracy and speed of support vector learning machines. In M. Mozer, M. Jordan, and T. Petsche, editors, *Advances in Neural Information Processing Systems 9*, pages 375–381, Cambridge, MA, 1997. MIT Press.

[88] C. J. C. Burges and V. Vapnik. A new method for constructing artificial neural networks. Interim technical report, ONR contract N00014-94-c-0186, AT&T Bell Laboratories, 1995.

[89] B. Carl. Inequalities of Bernstein-Jackson-type and the degree of compactness of operators in Banach spaces. *Ann. de l'Institut Fourier*, 35(3):79–118, 1985.

[90] B. Carl and I. Stephani. *Entropy, compactness, and the approximation of operators*. Cambridge University Press, Cambridge, UK, 1990.

[91] O. Catoni. Gibbs estimators. *Probability Theory and Related Fields*, 2001. Forthcoming.

[92] O. Catoni. Universal aggregation rules with sharp oracle inequalities. *Annals of Statistics*, 2001. Forthcoming.

[93] G. Cauwenberghs and T. Poggio. Incremental and decremental support vector machine learning. In *Advances in Neural Processing Systems*, 2001.

[94] G. J. Chaitin. On the length of programs for computing finite binary sequences. *Journal of the ACM*, 13(4):547–569, October 1966.

[95] A. Chalimourda, B. Schölkopf, and A. J. Smola. Choosing ν in support vector regression with different noise models — theory and experiments. In *Proceedings of the International Joint Conference on Neural Networks*, Como, Italy, 2000.

[96] C.-C. Chang, C.-W. Hsu, and C.-J. Lin. The analysis of decomposition methods for support

vector machines. *IEEE Transactions on Neural Networks*, 11(4):1003–1008, 2000.

[97] C.-C. Chang and C.-J. Lin. IJCNN 2001 challenge: generalization ability and text decoding. In *Proceedings of the International Joint Conference on Neural Networks*, Washington, DC, 2001. IEEE Press.

[98] C.-C. Chang and C.-J. Lin. Training ν-support vector classifiers: Theory and algorithms. *Neural Computation*, 13(9):2119–2147, 2001.

[99] O. Chapelle, P. Haffner, and V. Vapnik. SVMs for histogram-based image classification. *IEEE Transactions on Neural Networks*, 10(5), 1999.

[100] O. Chapelle and B. Schölkopf. Incorporating invariances in nonlinear SVMs. Submitted to NIPS'01. Earlier version presented at the NIPS'00 workshop on Learning with Kernels, 2001.

[101] O. Chapelle and V. Vapnik. Model selection for support vector machines. In S. A. Solla, T. K. Leen, and K.-R. Müller, editors, *Advances in Neural Information Processing Systems 12*. MIT Press, 2000.

[102] O. Chapelle, V. Vapnik, O. Bousquet, and S. Mukherjee. Choosing kernel parameters for support vector machines. *Machine Learning*, 2002. Forthcoming.

[103] O. Chapelle, V. Vapnik, and J. Weston. Transductive inference for estimating values of functions. In S. Solla, T. Leen, and K.-R. Müller, editors, *Advances in Neural Information Processing Systems 12*. MIT press, 2000.

[104] S. Chen, D. Donoho, and M. Saunders. Atomic decomposition by basis pursuit. *SIAM Journal of Scientific Computing*, 20(1):33–61, 1999.

[105] S. Chen and C. J. Harris. Design of the optimal separating hyperplane for the decision feedback equalizer using support vector machines. In *IEEE International Conference on Acoustic, Speech, and Signal Processing*, Istanbul, Turkey, 2000.

[106] V. Cherkassky and F. Mulier. *Learning from Data*. Wiley, New York, 1998.

[107] H. Chernoff. A measure of asymptotic efficiency of tests of a hypothesis based on the sum of observations. *Annals of Mathematical Statistics*, 23:493–507, 1952.

[108] R. Collobert and S. Bengio. Support vector machines for large-scale regression problems. IDIAP-RR 00-17, IDIAP, 2000. Description of SVM Torch Regression Code.

[109] D. Cook, A. Buja, and J. Cabrera. Projection pursuit indices based on orthonormal function expansions. *Journal of Computational and Graphical Statistics*, 2:225–250, 1993.

[110] J. W. Cooley and J. W. Tukey. An algorithm for machine calculation of complex Fourier series. *Mathematics of Computation*, 19:297–301, 1965.

[111] C. Cortes and V. Vapnik. Support vector networks. *Machine Learning*, 20:273–297, 1995.

[112] R. Courant and D. Hilbert. *Methoden der mathematischen Physik*. Springer-Verlag, Berlin, 4th edition, 1993.

[113] T. M. Cover. Geometrical and statistical properties of systems of linear inequalities with applications in pattern recognition. *IEEE Transactions on Electronic Computers*, 14:326–334, 1965.

[114] T. M. Cover and J. A. Thomas. *Elements of Information Theory*. Wiley, New York, 1991.

[115] D. Cox and F. O'Sullivan. Asymptotic analysis of penalized likelihood and related estimators. *Annals of Statistics*, 18:1676–1695, 1990.

[116] T. F. Cox and M. A. A. Cox. *Multidimensional Scaling*. Chapman and Hall, London, 1994.

[117] CPLEX Optimization Inc. Using the CPLEX callable library. Manual, 1994.

[118] H. Cramér. *Mathematical Methods of Statistics*. Princeton University Press, 1946.

[119] K. Crammer and Y. Singer. On the learnability and design of output codes for multiclass problems. In N. Cesa-Bianchi and S. Goldman, editors, *Proceedings of the 13th Conference on Computational Learning Theory (COLT'2000)*, pages 35–46, San Francisco, CA, 2000. Morgan Kaufmann.

[120] M. Crampin and F. A. E. Pirani. *Applicable Differential Geometry*. Cambridge University Press, Cambridge, UK, 1986.

[121] N. A. C. Cressie. *Statistics for Spatial Data*. J. Wiley and Sons, New York, 1993.

[122] D. J. Crisp and C. J. C. Burges. A geometric interpretation of ν-SVM classifiers. In S. A. Solla, T. K. Leen, and K.-R. Müller, editors, *Advances in Neural Information Processing Systems 12*. MIT Press, 2000.

[123] N. Cristianini, C. Campbell, and J. Shawe-Taylor. Dynamically adapting kernels in support

vector machines. In M. S. Kearns, S. A. Solla, and D. A. Cohn, editors, *Advances in Neural Information Processing Systems*, volume 11. MIT Press, Cambridge, MA, 1999.

[124] N. Cristianini, A. Elisseeff, and J. Shawe-Taylor. On optimizing kernel alignment. Technical Report 2001-087, NeuroCOLT, 2001.

[125] N. Cristianini and J. Shawe-Taylor. *An Introduction to Support Vector Machines*. Cambridge University Press, Cambridge, UK, 2000.

[126] N. Cristianini, J. Shawe-Taylor, and H. Lodhi. Latent semantic kernels. In *Proceedings of the 18th International Conference on Machine Learning*, San Francisco, 2001. Morgan Kaufman.

[127] F. Critchley. Multidimensional scaling: a short critique and a new method. In L. C. A. Corsten and J. Hermans, editors, *COMPSTAT*. Physica-Verlag, Vienna, 1978.

[128] L. Csató and M. Opper. Sparse representation for Gaussian process models. In T. K. Leen, T. G. Dietterich, and V. Tresp, editors, *Advances in Neural Information Processing Systems 13*. MIT Press, 2001.

[129] F. Cucker and S. Smale. On the mathematical foundations of learning. *Bulletin of the American Mathematical Society*, pages 1–50, January 2002.

[130] G. B. Dantzig. *Linear Programming and Extensions*. Princeton Univ. Press, Princeton, NJ, 1962.

[131] C. Dawson. The effectiveness of leave-one-out approximations for use with support vector machines. Master's thesis, Australian National University, 2001.

[132] G. Deco and D. Obradovic. *An Information-Theoretic Approach To Neural Computing*. Springer, Berlin, 1996.

[133] D. DeCoste and M. C. Burl. Distortion-invariant recognition via jittered queries. In *Proceedings IEEE Conference on Computer Vision and Pattern Recognition*, 2000.

[134] D. DeCoste and B. Schölkopf. Training invariant support vector machines. *Machine Learning*, 46:161–190, 2002. Also: Technical Report JPL-MLTR-00-1, Jet Propulsion Laboratory, Pasadena, CA, 2000.

[135] A. P. Dempster, N. M. Laird, and D. B. Rubin. Maximum Likelihood from Incomplete Data via the EM Algorithm. *Journal of the Royal Statistical Society B*, 39(1):1–22, 1977.

[136] L. Devroye, L. Györfi, and G. Lugosi. *A Probabilistic Theory of Pattern Recognition*, volume 31 of *Applications of mathematics*. Springer, New York, 1996.

[137] L. Devroye and G. Lugosi. *Combinatorial Methods in Density Estimation*. Springer, 2001.

[138] L. Devroye and G. L. Wise. Detection of abnormal behaviour via nonparametric estimation of the support. *SIAM Journal on Applied Mathematics*, 38(3):480–488, 1980.

[139] P. Diaconis and D. Freedman. Asymptotics of graphical projection pursuit. *Annals of Statistics*, 12(3):793–815, 1984.

[140] K. I. Diamantaras and S. Y. Kung. *Principal Component Neural Networks*. Wiley, New York, 1996.

[141] R. Dietrich, M. Opper, and H. Sompolinsky. Support vectors and statistical mechanics. In A. J. Smola, P. L. Bartlett, B. Schölkopf, and D. Schuurmans, editors, *Advances in Large Margin Classifiers*, pages 359–367, Cambridge, MA, 2000. MIT Press.

[142] T. G. Dietterich and G. Bakiri. Solving multi-class learning problems via error-correcting output codes. *Journal of Artificial Intelligence Research*, 2:263–286, 1995.

[143] C. Domingo and O. Watanabe. MadaBoost: a modification of AdaBoost. In *Proceedings of the 13th Annual Conference on Computational Learning Theory, COLT'00*, pages 180–189, 200.

[144] J. J. Dongarra and L. S. Blackford. ScaLAPACK tutorial. *Lecture Notes in Computer Science*, 1184:204–215, 1996.

[145] J. J. Dongarra, J. Du Croz, S. Duff, and S. Hammarling. A set of level 3 basic linear algebra subprograms. *ACM Transactions on Mathematical Software*, 16:1–17, 1990.

[146] J. J. Dongarra and R. C. Whaley. LAPACK working note 94: A user's guide to the BLACS v1.0. Technical Report UT-CS-95-281, Department of Computer Science, University of Tennessee, March 1995.

[147] H. Drucker, C. J. C. Burges, L. Kaufman, A. J. Smola, and V. Vapnik. Support vector regression machines. In M. Mozer, M. Jordan, and T. Petsche, editors, *Advances in Neural Information Processing Systems 9*, pages 155–161, Cambridge, MA, 1997. MIT Press.

[148] H. Drucker, R. Schapire, and P. Simard. Boosting performance in neural networks. *International Journal of Pattern Recognition and Artificial Intelligence*, 7(4):705–719, 1993.

[149] H. Drucker, B. Shahrary, and D. C. Gibbon. Relevance feedback using support vector machines. In *Proceedings of the 18th International Conference on Machine Learning*. Morgan Kaufmann, 2001.

[150] H. Drucker, D. Wu, and V. Vapnik. Support vector machines for spam categorization. *IEEE Transactions on Neural Networks*, 10(5):1048–1054, 1999.

[151] S. Duane, A. D. Kennedy, B. J. Pendleton, and D. Roweth. Hybrid monte carlo. *Physics Letters B*, 195:216–222, 1995.

[152] R. O. Duda and P. E. Hart. *Pattern Classification and Scene Analysis*. Wiley, New York, 1973.

[153] R. O. Duda, P. E. Hart, and D. G. Stork. *Pattern Classification*. Wiley, New York, second edition, 2001.

[154] R. P. W. Duin, D. de Ridder, and D. M. J. Tax. Featureless pattern classification. *Kybernetika*, 34:399–404, 1998.

[155] S. Dumais. Using SVMs for text categorization. *IEEE Intelligent Systems*, 13(4), 1998. In: Trends and Controversies — Support Vector Machines.

[156] R. Durbin, S. Eddy, A. Krogh, and G. Mitchison. *Biological Sequence Analysis: Probabilistic models of proteins and nucleic acids*. Cambridge University Press, 1998.

[157] N. Dyn. Interpolation and approximation by radial and related functions. In C. K. Chui, L. L. Schumaker, and D. J. Ward, editors, *Approximation Theory, VI*, pages 211–234. Academic Press, New York, 1991.

[158] J. H. J. Einmal and D. M. Mason. Generalized quantile processes. *Annals of Statistics*, 20(2):1062–1078, 1992.

[159] L. Elden and L. Wittmeyer-Koch. *Numerical Analysis: An Introduction*. Academic Press, Cambridge, 1990.

[160] A. Elisseeff. *Etude de la complexité et de la capacité des systèmes d'apprentissage: SVM multi-classes, réseaux de régularisation et réseaux de neurones multi-couches*. PhD thesis, ENS Lyon, 2000.

[161] A. Elisseeff, Y. Guermeur, and H. Paugam-Moisy. Margin error and generalization capabilities of multi-class discriminant systems. NeuroCOLT Technical Report NC-TR-99-051, Royal Holloway College, University of London, UK, 1999.

[162] A. Elisseeff and J. Weston. Kernel methods for multi-labelled classification and categorical regression problems. Technical report, Biowulf Technologies, New York, 2001.

[163] L. Fahrmeir and G. Tutz. *Multivariate Statistical Modelling Based on Generalized Linear Models*. Springer–Verlag, 1994.

[164] K. Fan, I. Glicksburg, and A. J. Hoffman. Systems of inequalities involving convex functions. *American Mathematical Society Proceedings*, 8:617–622, 1957.

[165] W. Feller. *An Introduction to Probability Theory and its Applications*. John Wiley & Sons, New York, 2nd edition, 1971.

[166] T. S. Ferguson. *Mathematical Statistics: A Decision Theoretic Approach*. Academic Press, San Diego, 1967.

[167] M. Ferraro and T. M. Caelli. Lie transformation groups, integral transforms, and invariant pattern recognition. *Spatial Vision*, 8:33–44, 1994.

[168] M. C. Ferris and T. S. Munson. Interior point methods for massive support vector machines. Data Mining Institute Technical Report 00-05, Computer Sciences Department, University of Wisconsin, Madison, Wisconsin, 2000.

[169] S. Fine and K. Scheinberg. Efficient SVM training using low-rank kernel representation. Technical report, IBM Watson Research Center, New York, 2000.

[170] G. Fischer. *Lineare Algebra*. Vieweg, Braunschweig, Germany, 1975.

[171] R. A. Fisher. The use of multiple measurements in taxonomic problems. *Annals of Eugenics*, 7:179–188, 1936.

[172] G. Flake and S. Lawrence. Efficient SVM regression training with SMO. *Machine Learning*, 2002. Forthcoming.

[173] R. Fletcher. *Practical Methods of Optimization*. John Wiley & Sons, New York, 1989.

[174] Y. Freund and R. E. Schapire. Experiments with a new boosting algorithm. In *Proceedings of the 13th International Conference on Machine Learning*, pages 148–146. Morgan Kaufmann, 1996.

[175] Y. Freund and R. E. Schapire. Large margin classification using the perceptron algorithm. In J. Shavlik, editor, *Machine Learning: Proceedings of the Fifteenth International Conference*, San

Francisco, CA, 1998. Morgan Kaufmann.

[176] J. H. Friedman. Exploratory projection pursuit. *Journal of the American Statistical Association*, 82:249–266, 1987.

[177] J. H. Friedman. Regularized discriminant analysis. *Journal of the American Statistical Association*, 84:165–175, 1989.

[178] J. H. Friedman. Another approach to polychotomous classification. Technical report, Department of Statistics and Stanford Linear Accelerator Center, Stanford University, 1996.

[179] J. H. Friedman. Greedy function approximation: a gradient boosting machine. Technical report, Stanford University, 1999.

[180] J. H. Friedman, T. J. Hastie, and R. J. Tibshirani. Additive logistic regression: a statistical view of boosting. Technical report, Stanford University, Dept. of Statistics, 1998.

[181] J. H. Friedman and W. Stuetzle. Projection pursuit regression. *Journal of the American Statistical Association*, 76(376):817–823, December 1981.

[182] J. H. Friedman and J. W. Tukey. A projection pursuit algorithm for exploratory data analysis. *IEEE Transactions on Computers*, C-23(9):881–890, 1974.

[183] T.-T. Frieß, N. Cristianini, and C. Campbell. The kernel adatron algorithm: a fast and simple learning procedure for support vector machines. In J. Shavlik, editor, *15th International Conf. Machine Learning*, pages 188–196. Morgan Kaufmann Publishers, 1998.

[184] T.-T. Frieß and R. F. Harrison. Linear programming support vector machines for pattern classification and regression estimation and the set reduction algorithm. TR RR-706, University of Sheffield, Sheffield, UK, 1998.

[185] T.-T. Frieß and R. F. Harrison. A kernel-based adaline. In M. Verleysen, editor, *Proceedings ESANN*, pages 245–250, Brussels, 1999. D Facto.

[186] K. Fukunaga. *Introduction to Statistical Pattern Recognition*. Academic Press, San Diego, 2nd edition, 1990.

[187] G. Fung and O. L. Mangasarian. Data selection for support vector machine classifiers. In *Proceedings of KDD'2000*, 2000. also: Data Mining Institute Technical Report 00-02, University of Wisconsin, Madison.

[188] G. Fung and O. L. Mangasarian. Proximal support vector machine classifiers. In D. Lee, F. Provost, and R. Srikant, editors, *Proceedings KDD2001: Knowledge Discovery and Data Mining, August 26-29, 2001, San Francisco, CA*, pages 64–70, New York, 2000. Asscociation for Computing Machinery.

[189] G. Fung, O. L. Mangasarian, and A. J. Smola. Minimal kernel classifiers. Technical Report DMI-00-08, Data Mining Institute, University of Wisconsin, Madison, 2000. Submitted to *IEEE Transactions on Pattern Analysis and Machine Intelligence*.

[190] T. S. Furey, N. Duffy, N. Cristianini, D. Bednarski, M. Schummer, and D. Haussler. Support vector machine classification and validation of cancer tissue samples using microarray expression data. *Bioinformatics*, 16(10):906–914, 2000.

[191] E. Gardner. The space of interactions in neural networks. *Journal of Physics A*, 21:257–270, 1988.

[192] E. Gardner and B. Derrida. Optimal storage properties of neural network models. *Journal of Physics A*, 21:271–284, 1988.

[193] A. Gelman, J. B. Carlin, H. S. Stern, and D. B. Rubin. *Bayesian Data Analysis*. Chapman and Hall, London, 1995.

[194] C. Gentile. A new approximate maximal margin classification algorithm. In T. K. Leen, T. G. Dietterich, and V. Tresp, editors, *Advances in Neural Information Processing Systems 13*, pages 500–506. MIT Press, 2001.

[195] A. Gersho and R. M. Gray. *Vector quantization and signal compression*. Kluwer Academic Publishers, Boston, 1992.

[196] M. Gibbs. *Bayesian Gaussian Methods for Regression and Classification*. PhD thesis, University of Cambridge, 1997.

[197] M. Gibbs and D. J. C. Mackay. Efficient implementation of Gaussian processes. Technical report, Cavendish Laboratory, Cambridge, UK, 1997.

[198] M. Gibbs and D. J. C. Mackay. Variational Gaussian process classifiers. Technical report, Cavendish Laboratory, Cambridge, UK, 1998.

[199] M. Girolami. Mercer kernel based clustering in feature space. *IEEE Transactions on Neural*

Networks, 2001. To appear.

[200] M. Girolami. Orthogonal series density estimation and the kernel eigenvalue problem. *Neural Computation*, 2001. To appear.

[201] F. Girosi. On some extensions of radial basis functions and their applications in artificial intelligence. *Computers Math. Applic.*, 24(12):61–80, 1992.

[202] F. Girosi. An equivalence between sparse approximation and support vector machines. *Neural Computation*, 10(6):1455–1480, 1998.

[203] F. Girosi and G. Anzellotti. Rates of convergence for radial basis functions and neural networks. In R. J. Mammone, editor, *Artificial Neural Networks for Speech and Vision*, pages 97–113, London, 1993. Chapman & Hall.

[204] F. Girosi, M. Jones, and T. Poggio. Priors, stabilizers and basis functions: From regularization to radial, tensor and additive splines. A.I. Memo No. 1430, MIT, 1993.

[205] F. Girosi, M. Jones, and T. Poggio. Regularization theory and neural networks architectures. *Neural Computation*, 7(2):219–269, 1995.

[206] H. Goldstein. *Classical Mechanics*. Addison-Wesley, Reading, MA, 1986.

[207] G. H. Golub and C. F. Van Loan. *Matrix Computations*. John Hopkins University Press, Baltimore, MD, 3rd edition, 1996.

[208] Y. Gordon, H. König, and C. Schütt. Geometric and probabilistic estimates for entropy and approximation numbers of operators. *Journal of Approximation Theory*, 49:219–239, 1987.

[209] I. S. Gradshteyn and I. M. Ryzhik. *Table of integrals, series, and products*. Academic Press, New York, 1981.

[210] T. Graepel, R. Herbrich, P. Bollmann-Sdorra, and K. Obermayer. Classification on pairwise proximity data. In M. S. Kearns, S. A. Solla, and D. A. Cohn, editors, *Advances in Neural Information Processing Systems*, volume 11, pages 438–444. MIT Press, Cambridge, MA, 1999.

[211] T. Graepel, R. Herbrich, and K. Obermayer. Bayesian transduction. In *Advances in Neural Information Processing Systems 12*. MIT Press, 1999.

[212] T. Graepel, R. Herbrich, B. Schölkopf, A. J. Smola, P. L. Bartlett, K. Müller, K. Obermayer, and R. C. Williamson. Classification on proximity data with LP-machines. In *Ninth International Conference on Artificial Neural Networks*, Conference Publications No. 470, pages 304–309, London, 1999. IEE.

[213] T. Graepel, R. Herbrich, and J. Shawe-Taylor. Generalisation error bounds for sparse linear classifiers. In *Proceedings of the Thirteenth Annual Conference on Computational Learning Theory (COLT) 2000*, pages 298–303, 2000.

[214] T. Graepel, R. Herbrich, and R. C. Williamson. From margin to sparsity. In T. K. Leen, T. G. Dietterich, and V. Tresp, editors, *Advances in Neural Information Processing Systems 13*, pages 210–216. MIT Press, 2001.

[215] T. Graepel and K. Obermayer. Fuzzy topographic kernel clustering. In W. Brauer, editor, *Proceedings of the 5th GI Workshop Fuzzy Neuro Systems '98*, pages 90–97, 1998.

[216] A. Gretton, A. Doucet, R. Herbrich, P. Rayner, and B. Schölkopf. Support vector regression for black-box system identification. In *Proceedings of the 11th IEEE Workshop on Statistical Signal Processing*, 2001.

[217] A. Gretton, R. Herbrich, B. Schölkopf, and P. J. W. Rayner. Bound on the leave-one-out error for 2-class classification using ν-SVMs. Technical report, University of Cambridge, 2001.

[218] P. Groeneboom and J. A. Wellner. *Information Bounds and Nonparametric Maximum Likelihood Estimation*, volume 19 of *DMV*. Springer Verlag, 1992.

[219] A. Guichardet. *Symmetric Hilbert spaces and related topics*, volume 261 of *Lecture Notes in Mathematics*. Springer-Verlag, 1972.

[220] Y. Guo, P. L. Bartlett, J. Shawe-Taylor, and R. C. Williamson. Covering numbers for support vector machines. In *Proceedings of the Twelfth Annual Conference on Computational Learning Theory, COLT'99*, pages 267–277, 1999.

[221] Y. Guo, P. L. Bartlett, A. J. Smola, and R. C. Williamson. Norm-based regularization of boosting. Submitted to *Machine Learning*, 2001.

[222] L. Gurvits. A note on a scale-sensitive dimension of linear bounded functionals in Banach spaces. In M. Li and A. Maruoka, editors, *Algorithmic Learning Theory ALT-97*, LNAI-1316, pages 352–363, Berlin, 1997. Springer.

[223] I. Guyon, B. Boser, and V. Vapnik. Automatic capacity tuning of very large VC-dimension classifiers. In S. J. Hanson, J. D. Cowan, and C. Lee Giles, editors, *Advances in Neural Information Processing Systems*, volume 5, pages 147–155. Morgan Kaufmann, San Mateo, CA, 1993.

[224] I. Guyon, J. Weston, S. Barnhill, and V. Vapnik. Gene selection for cancer classification using support vector machines. *Machine Learning*, 2002. Forthcoming. Also: Biowulf Technologies TR.

[225] P. C. Hansen. Analysis of discrete ill-posed problems by means of the *L*-curve. *SIAM Review*, 34(4):561–580, December 1992.

[226] W. Härdle. *Applied nonparametric regression*, volume 19 of *Econometric Society Monographs*. Cambridge University Press, 1990.

[227] W. Härdle. *Smoothing Techniques, With Implementations in S*. Springer, New York, 1991.

[228] S. Harmeling, A. Ziehe, M. Kawanabe, and K.-R. Müller. Kernel feature spaces and nonlinear blind source separation. In T.G. Dietterich, S. Becker, and Z. Ghahramani, editors, *Advances in Neural Information Processing Systems*, volume 14. MIT Press, 2002. To appear.

[229] J. A. Hartigan. Estimation of a convex density contour in two dimensions. *Journal of the American Statistical Association*, 82:267–270, 1987.

[230] T. J. Hastie, A. Buja, and R. J. Tibshirani. Penalized discriminant analysis. *Annals of Statistics*, 23:73–102, 1995.

[231] T. J. Hastie and W. Stuetzle. Principal curves. *Journal of the American Statistical Association*, 84(406):502–516, 1989.

[232] T. J. Hastie and R. J. Tibshirani. *Generalized Additive Models*, volume 43 of *Monographs on Statistics and Applied Probability*. Chapman & Hall, London, 1990.

[233] T. J. Hastie and R. J. Tibshirani. Classification by pairwise coupling. In M. I. Jordan, M. J. Kearns, and S. A. Solla, editors, *Advances in Neural Information Processing Systems*, volume 10. The MIT Press, 1998.

[234] D. Haussler. Convolutional kernels on discrete structures. Technical Report UCSC-CRL-99-10, Computer Science Department, University of California at Santa Cruz, 1999.

[235] S. Haykin. *Neural Networks : A Comprehensive Foundation*. Macmillan, New York, 2nd edition, 1998.

[236] P. Hayton, B. Schölkopf, L. Tarassenko, and P. Anuzis. Support vector novelty detection applied to jet engine vibration spectra. In T. K. Leen, T. G. Dietterich, and V. Tresp, editors, *Advances in Neural Information Processing Systems 13*, pages 946–952. MIT Press, 2001.

[237] M. A. Hearst, B. Schölkopf, S. Dumais, E. Osuna, and J. Platt. Trends and controversies — support vector machines. *IEEE Intelligent Systems*, 13:18–28, 1998.

[238] R. Herbrich. *Learning linear classifiers*. PhD thesis, TU Berlin, 2000. To be published by MIT Press, Cambridge, MA.

[239] R. Herbrich, T. Graepel, and C. Cambell. Bayes point machines: Estimating the Bayes point in kernel space. *IJCAI 99*, 1999.

[240] R. Herbrich, T. Graepel, and J. Shawe-Taylor. Sparsity vs. large margins for linear classifiers. In *Proceedings of the Thirteenth Annual Conference on Computational Learning Theory (COLT) 2000*, pages 304–308, 2000.

[241] R. Herbrich and R. C. Williamson. Algorithmic luckiness. Technical report, Microsoft Research, 2001. Submitted to *NIPS'2001*.

[242] M. Herbster. Learning additive models with fast evaluating kernels. In *Proceedings of the Fourteenth Annual Conference on Computational Learning Theory*, 2001.

[243] D. Hilbert. Grundzüge einer allgemeinen Theorie der linearen Integralgleichungen. *Nachrichten der Göttinger Akademie der Wissenschaften, Mathematisch-Physikalische Klasse*, pages 49–91, 1904.

[244] W. Hoeffding. Probability inequalities for sums of bounded random variables. *Journal of the American Statistical Association*, 58:13–30, 1963.

[245] A. E. Hoerl and R. W. Kennard. Ridge regression: biased estimation for nonorthogonal problems. *Technometrics*, 12:55–67, 1970.

[246] T. Hofmann and J. M. Buhmann. Pairwise data clustering by deterministic annealing. *IEEE Transactions on Pattern Analysis and Machine Intelligence*, 19(1):1–25, 1997.

[247] R. A. Horn and C. R. Johnson. *Matrix Analysis*. Cambridge University Press, Cambridge, 1985.

[248] H. Hotelling. Analysis of a complex of statistical variables into principal components. *Journal of Educational Psychology*, 24:417–441 and 498–520, 1933.

[249] S. Hua and Z. Sun. A novel method of protein secondary structure prediction with high segment overlap measure: support vector machine approach. *Journal of Molecular Biology*, 308:397–407, 2001.

[250] P. J. Huber. Robust statistics: a review. *Annals of Statistics*, 43:1041, 1972.

[251] P. J. Huber. *Robust Statistics*. John Wiley and Sons, New York, 1981.

[252] P. J. Huber. Projection pursuit. *Annals of Statistics*, 13(2):435–475, 1985.

[253] IBM Corporation. IBM optimization subroutine library guide and reference. *IBM Systems Journal*, 31, 1992. SC23-0519.

[254] I. A. Ibragimov and R. Z. Has'minskii. *Statistical Estimation — Asymptotic Theory*. Springer-Verlag, New York, 1981.

[255] J. Illingworth and J. Kittler. A survey of the Hough transform. *Computer Vision Graphics and Image Processing*, 44(1):87–116, October 1988.

[256] C. Iseli, C. V. Jongeneel, and P. Bucher. ESTScan: a program for detecting, evaluating, and reconstructing potential coding regions in EST sequences. In T. Lengauer, R. Schneider, P. Bork, D. Brutlag, J. Glasgow, H.-W. Mewes, and R. Zimmer, editors, *ISMB'99*, pages 138–148, Menlo Park, California 94025, August 1999. AAAI Press.

[257] T. S. Jaakkola, M. Diekhans, and D. Haussler. A discriminative framework for detecting remote protein homologies. *Journal of Computational Biology*, 7:95–114, 2000.

[258] T. S. Jaakkola and D. Haussler. Exploiting generative models in discriminative classifiers. In M. S. Kearns, S. A. Solla, and D. A. Cohn, editors, *Advances in Neural Information Processing Systems 11*, Cambridge, MA, 1999. MIT Press.

[259] T. S. Jaakkola and D. Haussler. Probabilistic kernel regression models. In *Proceedings of the 1999 Conference on AI and Statistics*, 1999.

[260] T. S. Jaakkola and M. I. Jordan. Computing upper and lower bounds on likelihoods in untractable networks. In *Proceedings of the 12th Conference on Uncertainty in AI*. Morgan Kaufman, 1996.

[261] T. S. Jaakkola, M. Meila, and T. Jebara. Maximum entropy discrimination. In S. A. Solla, T. K. Leen, and K.-R. Müller, editors, *Advances in Neural Information Processing Systems 12*. MIT Press, 2000.

[262] W. James and C. Stein. Estimation with quadratic loss. In *Proceedings of the Fourth Berkeley Symposium on Mathematics, Statistics and Probability*, volume 1, pages 361–380, Berkeley, 1960. University of California Press.

[263] T. Jebara and T. S. Jaakkola. Feature selection and dualities in maximum entropy discrimination. In *Uncertainty In Artificial Intelligence*, 2000.

[264] T. Jebara and A. Pentland. On reversing Jensen's inequality. In T. K. Leen, T. G. Dietterich, and V. Tresp, editors, *Neural Information Processing Systems NIPS 13*. MIT Press, 2001.

[265] T. Joachims. Text categorization with support vector machines: Learning with many relevant features. In Claire Nédellec and Céline Rouveirol, editors, *Proceedings of the European Conference on Machine Learning*, pages 137–142, Berlin, 1998. Springer.

[266] T. Joachims. Making large–scale SVM learning practical. In B. Schölkopf, C. J. C. Burges, and A. J. Smola, editors, *Advances in Kernel Methods — Support Vector Learning*, pages 169–184, Cambridge, MA, 1999. MIT Press.

[267] T. Joachims. Transductive inference for text classification using support vector machines. In I. Bratko and S. Dzeroski, editors, *Proceedings of the 16th International Conference on Machine Learning*, pages 200–209, San Francisco, 1999. Morgan Kaufmann.

[268] T. Joachims. Estimating the generalization performance of an SVM efficiently. In P. Langley, editor, *Proceedings of the 17th International Conference on Machine Learning*, pages 431–438, San Francisco, California, 2000. Morgan Kaufmann.

[269] F. John. Extremum problems with inequalities as subsidiary conditions. In K. O. Friedrichs, O. E. Neugebauer, and J. J. Stoker, editors, *Studies and Essays: Courant Anniversary Volume*, pages 187–204. Interscience Publishers, New York, NY, 1948.

[270] I. M. Johnstone. On the distribution of the largest principal component. Presented at the 5th world congress of the Bernoulli society, 2000.

[271] I. T. Jolliffe. *Principal Component Analysis*. Springer-Verlag, New York, New York, 1986.

[272] M. C. Jones and R. Sibson. What is projection pursuit? *Journal of the Royal Statistical Society A*,

150(1):1–36, 1987.

[273] M. I. Jordan and C. M. Bishop. *An Introduction to Probabilistic Graphical Models.* MIT Press, 2002.

[274] M. I. Jordan, Z. Ghahramani, T. S. Jaakkola, and L. K. Saul. An introduction to variational methods for graphical models. In *Learning in Graphical Models*, volume M.I. Jordan, pages 105–162. Kluwer, 1998.

[275] M. I. Jordan and R. Jacobs. Hierarchical mixtures of experts and the EM algorithm. *Neural Computation*, 6:181–214, 1994.

[276] N. Kambhatla and T. K. Leen. Fast non-linear dimension reduction. In J. D. Cowan, G. Tesauro, and J. Alspector, editors, *Advances in Neural Information Processing Systems 6. Proceedings of the 1993 Conference*, pages 152–159, San Francisco, CA, 1994. Morgan Kaufmann.

[277] N. Kambhatla and T. K. Leen. Dimension reduction by local principal component analysis. *Neural Computation*, 9(7):1493–1516, 1997.

[278] L. V. Kantorovich and V. I. Krylov. *Approximate Methods of Higher Analysis.* Noordhoff, Groningen, 1958.

[279] J. Karhunen and J. Joutsensalo. Generalizations of principal component analysis, optimization problems, and neural networks. *Neural Networks*, 8(4):549–562, 1995.

[280] K. Karhunen. Zur Spektraltheorie stochastischer Prozesse. *Annales Academiae Scientiarum Fennicae*, 37, 1946.

[281] S. Karlin. *Mathematical Methods and Theory in Games, Programming, and Economics*, volume I and II. Addison Wesley, Reading, MA, 1959.

[282] N. K. Karmarkar. A new polynomial–time algorithm for linear programming. *Proceedings of the 16th Annual ACM Symposium on Theory of Computing*, pages 302–311, 1984.

[283] W. Karush. Minima of functions of several variables with inequalities as side constraints. Master's thesis, Dept. of Mathematics, Univ. of Chicago, 1939.

[284] L. Kaufman. Solving the quadratic programming problem arising in support vector classification. In B. Schölkopf, C. J. C. Burges, and A. J. Smola, editors, *Advances in Kernel Methods — Support Vector Learning*, pages 147–168, Cambridge, MA, 1999. MIT Press.

[285] M. J. Kearns and D. Ron. Algorithmic stability and sanity-check bounds for leave-one-out cross-validation. *Neural Computation*, 11(6):1427–1453, 1999.

[286] M. J. Kearns and R. E. Schapire. Efficient distribution–free learning of probabilistic concepts. *Journal of Computer and System Sciences*, 48(3):464–497, 1994.

[287] M. J. Kearns, R. E. Schapire, and L. M. Sellie. Toward efficient agnostic learning. *Machine Learning*, 17(2):115–141, 1994.

[288] S. S. Keerthi. Efficient tuning of SVM hyperparameters using radius/margin bound and iterative algorithms. Cd-01-02, National University of Singapore, 2001.

[289] S. S. Keerthi and E. G. Gilbert. Convergence of a generalized SMO algorithm for SVM classifier design. Technical report, Dept. of Mechanical and Production Engineering, National University of Singapore, 2000.

[290] S. S. Keerthi, S. K. Shevade, C. Bhattacharyya, and K. R. K. Murthy. A fast iterative nearest point algorithm for support vector machine classifier design. Technical Report Technical Report TR-ISL-99-03, Indian Institute of Science, Bangalore, 1999. http://guppy.mpe.nus.edu.sg/~mpessk/npa_tr.ps.gz.

[291] S. S. Keerthi, S.K. Shevade, C. Bhattacharyya, and K.R.K. Murthy. Improvements to Platt's SMO algorithm for SVM classifier design. *Neural Computation*, 13:637–649, 2001.

[292] B. Kégl, A. Krzyżak, T. Linder, and K. Zeger. Learning and design of principal curves. *IEEE Transactions on Pattern Analysis and Machine Intelligence*, pages 281–297, 2000.

[293] B. Kégl, T. Linder, and G. Lugosi. Data-dependent margin-based generalization bounds for classification. In D. Helmbold and R. C. Williamson, editors, *Proceedings of the 14th Annual Conference on Computational Learning Theory, Amsterdam*, LNCS. Springer, 2001.

[294] K. I. Kim, K. Jung, S. H. Park, and H. J. Kim. Texture classification with kernel principal component analysis. *Electronics Letters*, 36(12):1021–1022, 2000.

[295] G. S. Kimeldorf and G. Wahba. A correspondence between Bayesian estimation on stochastic processes and smoothing by splines. *Annals of Mathematical Statistics*, 41:495–502, 1970.

[296] G. S. Kimeldorf and G. Wahba. Some results on Tchebycheffian spline functions. *Journal of Mathematical Analysis and Applications*, 33:82–95, 1971.

[297] M. Kirby and L. Sirovich. Application of the Karhunen-Loève procedure for the characterization of human faces. *IEEE Transactions on Pattern Analysis and Machine Intelligence*, 12(1):103–108, January 1990.

[298] J. Kivinen, A. J. Smola, and R. C. Williamson. Large margin classification for drifting targets. In *Advances in Neural Processing Systems*, 2001. Submitted.

[299] J. Kivinen, A. J. Smola, and R. C. Williamson. Online learning with kernel methods. In *Advances in Neural Processing Systems*, 2001. Submitted.

[300] J. Kivinen, M. K. Warmuth, and P. Auer. The perceptron algorithm versus Winnow: linear versus logarithmic mistake bounds when few input variables are relevant. *Artificial Intelligence*, 97:325–343, 1997.

[301] S. Klinke. Exploratory projection pursuit - the multivariate and discrete case. Discussion Paper 70, SFB 373, Humboldt-University of Berlin, 1995.

[302] T. Kohonen. Self-organized formation of topologically correct feature maps. *Biological Cybernetics*, 43:59–69, 1982.

[303] V. Kolchinskiĭ, D. Panchenko, and F. Lozano. Further explanation of the effectiveness of voting methods: The game between margins and weights. In D. Helmbold and R. C. Williamson, editors, *Proceedings of the 14th Annual Conference on Computational Learning Theory, Amsterdam*, LNCS. Springer, 2001.

[304] A. N. Kolmogorov. Stationary sequences in Hilbert spaces. *Moscow University Mathematics Bulletin*, 2:1–40, 1941.

[305] A. N. Kolmogorov. Three approaches to the quantitative definition of information. *Problems of Information Transmission*, 1:1–7, 1965.

[306] A. N. Kolmogorov and S. V. Fomin. *Functional Analysis.* Graylock Press, Albany, NY, 1961.

[307] H. König. *Eigenvalue Distribution of Compact Operators.* Birkhäuser, Basel, 1986.

[308] A. P. Korostelev and A. B. Tsybakov. *Minimax Theory of Image Reconstruction.* Springer, New York, 1993.

[309] A. Kowalczyk. Maximal margin perceptron. In A. J. Smola, P. L. Bartlett, B. Schölkopf, and D. Schuurmans, editors, *Advances in Large Margin Classifiers*, pages 75–113, Cambridge, MA, 2000. MIT Press.

[310] W. Krauth and M. Mézard. Learning algorithms with optimal stability in neural networks. *Journal of Physics A*, 20:L745–L752, 1987.

[311] U. Kreßel. Pairwise classification and support vector machines. In B. Schölkopf, C. J. C. Burges, and A. J. Smola, editors, *Advances in Kernel Methods — Support Vector Learning*, pages 255–268, Cambridge, MA, 1999. MIT Press.

[312] H. W. Kuhn and A. W. Tucker. Nonlinear programming. In *Proceedings of the 2nd Berkeley Symposium on Mathematical Statistics and Probabilistics*, pages 481–492, Berkeley, 1951. University of California Press.

[313] P. F. Lampert. Designing pattern categories with extremal paradigm information. In M. S. Watanabe, editor, *Methodologies of Pattern Recognition*, page 359. Academic Press, NY, 1969.

[314] J. Langford and M. Seeger. Bounds for averaging classifiers. CMU-CS 01-102, Carnegie Mellon University, 2001.

[315] N. Lawrence and B. Schölkopf. Estimating a kernel Fisher discriminant in the presence of label noise. In *Proceedings of the 18th International Conference on Machine Learning*, San Francisco, 2001. Morgan Kaufman.

[316] C. L. Lawson, R. J. Hanson, D. Kincaid, and F. T. Krogh. Basic linear algebra subprograms for FORTRAN usage. *ACM Transactions on Mathematical Software*, 5:308–323, 1979.

[317] Y. LeCun. A theoretical framework for backpropagation. In D. Touretzky, G. Hinton, and T. Sejnowski, editors, *Proceedings of the 1988 Connectionist Models Summer School*, pages 21–28, Palo Alto, June 1988. Morgan Kaufmann.

[318] Y. LeCun, B. Boser, J. S. Denker, D. Henderson, R. E. Howard, W. Hubbard, and L. J. Jackel. Backpropagation applied to handwritten zip code recognition. *Neural Computation*, 1:541–551, 1989.

[319] Y. LeCun, L. Bottou, Y. Bengio, and P. Haffner. Gradient-based learning applied to document recognition. *Proceedings of the IEEE*, 86:2278–2324, 1998.

[320] Y. LeCun, L. D. Jackel, L. Bottou, A. Brunot, C. Cortes, J. S. Denker, H. Drucker, I. Guyon, U. A.

Müller, E. Säckinger, P. Simard, and V. Vapnik. Comparison of learning algorithms for handwritten digit recognition. In F. Fogelman-Soulié and P. Gallinari, editors, *Proceedings ICANN'95 — International Conference on Artificial Neural Networks*, volume II, pages 53–60, Nanterre, France, 1995. EC2.

[321] Y. LeCun, L. D. Jackel, L. Bottou, C. Cortes, J. S. Denker, H. Drucker, I. Guyon, U. A. Müller, E. Säckinger, P. Simard, and V. Vapnik. Learning algorithms for classification: A comparison on handwritten digit recognition. *Neural Networks*, pages 261–276, 1995.

[322] W. S. Lee, P. L. Bartlett, and R. C. Williamson. The importance of convexity in learning with squared loss. *IEEE Transactions on Information Theory*, 44(5):1974–1980, 1998.

[323] Y. Lee, Y. Lin, and G. Wahba. Multicategory support vector machines. Technical Report 1040, Department of Statistics, University of Madison, Wisconsin, 2001.

[324] Y.-J. Lee and O. L. Mangasarian. SSVM: A smooth support vector machine. Technical Report 99-03, Data Mining Institute, Computer Sciences Department, University of Wisconsin, Madison, Wisconsin, September 1999. *Computational Optimization and Applications* 20(1), October 2001, to appear.

[325] Y.-J. Lee and O. L. Mangasarian. RSVM: Reduced support vector machines. Technical Report 00-07, Data Mining Institute, Computer Sciences Department, University of Wisconsin, Madison, Wisconsin, July 2000. Proceedings of the First SIAM International Conference on Data Mining, Chicago, April 5-7, 2001, CD-ROM Proceedings.

[326] E. Leopold and J. Kindermann. Text categorization with support vector machines: how to represent text in input space? *Machine Learning*, 2002. Forthcoming.

[327] M. S. Lewicki and T. J. Sejnowski. Learning nonlinear overcomplete representations for efficient coding. In M. I. Jordan, M. J. Kearns, and S. A. Solla, editors, *Advances in Neural Information Processing Systems*, volume 10. The MIT Press, 1998.

[328] S. Li, Q. Fu, L. Gu, B. Schölkopf, Y. Cheng, and H. Zhang. Kernel machine based learning for multi-view face detection and pose estimation. In *Proceedings of the International Conference on Computer Vision*, pages 674–679, 2001.

[329] Y. Li and P. M. Long. The relaxed online maximum margin algorithm. In S. A. Solla, T. K. Leen, and K.-R. Müller, editors, *Advances in Neural Information Processing Systems 12*, pages 498–504. MIT Press, 2000.

[330] C. J. Lin. On the convergence of the decomposition method for support vector machines. *IEEE Transactions on Neural Networks*, 2001. To appear.

[331] Y. Lin, Y. Lee, and G. Wahba. Support vector machines for classification in nonstandard situations. Technical Report 1016, Department of Statistics, University of Wisconsin, Madison, March 2000.

[332] S. P. Lloyd. Least squares quantization in PCM. *IEEE Transactions on Information Theory*, 28:129–137, 1982.

[333] H. Lodhi, J. Shawe-Taylor, N. Cristianini, and C. Watkins. Text classification using string kernels. Technical Report 2000-79, NeuroCOLT, 2000. Published in: T. K. Leen, T. G. Dietterich and V. Tresp (eds.), *Advances in Neural Information Processing Systems 13*, MIT Press, 2001.

[334] D. G. Luenberger. *Introduction to Linear and Nonlinear Programming*. Addison-Wesley, Reading, MA, 1973.

[335] A. Luntz and V. Brailovsky. On estimation of characters obtained in statistical procedure of recognition (in Russian). *Technicheskaya Kibernetica*, 3, 1969.

[336] I. J. Lustig, R. E. Marsten, and D. F. Shanno. On implementing Mehrotra's predictor-corrector interior point method for linear programming. Princeton Technical Report SOR 90-03., Dept. of Civil Engineering and Operations Research, Princeton University, 1990.

[337] H. Lütkepohl. *Handbook of Matrices*. Wiley, Chichester, 1996.

[338] D. J. C. MacKay. *Bayesian Modelling and Neural Networks*. PhD thesis, Computation and Neural Systems, California Institute of Technology, Pasadena, CA, 1991.

[339] D. J. C. MacKay. The evidence framework applied to classification networks. *Neural Computation*, 4:720–736, 1992.

[340] D. J. C. MacKay. Introduction to Gaussian processes. In C. M. Bishop, editor, *Neural Networks and Machine Learning*, pages 133–165. Springer-Verlag, Berlin, 1998.

[341] W. R. Madych and S. A. Nelson. Multivariate interpolation and conditionally positive definite functions II. *Mathematics of Computation*, 54(189):211–230, January 1990.

[342] S. Mallat and Z. Zhang. Matching Pursuit in a time-frequency dictionary. *IEEE Transactions on Signal Processing*, 41:3397–3415, 1993.

[343] O. L. Mangasarian. Linear and nonlinear separation of patterns by linear programming. *Operations Research*, 13:444–452, 1965.

[344] O. L. Mangasarian. Multi-surface method of pattern separation. *IEEE Transactions on Information Theory*, IT-14:801–807, 1968.

[345] O. L. Mangasarian. *Nonlinear Programming*. McGraw-Hill, New York, NY, 1969.

[346] O. L. Mangasarian. Minimum-support solutions of polyhedral concave programs. *Optimization*, 45:149–162, 1999. Also: Mathematical Programming Technical Report 97-05, Madison.

[347] O. L. Mangasarian. Generalized support vector machines. In A. J. Smola, P. L. Bartlett, B. Schölkopf, and D. Schuurmans, editors, *Advances in Large Margin Classifiers*, pages 135–146, Cambridge, MA, 2000. MIT Press.

[348] O. L. Mangasarian and D. R. Musicant. Lagrangian support vector machines. *Journal of Machine Learning Research*, 1:161–177, 2001. http://www.jmlr.org.

[349] L. Mason, J. Baxter, P. L. Bartlett, and M. Frean. Functional gradient techniques for combining hypotheses. In A. J. Smola, P. L. Bartlett, B. Schölkopf, and D. Schuurmans, editors, *Advances in Large Margin Classifiers*, pages 221–246, Cambridge, MA, 2000. MIT Press.

[350] D. Mattera, 1998. Personal communication.

[351] D. Mattera and S. Haykin. Support vector machines for dynamic reconstruction of a chaotic system. In B. Schölkopf, C. J. C. Burges, and A. J. Smola, editors, *Advances in Kernel Methods — Support Vector Learning*, pages 211–242, Cambridge, MA, 1999. MIT Press.

[352] D. Mattera, F. Palmieri, and S. Haykin. Simple and robust methods for support vector expansions. *IEEE Transactions on Neural Networks*, 10(5):1038–1047, 1999.

[353] D. A. McAllester. Some PAC-Bayesian theorems. In *Proceedings of the 11th Annual Conference on Computational Learning Theory*, pages 230–234. ACM Press, 1998.

[354] D. A. McAllester. PAC-Bayesian model averaging. In *Proceedings of the 12th Annual Conference on Computational Learning Theory*. ACM Press, 1999.

[355] P. McCullagh and J. A. Nelder. *Generalized Linear Models*. Chapman & Hall, London, 1983.

[356] C. McDiarmid. On the method of bounded differences. *Surveys in Combinatorics*, pages 148–188, 1989. Cambridge University Press.

[357] S. Mendelson. Learning relatively small classes. In *Conference on Computational Learning Theory COLT*, 2001. Submitted.

[358] S. Mendelson. Rademacher averages and phase transitions in Glivenko-Cantelli classes. *IEEE Transactions on Information Theory*, 2001. Submitted.

[359] J. Mercer. Functions of positive and negative type and their connection with the theory of integral equations. *Philosophical Transactions of the Royal Society, London*, A 209:415–446, 1909.

[360] C. A. Micchelli. Algebraic aspects of interpolation. *Proceedings of Symposia in Applied Mathematics*, 36:81–102, 1986.

[361] S. Mika. Nichtlineare Signalverarbeitung in Feature-Räumen. Diplomarbeit, Technische Universität Berlin, 1998.

[362] S. Mika, G. Rätsch, and K.-R. Müller. A mathematical programming approach to the kernel Fisher algorithm. In T. K. Leen, T. G. Dietterich, and V. Tresp, editors, *Advances in Neural Information Processing Systems 13*. MIT Press, 2001.

[363] S. Mika, G. Rätsch, J. Weston, B. Schölkopf, and K.-R. Müller. Fisher discriminant analysis with kernels. In Y.-H. Hu, J. Larsen, E. Wilson, and S. Douglas, editors, *Neural Networks for Signal Processing IX*, pages 41–48. IEEE, 1999.

[364] S. Mika, G. Rätsch, J. Weston, B. Schölkopf, A. J. Smola, and K.-R. Müller. Invariant feature extraction and classification in kernel spaces. In S. A. Solla, T. K. Leen, and K.-R. Müller, editors, *Advances in Neural Information Processing Systems 12*, pages 526–532. MIT Press, 2000.

[365] S. Mika, B. Schölkopf, A. J. Smola, K.-R. Müller, M. Scholz, and G. Rätsch. Kernel PCA and de-noising in feature spaces. In M. S. Kearns, S. A. Solla, and D. A. Cohn, editors, *Advances in Neural Information Processing Systems 11*, pages 536–542, Cambridge, MA, 1999. MIT Press.

[366] S. Mika, A. J. Smola, and B. Schölkopf. An improved training algorithm for kernel Fisher discriminants. In T. Jaakkola and T. Richardson, editors, *Artificial Intelligence and Statistics*, pages 98–104, San Francisco, CA, 2001. Morgan Kaufmann. Also: Microsoft Research TR-2000-77.

[367] M. L. Minsky and S. Papert. *Perceptrons*. MIT Press, Cambridge, MA, 1969.

[368] T. M. Mitchell. Version spaces: a candidate elimination approach to rule learning. In *Proceedings of the Fifth International Joint Conference on Artificial Intelligence*, pages 305–310, Cambridge, Massachusetts, 1977.

[369] J. J. More and G. Toraldo. On the solution of large quadratic programming problems with bound constraints. *SIAM Journal on Optimization*, 1(1):93–113, 1991.

[370] V. A. Morozov. *Methods for Solving Incorrectly Posed Problems*. Springer Verlag, 1984.

[371] S. Mukherjee, E. Osuna, and F. Girosi. Nonlinear prediction of chaotic time series using a support vector machine. In J. Principe, L. Gile, N. Morgan, and E. Wilson, editors, *Neural Networks for Signal Processing VII — Proceedings of the 1997 IEEE Workshop*, pages 511–520, New York, 1997. IEEE.

[372] S. Mukherjee, P. Tamayo, D. Slonim, A. Verri, T. Golub, J. P. Mesirov, and T. Poggio. Support vector machine classification of microarray data. Technical report, Artificial Intelligence Laboratory, Massachusetts Institute of Technology, 2000.

[373] C. Müller. *Analysis of Spherical Symmetries in Euclidean Spaces*, volume 129 of *Applied Mathematical Sciences*. Springer, New York, 1997.

[374] D. W. Müller. The excess mass approach in statistics. Beiträge zur Statistik, Universität Heidelberg, 1992.

[375] K.-R. Müller, S. Mika, G. Rätsch, K. Tsuda, and B. Schölkopf. An introduction to kernel-based learning algorithms. *IEEE Transactions on Neural Networks*, 12(2):181–201, 2001.

[376] K.-R. Müller, A. J. Smola, G. Rätsch, B. Schölkopf, J. Kohlmorgen, and V. Vapnik. Predicting time series with support vector machines. In W. Gerstner, A. Germond, M. Hasler, and J.-D. Nicoud, editors, *Artificial Neural Networks — ICANN'97*, pages 999–1004, Berlin, 1997. Springer Lecture Notes in Computer Science, Vol. 1327.

[377] N. Murata. An integral representation of functions using three-layered networks and their approximation bounds. *Neural Networks*, 9(6):947–956, 1996.

[378] N. Murata, K.-R. Müller, A. Ziehe, and S. Amari. Adaptive on-line learning in changing environments. In M. C. Mozer, M. I. Jordan, and T. Petsche, editors, *Advances in Neural Information Processing Systems*, volume 9, pages 599–605. The MIT Press, 1997.

[379] N. Murata, S. Yoshizawa, and S. Amari. Network information criterion—determining the number of hidden units for artificial neural network models. *IEEE Transactions on Neural Networks*, 5:865–872, 1994.

[380] B. A. Murtagh and M. A. Saunders. MINOS 5.4 user's guide. Technical Report SOL 83.20, Stanford University, 1993.

[381] B. K. Natarajan. Sparse approximate solutions to linear systems. *SIAM Journal of Computing*, 25(2):227–234, 1995.

[382] R. Neal. Priors for infinite networks. Technical Report CRG-TR-94-1, Dept. of Computer Science, University of Toronto, 1994.

[383] R. Neal. *Bayesian Learning in Neural Networks*. Springer Verlag, New York, 1996.

[384] R. Neal. Monte Carlo implementation of Gaussian process models for Bayesian regression and classification. Technical Report Technical Report 9702, Dept. of Statistics, 1997.

[385] D. Nolan. The excess mass ellipsoid. *Journal of Multivariate Analysis*, 39:348–371, 1991.

[386] A. B. J. Novikoff. On convergence proofs on perceptrons. In *Proceedings of the Symposium on the Mathematical Theory of Automata*, volume 12, pages 615–622. Polytechnic Institute of Brooklyn, 1962.

[387] E. Oja. A simplified neuron model as a principal component analyzer. *Journal of Mathematical Biology*, 15:267–273, 1982.

[388] N. Oliver, B. Schölkopf, and A. J. Smola. Natural regularization in SVMs. In A. J. Smola, P. L. Bartlett, B. Schölkopf, and D. Schuurmans, editors, *Advances in Large Margin Classifiers*, pages 51–60, Cambridge, MA, 2000. MIT Press.

[389] B. A. Olshausen and D. J. Field. Emergence of simple-cell receptive field properties by learning a sparse code for natural images. *Nature*, 381:607–609, 1996.

[390] T. Onoda, G. Rätsch, and K.-R. Müller. A non-intrusive monitoring system for household electric appliances with inverters. In *Proceedings the Second International ICSC Symposium on Neural Computation*, Berlin, 2000.

[391] M. Opper. On the annealed VC entropy for margin classifiers: A statistical mechanics study. In B. Schölkopf, C. J. C. Burges, and A. J. Smola, editors, *Advances in Kernel Methods — Support Vector Learning*, pages 117–126, Cambridge, MA, 1999. MIT Press.

[392] M. Opper and D. Haussler. Generalization performance of Bayes optimal classification algorithm for learning a perceptron. *Physical Review Letters*, 66:2677, 1991.

[393] M. Opper and W. Kinzel. Physics of generalization. In E. Domany J. L. van Hemmen and K. Schulten, editors, *Physics of Neural Networks III*. Springer Verlag, New York, 1996.

[394] M. Opper, W. Kinzel, J. Kleinz, and R. Nehl. On the ability of the optimal perceptron to generalize. *Journal of Physics A*, 23:581–586, 1990.

[395] M. Opper and O. Winther. Mean field methods for classification with Gaussian processes. In M. S. Kearns, S. A. Solla, and D. A. Cohn, editors, *Advances in Neural Information Processing Systems 11*, Cambridge, MA, 1999. MIT Press.

[396] M. Opper and O. Winther. Gaussian processes and SVM: mean field and leave-one-out. In A. J. Smola, P. L. Bartlett, B. Schölkopf, and D. Schuurmans, editors, *Advances in Large Margin Classifiers*, pages 311–326, Cambridge, MA, 2000. MIT Press.

[397] G. B. Orr and K.-R Müller. *Neural Networks: Tricks of the Trade*. LNCS 1524, Springer, Heidelberg, 1998.

[398] E. Osuna, R. Freund, and F. Girosi. An improved training algorithm for support vector machines. In J. Principe, L. Gile, N. Morgan, and E. Wilson, editors, *Neural Networks for Signal Processing VII — Proceedings of the 1997 IEEE Workshop*, pages 276–285, New York, 1997. IEEE.

[399] E. Osuna, R. Freund, and F. Girosi. Training support vector machines: An application to face detection. In *Proceedings IEEE Conference on Computer Vision and Pattern Recognition*, pages 130–136, 1997.

[400] E. Osuna and F. Girosi. Reducing the run-time complexity in support vector regression. In B. Schölkopf, C. J. C. Burges, and A. J. Smola, editors, *Advances in Kernel Methods — Support Vector Learning*, pages 271–284, Cambridge, MA, 1999. MIT Press.

[401] Z. Ovari. Kernels, eigenvalues and support vector machines. Honours thesis, Australian National University, Canberra, 2000.

[402] K. R. Parthasarathy and K. Schmidt. *Positive definite kernels, continuous tensor products, and central limit theorems of probability theory*, volume 272 of *Lecture Notes in Mathematics*. Springer-Verlag, Berlin, 1972.

[403] P. Pavlidis, J. Weston, J. Cai, and W. N. Grundy. Gene functional classification from heterogeneous data. In *Proceedings of the Fifth International Conference on Computational Molecular Biology*, pages 242–248, 2001.

[404] K. Pearson. On lines and planes of closest fit to points in space. *Philosophical Magazine*, 2:559–572, 1901.

[405] W. R. Pearson, T. Wood, Z. Zhang, and W. Miller. Comparison of DNA Sequences with Protein Sequences. *Genomics*, 46(1):24–36, November 1997.

[406] A. G. Pedersen and H. Nielsen. Neural Network Prediction of Translation Initiation Sites in Eukaryotes: Perspectives for EST and Genome analysis. In *ISMB'97*, volume 5, pages 226–233, 1997.

[407] F. Pérez-Cruz, P. L. Alarcón-Diana, A. Navia-Vázquez, and A. Artés-Rodríguez. Fast training of support vector classifiers. In T. K. Leen, T. G. Dietterich, and V. Tresp, editors, *Advances in Neural Information Processing Systems 13*. MIT Press, 2001.

[408] F. Pérez-Cruz and A. Artés-Rodríguez. A new optimizing procedure for ν-support vector regressor. In *Proceedings of the International Conference on Acoustics, Speech, and Signal Processing*, 2001.

[409] J. Platt. Fast training of support vector machines using sequential minimal optimization. In B. Schölkopf, C. J. C. Burges, and A. J. Smola, editors, *Advances in Kernel Methods — Support Vector Learning*, pages 185–208, Cambridge, MA, 1999. MIT Press.

[410] J. Platt. Probabilities for SV machines. In A. J. Smola, P. L. Bartlett, B. Schölkopf, and D. Schuurmans, editors, *Advances in Large Margin Classifiers*, pages 61–73, Cambridge, MA, 2000. MIT Press.

[411] J. C. Platt, N. Cristianini, and J. Shawe-Taylor. Large margin DAGs for multiclass classification. In S. A. Solla, T. K. Leen, and K.-R. Müller, editors, *Advances in Neural Information Processing Systems 12*, pages 547–553. MIT Press, 2000.

[412] T. Poggio. On optimal nonlinear associative recall. *Biological Cybernetics*, 19:201–209, 1975.

[413] T. Poggio and T. Vetter. Recognition and structure from one 2D model view: observations on prototypes, object classes and symmetries. A.I. Memo No. 1347, Artificial Intelligence Laboratory, Massachusetts Institute of Technology, 1992.

[414] E. Polak. *Computational Methods in Optimization*. Academic Press, New York, 1971.

[415] D. Pollard. *Convergence of stochastic processes*. Springer-Verlag, Berlin, 1984.

[416] W. Polonik. Measuring mass concentrations and estimating density contour clusters — an excess mass approach. *Annals of Statistics*, 23(3):855–881, 1995.

[417] W. Polonik. Minimum volume sets and generalized quantile processes. *Stochastic Processes and their Applications*, 69:1–24, 1997.

[418] M. Pontil, R. Rifkin, and T. Evgeniou. From regression to classification in support vector machines. In M. Verleysen, editor, *Proceedings ESANN*, pages 225–230, Brussels, 1999. D Facto.

[419] M. Pontil and A. Verri. Support vector machines for 3D object recognition. *IEEE Transactions on Pattern Analysis and Machine Intelligence*, 20:637–646, 1998.

[420] M. J. D. Powell. Radial basis functions for multivariable interpolation: a review. In J. C. Mason and M. G. Cox, editors, *Algorithms for Approximation*. Clarendon Press, Oxford, 1987.

[421] M. J. D. Powell. Truncated Laurent expansions for the fast evaluation of thin plate splines. *Numerical Algorithms*, 5:99–120, 1993.

[422] M. J. D. Powell. A new iterative algorithm for thin plate spline interpolation in two dimensions. *Annals of Numerical Mathematics*, 4:519–527, 1997.

[423] W. H. Press, S. A. Teukolsky, W. T. Vetterling, and B. P. Flannery. *Numerical Recipes in C: The Art of Scientific Computing*. Cambridge University Press, Cambridge, 2nd edition, 1992. ISBN 0-521-43108-5.

[424] K. Psounis, B. Prabhakar, and D. Engler. A randomized cache replacement scheme approximating LRU. In *Conference on Information Sciences and Systems*, volume 34, Princeton University, March 2000.

[425] C. R. Rao. *Linear Statistical Inference and its Applications*. Wiley, New York, 1973.

[426] C. Rasmussen. *Evaluation of Gaussian Processes and Other Methods for Non-Linear Regression*. PhD thesis, Department of Computer Science, University of Toronto, 1996. ftp://ftp.cs.toronto.edu/pub/carl/thesis.ps.gz.

[427] G. Rätsch. Ensemble-Lernmethoden zur Klassifikation. Diplomarbeit, Universität Potsdam, 1998.

[428] G. Rätsch, T. Onoda, and K.-R. Müller. Soft margins for AdaBoost. *Machine Learning*, 42(3):287–320, 2001. Also: NeuroCOLT Technical Report 1998-021.

[429] M. Reed and B. Simon. *Methods of modern mathematical physics. Vol. 1: Functional Analysis*. Academic Press, San Diego, 1980.

[430] P. Riegler and H. S. Seung. Vapnik-Chervonenkis entropy of the spherical perceptron. *Physical Review E*, 55:3283–3287, 1997.

[431] F. Riesz and B. S. Nagy. *Functional Analysis*. Frederick Ungar Publishing Co., 1955.

[432] B. D. Ripley. *Pattern Recognition and Neural Networks*. Cambridge University Press, Cambridge, 1996.

[433] J. Rissanen. Modeling by shortest data description. *Automatica*, 14:465–471, 1978.

[434] H. J. Ritter, T. M. Martinetz, and K. J. Schulten. *Neuronale Netze: Eine Einführung in die Neuroinformatik selbstorganisierender Abbildungen*. Addison-Wesley, Munich, Germany, 1990.

[435] R. T. Rockafellar. *Convex Analysis*, volume 28 of *Princeton Mathematics Series*. Princeton University Press, 1970.

[436] S. Romdhani, S. Gong, and A. Psarrou. A multiview nonlinear active shape model using kernel PCA. In *Proceedings of BMVC*, pages 483–492, Nottingham, UK, 1999.

[437] S. Romdhani, B. Schölkopf, P. Torr, and A. Blake. Fast face detection, using a sequential reduced support vector evaluation. TR 73, Microsoft Research, Redmond, WA, 2000. Published as: Computationally efficient face detection, *Proceedings of the International Conference on Computer Vision 2001*, pp. 695–700.

[438] D. Roobaert and M. M. Van Hulle. View-based 3d object recognition with support vector machines. In Y.-H. Hu, J. Larsen, E. Wilson, and S. Douglas, editors, *Neural Networks for Signal*

Processing IX. IEEE, 1999.

[439] F. Rosenblatt. The perceptron: A probabilistic model for information storage and organization in the brain. *Psychological Review*, 65(6):386–408, 1958.

[440] R. Rosipal, M. Girolami, and L. Trejo. Kernel PCA feature extraction of event-related potentials for human signal detection performance. In Malmgren, Borga, and Niklasson, editors, *Proceedings of the International Conference on Artificial Neural Networks in Medicine and Biology*, pages 321–326, 2000.

[441] R. Rosipal, M. Girolami, L. Trejo, and A. Cichocki. Kernel PCA for feature extraction and de-noising in non-linear regression. *Neural Computing & Applications*, 2001. To appear.

[442] V. Roth and V. Steinhage. Nonlinear discriminant analysis using kernel functions. In S. A. Solla, T. K. Leen, and K.-R. Müller, editors, *Advances in Neural Information Processing Systems 12*, pages 568–574. MIT Press, 2000.

[443] S. Roweis. EM algorithms for PCA and SPCA. In M. Jordan, M. Kearns, and S. Solla, editors, *Advances in Neural Information Processing Systems 10*, pages 626–632, Cambridge, MA, 1998. MIT Press.

[444] S. Roweis and Z. Ghahramani. A unifying review of linear Gaussian models. *Neural Computation*, 11(2), 1999.

[445] S. Roweis and L. Saul. Nonlinear dimensionality reduction by locally linear embedding. *Science*, 290:2323–2326, 2000.

[446] H. Rowley, S. Baluja, and T. Kanade. Neural network-based face detection. *IEEE Transactions on Pattern Analysis and Machine Intelligence*, 20:23–38, 1998.

[447] L. A. Rubel. A universal differential equation. *Bulletin of the American Mathematical Society*, 4(3):345–349, 1997.

[448] W. Rudin. *Functional Analysis*. McGraw-Hill, New York, 1973.

[449] P. Ruján. A fast method for calculating the perceptron with maximal stability. *Journal de Physique I France*, 3:277–290, 1993.

[450] P. Ruján. Playing billiard in version space. *Neural Computation*, 9:99–122, 1997.

[451] P. Ruján and M. Marchand. Computing the Bayes kernel classifier. In A. J. Smola, P. L. Bartlett, B. Schölkopf, and D. Schuurmans, editors, *Advances in Large Margin Classifiers*, pages 329–347, Cambridge, MA, 2000. MIT Press.

[452] D. E. Rumelhart, G. E. Hinton, and R. J. Williams. Learning representations by back-propagating errors. *Nature*, 323(9):533–536, 1986.

[453] M. Rychetsky, J. Shawe-Taylor, and M. Glesner. Direct Bayes point machines. In P. Langley, editor, *Proceedings of the 17th International Conference on Machine Learning*, San Francisco, 2000. Morgan Kaufman.

[454] T. W. Sager. An iterative method for estimating a multivariate mode and isopleth. *Journal of the American Statistical Association*, 74(366):329–339, 1979.

[455] S. Saitoh. *Theory of Reproducing Kernels and its Applications*. Longman Scientific & Technical, Harlow, England, 1988.

[456] S. L. Salzberg. A method for identifying splice sites and translational start sites in eukaryotic mRNA. *Computational Applied Bioscience*, 13(4):365–376, 1997.

[457] T. D. Sanger. An optimality principle for unsupervised learning. In D. S. Touretzky, editor, *Advances in Neural Information Processing Systems I*. Morgan Kaufmann Publishers, Carnegie Mellon University, 1989.

[458] N. Sauer. On the density of families of sets. *Journal of Combinatorial Theory*, 13:145–147, 1972.

[459] C. Saunders, M. O. Stitson, J. Weston, L. Bottou, B. Schölkopf, and A. J. Smola. Support vector machine reference manual. Technical Report CSD-TR-98-03, Department of Computer Science, Royal Holloway, University of London, Egham, UK, 1998. SVM available at http://svm.dcs.rhbnc.ac.uk/.

[460] R. Schapire, Y. Freund, P. L. Bartlett, and W. S. Lee. Boosting the margin: A new explanation for the effectiveness of voting methods. *Annals of Statistics*, 26:1651–1686, 1998.

[461] T. Scheffer and R. Herbrich. Unbiased assessment of learning algorithms. In *Proceedings of the International Joint Conference on Artificial Intelligence*, pages 798–803, 1997.

[462] M. Schmidt. Identifying speakers with support vectors networks. In *Proceedings of Interface '96*, Sydney, 1996.

[463] M. Schmidt and H. Gish. Speaker identification via support vector classifiers. In *Proceedings ICASSP'96*, pages 105–108, Atlanta, GA, 1996.

[464] I. J. Schoenberg. Metric spaces and completely monotone functions. *Annals of Mathematics*, 39:811–841, 1938.

[465] I. J. Schoenberg. Metric spaces and positive definite functions. *Transactions of the American Mathematical Society*, 44:522–536, 1938.

[466] I. J. Schoenberg. Positive definite functions on spheres. *Duke Mathematical Journal*, 9:96–108, 1942.

[467] B. Schölkopf. *Support Vector Learning*. R. Oldenbourg Verlag, München, 1997. Doktorarbeit, Technische Universität Berlin. Available from http://www.kyb.tuebingen.mpg.de/~bs.

[468] B. Schölkopf. The kernel trick for distances. TR MSR 2000 - 51, Microsoft Research, Redmond, WA, 2000. Published in: T. K. Leen, T. G. Dietterich and V. Tresp (eds.), *Advances in Neural Information Processing Systems 13*, MIT Press, 2001.

[469] B. Schölkopf, P. L. Bartlett, A. J. Smola, and R. Williamson. Shrinking the tube: a new support vector regression algorithm. In M. S. Kearns, S. A. Solla, and D. A. Cohn, editors, *Advances in Neural Information Processing Systems 11*, pages 330–336, Cambridge, MA, 1999. MIT Press.

[470] B. Schölkopf, C. Burges, and V. Vapnik. Extracting support data for a given task. In U. M. Fayyad and R. Uthurusamy, editors, *Proceedings, First International Conference on Knowledge Discovery & Data Mining*, Menlo Park, 1995. AAAI Press.

[471] B. Schölkopf, C. Burges, and V. Vapnik. Incorporating invariances in support vector learning machines. In C. von der Malsburg, W. von Seelen, J. C. Vorbrüggen, and B. Sendhoff, editors, *Artificial Neural Networks — ICANN'96*, pages 47–52, Berlin, 1996. Springer Lecture Notes in Computer Science, Vol. 1112.

[472] B. Schölkopf, C. J. C. Burges, and A. J. Smola. *Advances in Kernel Methods — Support Vector Learning*. MIT Press, Cambridge, MA, 1999.

[473] B. Schölkopf, R. Herbrich, A. J. Smola, and R. C. Williamson. A generalized representer theorem. Technical Report 2000-81, NeuroCOLT, 2000. Published in *Proceedings COLT'2001*, Springer Lecture Notes in Artificial Intelligence, 2001.

[474] B. Schölkopf, S. Mika, C. Burges, P. Knirsch, K.-R. Müller, G. Rätsch, and A. J. Smola. Input space vs. feature space in kernel-based methods. *IEEE Transactions on Neural Networks*, 10(5):1000–1017, 1999.

[475] B. Schölkopf, J. Platt, J. Shawe-Taylor, A. J. Smola, and R. C. Williamson. Estimating the support of a high-dimensional distribution. TR 87, Microsoft Research, Redmond, WA, 1999. http://www.research.microsoft.com/scripts/pubs/view.asp?TR_ID=MSR-TR-99-87. Abbreviated version published in *Neural Computation*, 13(7), 2001.

[476] B. Schölkopf, J. Platt, and A. J. Smola. Kernel method for percentile feature extraction. TR 22, Microsoft Research, Redmond, WA, 2000.

[477] B. Schölkopf, J. Shawe-Taylor, A. J. Smola, and R. C. Williamson. Kernel-dependent support vector error bounds. In *Ninth International Conference on Artificial Neural Networks*, Conference Publications No. 470, pages 103–108, London, 1999. IEE.

[478] B. Schölkopf, P. Simard, A. J. Smola, and V. Vapnik. Prior knowledge in support vector kernels. In M. Jordan, M. Kearns, and S. Solla, editors, *Advances in Neural Information Processing Systems 10*, pages 640–646, Cambridge, MA, 1998. MIT Press.

[479] B. Schölkopf, A. J. Smola, and K.-R. Müller. Nonlinear component analysis as a kernel eigenvalue problem. Technical Report 44, Max-Planck-Institut für biologische Kybernetik, 1996.

[480] B. Schölkopf, A. J. Smola, and K.-R. Müller. Kernel principal component analysis. In B. Schölkopf, C. J. C. Burges, and A. J. Smola, editors, *Advances in Kernel Methods - Support Vector Learning*, pages 327–352. MIT Press, Cambridge, MA, 1999. Short version appeared in *Neural Computation* 10:1299–1319, 1998.

[481] B. Schölkopf, A. J. Smola, R. C. Williamson, and P. L. Bartlett. New support vector algorithms. *Neural Computation*, 12:1207–1245, 2000.

[482] B. Schölkopf, K. Sung, C. Burges, F. Girosi, P. Niyogi, T. Poggio, and V. Vapnik. Comparing support vector machines with Gaussian kernels to radial basis function classifiers. *IEEE Transactions on Signal Processing*, 45:2758–2765, 1997.

[483] I. Schur. Bemerkungen zur Theorie der beschränkten Bilinearformen mit unendlich vielen Veränderlichen. *Journal für die Reine und Angewandte Mathematik*, 140:1–29, 1911.

[484] J. Schürmann. *Pattern Classification: a unified view of statistical and neural approaches.* Wiley, New York, 1996.

[485] G. Schwarz. Estimating the dimension of a model. *Annals of Statistics*, 6:461–464, 1978.

[486] M. Seeger. Bayesian methods for support vector machines and Gaussian processes. Master's thesis, University of Edinburgh, Division of Informatics, 1999.

[487] J. Segman, J. Rubinstein, and Y. Y. Zeevi. The canonical coordinates method for pattern deformation: Theoretical and computational considerations. *IEEE Transactions on Pattern Analysis and Machine Intelligence*, 14:1171–1183, 1992.

[488] B. Seifert, T. Gasser, and A. Wolf. Nonparametric estimation of residual variance revisited. *Biometrika*, 80:373–383, 1993.

[489] J. A. Sethian. *Level Set Methods and Fast Marching Methods.* Cambridge Monograph on Applied and Computational Mathematics. Cambridge University Press, 1999.

[490] A. Shashua. On the relationship between the support vector machine for classification and sparsified Fisher's linear discriminant. *Neural Processing Letters*, 9(2):129–139, 1999.

[491] J. Shawe-Taylor, P. L. Bartlett, R. C. Williamson, and M. Anthony. Structural risk minimization over data-dependent hierarchies. *IEEE Transactions on Information Theory*, 44(5):1926–1940, 1998.

[492] J. Shawe-Taylor and N. Cristianini. Margin distribution and soft margin. In A. J. Smola, P. L. Bartlett, B. Schölkopf, and D. Schuurmans, editors, *Advances in Large Margin Classifiers*, pages 349–358, Cambridge, MA, 2000. MIT Press.

[493] S. Shelah. A combinatorial problem; stability and order for models and theories in infinitary languages. *Pacific Journal of Mathematics*, 41:247–261, 1972.

[494] S. K. Shevade, S. S. Keerthi, C. Bhattacharyya, and K. R. K. Murthy. Improvements to SMO algorithm for SVM regression. Technical Report CD-99-16, Dept. of Mechanical and Production Engineering, Natl. Univ. Singapore, Singapore, 1999.

[495] K. Sim. Context kernels for text categorization. Master's thesis, Australian National University, 2001.

[496] P. Simard, Y. LeCun, and J. Denker. Efficient pattern recognition using a new transformation distance. In S. J. Hanson, J. D. Cowan, and C. L. Giles, editors, *Advances in Neural Information Processing Systems 5. Proceedings of the 1992 Conference*, pages 50–58, San Mateo, CA, 1993. Morgan Kaufmann.

[497] P. Simard, B. Victorri, Y. LeCun, and J. Denker. Tangent prop — a formalism for specifying selected invariances in an adaptive network. In J. E. Moody, S. J. Hanson, and R. P. Lippmann, editors, *Advances in Neural Information Processing Systems 4*, San Mateo, CA, 1992. Morgan Kaufmann.

[498] Y. Singer. Leveraged vector machines. In S. A. Solla, T. K. Leen, and K.-R. Müller, editors, *Advances in Neural Information Processing Systems 12*, pages 610 – 616. MIT Press, 2000.

[499] J. Skilling. *Maximum Entropy and Bayesian Methods.* Cambridge University Press, 1988.

[500] M. Slater. A note on Motzkin's transposition theorem. *Econometrica*, 19:185–186, 1951.

[501] A. J. Smola. Regression estimation with support vector learning machines. Diplomarbeit, Technische Universität München, 1996.

[502] A. J. Smola. *Learning with Kernels.* PhD thesis, Technische Universität Berlin, 1998. GMD Research Series No. 25.

[503] A. J. Smola and P. L. Bartlett. Sparse greedy Gaussian process regression. In T. K. Leen, T. G. Dietterich, and V. Tresp, editors, *Advances in Neural Information Processing Systems 13*. MIT Press, 2001.

[504] A. J. Smola, P. L. Bartlett, B. Schölkopf, and D. Schuurmans. *Advances in Large Margin Classifiers.* MIT Press, Cambridge, MA, 2000.

[505] A. J. Smola, A. Elisseeff, B. Schölkopf, and R. C. Williamson. Entropy numbers for convex combinations and MLPs. In A. J. Smola, P. L. Bartlett, B. Schölkopf, and D. Schuurmans, editors, *Advances in Large Margin Classifiers*, pages 369–387, Cambridge, MA, 2000. MIT Press.

[506] A. J. Smola, T. Frieß, and B. Schölkopf. Semiparametric support vector and linear programming machines. NeuroCOLT Technical Report NC-TR-98-021, Royal Holloway College, University of London, UK, 1998.

[507] A. J. Smola, T. Frieß, and B. Schölkopf. Semiparametric support vector and linear programming machines. In M. S. Kearns, S. A. Solla, and D. A. Cohn, editors, *Advances in Neural Information*

Processing Systems 11, pages 585–591, Cambridge, MA, 1999. MIT Press.

[508] A. J. Smola, O. Mangasarian, and B. Schölkopf. Sparse kernel feature analysis. Technical Report 99-04, Data Mining Institute, University of Madison, Wisconsin, 1999. ftp://ftp.cs.wisc.edu/dmi/tech-reports/99-04.ps; *Neural Computation*. Submitted.

[509] A. J. Smola, S. Mika, B. Schölkopf, and R. C. Williamson. Regularized principal manifolds. *Journal of Machine Learning Research*, 1:179–209, 2001. http://www.jmlr.org.

[510] A. J. Smola, N. Murata, B. Schölkopf, and K.-R. Müller. Asymptotically optimal choice of ε-loss for support vector machines. In L. Niklasson, M. Bodén, and T. Ziemke, editors, *Proceedings of the 8th International Conference on Artificial Neural Networks*, Perspectives in Neural Computing, pages 105–110, Berlin, 1998. Springer Verlag.

[511] A. J. Smola, Z. L. Óvári, and R. C. Williamson. Regularization with dot-product kernels. In *Advances in Neural Information Processing Systems*, 2000.

[512] A. J. Smola and B. Schölkopf. On a kernel-based method for pattern recognition, regression, approximation and operator inversion. *Algorithmica*, 22:211–231, 1998.

[513] A. J. Smola and B. Schölkopf. Sparse greedy matrix approximation for machine learning. In P. Langley, editor, *Proceedings of the 17th International Conference on Machine Learning*, pages 911–918, San Francisco, 2000. Morgan Kaufman.

[514] A. J. Smola and B. Schölkopf. A tutorial on support vector regression. *Statistics and Computing*, 2001. Forthcoming. Also: NeuroCOLT Technical Report NC-TR-98-030.

[515] A. J. Smola, B. Schölkopf, and K.-R. Müller. The connection between regularization operators and support vector kernels. *Neural Networks*, 11:637–649, 1998.

[516] A. J. Smola, B. Schölkopf, and K.-R. Müller. General cost functions for support vector regression. In T. Downs, M. Frean, and M. Gallagher, editors, *Proc. of the Ninth Australian Conf. on Neural Networks*, pages 79–83, Brisbane, Australia, 1998. University of Queensland.

[517] A. J. Smola, B. Schölkopf, and G. Rätsch. Linear programs for automatic accuracy control in regression. In *Ninth International Conference on Artificial Neural Networks*, Conference Publications No. 470, pages 575–580, London, 1999. IEE.

[518] A. J. Smola, J. Shawe-Taylor, B. Schölkopf, and R. C. Williamson. The entropy regularization information criterion. In S. A. Solla, T. K. Leen, and K.-R. Müller, editors, *Advances in Neural Information Processing Systems 12*, pages 342–348. MIT Press, 2000.

[519] A. J. Smola and U. von Luxburg. Stability of posterior estimates for kernels. In *Neural Information Processing Systems*, 2001. Submitted.

[520] I. H. Sneddon. *The Use of Integral Transforms*. McGraw–Hill, New York, 1972.

[521] P. Sollich. Probabilistic interpretation and Bayesian methods for support vector machines. In *ICANN'99 - Ninth International Conference on Artificial Neural Networks*, Conference Publications No. 470, pages 91–96, London, 1999. The Institution of Electrical Engineers.

[522] R. J. Solomonoff. A formal theory of inductive inference. *Information and Control*, 7:1–22, 224–254, 1964.

[523] E. D. Sontag. VC dimension of neural networks. In C. M. Bishop, editor, *Neural Networks and Machine Learning*, pages 69–94. Springer-Verlag, Berlin, 1998.

[524] A. Soshnikov. Universality at the edge of the spectrum in Wigner random matrices. *Comm. Math. Phys.*, 207:697–733, 1999.

[525] D. J. Spiegelhalter and S. L. Lauritzen. Sequential updating of conditional probabilities on directed graphical structures. *Networks*, 20:579–605, 1990.

[526] I. Steinwart. Some estimates for the entropy numbers of convex hulls with finitely many extreme points. Technical report, University of Jena, 1999.

[527] I. Steinwart. On the generalization ability of support vector machines. Technical report, University of Jena, 2001.

[528] S. Still, B. Schölkopf, K. Hepp, and R. J. Douglas. Four-legged walking gait control using a neuromorphic chip interfaced to a support vector learning algorithm. In T. K. Leen, T. G. Dietterich, and V. Tresp, editors, *Advances in Neural Information Processing Systems 13*, pages 741–747. MIT Press, 2001.

[529] M. Stitson, A. Gammerman, V. Vapnik, V. Vovk, C. Watkins, and J. Weston. Support vector regression with ANOVA decomposition kernels. In B. Schölkopf, C. J. C. Burges, and A. J. Smola, editors, *Advances in Kernel Methods — Support Vector Learning*, pages 285–292, Cambridge, MA, 1999. MIT Press.

[530] J. Stoer and R. Bulirsch. *Introduction to Numerical Analysis.* Springer Verlag, New York, second edition, 1993.

[531] D. Stoneking. Improving the manufacturability of electronic designs. *IEEE Spectrum*, 36(6):70–76, June 1999.

[532] J. A. K. Suykens and J. Vandewalle. Least squares support vector machine classifiers. *Neural Processing Letters*, 9:293–300, 1999.

[533] D. F. Swayne, D. Cook, and A. Buja. Xgobi. http://www.research.att.com/areas/stat/xgobi.

[534] L. Tarassenko, P. Hayton, N. Cerneaz, and M. Brady. Novelty detection for the identification of masses in mammograms. In *Proceedings Fourth IEE International Conference on Artificial Neural Networks*, pages 442–447, Cambridge, 1995.

[535] D. M. J. Tax and R. P. W. Duin. Data domain description by support vectors. In M. Verleysen, editor, *Proceedings ESANN*, pages 251–256, Brussels, 1999. D Facto.

[536] L.-N. Teow and K.-F. Loe. Handwritten digit recognition with a novel vision model that extracts linearly separable features. In *Proceedings IEEE Conference on Computer Vision and Pattern Recognition*, 2000.

[537] V. M. Tikhomirov. Diameters of sets in function spaces and the theory of best approximations. *Russian Mathematical Surveys*, 15(3):75–111, 1960.

[538] A. N. Tikhonov and V. Y. Arsenin. *Solution of Ill–Posed Problems.* Winston, Washington, DC, 1977.

[539] M. Tipping. The relevance vector machine. *Journal of Machine Learning Research*, 1:211–244, 2001.

[540] M. Tipping. Sparse kernel principal component analysis. In T. K. Leen, T. G. Dietterich, and V. Tresp, editors, *Advances in Neural Information Processing Systems 13*. MIT Press, 2001.

[541] M. Tipping and B. Schölkopf. A kernel approach for vector quantization with guaranteed distortion bounds. In T. Jaakkola and T. Richardson, editors, *Artificial Intelligence and Statistics*, pages 129–134, San Francisco, CA, 2001. Morgan Kaufmann.

[542] S. Tong and D. Koller. Support vector machine active learning with applications to text classification. In P. Langley, editor, *Proceedings of the 17th International Conference on Machine Learning*, San Francisco, California, 2000. Morgan Kaufmann.

[543] W. S. Torgerson. *Theory and Methods of Scaling.* Wiley, New York, 1958.

[544] C. A. Tracy and H. Widom. Universality of the distribution functions of random matrix theory. In M. T. Batchelor and L. T. Wille, editors, *Statistical Physics on the Eve of the 21st Century*, pages 230–239. World Sci. Publishing, 1999.

[545] T. Trafalis and A. Malysche. An analytic center machine. *Machine Learning*, 2002. Forthcoming.

[546] V. Tresp. A Bayesian committee machine. *Neural Computation*, 12(11):2719–2741, 2000.

[547] K. Tsuda. Support vector classifier with asymmetric kernel function. In M. Verleysen, editor, *Proceedings ESANN*, pages 183–188, Brussels, 1999. D Facto.

[548] K. Tsuda, M. Kawanabe, G. Rätsch, S. Sonnenburg, and K.R. Müller. A new discriminative kernel from probabilistic models. In T.G. Dietterich, S. Becker, and Z. Ghahramani, editors, *Advances in Neural Information Processing Systems*, volume 14. MIT Press, 2002. To appear.

[549] K. Tsuda, G. Rätsch, S. Mika, and K.-R. Müller. Meta learning: Learning to predict the leave-one-out error. Preprint, 2000.

[550] A. B. Tsybakov. On nonparametric estimation of density level sets. *Annals of Statistics*, 25(3):948–969, 1997.

[551] A. B. Tsybakov. Optimal aggregation of classifiers in statistical learning. Preprint of laboratoire de probabilité et modelès aléatoires, Université Paris 6 / Paris 7, 2001. http://www.proba.jussieu.fr/preprints.html. Submitted to Annals of Statistics.

[552] M. Unser, A. Aldroubi, and M. Eden. Fast B-spline transforms for continuous image representation and interpolation. *IEEE Transactions on Pattern Analysis and Machine Intelligence*, PAMI-13(3):277–285, March 1991.

[553] H. Uzawa. The Kuhn-Tucker theorem in concave programming. In K. J. Arrow, L. Hurwicz, and H. Uzawa, editors, *Studies in Linear and Nonlinear Programming*, pages 32–37. Stanford University Press, 1958.

[554] A. W. van der Vaart and J. A. Wellner. *Weak Convergence and Empirical Processes.* Springer, 1996.

[555] R. J. Vanderbei. *Linear Programming: Foundations and Extensions.* Kluwer Academic Publishers, Hingham, MA, 1997.

[556] R. J. Vanderbei. LOQO user's manual — version 3.10. Technical Report SOR-97-08, Princeton University, Statistics and Operations Research, 1997. Code available at http://www.princeton.edu/~rvdb/.

[557] R. J. Vanderbei, A. Duarte, and B. Yang. An algorithmic and numerical comparison of several interior-point methods. Technical Report SOR-94-05, Program in Statistics and Operations Research, Princeton University, 1994.

[558] P. Vannerem, K.-R. Müller, A. J. Smola, B. Schölkopf, and S. Söldner-Rembold. Classifying LEP data with support vector algorithms. In *Proceedings of AIHENP'99*, 1999.

[559] V. Vapnik. *Estimation of Dependences Based on Empirical Data [in Russian]*. Nauka, Moscow, 1979. (English translation: Springer Verlag, New York, 1982).

[560] V. Vapnik. *Estimation of Dependences Based on Empirical Data*. Springer-Verlag, Berlin, 1982.

[561] V. Vapnik. *The Nature of Statistical Learning Theory*. Springer, NY, 1995.

[562] V. Vapnik. *Statistical Learning Theory*. Wiley, NY, 1998.

[563] V. Vapnik. Three remarks on the support vector method of function estimation. In B. Schölkopf, C. J. C. Burges, and A. J. Smola, editors, *Advances in Kernel Methods — Support Vector Learning*, pages 25–42, Cambridge, MA, 1999. MIT Press.

[564] V. Vapnik. Lecture given at the dagstuhl seminar on inference principles and model selection, 2001.

[565] V. Vapnik and O. Chapelle. Bounds on error expectation for SVM. In A. J. Smola, P. L. Bartlett, B. Schölkopf, and D. Schuurmans, editors, *Advances in Large Margin Classifiers*, pages 261–280, Cambridge, MA, 2000. MIT Press.

[566] V. Vapnik and A. Chervonenkis. A note on one class of perceptrons. *Automation and Remote Control*, 25, 1964.

[567] V. Vapnik and A. Chervonenkis. Uniform convergence of frequencies of occurrence of events to their probabilities. *Dokl. Akad. Nauk SSSR*, 181:915–918, 1968.

[568] V. Vapnik and A. Chervonenkis. On the uniform convergence of relative frequencies of events to their probabilities. *Theory of Probability and its Applications*, 16(2):264–280, 1971.

[569] V. Vapnik and A. Chervonenkis. Ordered risk minimization. *Automation and Remote Control*, 35:1226–1235, 1403–1412, 1974.

[570] V. Vapnik and A. Chervonenkis. *Theory of Pattern Recognition [in Russian]*. Nauka, Moscow, 1974. (German Translation: W. Wapnik & A. Tscherwonenkis, *Theorie der Zeichenerkennung*, Akademie–Verlag, Berlin, 1979).

[571] V. Vapnik and A. Chervonenkis. The necessary and sufficient conditions for consistency in the empirical risk minimization method. *Pattern Recognition and Image Analysis*, 1(3):283–305, 1991.

[572] V. Vapnik, S. Golowich, and A. J. Smola. Support vector method for function approximation, regression estimation, and signal processing. In M. Mozer, M. Jordan, and T. Petsche, editors, *Advances in Neural Information Processing Systems 9*, pages 281–287, Cambridge, MA, 1997. MIT Press.

[573] V. Vapnik and A. Lerner. Pattern recognition using generalized portrait method. *Automation and Remote Control*, 24:774–780, 1963.

[574] N. Vayatis and R. Azencott. Distribution-dependent Vapnik-Chervonenkis bounds. In P. Fischer and H. U. Simon, editors, *Proceedings of the 4th European Conference on Computational Learning Theory*, volume 1572 of *LNAI*, pages 230–240, Berlin, 1999. Springer.

[575] T. Vetter and T. Poggio. Linear object classes and image synthesis from a single example image. *IEEE Transactions on Pattern Analysis and Machine Intelligence*, 19(7):733–742, 1997.

[576] T. Vetter, T. Poggio, and H. Bülthoff. The importance of symmetry and virtual views in three-dimensional object recognition. *Current Biology*, 4:18–23, 1994.

[577] P. Vincent and Y. Bengio. Kernel matching pursuit. Technical Report 1179, Département d'Informatique et Recherche Opérationnelle, Université de Montréal, 2000. Presented at Snowbird'00.

[578] G. Wahba. *Spline Models for Observational Data*, volume 59 of *CBMS-NSF Regional Conference Series in Applied Mathematics*. SIAM, Philadelphia, 1990.

[579] G. Wahba. Support vector machines, reproducing kernel Hilbert spaces and the randomized GACV. In B. Schölkopf, C. J. C. Burges, and A. J. Smola, editors, *Advances in Kernel Methods — Support Vector Learning*, pages 69–88, Cambridge, MA, 1999. MIT Press.

[580] G. Wahba, X. Lin, F. Gao, D. Xiang, R. Klein, and B. Klein. The bias-variance tradeoff and the randomized GACV. In M. S. Kearns, S. A. Solla, and D. A. Cohn, editors, *Advances in Neural Information Processing Systems*, volume 11, pages 620–626. MIT Press, Cambridge, MA, 1999.

[581] L. A. Wainstein and V. D. Zubakov. *Extraction of Signals from Noise.* Prentice-Hall, 1962. Translated from the Russian by R. A. Silverman.

[582] A. Wald. *Statistical Decision Functions.* Wiley, New York, 1950.

[583] C. S. Wallace and D. M. Boulton. An information measure for classification. *Computer Jrnl.*, 11(2):185–194, August 1968.

[584] M. K. Warmuth, G. Rätsch, M. Mathieson, J. Liao, and C. Lemmen. Active learning in the drug discovery process. In T.G. Dietterich, S. Becker, and Z. Ghahramani, editors, *Advances in Neural Information Processing Systems*, volume 14. MIT Press, 2002. To appear.

[585] C. Watkins. Dynamic alignment kernels. In A. J. Smola, P. L. Bartlett, B. Schölkopf, and D. Schuurmans, editors, *Advances in Large Margin Classifiers*, pages 39–50, Cambridge, MA, 2000. MIT Press.

[586] G. N. Watson. *A Treatise on the Theory of Bessel Functions.* Cambridge University Press, Cambridge, UK, 2 edition, 1958.

[587] H. L. Weinert. *Reproducing Kernel Hilbert Spaces.* Hutchinson Ross, Stroudsburg, PA, 1982.

[588] P. J. Werbos. *Beyond Regression: New Tools for Prediction and Analysis in the Behavioral Sciences.* PhD thesis, Harvard University, 1974.

[589] J. Weston. Leave-one-out support vector machines. In *Proceedings of the International Joint Conference on Artificial Intelligence*, Sweden, 1999.

[590] J. Weston, A. Elisseeff, and B. Schölkopf. Use of the ℓ_0-norm with linear models and kernel methods. Technical report, Biowulf Technologies, New York, 2001.

[591] J. Weston, A. Gammerman, M. Stitson, V. Vapnik, V. Vovk, and C. Watkins. Support vector density estimation. In B. Schölkopf, C. J. C. Burges, and A. J. Smola, editors, *Advances in Kernel Methods — Support Vector Learning*, pages 293–306, Cambridge, MA, 1999. MIT Press.

[592] J. Weston and R. Herbrich. Adaptive margin support vector machines. In A. J. Smola, P. L. Bartlett, B. Schölkopf, and D. Schuurmans, editors, *Advances in Large Margin Classifiers*, pages 281–295, Cambridge, MA, 2000. MIT Press.

[593] J. Weston and C. Watkins. Multi-class support vector machines. In M. Verleysen, editor, *Proceedings ESANN*, Brussels, 1999. D Facto.

[594] H. White. Parametric statistical estimation with artificial neural networks: a condensed discussion. In V. Cherkassky, J. H. Friedman, and H. Wechsler, editors, *From Statistics to Neural Networks*, NATO ASI Series. Springer, Berlin, 1994.

[595] H. Widom. Asymptotic behaviour of eigenvalues of certain integral operators. *Archive for Rational Mechanics and Analysis*, 17:215–229, 1964.

[596] C. K. I. Williams. Prediction with Gaussian processes: From linear regression to linear prediction and beyond. In M. I. Jordan, editor, *Learning and Inference in Graphical Models*. Kluwer, 1998.

[597] C. K. I. Williams, 2000. Personal Communication.

[598] C. K. I. Williams. On a connection between kernel PCA and metric multidimensional scaling. In T. K. Leen, T. G. Dietterich, and V. Tresp, editors, *Advances in Neural Information Processing Systems 13*. MIT Press, 2001.

[599] C. K. I. Williams. Personal communication., 2001.

[600] C. K. I. Williams and D. Barber. Bayesian classification with Gaussian processes. *IEEE Transactions on Pattern Analysis and Machine Intelligence*, 12(20), 1998.

[601] C. K. I. Williams and C. E. Rasmussen. Gaussian processes for regression. In D. S. Touretzky, M. C. Mozer, and M. E. Hasselmo, editors, *Advances in Neural Information Processing Systems (NIPS) 8*, pages 514–520. MIT Press, 1996.

[602] C. K. I. Williams and M. Seeger. The effect of the input density distribution on kernel-based classifiers. In P. Langley, editor, *Proceedings of the 17th International Conference on Machine Learning*, pages 1159–1166, San Francisco, California, 2000. Morgan Kaufmann.

[603] C. K. I. Williams and M. Seeger. Using the Nyström method to speed up kernel machines. In T. K. Leen, T. G. Dietterich, and V. Tresp, editors, *Advances in Neural Information Processing Systems NIPS'2000*. MIT Press, 2001.

[604] R. C. Williamson, J. Shawe-Taylor, B. Schölkopf, and A. J. Smola. Sample-based generalization

bounds. *IEEE Transactions on Information Theory*, 1999. Submitted. Also: NeuroCOLT Technical Report NC-TR-99-055.

[605] R. C. Williamson, A. J. Smola, and B. Schölkopf. Entropy numbers of linear function classes. In N. Cesa-Bianchi and S. Goldman, editors, *Proceedings of the 13th Annual Conference on Computational Learning Theory*, pages 309–319, San Francisco, 2000. Morgan Kaufman.

[606] R. C. Williamson, A. J. Smola, and B. Schölkopf. Generalization bounds for regularization networks and support vector machines via entropy numbers of compact operators. *IEEE Transactions on Information Theory*, 2001. Forthcoming.

[607] P. Wolfe. A duality theorem for nonlinear programming. *Quarterly of Applied Mathematics*, 19:239–244, 1961.

[608] D. H. Wolpert. The lack of a priori distinctions between learning algorithms. *Neural Computation*, 8(7):1341–1390, 1996.

[609] J. Xu, X. Zhang, and Y. Li. Kernel MSE algorithm: a unified framework for KFD, LS-SVM and KRR. In *Proceedings of the International Joint Conference on Neural Networks*, Washington, DC, 2001. IEEE Press.

[610] L. Xu and M. Jordan. On convergence properties of the EM algorithm for Gaussian mixtures. *Neural Computation*, 8:129–151, 1996.

[611] C.-H. Yeang, S. Ramaswamy, P. Tamayo, S. Mukherjee, R. M. Rifkin, M. Angelo, M. Reich, E. Lander, J. Mesirov, and T. Golub. Molecular classification of multiple tumor types. *Bioinformatics*, 17:S316–S322, 2001. ISMB'01 Supplement.

[612] A. Yuille and N. Grzywacz. The motion coherence theory. In *Proceedings of the International Conference on Computer Vision*, pages 344–354, Washington, D.C., December 1988. IEEE Computer Society Press.

[613] T. Zhang. Approximation bounds for some sparse kernel regression algorithms. Technical report, IBM Watson Research Center, Yorktown Heights, NY, 2001.

[614] T. Zhang. A general greedy approximation algorithm with applications. In *Neural Information Processing Systems 2001*, 2001. Submitted.

[615] T. Zhang. Leave-one-out cross validation bound for kernel methods with applications in learning. In D. Helmbold and R. C. Williamson, editors, *Proceedings of the Conference on Computational Learning Theory*, 2001.

[616] X. Zhang. Using class-center vectors to build support vector machines. In *Proceedings of NNSP'99*, 1999.

[617] A. Zien, G. Rätsch, S. Mika, B. Schölkopf, T. Lengauer, and K.-R. Müller. Engineering support vector machine kernels that recognize translation initiation sites. *Bioinformatics*, 16(9):799–807, 2000.

[618] G. Zoutendijk. *Methods of Feasible Directions: a Study in Linear and Non-linear Programming*. Elsevier, 1970.

Index

Notation and Symbols

$\mathbb{R}$	the set of reals
$\mathbb{N}$	the set of natural numbers, $\mathbb{N} = \{1, 2, \ldots\}$
$\mathcal{X}$	the input domain
N	(used if $\mathcal{X}$ is a vector space) dimension of $\mathcal{X}$
x_i	input patterns
y_i	target values $y_i \in \mathbb{R}$, or (in pattern recognition) classes $y_i \in \{\pm 1\}$
m	number of training examples
$[m]$	compact notation for $\{1, \ldots, m\}$
i, j	indices, by default running over $[m]$
X	a sample of input patterns, $X = (x_1, \ldots, x_m)$
Y	a sample of output targets, $Y = (y_1, \ldots, y_m)$
$\mathcal{H}$	feature space
Φ	feature map, $\Phi : \mathcal{X} \to \mathcal{H}$
$\mathbf{x}_i$	a vector with entries $[\mathbf{x}_i]_j$; usually a mapped pattern in $\mathcal{H}$, $\mathbf{x}_i = \Phi(x_i)$
$\mathbf{w}$	weight vector in feature space
b	constant offset (or threshold)
k	(positive definite) kernel
K	kernel matrix or Gram matrix, $K_{ij} = k(x_i, x_j)$
$\mathbf{E}[\xi]$	expectation of a random variable ξ (Section B.1.3)
$\mathrm{P}\{\cdot\}$	probability of a logical formula
$\mathrm{P}(C)$	probability of a set (event) C
$p(x)$	density evaluated at $x \in \mathcal{X}$
$\mathcal{N}(\varepsilon, \mathcal{F}, d)$	covering number of a set $\mathcal{F}$ in the metric d with precision ε
$\mathcal{N}(\mu, \sigma)$	normal distribution with mean μ and variance σ
ε	parameter of the ε-insensitive loss function
α_i	Lagrange multiplier or expansion coefficient
β_i	Lagrange multiplier
$\boldsymbol{\alpha}, \boldsymbol{\beta}$	vectors of Lagrange multipliers
ξ_i	slack variables
$\boldsymbol{\xi}$	vector of all slack variables
Q	Hessian of a quadratic program

$\langle \mathbf{x}, \mathbf{x}' \rangle$	dot product between $\mathbf{x}$ and $\mathbf{x}'$
$\|\cdot\|$	2-norm, $\|\mathbf{x}\| := \sqrt{\langle \mathbf{x}, \mathbf{x} \rangle}$
$\|\cdot\|_p$	p-norm , $\|x\|_p := \left(\sum_{i=1}^N \|x_i\|^p\right)^{1/p}$, $N \in \mathbb{N} \cup \{\infty\}$
$\|\cdot\|_\infty$	∞-norm , $\|x\|_\infty := \max_{i=1}^N \|x_i\|$ on $\mathbb{R}^N$, $\|x\|_\infty := \sup_{i=1}^\infty \|x_i\|$ on ℓ_∞
ln	logarithm to base e
$\log_2$	logarithm to base 2
f	a function $\mathcal{X} \to \mathbb{R}$ or $\mathcal{X} \to \{\pm 1\}$
$\mathcal{F}$	a family of functions
$\rho_f(x, y)$	margin of function f on the example (x, y), i.e., $y \cdot f(x)$
ρ_f	margin of f on the training set, i.e., $\min_{i=1}^m \rho_f(x_i, y_i)$
h	VC dimension
C	regularization parameter in front of the empirical risk term
λ	regularization parameter in front of the regularizer
$x \in [a, b]$	interval $a \leq x \leq b$
$x \in (a, b]$	interval $a < x \leq b$
$x \in (a, b)$	interval $a < x < b$
A^{-1}	inverse matrix (in some cases, pseudo-inverse)
$A^\top$	transposed matrix (or vector)
A^*	adjoint matrix (or: operator, vector), i.e., transposed and complex conjugate
$(x_j)_j$ or (x_j)	shorthand for a sequence $(x_j) = (x_1, x_2, \ldots)$
ℓ_p	sequence spaces, $1 \leq p \leq \infty$ (Section B.3.1)
$L_p(\mathcal{X})$	function spaces, $1 \leq p \leq \infty$ (Section B.3.1)
I_A	characteristic (or indicator) function on a set A i.e., $I_A(x) = 1$ if $x \in A$ and 0 otherwise
$\mathbf{1}$	unit matrix, or identity map ($\mathbf{1}(x) = x$ for all x)
$\|C\|$	cardinality of a set C (for finite sets, the number of elements)
Υ	regularization operator
δ_{ij}	Kronecker δ (Section B.2.1)
δ_x	Dirac δ, satisfying $\int \delta_x(y) f(y) dy = f(x)$
$O(g(n))$	a function $f(n)$ is said to be $O(g(n))$ if there exists a constant C such that $\|f(n)\| \leq Cg(n)$ for all n
$o(g(n))$	a function is said to be $o(g(n))$ if there exists a constant c such that $\|f(n)\| \geq cg(n)$ for all n
rhs/lhs	shorthand for "right/left hand side"
■	the end of a proof
•	easy problem
••	intermediate problem
•••	difficult problem
○○○	open problem

Printed in the United States
by Baker & Taylor Publisher Services